www.wadsworth.com

American GOVERNMENT AND POLITICS Today

1999–2000 EDITION

Steffen W. Schmidt Iowa State University

Mack C. Shelley Iowa State University

Barbara A. Bardes University of Cincinnati

West / Wadsworth
I(T)P® An International Thomson Publishing Company

Belmont, CA • Albany, NY • Boston • Cincinnati • Johannesburg • London • Madrid • Melbourne
Mexico City • New York • Pacific Grove, CA • Scottsdale, AZ • Singapore • Tokyo • Toronto

Publisher: Clark Baxter
Senior Development Editor: Sharon Adams Poore
Editorial Assistant: Melissa Gleason
Marketing Manager: Jay Hu
Project Editor: Sandra Craig
Print Buyer: Barbara Britton
Permissions Editor: Robert Kauser
Production and Illustrations: Bill Stryker
Text and Cover Design: Doug Abbott
Photo research: Megan Ryan and Bill Stryker
Copy Editor: Patricia Lewis
Cover Photographs: The White House © Richard Ellis/Sygma; people holding flag © Lynn Johnson/Black Star
Compositor: Parkwood Composition Service
Printer: Von Hoffmann

Printed in the United States of America
2 3 4 5 6 7 8 9 10

For more information, contact Wadsworth Publishing Company, 10 Davis Drive, Belmont, CA 94002, or electronically at
http://www.wadsworth.com

International Thomson Publishing Europe
Berkshire House
168–173 High Holborn
London, WC1V 7AA, United Kingdom

International Thomson Editores
Seneca, 53
Colonia Polanco
11560 México D.F. México

Nelson ITP, Australia
102 Dodds Street
South Melbourne
Victoria 3205 Australia

International Thomson Publishing Asia
60 Albert Street
#15-01 Albert Complex
Singapore 189969

Nelson Canada
1120 Birchmount Road
Scarborough, Ontario
Canada M1K 5G4

International Thomson Publishing Japan
Hirakawa-cho Kyowa Building, 3F
2-2-1 Hirakawa-cho, Chiyoda-ku
Tokyo 102, Japan

International Thomson Publishing Southern Africa
Building 18, Constantia Square
138 Sixteenth Road, P.O. Box 2459
Halfway House, 1685 South Africa

Library of Congress Cataloging-in-Publication Data

Schmidt, Steffen W.
    American government and politics today / Steffen W. Schmidt,
    Mack C. Shelley II, Barbara A. Bardes. 1999–2000 ed.
    Includes index.
ISBN: 0–534–55314–1
ISSN: 1079–0071
1999–2000 EDITION
    1. United States—Politics and government. I. Shelley, Mack C. 1950-   II. Bardes, Barbara A.   III. Title
JK274.S428   2000
320.973–dc20

Contents in Brief

Contents

CHAPTER 2 The Constitution 31

Civil Rights and Liberties 111

CHAPTER 4   Civil Liberties   113

People and
Politics 213

PART
3

CHAPTER 7 Public Opinion 215

CHAPTER 10 Campaigns, Candidates, and Elections 305

Political Institutions 375

PART 4

CHAPTER 12 The Congress 377

POLITICS AND ETHICS
Congress Examines Its Own for
Improprieties 411

CHAPTER 13 The Presidency 417

**POLITICS AND
COMPARATIVE SYSTEMS**
Filling the Ceremonial Role 421

POLITICS WIRED
Should the Executive Have the
Key to the Internet? 429

CRITICAL PERSPECTIVE
Is Congress Yielding Too Much
Power to the Presidency? 434

POLITICS AND ETHICS
The President and the
Independent Counsel 440

CHAPTER 14 The Bureaucracy 453

Public Policy 513

PART 5

CHAPTER 17 Economic Policy 547

State and Local Politics 603

Local Government 605

Features of Special Interest

Critical perspectives

Politics and . . .

Politics wired

MORE . . .

Politics wired, continued

Elections '98

Preface

As this edition of *American Government and Politics Today* goes to press, the man who sits in the Oval Office finds himself under siege. After months of speculation about President Clinton's relationship with a White House intern, Monica Lewinsky, the independent counsel investigating the affair submitted his report to Congress in September 1998. Congress, in turn, decided to share the report's contents with the public and posted it on the Internet. As the impact of the report and its supporting documents reached the media, the politicians, and the public, the American people struggled with the question of how their constitutional processes and their values should apply to this situation.

As in the past, Americans want stability in their institutions. This is one explanation for the public's continued approval, through most of 1998, of the president's job performance. Yet under the Constitution, it is up to Congress to decide what action should be taken. Congress's decision could bring drastic change to the executive branch. Not only might the president himself be removed from office or forced to resign, but the office of the presidency could be weakened by the politicization of the process. In addition, media coverage of the scandal and the Starr documents seemed to show there are no longer any rules about what can be printed or posted on the Internet. Such free-wheeling journalism may weaken trust in the press as well as in the institutions of government.

American citizens have always considered themselves secure in their homes and places of work and leisure activities. Terrorism was something that happened somewhere else. This is no longer true. Domestic terrorism on a grand scale has already occurred with the bombing of a federal building in Oklahoma City, and to a lesser extent with a bomb blast at the Olympic games in Atlanta. The more recent bombings of U.S. embassies in Kenya and Tanzania only served to reinforce the stark reality of today—terrorism is a U.S. problem. Americans and their leaders now face a serious question: How can terrorism be contained (there is little hope that it will ever be eliminated) without seriously impinging on Americans' constitutional rights?

These are only two of the numerous political issues facing this country today. Campaign-financing reform is still pending. New demands are being heard about solving the present and future problems related to Social Security, Medicare, Medicaid, and health care in general. While the 1990s were a period of relative prosperity for Americans, that decade left the nation with a plethora of political issues that must now be faced.

1998 Election Results Included and Analyzed

Our combined teaching experience has been that students respond to up-to-date information about political events. Consequently, we have included all relevant results of the November 1998 congressional elections. In addition, we have analyzed these results in terms of how they will affect our political processes at the national level in the following two years. While we have updated all of the text to be consistent with these election results, in particular we have added the following features:

● *More Divided Government* (Chapter 1).
● *Trends in Federalism* (Chapter 3).

- *Political Leadership by Women* (Chapter 5).
- *The Accuracy of the 1998 Polls* (Chapter 7).
- *Interest Groups: The Candidates of Choice* (Chapter 8).
- *Partisan Trends in the 1998 Elections* (Chapter 9).
- *Why Voters Voted as They Did in 1998* (Chapter 10).
- *The Role of the Media in the '98 Elections* (Chapter 11).
- *Congressional Characteristics after the '98 Elections* (Chapter 12).
- *Party Control of Congress after the 1998 Elections* (Chapter 12).

The Interactive Focus of This Text

Whether it be the problems that face Bill Clinton, election results, or terrorism, we constantly strive to involve the student reader in the analysis. We make sure that the reader comes to understand that politics is not an abstract process but a very human enterprise, one involving interaction among individuals from all walks of life. We encourage the reader to think critically. Virtually all of the features included in this text end with serious "For Critical Analysis" questions. We stress how different outcomes can affect students' civil rights and liberties, employment opportunities, and economic welfare. We further encourage interacting with the political system by ending each chapter with a feature titled *Toward Active Citizenship*. In addition, there is available with this edition a new, free student-oriented supplement called *Thinking Globally, Acting Locally*. This supplement is designed to help students get involved and become active citizens.

Smartbox—A New Interactive Loose-Leaf Package

For the first time ever, this edition of *American Government and Politics Today* can be ordered as a "Smartbox." The Smartbox contains the following:

- A loose-leaf version of the text.
- A fully interactive CD-ROM called *America at Odds*.
- An electronic study guide.
- *American Government Internet Activities*.
- An InfoTrac password (discussed below).
- *Readings in American Government*.

The Most Complete Web Connection

Not only has the political world been changing rapidly, but so, too, has the way in which information throughout the world is disseminated. We continue to make sure that our text leads the industry in terms of its integration with the World Wide Web. For this edition you will find the following Web-based resources:

- **The Wadsworth Political Science Resource Center**—at

  http://politicalscience.wadsworth.com

  Here students will find information on how to better surf the Web, links to general political Web sites, a career center, election updates, a discussion forum, and Monthly News Online.

● **A text-specific site for this book**—accessible through the Wadsworth Political Science Resource Center's site. The text-specific Web site includes:

  ■ A *quarterly e-zine,* which has topical essays with related links and discussion questions.

  ■ For each chapter, *links to other relevant sites,* including those with audio and video.

  ■ A link to the *interactive Web site* for the CD-ROM *(America at Odds).*

  ■ *Interactive quizzes* for which the students can submit answers to their professors via email.

  ■ An *online discussion forum* for students and professors.

  ■ *Chapter outlines and objectives* for the student to use.

  ■ For telecourse users, *links to the master telecourse site.*

  ■ *A Citizen's Survival Guide.*

● **Interactive quizzing on the CD-ROM** *(America at Odds)*—as well as links to relevant Web sites and a discussion forum for each of the twenty issues covered on the CD-ROM.

● **InfoTrac College Edition**—an online search engine that will take the student to exactly where he or she needs to go to find relevant information, including full-text articles in important political science journals and other sources. A special icon in the margin indicates that InfoTrac will provide information and links relating to the particular topic being discussed in the text.

● **Logging On**—a section at the end of each chapter that lists and briefly describes important Web sites relating to topics covered in the chapter.

● **Using the Internet for Political Analysis**—a feature concluding each chapter that takes the student through specific exercises on how to use the World Wide Web for a better understanding of American government.

● *American Government Internet Activities*—a free booklet that takes the student on a grand tour of numerous Web sites, each related to a specific major topic in American government studies. The student is asked to perform exercises on the Web for each topic covered.

● **Online testing**—which allows instructors to provide and grade examinations online, using *World Class Testing Tools.*

● **WESTLAW**—a leading legal research service that can now be accessed via the Web. Qualified adopters can obtain free WESTLAW hours.

Special Pedagogical Aids and High-Interest Features

The 1999–2000 Edition of *American Government and Politics Today* contains numerous pedagogical aids and high-interest features to assist both students and instructors in the learning/teaching process. The following list summarizes the special elements that can be found in each chapter.

● *Chapter Outline*—a preview of the contents of the chapter.

● *What If . . .* —a discussion of a hypothetical situation that begins with a "Background" section and concludes with "For Critical Analysis" questions.

● *Margin Definitions*—for all important terms.

● *Did You Know . . . ?*—margin features presenting various facts and figures that add relevance, humor, and some fun to the learning process.

● *Politics Wired*—a new feature about politics and the Internet.

- *E-mail Messages from the Past*—a new feature that could have been . . .
- *Critical Perspective*—a critical examination of a current issue or theory relating to a topic covered in the chapter.
- *Issues for the New Century*—a concluding section on issues in American politics that are yet to be resolved.
- *Toward Active Citizenship*—a chapter-ending feature showing the student some specific ways in which he or she can become actively involved in American politics.
- *Key Terms*—a chapter-ending list, with page numbers, of all terms in the chapter that were boldfaced and defined in the margins.
- *Chapter Summary*—a point-by-point summary of the chapter text.
- *Selected Print and Electronic Resources*—including suggested readings as well as media resources.
- *Logging On*—a list and brief description of relevant and important Web sites.
- *Using the Internet for Political Analysis*—a specific Internet exercise.

International Coverage Integrated Throughout

In addition to a chapter covering foreign policy, we include a special feature, titled *Politics and Comparative Systems,* that focuses on specific developments, events, or government structures in other nations of the world. Nearly every chapter of the text contains one of these features.

The Annotated U.S. Constitution, the Annotated *Federalist Papers,* and Other Appendices

Because we know that this book serves as a reference, we have included important documents for the student of American government to have close at hand. In this edition, we have placed the fully annotated Constitution at the end of Chapter 2, as an appendix to that chapter. New to this edition is an annotated version of *Federalist Papers* Nos. 10, 51, and 78. In addition, we have included the following appendices:

- The Declaration of Independence.
- How to Read Case Citations and Find Court Decisions (which in the previous edition appeared at the end of Chapter 2).
- Presidents of the United States.
- Justices of the U.S. Supreme Court in the Twentieth Century.
- Party Control of Congress in the Twentieth Century.
- Spanish Equivalents for Important Terms in American Government.

A Complete Supplements Package

We are proud to be the authors of a text that has the most complete, accessible, and fully integrated supplements package on the market. The text, along with the supplements listed below, constitute a total learning/teaching package for you and your students. For further information on any of these supplements, contact your West/Wadsworth/ITP sales representative.

Printed Supplements

- *Study Guide.*
- *Instructor's Manual.*
- *Test Bank.*
- *American Government Internet Activities.*
- *Readings in American Government.*
- *An Introduction to Critical Thinking and Writing in American Politics.*
- *Handbook of Selected Court Cases.*
- *Thinking Globally, Acting Locally.*
- *Handbook of Selected Legislation and Other Documents.*
- *College Survival Guide.*
- *Supplementary government texts for California, Florida, and Texas.*
- *Custom Telecourse Study Guide.*
- *Custom Telecourse Instructor's Guide.*

Computerized and Multimedia Resources

- *Transparency Acetates Package.*
- *PowerPoint Presentation Program*–for Windows and Macintosh.
- *World Class Testing Tools*–for test creation, delivery, and classroom management.
- *CD-ROM (America at Odds)*–covers twenty current political issues.
- *InfoTrac College Edition.*
- *Electronic Study Guide.*
- *Your Research: Data Analysis for American Government*–includes software, data sets, and workbook
- *WESTLAW*–free to qualified adopters.
- *Political Science Video Library.*
- *CNN Videos.*
- *Grade Improvement Video.*

For Users of the Previous Edition

As usual, we thank you for your past support of our work. We have made numerous changes to this text for the 1999–2000 Edition, many of which we list below. We have rewritten much of the text, added numerous new features, and updated it to reflect the results of the November 1998 elections.

New Special Features

- *Politics Wired.*
- *E-Mail Messages from the Past.*
- *Using the Internet for Political Analysis.*
- *Media Resources*–in the chapter-ending section listing selected print and electronic resources.
- *Elections '98.*

New *What If . . .* Features

- "What If . . . Every Citizen Were Required to Be on the Internet?" (Chapter 1).
- "What If . . . Constitutional Interpretation Never Changed?" (Chapter 2).
- "What If . . . States Had to Meet National Education Standards?" (Chapter 3).

- "What If . . . The Internet Were Censored?" (Chapter 4).
- "What If . . . Resident Aliens Had the Right to Vote?" (Chapter 5).
- "What If . . . Children Had a Bill of Rights?" (Chapter 6).
- "What If . . . Courts Used Public Opinion Polls to Decide Cases?" (Chapter 7).
- "What If . . . Foreign Interest Groups Were Banned?" (Chapter 8).
- "What If . . . The Government Subsidized Third Parties?" (Chapter 9).
- "What If . . . 'Soft Money' Were Banned?" (Chapter 10).
- "What If . . . Everyone Could Be a Broadcaster?" (Chapter 11).
- "What If . . . The President Were Required to Answer Questions Live on Television?" (Chapter 13).
- "What If . . . There Were a Freeze on Regulations?" (Chapter 14).
- "What If . . . Federal Judges Were Elected?" (Chapter 15).
- "What If . . . All Citizens Could Vote on Policy Issues?" (Chapter 16).
- "What If . . . Social Security Went Bankrupt?" (Chapter 17).
- "What If . . . There Were No Foreign Aid?" (Chapter 18).
- "What If . . . All States Allowed School Choice?" (Chapter 19).

New *Critical Perspectives*

- Chapter 1: "What Do Americans Believe?"
- Chapter 2: "Does It Matter What the Founders Thought?"
- Chapter 3: "Local Consequences of Federal Mandates."
- Chapter 4: "Can Privacy Rights Survive in Cyberspace?"
- Chapter 5: "The Continuing Debate over Multiculturalism in America."
- Chapter 6: "Who Really Has Benefited from Affirmative Action?"
- Chapter 7: "The Politics of Using a Poll to Conduct the Census."
- Chapter 8: "Are Labor Unions Getting Stronger of Weaker?"
- Chapter 9: "What Role Do Political Parties Play Today?"
- Chapter 10: "Why Can't We Reform Campaign Financing?"
- Chapter 11: "Bias in the Media—The Corporate Perspective."
- Chapter 13: "Is Congress Yielding Too Much Power to the Presidency?"
- Chapter 14: "Is the Federal Government Becoming Top-Heavy?"
- Chapter 15: "The Politicization of the Judicial Appointment Process."
- Chapter 16: "Is there a Net Cost to Immigration?"
- Chapter 17: "The Global Economy: Facts and Fallacies."
- Chapter 18: "The Silent Weapons—Chemical and Biological Warfare."
- Chapter 19: "Can States Control Betting on the Internet?"

Significant Changes within Chapters

Each chapter contains new features, updated information and tabular data, and whenever feasible, the most current information available on the problems facing President Clinton. Here we list other significant changes made to each chapter.

- Chapter 1—now includes a description of the dominant culture and the pervasive influence of that perspective in data and documents relating to American government and politics.
- Chapter 3—has been reorganized and revised generally to streamline coverage; a discussion of vertical checks and balances has been included, as has a section on competitive federalism.
- Chapter 4—the section discussing establishment-clause issues has been largely rewritten.
- Chapters 5 and 6—both chapters have been extensively revised and, to a

great extent, rewritten. Chapter 5 now focuses primarily on the struggle of African Americans and women for equality; Chapter 6 covers affirmative action; bilingual education; discrimination based on age, disability, and gender preferences; and the rights and status of juveniles.

- Chapter 10—has new sections on issue advocacy and voting by mail.
- Chapter 11—has a new section on talk-show politics.
- Chapter 12—the sections on candidates for congressional elections and how a bill becomes a law have been largely rewritten.
- Chapter 14—the discussions of bureaucratic reform measures and iron triangles have been extensively revised.
- Chapter 15—has been virtually rewritten.
- Chapter 16—has been extensively revised to include a discussion of the 1996 Welfare Reform Act in reference to the policymaking process, as well as new sections on poverty and children, homelessness, and crime.
- Chapter 17—now includes sections discussing the privatization of Social Security and the budget surplus.
- Chapter 18—has a new section on U.S.–China relations, plus coverage of the 1998 bombings of the U.S. embassies in Africa.

Changes to Appendices

- Annotations added to the *Federalist Papers.*
- The Constitution was moved to the end of Chapter 2.
- The former appendix to Chapter 2 ("How to Read Case Citations and and Find Court Decisions") now appears at the end of the book as Appendix B.
- The Citizen's Survival Guide is now posted on the text's Web site.

New Print Supplements

- *Thinking Globally, Acting Locally.*
- *Custom Telecourse Study Guide.*
- *Custom Telecourse Instructor's Guide.*
- Florida government supplement.

New Multimedia Supplements

- Smartbox—the text plus the CD-ROM (*America at Odds*), electronic study guide, InfoTrac password, Internet exercises, and readings.
- *America at Odds*—a fully interactive CD-ROM.
- *Electronic Study Guide.*
- *PowerPoint Presentation Program.*
- *World Class Testing Tools.*
- CNN Videos.
- Grade Improvement Video.
- New Web resources.
- Online testing.
- Online quizzes.
- Monthly News Online.
- Wadsworth Political Science Resource Center.
- Quarterly e-zine.
- InfoTrac College Edition.
- WESTLAW on the Web.

Acknowledgments

Since we started this project a number of years ago, a sizable cadre of individuals has helped us in various phases of the undertaking. The following academic reviewers offered numerous constructive criticisms, comments, and suggestions during the preparation of all previous editions:

Danny M. Adkison
Oklahoma State University

Sharon Z. Alter
William Rainey Harper College, Illinois

William Arp III
Louisiana State University

Kevin Bailey
North Harris Community College, Texas

Dr. Charles T. Barber
University of Southern Indiana, Evansville,

Clyde W. Barrow
Texas A&M University

David C. Benford, Jr.
Tarrant County Junior College

John A. Braithwaite
Coastline College

Lynn R. Brink
North Lake College, Irving, Texas

Barbara L. Brown
Southern Illinois University at Carbondale

Kenyon D. Bunch
Fort Lewis College, Durango, Colorado

Ralph Bunch
Portland State University, Oregon

Carol Cassell
University of Alabama

Frank J. Coppa
Union County College, Cranford, New Jersey

Robert E. Craig
University of New Hampshire

Doris Daniels
Nassau Community College, New York

Carolyn Grafton Davis
North Harris County College, Texas

Marshall L. DeRosa
Louisiana State University, Baton Rouge

Michael Dinneen
Tulsa Junior College, Oklahoma

Gavan Duffy
University of Texas at Austin

George C. Edwards III
Texas A&M University

Mark C. Ellickson
Southwestern Missouri State University, Springfield

Larry Elowitz
Georgia College

John W. Epperson
Simpson College, Indianola, Indiana

Daniel W. Fleitas
University of North Carolina at Charlotte

Elizabeth N. Flores
Del Mar College, Texas

Joel L. Franke
Blinn College, Brenham, Texas

Barry D. Friedman
North Georgia College

Robert S. Getz
SUNY–Brockport, New York

Kristina Gilbert
Riverside Community College, California

William A. Giles
Mississippi State University

Donald Gregory
Stephen F. Austin State University

Forest Grieves
University of Montana

Dale Grimnitz
Normandale Community College, Bloomington, Minnesota

Stefan D. Haag
Austin Community College, Texas

Jean Wahl Harris
University of Scranton, Pennsylvania

David N. Hartman
Rancho Santiago College, Santa Ana, California

Robert M. Herman
Moorpark College, California

Richard J. Herzog
Stephen F. Austin State University, Nacogdoches, Texas

Paul Holder
McClennan Community College, Waco, Texas

Michael Hoover
Seminole Community College, Sanford, Florida

J. C. Horton
San Antonio College, Texas

Robert Jackson
Washington State University

Willoughby Jarrell
Kennesaw College, Georgia

Loch K. Johnson
University of Georgia

Donald L. Jordan
United States Air Force Academy, Colorado

John D. Kay
Santa Barbara City College, California

Charles W. Kegley
University of South Carolina

Bruce L. Kessler
Shippensburg University, Pennsylvania

Nancy B. Kral
Tomball College, Texas

Dale Krane
Mississippi State University

Samuel Krislov
University of Minnesota

William W. Lamkin
Glendale Community College

Harry D. Lawrence
Southwest Texas Junior College, Uvaide, Texas

Ray Leal
Southwest Texas State University, San Marcos

Sue Lee
Center for Telecommunications, Dallas County Community College District

Carl Lieberman
University of Akron, Ohio

Orma Linford
Kansas State University

Eileen Lynch
Brookhaven College, Texas

James D. McElyea
Tulsa Junior College, Oklahoma

William P. McLauchlan
Purdue University, Indiana

William W. Maddox
University of Florida

S. J. Makielski, Jr.
Loyola University, New Orleans

Jarol B. Manheim
George Washington University

J. David Martin
Midwestern State University, Texas

Bruce B. Mason
Arizona State University

Steve J. Mazurana
University of Northern Colorado

Thomas J. McGaghie
Kellogg Community College, Michigan

Stanley Melnick
Valencia Community College, Florida

Robert Mittrick
Luzurne County Community College, Pennsylvania

Helen Molanphy
Richland College, Texas

Keith Nicholls
University of Alabama

Stephen Osofsky
Nassau Community College, New York

John P. Pelissero
Loyola University of Chicago

Neil A. Pinney
Western Michigan University

George E. Pippin
Jones County Community College,
Mississippi

Walter V. Powell
Slippery Rock University, Pennsylvania

Michael A. Preda
Midwestern State University, Texas

Charles Prysby
University of North Carolina

Donald R. Ranish
Antelope Valley College, California

John D. Rausch
Fairmont State University, West Virginia

Curt Reichel
University of Wisconsin

Russell D. Renka
Southeast Missouri State University

Paul Rozycki
Charles Stewart Mott Community College,
Flint, Michigan

Eleanor A. Schwab
South Dakota State University

Len Shipman
Mount San Antonio College, California

Scott Shrewsbury
Mankato State University, Minnesota

Michael W. Sonnlietner
Portland Community College, Oregon

Gilbert K. St. Clair
University of New Mexico

Carol Stix
Pace University, Pleasantville,
New York

Gerald S. Strom
University of Illinois at Chicago

John R. Todd
North Texas State University

Ron Velton
Grayson County College, Texas

Benjamin Walter
Vanderbilt University, Tennessee

B. Oliver Walter
University of Wyoming

Mark J. Wattier
Murray State University, Kentucky

Thomas L. Wells
Old Dominion University, Virginia

Jean B. White
Weber State College, Utah

Lance Widman
El Camino College, California

Allan Wiese
Mankato State University, Minnesota

J. David Woodard
Clemson University, South Carolina

Robert D. Wrinkle
Pan American University, Texas

The 1999–2000 Edition of this text is the result of our working closely with reviewers who each offered us penetrating criticisms, comments, and suggestions for how to improve the text. Although we haven't been able to take account of all requests, each of the reviewers listed below will see many of his or her suggestions taken to heart.

Evelyn Ballard
Houston Community College

David S. Bell
Eastern Washington University

Richard G. Buckner
Santa Fe Community College

Frank J. Coppa
Union County College, Cranford, New Jersey

Paul B. Davis
Truckee Meadows Community College,
Nevada

Richard D. Davis
Brigham Young University

Ron Deaton
Prince George's Community College,
Maryland

Jason F. Kirksey
Oklahoma State University

James J. Lopach
University of Montana

Thomas Louis Masterson
Butte College, California

James Morrow
Tulsa Community College

Mark E. Priewe
University of Texas at San Antonio

Bhim Sandhu
West Chester University, Pennsylvania

Pauline Schloesser
Texas Southern University

In preparing this edition of *American Politics and Government Today,* we were the beneficiaries of the expert guidance of a skilled and dedicated team of publishers and editors. We would like, first of all, to thank Susan Badger, the president of Wadsworth Publishing Company, for the support she has shown for this project. We have benefited greatly from the editorial supervision and encouragement given by Clark Baxter, publisher. Sharon Adams Poore, our senior developmental editor, also deserves our thanks for her efforts in coordinating reviews and in guaranteeing the timely publication of all supplemental materials. Additionally, our appreciation goes to Jay Hu, our marketing manager at Wadsworth, for his many efforts on our behalf. We are also grateful to Bill Stryker and his colleagues—Doug Abbott, Megan Ryan, and Ann Borman—for a striking design and for making it possible to get the text out on time. In addition, our gratitude goes to all of those who worked on the various supplements offered with this text and to Jenny Burke, who coordinates the Web site and other multimedia offerings.

Many other people helped during the research and editorial stages of this edition as well. Lavina Leed Miller skillfully coordinated the authors' efforts and provided editorial and research assistance from the outset of the project through its final stages. Pat Lewis's copyediting abilities contributed greatly to the book, as did the proofreading abilities of Suzie DeFazio. The indexing skills of Bob Marsh will not go unnoticed. We also thank Sherri Downing-Alfonso and Roxie Lee for their proofreading and other assistance, which helped us to meet our ambitious publishing schedule, and Sue Jasin of K&M Consulting for her contributions to the smooth running of the project.

Any errors, of course, remain our own. We welcome comments from instructors and students alike. Suggestions that we have received on previous editions have helped us to improve this text and to adapt it to the changing needs of instructors and students.

Steffen Schmidt
Mack Shelley
Barbara Bardes

About the Authors

Steffen W. Schmidt

Steffen W. Schmidt is a professor of political science at Iowa State University. He grew up in Colombia, South America, and studied in Colombia, Switzerland, and France. He obtained his Ph.D. from Columbia University, New York, in public law and government.

Schmidt has published six books and over seventy articles in scholarly journals. He is also the recipient of numerous prestigious teaching prizes, including the Amoco Award for Lifetime Career Achievement in Teaching and the Teacher of the Year award. He is a pioneer in the use of Web-based and real-time video courses and is a member of the American Political Science Association's section on Computers and Multimedia. He is on the editorial board of the *Political Science Educator*.

Schmidt has a political talk show on WOI radio, where he is known as Dr. Politics. The show has been broadcast live from various U.S. and international venues.

Schmidt likes to snow ski, ride hunter jumper horses, and race sailboats.

Mack C. Shelley II

Mack C. Shelley II is a professor of political science and statistics at Iowa State University. After receiving his Bachelor's degree from American University in Washington, D.C., he went on to graduate studies at the University of Wisconsin at Madison, where he received a Master's degree and a Ph.D. He taught for two years at Mississippi State University prior to arriving at Iowa State in 1979.

Shelley has published numerous articles, books, and monographs on public policy In1993, he was elected co-editor of the *Policy Studies Journal*. His published books include *The Permanent Majority: The Conservative Coalition in the United States Congress; Biotechnology and the Research Enterprise: A Guide to the Literature* (with William F. Woodman and Brian J. Reichel); and *American Public Policy: The Contemporary Agenda* (with Steven G. Koven and Bert E. Swanson).

In his spare time, Shelley has been known to participate in softball, bowling (he was on two championship faculty teams), and horseback riding. When his son was given a pool table for his fourteenth birthday, he took up that game as a pastime.

Barbara A. Bardes

Barbara A. Bardes is a professor of political science and Dean of Raymond Walters College at the University of Cincinnati. She received her Bachelor of Arts degree and Master of Arts degree from Kent State University, and her Ph.D. from the University of Cincinnati. She held a faculty position at Loyola University in Chicago for many years before returning to Cincinnati, her home town, as a college administrator.

Bardes has written articles on public opinion and foreign policy, and on women and politics. She has authored *Thinking about Public Policy and Declarations of Independence: Women and Political Power in Nineteenth Century American Novels.* Currently, she is writing a book on public opinion and American politics.

Bardes's home is located in a very small hamlet in Kentucky called Rabbit Hash, famous for its 150-year-old General Store. Her hobbies include travel, gardening, needlework, and antique collecting.

The American System

PART 1

chapter 1

American Government and Politics: Stability and Change

3

Every Citizen Were Required to Be on the Internet?

BACKGROUND

By 1999, almost half of all American households could access the Internet, and most white-collar employees had some access to the Internet from their workplaces. Many of the nation's leading newspapers and media outlets put their stories on the Web. Investors tracked their stock and bond portfolios through the Internet, and many companies were created specifically to sell their products online. The government uses the Internet to make information available on many subjects, and the Internal Revenue Service (IRS) has begun to accept tax returns filed electronically. It is clear that the speed and effectiveness of the Web is making it part of everyday life for many Americans.

WHAT IF EVERY CITIZEN WERE REQUIRED TO BE ON THE INTERNET?

Suppose that the government required that each household or individual be able to access the Internet and gave tax incentives or other support to make this possible. American citizens would have instant access to information that would make their lives safer and healthier: they could read reports on health research, car safety, environmental issues, food and nutrition, exercise programs, child-rearing studies, and other issues important to their families. They would have access to the greatest libraries and museums in the world, including the Library of Congress and the Smithsonian Institution. The full array of government regulations and forms would be accessible to all citizens, including passport applications, IRS forms, and Social Security account information. Having all of these resources available through the Internet would be especially helpful to senior citizens, persons with disabilities, and those who live in rural areas without government offices.

ENHANCED CITIZEN PARTICIPATION

If everyone were required to be connected to the Internet, it would be easy for people to register to vote and, if security issues are resolved, to cast their ballots in elections from home. This easy access to participation in the political system should increase the turnout in elections.

It also would be easy for citizens to contact elected and appointed government officials directly. Today's massive lobbying campaigns, which send thousands of postcards to government offices, would be replaced by massive e-mail campaigns. Individuals could contact the office of their senator or legislator with an e-mail message and then expect a quick response to their personal concerns and issues. Today, there are many online chat rooms where people debate policy issues. Imagine the level of activity in policy debate that could take place if all Americans were connected. Of course, given the anonymity of the Internet, there would be many "engineered" campaigns with computer-generated letters sent to officials and, very likely, even "fake" policy debates constructed to derail political issues.

INCREASED GOVERNMENT INTRUSION

Although connecting to the Internet could enhance citizens' participation in and knowledge of government, it could also entail some significant costs, especially in the realm of privacy. Technology has developed to the point that it would be relatively simple for the government to record and view all e-mail sent and received by individuals through the Internet, record and archive all requests submitted by individuals for information from any Web site, and search for any financial or other personal records that people keep on their computers. Although most software for the Internet contains encryption codes that secure your communications, the government has tried repeatedly to gain access to the keys to all such secret codes for the stated purpose of thwarting crime and terrorism. Obviously, if the government required every citizen to be linked to the Internet, enormous issues involving privacy rights and other personal freedoms enjoyed by individuals in the United States would have to be addressed before such a requirement would be accepted by most Americans.

FOR CRITICAL ANALYSIS

1. What kinds of information or services do you think people would want from the government through the Internet?
2. Considering how you as an individual might use a computer and the Internet, what kinds of activities and information on the computer do you regard as personal and private? How can that privacy be protected in the future?

Politics is about change—changes in policies and laws to enable a society to cope with internal or external forces that affect people's lives. Politics is about the debates and struggles within a community to meet the demands of the people and further the interests of society. People may seek changes—in the law, in the structure of government, or in the officials who lead the government—as a result of external forces, such as war or worldwide economic shifts. People may seek such changes as a result of technological advances, such as the Internet (discussed in the *What If . . .* opening this chapter), or as a result of internal forces, such as the growing belief that the post–World War II welfare system was not working.

Politics is also about stability. Stability in law, in economic relationships, and in social customs must exist so that individuals and groups can plan for the future and manage their affairs. The United States as a democratic society is constantly balancing the need for change to meet new conditions in the world with the need for stability in the nation and the lives of its people.

As one of the older democratic societies, the United States has a very stable form of government. Many nations in the world, however, are undergoing extreme changes as they try to define their future structures and political systems. Among the nations undergoing the most drastic changes are Russia and the other states of the former Soviet Union, South Africa after apartheid, and many of the turbulent economies of Southeast Asia.

In this chapter, we will discuss some of the questions and principles that are fundamental to the construction of any political system. Part of the excitement of the American political system is that these issues and principles continue to be debated in the United States as we attempt to balance the forces of stability with the forces of change.

Political Change in the United States

Due to our electoral system, Americans have the opportunity to change the balance of power in their national government every two years. In 1994, Americans chose to replace a Congress controlled by Democrats with Republican majorities in both the House of Representatives and the Senate. The result was **divided government,** with a president from one party and a Congress controlled by the other major party. Americans reelected Bill Clinton as president in 1996 and returned a Republican majority to Congress.

Divided Government

A situation that exists when political party control over the government is divided—for example, when the president is a Democrat and Congress is controlled by Republicans.

U.S. soldiers of the NATO-led peace forces in Bosnia watch the broadcast of the videotape of President Bill Clinton giving testimony to the grand jury in September 1998. The president's testimony concerned his relationship with White House intern Monica Lewinsky.

elections '98

More Divided Government

In 1998, the voters continued to support divided government, maintaining a Republican Congress while clearly approving the leadership of President clinton as the chief executive. Although the Republicans had hoped to gain a large number of seats in the House and the Senate by reminding the voters of the Lewinski scandal, their strategy failed on eletion day. Instead of electing more Republicans to Congress, voters added five Democrats to the House of Representatives. Polls taken during the campaign showed that a majority of Americans did not want the president to be impeached or removed from office. Republicans were thought to have lost support because of their focus on the scandal.

What does this succession of decisions say about Americans and political change? It would appear that as Americans approached the third millennium, they were strongly seeking only moderate change in their governmental system. They were counting on the Republican Congress to limit the actions of a Democratic president, but they still wanted that president to press forward with his agenda.

In terms of government policies, the divided government of the 1990s turned out to be quite effective. In 1999, Americans found themselves living in an incredibly prosperous time, with low inflation and low unemployment rates. The government was faced with a surplus in its budget for the first time in many decades. During the Clinton years, Americans had supported massive policy changes in the welfare system, in telecommunications laws, and in farm policy. Neither the American public nor the politicians, however, seemed ready to push for serious policy changes in campaign financing, in the Social Security or Medicare system, or in the health-care system. These issues continued to hover on the agenda, waiting for their place in the political debate.

The willingness of Americans to debate new initiatives and to demand changes in the way the government works is at the core of our democratic nation. Change—even revolutionary change—is a tribute to the success of a political system. As Abraham Lincoln put it, "This country with all its institutions, belongs to the people who inhabit it. Whenever they shall grow weary of the existing government, they can exercise their Constitutional right of amending it, or the revolutionary right to dismember or overthrow it."[1]

In the chapters that follow, we will look more closely at the **institutions** of our government and how they have changed over the decades. We will examine how the political processes of the nation work to accomplish those changes. To begin, we will look at why political institutions and processes are necessary in any society and what purposes they serve.

INFOTRAC ®
COLLEGE EDITION

"Stormy Season Ahead"

Institution
A long-standing, identifiable structure or association that performs certain functions for society.

What Is Politics?

Why do nations and people struggle so hard to establish a form of government and continue to expend so much effort in politics to keep that government functioning? Politics and forms of government are probably as old as human society. There are many definitions of politics, but all try to explain how human beings regulate conflict within their society. As soon as humans began to live in groups, particularly groups that were larger than their immediate families, they found that they needed to establish rules about behavior, property, the privileges

---

[1]*Oxford Dictionary of Quotations,* 3d ed. (Oxford, England: Oxford University Press, 1980), p. 314.

of individuals and groups, and how people would survive together. **Politics** can best be understood as the process of, as Harold Lasswell put it, "who gets what, when, and how."[2] To another social scientist, David Easton, politics should be defined as the "authoritative allocation of values."[3] Politics, then, is the struggle or process engaged in by human beings to decide which members of society get benefits or privileges and which are excluded from certain benefits or privileges.

In the early versions of human society, the tribe or village, politics was relatively informal. Tribal elders or hereditary chiefs were probably vested with the power to decide who married whom, who was able to build a hut on the best piece of land, and which young people succeeded them into the positions of leadership. Other societies were "democratic" from the very beginning, giving their members some form of choice of leadership and rules. Early human societies rarely had the concept of property, so few rules were needed to decide who owned which piece of property or who inherited that piece. The concepts of property and inheritance are much more modern. As society became more complex and humans became settled farmers rather than hunters and gatherers, the problems associated with property, inheritance, sales and exchanges, kinship, and rules of behavior became important to resolve. Politics developed into the process by which some of these questions were answered.

Inevitably, conflicts arise in society, because members of a group are distinct individuals with unique needs, values, and perspectives. At least three different kinds of conflicts that may require the need for political processes arise in a society:

1. People may differ over their beliefs, either religious or personal, or over basic issues of right and wrong. The kind of debate that has arisen in recent years on abortion is an example of this kind of conflict.
2. People within a society may differ greatly in their perception of what the society's goals should be. For example, Americans disagree over whether the national government should set national standards for education or whether the direction for schools should come primarily from local school boards and communities—an issue we discuss in Chapter 3.
3. People compete for scarce resources; jobs, income, and property are examples. The question of who will pay for Medicare benefits, for instance, is really a discussion of whether younger people will pay for the health care of the older persons in the society or whether retirees must pay more for this health insurance.

The Need for Government and Power

If *politics* refers to conflict and conflict resolution, **government** refers to the structures by which the decisions are made that resolve conflicts or allocate values. In early human societies, such as families and small tribes, there was no need for formal structures of government. Decisions were made by acknowledged leaders in those societies. In families, all members may meet together to decide values and priorities. Where there is a community that makes decisions and allocates values through informal rules, politics exists—but not government. Within most contemporary societies, these activities continue in many forms. For example, when a church decides to build a new building or hire a new minister, that decision may be made politically, but there is in fact no government.

DID YOU KNOW...
That the word *politkos* (pertaining to citizen or civic affairs) was used by the Greeks thousands of years ago and that the English word politics entered the language around 1529?

Politics
According to David Easton, the "authoritative allocation of values" for a society; according to Harold Lasswell, "who gets what, when, and how" in a society.

Government
A permanent structure (institution) composed of decision makers who make society's rules about conflict resolution and the allocation of resources and who possess the power to enforce those rules.

---

[2]Harold Lasswell, *Politics: Who Gets What, When and How* (New York: McGraw-Hill, 1936).
[3]David Easton, *The Political System* (New York: Knopf, 1953).

Politics can be found in schools, social groups, and any other organized group. When a society, however, reaches a certain level of complexity, it becomes necessary to establish a permanent or semipermanent group of individuals to act for the whole, to become the government.

Governments range in size from the volunteer city council and one or two employees of a small town to the massive and complex structures of the U.S. government or those of any other large, modern nation. Generally, governments not only make the rules but also implement them through the use of police, judges, and other government officials.

Authority and Legitimacy

In addition to instituting and carrying out laws regulating individual behavior, such as traffic laws and criminal laws, most modern governments also attempt to carry out public policies that are intended to fulfill specific national or state goals. For example, a state may decide that its goal is to reduce teenage consumption of alcohol and the driving accidents caused by such behavior. To do that, the state may institute extremely strong penalties for drinking, along with a statewide education program for teenagers and younger children about the dangers of drinking and driving. The U.S. government has instituted and attempted to implement a series of environmental laws meant to improve air and water quality. Environmental laws have required citizens to follow certain rules, such as using unleaded gasoline. The federal air-quality regulations have also forced car manufacturers to produce more fuel-efficient vehicles and, in some urban areas, have required citizens to take their vehicles through pollution-inspection stations to see if their cars meet government standards.

Why do citizens obey these laws and subject themselves to these regulations? One reason citizens obey government is that it has the **authority** to make such laws. By authority, we mean the ultimate right to enforce compliance with decisions. Americans also believe the laws should be obeyed because they possess **legitimacy**—that is, they are appropriate and rightful. The laws have been made according to the correct and accepted political process by representatives of the people. Therefore, they are accepted by the people as legitimate and having political authority.

The Question of Power

Another and perhaps more basic answer as to why we comply with the laws and rules of the government is that we understand that government has the **power** to enforce the law. We obey environmental laws and pay taxes in part because we acknowledge the legitimacy of the law. We also know that the government has the power to coerce our compliance with the law. Governments differ in the degree to which they must rely on coercion to gain **compliance** from their citizens. In authoritarian nations, the use of force is far more common than in democratic nations, in which most citizens comply with the law because they accept the authority of the government and its officials. In authoritarian or **totalitarian regimes,** the will of the government is imposed frequently and is upheld by the use of force.

The concept of power also involves the ability of one individual or a group to influence the actions of another individual or group of individuals. We frequently speak of the power of the president to convince Congress to pass laws, or the power of the American Association of Retired Persons to influence legislation. We also speak frequently of the power of money to influence political decisions. These uses of power are informal and involve using rewards for com-

Authority
The features of a leader or an institution that compel obedience, usually because of ascribed legitimacy. For most societies, government is the ultimate authority.

Legitimacy
A status conferred by the people on the government's officials, acts, and institutions through their belief that the government's actions are an appropriate use of power by a legally constituted governmental authority following correct decision-making policies. These actions are regarded as rightful and entitled to compliance and obedience on the part of citizens.

Power
The ability to cause others to modify their behavior and to conform to what the power holder wants.

Compliance
The act of accepting and carrying out authorities' decisions.

Totalitarian Regime
A form of government that controls all aspects of the political and social life of a nation. All power resides with the government. The citizens have no power to choose the leadership or policies of the country.

pliance rather than the threat of coercion. More often than not, political power in the government is a matter of influence and persuasion rather than coercion.

Who Governs?

One of the most fundamental questions of politics has to do with which person or groups of people control society through the government. Who possesses the power to make decisions about who gets what and how the benefits of the society are distributed among the people?

Sources of Political Power

At one extreme is a society governed by a totalitarian regime. In such a political system, a small group of leaders or a single individual—a dictator—makes all political decisions for the society. Every aspect of political, social, and economic life is controlled by the government. The power of the ruler is total (thus, the term *totalitarianism*).

Many of our terms for describing the distribution of political power are derived from the ancient Greeks, who were the first Western people to study politics systematically. A society in which political decisions were controlled by a small group was called an **oligarchy,** meaning rule by a few members of the **elite,** who generally benefited themselves. Another form of rule by the few was known as **aristocracy,** meaning rule by the most virtuous, most talented, or the best suited to the position. Later, in European history, aristocracy meant rule by the titled or the upper classes. In contrast to such a top-down form of control was the form known as **anarchy,** or the condition of no government. Anarchy exists when each individual makes his or her own rules for behavior, and there are no laws and no government.

The Greek term for rule by the people was **democracy.** Although most Greek philosophers were not convinced that democracy was the best form of government, they understood and debated the possibility of such a political system. Within the limits of their culture, some of the Greek city-states operated as democracies.

Oligarchy
Rule by a few members of the elite, who generally make decisions to benefit their own group.

Elite
An upper socioeconomic class that controls political and economic affairs.

Aristocracy
Rule by the best suited, through virtue, talent, or education; in later usage, rule by the upper class.

Anarchy
The condition of having no government and no laws. Each member of the society governs himself or herself.

Democracy
A system of government in which ultimate political authority is vested in the people. Derived from the Greek words *demos* ("the people") and *kratos* ("authority").

This town meeting in New Hampshire allows every citizen of the town to vote directly and in person for elected officials, for proposed policies, and, in some cases, for the town budget. To be effective, such a form of direct democracy requires that the citizens stay informed about local politics, attend town meetings, and devote time to discussion and decision making.

Direct Democracy as a Model

From the ancient Greek city-states comes a model for governance that has framed the modern debate over whether the people can make decisions about their own government and laws. The Athenian system of government is usually considered the model for **direct democracy** because the citizens of that community debated and voted directly on all laws, even those put forward by the ruling council of the city. The most important feature of Athenian democracy was that the **legislature** was composed of all of the citizens. Women, foreigners, and slaves, however, were excluded because they were not citizens. The outstanding feature of this early form of government was that it required a high level of participation from every citizen; that participation was seen as benefiting the individual and the city-state. The Athenians recognized that although a high level of participation might lead to instability in government, citizens, if informed about the issues, could be trusted to make decisions about the laws governing their community. (See the feature *E-Mail Messages from the Past* for some comments on democracy from the Athenian philosopher Plato.)

Direct democracy also has been practiced in some Swiss cantons and, in the United States, in New England town meetings and in some midwestern township meetings. At New England town meetings, which can include all of the voters who live in the town, important decisions are made for the community—such as levying taxes, hiring city officials, and deciding local ordinances—by majority vote. Some states provide a modern adaptation of direct democracy for their citizens; in most states, representative democracy is supplemented by the **initiative** or the **referendum**—a process by which the people may vote directly on laws or constitutional amendments. The **recall** process, which is available in over one-third of the states, allows the people to vote to remove an official from state office.

The Dangers of Direct Democracy

Although they were aware of the Athenian model, the framers of the U.S. Constitution—for the most part—were opposed to such a system. For many centuries preceding this country's establishment, any form of democracy was considered to be dangerous and to lead to instability. But in the eighteenth and

Direct Democracy
A system of government in which political decisions are made by the people directly, rather than by their elected representatives; probably possible only in small political communities.

Legislature
A government body primarily responsible for the making of laws.

Initiative
A procedure by which voters can propose a law or a constitutional amendment.

Referendum
An act of referring legislative (statutory) or constitutional measures to the voters for approval or disapproval.

Recall
A procedure allowing the people to vote to dismiss an elected official from state office before his or her term has expired.

INFOTRAC®
COLLEGE EDITION

"Too Much Democracy"

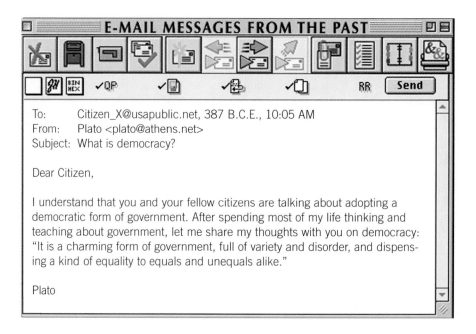

E-MAIL MESSAGES FROM THE PAST

To: Citizen_X@usapublic.net, 387 B.C.E., 10:05 AM
From: Plato <plato@athens.net>
Subject: What is democracy?

Dear Citizen,

I understand that you and your fellow citizens are talking about adopting a democratic form of government. After spending most of my life thinking and teaching about government, let me share my thoughts with you on democracy: "It is a charming form of government, full of variety and disorder, and dispensing a kind of equality to equals and unequals alike."

Plato

nineteenth centuries, the idea of government based on the **consent of the people** gained increasing popularity. Such a government was the main aspiration of the American and French revolutions, as well as of many subsequent ones. The masses, however, were considered to be too uneducated to govern themselves, too prone to the influence of demagogues (political leaders who manipulate popular prejudices), and too likely to abrogate minority rights.

James Madison defended the new scheme of government set forth in the U.S. Constitution, while warning of the problems inherent in a "pure democracy":

> A common passion or interest will, in almost every case, be felt by a majority of the whole . . . and there is nothing to check the inducements to sacrifice the weaker party or an obnoxious individual. Hence it is that such democracies have ever been spectacles of turbulence and contention, and have ever been found incompatible with personal security or the rights of property; and have in general been as short in their lives as they have been violent in their deaths.[4]

Like many other politicians of his time, Madison feared that pure, or direct, democracy would deteriorate into mob rule. What would keep the majority of the people, if given direct decision-making power, from abusing the rights of minority groups?

Representative Democracy

The framers of the U.S. Constitution chose to craft a **republic,** meaning a government in which the power rests with the people, who elect representatives to govern them and to make the laws and policies. To eighteenth-century Americans, the idea of a republic also meant a government based on common beliefs and virtues that would be fostered within small communities. The rulers were to be amateurs—good citizens—who would take turns representing their fellow citizens, in a way similar to the Greek model.[5]

To allow for change while ensuring a measure of stability, the U.S. Constitution creates a form of republican government known as a **representative democracy.** The people hold the ultimate power over the government through the election process, but policy decisions are all made by elected officials. Even this distance between the people and the government was not sufficient. Other provisions in the Constitution made sure that the Senate and the president would be selected by political elites rather than by the people, although later changes to the Constitution allowed the voters to elect members of the Senate directly. This modified form of democratic government came to be widely accepted throughout the Western world as a compromise between the desire for democratic control and the needs of the modern state. The feature at the end of the chapter, *Toward Active Citizenship,* suggests some ways for you to explore how representative democracies work.

Principles of Democratic Government.   All representative democracies rest on the rule of the people as expressed through the election of government officials. In the 1790s, only free white males were able to vote, and in some states, they had to be property owners as well. Women did not receive the right to vote in national elections in the United States until 1920, and the right to vote was not really secured by African Americans until the 1960s. Today, **universal suffrage** is the rule.

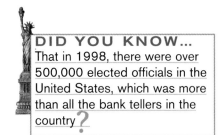

Consent of the People
The idea that governments and laws derive their legitimacy from the consent of the governed.

Republic
The form of government in which sovereignty rests with the people, who elect agents to represent them in lawmaking and other decisions.

Representative Democracy
A form of government in which representatives elected by the people make and enforce laws and policies.

Universal Suffrage
The right of all adults to vote for their representatives.

---

[4]James Madison, in Alexander Hamilton, James Madison, and John Jay, *The Federalist Papers,* No. 10 (New York: Mentor Books, 1964), p. 81. See Appendix D.
[5]See Chapter 2 for a discussion of the founders' ideas.

Granting every person the right to participate in the election of officials recognizes the equal voting power of each citizen. This emphasis on the equality of every individual before the law is central to the American system. Because everyone's vote counts equally, the only way to make fair decisions is by some form of **majority** will. But to ensure that **majority rule** does not become oppressive, modern democracies also provide guarantees of minority rights. If certain democratic principles did not protect minorities, the majority might violate the fundamental rights of members of certain groups, especially groups that are unpopular or dissimilar to the majority population. In the past, the majority has imposed such limitations on African Americans, Native Americans, and Japanese Americans, to name only a few.

One way to guarantee the continued existence of a representative democracy is to hold free, competitive elections. Thus, the minority always has the opportunity to win elective office. For such elections to be totally open, freedom of the press and speech must be preserved so that opposition candidates may present their criticisms of the government.

Constitutional Democracy.   Another key feature of Western representative democracy is that it is based on the principle of **limited government.** Not only is the government dependent on **popular sovereignty,** but the powers of the government are also clearly limited, either through a written document or through widely shared beliefs. The U.S. Constitution sets down the fundamental structure of the government and the limits to its activities. Such limits are intended to prevent political decisions based on the whims or ambitions of individuals in government rather than on constitutional principles.

Do We Have a Democracy?

The sheer size and complexity of American society seem to make it unsuitable for direct democracy on a national scale. Some scholars suggest that even representative democracy is difficult to achieve in any modern state. They point to the low level of turnout for presidential elections and the even lower turnout for local ones. Polling data have shown that many Americans

Majority
More than 50 percent.

Majority Rule
A basic principle of democracy asserting that the greatest number of citizens in any political unit should select officials and determine policies.

Limited Government
A form of government based on the principle that the powers of government should be clearly limited either through a written document or through wide public understanding; characterized by institutional checks to ensure that government serves the public rather than private interests.

Popular Sovereignty
The concept that ultimate political authority rests with the people.

Volunteers register voters in the Spanish Harlem section of New York City. By setting up a table in the neighborhood, the election officials make registration more convenient for voters as well as less threatening. Both political parties often conduct voter registration drives in the months before general elections.

are neither particularly interested in politics nor well informed. Few are able to name the persons running for Congress in their districts, and even fewer can discuss the candidates' positions. Members of Congress claim to represent their constituents, but few constituents follow the issues, much less communicate their views to their representatives. For the average citizen, the national government is too remote, too powerful, and too bureaucratic to be influenced by one vote.

Democracy for the Few

If ordinary citizens are not really making policy decisions with their votes, who is? One answer suggests that elites really govern the United States. Proponents of **elite theory** see society much as Alexander Hamilton did, who said,

> All communities divide themselves into the few and the many. The first are the rich and the wellborn, the other the mass of the people. . . . The people are turbulent and changing; they seldom judge or determine right. Give therefore to the first class a distinct, permanent share in the government. They will check the unsteadiness of the second, and as they cannot receive any advantage by a change, they therefore will ever maintain good government.

Elite theory describes an American mass population that is uninterested in politics and that is willing to let leaders make the decisions. Some versions of elite theory posit a small, cohesive elite class that makes almost all the important decisions regarding the nation,[6] whereas others suggest that voters choose among competing elites. New members of the elite are recruited through the educational system so that the brightest children of the masses allegedly have the opportunity to join the elite stratum.

In such a political system, the primary goal of the government is stability, because elites do not want any change in their status. Major social and economic change only takes place if elites see their resources threatened. This selfish interest of the elites does not mean, however, that they are necessarily undemocratic or always antiprogressive. Whereas some policies, such as favorable tax-avoidance laws, may be perceived as elitist in nature, other policies benefit many members of the public. Political scientists Thomas Dye and Harmon

Elite Theory
A perspective holding that society is ruled by a small number of people who exercise power in their self-interest.

[6]Michael Parenti, *Democracy for the Few*, 7th ed. (New York: St. Martin's Press, 1995).

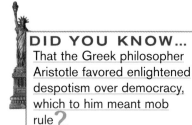

Ziegler propose that American elites are more devoted to democratic principles and rights than are most members of the mass public.[7]

Many observers contend that economic and social developments in the last several years have strengthened the perception that America is governed by an elite, privileged group. These observers believe that "the rich get richer and the poor get poorer" in this country and that, as a consequence, more and more Americans are becoming alienated from the political process. There is now an underclass of Americans that has little say in government and has little hope of being able to in the future—because the possibility of joining the elite stratum is so remote. Wealthier citizens have educational opportunities that poorer individuals believe they cannot afford. Moreover, as you will read in Chapter 10, political campaigns are expensive, and campaign costs have increased steadily each year. Today, candidates for political office, unless they can raise campaign funds from wealthy supporters or interest groups, have to drop out of the race—or not enter it in the first place. Some predict that if present trends continue, we will indeed have a "democracy for the few."

Democracy for Groups

A different school of thought looks at the characteristics of the American electorate and finds that our form of democracy is based on group interests. Even if the average citizen cannot keep up with political issues or cast a deciding vote in any election, the individual's interests will be protected by groups that represent him or her.

Theorists who subscribe to **pluralism** as a way of understanding American politics believe that people are naturally social and inclined to form associations. In the pluralists' view, politics is the struggle among groups to gain benefits for their members. Given the structures of the American political system, group conflicts tend to be settled by compromise and accommodation so that each interest is satisfied to some extent.[8]

Pluralism
A theory that views politics as a conflict among interest groups. Political decision making is characterized by bargaining and compromise.

Pluralists see public policy as resulting from group interactions carried out within Congress and the executive branch. Because there are a multitude of interests, no one group can dominate the political process. Furthermore, because most individuals have more than one interest, conflict among groups does not divide the nation into hostile camps.

There are a number of flaws in some of the basic assumptions of this theory. Among these are the relatively low number of people who formally join interest groups, the real disadvantages of pluralism for the poorer citizens, and the belief that group decision making always reflects the best interests of the nation.

With these flaws in mind, critics see a danger that groups may become so powerful that all policies become compromises crafted to satisfy the interests of the largest groups. The interests of the public as a whole, then, cannot be considered. Critics of pluralism have suggested that a democratic system can be virtually paralyzed by the struggle between interest groups. This struggle results in a condition sometimes called **hyperpluralism**, meaning that groups and their needs control the government and decision making rather than the government's acting for the good of the nation.

Hyperpluralism
A situation that arises when interest groups become so powerful that they dominate the political decision-making structures, rendering any consideration of the greater public interest impossible.

Both pluralism and elite theory attempt to explain the real workings of American democracy. Neither approach is complete, nor can either be proved. Viewing the United States as run by elites reminds us that the founders themselves were not great defenders of the mass public. In contrast, the pluralist view underscores both the advantages and the disadvantages of Americans' inclina-

[7]Thomas Dye and Harmon Ziegler, *The Irony of Democracy,* 10th ed. (Duxbury, Mass.: Wadsworth, 1996).
[8]David Truman, *The Governmental Process* (New York: Knopf, 1951); and Robert Dahl, *Who Governs?* (New Haven, Conn.: Yale University Press, 1961).

tion to join, to organize, and to pursue benefits for themselves. It points out all of the places within the American political system in which interest groups find it comfortable to work. With this knowledge, the system can be adjusted to keep interest groups within the limits of the public good.

Ideas and Politics: Political Culture

The writers of the American constitution believed that the structures they had created would provide for both democracy and a stable political system. They also believed that the nation would be sustained by its **political culture**—a concept defined as a patterned set of ideas, values, and ways of thinking about government and politics. In fact, one of the roles that the founders assigned to women in the early years of the republic was to be the guardians of the political culture and the teachers of our fundamental beliefs to generations of children.

There is considerable consensus among American citizens about certain concepts basic to the U.S. political system. Given that the vast majority of Americans are descendants of immigrants having diverse cultural and political backgrounds, how can we account for this consensus? Primarily, it is the result of **political socialization**—the process by which such beliefs and values are transmitted to new immigrants and to our children. The nation depends on several different agents to transmit to children and newcomers to our nation the precepts of our national culture.

The most obvious source of political socialization is the family. Parents teach their children about the value of participating in the political system through their example and through their approval. One of the primary functions of the public education system in the United States is to teach the values of the political culture to students through history courses, through discussions of political issues, and through the rituals of pledging allegiance to the flag and celebrating national holidays. Traditionally, political parties also have played a role in political socialization as a way to bring new voters to their ranks.

Before we discuss some of the most fundamental concepts of the American political culture, it is important to note that these values can be considered those of the **dominant culture.** The dominant culture in the United States has its roots in Western European civilization. From that civilization, American politics has inherited a bias toward individualism, private property, Judeo-Christian ethics, and, to some extent, the male domination of societal decisions. As the descendants of more recent immigrant groups, especially those from Asian and Islamic nations, become part of the American mainstream, there will be more challenges to the dominant culture. Other cultural heritages honor community or family over individualism and sometimes place far less emphasis on materialism. Additionally, changes in our own society have brought about the breakdown of some values, such as sanctity of the family structure, and the acceptance of others, such as women pursuing careers in the workplace.

Political Culture
The collection of beliefs and attitudes toward government and the political process held by a community or nation.

Political Socialization
The process through which individuals learn a set of political attitudes and form opinions about social issues. The family and the educational system are two of the most important forces in the political socialization process.

Dominant Culture
The values, customs, language, and ideals established by the group or groups in a society that traditionally have controlled politics and government institutions in that society.

The Fundamental Values

Some nations are very homogeneous, with most of their citizens having the same ethnic and religious background and sharing a common history. Achieving consensus on the basic values of the political culture is fairly easy in these nations. Because the United States is a nation of immigrants, socializing people into the political culture is an important function of the society. Over the two hundred years of its history, however, the people of the United States have formed a deep commitment to certain values and ideas. Among these are liberty, equality, and property.

Certain groups within the United States insist on maintaining their own cultural beliefs and practices. The Amish, pictured here, are descended from German religious sects and live in close communities in Pennsylvania, Ohio, Indiana, and Illinois, as well as in other states. The more conservative Amish groups do not use modern conveniences, such as automobiles or electricity, and have resisted immunizations and mandatory schooling for their children.

Liberty
The greatest freedom of individuals that is consistent with the freedom of other individuals in the society.

Liberty. The term **liberty** can be defined as the greatest freedom of individuals that is consistent with the freedom of other individuals in the society. In the United States, our civil liberties include religious freedom—both the right to practice whatever religion one chooses and freedom from any state-imposed religion. Our civil liberties also include freedom of speech—the right to express our opinions freely on matters, including government actions. Freedom of speech is perhaps one of our most prized liberties, because a democracy could not endure without it. These and other basic guarantees of liberty are not found in the body of the U.S. Constitution but in the Bill of Rights, the first ten amendments to the Constitution.

The process of ensuring liberty for all Americans did not end with the adoption of the Bill of Rights but has continued throughout our history. Political issues often turn on how a particular liberty should be interpreted or the extent to which it should be limited in the interests of society as a whole. Some of the most emotionally charged issues today, for example, have to do with whether our civil liberties include the liberty to have an abortion or (for terminally ill persons) to commit assisted suicide.

Equality
A concept that all people are of equal worth.

Equality. The Declaration of Independence states, "All men are created equal." Today, that statement has been amended by the political culture to include groups other than white males—women, African Americans, Native Americans, Asian Americans, and others. The definition of **equality,** however, has been disputed by Americans since the Revolution.[9] Does equality mean simply political equality—the right to register to vote, to cast a ballot, and to run for political office? Does equality mean equal opportunity for individuals to develop their talents and skills? If the latter is the meaning of equality, what should the United States do to ensure equal opportunities for those who are born poor, disabled, or female? As you will read in later chapters of this book, much of America's politics has concerned just such questions. Although most Americans believe strongly that all persons should have the opportunity to fulfill their potential, many disagree about whether it is the government's responsibility to eliminate economic and social differences. Interestingly, the Internet had provided

[9]Richard J. Ellis, "Rival Visions of Equality in American Political Culture," *Review of Politics,* Vol. 54 (Spring 1992), p. 254.

Americans with a forum in which all are equal—regardless of race, color, ethnic origin, gender, economic status, and the like (see the feature *Politics Wired: Anonymous, but Democratic, Debate?*).

Property. Many Americans probably remember that the "unalienable rights" asserted in the Declaration of Independence are the rights to "life, liberty, and the pursuit of happiness." The inspiration for that phrase, however, came from the writings of an English philosopher, John Locke (1632–1704), who stated that people's rights were to life, liberty, and **property**. In American political culture, the pursuit of happiness and property are considered to be closely related. Americans place great value on owning land, on acquiring material possessions, and on the monetary value of jobs. Property can be seen as giving its owner political power and the liberty to do whatever he or she wants. At the same time, the ownership of property immediately creates inequality in society. The desire to own property, however, is so widespread among all classes of Americans that socialist movements, which advocate the redistribution of wealth and property, have had a difficult time securing a wide following here.

Democracy, liberty, equality, and property—these concepts lie at the core of American political culture. Other issues—such as majority rule, popular sovereignty, and **fraternity**—are closely related to them. These fundamental principles are so deeply ingrained in U.S. culture that most Americans rarely question them. (See this chapter's *Critical Perspective* on pages 18 and 19 for a further discussion of what Americans believe.)

The Stability of the Culture

Political culture plays an important role in holding society together, because the system of ideas at the core of that culture must persuade people to support the existing political process through their attitudes and participation. If people

DID YOU KNOW...
That the Pledge of Allegiance was written by two journalists as a promotional stunt for a children's magazine, *Youth's Companion,* to be recited by children on Columbus Day in 1892?

Property
Anything that is or may be subject to ownership. As conceived by the political philosopher John Locke, the right to property is a natural right superior to human law (laws made by government).

Fraternity
From the Latin *fraternus* (brother), a term that came to mean, in the political philosophy of the eighteenth century, the condition in which each individual considers the needs of all others; a brotherhood. In the French Revolution of 1789, the popular cry was "liberty, equality, and fraternity."

POLITICS WIRED

Anonymous, but Democratic, Debate?

By most measures, more than 40 percent of American homes are connected to the Internet through personal computers and telephone modems. Millions of other Americans can access the Internet through libraries, schools, and universities. One phenomenon of the World Wide Web is the "chat room," in which individuals can "discuss" any issue anonymously by using a moniker or an Internet nickname. Most private commercial services, such as America Online, set up chat rooms for individuals based on hobbies or other common topics. Some chat rooms are geared toward adults, while others are geared toward all ages of participants.

One of the most fascinating aspects of Web anonymity is that many people are willing to share opinions about extremely sensitive topics—such as sex, drugs, racism, and religion—that they would not share in face-to-face discussions. Internet users are protected from the reactions of their "conversational" partners by distance, anonymity, and the fact that there are no facial or body signals to observe in the group. When America Online opened a special site called "Race Relations in Black and White," it attracted more than three thousand messages in one month. Children spoke to their elders, and whites and African Americans expressed their views on race in America.

Such public debate about hot topics is undoubtedly valuable to a free society. Of course, everyone cannot join in, because the benefit is restricted to the participants. And it cannot truly be said to meet the ideals of a direct democracy like that of ancient Athens in Greece, because the participants are masked by the nature of the Internet: although anonymity allows participants to be free from embarrassment, it also means that they cannot be held accountable for their views.

FOR CRITICAL ANALYSIS

Do you think that online discussions about political topics can have an impact on the political system?

Critical perspective

What Do Americans Believe?

Although it is fairly easy to articulate the ideals and values that are "shared" within the American political culture, obviously there are great differences within the American people over how these values are applied to political issues. In fact, given the wide variety of subcultures, ethnic groups, religious denominations and adherents, and generations that share this society, how much support is there within the public for the basic tenets of the American political dream?

Do We Believe in Liberty, Equality, and the Pursuit of Happiness?

According to the 1996 Survey of American Political Culture,* Americans as a whole show very strong support for the basic ideals of American culture. On the question of liberty, 74 percent of those surveyed said that it was essential to teach our children that "our founders limited the power of government so government would not intrude too much into the lives of its citizens." Additionally, 83 percent believed that it is essential to teach that "American democracy is only as strong as the virtue of its citizens."

The belief in equality for all Americans remains strong. In a 1994 survey, more than 70 percent of those polled said that they personally believed in the Declaration of Independence's proclamation of equality of all Americans. The 1996 political culture survey found that 83 percent of the respondents believed that it was essential to teach our children that "with hard work and perseverance, anyone can succeed in America," and 90 percent said that it was an essential or very important obligation of every American citizen to "treat . . . all people equally regardless of race or ethnic background." Americans have considerable doubt about whether this principle

*The public opinion data cited above are found in the following articles: "American Opinion in the 1990s," *The Public Perspective*, February/March 1998; "Americans Rate Their Society and Chart Its Values," *The Public Perspective*, February/March 1997; and "Americans' Ideas and Ideals," *The Public Perspective*, April/May 1995.

actually is honored in the United States, however. In a 1995 survey, 51 percent stated that most Americans do not have an equal chance to succeed in life, and 49 percent said that they do have such a chance. Additionally, only 60 percent of Americans believe that black Americans have an equal chance to succeed, and just 62 percent see the same kind of opportunity for women (1995).

If we define "the pursuit of happiness" as everyone succeeding, it is clear that this is a closely held value for most Americans (remember, 83 percent want this taught to children). A 1998 survey comparing the views of immigrants to native-born Americans found that 85 percent of all adults believed that "people who work hard to better themselves can get ahead in this country"; immigrants subscribed to this belief at the rate of 93 percent. For many Americans, this belief that all persons can get ahead is rooted in individual responsibility. While 49 percent feel that the poor have hard lives, 62 percent believe that the cause of poverty is that "people are not doing enough to help themselves out of poverty." Only 31 percent of Americans view people's circumstances as the cause of their poverty.

Are These Values Being Transmitted?

As noted in the text, the values that are the foundation of American political culture need to be transmitted to the next generation in order for the culture to survive over time. The agents of political socialization include families, schools, peers, and the media. Surveys of the public show that moral values have changed fairly substantially since World War II, with premarital sex and living together before marriage now widely accepted by those under sixty years of age. A majority of Americans approve of sex education in the schools and of making birth control available to teenagers.

Political values show none of this generational change. As the accompanying table indicates, when asked about the essential obligations of American citizenship, Americans between the ages of

begin to doubt the ideas underlying the culture, they will not transmit those beliefs to their children or support the existing political processes.

Consider that some subgroups, such as Native Americans and the Amish, have made concerted efforts to preserve their language or cultural practices. Many immigrant groups, including Hispanics, Asian Americans, and Caribbean Americans, maintain their language or cultural values within American cities and states. The question is whether these subgroups also subscribe to the values of the American political culture.

Critical perspective

What Do Americans Believe?—continued

eighteen and thirty-four give responses almost identical to those of the general adult population. Not only do younger and older Americans agree about the most important obligations, but they place them in exactly the same order of priority.

YOUTH ENDORSE SAME VALUES AS ALL AMERICANS

The table below compares the responses of younger Americans to all age groups when asked whether each of a series of statements was "an essential obligation of all Americans."

STATEMENT	18 TO 34 YR OLDS	ALL AGES SURVEYED
	(PERCENT SAYING ESSENTIAL OR VERY IMPORTANT OBLIGATION)	
Treating all people equally regardless of race or ethnic background	90%	90%
Reporting a crime one witnessed	89%	89%
Taking action if you hear someone screaming or being attacked	87%	88%
Being able to speak and read English	84%	86%
Voting in elections	80%	82%
Working to reduce inequality/injustice	83%	83%
Being civil to those with whom we disagree	78%	80%
Keeping fully informed about the news and public issues	69%	72%
Donating blood or organs for medical needs	56%	57%
Volunteering time to community service	56%	58%

SOURCE: "The 1996 Survey of American Political Culture," conducted by the Gallup Organization in 1996 and reported in *The Public Perspective*, February/March 1997, pp. 14–15.

What Is the Proper Role for the Government?

As noted in this chapter, the American system of government is a careful balance of democratic principles that allow for change and a set of government institutions that aim to create stability in the political system. Today, Americans have relatively little faith in the government's ability to solve the nation's problems. While 83 percent believe that the United States has the best system of government in the world, 67 percent say that it works well but needs some changes. When asked about their satisfaction with the system, 57 percent are mostly or very unsatisfied with the country's political system. In general, Americans believe that government has too much power (66 percent), should cut spending (83 percent), and should not attempt to redistribute wealth or provide jobs for all. Finally, Americans do believe that a decline in moral and ethical standards among people in politics and government is a major problem for government today.

What should we make of these measures of support for the system? Support for the basic values in the American political culture is strong, but contained within that support is an awareness among the American public that we are not living up to the promises of that system. The society is widely regarded as suffering from a decline in morality and values, and the government is seen as more of a problem than a solution. Such a gap between our beliefs and the facts of the situation can make Americans distrustful of the system or strongly interested in reform.

FOR CRITICAL ANALYSIS

1. Do you agree that "with hard work and perseverance, anyone can succeed in America"? Why or why not?
2. With respect to morality and values, why is the government seen as "more of a problem than a solution"?

Studies of immigrant groups and ethnic subgroups generally have shown that they are as supportive of the concepts of American political culture as other Americans are. For example, when asked if they would rather live in the United States than anywhere else, 95 percent of whites said the United States, as did 87 percent of African American respondents and 92 percent of Hispanics. Some surveys have shown that immigrants are even more enthusiastic about American values than native-born respondents. As shown in Figure 1–1 on the next page, immigrants are less supportive of holding on to their own culture than are adults in the general population.

FIGURE 1-1

Immigrants Adopt American Culture

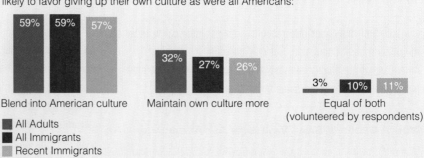

In a recent Gallup poll, those surveyed were asked to respond to the following question: "Which do you think is better for the United States—to encourage immigrants to blend into American culture by giving up some important aspects of their own culture or to encourage immigrants to maintain their own culture more strongly, even if that means they do not blend in as well?" Responses indicated that the most recent immigrants were almost as likely to favor giving up their own culture as were all Americans:

59% 59% 57%

32% 27% 26%

3% 10% 11%

Blend into American culture   Maintain own culture more   Equal of both (volunteered by respondents)

■ All Adults
■ All Immigrants
■ Recent Immigrants

SOURCE: Survey by the Gallup Organization for CNN/*USA Today,* reported in *The Public Perspective,* February/March 1998, p. 52.

The Changing Face of America

The face of America is changing as its citizens age, become more diverse, and generate new needs for laws and policies. Long a nation of growth, the United States has become a middle-aged nation with a low birthrate and an increasing number of older citizens who want services from the government. The 1990 census showed that between 1980 and 1990, the U.S. population grew only 9.8 percent, the second lowest rate of growth in the history of taking such measurements.

Several aspects of this population trend have significant political consequences. As Figure 1–2 shows, the population is aging quickly; the median age

Hispanic Americans join together to support a political candidate. Like other ethnic groups, these Hispanic voters seek to have their concerns heard by the candidates. In return, political candidates try to show their appreciation for the culture of the ethnic voters by delivering speeches in their language or promising more benefits for the group.

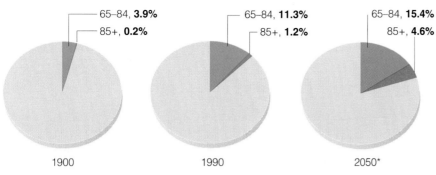

65–84, **3.9%**
85+, **0.2%**

65–84, **11.3%**
85+, **1.2%**

65–84, **15.4%**
85+, **4.6%**

1900   1990   2050*

SOURCE: U.S. Census Bureau, 1998.

FIGURE 1-2

Elderly Population by Age

(the age at which half the people are older and half are younger) will reach thirty-five by the year 2000. Even more startling is the fact that almost 13 percent of the population is now sixty-five years old or older. By the year 2030, more than 20 percent of the population will be retired or approaching retirement. If the current retirement and pension systems remain in place, including Social Security, a very large proportion of each worker's wages will have to be deducted to support benefits for the retired.

Ethnic Change

The ethnic character of the United States is also changing. Whites have a very low birthrate, whereas African Americans and Hispanics have more children per family. As displayed in Figure 1–3, including the effects of immigration, the proportion of whites has decreased, and the proportions of Hispanics, African Americans, and Asian Americans have increased.

Although studies show that the various groups in this country share many common values, conflicts between ethnic and racial groups also exist. These

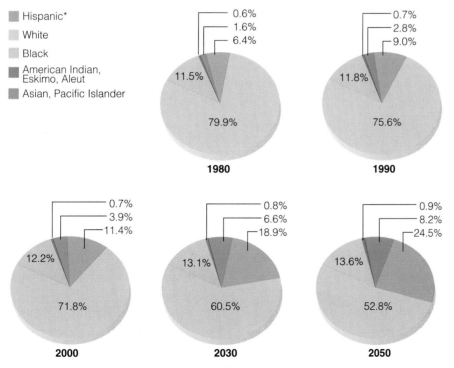

■ Hispanic*
  White
  Black
■ American Indian, Eskimo, Aleut
■ Asian, Pacific Islander

0.6%
1.6%
6.4%
11.5%
79.9%
1980

0.7%
2.8%
9.0%
11.8%
75.6%
1990

0.7%
3.9%
11.4%
12.2%
71.8%
2000

0.8%
6.6%
18.9%
13.1%
60.5%
2030

0.9%
8.2%
24.5%
13.6%
52.8%
2050

FIGURE 1-3

Distribution of the U.S. Population by Race and Hispanic Origin, 1980 to 2050

* Persons of Hispanic origin can be of any race. Data for 2000 and beyond are estimates.

SOURCE: U.S. Census Bureau.

Each year thousands of immigrants are sworn in as new U.S. citizens. The U.S. Constitution in Article II, Section 8, declares that Congress shall have the power to "establish a uniform Rule of Naturalization." Naturalization is the process by which individuals who are not yet citizens become U.S. citizens. Such individuals are called naturalized citizens as opposed to native-born citizens. There are myriad requirements to become a naturalized citizen. Because it is often difficult to do so, many immigrants remain in this country without proper documentation.

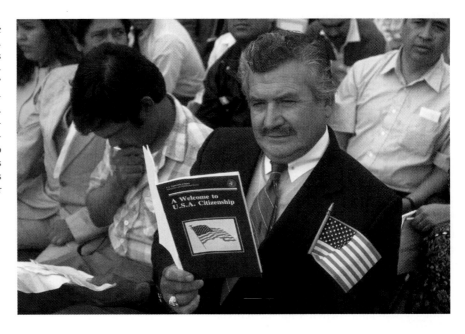

I N F O T R A C ®
COLLEGE EDITION

"More to Come Costs of Immigration"

FIGURE 1-4

Immigration as a Percentage of Total U.S. Population Growth, 1901 to Present

conflicts all too often erupt into "hate speech" or "hate crimes," which pose an increasing threat to political stability. There is no reason to assume that these and other divisive forces at work in our society cannot be overcome, but there is also no reason to ignore them. Consider, for example, the results of a recent *Newsweek* poll, in which respondents were asked the following question: "One hundred years from today, will the United States still exist as one nation?" Forty-eight percent of the African American respondents answered "No" to this question, as did 26 percent of white respondents and 38 percent of Hispanic respondents.

Immigrants are also likely to shape American politics in the future. Few Americans think of the current period in our history as being as volatile as the early years of the twentieth century, when millions of Europeans immigrated to the United States. Yet, as Figure 1–4 shows, the percentage of population growth attributed to immigration was about as high by 1990 as it was before World War I. In 1998, more than 1.7 million persons immigrated to the United States legally,

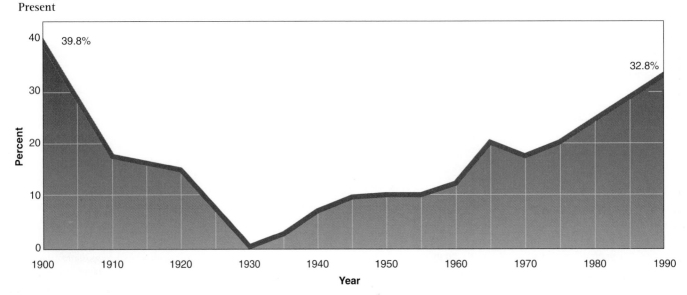

SOURCE: U.S. Immigration and Naturalization Service, Population Reference Bureau, *Population Bureau (1986),* and U.S. Bureau of the Census, *1990 Census Profile (1991),* as cited in *Universal Almanac 1996* (Kansas City, Mo.: Andrews and McMeel, 1996).

with the greatest number coming from Mexico, but sizable numbers from Asian nations as well. These changes are placing strain on the cohesiveness of U.S. political culture and on the willingness of citizens to support the political structures of the nation.

Other Trends

Other changes in the face of America have more to do with our changing society. More Americans continue to fill the urban places of the nation in comparison with rural areas. By 1999, more than 75 percent of the population lived in an urban environment. Women continued to increase their participation in the educational system. By the beginning of this decade, as many women as men had completed their high school educations, and the percentage of women who had completed college continued to grow.

Change also continues in the structure of American families, although the traditional two-parent family is still very strong. Just twenty years ago, more than 85 percent of children lived in a two-parent family. Today, 71 percent of children under age eighteen live in two-parent families, and 25 percent live with only one parent. About one-fourth of the children of one-parent families live in poverty.

Other changes also have consequences for social policies. Although the national government has been committed to ending poverty since the mid-1960s, 13.5 percent of all Americans still live in households that have incomes below the official poverty line. Although this number is large, it is below the 22 percent figure recorded in 1960. Far more alarming is the trend in prison populations. Since 1980, the number of persons incarcerated in state and federal prisons has increased from about a half a million to more than 1.7 million.

Also emerging as a part of the American landscape are citizens' militias or "patriot" groups. While members of these groups might say that they are proud to be Americans, many in these groups view the national government as the enemy—not the protector—of civil rights and liberties. Animosity toward the national government, for whatever reason, is thought to have motivated the 1995 bombing of the Oklahoma City Alfred P. Murrah Federal Building and some other terrorist acts against government bureaucrats, particularly in the West. Finally, recent national surveys have found that about one-fifth of all Americans are barely literate and have difficulty dealing with simple documents.

Each of these statistics raises political questions for the society as a whole. These facts challenge voters and their representatives to change policies in order to reduce poverty, crime, and illiteracy—if society can agree on how to accomplish these tasks. Another challenging problem of our time is terrorism, as discussed in this chapter's *Politics and Ideology*.

Ideas and Politics: Ideology

An **ideology** is a closely linked set of beliefs about the goal of politics and the most desirable political order. True ideologies are well-organized theories that can guide virtually every decision that an individual or society can make. As discussed on page 25 in this chapter's *Politics and Comparative Systems: Competing Visions of Power,* the major ideologies of our time are usually represented as a continuum from far left to far right according to their views of the power of government. Few Americans, however, derive their views on politics from the more extreme ideologies. In fact, the U.S. political spectrum has been dominated for decades by two relatively moderate ideological positions: **liberalism** and **conservatism.**

For Americans, terrorism always seemed to be a problem for other countries. Recently, though, terrorism on American soil has occurred, such as the 1995 bombing of the Alfred P. Murrah Federal Building in Oklahoma City. A crude, but effective, home-made bomb was detonated at the base of this building, killing 168 persons and injuring hundreds of others. It is thought that those convicted of the crime were affiliated with a local militia group.

Ideology
A comprehensive and logically ordered set of beliefs about the nature of people and about the institutions and role of government.

Liberalism
A set of beliefs that includes the advocacy of positive government action to improve the welfare of individuals, support for civil rights, and tolerance for political and social change.

Conservatism
A set of beliefs that includes a limited role for the national government in helping individuals, support for traditional values and lifestyles, and a cautious response to change.

POLITICS and Ideology

Beyond Ideology: Terrorism

One of the most troubling aspects of political ideology is that, if carried to an extreme, it can lead to violent acts that destroy the life, liberty, and property of others. Terrorism, to a significant extent, is linked to extremist political views. Sometimes, these views are held by a group. For example, if a bomb explodes in London, people assume that it is probably the work of the Irish Republican Army. The numerous bombings in Paris in 1995 were almost all tied to Algerian extremists. The killing of Israeli athletes during the 1972 Olympics in Munich, Germany, was connected to long-standing Palestine-Israel hostilities. Terrorist acts also have been sponsored by national governments, particularly by the Middle Eastern nations of Libya, Iraq, Iran, and the Sudan. Still other terrorist acts have been the work of a single individual, such as the Unabomber, a loner who conducted an almost two-decade reign of terror in the United States.

Traditionally, the United States has been a relatively safe haven from terrorism, with fewer terrorist incidents than any nation in the world. Since 1993, however, when a powerful terrorist bomb exploded in New York's World Trade Center, a rash of terrorist acts has occurred in this country. The bombing of the Oklahoma City Alfred P. Murrah Federal Building in 1995 killed 168 persons and injured hundreds of others. A pipe bomb hidden in a knapsack exploded at a public concert held to celebrate the Olympics in Atlanta, Georgia, killing two persons and injur-

President Clinton eulogizes the slain Capitol police officers who were killed in 1998 by a gunman who pushed past the security gate.

ing more than one hundred others.

The August 1998 bombing of two U.S. embassies in Africa underscored the urgent need to find solutions to the problem of terrorism. The bombings killed over 250 people, including 12 Americans, and injured more than 5,500 others.

Congress began to take action in 1996, when it provided $1 billion over four years to combat terrorism. Congress also modified immigration and political-asylum rules in an attempt to make it more difficult for potential terrorists to enter this country. Congress has considered an antiterrorism bill that would tighten airport security and allow suspected terrorists to be prosecuted under federal racketeering laws.

Law-enforcement agencies have responded to terrorist

attacks with swift investigations, arrests, and prosecutions. The individuals responsible for the World Trade Center bombing have been tried and convicted. Timothy McVeigh was convicted and sentenced to death in 1997 for the execution of the Oklahoma City bombing although his accused accomplice, Terry Nichols, received a life sentence. The unilateral terrorist campaign waged against professors and corporate leaders by the Unabomber came to a halt when Theodore Kaczynsky was arrested and then pled guilty to his crimes in 1998.

On August 20, 1998, less than three weeks after the American embassies in Africa were bombed, the United States retaliated with force. In an unprecedented move, President Clinton ordered Tomahawk cruise missile air strikes against terrorist camps

in Afghanistan and Sudan. The camps were apparently operated by groups loyal to Osama bin Laden, a wealthy Saudi Arabian exile who was thought to be responsible for the embassy bombings, as well as for other terrorist acts against the United States in the past ten years.

Combating terrorism is difficult because, typically, terrorist acts are random, diverse and unpredictable. Additionally, effective attempts to curb terrorism may involve trading off certain civil liberties, particularly the right to privacy.

FOR CRITICAL ANALYSIS

What liberties and privacy rights would you be willing to sacrifice in order to achieve protection against terrorist acts?

POLITICS and Comparative Systems

Competing Visions of Power

Political ideologies offer their adherents well-organized theories. These theories propose goals for the society and the political means by which those goals can be achieved. At the core of every political ideology is a set of values that guides its theory of governmental power. If we compare political ideologies on the basis of how much power the government should have within a society, we can array them on a continuum from left to right, as shown in the first box below.

For each of these ideological positions, the amount of power granted to the government is intended to achieve a certain set of goals within the society, and the perfect society would completely achieve these values. The values are arrayed in the second box below.

In the United States, there are adherents of each of these ideological positions. Given widely shared cultural values, however, only two of these belief systems consistently have played a central part in American political debates: liberalism and conservatism.

FOR CRITICAL ANALYSIS

What kinds of activities do you believe the government should control? When is government action most effective? Does answering those questions help you identify with one of the ideological positions described below?

How Much Power Should the Government Have?

MARXISM-LENINISM	SOCIALISM	LIBERALISM	CONSERVATISM	LIBERTARIANISM
Central control of economy and political system.	Active government control of major economic sectors.	Positive government action in economy and to achieve social goals.	Positive government action to support capitalism; action to uphold certain values.	Government action only for defense; almost no regulation of economy or individual behavior.

What Values Should the Government Pursue?

MARXISM-LENINISM	SOCIALISM	LIBERALISM	CONSERVATISM	LIBERTARIANISM
Total equality and security; unity and solidarity.	Economic equality; community.	Political liberty; economic security; equal opportunity.	Political liberty; economic liberty; order.	Total political and economic liberty for individuals.

American liberals believe that government should take strong positive action to solve the nation's economic and social problems. They believe that it is the obligation of the government to enhance opportunities for the economic and social equality of all individuals. Liberals tend to support programs to reduce poverty, to endorse progressive taxation to redistribute income from wealthier classes to the poorer, and to rely on government regulation to guide the activities of business and the economy.

Conservatives take a quite different approach to the role of government in the economy, believing that the private sector probably can outperform the government in almost any activity. Believing that the individual is primarily responsible for his or her own well-being, conservatives are less supportive of government initiatives to redistribute income or to craft programs that will change the status of individuals.

In the moral sphere, conservatives tend to support more government regulation of social values and moral decisions than do liberals. Thus, conservatives tend to oppose gay rights legislation and propose stronger curbs on pornography. Liberals usually show greater tolerance for different life choices and oppose government attempts to regulate personal behavior and morals.

Individuals in the society may not accept the full range of either liberal or conservative views. It is not unusual for Americans to be quite liberal on economic issues and supportive of considerable government intervention in the economy while holding conservative views on moral and social issues. Such a

INFOTRAC ®
COLLEGE EDITION

"America Fights Back Clinton Raises the Stakes"

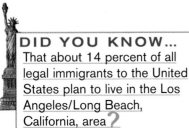

mixture of views makes it difficult for American political parties to identify themselves solely with either a conservative or liberal viewpoint, because such a position may cost them votes on specific issues.

There are also smaller groups of Americans who consider themselves to be communists, socialists, or libertarians, but these groups play a minor role in the national political arena. The limited role played by these and other alternative political perspectives is reinforced by the fact that they receive little positive exposure in classrooms, the media, or public discourse.

America's Politics: Issues for the New Century

Although the U.S. government is one of the oldest democratic regimes in the world and its Constitution remains relatively unchanged more than two hundred years after it was written, the U.S. political system has been dynamic since its founding. As you will read in the chapters that follow, Americans have changed their ideas about who votes and who controls the government, expanded their list of rights and liberties, originated and then revised a number of political parties, and significantly altered their view of the role of the national government in their lives and businesses.

Like the people of the nations of Eastern Europe and the former Soviet republics, the citizens of the United States have often pressed to make their government more responsive to the needs of the society and more effective in its functioning. What makes Americans different from the people of those other nations is a long and stable history that encourages them to try to modify the political structures and processes rather than invent totally new ones. Changing the political machinery has brought changes in the past—witness the social legislation of the New Deal in the 1930s and the Great Society in the 1960s—and Americans generally believe that significant change can occur again.

What are some of the American political tasks that remain unfinished as we enter the new century? Clearly, Americans struggle to keep a cohesive society as people become more diverse in terms of ethnic and racial backgrounds, generational expectations, and economic level. How can a wider range of Americans participate in the political process and make the process work for them? What kinds of institutions and policies can meet the demands of world markets, the needs of an aging population, the expectations of a society with instant media access, and the hopes of the youngest generations for jobs and opportunities similar to those given to their parents and grandparents? Many alternatives are up for debate: the decentralization of power to the states, new approaches to welfare and education reform, universal access to the Internet to connect all Americans, and hundreds more.

The remainder of this book will examine the roots and structures of contemporary American government and politics, with particular attention to the ways in which they have changed over time. At the end of each chapter, we will consider the issues that face the United States at the beginning of the twenty-first century—whether those issues involve the expansion of civil liberties or attempts to curb the power of interest groups. Without a doubt, there is enough unfinished business to last many decades. Also without a doubt, Americans will make political changes as they see fit.

TOWARD ACTIVE CITIZENSHIP

SEEING DEMOCRACY IN ACTION

One way to begin understanding the American political system is to observe a legislative body in action. There are thousands of elected legislatures in the United States at all levels of government. You might choose to visit the city council, a school board, the township board of trustees, the state legislature, or the U.S. Congress. Before attending a business session of the legislature, try to find out how the members are elected. Are they chosen by the "at-large" method of election so that each member represents the whole community, or are they chosen by specific geographic districts or wards? Some other questions you might want to ask are these: Is there a chairperson or official leader who controls the meetings and who may have more power than the other leaders? What are the responsibilities of this legislature? Are the members paid political officials, or do they volunteer their services? Do the officials serve as full-time or part-time employees?

When you visit the legislature, keep in mind the theory of representative democracy. The legislators or council members are elected to represent their constituents (those who voted them into office). Observe how often the members refer to their constituents or to the special needs of their community or electoral district. Listen carefully for the sources of conflict within a community. If there is a debate, for example, over a zoning proposal that involves the issue of land use, try to figure out why some members oppose the proposal. Perhaps the greatest sources of conflict in local government are questions of taxation and expenditure. It is important to remember that the council or board is also supposed to be working toward the good of the whole; listen for discussions of the community's priorities.

If you want to follow up on your visit and learn more about representative government in action, try to get a brief interview with one of the members of the council or board. In general, legislators are very willing to talk to students, particularly students who also are voters. Ask the member how he or she sees the job of representative. How can the wishes of the constituents be identified? How does the representative balance the needs of the ward or district with the good of the whole community? You also might ask the member how he or she keeps in touch with constituents and informs them of the activities of the council or board.

For a different view of democracy in action, watch the activities of the House of Representatives or Senate on one of the C-SPAN channels on cable television. These public television channels show speeches and actions on the floor of both chambers, broadcast committee hearings when possible, and televise interviews with government officials and the journalists who cover government and politics. If you watch the action on the floor of the House, for example, notice how few members actually are present. Is the member addressing his or her colleagues, or the voters back home? Why do you think members use large charts and graphs? Most observers of Congress believe that members dress differently and use a different speaking style since the proceedings have been televised.

Think about the advantages and disadvantages of representative democracy. Do you think the average citizen would take the time to consider all of the issues that representatives must debate? Do you think that, on the whole, the elected representatives act responsibly for their constituents?

To find out when and where the local legislative bodies meet, look up the number of the city hall or county building in the telephone directory, and call the clerk of council. You might also check cable television listings. In many communities, city council meetings and county board meetings can be seen on public access channels. For information on the structure of your local government, contact the local chapter of the League of Women Voters.

Many cities and almost all state governments have Internet Web sites to investigate. Take a look at some of these, and consider the usefulness of the information provided there to the average citizen.

Key terms

anarchy 9	government 7	political culture 15
aristocracy 9	hyperpluralism 14	political socialization 15
authority 8	ideology 23	politics 7
compliance 8	initiative 10	popular sovereignty 12
consent of the people 11	institution 6	power 8
conservatism 23	legislature 10	property 17
democracy 9	legitimacy 8	recall 10
direct democracy 10	liberalism 23	referendum 10
divided government 5	liberty 16	representative democracy 11
dominant culture 15	limited government 12	republic 11
elite 9	majority 12	totalitarian regime 8
elite theory 13	majority rule 12	universal suffrage 11
equality 16	oligarchy 9	
fraternity 17	pluralism 14	

Chapter summary

1 The willingness of Americans to debate new initiatives and to demand changes in the way the government works is at the core of our democratic nation. Americans worked hard to establish this form of government and continue to expend effort in politics to keep it functioning.

2 *Politics* was defined by Harold Lasswell as the process of "who gets what, when, and how" in a society. David Easton defined it as the "authoritative allocation of values" in a society. The prerogative of government to make allocative decisions is based on authority, legitimacy, and power. Sources of power include direct democracy, a system of government in which political decisions are made by the people directly.

3 Fearing the problems of a direct democracy, the framers of the Constitution set up a representative, or indirect, democracy. The people control the government through the election of representatives. Decisions are made by majority rule, although the rights of minorities are protected.

4 Some scholars believe that most of the power in our society is held by elite leaders who actively influence political decisions, while the masses are apathetic. The pluralist viewpoint, in contrast, suggests that groups that represent the different interests of the people struggle for political power. In pluralist theory, the political process is characterized by bargaining and compromise between groups.

5 The American political system is characterized by a set of cultural beliefs that includes liberty, equality, and property. These beliefs are passed on to each generation of Americans through the process of political socialization.

6 The face of America is changing as the population ages and becomes more ethnically diverse. Other changes—including the urbanization of the population, the growing number of women in the workforce, and poverty—are also altering the face of the nation.

7 Americans' ideas about how government should act in their lives vary widely. These views may be included in liberal, conservative, or other ideological positions. Certain ideology, when carried to an extreme, can lead to terrorist acts.

Selected print and electronic resources

SUGGESTED READINGS

Brinkley, Alan. *Liberalism and Its Discontents.* Cambridge, Mass.: Harvard University Press, 1998. The author explores how cultural changes and alternative political traditions have undermined the liberal tradition.

Lasswell, Harold. *Politics: Who Gets What, When and How.* New York: McGraw-Hill, 1936. This classic work defines the nature of politics.

Stanley, Harold W., and Richard G. Niemi. *Vital Statistics on American Politics,* 6th ed. Washington, D.C.: Congressional Quarterly Press, 1997. This valuable reference work contains over two hundred tables and figures on a wide range of topics covering almost all aspects of American politics.

Tocqueville, Alexis de. *Democracy in America.* Edited by Phillips Bradley. New York: Vintage Books, 1945. Life in the United States was described by a French writer who traveled through the nation in the 1820s.

Will, George F. *The Woven Figure: Conservatism and America's Fabric, 1994–1997*. New York: Scribner, 1997. In a series of essays, this well-known conservative political columnist offers an honest analysis of both the strong points and the flaws of American conservativism.

Wolfe, Alan. *One Nation, After All: How the Middle Class Really Think about God, Country, and Family*. New York: Viking Press, 1998. Based on the results of a survey he conducted, sociologist Alan Wolfe concludes that middle-class Americans are far less polarized politically, far less judgmental, and much more tolerant and willing to compromise than is often thought.

MEDIA RESOURCES

All Things Considered—A daily broadcast of National Public Radio that provides extensive coverage of political, economic, and social news stories.

Mr. Smith Goes to Washington—A classic movie, produced in 1939, starring Jimmy Stewart as the honest citizen who goes to Congress trying to represent his fellow citizens. The movie dramatizes the clash between representing principles and representing corrupt interests.

Logging on

The World Wide Web is becoming a virtual library, a telephone directory, a contact source, and a vehicle to improve your learning and understanding of issues. It therefore is important that you become familiar with Web resources. To help you do this, we have included *Logging On* sections at the end of each chapter in this book. Each of these sections contains a list of Internet addresses, or uniform resource locators (URLs), followed by an Internet exercise. The URLs will help you find information on topics covered within the chapters, as well as on related topics that you might find interesting. We hope this feature will lead you to some of the most interesting and productive Web locations.

The Internet should be approached with care. You should be very careful in giving out information about yourself. You also need to use good judgment because the reliability or intent of any given Web site is often unknown. Some sites are more concerned with accuracy than others, and some sites are updated to include current information, while others are not. Also, realize that sites come and go continually, so some of the Web sites that we include in these *Logging On* features may not exist by the time you read this book.

We also have a powerful and interesting Web site for the textbook, which you can find at

www.schmidt.politics.wadsworth.com/

This site has many features directly related to the textbook, including the site's most popular item—the test-review questions.

You will also want to check out the Wadsworth Political Science Resource Center for additional information and learning opportunities. The URL for this site is

politicalscience.wadsworth.com/

Finally, you may want to visit the home page of Dr. Politics—offered by Steffen Schmidt, one of the authors of this book—for some interesting ideas and activities relating to American government and politics. Go to

www.public.iastate.edu/~sws/ homepage.html

For discussion of current public-policy issues that are facing the American political system, try the resources at the Institute for Philosophy and Public Policy at

www.puaf.umd.edu/ippp/

Information about the rules and requirements for immigration and citizenship can be found at the Web site of the U.S. Immigration and Naturalization Service:

www.ins.usdoj.gov

For a basic "front door" to almost all U.S. government Web sites, click onto the very useful site maintained by the University of Michigan:

www.lib.umich.edu/libhome/Documents.center/ govweb.html

Using the internet for political analysis

The Internet is an excellent place for political organizations and interest groups to advertise their positions and to try to increase the number of Americans who support their causes. Take a look at the Web sites of two of the most prominent political "think tanks" and then try to identify the differences between their positions on one or two critical issues. The two Web sites to visit are the following:

The Heritage Foundation, at **www.heritage.org**

People for the American Way, at **www.pfaw.org**

Take note of the policies that are discussed at each site and try to figure out the "liberal" and "conservative" points of view on at least two topics.

chapter 2

The Constitution

¿what if

Constitutional Interpretation Never Changed?

BACKGROUND

OUR CONSTITUTION IS THE OLDEST WRITTEN CONSTITUTION IN THE WORLD TODAY. ONE OF THE REASONS IT HAS ENDURED IS THAT THE FRAMERS USED BROAD ENOUGH LANGUAGE TO ALLOW ROOM FOR INTERPRETATION. THE U.S. SUPREME COURT HAS BECOME THE ULTIMATE DECISION MAKER WHEN IT COMES TO DECIDING WHAT THE SEVEN THOUSAND WORDS IN OUR CONSTITUTION MEAN AND HOW THEY SHOULD BE APPLIED. BUT THE VIEWS OF THE JUSTICES OF THE SUPREME COURT HAVE CHANGED OVER TIME AS SOCIETY HAS CHANGED. AND SOCIETY HAS CHANGED, AT LEAST IN PART, BECAUSE OF CHANGES IN TECHNOLOGY ISSUES CONCERNING TELEPHONE CONVERSATIONS AND TRANSMISSION OF IDEAS OVER THE INTERNET CERTAINLY WERE NOT EVEN PIPE DREAMS TWO HUNDRED YEARS AGO. BECAUSE THE PRINCIPLES IN OUR CONSTITUTION ARE BROADLY EXPRESSED, THE SUPREME COURT HAS BEEN ABLE TO APPLY THOSE PRINCIPLES TO MEET THE NEEDS OF NEW GENERATIONS. BECAUSE OF ITS FLEXIBILITY AND ADAPTABILITY, OUR CONSTITUTION IS OFTEN REFERRED TO AS A "LIVING CONSTITUTION."

WHAT IF CONSTITUTIONAL INTERPRETATION NEVER CHANGED?

Some students of our Constitution believe that the way the Constitution is interpreted and applied should never change. Assume for a moment that whatever was in the minds of the framers some two hundred years ago remained the backbone of present-day views of the supreme law of the land. What kind of society would we have?

A RESTRICTED VIEW OF THE COMMERCE CLAUSE

Consider first the commerce clause. That clause, which is found in Article I, Section 8, of the Constitution, states that "Congress shall have the power" to "regulate Commerce . . . among the several States." The key to understanding the commerce clause is that it presumably concerns only *interstate* commerce—what goes on between and among the several states. The clause says nothing about Congress regulating activities within states (*intrastate* commerce).

The interpretation of the power of the national government to regulate all commerce has clearly changed since the framers first penned the above words. Over time, the Supreme Court has interpreted the commerce clause to mean that Congress has the power to regulate not only interstate commerce, but also any intrastate commerce that has a "substantial effect" on interstate commerce.

If the Supreme Court had not interpreted the commerce clause so expansively, our nation would be vastly different today. Many of the regulatory activities of the national government would not exist. Indeed, the national government would be a fraction of its size (but perhaps the state and local governments would be larger).

CIVIL RIGHTS AND LIBERTIES

The first ten amendments to the Constitution, the Bill of Rights, lay out the basic rights that all citizens shall enjoy. Many of the crucial issues with respect to our personal rights and liberties were not even conceived of two hundred years ago. Consider the Fourth Amendment right to be free of unreasonable searches and seizures. Originally, searches and seizures had to do with physical elements, items that could be touched or seen. In today's wired world, however, searches and seizures can take the form of police surveillance via electronic means. Over time, the Supreme Court has held that unless certain requirements are met, electronic surveillance constitutes an unreasonable search, in violation of the Fourth Amendment. If the original interpretations of this amendment were still followed, we would probably have much less protection against electronic surveillance.

Consider privacy rights. The framers did not mention a right to privacy in the Bill of Rights. Rather, modern-day interpretations have concluded that a right to privacy is implied by several of the first ten amendments to the Constitution. Further, consider such issues as abortion and assisted suicide. It is almost impossible to imagine how the Constitution as interpreted two hundred years ago could apply to these issues.

Finally, consider that the Declaration of Independence promised equality. Yet the Constitution implicitly acknowledged the institution of slavery and gave full political rights only to property-owning white males. The majority of Americans, including women and Native Americans, had no such rights. Had we stayed with the meaning of the Constitution as it was originally understood, certainly most of the political and civil rights enjoyed by the majority of American citizens today would not exist.

FOR CRITICAL ANALYSIS

1. What is the alternative to a "living" Constitution?
2. Why was privacy not as significant an issue two hundred years ago as it is today?

32

We the People of the United States, in Order to form a more perfect Union, establish Justice, insure domestic Tranquillity, provide for the common defence, promote the general Welfare, and secure the Blessings of Liberty to ourselves and our Posterity, do ordain and establish this Constitution for the United States of America.

Every schoolchild in America has at one time or another been exposed to these famous words from the Preamble to the U.S. Constitution. The document itself is remarkable. The U.S. Constitution, compared with others in the states and in the world, is relatively short. Because amending it is difficult (as you will see later in this chapter), it also has relatively few amendments. Perhaps even more remarkable is the fact that it has remained largely intact for over two hundred years. In large part, this is because the principles set forth in the Constitution are sufficiently broad that they can be adapted to meet the needs of a changing society—as you learned in this chapter's *What If* . . . .

How and why this Constitution was created is a story that has been told and retold. It is worth repeating, because the historical and political context in which this country's governmental machinery was formed is essential to understanding American government and politics today. The Constitution was not the result of completely creative thinking. Many of its provisions were grounded in contemporary political philosophy. The delegates to the Constitutional Convention in 1787 brought with them two important sets of influences: their political culture and their political experience. In the years between the first settlements in the New World and the writing of the Constitution, Americans had developed a political philosophy about how people should be governed and had tried out numerous forms of government. These experiences gave the founders the tools with which they constructed the Constitution.

DID YOU KNOW...
That the first English claim to territory in North America was made by John Cabot, on behalf of King Henry VII, on June 24, 1497?

Initial Colonizing Efforts

The first British outpost in North America was set up by Sir Walter Raleigh in the 1580s for the purpose of harassing the Spanish treasure fleets. The group, known as the Roanoke Island Colony, stands as one of history's great mysteries: After a three-year absence to resupply the colony, Raleigh's captain, John White, returned in 1590 to find signs that the colony's residents apparently had moved

The first British settlers who landed on the North American continent faced severe tests of endurance. This woodcut depicts a cold existence for the settlers in the late 1500s and early 1600s.

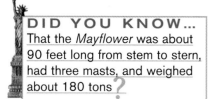

Representative Assembly
A legislature composed of individuals who represent the population.

north to Chesapeake Bay. White was unable to search further, and no evidence of the fate of the "lost colony" has ever been recorded. Local legends in North Carolina maintain that the lost colonists survived and intermarried with the Native Americans, and that their descendants live in the region today. Recent climatological studies may have helped to solve the mystery, however. Scientists at the University of Arkansas, based on the rings of ancient cypress trees still growing in the swamps of that area, concluded that the most extreme drought season during the trees' eight-hundred-year history coincided with the attempted settlement on Roanoke Island and lasted for three years.[1]

In 1607, the British government sent over a group of farmers to establish a trading post, Jamestown, in what is now Virginia. The Virginia Company of London was the first to establish successfully a permanent British colony in the Americas. The king of England gave the backers of this colony a charter granting them "full power and authority" to make laws "for the good and welfare" of the settlement. The colonists at Jamestown instituted a **representative assembly**, setting a precedent in government that was to be observed in later colonial adventures.

Jamestown was not a commercial success. Of the 105 men who landed, 67 died within the first year. But 800 new arrivals in 1609 added to their numbers. By the spring of the next year, frontier hazards had cut their numbers to 60. Of the 6,000 people who left England for Virginia between 1607 and 1623, 4,800 of them perished. The historian Charles Andrews has called this the "starving time for Virginia."[2] The climatological researchers just mentioned suggest that his "starving time" may have been brought about by another severe drought in the Jamestown area, which lasted from 1607 to 1612.

Separatists, the Mayflower, and the Compact

The first New England colony was established in 1620. A group of mostly extreme Separatists, who wished to break with the Church of England, came over on the ship *Mayflower* to the New World, landing at Plymouth (Massachusetts). Before going on shore, the adult males—women were not considered to have any

[1]D. W. Stahle et al., "The Lost Colony and Jamestown Droughts," *Science*, April 24, 1998.
[2]Charles M. Andrews, *The Colonial Period of American History*, Vol. 1 (New Haven, Conn.: Yale University Press, 1934), p. 110.

The signing of the compact aboard the *Mayflower*. In 1620, the Mayflower Compact was signed by almost all of the men aboard the ship *Mayflower*, just before disembarking at Plymouth, Massachusetts. It stated, "We . . . covenant and combine ourselves together into a civil body politick . . . ; and by vertue hearof to enact, constitute, and frame such just and equal laws . . . as shall be thought [necessary] for the generall good of the Colonie."

political status—drew up the Mayflower Compact, which was signed by forty-one of the forty-four men aboard the ship on November 21, 1620. The reason for the compact was obvious. This group was outside the jurisdiction of the Virginia Company of London, which had chartered their settlement in Virginia, not Massachusetts. The Separatist leaders feared that some of the *Mayflower* passengers might conclude that they were no longer under any obligations of civil obedience. Therefore, some form of public authority was imperative. As William Bradford (a printer and editor in Philadelphia) recalled in his accounts, there were "discontented and mutinous speeches that some of the strangers amongst them had let fall from them in the ship; That when they came a shore they would use their owne libertie; for none had power to command them."[3]

The compact was not a constitution. It was a political agreement in which the signers agreed to create and submit to the authority of a government, pending the receipt of a royal charter. The Mayflower Compact's historical and political significance is twofold: it depended on the consent of the affected individuals, and it served as a prototype for similar compacts in American history. According to Samuel Eliot Morison, the compact proved the determination of the English immigrants to live under the rule of law, based on the *consent of the people.*[4]

More Colonies, More Government

Another outpost in New England was set up by the Massachusetts Bay Colony in 1630. Then followed Rhode Island, Connecticut, New Hampshire, and others. By 1732, the last of the thirteen colonies, Georgia, was established. During the colonial period, Americans developed a concept of limited government, which followed from the establishment of the first colonies under Crown charters. Theoretically, London governed the colonies. In practice, owing partly to the colonies' distance from London, the colonists exercised a large measure of self-government. The colonists were able to make their own laws, as in the Fundamental Orders of Connecticut in 1639. The Massachusetts Body of Liberties in 1641 supported the protection of individual rights and was made a part of colonial law. In 1682, the Pennsylvania Frame of Government was passed. Along with the Pennsylvania Charter of Privileges of 1701, it established the rationale for our modern Constitution and Bill of Rights. All of this legislation enabled the colonists to acquire crucial political experience. After independence was declared in 1776, the states quickly set up their own constitutions.

British Restrictions and Colonial Grievances

The conflict between Britain and the American colonies, which ultimately led to the Revolutionary War, began in the 1760s when the British government decided to raise revenues by imposing taxes on the American colonies. Policy advisers to Britain's young King George III, who ascended the throne in 1760, decided that it was only logical to require the American colonists to help pay the costs of Britain's defending them during the French and Indian War (1756–1763). The colonists, who had grown accustomed to a large degree of self-government and independence from the British Crown, viewed the matter differently.

---

[3]John Camp, *Out of the Wilderness: The Emergence of an American Identity in Colonial New England* (Middleton, Conn.: Wesleyan University Press, 1990).

[4]See Morison's "The Mayflower Compact" in Daniel J. Boorstin, ed., *An American Primer* (Chicago: University of Chicago Press, 1966), p. 18.

DID YOU KNOW...
That during the Revolutionary War, while 9,000 American colonists took up arms against Britain, 8,000 "Loyalists" fought alongside the British?

MILESTONES IN EARLY U.S. POLITICAL HISTORY

1585 British outpost set up on Roanoke Island.
1607 Jamestown established; Virginia Company lands settlers.
1620 Mayflower Compact signed.
1630 Massachusetts Bay Colony set up.
1639 Fundamental Orders of Connecticut adopted.
1641 Massachusetts Body of Liberties adopted.
1682 Pennsylvania Frame of Government passed.
1701 Pennsylvania Charter of Privileges written.
1732 Last of the thirteen colonies established.
1756 French and Indian War declared.
1765 Stamp Act; Stamp Act Congress meets.
1774 First Continental Congress.
1775 Second Continental Congress; Revolutionary War begins.
1776 Declaration of Independence signed.
1777 Articles of Confederation drafted.
1781 Last state signs Articles of Confederation.
1783– "Critical period" in U.S.
1789   history; weak national government.
1786 Shays's Rebellion.
1787 Constitutional Convention.
1788 Ratification of Constitution.
1791 Ratification of Bill of Rights.

King George III (1738–1820) was king of Great Britain and Ireland from 1760 until his death on January 29, 1820. Under George III, the first attempt to tax the American colonies was made. Ultimately, the American colonies, exasperated at renewed attempts at taxation, proclaimed their independence on July 4, 1776.

First Continental Congress
The first gathering of delegates from twelve of the thirteen colonies, held in 1774.

Second Continental Congress
The 1775 congress of the colonies that established an army.

In 1764, the Sugar Act was passed. Many colonists were unwilling to pay the required tax. Further regulatory legislation was to come. In 1765, the British Parliament passed the Stamp Act, providing for internal taxation, or, as the colonists' Stamp Act Congress assembled in 1765 called it, "taxation without representation." The colonists boycotted the Stamp Act. The success of the boycott (the Stamp Act was repealed a year later) generated a feeling of unity within the colonies. The British, however, continued to try to raise revenues in the colonies. When duties on glass, lead, paint, and other items were passed in 1767, the colonists boycotted the purchase of English commodities in return. The colonists' fury over taxation climaxed in the Boston Tea Party: colonists dressed as Mohawk Indians dumped almost 350 chests of British tea into the Boston Harbor as a gesture of tax protest. In retaliation, the British Parliament passed the Coercive Acts (the "Intolerable Acts") in 1774, which closed Boston Harbor and placed the government of Boston under direct British control. The colonists were outraged—and they responded.

The Colonial Response: The Continental Congresses

New York, Pennsylvania, and Rhode Island proposed the convening of a colonial congress. The Massachusetts House of Representatives requested that all colonies hold conventions to select delegates to be sent to Philadelphia for such a congress. The **First Continental Congress** was held at Carpenter's Hall on September 5, 1774. It was a gathering of delegates from twelve of the thirteen colonies (Georgia did not attend until 1775). At that meeting, there was little talk of independence. The Congress passed a resolution requesting that the colonies send a petition to King George III expressing their grievances. Resolutions were also passed requiring that the colonies raise their own troops and boycott British trade. The British government condemned the Congress's actions, treating them as open acts of rebellion.

The delegates to the First Continental Congress declared that in every county and city, a committee was to be formed whose mission was to spy on the conduct of friends and neighbors and to report to the press any violators of the trade ban. The formation of these committees was an act of cooperation among the colonies, which represented a step toward the creation of a national government.

By the time the **Second Continental Congress** met in May 1775 (this time all of the colonies were represented), fighting already had broken out between the British and the colonists. One of the main actions of the Second Congress was to establish an army. It did this by declaring the militia that had gathered around Boston an army and naming George Washington as commander in chief. The participants in that Congress still attempted to reach a peaceful settlement with the British Parliament. One declaration of the Congress stated explicitly that "we have not raised armies with ambitious designs of separating from Great Britain, and establishing independent states." But by the beginning of 1776, military encounters had become increasingly frequent.

Public debate was acrimonious. Then Thomas Paine's *Common Sense* appeared in Philadelphia bookstores. The pamphlet was a colonial best seller. (To do relatively as well today, a book would have to sell between eight and ten million copies in its first year of publication.) Many agreed that Paine did make common sense when he argued that

> a government of our own is our natural right: and when a man seriously reflects on the precariousness of human affairs, he will become convinced, that it is infinitely wiser and safer, to form a constitution of our own in a cool and deliberate

manner, while we have it in our power, than to trust such an interesting event to time and chance.[5]

Students of Paine's pamphlet point out that his arguments were not new—they were common in tavern debates throughout the land. Rather, it was the near poetry of his words—which were at the same time as plain as the alphabet—that struck his readers.

Declaring Independence

The Resolution of Independence

On April 6, 1776, the Second Continental Congress voted for free trade at all American ports for all countries except Great Britain. This act could be interpreted as an implicit declaration of independence. The next month, the Congress suggested that each of the colonies establish state governments unconnected to Britain. Finally, on July 2, the Resolution of Independence was adopted by the Second Continental Congress:

> RESOLVED, That these United Colonies are, and of right ought to be free and independent States, that they are absolved from allegiance to the British Crown, and that all political connection between them and the state of Great Britain is, and ought to be, totally dissolved.

The actual Resolution of Independence was not legally significant. On the one hand, it was not judicially enforceable, for it established no legal rights or duties. On the other hand, the colonies were already, in their own judgment, self-governing and independent of Britain. Rather, the Resolution of Independence and the subsequent Declaration of Independence were necessary to establish the legitimacy of the new nation in the eyes of foreign governments, as well as in the eyes of the colonists themselves. What the new nation needed most was supplies for its armies and a commitment of foreign military aid. Unless it appeared in the eyes of the world as a political entity separate and independent from Britain, no foreign government would enter into a contract with its leaders.

"You know, the idea of taxation with representation doesn't appeal to me very much either."

Drawing by Handelsman; © 1970 The New Yorker Magazine, Inc.

July 4, 1776—The Declaration of Independence

By June 1776, Thomas Jefferson already was writing drafts of the Declaration of Independence in the second-floor parlor of a bricklayer's house in Philadelphia. On adoption of the Resolution of Independence, Jefferson had argued that a declaration putting forth clearly the causes that compelled the colonies to separate from England was necessary. The Second Congress assigned the task to him, and he completed his work on the declaration, which enumerated the colonists' major grievances against England. Some of his work was amended to gain unanimous acceptance (for example, his condemnation of the slave trade was eliminated to satisfy Georgia and North Carolina), but the bulk of it was passed intact on July 4, 1776. On July 19, the modified draft became "the unanimous declaration of the thirteen United States of America." On August 2, it was signed by the members of the Second Continental Congress.

A revolutionary concept of the Declaration was the assumption, inspired by the ideas of the English political philosopher John Locke (1632–1704), that people have **natural rights** ("unalienable Rights"), including the rights to "life, liberty, and the pursuit of happiness." Governments are established to secure these rights, and

Natural Rights
Rights held to be inherent in natural law, not dependent on governments. John Locke stated that natural law, being superior to human law, specifies certain rights of "life, liberty, and property." These rights, altered to become "life, liberty, and the pursuit of happiness," are asserted in the Declaration of Independence.

---

[5]*The Political Writings of Thomas Paine,* Vol. 1 (Boston: J. P. Mendum Investigator Office, 1870), p. 46.

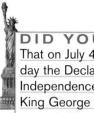
governments derive their power "from the consent of the governed."[6] The Declaration claimed that whenever government "becomes destructive to these ends, it is the Right of the People to alter or to abolish it, and to institute a new government."

After setting forth these basic principles of government, the Declaration of Independence goes on to justify the colonists' revolt against Britain. Much of the remainder of the document is a list of what "He" (King George III) had done to deprive the colonists of their rights. (See Appendix A for the text of the Declaration of Independence.)

Once it had fulfilled its purpose of legitimating the American Revolution, the Declaration of Independence was all but forgotten for many years. According to scholar Pauline Maier, the Declaration did not become enshrined as what she calls "American Scripture" until the nineteenth century.[7]

The Rise of Republicanism

Although the colonists had formally declared independence from Britain, the fight to gain actual independence continued for five more years—until the British General Cornwallis surrendered at Yorktown in 1781. In 1783, after Britain formally recognized the independent status of the United States in the Treaty of Paris, Washington disbanded the army. During these years of military struggles, the states faced the additional challenge of creating a system of self-government for an independent United States.

Some colonists in the middle and lower southern colonies had demanded that independence be preceded by the formation of a strong central government. But the anti-Royalists in New England and Virginia, who called themselves Republicans, were against a strong central government. They opposed monarchy, executive authority, and virtually any form of restraint on the power of local groups. These so-called Republicans were a major political force from 1776

[6]Not all scholars believe that Jefferson was truly influenced by Locke. For example, Jay Fliegelman states that "Jefferson's fascination with Homer, Ossian, Patrick Henry, and the violin is of greater significance than his indebtedness to Locke." Jay Fliegelman, *Declaring Independence: Jefferson, Natural Language, and the Culture of Performance* (Stanford, Calif.: Stanford University Press, 1993).
[7]See Pauline Maier, *American Scripture: Making the Declaration of Independence* (New York: Knopf, 1997).

Members of the Second Continental Congress adopted the Declaration of Independence on July 4, 1776. Minor changes were made in the document in the following two weeks. On July 19, the modified draft became the "unanimous declaration of the thirteen United States of America." On August 2, the members of the Second Continental Congress signed it. The first official printed version carried only the signatures of the Congress's president, John Hancock, and its secretary, Charles Thompson.

to 1780. Indeed, they almost prevented victory over the British by their unwillingness to cooperate with any central authority.

During this time, all of the states adopted written constitutions. Eleven of the constitutions were completely new. Two of them—those of Connecticut and Rhode Island—were old royal charters with minor modifications. Republican sentiment led to increased power for the legislatures. In Pennsylvania and Georgia, **unicameral** (one-body) **legislatures** were unchecked by executive or judicial authority. Basically, the Republicans attempted to maintain the politics of 1776. In almost all states, the legislature was predominant.

The Articles of Confederation: Our First Form of Government

The fear of a powerful central government led to the passage of the Articles of Confederation. The term **confederation** is important; it means a voluntary association of *independent* **states,** in which the member states agree to only limited restraints on their freedom of action. As a result, confederations seldom have an effective executive authority.

In June 1776, the Second Continental Congress began the process of drafting what would become the Articles of Confederation. The final form of the Articles was achieved by November 15, 1777. It was not until March 1, 1781, however, that the last state, Maryland, agreed to ratify what was called the Articles of Confederation and Perpetual Union. Well before the final ratification of the Articles, however, many of them were implemented: the Continental Congress and the thirteen states conducted American military, economic, and political affairs according to the standards and the form specified by the Articles.[8]

Under the Articles, the thirteen original colonies, now states, established on March 1, 1781, a government of the states—the Congress of the Confederation. The Congress was a unicameral assembly of so-called ambassadors from each state, with each state possessing a single vote. Each year, the Congress would choose one of its members as its president, but the Articles did not provide for a president of the United States. The Congress was authorized in Article X to appoint an executive committee of the states "to execute in the recess of Congress, such of the powers of Congress as the United States, in Congress assembled, by the consent of nine [of the thirteen] states, shall from time to time think expedient to vest with them." The Congress was also allowed to appoint other committees and civil officers necessary for managing the general affairs of the United States. In addition, the Congress could regulate foreign affairs and establish coinage and weights and measures. But it lacked an independent source of revenue and the necessary executive machinery to enforce its decisions throughout the land. Article II of the Articles of Confederation guaranteed that each state would retain its sovereignty. Figure 2–1 illustrates the structure of the government under the Articles of Confederation; Table 2–1 on page 40 summarizes the powers—and the lack of powers—of Congress under that system.

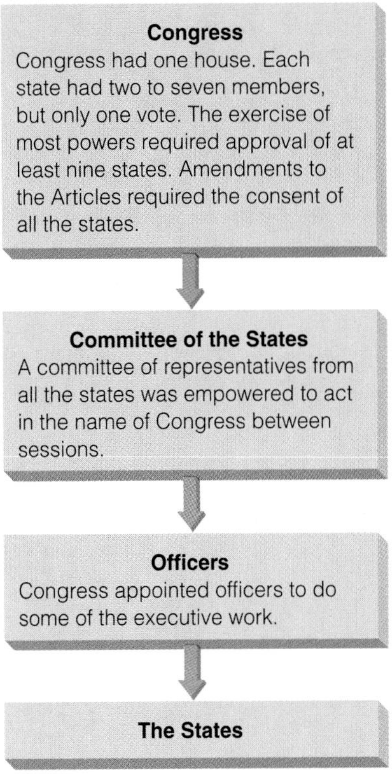

Accomplishments under the Articles

Although the Articles of Confederation had many defects, there were also some accomplishments during the eight years of their existence. Certain states' claims to western lands were settled. Maryland had objected to the claims of Massachusetts, New York, Connecticut, Virginia, the Carolinas, and Georgia. It

[8]Robert W. Hoffert, *A Politics of Tensions: The Articles of Confederation and American Political Ideas* (Niwot, Colo.: University Press of Colorado, 1992).

Unicameral Legislature
A legislature with only one legislative body, as compared with a bicameral (two-house) legislature, such as the U.S. Congress. Nebraska is the only state in the union with a unicameral legislature.

Confederation
A political system in which states or regional governments retain ultimate authority except for those powers they expressly delegate to a central government. A voluntary association of independent states, in which the member states agree to limited restraints on their freedom of action.

State
A group of people occupying a specific area and organized under one government; may be either a nation or a subunit of a nation.

FIGURE 2-1

The Structure of the Confederal Government under the Articles of Confederation

Congress
Congress had one house. Each state had two to seven members, but only one vote. The exercise of most powers required approval of at least nine states. Amendments to the Articles required the consent of all the states.

↓

Committee of the States
A committee of representatives from all the states was empowered to act in the name of Congress between sessions.

↓

Officers
Congress appointed officers to do some of the executive work.

↓

The States

TABLE 2-1

Powers of the Congress of the Confederation

CONGRESS HAD POWER TO	CONGRESS LACKED POWER TO
■ Declare war and make peace. ■ Enter into treaties and alliances. ■ Establish and control armed forces. ■ Requisition men and money from states. ■ Regulate coinage. ■ Borrow money and issue bills of credit. ■ Fix uniform standards of weight and measurement. ■ Create admiralty courts. ■ Create a postal system. ■ Regulate Indian affairs. ■ Guarantee citizens of each state the rights and privileges of citizens in the several states when in another state. ■ Adjudicate disputes between states upon state petition.	■ Provide for effective treaty-making power and control foreign relations; it could not compel states to respect treaties. ■ Compel states to meet military quotas; it could not draft soldiers. ■ Regulate interstate and foreign commerce; it left each state free to set up its own tariff system. ■ Collect taxes directly from the people; it had to rely on states to collect and forward taxes. ■ Compel states to pay their share of government costs. ■ Provide and maintain a sound monetary system or issue paper money; this was left up to the states, and monies in circulation differed tremendously in value.

was only after these states consented to give up their land claims to the United States as a whole that Maryland signed the Articles of Confederation. Another accomplishment under the Articles was the passage of the Northwest Ordinance of 1787, which established a basic pattern of government for new territories north of the Ohio River.

Weaknesses of the Articles

Although Congress had the legal right to declare war and to conduct foreign policy, it did not have the right to demand revenues from the states. It could only *ask* for them. Additionally, the actions of Congress required the consent of nine states. Any amendments to the Articles required the unanimous consent of the Congress and confirmation by every state legislature. Furthermore, the Articles did not create a national system of courts.

Basically, the functioning of the government under the Articles depended on the goodwill of the states. Article III of the Articles simply established a "league of friendship" among the states—no national government was intended.

Probably the most fundamental weakness of the Articles, and the most basic cause of their eventual replacement by the Constitution, concerned the lack of power to raise money for the militia. The Articles lacked any language giving Congress coercive power to raise money (by levying taxes) to provide adequate support for the military forces controlled by Congress. When states refused to send money to support the government (not one state met the financial requests made by Congress under the Articles), Congress resorted to selling off western lands to speculators or issuing bonds that sold for less than their face value. Due to a lack of resources, the Continental Congress was forced to disband the army, even in the face of serious Spanish and British military threats.

Shays's Rebellion and the Need for Revision of the Articles

Because of the weaknesses of the Articles of Confederation, the central government could do little to maintain peace and order in the new nation. The states bickered among themselves and increasingly taxed each other's goods. At times they prevented trade altogether. By 1784, the country faced a serious economic depression. Banks were calling in old loans and refusing to give new ones. People who could not pay their debts were often thrown into prison.

By 1786, in Concord, Massachusetts, the scene of one of the first battles of the Revolution, there were three times as many people in prison for debt as there were for all other crimes combined. In Worcester County, Massachusetts, the ratio was even higher—twenty to one. Most of the prisoners were small farmers who could not pay their debts owing to the disorganized state of the economy.

In August 1786, mobs of musket-bearing farmers led by former revolutionary captain Daniel Shays seized county courthouses and disrupted the trials of the debtors in Springfield, Massachusetts. Shays and his men then launched an attack on the federal arsenal at Springfield, but they were repulsed. Shays's Rebellion demonstrated that the central government could not protect the citizenry from armed rebellion or provide adequately for the public welfare. The rebellion spurred the nation's political leaders to action. As John Jay wrote to Thomas Jefferson, clearly "changes were necessary" (see the feature *E-Mail Messages from the Past*).

Drafting the Constitution

The Annapolis Convention

The Virginia legislature called for a meeting of all the states to be held at Annapolis, Maryland, on September 11, 1786—ostensibly to discuss commercial problems only. It was evident to those in attendance (including Alexander Hamilton and James Madison) that the national government had serious weaknesses that had to be addressed if it were to survive. Among the important

E-MAIL MESSAGES FROM THE PAST

To: Thomas.Jefferson@earlynet.fr, October 28, 1786, 8:28 AM
From: John Jay <jjay@usapast.gov>
Subject: Rebellion in Massachusetts
X-attachments:

Sir:

The inefficacy of our Government becomes daily more and more apparent. . . . A Spirit of Licentiousness has infected Massachusetts, which appears more formidable than some at first apprehended. . . . The public Papers herewith [attached] contain everything generally known about these Matters. A Reluctance to Taxes, an Impatience of Government, a Rage for Property, and little Regard to the Means of acquiring it, together with a Desire of Equality in all Things, seem to actuate the Mass of those who are uneasy in their Circumstances. . . . In short, my Dr. Sir; we are in a very unpleasant Situation. Changes are Necessary, but what they ought to be, what they will be, and how and when to be produced, are arduous Questions. I feel for the Cause of Liberty. . . . If it should not take Root in this Soil[,] Little Pains will be taken to cultivate it in any other.

Yours,

John Jay

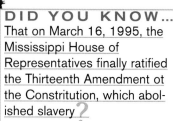

problems to be solved were the relationship between the states and the central government, the powers of the national legislature, the need for executive leadership, and the establishment of policies for economic stability.

At this Annapolis meeting, a call was issued to all of the states for a general convention to meet in Philadelphia in May 1787 "to consider the exigencies of the union." When the Republicans, who favored a weak central government, realized that the Philadelphia meeting would in fact take place, they approved the convention in February 1787. They made it explicit, however, that the convention was "for the sole and express purpose of revising the Articles of Confederation." Those in favor of a stronger national government—the Federalists, as they were to be called—had different ideas.

The Philadelphia Convention

The designated date for the opening of the convention was May 14, 1787. Because few of the delegates had actually arrived in Philadelphia by that time, however, it was not formally opened in the East Room of the Pennsylvania State House until May 25.[9] Fifty-five of the seventy-four delegates chosen for the convention actually attended the convention. (Of those fifty-five, only about forty played active roles at the convention.) Rhode Island was the only state that refused to send delegates.

The Working Environment

The conditions under which the delegates worked for 115 days were far from ideal and were made even worse by the necessity of maintaining total secrecy. The framers of the Constitution felt that if public debate were started on particular positions, delegates would have a more difficult time compromising or backing down to reach agreement. Consequently, the windows were usually shut in the East Room of the State House. Summer quickly arrived, and the air became heavy, humid, and hot by noon of each day. Also, when the windows were open, flies swarmed into the room. The delegates did, however, have a nearby tavern and inn to which they retired each evening. The Indian Queen became the informal headquarters of the delegates.

Factions among the Delegates

We know much about the proceedings at the convention because James Madison kept a daily, detailed personal journal. A majority of the delegates were strong nationalists—they wanted a central government with real power, unlike the central government under the Articles of Confederation. George Washington and Benjamin Franklin preferred limited national authority based on a separation of powers. They were apparently willing to accept any type of national government, however, as long as the other delegates approved it. A few advocates of a strong central government, led by Gouverneur Morris of Pennsylvania and John Rutledge of South Carolina, distrusted the ability of the common people to engage in self-government.

Among the nationalists were several monarchists, including Alexander Hamilton, who was chiefly responsible for the Annapolis Convention's call for the Constitutional Convention. In a long speech on June 18, he presented his views: "I have no scruple in declaring . . . that the British government is the best in the world and that I doubt much whether anything short of it will do in America."

Elbridge Gerry (1744–1814), from Massachusetts, was a patriot during the Revolution. He was a signatory of the Declaration of Independence and later became governor of Massachusetts (1810–1812). He became James Madison's new vice president when Madison was reelected in December 1812.

---

[9]The State House was later named Independence Hall. This was the same room in which the Declaration of Independence had been signed eleven years earlier.

George Washington presided over the Constitutional Convention of 1787. Although the convention was supposed to have started on May 14, 1787, few of the delegates had actually arrived in Philadelphia by that date. It formally opened in the East Room of the Pennsylvania State House (later named Independence Hall) on May 25. Only Rhode Island did not send any delegates.

Another important group of nationalists were of a more democratic stripe. Led by James Madison of Virginia and James Wilson of Pennsylvania, these democratic nationalists wanted a central government founded on popular support.

Still another faction consisted of nationalists who were less democratic in nature and who would support a central government only if it were founded on very narrowly defined republican principles. This group was made up of a relatively small number of delegates, including Edmund Randolph and George Mason of Virginia, Elbridge Gerry of Massachusetts, and Luther Martin and John Francis Mercer of Maryland.

Most of the other delegates from Maryland, New Hampshire, Connecticut, New Jersey, and Delaware were concerned about only one thing—claims to western lands. As long as those lands became the common property of all of the states, they were willing to support a central government.

Finally, there was a group of delegates who were totally against a national authority. Two of the three delegates from New York quit the convention when they saw the nationalist direction of its proceedings.

James Madison (1751–1836) contributed to the colonial cause by bringing to it a deep understanding of government and political philosophy. These resources first proved valuable in 1776, when he helped to draft the constitution for the new state of Virginia. Madison was prominent in disestablishing the Anglican Church when he was a representative of his county in the Virginia legislature from 1784 to 1786. At the Annapolis Convention, he supported New Jersey's motion to hold a federal constitutional convention the following year. Madison earned the title "master builder of the Constitution" because of his persuasive logic during the Constitutional Convention. His contributions to the *Federalist Papers* showed him to be a brilliant political thinker and writer.

Politicking and Compromises

The debates at the convention started on the first day. James Madison had spent months reviewing European political theory. When his Virginia delegation arrived ahead of most of the others, it got to work immediately. By the time George Washington opened the convention, Governor Edmund Randolph of Virginia was immediately able to present fifteen resolutions. In retrospect, this was a masterful stroke on the part of the Virginia delegation. It set the agenda for the remainder of the convention—even though, in principle, the delegates had been sent to Philadelphia for the sole purpose of amending the Articles of Confederation. They had not been sent to write a new constitution.

The Virginia Plan. Randolph's fifteen resolutions proposed an entirely new national government under a constitution. It was, however, a plan that favored the large states, including Virginia. Basically, it called for the following:

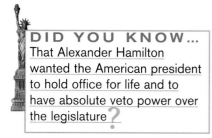

Bicameral Legislature
A legislature made up of two chambers, or parts. The U.S. Congress, composed of the House of Representatives and the Senate, is a bicameral legislature.

1. A **bicameral** (two-house) **legislature,** with the lower house chosen by the people and the smaller upper house chosen by the lower house from nominees selected by state legislatures. The number of representatives would be proportional to a state's population, thus favoring the large states. The legislature could void any state laws.
2. The creation of an unspecified national executive, elected by the legislature.
3. The creation of a national judiciary appointed by the legislature.

It did not take long for the smaller states to realize they would fare poorly under the Virginia plan, according to which Virginia, Massachusetts, and Pennsylvania would form a majority in the national legislature. The debate on the plan dragged on for a number of weeks. It was time for the small states to come up with their own plan.

The New Jersey Plan.　On June 15, lawyer William Paterson of New Jersey offered an alternative plan. After all, argued Paterson, under the Articles of Confederation all states had equality; therefore, the convention had no power to change this arrangement. He proposed the following:

1. The fundamental principle of the Articles of Confederation—one state, one vote—would be retained.
2. Congress would be able to regulate trade and impose taxes.
3. All acts of Congress would be the supreme law of the land.
4. Several people would be elected by Congress to form an executive office.
5. The executive office would appoint a Supreme Court.

Basically, the New Jersey plan was simply an amendment of the Articles of Confederation. Its only notable feature was its reference to the **supremacy doctrine,** which was later included in the Constitution.

Supremacy Doctrine
A doctrine that asserts the superiority of national law over state or regional laws. This principle is rooted in Article VI of the Constitution, which provides that the Constitution, the laws passed by the national government under its constitutional powers, and all treaties constitute the supreme law of the land.

Great Compromise
The compromise between the New Jersey and the Virginia plans that created one chamber of the Congress based on population and one chamber that represented each state equally; also called the Connecticut Compromise.

The "Great Compromise."　The delegates were at an impasse. Most wanted a strong national government and were unwilling even to consider the New Jersey plan. But when the Virginia plan was brought up again, the small states threatened to leave. It was not until July 16 that the **Great Compromise** was achieved. Roger Sherman of Connecticut proposed the following:

1. A bicameral legislature in which the House of Representatives would be apportioned according to the number of free inhabitants in each state, plus three-fifths of the slaves.
2. An upper house, the Senate, which would have two members from each state elected by the state legislatures.

This plan, also called the Connecticut Compromise because of the role of the Connecticut delegates in the proposal, broke the deadlock. It did exact a political price, however, because it permitted each state to have equal representation in the Senate. Having two senators represent each state in effect diluted the voting power of citizens living in more heavily populated states and gave the smaller states disproportionate political powers. But the Connecticut Compromise resolved the large-state/small-state controversy. In addition, the Senate acted as part of a checks-and-balances system against the House, which many feared would be dominated by, and responsive to, the masses.

INFOTRAC ®
COLLEGE EDITION

"The Legacy of Slavery Lingers"

The Three-Fifths Compromise.　The Great Compromise also settled another major issue—how to deal with slaves in the representational scheme. Slavery was legal everywhere except in Massachusetts, but it was concentrated in the South. The South wanted slaves to be counted equally in determining representation in Congress. Delegates from the northern states objected. Sherman's three-fifths compromise solved the issue, satisfying those northerners who felt that slaves should not be counted at all and those southerners who wanted them to be counted as free whites. Actually, Sherman's Connecticut plan spoke of three-fifths of "all other persons" (and that is the language in the Constitution itself). It is not hard to figure out, though, who those other persons were.

The slavery issue was not completely eliminated by the three-fifths compromise. Many delegates were opposed to slavery and wanted it banned entirely in the United States. Charles Pinckney of South Carolina led strong southern opposition to the idea of a ban on slavery. Finally, the delegates agreed that Congress could limit the importation of slaves after 1808. The compromise meant that the issue of slavery itself was never addressed. The South won twenty years of unrestricted slave trade and a requirement that escaped slaves in free states be returned to their owners in slave states.

Other Issues. The agrarian South and the mercantile North were in conflict. The South was worried that the northern majority in Congress would pass legislation unfavorable to its economic interests. Because the South depended on exports of its agricultural products, it feared the imposition of export taxes. In return for acceding to the northern demand that Congress be given the power to regulate commerce among the states and with other nations, the South obtained a promise that export taxes would not be imposed. Even today, such taxes are prohibited. The United States is one of the few countries that does not tax its exports.

There were other disagreements. The delegates could not decide whether to establish only a Supreme Court or to create lower courts as well. They deferred the issue by mandating a Supreme Court and allowing Congress to establish lower courts. They also disagreed over whether the president or the Senate would choose the Supreme Court justices. A compromise was reached with the agreement that the president would nominate the justices and the Senate would confirm the nominations.

These compromises, as well as others, resulted from the recognition that if one group of states refused to ratify the Constitution, it was doomed.

An American slave market as depicted in a painting from the nineteenth century. The writers of the Constitution did not ban slavery in the United States but did agree to limit the importation of new slaves after 1808. Nowhere are the words slavery or slaves used in the Constitution. Instead, the Constitution uses such language as "no person held in service" and "all other persons."

Separation of Powers
The principle of dividing governmental powers among the executive, the legislative, and the judicial branches of government.

Madisonian Model
A structure of government proposed by James Madison in which the powers of the government are separated into three branches: executive, legislative, and judicial.

Checks and Balances
A major principle of the American governmental system whereby each branch of the government exercises a check on the actions of the others.

Electoral College
A group of persons called electors selected by the voters in each state and Washington, D.C.; this group officially elects the president and vice president of the United States. The number of electors in each state is equal to the number of each state's representatives in both houses of Congress. The Twenty-third Amendment to the Constitution permits Washington, D.C., to have as many electors as a state of comparable population.

Working toward Final Agreement

The Connecticut Compromise was reached by mid-July. The makeup of the executive branch and the judiciary, however, was left unsettled. The remaining work of the convention was turned over to a five-man Committee of Detail, which presented a rough draft of the Constitution on August 6. It made the executive and judicial branches subordinate to the legislative branch.

The Madisonian Model.   The major issue of **separation of powers** had not yet been resolved. The delegates were concerned with structuring the government to prevent the imposition of tyranny—either by the majority or by a minority. It was Madison who proposed a governmental scheme—sometimes called the **Madisonian model**—to achieve this: the executive, legislative, and judicial powers of government were to be separated so that no one branch had enough power to dominate the others. The separation of powers was by function, as well as by personnel, with Congress passing laws, the president enforcing and administering laws, and the courts interpreting laws in individual circumstances.

Each of the three branches of government would be independent of the others, but they would have to cooperate to govern. According to Madison, in *Federalist Paper* No. 51 (see Appendix D), "the great security against a gradual concentration of the several powers in the same department consists in giving to those who administer each department the necessary constitutional means and personal motives to resist encroachments of the others."

The "constitutional means" Madison referred to is a system of **checks and balances** through which each branch of the government can check the actions of the other branches. For example, Congress can enact laws, but the president has veto power over congressional acts. The Supreme Court has the power to declare acts of Congress and of the executive branch unconstitutional, but the president appoints the justices of the Supreme Court, with the advice and consent of the Senate. (The Supreme Court's power to declare acts unconstitutional was not mentioned in the Constitution, although arguably the framers assumed that the Court would have this power—see the discussion of judicial review later in this chapter.) Figure 2–2 outlines these checks and balances.

The Executive.   Some delegates favored a plural executive made up of representatives from the various regions. This was abandoned in favor of a single chief executive. Some argued that Congress should choose the executive. To make the presidency completely independent of the proposed Congress, however, an **electoral college** was adopted, probably at James Wilson's suggestion. To be sure, the electoral college created a cumbersome presidential election process (see Chapter 10). It could even result in a candidate who came in second in the popular vote becoming president by being the top vote getter in the electoral college. The electoral college insulated the president, however, from direct popular control. The seven-year single term that some of the delegates had proposed was replaced by a four-year term and the possibility of reelection.

The Final Document

On September 17, 1787, the Constitution was approved by thirty-nine delegates. Of the fifty-five who had attended originally, only forty-two remained. Only three delegates refused to sign the Constitution. Others disapproved of at least parts of it but signed anyway to begin the ratification debate.

The Constitution that was to be ratified established the following fundamental principles:

FIGURE 2-2

Checks and Balances

The major checks and balances among the three branches are illustrated here. Some of these checks are not mentioned in the Constitution, such as judicial review—the power of the courts to declare federal or state acts unconstitutional—or the president's ability to refuse to enforce judicial decisions or congressional legislation. Checks and balances can be thought of as a confrontation of powers or responsibilities. Each branch checks the action of another; two branches in conflict have powers that can result in balances or stalemates, requiring one branch to give in or both to reach a compromise.

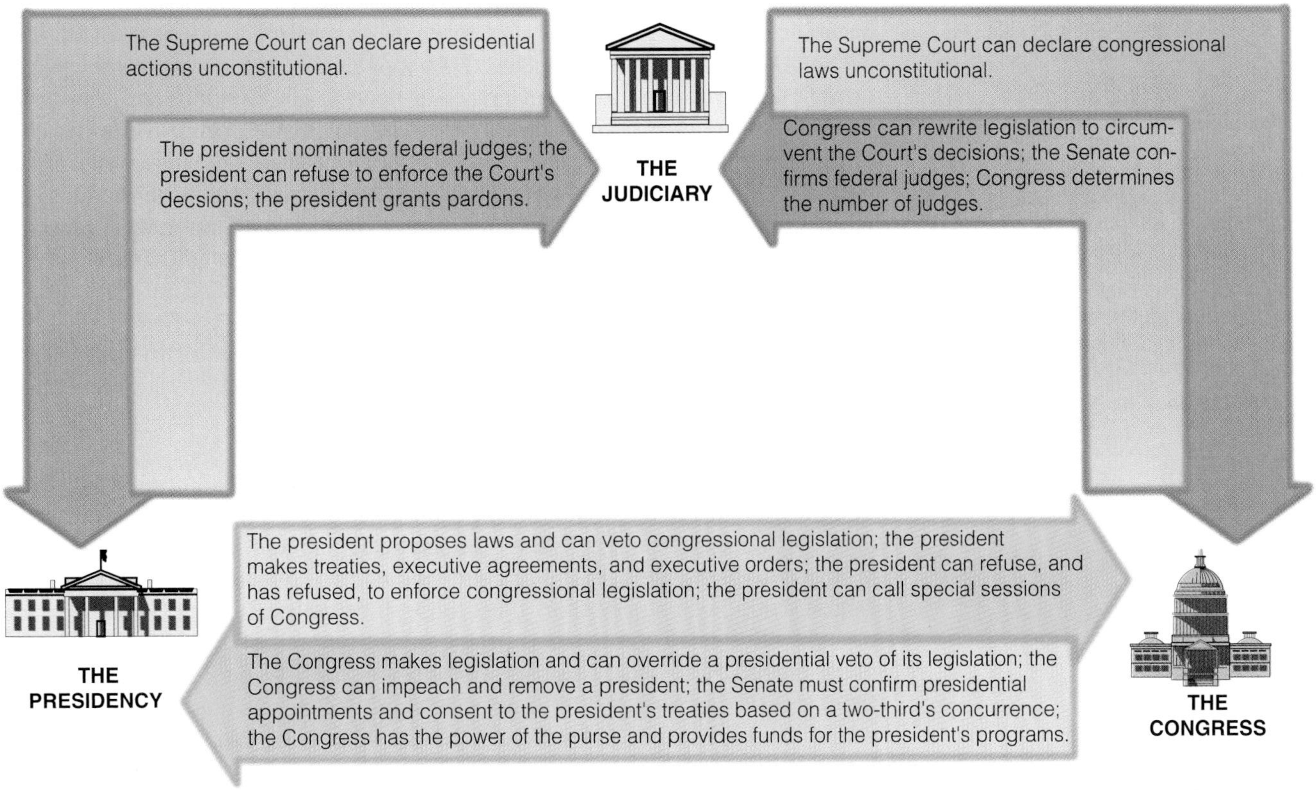

The Supreme Court can declare presidential actions unconstitutional.

The president nominates federal judges; the president can refuse to enforce the Court's decsions; the president grants pardons.

THE JUDICIARY

The Supreme Court can declare congressional laws unconstitutional.

Congress can rewrite legislation to circumvent the Court's decisions; the Senate confirms federal judges; Congress determines the number of judges.

THE PRESIDENCY

The president proposes laws and can veto congressional legislation; the president makes treaties, executive agreements, and executive orders; the president can refuse, and has refused, to enforce congressional legislation; the president can call special sessions of Congress.

The Congress makes legislation and can override a presidential veto of its legislation; the Congress can impeach and remove a president; the Senate must confirm presidential appointments and consent to the president's treaties based on a two-third's concurrence; the Congress has the power of the purse and provides funds for the president's programs.

THE CONGRESS

1. Popular sovereignty, or control by the people.
2. A republican government in which the people choose representatives to make decisions for them.
3. Limited government with written laws, in contrast to the powerful monarchical English government against which the colonists had rebelled.
4. Separation of powers, with checks and balances among branches to prevent any one branch from gaining too much power.
5. A federal system that allowed for states' rights, because the states feared too much centralized control (the federal system of government created by the Constitution is discussed in detail in Chapter 3).

The Difficult Road to Ratification

The founders knew that **ratification** of the Constitution was far from certain. Indeed, because it was almost guaranteed that many state legislatures would not ratify it, the delegates agreed that each state should hold a special convention. Elected delegates to these conventions would discuss and vote on the Constitution. Further departing from the Articles of Confederation, the delegates agreed that as soon as nine states (rather than all thirteen) approved the Constitution, it would take effect, and Congress could begin to organize the new government.

Ratification
Formal approval.

48

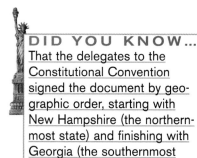

DID YOU KNOW...
That the delegates to the Constitutional Convention signed the document by geographic order, starting with New Hampshire (the northernmost state) and finishing with Georgia (the southernmost state)?

Federalist
The name given to one who was in favor of the adoption of the U.S. Constitution and the creation of a federal union with a strong central government.

Anti-Federalist
An individual who opposed the ratification of the new Constitution in 1787. The Anti-Federalists were opposed to a strong central government.

The Federalists Push for Ratification

The two opposing forces in the battle over ratification were the Federalists and the Anti-Federalists. The **Federalists**—those in favor of a strong central government and the new Constitution—had an advantage over their opponents, the **Anti-Federalists,** who wanted to prevent the Constitution as drafted from being ratified. In the first place, the Federalists had assumed a positive name, leaving their opposition the negative label of *Anti*-Federalist.[10] More important, the Federalists had attended the Constitutional Convention and knew of all the deliberations that had taken place. Their opponents had no such knowledge, because those deliberations had not been open to the public. Thus, the Anti-Federalists were at a disadvantage in terms of information about the document. The Federalists also had time, power, and money on their side. Communications were slow. Those who had access to the best communications were Federalists—mostly wealthy bankers, lawyers, plantation owners, and merchants living in urban areas, where communication was better. The Federalist campaign was organized relatively quickly and effectively to elect Federalists as delegates to the state ratifying conventions.

The Anti-Federalists, however, had at least one strong point in their favor: they stood for the status quo. In general, the greater burden is placed on those advocating change.

The Federalist Papers.   In New York, opponents of the Constitution were quick to attack it. Alexander Hamilton answered their attacks in newspaper columns over the signature "Caesar." When the Caesar letters had little effect, Hamilton switched to the pseudonym Publius and secured two collaborators—John Jay and James Madison. In a very short time, those three political figures wrote a series of eighty-five essays in defense of the Constitution and of a republican form of government. These widely read essays appeared in New York newspapers from October 1787 to August 1788 and were reprinted in the newspapers of other states. Although we do not know for certain who wrote every one, it is apparent that Hamilton was responsible for about two-thirds of the essays. These included the most important ones interpreting the Constitution, explaining the various powers of the three branches, and presenting a theory of judicial review. Madison's *Federalist Paper* No. 10 (see Appendix D), however, is considered a classic in political theory; it deals with the nature of groups—or factions, as he called them. In spite of the rapidity with which *The Federalist Papers* were written, they are considered by many to be perhaps the best example of political theorizing ever produced in the United States.[11]

The Anti-Federalist Response.   The Anti-Federalists used such pseudonyms as Montezuma and Philadelphiensis in their replies. Many of their attacks against the Constitution were also brilliant. They claimed that it was a document written by aristocrats and would lead to aristocratic tyranny. More important, the Anti-Federalists believed that the Constitution would create an overbearing and overburdening central government inimical to personal liberty. (The Constitution said nothing about freedom of the press, freedom of religion, or any other individual liberty.) They wanted to include a list of guaranteed liberties, or a bill of rights. Finally, the Anti-Federalists decried the weakened power of the states.

---

[10] There is some irony here. At the Constitutional Convention, those opposed to a strong central government pushed for a federal system because such a system would allow states to retain some of their sovereign rights (see Chapter 3). The label *Anti-Federalists* thus contradicted their essential views.
[11] Some scholars believe that *The Federalist Papers* played only a minor role in securing ratification of the Constitution. Even if this is true, they still have lasting value as an authoritative explanation of the Constitution.

The Anti-Federalists cannot be dismissed as a bunch of unpatriotic extremists. They included such patriots as Patrick Henry and Samuel Adams. They were arguing what had been the most prevalent view of the time. This view derived from the French political philosopher Montesquieu (1689–1755), who believed that liberty was only safe in relatively small societies governed by direct democracy or by a large legislature with small districts. The Madisonian view favoring a large republic, particularly expressed in *Federalist Papers* No. 10 and No. 51 (see Appendix D), was actually the more *un*popular view of the time. Madison was probably convincing because citizens were already persuaded that a strong national government was necessary to combat foreign enemies and to prevent domestic insurrections. Still, some researchers believe it was mainly the bitter experiences with the Articles of Confederation, rather than Madison's arguments, that created the setting for the ratification of the Constitution.[12]

The March to the Finish

The struggle for ratification continued. Strong majorities were procured in Delaware, Pennsylvania, New Jersey, Georgia, and Connecticut. After a bitter struggle in Massachusetts, that state ratified the Constitution by a narrow margin on February 6, 1788. By the spring, Maryland and South Carolina had ratified by sizable majorities. Then on June 21 of that year, New Hampshire became the ninth state to ratify the Constitution. Although the Constitution was formally in effect, this meant little without Virginia and New York, the latter not ratifying for yet another month. (See Table 2–2.)

The Bill of Rights

Ratification of the U.S. Constitution in several important states would not have occurred if the Federalists had not assured the states that amendments to the Constitution would be passed to protect individual liberties against incursions

---

[12]Of particular interest is the view of the Anti-Federalist position contained in Herbert J. Storing, *What the Anti-Federalists Were For* (Chicago: University of Chicago Press, 1981). Storing also edited seven volumes of the Anti-Federalist writings, *The Complete Anti-Federalist* (Chicago: University of Chicago Press, 1981). See also Josephine F. Pacheco, *Antifederalism: The Legacy of George Mason* (Fairfax, Va.: George Mason University Press, 1992).

TABLE 2-2

Ratification of the Constitution

STATE	DATE	VOTE FOR–AGAINST
Delaware	Dec. 7, 1787	30–0
Pennsylvania	Dec. 12, 1787	43–23
New Jersey	Dec. 18, 1787	38–0
Georgia	Jan. 2, 1788	26–0
Connecticut	Jan. 9, 1788	128–40
Massachusetts	Feb. 6, 1788	187–168
Maryland	Apr. 28, 1788	63–11
South Carolina	May 23, 1788	149–73
New Hampshire	June 21, 1788	57–46
Virginia	June 25, 1788	89–79
New York	July 26, 1788	30–27
North Carolina	Nov. 21, 1789*	194–77
Rhode Island	May 29, 1790	34–32

*Ratification was originally defeated on August 4, 1788, by a vote of 184–84.

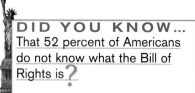

by the national government. Many of the recommendations of the state ratifying conventions included specific rights that were considered later by James Madison as he labored to draft what became the Bill of Rights. An important right was the right to free speech (see the feature *Politics Wired: The Internet and Free Speech*). (Although called the Bill of Rights, essentially the first ten amendments to the Constitution were a "bill of limits," because the amendments limited the powers of the national government in regard to the rights and liberties of individuals.)

Ironically, a year earlier Madison had told Jefferson, "I have never thought the omission [of the Bill of Rights] a material defect" of the Constitution. But Jefferson's enthusiasm for a bill of rights apparently influenced Madison, as did his desire to gain popular support for his election to Congress. He promised in his campaign letter to voters that, once elected, he would force Congress to "prepare and recommend to the states for ratification, the most satisfactory provisions for all essential rights."

Madison had to cull through more than two hundred state recommendations. It was no small task, and in retrospect he chose remarkably well. One of the rights appropriate for constitutional protection that he left out was equal protection under the laws—but that was not commonly regarded as a basic right at that time. It wasn't until 1868 that an amendment guaranteeing that no state shall deny equal protection to any person was ratified. (The Supreme Court has applied this guarantee to certain actions of the federal government as well.)

The final number of amendments that Madison and a specially appointed committee came up with was seventeen. Congress tightened the language somewhat and eliminated five of the amendments. Of the remaining twelve, two—dealing with the apportionment of representatives and the compensation of the

POLITICS **W I R E D**

The Internet and Free Speech

One of the most important rights of Americans is freedom of speech. Yet, even now, more than two hundred years after the U.S. Bill of Rights was ratified, citizens in some countries do not enjoy this right. Will widespread use of the Internet alter this situation? Some contend that it will.

Consider the People's Republic of China. There, the government prohibits subversive speech against the socialist system or speech that might harm national unity or the "spiritual civilization" that China's political leaders are attempting to build. Enter the Internet. On the one hand, Chinese leaders would like to take advantage

of the benefits of the Internet—particularly, the easier exchange of academic, scientific, and business and technical information. On the other hand, they do not want Chinese citizens to be exposed to Western influences that are contrary to the government's political and cultural goals. How do officials promote what they see as good uses of the Internet and at the same time restrict other uses?

To date, the Chinese government has employed two methods to control Internet use. One method is to use filtering software to block electronic pathways to any

objectionable sites—including the sites of such Western news organizations as CNN and *Time* magazine. The other method is to monitor the online activities of Internet users. Neither of these methods is foolproof, and the Chinese government may be fighting a losing battle. For example, even today, when only an estimated 250,000 people in China are online, it is difficult to monitor all of these users' activities. By the year 2002, when an estimated ten million people (or more) in China will be using the Internet, it may be impossible to do so.

Some believe that the Internet, by exposing Chinese citizens to a variety of views

on politics and culture, will eventually transform China. According to Steven Calcotte, a technology consultant in Beijing, it already is. Calcotte concluded that the first graduates from Beijing University to have had access to e-mail and the Internet have a much different outlook than previous graduates had.*

FOR CRITICAL ANALYSIS

Some argue that the Internet is a valuable weapon in the struggle for democracy. Could it also be used to restrict freedoms?

*The Economist, February 7, 1998, p. 43.

members of Congress—were not ratified immediately by the states. Eventually, Supreme Court decisions led to legislative reforms relating to apportionment. The amendment relating to compensation of members of Congress was ratified 203 years later—in 1992!

On December 15, 1791, the national Bill of Rights was adopted when Virginia agreed to ratify the ten amendments. The basic structure of American government had already been established. Now the fundamental rights and liberties of individuals were protected, at least in theory, at the national level. The proposed amendment that Madison characterized as "the most valuable amendment in the whole lot"—which would have prohibited the states from infringing on the freedoms of conscience, press, and jury trial—had been eliminated by the Senate. Thus, the Bill of Rights as adopted did not limit state power, and individual citizens had to rely on the guarantees contained in the particular state constitution or state bill of rights. The country had to wait until the violence of the Civil War before significant limitations on state power in the form of the Fourteenth Amendment became part of the national Constitution.

On ratification, the Bill of Rights became part of the U.S. Constitution. Because of the success of the American experiment in self-government, the U.S. Constitution has served as a model for many other nations (see the feature *Politics and Comparative Systems: Writing the World's Constitutions*).

The Motives of the Framers

In 1913, historian Charles Beard published *An Economic Interpretation of the Constitution of the United States,* charging that the Constitution had been produced primarily by wealthy property owners who desired a stronger government

POLITICS and Comparative Systems

Writing the World's Constitutions

The U.S. Constitution is now the oldest written constitution in the world. Scholars point out that one of the reasons the Constitution has withstood the test of time is its brevity. Its twenty or so pages (including amendments) set forth broad principles of government and do not give details on how those principles should be applied to specific situations. The founders realized that if a constitution formalizes in writing the particular views of its time, it will not serve a future age when those views give way to others.

The U.S. Constitution is also the most imitated consti-

tution in the world, having served as a model for constitutions in at least 174 countries. Many of these constitutions, including those in the republics of the former Soviet Union, have been drafted with the help of U.S. constitutional experts.

One of the challenges encountered by these scholars is trying to convince other nations that brevity in a constitution can be a good thing. People today want their constitutions to provide for every contingency, claims Martin Garbus, a New York expert on the First Amendment who helped the Czechs and Slovaks write

new constitutions. The trend today in constitutional writing seems to be away from brevity and toward comprehensiveness. This trend has had the obvious result: the world's constitutions are getting longer. South Africa's new constitution is 150 pages, and that of Brazil exceeds 200 pages. India has gone even further: its constitution fills more than 500 pages.

Ultimately, what constitutions do or do not include may not be all that important. After all, Iraq's bill of rights proclaims all kinds of freedoms, but that may not mean much. As Judge

Learned Hand once said, "Liberty lies in the hearts of men and women; when it dies there, no constitution, no law, no court can ever do much to help it." In the long run, what has made the U.S. Constitution endure is not only its words and the principles it expresses but also the American tradition of liberty.

FOR CRITICAL ANALYSIS

Which do you think is more important in determining whether a representative government will endure, a written constitution or a national tradition of liberty?

able to protect their property rights.[13] Beard also claimed that the Constitution had been imposed by undemocratic methods to prevent democratic majorities from exercising real power. He pointed out that there was never any popular vote on whether to hold a constitutional convention in the first place. Furthermore, even if such a vote had been taken, state laws generally restricted voting rights to property-owning white males, meaning most people in the country (white males without property, women, Native Americans, and slaves) were not eligible to vote.

Beard's thesis gave rise to a long-standing debate over the purpose of the Constitution. Was it designed to protect all of the people against the power of government and their own excesses? Or was it written to serve the interests of the people and groups that wielded economic power in the United States after the Revolution? Recall from Chapter 1 that the *elite theory* of American government assumes that our democracy is in essence an oligarchy in which decisions are made by an elite group—or competing elite groups—of wealthy and powerful individuals. Beard's thesis accords with this view.

Were the delegates to the Constitutional Convention an elite group? Was the Constitution truly favored by a majority of Americans? We look at these questions here. A further issue, discussed in this chapter's *Critical Perspective,* is whether the motives of the framers even matter in today's world.

[13]Charles A. Beard, *An Economic Interpretation of the Constitution of the United States* (New York: Macmillan, 1913; New York: Free Press, 1986).

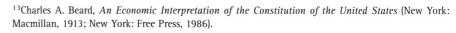

Critical│perspective

Does It Matter What the Founders Thought?

Much of the legal debate today over constitutional issues concerns the original meaning of the Constitution. Some argue that the founders' intent is of critical importance in interpreting the Constitution. Others contend that if the Supreme Court always applied constitutional provisions in light of what the founders thought, the Constitution could not be adapted to today's world–which is far different from that of the founders. In any event, the political dimensions of this debate have had grave consequences. For example, how the founders viewed the concept of federalism has had an impact on the issue of states' rights. After all, the Civil War was, in part, fought over this issue. In the 1990s, the issue of states' rights became prominent again.

The Founders' Intentions Are Not Really Relevant

Consider the founders' view of democracy. They wanted the general public to be somewhat distant from the government. Hence, they created a representative democracy, not a direct democracy. They also did not override state laws that restricted the vote to property-owning white males. Additionally, they instituted the electoral college so that the public could not elect presidents directly. According to one historian, the founders thought that even the electoral college system gave the public too much power. Yet they were apparently not too worried because they felt that the electors would often be deadlocked, in which case it would be up to the House of Representatives to decide who would be president. James Madison thought the House would have to decide the issue in nine out of every ten elections. George Mason believed a deadlock would occur in forty-nine out of every fifty elections.*

Indeed, even the word *democracy* seemed distasteful to the founders. Historian Charles Beard pointed out that the term was used by conservatives to smear their opponents as late as the mid-1800s. Certainly, the founders rarely–if ever–publicly identified themselves as Democrats. Even Thomas Jefferson, many of whose supporters called themselves Democrats or Democratic Republicans, stated in his 1801 inaugural address, "We are all Republicans–we are all Federalists" (not "We are all Democratic Republicans–we are all Federalists"). So, if the founders' views on democracy had prevailed over time, we certainly would not have the democratic form of government we have today.

Consider in addition the founders' view on equality, which are much different than those today. They readily accepted inequality in wealth and property. They were not remotely prepared for the concept of equality as it is understood by most Americans today. Even

*Richard Shenkman, *Legends, Lives & Cherished Myths of American History* (New York: Harper and Row, 1989), pp. 22–23.

Who Were the Delegates?

Who were the fifty-five delegates to the Constitutional Convention? They certainly did not represent a cross section of eighteenth-century American society. Indeed, most were members of the upper class. Consider the following facts:

1. Thirty-three were members of the legal profession.
2. Three were physicians.
3. Almost 50 percent were college graduates.
4. Seven were former chief executives of their respective states.
5. Six were large plantation owners.
6. Eight were important businesspersons.

They were also relatively young by today's standards: James Madison was thirty-six, Alexander Hamilton was only thirty-two, and Jonathan Dyton of New Jersey was twenty-six. The venerable Benjamin Franklin, however, was eighty-one and had to be carried in on a portable chair borne by four prisoners from a local jail. Not counting Franklin, the average age was just over forty-two.

Additionally, all of the delegates were white and male. In contrast, some of the demographics of the 535 members of the 106th Congress, which took office

Critical perspective

Does It Matter What the Founders Thought?–continued

Jefferson, who advocated freedom for the slaves, did not free his own slaves. Do we really want the views of these individuals to shape our interpretations and applications of the Constitution today?

The Founders' Intentions Should Be Heeded

Three constitutional and political scholars, Alan Brinkley, Kathleen M. Sullivan, and Nelson W. Polsby, argue that the Constitution should be read as it was written, no more no less.[†] In particular, they argue against the current trend toward devolution–the transfer of certain central government powers to the states (see Chapter 3). Many of those who support devolution argue that the framers did not intend the national government to have such extensive powers. Therefore, some powers should be "returned" to state governments. Brinkley, Sullivan, and Polsby, however, argue that such devolution is contrary to the intentions of the founders.

Sullivan, for example, points out that in *Federalist Paper* No. 10 Madison warned against the divisive forces of faction. As a counter to this, Madison argued that we needed to "extend the sphere" of government to national dimensions in order to keep the destructive power of factionalism in check. Madison believed that smaller, homogeneous governmental units were more vulnerable to the tyranny of

local majorities. Therefore, according to Sullivan, the attempts to decentralize the national government's powers today are not consistent with the founders' views. Such attempts are also dangerous for the nation. If more and more powers were to be transferred to state and local governments, the United States would become a "Balkanized republic, with 50 semi-autonomous governments." The result would be an accentuation of "the regional, economic, religious, ethnic, and racial differences that already divide us."

In sum, these scholars argue that enfeebling the federal government is not consistent with what the founders wanted. The result would be a national government with too little power to manage the economy, protect the environment, and address important social issues.

FOR CRITICAL ANALYSIS

1. Is there any way to reconcile the view of those in favor of devolution (transferring more power to the states) with the view held by Brinkley, Sullivan, and Polsby?
2. If a new Constitution were drafted today, would the courts, politicians, and political scientists have more or less difficulty understanding the views of those who wrote it than in understanding the views of the framers of our existing Constitution? Why or why not?

[†]Alan Brinkley et al., *The New Federalist Papers: Essays in Defense of the Constitution* (New York: W. W. Norton and Co., 1997).

in January 1999, are as follows: 39 are African Americans, 20 are Hispanics, and 65 are women.

Was the Constitution Truly Favored by the Majority?

Political scientists and historians still debate whether the Constitution actually was favored by a popular majority. The delegates at the various state ratifying conventions had been selected by only 150,000 of the approximately 4 million citizens of that time. That does not seem very democratic—at least not by today's standards. (On election day in 1996, for example, 91.4 million persons—of 185 million people of voting age—voted in the presidential election.) Even Federalist John Marshall believed that in some of the adopting states a majority of the people opposed the Constitution.[14] Indeed, some historians have suggested that if a Gallup poll could have been taken at that time, the Anti-Federalists would probably have outnumbered the Federalists.[15]

We have to realize, however, that at that time transportation and communication were rudimentary and slow. It would have been difficult to discover the true state of popular opinion, even if the leaders of the new nation had been concerned enough to do so.

Altering the Constitution: The Formal Amendment Process

The U.S. Constitution consists of 7,000 words. It is shorter than every state constitution except that of Vermont, which has 6,880 words. One of the reasons the federal Constitution is short is that the framers intended it to be only a framework for governing, to be interpreted by succeeding generations. One of the reasons it has remained short is because the formal amending procedure does not allow for changes to be made easily. Article V of the Constitution outlines the way in which amendments may be proposed and ratified (see Figure 2–3).

Two formal methods of proposing an amendment to the Constitution are available: (1) a two-thirds vote in each house of Congress or (2) a national con-

INFOTRAC®
COLLEGE EDITION

"Keep Your Amendments Off My Constitution"

---

[14]Beard, *An Economic Interpretation of the Constitution*, p. 299.
[15]Jim Powell, "James Madison—Checks and Balances to Limit Government Power," *The Freeman*, March 1996, p. 178.

FIGURE 2-3

The Formal Constitutional Amending Procedure

There are two ways of proposing amendments to the U.S. Constitution and two ways of ratifying proposed amendments. Among the four possibilities, the usual route has been proposal by Congress and ratification by state legislatures.

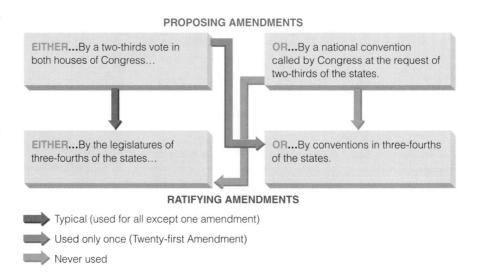

PROPOSING AMENDMENTS

EITHER...By a two-thirds vote in both houses of Congress...

OR...By a national convention called by Congress at the request of two-thirds of the states.

EITHER...By the legislatures of three-fourths of the states...

OR...By conventions in three-fourths of the states.

RATIFYING AMENDMENTS

Typical (used for all except one amendment)

Used only once (Twenty-first Amendment)

Never used

vention that is called by Congress at the request of two-thirds of the state legislatures (the second method has never been used).

Ratification can occur by one of two methods: (1) by a positive vote in three-fourths of the legislatures of the various states or (2) by special conventions called in the states for the specific purpose of ratifying the proposed amendment and a positive vote in three-fourths of them. The second method has been used only once, to repeal Prohibition. That situation was exceptional because it involved an amendment (the Twenty-first) to repeal an amendment (the Eighteenth, which had created Prohibition). State conventions were necessary for repeal of the Eighteenth Amendment because the "pro-dry" legislatures in the more conservative states would never have passed the repeal. (Note that Congress determines the method of ratification to be used by all states for each proposed constitutional amendment.)

Many Amendments Proposed, Few Accepted

Congress has considered more than eleven thousand amendments to the Constitution. Only thirty-three have been submitted to the states after having been approved by the required two-thirds vote in each chamber of Congress, and only twenty-seven have been ratified (see Table 2–3). It should be clear that the process is much more difficult than a graphic depiction such as Figure 2–3 can indicate. Because of competing social and economic interests, the requirement that two-thirds of both the House and Senate approve the amendments is difficult to achieve. Thirty-four senators, representing only seventeen sparsely populated states, could block any amendment. For example, the Republican-controlled House approved the Balanced Budget Amendment within the first one hundred days of the 104th Congress in 1995, but it was defeated in the Senate by one vote.

After approval by Congress, the process becomes even more arduous. Three-fourths of the state legislatures must approve the amendment. Only those

TABLE 2-3

Amendments to the Constitution

Amendments	Subject	Year Adopted	Time Required for Ratification
1st–10th	The Bill of Rights	1791	2 years, 2 months, 20 days
11th	Immunity of states from certain suits	1795	11 months, 3 days
12th	Changes in electoral college procedure	1804	6 months, 3 days
13th	Prohibition of slavery	1865	10 months, 3 days
14th	Citizenship, due process, and equal protection	1868	2 years, 26 days
15th	No denial of vote because of race, color, or previous condition of servitude	1870	11 months, 8 days
16th	Power of Congress to tax income	1913	3 years, 6 months, 22 days
17th	Direct election of U.S. senators	1913	10 months, 26 days
18th	National (liquor) prohibition	1919	1 year, 29 days
19th	Women's right to vote	1920	1 year, 2 months, 14 days
20th	Change of dates for congressional and presidential terms	1933	10 months, 21 days
21st	Repeal of the Eighteenth Amendment	1933	9 months, 15 days
22d	Limit on presidential tenure	1951	3 years, 11 months, 3 days
23d	District of Columbia electoral vote	1961	9 months, 13 days
24th	Prohibition of tax payment as a qualification to vote in federal elections	1964	1 year, 4 months, 9 days
25th	Procedures for determining presidential disability, presidential succession, and filling a vice presidential vacancy	1967	1 year, 7 months, 4 days
26th	Prohibition of setting minimum voting age above eighteen in any election	1971	3 months, 7 days
27th	Prohibition of Congress's voting itself a raise that takes effect before the next election	1992	203 years

A rally at the U.S. Capitol supporting a constitutional amendment to outlaw the desecration of the American flag.

amendments that have wide popular support across parties and in all regions of the country are likely to be approved.

Why was the amendment process made so difficult? The framers feared that a simple amendment process could lead to a tyranny of the majority, which could pass amendments to oppress disfavored individuals and groups. The cumbersome amendment process does not seem to stem the number of amendments that are proposed each year in Congress, however, particularly in recent years (see the feature *Politics and the Constitution: Amendment Fever?*). For some ideas on how you can become involved in the amendment process, see the *Toward Active Citizenship* feature at the end of this chapter.

Limits on Ratification

A reading of Article V of the Constitution reveals that the framers of the Constitution specified no time limit on the ratification process. The Supreme Court has held that Congress can specify a time for ratification as long as it is "reasonable." Since 1919, most proposed amendments have included a requirement that ratification be obtained within seven years. This was the case with the proposed Equal Rights Amendment. When three-fourths of the states had not ratified in time, Congress extended the limit for an additional three years and three months. That extension expired on June 30, 1982, and the amendment still had not been ratified. Another proposed amendment, which would have guaranteed congressional representation to the District of Columbia, fell far short of the thirty-eight state ratifications needed before its August 22, 1985, deadline.

On May 7, 1992, the Michigan state legislature became the thirty-eighth state to ratify the Twenty-seventh Amendment (on congressional compensation)—one of the two "lost" amendments of the twelve that originally were sent to the states in 1789. Because most of the amendments proposed in recent years have been given a time limit of only seven years by Congress, it was questionable for a while whether the amendment would become effective even if the necessary number of states ratified it. Is 203 years too long a lapse of time between the proposal and the final ratification of an amendment? It apparently was not, because the amendment was certified as legitimate by archivist Don Wilson of the National Archives on May 18, 1992.

POLITICS and the Constitution

Amendment Fever?

In the past few years, numerous constitutional amendments have been proposed in Congress. They include, for example, amendments to prohibit flag burning, to allow prayer in the schools, to limit the term of members of Congress, to ban abortion, to balance the budget, and to reform campaign financing.

Should Americans be at all concerned about this "amendment fever," as constitutional expert Kathleen Sullivan calls it? Some scholars think so. They are concerned that such unrestrained attempts to amend the Constitution are threatening the stability of the Constitution. The amendment process, they claim, is being used as a political tool by members of Congress who want to show their positions on various issues, such as abortion. After all, it is relatively easy to propose a constitutional amendment in Congress. All a member has to do is make a resolution, which then goes to a committee where it is recorded (and often forgotten).

Recently, about sixty former public officials, scholars, and attorneys formed a group called Citizens for the Constitution. The group's goal is to educate the public on the danger of continuing, unrestrained attempts to amend the Constitution.

According to one of the group's members, former federal judge Abner Mikva, "Our Constitution is a carefully crafted charter meant to set forth fundamental political ideals and a framework for governance. It should not be menaced by an amendment-of-the-week assault." The group believes, as did James Madison, that the amendment process should be used only "for certain great and extraordinary occasions"—and not to attain goals that can be addressed through simple legislation.

Others are not so worried about the profusion of proposed amendments. The founders, they argue, ensured that constitutional amendments would be few and far between by making the amendment process so cumbersome. The facts, they say, speak for themselves: only seventeen of the more than eleven thousand amendments that have been proposed since the ratification of the Bill of Rights have survived the amendment process and actually become a part of our Constitution.

FOR CRITICAL ANALYSIS

Do you agree with Citizens for the Constitution that the political use of amendment proposals is threatening the stability of the Constitution? Why or why not?

The National Convention Provision

The Constitution provides that a national convention requested by the legislatures of two-thirds of the states can propose a constitutional amendment. Congress has received approximately 400 convention applications since the Constitution was ratified; every state has applied at least once. Less than 20 applications were submitted during the Constitution's first hundred years, but more than 150 have been filed in the last two decades. No national convention has been held since 1787, and many national political and judicial leaders are uneasy about the prospect of convening a body that conceivably could do as the Constitutional Convention did—create a new form of government. The state legislative bodies that originate national convention applications, however, appear not to be uncomfortable with such a constitutional modification process; more than 230 state constitutional conventions have been held.

Informal Methods of Constitutional Change

Formal amendments are one way of changing our Constitution, and, as is obvious by their small number, they have not been resorted to very frequently. If we discount the first ten amendments (the Bill of Rights), which passed soon after the ratification of the Constitution, there have been only seventeen formal alterations of the Constitution in the more than two hundred years of its existence.

But looking at the sparse number of formal constitutional changes gives us an incomplete view. The brevity and ambiguity of the original document have permitted great changes in the Constitution by way of changing interpretations over time. As the United States grew, both in population and territory, new social and political realities emerged. Congress, presidents, and the courts found it necessary to interpret the Constitution's provisions in light of these new realities. The Constitution has proved to be a remarkably flexible document, adapting itself time and again to new events and concerns.

Congressional Legislation

The Constitution gives Congress broad powers to carry out its duties as the nation's legislative body. For example, Article I, Section 8, of the Constitution gives Congress the power to regulate foreign and interstate commerce. Although there is no clear definition of foreign commerce or interstate commerce in the Constitution, Congress has cited the *commerce clause* as the basis for passing thousands of laws that have defined the meaning of foreign and interstate commerce. Similarly, Article III, Section 1, states that the national judiciary shall consist of one supreme court and "such inferior courts, as Congress may from time to time ordain and establish." Through a series of acts, Congress has used this broad sanction to establish the federal court system of today.

Presidential Actions

Even though the Constitution does not expressly authorize the president to propose bills or even budgets to Congress, presidents since the time of Woodrow Wilson (who served as president from 1913 to 1921) have proposed hundreds of bills to Congress each year. Presidents have also relied on their Article II authority as commander in chief of the nation's armed forces to send American troops abroad into combat, although the Constitution provides that Congress has the power to declare war. Presidents have also conducted foreign affairs by the use of **executive agreements,** which are legally binding documents made between the president and a foreign head of state. The Constitution does not mention such agreements.

Executive Agreement
A binding international agreement made between chiefs of state that does not require legislative sanction.

Judicial Review

Another way of changing the Constitution—or of making it more flexible—is through the power of judicial review. **Judicial review** refers to the power of U.S. courts to invalidate actions undertaken by the legislative and executive branches of government. A state court, for example, may rule that a statute enacted by the state legislature is unconstitutional. Federal courts (and ultimately, the United States Supreme Court) may rule unconstitutional not only acts of Congress and decisions of the national executive branch but also state statutes, state executive actions, and even provisions of state constitutions.

The Constitution does not specifically mention the power of judicial review. Those in attendance at the Constitutional Convention, however, probably expected that the courts would have some authority to review the legality of acts by the executive and legislative branches. Indeed, Alexander Hamilton, in *Federalist Paper* No. 78 (see Appendix D), explicitly outlined the concept of judicial review. Whether the power of judicial review can be justified constitutionally is a question we explore in Chapter 15, in the context of the role of the judiciary. For now, suffice it to say that in 1803, the Supreme Court claimed this power for itself in *Marbury v. Madison*,[16] in which the Supreme Court ruled that a particular provision of an act of Congress was unconstitutional.

Judicial Review
The power of the Supreme Court or any court to declare unconstitutional federal or state laws and other acts of government.

[16]1 Cranch 137 (1803). (See Appendix B for information on how court decisions are referenced.) See the *Politics and the Law* in Chapter 15 for a discussion of the *Marbury v. Madison* case and its significance.

Through the process of judicial review, the Supreme Court adapts the Constitution to modern situations. Electronic technology, for example, did not exist when the Constitution was ratified. Nonetheless, in this century the Supreme Court used the Fourth Amendment guarantees against unreasonable searches and seizures to place limits on wiretapping and other electronic eavesdropping methods by government officials. Additionally, the Supreme Court has changed its interpretation of the Constitution in accordance with changing times. It ruled in 1896 that "separate-but-equal" public facilities for African Americans were constitutional; but by 1954 the times had changed, and the Supreme Court reversed that decision.[17] Woodrow Wilson summarized the Supreme Court's work when he described it as "a constitutional convention in continuous session." Basically, the law is what the Supreme Court says it is at any point in time.

Interpretation, Custom, and Usage

The Constitution has also been changed through its interpretation by both Congress and the president. Originally, the president had a staff consisting of personal secretaries and a few others. Today, because Congress delegates specific tasks to the president and the chief executive assumes political leadership, the executive office staff alone has increased to several thousand persons. The executive branch provides legislative leadership far beyond the intentions of the Constitution.

Changes in the ways of doing political business have also altered the Constitution. The Constitution does not mention political parties, yet these informal, "extraconstitutional" organizations make the nominations for offices, run the campaigns, organize the members of Congress, and in fact change the election system from time to time. The emergence and evolution of the party system, for example, have changed the way of electing the president. The Constitution calls for the electoral college to choose the president. Today, the people vote for electors who are pledged to the candidate of their party, effectively choosing the president themselves. Perhaps most strikingly, the Constitution has been adapted from serving the needs of a small, rural republic with no international prestige to providing a framework of government for an industrial giant with vast geographic, natural, and human resources.

The Constitution:
Issues for the New Century

The U.S. Constitution has been called a "living" constitution because the framers embodied it with sufficient flexibility that its meaning and application could change as the nation and its people changed. As we fully develop the age of technology, information, and communication, this inherent flexibility undoubtedly will be pushed to its limits at times. For example, how can our constitutional right to free speech be applied to electronic communications via the Internet? How can privacy rights be protected in an electronic age? Furthermore, how can any state or national law protect rights in an electronic jurisdiction that is essentially international in scope?

A further issue involves striking a balance between the rights of the fifty sovereign states and the powers of the national government. This has never been easy, and during the 1860s, the nation resorted to civil war to resolve the issue.

DID YOU KNOW...
That some of the framers of the Constitution were influenced by Native American political values, particularly those of the Iroquois Confederacy (the Iroquois concluded a treaty in 1520 that contained wording ["We, the people, to form a union, to establish peace, equity, and order . . . "] very similar to the Preamble to the U.S. Constitution)?

---

[17]*Brown v. Board of Education of Topeka,* 347 U.S. 483 (1954).

Citizens protest the availability of pornography on the Internet. How should the First Amendment's guarantee of freedom of speech be applied to materials available on the World Wide Web?

INFOTRAC ®
COLLEGE EDITION

"Proposed Religious Freedom Amendment"

As we enter the twenty-first century, there again seems to be a growing movement toward states' rights and away from national government involvement. We examine the challenges posed by a federal form of government—and how those challenges have been dealt with in the past—in Chapter 3. We return to this theme again in later chapters of this text.

A serious constitutional issue currently facing Congress has to do with the possible impeachment of President Clinton. Kenneth Starr, the independent counsel who investigated the president's relationship with White House intern Monica Lewinsky (see Chapter 13), submitted a report on his findings to Congress in the fall of 1998. In his report, he set forth a number of "grounds for impeachment," including perjury (in testimony given in relation to the Lewinsky affair) and obstruction of justice. Shortly thereafter, the House of Representatives voted to launch an investigation into the charges against Clinton.

Depending on the outcome of the investigation, the House may or may not decide to go forward with impeachment proceedings (see Chapters 12 and 13 for details on the impeachment process). If it does, an important constitutional question may eventually have to be decided: Do the charges against Clinton—including perjury and obstruction of justice—constitute grounds for impeachment under the Constitution? According to Article II, Section 4, of the Constitution, a president (or any other civil officer of the United States) "shall be removed from Office on Impeachment for, and Conviction of, Treason, Bribery, or other high Crimes and Misdemeanors." Given that Clinton has not been charged with committing treason or bribery, the question that would have to be decided is whether Clinton's offenses constitute "high Crimes and Misdemeanors."

These are just a few of the issues on today's horizon that can only be resolved through constitutional interpretation. Throughout this book, you will read about many more.

T O W A R D   A C T I V E   C I T I Z E N S H I P

HOW CAN YOU AFFECT THE U.S. CONSTITUTION?

The Constitution is an enduring document that has survived more than two hundred years of turbulent history. It is also a changing document, however. Twenty-seven amendments have been added to the original Constitution. How can you, as an individual, actively help to rewrite the Constitution?

One of the best ways is to work for (or against) a constitutional amendment. At the time of this writing, national coalitions of interest groups are supporting or opposing proposed amendments concerning prayer in the schools and antiabortion laws. If you want an opportunity to change the Constitution—or to assure that it is not changed—you could work for or with one of the alliances of groups interested in the fate of these amendments.

The following contacts should help you get started on efforts to affect the U.S. Constitution directly.

School Prayer Amendment

The proposed school prayer amendment, or Religious Freedom Amendment, would allow for student-sponsored prayer in public schools.

Supporters of the amendment claim that it is necessary to correct Supreme Court rulings that have strayed from the meaning of both the establishment clause and the free exercise clause. To learn more about the arguments in favor of the school prayer amendment, you can contact the Christian Coalition, 1801-L Sara Drive, Chesapeake, VA 23320 (757-424-2630). You can access its Web site at

www.cc.org/

Critics of the amendment claim that the amendment would allow students to impose their religious beliefs on classmates by holding prayers at mandatory school events. For information on this position, contact the American Civil Liberties Union (ACLU), 125 Broad St., 18th Floor, New York, NY 10004 (202-544-1681). The ACLU is online at

www.aclu.org/

Abortion

One of the organizations whose primary goal is to secure the passage of the Human Life Amendment is the American Life League, P.O. Box 1350, Stafford, VA 22555 (703-690-2049). It can be reached online at

www.all.org/

The Human Life Amendment would recognize in law the "personhood" of the unborn, secure human rights protections for the fetus from the time of fertilization, and prohibit abortion under any circumstances.

A political action and information organization working on behalf of "pro-choice" issues—that is, the right of women to have control over reproduction—is the National Abortion and Reproductive Rights Action League, 1156 15th St. N.W., Suite 700, Washington, DC 20005 (202-973-3000). Its URL is

www.naral.org/

This organization has roughly 500,000 members.

Key terms

Chapter summary

1 An early effort by Great Britain to establish North American colonies was unsuccessful. The first English colonies were established at Jamestown in 1607 and Plymouth in 1620. The Mayflower Compact created the first formal government. By the mid-1700s, other British colonies had been established along the Atlantic seaboard from Georgia to Maine.

2 In 1763, the British tried to reassert control over their increasingly independent-minded colonies through a series of taxes and legislative acts. The colonists responded with boycotts of British products and protests. Representatives of the colonies formed the First Continental Congress in 1774. The delegates sent a petition to the king of England expressing their grievances. The Second Continental Congress established an army in 1775 to defend colonists against any attacks by British soldiers.

3 On July 4, 1776, the Second Continental Congress approved the Declaration of Independence. Perhaps the most revolutionary aspects of the Declaration were its assumptions that people have natural rights to life, liberty, and the pursuit of happiness; that governments derive their power from the consent of the governed; and that people have a right to overthrow oppressive governments. During the Revolutionary War, all of the colonies adopted written constitutions that severely curtailed the power of executives, thus giving their legislatures predominant powers. By the end of the Revolutionary War, the states had signed the Articles of Confederation, creating a weak central government with few powers. The Articles proved to be unworkable because the national government had no way to assure compliance by the states with such measures as securing tax revenues.

4 General dissatisfaction with the Articles of Confederation prompted delegates to call the Philadelphia Convention in 1787. Although the delegates originally convened with the idea of amending the Articles, the discussions soon focused on creating a constitution for a new form of government. The Virginia plan and the New Jersey plan were offered but did not garner widespread support. A compromise offered by the state of Connecticut helped to break the large-state/small-state disputes dividing the delegates. The final version of the Constitution provided for the separation of powers and for checks and balances.

5 Fears of a strong central government prompted the addition of the Bill of Rights to the Constitution. The Bill of Rights secured a wide variety of freedoms for Americans, including the freedoms of religion, speech, and assembly. It was initially applied only to the federal government, but amendments to the Constitution following the Civil War made it clear that the Bill of Rights also applied to the states.

6 An amendment to the Constitution may be proposed by either a two-thirds vote in each house of Congress or by a national convention called by Congress at the request of two-thirds of the state legislatures. Ratification can occur by either a positive vote in three-fourths of the legislatures of the various states or by special conventions called in the states for the specific purpose of ratifying the proposed amendment and a positive vote in three-fourths of these state conventions. Informal methods of constitutional change include congressional legislation, presidential actions, judicial review, and changing interpretations of the Constitution.

Selected print and electronic resources

SUGGESTED READINGS

Casper, Gerhard. *Separating Power: Essays on the Founding Period.* Cambridge, Mass.: Harvard University Press, 1997. The author argues that the founders had not fully worked through their principles of constitutional government. Therefore, when scholars and judges try to interpret the Constitution by looking at the intentions of the framers, they run into difficulty.

Hamilton, Alexander, James Madison, and John Jay. *The Federalist Papers.* Cambridge, Mass.: Harvard University Press, 1961. The complete set of columns from the *New York Packet* defending the new Constitution is presented.

Holder, Angela Roddey, and John T. Roddey Holder. *The Meaning of the Constitution.* 3d ed. Hauppauge, N.Y.: Barron's Educational Series, Inc., 1997. This slim book brings the Constitution to life by giving examples of how each article and amendment apply to the world of everyday life and politics. An excellent resource for understanding the key role that the Constitution plays in the American political system.

Maier, Pauline. *American Scripture: Making the Declaration of Independence.* New York: Knopf, 1997. Mater offers an analysis of the Declaration of Independence, the context in which it was written, and its significance in American political life as "American Scripture." Her book has been acclaimed as the most scholarly and insightful work on this topic to appear in the last seventy-five years.

MEDIA RESOURCES

In the Beginning—A Bill Moyers program that features discussions with three prominent historians about the roots of the Constitution and its impact on our society.

John Locke—A video exploring the character and principal views of John Locke.

Where America Began—A video tour of American colonial history, including Jamestown, Williamsburg, and Yorktown.

Logging on

For U.S. founding documents, including the Declaration of Independence, the U.S. Constitution, scanned originals of the U.S. Constitution, and *The Federalist Papers,* go to Emory University School of Law's Web site at

www.law.emory.edu/FEDERAL/

The University of Oklahoma Law Center has a number of U.S. historical documents online, including many of those discussed in this chapter. Go to

www.law.uoknor.edu/ushist.html

The National Constitution Center provides information on the Constitution—including its history, current debates over constitutional provisions, and news articles—at the following site:

members.constitutioncenter.org/

A study aid for the U.S. Constitution is available at the following Web site, which has links to many different views for each segment of the Constitution:

members.aol.com/tcnbp/index.htm

If you want to look at state constitutions, go to

www.findlaw.com/casecode/state.html

To find constitutions for other countries, go to

www.uni-wuerzburg.de/law/home.html

Using the Internet for political analysis

As noted in this chapter, the U.S. Constitution is one of the most concise in the world. It clearly reflects the basic values of the framers in its emphasis on republican government, liberty, and limited government. Take a look at some modern constitutions at the following site, which is maintained by Washburn University School of Law:

lawlib.wuacc.edu/washlaw/forint/forintmain.html

Choose at least two constitutions from non-Western nations—that is, from Africa, Asia, or the Middle East. Compare these constitutions to that of the United States in terms of guarantees of the people's rights and liberties, the power of the central government, and the relationship between religion and the government.

The Constitution of the United States of America*

The Preamble

We the People of the United States, in Order to form a more perfect Union, establish Justice, insure domestic Tranquility, provide for the common defence, promote the general Welfare, and secure the Blessings of Liberty to ourselves and our Posterity, do ordain and establish this Constitution for the United States of America.

The Preamble declares that "We the People" are the authority for the Constitution (unlike the Articles of Confederation, which derived their authority from the states). The Preamble also sets out the purposes of the Constitution.

Article I. (Legislative Branch)

The first part of the Constitution is called Article 1; it deals with the organization and powers of the lawmaking branch of the national government, the Congress.

Section 1. Legislative Powers

All legislative Powers herein granted shall be vested in a Congress of the United States, which shall consist of a Senate and House of Representatives.

Section 2. House of Representatives

Clause 1: Composition and Election of Members. The House of Representatives shall be composed of Members chosen every second Year by the People of the several States, and the Electors in each State shall have the Qualifications requisite for Electors of the most numerous Branch of the State Legislature.

Each state has the power to decide who may vote for members of Congress. Within each state, those who may vote for state legislators may also vote for members of the House of Representatives (and, under the Seventeenth Amendment, for U.S. senators). When the Constitution was written, nearly all states limited voting rights to white male property owners or taxpayers at least twenty-one years old. Subsequent amendments granted voting power to African American men, all women, and eighteen-year-olds.

Clause 2: Qualifications. No Person shall be a Representative who shall not have attained to the Age of twenty five Years, and been seven Years a Citizen of the United States, and who shall not, when elected, be an Inhabitant of that State in which he shall be chosen.

Each member of the House must (1) be at least twenty-five years old, (2) have been a U.S. citizen for at least seven years, and (3) be a resident of the state in which she or he is elected.

Clause 3: Apportionment of Representatives and Direct Taxes. Representatives [and direct Taxes][1] shall be apportioned among the several States which may be included within this Union, according to their respective Numbers [which shall be determined by adding to the whole Number of free Persons, including those bound to Service for a Term of Years, and excluding Indians not taxed, three fifths of all other Persons].[2] The actual Enumeration shall be made within three Years after the first Meeting of the Congress of the United States, and within every subsequent Term of ten Years, in such Manner as they shall by Law direct. The Number of Representatives

---

*The spelling, capitalization, and punctuation of the original have been retained here. Brackets indicate passages that have been altered by amendments to the Constitution.

---

[1]Modified by the Sixteenth Amendment.
[2]Modified by the Fourteenth Amendment.

shall not exceed one for every thirty Thousand, but each State shall have at Least one Representative; and until such enumeration shall be made, the State of New Hampshire shall be entitled to chuse three, Massachusetts eight, Rhode Island and Providence Plantations one, Connecticut five, New York six, New Jersey four, Pennsylvania eight, Delaware one, Maryland six, Virginia ten, North Carolina five, South Carolina five, and Georgia three.

A state's representation in the House is based on the size of its population. Population is counted in each decade's census, after which Congress reapportions House seats. Since early in the twentieth century, the number of seats has been limited to 435.

Clause 4: Vacancies.   When vacancies happen in the Representation from any State, the Executive Authority thereof shall issue Writs of Election to fill such Vacancies.

The "Executive Authority" is the state's governor. When a vacancy occurs in the House, the governor calls a special election to fill it.

Clause 5: Officers and Impeachment.   The House of Representatives shall chuse their Speaker and other Officers; and shall have the sole Power of Impeachment.

The power to impeach is the power to accuse. In this case, it is the power to accuse members of the executive or judicial branch of wrongdoing or abuse of power. Once a bill of impeachment is issued, the Senate holds the trial.

Section 3. The Senate
Clause 1: Term and Number of Members.   The Senate of the United States shall be composed of two Senators from each State [chosen by the Legislature thereof],[3] for six Years; and each Senator shall have one Vote.

Every state has two senators, each of whom serves for six years and has one vote in the upper chamber. Since the Seventeenth Amendment in 1913, all senators are elected directly by voters of the state during the regular election.

Clause 2: Classification of Senators.   Immediately after they shall be assembled in Consequence of the first Election, they shall be divided as equally as may be into three Classes. The Seats of the Senators of the first Class shall be vacated at the Expiration of the second Year, of the second Class at the Expiration of the fourth Year, and of the third Class at the Expiration of the sixth Year, so that one third may be chosen every second Year; [and if Vacancies happen by Resignation, or otherwise, during the

Recess of the Legislature of any State, the Executive thereof may make temporary Appointments until the next Meeting of the Legislature, which shall then fill such Vacancies].[4]

One-third of the Senate's seats are open to election every two years (unlike the House, all of whose members are elected simultaneously).

Clause 3: Qualifications.   No Person shall be a Senator who shall not have attained to the Age of thirty Years, and been nine Years a Citizen of the United States, and who shall not, when elected, be an Inhabitant of that State for which he shall be chosen.

Every senator must be at least thirty years old, a citizen of the United States for a minimum of nine years, and a resident of the state in which he or she is elected.

Clause 4: The Role of the Vice President.   The Vice President of the United States shall be President of the Senate, but shall have no Vote, unless they be equally divided.

The vice president presides over meetings of the Senate but cannot vote unless there is a tie. The Constitution gives no other official duties to the vice president.

Clause 5: Other Officers.   The Senate shall chuse their other Officers, and also a President pro tempore, in the Absence of the Vice President, or when he shall exercise the Office of President of the United States.

The Senate votes for one of its members to preside when the vice president is absent. This person is usually called the president pro tempore because of the temporary situation of the position.

Clause 6: Impeachment Trials.   The Senate shall have the sole Power to try all Impeachments. When sitting for that Purpose, they shall be on Oath or Affirmation. When the President of the United States is tried, the Chief Justice shall preside: And no Person shall be convicted without the Concurrence of two thirds of the Members present.

The Senate conducts trials of officials that the House impeaches. The Senate sits as a jury, with the vice president presiding if the president is not on trial.

Clause 7: Penalties for Conviction.   Judgment in Cases of Impeachment shall not extend further than to removal from Office, and disqualification to hold and enjoy any Office of honor, Trust, or Profit under the United States:

---

[3]Repealed by the Seventeenth Amendment.

[4]Modified by the Seventeenth Amendment.

but the Party convicted shall nevertheless be liable and subject to Indictment, Trial, Judgment, and Punishment, according to Law.

On conviction of impeachment charges, the Senate can only force an official to leave office and prevent him or her from holding another office in the federal government. The individual, however, can still be tried in a regular court.

Section 4. Congressional Elections: Times, Manner, and Places

Clause 1: Elections. The Times, Places and Manner of holding Elections for Senators and Representatives, shall be prescribed in each State by the Legislature thereof; but the Congress may at any time by Law make or alter such Regulations, except as to the Places of chusing Senators.

Congress set the Tuesday after the first Monday in November in even-numbered years as the date for congressional elections. In states with more than one seat in the House, Congress requires that representatives be elected from districts within each state. Under the Seventeenth Amendment, senators are elected at the same places as other officials.

Clause 2: Sessions of Congress. [The Congress shall assemble at least once in every Year, and such Meeting shall be on the first Monday in December, unless they shall by Law appoint a different Day.][5]

Congress has to meet every year at least once. The regular session now begins at noon on January 3 of each year, subsequent to the Twentieth Amendment, unless Congress passes a law to fix a different date. Congress stays in session until its members vote to adjourn. Additionally, the president may call a special session.

Section 5. Powers and Duties of the Houses

Clause 1: Admitting Members and Quorum. Each House shall be the Judge of the Elections, Returns, and Qualifications of its own Members, and a Majority of each shall constitute a Quorum to do Business; but a smaller Number may adjourn from day to day, and may be authorized to compel the Attendance of absent Members, in such Manner, and under such Penalties as each House may provide.

Each chamber may exclude or refuse to seat a member-elect.

The quorum rule requires that 218 members of the House and 51 members of the Senate be present in order to conduct business. This rule is normally not enforced in the handling of routine matters.

---

[5]Changed by the Twentieth Amendment.

Clause 2: Rules and Discipline of Members. Each House may determine the Rules of its Proceedings, punish its Members for disorderly Behaviour, and, with the Concurrence of two thirds, expel a Member.

The House and the Senate may adopt their own rules to guide their proceedings. Each may also discipline its members for conduct that is deemed unacceptable. No member may be expelled without a two-thirds majority vote in favor of expulsion.

Clause 3: Keeping a Record. Each House shall keep a Journal of its Proceedings, and from time to time publish the same, excepting such Parts as may in their Judgment require Secrecy; and the Yeas and Nays of the Members of either House on any question shall, at the Desire of one fifth of those Present, be entered on the Journal.

The journals of the two houses are published at the end of each session of Congress.

Clause 4: Adjournment. Neither House, during the Session of Congress, shall, without the Consent of the other, adjourn for more than three days, nor to any other Place than that in which the two Houses shall be sitting.

Congress has the power to determine when and where to meet, provided, however, that both houses meet in the same city. Neither house may recess in excess of three days without the consent of the other.

Section 6. Rights of Members

Clause 1: Compensation and Privileges. The Senators and Representatives shall receive a Compensation for their services, to be ascertained by Law, and paid out of the Treasury of the United States. They shall in all Cases, except Treason, Felony and Breach of the Peace, be privileged from Arrest during their Attendance at the Session of their respective Houses, and in going to and returning from the same; and for any Speech or Debate in either House, they shall not be questioned in any other Place.

Congressional salaries are to be paid by the U.S. Treasury rather than by the members' respective states. The original salaries were $6 per day; in 1857 they were $3,000 per year. Both representatives and senators currently are paid $136,700 each year.

Treason is defined in Article III, Section 3. A felony is any serious crime. A breach of the peace is any indictable offense less than treason or a felony. Members cannot be arrested for things they say during speeches and debates in Congress. This immunity applies to the Capitol Building itself and not to their private lives.

Clause 2: Restrictions. No Senator or Representative shall, during the Time for which he was elected, be appointed to any civil Office under the Authority of the United States, which shall have been created, or the Emoluments whereof shall have been encreased during such time; and no Person holding any Office under the United States, shall be a Member of either House during his Continuance in Office.

During the term for which a member was elected, he or she cannot concurrently accept another federal government position.

Section 7. Legislative Powers: Bills and Resolutions

Clause 1: Revenue Bills. All Bills for raising Revenue shall originate in the House of Representatives; but the Senate may propose or concur with Amendments as on other Bills.

All tax and appropriation bills for raising money have to originate in the House of Representatives. The Senate, though, often amends such bills and may even substitute an entirely different bill.

Clause 2: The Presidential Veto. Every Bill which shall have passed the House of Representatives and the Senate, shall, before it becomes a Law, be presented to the President of the United States; If he approve he shall sign it, but if not he shall return it, with his Objections to the House in which it shall have originated, who shall enter the Objections at large on their Journal, and proceed to reconsider it. If after such Reconsideration two thirds of that House shall agree to pass the Bill, it shall be sent together with the Objections, to the other House, by which it shall likewise be reconsidered, and if approved by two thirds of that House, it shall become a Law. But in all such Cases the Votes of both Houses shall be determined by Yeas and Nays, and the Names of the Persons voting for and against the Bill shall be entered on the Journal of each House respectively. If any Bill shall not be returned by the President within ten Days (Sundays excepted) after it shall have been presented to him, the Same shall be a Law, in like Manner as if he had signed it, unless the Congress by their Adjournment prevent its Return in which Case it shall not be a Law.

When Congress sends the president a bill, he or she can sign it (in which case it becomes law) or send it back to the house in which it originated. If it is sent back, a two-thirds majority of each house must pass it again for it to become law. If the president neither signs it nor sends it back within ten days, it becomes law anyway, unless Congress adjourns in the meantime.

Clause 3: Actions on Other Matters. Every Order, Resolution, or Vote to which the Concurrence of the Senate and House of Representatives may be necessary (except on a question of Adjournment) shall be presented to the President of the United States; and before the Same shall take Effect, shall be approved by him, or being disapproved by him, shall be repassed by two thirds of the Senate and House of Representatives, according to the Rules and Limitations prescribed in the Case of a Bill.

The president must either sign or veto everything that Congress passes, except votes to adjourn and resolutions not having the force of law.

Section 8. The Powers of Congress

Clause 1: Taxing. The Congress shall have Power To lay and collect Taxes, Duties, Imposts and Excises, to pay the Debts and provide for the common Defence and general Welfare of the United States; but all Duties, Imposts and Excises shall be uniform throughout the United States;

Duties are taxes on imports and exports. Impost is a generic term for tax. Excises are taxes on the manufacture, sale, or use of goods.

Clause 2: Borrowing. To borrow Money on the credit of the United States;

Congress has the power to borrow money, which is normally carried out through the sale of U.S. treasury bonds on which interest is paid. Note that the Constitution places no limit on the amount of government borrowing.

Clause 3: Regulation of Commerce. To regulate Commerce with foreign Nations, and among the several States, and with the Indian Tribes;

This is the commerce clause, which gives to the Congress the power to regulate interstate and foreign trade. Much of the activity of Congress is based on this clause.

Clause 4: Naturalization and Bankruptcy. To establish a uniform Rule of Naturalization, and uniform Laws on the subject of Bankruptcies throughout the United States;

Only Congress may determine how aliens can become citizens of the United States. Congress may make laws with respect to bankruptcy.

Clause 5: Money and Standards. To coin Money, regulate the Value thereof, and of foreign Coin, and fix the Standard of Weights and Measures;

Congress mints coins and prints and circulates paper money. Congress can establish uniform measures of time, distance, weight, and so on. In 1838, Congress adopted the English system of weights and measurements as our national standard.

Clause 6: Punishing Counterfeiters. To provide for the Punishment of counterfeiting the Securities and current Coin of the United States;

Congress has the power to punish those who copy American money and pass it off as real. Currently, the fine is up to $5,000 and/or imprisonment for up to fifteen years.

Clause 7: Roads and Post Offices. To establish Post Offices and post Roads;

Post roads include all routes over which mail is carried— highways, railways, waterways, and airways.

Clause 8: Patents and Copyrights. To promote the Progress of Science and useful Arts, by securing for limited Times to Authors and Inventors the exclusive Right to their respective Writings and Discoveries;

Authors' and composers' works are protected by copyrights established by copyright law, which currently is the 1978 Copyright Act. Copyrights are valid for the life of the author or composer plus fifty years. Inventors' works are protected by patents, which vary in length of protection from three and a half to seventeen years. A patent gives a person the exclusive right to control the manufacture or sale of her or his invention.

Clause 9: Lower Courts. To constitute Tribunals inferior to the supreme Court;

Congress has the authority to set up all federal courts, except the Supreme Court, and to decide what cases those courts will hear.

Clause 10: Punishment for Piracy. To define and punish Piracies and Felonies committed on the high Seas, and Offences against the Law of Nations;

Congress has the authority to prohibit the commission of certain acts outside U.S. territory and to punish certain violations of international law.

Clause 11: Declaration of War. To declare War, grant Letters of Marque and Reprisal, and make Rules concerning Captures on Land and Water;

Only Congress can declare war, although the president, as commander in chief, can make war without Congress's formal declaration. Letters of marque and reprisal authorized private parties to capture and destroy enemy ships in wartime. Since the middle of the nineteenth century, international law has prohibited letters of marque and reprisal, and the United States has honored the ban.

Clause 12: The Army. To raise and support Armies, but no Appropriation of Money to that Use shall be for a longer Term than two Years;

Congress has the power to create an army; the money used to pay for it must be appropriated for no more than two-year intervals. This latter restriction gives ultimate control of the army to civilians.

Clause 13: Creation of a Navy. To provide and maintain a Navy;

This clause allows for the maintenance of a navy. In 1947, Congress created the U.S. Air Force.

Clause 14: Regulation of the Armed Forces. To make Rules for the Government and Regulation of the land and naval Forces;

Congress sets the rules for the military mainly by way of the Uniform Code of Military Justice, which was enacted in 1950 by Congress.

Clause 15: The Militia. To provide for calling forth the Militia to execute the Laws of the Union, suppress Insurrections and repel Invasions;

The militia is known today as the National Guard. Both Congress and the president have the authority to call the National Guard into federal service.

Clause 16: How the Militia Is Organized. To provide for organizing, arming, and disciplining the Militia, and for governing such Part of them as may be employed in the Service of the United States, reserving to the States respectively, the Appointment of the Officers, and the Authority of training the Militia according to the discipline prescribed by Congress;

This clause gives Congress the power to "federalize" state militia (National Guard). When called into such service, the National Guard is subject to the same rules that Congress has set forth for the regular armed services.

Clause 17: Creation of the District of Columbia. To exercise exclusive Legislation in all Cases whatsoever, over such District (not exceeding ten Miles square) as may, by Cession of particular States, and the Acceptance of Congress, become the Seat of the Government of the United States, and to exercise like Authority over all Places purchased by the Consent of the Legislature of the State in which the Same shall be, for the Erection of Forts, Magazines, Arsenals, dock-Yards, and other needful Buildings;—And

Congress established the District of Columbia as the national capital in 1791. Virginia and Maryland had granted land for the District, but Virginia's grant was returned because it was believed it would not be needed. Today, the District covers sixty-nine square miles.

Clause 18: The Elastic Clause. To make all Laws which shall be necessary and proper for carrying into Execution the foregoing Powers, and all other Powers vested by this Constitution in the Government of the United States, or in any Department or Officer thereof.

This clause—the necessary and proper clause, or the elastic clause—grants no specific powers, and thus it can be stretched to fit different circumstances. It has allowed Congress to adapt the government to changing needs and times.

Section 9. The Powers Denied to Congress
Clause 1: Question of Slavery. The Migration or Importation of such Persons as any of the States now existing shall think proper to admit, shall not be prohibited by the Congress prior to the Year one thousand eight hundred and eight, but a Tax or duty may be imposed on such Importation, not exceeding ten dollars for each Person.

"Persons" referred to slaves. Congress outlawed the slave trade in 1808.

Clause 2: Habeas Corpus. The privilege of the Writ of Habeas Corpus shall not be suspended, unless when in Cases of Rebellion or Invasion the public Safety may require it.

A writ of habeas corpus is a court order directing a sheriff or other public officer who is detaining another person to "produce the body" of the detainee so the court can assess the legality of the detention.

Clause 3: Special Bills. No Bill of Attainder or ex post facto Law shall be passed.

A bill of attainder is a law that inflicts punishment without a trial. An ex post facto law is a law that inflicts punishment for an act that was not illegal when it was committed.

Clause 4: Direct Taxes. [No Capitation, or other direct, Tax shall be laid, unless in Proportion to the Census or Enumeration herein before directed to be taken.][6]

A capitation is a tax on a person. A direct tax is a tax paid directly to the government, such as a property tax. This

clause was intended to prevent Congress from levying a tax on slaves per person and thereby taxing slavery out of existence.

Clause 5: Export Taxes. No Tax or Duty shall be laid on Articles exported from any State.

Congress may not tax any goods sold from one state to another or from one state to a foreign country. (Congress does have the power to tax goods that are bought from other countries, however.)

Clause 6: Interstate Commerce. No Preference shall be given by any Regulation of Commerce or Revenue to the Ports of one State over those of another: nor shall Vessels bound to, or from, one State, be obliged to enter, clear, or pay Duties in another.

Congress may not treat different ports within the United States differently in terms of taxing and commerce powers. Congress may not tax goods sent from one state to another. Finally, Congress may not give one state's port a legal advantage over those of another state.

Clause 7: Treasury Withdrawals. No Money shall be drawn from the Treasury, but in Consequence of Appropriations made by Law; and a regular Statement and Account of the Receipts and Expenditures of all public Money shall be published from time to time.

Federal funds can be spent only as Congress authorizes. This is a significant check on the president's power.

Clause 8: Titles of Nobility. No Title of Nobility shall be granted by the United States: And no Person holding any Office of Profit or Trust under them, shall, without the Consent of the Congress, accept of any present, Emolument, Office, or Title, of any kind whatever, from any King, Prince, or foreign State.

On no person in the United States may be bestowed a title of nobility, such as a duke or duchess. This clause also discourages bribery of American officials by foreign governments.

Section 10. Those Powers Denied to the States
Clause 1: Treaties and Coinage. No State shall enter into any Treaty, Alliance, or Confederation; grant Letters of Marque and Reprisal; coin Money; emit Bills of Credit; make any Thing but gold and silver Coin a Tender in Payment of Debts; pass any Bill of Attainder, ex post facto Law, or Law impairing the Obligation of Contracts, or grant any Title of Nobility.

Prohibiting state laws "impairing the Obligation of Contracts" was intended to protect creditors. (Shays's Rebellion—an attempt to prevent courts from giving effect

---

[6]Modified by the Sixteenth Amendment.

to creditors' legal actions against debtors—occurred only one year before the Constitution was written.)

Clause 2: Duties and Imposts. No State shall, without the Consent of the Congress, lay any Imports or Duties on Imports or Exports, except what may be absolutely necessary for executing its inspection Laws; and the net Produce of all Duties and Imposts, laid by any State on Imports or Exports, shall be for the Use of the Treasury of the United States; and all such Laws shall be subject to the Revision and Controul of the Congress.

Only Congress can tax imports. Further, the states cannot tax exports.

Clause 3: War. No State shall, without the Consent of Congress, lay any Duty of Tonnage, keep Troops, or Ships of War in time of Peace, enter into any Agreement or Compact with another State, or with a foreign Power or engage in War, unless actually invaded, or in such imminent Danger as will not admit of delay.

A duty of tonnage is a tax on ships according to their cargo capacity. No states may effectively tax ships according to their cargo unless Congress agrees. Additionally, this clause forbids any state to keep troops or warships during peacetime or to make a compact with another state or foreign nation unless Congress so agrees. States can, in contrast, maintain a militia, but its use has to be limited to internal disorders that occur within a state—unless, of course, the militia is called into federal service.

Article II. (Executive Branch)

Section 1. The Nature and Scope of Presidential Power

Clause 1: Four-Year Term. The executive Power shall be vested in a President of the United States of America. He shall hold his Office during the Term of four Years, and, together with the Vice President, chosen for the same Term, be elected, as follows.

The president has the power to carry out laws made by Congress, called the executive power. He or she serves in office for a four-year term after election. The Twenty-second Amendment limits the number of times a person may be elected president.

Clause 2: Choosing Electors from Each State. Each State shall appoint, in such Manner as the Legislature thereof may direct, a Number of Electors, equal to the whole Number of Senators and Representatives to which the State may be entitled in the Congress; but no Senator or Representative, or Person holding an Office of Trust or Profit under the United States, shall be appointed an Elector.

The "Electors" are more commonly known as the "electoral college." The president is elected by electors—that is, representatives chosen by the people—rather than by the people directly.

Clause 3: The Former System of Elections. [The Electors shall meet in their respective States, and vote by Ballot for two Persons, of whom one at least shall not be an Inhabitant of the same State with themselves. And they shall make a List of all the Persons voted for, and of the Number of Votes for each; which List they shall sign and certify, and transmit sealed to the Seat of the Government of the United States, directed to the President of the Senate. The President of the Senate shall, in the Presence of the Senate and House of Representatives, open all the Certificates, and the Votes shall then be counted. The Person having the greatest Number of Votes shall be the President, if such Number be a Majority of the whole Number of Electors appointed; and if there be more than one who have such Majority, and have an equal Number of Votes, then the House of Representatives shall immediately chuse by Ballot one of them for President; and if no Person have a Majority, then from the five highest on the List the said House shall in like Manner chuse the President. But in chusing the President, the Votes shall be taken by States, the Representation from each State having one Vote; A quorum for this Purpose shall consist of a Member or Members from two thirds of the States, and a Majority of all the States shall be necessary to a Choice. In every Case, after the Choice of the President, the Person having the greater Number of Votes of the Electors shall be the Vice President. But if there should remain two or more who have equal Votes, the Senate shall chuse from them by Ballot the Vice President.][7]

The original method of selecting the president and vice president was replaced by the Twelfth Amendment. Apparently, the framers did not anticipate the rise of political parties and the development of primaries and conventions.

Clause 4: The Time of Elections. The Congress may determine the Time of chusing the Electors, and the Day on which they shall give their Votes; which Day shall be the same throughout the United States.

Congress set the Tuesday after the first Monday in November every fourth year as the date for choosing electors. The electors cast their votes on the Monday after the second Wednesday in December of that year.

Clause 5: Qualifications for President. No person except a natural born Citizen, or a Citizen of the United States, at the time of the Adoption of this Constitution,

---

[7]Changed by the Twelfth Amendment.

shall be eligible to the Office of President; neither shall any Person be eligible to that Office who shall not have attained to the Age of thirty five Years, and been fourteen Years a Resident within the United States.

The president must be a natural-born citizen, be at least thirty-five years of age when taking office, and have been a resident within the United States for at least fourteen years.

Clause 6: Succession of the Vice President. [In Case of the Removal of the President from Office, or of his Death, Resignation or Inability to discharge the Powers and Duties of the said Office, the same shall devolve on the Vice President, and the Congress may by Law provide for the Case of Removal, Death, Resignation or Inability, both of the President and Vice President, declaring what Officer shall then act as President, and such Officer shall act accordingly, until the Disability be removed, or a President shall be elected.][8]

This former section provided for the method by which the vice president was to succeed to the presidency, but its wording is ambiguous. It was replaced by the Twenty-fifth Amendment.

Clause 7: The President's Salary. The President shall, at stated Times, receive for his Services, a Compensation, which shall neither be encreased nor diminished during the Period for which he shall have been elected, and he shall not receive within that Period any other Emolument from the United States, or any of them.

The president maintains the same salary during each four-year term. Moreover, she or he may not receive additional cash payments from the government. Originally set at $25,000 per year, it is currently $200,000 a year plus a $50,000 taxable expense account.

Clause 8: The Oath of Office. Before he enter on the Execution of his Office, he shall take the following Oath or Affirmation: "I do solemnly swear (or affirm) that I will faithfully execute the Office of President of the United States, and will to the best of my Ability, preserve, protect and defend the Constitution of the United States."

The president is "sworn in" prior to beginning the duties of the office. Currently, the taking of the oath of office occurs on January 20, following the November election. The ceremony is called the inauguration. The oath of office is administered by the chief justice of the United States Supreme Court.

Section 2. Powers of the President
Clause 1: Commander in Chief. The President shall be Commander in Chief of the Army and Navy of the United States, and of the Militia of the several States, when called into the actual Service of the United States; he may require the Opinion, in writing, of the principal Officer in each of the executive Departments, upon any Subject relating to the Duties of their respective Offices, and he shall have Power to grant Reprieves and Pardons for Offences against the United States, except in Cases of Impeachment.

The armed forces are placed under civilian control because the president is a civilian, but still commander in chief of the military. The president may ask for the help of the heads of each of the executive departments (thereby creating the cabinet). The cabinet members are chosen by the president with the consent of the Senate, but they can be removed without Senate approval.

The president's clemency powers extend only to federal cases. In those cases, he or she may grant a full or conditional pardon, or reduce a prison term or fine.

Clause 2: Treaties and Appointment. He shall have Power, by and with the Advice and Consent of the Senate, to make Treaties, provided two thirds of the Senators present concur; and he shall nominate, and by and with the Advice and Consent of the Senate, shall appoint Ambassadors, other public Ministers and Consuls, Judges of the supreme Court, and all other Officers of the United States, whose Appointments are not herein otherwise provided for, and which shall be established by Law; but the Congress may by Law vest the Appointment of such inferior Officers, as they think proper, in the President alone, in the Courts of Law, or in the Heads of Departments.

Many of the major powers of the president are identified in this clause, including the power to make treaties with foreign governments (with the approval of the Senate by a two-thirds vote) and the power to appoint ambassadors, Supreme Court justices, and other government officials. Most such appointments require Senate approval.

Clause 3: Vacancies. The President shall have Power to fill up all Vacancies that may happen during the Recess of the Senate, by granting Commissions which shall expire at the end of their next Session.

The president has the power to appoint temporary officials to fill vacant federal offices without Senate approval if the Congress is not in session. Such appointments expire automatically at the end of Congress's next term.

Section 3. Duties of the President
He shall from time to time give to the Congress Information of the State of the Union, and recommend to their Consideration such Measures as he shall judge necessary and expedient; he may, on extraordinary Occasions, convene both Houses, or either of them, and in Case of

---

[8]Modified by the Twenty-fifth Amendment.

Disagreement between them, with Respect to the Time of Adjournment, he may adjourn them to such Time as he shall think proper; he shall receive Ambassadors and other public Ministers; he shall take Care that the Laws be faithfully executed, and shall Commission all the Officers of the United States.

Annually, the president reports on the state of the union to Congress, recommends legislative measures, and proposes a federal budget. The State of the Union speech is a statement not only to Congress but also to the American people. After it is given, the president proposes a federal budget and presents an economic report. At any time he or she so chooses, the president may send special messages to Congress while it is in session. The president has the power to call special sessions, to adjourn Congress when its two houses do not agree for that purpose, to receive diplomatic representatives of other governments, and to ensure the proper execution of all federal laws. The president further has the ability to empower federal officers to hold their positions and to perform their duties.

Section 4. Impeachment

The President, Vice President and all civil Officers of the United States, shall be removed from Office on Impeachment for, and Conviction of, Treason, Bribery, or other high Crimes and Misdemeanors.

Treason denotes giving aid to the nation's enemies. The definition of high crimes and misdemeanors is usually given as serious abuses of political power. In either case, the president or vice president may be accused by the House (called an impeachment) and then removed from office if convicted by the Senate. (Note that impeachment does not mean removal, but rather the state of being accused of treason or high crimes and misdemeanors.)

Article III. (Judicial Branch)

Section 1. Judicial Powers, Courts, and Judges

The judicial Power of the United States, shall be vested in one supreme Court, and in such inferior Courts as the Congress may from time to time ordain and establish. The Judges, both of the supreme and inferior Courts, shall hold their Offices during good Behaviour, and shall, at stated Times, receive for their Services a Compensation, which shall not be diminished during their Continuance in Office.

The Supreme Court is vested with judicial power, as are the lower federal courts that Congress creates. Federal judges serve in their offices for life unless they are impeached and convicted by Congress. The payment of federal judges may not be reduced during their time in office.

Section 2. Jurisdiction

Clause 1: Cases under Federal Jurisdiction. The judicial Power shall extend to all Cases, in Law and Equity, arising under this Constitution, the Laws of the United States, and Treaties made, or which shall be made, under their Authority;—to all Cases affecting Ambassadors, other public Ministers and Consuls;—to all Cases of admiralty and maritime Jurisdiction;—to Controversies to which the United States shall be a Party;—to Controversies between two or more States; [—between a State and Citizens of another State;—][9] between Citizens of different States;—between Citizens of the same State claiming Lands under Grants of different States, [and between a State, or the Citizens thereof, and foreign States, Citizens or Subjects.][10]

The federal courts take on cases that concern the meaning of the U.S. Constitution, all federal laws, and treaties. They also can take on cases involving citizens of different states and citizens of foreign nations.

Clause 2: Cases for the Supreme Court. In all Cases affecting Ambassadors, other public Ministers and Consuls, and those in which a State shall be a Party, the supreme Court shall have original Jurisdiction. In all the other Cases before mentioned, the supreme Court shall have appellate Jurisdiction, both as to Law and Fact, with such Exceptions, and under such Regulations as the Congress shall make.

In a limited number of situations, the Supreme Court acts as a trial court and has original jurisdiction. These cases involve a representative from another country or involve a state. In all other situations, the cases must first be tried in the lower courts and then can be appealed to the Supreme Court. Congress may, however, make exceptions. Today the Supreme Court acts as a trial court of first instance on rare occasions.

Clause 3: The Conduct of Trials. The Trial of all Crimes, except in Cases of Impeachment, shall be by Jury; and such Trial shall be held in the State where the said Crimes shall have been committed; but when not committed within any State, the Trial shall be at such Place or Places as the Congress may by Law have directed.

Any person accused of a federal crime is granted the right to a trial by jury in a federal court in that state in which the crime was committed. Trials of impeachment are an exception.

Section 3. Treason

Clause 1: The Definition of Treason. Treason against the United States, shall consist only in levying War against

---

[9]Modified by the Eleventh Amendment.
[10]Modified by the Eleventh Amendment.

them, or, in adhering to their Enemies, giving them Aid and Comfort. No Person shall be convicted of Treason unless on the Testimony of two Witnesses to the same overt Act, or on Confession in open Court.

Treason is the making of war against the United States or giving aid to its enemies.

Clause 2: Punishment. The Congress shall have Power to declare the Punishment of Treason, but no Attainder of Treason shall work Corruption of Blood, or Forfeiture except during the Life of the Person attainted.

Congress has provided that the punishment for treason ranges from a minimum of five years in prison and/or a $10,000 fine to a maximum of death. "No Attainder of Treason shall work Corruption of Blood" prohibits punishment of the traitor's heirs.

Article IV. (Relations among the States)

Section 1. Full Faith and Credit
Full Faith and Credit shall be given in each State to the public Acts, Records, and judicial Proceedings of every other State. And the Congress may by general Laws prescribe the Manner in which such Acts, Records and Proceedings shall be proved, and the Effect thereof.

All states are required to respect one another's laws, records, and lawful decisions. There are exceptions, however. A state does not have to enforce another state's criminal code. Nor does it have to recognize another state's grant of a divorce if the person obtaining the divorce did not establish legal residence in the state in which it was given.

Section 2. Treatment of Citizens
Clause 1: Privileges and Immunities. The Citizens of each State shall be entitled to all Privileges and Immunities of Citizens in the several States.

A citizen of a state has the same rights and privileges as the citizens of another state in which he or she happens to be.

Clause 2: Extradition. A Person charged in any State with Treason, Felony, or other Crime, who shall flee from Justice, and be found in another State, shall on Demand of the executive Authority of the State from which he fled, be delivered up, to be removed to the State having Jurisdiction of the Crime.

Any person accused of a crime who flees to another state must be returned to the state in which the crime occurred.

Clause 3: Fugitive Slaves. [No Person held to Service or Labour in one State, under the Laws thereof, escaping

into another, shall, in Consequence of any Law or Regulation therein, be discharged from such Service or Labour, but shall be delivered up on Claim of the Party to whom such Service or Labour may be due.][11]

This clause was struck down by the Thirteenth Amendment, which abolished slavery in 1865.

Section 3. Admission of States
Clause 1: The Process. New States may be admitted by the Congress into this Union; but no new State shall be formed or erected within the Jurisdiction of any other State; nor any State be formed by the Junction of two or more States, or Parts of States, without the Consent of the Legislatures of the States concerned as well as of the Congress.

Only Congress has the power to admit new states to the union. No state may be created by taking territory from an existing state unless the state's legislature so consents.

Clause 2: Public Land. The Congress shall have Power to dispose of and make all needful Rules and Regulations respecting the Territory or other Property belonging to the United States; and nothing in this Constitution shall be so construed as to Prejudice any Claims of the United States, or of any particular State.

The federal government has the exclusive right to administer federal government public lands.

Section 4. Republican Form of Government
The United States shall guarantee to every State in this Union a Republican Form of Government, and shall protect each of them against Invasion; and on Application of the Legislature, or of the Executive (when the Legislature cannot be convened) against domestic Violence.

Each state is promised a form of government in which the people elect their representatives, called a republican form. The federal government is bound to protect states against any attack by foreigners or during times of trouble within a state.

Article V. (Methods of Amendment)
The Congress, whenever two thirds of both Houses shall deem it necessary, shall propose Amendments to this Constitution, or on the Application of the Legislatures of two thirds of the several States, shall call a Convention for proposing Amendments, which, in either Case, shall be valid to all Intents and Purposes, as Part of this Constitution, when ratified by the Legislatures of three fourths of the several States, or by Conventions in three

---

[11]Repealed by the Thirteenth Amendment.

fourths thereof, as the one or the other Mode of Ratification may be proposed by the Congress; Provided that no Amendment which may be made prior to the Year One thousand eight hundred and eight shall in any Manner affect the first and fourth Clauses in the Ninth Section of the First Article; and that no State, without its Consent, shall be deprived of its equal Suffrage in the Senate.

Amendments may be proposed in either of two ways: a two-thirds vote of each house (Congress) or at the request of two-thirds of the states. Ratification of amendments may be carried out in two ways: by the legislatures of three-fourths of the states or by the voters in three-fourths of the states. No state may be denied equal representation in the Senate.

Article VI. (National Supremacy)

Clause 1: Existing Obligations.   All Debts contracted and Engagements entered into, before the Adoption of this Constitution shall be as valid against the United States under this Constitution, as under the Confederation.

During the Revolutionary War and the years of the Confederation, Congress borrowed large sums. This clause pledged that the new federal government would assume those financial obligations.

Clause 2: Supreme Law of the Land.   This Constitution, and the Laws of the United States which shall be made in Pursuance thereof; and all Treaties made, or which shall be made, under the Authority of the United States, shall be the supreme Law of the Land; and the Judges in every State shall be bound thereby, any Thing in the Constitution or Laws of any State to the Contrary notwithstanding.

This is typically called the supremacy clause; it declares that federal law takes precedence over all forms of state law. No government, at the local or state level, may make or enforce any law that conflicts with any provision of the Constitution, acts of Congress, treaties, or other rules and regulations issued by the president and his or her subordinates in the executive branch of the federal government.

Clause 3: Oath of Office.   The Senators and Representatives before mentioned, and the Members of the several State Legislatures, and all executive and judicial Officers, both of the United States and of the several States, shall be bound by Oath or Affirmation, to support this Constitution; but no religious Test shall ever be required as a Qualification to any Office or public Trust under the United States.

Every federal and state official must take an oath of office promising to support the U.S. Constitution. Religion may not be used as a qualification to serve in any federal office.

Article VII. (Ratification)

The Ratification of the Conventions of nine States shall be sufficient for the Establishment of this Constitution between the States so ratifying the Same.

Nine states were required to ratify the Constitution. Delaware was the first and New Hampshire the ninth.

Done in Convention by the Unanimous Consent of the States present the Seventeenth Day of September in the Year of our Lord one thousand seven hundred and Eighty seven and of the Independence of the United States of America the Twelfth. In witness whereof we have hereunto subscribed our Names,

Go. WASHINGTON
Presid't. and deputy from Virginia

Attest
WILLIAM JACKSON
Secretary

DELAWARE
Geo. Read
Gunning Bedfordjun
John Dickinson
Richard Basset
Jaco. Broom

MASSACHUSETTS
Nathaniel Gorham
Rufus King

CONNECTICUT
Wm. Saml. Johnson
Roger Sherman

NEW YORK
Alexander Hamilton

NEW JERSEY
Wh. Livingston
David Brearley.
Wm. Paterson.
Jona. Dayton

PENNSYLVANIA
B. Franklin
Thomas Mifflin
Robt. Morris
Geo. Clymer
Thos. FitzSimons
Jared Ingersoll
James Wilson.
Gouv. Morris

NEW HAMPSHIRE
John Langdon
Nicholas Gilman

MARYLAND
James McHenry
Dan of St. Thos. Jenifer
Danl. Carroll.

VIRGINIA
John Blair
James Madison Jr.

NORTH CAROLINA
Wm. Blount
Richd. Dobbs Spaight.
Hu. Willaimson

SOUTH CAROLINA
J. Rutledge
Charles Cotesworth Pinckney
Charles Pinckney
Pierce Butler

GEORGIA
William Few
Abr. Baldwin

Articles in addition to, and amendment of the Constitution of the United States of America, proposed by Congress and ratified by the Legislatures of the several states, pursuant to the Fifth Article of the original Constitution.

Amendments to the Constitution of the United States

The Bill of Rights[12]

Amendment I.
Religion, Speech, Assembly, and Petition

Congress shall make no law respecting an establishment of religion, or prohibiting the free exercise thereof; or abridging the freedom of speech, or of the press; or the right of the people peaceably to assemble, and to petition the Government for a redress of grievances.

Congress may not create an official church or enact laws limiting the freedom of religion, speech, the press, assembly, and petition. These guarantees, like the others in the Bill of Rights (the first ten amendments), are not absolute—each may be exercised only with regard to the rights of other persons.

Amendment II.
Militia and the Right to Bear Arms

A well regulated Militia, being necessary to the security of a free State, the right of the people to keep and bear Arms, shall not be infringed.

To protect itself, each state has the right to maintain a volunteer armed force. States and the federal government regulate the possession and use of firearms by individuals.

Amendment III.
The Quartering of Soldiers

No Soldier shall, in time of peace be quartered in any house, without the consent of the Owner, nor in time of war, but in a manner to be prescribed by law.

Before the Revolutionary War, it had been common British practice to quarter soldiers in colonists' homes. Military troops do not have the power to take over private houses during peacetime.

Amendment IV.
Searches and Seizures

The right of the people to be secure in their persons, houses, papers, and effects, against unreasonable searches and seizures, shall not be violated, and no Warrants shall issue, but upon probable cause, supported by Oath or affirmation, and particularly describing the place to be searched, and the persons or things to be seized.

Here the word warrant means "justification" and refers to a document issued by a magistrate or judge indicating the name, address, and possible offense committed. Anyone asking for the warrant, such as a police officer, must be able to convince the magistrate or judge that an offense probably has been committed.

Amendment V.
Grand Juries, Self-incrimination, Double Jeopardy, Due Process, and Eminent Domain

No person shall be held to answer for a capital, or otherwise infamous crime, unless on a presentment or indictment of a Grand Jury, except in cases arising in the land or naval forces, or in the Militia, when in actual service in time of War or public danger; nor shall any person be subject for the same offence to be twice put in jeopardy of life or limb; nor shall be compelled in any criminal case to be a witness against himself, nor be deprived of life, liberty, or property, without due process of law; nor shall private property be taken for public use, without just compensation.

There are two types of juries. A grand jury considers physical evidence and the testimony of witnesses, and decides whether there is sufficient reason to bring a case to trial. A petit jury hears the case at trial and decides it. "For the same offence to be twice put in jeopardy of life or limb" means to be tried twice for the same crime. A person may not be tried for the same crime twice or forced to give evidence against herself or himself. No person's right to life, liberty, or property may be taken away except by lawful means, called the due process of law. Private property taken for use in public purposes must be paid for by the government.

Amendment VI.
Criminal Court Procedures

In all criminal prosecutions, the accused shall enjoy the right to a speedy and public trial, by an impartial jury of the State and district wherein the crime shall have been committed, which district shall have been previously ascertained by law, and to be informed of the nature and cause of the accusation; to be confronted with the witnesses against him; to have compulsory process for obtaining wit-

---

[12]On September 25, 1789, Congress transmitted to the state legislatures twelve proposed amendments, two of which, having to do with congressional representation and congressional pay, were not adopted. The remaining ten amendments became the Bill of Rights. In 1992, the amendment concerning congressional pay was adopted as the Twenty-seventh Amendment.

nesses in his favor, and to have the Assistance of Counsel for his defence.

Any person accused of a crime has the right to a fair and public trial by a jury in the state in which the crime took place. The charges against that person must be so indicated. Any accused person has the right to a lawyer to defend him or her and to question those who testify against him or her, as well as the right to call people to speak in his or her favor at trial.

Amendment VII.
Trial by Jury in Civil Cases

In Suits at common law, where the value in controversy shall exceed twenty dollars, the right of trial by jury shall be preserved, and no fact tried by jury, shall be otherwise re-examined in any Court of the United States, than according to the rules of the common law.

A jury trial may be requested by either party in a dispute in any case involving more than $20. If both parties agree to a trial by a judge without a jury, the right to a jury trial may be put aside.

Amendment VIII.
Bail, Cruel and Unusual Punishment

Excessive bail shall not be required, nor excessive fines imposed, nor cruel and unusual punishments inflicted.

Bail is that amount of money that a person accused of a crime may be required to deposit with the court as a guarantee that she or he will appear in court when requested. The amount of bail required or the fine imposed as punishment for a crime must be reasonable compared with the seriousness of the crime involved. Any punishment judged to be too harsh or too severe for a crime shall be prohibited.

Amendment IX.
The Rights Retained by the People

The enumeration in the Constitution, of certain rights, shall not be construed to deny or disparage others retained by the people.

Many civil rights that are not explicitly enumerated in the Constitution are still held by the people.

Amendment X.
Reserved Powers of the States

The powers not delegated to the United States by the Constitution, nor prohibited by it to the States, are reserved to the States respectively, or to the people.

Those powers not delegated by the Constitution to the federal government or expressly denied to the states belong to

the states and to the people. This clause in essence allows the states to pass laws under its "police powers."

Amendment XI
(Ratified on February 7, 1795).
Suits Against States

The Judicial power of the United States shall not be construed to extend to any suit in law or equity, commenced or prosecuted against one of the United States by Citizens of another State, or by Citizens or Subjects of any Foreign State.

This amendment has been interpreted to mean that a state cannot be sued in federal court by one of its citizens, by a citizen of another state, or by a foreign country.

Amendment XII
(Ratified on June 15, 1804).
Election of the President

The Electors shall meet in their respective states, and vote by ballot for President and Vice-President, one of whom, at least, shall not be an inhabitant of the same State with themselves; they shall name in their ballots the person voted for as President, and in distinct ballots the person voted for as Vice-President, and they shall make distinct lists of all persons voted for as President, and of all persons voted for as Vice-President, and of the number of votes for each, which lists they shall sign and certify, and transmit sealed to the seat of the government of the United States, directed to the President of the Senate;–The President of the Senate shall, in the presence of the Senate and House of Representatives, open all the certificates and the votes shall then be counted;–The person having the greatest number of votes for President, shall be the President, if such number be a majority of the whole number of Electors appointed; and if no person have such majority, then from the persons having the highest numbers not exceeding three on the list of those voted for as President, the House of Representatives shall choose immediately, by ballot, the President. But in choosing the President, the votes shall be taken by States, the representation from each State having one vote; a quorum for this purpose shall consist of a member or members from two-thirds of the States, and a majority of all States shall be necessary to a choice. [And if the House of Representatives shall not choose a President whenever the right of choice shall devolve upon them, before the fourth day of March next following, then the Vice-President shall act as President, as in the case of the death or other constitutional disability of the President.][13]– The person having the greatest number of votes as Vice-President, shall be the Vice-President, if such number be a

---

[13]Changed by the Twentieth Amendment.

majority of the whole number of Electors appointed, and if no person have a majority, then from the two highest numbers on the list, the Senate shall choose the Vice President; a quorum for the purpose shall consist of two-thirds of the whole number of Senators, and a majority of the whole number shall be necessary to a choice. But no person constitutionally ineligible to the office of President shall be eligible to that of Vice-President of the United States.

The original procedure set out for the election of president and vice president in Article II, Section 1, resulted in a tie in 1800 between Thomas Jefferson and Aaron Burr. It was not until the next year that the House of Representatives chose Jefferson to be president. This amendment changed the procedure by providing for separate ballots for president and vice president.

Amendment XIII
(Ratified on December 6, 1865).
Prohibition of Slavery

Section 1.
Neither slavery nor involuntary servitude, except as a punishment for crime whereof the party shall have been duly convicted, shall exist within the United States, or any place subject to their jurisdiction.

Some slaves had been freed during the Civil War. This amendment freed the others and abolished slavery.

Section 2.
Congress shall have power to enforce this article by appropriate legislation.

Amendment XIV
(Ratified on July 9, 1868).
Citizenship, Due Process, and Equal Protection of the Laws

Section 1.
All persons born or naturalized in the United States, and subject to the jurisdiction thereof, are citizens of the United States and of the State wherein they reside. No State shall make or enforce any law which shall abridge the privileges or immunities of citizens of the United States; nor shall any State deprive any person of life, liberty, or property, without due process of law; nor deny to any person within its jurisdiction the equal protection of the laws.

Under this provision, states cannot make or enforce laws that take away rights given to all citizens by the federal government. States cannot act unfairly or arbitrarily toward, or discriminate against, any person.

Section 2.
Representatives shall be apportioned among the several States according to their respective numbers, counting the whole number of persons in each State, excluding Indians not taxed. But when the right to vote at any election for the choice of electors for President and Vice President of the United States, Representatives in Congress, the Executive and Judicial officers of a State, or the members of the Legislature thereof, is denied to any of the male inhabitants of such State, being [twenty-one][14] years of age, and citizens of the United States, or in any way abridged, except for participation in rebellion, or other crime, the basis of representation therein shall be reduced in the proportion which the number of such male citizens shall bear to the whole number of male citizens twenty-one years of age in such State.

Section 3.
No person shall be a Senator or Representative in Congress, or elector of President and Vice President, or hold any office, civil or military, under the United States, or under any State, who having previously taken an oath, as a member of Congress, or as an officer of the United States, or as a member of any State legislature, or as an executive or judicial officer of any State, to support the Constitution of the United States, shall have engaged in insurrection or rebellion against the same, or given aid or comfort to the enemies thereof. But Congress may by a vote of two-thirds of each House, remove such disability.

This provision forbade former state or federal government officials who had acted in support of the Confederacy during the Civil War to hold office again. It limited the president's power to pardon those persons. Congress removed this "disability" in 1898.

Section 4.
The validity of the public debt of the United States, authorized by law, including debts incurred for payment of pensions and bounties for services in suppressing insurrection or rebellion, shall not be questioned. But neither the United States nor any State shall assume or pay any debt or obligation incurred in aid of insurrection or rebellion against the United States, or any claim for the loss or emancipation of any slave, but all such debts, obligations and claims shall be held illegal and void.

Section 5.
The Congress shall have power to enforce, by appropriate legislation, the provisions of this article.

---

[14]Changed by the Twenty-sixth Amendment.

Amendment XV
(Ratified on February 3, 1870).
The Right to Vote

Section 1.

The right of citizens of the United States to vote shall not be denied or abridged by the United States or by any State on account of race, color, or previous condition of servitude.

No citizen can be refused the right to vote simply because of race or color or because that person was once a slave.

Section 2.

The Congress shall have power to enforce this article by appropriate legislation.

Amendment XVI
(Ratified on February 3, 1913).
Income Taxes

The Congress shall have power to lay and collect taxes on incomes, from whatever source derived, without apportionment among the several States, and without regard to any census or enumeration.

This amendment allows Congress to tax income without sharing the revenue so obtained with the states according to their population.

Amendment XVII
(Ratified on April 8, 1913).
The Popular Election of Senators

The Senate of the United States shall be composed of two Senators from each State, elected by the people thereof, for six years; and each Senator shall have one vote. The electors in each State shall have the qualifications requisite for electors of the most numerous branch of the State legislatures.

When vacancies happen in the representation of any State in the Senate, the executive authority of such State shall issue writs of election to fill such vacancies: *Provided,* That the legislature of any State may empower the executive thereof to make temporary appointments until the people fill the vacancies by election as the legislature may direct.

This amendment shall not be so construed as to affect the election or term of any Senator chosen before it becomes valid as part of the Constitution.

This amendment modified portions of Article I, Section 3, that related to election of senators. Senators are now elected by the voters in each state directly. When a vacancy

occurs, either the state may fill the vacancy by a special election, or the governor of the state involved may appoint someone to fill the seat until the next election.

Amendment XVIII
(Ratified on January 16, 1919).
Prohibition.

Section 1.

After one year from the ratification of this article the manufacture, sale, or transportation of intoxicating liquors within, the importation thereof into, or the exportation thereof from the United States and all territory subject to the jurisdiction thereof for beverage purposes is hereby prohibited.

Section 2.

The Congress and the several States shall have concurrent power to enforce this article by appropriate legislation.

Section 3.

This article shall be inoperative unless it shall have been ratified as an amendment to the Constitution by the legislatures of the several States, as provided in the Constitution, within seven years from the date of the submission hereof to the States by the Congress.[15]

This amendment made it illegal to manufacture, sell, and transport alcoholic beverages in the United States. It was repealed by the Twenty-first Amendment.

Amendment XIX
(Ratified on August 18, 1920).
Women's Right to Vote.

The right of citizens of the United States to vote shall not be denied or abridged by the United States or by any State on account of sex.

Congress shall have power to enforce this article by appropriate legislation.

Women were given the right to vote by this amendment, and Congress was given the power to enforce this right.

Amendment XX
(Ratified on January 23, 1933).
The Lame Duck Amendment

Section 1.

The terms of the President and Vice President shall end at noon on the 20th day of January, and the terms of Senators and Representatives at noon on the 3d day of

---

[15]The Eighteenth Amendment was repealed by the Twenty-first Amendment.

January, of the years in which such terms would have ended if this article had not been ratified; and the terms of their successors shall then begin.

This amendment modified Article I, Section 4, Clause 2, and other provisions relating to the president in the Twelfth Amendment. The taking of the oath of office was moved from March 4 to January 20.

Section 2.

The Congress shall assemble at least once in every year, and such meeting shall begin at noon on the 3d day of January, unless they shall by law appoint a different day.

Congress changed the beginning of its term to January 3. The reason the Twentieth Amendment is called the Lame Duck Amendment is because it shortens the time between when a member of Congress is defeated for reelection and when he or she leaves office.

Section 3.

If, at the time fixed for the beginning of the term of the President, the President elect shall have died, the Vice President elect shall become President. If a President shall not have been chosen before the time fixed for the beginning of his term, or if the President elect shall have failed to qualify, then the Vice President elect shall act as President until a President shall have qualified; and the Congress may by law provide for the case wherein neither a President elect nor a Vice President elect shall have qualified, declaring who shall then act as President, or the manner in which one who is to act shall be selected, and such person shall act accordingly until a President or Vice President shall have qualified.

This part of the amendment deals with problem areas left ambiguous by Article II and the Twelfth Amendment. If the president dies before January 20 or fails to qualify for office, the presidency is to be filled in the order given in this section.

Section 4.

The Congress may by law provide for the case of the death of any of the persons from whom the House of Representatives may choose a President whenever the rights of choice shall have devolved upon them, and for the case of the death of any of the persons from whom the Senate may choose a Vice President whenever the right of choice shall have devolved upon them.

Congress has never created legislation subsequent to this section.

Section 5.

Sections 1 and 2 shall take effect on the 15th day of October following the ratification of this article.

Section 6.

This article shall be inoperative unless it shall have been ratified as an amendment to the Constitution by the legislatures of three-fourths of the several States within seven years from the date of its submission.

Amendment XXI
(Ratified on December 5, 1933).
The Repeal of Prohibition.

Section 1.

The eighteenth article of amendment to the Constitution of the United States is hereby repealed.

Section 2.

The transportation or importation into any State, Territory, or possession of the United States for delivery or use therein of intoxicating liquors, in violation of the laws thereof, is hereby prohibited.

Section 3.

This article shall be inoperative unless it shall have been ratified as an amendment to the Constitution by conventions in the several States, as provided in the Constitution, within seven years from the date of the submission hereof to the States by the Congress.

The amendment repealed the Eighteenth Amendment but did not make alcoholic beverages legal everywhere. Rather, they remained illegal in any state that so designated them. Many such "dry" states existed for a number of years after 1933. Today, there are still "dry" counties within the United States, in which alcoholic beverages are illegal.

Amendment XXII
(Ratified on February 27, 1951).
Limitation of Presidential Terms.

Section 1.

No person shall be elected to the office of the President more than twice, and no person who has held the office of President, or acted as President, for more than two years of a term to which some other person was elected President shall be elected to the office of President more than once. But this Article shall not apply to any person holding the office of President when this Article was proposed by the Congress, and shall not prevent any person who may be holding the office of President, or acting as President, during the term within which this Article becomes operative from holding the office of President or acting as President during the remainder of such term.

Section 2.

This article shall be inoperative unless it shall have been ratified as an amendment to the Constitution by the legislatures of three-fourths of the several States within seven years from the date of its submission to the States by the Congress.

No president may serve more than two elected terms. If, however, a president has succeeded to the office after the halfway point of a term in which another president was originally elected, then that president may serve for more than eight years, but not to exceed ten years.

Amendment XXIII
(Ratified on March 29, 1961).
Presidential Electors for
the District of Columbia.

Section 1.

The District constituting the seat of Government of the United States shall appoint in such manner as the Congress may direct:

A number of electors of President and Vice President equal to the whole number of Senators and Representatives in Congress to which the District would be entitled if it were a State, but in no event more than the least populous State; they shall be in addition to those appointed by the States, but they shall be considered, for the purposes of the election of President and Vice President, to be electors appointed by a State; and they shall meet in the District and perform such duties as provided by the twelfth article of amendment.

Section 2.

The Congress shall have power to enforce this article by appropriate legislation.

Citizens living in the District of Columbia have the right to vote in elections for president and vice president. The District of Columbia has three presidential electors, whereas before this amendment it had none.

Amendment XXIV
(Ratified on January 23, 1964).
The Anti–Poll Tax Amendment.

Section 1.

The right of citizens of the United States to vote in any primary or other election for President or Vice President, for electors for President or Vice President, or for Senator or Representative in Congress, shall not be denied or abridged by the United States, or any State by reason of failure to pay any poll tax or other tax.

Section 2.

The Congress shall have power to enforce this article by appropriate legislation.

No government shall require a person to pay a poll tax in order to vote in any federal election.

Amendment XXV
(Ratified on February 10, 1967).
Presidential Disability and Vice Presidential
Vacancies.

Section 1.

In case of the removal of the President from office or of his death or resignation, the Vice President shall become President.

Whenever a president dies or resigns from office, the vice president becomes president.

Section 2.

Whenever there is a vacancy in the office of the Vice President, the President shall nominate a Vice President who shall take office upon confirmation by a majority vote of both Houses of Congress.

Whenever the office of the vice presidency becomes vacant, the president may appoint someone to fill this office, provided Congress consents.

Section 3.

Whenever the President transmits to the President pro tempore of the Senate and the Speaker of the House of Representatives his written declaration that he is unable to discharge the powers and duties of his office, and until he transmits to them a written declaration to the contrary, such powers and duties shall be discharged by the Vice President as Acting President.

Whenever the president believes she or he is unable to carry out the duties of the office, she or he shall so indicate to Congress in writing. The vice president then acts as president until the president declares that she or he is again able to properly carry out the duties of the office.

Section 4.

Whenever the Vice President and a majority of either the principal officers of the executive departments or of such other body as Congress may by law provide, transmit to the President pro tempore of the Senate and the Speaker of the House of Representatives their written declaration that the President is unable to discharge the powers and duties of his office, the Vice President shall immediately assume the powers and duties of the office as Acting President.

Thereafter, when the President transmits to the President pro tempore of the Senate and the Speaker of the House of Representatives his written declaration that no inability exists, he shall resume the powers and duties of his office unless the Vice President and a majority of either the principal officers of the executive department or of such other body as Congress may by law provide, transmit within four days to the President pro tempore of the Senate and the Speaker of the House of Representatives their written declaration that the President is unable to discharge the powers and duties of his office. Thereupon Congress shall decide the issue, assembling within forty-eight hours for that purpose if not in session. If the Congress, within twenty-one days after receipt of the latter written declaration, or, if Congress is not in session, within twenty-one days after Congress is required to assemble, determines by two-thirds vote of both Houses that the President is unable to discharge the powers and duties of his office, the Vice President shall continue to discharge the same as Acting President; otherwise, the President shall resume the powers and duties of his office.

Whenever the vice president and a majority of the members of the cabinet believe that the president cannot carry out his or her duties, they shall so indicate in writing to Congress. The vice president shall then act as president. When the president believes that she or he is able to carry out her or his duties again, she or he shall so indicate to the Congress. If, though, the vice president and a majority of the Cabinet do not agree, Congress must decide by a two-thirds vote within three weeks who shall act as president.

Amendment XXVI
(Ratified on July 1, 1971).
The Eighteen-Year-Old Vote.

Section 1.
The right of citizens of the United States, who are eighteen years of age or older, to vote shall not be denied or abridged by the United States or by any State on account of age.

No one over eighteen years of age can be denied the right to vote in federal or state elections by virtue of age.

Section 2.
The Congress shall have power to enforce this article by appropriate legislation.

Amendment XXVII
(Ratified on May 7, 1992).
Congressional Pay.

No law varying the compensation for the services of the Senators and Representatives shall take effect, until an election of representatives shall have intervened.

This amendment allows the voters to have some control over increases in salaries for congressional members. Originally submitted to the states for ratification in 1789, it was not ratified until 203 years later, in 1992.

Federalism

States Had to Meet National Education Standards?

BACKGROUND

ACHIEVEMENT TEST SCORES OF AMERICAN STUDENTS IN JUNIOR HIGH AND HIGH SCHOOL CONTINUE TO LAG BEHIND THOSE IN MANY OTHER COUNTRIES. IN MATH PARTICULARLY, U.S. EIGHTH GRADERS RECENTLY TESTED WELL BELOW EIGHTH GRADERS IN JAPAN, FRANCE, CANADA, GERMANY, NEW ZEALAND, AND BRITAIN. OUR GRADUATING HIGH SCHOOL SENIORS SEEM TO LACK THE SKILLS AND TRAINING THAT ARE REQUIRED IN TODAY'S COMPETITIVE WORLD. ONE SUGGESTION FOR IMPROVING EDUCATIONAL ATTAINMENT IN AMERICA IS THE IMPOSITION OF NATIONAL TESTING STANDARDS ON ALL OF THE STATES. BUT THIS RUNS COUNTER TO THE TYPICAL VIEW OF OUR FEDERAL SYSTEM, IN WHICH STATE AND LOCAL GOVERNMENTS, NOT WASHINGTON, D.C., HAVE ALWAYS BEEN IN CHARGE OF EDUCATION.

WHAT IF STATES HAD TO MEET NATIONAL EDUCATION STANDARDS?

National education standards can be effective only if there is national testing. That is exactly what President Clinton outlined in his State of the Union Address in 1997. The goal of the national program would be to set standards based on the best thinking of educators and experts in each field. These standards would serve as academic benchmarks to which

states and local school districts could aspire.

One thing is certain: any type of national testing will show what we already know—that student achievement is lower in some states than in others. Thus, if states had to meet national education standards, many of the poorer states, such as Mississippi, would find themselves facing a dilemma: How could they raise student achievement to meet the new standards?

Very likely, we would see an increase in "test-oriented" teaching—a practice that, according to many parents and educators, interferes with effective teaching and learning. Consider, too, that the states that rank very high in educational achievement also engage in relatively little statewide testing of their students. Some of these states contend that greater school choice, not more testing, is the way to improve education. Other states have shown that setting up "charter" schools, which have fewer restrictions and more parental involvement, has improved student achievement. Some other states, such as Iowa and Minnesota, raised the quality

of their schools by setting tougher standards for teacher education and licensing.

THERE IS MUCH SUPPORT FOR NATIONAL STANDARDS

Public opinion polls show widespread support for national standards and testing based on a challenging and rigorous curriculum. Many claim that national education standards would further educational achievement in the United States.

The implementation of national education standards would also make American education more uniform. As it is, educational achievement varies greatly from one state and locality to another. This makes it difficult for, say, a prospective employer to predict with any accuracy what a high school graduate has or has not learned.

THE POSSIBILITY OF NATIONAL CONTROL

It is possible that national testing, even if it were voluntary, could lead to a national curriculum. Such educational uniformity is unknown in the United States, although in countries with unitary systems of government (explained in this chapter), national curricula are common. This is true in France, for example.

Many advocates of states' rights and the separation of decision making at the local level from Washington, D.C., are against national tests. They believe that education should remain under the control of state and local authorities, as it always has been. Particularly, they argue, curriculum decisions should be made by local school boards, which are influenced by involved parents and teachers in each community.

FOR CRITICAL ANALYSIS

1. In which subject areas do you think national education standards would be most likely to undercut or challenge local control over what schools teach?

2. "While U.S. student achievement is perhaps dismal, U.S. workers remain the highest paid in the world and U.S. standards of living are rising." Analyze this quotation with respect to whether national education standards are necessary.

There are many separate governments in this country. One national government and fifty state governments, plus local governments, create a grand total of more than 83,000 governments in all! The breakdown can be seen in Table 3-1. Those 83,000 governments are operated by about 500,000 elected officeholders.

Visitors from France or Spain are often awestruck by the complexity of our system of government. Consider that a criminal action can be defined by state law, by national law, or by both. Thus, a criminal suspect can be prosecuted in the state court system or in the federal court system (or both). Often, economic regulation over exactly the same matter exists at the local level, the state level, and the national level—generating multiple forms to be completed, multiple procedures to be followed, and multiple laws to be obeyed. Numerous programs are funded by the national government but administered by state and local governments.

There are various ways of ordering relations between central governments and local units. *Federalism* is one of these ways. Understanding federalism and how it differs from other forms of government is important in understanding the American political system. Indeed, many political issues today, including the one discussed in this chapter's opening *What If . . .* , would not arise if we did not have a federal form of government in which governmental authority is divided between the central government and various subunits.

Three Systems of Government

There are basically three ways of ordering relations between central governments and local units: (1) a unitary system, (2) a confederal system, and (3) a federal system. The most popular, both historically and today, is the unitary system.

A Unitary System

A **unitary system** of government is the easiest to define. Unitary systems allow ultimate governmental authority to rest in the hands of the national, or central, government. Consider a typical unitary system—France. There are departments and municipalities in France. Within the departments and the municipalities are

Unitary System
A centralized governmental system in which local or subdivisional governments exercise only those powers given to them by the central government.

TABLE 3-1

The Number of Governments in the United States Today

With more than 83,000 separate governmental units in the United States today, it is no wonder that intergovernmental relations in the United States are so complicated. Actually, the number of school districts has decreased over time, but the number of special districts created for single purposes, such as flood control, has increased from only about 8,000 during World War II to nearly 30,000 today.

Federal government		1
State governments		50
Local governments		83,149
Counties	3,042	
Municipalities	19,205	
(mainly cities or towns)		
Townships	16,691	
(less extensive powers)		
Special districts	29,483	
(water, sewer, and so on)		
School districts	14,728	
TOTAL		83,200

SOURCE: U.S. Department of Commerce, *Statistical Abstract of the United States, 1997* (Washington, D.C.: U.S. Government Printing Office, 1997).

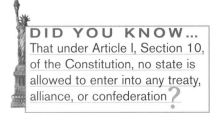

separate government entities with elected and appointed officials. So far, the French system appears to be very similar to the U.S. system, but the similarity is only superficial. Under the unitary French system, the decisions of the governments of the departments and municipalities can be overruled by the national government. The national government also can cut off the funding of many departmental and municipal government activities. Moreover, in a unitary system such as that in France, all questions related to education, police, the use of land, and welfare are handled by the national government.[1] Great Britain, Sweden, Israel, Egypt, Ghana, and the Philippines also have unitary systems of government, as do most countries today.

A Confederal System

Confederal System
A system of government consisting of a league of independent states, each having essentially sovereign powers. The central government created by such a league has only limited powers over the states.

You were introduced to the elements of a **confederal system** of government in Chapter 2, when we examined the Articles of Confederation. A confederation is the opposite of a unitary governing system. It is a league of independent states in which a central government or administration handles only those matters of common concern expressly delegated to it by the member states. The central governmental unit has no ability to make laws directly applicable to individuals unless the member states explicitly support such laws. The United States under the Articles of Confederation and the Confederate States during the American Civil War were confederations.

There are few, if any, confederations in the world today that resemble those that existed in the United States. Switzerland is a confederation of twenty-three sovereign cantons, and several republics of the former Soviet Union formed the Commonwealth of Independent States. Countries also have formed organizations with one another for limited purposes: military/peacekeeping, as in the case of the North Atlantic Treaty Organization or the United Nations; or economic, as in the case of the European Union (formerly the European Community) or the economic unit created by the North American Free Trade Agreement. These organizations, however, are not true confederations.

A Federal System

Federal System
A system of government in which power is divided by a written constitution between a central government and regional, or subdivisional, governments. Each level must have some domain in which its policies are dominant and some genuine political or constitutional guarantee of its authority.

The **federal system** lies between the unitary and confederal forms of government. In a federal system, authority is divided, usually by a written constitution, between a central government and regional, or subdivisional, governments (often called constituent governments). The central government and the constituent governments both act directly on the people through laws and through the actions of elected and appointed governmental officials. Within each government's sphere of authority, each is supreme, in theory. Contrast a federal system to a unitary one in which the central government is supreme and the constituent governments derive their authority from it. Australia, Canada, Mexico, India, Brazil, and Germany are examples of nations with federal systems. See Figure 3–1 for a comparison of the three systems.

Why Federalism?

Why did the United States develop in a federal direction? We look here at that question as well as at some of the arguments for and against a federal form of government.

[1]In the past decade, legislation has altered somewhat the unitary character of the French political system.

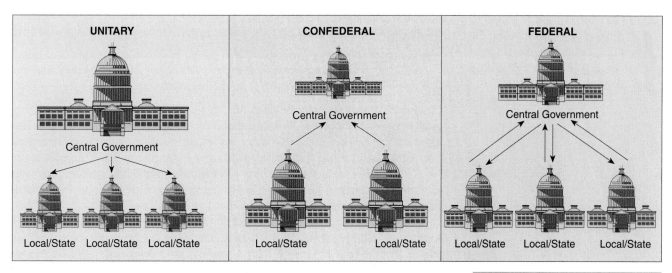

The Flow of Power in Three Systems of Government

In a unitary system, the flow of power is from the central government to the local and state governments. In a confederal system, the flow of power is in the opposite direction—from the state and local governments to the central government. In a federal system, the flow of power, in principle, goes both ways.

A Practical Solution

As you saw in Chapter 2, the historical basis of the federal system was laid down in Philadelphia at the Constitutional Convention, where strong national government advocates opposed equally strong states' rights advocates. This dichotomy continued through to the ratifying conventions in the several states. The resulting federal system was a compromise. The supporters of the new constitution were political pragmatists—they realized that without a federal arrangement, there would be no ratification of the new Constitution. The appeal of federalism was that it retained state traditions and local power while establishing a strong national government capable of handling common problems.

Even if the colonial leaders had agreed on the desirability of a unitary system, the problems of size and regional isolation would have made such a system difficult operationally. At the time of the Philadelphia Convention, the thirteen colonies taken together were larger geographically than England or France. Slow travel and communication, combined with geographic spread, contributed to the isolation of many regions within the colonies. For example, it could take up to several weeks for all of the colonies to be informed about one particular political decision.

Other Arguments for Federalism

The arguments for federalism in the United States and elsewhere involve a complex set of factors, some of which we already have noted. First, for big countries, such as the United States, India, and Canada, federalism allows many functions to be "farmed out" by the central government to the states or provinces. The lower levels of government, accepting these responsibilities, thereby can become the focus of political dissatisfaction rather than the national authorities. Second, even with modern transportation and communications systems, the sheer geographic or population size of some nations makes it impractical to locate all political authority in one place. Finally, federalism brings government closer to the people. It allows more direct access to, and influence on, government agencies and policies, rather than leaving the population restive and dissatisfied with a remote, faceless, all-powerful central authority.

In the United States, federalism historically has yielded many benefits. State governments long have been a training ground for future national leaders. Presidents Ronald Reagan and Bill Clinton made their political mark as state governors. The states themselves have been testing grounds for new government initiatives. As United States Supreme Court justice Louis Brandeis once observed:

> It is one of the happy incidents of the federal system that a single courageous state may, if its citizens choose, serve as a laboratory and try novel social and economic experiments without risk to the rest of the country.[2]

Examples of programs pioneered at the state level include unemployment compensation, which began in Wisconsin, and air-pollution control, which was initiated in California. Currently, states are experimenting with policies ranging from educational reforms to the medical use of marijuana. Since the passage of the 1996 Welfare Reform Act, which gave more control over welfare programs to state governments, states are also experimenting with different methods of delivering welfare assistance.

Additionally, the American way of life always has been characterized by a number of political subcultures, which divide along the lines of race and ethnic origin, wealth, education, and, more recently, age, degree of religious fundamentalism, and sexual preference. The existence of diverse political subcultures would appear to be at odds with a political authority concentrated solely in a central government. Had the United States developed into a unitary system, the various political subcultures certainly would have been less able to influence government behavior (relative to their own regions and interests) than they have been, and continue to be, in our federal system.

Arguments against Federalism

Not everyone thinks federalism is such a good idea. Some see it as a way for powerful state and local interests to block progress and impede national plans. Others see dangers in the expansion of national powers at the expense of the states. President Ronald Reagan said, "The Founding Fathers saw the federalist system as constructed something like a masonry wall. The States are the bricks, the national government is the mortar. . . . Unfortunately, over the years, many people have increasingly come to believe that Washington is the whole wall."[3]

Smaller political units are more likely to be dominated by a single political group, and the dominant groups in some cities and states have resisted implementing equal rights for all minority groups. (This was essentially the argument that James Madison put forth in *Federalist Paper* No. 10, which you can read in Appendix D of this text.) Others point out, however, that the dominant factions in other states have been more progressive than the national government in many areas, such as the environment.

The Constitutional Basis for American Federalism

No mention of the designation "federal system" can be found in the U.S. Constitution. Nor is it possible to find a systematic division of governmental authority between the national and state governments in that document. Rather, the Constitution sets out different types of powers (see Figure 3–2). These powers can be classified as (1) the powers of the national government, (2) the powers of

Air pollution in Los Angeles, California. Air-pollution control was initiated in California to cope with the threatening conditions produced by the enormous population in the area and the famous congestion of automobile traffic.

---

[2]*New State Ice Co. v. Liebmann*, 285 U.S. 262 (1932).

[3]Text of the address by the president to the National Conference of State Legislatures, Atlanta, Georgia (Washington, D.C.: The White House, Office of the Press Secretary, July 30, 1981), as quoted in Edward Millican, *One United People: The Federalist Papers and the National Idea* (Lexington, Ky.: The University Press of Kentucky, 1990).

the states, and (3) prohibited powers. The Constitution also makes it clear that if a state or local law conflicts with a national law, the national law will prevail.

Powers of the National Government

The powers delegated to the national government include both expressed and implied powers, as well as the special category of inherent powers. Most of the powers expressly delegated to the national government are found in Article I, Section 8, of the Constitution. These **enumerated powers** include coining money, setting standards for weights and measures, making uniform naturalization laws, admitting new states, establishing post offices, and declaring war. Another important enumerated power is the power to regulate commerce among the states—a topic we deal with later in this chapter.

The implied powers of the national government are also based on Article I, Section 8, which states that the Congress shall have the power

> [t]o make all laws which shall be necessary and proper for carrying into Execution the foregoing Powers, and all other Powers vested by this Constitution in the Government of the United States, or in any Department or Officer thereof.

Enumerated Powers
Powers specifically granted to the national government by the Constitution. The first seventeen clauses of Article I, Section 8, specify most of the enumerated powers of Congress.

FIGURE 3-2

The American Federal System—The Division of Powers between the National Government and the State Governments
Here we look at the constitutional powers of both the national government and the state governments together. Then we look at the powers denied by the Constitution to each level of government.

SELECTED CONSTITUTIONAL POWERS

National Government

EXPRESSED
- To coin money
- To conduct foreign relations
- To regulate interstate commerce
- To levy and collect taxes
- To declare war
- To raise and support the military
- To establish post offices
- To establish courts inferior to the Supreme Court
- To admit new states

IMPLIED
"To make all Laws which shall be necessary and proper for carrying into Execution the foregoing Powers, and all other Powers vested by this Constitution in the Government of the United States, or in any Department or Officer thereof."
(Article 1, Section 8, Clause 18)

National and State Governments

CONCURRENT
- To levy and collect taxes
- To borrow money
- To make and enforce laws
- To establish courts
- To provide for the general welfare
- To charter banks and corporations

State Governments

RESERVED TO THE STATES
- To regulate intrastate commerce
- To conduct elections
- To provide for public health, safety, and morals
- To establish local governments
- To ratify amendments to the federal constitution
- To establish a state militia

SELECTED POWERS DENIED BY THE CONSTITUTION

National Government

- To tax articles exported from any state
- To violate the Bill of Rights
- To change state boundaries
- To suspend the right of *habeas corpus*
- To make ex post facto laws
- To subject officeholders to a religious test

National and State Governments

- To grant titles of nobility
- To permit slavery
- To deny citizens the right to vote because of race, color, or previous servitude
- To deny citizens the right to vote because of gender

State Governments

- To tax imports or exports
- To coin money
- To enter into treaties
- To impair obligations of contracts
- To abridge the privileges or immunities of citizens or deny due process and equal protection of the laws

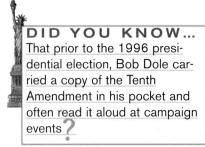

Elastic Clause, or Necessary and Proper Clause
The clause in Article I, Section 8, that grants Congress the power to do whatever is necessary to execute its specifically delegated powers.

INFOTRAC ®
COLLEGE EDITION

"Earthquake Victims Hit the Jackpot"

Police Power
The authority to legislate for the protection of the health, morals, safety, and welfare of the people. In the United States, most police power is a reserved power of the states.

Concurrent Powers
Powers held jointly by the national and state governments.

This clause is sometimes called the **elastic clause,** or the **necessary and proper clause,** because it provides flexibility to our constitutional system. It gives Congress all of those powers that can be reasonably inferred but that are not expressly stated in the brief wording of the Constitution. The clause was first used in the Supreme Court decision of *McCulloch v. Maryland*[4] (discussed later in this chapter) to develop the concept of implied powers. Through this concept, the national government has succeeded in strengthening the scope of its authority to meet the numerous problems that the framers of the Constitution did not, and could not, anticipate.

A special category of national powers that is not implied by the necessary and proper clause consists of what have been labeled the inherent powers of the national government. These powers derive from the fact that the United States is a sovereign power among nations, and as such, its national government must be the only government that deals with other nations. Under international law, it is assumed that all nation-states, regardless of their size or power, have an *inherent* right to ensure their own survival. To do this, each nation must have the ability to act in its own interest among and with the community of nations—by, for instance, making treaties, waging war, seeking trade, and acquiring territory. The national government has these powers whether or not they have been enumerated in the Constitution. Some constitutional scholars categorize inherent powers as a third type of power, completely distinct from the delegated powers (both expressed and implied) of the national government.

Powers of the State Governments

The Tenth Amendment states that the powers not delegated to the United States by the Constitution, nor prohibited by it to the states, are reserved to the states, or to the people. These are the reserved powers that the national government cannot deny to the states. Because these powers are not expressly listed—and because they are not limited to powers that are expressly listed—there is sometimes a question as to whether a certain power is delegated to the national government or reserved to the states. State powers have been held to include each state's right to regulate commerce within its borders and to provide for a state militia. States also have the reserved power to make laws on all matters not prohibited to the states by the national or state constitutions and not expressly, or by implication, delegated to the national government. The states also have **police power**—the authority to legislate for the protection of the health, morals, safety, and welfare of the people. Their police power enables states to pass laws governing such activities as crimes, marriage, contracts, education, traffic laws, and land use.

The ambiguity of the Tenth Amendment has allowed the reserved powers of the states to be defined differently at different times in our history. When there is widespread support for increased regulation by the national government, the Tenth Amendment tends to recede into the background. When the tide turns the other way, as it has in recent years (see the discussion of the new federalism later in this chapter), the Tenth Amendment is resurrected to justify arguments supporting increased states' rights.

Concurrent Powers

In certain areas, the states share **concurrent powers** with the national government. Most concurrent powers are not specifically stated in the Constitution; they are only implied. An example of a concurrent power is the power to tax.

---

[4] 4 Wheaton 316 (1819).

The police power of the states includes the power to create and enforce traffic laws and to regulate commerce within their borders.

The types of taxation are divided between the levels of government. States may not levy a tariff (a set of taxes on imported goods); the federal government may not tax real estate; and neither may tax the facilities of the other. If the state governments did not have the power to tax, they would not be able to function other than on a ceremonial basis. Other concurrent powers include the power to borrow money, to establish courts, and to charter banks and corporations. Concurrent powers are normally limited to the geographic area of the state and to those functions not delegated by the Constitution exclusively to the national government—such as the coinage of money and the negotiation of treaties.

Prohibited Powers

The Constitution prohibits or denies a number of powers to the national government. For example, the national government has expressly been denied the power to impose taxes on goods sold to other countries (exports). Moreover, any power not delegated expressly or implicitly to the federal government by the Constitution is prohibited to it. For example, the national government cannot create a national public school system. The states are also denied certain powers. For example, no state is allowed to enter into a treaty on its own with another country.

The Supremacy Clause

The supremacy of the national constitution over subnational laws and actions can be found in the **supremacy clause** of the Constitution. The supremacy clause (Article VI, Clause 2) states the following:

> This Constitution and the Laws of the United States which shall be made in Pursuance thereof; and all Treaties made . . . under the Authority of the United States, shall be the supreme Law of the Land; and the Judges in every State shall be bound thereby, any Thing in the Constitution or Laws of any State to the Contrary notwithstanding.

In other words, states cannot use their reserved or concurrent powers to thwart national policies. All national and state officers, as well as judges, must

Supremacy Clause
The constitutional provision that makes the Constitution and federal laws superior to all conflicting state and local laws.

be bound by oath to support the Constitution. Hence, any legitimate exercise of national governmental power supersedes any conflicting state action.[5] Of course, deciding whether a conflict actually exists is a judicial matter, as you will soon read about in the case of *McCulloch v. Maryland.*

National government legislation in a concurrent area is said to *preempt* (take precedence over) conflicting state or local laws or regulations in that area. One of the ways in which the national government has extended its powers, particularly during the twentieth century, is through the preemption of state and local laws by national legislation. Consider that in the first decade of the twentieth century, fewer than 20 national laws preempted laws and regulations issued by state and local governments. By the end of the century, this number had risen to nearly 120.

Some political scientists believe that national supremacy is critical for the longevity and smooth functioning of a federal system. Nonetheless, the application of this principle has been a continuous source of conflict. Indeed, as you will see, the most extreme result of this conflict was the Civil War.

Vertical Checks and Balances

Recall from Chapter 2 that one of the concerns of the founders was to prevent the national government from becoming too powerful. For that reason, they divided the government into three branches—legislative, executive, judicial. They also created a system of checks and balances that allowed each branch to check the actions of the other branches. The federal form of government created by the founders also involves checks and balances. These are sometimes called "vertical" checks and balances because they involve relationships between the states and the national government.

For example, the reserved powers of the states act as a check on the national government. Additionally, the states' interests are represented in the national legislature (Congress), and the citizens of the various states determine who will head the executive branch (the presidency). The founders also made it impossible for the central government to change the Constitution without the states' consent, as you read in Chapter 2. Finally, national programs and policies are administered by the states, which gives the states considerable control over the ultimate shape of those programs and policies.

The national government, in turn, can check state policies by exercising its constitutional powers under the clauses just discussed, as well as under the commerce clause (to be discussed later). Furthermore, the national government can influence state policies indirectly through federal grants, as you will learn later in this chapter.

Horizontal Federalism

So far we have examined only the relationship between central and state governmental units. The states, however, have numerous commercial, social, and other dealings among themselves. These interstate activities, problems, and policies make up what can be called **horizontal federalism.** The national Constitution imposes certain "rules of the road" on horizontal federalism, which have had the effect of preventing any one state from setting itself apart from the other states. The three most important clauses relating to horizontal federalism in the Constitution, all taken from the Articles of Confederation, require each state to do the following:

Horizontal Federalism
Activities, problems, and policies that require state governments to interact with one another.

---

[5]An excellent example of this is President Dwight Eisenhower's disciplining of Arkansas governor Orval Faubus by federalizing the National Guard to enforce the court-ordered desegregation of Little Rock High School.

1. Give full faith and credit to every other state's public acts, records, and judicial proceedings (Article IV, Section 1).
2. Extend to every other state's citizens the privileges and immunities of its own citizens (Article IV, Section 2).
3. Agree to return persons who are fleeing from justice in another state back to their home state when requested to do so (Article IV, Section 2).

Additionally, states may enter into agreements called **interstate compacts**—if consented to by Congress. In reality, congressional consent is necessary only if such a compact increases the power of the contracting states relative to other states (or to the national government). Typical examples of interstate compacts are the establishment of the Port Authority of New York and New Jersey by the states of New York and New Jersey and the regulation of the production of crude oil and natural gas by the Interstate Oil and Gas Compact of 1935.

Interstate Compact
An agreement between two or more states. Agreements on minor matters are made without congressional consent, but any compact that tends to increase the power of the contracting states relative to other states or relative to the national government generally requires the consent of Congress. Such compacts serve as a means by which states can solve regional problems.

Defining Constitutional Powers—The Early Years

Recall from Chapter 2 that constitutional language, to be effective and to endure, must have some degree of ambiguity. Certainly, the powers delegated to the national government and the powers reserved to the states contain elements of ambiguity, thus leaving the door open for different interpretations of federalism. Disputes over the boundaries of national versus state powers have characterized this nation from the beginning. In the early 1800s, the most significant disputes arose over differing interpretations of the implied powers of the national government under the necessary and proper clause and the respective powers of the national government and the states in regard to commerce.

Although political bodies at all levels of government play important roles in the process of settling such disputes, ultimately it is the Supreme Court that casts the final vote. As might be expected, the character of the referee will have an impact on the ultimate outcome of any boundary dispute. From 1801 to 1835, the Supreme Court was headed by Chief Justice John Marshall, a Federalist who advocated a strong central government. We look here at two cases decided by the Marshall Court: *McCulloch v. Maryland*[6] and *Gibbons v. Ogden*.[7] Both cases are considered milestones in the movement toward national government supremacy.

Interstate compacts have long been used as a way to address issues that affect more than one state. An interstate compact between New York and New Jersey in 1921 created the Port Authority of New York and New Jersey to develop and maintain harbor facilities in that area, including the Port Authority Bus Terminal shown here. Today, there are over two hundred interstate compacts.

McCulloch v. Maryland (1819)

The U.S. Constitution says nothing about establishing a national bank. Nonetheless, at different times Congress chartered two banks—the First and Second Banks of the United States—and provided part of their initial capital; they were thus national banks. The government of Maryland imposed a tax on the Second Bank's Baltimore branch in an attempt to put that branch out of business. The branch's cashier, James William McCulloch, refused to pay the Maryland tax. When Maryland took McCulloch to its state court, the state of Maryland won. The national government appealed the case to the Supreme Court.

One of the issues before the Court was whether the national government had the implied power, under the necessary and proper clause, to charter a bank and contribute capital to it. The other important question before the Court was the following: If the bank was constitutional, could a state tax it? In other words,

[6]4 Wheaton 316 (1819).
[7]9 Wheaton 1 (1824).

John Marshall (1755–1835) was the fourth chief justice of the Supreme Court. When Marshall took over, the Court had little power and almost no influence over the other two branches of government. Some scholars have declared that Marshall is the true architect of the American constitutional system, because he single-handedly gave new power to the Constitution. Early in his career, he was an attorney and was elected to the first of four terms in the Virginia Assembly. He was instrumental in the fight to ratify the Constitution in Virginia. Prior to being named to the Supreme Court, he won a seat in Congress in 1799 and in 1800 became secretary of state to John Adams.

Commerce Clause
The section of the Constitution in which Congress is given the power to regulate trade among the states and with foreign countries.

Injunction
An order issued by a court to compel or restrain the performance of an act by an individual or entity.

was a state action that conflicted with a national government action invalid under the supremacy clause?

Chief Justice John Marshall held that if establishing such a national bank aided the national government in the exercise of its designated powers, then the authority to set up such a bank could be implied. To Marshall, the necessary and proper clause embraced "all means which are appropriate" to carry out "the legitimate ends" of the Constitution. Only when such actions are forbidden by the letter and spirit of the Constitution are they thereby unconstitutional. Having established this doctrine of implied powers, Marshall then answered the other important question before the Court and established the doctrine of national supremacy. Marshall stated that no state could use its taxing power to tax an arm of the national government. If it could, "the declaration that the Constitution . . . shall be the supreme law of the land, is empty and unmeaning declamation."

Marshall's decision enabled the national government to grow and to meet problems that the Constitution's framers were unable to foresee. Today, practically every expressed power of the national government has been expanded in one way or another by use of the necessary and proper clause.

Gibbons v. Ogden (1824)

One of the more important parts of the Constitution included in Article I, Section 8, is the so-called **commerce clause,** in which Congress is given the power "[t]o regulate Commerce with foreign Nations, and among the several States, and with the Indian Tribes." The meaning of this clause was at issue in *Gibbons v. Ogden.*

The background to the case was as follows. Robert Fulton and Robert Livingston secured a monopoly on steam navigation on the waters in New York State from the New York legislature in 1803. They licensed Aaron Ogden to operate steam-powered ferryboats between New York and New Jersey. Thomas Gibbons, who had obtained a license from the U.S. government to operate boats in interstate waters, decided to compete with Ogden, but he did so without New York's permission. Ogden sued Gibbons. The New York state courts granted Ogden an **injunction,** prohibiting Gibbons from operating in New York waters. Gibbons appealed to the Supreme Court.

There were actually several issues before the Court in this case. The first issue had to do with how the term *commerce* should be defined. New York's highest court had defined the term narrowly to mean only the shipment of goods, or the interchange of commodities, *not* navigation or the transport of people. The second issue was whether the national government's power to regulate interstate commerce extended to commerce within a state (*intra*state commerce) or was limited strictly to commerce among the states (*inter*state commerce). The third issue was whether the power to regulate interstate commerce was a concurrent power (as the New York court had concluded) or an exclusive national power.

Marshall defined *commerce* as *all* commercial intercourse—all business dealings—including navigation and the transport of people. Marshall also held that the commerce power of the national government could be exercised in state jurisdictions, even though it cannot reach *solely* intrastate commerce. Finally, Marshall emphasized that the power to regulate interstate commerce was an *exclusive* national power. Marshall held that because Gibbons was duly authorized by the national government to navigate in interstate waters, he could not be prohibited from doing so by a state court.

Marshall's expansive interpretation of the commerce clause in *Gibbons v. Ogden* allowed the national government to exercise increasing authority over all areas of economic affairs throughout the land. Congress did not immediately exploit this broad grant of power. In the 1930s and subsequent decades, however, the commerce clause became the primary constitutional basis for national government regulation—as you will read later in this chapter. (Note that by holding that Congress had the exclusive power to regulate commerce, Chief Justice Marshall enabled the commerce clause to be used in the future as a check against state laws and regulations that overreach their borders. For a discussion of this aspect of the commerce clause, see the feature *Politics Wired: Does State Regulation of the Internet Violate the Commerce Clause?*)

States' Rights and the Resort to Civil War

We usually think of the Civil War simply as the fight to free the slaves, but that issue was closely intertwined with another one. (See the feature *E-Mail Messages from the Past* on page 96). At the heart of the controversy that led to the Civil War was the issue of national government supremacy versus the rights

POLITICS WIRED

Does State Regulation of the Internet Violate the Commerce Clause?

Recently, several states have enacted laws regulating Internet transactions. For example, the Georgia legislature has enacted a law prohibiting Internet users from "falsely identifying" themselves online. Similar legislation is pending in California. Texas and Florida have concluded that law firm Web pages, including those of out-of-state firms, are subject to the rules of professional conduct applicable to attorney advertising in Texas and Florida, respectively. Many other states have been attempting to apply traditional laws to communications taking place over the Internet.

States, as part of their reserved powers, have the ability to regulate activities within their borders. But state attempts to regulate transactions on the Internet, where geographical borders do not exist, pose special problems. Consider an example. Suppose that the state securities bureau of New Jersey wants to protect New Jersey citizens against fraudulent

online investment schemes. To do this, the bureau issues a regulation making it illegal for any person to offer securities (corporate stocks) online to people in New Jersey unless that person has registered as a broker in New Jersey and has complied with that state's disclosure requirements and other securities laws. In effect, New Jersey has "exported" its regulatory scheme to all of the other states. Every person in the United States who offers securities online either must comply with New Jersey's regulations or risk being haled into court in New Jersey for violating its securities laws.

Traditionally, the courts have viewed state laws that regulate activities beyond their borders through the lens of the commerce clause of the Constitution. That clause, as interpreted by the Supreme Court, grants to Congress the exclusive power to regulate interstate commerce. In its negative ("dormant") aspect,

the commerce clause also limits the ability of the states to pass laws that restrict the free flow of interstate commerce. For example, the Supreme Court has held that state laws limiting the length of trucks or trains traveling within their borders violate the commerce clause because the restrictions substantially burden interstate commerce.

Certainly, the Internet, like a truck or a train, is an instrument of commerce. For this reason, some scholars argue that the courts should subject state laws regulating the Internet to a commerce clause analysis.* To date, at least one court has done so. In 1997, a federal court invalidated a New York law that made it a crime to use a computer to disseminate obscene material to minors. The court stated that New York, by passing the act, had "deliberately imposed its legislation on the Internet and, by doing

so, projected its law into other states whose citizens use the Net. This encroachment upon the authority which the Constitution specifically confers upon the federal government and upon the sovereignty of New York's sister states is *per se* [in itself] violative of the Commerce Clause."[†]

The Internet, because of its unique nature, understandably has posed unique problems for virtually all aspects of American law and government. Clearly, federalism is no exception.

FOR CRITICAL ANALYSIS

Given that the Internet is a global network, is it possible for any government—national or state—anywhere in the world to regulate this new "instrument of commerce" effectively?

[†]*American Libraries Association v. Pataki,* 969 F.Supp. 160 (S.D.N.Y. 1997).

*See, for example, Dan L. Burk, "How State Regulation of the Internet Violates the Commerce Clause," *The Cato Journal,* Vol. 17, No. 2 (Fall 1997).

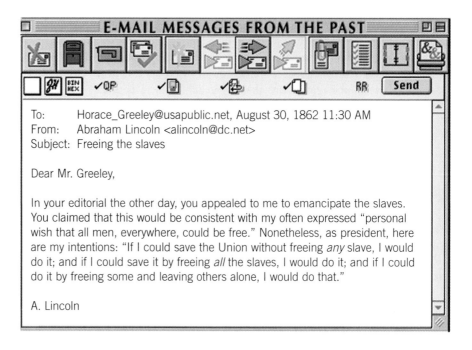

E-MAIL MESSAGES FROM THE PAST

To: Horace_Greeley@usapublic.net, August 30, 1862 11:30 AM
From: Abraham Lincoln <alincoln@dc.net>
Subject: Freeing the slaves

Dear Mr. Greeley,

In your editorial the other day, you appealed to me to emancipate the slaves.
You claimed that this would be consistent with my often expressed "personal
wish that all men, everywhere, could be free." Nonetheless, as president, here
are my intentions: "If I could save the Union without freeing *any* slave, I would
do it; and if I could save it by freeing *all* the slaves, I would do it; and if I could
do it by freeing some and leaving others alone, I would do that."

A. Lincoln

of the separate states. Essentially, the Civil War brought to an ultimate and violent climax the ideological debate that had been outlined by the Federalist and Anti-Federalist parties even before the Constitution was ratified.

The Shift Back to States' Rights

As we have seen, while John Marshall was chief justice of the Supreme Court, he did much to increase the power of the national government and to reduce that of the states. During the Jacksonian era (1829–1837), however, a shift back to states' rights began. The question of the regulation of commerce became one of the major issues in federal-state relations. The business community preferred state regulation (or, better yet, no regulation) of commerce.

The Civil War was not fought over just the question of slavery. Rather, the supremacy of the national government was at issue. Had the South won, presumably any state or states would have the right to secede from the Union.

When Congress passed a tariff in 1828, the state of South Carolina attempted to nullify the tariff (render it void), claiming that in cases of conflict between a state and the national government, the state should have the ultimate authority over its citizens. The concept of **nullification** eventually was used by others to justify the **secession** of the southern states from the Union.

War and the Growth of the National Government

The ultimate defeat of the South permanently ended any idea that a state within the Union can successfully claim the right to secede. Ironically, the Civil War—brought about in large part because of the South's desire for increased states' rights—resulted in the opposite: an increase in the political power of the national government.

Thousands of new employees were hired to run the Union war effort and to deal with the social and economic problems that had to be handled in the aftermath of war. A billion-dollar ($1.3 billion, which is over $11 billion in today's dollars) national government budget was passed for the first time in 1865 to cover the increased government expenditures. The first (temporary) income tax was imposed on citizens to help pay for the war. Both the increased national government spending and the nationally imposed income tax were precursors to the expanded role of the national government in the American federal system.[8] Civil liberties were curtailed in the Union and in the Confederacy in the name of the wartime emergency. The distribution of pensions and widow's benefits also boosted the national government's social role. The North's victory set the nation on the path to a modern industrial economy and society.

The Continuing Dispute over the Division of Power

Although the outcome of the Civil War firmly established the supremacy of the national government and put to rest the idea that a state could secede from the Union, the war by no means ended the debate over the division of powers between the national government and the states. The debate can be viewed as progressing through at least three stages since the Civil War: dual federalism, cooperative federalism, and the new federalism.

Dual Federalism

During the decades following the Civil War, the prevailing doctrine was that of **dual federalism**—a doctrine that emphasizes a distinction between federal and state spheres of government authority. Various images have been used to describe different configurations of federalism over time. Dual federalism is commonly depicted as a layer cake, because the state governments and the national government are viewed as separate entities, like separate layers in a cake.

Generally, in the decades following the Civil War the states exercised their police powers to regulate affairs within their borders, such as intrastate commerce, and the national government stayed out of purely local affairs. The courts tended to support the states' rights to exercise their police powers and concurrent powers in regard to the regulation of intrastate activities. For example, in 1918, the Supreme Court ruled that a 1916 federal law banning child labor was

---

DID YOU KNOW...
That Abraham Lincoln, the "Great Emancipator," claimed on taking office that he would not attack slavery as an institution and that he even wanted a constitutional amendment to make the right to own slaves irrevocable?

Nullification
The act of nullifying, or rendering void. Prior to the Civil War, southern supporters of states' rights claimed that a state had the right to declare a national law to be null and void and therefore not binding on its citizens, on the assumption that ultimate sovereign authority rested with the several states.

Secession
The act of formally withdrawing from membership in an alliance; the withdrawal of a state from the federal Union.

Dual Federalism
A system of government in which the states and the national government each remain supreme within their own spheres. The doctrine looks on nation and state as coequal sovereign powers. It holds that acts of states within their reserved powers are legitimate limitations on the powers of the national government.

---

[8]The future of the national government's powerful role was cemented with the passage of the Sixteenth Amendment (ratified in 1913), which authorized the federal income tax.

In the 1800s, very young children worked in coal mines. Today, child-labor laws prohibit employers from hiring such young workers. Some argue that even in the absence of child-labor laws, few, if any, children would still be working in the mines, because the United States is a much richer country than it was a hundred years ago. Presumably, today's parents, no longer at subsistence income levels, would opt to have their children go to school.

unconstitutional because it attempted to regulate a local problem.[9] In the 1930s, however, the doctrine of dual federalism receded into the background as the nation attempted to deal with the Great Depression.

Cooperative Federalism

Franklin D. Roosevelt was inaugurated on March 4, 1933, as the thirty-second president of the United States. In the previous year, nearly 1,500 banks had failed (and 4,000 more would fail in 1933). Thirty-two thousand businesses closed down, and one-fourth of the labor force was unemployed. The national government had been expected to do something about the disastrous state of the economy. But for the first three years of the Great Depression, the national government did very little. That changed with the new Democratic administration's energetic intervention in the economy. FDR's "New Deal" included numerous government spending and welfare programs, in addition to voluminous regulations relating to economic activity.

Some political scientists have labeled the era since 1937 as an era characterized by **cooperative federalism,** in which the states and the national government cooperate in solving complex common problems. The New Deal programs of Franklin Roosevelt, for example, often involved joint action between the national government and the states. Federal grants (discussed later) were given to the states to help pay for public works projects, housing assistance, Aid to Families with Dependent Children, unemployment compensation, and other programs. The states, in turn, were required to implement the programs and pay for at least some of the costs involved. The pattern of national-state relationships during these years gave rise to a new metaphor for federalism—that of a marble cake.

Others see the 1930s as the beginning of an era of national supremacy, in which the power of the states has been consistently diminished. Certainly, the 1960s and 1970s saw an even greater expansion of the national government's

Cooperative Federalism
The theory that the states and the national government should cooperate in solving problems.

---

[9]*Hammer v. Dagenhart,* 247 U.S. 251 (1918). This decision was overruled in *United States v. Darby,* 312 U.S. 100 (1940).

This housing development in Minnesota was one of the many projects sponsored by the New Deal's Works Progress Administration (WPA) in the 1930s. The federal government's efforts to alleviate unemployment (in this case, among construction workers) during the Great Depression signaled a shift from dual federalism to cooperative federalism.

role in domestic policy. The "Great Society" program of Lyndon Johnson's administration (1963–1969) created the Job Corps, Operation Head Start, Volunteers in Service to America (VISTA), Medicaid, and Medicare. The Civil Rights Act of 1964 prohibited discrimination in public accommodations, employment, and other areas on the basis of race, color, national origin, religion, or gender. The economy was regulated further in the 1970s by national laws protecting consumers, employees, and the environment. Today, few activities are beyond the reach of the regulatory arm of the national government.

The evolving pattern of national-state-local government relationships during the 1960s gave rise to yet another metaphor—**picket-fence federalism**, a concept devised by political scientist Terry Sanford. The horizontal boards in the fence represent the different levels of government (national, state, and local), while the vertical pickets represent the various programs and policies in which each level of government is involved. Officials at each level of government work together to promote and develop the policy represented by each picket.

Federal Grants-in-Aid. As part of the system of cooperative federalism, the national government gives back to the states (and local governments) a significant amount of the tax dollars it collects—an estimated $255 billion a year in fiscal year 1998. Federal grants typically have taken the form of **categorical grants-in-aid**, which are grants to state and local governments designed for very specific programs or projects. For some of the categorical grant programs, the state and local governments must put up a share of the money, usually called **matching funds.** For other types of programs, the funds are awarded according to a formula that takes into account the relative wealth of the state, a process known as **equalization.**

Grants-in-aid in the form of land grants were given to the states even before the ratification of the Constitution. Cash grants-in-aid started in 1808, when Congress gave money to the states to pay for the state militias. It was not until the twentieth century, however, that the federal grants-in-aid program became significant. Grants-in-aid and the restrictions and regulations that accompany them started to mushroom during Roosevelt's administration. The major growth began in the 1960s, however, when the dollar amount of grants-in-aid quadrupled to help pay for the Great Society programs of the Johnson administration. Grants

Picket-Fence Federalism
A model of federalism in which specific programs and policies (depicted as vertical pickets in a picket fence) involve all levels of government—national, state, and local (depicted by the horizontal boards in a picket fence).

Categorical Grants-in-Aid
Federal grants-in-aid to states or local governments that are for very specific programs or projects.

Matching Funds
For many categorical grant programs, money that the state must provide to "match" the federal funds. Some programs require the state to raise only 10 percent of the funds, whereas others approach an even share.

Equalization
A method for adjusting the amount of money that a state must provide to receive federal funds. The formula used takes into account the wealth of the state or its ability to tax its citizens.

President Johnson displays his signature on the War on Poverty Bill after he signed it into law in a ceremony in the Rose Garden at the White House on August 20, 1964.

became available in numerous areas, including the fields of education, pollution control, conservation, recreation, and highway construction and maintenance.

Nowhere can the shift toward a greater role for the central government in the United States be seen better than in the shift toward increased central government spending as a percentage of total government spending. Figure 3–3 shows that in 1929, on the eve of the Great Depression, local governments accounted for 60 percent of all government outlays, whereas the federal government accounted for only 17 percent. After Roosevelt's New Deal had been in place for several years during the Great Depression, local governments gave up half their share of the government spending pie, dropping to 30 percent, and the federal government increased its share to 47 percent. Estimates are that in 1998, the federal government accounts for about 66 percent of all government spending.

By attaching conditions to federal grants, the national government has been able to exercise substantial control over matters that traditionally have fallen under the purview of state governments. If a state does not comply with a particular requirement, the national government may withhold federal funds for other programs. A classic example of the power of the federal government to sanction the states for lack of compliance occurred during the administration of Ronald Reagan (1981–1989). Reagan threatened to withhold federal highway funds unless the states raised the minimum drinking age to twenty-one years.

Cooperative Federalism and the Supreme Court. The full effect of Chief Justice John Marshall's broad interpretation of the commerce clause has only been realized in the twentieth century. In particular, the commerce clause has been used to justify national regulation of virtually any activity, even what would appear to be a purely local activity. For example, in 1942, the Supreme Court held that wheat production by an individual farmer intended wholly for consumption on his own farm was subject to federal regulation—because the home consumption of wheat reduced the demand for wheat and thus could have a substantial effect on interstate commerce.[10]

The commerce clause has also been used to validate congressional legislation even in what would seem to be social and moral matters—concerns traditionally

[10]*Wickard v. Filburn,* 317 U.S. 111 (1942).

FIGURE 3-3

The Shift toward Central Government Spending

Before the Great Depression, local governments accounted for 60 percent of all government spending, with the federal government accounting for only 17 percent. By 1960, federal government spending was up to 64 percent, local governments accounted for only 19 percent, and the remainder was spent by state governments. The estimate for 1998 is that the federal government accounts for 66 percent and local governments for 15.5 percent.

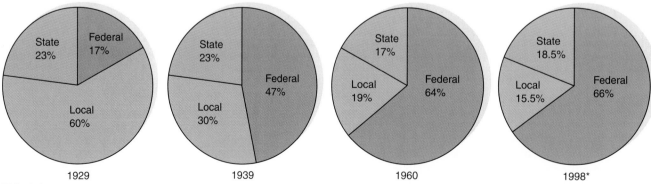

| 1929 | 1939 | 1960 | 1998* |

1929: State 23%, Federal 17%, Local 60%
1939: State 23%, Federal 47%, Local 30%
1960: State 17%, Local 19%, Federal 64%
1998*: State 18.5%, Local 15.5%, Federal 66%

*Estimated

SOURCE: U.S. Department of Commerce, Bureau of the Census, *Government Finances* (Washington, D.C.: U.S. Government Printing Office, 1998).

regulated by the states. For example, in 1964 a small hotel in Georgia challenged the constitutionality of the Civil Rights Act of that year, claiming that Congress had exceeded its authority under the commerce clause by regulating local, intrastate affairs. The Supreme Court held that the 1964 act was constitutional, concluding that "[i]f it is interstate commerce that feels the pinch, it does not matter how local the operation that applies the squeeze."[11] By 1980, the Supreme Court acknowledged that the commerce clause had "long been interpreted to extend beyond activities actually in interstate commerce to reach other activities, while wholly local in nature, which nevertheless substantially affect interstate commerce."[12]

The New Federalism

The third phase of federalism was labeled the **new federalism** by President Richard Nixon (1969–1974). Its goal is to restore to the states some of the powers that have been exercised by the national government since the 1930s. The word *devolution*—which means the transfer of powers to political subunits—is often used in connection with this approach to federalism. (For devolutionary trends in other countries, see the feature *Politics and Comparative Systems: Can Devolution Lead to Stronger Unions?*)

Tools of the New Federalism—Block Grants.   One of the major tools of the new federalism is the block grant. **Block grants** place fewer restrictions on grants-in-

New Federalism
A plan both to limit the national government's power to regulate and to restore power to state governments. Essentially, the new federalism is designed to give the states greater ability to decide for themselves how government revenues should be spent.

Block Grants
Federal programs that provide funds to state and local governments for general functional areas, such as criminal justice or mental-health programs.

[11]*Heart of Atlanta Motel v. United States*, 379 U.S. 241 (1964).
[12]*McLain v. Real Estate Board of New Orleans, Inc.*, 444 U.S. 232 (1980).

POLITICS and Comparative Systems

Can Devolution Lead to Stronger Unions?

Since the end of World War II in 1945, the number of independent countries has grown tremendously. Given that the earth's land surface has not changed in size, this means that more and more of the world's countries are smaller. Indeed, according to Harvard economics professor Alberto Alesina, half of the world's countries now have smaller populations than the state of Massachusetts.*

One reason for this proliferation of small countries is, of course, the end of colonial rule in such areas as sub-Saharan Africa, which now contains forty-eight independent countries. Additionally, the dissolution of the

*The Economist, January 3, 1998, p. 56.

Soviet Union in the early 1990s led to a political makeover of the map of Eastern Europe. The Soviet Union itself became fifteen independent nations. Czechoslovakia became the Czech Republic and Slovakia. Yugoslavia split into several separate nations: Bosnia-Herzegovina, Macedonia, Croatia, Slovenia, and Montenegro.

Generally, the idea that "smaller is better" seems to be increasingly prevalent, and separatist groups abound in today's world. Scottish nationalists want to become independent of the United Kingdom. Many citizens of Quebec would like to declare

independence from Canada and become self-governing. Native Hawaiians seek sovereign status. Some citizens of Texas would like to see that state become an independent nation. In part, this urge toward separatism is fueled by the desire of groups to achieve cultural or racial homogeneity.

Can devolution—the transfer of powers from the central government to political subunits within a nation—defuse the urge toward separatism? Some observers contend that it can. They point to the success of devolution in Germany, which since World War II has given significant powers to its sixteen *Länder* (states). Even though some of

these states were once self-governing "kingdoms," none of them has shown a desire to secede from the German union (Germany). As another example, France, traditionally a highly centralized nation, has reduced separatist dangers by giving more authority to its political subunits. Similar devolutionary efforts by the governments of Italy and Spain have helped to hold those nations together.

FOR CRITICAL ANALYSIS

How is it possible that devolution could help to make a national union stronger, rather than weaker?

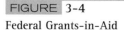

INFOTRAC ®
COLLEGE EDITION

"Constitutional
Federalism - Conditions"

aid given to state and local governments by grouping a number of categorical grants under one broad purpose. Governors and mayors generally prefer block grants because they give the states more flexibility in how the money is spent.

Out of the numerous block grants that were proposed from 1966 until the election of Ronald Reagan in 1980, only five were actually legislated. At the Reagan administration's urging, Congress increased the number to nine. By the beginning of the 1990s, such block grants accounted for slightly over 10 percent of all federal aid programs. With the Republican sweep of Congress in the 1994 elections, block grants again became the focus of attention. Republicans proposed reforming welfare and a number of other federal programs by transforming the categorical grants-in-aid to block grants and transferring more of the policymaking authority to the states. Congress succeeded, in part, in achieving these goals when it passed the welfare reform bill of 1996 (discussed in Chapter 16).

Although state governments desire block grants, Congress generally prefers categorical grants so that the expenditures are targeted according to congressional priorities. These priorities include programs, such as those for disadvantaged groups and individuals, that significantly benefit many voters. As you can see in Figure 3–4, federal grants-in-aid grew rapidly during the Nixon and Ford

FIGURE 3-4

Federal Grants-in-Aid

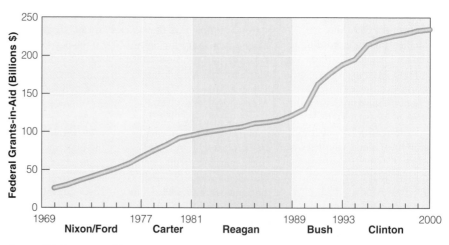

SOURCES: U.S. Department of Commerce, *Statistical Abstract of the United States* (Washington D.C.: U.S. Government Printing Office, 1997). Data for 1998 and beyond are projected.

administrations, as well as during the Carter administration. The rate of growth slowed considerably during the Reagan administration, only to speed up again under Presidents Bush and Clinton.

Trends in Federalism

In a number of states, the 1998 midterm election saw voters approving ballot measures that expressed their desire for state policies that differ from those pursued by the national government. Voters in Washington joined those in California in outlawing any preferential treatment in college admissions or contracts by the state government. Such actions are more drastic than any yet required by the United States Supreme Court. In five of the western states, voters also approved the use of marijuana for medicinal uses, possibly placing doctors and patients in those states in violation of federal drug laws. While such laws may be struck down later in a federal court, the voters clearly believed that they had the right to make laws specific to their state's own situation.

Federal Mandates.   A major obstacle faced by those who favor returning power to the states concerns **federal mandates**—requirements in federal legislation that force states and municipalities to comply with certain rules. Examples of recent federal mandates are minimum water purity requirements for specific localities and requirements for access by persons with physical disabilities to public buildings, sidewalks, and other areas. As mentioned earlier, under the supremacy clause of the Constitution, federal laws preempt conflicting state and local laws.

No accurate analysis exists of the overall costs state and local governments have incurred as a result of federal mandates. Certain mandates, however, clearly are very costly. For example, one mandate involves eligibility for Medicaid. Medicaid is the federally subsidized, state-run health-care program for low-income Americans. The estimated cost of the programs for the states was over $70 billion in 1997. Table 3–2 shows the projected cost to the states of other federal mandates through 1998. (See this chapter's *Critical Perspective* for a discussion of the consequences of federal mandates for local governments.)

Federal Mandate
A requirement in federal legislation that forces states and municipalities to comply with certain rules.

INFOTRAC ®
COLLEGE EDITION

"Cities Skeptical about Justice Bill"

TABLE 3-2

The Projected Cost of Federal Mandates to the States through 1998

MANDATE	FISCAL YEARS 1994–1998 PROJECTED TOTAL COSTS (IN BILLIONS OF DOLLARS)
Underground storage tank regulations	1.0
Clean Water Act/wetlands	29.3
Clean Air Act	3.7
Solid waste disposal	5.5
Safe Drinking Water Act	8.6
Asbestos removal	.7
Lead-based paint	1.6
Endangered species	.2
Americans with Disabilities Act	2.2
Fair Labor Standards Act*	1.1
TOTAL	53.9

*Exempt employee and other costs.

SOURCE: National Association of Towns and Townships.

Critical perspective

Local Consequences of Federal Mandates

The 104th Congress passed a law, the Unfunded Mandates Reform Act of 1995, designed to alleviate the problem of unfunded federal mandates. Closer analysis of this legislation, however, shows that it has had little impact. Indeed, the growth in federal mandates appears to be about the same whether Republicans or Democrats dominate Congress and seems to be unaffected by whether a Republican or Democrat is president. All in all, the National Conference of State Legislators has identified almost two hundred unfunded mandates that have been imposed on the states.

Some Estimated Costs to Local Communities

The costs of federal mandates to local communities are extensive. Consider the following examples:

■ According to Ohio governor George V. Voinovich, seventeen cents of every state and local tax dollar paid by Ohio residents are spent on federal mandates.

■ A typical U.S. business must sort through and fill out about one hundred information booklets and forms concerning federal regulations. The time cost involved in these actions is usually ignored. Some businesses have seen large increases in their start-up costs because of federal mandates. For example, a single dry cleaner's start-up costs have increased by over $100,000.

■ Fairfax County, Virginia, reports that half of its nonschool budget is used for programs and mandates imposed by Congress (and by the state government) for which the county receives no funds.

■ According to Price Waterhouse, an accounting firm, and the U.S. Conference of Mayors, the top three hundred cities in America paid over $50 billion to comply with federal mandates just during the period from 1994 to 1998. The Environmental Protection Agency (EPA) has estimated that state and local governments must spend about $40 billion a year to comply just with its environmental mandates. This figure was developed before the EPA imposed new standards on particulate levels and ozone. According to some researchers, these standards alone may impose $30 to $40 billion a year in additional costs.

■ Many schools have had to be temporarily shut down to comply with the Asbestos Hazard Emergency Response Act. In the first five years after the act was passed, state and local governments spent over $6 billion to remove asbestos. Full compliance for all schools may cost more than $100 billion.

The Problem of Regulatory Inflexibility

Although local conditions are not always the same, federal mandates typically impose the same requirements on all state and local governments. This creates regulatory inflexibility that can make achieving the goal of a mandate costlier than necessary. For example, the Americans with Disabilities Act (ADA) of 1990 requires, among other things, that all public buildings and public services be accessible to persons with disabilities. Yet local governments, especially smaller communities, have little say in how such accommodations should be made. For instance, even though it might be cheaper to transport persons using wheelchairs via taxis, the local government may be required to add special wheelchair lifts to all city buses instead.

Another example of this inflexibility is a mandate of the federal Safe Drinking Water Act. This act requires the EPA, every three years, to identify twenty-five new substances that localities must test for in their water supplies. Cities across America have to bear this cost, even though some of the substances they must test for have been banned for decades.

Regulatory inflexibility can impose burdens on local governments in other ways. Consider the situation in which Anchorage, Alaska, found itself when trying to comply with a requirement of the Clean Water Act. That act required local governments to remove 30 percent of solid materials from sewage water. But Anchorage's sewage did not contain that much solid material, so the city could not remove it. Nevertheless, if Anchorage did not remove some materials, it would face penalties for failure to comply with the requirement. (Eventually, the city solved the problem by dumping five thousand pounds of fish waste, supplied by two local fish processors, into the sewer system and then removing it.)

Critics of federal mandates argue that most of them should not be applied with the same rules and regulations across all cities and states. After all, they claim, if the founders had wanted uniformity in government programs and policies across the nation, they would have established a unitary, rather than a federal, system of government.

FOR CRITICAL ANALYSIS
1. What are the benefits of uniform federal mandates?
2. What administrative problems would arise if states and municipalities were allowed to submit alternative ways to satisfy the goals of federal mandates, rather than following the methods outlined in such mandates?

One of the major "planks" in the Republican platform of 1994 was a promise to end unfunded mandates to state and local governments. By March 1995, the Republican-controlled 104th Congress had indeed succeeded in passing a bill to regulate the use of such federal mandates. On close analysis, however, the 1995 legislation was mostly symbolic; it accomplished little actual change in the use of unfunded federal mandates. To a great extent, this is because, although the Republicans had sought to repeal previously legislated mandates dealing with such matters as civil rights and discrimination, the compromise bill that President Clinton signed exempts these matters. The act also exempts legislation concerning such issues as constitutional rights, voting rights, and national security. In short, the act exempts the matters that account for many of the most costly unfunded mandates imposed on state and local governments during the last decade.

The Supreme Court and the New Federalism.   Many supporters of the new federalism argue that the national government has exceeded the regulatory powers granted to it by the Constitution. In fact, one of the rallying cries of the new federalism has been that the national government has gone too far in the direction of exercising powers reserved to the states under the Tenth Amendment to the Constitution. To a limited extent, the federal courts have agreed with this contention.

In 1992, for example, the United States Supreme Court held that requirements imposed on the state of New York under a federal law regulating low-level radioactive waste were inconsistent with the Tenth Amendment and thus unconstitutional. According to the Court, the act's "take title" provision, which required states to accept ownership of waste or regulate waste according to Congress's instructions, exceeded the enumerated powers of Congress. Although Congress can regulate the handling of such waste, "it may not conscript state governments as its agents" in an attempt to enforce a program of federal regulation.[13]

In 1997, the Court revisited this Tenth Amendment issue. In *Printz v. United States,*[14] the Court struck down the provisions of the federal Brady Handgun Violence Prevention Act of 1993 that required state employees to check the backgrounds of prospective handgun purchasers. Said the Court:

> [T]he federal government may neither issue directives requiring the States to address particular problems, nor command the States' officers, or those of their political subdivisions, to administer or enforce a federal regulatory program.

The Court held that the provisions violated "the very principle of separate state sovereignty," which was "one of the Constitution's structural protections of liberty."

The Supreme Court has also been reining in the powers of the national government under the commerce clause. In a widely publicized 1995 case, *United States v. Lopez,*[15] the Supreme Court held that Congress had exceeded its constitutional authority under the commerce clause when it passed the Gun-Free School Zones Act in 1990. The Court stated that the act, which banned the possession of guns within one thousand feet of any school, was unconstitutional because it attempted to regulate an area that had "nothing to do with commerce, or any sort of economic enterprise." This marked the first time in sixty years that the Supreme Court had placed a limit on the national government's authority under the commerce clause.

DID YOU KNOW... That the city of Columbus, Ohio, estimates that its cost of meeting federal environmental mandates will increase to 23 percent of the city's budget by the year 2000 and that part of this cost goes for testing city drinking water for fifty-two different pesticides—including those used only on pineapples and rice, neither of which is grown in Ohio?

---

[13]*New York v. United States,* 505 U.S. 144 (1992).
[14]117 S.Ct. 2157 (1997).
[15]514 U.S. 549 (1995).

These and several other cases curbing national government authority[16] would seem to indicate that the federal courts are reversing their position in regard to the constitutional powers of the national government. Note, though, that just a few days after the *Lopez* case was decided, the Supreme Court again declared that what appeared (to many) to be fundamentally local activities sufficiently affected interstate commerce to be subject to federal legislation.[17]

Competitive Federalism—
An Alternative Model

The most common conception of federalism focuses on national-state relationships—that is, on the allocation of power between the national government based in Washington, D.C., and the fifty state governments. Under this common notion of federalism, state and local governments have come to be viewed as administrative units of the national government, put there to carry out the management of national programs more effectively. Several scholars have noted that the devolutionary legislation and "power to the states" agenda of the 1990s have not really upset this arrangement. They point out that even when the central government transfers certain responsibilities to state governments, it is the central government that makes the decision to do so. In other words, the central government "grants" such responsibilities to the states and determines their scope.

Competitive Federalism

A model of federalism in which states compete with one another in the provision of goods and services so as to attract "customers"—citizens from other states.

In recent years, an alternative model of federalism has emerged in which government relations are viewed from a more horizontal perspective. Political scientist Thomas R. Dye, a leading proponent of **competitive federalism,** believes that federalism should be viewed as a marketplace across states and municipalities in which state and local governments vie for "customers." Competition among governments would strengthen the allocative functions of government by allowing different jurisdictions to match government-provided goods and services with variations in citizen demand. Citizens could migrate to jurisdictions in which government policies and services best match their desires. For example, if the tax burdens in a particular state are too heavy, citizens can "vote with their feet" and move to another jurisdiction whose tax policies are more favorable to the citizens' interests.[18]

Those who argue in favor of competitive federalism suggest another benefit. Effective competition among governments creates an antidote to a central problem in representative governments—the "capture" of government by special interests. Legislation catering to special interest groups not only fails to reflect the interests of the majority of the voters but also places a significant burden on business and personal activities. Competition among governments, however, allows people to move to other jurisdictions. Those state and local governments that have been captured by special interests may end up losing constituents to other jurisdictions that are more responsive to voters' preferences.

Not surprisingly, supporters of competitive federalism argue in favor of giving state and local governments more responsibility for the welfare of their citizens. National government control over state and local politics—through federal mandates or conditions attached to federal grants, for example—would have to be strictly limited for competitive federalism to be effective.

---

[16]See, for example, *Seminole Tribe of Florida v. Florida,* 116 S.Ct. 1114 (1996); *City of Boerne v. Flores,* 117 S.Ct. 2365 (1997); and *Washington v. Glucksberg,* 117 S.Ct. 2258 (1997).

[17]*United States v. Robertson,* 514 U.S. 669 (1995).

[18]Thomas R. Dye, *American Federalism: Competition among Governments* (Lexington, Mass.: Lexington Books, 1990).

Federalism: Issues for the New Century

Essentially, the issue facing Americans as we enter the new century is how to deal with the problems that caused the growth of the national government in the first place. Even if the Great Depression had not occurred, we probably still would have witnessed a growth of national-level powers as the country became increasingly populated, industrial, interdependent with other countries, and a world power. With these changes, problems and situations that once were treated locally now have a profound impact on Americans hundreds or even thousands of miles away.

For example, if one state is unable to maintain an adequate highway system, the economy of the entire region may suffer. If another state maintains a substandard educational system, the quality of the work force, the welfare rolls, and the criminal justice agencies in other states may be affected. Environmental pollution does not respect state borders, nor do poverty, crime, and violence. National defense, space exploration, and an increasingly global economy also call for national—not state—action. So the ascendancy of national supremacy had a very logical and very real set of causes. Our more mobile, industrial, and increasingly interdependent nation demanded more uniform and consistent sets of rules, regulations, and governmental programs.

The new federalism presumes that state governments should exercise more authority over certain areas that came under national control during the 1930s and subsequent decades. The new federalism, however, has yet to become a reality. Its future success depends on whether certain political obstacles can be overcome. Cooperative federalism resulted in the growth of a national bureaucracy that became firmly entrenched and that seeks to perpetuate itself (see Chapter 14). The senators and representatives in Congress must heed the wishes of their constituents if they are to retain their positions. They must also heed the wishes of various interest groups (see Chapter 8). Even those groups that vote Republican may pressure Congress to pass national regulatory legislation if such regulation is in the groups' political interest.

Furthermore, state governments have grown in size during the twentieth century, as have state populations. As many local governments have realized, state governments find it difficult to create and implement, on a statewide basis, programs that address the diverse needs of different local communities. Indeed, by the late 1990s, many local governments had seized the initiative in dealing with such issues as crime, educational problems, and joblessness. In Chicago, the mayor took over the school system to improve educational performance. The mayor of Milwaukee introduced school vouchers. Mayors in some cities, such as New Orleans, imposed curfews. In the new century, local governments, along with state governments, may well become significant "laboratories" for experimental new programs and policies.

TOWARD ACTIVE CITIZENSHIP

WRITING LETTERS TO THE EDITOR

Just about every day an issue concerning federalism is discussed in the media. Advocates of decentralization—a shift of power from federal to state or local governments—argue that we must recognize the rights of states to design their own destinies and master their own fates. Advocates of centralization—more power to the national government—see the shift toward decentralization as undermining the national purpose, common interests, and responsibilities that bind us together in pursuit of national goals.

The big question is how much the national government should do for the people. Is it within the power of the national government to decide what the law should be on abortion? Before 1973, each state set its own laws without interference from the national government. Who should be responsible for the homeless? Should the national government subsidize state and local efforts to help them?

You may have valid, important points to make on these or other issues. One of the best ways to make your point is by writing an effective letter to the editor of your local newspaper (or even to a national newspaper such as the *New York Times*). First, you should familiarize yourself with the kinds of letters that are accepted by the newspapers to which you want to write. Then follow these rules for writing an effective letter:

1. Use a computer, and double-space the lines. If possible, use a spelling checker and grammar checker.

2. Your lead topic sentence should be short, to the point, and powerful.

3. Keep your thoughts on target—choose only one topic to discuss in your letter. Make sure it is newsworthy and timely.

4. Make sure your letters are concise; never let your letter exceed a page and a half in length (double-spaced).

5. If you know that facts were misstated or left out in current news stories about your topic, supply the facts. The public wants to know.

6. Don't be afraid to express moral judgments. You can go a long way by appealing to the readers' sense of justice.

7. Personalize the letter by bringing in your own experiences, if possible.

8. Sign your letter, and give your address (including your e-mail address, if you have one) and your telephone number.

9. Send your letter to the editorial office of the newspaper or magazine of your choice. Many publications now have e-mail addresses and home pages on the World Wide Web. The Web sites often give information on where you can send mail. Use these addresses, because more and more editors are "wired."

10. With appropriate changes, you can send your letter to other newspapers and magazines as well. Make sure, however, that the letters are not exactly the same. If your letter is not published, try again. Eventually, one will be.

Key terms

Chapter summary

1 There are three basic models for ordering relations between central governments and local units: (a) a unitary system (in which ultimate power is held by national government), (b) a confederal system (in which ultimate power is retained by the states), and (c) a federal system (in which governmental powers are divided between the national government and the states). A major reason for the creation of a federal system in the United States is that it reflected a compromise between the views of the Federalists (who wanted a strong national government) and those of the Anti-Federalists (who wanted the states to retain their sovereignty), thus making ratification of the Constitution possible.

2 The Constitution expressly delegated certain powers to the national government in Article I, Section 8. In addition to these expressed powers, the national government has implied and inherent powers. Implied powers are those that are reasonably necessary to carry out the powers expressly delegated to the national government. Inherent powers are those held by the national government by virtue of its being a sovereign state with the right to preserve itself.

3 The Tenth Amendment to the Constitution states that powers not delegated to the United States by the Constitution, nor prohibited by it to the states, are reserved to the states, or to the people. In certain areas, the Constitution provides for concurrent powers, such as the power to tax, which are powers that are held jointly by the national and state governments. The Constitution also denies certain powers to both the national government and the states.

4 The supremacy clause of the Constitution states that the Constitution, congressional laws, and national treaties are the supreme law of the land. States cannot use their reserved or concurrent powers to override national policies. Vertical checks and balances allow the states to influence the national government and vice versa.

5 The three most important clauses in the Constitution relating to horizontal federalism require that (a) each state give full faith and credit to every other state's public acts, records, and judicial proceedings; (b) each state extend to every other state's citizens the privileges and immunities of its own citizens; and (c) each state agree to return persons who are fleeing from justice to another state back to their home state when requested to do so.

6 Two landmark Supreme Court cases expanded the constitutional powers of the national government. Chief Justice John Marshall's expansive interpretation of the "necessary and proper" clause of the Constitution in *McCulloch v. Maryland* (1819) enhanced the implied power of the national government. Marshall's broad interpretation of the commerce clause in *Gibbons v. Ogden* (1824) further extended the constitutional regulatory powers of the national government.

7 At the heart of the controversy that led to the Civil War was the issue of national government supremacy versus the rights of the separate states. The notion of nullification eventually led to the secession of the Confederate states from the Union. But the effect of the South's desire for increased states' rights and the subsequent Civil War was an increase in the political power of the national government.

8 Since the Civil War, federalism has evolved through at least three phases: dual federalism, cooperative federalism, and the new federalism. In dual federalism, each of the states and the federal government remain supreme within their own spheres. The era since the Great Depression has sometimes been labeled one of cooperative federalism, in which states and the national government cooperate in solving complex common problems. Others view it as the beginning of an era of national supremacy, because from the era of Franklin Roosevelt to the present, the national government continually has expanded its regulatory powers and activities.

9 The goal of the *new federalism,* labeled as such by President Nixon, is to decentralize federal programs and return more decision-making authority to the states. A major tool of the new federalism is the block grant, which groups various categorical grants together and gives more authority to the states in respect to the use of federal funds. Curbing unfunded federal mandates is seen as yet another step on the road to a new federalism. The new federalism may take some time to build because of the numerous political obstacles to its implementation.

10 An alternative model of federalism, competitive federalism, has emerged in recent years. In competitive federalism, state and local governments compete with one another in the delivery of government-provided goods and services. Citizens show their preferences for specific government policies by "voting with their feet"—moving to jurisdictions that provide a more attractive mix of goods and services.

Selected print and electronic resources

SUGGESTED READINGS

Brinkley, Alan, et al. *The New Federalist Papers: Essays in Defense of the Constitution.* New York: W. W. Norton and Co., 1997. The authors of these essays argue that many of the current efforts to transfer national governmental powers to state and local governments are contrary to the Constitution and the intentions of the founders.

Donahue, John D. *Disunited States.* New York: Basic Books, 1997. The author analyzes current "devolutionary" politics and concludes that devolution may not be in the nation's best interests.

Hamilton, Alexander, James Madison, and John Jay. *The Federalist Papers.* Cambridge, Mass.: Harvard University Press, 1961. These essays remain an authoritative exposition of the founders' views of federalism.

Walker, David B. *The Rebirth of Federalism: Slouching toward Washington.* Chatham, N.J.: Chatham House, 1995. This history of American federalism offers an excellent analysis of federalism's current "feeble" condition. The book links the failure of true federalism to the decline of trust in the national government during the 1990s.

MEDIA RESOURCES

Can the States Do It Better?—A film in which various experts explore the debate over how much power the national government should have and use documentary film footage and other resources to illustrate historical instances of this debate.

Logging on

To learn the founders' views on federalism, you can access *The Federalist Papers* online at

www.law.emory.edu/FEDERAL/

The following site has links to U.S. state constitutions, *The Federalist Papers,* and international federations, such as the European Union:

www.constitution.org/cs_feder.htm

Project Vote Smart's Web site on current issues in American government offers a number of articles on federalism/states' rights. Go to

www.vote-smart.org/issues/
FEDERALISM_STATES_RIGHTS/

The following Web site of the Council of State Governments is a good source for information on state responses to federalism issues:

www.statesnews.org/

You can find a directory of numerous federalism links at

www.gmu.edu/

The Brookings Institution's policy analyses and recommendations on a variety of issues, including federalism, can be accessed at

www.brook.edu/

For a libertarian approach to issues relating to federalism, go to the Cato Institute's Web page at

www.cato.org/

Using the Internet for political analysis

Almost all state governments have made some part of their organizations and laws available electronically. Use the Internet to compare state issues and policies by pointing your browser to the site maintained by NASIRE, The National Association of State Information Resource Executives:

www.nasire.org/

Click on StateSearch, and then go to the pages for the Department of Parks or Environmental Resources (the name depends on the state). Compare the hot topics or "What's New" issues of at least two states from different regions of the country. What are the hot issues at the state level? How are those issues unique to that state? Can the state solve the problems alone, or is the issue national in scope? To what extent do you find evidence of national legislation in these state pages?

Civil Rights and Liberties

PART 2

chapter **4**

Civil Liberties

¿ what if

The Internet Were Censored?

BACKGROUND

THE INTERNET HAS BECOME THE GREATEST LIBRARY EVER. WITH THE GOOD COMES THE BAD, THOUGH. IN PARTICULAR, SOME CONCERNED CITIZENS WERE WORRIED THAT CHILDREN TOO EASILY CAN ACCESS WEB SITES CONTAINING INAPPROPRIATE MATERIALS, SUCH AS PORNOGRAPHY OR RACIST PROPAGANDA.

SO, THERE ARE SEVERAL POSSIBILITIES. ONE IS INDIRECT CENSORSHIP THROUGH FEDERAL OR STATE LAWS THAT CRIMINALIZE THE TRANSMISSION OF PORNOGRAPHIC MATERIALS ONLINE. ANOTHER POSSIBILITY IS FEDERAL OR STATE LAWS THAT REQUIRE THE USE OF SO-CALLED FILTERING PROGRAMS WHENEVER CHILDREN MIGHT BE INVOLVED. IN EITHER CASE, THE BATTLE LINES ARE DRAWN. CIVIL LIBERTARIAN GROUPS AND OTHER FREE SPEECH ADVOCATES WANT NO CENSORSHIP. CONCERNED PARENTS THINK DIFFERENTLY.

WHAT IF THE INTERNET WERE CENSORED?

There already has been one attempt—by the federal government—to censor the Internet. The Communications Decency Act of 1996 made it a criminal offense to make "patently offensive" and "indecent" speech available online to minors. The Supreme Court ruled this law unconstitutional because it infringed too much on speech protected under the First Amendment. Nevertheless, suppose that somehow Congress could overcome the Supreme

Court's objections. Assume that a law is passed that criminalizes the online transmission of speech harmful to minors. We can predict that if such a law were passed, an army of federal "Net watchers" would be needed to enforce it. Web sites are already growing at a daunting rate. There is no way that a government, even the federal government, can check every potentially pornographic Web site every day. But it could try, just as many state and local governments have attempted to "stomp out pornography" in printed and other forms.

Then, the following question inevitably arises: By what standard should pornography be judged? Traditionally, the Supreme Court has held that what does or does not constitute pornography is to be determined by local community standards. What would happen if this same approach were used as a "base line" for censoring materials on the Internet, which is worldwide? In effect, the most restrictive community standards would apply to every U.S. user of the Internet. After all, any site on the Web can be accessed from any community in the country. So, what you would be able to view on the Internet would have to satisfy the

decency and obscenity standards of our most restrictive community, wherever it may be in the United States.

AN ALTERNATIVE— REQUIRING FILTERING SOFTWARE

Filtering software denies users access to certain Web sites that are predetermined to be potentially indecent or obscene. Some institutions, such as libraries and state agencies, already have adopted some form of filtering software. What if children were prohibited by law from accessing the Internet from any system in a library, school, or other publicly run enterprise that did not have such filtering software? Certainly, if such a law were passed, filtering software would have to become much better and more effective than it is now. Some of the programs prevent access to any site that uses words depicting body parts. This means that a student in biology could not have access to bona fide educational programs.

The American Civil Liberties Union (ACLU) so far has actively opposed such filtering programs because they tend to prevent access to a large part of the Internet, so that too much censoring is going on—a clear violation of the First Amendment.

WE CANNOT CONTROL THE WORLD

Even if the American government did decide to criminalize pornography on the Internet, our government could do little to regulate Internet sites in other countries. After all, the U.S. government does not control the entire world but only what happens within its own borders, more or less. Given the ease with which anyone can set up a home page on a server thousands of miles from the shores of the United States, the possibility of truly stopping indecent material on the Web seems remote.

FOR CRITICAL ANALYSIS

1. What is the difference between the regulation of explicitly sexual material in magazines, which can be purchased in most jurisdictions by adults, and explicitly sexual materials on the Web?
2. "All filtering programs are not alike." Why not?

Most Americans believe that they have more individual freedom than virtually any other people on earth. For the most part, this opinion is accurate. The freedoms that we take for granted—religion, speech, press, and assembly—are relatively unknown in some parts of the world. In some nations today, citizens have little chance of living without government harassment if they choose to criticize openly, through speech or print, the government or its actions. Indeed, if the United States suddenly had the same rules, laws, and procedures about verbal and printed expression that exist in certain other countries, American jails would be filled overnight with transgressors. Few people would be discussing Internet censorship in hypothetical terms, as we do in the chapter-opening *What If . . . ,* because very likely such censorship would be a reality.

Civil Liberties and the Fear of Government

Remember from Chapter 2 that to obtain ratification of the Constitution by the necessary nine states, the Federalists had to deal with the colonists' fears of a too-powerful national government. The Bill of Rights was the result. These first ten amendments to the U.S. Constitution were passed by Congress on September 25, 1789, and ratified by three-fourths of the states by December 15, 1791. Linked directly to the strong prerevolutionary sentiment for natural rights was the notion that a right was first and foremost a *limitation* on any government's ruling power. Thus, when we speak of **civil liberties** in the United States, we are referring mostly to the specific limitations on government outlined in the Bill of Rights (although there are such limitations in the Constitution's main text itself, including the prohibition against *ex post facto* laws and others found in Section 9 of Article I).

As you read through these chapters, bear in mind that the Bill of Rights, like the rest of the Constitution, is relatively brief. The framers set forth broad guidelines, leaving it up to the courts to interpret these constitutional mandates and apply them to specific situations. Thus, judicial interpretations shape the true nature of the civil liberties and rights that we possess. Because judicial interpretations change over time, so do our liberties and rights. As you will read in the following pages, there have been numerous conflicts over the meaning of such simple phrases as *freedom of religion* and *freedom of the press*. To understand what freedoms we actually have, we need to examine how the courts—and particularly the Supreme Court—have resolved some of those conflicts. One important conflict has to do with whether the national Bill of Rights limited state governments as well as the national government.

Civil Liberties
Those personal freedoms that are protected for all individuals and that generally deal with individual freedom. Civil liberties typically involve restraining the government's actions against individuals.

"First They Come for the Libraries"

The Nationalization of the Bill of Rights

Most citizens do not realize that, as originally intended, the Bill of Rights limited only the powers of the national government. At the time the Bill of Rights was ratified, there was little concern over the potential of state governments to curb civil liberties. For one thing, state governments were closer to home and easier to control. For another, most state constitutions already had bills of rights. Rather, the fear was of the potential tyranny of the national government. The Bill of Rights begins with the words, "Congress shall make no law . . . ." It says nothing about *states* making laws that might abridge citizens' civil liberties.

State bills of rights were similar to the national one, but there were some differences. Furthermore, each state's judicial system interpreted the rights

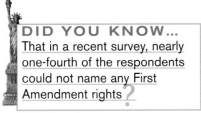

DID YOU KNOW...
That in a recent survey, nearly one-fourth of the respondents could not name any First Amendment rights?

differently. A citizen in one state, therefore, effectively had a different set of civil rights from a citizen in another state. It was not until after the Fourteenth Amendment was ratified in 1868 that civil liberties guaranteed by the national Constitution began to be applied to the states. Section 1 of that amendment provides, in part, as follows:

> No State shall . . . deprive any person of life, liberty, or property, without due process of law.

There was no question that the Fourteenth Amendment applied to state governments. For decades, however, the courts were reluctant to define the liberties spelled out in the national Bill of Rights as constituting "due process of law," which was protected under the Fourteenth Amendment. It was not until 1925, in *Gitlow v. New York,*[1] that the United States Supreme Court held that the Fourteenth Amendment protected the freedom of speech guaranteed by the First Amendment to the Constitution.

Incorporation Theory
The view that most of the protections of the Bill of Rights are applied against state governments through the Fourteenth Amendment's due process clause.

Only gradually, and never completely, did the Supreme Court accept the **incorporation theory**—the view that most of the protections of the Bill of Rights are incorporated into the Fourteenth Amendment's protection against state government. Table 4–1 shows the rights that the Court has incorporated into the Fourteenth Amendment and the case in which it first applied each protection. As you can see in that table, in the fifteen years following the *Gitlow* decision, the Supreme Court incorporated into the Fourteenth Amendment the other basic freedoms (of the press, assembly, the right to petition, and religion) guaranteed by the First Amendment. These and the later Supreme Court decisions listed in Table 4–1 have bound the fifty states to accept for their respective citizens most of the rights and freedoms that are set forth in the U.S. Bill of Rights. We now look at some of those rights and freedoms, beginning with the freedom of religion.

Freedom of Religion

In the United States, freedom of religion consists of two principal precepts as they are presented in the First Amendment. The first has to do with the separation of church and state, and the second guarantees the free exercise of religion.

[1]268 U.S. 652 (1925).

TABLE 4–1

Incorporating the Bill of Rights into the Fourteenth Amendment

YEAR	ISSUE	AMENDMENT INVOLVED	COURT CASE
1925	Freedom of speech	I	*Gitlow v. New York,* 268 U.S. 652.
1931	Freedom of the press	I	*Near v. Minnesota,* 283 U.S. 697.
1932	Right to a lawyer in capital punishment cases	VI	*Powell v. Alabama,* 287 U.S. 45.
1937	Freedom of assembly and right to petition	I	*De Jonge v. Oregon,* 299 U.S. 353.
1940	Freedom of religion	I	*Cantwell v. Connecticut,* 310 U.S. 296.
1947	Separation of state and church	I	*Everson v. Board of Education,* 330 U.S. 1.
1948	Right to a public trial	VI	*In re Oliver,* 333 U.S. 257.
1949	No unreasonable searches and seizures	IV	*Wolf v. Colorado,* 338 U.S. 25.
1961	Exclusionary rule	IV	*Mapp v. Ohio,* 367 U.S. 643.
1962	No cruel and unusual punishment	VIII	*Robinson v. California,* 370 U.S. 660.
1963	Right to a lawyer in all criminal felony cases	VI	*Gideon v. Wainwright,* 372 U.S. 335.
1964	No compulsory self-incrimination	V	*Malloy v. Hogan,* 378 U.S. 1.
1965	Right to privacy	I	*Griswold v. Connecticut,* 381 U.S. 479.
1966	Right to an impartial jury	VI	*Parker v. Gladden,* 385 U.S. 363.
1967	Right to a speedy trial	VI	*Klopfer v. North Carolina,* 386 U.S. 213.
1969	No double jeopardy	V	*Benton v. Maryland,* 395 U.S. 784.

The Separation of Church and State

The First Amendment to the Constitution states, in part, that "Congress shall make no law respecting an establishment of religion." In the words of President Jefferson, the **establishment clause** was designed to create a "wall of separation of Church and State." (For Jefferson's views on religion and government, see the feature *E-Mail Messages from the Past*.) Perhaps Jefferson was thinking about the religious intolerance that characterized the first colonies. Although many of the American colonies were founded by groups in pursuit of religious freedom, nonetheless they were quite intolerant of religious beliefs that did not conform to those held by the majority of citizens within their own communities. Jefferson undoubtedly was also aware that state religions were the rule; among the original thirteen American colonies, nine of them had official religions.

As interpreted by the Supreme Court, the establishment clause in the First Amendment means at least the following:

> Neither a state nor the federal government can set up a church. Neither can pass laws which aid one religion, aid all religions, or prefer one religion over another. Neither can force nor influence a person to go to or to remain away from church against his will or force him to profess a belief or disbelief in any religion. No person can be punished for entertaining or professing religious beliefs or disbeliefs, for church attendance or nonattendance. No tax in any amount, large or small, can be levied to support any religious activities or institutions, whatever they may be called, or whatever form they may adopt to teach or practice religion. Neither a state nor the federal government can, openly or secretly, participate in the affairs of any religious organizations or groups and vice versa.[2]

The establishment clause covers all conflicts about such matters as the legality of state and local government aid to religious organizations and schools, allowing or requiring school prayers, and the teaching of evolution versus fundamentalist theories of creation.

Aid to Church-Related Schools. Throughout the United States, all property owners except religious, educational, fraternal, literary, scientific, and similar

---

[2]*Everson v. Board of Education,* 330 U.S. 1 (1947).

Establishment Clause
The part of the First Amendment prohibiting the establishment of a church officially supported by the national government. It is applied to questions of state and local government aid to religious organizations and schools, questions of the legality of allowing or requiring school prayers, and questions of the teaching of evolution versus fundamentalist theories of creation.

INFOTRAC®
COLLEGE EDITION

"Blocking the Exits"

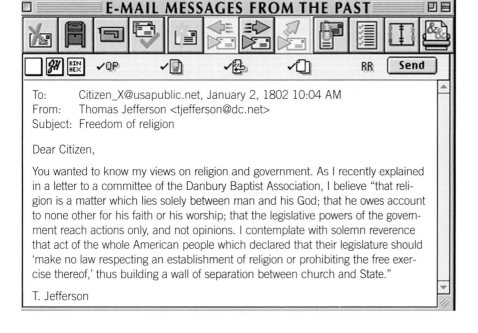

E-MAIL MESSAGES FROM THE PAST

To: Citizen_X@usapublic.net, January 2, 1802 10:04 AM
From: Thomas Jefferson <tjefferson@dc.net>
Subject: Freedom of religion

Dear Citizen,

You wanted to know my views on religion and government. As I recently explained in a letter to a committee of the Danbury Baptist Association, I believe "that religion is a matter which lies solely between man and his God; that he owes account to none other for his faith or his worship; that the legislative powers of the government reach actions only, and not opinions. I contemplate with solemn reverence that act of the whole American people which declared that their legislature should 'make no law respecting an establishment of religion or prohibiting the free exercise thereof,' thus building a wall of separation between church and State."

T. Jefferson

nonprofit institutions must pay property taxes. A large part of the proceeds of such taxes goes to support public schools. But not all school-age children attend public schools. Fully 12 percent attend private schools, of which 85 percent have religious affiliations. Numerous cases have reached the Supreme Court in which the Court has tried to draw a fine line between permissible public aid to students in church-related schools and impermissible public aid to religion.

These issues have arisen most often at the elementary and secondary levels. In a series of cases, the Supreme Court has allowed states to use tax funds for lunches, textbooks, diagnostic services for speech and hearing problems, standardized tests, and transportation for students attending church-operated elementary and secondary schools. In a number of cases, however, the Supreme Court has held state programs helping church-related schools to be unconstitutional. The Court has also denied state reimbursements to religious schools for field trips and for developing achievement tests.

In 1971, in *Lemon v. Kurtzman,*[3] the Court ruled that direct state aid could not be used to subsidize religious instruction. The Court in the *Lemon* case gave its most general statement on the constitutionality of government aid to religious schools, stating that the aid had to be secular in aim, that it could not have the primary effect of advancing or inhibiting religion, and that the government must avoid "an excessive government entanglement with religion." All laws under the establishment clause are now subject to the three-part *Lemon* test. How the test is applied, however, has varied over the years.

Issues concerning the use of public funds for church-related schools are likely to continue as state legislators search for new ways to improve the educational system in this country. One alternative to the current public educational system would allow students to use public funds for private schools, including church-operated schools. (See the feature entitled *Politics and the Constitution: Do School Vouchers Violate the Establishment Clause?*)

The Issue of School Prayer. Do the states have the right to promote religion in general, without making any attempt to establish a particular religion? That is the question in the issue of school prayer and was the precise question pre-

---

[3]403 U.S. 602 (1971).

Fundamentalists Vicki Frost and her husband challenged certain textbooks as being too secular and violating their freedom of religion. Other people have argued that public schools cannot teach about religion because that would be a violation of the establishment clause.

POLITICS and the Constitution
Do School Vouchers Violate the Establishment Clause?

Many parents are dismayed at what they perceive as the declining quality of their children's education in the public school system. Of course, there are alternatives—private schools or home-schooling—but these alternatives are costly. Furthermore, parents who send their children to private schools have to pay, in addition to private school tuition, the taxes that support the public school system. One of the proposals for making private schools more affordable for more Americans—and improving educational opportunities generally—is the voucher system. Under a voucher system, parents can use educational vouchers (state-issued credits) to "purchase" education at any school, private or public.

Supporters of voucher programs argue that such programs produce positive results. For example, one year after the Cleveland City School District initiated its pilot program utilizing vouchers, a study conducted by Harvard University found that test scores of participating students were meaningfully higher, and students' parents were overwhelmingly satis-

fied. A voucher program in Milwaukee showed similarly positive results.* Interestingly, in the Cleveland program—in which four out of every five students used the vouchers to attend private (predominantly Catholic) schools—the private schools produced better results at less than one-third of the cost of a public education. While the expenditure per pupil in Cleveland's public schools is roughly $6,500 a year, tuition at private schools costs, on average, about $2,000.

Opponents of vouchers argue, among other things, that allowing families to use state funds to pay for church-operated schools violates the establishment clause of the First Amendment. In 1997, an Ohio court of appeals ruled that the Cleveland program violates the establishment clause because it provides direct government funding to religious institutions.† The program was allowed to continue for one year, however, pending review by the Ohio Supreme Court.

*_Forbes_, October 13, 1997, p. 27.
†_Simmons-Harris v. Goff_, ___ Oh.App. ___ (1997). [This decision is not yet published in a reporter.]

Parents and students in Austin, Texas, advocate the adoption of legislation that would allow for school choice and a voucher system.

More recently, however, the Supreme Court of Wisconsin arrived at a different conclusion when reviewing a case challenging the constitutionality of a similar voucher program in Milwaukee. In the eyes of the Wisconsin high court, the Milwaukee program did not violate the First Amendment because, among other things, the program "had a secular purpose" and did not "have the primary effect of advancing religion."‡ Whether a voucher program recently approved by a Pennsylvania

‡_Jackson v. Benson_, 578 N.W.2d 602 (Wisc. 1998).

school board will pass constitutional muster remains to be seen. Very likely, the issue ultimately will have to be decided by the United States Supreme Court.

FOR CRITICAL ANALYSIS

With respect to the establishment clause, is there any significant difference between school vouchers and Pell grants—federal grants that offer disadvantaged students a state-funded college education at any institution of higher learning, public or private?

sented in 1962 in _Engel v. Vitale_,[4] the so-called Regents' Prayer case in New York. The State Board of Regents of New York had suggested that a prayer be spoken aloud in the public schools at the beginning of each day. The recommended prayer was as follows:

> Almighty God, we acknowledge our dependence upon Thee,
> And we beg Thy blessings upon us, our parents, our teachers, and our Country.

Such a prayer was implemented in many New York public schools.

The parents of a number of students challenged the action of the regents, maintaining that it violated the establishment clause of the First Amendment. At

---

[4]370 U.S. 421 (1962).

Children pray in school. Such in-school prayer is in violation of Supreme Court rulings based on the First Amendment. A Supreme Court ruling does not necessarily carry with it a mechanism for enforcement everywhere in the United States, however.

trial, the parents lost. The Supreme Court, however, ruled that the regents' action was unconstitutional because "the constitutional prohibition against laws respecting an establishment of a religion must mean at least that in this country it is no part of the business of government to compose official prayers for any group of the American people to recite as part of a religious program carried on by any government." The Court's conclusion was based in part on the "historical fact that governmentally established religions and religious persecutions go hand in hand." In *Abington School District v. Schempp*[5] (1963), the Supreme Court outlawed daily readings of the Bible and recitation of the Lord's Prayer in public schools.

Although the Supreme Court has ruled repeatedly against officially sponsored prayer and Bible-reading sessions in public schools, other means for bringing some form of religious expression into public education have been attempted. In 1983, the Tennessee legislature passed a bill requiring public school classes to begin each day with a minute of silence. Alabama also had a similar law. In *Wallace v. Jaffree*[6] (1985), the Supreme Court struck down as unconstitutional the Alabama law authorizing one minute of silence in all public schools for prayer or meditation. Applying the three-part *Lemon* test, the Court concluded that the law violated the establishment clause because it was "an endorsement of religion lacking any clearly secular purpose."

Since then, the lower courts have interpreted the Supreme Court's decision to mean that states can require a moment of silence in the schools as long as they make it clear that the purpose of the law is secular, not religious. For example, in 1997, a federal appellate court held that Georgia's "Moment of Quiet Reflection in Schools Act" did not violate the establishment clause because the act clearly stated that the moment of silence was "not intended to be and shall not be conducted as a religious service or exercise but shall be considered as an opportunity for a moment of silent reflection on the anticipated activities of the day."[7]

Recently, schools in several states have begun including courses that study the Bible as history. See the feature *Politics and Religion: Should the Bible Be Taught as History?* for a discussion of this issue.

Prayer outside the Classroom.   The courts have also dealt with cases involving prayer in public schools outside the classroom, particularly prayer during graduation ceremonies. In 1992, in *Lee v. Weisman*,[8] the Supreme Court held that it was unconstitutional for a school to invite a rabbi to deliver a nonsectarian prayer at graduation. The Court said nothing about *students* organizing and leading prayers at graduation ceremonies, however, and since then the lower courts have disagreed on this issue.

Forbidding the Teaching of Evolution.   For a good part of this century, certain religious groups, particularly in the southern states, have opposed the teaching of evolution in the schools. To these groups, evolutionary theory directly counters their religious belief that human beings did not evolve but were created fully formed, as described in the biblical story of the creation. State and local attempts to forbid the teaching of evolution, however, have not passed constitutional muster in the eyes of the United States Supreme Court. For example, in 1968, the Supreme Court held, in *Epperson v. Arkansas*,[9] that an Arkansas law prohibiting the teaching of evolution violated the establishment clause, because it imposed religious beliefs on students. The Louisiana legislature passed a law

[5]374 U.S. 203 (1963).
[6]472 U.S. 38 (1985).
[7]*Brown v. Gwinnett County School District,* 112 F.3d 1464 (1997).
[8]505 U.S. 577 (1992).
[9]393 U.S. 97 (1968).

POLITICS and Religion

Should the Bible Be Taught as History?

In recent years, yet another establishment clause issue has surfaced in the educational context: Should the Bible be taught as history? Recently, the Christian Coalition and sixteen other groups issued a statement calling on the schools to include the study of religion, when appropriate, as an important part of education. After all, these groups claim, the Judeo-Christian tradition is an essential component of Western culture. To be well educated, they argue, people need to understand this tradition and its influence on Western society and institutions. These groups believe that students should be taught how religion was one of the shaping forces of American history, beginning with the colonial period.

Even though *Bartlett's Quotations* devotes forty-two pages to quotations from the Bible, a number exceeded only by the sixty-three pages of quotations from Shakespeare, religion is conspicuously absent from the textbooks used in public schools. One study of over sixty public school texts found them "so devoid of reference to religion as to give the impression that it has ceased to exist in America." Even the religious motives of the Pilgrims went unmentioned.* Several public schools have attempted to remedy this situation by including biblical studies in their curricula. But does such instruction violate the separation of church and state

*Michael J. Gerson, "Public Schools Teach Bible as History," *U.S. News & World Report*, January 12, 1998, p. 24.

mandated by the establishment clause?

In early 1998, a test case came before a federal district court in Florida. At issue was a proposal by school officials in Lee County, Florida, to authorize an elective high school course on the Bible as history. The American Civil Liberties Union and other groups challenged the proposed program as unconstitutional. The court ruled that teaching the Old Testament did not violate the establishment clause because the course was adopted by the school board for secular reasons and teaches the Bible in a historical context. The course would have to be monitored closely, however, to ensure "that the classes are predominantly history classes, and are being taught in a permissibly objective

manner." The planned course in New Testament history, however, was constitutionally impermissible. The judge found it "difficult to conceive how the account of the resurrection or of miracles could be taught as secular history."

Certainly, one district court's decision will not resolve the controversy over Bible instruction in the public schools. Other courts may rule differently on the issue if the constitutionality of similar programs in other areas is challenged, as they likely will be.

FOR CRITICAL ANALYSIS

Is it possible to separate biblical instruction from religious indoctrination?

requiring the teaching of the biblical story of the creation alongside the teaching of evolution. In 1987, in *Edwards v. Aguillard,*[10] the Supreme Court declared that this law was unconstitutional, in part because it had as its primary purpose the promotion of a particular religious belief.

State and local groups in the so-called Bible Belt continue their efforts against the teaching of evolution. The Tennessee legislature recently considered a bill that would allow a school to fire any teacher who presents evolution as fact. A proposed amendment to the bill would also protect teachers who want to teach the biblical theories of the creation along with evolution. Alabama has approved a disclaimer to be inserted in biology textbooks, indicating that evolution is "a controversial theory some scientists present as a scientific explanation for the origin of living things." A school district in Georgia adopted a policy that creationism could be taught along with evolution. No doubt, these laws and policies will be challenged on constitutional grounds.

The Supreme Court's Current Approach to Church-State Issues.   Some claim that the current Supreme Court is lowering somewhat the barrier between church and state. In 1995, in *Rosenberger v. University of Virginia,*[11] the Court held that

---

[10]482 U.S. 578 (1987).
[11]515 U.S. 819 (1995).

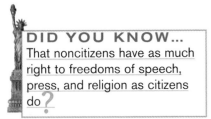

the University of Virginia violated the establishment clause when it refused to fund a Christian group's newsletter but granted funds to more than one hundred other student organizations. The Court ruled that the university's policy unconstitutionally discriminated against religious speech. The Court pointed out that the money came from student fees, not general taxes, and was used for the "neutral" payment of bills for student groups. Justice Souter, who dissented from the majority's conclusion, saw nothing neutral about the Court's decision. He stated, "The Court today, for the first time, approves direct funding of core religious activities by an arm of the state."

The willingness of the Court to accommodate religion was illustrated further in 1997, when the Court decided to review its 1985 decision in *Aguilar v. Felton*.[12] At issue in the *Aguilar* case was the use of federal funds to pay for special educational services for disadvantaged students attending religious schools. The Court held that using federal funds to provide such services on school property violated the establishment clause. When reviewing the *Aguilar* decision in 1997, however, the Court reversed its position. In *Agostini v. Felton*,[13] the Court held that *Aguilar* was "no longer good law." Why? What had happened between 1985 and 1997 to cause the Court to change its mind? Justice O'Connor answered this question in the *Agostini* opinion: What had changed since *Aguilar*, she stated, was "our understanding" of the establishment clause.

These decisions provide striking examples of how constitutional provisions, including the establishment clause, can be interpreted differently by different courts at different times. Note that between 1985 and 1997, the Court's makeup had changed considerably. In fact, six of the nine justices who participated in the 1997 decision were appointed *after* the 1985 decision.

The Free Exercise of Religious Beliefs

Free Exercise Clause
The provision of the First Amendment guaranteeing the free exercise of religion.

The First Amendment constrains Congress from prohibiting the free exercise of religion. Does this **free exercise clause** mean that no type of religious practice can be prohibited or restricted by government? Certainly, a person can hold any religious belief that he or she wants; or a person can have no religious belief. When, however, religious *practices* work against public policy and the public welfare, the government can act. For example, regardless of a child's or parent's religious beliefs, the government can require certain types of vaccinations. Similarly, although children of Jehovah's Witnesses are not required to say the Pledge of Allegiance at school, their parents cannot prevent them from accepting medical treatment (such as blood transfusions) if in fact their lives are in danger. Additionally, public school students can be required to study from textbooks chosen by school authorities.

The courts and lawmakers are constantly faced with a dilemma. On the one hand, no law may be made that requires someone to do something contrary to his or her religious beliefs or teachings, because this would interfere with the free exercise of religion. On the other hand, if certain individuals, because of their religious beliefs, are exempted from specific laws, then such exemptions might tend to favor religion and be contrary to the establishment clause. The original view of the Supreme Court was that although religious beliefs are protected by the law, acting on those beliefs may not be.

The extent to which government can regulate religious practices always has been subject to controversy. Certainly, it has been in the 1990s. For example, in 1990, in *Oregon v. Smith*,[14] the Supreme Court ruled that the state of Oregon

[12]473 U.S. 402 (1985).
[13]117 S.Ct. 1997 (1997).
[14]494 U.S. 872 (1990).

Here, a group of Hare Krishna adherents are crossing a street singing and playing drums and cymbals. This unfettered expression of their religious belief, and even the proselytization of their faith, is protected by the Constitution. Airport authorities, however, have been allowed to place physical restrictions on Hare Krishna groups to prevent them from approaching travelers. Often, they must stay behind a counter or other structure and not initiate contact with travelers unless invited to do so.

could deny unemployment benefits to two drug counselors who had been fired for using peyote, an illegal drug, in their religious services. The counselors had argued that using peyote was part of the practice of a Native American religion. Many criticized the decision as going too far in the direction of regulating religious practices.

In 1993, Congress responded to the public's criticism by passing the Religious Freedom Restoration Act (RFRA). One of the specific purposes of the act was to overturn the Supreme Court's decision in *Oregon v. Smith*. The act required national, state, and local governments to "accommodate religious conduct" unless the government could show that there was a *compelling* reason not to do so. Moreover, if the government did regulate a religious practice, it had to use the least restrictive means possible.

Many people felt that the RFRA went too far in the other direction—it accommodated practices that were contrary to the public policies of state governments. Proponents of states' rights complained that the act intruded into an area traditionally governed by state laws, not the national government. In 1997, in *City of Boerne v. Flores,*[15] the Supreme Court agreed and held that Congress had exceeded its constitutional authority when it passed the RFRA. According to the Court, the act's "sweeping coverage ensures its intrusion at every level of government, displacing laws and prohibiting official actions of almost every description and regardless of subject matter."

Freedom of Expression

Perhaps the most frequently invoked freedom that Americans have is the right to free speech and a free press without government interference. Each of us has the right to have our say, and all of us have the right to hear what others say. For the most part, Americans can criticize public officials and their actions without fear of reprisal or imprisonment by any branch of our government.

INFOTRAC ®
COLLEGE EDITION

"Why Was I Thrown Out of the Hall"

---

[15]117 S.Ct. 2157 (1997).

Permitted Restrictions on Expression

At various times, restrictions on expression have been permitted. A description of several such restrictions follows.

Clear and Present Danger.   When a person's remarks present a clear and present danger to the peace or public order, they can be curtailed constitutionally. Justice Oliver Wendell Holmes used this reasoning in 1919 when examining the case of a socialist who had been convicted for violating the Espionage Act. Holmes stated:

> The question in every case is whether the words are used in such circumstances and are of such a nature as to create a *clear and present danger* that they will bring about the substantive evils that Congress has a right to prevent. It is a question of proximity and degree. [Emphasis added.][16]

Clear and Present Danger Test

The test proposed by Justice Holmes for determining when government may restrict free speech. Restrictions are permissible, he argued, only when speech provokes a "clear and present danger" to the public order.

Thus, according to the **clear and present danger test,** expression may be restricted if evidence exists that such expression would cause a condition, actual or imminent, that Congress has the power to prevent. Commenting on this test, Justice Louis D. Brandeis in 1920 said, "Correctly applied, it will reserve the right of free speech . . . from suppression by tyrannists, well-meaning majorities, and from abuse by irresponsible, fanatical minorities."[17]

The Supreme Court modified the clear and present danger test in a 1951 case, *Dennis v. United States.*[18] At the time, there was considerable tension between the United States and the Soviet Union. The Soviet Union's government was run by the Communist party. Twelve members of the American Communist Party were convicted of violating a statute that made it a crime to conspire to teach, advocate, or organize the violent overthrow of any government in the United States. The Supreme Court affirmed the convictions, significantly modifying the clear and present danger test in the process. The Court applied a "grave and probable danger rule." Under this rule, "the gravity of the 'evil' discounted by its improbability justifies such invasion of free speech as is necessary to avoid the danger." This rule gave much less protection to free speech than did the clear and present danger test. (Concerns over national security have led the U.S. government not only to restrain free speech but also to curb other civil liberties as well—see the feature *Politics and Diversity: Civil Liberties versus National Security.*)

Bad-Tendency Rule

A rule stating that speech or other First Amendment freedoms may be curtailed if there is a possibility that such expression might lead to some "evil."

The Bad-Tendency Rule.   According to the **bad-tendency rule,** speech or other First Amendment freedoms may be curtailed if there is a possibility that such expression might lead to some "evil." In *Gitlow v. New York,*[19] a member of a left-wing group was convicted of violating New York state's criminal anarchy statute when he published and distributed a pamphlet urging the violent overthrow of the U.S. government. In its majority opinion, the Supreme Court held that although the First Amendment afforded protection against state incursions on freedom of expression, Gitlow could be punished legally in this particular instance because his expression would tend to bring about evils that the state had a right to prevent.

Prior Restraint

Restraining an action before the activity has actually occurred. It involves censorship, as opposed to subsequent punishment.

No Prior Restraint.   Restraining an activity before that activity has actually occurred is referred to as **prior restraint.** It involves censorship, as opposed to subsequent punishment. Prior restraint of expression would require, for example, a permit before a speech could be made, a newspaper published, or a movie

---

[16]*Schenck v. United States,* 249 U.S. 47 (1919).
[17]*Schaefer v. United States,* 251 U.S. 466 (1920).
[18]341 U.S. 494 (1951).
[19]268 U.S. 652 (1925).

POLITICS and Diversity

Civil Liberties versus National Security

One of the low points in American history occurred during World War II (1941–1945) when the U.S. government, in the interests of national security, curtailed the rights and liberties of numerous immigrants and citizens.

For example, after the Japanese bombed Pearl Harbor in 1941, the military anticipated that the Japanese might launch an invasion against the West Coast of the United States. Fearing that persons of Japanese ancestry might be disloyal to the United States, curfews were imposed on Japanese Americans living on the West Coast, and more than 112,000 persons of Japanese ancestry were evacuated from the West Coast and transported to "internment" camps. In a word, due to alleged mili-

tary necessity, Japanese Americans were deprived of their constitutional rights to equal protection under the law and procedural due process, as well as the rights to live and work where they wished and to move about freely.* Not until 1945 were all the internment camps closed and the prisoners freed.

While the suffering of these Japanese Americans has received fairly widespread attention, few are aware that other immigrant groups received similar treatment. Little attention has been given to the 600,000 Italian immigrants who were classified as "enemy aliens" during World

*The Supreme Court upheld these actions in *Hirabayashi v. United States*, 320 U.S. 81 (1943); and *Korematsu v. United States*, 323 U.S. 214 (1944).

War II. Those Italian Americans who had shown sympathy for Mussolini were temporarily banished from California. Others were not allowed to travel more than five miles from their homes. Dozens of Italian immigrants had their fishing boats confiscated by the Coast Guard, and about 10,000 Italian Americans were forced to leave their homes in California coastal communities and move inland. About 1,600 Italian Americans were relocated to Fort Missoula, Montana, and interned there, along with Japanese Americans. Additionally, more than 10,000 Germans and German Americans were moved to internment camps, as were some Bulgarians, Czechs,

Hungarians, and Romanians.†

In 1988, the U.S. government issued an apology to Japanese Americans, and Congress provided funds to compensate former Japanese American internees or their survivors—$1.25 billion for 65,000 people. Notably, the U.S. government has never apologized to, or compensated, immigrants from other nations who also populated the wartime internment camps.

FOR CRITICAL ANALYSIS

Can concerns over national security ever justify restrictions on civil liberties?

†James Brooke, "After Silence, Italians Recall the Internment," *The New York Times*, August 11, 1997, p. A8.

or TV show exhibited. Most, if not all, Supreme Court justices have been especially critical of any governmental action that imposes prior restraint on expression. The Court clearly expressed this attitude in *Nebraska Press Association v. Stuart*,[20] a case decided in 1976:

> A prior restraint on expression comes to this Court with a "heavy presumption" against its constitutionality. . . . The government thus carries a heavy burden of showing justification for the enforcement of such a restraint.

One of the most famous cases concerning prior restraint was *New York Times v. United States*[21] (1971), the so-called Pentagon Papers case. The *Times* and the *Washington Post* were about to publish the Pentagon Papers, an elaborate secret history of the U.S. government's involvement in the Vietnam War (1964–1975). The secret documents had been obtained illegally by a disillusioned former Pentagon official. The government wanted a court order to bar publication of the documents, arguing that national security was being threatened and that the documents had been stolen. The newspapers argued that the public had a right to know the information contained in the papers and that the press had the right to inform the public. The Supreme Court ruled six to three in favor of the newspapers' right to publish the information. This case affirmed the no prior restraint doctrine.

---

[20]427 U.S. 539 (1976). See also *Near v. Minnesota*, 283 U.S. 697 (1931).
[21]403 U.S. 713 (1971).

These individuals burn an American flag as a symbolic expression of their opposition to government policy. Would a constitutional amendment to prohibit such desecration of the American flag place unacceptable limitations on symbolic speech?

Symbolic Speech
Nonverbal expression of beliefs, which is given substantial protection by the courts.

Commercial Speech
Advertising statements, which have increasingly been given First Amendment protection.

The Protection of Symbolic Speech

Not all expression is in words or in writing. Gestures, movements, articles of clothing, and other forms of expressive conduct are considered **symbolic speech.** Such speech is given substantial protection today by our courts. For example, in 1989, in *Texas v. Johnson*,[22] the Supreme Court ruled that state laws that prohibited the burning of the American flag as part of a peaceful protest also violated the freedom of expression protected by the First Amendment. Congress responded by passing the Flag Protection Act of 1989, which was ruled unconstitutional by the Supreme Court in June 1990.[23] Congress and President Bush immediately pledged to work for a constitutional amendment to "protect our flag"—an effort that has yet to be successful.

In *R.A.V. v. City of St. Paul, Minnesota*[24] (1992), the Supreme Court ruled that a city statute banning bias-motivated disorderly conduct (in this case, the placing of a burning cross in another's front yard as a gesture of hate) was an unconstitutional restriction of speech. Freedom of speech can also apply to group-sponsored events. In 1995, the Supreme Court held that forcing the organizers of Boston's St. Patrick's Day parade to include gays and lesbians violated the organizers' freedom of speech.[25]

The Protection of Commercial Speech

Commercial speech is usually defined as advertising statements. Can advertisers use their First Amendment rights to prevent restrictions on the content of commercial advertising? Until the 1970s, the Supreme Court held that such speech was not protected at all by the First Amendment. By the mid-1970s, however, more and more commercial speech was brought under First Amendment protection. According to Justice Harry A. Blackmun, "Advertising, however tasteless and excessive it sometimes may seem, is nonetheless dissemination of information as to who is producing and selling what product for what reason and at what price."[26] Generally, the Supreme Court will consider a restriction on commercial speech valid as long as it (1) seeks to implement a substantial government interest, (2) directly advances that interest, and (3) goes no further than necessary to accomplish its objective.

Unprotected Speech: Obscenity

Numerous state and federal statutes make it a crime to disseminate obscene materials. Generally, the courts have not been willing to extend constitutional protections of free speech to what they consider obscene materials. But what is obscenity? Justice Potter Stewart once stated, in *Jacobellis v. Ohio*,[27] a 1964 case, that even though he could not define obscenity, "I know it when I see it." The problem, of course, is that even if it were agreed on, the definition of obscenity changes with the times. Victorians deeply disapproved of the "loose" morals of the Elizabethan Age. The works of Mark Twain and Edgar Rice Burroughs have at times been considered obscene (after all, Tarzan and Jane were not legally wedded).

The Supreme Court has grappled from time to time with the problem of specifying an operationally effective definition of obscenity. In 1973, in *Miller v.*

---

[22]488 U.S. 884 (1989).
[23]*United States v. Eichman*, 496 U.S. 310 (1990).
[24]505 U.S. 377 (1992).
[25]*Hurley v. Irish-American Gay, Lesbian and Bisexual Group of Boston*, 515 U.S. 557 (1995).
[26]*Virginia State Board of Pharmacy v. Virginia Citizens Consumer Council, Inc.*, 425 U.S. 748 (1976).
[27]378 U.S. 184 (1964).

California,[28] Chief Justice Warren Burger created a formal list of requirements that currently must be met for material to be legally obscene. Material is obscene if (1) the average person finds that it violates contemporary community standards; (2) the work taken as a whole appeals to a prurient interest in sex; (3) the work shows patently offensive sexual conduct; and (4) the work lacks serious redeeming literary, artistic, political, or scientific merit.

The problem, of course, is that one person's prurient interest is another person's medical interest or artistic pleasure. The Court went on to state that the definition of prurient interest would be determined by the community's standards. The Court avoided presenting a definition of obscenity, leaving this determination to local and state authorities. Consequently, the *Miller* case has had widely inconsistent applications.

Obscenity remains a constitutionally unsettled area. Many women's rights activists, often in alliance with religious fundamentalists, have pushed for antipornography laws on the basis that pornography violates women's rights. In regard to child pornography, the Supreme Court has upheld state laws making it illegal to sell materials showing sexual performances by minors. In 1990, in *Osborne v. Ohio,*[29] the Court ruled that states can outlaw the possession of child pornography in the home. The Court reasoned that the ban on private possession is justified because owning the material perpetuates commercial demand for it and for the exploitation of the children involved.

Public concern over access to pornographic materials via the Internet led Congress to enact the Communications Decency Act of 1996. The act imposed criminal penalties on those who made "indecent" materials available online to persons under the age of eighteen. In 1997, however, in *Reno v. American Civil Liberties Union,*[30] the Supreme Court held that the act was unconstitutional because it restrained too much protected adult speech. A basic problem with any attempt to regulate obscene speech on the Internet is that there are no "community standards" in that medium.

Unprotected Speech: Slander

Can you say anything you want about someone else? Not really. Individuals are protected from **defamation of character,** which is defined as wrongfully hurting a person's good reputation. The law has imposed a general duty on all persons to refrain from making false, defamatory statements about others. Breaching this duty orally involves the wrongdoing called **slander.** (Breaching it in writing involves the wrongdoing called *libel,* which is discussed later.

Legally, slander is the public uttering of a false statement that harms the good reputation of another. Slanderous public uttering means that the defamatory statements are made to, or within the hearing of, persons other than the defamed party. If one person calls another dishonest, manipulative, and incompetent when no one else is around, that does not constitute slander. The message is not communicated to a third party. If, however, a third party accidentally overhears defamatory statements, the courts have generally held that this constitutes a public uttering and therefore slander, which is prohibited.

Fighting Words and Hecklers' Veto

The Supreme Court has prohibited types of speech that tend to incite an immediate breach of peace. For example, public speakers may not use **fighting words.**

---

[28]413 U.S. 5 (1973).
[29]495 U.S. 103 (1990).
[30]117 S.Ct. 2329 (1997).

DID YOU KNOW...
That a local newspaper in Winchester, Indiana, refused to print a proposed antipornography ordinance because the newspaper considered the language of the ordinance too "obscene" to print?

Defamation of Character
Wrongfully hurting a person's good reputation. The law has imposed a general duty on all persons to refrain from making false, defamatory statements about others.

Slander
The public uttering of a false statement that harms the good reputation of another. The statement must be made to, or within the hearing of, persons other than the defamed party.

Fighting Words
Words that, when uttered by a public speaker, are so inflammatory that they could provoke the average listener to violence; the words are usually of a racial, religious, or ethnic type.

Hecklers' Veto
Boisterous and generally disruptive behavior by listeners to public speakers that, in effect, vetoes the public speakers' right to speak.

These may include racial, religious, or ethnic slurs that are so inflammatory that they will provoke the "average" listener to fight. Members of a crowd listening to a speech are prohibited from exercising a **hecklers' veto.** The boisterous and disruptive behavior of hecklers poses the threat of disruption or violence, so hecklers are vetoing the essential rights of the speaker.

Hate Speech

Some state universities have challenged the boundaries of the protection of free speech provided by the First Amendment with the issuance of campus speech and behavior codes. Such codes are designed to prohibit so-called hate speech–abusive speech attacking persons on the basis of their ethnicity, race, or other criteria. For example, a University of Michigan code banned "any behavior, verbal or physical, that stigmatizes or victimizes an individual on the basis of race, ethnicity, religion, sex, sexual orientation, creed, national origin, ancestry, age, marital status, handicap" or Vietnam-veteran status. A federal court found that the code violated students' First Amendment rights.[31] Although many people assert that such codes are necessary to stem violence on American campuses, the courts generally have held, as in the University of Michigan case, that they are unconstitutional restrictions on the right to free speech.

Campus speech and behavior codes raise a controversial issue: whether rights to free speech can (or should) be traded off to reduce violence in America. This issue extends to hate speech transmitted on the Internet as well, which is a growing concern for many Americans. Those who know how to navigate the online world can find information on virtually any topic, from how to build bombs to how to wage war against the government. Here again, the issue is whether free speech on the Internet should be restrained in the interests of protecting against violence.

At least one federal court has held that "hate speech" on the Internet is a criminal violation. That case, decided in 1998, involved an engineering student, Richard Machado, who had been attending the University of California's Irvine campus. After being expelled from the university for low grades, Machado sent e-mail messages to some sixty Asian students in which he threatened to "hunt down and kill" them. He was charged under a 1968 act making it a crime to interfere with federally protected activities, such as voting or attending a public school. The jury found that his actions violated that act.

Freedom of the Press

Freedom of the press can be regarded as a special instance of freedom of speech. Of course, at the time of the framing of the Constitution, the press meant only newspapers, magazines, and perhaps pamphlets. As technology has modified the ways in which we disseminate information, so too have the laws touching on freedom of the press been modified. What can and cannot be printed still occupies an important place in constitutional law, however.

Defamation in Writing

Libel
A written defamation of a person's character, reputation, business, or property rights. To a limited degree, the First Amendment protects the press from libel actions.

Libel is defamation in writing (or in pictures, signs, or films, or any other communication that has the potentially harmful qualities of written or printed words). As with slander, libel occurs only if the defamatory statements are observed by a third party. If one person writes another a private letter wrong-

---

[31]*Doe v. University of Michigan,* 721 F.Supp. 852 (1989).

fully accusing him or her of embezzling funds, that does not constitute libel. It is interesting that the courts have generally held that dictating a letter to a secretary constitutes communication of the letter's contents to a third party, and therefore, if defamation has occurred, the wrongdoer can be sued.

Newspapers are often involved in libel suits. *New York Times Co. v. Sullivan*[32] (1964) explored an important question about libelous statements made about **public figures**—public officials and employees who exercise substantial governmental power, as well as any persons who are generally in the public limelight. Sullivan, a commissioner of the city of Montgomery, Alabama, sued the New York Times Company for libel because it had printed an advertisement critical of the actions of the Montgomery police during the civil rights movement.

Although the lower courts held in Sullivan's favor, the Supreme Court reversed the judgment. It found that Alabama's libel laws as applied to public officials in the performance of their duty deprived critics of their rights of free speech under the First Amendment. Speaking for the Court, Justice William J. Brennan, Jr., stated that libel laws such as those in Alabama would inhibit the unfettered discussion of public issues. The Court indicated that only when a statement was made with **actual malice**—that is, with either knowledge of its falsity or a reckless disregard of the truth—against a public official could damages be obtained. If the Court had upheld the Alabama judgment, virtually any criticism of public officials could be suppressed.

In the *New York Times* case, the Supreme Court set a standard that has since been applied to public figures generally. Statements made about public figures, especially when they are made via a public medium, are usually related to matters of general public interest; they are made about people who substantially affect all of us. Furthermore, public figures generally have some access to a public medium for answering disparaging falsehoods about themselves, whereas private individuals do not. For these reasons, public figures have a greater burden of proof (they must prove that the statements were made in actual malice) in defamation cases than do private individuals.

A Free Press versus a Fair Trial: Gag Orders

Another major issue relating to freedom of the press concerns media coverage of criminal trials. The Sixth Amendment to the Constitution guarantees the right of criminal suspects to a fair trial. In other words, the accused have rights. The First Amendment guarantees freedom of the press. What if the two rights appear to be in conflict? Which one prevails?

Jurors certainly may be influenced by reading news stories about the trial in which they are participating. In the 1970s, judges increasingly issued **gag orders,** which restricted the publication of news about a trial in progress or even a pretrial hearing. In a landmark 1976 case, *Nebraska Press Association v. Stuart,*[33] the Supreme Court unanimously ruled that a Nebraska judge's gag order had violated the First Amendment's guarantee of freedom of the press. Chief Justice Warren Burger indicated that even pervasive adverse pretrial publicity did not necessarily lead to an unfair trial and that prior restraints on publication were not justified. Some justices even went so far as to indicate that gag orders are never justified.

In spite of the *Nebraska Press Association* ruling, the Court has upheld certain types of gag orders. In *Gannett Company v. De Pasquale*[34] (1979), for example, the highest court held that if a judge found a reasonable probability that news publicity would harm a defendant's right to a fair trial, the court could

Public Figures
Public officials, movie stars, and generally all persons who become known to the public because of their positions or activities.

Actual Malice
Actual desire and intent to see another suffer by one's actions. Actual malice in libel cases generally consists of intentionally publishing any written or printed statement that is injurious to the character of another with either knowledge of the statement's falsity or a reckless disregard for the truth.

Gag Order
An order issued by a judge restricting the publication of news about a trial in progress or a pretrial hearing in order to protect the accused's right to a fair trial.

---

[32]376 U.S. 254 (1964).
[33]427 U.S. 539 (1976).
[34]443 U.S. 368 (1979).

impose a gag rule: "Members of the public have no constitutional right under the Sixth and Fourteenth Amendments to *attend* criminal trials."

The *Nebraska* and *Gannett* cases, however, involved pretrial hearings. Could a judge impose a gag order on an entire trial, including pretrial hearings? In *Richmond Newspapers, Inc. v. Virginia*[35] (1980), the Court ruled that actual trials must be open to the public except under unusual circumstances.

Confidentiality and Reporters' Work Papers

Does freedom of the press mean that news reporters have a right to keep their sources and working papers confidential? To an extent, yes. Courts, however, have often claimed that this right must take second place to the needs of criminal prosecutors to obtain information. In several cases, for example, police officers have been permitted to search newspaper offices for documents related to cases under investigation.

One important case concerned the *Stanford Daily*. The campus newspaper of Stanford University had its offices searched by police officers with a search warrant. They were looking for photographs that would identify demonstrators who may have been responsible for injuries to the police. In this particular case, decided in 1978, the Supreme Court ruled that the protection of confidentiality, and therefore the protection of the First Amendment's guarantee of a free press, was less important under the specific circumstances than the needs of law enforcement agencies to secure information necessary for prosecution.[36]

Congress responded to the Supreme Court's *Stanford Daily* decision by enacting the Privacy Protection Act of 1980. This law applies to state as well as federal law enforcement personnel. It limits their power to obtain evidence from the news media by means of a search warrant and in many instances requires that they use a subpoena. Additionally, more than half of the states have enacted so-called shield laws. These laws protect reporters against having to reveal their sources and other confidential information. Nonetheless, some courts continue to give more weight to law enforcement needs than to news reporters' needs to keep their sources and notes confidential. For example, in 1993 a federal appeals court ruled that a reporter's material only had to be "relevant" to a case to have to be relinquished to parties in a federal criminal trial.[37]

Films, Radio, and TV

As was noted, only in a few cases has the Supreme Court upheld prior restraint of published materials. The Court's reluctance to accept prior restraint is less evident with respect to motion pictures. In the first half of the twentieth century, films were routinely submitted to local censorship boards. In 1968, the Supreme Court ruled that a film can be banned only under a law that provides for a prompt hearing at which the film is shown to be obscene. Today, few local censorship boards exist. Instead, the film industry regulates itself primarily through the industry's rating system.

Radio and television broadcasting has the most limited First Amendment protection. The reason that broadcasting initially received more limited protection than the printed media is that, at that time, the number of airwave frequencies was limited.

In 1934, the national government established the Federal Communications Commission (FCC) to regulate electromagnetic wave frequencies. No one has a

---

[35]448 U.S. 555 (1980).
[36]*Zurcher v. Stanford Daily*, 436 U.S. 547 (1978).
[37]*United States v. Cutler*, 6 F.3d 67 (2d Cir. 1993).

right to use the airwaves without a license granted by the FCC. The FCC grants licenses for limited periods and imposes numerous regulations on broadcasting. One of these regulations, called the **equal time rule**, requires any station that gives or sells airtime to a political candidate to make an equal amount of time available for purchase to all competing candidates. Another rule, sometimes referred to as the **personal attack rule**, provides that if a radio or television station is used to attack the honesty or integrity of a person, the station must see to it that the person attacked is afforded the fullest opportunity to respond. Perhaps the most controversial FCC rule was its **fairness doctrine**, which obligated owners of broadcast licenses to present "both" sides of significant public issues. The FCC abolished the fairness doctrine in 1987.

The FCC also can impose sanctions on those radio or TV stations broadcasting "filthy words," even if the words are not legally obscene. From 1993 through 1995, the FCC fined some radio stations that broadcast the talk show hosted by Howard Stern a total of more than $1.5 million for what the agency considered to be indecent radio programs. Also, the FCC has occasionally refused to renew licenses of broadcasters who presumably have not "served the public interest."

Equal Time Rule
A Federal Communications Commission regulation that requires broadcasting stations that give or sell air time to political candidates to make equal amounts of time available to all competing candidates.

Personal Attack Rule
A Federal Communications Commission regulation that requires broadcasting stations, if the stations are used to attack the honesty or integrity of persons, to allow the persons attacked the fullest opportunity to respond.

Fairness Doctrine
A Federal Communications Commission regulation affecting broadcasting media, which required that fair or equal opportunity be given to legitimate opposing political groups or individuals to broadcast their views.

The Right to Assemble and to Petition the Government

The First Amendment prohibits Congress from making any law that abridges "the right of the people peaceably to assemble and to petition the Government for a redress of grievances." Inherent in such a right is the ability of private citizens to communicate their ideas on public issues to government officials, as well as to other individuals. The Supreme Court has often put this freedom on a par with the freedom of speech and the freedom of the press. Nonetheless, it has allowed municipalities to require permits for parades, sound trucks, and demonstrations, so that public officials may control traffic or prevent demonstrations from turning into riots.

This became a major issue in 1977 when the American Nazi party wanted to march through the largely Jewish suburb of Skokie, Illinois. The American Civil

Radio "shock jock" Howard Stern apparently offended the sensitivities of the Federal Communications Commission (FCC). That regulatory body fined Stern's radio station owner hundreds of thousands of dollars for Stern's purportedly obscene outbursts on radio. The extent to which the FCC can regulate speech over the air involves the First Amendment. Today, both on the radio and on TV, what is considered permissive and acceptable would probably have been considered "obscene" three decades ago.

With their right to assemble and demonstrate protected by the Constitution, members of the modern Ku Klux Klan march in Wilmington, North Carolina. The police escort is charged with making sure that neither the marchers nor the observers provoke any violence.

Liberties Union defended the Nazis' right to march (in spite of its opposition to the Nazi philosophy). The Supreme Court let stand a lower court's ruling that the city of Skokie had violated the Nazis' First Amendment guarantees by denying them a permit to march.[38]

An issue that has surfaced in recent years is whether communities can prevent gang members from gathering together on the streets without violating their right of assembly, or associated rights. For example, in 1997, the city of Los Angeles sued a group of gang members under the city's "public nuisance" laws and convinced the court to issue an order preventing, among other things, the gang members from appearing in public together. The order likely will stand, because the California Supreme Court, in an earlier decision, had concluded that gang members' "associational rights" do not outweigh the right of society to peace and quiet and to be free from harm.

More Liberties under Scrutiny: Matters of Privacy

During the past several years, a number of civil liberties that relate to the right to privacy have become important social issues. Among the most important issues are those concerning sexual freedom, abortion, and the "right to die."

The Right to Privacy

No explicit reference is made anywhere in the Constitution to a person's right to privacy. The courts did not take a very positive approach toward the right to privacy until relatively recently. For example, during Prohibition, suspected bootleggers' telephones were routinely tapped, and the information obtained was used as a legal basis for prosecution. In *Olmstead v. United States*[39] (1928), the Supreme Court upheld such an invasion of privacy. Justice Louis Brandeis, a

---

[38] *Smith v. Collin,* 439 U.S. 916 (1978).
[39] 277 U.S. 438 (1928). This decision was overruled later in *Katz v. United States,* 389 U.S. 347 (1967).

champion of personal freedoms, strongly dissented to the majority decision in this case. He argued that the framers of the Constitution gave every citizen the right to be left alone. He called such a right "the most comprehensive of rights and the right most valued by civilized men."

In the 1960s, the highest court began to modify the majority view. In 1965, in *Griswold v. Connecticut,*[40] the Supreme Court overthrew a Connecticut law that effectively prohibited the use of contraceptives, holding that the law violated the right to privacy. Justice William O. Douglas formulated a unique way of reading this right into the Bill of Rights. He claimed that the First, Third, Fourth, Fifth, and Ninth Amendments created "penumbras, formed by emanations from those guarantees that help give them life and substance," and he went on to talk about zones of privacy that are guaranteed by these rights. When we read the Ninth Amendment, we can see the foundation for his reasoning: "The enumeration in the Constitution of certain rights, shall not be construed to deny or disparage others retained by the people." In other words, just because the Constitution, including its amendments, does not specifically talk about the right to privacy does not mean that this right is denied to the people.

Privacy Rights in an Information Age

An important privacy issue, created in part by new technology, is the amassing of information on individuals by government agencies and private businesses, such as marketing firms. The average American citizen has personal information filed away in dozens of agencies—such as the Social Security Administration and the Internal Revenue Service. Because of the threat of indiscriminate use of private information by nonauthorized individuals, Congress passed the Privacy Act in 1974. This was the first law regulating the use of federal government information about private individuals. Under the Privacy Act, every citizen has the right to obtain copies of personal records collected by federal agencies and to correct inaccuracies in such records. The ease with which personal information can be obtained by using the Internet for marketing and other purposes has led to unique challenges with regard to privacy rights. This chapter's *Critical Perspective* on pages 134 and 135 explores this issue.

Privacy Rights and Abortion

Historically, abortion was not a criminal offense before the "quickening" of the fetus (the first movement of the fetus in the uterus, usually between the sixteenth and eighteenth weeks of pregnancy). During the last half of the nineteenth century, however, state laws became more severe. By 1973, performance of an abortion was a criminal offense in most states.

Roe v. Wade. In *Roe v. Wade*[41] (1973), the United States Supreme Court accepted the argument that the laws against abortion violated "Jane Roe's" right to privacy under the Constitution. The Court did not answer the question about when life begins. It simply said that "the right to privacy is broad enough to encompass a woman's decision whether or not to terminate her pregnancy." The Court held that during the first trimester (three months) of pregnancy, abortion was an issue solely between a woman and her doctor. The state could not limit abortions except to require that they be performed by licensed physicians. During the second trimester, to protect the health of the mother, the state was

[40]381 U.S. 479 (1965).
[41]410 U.S. 113 (1973). Jane Roe was not the real name of the woman in this case. It is a common legal pseudonym used to protect a person's privacy.

Critical perspective

Can Privacy Rights Survive in Cyberspace?

A recent ad in a national publication offered the following service: "Will find anyone you want us to for $69.95." Before the age of the Internet, such an ad would never have appeared. Today, though, there are specialists who can use the Internet to find, well, just about anyone. They also can find information on just about anything and everybody, including individuals' unlisted phone numbers, addresses, driver's license numbers, car registrations, some medical records, military records, criminal records, and the like.

The computer age, coupled with the explosion of information available in cyberspace through the connecting of data banks worldwide, has created a troublesome corollary: an explosion in privacy issues.

We Are All Naked in Cyberspace

In her book *Naked in Cyberspace: How to Find Personal Information Online,** researcher Carole A. Lane made the following claim: "sitting at my computer, beginning with no more than your name and address, I can find out what you do for a living, the names and ages of your spouse and children, what kind of car you drive, the value of your house and how much taxes you pay on it." Lane is a paid Internet searcher and a member of the Association of Independent Information Professionals. She says that "real privacy as we have known it is fleeting."

Consider that if you go into Infospace on the Web, you will find your home address–if you have a listed phone number (as do 112 million Americans). If someone types in your name, that person receives a map of your neighborhood with a little "X" marking your residence. He or she even can get written directions to your house.

*Wilton, Conn.: Pemberton Press, 1997.

Not surprisingly, various government agencies and Congress have decided to investigate and legislate Internet privacy issues. For example, when staff members of U.S. senator Dianne Feinstein (D., Cal.) were able to find her Social Security number on the Internet in less than three minutes, she introduced the Personal Information Privacy Act of 1997. Had it passed, it would have made it tougher for businesses to sell Social Security numbers, unlisted phone numbers, and the like. To head off legislation of this sort, some of the major database companies have agreed voluntarily to impose greater restrictions on access to such sensitive information. Privacy groups are not satisfied, however. They point out that voluntary agreements cannot provide for punishment if they are violated.

Cookies Are Not Just for Eating

You may not know it, but every time you access a Web site, a "tag" may be left in your computer hard drive. Information about you is being stored on your own computer. This procedure is called using a "cookie." Every time you visit a Web site, the server on which it is stored and your computer have to communicate. This communication occurs through a language called http, or hypertext transfer protocol. Many times, the Web sites you access will send out an http command (the cookie) that tells your Internet browser to save part of that communication. So, the next time you visit the same Web site, the saved information is sent back. For the most part, cookies are used simply to tell each Web site how many times you have visited that site before. Cookies can also be used to store a log-in password or a credit-card number if you are buying items, such as CDs. That saves you time in the future because you do not have to key in your password and credit-card number.

INFOTRAC®
COLLEGE EDITION

"The World Wide Never Forgets"

allowed to specify the conditions under which an abortion could be performed. During the final trimester, the state could regulate or even outlaw abortions except when necessary to preserve the life or health of the mother.

After *Roe*, the Supreme Court issued decisions in a number of cases defining and redefining the boundaries of state regulation of abortion. During the 1980s, the Court twice struck down laws that required a woman who wished to have an abortion to undergo counseling designed to discourage abortions. In the late 1980s and early 1990s, however, the Court took a more conservative approach. Although the Court did not explicitly overturn the *Roe* decision, it upheld state laws that place restrictions on abortion rights. For example, in *Webster v.*

Critical perspective

Can Privacy Rights Survive in Cyberspace?—continued

Civil libertarians fear that cookies can too easily be used to track your Web-surfing habits. The Web sites that generate such cookies, however, argue that they are harmless. They simply help to enhance your Web surfing. Civil liberties groups are not so sure. They have founded the Electronic Frontier Foundation as well as the Electronic Privacy Information Center. Both groups have urged private controls over the use of cookies.

Netscape, IBM, and Verisign, Inc., have proposed an open-profiling standard. It would replace cookies with Web software that allows consumers to determine what sort of information they wish to share and with which Web sites.

Keeping Your Internet Service Provider Honest

Because Internet service providers (ISPs) are how you get on the Internet, they are the ones who can best protect your privacy. They are aided by the federal Electronic Communications Privacy Act (ECPA) of 1986, which protects you from unreasonable search and seizures of information by government officials. The electronic communications and personal information stored by your ISP are protected by the ECPA. For example, government officials are required to obtain a warrant if they wish to access the contents of communications held in electronic storage by your ISP.

Is There Really a Problem?

Not everybody believes that the age of cyberspace has brought about the death of privacy. Consider the use of cookies. Some believe that they are as mundane as the ticket you get from the dry cleaners. When you go to pick up your clothes, the dry cleaner matches up the tickets to ensure that you get the right clothing. That is similar to what a Web site does when it takes your cookies the next time you enter the site. Moreover, Web sites that request information are very explicit. The *New York Times* requires you to fill out a free registration form before you can have access to its site for the first time. You are asked for only your name, e-mail address, job, and salary, which is much less than you are asked when you fill out a typical credit application. In any event, if you want to access the *New York Times* site or any similar site that requests information, you always can lie to protect your privacy.

Recently, the Federal Trade Commission held four days of hearings about Internet privacy. Ironically, there have been no hearings about the privacy of medical and pharmaceutical records. Although these have nothing to do with the Internet, such records are very important in terms of privacy. Yet they go wholly unprotected under current federal law. They are shared routinely among insurers and employers with virtually no restrictions. Credit-card companies in the past, well before the Internet was popular, have sold and continue to sell a host of personal information. The cookie on your hard drive may be a speck of dust in comparison.

FOR CRITICAL ANALYSIS

1. What is the difference between privacy concerns stemming from Internet use and privacy concerns that occurred prior to the Internet?
2. What benefits do users derive from the easier access to personal information made possible by the Internet?

Reproductive Health Services[42] (1989), the Court upheld a Missouri statute that, among other things, banned the use of public hospitals or other taxpayer-supported facilities for performing abortions. And, in *Planned Parenthood v. Casey*[43] (1992), the Court upheld a Pennsylvania law that required preabortion counseling, a waiting period of twenty-four hours, and, for girls under the age of eighteen, parental or judicial permission. As a result, abortions are now more difficult to obtain in some states than others.

---

[42]492 U.S. 490 (1989).
[43]505 U.S. 833 (1992).

Pro-life groups increased their demonstrations against abortion facilities throughout the 1990s. The clash between the pro-choice and the pro-life forces have resulted in several individuals being killed. The Supreme Court has imposed restrictions on what pro-life groups could do in their demonstrations around abortion clinics.

The Controversy Continues. Abortion continues to be a divisive issue. Antiabortion forces continue to push for laws banning abortion, to endorse political candidates who support their views, and to organize protests. Because of several episodes of violence attending protests at abortion clinics, in 1994 Congress passed the Freedom of Access to Clinic Entrances Act. The act prohibits protesters from blocking entrances to such clinics. The Supreme Court ruled in 1993 that abortion protesters can be prosecuted under laws governing racketeering,[44] and in 1998 a federal court in Illinois convicted antiabortion protesters under these laws.

Antiabortion forces have as yet met with little success by arguing that these actions unconstitutionally restrain their right to free speech. In 1997, the Supreme Court upheld the constitutionality of prohibiting protesters from entering a fifteen-foot "buffer zone" around abortion clinics and from giving unwanted counseling to those entering the clinics.[45]

Privacy Rights and the "Right to Die"

The 1976 case involving Karen Ann Quinlan was one of the first publicized right-to-die cases.[46] The parents of Quinlan, a young woman who had been in a coma for nearly a year and who had been kept alive during that time by a respirator, wanted her respirator removed. In 1976, the New Jersey Supreme Court ruled that the right to privacy includes the right of a patient to refuse treatment and that patients unable to speak can exercise that right through a family member or guardian. In 1990, the Supreme Court took up the issue. In *Cruzan v. Director, Missouri Department of Health*,[47] the Court stated that a patient's life-sustaining treatment can be withdrawn at the request of a family member only if there is "clear and convincing evidence" that the patient did *not* want such treatment.

---

[44]*National Organization of Women v. Joseph Scheidler,* 509 U.S. 951 (1993).
[45]*Schenck v. ProChoice Network,* 117 S.Ct. 855 (1997).
[46]*In re Quinlan,* 70 N.J. 10 (1976).
[47]497 U.S. 261 (1990).

Since the 1976 *Quinlan* decision, most states have enacted laws permitting people to designate their wishes concerning life-sustaining procedures in "living wills" or durable health-care powers of attorney. These laws and the Supreme Court's *Cruzan* decision largely have resolved this aspect of the right-to-die controversy.

In the 1990s, however, another issue surfaced: Do privacy rights include the right of terminally ill people to end their lives through physician-assisted suicide? Until 1996, the courts consistently upheld state laws that prohibited this practice, either through specific statutes or under their general homicide statutes. In 1996, after two federal appellate courts ruled that state laws banning assisted suicide (in Washington and New York) were unconstitutional, the issue reached the Supreme Court. In 1997, in *Washington v. Glucksberg*,[48] the Court stated, clearly and categorically, that the liberty interest protected by the Constitution does not include a right to commit suicide, with or without assistance. To hold otherwise, said the Court, would be "to reverse centuries of legal doctrine and practice, and strike down the considered policy choice of almost every state."

In effect, the Supreme Court left the decision in the hands of the states. Since then, assisted suicide has been allowed in only one state—Oregon.

The Great Balancing Act: The Rights of the Accused versus the Rights of Society

The United States has one of the highest violent crime rates in the world. It is not surprising, therefore, that many citizens have extremely strong opinions about the rights of those accused of criminal offenses. When an accused person, especially one who has confessed to some criminal act, is set free because of an apparent legal "technicality," many people may feel that the rights of the accused are being given more weight than the rights of society and of potential or actual victims. Why, then, give criminal suspects rights? The answer is partly to avoid convicting innocent people, but mostly because all criminal suspects have the right to due process of law and fair treatment.

The courts and the police must constantly engage in a balancing act of competing rights. At the basis of all discussions about the appropriate balance is, of course, the U.S. Bill of Rights. The Fourth, Fifth, Sixth, and Eighth Amendments deal specifically with the rights of criminal defendants. (You will learn about some of your rights under the Fourth Amendment in the *Toward Active Citizenship* feature at the end of this chapter.)

Rights of the Accused

The basic rights of criminal defendants are outlined below. When appropriate, the specific constitutional provision or amendment on which a right is based also is given.

Limits on the Conduct of Police Officers and Prosecutors
- No unreasonable or unwarranted searches and seizures (Amend. IV).
- No arrest except on probable cause (Amend. IV).
- No coerced confessions or illegal interrogation (Amend. V).
- No entrapment.
- Upon questioning, a suspect must be informed of his or her rights.

---

[48]117 S.Ct. 2258 (1997).

Writ of *Habeas Corpus*

Habeas corpus means, literally, "you have the body." A writ of *habeas corpus* is an order that requires jailers to bring a person before a court or judge and explain why the person is being held in prison.

Defendant's Pretrial Rights

- Writ of *habeas corpus* (Article I, Section 9).
- Prompt arraignment (Amend. VI).
- Legal counsel (Amend. VI).
- Reasonable bail (Amend. VIII).
- To be informed of charges (Amend. VI).
- To remain silent (Amend. V).

Trial Rights

- Speedy and public trial before a jury (Amend. VI).
- Impartial jury selected from a cross section of the community (Amend. VI).
- Trial atmosphere free of prejudice, fear, and outside interference.
- No compulsory self-incrimination (Amend. V).
- Adequate counsel (Amend. VI).
- No cruel and unusual punishment (Amend. VIII).
- Appeal of convictions.
- No double jeopardy (Amend. V).

Extending the Rights of the Accused

During the 1960s, the Supreme Court, under Chief Justice Earl Warren, significantly expanded the rights of accused persons. In a case decided in 1963, *Gideon v. Wainwright*,[49] the Court held that if a person is accused of a felony and cannot afford an attorney, an attorney must be made available to the accused person at the government's expense. Although the Sixth Amendment to the Constitution provides for the right to counsel, the Supreme Court had established a precedent twenty-one years earlier in *Betts v. Brady*,[50] when it held that only criminal defendants in capital cases automatically had a right to legal counsel.

Three years later, the Court issued its decision in *Miranda v. Arizona*.[51] The case involved Ernesto Miranda, who was arrested and charged with the kidnapping and rape of a young woman. After two hours of questioning, Miranda con-

[49]372 U.S. 335 (1963).
[50]316 U.S. 455 (1942).
[51]384 U.S. 436 (1966).

This individual is being read his *Miranda* rights by the arresting officer. These rights were established in the 1966 case *Miranda v. Arizona*. The rights concern minimum procedural safeguards. They are also known as the *Miranda* warnings and include informing arrested persons prior to questioning (1) that they have the right to remain silent, (2) that anything they say may be used as evidence against them, and (3) that they have the right to the presence of an attorney.

More and more state and local governments have adopted so-called "Megan's laws," laws that inform citizens when criminal sexual offenders move into their neighborhood. Do such laws violate the rights of individuals who have "paid their debt to society," or do they rightfully forewarn a community of potential danger?

fessed and was later convicted. Miranda's lawyer appealed his conviction, arguing that the police had never informed Miranda that he had a right to remain silent and a right to be represented by counsel. The Court, in ruling in Miranda's favor, enunciated the *Miranda* rights that are now familiar to virtually all Americans:

> Prior to any questioning, the person must be warned that he has a right to remain silent, that any statement he does make may be used against him, and that he has a right to the presence of an attorney, either retained or appointed.

Many people, particularly police officials, complained that the *Miranda* ruling distorted the Constitution by placing the rights of criminal suspects above the rights of society as a whole. Others, however, agreed with the Court that criminal law enforcement would be more reliable if it were based on independently secured evidence rather than on confessions obtained under coercive interrogation conditions in the absence of counsel.

As part of a continuing attempt to balance the rights of criminal defendants against the rights of society, Congress and the courts subsequently have created several exceptions to the *Miranda* ruling. For example, the Omnibus Crime Control and Safe Streets Act of 1968 provided that in federal cases, a voluntary confession could be used as evidence even if the accused person was not informed of his or her rights. Even in cases that are not tried in federal courts, confessions have been allowed into evidence in certain circumstances. For example, in 1984 the Supreme Court held that when "public safety" required action (in this case, to find a loaded gun), police could interrogate the suspect before advising him of his right to remain silent.[52]

The Exclusionary Rule

At least since 1914, judicial policy has prohibited the admission of illegally seized evidence at trials in federal courts. This is the so-called **exclusionary rule.** Improperly obtained evidence, no matter how telling, cannot be used by

Exclusionary Rule
A policy forbidding the admission at trial of illegally seized evidence.

---

[52]*New York v. Quarles,* 467 U.S. 649 (1984).

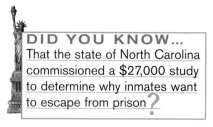

prosecutors. This includes evidence obtained by police in violation of a suspect's *Miranda* rights or of the Fourth Amendment. The Fourth Amendment protects against unreasonable searches and seizures and requires that a search warrant may be issued by a judge to a police officer only on probable cause (a demonstration of facts that permit a reasonable belief that a crime has been committed). The question that must be determined by the courts is what constitutes an "unreasonable" search and seizure.

The reasoning behind the exclusionary rule is that it forces police officers to gather evidence properly, in which case their due diligence will be rewarded by a conviction. The exclusionary rule has always had critics who argue that it permits guilty persons to be freed because of innocent errors.

This rule was first extended to state court proceedings in a 1961 Supreme Court decision, *Mapp v. Ohio*.[53] In this case, the Court overturned the conviction of Dollree Mapp for the possession of obscene materials. Police found pornographic books in her apartment after searching it without a search warrant and despite her refusal to let them in.

In 1984, the Supreme Court held that illegally obtained evidence could be admitted at trial if law enforcement personnel could prove that they would have obtained the evidence legally anyway.[54] In another case decided in the same year, the Court held that a police officer who used a technically incorrect search warrant form to obtain evidence had acted in good faith and therefore the evidence was admissible at trial. The Court thus created the "good faith" exception to the exclusionary rule.[55]

Other exceptions to the rule made by the courts during the 1980s and 1990s have tended to further weaken criminal defendants' rights and, according to many critics, have allowed law enforcement personnel to exercise power a little too arbitrarily. Who is to say, for example, whether a police officer was acting in "good faith" when obtaining evidence against a criminal suspect? Others argue that these exceptions have not altered the basic fact that the numerous rights of criminal defendants make justice difficult—if not impossible—to obtain (see the feature entitled *Politics and Criminal Justice* for a further discussion of this view).

The Death Penalty

Capital punishment remains one of the most debated aspects of our criminal justice system. Those in favor of the death penalty maintain that it serves as a deterrent to serious crime and satisfies society's need for justice and fair play. Those opposed to the death penalty do not believe it has any deterrent value and hold that it constitutes a barbaric act in an otherwise civilized society. Recent public opinion polls have demonstrated that a large majority of Americans favor using the death penalty more frequently, and thirty-eight states currently provide for the death penalty.

Cruel and Unusual Punishment?   Amendment VIII prohibits cruel and unusual punishment. Throughout history, "cruel and unusual" referred to punishments that were more serious than the crimes—the phrase referred to torture and to executions that prolonged the agony of dying. The Supreme Court never interpreted "cruel and unusual" to prohibit all forms of capital punishment in all circumstances. Indeed, a number of states had imposed the death penalty for a variety of crimes and allowed juries to decide when the condemned could be

---

[53]367 U.S. 643 (1961).
[54]*Nix v. Williams*, 467 U.S. 431 (1984).
[55]*Massachusetts v. Sheppard*, 468 U.S. 981 (1984).

POLITICS and Criminal Justice

Are Criminal Procedures Getting in the Way of Justice?

Criminal procedures are no longer an arcane series of rules known only to prosecutors, criminal defense attorneys, and judges. Indeed, in 1994 and 1995, as the O. J. Simpson trial unfolded before television cameras, vast numbers of Americans learned how procedural requirements affect the outcome of criminal proceedings.

The purpose of criminal procedural rules is, of course, to ensure that state prosecutors do not infringe on the constitutional rights of defendants, particularly the right to due process of law. After all, a criminal prosecution brings the force of the state, with all its resources, to bear against the individual. The *Miranda* requirements, the exclusionary rule, and other procedural rules are designed to safeguard the rights of individuals against the immense power of the state.

Many contend, however, that criminal procedures are getting in the way of truth and criminal justice. Certainly, New York state trial judge Harold J. Rothwax thinks so. In his book, *Guilty: The Collapse of Criminal Justice,** Rothwax contends that the *Miranda* requirements and court interpretations of the Fourth and Fifth Amendments have created a thicket of criminal procedures that has resulted in the "collapse of criminal justice" in this country. Even defendants who confess their guilt go free if they can prove that law enforcement officers violated a procedural requirement in some way, such as failing to read a criminal suspect his or her *Miranda* rights at the appropriate moment or obtaining evi-

*New York: Random House, 1996.

dence without a valid search warrant. Among other things, Rothwax proposes that the *Miranda* requirements be eliminated.

Rothwax is not alone in his concern about the collapse of criminal justice. Increasingly, other legal scholars and former judges are speaking out against the system. One of these critics is Burton S. Katz, a former prosecutor and judge in the California state court system. In his book, *Justice Overruled: Unmasking the Criminal Justice System,†* Katz blames the Supreme Court for creating a system of protections for criminal suspects that ties the hands of police officers and allows known criminals to go free. In what he refers to as a "broken criminal justice system," trials are turned into

†New York: Warner Books, 1997.

mockeries of justice.

Katz emphasizes that the many legal loopholes available to criminal defendants have resulted in a new phenomenon, which he calls "testi-lying." This occurs when law enforcement personnel, intent on getting a conviction, "bend the truth" about how evidence was gathered or whether the defendant was read his or her rights correctly. Katz also laments the abuse of the jury selection process and the increasing use of diminished-capacity defenses that allows killers to go free.

FOR CRITICAL ANALYSIS

If the Miranda *rules were abolished, as Judge Harold Rothwax proposes, would society be better or worse off? Explain.*

sentenced to death. Many believed, however, and in 1972 the Supreme Court agreed, in *Furman v. Georgia,*[56] that the imposition of the death penalty was random and arbitrary.

The Supreme Court's 1972 decision stated that the death penalty, as then applied, violated the Eighth and Fourteenth Amendments. It ruled that capital punishment is not necessarily cruel and unusual if the criminal has killed or attempted to kill someone. In its opinion, the Court invited the states to make more precise laws so that the death penalty would be applied more consistently. A majority of states have done so. By the 1990s, an increasing number of states were executing death-row inmates. Indeed, by 1998 convicted murderers were being executed at a rate of about one every five days. In the two decades prior to 1998, 432 convicted murderers were put to death. In 1998, about 3,200 convicts across the United States were awaiting execution.

Very likely, the number of executions will continue to rise as a result of a 1996 federal law that imposes a severe time limit on death-row appeals. The law also requires federal judges to hear these appeals and issue their opinions within a specified time period. Many are concerned that the shortened appeals process increases the possibility that innocent persons may be put to death. Since 1973,

[56]408 U.S. 238 (1972).

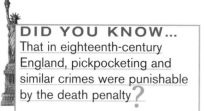

seventy-three people have been freed from death row after courts have found that they were wrongfully convicted. On average, it takes about seven years to exonerate someone on death row. In recent years, however, the time between conviction and execution has been shortened from an average of ten to twelve years to an average of six to eight years.

Sanity Issues. Issues surrounding the sanity of death-row inmates have come up in the last decade. In 1986, in *Ford v. Wainwright*,[57] the Supreme Court ruled that the U.S. Constitution bars states from executing convicted killers who have become insane while waiting on death row. Despite this ruling, in 1989, in *Penry v. Lynaugh*,[58] the Supreme Court held that mentally retarded persons may be executed for murder. In the same year, in *Stanford v. Kentucky*,[59] the Court found that defendants who were as young as sixteen years of age could be executed if they had committed a murder. Finally, in *Murray v. Giarratano*,[60] another case decided in 1989, the Court held that indigent death-row inmates have no constitutional right to a lawyer for a second round of state court appeals.

Racial Bias. The Supreme Court also must wrestle with issues involving racial discrimination and the death penalty. In *McClesky v. Kemp*[61] (1987), the Court considered statistical evidence regarding Georgia's death-sentencing process, which the defendant claimed was racially discriminatory. The Court held that some disparities are an inevitable part of the criminal justice system and do not necessarily violate the Constitution. The defendant had presented a statistical study based on more than two thousand murder cases that occurred in Georgia during the 1970s. The study purported to show that the death sentence was imposed more often on black defendants convicted of killing whites than on white defendants convicted of killing blacks. The Supreme Court decided that the statistics did not prove that race enters into capital sentencing decisions or

[57]477 U.S. 399 (1986).
[58]492 U.S. 302 (1989).
[59]492 U.S. 361 (1989).
[60]492 U.S. 1 (1989).
[61]481 U.S. 279 (1987).

People gather outside a Virginia penitentiary to keep vigil. They are protesting against the execution of a convict.

that it was a factor in the defendant's case. The Court stated that the unpredictability of jury decisions does not justify their condemnation, because it is the jury's function to make difficult judgments. The Court explained that any method for determining guilt or punishment has its weaknesses and the potential for misuse. Despite such imperfections, the Court concluded, constitutional guarantees are met when the method has been made as fair as possible.

Civil Liberties: Issues for the New Century

In the new century, the courts certainly will continue to grapple with several significant issues concerning First Amendment freedoms. One issue concerns the emerging use of the Internet for personal communications and business transactions. Adapting traditional legal concepts and doctrines to the realm of cyberspace—and establishing new laws and guidelines—will take time and will certainly elicit controversy. So will decisions as to whether the Internet should be regulated and who the regulators should be. "Hate speech" and disorderly protests will also force difficult trade-offs to be made between the constitutional guarantee of free speech and society's need to reduce violence.

The desire of many Americans to express publicly their religious beliefs presents an ongoing challenge to courts and legislators, who at some point will need to issue more definitive guidelines on such issues as school prayer, the teaching of evolution, and the use of public funds for education in church-related schools.

How to protect privacy rights in the online environment is an issue that will probably not disappear any time soon. The abortion issue also has yet to be resolved. Although the Supreme Court has upheld state laws banning assisted suicide, state legislators will continue to face controversial demands regarding this practice.

Finally, because crime continues to be a major problem in this country, the rights of accused persons probably will continue to be challenged. As American society looks for new ways to halt crime, it also must attempt to maintain some kind of balance between the rights of accused persons and the rights of those who suffer from criminal wrongdoing. If past experience is any indication, this challenge will continue to exist for generations to come.

TOWARD ACTIVE CITIZENSHIP

YOUR CIVIL LIBERTIES: SEARCHES AND SEIZURES

What happens if you are stopped by members of the police force? Your civil liberties protect you from having to provide information other than your name and address. Indeed, you are not really required to produce identification, although it is a good idea to show this to the officers. Normally, even if you have not been placed under arrest, the officers have the right to frisk you for weapons, and you must let them proceed. The officers cannot, however, check your person or your clothing further if, in their judgment, no weaponlike object is produced.

The officers may search you only if they have a search warrant or probable cause that they will likely find incriminating evidence if the search is conducted. Normally, it is unwise to resist physically the officers' attempt to search you if they do not have probable cause or a warrant; it is usually best simply to refuse orally to give permission for the search, preferably in the presence of a witness. Also, it is usually advisable to tell the officer as little as possible about yourself and the situation that is under investigation. Being polite and courteous, though firm, is better than acting out of anger or frustration and making the officers irritable. If you are arrested, it is best to keep quiet until you can speak with a lawyer.

If you are in your car and are stopped by the police, the same fundamental rules apply. Always be ready to show your driver's license and car registration quickly. You may be asked to get out of the car. The officers may use a flashlight to peer inside if it is too dark to see otherwise. None of this constitutes a search. A true search requires either a warrant or probable cause. No officer has the legal right to search your car simply to find out if you may have committed a crime. Police officers can conduct searches that are incident to lawful arrests, however.

If you are in your residence and a police officer with a search warrant appears, you should examine the warrant before granting entry. A warrant that is correctly made out will state the exact place or persons to be searched, a description of the object sought, and the date of the warrant (which should be no more than ten days old), and it will bear the signature of a judge or magistrate. If the search warrant is in order, you should not make any statement. If you believe the warrant to be invalid, you should make it clear orally that you have not consented to the search, preferably in the presence of a witness. If the warrant later is proved to be invalid, normally any evidence obtained will be considered illegal.

Officers who attempt to enter your home without a search warrant can do so only if they are pursuing a suspected felon into the house. Rarely is it advisable to give permission for a warrantless search. You, as the resident, must be the one to give permission if any evidence obtained is to be considered legal. The landlord, manager, or head of a college dormitory cannot give legal permission. A roommate, however, can give permission for a search of his or her room, which may allow the police to search those areas in which you have personal belongings.

If you find yourself a guest in a location that is being legally searched, you may be legally searched also. But unless you have been placed under arrest, you cannot be compelled to go to the police station or into a squad car.

If you would like to find out more about your rights and obligations under the laws of searches and seizures, you might wish to contact the following organizations:

The American Civil Liberties Union
125 Broad St., 18th Floor
New York, NY 10004
1-800-775-ACLU
www.aclu.org/

Legal Defense Fund
755 Riverpoint Dr., Suite 100
West Sacramento, CA 95605
1-800-882-9906

Key terms

actual malice 129	exclusionary rule 139	personal attack rule 131
bad-tendency rule 124	fairness doctrine 131	prior restraint 124
civil liberties 115	fighting words 127	public figures 129
clear and present danger test 124	free exercise clause 122	slander 127
commercial speech 126	gag order 129	symbolic speech 126
defamation of character 127	hecklers' veto 128	writ of *habeas corpus* 138
equal time rule 131	incorporation theory 116	
establishment clause 117	libel 128	

Chapter summary

1 To deal with American colonists' fears of a too-powerful national government, after the adoption of the U.S. Constitution, Congress proposed a Bill of Rights. These ten amendments to the Constitution were ratified by the states by the end of 1791. The amendments represent civil liberties—that is, they are limitations on the government.

2 Originally, the Bill of Rights limited only the power of the national government, not that of the states. Gradually, however, the Supreme Court accepted the incorporation theory under which no state can violate the Bill of Rights.

3 The First Amendment protects against government interference with the freedom of religion by requiring a separation of church and state and by guaranteeing the free exercise of religion. The separation of church and state is mandated in the establishment clause. Under this clause, the Supreme Court has ruled against officially sponsored prayer, Bible-reading sessions, and "meditation or silent reflection" for a religious purpose in public schools. The Court has also struck down laws forbidding the teaching of evolution or requiring the teaching of the biblical story of the creation. The government can provide financial aid to religious schools if the aid is secular in aim, the aid does not have the primary effect of advancing or inhibiting religion, and if the aid does not create "an excessive government entanglement with religion."

4 The First Amendment protects against government interference with the freedom of speech, which includes symbolic speech (expressive conduct). Restrictions are permitted when expression presents a clear and present danger to the peace or public order, or when expression has a bad tendency (that is, when it might lead to some "evil"). Expression may be restrained before it occurs, but such prior restraint has a "heavy presumption" against its constitutionality. Commercial speech (advertising) by businesses has received limited First Amendment protection. Speech that has not received First Amendment protection includes expression judged to be obscene, utterances con-

sidered to be slanderous, and speech constituting fighting words or a hecklers' veto.

5 The First Amendment protects against government interference with the freedom of the press, which can be regarded as a special instance of freedom of speech. Speech by the press that does not receive protection includes libelous statements made with actual malice. Publication of news about a criminal trial may be restricted by a gag order under unusual circumstances. The press may be asked to cooperate in criminal investigations by revealing its sources or providing other evidence in response to subpoenas or search warrants. In many states, shield laws protect reporters from having to reveal their sources and confidential information.

6 The First Amendment protects the right to assemble peaceably and to petition the government. Permits may be required for parades, sound trucks, and demonstrations to maintain the public order, and a permit may be denied to protect the public safety. To avoid government interference with freedom of association, an organization cannot be required to publish a list of its members.

7 Under the Ninth Amendment, rights not specifically mentioned in the Constitution are not denied to the people. Among these unspecified rights is a right to privacy, which has been implied through the First, Third, Fourth, Fifth, and Ninth Amendments. A major privacy issue today concerns the problem of protecting privacy rights in cyberspace. Questions concerning whether an individual's privacy rights include a right to have an abortion or a "right to die" also continue to elicit controversy. Another issue with serious implications is physician-assisted suicide. The Supreme Court has held that individuals do not have a constitutional right to commit physician-assisted suicide and has upheld state laws banning the practice.

8 The Constitution includes protections for the rights of persons accused of crimes. Under the Fourth Amendment, no one may be subject to an unreasonable search or seizure or arrested except on probable cause. Under the Fifth Amendment, an accused person has the right to remain silent. Under the Sixth Amendment, an accused person must be informed of the reason for his or her arrest. The accused also has the right to adequate counsel, even if he or she cannot afford an attorney, and the right to a prompt arraignment and a speedy and public trial before an impartial jury selected from a cross section of the com-munity. The exclusionary rule forbids the admission in court of illegally seized evidence. There is a "good faith exception" to the exclusionary rule: illegally seized evidence need not be thrown out owing to, for example, a technical defect in a search warrant. Under the Eighth Amendment, cruel and unusual punishment is prohibited. Whether the death penalty is cruel and unusual punishment continues to be debated.

Selected print and electronic resources

SUGGESTED READINGS

Fiss, Owen M. *The Irony of Free Speech.* Cambridge, Mass.: Harvard University Press, 1996. The author, a professor at Yale Law School, argues that the state "might become the friend, rather than the enemy, of freedom" by suppressing certain types of speech, such as hate speech and pornography.

Foster, James C., and Susan M. Leeson. *Constitutional Law: Cases in Context,* Englewood Cliffs, N.J.: Prentice-Hall, 1998. This comprehensive collection of Supreme Court constitutional law cases traces the effects of each case on the American political system.

Lewis, Anthony. *Gideon's Trumpet.* New York: Vintage, 1964. This classic work discusses the background and facts of *Gideon v. Wainwright,* the 1963 Supreme Court case in which the Court held that the state must make an attorney available for any person accused of a felony who cannot afford a lawyer.

Neumann, Milton, et al., eds. *Hate Speech on Campus: Cases, Case Studies, and Commentary.* Boston: Northeastern University Press, 1997. This collection of essays examines free speech issues and cases, including hate speech on university campuses.

MEDIA RESOURCES

The Chamber—A movie, based on John Grisham's novel by the same name, about a young lawyer who defends a man (his grandfather) who has been sentenced to death and faces imminent execution.

Execution at Midnight—A video presenting the arguments and evidence on both sides of the controversial death-penalty issue.

Gideon's Trumpet—An excellent 1980 film about the *Gideon v. Wainwright* case; Henry Fonda plays the role of the convicted petty thief, Clarence Earl Gideon.

May It Please the Court: The First Amendment—A set of audio-cassette recordings and written transcripts of the oral arguments made before the Supreme Court in sixteen key First Amendment cases. Participants in the recording include nationally known attorneys and several Supreme Court justices.

The People versus Larry Flynt—An R-rated 1996 film that clearly articulates the conflict between freedom of the press and how a community defines pornography.

Logging on

At Project Vote Smart's Web site, you can find discussions of major issues, including those involving civil liberties, abortion, and crime. Go to

www.vote-smart.org/issues/

The American Civil Liberties Union (ACLU), the leading civil liberties organization, provides an extensive array of information and links concerning civil rights issues at

www.aclu.org/

The Liberty Counsel describes itself as "a nonprofit religious civil liberties education and legal defense organization established to preserve religious freedom." The URL for its Web site is

www.lc.org/

Summaries and the full text of Supreme Court constitutional law decisions, plus a virtual tour of the Supreme Court, are available at

oyez.nwu.edu/

If you want to read historic Supreme Court decisions, you can find them, listed by name, at

supct.law.cornell.edu/supct/

The Center for Democracy and Technology (CDT) focuses on how developments in communications technology are affecting the constitutional liberties of Americans. You can access the CDT's site at

www.cdt.org/

For a copy of the statement by the American Library Association's Intellectual Freedom Committee concerning the use of filtering software and other issues relating to free speech on the Internet, go to

www.ala.org/alaorg/oif/filt_filt_res.html

Using the Internet for political analysis

Explore the freedom of religious expression that is available to all through the Internet. Use a search engine, such as Yahoo or Alta Vista, to search for Web sites sponsored by "mainline" religious groups and for sites offered by groups that subscribe to less common religious or quasi-religious beliefs or doctrines, such as Scientology, Satanism, atheism, Heaven's Gate, and Zoroastrianism.

Examine the home pages of at least three groups. List any of their views or beliefs that may violate current laws, be counter to current political practices, or otherwise have political implications. Do the groups acknowledge their differences with the state or with each other? How does an individual judge the validity or persuasiveness of this information?

Civil Rights: Equal Protection

¿ what if

Resident Aliens Had the Right to Vote?

BACKGROUND

ACCORDING TO U.S. LAW, THERE ARE SEVERAL CATEGORIES OF ALIENS, INCLUDING ILLEGAL ALIENS, WHO CAN BE DEPORTED IF CAUGHT; NON-RESIDENT ALIENS, WHO ARE STAYING FOR A LIMITED TIME FOR TOURISM OR BUSINESS; AND RESIDENT ALIENS. THOSE IN THE LATTER CATEGORY HAVE SO-CALLED GREEN CARDS. THEY ARE IN THE UNITED STATES AS PERMANENT RESIDENTS AND, AFTER A SPECIFIED TIME PERIOD, CAN APPLY FOR CITIZENSHIP. RESIDENT ALIENS MAY STAY IN THE UNITED STATES AS LONG AS THEY DESIRE AND ARE NOT REQUIRED TO SEEK CITIZENSHIP. UNDER CURRENT LAW, RESIDENT ALIENS HAVE VIRTUALLY ALL OF THE RIGHTS AFFORDED TO CITIZENS. ALIENS, HOWEVER, BECAUSE THEY ARE NOT CITIZENS, MAY NOT VOTE IN ANY PUBLIC ELECTION HELD ANYWHERE IN THE UNITED STATES.

WHAT IF RESIDENT ALIENS HAD THE RIGHT TO VOTE?

America is a land of immigrants. In general, except for Native Americans, we are all descended from immigrants who arrived in this country over the last five hundred years. According to the U.S. Census Bureau, as of 1998 over 26 million (over 9 percent) of this nation's residents were born in foreign countries. Of this number, according to the Immigration and Naturalization Service, 11 million are legal, permanent residents who are not yet citizens. What if a law were

passed that granted these residents aliens (but not illegal or nonresident aliens) the right to vote?

If all resident aliens were spread out equally throughout all jurisdictions in the United States, their ability to vote probably would have little impact on the political landscape. But resident aliens are most heavily concentrated in California (where 35.3 percent of all resident aliens are located), then New York (14.1 percent), followed by Texas and Florida (with about 7.5 percent each).

CALIFORNIA IS WHERE THE MAIN IMPACT WOULD BE FELT

Allowing resident aliens to vote would have the greatest impact in California. According to researcher Jorge G. Castañeda, over 55 percent of California's 6 million Latinos do not have citizenship; in Los Angeles this number is over 62 percent. Although Latinos constitute more than 26 percent of California's population, they cast only 10 percent of the votes. According to Castañeda, most of the policies for the state of California are decided by white, Anglo-Saxon, older, and wealthier Californians.

If the millions of Latinos without citizenship in California

could suddenly vote, politics might change in that state. Specifically, there might be less incentive to put anti-immigration initiatives, such as Proposition 187, on the ballot. That ballot initiative, which was declared unconstitutional by a federal court in 1997, would have denied numerous public services to illegal immigrants. Moreover, politicians in general in California would have to pay more attention to Latinos and their political wants and needs.

In New York, the impact of this new voting group would be of a different character. In that state, the more than 1.5 million legal permanent residents who do not have citizenship are not dominated by a single ethnic group, as in California. Therefore, politicians would not need to cater to the needs of an obvious, fairly well defined ethnic group of new voters with similar ethnic backgrounds.

In Texas and Florida, Hispanics do constitute the majority of resident aliens. But in each of these states, they number less than one million and therefore would not have as much of an impact at the ballot box.

WOULD THERE BE MORE HOSTILITY TOWARD IMMIGRANTS?

The rising immigration rates during the 1990s resulted in

increased hostility toward immigrants. In 1996, Congress made extremely harsh changes in the immigration law, denying welfare benefits to certain groups of immigrants and making it more difficult for other groups to enter the United States without visas. Even though some of the harsher provisions of the 1996 act were modified in 1997, current immigration law is much more restrictive than it has been in the past. If resident aliens were given the right to vote, and therefore influence the political allocation of government resources, some argue that anti-immigrant sentiment in this country would be intensified.

FOR CRITICAL ANALYSIS

1. If resident aliens work, send their children to public schools, and pay taxes, why shouldn't they be given the right to vote?

2. How is it possible to argue against immigration while living in a nation where virtually all citizens are descended from immigrants?

The topic of this chapter's opening *What if . . .* feature—the right of immigrants to vote—certainly was not an issue in the early years of this nation. Nor were the political rights of other large groups of Americans. In spite of the words set forth in the Declaration of Independence that "all Men are created equal," the majority of the population in those years had no political rights. As you learned in Chapter 2, the framers of the Constitution permitted slavery to continue (although many of the founders would have liked to abolish it—see the feature *Politics and Diversity: George Washington—No Longer a Hero?*). Slaves thus were excluded from the political process. Women also were excluded for the most part, as were Native Americans, African Americans who were not slaves, and even white men who did not own property. Indeed, it has taken this nation more than two hundred years to approach even a semblance of equality among all Americans.

Equality is at the heart of the concept of civil rights. Generally, the term **civil rights** refers to the rights of all Americans to equal treatment under the law, as provided for by the Fourteenth Amendment to the Constitution. Although the terms *civil rights* and *civil liberties* are sometimes used interchangeably, scholars tend to make a distinction between the two. As you learned in Chapter 4, civil liberties are basically *limitations* on government; they specify what the government *cannot* do. Civil rights, in contrast, specify what the government *must* do—to ensure equal protection and freedom from discrimination.

Essentially, the history of civil rights in America is the story of the struggle of various groups to be free from discriminatory treatment. In this chapter, we look at two movements that had significant consequences for the history of civil rights in America: the civil rights movement of the 1950s and 1960s and the women's movement, which began in the mid-1800s and continues today. Each of these movements resulted in legislation that secured important basic rights

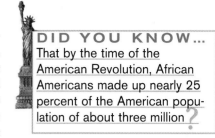

DID YOU KNOW...
That by the time of the American Revolution, African Americans made up nearly 25 percent of the American population of about three million?

Civil Rights
Generally, all rights rooted in the Fourteenth Amendment's guarantee of equal protection under the law.

POLITICS and Diversity

George Washington—No Longer a Hero?

In late 1997, the New Orleans school board changed the name of one of the schools in its district from George Washington Elementary to Charles Richard Drew Elementary. Drew was an African American physician who pioneered the use of blood plasma during World War II (1941–1945), saving the lives of countless soldiers. Why did the board change the school's name? The reason was that Washington owned slaves, and in 1992 the school board had decided to rename all of the schools in its district that had been named after persons who had owned slaves and "did not

believe in equal opportunity for all."

The school board's 1992 decision did not make the national headlines. But when the board attacked George Washington, the most venerable of all American national icons, the media responded. Critics of the board's decision pointed out that without Washington's effective leadership during the struggling years of the new nation, the new republic might not have survived. To be sure, Washington owned slaves, acknowledged the critics. But he also regarded slavery as

an evil institution—and he freed his slaves on his death. Other great leaders during the nation's early years—including Benjamin Franklin, John Quincy Adams, and Thomas Jefferson—were also against slavery. Yet each of these leaders put the Union first, and a Union could only be created if they agreed not to outlaw slavery.

Certainly, the members of the New Orleans school board were aware of the founders' many achievements. How, then, could they base their decision solely on the slavery issue? History has always been the province of those in

power, and on the New Orleans school board, those in power are African Americans. In most school districts in the nation, the school boards are dominated by white majorities, and they generally honor famous men and women of European American backgrounds.

FOR CRITICAL ANALYSIS

Should people and events of the past be judged by the standards of their own times or by present standards?

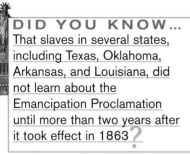

for all Americans—the right to vote and the right to equal protection under the laws. In the next chapter, we explore a question with serious implications for today's voters and policymakers: What should be the government's responsibility when equal protection under the law is not enough to ensure truly equal opportunities for Americans?

Note that numerous minorities in this nation have suffered—and some continue to suffer—from discrimination. Hispanics, Native Americans, Asian Americans, Arab Americans from Middle Eastern countries, and persons from India have all had to struggle for equal treatment, as have people from various island nations and other countries. The fact that these groups are not singled out for special attention in the following pages should not be construed to mean that their struggle for equality is any less significant than the struggles of those groups that we do discuss.

African Americans and the Consequences of Slavery in the United States

Article I, Section 2, of the U.S. Constitution states that congressional representatives are to be apportioned among the states according to their respective numbers. These numbers were to be obtained by adding to the total number of free persons "three fifths of all other Persons." The "other persons" were, of course, slaves. A slave was thus equal to three-fifths of a white person. As Abraham Lincoln stated sarcastically, "All men are created equal, except Negroes." Before 1863, the Constitution thus protected slavery and made equality impossible in the sense we use the word today. African American leader Frederick Douglass pointed out that "Liberty and Slavery—opposite as Heaven and Hell—are both in the Constitution."

The constitutionality of slavery was confirmed just a few years before the outbreak of the Civil War in the famous *Dred Scott v. Sanford*[1] case of 1857. The Supreme Court held that slaves were not citizens of the United States, nor were they entitled to the rights and privileges of citizenship. The Court also ruled that the Missouri Compromise, which banned slavery in the territories north of 36° 30' latitude (the southern border of Missouri), was unconstitutional. The *Dred Scott* decision had grave consequences. Most observers contend that the ruling contributed to making the Civil War inevitable.

Ending Constitutional Servitude

With the emancipation of the slaves by President Lincoln's Emancipation Proclamation in 1863 and the passage of the Thirteenth, Fourteenth, and Fifteenth Amendments during the Reconstruction period following the Civil War, constitutional inequality was ended.

The Thirteenth Amendment (1865) states that neither slavery nor involuntary servitude shall exist within the United States. The Fourteenth Amendment (ratified on July 9, 1868) tells us that *all* persons born or naturalized in the United States are citizens of the United States. It states, furthermore, that "[n]o State shall make or enforce any law which shall abridge the privileges or immunities of the citizens of the United States; nor shall any State deprive any person of life, liberty or property, without due process of law; nor deny to any person within its jurisdiction the equal protection of the laws." Note the use of the terms *citizen*

This portrait is of Dred Scott (1795–1858), an American slave who was born in South Hampton County, Virginia, and who later moved with his owner to the state of Illinois, where slavery was illegal. He was the nominal plaintiff in a test case that sought to obtain his freedom on the ground that he lived in the free state of Illinois. Although the Supreme Court ruled against him, he was soon emancipated and became a hotel porter in St. Louis.

---

[1] 19 Howard 393 (1857).

and *person* in this amendment. *Citizens* have political rights, such as the right to vote and run for political office. Citizens also have certain privileges or immunities (see Chapter 3). All *persons,* however, including legal *and* illegal immigrants, have a right to due process of law and equal protection under the law.

The Fifteenth Amendment seems equally impressive: "The right of citizens of the United States to vote shall not be denied or abridged by the United States or by any State on account of race, color, or previous condition of servitude." Pressure was brought to bear on Congress to include in the Fourteenth and Fifteenth Amendments a prohibition against discrimination based on sex, but with no success.

As we shall see, the words of these amendments had little immediate effect. Although slavery was legally and constitutionally ended, African American political and social inequality has continued to the present time. In the following sections, we discuss several landmarks in the struggle of African Americans to overcome this inequality.

The Civil Rights Acts of 1865 to 1875

At the end of the Civil War, President Lincoln's Republican party controlled the national government and most state governments, and the so-called Radical Republicans, with their strong antislavery stance, controlled that party. The Radical Republicans pushed through the Thirteenth, Fourteenth, and Fifteenth Amendments to the Constitution (the "Civil War amendments"). From 1865 to 1875, they succeeded in getting Congress to pass a series of civil rights acts that were aimed at enforcing these amendments. Even Republicans who were not necessarily sympathetic to a strong antislavery position wanted to undercut Democratic domination of the South. What better way to do so than to guarantee African American suffrage?

The first Civil Rights Act in the Reconstruction period that followed the Civil War was passed in 1866 over the veto of President Andrew Johnson. That act extended citizenship to anyone born in the United States and gave African Americans full equality before the law. The act further authorized the president to enforce the law with national armed forces. Many considered the law to be unconstitutional, but such problems disappeared in 1868 with the adoption of the Fourteenth Amendment.

Abraham Lincoln reads the Emancipation Proclamation on July 22, 1862. The Emancipation Proclamation did not abolish slavery (that was done by the Thirteenth Amendment, in 1865), but it ensured that slavery would be abolished if and when the North won the Civil War. After the Battle of Antietam on September 17, 1862, Lincoln publicly announced the Emancipation Proclamation and declared that all slaves residing in states that were still in rebellion against the United States on January 1, 1863, would be freed once those states came under the military control of the Union Army.

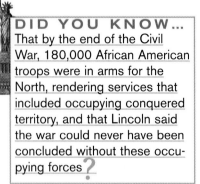

Among the six other civil rights acts in the nineteenth century, one of the more important ones was the Enforcement Act of May 31, 1870, which set out specific criminal sanctions for interfering with the right to vote as protected by the Fifteenth Amendment and by the Civil Rights Act of 1866. Equally important was the Civil Rights Act of April 20, 1872, known as the Anti–Ku Klux Klan Act. This act made it a federal crime for anyone to use law or custom to deprive an individual of his or her rights, privileges, and immunities secured by the Constitution or by any federal law. Section 2 of that act imposed detailed penalties or damages for violation of the act.

The last of these early civil rights acts, known as the Second Civil Rights Act, was passed on March 1, 1875. It declared that everyone is entitled to full and equal enjoyment of public accommodations, theaters, and other places of public amusement, and it imposed penalties for violators. This act, however, was virtually nullified by the *Civil Rights Cases* of 1883 discussed below.

The civil rights acts of the 1870s are of special interest, because they were an indication that congressional power or authority applied both to official, or government, action and to private action. The theory behind the acts was that if a state government failed to act, Congress could act in its absence. Thus, Congress could legislate directly against private individuals who were violating the constitutional rights of other individuals when state officials failed to protect those rights. At the time, this was a novel theory. It was not implemented in practice until the 1960s.

The Ineffectiveness of the Civil Rights Laws

The Reconstruction statutes, or civil rights acts, ultimately did little to secure equality for African Americans in their civil rights. Both the *Civil Rights Cases* and the case of *Plessy v. Ferguson* effectively nullified these acts. Additionally, various voting barriers were erected that prevented African Americans from exercising their right to vote.

The *Civil Rights Cases*. The Supreme Court invalidated the 1875 Civil Rights Act when it held, in the *Civil Rights Cases*[2] of 1883, that the enforcement clause of the Fourteenth Amendment (which states that "[n]o State shall make or enforce any law which shall abridge the privileges or immunities of citizens") was limited to correcting actions by states in their official acts; thus, the discriminatory acts of *private* citizens were not illegal. ("Individual invasion of individual rights is not the subject matter of the Amendment.") The 1883 Supreme Court decision met with widespread approval throughout most of the United States.

In a dissenting opinion, Justice John Marshall Harlan contended that the Thirteenth Amendment gave Congress broad powers to enact laws to ensure the rights of former slaves. According to Justice Harlan, the freedom conferred by that amendment included the freedom from all "badges of slavery."

Twenty years after the Civil War, the nation was all too willing to forget about the Civil War amendments and the civil rights legislation of the 1860s and 1870s. The other civil rights laws that the Court specifically did not invalidate became dead letters in the statute books, although they were never repealed by Congress. At the same time, many former proslavery secessionists had regained political power in the southern states. In the last decades of the nineteenth century, these racists enacted the Jim Crow laws, which will be discussed next in relation to the separate-but-equal doctrine.

---

[2] 109 U.S. 3 (1883).

Plessy v. Ferguson: **Separate but Equal.** A key decision during this period concerned Homer Plessy, a Louisiana resident who was one-eighth African American. In 1892, he was riding in a train from New Orleans when the conductor made him leave the car, which was restricted to whites, and directed him to a car for nonwhites. At that time, Louisiana had a statute providing for separate railway cars for whites and African Americans.

Plessy went to court, claiming that such a statute was contrary to the Fourteenth Amendment's equal protection clause. In 1896, the United States Supreme Court rejected Plessy's contention. The Court concluded that the Fourteenth Amendment "could not have been intended to abolish distinctions based upon color, or to enforce social . . . equality." The Court indicated that segregation alone did not violate the Constitution: "Laws permitting, and even requiring their separation in places where they are liable to be brought into contact do not necessarily imply the inferiority of either race to the other."[3] So was born the **separate-but-equal doctrine.**

The only justice to vote against this decision was John Marshall Harlan, a former slaveholder. He stated in his dissent, "Our Constitution is color-blind, and neither knows nor tolerates classes among citizens." Justice Harlan also predicted that the separate-but-equal doctrine would "in time prove to be . . . as pernicious as the decision . . . in the Dred Scott Case."

For more than half a century, the separate-but-equal doctrine was accepted as consistent with the equal protection clause in the Fourteenth Amendment. In practical terms, the separate-but-equal doctrine effectively nullified that clause. *Plessy v. Ferguson* became the judicial cornerstone of racial discrimination throughout the United States. Even though *Plessy* upheld segregated facilities in railway cars only, it was assumed that the Supreme Court was upholding segregation everywhere as long as the separate facilities were equal. The result was a system of racial segregation, particularly in the South, that required separate drinking fountains; separate seats in theaters, restaurants, and hotels; separate public toilets; and separate waiting rooms for the two races—collectively known as Jim Crow laws. "Separate" was indeed the rule, but "equal" was never enforced, nor was it a reality.

Voting Barriers. The brief enfranchisement of African Americans ended after 1877, when the federal troops that occupied the South during the Reconstruction era were withdrawn. Southern politicians regained control of state governments and, using everything except race as a formal criterion, passed laws that effectively deprived African Americans of the right to vote. By using the ruse that political party primaries were private, southern whites were allowed to exclude African Americans. The **white primary** was upheld by the Supreme Court until 1944 when, in *Smith v. Allwright,*[4] the Court found it to be a violation of the Fifteenth Amendment.

Another barrier to African American voting was the **grandfather clause,** which restricted the voting franchise to those who could prove that their grandfathers had voted before 1867. **Poll taxes** required the payment of a fee to vote; thus, poor African Americans—as well as poor whites—who could not afford to pay the tax were excluded from voting. Not until the Twenty-fourth Amendment to the Constitution was ratified in 1964 was the poll tax eliminated as a precondition to voting. **Literacy tests** also were used to deny the vote to African Americans. Such tests asked potential voters to read, recite, or interpret complicated texts, such as a section of the state constitution, to the satisfaction of local registrars.

---

[3]*Plessy v. Ferguson,* 163 U.S. 537 (1896).
[4]321 U.S. 649 (1944).

Jim Crow laws required the segregation of the races, particularly in public facilities such as this theater. The name "Jim Crow" originates from a nineteenth-century vaudeville character who was called Jim (which was a common name) Crow (for a black-colored bird). Thus, the name "Jim Crow" was applied to laws and practices affecting African Americans.

Separate-but-Equal Doctrine
The doctrine holding that segregation in schools and public accommodations does not imply that one race is superior to another; and that separate-but-equal facilities do not violate the equal protection clause.

White Primary
A state primary election that restricts voting to whites only; outlawed by the Supreme Court in 1944.

Grandfather Clause
A device used by southern states to exempt whites from state taxes and literacy laws originally intended to disfranchise African American voters. It restricted the voting franchise to those who could prove that their grandfathers had voted before 1867.

Poll Tax
A special tax that must be paid as a qualification for voting. The Twenty-fourth Amendment to the Constitution outlawed the poll tax in national elections, and in 1966 the Supreme Court declared it unconstitutional in all elections.

Literacy Test
A test administered as a precondition for voting, often used to prevent African Americans from exercising their right to vote.

The End of the Separate-but-Equal Doctrine

A successful attack on the separate-but-equal doctrine began with a series of lawsuits in the 1930s to admit African Americans to state professional schools. By 1950, the Supreme Court had ruled that African Americans who were admitted to a state university could not be assigned to separate sections of classrooms, libraries, and cafeterias. In 1951, Oliver Brown decided that his eight-year-old daughter, Linda Carol Brown, should not have to go to an all-nonwhite elementary school twenty-one blocks from her home, when there was a white school only seven blocks away. The National Association for the Advancement of Colored People (NAACP), formed in 1909, decided to help Oliver Brown. The results were monumental in their impact on American society. Actually, a series of cases, first argued in 1952, contested state laws permitting or requiring the establishment of separate school facilities based on race. Following the death of Chief Justice Frederick M. Vinson and his replacement by Earl Warren, the Supreme Court asked for rearguments.

Brown v. Board of Education of Topeka. The 1954 unanimous decision in *Brown v. Board of Education of Topeka*[5] established that public school segregation of races violates the equal protection clause of the Fourteenth Amendment. Concluding that separate schools are inherently unequal, Chief Justice Warren stated that "to separate [African Americans] from others of similar age and qualifications solely because of their race generates a feeling of inferiority as to their status in the community that may affect their hearts and minds in a way unlikely ever to be undone." Warren said that separation implied inferiority, whereas the majority opinion in *Plessy v. Ferguson* had said the opposite.

"With All Deliberate Speed." The following year, in *Brown v. Board of Education*[6] (sometimes called the second *Brown* decision), the Court asked for rearguments concerning the way in which compliance with the 1954 decision should be undertaken. The Supreme Court declared that the lower courts must ensure that African Americans would be admitted to schools on a nondiscriminatory basis "with all deliberate speed." The high court told lower federal courts that they had to take an activist role in society. The district courts were to consider devices in their desegregation orders that might include "the school transportation system, personnel, [and] revision of school districts and attendance areas into compact units to achieve a system of determining admission to the public schools on a nonracial basis."

Reactions to School Integration

One unlooked-for effect of the "all deliberate speed" decision was that the term *deliberate* was used as a loophole by some officials, who were able to delay desegregation by showing that they were indeed acting with all deliberate speed but still were unable to desegregate. Another reaction to court-ordered desegregation was "white flight." In some school districts, the public school population became 100 percent nonwhite when white parents sent their children to newly established private schools, sometimes known as "segregation academies."

The white South did not let the Supreme Court ruling go unchallenged. Arkansas's Governor Orval Faubus used the state's National Guard to block the integration of Central High School in Little Rock in September 1957. The federal court demanded that the troops be withdrawn. Finally, President Dwight

---

[5]347 U.S. 483 (1954).
[6]349 U.S. 294 (1955).

After the *Brown* decision, aggressive white reaction followed for a number of years, particularly with respect to the attempt to desegregate the school system in Little Rock, Arkansas. After the local school board secured approval of the federal courts for desegregation, Governor Orval Faubus sent in the state's National Guard to preserve order when a handful of African American students entered Little Rock Central High School on September 2, 1957. The National Guard was withdrawn after a few weeks and replaced by a white mob. President Dwight Eisenhower sent in five hundred soldiers on September 24, many of whom remained there for the rest of the school year.

Eisenhower had to federalize the Arkansas National Guard and send it to quell the violence. Central High became integrated.

The universities in the South, however, remained segregated. When James Meredith, an African American student, attempted to enroll at the University of Mississippi in Oxford in 1962, violence flared there, as it had in Little Rock. Two men were killed, and a number of people were injured in campus rioting. President John Kennedy sent federal marshals and ordered federal troops to maintain peace and protect Meredith. One year later, George Wallace, governor of Alabama, promised "to stand in the schoolhouse door" to prevent two African American students from enrolling at the University of Alabama in Tuscaloosa. Wallace was forced to back down when Kennedy federalized the Alabama National Guard.

An Integrationist Attempt at a Cure: Busing

In most parts of the United States, residential concentrations by race have made it difficult to achieve racial balance in schools. Although it is true that a number of school boards in northern districts created segregated schools by drawing school district lines arbitrarily, the residential concentration of African Americans and other minorities in well-defined geographic locations has contributed to the difficulty of achieving racial balance. This concentration results in *de facto* **segregation.**

Court-Ordered Busing. The obvious solution to both *de facto* and **de jure segregation** seemed to be transporting some African American schoolchildren to white schools and some white schoolchildren to African American schools. Increasingly, the courts ordered school districts to engage in such **busing** across neighborhoods. Busing led to violence in some northern cities, such as in south Boston, where African American students were bused into blue-collar Irish Catholic neighborhoods. Indeed, busing was unpopular with many groups. In the mid-1970s, almost 50 percent of African Americans interviewed were opposed to busing, and approximately three-fourths of the whites interviewed held the same opinion. Nonetheless, through the next decade, the Supreme Court fairly consistently came down on the side of upholding busing plans in the cases it decided.

De Facto Segregation
Racial segregation that occurs because of past social and economic conditions and residential patterns.

De Jure Segregation
Racial segregation that occurs because of laws or administrative decisions by public agencies.

Busing
The transportation of public school students from areas where they live to schools in other areas to eliminate school segregation based on residential patterns.

To remedy *de facto* segregation, the courts often imposed busing requirements on school districts. Busing meant transporting children of white neighborhoods to nonwhite schools, and vice versa. Busing has been one of the most controversial domestic policies in the history of this country. Initially, bused students had to be escorted by police because of potential violence. This scene was photographed in Boston in the 1970s.

Changing Directions. In an apparent reversal of previous decisions, the Supreme Court in June 1986 allowed the Norfolk, Virginia, public school system to end fifteen years of court-ordered busing of elementary schoolchildren.[7] The Norfolk school board supported the decision because of a drop in enrollment from 32,500 whites attending public schools in 1970, when busing was ordered, to fewer than 14,000 in 1985.

In 1991, the Supreme Court held, in *Board of Education v. Dowell,*[8] that a school board only needs to show that it has complied in "good faith" with a desegregation decree. In *Dowell,* the Supreme Court instructed a lower court administering the decree that if school racial concentration was a product of residential segregation that resulted from "private decision making and economics," its effects may be ignored entirely.

In *Freeman v. Pitts,*[9] decided in 1992, the Supreme Court also stressed the importance of "local control over the education of children." In *Freeman,* a Georgia school district, which had once been segregated by law and was operating under a federal district court–administered desegregation decree, was allowed to regain partial control over its schools, although it was judged to have not complied with certain aspects of the decree. In 1995, the Supreme Court ruled in *Missouri v. Jenkins*[10] that the state of Missouri could stop spending money to attract a multiracial student body in urban school districts through major educational improvements. This decision dealt a potentially fatal blow to the use of magnet schools for racial integration. (See this chapter's feature entitled *Politics and Race: Central High, Revisited* for a discussion of the resegregation of schools and the search for alternatives to integration in the ongoing quest for equal educational opportunities.)

---

[7]*Riddick v. School Board of City of Norfolk,* 627 F.Supp. 814 (E.D.Va. 1984); *certiorari* denied, 479 U.S. 938 (1986)—see Chapter 15 for a discussion of the meaning of the term *certiorari.*
[8]498 U.S. 237 (1991).
[9]503 U.S. 467 (1992).
[10]515 U.S. 70 (1995).

POLITICS and Race

Central High, Revisited

Central High School in Little Rock, Arkansas, was once an all-white school. That ended in 1957, when the federal government forced the school's integration. Now, some forty years later, 58 percent of Central High's students are African Americans, and white students constitute 39 percent. But according to news correspondent Julian Barnes, these figures conceal a "troubling modern reality"; like many other schools that appear to be integrated, Central High is highly segregated within its doors.

Honors classes, for example, are attended predominantly by white students and taught by white teachers. Of the thirty-two honors classes, only five are taught by blacks. Blacks typically sign up for the "regular" courses. According to Barnes, this segregation in the classrooms reinforces self-segregation in other areas of school life. Blacks tend to use the front doors when entering the school; whites prefer the side door, near the parking lot. Most of the black students eat lunch inside the school, near the hot lunch area, while white students eat outside near the concession stand.*

*Julian E. Barnes, "Segregation, Now," *U.S. News & World Report*, September 22, 1997, pp. 22–28.

This is a scene from an urban American high school during lunch break. *De facto* segregation often results in schools that have a predominance of nonwhite students. Here, one table is occupied by African American students, another by Hispanics.

Other schools around the nation are becoming segregated also, some internally like Central High, but many others because of *de facto* segregation. The rapid decline in the relative proportion of whites who live in big cities and high minority birthrates have increased the minority presence in those urban areas. Today, one out of every three African American and Hispanic students goes to a school with more than 90 percent minority enrollment.

In the largest U.S. cities, fifteen out of sixteen African American and Hispanic students go to schools with almost no whites.

Generally, in the late 1990s Americans are taking another look at what desegregation means. The attempt to integrate the schools, particularly through busing, has largely failed to improve educational resources and achievement for African American children. The goal of racially balanced schools envisioned in the 1954

Brown v. Board of Education of Topeka decision now seems to be giving way to the goal of better educated children, even if that means educating them in segregated schools.

FOR CRITICAL ANALYSIS

Should honors classes that divide students along racial lines be abolished? If Central High abolished its honors classes, what might result?

The Civil Rights Movement

The *Brown* decision applied only to public schools. Not much else in the structure of existing segregation was affected. In December 1955, a forty-three-year-old African American woman, Rosa Parks, boarded a public bus in Montgomery, Alabama. When the bus became crowded and several white people stepped aboard, Parks was asked to move to the rear of the bus, the "colored" section. She refused, was arrested, and was fined $10; but that was not the end of the

Rosa Parks was born on February 4, 1913, in Tuskegee, Alabama. She was active in the Montgomery Voters' League and the NAACP League Council. After she instigated the successful boycott of the Montgomery bus system, she was fired from her job and moved to Detroit. In 1987, she founded the Rosa Raymond Parks Institute for Self-Development, offering guidance to disadvantaged African Americans.

matter. For an entire year, African Americans boycotted the Montgomery bus line. The protest was headed by a twenty-seven-year-old Baptist minister, Dr. Martin Luther King, Jr. During the protest period, he went to jail, and his house was bombed. In the face of overwhelming odds, however, King won. In 1956, the federal district court issued an injunction prohibiting the segregation of buses in Montgomery. The era of civil rights protests had begun.

King's Philosophy of Nonviolence

The following year, in 1957, King formed the Southern Christian Leadership Conference (SCLC). King's philosophy of nonviolent civil disobedience was influenced, in part, by Mahatma Gandhi's (1869–1948) life and teachings. Gandhi had led Indian resistance to the British colonial system from 1919 to 1947. He used tactics such as demonstrations and marches, as well as purposeful, public disobedience to unjust laws, while remaining nonviolent. King's followers successfully used these methods to widen public acceptance of their case.

For the next decade, African Americans and sympathetic whites engaged in sit-ins, freedom rides, and freedom marches. In the beginning, such demonstrations were often met with violence, but the contrasting image of nonviolent African Americans and violent, hostile whites created strong public support for the civil rights movement. When African Americans in Greensboro, North Carolina, were refused service at a Woolworth's lunch counter, they organized a sit-in that was aided day after day by sympathetic whites and other African Americans. Enraged customers threw ketchup on the protestors. Some spat in their faces. The sit-in movement continued to grow, however. Within six months of the first sit-in the Greensboro Woolworth's, hundreds of lunch counters throughout the South were serving African Americans.

The sit-in technique was also successfully used to integrate interstate buses and their terminals, as well as railroads engaged in interstate transportation. Although buses and railroads that were engaged in interstate transportation were prohibited by law from segregating African Americans from whites, they stopped doing so only after the sit-in protests.

The civil rights movement gathered momentum in the 1960s. One of the most famous of the violence-plagued protests occurred in Birmingham, Alabama, in the spring of 1963, when Police Commissioner Eugene "Bull" Connor unleashed police dogs and used electric cattle prods against the protesters. The object of the protest had been to provoke a reaction by local officials so that the federal government would act. People throughout the country viewed the event on national television with indignation and horror. King himself was thrown in jail, and it was during this period that he wrote his famous "Letter from a Birmingham Jail."[11] (See the feature *E-Mail Messages from the Past* on page 161 for an excerpt from this letter.)

The media coverage of the Birmingham protest and the violent response it elicited played a key role in the process of ending Jim Crow conditions in the United States. The ultimate result was the most important civil rights act in the nation's history, the Civil Rights Act of 1964 (to be discussed shortly).

King's March on Washington

In August 1963, King organized the massive March on Washington for Jobs and Freedom. Before nearly a quarter-million white and African American spectators and millions watching on television, King told the world his dream:

---

[11] A copy of this letter is included in Andrew Carroll, *Letters of a Nation: A Collection of Extraordinary Letters* (New York: Kodansha International, 1997), pp. 208–226.

Dr. Martin Luther King, Jr., at the August 1963 March on Washington for Jobs and Freedom.

I have a dream that my four little children will one day live in a nation where they will not be judged by the color of their skin but by the content of their character. . . . When we let freedom ring, when we let it ring from every village and every hamlet, from every state and every city, we will be able to speed up that day when all God's children, black men and white men, Jews and Gentiles, Protestants and Catholics, will be able to join hands and sing in the words of that old Negro Spiritual, "Free at last! Free at last! Thank God almighty, we are free at last!"

King's dream was not to be realized immediately, however. Eighteen days after his famous speech, four African American girls attending Bible class in the basement room of the Sixteenth Street Baptist Church in Birmingham, Alabama, were killed by a bomb explosion.

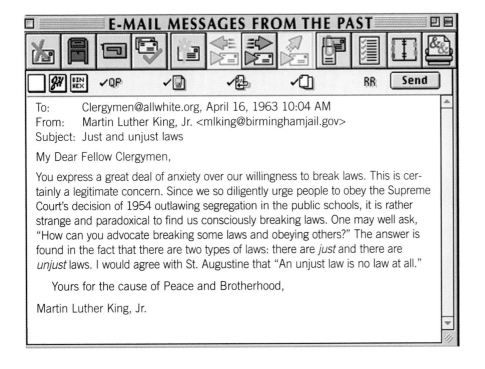

E-MAIL MESSAGES FROM THE PAST

To: Clergymen@allwhite.org, April 16, 1963 10:04 AM
From: Martin Luther King, Jr. <mlking@birminghamjail.gov>
Subject: Just and unjust laws

My Dear Fellow Clergymen,

You express a great deal of anxiety over our willingness to break laws. This is certainly a legitimate concern. Since we so diligently urge people to obey the Supreme Court's decision of 1954 outlawing segregation in the public schools, it is rather strange and paradoxical to find us consciously breaking laws. One may well ask, "How can you advocate breaking some laws and obeying others?" The answer is found in the fact that there are two types of laws: there are *just* and there are *unjust* laws. I would agree with St. Augustine that "An unjust law is no law at all."

Yours for the cause of Peace and Brotherhood,

Martin Luther King, Jr.

Police-dog attacks, cattle prods, high-pressure water hoses, beatings, bombings, and the March on Washington—all of these events led to an environment in which Congress felt compelled to act on behalf of African Americans. The second era of civil rights acts, sometimes referred to as the second Reconstruction period, was under way.

Modern Civil Rights Legislation

In the wake of the Montgomery bus boycott, public sentiment for stronger civil rights legislation put pressure on Congress and President Dwight Eisenhower to act. The action taken was relatively symbolic. The Civil Rights Act of 1957 established a Civil Rights Commission and a new Civil Rights Division within the Justice Department. (President Ronald Reagan tried to abolish the commission in 1983; Congress extended its life for another twenty years, after working out a compromise in which the president and congressional leaders would select its members.) The Civil Rights Act of 1960 provided that whenever a pattern or practice of discrimination was documented, the Justice Department could bring suit, even against a state. The act also set penalties for obstructing a federal court order by threat of force and for illegally using and transporting explosives. But the 1960 Civil Rights Act, as well as that of 1957, had little substantive impact.

The same cannot be said about the Civil Rights Acts of 1964 and 1968 or the Voting Rights Act of 1965 (discussed next). Those acts marked the assumption by Congress of a leading role in the enforcement of the constitutional notion of equality for *all* Americans, as provided by the Fourteenth and Fifteenth Amendments.

The Civil Rights Act of 1964

As the civil rights movement mounted in intensity, equality before the law came to be "an idea whose time has come," in the words of conservative Senate Minority Leader Everett Dirksen. The Civil Rights Act of 1964, the most far-reaching bill on civil rights in modern times, forbade discrimination on the basis of race, color, religion, gender, and national origin. The major provisions of the act were as follows:

In 1963, a historic civil rights bill was before Congress. Many opposed the bill as too radical. To galvanize senators and representatives to pass the bill, Martin Luther King, Jr., organized the March on Washington for Jobs and Freedom. On August 28, 1963, nearly a quarter-million Americans appeared in Washington to call for its passage. At the time, it was the largest demonstration in the capital's history.

1. It outlawed arbitrary discrimination in voter registration.
2. It barred discrimination in public accommodations, such as hotels and restaurants, whose operations affect interstate commerce.
3. It authorized the federal government to sue to desegregate public schools and facilities.
4. It expanded the power of the Civil Rights Commission and extended its life.
5. It provided for the withholding of federal funds from programs administered in a discriminatory manner.
6. It established the right to equality of opportunity in employment.

Several factors led to the passage of the 1964 act. As noted earlier, there had been a dramatic change in the climate of public opinion owing to violence perpetrated against protesting African Americans and whites in the South. Second, the assassination of President John F. Kennedy in 1963 had, according to some, a significant effect on the national conscience. Many believed the civil rights program to be the legislative tribute that Congress paid to the martyred Kennedy. The act was passed in Congress only after the longest **filibuster** in the history of the Senate (eighty-three days) and only after **cloture** was imposed for the first time to cut off a civil rights filibuster.

Title VII of the Civil Rights Act of 1964 is the cornerstone of employment-discrimination law. It prohibits discrimination in employment based on race, color, religion, gender, or national origin. Under Title VII, executive orders were issued that banned employment discrimination by firms that received any federal funding. The 1964 Civil Rights Act created a five-member commission, the **Equal Employment Opportunity Commission (EEOC)**, to administer Title VII.

The EEOC can issue interpretive guidelines and regulations, but these do not have the force of law. Rather, they give notice of the commission's enforcement policy. The EEOC also has investigatory powers. It has broad authority to require the production of documentary evidence, to hold hearings, and to **subpoena** and examine witnesses under oath.

The Civil Rights Act of 1968 and Other Housing-Reform Legislation

Martin Luther King, Jr., was assassinated on April 4, 1968. Nine days after King's death, President Johnson signed the Civil Rights Act of 1968, which forbade discrimination in most housing and provided penalties for those attempting to interfere with individual civil rights (giving protection to civil rights workers, among others). Subsequent legislation added enforcement provisions to the federal government's rules pertaining to discriminatory mortgage-lending practices. Today, all lenders must report to the federal government the race, gender, and income of all mortgage-loan seekers, along with the final decision on their loan applications.

The Voting Rights Act of 1965

As late as 1960, only 29.1 percent of African Americans of voting age were registered in the southern states, in stark contrast to 61.1 percent of whites. In 1965, Martin Luther King, Jr., took action to change all that. Selma, the seat of Dallas County, Alabama, was chosen as the site to dramatize the voting-rights problem. In Dallas County, only 2 percent of eligible African Americans had registered to vote by the beginning of 1965. King organized a fifty-mile march from Selma to the state capital in Montgomery. He didn't get very far. Acting on orders of Governor George Wallace to disband the marchers, state troopers did so with a vengeance—with tear gas, night sticks, and whips.

INFOTRAC®
COLLEGE EDITION

"Clinton Opens School Doors for Little Rock Nine"

Filibuster
In the Senate, unlimited debate to halt action on a particular bill.

Cloture
A method invoked to close off debate and to bring the matter under consideration to a vote in the Senate.

Equal Employment Opportunity Commission (EEOC)
A commission established by the 1964 Civil Rights Act to (1) end discrimination based on race, color, religion, gender, or national origin in conditions of employment and (2) promote voluntary action programs by employers, unions, and community organizations to foster equal job opportunities.

Subpoena
A legal writ requiring a person's appearance in court to give testimony.

Once again the national government was required to intervene to force compliance with the law. President Lyndon Johnson federalized the National Guard, and the march continued. During the march, the president went on television to address a special joint session of Congress urging passage of new legislation to ensure African Americans the right to vote. The events during the Selma march and Johnson's dramatic speech, in which he invoked the slogan of the civil rights movement ("We shall overcome"), were credited for the swift passage of the Voting Rights Act of 1965.

Provisions of the Voting Rights Act of 1965. The Voting Rights Act of 1965 had two major provisions. The first one outlawed discriminatory voter-registration tests. The second major section authorized federal registration of persons and federally administered voting procedures in any political subdivision or state that discriminated electorally against a particular group. In part, the act provided that certain political subdivisions could not change their voting procedures and election laws without federal approval. The act targeted counties, mostly in the South, in which less than 50 percent of the eligible population was registered to vote. Federal voter registrars were sent to these areas to register African Americans who had been restricted by local registrars. Within one week after the act was passed, forty-five federal examiners were sent to the South. A massive voter-registration drive covered the country.

Increased Political Participation by African Americans. As a result of the Voting Rights Act of 1965, its amendments, and the large-scale voter-registration drives in the South, the number of African Americans registered to vote climbed dramatically. By 1980, 55.8 percent of African Americans of voting age in the South were registered. By the 1996 presidential elections, 63.5 percent of voting-age African Americans were registered to vote, which was just slightly less than the 67.7 percent of voting-age whites who were registered to vote.

By 1998, there were about 8,000 African American elected officials in the United States, including the mayors of Atlanta, Detroit, and the District of Columbia. Today, there are thirty-nine African Americans in Congress. In 1984, the Reverend Jesse Jackson became the first African American candidate to

Reverend Jesse Jackson (shown marching with Patricia Ireland, president of the National Organization for Women) is one example of the increased political participation of African Americans.

compete seriously for the presidential nomination. In 1989, Virginia became the first state to elect an African American governor. In the same year, General Colin Powell became the first African American to be appointed chairman of the Joint Chiefs of Staff. In 1991, Clarence Thomas became a justice of the Supreme Court, replacing Thurgood Marshall, the first African American justice.

DID YOU KNOW...
That in 1790, according to census data, only two out of every five Americans were of English origin?

Voting Rights for Other Minorities

As mentioned earlier, the civil rights movement was primarily focused on the rights of African Americans. Yet the legislation resulting from the movement ultimately has benefited virtually all minority groups. The Civil Rights Act of 1964, for example, prohibits discrimination against any person because of race, color, or national origin. Subsequent amendments to the Voting Rights Act of 1965 extended its protections to other minorities, including Hispanic Americans, Asian Americans, Native Americans, and Native Alaskans. To further protect the voting rights of minorities, the act now provides that states must make available bilingual ballots in counties where 5 percent or more of the population speaks a language other than English.

The political participation of other minority groups in the United States has also been increasing. Hispanics are gaining political power in several states. By the late 1990s, over 5 percent of the legislative seats in Arizona, California, Colorado, Florida, New Mexico, and Texas were held by legislators of Hispanic ancestry. At the national level, the percentage of Hispanics in Congress is somewhat lower—they constitute about 3 percent of that institution's members. There is also a Native American in Congress—Senator Ben Nighthorse Campbell (Rep., Colo.), who was elected to the Senate in 1992 after having served in the House from 1987 to 1992.

Even though political participation by minorities has increased dramatically since the 1960s, the number of political offices held by members of minority groups remains disproportionately low compared to their numbers in the overall population.

Melting Pot or Multicultural Mix?

Time and again, this nation has been challenged and changed—and culturally enriched—by immigrant groups. In the 1990s, immigration rates were higher than they had been since the early twentieth century, when they reached their peak. Today, about one million people a year immigrate to this country, and, as mentioned in this chapter's *What If . . .* , those who were born on foreign soil now constitute over 9 percent of the U.S. population.

All of these immigrants have faced the challenges involved in living in a new and different political and cultural environment. Most of them have had to overcome language barriers, and many had to deal with discrimination in one form or another because of their color, their inability to speak English fluently, or their customs. The civil rights legislation passed during and since the 1960s has done much to counter the effects of prejudice against immigrant groups by ensuring that they obtain equal rights under the law.

One of the questions facing scholars and political leaders today concerns the relationships between the majority and the many minority ethnic groups in the United States. Specifically, does this pattern sustain the traditional idea of America as a melting pot?

INFOTRAC ®
COLLEGE EDITION

"Don't Slam the Lid on the Melting Pot"

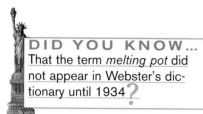

The Melting Pot

No one really knows when American society was first described as a *melting pot,* although the phrase was made popular by a 1908 play of that name by Israel Zangwill. The concept, however, has a long history. Certainly, the founders of this nation hinted at the idea of a melting pot when they created our national motto, *e pluribus unum* (Latin for "one out of many"). In 1782, the notion was expressed clearly by J. Hector St. John de Crèvecoeur, a naturalized citizen of New York, when he wrote that in America "individuals of all nations are melted into a new race of men."[12]

The melting-pot image appealed strongly to immigrants in the past, particularly to the millions of individuals from Europe and Eastern Europe who came to the United States in the late 1800s and early 1900s. Those immigrants felt that assimilation—adopting the language and political values of the dominant cultural group—was an essential first step toward achieving freedom and economic security in their new country.

Today, however, many question whether the melting pot is an adequate metaphor for American society. Indeed, some scholars question whether the metaphor was ever appropriate. Some contend that the melting-pot metaphor applies only to European immigrants to this nation. Those groups, in time, cast off their ties to their native countries and identified themselves primarily as "Americans." African Americans, however, were not included in this vision. Nor were Native Americans or the Japanese and Chinese groups who had immigrated to the United States in the late nineteenth and early twentieth centuries.

Ethnic Separatism

An alternative perception of America views the nation not as a melting pot of different cultures but as a country of many separate cultures, each having its own distinct cultural identity. In this vision of America, the dominant ethnic group—white descendants of Europeans—is just one of many groups in what Ben

---

[12]*Letters from an American Farmer* (London: Thomas Davis & Lockyear Davis, 1782), pp. 51–52.

In Los Angeles, Mexican Americans celebrate Cinco de Mayo. Is America a nation of many ethnic cultures existing separately, or is it a melting pot of diverse cultures?

Wattenberg of the American Enterprise Institute calls the world's first "universal nation." According to Wattenberg, this "old guard" white majority will no longer dominate American political life in the future.

Consider that since 1977, four out of five immigrants have come from Latin America or Asia. If current rates continue, Hispanics will overtake African Americans as the nation's largest minority by the year 2010. By the year 2030, African Americans and Hispanics together will constitute 30 percent of the population. If Hispanics and African Americans can form coalitions, perhaps with Asian Americans, their political strength can be increased dramatically, for they will have the numerical strength to make significant changes. African American leader Jesse Jackson attempted to form a coalition of minorities during his 1984 and 1988 presidential campaigns. These campaigns focused on and were supported by a "Rainbow Coalition" of African Americans, Hispanics, Native Americans, women, and other underrepresented groups. (See this chapter's *Critical Perspective: The Continuing Debate over Multiculturalism in America* on pages 168 and 169 for a further discussion of the implications of ethnic separatism.)

> **DID YOU KNOW...**
> That in 1916, four years before the Nineteenth Amendment gave women the right to vote, Jeannette Rankin became the first woman to be elected to the U.S. House of Representatives?

Women's Struggle for Equal Rights

Like African Americans and other minorities, women also have had to struggle for equality. During the first phase of this struggle, the primary goal of women was to obtain the right to vote. Some women had hoped that the founders would provide such a right in the Constitution. In 1776, Abigail Adams wrote to her husband, John Adams, the following words in reference to new laws that would be necessary if a Declaration of Independence was issued:

> I desire you would remember the ladies. . . . If particular care and attention is not paid to the ladies, we are determined to foment a rebellion and will not hold ourselves bound by any laws in which we have no voice or representation.[13]

Despite this request, the founders did not include in the Constitution a provision guaranteeing women the right to vote. Nor did it deny to women—or to any others—this right. Rather, the founders left it up to the states to decide such issues, and, as stated earlier, by and large, the states limited the franchise to adult white males who owned property. That only property owners could vote apparently did not seem unusual to the founders. The prevailing view seems to have been that "the people who own the country ought to govern it," as John Jay phrased it.

Early Women's Political Movements

The first political cause in which women became actively engaged was the slavery abolition movement. Even male abolitionists felt that women should not take an active role on the subject in public, however. When the World Antislavery Convention was held in London in 1840, women delegates were barred from active participation. Responding partly to this rebuff, two American delegates, Lucretia Mott and Elizabeth Cady Stanton, returned from that meeting with plans to work for women's rights in the United States.

In 1848, Mott and Stanton organized the first women's rights convention in Seneca Falls, New York. The three hundred people who attended approved a Declaration of Sentiments: "We hold these truths to be self-evident: that all men

Elizabeth Cady Stanton (1815–1902) was a social reformer and a women's suffrage leader. At her wedding to Henry B. Stanton in 1840, she insisted on dropping the word "obey" from the marriage vows. She wrote *The History of Women's Suffrage,* which was published in 1886.

---

[13]As quoted in Lewis D. Eigen and Jonathan P. Siegel, *The Macmillan Dictionary of Political Quotations* (New York: Macmillan, 1993), p. 324.

Critical perspective

The Continuing Debate over Multiculturalism in America

As mentioned elsewhere, traditionally American society has been viewed as a melting pot of different cultural "ingredients" brought to these shores by countless immigrants. Since the 1960s, however, proponents of multiculturalism, or ethnic pluralism, have contended that the melting-pot metaphor should be replaced by another that more accurately reflects the diversity of American society. They claim that the ethnic pluralism of America is better represented as a "salad bowl" or a "glorious mosaic" in which various ethnic groups form parts of the whole while retaining their distinctive qualities and cultural characteristics.

Ethnic pluralism has been defined in many ways, but according to political scientist Jim Sidanius and his co-researchers, the term has come to imply that (1) ethnic subgroups in a nation maintain their distinctiveness rather than "dissolving into a unitary ethnicity of nationhood"; (2) all ethnic groups are considered co-equal partners in society, so no one group is dominant; and (3) people can simultaneously maintain a positive commitment both to an ethnic particularism and to the larger political community.*

A threshold issue in the debate over multiculturalism has to do with whether it is necessarily a divisive force. Does a positive commitment to one's ethnic group mean that one cannot have an equally positive commitment to the larger political community? A related issue focuses on the implications of the multiculturalists' approach to history.

Is Ethnic Allegiance a Disunifying Force in America?

Many contend that strong ethnic ties necessarily weaken allegiance to "American" political and cultural values. There is a certain logic

*Jim Sidanius et al., "The Interface between Ethnic and National Attachment: Ethnic Pluralism or Ethnic Dominance," *Public Opinion Quarterly*, Spring 1997, pp. 102–133.

to this argument; at its heart is the assumption that no one can serve two masters simultaneously. Recent studies, though, have challenged this assumption.

Based on an extensive study of Mexican Americans, researchers R. O. de la Garza, A. Falcon, and F. C. Garcia concluded that there is little evidence that ethnic allegiance leads to less patriotism. They discovered that Mexican Americans were no less patriotic than Euro-Americans. If anything, they concluded, there was a positive relationship between attachment to one's Mexican American heritage and attachment to the United States as a whole. Their conclusion was that, rather than disunifying America, "American ethnics use ethnicity to create resources such as group solidarity and political organizations to facilitate their full participation in American society."†

The group of researchers led by Jim Sidanius, referred to above, examined multiculturalism from a "group dominance" perspective. Their research showed that the feeling of "belongingness" to the nation as a whole is most strongly and positively associated with membership in dominant ethnic groups. They discovered that patriotism increased as a function of ethnic attachment among European Americans, as well as among most Latinos, but that patriotism decreased as a function of ethnic attachment among African Americans. They also found that Latinos in the southern California area (but not elsewhere in the nation) were similar to African Americans—the closer the ethnic attachment, the less patriotic they were. The authors suggested that this might be because of the hostility of the dominant group toward immigrants, most of whom are Latinos, in southern California.

†R. O. de la Garza, A. Falcon, and F. C. Garcia, "Will the Real Americans Please Stand Up: Anglo and Mexican-American Support of Core American Political Values," *American Journal of Political Science*, Vol. 40 (May 1996), pp. 335–351.

and women are created equal." (For some of the views held by Lucretia Mott, see the feature *E-Mail Messages from the Past* on page 170.) In the following twelve years, groups of feminists held seven conventions in different cities in the Midwest and East. With the outbreak of the Civil War, however, advocates of women's rights were urged to put their support behind the war effort, and most agreed.

The Suffrage Issue and the Fifteenth Amendment. "The right of citizens of the United States to vote shall not be denied or abridged by the United States or

Critical perspective

The Continuing Debate over Multiculturalism in America—continued

The Rewriting of History

One of the goals of multiculturalism is to revise—if not replace—the "dead white male" view of history. Advocates of multiculturalism believe that children should learn not only about other countries and cultures but also about the contributions of various groups that traditionally have been neglected in the writing of history.

Opponents of multiculturalism claim that it results in undiscriminating cultural relativism because it encourages a view of history in which all cultures are given equal weight. The foundations of Western civilization, they claim, are presented as being no more or less important to a study of American traditions than are the foundations of African, Middle Eastern, or Asian civilizations. Such an approach, say these opponents, distorts the past by playing down some of the greatest achievements of Western Europeans and Americans and promoting beyond their ultimate value the accomplishments of other groups.

Multiculturalism versus "The American Creed"

One of the harshest critics of multiculturalism is Samuel P. Huntington. In his widely read book *The Clash of Civilizations and the Remaking of World Order*,‡ Huntington states that American national identity has been defined politically "by the principles of the American Creed on which Americans overwhelmingly agree (liberty, democracy, individualism, equality before the law, constitutionalism, private property)." These principles are rooted in the Western cultural and political tradition. Therefore, multiculturalists who would divest America of its "sinful" European inheritance are undermining the American Creed.

‡New York: Simon & Schuster, 1996.

Huntington claims that ethnic separatism in any country will ultimately lead to internal strife and disunion. He points out that the founders of this nation were wary of the potential instability that could be brought about by conflicts between different groups, or factions, in American society. This fear was shared by later American leaders, including President Theodore Roosevelt (1901–1909), who once said that "the absolutely certain way of bringing this nation to ruin, of preventing all possibility of its continuing as a nation at all would be to permit it to become a tangle of squabbling nationalities." According to Huntington, no country that lacks a core cultural heritage can long endure as a coherent society:

> A multicivilization in the United States will not be the United States; it will be the United Nations. . . . Rejection of the [American] creed and of Western civilization means the end of the United States of America as we have known it. It also means effectively the end of Western civilization. . . . The future of the United States and of the West depends upon Americans reaffirming our commitment to Western civilization. Domestically this means rejecting the devisive siren calls of multiculturalism.§

FOR CRITICAL ANALYSIS

1. Can you think of any federal legislation that promotes ethnic pluralism?

2. Does the research showing increased patriotism among more ethnically conscious groups necessarily contradict Huntington's view of the multiculturalists' potential harm to American society? Explain.

§*Ibid.*, p. 307.

by any State on account of race, color, or previous condition of servitude." So reads Section 1 of Amendment XV to the Constitution, which was ratified in 1870. The campaign for the passage of this amendment split the women's **suffrage** movement. Militant feminists wanted to add "sex" to "race, color, or previous condition of servitude." Other feminists, along with many men, opposed this view; they wanted to separate African American suffrage and women's suffrage to ensure the passage of the amendment. So, although the African American press supported the women's suffrage movement, it became separate from the racial equality movement. Still, some women attempted to

Suffrage
The right to vote; the franchise.

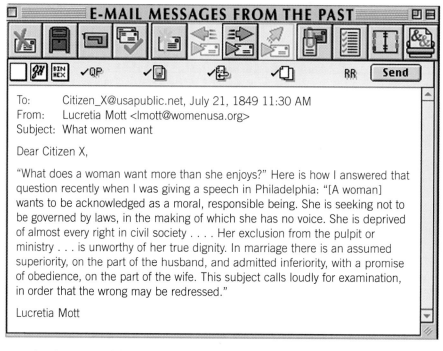

E-MAIL MESSAGES FROM THE PAST

To: Citizen_X@usapublic.net, July 21, 1849 11:30 AM
From: Lucretia Mott <lmott@womenusa.org>
Subject: What women want

Dear Citizen X,

"What does a woman want more than she enjoys?" Here is how I answered that question recently when I was giving a speech in Philadelphia: "[A woman] wants to be acknowledged as a moral, responsible being. She is seeking not to be governed by laws, in the making of which she has no voice. She is deprived of almost every right in civil society . . . . Her exclusion from the pulpit or ministry . . . is unworthy of her true dignity. In marriage there is an assumed superiority, on the part of the husband, and admitted inferiority, with a promise of obedience, on the part of the wife. This subject calls loudly for examination, in order that the wrong may be redressed."

Lucretia Mott

vote in the years following the Civil War. One, Virginia Louisa Minor, was arrested and convicted in 1872. She appealed to the Supreme Court, but the Court upheld her conviction.[14]

Women's Suffrage Associations.   Susan B. Anthony and Elizabeth Cady Stanton formed the National Woman Suffrage Association in 1869. According to their view, women's suffrage was a means to achieve major improvements in the economic and social situation of women in the United States. In other words, the vote was to be used to obtain a larger goal. Lucy Stone, however, felt that the vote was the only major issue. Members of the American Woman Suffrage Association, founded by Stone and others, traveled to each state, addressed state legislatures, wrote, published, and argued their convictions. They achieved only limited success. In 1890, the two organizations quit battling and joined forces. The National American Woman Suffrage Association had only one goal—the enfranchisement of women—but it made little progress.

By the early 1900s, small radical splinter groups were formed, such as the Congressional Union, headed by Alice Paul. This organization worked solely for the passage of an amendment to the U.S. Constitution. Willing to use "unorthodox" means to achieve its goal, this group and others took to the streets. There were parades, hunger strikes, arrests, and jailings. Finally, in 1920, seventy-two years after the Seneca Falls convention, the Nineteenth Amendment was passed: "The right of citizens of the United States to vote shall not be denied or abridged by the United States or by any State on account of sex." Women were thus enfranchised. Although today it may seem that the United States was slow to give women the vote, it was really not too far behind the rest of the world (see Table 5–1).

The Modern Women's Movement

After women gained the right to vote in 1920, there was little organized political activity by women until the 1960s. The civil rights movement of that decade

Susan B. Anthony (1820–1906) was a leader of the women's suffrage movement who was also active in the antialcohol and antislavery movements. In 1869, with Elizabeth Cady Stanton, she founded the National Woman Suffrage Association. In 1888, she organized the International Council of Women and, in 1904, the International Women's Suffrage Alliance, in Berlin.

---

[14]*Minor v. Happersett*, 21 Wall. 162 (1874). The Supreme Court reasoned that the right to vote was a privilege of state, not federal, citizenship. The Court did not consider privileges of state citizenship to be protected by the Fourteenth Amendment.

TABLE 5-1

Years, by Country, in Which Women Gained the Right to Vote

1893: New Zealand	1919: Germany	1945: Italy	1953: Mexico
1902: Australia	1920: United States	1945: Japan	1956: Egypt
1913: Norway	1930: South Africa	1947: Argentina	1963: Kenya
1918: Britain	1932: Brazil	1950: India	1971: Switzerland
1918: Canada	1944: France	1952: Greece	1984: Yemen

SOURCE: Center for the American Woman and Politics, 1995.

resulted in a growing awareness of rights for all groups, including women. Additionally, the publication of Betty Friedan's *The Feminine Mystique* in 1963 focused national attention on the unequal status of women in American life.

In 1966, Friedan and others who were dissatisfied with the lack of aggressive action against gender discrimination by the then-largest women's organizations— the National Federation of Business and Professional Women's Clubs and the League of Women Voters—formed the National Organization for Women (NOW). NOW immediately adopted a blanket resolution designed "to bring women into full participation in the mainstream of American society *now*, exercising all the privileges and responsibilities thereof in truly equal partnership with men."

NOW has been in the forefront of what is often called the *feminist movement*. Historian Nancy Cott contends that the word *feminism* first began to be used around 1910. At that time, it meant, as it does today, a "complete social revolution"—a radical notion that gained little support among members of the suffrage movement. It is difficult to measure the support for **feminism** today because the term means different things to different people. When the dictionary definition of a feminist—"someone who supports political, economic, and social equality for women"—was read to respondents in a recent survey, however, 67 percent labeled themselves as feminists.[15]

The initial focus of the modern women's movement was not on expanding the political rights of women. Rather, leaders of NOW and other liberal women's rights advocates sought to eradicate gender inequality through a constitutional amendment.

Feminism
The movement that supports political, economic, and social equality for women.

The Equal Rights Amendment.   The proposed Equal Rights Amendment (ERA), which was first introduced in Congress in 1923 by leaders of the National Women's Party, states as follows: "Equality of rights under the law shall not be denied or abridged by the United States or by any state on account of sex." For years the amendment was not even given a hearing in Congress, but finally it was approved by both chambers and sent to the state legislatures for ratification on March 22, 1972.

As was noted in Chapter 2, any constitutional amendment must be ratified by the legislatures (or conventions) in three-fourths of the states before it can become law. Since the early 1900s, most proposed amendments have required that ratification occur within seven years of Congress's adoption of the amendment. The necessary thirty-eight states failed to ratify the amendment within the seven-year period specified by Congress, even though it was supported by numerous national party platforms, six presidents, and both chambers of Congress. To date, efforts to reintroduce the amendment have not succeeded.

During the national debate over the ratification of the ERA, a women's countermovement emerged. Many women perceived the goals pursued by NOW and other liberal women's organizations as a threat to their way of life. At the head of the countermovement was Republican Phyllis Schlafly and her conservative organization, Eagle Forum. Eagle Forum's "Stop-ERA" campaign found significant

---

[15]Nancy E. McGlen and Karen O'Connor, *Women, Politics, and American Society*, 2d ed. (Upper Saddle River, N.J.: Prentice Hall, 1998), p. 11.

support among fundamentalist religious groups and various other conservative organizations. The campaign was effective in blocking the ratification of the ERA.

Challenging Gender Discrimination in the Courts.   When the ERA failed to be ratified, women's rights organizations began to refocus their efforts. Although NOW continued to press for the ERA, other groups challenged discriminatory statutes and policies in the federal courts, contending that they violated the Fourteenth Amendment's equal protection clause. Since the 1970s, the Supreme Court has tended to scrutinize gender classifications closely and has invalidated a number of such statutes and policies. For example, in 1977 the Court held that police and firefighting units cannot establish arbitrary rules, such as height and weight requirements, that tend to preclude women from joining those occupations.[16] In 1983, the Court ruled that insurance companies cannot charge different rates for women and men.[17]

A question that the Court has not ruled on is whether women should be allowed to participate in military combat. Generally, the Supreme Court has left this decision up to Congress and the Department of Defense. Although recently women have been allowed to serve as combat pilots and on naval warships, to date they have not been allowed to join infantry combat units. In regard to military training institutes, however, the Supreme Court held in 1996 that the state-financed Virginia Military Institute's policy of accepting only males violated the equal protection clause.[18]

Expanding Women's Political Opportunities.   Following the failure of the ERA, in addition to fighting discrimination in the courts, the women's movement began to work for increased representation in government. Several women's political organizations that are active today concentrate their efforts on getting women elected to political offices. These organizations include the national Women's Political Caucus, the Coalition for Women's Appointments, the Fund for a Feminist Majority, and Black Women Organized for Action.

A variety of women's political action committees, or PACs (see Chapter 10), have also been created and are now important sources of financial support for

[16]*Dothard v. Rawlinson,* 433 U.S. 321 (1977).
[17]*Arizona v. Norris,* 463 U.S. 1073 (1983).
[18]*United States v. Virginia,* 518 U.S. 515 (1996).

A female cadet begins her training at the Virginia Military Institute. In 1996, the Supreme Court ruled that the institute's policy of accepting only males violated the equal protection clause of the Constitution.

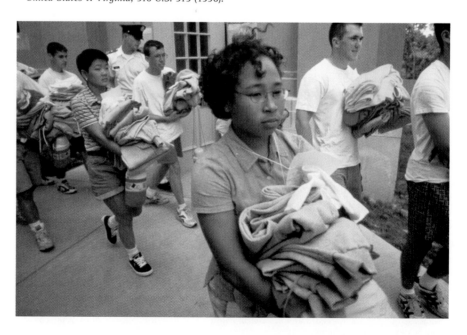

women candidates. The largest of these PACs is EMILY's List (EMILY stands for "Early Money Is Like Yeast—It Makes the Dough Rise"). This PAC supports Democratic women candidates for congressional offices and governorships. Founded in 1985, EMILY's List now has nearly 70,000 members who contribute funds to be used for political campaigns.

Women in Politics Today

The efforts of women's rights advocates and organizations have helped to increase the number of women holding political offices in all areas of government. The men's club atmosphere still prevails in Congress, however, and no woman has yet held one of the major congressional leadership positions. But the number of women holding congressional seats has increased significantly in recent years. Elections during the 1990s brought more women to Congress than either the Senate or the House had seen before. After the 1998 elections, there were fifty-six women in the House and nine in the Senate. (See the feature *Elections '98: Political Leadership by Women* for further details on women in today's Congress.)

DID YOU KNOW...
That a student complained to University of Oregon officials that the university's motto, *Mens Agitat Molem* (which roughly translated from the Latin means "Mind over Matter"), was sexist and suggested that it be changed to *Mens and Womens Agitat Molem*?

Political Leadership by Women

elections '98

Although the 1998 elections saw the defeat of Senator Carol Moseley-Braun, the only African American woman in the U.S. Senate, the elections showed the growing strength of women as candidates for state and national office. Despite the defeat of Moseley-Braun, fifty-six women were elected to the House of Representatives, and four women won senatorial elections. Three women—Barbara Mikulski, Barbara Boxer, and Patty Murray—were reelected to the Senate, while Blanche Lincoln of Arkansas became a new member of that chamber. One Senate race and several House races pitted Republican and Democratic female candidates against each other.

In races for state offices, the number of women candidates continued to increase. Perhaps the most striking outcome of the 1998 elections at the state level was in Arizona. There, the top five state offices—governor, attorney general, treasurer, secretary of state, and superintendent of public instruction—were all won by women. Interestingly, four of the women were Republicans, while one was elected as a Democrat. It appeared that most Arizona voters took little notice of the fact that the leading candidates were all female.

Although no woman has yet been nominated for president by a major political party, a recent Gallup poll found that 92 percent of women and 88 percent of men said that they would vote for a qualified woman for president if she was nominated by their party. Additionally, an increasing number of women are being appointed to cabinet posts. Franklin Roosevelt appointed the first woman to a cabinet post—Frances Perkins, who was secretary of labor from 1933 to 1945. In 1969, President Richard Nixon declared that "a woman can and should be able to do any political job that a man can do." But by the time of his resignation in 1974, he had not appointed a woman to the cabinet. His successor, Gerald Ford (1974–1977), however, appointed a woman as secretary of housing

On January 23, 1997, Madeleine K. Albright was sworn in as secretary of state. She became not only the first woman to hold that post but also the highest-ranking woman in the executive branch of the U.S. government.

Gender Discrimination
Any practice, policy, or procedure that denies equality of treatment to an individual or to a group because of gender.

and urban development, and each subsequent president has appointed at least two women to head cabinet departments. President Bill Clinton appointed four women to his cabinet, more than any previous president. One of Clinton's appointees, Secretary of State Madeleine Albright, became the first woman ever to hold an "inner" cabinet post.

Increasingly, women are sitting on federal judicial benches as well. President Ronald Reagan was credited with a historical first when he appointed Sandra Day O'Connor to the Supreme Court in 1981. President Clinton, during his first term, appointed another woman, Ruth Bader Ginsburg, to the Court.

Women have had more success in gaining political offices in state legislatures and local governments. Several women have been elected to governorships, and by 1998, of the 7,424 state legislators, 1,607 (22 percent) were women. In some states, including Washington, Colorado, and Nevada, over one-third of the legislative seats now are held by women. In New Hampshire, not only are 31 percent of the legislators women but so also are the governor (Democrat Jeanne Shaheen) and the speaker of the House (Republican Donny Sytek). Additionally, Chicago, Houston, and San Francisco have had women mayors, as have 17 percent of U.S. cities with populations of more than thirty thousand.

For all their achievements in the political arena, however, the number of women holding political offices remains disproportionately low compared to their participation as voters. As Table 5–2 indicates, the absolute turnout of female voters nationally is higher than that of male voters.

Gender-Based Discrimination in the Workplace

Traditional cultural beliefs concerning the proper role of women in society continue to be evident not only in the political arena but also in the workplace. Since the 1960s, however, women have gained substantial protection against discrimination by laws mandating equal employment opportunities and equal pay.

Title VII of the Civil Rights Act of 1964

Title VII of the Civil Rights Act of 1964 prohibits **gender discrimination** in the employment context and has been used to strike down employment policies that discriminate against employees on the basis of gender. Even so-called protective policies have been held to violate Title VII if they have a discriminatory effect. In 1991, for example, the Supreme Court held that a fetal protection policy established by Johnson Controls, Inc., the country's largest producer of automobile batteries, violated Title VII. The policy required all women of childbearing age working in jobs that entailed periodic exposure to lead or other hazardous

TABLE 5-2

Voting and Registration

	Persons of Voting Age (Millions)	Persons Reporting They Registered (Millions)	Persons Reporting They Voted (Percentage)
Voting participation by females has recently been equal to, or greater than, voting participation by males. In both percentage and absolute terms, more females than males voted and registered in 1996.			
Male	92.6	59.6	52.8
Female	101.0	68.0	55.5

SOURCE: U.S. Bureau of the Census, 1997.

materials to prove that they were infertile or to transfer to other positions. Women who agreed to transfer often had to accept cuts in pay and reduced job responsibilities. The Court concluded that women who are "as capable of doing their jobs as their male counterparts may not be forced to choose between having a child and having a job."[19]

In 1978, Congress amended Title VII to expand the definition of gender discrimination to include discrimination based on pregnancy. Women affected by pregnancy, childbirth, or related medical conditions must be treated—for all employment-related purposes, including the receipt of benefits under employee-benefit programs—the same as other persons not so affected but similar in ability to work.

Sexual Harassment

The Supreme Court has also held that Title VII prohibits **sexual harassment** in the workplace. Sexual harassment occurs when job opportunities, promotions, salary increases, and so on are given in return for sexual favors. A special form of sexual harassment, called hostile-environment harassment, occurs when an employee is subjected to sexual conduct or comments that interfere with the employee's job performance or are so pervasive or severe as to create an intimidating, hostile, or offensive environment. (Increasingly, other nations are passing laws to protect women from sexual harassment in the workplace. See the feature *Politics and Comparative Systems: Sexual Harassment—A Worldwide Problem*.)

[19]*United Automobile Workers v. Johnson Controls, Inc.*, 499 U.S. 187 (1991).

Sexual Harassment
Unwanted physical or verbal conduct or abuse of a sexual nature that interferes with a recipient's job performance, creates a hostile environment, or carries with it an implicit or explicit threat of adverse employment consequences.

INFOTRAC®
COLLEGE EDITION

"Groping toward Sanity"

POLITICS and Comparative Systems

Sexual Harassment—A Worldwide Problem

The problem of sexual harassment in the workplace is not confined to the United States. Indeed, it is a worldwide problem for women workers. In some countries, there is no legal protection against any form of employment discrimination. Egypt and Turkey, for example, have no laws requiring any form of equal employment opportunity. In Argentina, employment discrimination is not a political issue or a practice prohibited by law. Similarly, in Brazil, equal employment opportunity is not a factor in employment relationships. Even in those countries that do have laws prohibiting discriminatory employment practices, including gender-based discrimination, those laws often do not specifically include sexual harassment as a discriminatory practice.

Several countries recently have attempted to remedy this omission by passing new laws or amending others to specifically prohibit sexual harassment in the workplace. Japan, for example, recently amended its Equal Employment Opportunity Law to include a provision making sexual harassment illegal. The revised law went into effect in 1999. In early 1998, Thailand passed its first sexual-harassment law. The European Union, which some years ago outlawed gender-based discrimination, is now considering a proposal that would specifically identify sexual harassment as a form of discrimination.

Clearly, such laws will benefit women in the future, but in the meantime, old traditions die hard. In Germany, for example, a country known for its conservative and male-dominated culture, the topic of sexual harassment is more or less taboo. "We're trying to pretend that the problem isn't there," claims one employment specialist in that country. Women's support groups throughout Europe contend that corporations in European countries tend to view sexual harassment with "quiet tolerance." They contrast this attitude with that of most major U.S. corporations, which have implemented specific procedures to deal with harassment claims.

The tendency to ignore the problem of sexual harassment is widespread among employees as well as employers. Consider the results of a recent survey taken by the Japanese Ministry of Labor: although over 60 percent of the women respondents claimed that they had experienced at least one act of sexual harassment, less than 1 percent of those women complained to their unions about the matter.

FOR CRITICAL ANALYSIS

Why do you think U.S. corporations are more aggressive than European companies in taking steps to prevent sexual harassment in the workplace?

The problem of sexual harassment received widespread attention in the national media in 1991, when law professor Anita Hill charged that Supreme Court nominee Clarence Thomas had sexually harassed her when they both had worked at the Equal Employment Opportunity Commission (EEOC). Although Thomas was appointed to the Court, Hill's allegations caused a national furor and resulted in a dramatic increase in sexual-harassment claims.

Definitional Problems. One of the questions faced by employers and employees—as well as the courts—is deciding the point at which offensive conduct in the workplace is so "pervasive or severe" as to create a hostile working environment. In 1993, in *Harris v. Forklift Systems, Inc.,*[20] the Supreme Court attempted to give some guidelines on this issue, as well as on another question: Must a worker claiming to be a victim of hostile-environment harassment establish that the offensive conduct gave rise to serious emotional or psychological effects? Justice O'Connor answered both questions by stating, "So long as the environment would reasonably be perceived, and is perceived, as hostile or abusive, there is no need for it also to be psychologically injurious."

Many have complained that the Court's 1993 decision failed to provide the lower courts with a definitive standard by which to judge hostile-environment claims. Essentially, in some cases, a hostile environment exists whenever an employee claims it exists. According to William Petrocelli, the author of *Sexual Harassment on the Job,*[21] "If you feel you've been sexually harassed, then you have been." Some courts have held that just one incident of sexually offensive conduct—such as a sexist remark by a co-worker or a photo on an employer's desk of his bikini-clad wife—can create a hostile environment.

The Court's Recent Decisions Concerning Harassment. In 1998, in *Faragher v. City of Boca Raton,*[22] the Court addressed another important question: Should an employer be held liable for its supervisor's sexual harassment of an employee even though the employer was unaware of the harrassment? The Court ruled that the employer in this case was liable but stated that the employer might have avoided such liability if it had taken reasonable care to prevent harassing behavior—which the employer had not done. In another case, *Burlington Industries v. Ellerth,*[23] the Court similarly held that an employer was liable for sexual harassment caused by a supervisor's actions even though the employee had suffered no tangible job consequences as a result of those actions. Again, the Court emphasized that a key factor in holding the employer liable was whether the employer had exercised reasonable care to prevent and correct promptly any sexually harassing behavior.

In another 1998 case, *Oncale v. Sundowner Offshore Services, Inc.,*[24] the Supreme Court addressed a further issue: Should Title VII protection be extended to cover situations in which individuals are harassed by members of the same sex? The Court answered this question in the affirmative. (An emerging issue that sooner or later will probably have to be addressed by the high court has to do with Internet communications and harassment—a topic explored in the feature *Politics Wired: Sexual Harassment Goes Online.*)

Politics and Sexual Harassment—*Jones v. Clinton*. In view of the latitude given by many courts to sexual-harassment claimants, the court's recent decision in the *Jones v. Clinton* case seems, as one observer stated, "strikingly retro."

Paula Corbin Jones, a state employee of Arkansas during Bill Clinton's governorship, filed a lawsuit for sexual harassment that had occurred years before. The Supreme Court upheld her right to proceed with a suit against a sitting president, but the suit was later dismissed by the presiding judge in the lower federal court.

[20]510 U.S. 17 (1993).
[21]William Petrocelli and Barbara Kate Repa, *Sexual Harassment on the Job: What It Is and How to Stop It,* 3d ed. (Berkeley, Calif.: Nolo Press, 1998).
[22]118 S.Ct. 2275 (1998).
[23]118 S.Ct. 2257 (1998).
[24]118 S.Ct. 998 (1998).

POLITICS WIRED

Sexual Harassment Goes Online

Today's "wired" workplace has made life easier in many ways for employers and employees alike. But it has also presented some problems. A significant problem is that employees who access Web sites containing sexually explicit materials, racist cartoons, and pornographic images can create a hostile environment for their co-workers. You can probably imagine how this might happen. A woman may walk by a co-worker's desk and see some images on that worker's computer that she finds objectionable. An employee may download materials from a pornographic site to the company's computer system, which another employee accidentally views. A worker might print out a sexually explicit image and forget to remove it from the printer before a co-worker happens to see it.

Just one successful suit for harassment against a small company can bankrupt that firm. Even if the worker does not succeed in the suit, the legal fees incurred in defending against the claim—and the possible harm to the firm's reputation—could be devastating for the firm's balance sheet. It should therefore come as no surprise that employers are anxious to prevent hostile environments in their workplaces. Increasingly, employers are removing potentially offensive photos and posters from desks and walls, establishing harassment policies, and training employees in what constitutes sexual harassment and what procedures to follow if an employee experiences harassment. They are also taking steps to prevent liability for sexual harassment that results from Internet use.

One tactic being used by some employers is to monitor their employees' e-mail and the sites they access on the Internet. Another tactic is to install filtering software to prevent employees from accessing certain sites. Still another is to prohibit all but certain employees from accessing the Internet. In the private sector, such an invasion of employee privacy is generally considered legal, as long as the employees are informed of—and consent to—such actions. Attempts by government employers to constrain speech on the Internet, however, have run into constitutional problems.

Consider a law passed by the state of Virginia to protect state employees from a hostile work environment. The law prohibited employees of state agencies (including institutions of higher learning) from using any "agency-owned or agency-leased computer equipment to access, download, print, or store any information infrastructure files or services having sexually explicit content," unless authorized to do so by an agency head. Some university researchers challenged the law, claiming that it interfered with their research and teaching and that it unconstitutionally restricted free speech. The court agreed that the law was unconstitutional, holding that the statute imposed restrictions on speech beyond what was necessary to prevent a sexually hostile work environment.*

FOR CRITICAL ANALYSIS

Can you think of any other ways in which Internet use in the workplace could create a hostile environment?

*Urofsky v. Allen, 995 F.Supp. 634 (E.D.Va. 1998).

Paula Corbin Jones brought a lawsuit against President Clinton in 1994, accusing the president of sexually harassing her when she was an employee of the state of Arkansas and he was the governor. She claimed that he made unwanted sexual advances and acted in an obscene manner. A threshold issue in the suit—whether a civil suit could be brought against a sitting president for conduct that occurred before taking office as president—was decided in the affirmative by the Supreme Court in 1997.[25]

When the suit went forward in a federal district court in Little Rock, Arkansas, President Clinton asked Judge Susan Webber Wright to dismiss the suit. The president argued that even if the actions Jones complained about were true, they did not amount to hostile-environment harassment. The judge agreed and threw out the lawsuit. While she found the president's alleged behavior to be "boorish and offensive," the judge concluded that Jones had "failed to demonstrate that she has a case and the court therefore finds that there are no genuine issues for trial."[26] Jones has since appealed the district court's decision.

Many were surprised at the reluctance of the National Organization for Women (NOW) to speak out as forcefully against the Democratic president as it has against other public figures on the conservative side of the political spectrum.

---

[25]*Jones v. Clinton,* 117 S.Ct. 1636 (1997).
[26]*Jones v. Clinton,* 990 F.Supp. 657 (E.D.Ark. 1998).

Comparable Worth
The idea that compensation should be
based on the worth of the job to an
employer and that factors unrelated to
the worth of a job, such as the sex of
the employee, should not affect
compensation.

In sworn testamony given in relation to
Paula Jones's sexual-harassment lawsuit,
President Clinton denied having had sexual
relations with White House intern Monica
Lewinsky, shown here. Clinton also made
public denials of any affair with Lewinsky.
By the fall of 1998, it became clear that his
denials were false, and many people—including several Democrats in Congress—questioned not only his moral integrity but
whether he should continue to hold the
nation's highest office.

During the Senate hearings prior to Justice Clarence Thomas's appointment to the
Supreme court, NOW strongly supported Anita Hill's position. Similarly, when
allegations of sexual misconduct on the part of Republican senator Bob
Packwood of Oregon came to light in 1995, NOW and other women's organizations were in the forefront of those pushing for action on the matter. Packwood
eventually was forced to resign after the Senate Ethics Committee investigated
the claims against him and recommended his expulsion from the Senate.
Claiming that NOW's position in the *Jones v. Clinton* case was hypocritical, some
NOW members called for the resignation of NOW's national officers, including
the organization's president, Patricia Ireland.

Ireland, in a press release issued April 22, 1998, defended her position by
claiming that the "overwhelming consensus of our chapters, states, and national
board" was not to support Jones in her appeal of the district court's ruling.
Among other things, Ireland stated that NOW's leaders were "disinclined to work
with the disreputable right wing organizations and individuals advancing her
cause, who themselves have a longstanding political interest in undermining our
movement to strengthen women's rights and weakening the laws that protect
those rights." Although Ireland reaffirmed NOW's concern with sexual harassment as an issue in our society, the organization claimed not to take a political
position on the *Jones* case itself.

Wage Discrimination

By 1999, women constituted close to 50 percent of the U.S. labor force, and that
number continues to grow. By the year 2010, women will approach a majority
of U.S. workers. Although Title VII and other legislation since the 1960s have
mandated equal employment opportunities for men and women, women continue to earn less, on average, than men do. Currently, for every dollar earned
by men, women earn about seventy-eight cents.

The Equal Pay Act of 1963.   The issue of wage discrimination was first
addressed during World War II (1941–1945), when the War Labor Board issued
an "equal pay for women" policy. In implementing the policy, the board often
evaluated jobs for their comparability and required equal pay for comparable
jobs. The board's authority ended with the war. Supported by the next three
presidential administrations, the Equal Pay Act was finally enacted in 1963 as
an amendment to the Fair Labor Standards Act of 1938.

Basically, the Equal Pay Act requires employers to pay equal pay for substantially equal work. In other words, males cannot be paid more than females
who perform essentially the same job. The Equal Pay Act did not address the fact
that certain types of jobs traditionally held by women pay lower wages than the
jobs usually held by men. For example, more women than men are secretaries,
sales clerks, and nurses, whereas more men than women are construction workers, truck drivers, and plumbers. Even if all secretaries performing substantially
similar jobs for a company earned the same salaries, they would still be earning
less than the company's truck drivers.

Comparable Worth, or Pay Equity.   The concept of **comparable worth,** or pay
equity, is that women should receive equal pay not just for equal (that is, the
same) work but also for work requiring comparable skill, effort, and responsibility. The comparable worth doctrine attempts to redress the effects of traditional "women's work" being undervalued and underpaid.

In 1981, the Supreme Court ruled that female workers could sue under Title
VII even if they were not performing the same jobs as men.[27] By the late 1990s,

[27]*Washington County, Oregon v. Gunther,* 452 U.S. 161 (1981).

about half of the states had adjusted the pay of state government employees. The state of Washington closed the pay gap most successfully, reducing the difference in average pay between men and women to 5 percent.

The problem with comparable worth is that wages in the United States traditionally have been determined by the forces of supply and demand in the labor market. If pay scales based on comparable worth were implemented, what criteria would be used to determine the value of particular jobs? To date, this question has not been resolved satisfactorily—although, as mentioned, several state governments have modified their pay scales to reduce the "gender gap" with respect to wages.

The Glass Ceiling. Although increased numbers of women are holding jobs in professions or business enterprises that were once dominated by men, few women hold top positions in their firms. Less than 10 percent of the Fortune 500 companies in America—America's leading corporations—have a woman as one of their five highest-paid executives. Because the barriers faced by women in the corporate world are subtle and not easily pinpointed, they have been referred to as "the glass ceiling."

Clearly, age-old perceptions of the proper role of women in society make it difficult for women to compete effectively in the corporate and professional world. The view that a "woman's place is in the home" continues to be remarkably widespread. According to a recent poll, 57 percent of Americans completely or mostly agree that "it is generally better for society if the man is the achiever outside the home and the woman takes care of the home and family." Women professionals and executives probably will continue to encounter glass ceilings in their workplaces until Americans reach some kind of a consensus on what role women should play in our society.

Civil Rights—Equal Protection: Issues for the New Century

To be sure, since the 1950s the gains of African Americans, other minorities, and women have been impressive. The civil rights movement and the legislation it prompted have done much to make equal protection of the laws a reality for minority groups. Nevertheless, these groups remain underrepresented in politics, particularly at the national level. One of the challenges for the new century is how to promote greater political participation among minority groups in American society.

Certainly, the debate over the implications of ethnic separatism and pluralism will continue into the new century. If, as one scholar suggests, ethnic separatism reflects a reality of racial divisiveness in this country, particularly with respect to African Americans, then maintaining a "national" identity and culture may be difficult indeed.[28]

We also can predict that controversy over the role that women should play in our society will continue to foster both private and public debate in the new century. Certainly, some liberal women's organizations will continue to work toward the goal of complete gender equality in American life, and others will push for more equality in political representation. Just as certainly, they will encounter opposition from conservative groups, including a number of women's organizations. Finally, although women have much more protection today against gender discrimination in the workplace, the "glass ceiling" will probably remain in place for many years to come.

---

[28]Nathan Glazer, *We Are All Multiculturalists Now* (Cambridge, Mass.: Harvard University Press, 1997).

TOWARD ACTIVE CITIZENSHIP

CITIZENSHIP AND IMMIGRANT RIGHTS

A great debate has taken place in recent years over the issue of immigrant rights. The questions have included whether illegal immigrants can become citizens, whether employers are liable for hiring illegal immigrants, and whether the economy can absorb so many new workers.

Many organizations are concerned with the way in which illegal immigrants are treated by federal and state police and immigration officials. Such groups want to maintain the nation's commitment to relatively free entry to people of all racial, ethnic, religious, political, and economic backgrounds. Their goals are fair immigration rules, greater protection for resident illegal aliens, and a more pluralistic and tolerant culture.

You can become involved in this national controversy over immigration and citizenship policy in a number of ways. You can pay attention to the often contradictory policies that are proposed in Congress to deal with the problem. If you feel deeply enough about this issue, you might wish to join action organizations that lobby through influencing public opinion or by exerting direct pressure on Congress and the executive branch. You can also lobby your local government to enact laws allowing aliens fleeing persecution to live in your community.

The following groups are generally in favor of the right to immigrate and immigrants' rights:

National Network for Immigrant and Refugee Rights
310 Eighth St., Suite 307
Oakland, CA 94607
510-465-1984

www.nnirr.org/

National Immigrants' Rights Project
American Civil Liberties Union
132 West 43d St.
New York, NY 10036
212-944-9800

www.aclu.org/issues/immigrant/hmir.html

Groups that usually support stricter enforcement of existing immigration laws or a more homogeneous culture include the following:

Federation for American Immigration Reform
1666 Connecticut Ave. N.W., Suite 400
Washington, DC 20036
202-328-7004

www.fairus.org/

U.S. English
1747 Pennsylvania Ave. N.W., Suite 1100
Washington, DC 20006
202-833-0100

www.us-english.org/

Key terms

busing 157

civil rights 151

cloture 163

comparable worth 178

de facto segregation 157

de jure segregation 157

Equal Employment Opportunity
   Commission (EEOC) 163

feminism 171

filibuster 163

gender discrimination 174

grandfather clause 155

literacy test 155

poll tax 155

separate-but-equal doctrine 155

sexual harassment 175

subpoena 163

suffrage 169

white primary 155

Chapter summary

1 The civil rights movement started with the struggle by African Americans for equality. Before the Civil War, African Americans were slaves, and slavery was protected by the Constitution and the Supreme Court. African Americans were not considered citizens or entitled to the rights and privileges of citizenship. In 1863 and during the years after the Civil War, the Emancipation Proclamation and the Thirteenth, Fourteenth, and Fifteenth Amendments (the "Civil War amendments") legally and constitutionally ended slavery. From 1865 to 1875, to enforce the Civil War amendments, Congress passed a number of laws (civil rights acts). African Americans gained citizenship, the right to vote, equality before the law, and protection from deprivation of these rights.

2 Politically and socially, African American inequality continued. The *Civil Rights Cases* (1883) and *Plessy v. Ferguson* (1896) effectively nullified the civil rights acts of 1865 to 1875. In the *Civil Rights Cases,* the Supreme Court held that the Fourteenth Amendment did not apply to private invasions of individual rights. In *Plessy,* the Court upheld the separate-but-equal doctrine, declaring that segregation did not violate the Constitution. African Americans were excluded from the voting process through poll taxes, grandfather clauses, white primaries, and literacy tests.

3 Legal segregation was declared unconstitutional by the Supreme Court in *Brown v. Board of Education of Topeka* (1954), in which the Court stated that separation implied inferiority. In *Brown v. Board of Education* (1955), the Supreme Court ordered federal courts to ensure that public schools were desegregated "with all deliberate speed." Segregationists resisted with legal tactics, violence, and "white flight." Integrationists responded with court orders, federal marshals, and busing. Also in 1955, the modern civil rights movement began with a boycott of segregated public transportation in Montgomery, Alabama. Of particular impact was the Civil Rights Act of 1964. The act bans discrimination on the basis of race, color, religion, gender, or national origin in employment and public accommodations. The act created the Equal Employment Opportunity Commission to administer the act.

4 The Voting Rights Act of 1965 outlawed discriminatory voter-registration tests and authorized federal registration of persons and federally administered procedures in any state or political subdivision evidencing electoral discrimination or low registration rates. Subsequent amendments to this act extended its protections to other minorities. As a result of the Voting Rights Act, its amendments, and federal registration drives, African American political participation increased dramatically.

5 The protective legislation passed during and since the 1960s applies not only to African Americans but to other ethnic groups as well. Other minorities have also been increasingly represented in national and state politics, although they have yet to gain representation proportionate to their numbers in the U.S. population.

6 America has always been a land of immigrants and continues to be so. Today, more than one million immigrants from other nations enter the United States each year, and nearly 9 percent of the U.S. population consists of foreign-born persons. The civil rights legislation of the 1960s and later has helped immigrants to overcome some of the effects of prejudice and discrimination against them. Whether the United States is a "melting pot" or a nation best characterized by ethnic separatism or pluralism continues to be debated.

7 In the early history of the United States, women were considered citizens, but by and large they had no political rights. After the first women's rights convention in 1848, the women's movement gained momentum. Women's organizations continued to work toward the goal of the enfranchisement of women. Progress was slow, and it was not until 1920, when the Nineteenth Amendment was ratified, that women finally obtained the right to vote.

8 The modern women's movement began in the 1960s in the wake of the civil rights movement. The National Organization for Women (NOW) was formed in 1963 to bring about complete equality for women in all walks of life. When the efforts to secure the ratification of the Equal Rights Amendment failed, the women's movement began to focus on other methods—including litigation and increasing the political representation of women—to further the goal of gender equality. Although women have found it difficult to gain positions of political leadership, their numbers in Congress and in state and local government bodies have increased significantly in the 1990s.

9 Women continue to struggle against gender discrimination in the employment context. Federal government efforts to eliminate gender discrimination in the workplace include Title VII of the Civil Rights Act of 1964, which prohibits, among other things, gender-based discrimination. Title VII has been used to invalidate even "protective" laws or policies, such as fetal protection policies. The Supreme Court has upheld the right of women to be free from sexual harassment on the job, but defining what constitutes sexual harassment, particularly hostile-environment sexual harassment, continues to be a problem. Wage discrimination also continues to be a problem for women, as does the "glass ceiling" that prevents them from rising to the top of their business or professional firms.

Selected print and electronic resources

SUGGESTED READINGS

McGlen, Nancy E., and Karen O'Connor. *Women, Politics, and American Society.* 2d ed. Upper Saddle River, N.J.: Prentice Hall, 1998. This is an excellent history of the women's movement in the United States.

Rhode, Deborah L. *Speaking of Sex: The Denial of Gender Inequality.* Cambridge, Mass.: Harvard University Press, 1997. The author, using scholarly research, tells why women and men are still not equal.

Sniderman, Paul M., and Edward G. Carmines. *Reaching beyond Race.* Cambridge, Mass.: Harvard University Press, 1997. In this text, the authors show that prejudice, although by no means gone, has lost its power to dominate the political thinking of white Americans.

Woodward, C. Vann. *The Strange Career of Jim Crow.* New York: Oxford University Press, 1957. This is the classic study of segregation in the southern United States.

MEDIA RESOURCES

Beyond the Glass Ceiling—A CNN-produced program showing the difficulties women face in trying to rise to the top in corporate America.

Dr. Martin Luther King: A Historical Perspective—One of the best documentaries on the civil rights movement, focusing on the life and times of Martin Luther King, Jr.

Frederick Douglass—A documentary about the man who escaped slavery to become a world-famous orator, journalist, diplomat, abolitionist, and civil rights advocate in the mid-1800s.

I Have a Dream—Another film on Martin Luther King, Jr., this one focusing on the 1963 march on Washington and King's "I have a dream" speech, which some consider to be one of the greatest speeches of all time.

Separate but Equal—A video focusing on Thurgood Marshall, the lawyer (and later Supreme Court justice) who took the struggle for equal rights to the Supreme Court, and on the rise and demise of segregation in America.

Logging on

There are an incredible number of resources on the World Wide Web relating to civil rights—and particularly the problem of discrimination. One of the most active and visible civil rights organizations today is the American Civil Liberties Union. You can access its Web site at

www.aclu.org/

An extensive collection of information on Martin Luther King, Jr., is offered by the Martin Luther King Papers Project at Stanford University. If you wish to check out these papers, go to

www.stanford.edu/group/King/

If you are interested in learning more about the Equal Employment Opportunity Commission (EEOC) or want to find out how to file a complaint with that agency, go to

www.eeoc.gov/

The National Association for the Advancement of Colored People (NAACP) is online at

www.naacp.org/

For information on the League of Latin American Citizens (LULAC), go to

www.mundo.com/lulac.html

The URL for Women's Web World, which provides information on empowerment and equality for women, is

www.feminist.org/

If you wish to contact the National Organization for Women (NOW) or check out the resources and links it offers, go to

www.now.org/

Using the Internet for political analysis

Sometimes, given all of the laws that have been passed and court cases decided, it may seem that all of the basic issues concerning equality for American citizens have been resolved. To test that assumption, take a look at one of the following Web sites and identify at least two or three issues of equal treatment that remain to be resolved.

LatinoLink, at **www.latinolink.com/**
NAACP Online, at **www.naacp.org/**
Feminist Majority Online, at **www.feminist.org/**

Civil Rights: Beyond Equal Protection

BACKGROUND

CURRENTLY CHILDREN DO NOT HAVE A SPECIFIC BILL OF RIGHTS THAT APPLIES TO THEM. ALTHOUGH THEY ENJOY MANY OF THE PROTECTIONS AFFORDED BY THE CONSTITUTION, FOR THE MOST PART CHILDREN'S RIGHTS ARE MORE LIMITED THAN THOSE OF ADULTS. FOR EXAMPLE, NOT UNTIL 1967 DID JUVENILES HAVE A GUARANTEED RIGHT TO COUNSEL WHEN ACCUSED OF A CRIME.* MINORS HAVE A RIGHT TO FREE SPEECH, BUT IT IS LIMITED, PARTICULARLY WITH REGARD TO THEIR SCHOOL ACTIVITIES.† FINALLY, CHILDREN HAVE THE RIGHT TO BE FREE OF PHYSICAL ABUSE.

SOME HAVE SUGGESTED THAT A MORE COMPLETE CHILDREN'S BILL OF RIGHTS IS NEEDED. INDEED, IN 1989 THE UNITED NATIONS GENERAL ASSEMBLY ADOPTED THE UNITED NATIONS CONVENTION ON THE RIGHTS OF CHILDREN, WHICH SINCE THEN HAS BEEN RATIFIED BY MOST OF THE WORLD'S NATIONS (BUT NOT BY THE UNITED STATES). THOSE NATIONS THAT SIGN AND RATIFY THE CONVENTION COMMIT THEMSELVES TO FURNISHING THE BASIC ELEMENTS OF NUTRITION, EDUCATION, AND HEALTH TO ALL CHILDREN.

WHAT IF CHILDREN HAD A BILL OF RIGHTS?

First we must establish what would be in a children's bill of rights. Using the United Nations Convention on the Rights of Children as a starting point, we can assume that such a bill of

*In re Gault, 387 U.S. 1 (1967).

†Hazelwood School District v. Kuhlmeier, 484 U.S. 260 (1988).

rights, at a minimum, would give children the right to the following:

• Nutritious food.
• Preventive health care.
• A quality education.
• A clean environment.
• Free speech, privacy, and other constitutional rights that adults enjoy.
• Freedom from physical and mental abuse.
• Freedom from harassment.
• Freedom from physical constraint.

WHAT THESE RIGHTS MIGHT MEAN

If children had a bill of rights setting forth the above guarantees, major issues would arise. Consider the right to a quality education. Some proponents of a children's bill of rights argue that this is the most important right that we can give them. There is definitely a correlation between the amount of education a person has and that person's economic prospects and lifetime income. Also, surveys indicate that those with more education tend to participate to a greater degree in government through voting.

But what does it mean to guarantee a quality education to all children? The federal government might have to step in to legislate equal expenditures per student

across all fifty states. Taxes might have to be raised to pay for additional educational resources in the low-spending states.

The right to preventive health care would also involve the government. Those children who are considered "at risk" would create additional funding issues. Would the federal government or the state governments be involved here? In any event, improvement of health care for all children would definitely require higher taxes, too.

GOING TO COURT

If a children's bill of rights were a reality, presumably children would be allowed to sue to enforce their rights. And, if a child were too young to do so, a grandparent, neighbor, or friend of the family might be able to sue on behalf of the very young child. Litigation would increase dramatically. Already, litigation has increased as children have attempted to gain the right to choose which parent they live with after a divorce. Much more litigation would be guaranteed if children had a bill of rights.

Presumably, the existence of such a bill of rights would diminish parental authority. Severe discipline could cause a child to claim physical or

mental abuse and "report" on the parents. Indeed, this is one of the reasons that the opponents of the United Nations Convention on the Rights of Children have prevented it from being ratified—they believe that such a bill of rights for children would allow child-advocacy lawyers to assert children's rights against their parents.

FOR CRITICAL ANALYSIS

1. If children had a right to a clean environment, could they sue to prevent their parents from smoking in the house?
2. If children had an unlimited right to free speech, would that mean that they could say anything they want at the dinner table without fear of reprimand from their parents?
3. What other reasons can you think of that might explain why the United States has not yet ratified the United Nations Convention on the Rights of Children?

Remember from the previous chapter that the Civil Rights Act of 1964 prohibited discrimination against any person on the basis of race, color, national origin, religion, or gender. The act also established the right to equal opportunity in employment. A basic problem remained, however: minority groups and women, because of past discrimination, often lacked the education and skills to compete effectively in the marketplace. In 1965, the federal government attempted to remedy this problem by implementing the concept of affirmative action. **Affirmative action** policies give special preferences in educational admissions and employment decisions to groups that have been discriminated against in the past.

Affirmative action policies, by giving special treatment to some groups and not others in an attempt to "level the playing field," go beyond a strict interpretation of the equal protection clause of the Fourteenth Amendment. So do a number of other laws and programs established by the government during and since the 1960s. Bilingual education programs were launched in the 1960s to give special educational assistance to non-English-speaking immigrants, particularly Hispanics. In 1967, Congress passed legislation designed to assist older Americans in the workplace, who traditionally have suffered from discriminatory treatment. In 1990, Congress enacted a law mandating that the needs of persons with disabilities be accommodated in all public facilities as well as in the workplace. Some state and local governments have passed special laws protecting the rights of yet another group—gay males and lesbians. (For suggestions on how you can avail yourself of these laws if you feel you are being discriminated against, see the feature *Toward Active Citizenship* at the end of this chapter.)

In this chapter, we explore the controversy engendered by affirmative action policies and bilingual education programs. We then look at the gains that have been made by older Americans, persons with disabilities, and gay men and lesbians in their struggle for equal treatment. We conclude the chapter with a discussion of the issue touched on in this chapter's opening *What If . . .* feature: the rights and status of children in American society.

Affirmative Action

A policy in job hiring that gives special consideration or compensatory treatment to traditionally disadvantaged groups in an effort to overcome present effects of past discrimination.

Affirmative Action

In 1965, President Lyndon Johnson ordered that affirmative action policies be undertaken to remedy the effects of past discrimination. All government agencies,

Students at the University of California demonstrate their disagreement with the university's stand on affirmative action. In 1997, the university's board of regents voted to end its affirmative action policy, which had long influenced the university's admissions decisions.

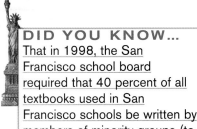

INFOTRAC®
COLLEGE EDITION

"In Search of Fairness"

Reverse Discrimination
The charge that affirmative action programs requiring preferential treatment or quotas discriminate against those who do not have minority status.

including those of state and local governments, were required to implement such policies. Additionally, affirmative action requirements were imposed on companies that sell goods or services to the federal government and on institutions that receive federal funds. Affirmative action policies were also required whenever an employer had been ordered to develop such a plan by a court or by the Equal Employment Opportunity Commission because of evidence of past discrimination. Finally, labor unions that had been found to discriminate against women or minorities in the past were required to establish and follow affirmative action plans.

Affirmative action programs have been controversial because they sometimes result in discrimination against majority groups, such as white males (or discrimination against other minority groups that may not be given preferential treatment under a particular affirmative action program). At issue in the current debate over affirmative action programs is whether such programs, because of their inherently discriminatory nature, violate the equal protection clause of the Fourteenth Amendment to the Constitution.

The *Bakke* Case

An early case addressing this issue involved an affirmative action program implemented by the University of California at Davis. Allan Bakke, a Vietnam War veteran and engineer who had been turned down for medical school at the Davis campus of the University of California, discovered that his academic record was better than those of some of the minority applicants who had been admitted to the program. He sued the University of California regents, alleging **reverse discrimination.** The UC–Davis Medical School had held sixteen places out of one hundred for educationally "disadvantaged students" each year, and the administrators at that campus admitted to using race as a criterion for admission for these particular minority slots. At trial in 1974, Bakke said that his exclusion from medical school violated his rights under the Fourteenth Amendment's provision for equal protection of the laws. The trial court agreed. On appeal, the California Supreme Court agreed also. Finally, the regents of the university appealed to the United States Supreme Court.

On June 28, 1978, the Supreme Court handed down its decision in *Regents of the University of California v. Bakke.*[1] The Court did not actually rule against affirmative action programs but did hold that Bakke must be admitted to the UC–Davis Medical School because its admission policy had used race as the sole criterion for the sixteen "minority" positions. But Justice Lewis Powell, speaking for the Court, indicated that race can be considered "as a factor" among others in admissions (and presumably hiring) decisions. In other words, it is legal to give special consideration to "afflicted minority groups" in an effort to remedy past discrimination. Race can be one of many criteria for admission, but not the only one. So affirmative action programs, but not specific quota systems, were upheld as constitutional.

Further Limitations on Affirmative Action

A number of cases decided during the 1980s placed even further limits on affirmative action programs. In 1984, for example, in *Firefighters Local Union No. 1784 v. Stotts,*[2] the Supreme Court said that the layoffs of Memphis firefighters had to be done on the basis of seniority unless there were African American employees who could prove they were victims of racial bias. In 1989, the

[1]438 U.S. 265 (1978).
[2]467 U.S. 561 (1984).

Supreme Court considered whether whites could challenge employment decisions made on the basis of an earlier judgment that included goals for hiring African Americans as firefighters in the city of Birmingham, Alabama. White firefighters who had not been parties in the earlier proceedings alleged that because of their race, they were being denied promotions in favor of less qualified African Americans. The Supreme Court held that the white firefighters could challenge those employment decisions.[3] In another 1989 decision, the Court invalidated a local government minority-preference program, ruling that it violated the equal protection clause. This decision signaled to dozens of cities and states that hundreds of affirmative action programs might also be invalid.[4]

In regard to racial discrimination, the Court made it harder for minority workers to sue employers.[5] In 1993, the Court used *Bakke* as a precedent for deciding that a policy of the city of Jacksonville, Florida, requiring that 10 percent of funds spent on city contracts be set aside annually for minority business enterprises, improperly discriminated against white contractors.[6]

The Civil Rights Act of 1991

By 1990, civil rights activists were arguing that the conservative rulings of the Supreme Court made it difficult for victims of employment discrimination to prove their cases. Believing that the courts could not be counted on to expand civil rights protections, some activists turned to Congress. Congress responded with the Civil Rights Act of 1991, which effectively overturned some of the conservative rulings and made it easier for workers to sue employers. The act consisted of amendments to Title VII of the Civil Rights Act of 1964 and other laws prohibiting discrimination. More than anything, the act clarified for the courts some of the ambiguities in the provisions of those earlier laws. The act did not, and could not, make any pronouncements on the *constitutionality* of affirmative action programs. That is the Supreme Court's job.

Court Decisions in the 1990s

As the twentieth century drew to a close, the Court went even further than *Bakke* and subsequent cases in questioning the constitutional validity of affirmative action programs. For example, in a 1995 case, *Adarand Constructors, Inc. v. Peña,*[7] the Supreme Court held that any federal, state, or local affirmative action program that uses racial or ethnic classifications as the basis for making decisions is subject to "strict scrutiny" by the courts. Under a strict-scrutiny analysis, to be constitutional, a discriminatory law or action must be narrowly tailored to meet a *compelling* government interest. In effect, the Court's opinion in *Adarand* means that an affirmative action program cannot make use of quotas or preferences for unqualified persons, and once the program has succeeded, it must be changed or dropped.

In 1996, a federal appellate court issued a decision that also has far-reaching implications. In *Hopwood v. State of Texas,*[8] two white law school applicants sued the University of Texas School of Law in Austin, alleging that they were denied admission because of the school's affirmative action program. The program allowed admissions officials to take race and other factors into consideration

---

[3]*Martin v. Wilks,* 490 U.S. 755 (1989).
[4]*Richmond v. J. A. Croson Co.,* 488 U.S. 469 (1989).
[5]*Wards Cove Packing Co. v. Atonio,* 490 U.S. 642 (1989).
[6]*Northwestern Florida Chapter of the Association of General Contractors of America v. Jacksonville, Florida,* 508 U.S. 656 (1993).
[7]515 U.S. 200 (1995).
[8]84 F.3d 720 (5th Cir. 1996).

when determining which students would be admitted. The federal appellate court held that the program violated the equal protection clause because it discriminated in favor of minority applicants. Significantly, the court directly challenged the *Bakke* decision by stating that the use of race even as a means of achieving diversity on college campuses "undercuts the Fourteenth Amendment." The Supreme Court declined to hear the case, thus letting the lower court's decision stand.

Since the *Hopwood* decision, the Supreme Court has refused to hear several other appeals concerning affirmative action. An exception in this respect was the Court's decision, in 1997, to review a case brought by Sharon Taxman, a white business education schoolteacher in Piscataway, New Jersey. When the Piscataway School Board had to choose between laying off Taxman or an African American teacher, Debra Williams, the board dismissed Taxman. Both teachers were equally qualified, and the board's only reason for deciding to dismiss Taxman instead of Williams was to further its goal of creating a diverse workforce. Before the Court could decide the matter, however, Taxman agreed to settle the case out of court. About 70 percent of the $433,500 settlement she received was funded by civil rights groups. (These groups feared that if the case reached the Supreme Court, the Court might hold in favor of Taxman, thus virtually ending similar affirmative action programs throughout the nation.)

During the early months of 1998, the issue remained unsettled as the Court declined to hear several cases involving affirmative action. The Court let stand decisions in the lower courts that invalidated two minority set-aside programs in Dade County, Florida. The Court also rejected an appeal by a former Nevada college professor who said that she was discriminated against because she is white. (In contrast to the U.S. Supreme Court's reluctance to support broadly tailored affirmative action programs, the highest court in the European Union seems to be taking the opposite position—see the feature *Politics and Comparative Systems: Affirmative Action in the European Union.*)

California's Proposition 209

In 1996, by a ballot initiative known as Proposition 209, a majority of California voters approved a constitutional amendment that ended all state-sponsored

Citizens in California demonstrate their opposition to Proposition 209, the ballot initiative that ended all state-sponsored affirmative action programs in the state. Why are affirmative action programs more controversial today than they were a decade or so ago?

POLITICS and Comparative Systems

Affirmative Action in the European Union

Like the United States, countries throughout Europe have instituted affirmative action laws and policies designed to remedy the effects of past discrimination, particularly against women. When such laws or policies are challenged, the ultimate decision maker is the European Court of Justice—the highest court in the European Union (EU), which is located in Luxembourg.

For a time, women's rights groups in Europe feared that affirmative action programs might not survive because of a 1995 ruling by the European Court of Justice in which the court invalidated an affirmative action law enacted by the German state of Bremen.

The court held that "[n]ational rules which guarantee women absolute and unconditional priority for appointment or promotion go beyond promoting equal opportunities, and overstep the limits of EU law."*

In a landmark 1997 decision, however, the court upheld an affirmative action law enacted by another German state. That law said that where "there are fewer women than men in the particular higher-grade post in the career bracket, women are to be given priority for promotion in the event of equal

The New York Times, October 18, 1995, p. A11.

suitability, competence and professional performance, unless reasons specific to an individual [male] candidate tilt the balance in his favor." The court held that this law was valid because, unlike the Bremen law in the 1995 case, it did not completely exclude men. The court went on to explain that affirmative action was a valid attempt to remedy past and present discrimination against women. "Even where male and female candidates are equally qualified," stated the court, "male candidates tend to be promoted in preference to female candidates, particularly because of prejudices and stereotypes concerning the

role and capacities of women in working life."[†]

FOR CRITICAL ANALYSIS

In contrast to the United States, affirmative action policies in Europe seem to be focused primarily on remedying the effects of discrimination against women and not discrimination against other groups. How might you explain this difference between U.S. and European affirmative action laws?

[†]Leyla Linton, "EU Court Upholds Hiring Preferences," *The National Law Journal,* November 24, 1997, p. A14.

affirmative action programs in that state. The law was immediately challenged in court by civil rights groups and others. These groups claimed that the law violated the Fourteenth Amendment by denying racial minorities and women the equal protection of the law. In 1997, however, a federal appellate court upheld the constitutionality of the amendment. Thus, affirmative action is now illegal in California in all state-sponsored institutions, including state agencies and educational institutions.

The initial fear that the law banning affirmative action would lower minority enrollment in institutions of higher education seemed to be confirmed in the first year after the law went into effect. According to statistics released in early 1998, the number of African Americans admitted to the University of California (UC) at Berkeley fell by 57 percent and the number of Latinos by 40 percent. At the University of California at Los Angeles (UCLA), admission statistics showed a 43 percent decline for African Americans and a 33 percent decline for Latinos. When admission figures for the whole nine-campus University of California system were examined, however, a more encouraging picture emerged: the drop in admissions for all minorities was less than two percentage points.

Since 1996, other states have been considering similar laws, but as yet none has been placed on a state ballot. In 1997, when the issue was put to citizens of Houston, Texas, they voted to retain affirmative action programs in that city.

Will Affirmative Action Survive?

The efforts of conservative interest groups and negative publicity have led many to believe that affirmative action policies have not resulted in equal protection of the laws for *most* Americans, including various minority groups that do not qual-

FIGURE 6-1

Support for Affirmative Action
Programs by Group

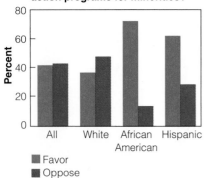

Do you favor or oppose affirmative
action programs for minorities?

■ Favor
■ Oppose

Source: *Wall Street Journal*/CBS News poll
conducted December 4–8, 1997.

INFOTRAC ®
COLLEGE EDITION

**"Two Languages Are Better
Than One"**

ify for special affirmative action preferences. Many groups contend that the time has come for a "colorblind" society in which racial and ethnic differences should not mandate decisions made by business firms, government agencies, and educational institutions in our society. (See this chapter's *Critical Perspective* for a discussion of a recent scholarly examination of this issue.)

Nevertheless, affirmative action continues to receive widespread support. Certainly, the Clinton administration is in favor of retaining such policies, perhaps with some modifications, and the Supreme Court, as already indicated, has not yet issued a blanket decision on the matter. As you can see in Figure 6–1, affirmative action finds significant support among African Americans and Hispanics, while whites are fairly divided on the issue. Significantly, in a recent *New York Times*/CBS News poll asking respondents what they thought should be done about affirmative action policies, 24 percent of those surveyed thought that the policies should be left as they are, and 43 percent thought they should be kept, but changed. Only 25 percent thought they should be abandoned entirely.

Bilingual Education

The continuous influx of immigrants into this country presents an ongoing challenge—how to overcome language barriers, particularly in the schools. From 1990 to 2010, the number of minority children is expected to grow from 19 million to 23 million. Currently, in one high school in a Los Angeles suburb, more than thirty languages are spoken. This trend toward cultural diversity will continue.

Educators thus are faced with the question of how to best educate children who do not speak English or who do not speak it very well. Should attempts be made to educate these children in their native languages through bilingual education programs? Should students be taught only in English? Or should they be placed in short-term "English-immersion" programs prior to entering regular classes? Since the 1960s, many have contended that bilingual education programs offer the best solution to the language problems facing immigrants.

Accommodating Diversity with Bilingual Education

Bilingual education programs teach children in their native language while also teaching them English. To some extent, bilingual education programs are the result of the government policies favoring multiculturalism that grew out of the civil rights movement. As discussed in Chapter 5, multiculturalism involves the belief that the government should accommodate the needs of different cultural groups and should protect and encourage ethnic and cultural differences.

Children attending classes taught in English were frequently encouraged by their teachers as well as their parents to speak English as much as possible, both at school and at home. Children who did so felt distanced from their grandparents and family members who spoke no English and, as a result, from their ethnic backgrounds. Bilingual education was premised on the hope that over time, Hispanic children would become truly bilingual without having to sacrifice their close family relationships and cultural heritage.

Congress authorized bilingual education programs in 1968 when it passed the Bilingual Education Act, which was intended primarily to help Hispanic children learn English. In a 1974 case, *Lau v. Nichols*,[9] the Supreme Court bolstered the claim that children have a right to bilingual education. In that case, the Court

---

[9]414 U.S. 563 (1974).

Critical perspective

Who Really Has Benefited from Affirmative Action?

In 1968, the Kerner Commission on Civil Disorders released a report on race relations following riots in several inner cities. The report stated that segregation was accelerating and that America was evolving into two societies. More recently, the idea that racial divisiveness between black and white Americans is increasing has been emphasized by a number of publications, including Andrew Hacker's provocatively titled book *Two Nations: Black and White, Separate, Hostile, Unequal.**

Affirmative action programs have now been in effect for several decades. As mentioned in this chapter, their goal has been to redress the harm done through any racial prejudices in the past. Have affirmative action programs resulted in much progress? Is the current controversy over them misplaced? Are they necessary to prevent us from becoming "two nations," as suggested by the Kerner Commission and others? The answer, according to Stephen Thernstrom of Harvard University and Abigail Thernstrom of the Manhattan Institute, is a resounding no.

Most Black Progress Occurred before Affirmative Action, According to These Critics

In their recently published book, *America in Black and White: One Nation, Indivisible,*† the Thernstroms take issue with the notion that racism in America is permanent. They bolster their view with an impressive collection of data. Among other things, these data show that black and white high school student graduation rates are about the same today. Economically, 40 percent of the nation's black citizens consider themselves members of the middle class, and statistics show that black married couples earn only slightly less, on average, than their white counterparts. As far as unemployment goes, about 93 percent of blacks in the labor force have jobs. Residential segregation also has dropped dramatically since World War II, and between 1970 and 1995 the number of African Americans living in suburban communities nearly doubled.

Additionally, on the basis of interview surveys, the Thernstroms argue that there has been a change in the thinking of both whites and blacks with respect to racial relations. Today, about 70 percent of both blacks and whites claim to have a "good friend" of the other race.

*New York: Ballantine Books, 1995.
†New York: Simon & Schuster, 1997.

In other words, according to these researchers, the focus on the black underclass has improperly defined our notion of black America. It has resulted in a misleading picture. According to the Thernstroms:

> Over the last half century, the position of African Americans thus improved dramatically by just about every possible measure of social and economic achievement. . . . Much of the change took place before the civil rights movement.

A Critical View of Affirmative Action

These researchers specifically contend that greater advances for African Americans occurred in the two decades prior to the civil rights movement than in the years since then. Hence, preferences (affirmative action), not their elimination, threaten progress. The Thernstroms point out that racist whites have always said that blacks were defined by their color. Racial preferences, according to these authors, seem to validate that view. But this is the wrong foundation on which to build a better society for both blacks and whites.

Accordingly, the Thernstroms call for an end to all policies and procedures that generate racial preferences, including race-norming of test scores and affirmative action. After all, they contend, the inequalities that currently exist between black and white economic achievement result mostly from differences in educational attainment, fatherless families, and the crime rate. While admitting that racial preferences helped more blacks enter law and medical schools, the authors point out that lawyers and physicians are a tiny fraction of the black middle class.

As an alternative to affirmative action, the authors urge a colorblind set of public policies. They argue that racial preferences cannot rescue a high school dropout who cannot "cut it" in the modern world of work. The solution is not in preferences, they say, but in attacking the three serious problems facing the black community—lack of educational achievement, dysfunctional family structures, and crime.

FOR CRITICAL ANALYSIS

1. In reality, affirmative action programs affect a very small number of minority members, women, and white males. Why, then, do such programs generate so much heated debate?

2. The Thernstroms' work has been aggressively attacked by proponents of racial preferences. What are some of the arguments that might be used in such attacks?

Bilingual education in the fourth grade at the Walnut Creek Elementary school in Austin, Texas.

ordered a California school district to provide special programs for Chinese students with language difficulties if a substantial number of these children attended school in the district. Today, most bilingual education programs are for Hispanic American children, particularly in areas of the country, such as California and Texas, where there are large numbers of Hispanic residents.

The Current Controversy over Bilingual Education

Bilingual education programs always have been controversial, and today they are increasingly coming under attack. Ironically, some of the strongest critics of bilingual programs are parents of Hispanic children who have been in such programs. These parents feel that bilingual programs have hindered their children's ability to learn English quickly and therefore are a detriment to learning and academic advancement. Many believe that their children would fare better in regular classrooms. Another desirable option for many educators and parents are "English-immersion" programs in which students are given intensive instruction in English for a limited period of time and then placed in regular classrooms.

Other critics of bilingual education include those opposed to multiculturalist policies, "America-firsters," and "English-only" advocates. They believe that government policies should emphasize the unity, not the diversity, of American culture. One way to do this is by helping the children of immigrants learn, as quickly as possible, the English language—a basic unifying element in American culture. In response to pressure from these groups, as well as for other reasons, nearly half of the states have passed "English-only" laws that require all official speech to be in English. Congress is also considering a bill that would make English the official language of the U.S. government.

For many, however, the primary focus of their criticism of bilingual programs is simply education. Do bilingual education programs hinder Hispanic children's chances of success in a world dominated by the English language? Or is bilingual education essential for integrating English-speaking and non-English-speaking children into an increasingly multicultural nation?

Voters in California answered these questions when they passed a ballot measure, in June 1998, that called for the end of bilingual education programs in that state. The law allows schools to implement "English-immersion" programs for Spanish-speaking children, who later will go into regular classrooms. (The new California law was immediately challenged in court on the ground that it unconstitutionally discriminated against non-English-speaking groups. A federal district court, however, concluding that the new law did not violate the equal protection clause, refused to prevent the law's implementation.) Eventually, voters in other states, particularly those that have large Hispanic populations, also will have to decide this question at the polls.

Special Protection for Older Americans

Americans are getting older. In colonial times, about half the population was under the age of sixteen. In 1990, the number of people under the age of sixteen was fewer than one in four, and half were thirty-three or older. By the year 2050, at least half could be thirty-nine or older.

Today, nearly 34 million Americans (over 12 percent of the population) are aged sixty-five or over. As can be seen in Figure 6–2, by the year 2020, this figure is projected to reach 53.6 million. From 2010 to 2030, the Bureau of the Census predicts that the portion of the population over age sixty-five will grow

76 percent, while the population under age sixty-five will increase only 6.5 percent (see Figure 6–2).

Senior citizens face a variety of problems unique to their group. One problem that seems to endure, despite government legislation designed to prevent it, is age discrimination in employment. Others include health care and income security. Since the 1930s, the government has established programs, such as Social Security and Medicare, designed to protect the health and welfare of older Americans. Although we touch on these public benefits in this section, they are explored more fully in Chapters 16 and 17.

Age Discrimination in Employment

Age discrimination is potentially the most widespread form of discrimination, because anyone—regardless of race, color, national origin, or gender—could be a victim at some point in life. The unstated policies of some companies not to hire or to demote or dismiss people they feel are "too old" have made it difficult for some older workers to succeed in their jobs or continue with their careers. Additionally, older workers have fallen victim at times to cost-cutting efforts by employers. To reduce operational costs, companies may replace older, higher-salaried workers with younger, lower-salaried workers.

The Age Discrimination in Employment Act of 1967. In an attempt to protect older employees from such discriminatory practices, Congress passed the Age Discrimination in Employment Act (ADEA) in 1967. The act, which applies to employers, employment agencies, and labor organizations and covers individuals over the age of forty, prohibits discrimination against individuals on the basis of age unless age is shown to be a bona fide occupational qualification reasonably necessary to the normal operation of the particular business.

Specifically, it is against the law to discriminate by age in wages, benefits, hours worked, or availability of overtime. Employers and unions may not discriminate in providing fringe benefits, such as education or training programs, career development, sick leave, and vacations. It is a violation of the act to publish notices or advertisements indicating an age-preference limitation or

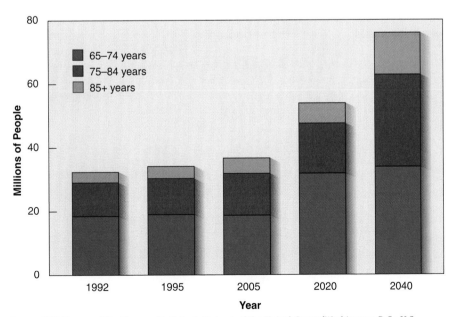

FIGURE 6-2

Population Projections: Persons Aged 65 or Older (in Millions)

As shown here, the number of Americans who will be sixty-five years of age or older will grow dramatically during the next century. The number will double between 2005 and 2040. These older Americans will increase their political power as their numbers increase.

SOURCE: U.S. Bureau of the Census, *Statistical Abstract of the United States* (Washington, D.C.: U.S. Government Printing Office, 1997).

discrimination based on age. Even advertisements that imply a preference for youthful workers over older workers are in violation of the law. Requesting age on an application is not illegal but may be closely scrutinized in light of the employer's hiring practices.

To succeed in a suit for age discrimination, an employee must prove that the employer's action, such as a decision to fire the employee, was motivated, at least in part, by age bias. Proof that qualified older employees are generally discharged before younger employees or that co-workers continually made unflattering age-related comments about the discharged worker may be enough. In 1996, the Supreme Court held that even if an older worker is replaced by a younger worker falling under the protection of the ADEA—that is, by a younger worker who is also over the age of forty—the older worker is entitled to bring a suit under the ADEA. The Court stated that the issue in all ADEA cases is whether age discrimination has in fact occurred, regardless of the age of the replacement worker.[10]

Mandatory Retirement. The ADEA, as initially passed, did not address one of the major problems facing older workers—**mandatory retirement** rules, which required employees to retire when they reached a certain age. Mandatory retirement rules often meant that competent, well-trained employees who wanted to continue working were unable to do so. In 1978, in an amendment to the ADEA, Congress prohibited mandatory retirement rules with respect to most employees under the age of seventy. Many states had already passed similar statutes. In 1986, Congress outlawed mandatory retirement rules entirely for all but a few selected occupations, such as firefighting.

Mandatory Retirement
Forced retirement when a person reaches a certain age.

Age, Political Participation, and Public Benefits

If we use voter participation as a measure of political involvement, it is clear that voter participation increases with age. Table 6–1 shows that, of the six age categories listed, the over-sixty-five age group ranks first in voter registration and in actual turnout on election day. Whereas approximately 54.2 percent of

[10]*O'Connor v. Consolidated Coil Caterers Corp.,* 116 S.Ct. 1307 (1996).

The Gray Panthers is a politically active organization that promotes policies and actions that are of special interest to senior citizens.

TABLE 6-1

Voter Participation by Age Group

Voter participation generally is positively correlated with age. The lowest participation is by persons eighteen to twenty years old, and the highest is by those aged sixty-five and over.			
AGE GROUP	**NUMBER OF OF PERSONS (MILLIONS)**	**PERCENTAGE REPORTING THEY REGISTERED**	**PERCENTAGE REPORTING THEY VOTED**
18–20	10.7	45.6	31.2
21–24	13.8	51.2	33.4
25–44	83.4	61.9	49.2
45–64	53.7	73.5	64.4
65 and over	31.9	77.0	67.0

SOURCE: U.S. Bureau of the Census, *Statistical Abstract of the United States* (Washington, D.C.: U.S. Government Printing Office, 1997). Data are for 1996.

all persons of voting age claim to have voted, in the over-sixty-five category, the voting rate is 67.0 percent.

Older Americans work for their interests through a number of large and effective political associations. The largest group is the American Association of Retired Persons (AARP), for those aged fifty and older. Founded in 1958, it has a current membership of more than thirty-three million. The AARP and the National Retired Teachers' Association have united in a powerful joint effort to ensure beneficial treatment for older Americans by lobbying for legislation at the federal and state levels. They use the same staff in Washington and provide almost the same services to their members, including low-priced group insurance and travel programs.

Because of their voting and lobbying power, Americans over the age of sixty-five receive a disproportionate share of government spending. Almost half of the entire federal budget is spent on Medicare and Social Security. Medicare costs recently have risen at about twice the rate of inflation for the economy as a whole. Many programs, such as Medicare and Social Security, have been tied legislatively to external factors so that spending on them has become, to a large degree, uncontrollable and automatic. Indeed, there is growing concern over whether the government is allocating too many resources to seniors and not enough to the welfare of younger Americans (see the feature *Politics and Ethics: Generational Warfare* on page 198).

Securing Rights for Persons with Disabilities

Like older Americans, persons with disabilities did not fall under the protective umbrella of the Civil Rights Act of 1964. Remember from Chapter 5 that the 1964 act prohibited discrimination against any person on the basis of race, color, national origin, religion, or gender. As just noted, Congress addressed the problem of age discrimination in 1967. By the 1970s, Congress also began to pass legislation to protect Americans with disabilities. In 1973, Congress passed the Rehabilitation Act, which prohibited discrimination against persons with disabilities in programs receiving federal aid. A 1978 amendment to the act established the Architectural and Transportation Barriers Compliance Board. Regulations for ramps, elevators, and the like in all federal buildings were implemented. Congress passed the Education for All Handicapped Children Act in 1975. It guarantees that all children with disabilities will receive an "appropriate" education. The

POLITICS and Ethics

Generational Warfare

In the past, older Americans were considered a disadvantaged group in American society. For example, in 1959, 35 percent were living below the poverty level. During the 1960s and 1970s, older Americans continued to be disproportionately poor. Today, however, less than 10 percent of senior citizens live below the poverty level. Nevertheless, as mentioned in the text, older Americans continue to receive a disproportionate share of government benefits through such programs as Medicare and Social Security.

Politicians frequently point out that "the youth of America is the future of America." Why, then, do Americans generally vote in favor of funding programs that benefit seniors rather than young people?

One reason is that, as shown in Table 6–1 on page 197, older Americans wield considerable voting power. Another reason is that older Americans are represented by one of the largest and most powerful interest groups in the nation—the American Association of Retired Persons (AARP).

A few years ago, Congress passed a law that required seniors whose income exceeded a certain amount to pay for part of their Medicare coverage. The AARP fought back with a vigorous lobbying campaign, and the law was repealed. The fact is, any politician who wants to be reelected has a strong incentive *not* to back legislation that is adverse to the inter-

ests of older Americans. For the same reasons, older Americans also wield substantial political influence at the state level.

Clearly, the future of this country is in the hands of American youth. Yet if the trend toward increasing the proportion of government resources going to seniors continues, children in the future may not be equipped to deal with the increasingly complex political and economic problems facing American government. Consider that child abuse is a growing problem; violent crime by teenagers and even preteens is a source of widespread concern; and increasingly, the nation is challenged to provide its youth with a quality education. At

the same time, the number of voters who have children under the age of eighteen is decreasing, and voter turnout among younger Americans who are eligible to vote is low.

At its heart, this issue poses an ethical question: Given that seniors, as a group, are wealthier than they have ever been, how can the government justify such a large percentage of its resources going to them instead of to younger persons who have greater needs?

FOR CRITICAL ANALYSIS

Is there anything that younger Americans can do to secure more resources for

most significant federal legislation with respect to the rights of persons with disabilities, however, is the Americans with Disabilities Act (ADA), which Congress passed in 1990.

The Americans with Disabilities Act of 1990

The ADA requires that all public buildings and public services be accessible to persons with disabilities. The act also mandates that employers must reasonably accommodate the needs of workers or potential workers with disabilities.

Physical access means ramps; handrails; wheelchair-accessible restrooms, counters, drinking fountains, telephones, and doorways; and more accessible mass transit. In addition, other steps must be taken to comply with the act. Car-rental companies must provide cars with hand controls for disabled drivers. Telephone companies are required to have operators to pass on messages from speech-impaired persons who use telephones with keyboards.

The ADA requires employers to "reasonably accommodate" the needs of persons with disabilities unless to do so would cause the employer to suffer an "undue hardship." The ADA defines persons with disabilities as persons who have physical or mental impairments that "substantially limit" their everyday activities. Health conditions that have been considered disabilities under federal law include blindness, alcoholism, heart disease, cancer, muscular dystrophy, cerebral palsy, paraplegia, diabetes, acquired immune deficiency syndrome (AIDS), and, most recently, the human immunodeficiency virus (HIV) that causes AIDS.

President George Bush signs the 1990 Americans with Disabilities Act. The act requires corporations and public institutions to implement access for disabled Americans and requires employers to accommodate workers with disabilities.

The ADA does not require that *unqualified* applicants with disabilities be hired or retained. If a job applicant or an employee with a disability, with reasonable accommodation, can perform essential job functions, however, then the employer must make the accommodation. Required accommodations may include installing ramps for a wheelchair, establishing more flexible working hours, creating or modifying job assignments, and creating or improving training materials and procedures.

Interpreting and Applying the ADA

The ADA has been controversial, not because of its goal—preventing discrimination against persons with disabilities—but because of the difficulties involved in interpreting and applying the act's provisions. For example, what constitutes a physical or mental impairment? At what point does such an impairment "substantially limit" a "major life activity," and what constitutes a major life activity? Finally, what exactly is required to "reasonably accommodate" persons with disabilities, and at what point does accommodation constitute an "undue hardship" for employers?

The courts have had to address these questions, and the outcome of any particular case is not always predictable. For example, in one case an employee came to work toting a loaded gun. The employer, who, like all employers, was required by law to maintain a safe workplace for employees, fired the employee on the spot. The employee took the employer to court, and the jury concluded that the employee's behavior was the result of a mental impairment. Therefore, the employer should not have fired him but accommodated his disability in some way, such as by giving him a leave of absence.

In 1998, the United States Supreme Court for the first time took up a case involving the interpretation of the ADA. The issue was whether HIV, the virus that causes AIDS, could qualify as a disability under the act. The Court held that an HIV infection, even though it has not yet been evidenced by any physical symptoms, is a physical impairment that substantially limits the major life activity of existence. Therefore, persons infected with HIV fall under the protection of the ADA and must be accommodated—unless to do so would constitute a "direct threat" to others.[11]

---

[11]*Bragdon v. Abbott*, 118 S.Ct. 2196 (1998).

As a political force, the disabled have emerged as a significant group. Persons with disabilities have held numerous demonstrations, demanding to have their rights upheld in the work force and in society.

An ADA case that received widespread media attention in 1998 involved Casey Martin, a professional golfer. Martin has a congenital deformity of his right leg, and the simple act of walking is very dangerous—it could cause a fractured bone or a hemorrhage in that leg. Martin could do everything well in the game of golf except walk to and from his shots. When he asked the Professional Golfers' Association (PGA) to let him use a golf cart rather than walk in a PGA tournament, however, PGA officials denied his request—it was against the association's rules. Martin claimed that the PGA was obligated, under the ADA, to accommodate his disability. The PGA argued that it was a private organization and therefore not subject to the ADA. When the case reached a federal court, no one could predict with certainty how the court would rule. As it turned out, the court held in Martin's favor.[12]

Uncertainty in how the act will be applied creates special problems for employers, business owners, and other organizations that must comply with the act's requirements. Despite the ADA's shortcomings, however, many persons suffering from disabilities have benefited from the act, as well as from the changing social attitudes toward them that the act has helped to foster. And a significant number of people with disabilities take advantage of the act's protective provisions. As you can see in Figure 6–3, nearly one-fourth of the complaints filed with the Equal Employment Opportunity Commission in a recent year were for disability-based discrimination.

The Rights and Status of Gay Males and Lesbians

On June 27, 1969, patrons of the Stonewall Inn, a New York City bar popular with gays and lesbians, responded to a police raid by throwing beer cans and bottles because they were angry at what they felt was unrelenting police harassment. In the ensuing riot, which lasted two nights, hundreds of gays and lesbians fought with police. Before Stonewall, the stigma attached to homosexual-

FIGURE 6-3

Charges Filed with the EEOC Alleging Discrimination

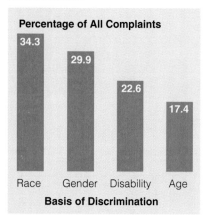

Percentage of All Complaints

34.3	29.9	22.6	17.4
Race	Gender	Disability	Age

Basis of Discrimination

SOURCE: Equal Employment Opportunity Commission, 1997.

---

[12]*Martin v. PGA, Inc.,* __ F.Supp.__ (D.Ore. 1998).

ity and the resulting fear of exposure had tended to keep most gays and lesbians acquiescent. In the months immediately after Stonewall, however, "gay power" graffiti began to appear in New York City. The Gay Liberation Front and the Gay Activist Alliance were formed, and similar groups sprang up in other parts of the country. Thus Stonewall has been called "the shot heard round the homosexual world."

The Stonewall incident marked the beginning of the movement for gay and lesbian rights. Since then, gay men and lesbians have formed thousands of organizations to exert pressure on legislatures, the media, schools, churches, and other organizations to recognize their right to equal treatment. One of the largest gay rights groups today is the Human Rights Campaign Fund, whose goal is to see federal gay rights laws passed. Another major group is the National Gay and Lesbian Task Force, which works toward the repeal of state sodomy laws (laws prohibiting certain forms of sexual activity, including homosexual relationships). The American Civil Liberties Union also actively promotes laws protecting gays and lesbians, as do several other liberal civil rights organizations.

To a great extent, lesbian and gay groups have succeeded in changing public opinion—and state and local laws—relating to their status and rights. Nevertheless, they continue to struggle against age-old biases against homosexuality, often rooted in deeply held religious beliefs, and the rights of gay men and lesbians remain an extremely divisive issue in American society.

State and Local Laws against Gays

Prior to the Stonewall incident in 1969, forty-nine states had sodomy laws (Illinois, which had repealed its sodomy law in 1962, was the only exception). During the 1970s and 1980s, more than half of these laws were either repealed or struck down by the courts. Several state and local governments have gone further in their efforts to protect gay and lesbian rights. Today, ten states[13] and 165 cities and counties have special laws protecting lesbians and gay men against discrimination in employment, housing, public accommodations, and credit.

The trend toward repealing state anti-gay laws ended in 1986 with the Supreme Court's decision in *Bowers v. Hardwick*.[14] In that case, the Court upheld, by a five-to-four vote, a Georgia law that made homosexual conduct between two adults a crime. Justice Byron White, writing for the majority, stated that "we are quite unwilling" to "announce . . . a fundamental right to engage in homosexual sodomy." Since that decision, no state has repealed its sodomy law.

In a 1996 case, *Romer v. Evans*,[15] the Supreme Court issued a decision that had a significant impact on the rights of gays and lesbians. The case involved a Colorado state constitutional amendment that invalidated all existing state and local laws protecting homosexuals from discrimination. The Supreme Court held that the amendment violated the equal protection clause of the Constitution because it denied to homosexuals in Colorado—but to no other Colorado residents—"the right to seek specific protection of the law." The Court stated that the equal protection clause simply does not permit Colorado to make homosexuals "unequal to everyone else."

Despite the Supreme Court's ruling in *Romer v. Evans*, a federal appellate court in 1997 upheld an anti-gay amendment to Cincinnati's city charter that was similar to Colorado's constitutional amendment. Because all U.S. courts are obligated to abide by Supreme Court decisions (see Chapter 15), critics called the

---

[13]California, Connecticut, Hawaii, Massachusetts, Minnesota, New Hampshire, New Jersey, Rhode Island, Vermont, and Wisconsin. Maine also had a law protecting gay and lesbian rights until February 1998, when the law was repealed in a referendum.

[14]478 U.S. 186 (1986).

[15]517 U.S. 620 (1996).

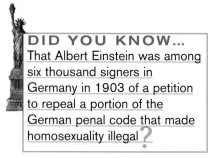

federal appellate court's decision a "renegade ruling" that had no legal basis. According to the court's opinion, however, all that the *Romer* decision meant was that a city has a right to create an ordinance protecting gay rights, and if it chooses to do so, the state cannot nullify it. The Supreme Court did not rule that cities *must* create such laws.[16]

The Gay Community and Politics

Politicians at the national level have not overlooked the potential significance of homosexual issues in American politics. While conservative politicians generally have been critical of securing gay and lesbian rights, liberals, by and large, have been speaking out for gay rights in the last two decades. In 1980, the Democratic platform included a gay plank for the first time. Walter Mondale, former vice president of the United States and the Democratic Party nominee for president in 1984, addressed a gay convention and openly bid for the political support of gays and lesbians. The gay community also supported Jesse Jackson's 1988 bid for the presidency and Jackson's Rainbow Coalition.

President Clinton, who has long embraced much of the gay rights agenda, recently became the first sitting president to address a gay rights organization. In late 1997, in a speech intentionally reminiscent of Harry Truman's 1947 speech to an African American civil rights organization, Clinton pledged his support for equal rights for gay and lesbian Americans at a fund-raiser sponsored by the Human Rights Campaign Fund.

Several laws at the national level have also been changed in the past two decades. Among other things, the government has lifted the ban on hiring gays and lesbians and voided a 1952 law prohibiting gays and lesbians from immigrating to the United States. Currently, Congress is considering a bill that would bar workplace discrimination based on sexual orientation.

Gay Men and Lesbians in the Military

The U.S. Department of Defense traditionally has viewed homosexuality as incompatible with military service. Supporters of gay and lesbian rights have attacked this policy in recent years, and in 1993 the policy was modified. In that year, President Bill Clinton announced that a new policy, generally characterized as "don't ask, don't tell," would be in effect. Enlistees would not be asked about their sexual orientation, and gays and lesbians would be allowed to serve in the military as long as they did not declare that they were gay or lesbian, or commit homosexual acts. Military officials endorsed the new policy, after opposing it initially, but supporters of gay rights were not enthusiastic. Clinton had promised during his presidential campaign to repeal outright the long-standing ban.

Several gays and lesbians who have been discharged from military service have protested their discharges by bringing suit against the Defense Department. In one case, a former Navy lieutenant, Paul Thomasson, was dismissed from the service in 1995 after stating "I am gay" in a letter to his commanding admiral. In 1996, a federal appellate court reviewed the case and concluded that the courts should defer, as they traditionally have, to the other branches of government, especially in military policy. A dissenting judge wrote that Thomasson was being punished for "nothing more than an expression of his state of mind."[17]

At issue in these cases are the constitutional rights to free speech, privacy, and the equal protection of the laws. (See this chapter's *Politics Wired* for a discussion of an unusual case involving military policy and online privacy rights.)

---

[16]*Equality Foundation of Greater Cincinnati v. City of Cincinnati* (6th Cir. 1998); unpublished opinion.
[17]*Thomasson v. Perry*, 80 F.3d 915 (4th Cir. 1996).

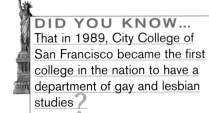

Because the lower courts are in disagreement, it is likely that the Supreme Court will rule on the matter in the future.

Same-Sex Marriages and Child-Custody Issues

Perhaps one of the most sensitive political issues with respect to the rights of gay and lesbian couples is whether they should be allowed to marry, just as heterosexual couples are. The controversy over this issue was fueled in 1993 by a Hawaii Supreme Court ruling that denying marriage licenses to gay couples may violate the equal protection clause of the Hawaii constitution. The court stated that unless Hawaii could offer a "compelling" reason to maintain this discriminatory practice, it must be abandoned. The Hawaii Supreme Court then sent the case back to the trial court to determine if the state did indeed have such a compelling reason. In 1996, the trial court ruled that the state had failed to meet this burden, and therefore the ban on same-sex marriages violates the state constitution.

There is a strong possibility that the lawsuit will compel Hawaii to begin allowing lesbians and gay men to marry. If that happens, other states will have to decide whether to treat persons who are legally married in Hawaii as married couples in their states as well. Opponents of gay rights have pushed for state laws banning same-sex marriages, and to date at least sixteen states have enacted such laws, and two state governors have signed executive orders preventing same-sex marriages. Many other states are considering similar laws. In 1996, Congress passed the Defense of Marriage Act, which bans federal recognition of

POLITICS WIRED

Gays, the Military, and the Privacy of Online Communications

Suppose that a naval officer had an account with America Online (AOL) and on the AOL profile page gave his name as "Tim," his location as "Hawaii," and his marital status as "gay." Further suppose that a recipient of e-mail from "Tim," unsure of the sender's identity, checked his profile page and forwarded the information to his superior officers. If a Navy investigator called AOL anonymously and learned that the "Tim" on the profile page was Senior Petty Officer Timothy R. McVeigh,* would this knowledge serve as grounds

*This is *not* the Timothy McVeigh who was convicted for the 1995 bombing of the Alfred P. Murrah Federal Building in Oklahoma City.

to accuse McVeigh of "sodomy and indecent acts"?

Certainly, the Navy officials investigating McVeigh thought it was. Under the military's "don't ask, don't tell" policy, publicly declaring that one is gay is the same as performing prohibited homosexual acts and is thus grounds for discharge. Navy officials, concluding that the information that McVeigh included on his AOL profile page constituted a public declaration that he was gay, ordered McVeigh's dismissal from the Navy.

McVeigh challenged the dismissal, claiming that because he had never said publicly that he was gay the

Navy had no right to ask about his sexual orientation. Further, he argued that the Navy had violated a 1986 federal privacy law governing electronic communications by obtaining information from AOL without a warrant or a court order. In early 1998, federal court judge Stanley Sporkin agreed and ordered the Navy to reinstate McVeigh.

McVeigh's case, which received widespread publicity, raises troublesome questions not only about the Navy's intrusion into McVeigh's privacy but also about privacy rights in the online world generally. Judge Sporkin emphasized the tenuousness of privacy rights in his decision. He stated that electronic

privacy laws must be applied strictly in these days of "big brother" because through technology, "the privacy interests of individuals from all walks of life are being ignored or marginialized."[†]

FOR CRITICAL ANALYSIS

What if McVeigh had stated in an e-mail message to a friend or other person that he was gay? As far as the military's "don't ask, don't tell" policy is concerned, would this constitute a "public declaration" that he was a homosexual?

[†]*Timothy R. McVeigh v Cohen*, 983 F.Supp. 215 (D.C. 1998).

Gay men and lesbians demonstrate in New York City's Bryant Park in favor of same-sex marriages. They want the state of New York to legalize such marriages.

INFOTRAC®
COLLEGE EDITION

"Is the Air Force Asking and Telling"

lesbian and gay couples and allows state governments to ignore same-sex marriages performed in other states.

Another legal challenge faced by gay couples is the difficulty they have obtaining child-custody rights. Courts around the country are wrestling with how much weight, if any, should be given to a parent's sexual orientation when deciding which of two parents should have custody. The courts are split on the issue. In about half the states, courts have held that a parent's sexual orientation should not be a significant factor in determining child custody. Courts in other states, however, tend to give more weight to sexual orientation. In one case, a court even went so far as to award custody to a father because the child's mother was a lesbian, even though the father had served eight years in prison for killing his first wife.

The Rights and Status of Juveniles

Approximately seventy-six million Americans—almost 30 percent of the total population—are under twenty-one years of age. The definition of children ranges from persons under age sixteen to persons under age twenty-one. However defined, children in the United States have the fewest rights and protections, as indicated in the chapter-opening *What If . . .* feature.

The reason for this lack is the common presumption of society and its lawmakers that children are basically protected by their parents. This is not to say that children are the exclusive property of the parents. Rather, an overwhelming case in favor of *not* allowing parents to control the actions of their children must be presented before children can be given authorization to act without parental consent (or before the state can be given authorization to act on children's behalf without regard to their parents' wishes).

Supreme Court decisions affecting children's rights of today began a process of slow evolution with *Brown v. Board of Education of Topeka*, the landmark civil rights case of 1954 discussed in Chapter 5. In *Brown*, the Court granted children the status of rights-bearing persons. In 1967, in *In re Gault*,[18] the Court

---

[18]387 U.S. 1 (1967).

expressly held that children have a constitutional right to be represented by counsel at the government's expense in a criminal action. Five years later, the Court acknowledged that "children are 'persons' within the meaning of the Bill of Rights. We have held so over and over again."[19]

Supreme Court decisions affecting the rights of children have also touched on another very controversial issue: abortion. In 1976, the Court recognized a girl's right to have an abortion without consulting her parents.[20] More recently, however, the Court has allowed state laws to dictate whether consent must be obtained by the child.

Voting Rights and the Young

The Twenty-sixth Amendment to the Constitution, ratified on July 1, 1971, reads as follows:

> The right of citizens of the United States, who are eighteen years of age or older, to vote shall not be denied or abridged by the United States or by any State on account of age.

Before this amendment was ratified, the age at which citizens could vote was twenty-one. Why did the Twenty-sixth Amendment specify age eighteen? Why not seventeen or sixteen? And why did it take until 1971 to allow those between the ages of eighteen and twenty-one to vote?

There are no easy answers to such questions. One cannot argue simply that those under twenty-one, or those under eighteen, are "incompetent." Incompetent at what? Certainly, one could find a significant number of seventeen-year-olds who can understand the political issues presented to them as well as can many adults eligible to vote. One of the arguments used for granting suffrage to eighteen-year-olds was that, because they could be drafted to fight in the country's wars, they had a stake in public policy. At the time, the example of the Vietnam War (1964–1975) was paramount.

Have eighteen- to twenty-year-olds used their right to vote? Yes and no. Immediately after the passage of the Twenty-sixth Amendment, the percentage of eighteen- to twenty-year-olds registering to vote was 58 percent (in 1972), and 48.4 percent reported that they had voted. But by the 1996 presidential election, of the 10.7 million Americans in the eighteen-to-twenty voting age bracket, 45.6 percent were registered, and 31.2 percent reported that they had voted. Contrast this turnout with that of Americans who are aged sixty-five or older. Of the 31.9 million people in this age group, 77 percent were registered to vote, and 67 percent turned out to vote in the 1996 elections. (Some of the consequences of this age disparity in voting were explored in this chapter's *Critical Perspective.*)

The Rights of Children in Civil and Criminal Proceedings

Children today have limited rights in civil and criminal proceedings in our judicial system. Different procedural rules and judicial safeguards apply in civil and criminal laws. **Civil law** relates in part to contracts among private individuals or companies. **Criminal law** relates to crimes against society that are defined by society acting through its legislatures.

Civil Rights of Juveniles. Children are defined exclusively by state law with respect to private contract negotiations, rights, and remedies. The legal definition

---

[19] *Wisconsin v. Yoder,* 406 U.S. 205 (1972).
[20] *Planned Parenthood of Central Missouri v. Danforth,* 428 U.S. 52 (1976).

DID YOU KNOW...
That the United Nations Convention on the Rights of Children calls for the provision of effective legal assistance for children so that their interests can be "heard directly"?

Civil Law
The law regulating conduct between private persons over noncriminal matters. Under civil law, the government provides the forum for the settlement of disputes between private parties in such matters as contracts, domestic relations, and business relations.

Criminal Law
The law that defines crimes and provides punishment for violations. In criminal cases, the government is the prosecutor, because crimes are against the public order.

Majority

Full age; the age at which a person is entitled by law to the right to manage his or her own affairs and to the full enjoyment of civil rights.

Necessaries

In contract law, necessaries include whatever is reasonably necessary for suitable subsistence as measured by age, state, condition in life, and so on.

of **majority** varies from eighteen to twenty-one years of age, depending on the state. If an individual is legally a minor, as a rule, that person cannot be held responsible for contracts that he or she forms with others. In most states, only contracts entered into for so-called **necessaries** (things necessary for subsistence, as determined by the courts) can be enforced against minors. Also, when minors engage in negligent behavior, typically their parents are liable. If, for example, a minor destroys a neighbor's fence, the neighbor may bring suit against the child's parent but not against the child.

Civil law encompasses an area that has recently broken new ground in children's rights: child custody. Child-custody rulings have traditionally given little weight to the wishes of the child. Courts have maintained their right to act on behalf of the child's "best interests" but have sometimes been constrained from doing so by the "greater" rights possessed by adults. For instance, a widely publicized Michigan Supreme Court ruling awarded legal custody of a two-and-a-half-year-old Michigan resident to an Iowa couple, the child's biological parents. A Michigan couple, who had cared for the child since shortly after its birth and who had petitioned to adopt the child, lost out in the custody battle. The court clearly said that the law had allowed it to consider only parents' rights and not the child's best interests.

Children's rights and their ability to articulate their rights for themselves in custody matters were strengthened, however, by several well-publicized rulings in which older children were involved. In 1992, an eleven-year-old Florida boy filed suit in his own name, assisted by his own privately retained legal counsel, to terminate his relationship with his biological parents and to have the court affirm his right to be adopted by foster parents. The court granted his request, although it did not agree procedurally with the method by which the boy initiated the suit.[21] The news media characterized the case as the first instance in which a minor child had "divorced" himself from his parents. In 1992, a New York court recognized the rights of an eleven-year-old boy to dismiss a court-appointed attorney and retain a lawyer of his own choosing to represent his interests in a court battle his parents were waging over his custody. In 1993, a court ruled in favor of a fourteen-year-old Florida girl, who had been mistakenly switched at birth and given to the wrong couple. She sued to have a court declare her legally to be the child of her nonbiological parents.[22]

Criminal Rights of Juveniles.   One of the main requirements for an act to be criminal is intent. The law has given children certain defenses against criminal prosecution because of their presumed inability to have criminal intent. Under the **common law,** children up to seven years of age were considered incapable of committing a crime, because they did not have the moral sense to understand that they were doing wrong. Children between the ages of seven and fourteen were also presumed to be incapable of committing a crime, but this presumption could be challenged by showing that the child understood the wrongful nature of the act. Today, states vary in their approaches. Most states retain the common law approach, although age limits vary from state to state. Other states have simply set a minimum age for criminal responsibility.

All states have juvenile court systems that handle children below the age of criminal responsibility who commit delinquent acts. The aim of juvenile courts is allegedly to reform rather than to punish. In states that retain the common law approach, children who are above the minimum age but are still juveniles can be turned over to the criminal courts if the juvenile court determines that they should be treated as adults. Children still do not have the right to trial by

Common Law

Judge-made law that originated in England from decisions shaped according to prevailing customs. Decisions were applied to similar situations and thus gradually became common to the nation.

---

[21]*Kingsley v. Kingsley,* 623 So.2d 780 (Fla.App. 1993).
[22]*The New York Times,* August 19, 1993, p. 16.

This juvenile is being arrested in the same way as an adult would be, but he does not have the rights under criminal law of an adult. Juveniles normally receive less severe punishment than adults do for similar crimes, however.

jury or to post bail. Also, in most states parents can still commit their minor children to state mental institutions without allowing the child a hearing.

Although minors still do not usually have the full rights of adults in criminal proceedings, they have certain advantages. In felony, manslaughter, murder, armed robbery, and assault cases, juveniles usually are not tried as adults. They may be sentenced to probation or "reform" school for a relatively few years regardless of the seriousness of their crimes. Most states, however, allow juveniles to be tried as adults (often at the discretion of the judge) for certain crimes, such as murder. When they are tried as adults, they are treated to due process of law and tried for the crime, rather than being given the paternalistic treatment reserved for the juvenile delinquent.

Juveniles who are tried as adults may also face adult penalties, including the death penalty. Currently, about seventy people are on the nation's death rows for crimes that they committed when they were sixteen or seventeen. Today, there is talk of allowing the execution of even younger people who commit murders. In 1997, after two thirteen-year-olds beat a Sacramento man to death, California governor Pete Wilson said that the death penalty "has to be a possibility" in such cases. Texas state representative Jim Pitts recently said that he would lower the age at which a child can be sentenced to death for murder to eleven. This statement came on the heels of a shooting event at a school in Jonesboro, Arkansas, in which two boys, aged eleven and thirteen, killed four students and a teacher.

What to do about crime committed by juveniles is a pressing problem for today's political leaders. One approach to the problem is to treat juveniles as adults, which more and more judges seem to be doing. There appears to be widespread public support for this approach, as well as for lowering the age at which juveniles should receive adult treatment in criminal proceedings. According to an NBC/*Wall Street Journal* poll released in April 1998, two-thirds of U.S. adults think that juveniles under the age of thirteen who commit murder should be tried as adults. Another approach is to hold parents responsible for the crimes of their minor children (a minority of the states do so under so-called parental-responsibility laws). These are contradictory approaches, to be sure. Yet they perhaps reflect the divided opinion in our society concerning the rights of children versus the rights of parents.

Civil Rights— Beyond Equal Protection: Issues for the New Century

As the twentieth century draws to a close, the future of civil rights in the United States remains somewhat cloudy. Certainly, the controversy over affirmative action policies has not been resolved one way or the other, and America's political leaders and the courts will continue to address this issue in the coming years. Whether bilingual education programs help or hinder the education of immigrant children is another issue that will extend into the foreseeable future.

The expanding proportion of the American population that is over the age of sixty-five will also lead to political and economic conflicts in the future. As senior citizens become a larger percentage of the population, their political power will continue to grow. Undoubtedly, they will clash repeatedly with those who propose cutting or modifying benefits for older Americans or changing the way in which current programs benefiting seniors, such as Social Security and Medicare, are administered. Additionally, persons with disabilities, their employers, and the courts will continue to struggle with what exactly the Americans with Disabilities Act does and does not require.

Although no nation is capable of legislating morality, our government does have a responsibility to create an environment that does not allow state-sanctioned discrimination against any person. Yet gay men and lesbians continue to be subject to anti-gay laws and other discriminatory actions. Clearly, the struggle for equal treatment waged by this group of Americans is far from over.

Finally, the debate over the rights of children has been intensified in recent years by the increase in violent crime committed by teenagers and preteens and the increased awareness of the extent of child abuse in this nation. We can be sure that the controversy over the welfare and rights of children will continue for years to come.

TOWARD ACTIVE CITIZENSHIP

DEALING WITH DISCRIMINATION

When you apply for a job, you may be subjected to a variety of possibly discriminatory practices—based on your race, color, gender, religion, age, national origin, sexual preference, or disability. You may also be subjected to a battery of tests, some of which you may feel are discriminatory. At both state and federal levels, the government has continued to examine the fairness and validity of criteria used in job-applicant screening. If you believe that you have been discriminated against by a potential employer, you may wish to consider the following steps:

1. Evaluate your own capabilities, and determine if you are truly qualified for the position.
2. Analyze the reasons that you were turned down (or dismissed). Do you feel that others would agree with you that you have been the object of discrimination, or would they uphold your employer's claim?
3. If you still believe that you have been unfairly treated, you have recourse to several agencies and services.

You should first speak to the personnel director of the company and politely explain that you feel you have not been adequately evaluated. If asked, explain your concerns clearly. If necessary, go into explicit detail, and indicate that you feel that you may have been discriminated against. If a second evaluation is not forthcoming, contact the local branch of your state employment agency. If you still do not obtain adequate help, contact one or more of the following agencies, usually found by looking in your telephone directory under "State Government" listings.

1. If a government entity is involved, a state ombudsman or citizen aide who will mediate may be available.
2. You may wish to contact the state civil rights commission, which will at least give you advice even if it does not wish to take up your case.
3. The state attorney general's office will normally have a division dealing with discrimination and civil rights.
4. There may be a special commission or department specifically set up to help you, such as a women's status commission or a commission on Hispanics or Asian Americans. If you are a woman or a member of such a minority, contact these commissions.
5. Finally, at the national level, you can contact the American Civil Liberties Union, 132 West 43d St., New York, N.Y. 10036, 212-944-9800, or check

www.aclu.org

You can also contact the most appropriate federal agency: the Equal Employment Opportunity Commission, 1801 L St. N.W., Washington, DC 20507, 202-663-4900, or go to

www.eeoc.gov/

Key terms

affirmative action 187

civil law 205

common law 206

criminal law 205

majority 206

mandatory retirement 196

necessaries 206

reverse discrimination 188

Chapter summary

1 Affirmative action programs have been controversial because they can lead to reverse discrimination against majority groups or even other minority groups. In an early case on the issue, *Regents of the University of California v. Bakke* (1978), the Supreme Court held that using race as the sole criterion for admission to a university is improper. Since *Bakke* a number of Supreme Court decisions have further limited affirmative action programs. Recent Supreme Court decisions, particularly *Adarand Constructors, Inc. v. Peña,* and decisions by the lower courts that the Supreme Court has let stand, such as *Hopwood v. State of Texas,* have led some observers to conclude that it will be difficult in the future for any affirmative action program to pass constitutional muster. California voters banned state-sponsored affirmative action in that state in a 1996 ballot initiative known as Proposition 209, which was upheld as constitutional by a federal appellate court. Whether affirmative action programs will survive the current backlash against them remains to be seen.

2 Bilingual education programs, like affirmative action, have come under attack in recent years by "America-firsters," "English-only" advocates, and critics of multiculturalism. The major criticism against bilingual education programs, however, is that they impede children's ability to learn English quickly and succeed academically.

3 Problems associated with aging and retirement are becoming increasingly important as the number of older persons in the United States increases. Many older Americans have lost their jobs due to age bias and cost-cutting efforts by business firms. The Age Discrimination in Employment Act of 1967 prohibits job-related discrimination against individuals over the age of forty on the basis of age, unless age is shown to be a bona fide occupational qualification reasonably necessary to the normal operation of the business. Amendments to the act prohibit mandatory retirement except in a few selected professions. As a group, older people contribute significantly to American political life, ranking first in voter registration and turnout and being well represented in Congress. Through a variety of organizations, older Americans lobby effectively at both the federal and state levels.

4 In 1973, Congress passed the Rehabilitation Act, which prohibits discrimination against persons with disabilities in programs receiving federal aid. Regulations implementing the act provide for ramps, elevators, and the like in all federal buildings. The Education for All Handicapped Children Act (1975) provides that all children with disabilities receive an "appropriate" education. The Americans with Disabilities Act of 1990 prohibits job discrimination against persons with physical and mental disabilities, requiring that positive steps be taken to comply with the act's requirements. The act also requires expanded access to public facilities, including transportation, and to services offered by such private concerns as car-rental and telephone companies.

5 Gay and lesbian rights groups, which first began to form in 1969, now number in the thousands. These groups work to promote laws protecting gay men and lesbians from discrimination and to repeal anti-gay laws. Since 1969, sodomy laws have been repealed in more than half of the states, and ten states and 165 cities and counties now have laws prohibiting discrimination based on sexual orientation. Gay men and lesbians are no longer barred from federal employment or from immigrating to this country, and Congress is currently considering a bill that would ban employment discrimination against gay men and lesbians. Since 1980, liberal Democrats at the national level have supported gay and lesbian rights and sought electoral support from these groups. The military's "don't ask, don't tell" policy has fueled extensive controversy, as have same-sex marriages and child-custody issues.

6 Although children form a large group of Americans, they have the fewest rights and protections, in part because it is commonly presumed that parents protect their children. The Twenty-sixth Amendment grants the right to vote to those aged eighteen or older. In most states, only contracts entered into for necessaries can be enforced against minors. When minors engage in negligent acts, their parents may be held liable. Minors have some defense against criminal prosecution because of their presumed inability to have criminal intent at certain ages. For those below the age of criminal responsibility, there are state juvenile courts. When minors are tried as adults, they receive all of

Selected print and electronic resources

SUGGESTED READINGS

Bolick, Clint. *The Affirmative Action Fraud: Can We Restore the American Civil Rights Vision?* Washington, D.C.: The Cato Institute, 1996. Bolick argues that race-based preferences have dramatically widened the racial divide in the United States.

Lawrence, Charles R., III, and Mari J. Matsuda. *We Won't Go Back: Making the Case for Affirmative Action.* St. Charles, Ill.: Houghton Mifflin, 1997. The authors look at how affirmative action policies have benefited people. They focus on the human side of the debate over this divisive issue and include in their book a variety of stories showing how these policies have affected the everyday lives of numerous Americans.

Leone, Bruno, et al., eds. *Child Welfare: Opposing Viewpoints.* San Diego, Calif.: Greenhaven Press, 1998. This "issues" book presents opposing viewpoints on various aspects of child welfare.

Roemer, John E. *Equality of Opportunity.* Cambridge, Mass.: Harvard University Press, 1998. Roemer examines the two positions in the affirmative action debate and concludes that both emphasize equal opportunity; they differ over whether equal opportunity should be required before or after the competition (such as for jobs) starts.

Sleeper, Jim. *Liberal Racism.* New York: Viking Press, 1997. This book offers a liberal's perspective on why racial preferences should be eliminated.

MEDIA RESOURCES

Affirmative Action: The History of an Idea—This program explores the historical roots of affirmative action and the current debate over its usefulness.

Shot by a Kid—A film documenting the relationship among children, guns, and violence in four major cities of the United States.

Logging on

For information on, and arguments in support of, affirmative action and the rights of the groups discussed in this chapter, a good source is the American Civil Liberties Union's Web site

www.aclu.org/

The National Organization for Women (NOW) offers online information and updates on the status of women's rights, including affirmative action cases involving women. Go to

www.now.org/

An excellent source for information on discrimination based on age and disability is the Equal Employment Opportunity Commission's Web site at

www.eeoc.gov/

You can find information on the Americans with Disabilities Act (ADA) of 1990, including the act's text, at

janweb.icdi.wvu.edu/kinder

You can access the Web site of the Human Rights Campaign Fund, the nation's largest gay and lesbian political organization, at

www.hrc.org/

If you are interested in children's rights and welfare, a good starting place is the Web site of the Child Welfare Institute. Go to

www.gocwi.org/

Using the Internet for political analysis

Imagine that you are the owner of a new franchise business and are hiring your first employees. Several of the applicants are over the age of sixty-five, and one of them tells you that she has impaired hearing but has a good hearing aid to assist her.

Using one of the Web sites given in the next column, look up Labor and Employment Law and develop some guidelines for your hiring practices that will not violate laws prohibiting discrimination against older Americans and workers with disabilities. Consider the information

that you find on the Web. To what extent would you rely on this information when you write an employment manual? What other resources might you also check?

FindLaw, at **www.findlaw.com/**
U.S. House of Representatives Law Library, at **law.house.gov/**
Legal Resource Guide, at **www.ilrg.com/**

People and Politics

PART 3

chapter **7**

Public Opinion

Courts Used Public Opinion Polls to Decide Cases?

BACKGROUND

IN THE UNITED STATES, THE GUILT OR INNOCENCE OF ANYONE ON TRIAL IS DETERMINED EITHER BY A JUDGE OR A PANEL OF JUDGES OR, ACCORDING TO ANCIENT BRITISH PRACTICE, A JURY OF THAT PERSON'S PEERS. THE JURY SYSTEM WAS DEVELOPED TO ASSURE ORDINARY PEOPLE THE OPPORTUNITY TO GET A FAIR HEARING FROM OTHER MEMBERS OF SOCIETY. TODAY, THE JURY POOL—A GROUP OF THOSE ELIGIBLE TO BE CHOSEN TO SIT ON A JURY—NORMALLY IS A RANDOM SELECTION OF INDIVIDUALS WHO ARE REGISTERED TO VOTE.

WITH THE ADVENT OF TELEVISED TRIALS AND EXTENSIVE MEDIA COVERAGE OF HIGH-PROFILE CASES, THE POSSIBILITY ARISES THAT THE JURY OR JUDGE MAY BE INFLUENCED BY MEDIA COMMENTARY OR BY REPORTED PUBLIC OPINION ABOUT GUILT OR INNOCENCE. PERHAPS IT WOULD BE FAIRER TO A PERSON ON TRIAL TO HAVE HIS OR HER CASE DECIDED BY A SCIENTIFICALLY CONDUCTED POLL OF PUBLIC OPINION.

WHAT IF COURTS USED PUBLIC OPINION POLLS TO DECIDE CASES?

Given that relatively few individuals ever commit the time to serve on a jury, scientifically selecting a sample of adult Americans to decide the outcome of a trial might provide a much more representative group to listen to the evidence presented in the court and then make a decision. To give some validity to the opinions, the sample would be much larger than a jury—say, at least 1,200 persons. The opinions expressed by the jury, then, would represent the opinions of all the people living in that jurisdiction and, perhaps more importantly, would include the views of individuals who are excluded from jury duty by employment, infirmity, or their own choice.

How would the public gain enough information to make a decision about a trial? Some trials, of course, are televised. Persons selected to be polled could be asked to watch news summaries of the trial or the trial itself. Or, those charged with devising the poll could give the individuals enough information in the survey to enable them to have an opinion. Today, many prosecutors and defense attorneys use similar kinds of polling to find out what kind of jurors are most likely to be favorable to their clients or how much of an award might be expected if their clients are successful in their suits. Polling "tests" the community's opinion before and during trials. Although today's jurors often are asked not to watch news about their trials, inevitably jurors have seen public opinion polls about cases such as that of O. J. Simpson before they begin serving on the jury.

Using a poll of public opinion to try cases would lead to radical changes in the roles of the court, the judge, and the attorneys. The judge might need to coordinate the design of the survey and supervise the provision of information by the attorneys from both sides. There would be little use for charismatic attorneys in the courtroom. Instead, attorneys would likely spend even more time on television trying to shape community opinion.

CAN THE PUBLIC JUDGE A TRIAL?

There is a lot of evidence about how the public follows high-profile trials such as that of O. J. Simpson or the British nanny, Louise Woodward. Even though most Americans do not follow the actual transcripts of such trials and may not be knowledgeable about the points of law raised in the courtroom, Americans are quite willing to form opinions about guilt or innocence and to tell them to the pollster. One of the shortcomings of any public opinion poll is the tendency of respondents to answer any question asked whether they have sufficient information to have an opinion or not. Sometimes, respondents just want to end the interview politely, so they answer the questions.

In addition, polls generally indicate that over the months of a trial, public views tend to be less than stable. The wording of questions can also make a difference in the results obtained by surveys.

FOR CRITICAL ANALYSIS

1. Can you think of some cases, such as those against the tobacco industry or those dealing with asbestos, that might be suitable to be decided by public opinion?
2. Why might some defendants think that they might have a better chance in the court of public opinion than in a real courtroom? What could they do to sway public opinion to their advantage?

Public opinion polls can give voice to the preferences of the people between elections. These preferences may relate to the distribution of power between the national government and the states, and the future role of the nation in the world. Furthermore, public opinion, whether expressed through scientifically conducted opinion polls or directly over the Internet, can reflect the public's views on specific policy actions in a way that elections cannot. What role, then, does public opinion play in the changing American political system? Is it truly the voice of the people, or is it an instrument to be manipulated by politicians and interest groups? Can political leaders count on public opinion to provide guidance on their actions, or are the results of most opinion polls too ephemeral to be useful? (For George Washington's views on public opinion, see the feature *E-Mail Messages from the Past*.)

The very character of public opinion polls may limit their usefulness. After all, the pollster wrote the questions, called the respondents, and perhaps forwarded the results to the politicians. Public opinion, as gathered by polls, is not equivalent to constituents' letters to their representatives or to ballots cast in an election. In fact, polls may be flawed in a number of ways. As the chapter-opening *What If . . .* suggests, however, polls have become a frequent component of the political and judicial process.

INFOTRAC ®
COLLEGE EDITION

"Preparing for Trial: An Uncommon Approach"

How Powerful Is Public Opinion?

At various times in the recent history of the United States, public opinion has played a powerful role in presidential politics. Beginning in 1965, public opinion became strongly divided over the Vietnam War (1964–1975). Numerous public expressions of opposition to the war took place, as measured by the polls and demonstrations in many cities. By 1968, when Lyndon Johnson was preparing to run for another term, public opinion against the war was expressed through a surge of support for antiwar candidate Senator Eugene McCarthy in the New Hampshire primary. Faced with public disapproval, Johnson dropped out of the race.

As the scandal surrounding the 1972 **Watergate break-in** unfolded, revealing the role of President Richard Nixon through congressional hearings and tape

Watergate Break-in
The 1972 illegal entry into the Democratic National Committee offices by participants in Richard Nixon's reelection campaign.

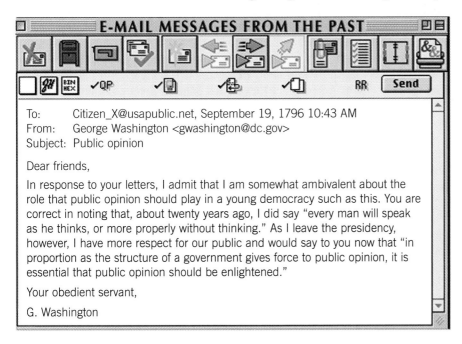

E-MAIL MESSAGES FROM THE PAST

To: Citizen_X@usapublic.net, September 19, 1796 10:43 AM
From: George Washington <gwashington@dc.gov>
Subject: Public opinion

Dear friends,

In response to your letters, I admit that I am somewhat ambivalent about the role that public opinion should play in a young democracy such as this. You are correct in noting that, about twenty years ago, I did say "every man will speak as he thinks, or more properly without thinking." As I leave the presidency, however, I have more respect for our public and would say to you now that "in proportion as the structure of a government gives force to public opinion, it is essential that public opinion should be enlightened."

Your obedient servant,

G. Washington

Those who wish to have legislation passed often muster the forces of public opinion to help convince Congress to pass it. Here you see citizens voicing their opinions on health-care reform.

Public Opinion
The aggregate of individual attitudes or beliefs shared by some portion of the adult population. There is no one public opinion, because there are many different "publics."

recordings from his office, a similar groundswell of opinion against the president occurred. In this case, the disastrous fall in the president's approval ratings to less than 25 percent coincided with the decision by the House Judiciary Committee to initiate impeachment proceedings against the president. Nixon, facing an impeachment trial, resigned from office.

Public opinion polls also can be seen as a measure of a president's strength. As charges about his personal life were debated openly in the media, President Clinton's presidential approval rating climbed to the highest point in his presidency. Given the surge of positive public opinion, even his strongest critics in Congress at that time felt that they could not wage political attacks on Clinton or consider impeachment proceedings against him. They believed that their own popularity would suffer if they did.

In most situations, legislators, politicians, and presidents use public opinion to shore up their own arguments. It provides a kind of evidence for their own point of view. If the results of polls do not support their positions, they can either commission their own polls or ignore the polls. Politicians find it more difficult to use public opinion on complex issues, such as changes in Medicare or welfare reform, because such complicated issues cannot be discussed fully in a poll. People will give opinions when asked, but poll questions do not really provide the opportunity for discussion and dialogue. Public opinion is more likely to be unfavorable when it comes to the use of troops overseas, but presidents who are able to limit the casualties among American troops sent on a military mission have much more freedom from the constraints of public opinion. President Clinton was able to secure such freedom with the almost casualty-free missions of American troops in both Haiti and Bosnia. Public opinion, then, is neither all powerful nor powerless.

Defining Public Opinion

There is no one public opinion, because there are many different "publics." In a nation of over 270 million people, there may be innumerable gradations of opinion on an issue. What we do is describe the distribution of opinions among the public about a particular question. Thus, we define **public opinion** as the aggregate of individual attitudes or beliefs shared by some portion of the adult population.

Often, the public holds quite a range of opinions on a topic, making it difficult to discern what kinds of policies most Americans might support. For example, as Congress debated passing legislation to regulate the tobacco industry, frequent polls asked Americans their views on such policies. Most polls showed that the majority of Americans believed that smoking-related illnesses were the fault of the smokers themselves (67 percent), rather than of the companies (19 percent), yet Americans were divided evenly on whether private suits against the companies by those who had such illnesses should be limited. Americans generally approved of having tobacco companies help pay for health insurance for poor children but were not sure whether those companies should be banned from sponsoring sporting events.

How is public opinion made known in a democracy? In the case of the Vietnam War, it was made known by numerous antiwar protests, countless articles in magazines and newspapers, and continuing electronic media coverage of antiwar demonstrations. Normally, however, public opinion becomes known in a democracy through elections and, in some states, initiatives or referenda (see Chapter 19). Other ways are through lobbying and interest group activities, which are also used to influence public opinion (see Chapter 8). In the age of the Internet, citizens increasingly are able to send their opinions to government officials electronically.

Consensus and Division

There are very few issues on which most Americans agree. The more normal situation is for opinion to be distributed among several different positions. Looking at the distribution of opinion can tell us how divided the public is on a question and give us some indication of whether compromise is possible. The distribution of opinion can also tell us how many individuals have not thought enough about an issue to hold an opinion.

When a large proportion of the American public appears to express the same view on an issue, we say that a **consensus** exists, at least at the moment the poll was taken. Figure 7–1 shows the pattern of opinion that might be called consensual. Issues on which the public holds widely differing attitudes result in **divisive opinion** (Figure 7–2). If there is no possible middle position on such issues, we expect that the division will continue to generate political conflict.

Figure 7–3 shows a distribution of opinion indicating that most Americans either have no information about the issue or are not interested enough in the issue to formulate a position. Politicians may feel that the lack of knowledge gives them more room to maneuver, or they may be wary of taking any action for fear that opinion will crystallize after a crisis.

Public opinion can be defined most clearly by its effect. As political scientist V. O. Key, Jr., said, public opinion is what governments "find it prudent to heed."[1] This means that for public opinion to be effective, enough people have to hold a particular view with such strong conviction that a government feels its actions should be influenced by that view.

An interesting question arises as to when *private* opinion becomes *public* opinion. Everyone probably has a private opinion about the competence of the president, as well as private opinions about more personal concerns, such as the state of a neighbor's lawn. We say that private opinion becomes public opinion when the opinion is publicly expressed and if the opinion concerns public issues. When someone's private opinion becomes so strong that the individual is willing to go to the polls to vote for or against a candidate or an issue—or is willing to

[1]V. O. Key, Jr., *Public Opinion and American Democracy* (New York: Knopf, 1961), p. 10.

Consensus
General agreement among the citizenry on an issue.

Divisive Opinion
Public opinion that is polarized between two quite different positions.

FIGURE 7–1
Consensus Opinion

Question: Do you think it is morally acceptable to clone human beings?

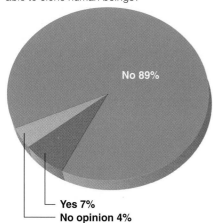

SOURCE: Survey by Yankelovich Partners, Inc., for *Time*/CNN, February 26–27, 1997.

FIGURE 7–2
Divisive Opinion

Question: Do you think it would be a good thing or a bad thing for the tobacco companies in this country to be driven out of business by a lawsuit?

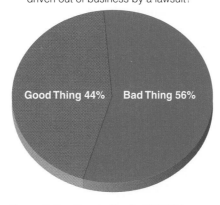

SOURCE: Gallup Organization for CNN/*USA Today*, May 6–7, 1997.

FIGURE 7–3
Nonopinion

Question: Do you favor or oppose NAFTA (North American Free Trade Agreement) or don't you know enough about NAFTA to say?

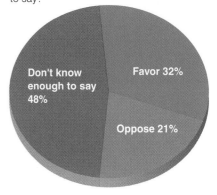

SOURCE: Survey by CBS News/*New York Times*, August 3–5, 1996.

Union members protest a cut in benefits. A strike can be seen as an expression of public opinion, but if the union does not get support from others, politicians will feel little effect.

participate in a demonstration, to discuss the issue at work, to speak out on local television or a radio talk show, or to participate in the political process in any one of a dozen other ways—then that opinion becomes public opinion.

The Qualities of Public Opinion

At the beginning of the Vietnam War in the 1960s, public opinion about its conduct was not very clear, like a camera that is not focused. As the war progressed and U.S. involvement deepened, public opinion became increasingly clarified. In that case, as in most cases, public opinion has identifiable qualities that change over time. Political scientists have identified some qualities to describe public opinion: (1) intensity, (2) fluidity, (3) stability, (4) relevance, and (5) political knowledge.

Intensity.   How strongly people are willing to express their private opinions determines the **intensity** of public opinion. Consider an example that was in the news regularly for a time—the state of democracy in Haiti. Most Americans did not have strong opinions about the future of democracy in this island nation. They did, however, have more intense opinions about whether American troops should remain in Haiti to keep the peace. Opinions were even more intense about whether Haitians should be allowed to immigrate to the United States in large numbers. Intense opinions held by such groups as the voters of Florida can have a much greater impact on national politics than their numbers would suggest.

Intensity
The strength of a position for or against a public policy or an issue. Intensity is often critical in generating public action; an intense minority can often win on an issue of public policy over a less intense majority.

Fluidity.   Public opinion can change drastically in a very short period of time. When this occurs, we say that public opinion is fluid. At the end of World War II, for example, the American people were about evenly divided in their opinions of the U.S. wartime ally, the Soviet Union. A 1945 Roper poll showed that about 39 percent of Americans saw the Soviets as peace loving, whereas 38 percent felt they were aggressive. During the years of the Cold War (1947 to, roughly, 1985), American opinion about the aims of the Soviet Union was very consistent. Between 13 and 17 percent of the American people believed that the Soviet Union was peace loving, and more than 60 percent saw it as aggressive. As Americans witnessed first the opening of the Soviet Union to Western influences and then the breakdown of the Soviet Union, American opinion about the Soviet Union changed quickly. Between 1985 and 1990, the number of Americans who saw the Soviet Union as peace loving increased from 17 to 43 percent.[2] And by 1996, only 12 percent of Americans saw Russia as an enemy of the United States. The **fluidity** of American opinion was a response to the rapidly changing conditions in the Soviet Union and world politics. Such fluidity in public opinion reflects public awareness of government policy and in turn influences government decision making.

Stability. Many individual opinions remain constant over a lifetime. Taken together, individual opinions that constitute public opinion may also be extremely stable, persisting for many years. Consider the effect of the Civil War on political attitudes in the South. In the eyes of southerners, the Republicans under Abraham Lincoln were responsible for the Civil War and the ensuing humiliations experienced by a defeated South. Consequently, the South became strongly Democratic. Until the post–World War II period, it was called the **Solid South,** because Democratic candidates nearly always won. We can say that public opinion in the South in favor of Democrats and against Republicans had great **stability.**

Relevance. Relevant public opinion for most people is simply public opinion that deals with issues concerning them. If a person has a sick parent who is having trouble meeting medical bills, then public opinion that is focused on the issues of Medicare or Medicaid will be relevant for that person. If another person likes to go hunting with his or her children, gun control becomes a relevant political issue. Of course, **relevance** changes according to events. Public concern about inflation, for example, was at an all-time low during the late 1980s and most of the 1990s. Why? Because the United States had relatively little inflation during that period. Public opinion about the issue of unemployment certainly was relevant during the Great Depression of the 1930s, but not in the 1960s, when the nation experienced 102 months of almost uninterrupted economic growth from 1961 to 1969, or in the late 1990s, when unemployment reached a thirty-year low.

---

[2]*The Public Perspective,* August/September, 1997, p. 30.

Fluidity
The extent to which public opinion changes over time.

Solid South
A term describing the tendency of the post–Civil War southern states to vote for the Democratic Party. (Voting patterns in the South have changed, though.)

Stability
The extent to which public opinion remains constant over a period of time.

Relevance
The extent to which an issue is of concern at a particular time. Issues become relevant when the public views them as pressing or of direct concern to daily life.

Reprinted with special permission of King Features Syndicate.

Certain popular books or spectacular events can make a particular issue relevant. A succession of violent acts—including the bombing of the Alfred P. Murrah Federal Building in Oklahoma City in 1995, the bombing of an American military compound in Saudi Arabia in 1996, and the bombing of the American embassies in the African countries of Kenya and Tanzania in 1998—made violence and terrorism increasingly relevant for many citizens in the late 1990s.

Political Knowledge.   People are more likely to base their opinions on knowledge about an issue if they have strong feelings about the topic. Just as relevance and intensity are closely related to having an opinion, individuals who are strongly interested in a question will probably take the time to read about it.

Looking at the population as a whole, the level of political information is modest. Survey research tells us that slightly less than 29 percent of adult Americans can give the name of their congresspersons, and just 25 percent can name both U.S. senators from their states. Only 34 percent of adults know that Congress declares war,[3] though almost 70 percent know the majority party in Congress. What these data tell us is that Americans do not expend much effort remembering political facts that may not be important to their daily lives.

Americans are also likely to forget political information quite quickly. Facts that are of vital interest to citizens in a time of crisis lose their significance after the crisis has passed. In the 1985 *New York Times*/CBS News Survey on Vietnam, marking the tenth anniversary of the end of that conflict, 63 percent of those questioned knew that the United States sided with the South Vietnamese in that conflict. Only 27 percent remembered, however, which side in that conflict launched the Tet offensive, which was a major political defeat for American and South Vietnamese forces.

If political information is perceived to be of no use to an individual or is painful to recall, it is not surprising that facts are forgotten. It is disconcerting to learn, however, that Americans have little or no information about policy decisions that have the potential to change our world. In June 1997, for example, 40 percent of Americans had not heard that Hong Kong was reverting to rule by China, and in 1997, as Congress was considering whether to admit new nations to the North Atlantic Treaty Organization (NATO) at a cost of billions of dollars to the United States, 71 percent of those questioned had heard not very much or nothing at all about the expansion of NATO.[4] Politicians can use this lack of interest to justify either voting as they see fit or opposing any initiative.

Measuring Public Opinion: Polling Techniques

The History of Opinion Polls

Although some idea of public opinion can be discovered by asking persons we know for their opinions or by reading the "Letters to the Editor" sections in newspapers, most descriptions of the distribution of opinions are based on **opinion polls.** During the 1800s, certain American newspapers and magazines spiced up their political coverage by doing face-to-face straw polls (unofficial polls indicating the trend of political opinion) or mail surveys of their readers' opinions. In this century, the magazine *Literary Digest* further developed the technique of opinion polls by mailing large numbers of questionnaires to indi-

Opinion Poll
A method of systematically questioning a small, selected sample of respondents who are deemed representative of the total population. Opinion polls are widely used by government, business, university scholars, political candidates, and voluntary groups to provide reasonably accurate data on public attitudes, beliefs, expectations, and behavior.

---

[3]Michael X. Delli Carpini and Scott Keeter, "The Public's Knowledge of Politics," in J. David Dennamar, ed., *Public Opinion, the Press, and Public Policy* (Westport, Conn.: Praeger, 1992), p. 29.
[4]*The Public Perspective,* August/September 1997, p. 10.

viduals, many of whom were its own subscribers. From 1916 to 1936, more than 70 percent of the magazine's election predictions were accurate.

Literary Digest's polling activities suffered a major setback in 1936, however, when the magazine predicted, based on more than two million returned questionnaires, that Republican candidate Alfred Landon would win over Democratic candidate Franklin D. Roosevelt. Landon won in only two states. A major problem with the *Digest*'s polling technique was its continuing use of nonrepresentative respondents. In 1936, at the bottom of the Great Depression, the magazine's subscribers were, for one thing, considerably more affluent than the average American.

Several newcomers to the public opinion poll industry accurately predicted Roosevelt's landslide victory. The organizations of these newcomers are still active in the poll-taking industry today: the Gallup poll of George Gallup, and the Roper poll founded by Elmo Roper. Gallup and Roper, along with Archibald Crossley, developed the modern polling techniques of market research. Using personal interviews with small samples of selected voters (less than a few thousand), they showed that they could predict with accuracy the behavior of the total voting population. We shall see how this is possible.

Government officials during World War II were keenly interested in public opinion about the war effort and about the increasing number of restrictions placed on civilian activities. Improved methods of sampling were used, and by the 1950s, a whole new science of survey research was developed, which soon spread to Western Europe, Israel, and other countries. Survey research centers sprang up throughout the United States, particularly at universities. Some of these survey groups are the American Institute of Public Opinion at Princeton, New Jersey; the National Opinion Research Center at the University of Chicago; and the Survey Research Center at the University of Michigan.

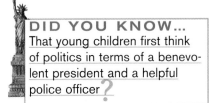

Sampling Techniques

How can interviewing fewer than two thousand voters tell us what tens of millions of voters will do? Clearly, it is necessary that the sample of individuals be representative of all voters in the population. Consider an analogy. Let's say we have a large jar containing ten thousand pennies of various dates, and we want to know how many pennies were minted within certain decades (1950–1959, 1960–1969, and so on). One way to estimate the distribution of the dates on the pennies—without examining all ten thousand—is to take a representative sample. This sample would be obtained by mixing the pennies up well and then removing a handful of them—perhaps one hundred pennies. The distribution of dates might be as follows:

- *1950–1959: 5 percent.*
- *1960–1969: 5 percent.*
- *1970–1979: 20 percent.*
- *1980–1989: 30 percent.*
- *1990–present: 40 percent.*

If the pennies are very well mixed within the jar, and if you take a large enough sample, the resulting distribution would probably approach the actual distribution of the dates of all ten thousand coins.

The most important principle in sampling, or poll taking, is randomness. Every penny or every person should have a known chance, and especially an *equal chance,* of being sampled. If this happens, then a small sample should be representative of the whole group, both in demographic characteristics (age, religion, race, living area, and the like) and in opinions. The ideal way to sample the voting population of the United States would be to put all voter names into

This woman is participating in a *Los Angeles Times* exit poll after casting her vote in the 1996 election.

"Should the Census Bureau Use Statistical Sampling"

a jar—or a computer—and randomly sample, say, two thousand of them. Because this is too costly and inefficient, pollsters have developed other ways to obtain good samples. One of the most interesting techniques is simply to choose a random selection of telephone numbers and interview the respective households. This technique produces a relatively accurate sample at a low cost.

To ensure that the random samples include respondents from relevant segments of the population—rural, urban, Northeast, South, and so on—most survey organizations randomly choose, say, urban areas that they will consider as representative of all urban areas. Then they randomly select their respondents within those areas. A generally less accurate technique is known as *quota sampling*. For this type of poll, survey researchers decide how many persons of certain types they need in the survey—such as minorities, women, or farmers—and then send out interviewers to find the necessary number of these types. This method is often not only less accurate, but it also may be biased if, say, the interviewer refuses to go into certain neighborhoods or will not interview after dark.

Generally, the national survey organizations take great care to select their samples randomly, because their reputations rest on the accuracy of their results. Usually, the Gallup or Roper polls interview about 1,500 individuals, and their results have a very high probability of being correct—within a margin of 3 percent. The accuracy with which the Gallup poll has predicted national election results is reflected in Table 7–1. (One of the problems with polling via the Internet is the difficulty of obtaining scientific samples—see the feature *Politics Wired: Polling in Cyberspace*.)

Similar sampling techniques are used in many other, nonpolitical situations. For the Nielsen ratings of television programs, for example, representative households are selected by the A. C. Nielsen Company, and a machine is attached

POLITICS WIRED

Polling in Cyberspace

Given the millions of Americans who are now able to access the World Wide Web, conducting public opinion polling on the Internet would seem to be an easy and efficient way to reach a very large sample of Americans and thus to obtain more accurate and more representative polling results.

Not surprisingly, polling on the Internet is a rapidly growing enterprise, and many Web sites encourage the expression of individual opinions on political issues. These sites range from nonpartisan sites maintained by organizations that are trying to increase participation, to the White House and the national party sites, to sites maintained by newspapers, such as *USA Today*.

Polling on the Web may seem like a good idea, but at this point it is extremely vulnerable to sampling error and manipulation. For one thing, not all Americans are represented equally on the Internet: recent studies have shown that Americans who are poor or members of minority groups are less likely than others to use the Internet. Also, not all Americans who can access the Web do so, nor are all likely to be "tuned in" when the poll is taken.

Probably the biggest problem with polling on the Internet is the amount of bias in any results that are published. Because sending your views to your favorite political party or newspaper is virtually free and takes little effort, opinions likely will be skewed toward those of the group sponsoring the poll. People will write to those who agree with them. Indeed, to improve the poll numbers, groups of people who are intensely interested in an issue will send their collective views thousands of times to those who agree with them.

At this point, polling on the Internet is useful only when the poll is used to find

a targeted audience and, most likely, to ask this audience questions related to the issues they have in common. Even with a limited group, such as computer executives, no one as yet has solved the problem of how to obtain a scientific sample of users to poll.

FOR CRITICAL ANALYSIS

How should the president of the United States or the speaker of the House of Representatives weigh the thousands of opinions on important issues that are received via the Internet?

to each household's television set. The machine monitors viewing choices twenty-four hours a day and transmits this information to the company's central offices. A one-point drop in a Nielsen rating can mean a loss of revenue of millions of dollars to a television network. A one-point drop indicates that about 800,000 fewer viewers are watching a particular show. As a result, advertisers

TABLE 7-1

Gallup Poll Accuracy Record

YEAR	GALLUP FINAL SURVEY		ELECTION RESULTS		DEVIATION*
1996	52.0%	CLINTON	49.0%	CLINTON	−3.0
1994	58.0	Republican	51.0	Republican	+7.0
1992†	49.0	CLINTON	43.2	CLINTON	+5.8
1990	54.0	Democratic	54.1	Democratic	−0.1
1988	56.0	BUSH	53.9	BUSH	−2.1
1984	59.0	REAGAN	59.1	REAGAN	−0.1
1982	55.0	Democratic	56.1	Democratic	−1.1
1980	47.0	REAGAN	50.8	REAGAN	−3.8
1978	55.0	Democratic	54.6	Democratic	+0.4
1976	48.0	CARTER	50.0	CARTER	−2.0
1974	60.0	Democratic	58.9	Democratic	+1.1
1972	62.0	NIXON	61.8	NIXON	+0.2
1970	53.0	Democratic	54.3	Democratic	−1.3
1968	43.0	NIXON	43.5	NIXON	−0.5
1966	52.5	Democratic	51.9	Democratic	+0.6
1964	64.0	JOHNSON	61.3	JOHNSON	+2.7
1962	55.5	Democratic	52.7	Democratic	+2.8
1960	51.0	KENNEDY	50.1	KENNEDY	+0.9
1958	57.0	Democratic	56.5	Democratic	+0.5
1956	59.5	EISENHOWER	57.8	EISENHOWER	+1.7
1954	51.5	Democratic	52.7	Democratic	−1.2
1952	51.0	EISENHOWER	55.4	EISENHOWER	−4.4
1950	51.0	Democratic	50.3	Democratic	+0.7
1948	44.5	TRUMAN	49.9	TRUMAN	−5.4
1946	58.0	Republican	54.3	Republican	+3.7
1944	51.5	ROOSEVELT	53.3	ROOSEVELT	−1.8
1942	52.0	Democratic	48.0	Democratic	+4.0
1940	52.0	ROOSEVELT	55.0	ROOSEVELT	−3.0
1938	54.0	Democratic	50.8	Democratic	+3.2
1936	55.7	ROOSEVELT	62.5	ROOSEVELT	−6.8

Note: No congressional poll done in 1986.
*Average deviation for 30 national elections: 2.4 percent.

TREND IN DEVIATION:
Elections	Average Error
1936–1950	3.6
1952–1996	2.0

† The Ross Perot candidacy created an additional source of error in estimating the 1992 presidential vote. There was no historical precedent for Perot, an independent candidate who was accorded equal status to the major party nominees in the presidential debates and had a record advertising budget. Gallup's decision to allocate none of the undecided vote to Perot, based on past performance of third party and independent candidates, resulted in the overestimation of Clinton's vote.

SOURCE: *The Gallup Poll Monthly,* November 1992; *Time,* November 21, 1994; *Wall Street Journal,* November 6, 1996.

are unwilling to pay as much for viewing time. Indeed, in many cases advertising rates are based solely on Nielsen ratings. When you consider that only about three thousand families have that little machine attached to their television sets, it is apparent that the science of selecting representative samples has come a long way—at least far enough to convince major advertisers to accept advertising fees based on the results of those samples. (For a discussion of whether polls should be used in conducting the national census, see this chapter's *Critical Perspective*.)

Problems with Polls

Public opinion polls are, as noted above, snapshots of the opinions and preferences of the people at a specific moment in time and as expressed in response to a specific question. Given that definition, it is fairly easy to understand situations in which the polls are wrong. For example, opinion polls leading up to the 1980 presidential election showed President Jimmy Carter defeating challenger Ronald Reagan. Only a few analysts noted the large number of

Critical perspective

The Politics of Using a Poll to Conduct the Census

As you are aware, the federal government conducts a census of all the households and individuals in the nation at the beginning of each decade. The last decennial census was taken in 1990; the next one will be taken in the year 2000. The U.S. Constitution requires that a census be taken for the purpose of determining how congressional districts are to be reapportioned among the states. Since the number of seats in the House of Representatives was limited to 435 in the Reapportionment Act of 1929, the number of representatives for each state is recalculated after each decennial census. As you will read in Chapter 12, Congress assigns legislative seats in Congress to each state based on the census count, but the redrawing of the actual boundaries of congressional districts is left to the states.

The Controversy over Census Counts

The last three census counts have given rise to considerable controversy. Members of minority groups and mayors of large cities claimed that the censuses undercounted their populations. Such undercounts might be due to a reluctance of census personnel to go into urban neighborhoods, the relative lack of minority census takers, a lack of trust in the government among certain groups, language barriers in immigrant neighborhoods, and possibly a lack of competence within the census operation.

In any event, an undercount can have extremely serious political and financial consequences. One consequence of an undercount might be the loss of a congressional district by a state and its local governments. Another is the loss of federal funds and programs that are tied to census data. Following recent census counts, urban areas appeared to be losing their congressional seats to suburban areas and to states with significant population growth.

The U.S. Census Bureau actually uses scientific polling to conduct much of its business—except for the decennial census. Monthly polls are used to produce updated estimates of the population. The bureau also uses polling for many other projects required by law. To add fuel to the debate over the census, these other "counts," relying on survey research and the technique of "sampling" the population, have supported the argument that some groups were undercounted in recent decennial censuses. After the 1990 census, the bureau recommended adjusted "counts" to correct for undercounting in some areas.

What If Polling Techniques Were Used in the Year 2000 Census?

To improve the process for the year 2000, the Census Bureau proposed using the standard mail and personal survey for 90 percent of the count and then using a scientific poll for the other 10 percent of the survey. The bureau suggested that this approach would give the best possible count, lessen the need to "adjust" counts, "undecided" respondents to poll questions a week before the election. Those voters shifted massively to Reagan at the last minute, and Reagan won the election.

The famous photo of Harry Truman showing the front page that declared his defeat (see page 228) is another tribute to the weakness of polling. Again, the poll that predicted his defeat was taken more than a week before election day.

Polls may also report erroneous results because the pool of respondents was not chosen in a scientific manner. That is, the form of sampling and the number of people sampled may be too small to overcome **sampling error,** which is the difference between the sample results and the true result if the entire population had been interviewed. The sample would be biased, for example, if the poll interviewed people by telephone and did not correct for the fact that more women than men answer the telephone and that some populations (college students and very poor individuals, for example) cannot be found so easily by telephone. Unscientific mail-in polls, telephone call-in polls, and polls completed by the workers in a campaign office are usually biased and do not give an accurate picture of the public's views.

Sampling Error
The difference between a sample's results and the true result if the entire population had been interviewed.

Critical perspective

The Politics of Using a Poll to Conduct the Census—continued

and reduce the number of federal court cases that were generated by the adjusting procedure.

Many members of Congress were appalled by the proposal. The director of the bureau resigned amidst the conflict over the new method. Republicans were portrayed as opposing sampling as a method because it might aid groups that were traditionally Democratic voters. Other members of Congress attacked the use of polling because of its other uses. Some experts wondered if using polling might further undermine trust in the process and encourage some individuals to avoid the census because they would be "counted" through the polling process. Other experts charged that those who opposed using a sampling process were antiscientific.

What difference would it make if the census were conducted by polling techniques? If the poll were scientifically conducted and used a large enough sample, say, 100,000 households, it would probably be more accurate than the door-to-door count. The poll would also be less expensive and more efficient. Because it would be a sample, however, it might provide a less accurate description of the population of each individual community. For example, what would happen if the census suggested that several dozen Asian Americans lived in a particular city or county but no county official or local government worker could ever find more than one or two? Would the county be subjected to scrutiny because the supposed

number of Asian Americans never materialized?

At the same time, states probably would be well served by a census conducted in this way. The counts would probably be more accurate than under the older method, and the states would be apportioned the correct number of congressional districts with far greater certainty.

Ultimately, this issue will be decided by the courts. In 1998, a federal court held that using sampling techniques violates the Constitution's requirement for an enumeration. If, on appeal, the Supreme Court agrees with the lower court, then a constitutional amendment would be necessary to allow the use of polls in taking the census.

If you are interested in more information about the debate over the 2000 census and the report of the House committee that dealt with this topic, look for House Report 821 at

www.thomas.loc.gov/cp104

FOR CRITICAL ANALYSIS

1. Why would a scientific poll be more accurate than the door-to-door census of the past? Would you trust the results of such a poll?
2. Think about your state. How would an accurate count of the population be advantageous or disadvantageous to your state in the next decade?

President Harry S. Truman holds up the front page of the *Chicago Daily Tribune* issue that predicted his defeat on the basis of a Gallup poll. The poll had indicated that Truman would lose the 1948 contest for his reelection by a margin of 55.5 to 44.5 percent. Gallup's poll was completed more than two weeks before the election, so it missed the undecided voters. Truman won the election with 49.9 percent of the vote.

As poll takers get close to election day, they become even more concerned about their sample of respondents. Some pollsters continue to interview eligible voters, meaning those over eighteen and registered to vote. Many others use a series of questions in the poll and other weighting methods to try to identify "likely voters" so that they can be more accurate in their election-eve

POLITICS and Technology

The Interviewer Becomes a Machine

As you have read in this chapter, public opinion pollsters began to develop a scientific basis for sampling the population and asking questions in the late 1930s and during World War II (1941–1945). For several decades after the war, good polls were conducted only by sending out individual interviewers to people's homes. The homes were chosen by complicated national sampling techniques, and numerous methodologies were developed to assure a good sample from within each household.

In the 1960s, the methods for conducting a telephone sample were perfected. Not only could the pollsters use a random sample of telephone numbers to locate their households, but they also could conduct the interviews by telephone, thus cutting costs and assuring their physical security.

The next step in polling technology was computer-assisted telephone interviewing, or CATI. After a computer dials a respondent's telephone number, the interviewer reads the questions from the computer screen and enters the respondent's answers directly into the computer, where they can be analyzed almost instantly. This development cut costs further and made possible "overnight" polls—polls conducted immediately after debates and during crises.

Technology is now close to eliminating the interviewer altogether. With CATS—completely automated telephone surveying—computers and a type of voicemail system are used to complete the entire interview. The computer makes the call, a recording asks the questions, and the respondent is asked to use his or her touch-tone phone to give responses. Again, the data can be analyzed instantly because they are entered directly into the computer. The pollster who developed CATS, Jay Leve, believes that the system is just as reliable as human interviewers in getting a sample and actually improves on human techniques by eliminating certain interview biases. For example, respondents will not answer the way that they think the interviewer expects or desires them to. The technology bears the commercial name, Bullet Poll. So far, it has been used to conduct more than two thousand surveys in major market areas.

Obviously, this type of technology makes it possible for a company, candidate, or television station to take virtually instant polls and then use them to advantage—on the evening news, for example.

FOR CRITICAL ANALYSIS

Do you think that people respond as thoughtfully to a recorded poll as to a live interviewer?

predictions. When a poll changes its method from reporting the views of eligible voters to reporting those of likely voters, the results are likely to change dramatically.

Finally, it makes sense to expect that the results of a poll will depend on the questions that are asked. Depending on what question is asked, voters could be said either to support a particular proposal or to oppose it. Furthermore, respondents' answers are also influenced by the order in which questions are asked, the types of answers they are allowed to choose, and in some cases, by their interaction with the interviewer. To some extent, people try to please the interviewer. They answer questions about which they have no information and avoid some answers to try to measure up to the interviewer's expectations. (See the feature entitled *Politics and Technology: The Interviewer Becomes a Machine* on the previous page for a discussion of a new polling technique that eliminates the effects of the interviewer's expectations in polling.) Most recently, some campaigns have been using "push polls," in which the respondents are given misleading information in the questions asked to get them to vote against a candidate. Obviously, the answers given are likely to be influenced by such techniques. For a further discussion of push polls, see the feature below entitled *Politics and Ethics: Polls That Mislead*.

Because of these problems, you need to be especially careful when evaluating poll results. For some suggestions on how to be a critical consumer of public opinion polls, see the feature *Toward Active Citizenship* at the end of this chapter.

POLITICS and Ethics

Polls That Mislead

Pollsters long have known that the wording of questions can influence the response that a person gives. Different question wordings can provoke extensive political debate about the actual preferences of the public. When President Clinton and the congressional Republicans were unable to resolve their differences over the budget for more than six months, Democrats were cheered by poll results that showed that the majority of Americans opposed "cutting funding for Medicare." Republicans countered by showing poll results that indicated that many Americans supported "decreasing the growth in funding for Medicare." Both parties were depending on question wording for building a case for their own positions.

A far more deliberate use of question wording has surfaced recently in election campaigns. In the weeks before a primary or general election, voters are interviewed in what seems to be a legitimate poll. One or more of the questions in the poll, however, gives the respondent false or misleading information about the opposing candidate in an effort to influence the respondent's vote. Such surveys have become known as "push polls," because they are intended to push the voter to the candidate whose campaign sponsored the poll.

Sometimes the information given in the question is simply misleading, while on other occasions it has been closer to scandal or gossip. In another variation, push polls can be used to start rumors about a candidate at a time very close to the election when rebuttal of the information is almost impossible.

The prevalence of push polling in early 1996 led to a statement by the American Association for Public Opinion Research condemning such polls and labeling them marketing ploys. It also led to the introduction of legislation in Virginia to regulate polls by requiring the disclosure of the candidate sponsoring the polls. By the middle of 1996, both major political parties had issued a statement saying that they would not engage in such polls. Similar tactics also may be used by polls about commercial products or any other topic, however. The ultimate result will be a further weakening of public confidence in any poll.

FOR CRITICAL ANALYSIS

How can you tell whether a survey question is worded "neutrally" or whether it might be biased toward a particular response?

elections '98

The Accuracy of the 1998 Polls

Polling the public played a critical role in the strategic decisions of the parties in 1998. Democrats running for Congress relied on the polling data showing that Americans were tired of the Clinton scandal and focused their campaign on such issues as education and Social Security. The Republicans chose to run ads reminding the voters of the scandal in the last week before the election, an ad campaign that appeared to backfire on election day.

As the election neared, pollsters tried to forecast the outcome of the congressional and state races, correcting their estimates for an expected level of turnout. Most pollsters predicted low voter turnout and tried to base their predictions on a "likely voter" model. Early polling results showed that more people planned to vote for Republicans for Congress than for Democrats. In the last week before election day, however, the polls began to show the opposite—that more people planned to vote for Democrats (48 percent) than for Republicans (45 percent). Because of their inability to truly predict turnout, pollsters were less accurate in the statewide races than they were on the national level.

How Opinion Is Formed

Political Socialization
The process by which individuals acquire political beliefs and attitudes.

Most Americans are willing to express opinions on political issues when asked. How do individuals acquire these opinions and attitudes? Most views that are expressed as political opinions are acquired through a process known as **political socialization.** By this we mean that individuals acquire their political attitudes, often including their party identification, through relationships with their families, friends, and co-workers. The most important influences in this process are the following: (1) the family, (2) the educational environment and achievement of the individual, (3) peers, (4) religion, (5) economic status and occupation, (6) political events, (7) opinion leaders, (8) the media, and (9) race and other demographic traits. We discuss each of these influences below, as well as the relatively recent phenomenon of the gender gap.

The Importance of the Family

The family is the most important force in political socialization. Not only do our parents' political attitudes and actions affect our adult opinions, but the family also links us to other socialization forces. We acquire our ethnic identity, our notion of social class, our educational opportunities, and our early religious beliefs from our families. Each of these factors can also influence our political attitudes.

How do parents transmit these attachments? Studies suggest that the influence of parents is due to two factors: communication and receptivity. Parents communicate their feelings and preferences to children constantly. Because children have such a strong need for parental approval, they are very receptive to their parents' views.[5]

---

[5]Robert S. Erikson and Kent L. Tedin, *American Public Opinion: Its Origins, Content and Impact,* 5th ed. (Boston: Allyn and Bacon, 1995), p. 125.

The clearest legacy of the family is partisan identification. If both parents identify with one party, there is a strong likelihood that the children will begin political life with the same party preference. In their classic study of political attitudes among adolescents, M. Kent Jennings and Richard G. Niemi probed the partisan attachments of high school seniors and their parents during the mid-1960s.[6] They found that Democratic parents tend to produce Democratic children about two-thirds of the time, and independent and Republican parents both transmit their beliefs about parties only slightly less well. There is still a sizable amount of cross-generational slippage, however. In all, Jennings and Niemi found that 59 percent of the children agreed with their parents' party ties.

In a 1973 reinterview of the same children and their parents, Jennings and Niemi found that the younger people had become notably more independent of partisan ties, whereas their parents had experienced very little change.[7] By 1973, a majority of the children had deviated from their parents' partisanship.

Educational Influence on Political Opinion

From the early days of the republic, schools were perceived to be important transmitters of political information and attitudes. Children in the primary grades learn about their country mostly in patriotic ways. They learn to salute the flag, to say the Pledge of Allegiance, and to celebrate national holidays. Later, in the middle grades, children learn more historical facts and come to understand the structure of government and the functions of the president, judges, and Congress. By high school, students have a more complex understanding of the political system, may identify with a political party, and may take positions on issues.

Generally, education is closely linked to political participation. The more education a person receives, the more likely it is that the person will be interested in politics, be confident in his or her ability to understand political issues, and be an active participant in the political process.

Peers and Peer Group Influence

Once a child enters school, the child's friends become an important influence on behavior and attitudes. As young children, and later as adults, friendships and associations in **peer groups** are influential on political attitudes. We must, however, separate the effects of peer group pressure on opinions and attitudes in general from peer group pressure on political opinions. For the most part, associations among peers are nonpolitical. Political attitudes are more likely to be shaped by peer groups when the peer groups are involved directly in political activities.

Individuals who join interest groups based on ethnic identity may find, for example, a common political bond through working for the group's civil liberties and rights. African American activist groups may consist of individuals who join together to support government programs that will aid the African American population. Members of a labor union may feel strong political pressure to support certain pro-labor candidates.

Religious Influence

Religious associations tend to create definite political attitudes, although why this occurs is not clearly understood. Surveys show that Roman Catholic respondents

Patriotism is instilled in children through the process of political socialization. The child in this picture knows that her parents approve of this display of support for their political beliefs.

Peer Group

A group consisting of members sharing common relevant social characteristics. These groups play an important part in the socialization process, helping to shape attitudes and beliefs.

INFOTRAC ®
COLLEGE EDITION

"Political Socialization in the Classroom Revisited"

---

[6]M. Kent Jennings and Richard G. Niemi, *The Political Character of Adolescence: The Influence of Families and Schools* (Princeton, N.J.: Princeton University Press, 1974).

[7]M. Kent Jennings and Richard G. Niemi, *Generations and Politics* (Princeton, N.J.: Princeton University Press, 1981).

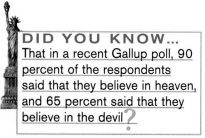

tend to be more liberal on economic issues than are Protestants. Apparently, Jewish respondents are more liberal on all fronts than either Catholics or Protestants. In terms of voting behavior, it has been observed that northern white Protestants are more likely to vote Republican, whereas northern white Roman Catholics more often vote Democratic; everywhere in the United States, Jews mostly vote Democratic. The increase in fundamentalist or evangelical Protestants has had a political impact. A recent study by the Pew Center for the People and the Press found that 42 percent of white evangelical Protestants are Republican. Less than ten years ago, this figure was 35 percent.

These associations between religious background and political attitudes are partly derived from the ethnic background of certain religious groups and the conditions at the time their forebears immigrated to the United States. Germans who immigrated before the Civil War tended to be Republican regardless of their religious backgrounds, whereas Eastern European Catholics, who arrived in the late nineteenth century, adopted the Democratic identity of the cities in which they made their homes.

Sometimes a candidate's religion enters the political picture, as it did in the 1960 presidential election contest between Democrat John Kennedy and Republican Richard Nixon. The fact that Kennedy was a Catholic—the second Catholic to be nominated by a major party—polarized many voters. Among northern whites, Kennedy was supported by 83 percent of voting Catholics and by 93 percent of Jewish voters but by only 28 percent of the Protestants who voted.

The Influence of Economic Status and Occupation

How wealthy you are and the kind of job you hold are also associated with your political views. Social-class differences emerge on a wide range of issues. Poorer people are more inclined to favor government social-welfare programs but are likely to be conservative on social issues such as abortion. The upper middle class is more likely to hold conservative economic views but to be tolerant of social change. People in lower economic strata also tend to be more isolationist on foreign policy issues and are more likely to identify with the Democratic Party and vote for Democratic candidates. Support for civil liberties and tolerance of different points of view tend to be greater among those with higher social status and lower among those with lower social status. Probably, it is educational differences more than the pattern of life at home or work that account for this.

The Influence of Political Events

People's political attitudes may be shaped by political events and the nation's reactions to them. In the 1960s and 1970s, the war in Vietnam—including revelations about the secret bombing in Cambodia—and the Watergate break-in and subsequent cover-up fostered widespread cynicism toward government. In one study of the impact of the Watergate scandal of 1972, Christopher Arterton found that schoolchildren changed their image of President Nixon from a "benevolent" to a "malevolent" leader as the scandal unfolded. Negative views also increased about other aspects of politics and politicians. Members of that age group moderated their views, however, as they matured.[8]

When events produce a long-lasting political impact, **generational effects** result. Voters who grew up in the 1930s during the Great Depression were likely to form lifelong attachments to the Democratic Party, the party of Franklin D.

Generational Effect
A long-lasting effect of events of a particular time period on the political opinions or preferences of those who came of political age at that time.

---

[8]Christopher F. Arterton, "The Impact of Watergate on Children's Attitudes toward Authority," *American Political Science Review*, Vol. 89 (June 1974), pp. 269–288.

Roosevelt. There was some evidence that the years of economic prosperity under Ronald Reagan during the 1980s may have influenced young adults to identify with the Republican Party. A 1990 poll showed that 52 percent of thirteen- to seventeen-year-olds thought of themselves as Republicans, whereas 32 percent of this age group thought of themselves as Democrats. Although the number of younger voters identifying themselves as Republicans declined in 1992, the group that voted for the first time in 1995 were more likely to be Republican.[9]

Opinion Leaders' Influence

We are all influenced by those with whom we are closely associated or whom we hold in great respect—friends at school, family members and other relatives, teachers, and so on. In a sense, these people are **opinion leaders,** but on an informal level; that is, their influence over us is not necessarily intentional or deliberate. We are also influenced by formal opinion leaders, such as presidents, lobbyists, congresspersons, or news commentators, who have as part of their jobs the task of swaying people's views. Their interest lies in defining the political agenda in such a way that discussions about policy options will take place on their terms.

Opinion Leader
One who is able to influence the opinions of others because of position, expertise, or personality. Such leaders help to shape public opinion.

Media Influence

Clearly, the **media**—newspapers, television, radio broadcasts, and Internet sources—strongly influence public opinion. This is because the media inform the public about the issues and events of our times and thus have an agenda-setting effect. In other words, to borrow from Bernard Cohen's classic statement on the media and public opinion, the media may not be successful in telling people what to think, but they are "stunningly successful in telling their audience what to think about."[10]

Media
The technical means of communication with mass audiences.

Today, many contend that the media's influence on public opinion is increasing to the point that the media are as influential as the family in regard to public opinion. For example, in her analysis of the role played by the media in American politics,[11] media scholar Doris A. Graber points out that high school students, when asked where they obtain the information on which they base their attitudes, mention the mass media far more than their families, friends, and teachers. This trend, combined with the increasing popularity of more populist and interactive news sources, such as talk shows and the Internet, may significantly alter the nature of the media's influence on public debate in the future. (See Chapter 11 for a more detailed analysis of the role of the media in American political life.)

The Influence of Demographic Traits

African Americans show a much stronger commitment than do whites to steady or more rapid racial desegregation. African Americans tend to be more liberal than whites on social-welfare issues, civil liberties, and even foreign policy. Party preference and voting among African Americans since the 1930s have supported the Democrats very heavily.

It is somewhat surprising that a person's chronological age has comparatively little impact on political preferences. Still, young adults are somewhat more

---

[9]*America at the Polls 1996* (Storrs, Conn.: Roper Center, 1997), pp. 56–57.

[10]*The Press and Foreign Policy* (Princeton, N.J.: Princeton University Press, 1963), p. 81.

[11]See Doris A. Graber, *Mass Media and American Politics,* 5th ed. (Washington, D.C.: Congressional Quarterly Books, 1997).

Nation of Islam leader Louis Farrakhan and his supporters organized the Million Man March on Washington in 1995. The march, pictured here, can be seen as an expression of public opinion by a group of African Americans. The participants expressed their belief in the importance of individual responsibility, family responsibility, and dedication to the greater community.

liberal than older people on most issues, and they are considerably more progressive on such issues as marijuana legalization, pornography, civil disobedience, and racial and sexual equality.

Finally, attitudes vary from region to region, although such patterns probably are accounted for mostly by social class and other differences. Regional differences are relatively unimportant today. There is still a tendency for the South and the East to be more Democratic than the West and the Midwest. More important than region is a person's residence—urban, suburban, or rural. Big cities tend to be more liberal and Democratic because of their greater concentration of minorities and newer ethnic groups. Smaller communities are more conservative and, outside the South, more Republican.

The Gender Gap

Gender Gap

A term most often used to describe the difference between the percentage of votes a candidate receives from women and the percentage of votes the candidate receives from men. The term came into use after the 1980 presidential election.

Until the 1980s, there was little evidence that men's and women's political attitudes were very different. The election of Ronald Reagan in 1980, however, soon came to be associated with a **gender gap**. In a May 1983 Gallup poll, 43 percent of the women polled approved of Reagan's performance in office and 44 percent disapproved, versus 49 percent of men who approved and 41 percent who disapproved.

In the 1988 election, the gender gap reappeared, but in a modified form. Although the Democrats hoped that women's votes would add significantly to their totals, a deep split between men and women did not occur. The final polls showed that 54 percent of the men voted for George Bush, as did 50 percent of the women. The 1992 presidential election again found women more likely than men to vote for the Democrats: 46 percent of women voted for Bill Clinton, compared with 41 percent of the men. Additionally, women were less likely to vote for independent candidate H. Ross Perot than were men. Throughout his first term, Clinton continued to get higher approval marks from women than from men, and women were more supportive of him through the personal scandal periods of his second term.

Women also appear to hold different attitudes from their male counterparts on a range of issues other than presidential preferences. They are much more likely to oppose capital punishment, as well as the use of force abroad. Studies have also shown that women are more concerned about risks to the environment, more supportive of social welfare, and more supportive of extending civil rights to gay men and lesbians than are men. These differences of opinion appear to be growing and may become an important factor in future elections at national and local levels.[12]

Political Culture and Public Opinion

Americans are divided into a multitude of ethnic, religious, regional, and political subgroups. In many cases, members of these groups hold a particular set of opinions about government policies, about the goals of the society, and about the rights of their group and the rights of others. Given the diversity of American society and the wide range of opinions contained within it, how is it that the political process continues to function without being stalemated by conflict and dissension?

One explanation is rooted in the concept of the American political culture, which can be described as a set of attitudes and ideas about the nation and the government. As discussed in Chapter 1, our political culture is widely shared by Americans of many different backgrounds. To some extent, it consists of symbols, such as the American flag, the Liberty Bell, and the Statue of Liberty. The elements of our political culture also include certain shared beliefs about the most important values in the American political system, including (1) liberty, equality, and property; (2) support for religion; and (3) community service and personal achievement. The structure of the government—particularly federalism, the political parties, the powers of Congress, and popular rule—were also found to be important values.[13]

The political culture provides a general environment of support for the political system. If the people share certain beliefs about the system and a reservoir of good feeling exists toward the institutions of government, the nation will be better able to weather periods of crisis, such as Watergate. This foundation of goodwill may combat cynicism and increase the level of participation in elections as well. During the 1960s and 1970s, survey research showed that the overall level of **political trust** declined steeply. A considerable proportion of Americans seemed to feel that they could not trust government officials and that they could not count on officials to care about the ordinary person. This index of political trust reached an all-time low in 1992, reflecting Americans' cynicism about the government and the presidential election campaign (see Table 7–2).

INFOTRAC®
COLLEGE EDITION

"America's Civic Condition"

Political Trust
The degree to which individuals express trust in the government and political institutions, usually measured through a specific series of survey questions.

---

[12]Jody Newman, "The Gender Story: Women as Voters and Candidates in the 1996 Elections," in *America at the Polls 1996* (Storrs, Conn.: Roper Center, 1997), pp. 102–103.
[13]Donald Devine, *Political Culture of the United States* (Boston: Little, Brown, 1972).

TABLE 7-2

Trends in Political Trust

QUESTION: How much of the time do you think you can trust the government in Washington to do what is right—just about always, most of the time, or only some of the time?

	1964	1968	1972	1974	1976	1978	1980	1982	1984	1986	1988	1990	1992	1994	1996	1998
Percentage saying:																
Always/Most of the time	76	61	53	36	33	29	25	32	46	42	44	27	23	20	25	34
Some of the time	22	36	45	61	63	67	73	64	51	55	54	73	75	79	71	66

SOURCE: *New York Times*/CBS News Surveys; the University of Michigan Survey Research Center, National Election Studies; and the Pew Research Center for the People and the Press.

Public Opinion about Government

A vital component of public opinion in the United States is the considerable ambivalence with which the public regards many major national institutions. Table 7–3 shows trends from 1973 to 1997 in Gallup public opinion polls asking respondents, at regularly spaced intervals, how much confidence they had in the institutions listed. Over the years, military and religious organizations have ranked highest, but note the decline in confidence in churches following the numerous scandals concerning television evangelists in the late 1980s. Note also the heightened regard for the military after the war in the Persian Gulf in 1991. Not only did the Gulf War give a temporary boost to President Bush's popularity, but it also seemed to inspire patriotism and support for the military throughout the nation. Table 7–3 shows that in 1991, the public had more confidence in the military than it did in the church or organized religion, in newspapers, or in any institution of government.

The United States Supreme Court, which many people do not see as a particularly political institution, although it is clearly involved in decisions with vitally

TABLE 7-3

Confidence in Institutions Trend

QUESTION: I am going to read a list of institutions in American society. Would you please tell me how much confidence you, yourself, have in each one—a great deal, quite a lot, some, or very little?

	PERCENTAGE SAYING "GREAT DEAL" OR "QUITE A LOT"												
	1973	1975	1977	1979	1981	1983	1985	1987	1989	1991	1993	1995	1997
Church or organized religion	66%	68%	65%	65%	64%	62%	66%	61%	52%	56%	53%	57%	56%
Military	NA	58	57	54	50	53	61	61	63	69	67	64	60
U.S. Supreme Court	44	49	46	45	46	42	56	52	46	39	43	44	50
Banks and banking	NA	NA	NA	60	46	51	51	51	42	30	38	43	41
Public schools	58	NA	54	53	42	39	48	50	43	35	39	40	40
Congress	42	40	40	34	29	28	39	NA	32	18	19	21	22
Newspapers	39	NA	NA	51	35	38	35	31	NA	32	31	30	35
Big business	26	34	33	32	20	28	31	NA	NA	22	23	21	28
Television	37	NA	NA	38	25	25	29	28	NA	24	21	33	34
Organized labor	30	38	39	36	28	26	28	26	NA	22	26	26	23

NA = Not asked.

SOURCE: *The Gallup Report*, July 1997.

important consequences for the nation, also scored well, as did banks and banking until recently. A series of unpopular Supreme Court decisions from 1989 to 1991 and the savings and loan scandals of about the same time caused the public's confidence in both of those institutions to drop significantly by 1991. Even less confidence is expressed in newspapers, big business, television, and organized labor, all of which certainly are involved directly or indirectly in the political process. In 1991, following a scandal involving congressional banking practices and other embarrassments, confidence in Congress fell to a record low of 18 percent. (Note that the decreasing confidence in Congress has been paralleled by an increasing confidence in the ability of state and local institutions.) Scandal does not always lead to a decline in approval ratings, however—see the feature *Politics and Polling: Can Scandal Bring Popularity?*

Although people may not have much confidence in government institutions, they nonetheless turn to government to solve what they perceive to be the major problems facing the country. Table 7–4, which is based on Gallup polls conducted

POLITICS and Polling

Can Scandal Bring Popularity?

As President Clinton began his second term in office, personal scandals seemed to take up more and more of his time. Paula Jones won the right to sue him for alleged misconduct that took place before he became president. Independent Counsel Kenneth Starr continued to investigate the Whitewater savings and loan issue. And, in January 1998, allegations arose that the president had had an affair with a White House intern, Monica Lewinsky, and then lied about it under oath. Judge Starr pursued his investigation of these claims with vigor.

The media attacked these stories with tremendous

energy, reporting on a daily basis stories, myths, facts, and any event they could find to talk about. The White House simply denied any wrongdoing and said no more. What occurred at this time baffled many political analysts: the president's job approval rating, as measured by public opinion polls, rose dramatically. A Gallup poll taken on April 1, 1998, showed a 67 percent favorable rating. The same poll indicated that although 50 percent of the people surveyed believed that what had happened between the president and Paula Jones was sexual harassment, 67 percent said that investigations of the president's per-

sonal life should stop.

What these kinds of data show is that people have very complex opinions about such issues. Some commentators suggest that people worry that if the president is under attack, the economy might falter and people could suffer. Others note that most people do not want to talk or think about the president's private life. Still others suggest that there is a "rally" effect for the president as the symbol of the nation, with those who attack the president seen as attacking the nation. Finally, as Everett Carll Ladd points out, the public was

very reluctant to criticize President Nixon in the months after the Watergate scandal began to be investigated; when his job approval ratings fell, the decline was due to a terrible economy. Ladd suggests that the key to job approval ratings is the health of the economy and that of the nation, not the problems of the president.*

FOR CRITICAL ANALYSIS

In your opinion, would the nation be better or worse off if the president's private life were not subject to scrutiny by the media, court judges, other government officials, and the public generally?

*Everett Carll Ladd, "Nixon, Clinton and the Polls," *The Wall Street Journal,* April 1, 1998, p. A18.

Do you approve or disapprove of the way Bill Clinton is handling his job as president?	
Approve	67%
Disapprove	28%
No opinion	5%

Was the Clinton/Jones incident sexual harassment?	
Yes	50%
No	43%
No opinion	7%

Should the investigations into sexual allegations involving Bill Clinton continue or should they stop now?	
Continue	31%
Stop now	67%
No opinion	2%

TABLE   7-4

Most Important Problem Trend, 1975 to Present

1998	Crime, violence	1986	Unemployment, budget deficit
1997	Crime, violence	1985	Fear of war, unemployment
1996	Budget deficit	1984	Unemployment, fear of war
1995	Crime, violence	1983	Unemployment, high cost of living
1994	Crime, violence, health care	1982	Unemployment, high cost of living
1993	Health care, budget deficit	1981	High cost of living, unemployment
1992	Unemployment, budget deficit	1980	High cost of living, unemployment
1991	Economy	1979	High cost of living, energy problems
1990	War in Middle East	1978	High cost of living, energy problems
1989	War on drugs	1977	High cost of living, unemployment
1988	Economy, budget deficit	1976	High cost of living, unemployment
1987	Unemployment, economy	1975	High cost of living, unemployment

SOURCE: *New York Times*/CBS News Poll, January 1996; *Gallup Report*, 1998.

over the years 1975 to 1998, shows that the leading problems clearly have changed over time. The public tends to emphasize problems that are immediate. It is not at all unusual to see fairly sudden, and even apparently contradictory, shifts in public perceptions of what government should do. In recent years, unemployment, crime, and the budget deficit reached the top of the problems list.

This gives rise to a critically important question: Is government really responsive to public opinion? A study by political scientists Benjamin I. Page and Robert Y. Shapiro suggests that in fact the national government is very responsive to the public's demands for action.[14] In looking at changes in public opinion poll results over time, Page and Shapiro show that when the public supports a policy change, the following occurs: policy changes in a direction congruent with the change in public opinion 43 percent of the time, policy changes in a direction opposite to the change in opinion 22 percent of the time, and policy does not change at all 33 percent of the time. So, overall, the national government could be said to respond to changes in public opinion about two-thirds of the time. Page and Shapiro also show, as should be no surprise, that when public opinion changes more dramatically—say, by 20 percentage points rather than by just 6 or 7 percentage points—government policy is much more likely to follow changing public attitudes.

The Spectrum of Political Beliefs

Political candidates and officeholders in the United States frequently are identified as liberals or conservatives. These terms refer loosely to a spectrum of political beliefs that commonly are arrayed on a continuum from left to right. Each of the terms has changed its meaning from its origins and continues to change as the issues of political debate change. In the United States, however, the terms most frequently refer to sets of political positions that date from the Great Depression.

Liberals are most commonly understood to embrace national government solutions to public problems, to believe that the national government should intervene in the economy to ensure its health, to support social-welfare programs to assist the disadvantaged, and to be tolerant of social change. Today, liberals are often identified with policies supporting women's rights and civil rights, and opposing increased defense spending.

[14]See the extensive work of Page and Shapiro in Benjamin I. Page and Robert Y. Shapiro, *The Rational Public: Fifty Years of Trends in Americans' Policy Preferences* (Chicago: University of Chicago Press, 1992).

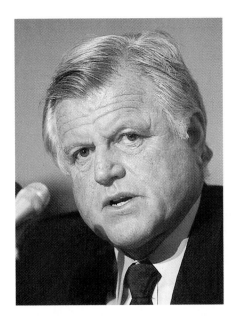 

Senator Edward Kennedy (left) of Massachusetts has been a liberal voice throughout his tenure in Congress. Patrick Buchanan (right), who opposed President George Bush during the Republican presidential primaries in 1992 and Robert Dole in 1996, is an outspoken conservative. Buchanan has built a career in television as a political commentator.

In contrast, conservatives usually feel that the national government has grown too large, that the private sector needs less interference from the government, that social-welfare programs should be limited, that state and local governments should be able to make their own decisions, and that the nation's defense should be strengthened. Some conservatives express grave concerns about the decline of family life and traditional values in this country; they would not be tolerant of gay rights laws, for example. Senator Edward Kennedy and 1992 and 1996 presidential candidate Pat Buchanan are examples of today's variety of liberalism and conservatism, respectively.

When asked, Americans usually are willing to identify themselves on the liberal-conservative spectrum. More individuals are likely to consider themselves moderates than as liberals or conservatives. As Table 7–5 shows, although the

TABLE **7-5**

Ideological Self-identification, 1976 to Present

There has been relatively little change in the distribution of liberals and conservatives, even after the elections of self-described liberal or conservative presidents.

YEAR	LIBERAL	MODERATE	CONSERVATIVE	NO OPINION
1976	21%	41%	26%	12%
1977	21	38	29	12
1978	21	35	27	17
1979	21	42	26	12
1980	19	40	31	11
1981	18	43	30	9
1982	17	40	33	11
1984	17	41	31	11
1986	20	45	28	7
1988	18	45	33	4
1990	20	45	28	6
1992	19	41	34	6
1993	18	45	32	5
1994	18	48	34	0
1995	19	39	37	4
1996	17	45	34	4
1997	17	40	39	4

SOURCE: *Gallup Reports;* and *New York Times*/CBS News Surveys.

Ideologue
An individual whose political opinions are carefully thought out and relatively consistent with one another. Ideologues are often described as having a comprehensive world view.

number of moderates and conservatives has increased and the number of liberals has declined in the past two decades, there has not been a dramatic change in ideological self-identification since 1976.

Most Americans, however, do not fit into the categories as nicely as do Edward Kennedy or Pat Buchanan. Many political leaders, who are quite conscious of their philosophical views and who hold a carefully thought out and a more or less consistent set of political beliefs, can be described as **ideologues.** Partly because most citizens are not strongly interested in all political issues and partly because Americans have different stakes in politics, most people have mixed sets of opinions that do not fit into one ideological framework. Election research suggests that only a small percentage of all Americans, perhaps less than 10 percent, could be identified as ideologues. The rest of the public conceives of politics more in terms of the political parties or of economic well-being.

Some critics of the American political system have felt that elections would be more meaningful and that the nation could face important policy problems more effectively if Americans were more ideological in their thinking. Public opinion research suggests that for most Americans, political issues are not usually as important as events in their daily lives are. There is no evidence to suggest that forces are in place to turn Americans into highly motivated ideological voters.

Public Opinion and the Political Process

Surveys of public opinion, no matter what fascinating questions they ask or how quickly they get the answers, are not equivalent to elections in the United States. Because not all Americans are equally interested in politics or equally informed, public opinion polls can suggest only the general distribution of opinion on issues. Many times, only a few citizens have formulated preferences, and these preferences will be changed by events.

Politicians, whether in office or in the midst of a campaign, see public opinion as important to their careers. The president, members of Congress, governors, and other elected officials realize that strong support by the public as expressed in opinion polls is a source of power in dealing with other politicians. It is far more difficult for a senator to say no to the president if the president is immensely popular and if polls show approval of the president's policies. Public opinion also helps political candidates identify the most important concerns among the public and may help them shape their campaigns successfully. (For the public's views on the issue of campaign-financing reform, see the feature *Politics and Money: What the Polls Say about Campaign-Financing Reform.*)

Although opinion polls cannot give exact guidance on what the government should do in a specific instance, the opinions measured in polls do set an informal limit on government action. For example, consider the highly controversial issue of abortion. Most Americans are moderates on this issue; they do not approve of abortion as a means of birth control, but they do feel that it should be available under certain circumstances. Yet sizable groups of people express very intense feelings both for and against abortion. Given this distribution of opinion, most elected officials would rather not try to change policy to favor either of the extreme positions. To do so would clearly violate the opinion of the majority of Americans. In this case, as in many others, public opinion does not make public policy; rather, it restrains officials from taking truly unpopular actions. If officials do act in the face of public opposition, the consequences of such actions will be determined at the ballot box.

POLITICS and Money

What the Polls Say about Campaign-Financing Reform

Despite almost a year of congressional hearings and investigations by the Justice Department and others, the topic of campaign-financing abuse has not inspired the American public to demand reform. Both Republican and Democratic members of Congress have talked about reform for half a decade, but once again in 1998, all efforts to pass legislation to reform the system for financing campaigns failed. Polls of the American public find that most Americans would like to see campaign-financing reform but have little, if any, faith that this will happen. Furthermore, Gallup polling data showed that few expected the hearings to produce new information. Although more citizens said that the Democratic Party was unethical in the way that it raised funds in 1996 (35 percent) than said that the Republican Party was unethical (15 percent), only 21 percent of those surveyed believed that neither party was unethical. Further evidence of the public's lack of faith in the parties is shown in the answer to the question, "Do you think the Republican Party or the Democratic Party did anything unethical in the way it raised funds for the 1996 election?" Sixty-three percent believed that the Democratic Party did something unethical, and 55 percent said the same for the Republicans.

FOR CRITICAL ANALYSIS

Can you think of a scandal or incidence of wrongdoing so terrible that it might cause the public to demand campaign-financing reform?

Public Opinion: Issues for the New Century

Public opinion is a vital part of the political process—it identifies issues for resolution, provides for a public debate on the issues, gives policymakers some idea of what the voters prefer, and sets boundaries on those same policymakers. The polling industry, however, may be close to putting itself out of business either through public distrust or government regulation.

The science of polling provides powerful information to private and governmental bodies to manipulate the public, to influence markets and the economy, and to shape the public agenda. Yet there is no mechanism to sort out "accurate" and "scientific" polls from marketing devices. The explosion of polls and poll results has also alienated the public. Refusal rates for polls have soared to above 40 percent in some instances. This means that certain groups within the public are no longer willing to cooperate with the pollsters, thus weakening the samples.

At the same time that the public is wearying of the polls and paying less attention to them, the media are increasing their expenditures on them, polling on almost every conceivable issue. The real danger is that deliberation on the real effects of policies and their impact on society will be drowned out by poll results that substitute for public debate. Whether the answer is to regulate polls, to outlaw polls before elections or at some other point in time, or just to allow the polls to exhaust themselves, any change undoubtedly will provoke strong opposition from the media, as well as from those who see a challenge to First Amendment freedoms.

TOWARD ACTIVE CITIZENSHIP

BE A CRITICAL CONSUMER OF OPINION POLLS

Americans are inundated with the results of public opinion polls. The polls, often reported to us through television news, the newspaper, *Time, Newsweek,* or radio, purport to tell us a variety of things: whether the president's popularity is up or down, whether gun control is more popular now than previously, or who is leading the pack for the next presidential nomination.

What must be kept in mind with this blizzard of information is that not all poll results are equally good or equally believable. As a critical consumer, you need to be aware of what makes one set of public opinion poll results valid and other results useless or even dangerously misleading.

Selection of the Sample

How were the people who were interviewed selected? Pay attention only to opinion polls that are based on scientific, or random, samples, in which a known probability was used to select every person who was interviewed. These *probability samples,* as they are also called, can take a number of different forms. The simplest to understand is known as a *random sample,* in which everybody had a known, and possibly an equal, chance of being chosen to be interviewed. As a rule, do not give credence to the results of opinion polls that consist of shopping-mall interviews. The main problem with this kind of opinion taking, which is a special version of a so-called *accidental sample,* is that not everyone had an equal chance of being in the mall when the interview took place. Also, it is almost certain that the people in the mall are not a reasonable cross section of a community's entire population (shopping malls would tend to attract people who are disproportionately younger, female, mobile, and middle class).

Probability samples are useful (and nonprobability samples are not) for the following reason: when you know the odds that the particular sample would have been chosen randomly from a larger population, you can calculate the range within which the real results for the whole population would fall if everybody had been interviewed. Well-designed probability samples will allow the pollster to say, for example, that he or she is 95 percent sure that 61 percent of the public, plus or minus 4 percentage points, supports national health insurance. It turns out that if you want to become twice as precise about a poll result, you would need to collect a sample four times as large. This tends to make accurate polls quite expensive and difficult to collect. Typically, the Gallup organization seldom interviews more than about 1,500 respondents.

Interview Method

There are other important points to keep in mind when you see opinion poll results. How were people contacted for the poll—by mail, by telephone, in person in their homes, or in some other way? By and large, because of its lower cost, polling firms have turned more and more to telephone interviewing. This method usually can produce highly accurate results. Its disadvantage is that telephone interviews typically need to be short and to deal with questions that are fairly easy to answer. Interviews in person are better for getting useful information about why a particular response was given to a question. They take much longer to complete, however, and are not as useful if results must be generated quickly. Results from mailed questionnaires should be taken with a grain of salt. Usually, only a small percentage of people complete them and send them back.

Nonpolls

Be particularly critical of telephone "call-in" polls or "Internet polls." When viewers or listeners of television or radio shows are encouraged to call in their opinions to an 800 telephone number, the call is free, but the polling results are useless. Users of the Internet also have an easy way to make their views known. Only people who are interested in the topic will take the trouble to respond, however, and that group, of course, is not representative of the general public. Polls that use 900 numbers are perhaps even more misleading. The only respondents to those polls are those who care enough about the topic to pay for a call. Both types of polls are likely to be manipulated by interest groups or supporters of a political candidate, who will organize their supporters to make calls and reinforce their own point of view. Remember, when seeing the results of any poll, to take a moment and try to find out how the poll was conducted.

Key terms

consensus 219	intensity 220	political trust 235
divisive opinion 219	media 233	public opinion 218
fluidity 221	opinion leader 233	relevance 221
gender gap 234	opinion poll 222	sampling error 227
generational effect 232	peer group 231	Solid South 221
ideologue 240	political socialization 230	stability 221
		Watergate break-in 217

Chapter summary

1 Public opinion is the aggregate of individual attitudes or beliefs shared by some portion of the adult population. It has at least five special qualities: (a) intensity—the strength of an opinion; (b) fluidity—the extent to which opinion changes; (c) stability—the extent to which opinion remains constant; (d) relevance—the extent to which an issue is of concern at a particular time; and (e) political knowledge. Consensus issues are those on which most people agree, whereas divisive issues are those about which people strongly disagree.

2 Most descriptions of public opinion are based on the results of opinion polls. The accuracy of polls is based on sampling techniques that ensure randomness in the selection of respondents. Polls only measure opinions held on the day they are taken and will not reflect rapidly changing opinions. Certain methodological problems may reduce the accuracy of polls.

3 Opinions and attitudes are produced by a combination of socialization, information, and experience. Young peo-ple, for example, are likely to be influenced by their parents' political party identification. Education has an effect on opinions and attitudes, as do peer groups, religious affiliation, and economic status. Political events may have generational effects, shaping the opinions of a particular age group. Opinion leaders, the media, ethnicity, and gender also affect political views.

4 A political culture exists in the United States because so many Americans hold similar attitudes and beliefs about how the government and the political system should work. In addition, most Americans are able to identify themselves as liberals, moderates, or conservatives, even though they may not articulate a consistent philosophy of politics, or ideology.

5 Public opinion can play an important part in the political system by providing information to candidates, by indicating support or opposition to the president and Congress, and by setting limits on government action through public pressure.

Selected print and electronic resources

SUGGESTED READINGS

Asher, Herbert. *Polling and the Public: What Every Citizen Should Know.* 3d ed. Washington, D.C.: Congressional Quarterly Press, 1995. This brief introduction to the science of polling for the citizen as consumer pays special attention to the use of polls by the media and by political candidates.

Delli Carpini, Michael X., and Scott Keeter. *What Americans Know about Politics and Why It Matters.* New Haven, Conn.: Yale University Press, 1996. The authors provide an extensive discussion of all the known data about the amount of political knowledge possessed by Americans and how they come to possess it.

Erikson, Robert S., and Kent L. Tedin. *American Public Opinion: Its Origins, Content, and Impact.* 5th ed. New York: Macmillan, 1995. This book gives an overview of public opinion, its formation, and its distribution within the public. It also explores how public opinion influences public policy.

Fishkin, James S. *The Voice of the People: Public Opinion and Democracy.* New Haven, Conn.: Yale University Press, 1995. In this provocative work, Fishkin lays out his proposal for a deliberative poll and discusses the theoretical framework for using such a gathering for understanding public opinion on major issues.

Gaubatz, Kathlyn Taylor. *Crime in the Public Mind.* Ann Arbor, Mich.: University of Michigan Press, 1995. This volume explores in depth American attitudes toward criminals and the criminal justice system. The author compares the views of those who support "tougher" policies toward crime with those who oppose such policies.

Langston, Thomas S. *With Reverence and Contempt: How Americans Think about Their President.* Baltimore, Md.: Johns Hopkins University Press, 1995. This is a qualitative study of how Americans regard the president and the presidency. The author looks at the topic both historically and in terms of reforms that might improve the relationship between the people and the president.

Logging on

If you do a search on Yahoo using "Public AND Opinion," you'll get, among other things, some lists under "Government: Politics: Political Opinion: . . ." After the colon, they list different options: Conservative, Liberal/Progressive, or Libertarian. These contain numerous links to other sources.

Yale University Library, one of the great research institutions, has a Social Science Library and Information Services. If you want to roam around some library sources of public opinion data, this is an interesting site to visit. Go to

www.library.yale.edu/socsci/opinion/

According to its home page, the mission of National Election Studies (NES) "is to produce high quality data on voting, public opinion, and political participation that serves the research needs of social scientists, teachers, students, and policymakers concerned with understanding the theoretical and empirical foundations of mass politics in a democratic society." This is a good place to obtain information related to public opinion. Find it at

www.umich.edu/~nes/

There are quite a few Web sites dealing with public opinion that are worth a look. One of the best is that maintained by the Gallup polling organization at

www.gallup.com

The Gallup organization posts all of its own reports and polling results. The archive of past polls is excellent.

Using the Internet for political analysis

To sharpen your skills in using public opinion data, point your browser to one of the sites noted in the *Logging On* or to one maintained by one of the national newspapers. Pick a subject or topic on which the site maintains public opinion polling results (often you must use the Contents button for this). Then try to identify and consider the following types of information: First, how large was the sample, and how big is the "confidence" interval cited in the study? Do you know who commissioned the poll and to whom the results were given? Second, examine at least three questions and responses, and answer the following questions: How might the wording of the question have influenced the responses? How can you tell if the survey respondents had any information about the question asked? Was the number of respondents who couldn't answer the question significant? Can you tell if respondents could answer the question without much information? Finally, consider how much a political leader may or may not learn from this poll.

chapter **8**

Interest
Groups

BACKGROUND

EACH YEAR, LOBBYING EXPENDITURES BY FOREIGN CORPORATIONS, INTEREST GROUPS, AND FOREIGN GOVERNMENTS MOUNT. OFTEN, FOREIGN INTERESTS WORK TOGETHER WITH AMERICAN INTERESTS TO IMPROVE THEIR ECONOMIC OR POLITICAL FORTUNES. FOR EXAMPLE, TO INCREASE ITS SALES OF AIRPLANES TO CHINA, THE BOEING CORPORATION ALLIED ITSELF WITH THE CHINESE GOVERNMENT TO LOBBY FOR BETTER TRADE STATUS FOR CHINA. OFTEN, FOREIGN GOVERNMENTS AND INTERESTS HIRE RETIRED MEMBERS OF CONGRESS OR FORMER PRESIDENTIAL CANDIDATES TO REPRESENT THEIR VIEWS IN WASHINGTON. IT IS NOT UNUSUAL FOR THE EXPENDITURES OF JAPANESE INTERESTS, FOR EXAMPLE, TO TOP $60 MILLION IN A YEAR. ALTHOUGH MANY OF THE ISSUES THAT ARE THE SUBJECT OF INTERNATIONAL LOBBYING ARE OF EQUAL IMPORTANCE TO AMERICANS, IT IS POSSIBLE THAT FOREIGN INTERESTS CAN GAIN ADVANTAGES THROUGH LEGISLATION THAT DAMAGES THEIR

WHAT IF FOREIGN INTEREST GROUPS WERE BANNED?

One way to limit the influence of foreign governments on U.S. policymakers would be to ban foreign interest groups from lobbying U.S. government officials. What would happen if Congress did so?

Certainly, it would be far more difficult for other coun-

tries to influence U.S. policy-making. It would also free U.S. government officials from having to worry about the effect of legislation or other government actions on foreign countries or groups. But it would also create some problems.

For one thing, Congress would have to identify what, exactly, constitutes a foreign interest. As business has become more and more global, it is no longer easy to decide whether a company is foreign or domestic. An American company may have ownership rights in a foreign company, which in turn has a U.S. subsidiary. Is that a foreign or a domestic company? Furthermore, American companies with foreign operations are allowed to lobby foreign governments and even donate campaign contributions to political candidates in other countries. Would such activity also be banned in the interest of fairness?

AMERICAN INTERESTS WOULD BE AFFECTED, TOO

Banning foreign interests would also adversely affect a number of Americans. Often, the interests of American businesses, workers, or communities are closely tied to foreign

interests. It is not uncommon for American firms to purchase products from—or sell products to—businesses in other countries. Consider that the economic interests of the workers in the Boeing plant at Everett, Washington, are heavily dependent on their employer's ability to sell airplanes in foreign nations, such as China. These workers have every right to be represented in the halls of Congress to make the case for open trade with China or any other nation. But their case would be much stronger if they could join forces with foreign lobbies.

PROBLEMS WITH ENFORCEMENT

Finally, enforcing the ban could prove difficult. Consider the problem Congress has faced with foreign campaign contributions. Foreign corporations, nonresident aliens, and foreign governments are prohibited from making direct campaign contributions to American campaigns. This is because, in a sense, campaign contributions are a way for Americans to take part in the debate over who is to be elected. Congress has thus seen fit to exclude foreign interests to make sure that elected officials represent Americans.

As recent campaigns have shown, however, foreign

groups and individuals have found ways to transfer funds into the accounts of American voters and legal residents, who can then make the contributions. Although such transfers are illegal, they are difficult to identify. As you will read in this chapter, lobbyists use many *indirect* techniques to influence legislators. No doubt, foreign interests would find ways of skirting the ban on lobbying by resorting to indirect tactics that would be hard to identify and monitor.

FOR CRITICAL ANALYSIS

1. Can you think of particular issues or political questions on which the interests of a foreign nation truly would oppose American interests? Think of issues such as the price of oil or trade in computers.

2. How could the lobbying efforts of groups such as the American Jewish Committee or the Arab American Association, which represent American citizens, be restricted?

3. Should American corporations be required to reveal all contacts they have with foreign interests or partners in regard to legislation and public policy?

Facing lawsuits by the families of cancer patients and under attack by the governments of many of the states, the tobacco industry came to the bargaining table in 1997 to shape national legislation that would permit the tobacco companies to continue to market their products, although under strict regulations. By 1998, when legislation was under consideration by Congress, the tobacco manufacturers already had agreed to pay individual states billions of dollars to repay the costs of treating patients who suffered tobacco-related illnesses. The tobacco negotiations involved a combination of **lobbying** and **interest group** maneuvering for a settlement that could reach $500 billion over two decades. In April 1998, however, the tobacco companies pulled out of the tentative agreement.

The debate over the regulation of tobacco began more than thirty years ago, when it was first proposed that the health risks of smoking be identified. The range of interest groups participating in the debate has expanded greatly since those early days when the major groups were the tobacco companies and the federal government. Among the crowd at or near the table during the recent negotiations were the tobacco companies; the attorneys general of more than twenty states; the Food and Drug Administration; legislators; health groups, including the American Medical Association; children's groups; farmers; asbestos companies and drug companies; and hundreds of lawyers representing clients. Many of these groups also claimed to represent large segments of the American public–smokers, nonsmokers, and the taxpayers.

The tobacco negotiations presented complicated issues for the political system: If the price of tobacco were raised, would smoking among teens be reduced? Could regulating the advertising and availability of tobacco products reduce teen smoking? What would happen to the farmers who depended on the tobacco crop? Who should pay for the health costs of cigarette smoking? How would the settlement affect the industry and employees, the tax revenues of the government, health costs, and the general health of society? Knowing that Congress and the president eventually would have to agree to the final set of regulations and legal restrictions, the tobacco interests not only lobbied intensely but also poured large amounts of money into the political campaign war chests of members of Congress. Reports documented gifts of more than $4.5 million from tobacco companies to candidates and political parties during 1997. The tobacco industry also spent more than $58 million on lobbying activities during 1996 and 1997 as the negotiations for a settlement continued.

Lobbying
The attempt by organizations or by individuals to influence the passage, defeat, or contents of legislation and the administrative decisions of government.

Interest Group
An organized group of individuals sharing common objectives who actively attempt to influence policymakers in all three branches of the government and at all levels.

INFOTRAC®
COLLEGE EDITION

"Congress Snuffs out the Tobacco Bill"

Lobbying activity becomes most intensive the day a vote is being taken on an important issue. Here lobbyists are working frantically on the day that the North American Free Trade Agreement vote was taken. Not surprisingly, lobbyists are often found in the lobbies of Congress.

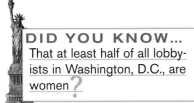
The Role of Interest Groups

As the negotiations for a tobacco settlement and for the future regulation of the industry demonstrate, the American system of government and politics provides a wealth of opportunities for those affected by government action to voice their views and to try to influence policymakers.

Interest groups take many forms. They include ordinary people who make their points in Congress and the statehouses of America. When a businessperson contacts her state representative about a proposed change in the law, she is lobbying the government. When farmers descend on Washington, D.C., in tractors or Americans with disabilities gather in the corridors of city hall, they are also interest groups lobbying their representatives. Protected by the First Amendment's guarantee of the right to assemble and petition the government for the redress of grievances, individuals have joined together in voluntary associations to try to influence the government ever since the Boston Tea Party (see Chapter 2), which involved, after all, an eighteenth-century trade issue.

As pluralist theories suggest, the structure of American government invites the participation of interest groups. The governmental system has many points of access or places in the decision-making process at which interest groups may focus an attack. If a bill opposed by a group passes the Senate, the lobbying efforts shift to the House of Representatives or to the president to seek a veto. If, in spite of all efforts, the legislation passes, the group may even lobby the executive agency or bureau that is supposed to implement the law and hope to influence the way in which the legislation is applied. In some cases, interest groups carry their efforts into the court system, either by filing lawsuits or filing briefs as "friends of the court." The constitutional features of separation of powers and checks and balances encourage interest groups in their efforts.

A Nation of Joiners?

Alexis de Tocqueville observed in 1834 that "in no country of the world has the principle of association been more successfully used or applied to a greater multitude of objectives than in America."[1] The French traveler was amazed at the degree to which Americans formed groups to solve civic problems, establish social relationships, and speak for their economic or political interests. Perhaps James Madison, when he wrote *Federalist Paper* No. 10 (see Appendix D), had already judged the character of his country's citizens similarly. He supported the creation of a large republic with several states to encourage the formation of many interests. The multitude of interests, in Madison's view, would work to discourage the formation of an oppressive larger minority or majority interest.

Surely, neither Madison nor de Tocqueville foresaw the formation of more than a hundred thousand associations in the United States. Poll data show that more than two-thirds of all Americans belong to at least one group or association. While the majority of these affiliations could not be classified as "interest groups" in the political sense, Americans do understand the principles of working in groups. As noted in Chapter 1, some scholars maintain that this penchant for group action supports a pluralist interpretation of American politics, in which most government policies become the work of group conflict and compromise. (The tobacco bill, discussed earlier, illustrates this principle.) Some critics might say that the drive to organize interests can go too far, resulting in "hyperpluralism," meaning that so many powerful interests are competing that no real policy change can take place. Furthermore, it is possible that interest

Alexis de Tocqueville (1805–1859), a French social historian and traveler, commented on Americans' predilection for joining groups.

---

[1]Alexis de Tocqueville, *Democracy in America*, Vol. 1, edited by Phillips Bradley (New York: Knopf, 1980), p. 191.

groups can become so powerful that the needs and demands of ordinary citizens can be ignored (see the discussion of interest groups and representative democracy later in this chapter).

Recently, American society has been faulted for a perceived decline in participation in group activities, a decline that may threaten society's ability to maintain itself. The debate over this issue is discussed in this chapter's feature entitled *Politics and Civic Participation: Is America's Social Fabric Coming Apart at the Seams?*

The Benefits of Interest Groups

One puzzle that has fascinated political scientists is why some people join interest groups, whereas many others do not. Everyone has some interest that could benefit from government action. For many groups, however, those remain unorganized interests, or latent interests.

According to the theory of Mancur Olson, it may be that it simply is not rational for individuals to join most groups. He introduces the idea of the "collective

POLITICS and Civic Participation

Is America's Social Fabric Coming Apart at the Seams?

During the 1990s, a common lament was that Americans were becoming apathetic about politics and disinterested in civic participation. Voter turnout was low. Surveys showed that Americans were increasingly distrustful of government officials and that confidence in major institutions, such as Congress, was declining.

In 1995, Robert D. Putnam of Harvard University published an influential essay in which he argued that Americans were becoming increasingly disconnected from their communities and from each other. Just as more people were "bowling alone" rather than joining bowling leagues, so were more Americans retreating into private spaces rather than getting involved in their communities. To bolster his thesis, Putnam pointed to the declining participation in such organizations as the

PTA, the Red Cross, and the Girl Scouts.*

Civic participation has always been the thread that holds our nation's social fabric together, and worried commentators echoed Putnam's fear that declining civic involvement could have dire results for our nation.

Despite these alarms, however, recent studies have shown that America is not falling apart at the seams. On the contrary, membership in organizations appears to be higher than previously reported, according to a study of civic involvement conducted by the University of Virginia's Center for Survey Research under the direction of the American

*See the following articles by Robert Putnam: "Tuning In, Tuning Out: The Strange Disappearance of Social Capital in America," *PS: Political Science and Politics,* December 1995, pp. 664–683; and "Bowling Alone, Revisited," *The Responsive Community,* Vol. 18 (Spring 1995), p. 33

Association of Retired Persons (AARP).†

The results of the AARP study, which were released in late 1997, clearly showed that "we're not a nation of civic slugs," as Constance Swank, who directed the project for the AARP, commented. In fact, 98 percent of those surveyed were involved in at least one activity that connected them to people outside their households: 78 percent visit with friends, 64 percent are engaged in religious activities, 61 percent pursue hobbies outside their households, 57 percent perform activities with teens and children, and 53 percent volunteer time. The average respondent claimed more than four memberships in more than three types of organizations, including religious organizations, health and sports clubs, professional trade groups,

†Thomas M. Guterbock and John C. Fries, *Maintaining America's Social Fabric: The AARP Survey of Civic Involvement* (University of Virginia: Center for Survey Research, December 1997).

school groups, and neighborhood groups. One-third of the respondents reported that they had worked with others to solve local problems, and eight out of ten respondents believed that they could solve local problems by acting in concert with others.

A not-too-rosy finding was that the youngest adults surveyed—those between the ages of eighteen and twenty-six—exhibited the least confidence in the government's ability to do what is right and the least involvement in their communities. A big unknown is whether the opinions and actions of this age group will change in the coming years.

FOR CRITICAL ANALYSIS

If a person stays informed on political issues and votes regularly at the polls, why should society be concerned if that person does not participate in any group activities?

good." This concept refers to any public benefit that, if available to any member of the community, cannot be denied to any other member, whether or not he or she participated in the effort to gain the good.

Although collective benefits are usually thought of as coming from such public goods as clean air or national defense, benefits are also bestowed by the government on subsets of the public. Price subsidies to dairy farmers and loans to college students are examples. Olson uses economic theory to propose that it is not rational for interested individuals to join groups that work for group benefits. In fact, it is often more rational for the individual to wait for others to procure the benefits and then share them.

If so little incentive exists for individuals to join together, why are there thousands of interest groups lobbying in Washington? According to the logic of collective action, if the contribution of an individual *will* make a difference to the effort, then it is worth it to the individual to join. Thus, smaller groups, which seek benefits for only a small proportion of the population, are more likely to enroll members who will give time and money to the cause. Larger groups, which represent general public interests (the women's movement or the American Civil Liberties Union, for example), will find it relatively more difficult to get individuals to join. People need an incentive—material or otherwise—to join.[2]

Solidary Incentives

Solidary Incentive
A reason or motive having to do with the desire to associate with others and to share with others a particular interest or hobby.

Interest groups offer **solidary incentives** for their members. Solidary incentives include companionship, a sense of belonging, and the pleasure of associating with others. Although originally the National Audubon Society was founded to save the snowy egret from extinction, most members join today to learn more about birds and to meet and share their pleasure with other individuals who enjoy bird watching as a hobby. Even though the incentive might be solidary for many members, this organization nonetheless also pursues an active political agenda, working to preserve the environment and to protect endangered species. Most members may not play any part in working toward larger, more national goals unless the organization can convince them to take political action or unless some local environmental issue arises.

Material Incentives

Material Incentive
A reason or motive having to do with economic benefits or opportunities.

For other individuals, interest groups offer direct **material incentives**. A case in point is the American Association of Retired Persons (AARP), which provides discounts, insurance plans, and organized travel opportunities for its members. Because of its exceptionally low dues ($8 annually) and the benefits gained through membership in the AARP, it has become the largest—and a very powerful—interest group in the United States. The AARP can claim to represent the interests of millions of senior citizens and can show that they actually have joined the group. For most seniors, the material incentives outweigh the membership costs.

Many other interest groups offer indirect material incentives for their members. Such groups as the American Dairy Association or the National Association of Automobile Dealers do not give discounts or freebies to their members, but they do offer indirect benefits and rewards by, for example, protecting the material interests of their members from government policymaking that is injurious to their industry or business.

---

[2]For further reading on this complex and interesting theory, see Mancur Olson, *The Logic of Collective Action* (Cambridge, Mass.: Harvard University Press, 1965).

Purposive Incentives

Interest groups also offer the opportunity for individuals to pursue political, economic, or social goals through joint action. Such **purposive incentives** offer individuals the satisfaction of taking action for the sake of their beliefs or principles. The individuals who belong to groups focusing on the abortion issue have joined those groups because they are concerned about the question of whether abortions should be made available to the public. People join such groups because they feel strongly enough about the issues to support the groups' work with money and time.

Purposive Incentive
A reason or motive having to do with ethical beliefs or ideological principles.

Interest Groups and Social Movements

Interest groups are often spawned by mass **social movements.** Such movements represent demands by a large segment of the population for change in the political, economic, or social system. Social movements are often the first expression of latent discontent with the contemporary system. They may be the authentic voice of weaker or oppressed groups in society that do not have the means or standing to organize as interest groups. For example, the women's movement of the nineteenth century suffered social disapproval from most mainstream political and social leaders. Because women were unable to vote or take an active part in the political system, it was difficult for women who desired greater freedoms to organize formal groups. After the Civil War, when more women became active in professional life, the first real women's rights group, the National Woman Suffrage Association, came into being.

African Americans found themselves in an even more disadvantaged situation after the end of the Reconstruction period. Not only were they unable to exercise political rights in many southern and border states, but also participation in any form of organization could lead to economic ruin, physical harassment, or even death. The civil rights movement of the 1950s and 1960s was clearly a social movement. Although several formal organizations worked to support the movement—including the Southern Christian Leadership Conference, the National Association for the Advancement of Colored People, and the Urban

Social Movement
A movement that represents the demands of a large segment of the public for political, economic, or social change.

President Clinton is shown here addressing the American Association of Retired Persons (AARP), which has become one of the most powerful lobbying groups in America. As the population grows older, a larger percentage of Americans are over the age of fifty. Any president knows the importance of keeping such an important interest group happy. Through its lobbying efforts, the AARP has been effective in preventing any significant reductions in Social Security benefits.

League—only a social movement could generate the kinds of civil disobedience that took place in hundreds of towns and cities across the country.

Social movements are often precursors of interest groups. They may generate interest groups with specific goals that successfully recruit members through the incentives the group offers. In the case of the women's movement of the 1960s, the National Organization for Women was formed out of a demand to end gender-segregated job advertising in newspapers.

Types of Interest Groups

Thousands of groups exist to influence government. Among the major types of interest groups are those that represent the main sectors of the economy—business, agricultural, government, and labor groups. In more recent years, a number of "public-interest" organizations have been formed to represent the needs of the general citizenry, including some "single-issue" groups. The interests of foreign governments and foreign businesses are also represented in the American political arena, as discussed in the chapter-opening *What If* feature. The membership of some major interest groups is shown in Table 8–1.

Economic Interest Groups

Numerous interest groups have been formed to promote economic interests. These groups include business, agricultural, labor, public employee, and professional organizations.

Business Interest Groups. Thousands of trade and business organizations attempt to influence government policies. Some groups target a single regulatory unit, whereas others try to effect major policy changes. Three large business groups are consistently effective: (1) the National Association of Manufacturers (NAM), (2) the U.S. Chamber of Commerce, and (3) the Business Roundtable. The annual budget of the NAM is more than $22 million, which it collects in dues from about 14,000 relatively large corporations. Sometimes called the National Chamber, the U.S. Chamber of Commerce represents more than 200,000 businesses. Dues from its members, which include about 4,000 local chambers of commerce, exceed $30 million a year. Separately, two hundred of the largest corporations in the United States send their chief executive officers to the Business Roundtable. This organization is based in New York, but it does its lobbying in Washington, D.C. Established in 1972, the Roundtable was designed to promote a more aggressive view of business interests in general, cutting across specific industries. Dues paid by the member corporations are determined by the companies' wealth.

Agricultural Interest Groups. American farmers and their workers represent about 2 percent of the U.S. population. In spite of this, farmers' influence on legislation beneficial to their interests has been enormous. Farmers have succeeded in their aims because they have very strong interest groups. They are geographically dispersed and therefore have many representatives and senators to speak for them. The American Farm Bureau Federation, established in 1919, has over 4.7 million members. It was instrumental in getting government guarantees of "fair" prices during the Great Depression in the 1930s.[3] Another important agricultural special interest organization is the National Farmers' Union (NFU).

---

[3]The Agricultural Adjustment Act of 1933 (declared unconstitutional) was replaced by the 1937 Agricultural Adjustment Act and later changed and amended several times.

TABLE 8-1

Characteristics of Selected Interest Groups

NAME (FOUNDED)	MEMBERS (INDIVIDUALS OR AS NOTED)
Business/Economic	
Business Roundtable (1972)	200 corporations
The Conference Board, Inc. (1916)	3,000 labor unions, colleges & universities, etc.
National Association of Manufacturers (1895)	14,000 companies
U.S. Chamber of Commerce (1912)	200,000 companies, state & local chambers of commerce, etc.
Civil/Constitutional Rights	
AIDS Coalition to Unleash Power (ACT UP–New York) (1987)	4,000 (NYC) + national branches
American Association of Retired Persons (1958)	33,000,000
American Civil Liberties Union (1920)	275,000
Amnesty International USA (1961)	over 1 million
Handgun Control, Inc. (1974)	380,000
Leadership Conference on Civil Rights, Inc. (1950)	80 national organizations
League of United Latin American Citizens (LULAC) (1929)	115,000
Mexican-American Legal Defense and Educational Fund (1968)	—
NAACP Legal Defense and Educational Fund, Inc. (1940)	—
National Abortion Rights Action League (1969)	500,000
National Association for the Advancement of Colored People (1909)	over 500,000
National Gay and Lesbian Task Force (1973)	18,000
National Organization for Women, Inc. (1966)	250,000
National Rifle Association of America (1871)	2,800,000
National Right to Life Committee, Inc. (1973)	—
National Urban League (1910)	1,600,000
Planned Parenthood Federation of America, Inc. (1916)	—
Women's Legal Defense Fund (1971)	1,500
Community/Grassroots	
The American Society for the Prevention of Cruelty to Animals (1866)	400,000
Association of Community Organizations for Reform Now (ACORN) (1970)	90,000
Mothers Against Drunk Driving (1980)	3,200,000
National Anti-Vivisection Society (1929)	—
Environmental	
Environmental Defense Fund (1967)	300,000
Greenpeace USA (1971)	2,100,000
Izaak Walton League of America (1922)	52,700
League of Conservation Voters (1970)	60,000
National Audubon Society (1905)	600,000
National Wildlife Federation (1936)	4,400,000
The Nature Conservancy (1951)	800,000
Sierra Club (1892)	550,000
The Wilderness Society (1935)	270,000
World Wildlife Fund (1948)	1,200,000
International Affairs	
American Israel Public Affairs Committee (1954)	55,000
Human Rights Watch (1978)	—
Accuracy in Media (1969)	25,000

SOURCE: Foundation for Public Affairs, *Public Interest Profiles 1995–1996* (Washington, D.C.: Congressional Quarterly Press, 1995), and authors' update.

Northwest Airline pilots picket at the Minneapolis airport during their 1998 strike.

Labor Movement

Generally, the full range of economic and political expression of working-class interests; politically, the organization of working-class interests.

Service Sector

The sector of the economy that provides services—such as food services, insurance, and education—in contrast to the sector of the economy that produces goods.

Labor Interest Groups.   Interest groups representing the **labor movement** date back to at least 1886 when the American Federation of Labor (AFL) was formed. In 1955, the AFL joined forces with the Congress of Industrial Organizations (CIO). Today, the combined AFL-CIO is an enormous union with a membership exceeding 13 million workers. In a sense, the AFL-CIO is a union of unions.

The political arm of the AFL-CIO is the Committee on Political Education (COPE). COPE's activities are funded by voluntary contributions from union members. COPE has been active in state and national campaigns since 1956.

Other unions are also active politically. One of the most widely known is the International Brotherhood of Teamsters, which was led by Jimmy Hoffa until his expulsion in 1967 because of alleged ties with organized crime. The Teamsters Union was established initially in 1903 and today has a membership of 1.3 million.

Another independent union is the Automobile, Aerospace, and Agricultural Implement Workers of America (formerly United Automobile Workers), founded in 1935. It now has a membership of 500,000. Also very active in labor lobbying is the United Mine Workers union, representing about 200,000 members.

The role of unions in American society has weakened in recent years, as witnessed by a decline in union membership (see Figure 8–1). (See this chapter's *Critical Perspective: Are Labor Unions Getting Stronger or Weaker?*) In the age of automation and with the rise of the **service sector,** blue-collar workers in basic industries (autos, steel, and the like) represent a smaller and smaller percentage of the total working population. Because of this decline in the industrial sector of the economy, national unions are looking to nontraditional areas for their membership, including migrant farm workers, service workers, and, most recently, public employees—such as police officers; fire-fighting personnel; and teachers, including college professors.

Public Employee Interest Groups.   The degree of unionization in the private sector has declined since 1965, but this has been offset partially by growth in the unionization of public employees. Figure 8–1 shows the growth in the public sector work force. With a total work force of more than 6.6 million, these unions are likely to continue expanding.

Both the American Federation of State, County, and Municipal Employees and the American Federation of Teachers are members of the AFL-CIO's Public Employee Department. Originally, the public employee unions started out as social and professional organizations. Over the years, they have become quite

FIGURE 8-1

Decline in Union Membership, 1948 to Present

As shown in this figure, the percentage of the total work force that is represented by labor unions has declined precipitously over the last two decades. Note, however, that in contrast to the decline in union membership in the private sector, the percentage of government workers who are unionized has increased significantly.

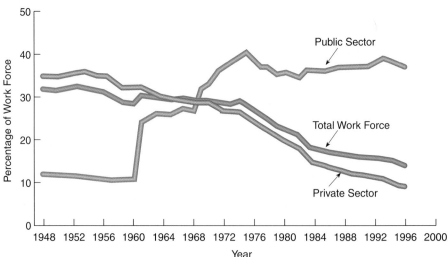

Source: Bureau of Labor Statistics, 1998.

Critical | perspective

Are Labor Unions Getting Stronger or Weaker?

The American trade union movement began in the early 1800s with the formation of organizations uniting workers in various crafts, such as carpenters and shoemakers. As the U.S. manufacturing system developed during the Civil War, more and more factories were established. After the Civil War, the union movement was fostered first by the Knights of Labor and then by the formation of the American Federation of Labor (AFL), a relatively nonideological movement that intended to organize skilled industrial workers. Strikes began to be successful.

Over the next hundred years, the labor movement grew enormously in both membership and political influence. The AFL continued to grow, spurred on by the founding of the United Mine Workers and the unions of the Congress of Industrial Organizations (CIO), which represented mass-production workers. As a result of supportive legislation passed during the administration of Franklin Roosevelt, the union movement expanded. By the end of World War II (1941–1945), unions included more than 15 million workers, representing more than one-third of the nonagricultural work force.

The Republican Congress of the postwar period placed some constraints on the labor movement with the Taft-Hartley Act of 1947. Since that time, the power of the labor unions has waxed and waned due to both internal and external tensions. Democratic administrations and Congresses generally have supported pro-union legislation, and John Kennedy gave public employees the right to join unions through an executive order in 1962. Republican administrations generally have been pro-employer in matters of labor legislation.

Regardless of the legislative and political climate, however, the growth of the service sector, high-tech industries, and the movement of factories to the nonunion South have greatly reduced labor's proportion of the workforce. Today, only 14.1 percent of workers (about 16 million workers) belong to unions. And the greatest successes in organizing have been in public sector jobs.

During the Reagan and Bush administrations, few union strikes were successful, and organizing efforts declined. The Republican congressional victory of 1994, however, seemed to put new life into the lobbying and political efforts of the union movement. Faced with a Congress that was quite anti-union in its political views, the AFL-CIO vowed to return a Democratic Congress to power in 1996 to support President Clinton. Labor unions taxed their members an extra assessment to raise $30 million for the campaign.

Coordinated advertisements were run across the country in support of Democratic candidates and in opposition to the Republican presidential candidate, Robert Dole. Although the business community took months to respond, eventually business interests raised even more money to support Republican candidates. It was clear, however, that the labor unions would respond to political challenges in the future.

The labor union movement also won a huge public relations victory with the successful Teamsters' strike against United Parcel Service (UPS) in 1997. Many small businesses and the U.S. Postal Service felt the brunt of that strike. UPS eventually settled with the Teamsters, apparently accepting labor's views on the use of part-time workers. The Teamsters' president, Ron Carey, and his staff definitely dominated the media coverage of the strike, effectively painting UPS as an unfair and uncaring employer.

Following the Teamsters' victory and the flexing of labor's political muscle, many commentators suggested that the labor movement was again on the rise in the United States. But the Teamsters' victory was soon undercut by the removal of Carey from office due to election fraud. Data released in 1998 showed a slight decline in overall union membership even as organizing efforts intensified. As the movement feared, the Republican Congress has pressured for legislation to control union expenditures on political campaigns. Similar laws are being considered in almost two dozen states.

In an era when the economy is robust, it is more difficult for unions to recruit workers. At the same time, employers continue to hire part-time workers with reduced benefits or no benefits, jobs are cut, and factories are moved to Mexico and other parts of the world. Whether the union movement will be a powerful political force in the future is an unanswered question.

FOR CRITICAL ANALYSIS

1. What kinds of employment issues are most likely to cause workers to join a union? Do labor unions seem to be addressing those issues today?
2. Do you agree that unions should be able to spend their funds (raised from members' dues) on political campaigns? Is such spending really in the members' interest?
3. How important is the political make-up of Congress to the growth or decline of unions in the United States?

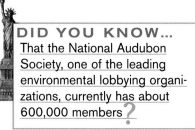

militant and are often involved in strikes. Many of these strikes are illegal, because certain public employees do not have the right to strike and essentially sign a contract so stating. In August 1981, the Professional Air Traffic Controllers Organization (PATCO) went on strike in defiance of a court order. President Ronald Reagan, convinced that public opinion was on his side, fired the strikers. Supervisors, nonstrikers, military personnel, and new trainees were rounded up to handle the jobs vacated by the 16,000 terminated air traffic controllers.

A powerful interest group lobbying on behalf of public employees is the National Education Association (NEA), a nationwide organization of about 2.3 million administrators, teachers, and others connected with education. The NEA lobbies intensively for increased public funding of education. The NEA sponsors regional and national conventions each year and has an extensive program of electronic media broadcasts, surveys, and the like.

Interest Groups of Professionals. Numerous professional organizations exist, including the American Bar Association, the Association of General Contractors of America, the Institute of Electrical and Electronic Engineers, the Screen Actors Guild, and others. Some professional groups, such as lawyers and doctors, are more influential than others due to their social status. Lawyers have a unique advantage—a large number of members of Congress share their profession. In terms of money spent on lobbying, however, one professional organization stands head and shoulders above the rest—the American Medical Association (AMA). Founded in 1947, it is now affiliated with more than 2,000 local and state medical societies and has a total membership of 285,000 and an administrative staff of 1,100. The AMA spent an estimated $2.8 million in 1996 presidential campaign contributions in its efforts to influence legislation.

Environmental Groups

Environmental interest groups are not new. We have already mentioned the National Audubon Society, which was founded in 1905 to protect the snowy egret from the commercial demand for hat decorations. The patron of the Sierra Club, John Muir, worked for the creation of national parks more than ninety

The *Rainbow Warrior,* the flagship of Greenpeace, is both a symbol for the environmental interest group and a resource that can be used for actions at sea to protect the environment. The *Rainbow Warrior* has acted to save dolphins, to protest oil spills, and to stop Japanese and Russian whaling.

years ago. But the blossoming of national environmental groups with mass memberships is a relatively recent phenomenon. Since the first Earth Day, organized in 1972, many interest groups have sprung up to protect the environment in general or unique ecological niches. The groups range from the National Wildlife Federation, with a membership of more than 4.4 million and an emphasis on education, to the fairly elite Environmental Defense Fund, with a membership of 300,000 and a focus on influencing federal policy. Other groups include the Nature Conservancy, which seeks members' contributions so the organization can buy up threatened natural areas and either give them to state or local governments or manage them itself, and the more radical Greenpeace Society and Earth First.

INFOTRAC®
COLLEGE EDITION

"Loggers vs. Greenpeace"

Public-Interest Groups

Public interest is a difficult term to define because, as we noted earlier, there are many publics in our nation of over 270 million. It is almost impossible for one particular public policy to benefit everybody, which makes it practically impossible to define the public interest. Nonetheless, over the past few decades, a variety of law and lobbying organizations have been formed "in the public interest."

Public Interest
The best interests of the collective, overall community; the national good, rather than the narrow interests of a self-serving group.

Nader Organizations.   The most well-known and perhaps the most effective public-interest groups are those organized under the leadership of consumer activist Ralph Nader. The story of Ralph Nader's rise to the top began after the publication, in 1965, of his book *Unsafe at Any Speed,* a lambasting critique of the purported attempt by General Motors (GM) to keep from the public detrimental information about GM's rear-engine Corvair. Partly as a result of Nader's book, Congress began to consider testimony in favor of an automobile safety bill. GM made a clumsy attempt to discredit Nader's background. Nader sued, the media exploited the story, and when GM settled out of court for $425,000, Nader became the recognized champion of consumer interests. Since then, Nader has turned over much of his income to the more than sixty public-interest groups that he has formed or sponsored. In recent years, Nader has opposed tort reform legislation, among other things.

Other Public-Interest Groups.   Partly in response to the Nader organizations, numerous conservative public-interest law firms have sprung up that are often pitted against the consumer groups in court. Some of these are the Mountain States Legal Defense Foundation, the Pacific Legal Foundation, the National Right-to-Work Legal Defense Foundation, the Washington Legal Foundation, and the Mid-Atlantic Legal Foundation.

One of the largest public-interest groups is Common Cause, founded in 1968, whose goal is to reorder national priorities toward "the public" and to make governmental institutions more responsive to the needs of the public. Anyone willing to pay dues of $20 a year can become a member. Members are polled regularly to obtain information about local and national issues requiring reassessment. Some of the activities of Common Cause have been (1) helping to ensure the passage of the Twenty-sixth Amendment (giving eighteen-year-olds the right to vote), (2) achieving greater voter registration in all states, (3) supporting the complete withdrawal of all U.S. forces from South Vietnam in the 1970s, and (4) promoting legislation that would limit campaign spending.

Other public-interest groups are active on a wide range of issues. The goal of the League of Women Voters, founded in 1920, is to educate the public on political matters. Although generally nonpartisan, it has lobbied for the Equal Rights Amendment and for government reform. The Consumer Federation of America is an alliance of about two hundred local and national organizations interested

Ralph Nader began the movement to create public-interest groups through the publication, in 1965, of his book *Unsafe at Any Speed,* which criticized General Motors for underplaying the dangers of its Corvair automobile. Since that time, he has founded a number of not-for-profit public interest groups that track business and governmental actions in specific policy arenas.

in consumer protection. The American Civil Liberties Union dates back to World War I, when, under a different name, it defended draft resisters. It generally enters into legal disputes related to Bill of Rights issues.

Special Interest Groups

Special interest groups, being narrowly focused, may be able to call more attention to their respective causes because they have simple and straightforward goals and because their members tend to care intensely about the issues. Thus, such groups can easily motivate their members to contact legislators or to organize demonstrations in support of their policy goals.

A number of interest groups focus on just one issue. The abortion debate has created various groups opposed to abortion (such as Right to Life) and groups in favor of abortion (such as the National Abortion Rights Action League). Other single-issue groups are the National Rifle Association, the Right to Work Committee (an anti-union group), and the Hudson Valley PAC (a pro-Israel group).

Other groups represent particular groups of Americans who share a common characteristic, such as age or ethnicity. Such interest groups lobby for legislation that may benefit their members in terms of rights or just represent a viewpoint.

The American Association of Retired Persons (AARP), as mentioned earlier, is one of the most powerful interest groups in Washington, D.C., and, according to some, the strongest lobbying group in the United States. It is certainly the nation's largest interest group, with a membership of over thirty-three million. The AARP has accomplished much for its members over the years. It played a significant role in the creation of Medicare and Medicaid, as well as in obtaining cost-of-living increases in Social Security payments. Today, though, the AARP is under attack. In part, this is because of the changed circumstances of today's older Americans. Whereas they were once among the poorer groups of our society, today they are, on average, among the country's wealthiest citizens. In other words, they no longer need special legislation to protect their welfare

Reprinted courtesy of Larry Wright and the *Detroit News.*

to the extent that they once did. Nonetheless, the AARP continues to pressure Congress for legislation that benefits this group of Americans.

Foreign Governments

Home-grown interests are not the only players in the game. Washington, D.C., is also the center for lobbying by foreign governments as well as private foreign interests. Large research and lobbying staffs are maintained by governments of the largest U.S. trading partners, such as Japan, South Korea, Canada, and the European Union (EU) countries. Even smaller nations, such as those in the Caribbean, engage lobbyists when vital legislation affecting their trade interests is considered. Frequently, these foreign interests hire former representatives or former senators to promote their positions on Capitol Hill. As indicated in the chapter-opening *What If . . .* feature, there is growing concern over the influence of foreign interests on U.S. politics.

Interest Group Strategies

Interest groups employ a wide range of techniques and strategies to promote their policy goals. Although few groups are successful at persuading Congress and the president to endorse their programs completely, many are able to prevent—or at least weaken—legislation injurious to their members from being considered. The key to success for interest groups is the ability to have access to government officials. To achieve this, interest groups and their representatives try to cultivate long-term relationships with legislators and government officials. The best of such relationships are based on mutual respect and cooperation. The interest group provides the official with excellent sources of information and assistance, and the official in turn gives the group opportunities to express its views.

The techniques used by interest groups may be divided into those that are direct and indirect. **Direct techniques** include all those ways in which the interest group and its lobbyists approach the officials personally to press their case. **Indirect techniques,** in contrast, include strategies that use the general public or individuals to influence the government for the interest group.

Direct Techniques

Lobbying, publicizing ratings of legislative behavior, and providing campaign assistance are the three main direct techniques used by interest groups.

Lobbying Techniques. As might be guessed, the term *lobbying* comes from the activities of private citizens regularly congregating in the lobbies of legislative chambers before a session to petition legislators. In the latter part of the nineteenth century, railroad and industrial groups openly bribed state legislators to pass legislation beneficial to their interests, giving lobbying a well-deserved bad name. Today, standard lobbying techniques still include buttonholing (detaining and engaging in conversation) senators and representatives in state capitols and in Washington, D.C., while they are moving from their offices to the voting chambers. Lobbyists, however, do much more than that.

Lobbyists engage in an array of activities to influence legislation and government policy. These include, at a minimum, the following:

The job of lobbyists never stops. These Washington lobbyists are scrutinizing news reports to ascertain the positions of members of Congress on policy issues that will have an impact on those interests that the lobbyists represent. While many critics of lobbyists and interest groups argue that they distort the actions of our government, the First Amendment prohibits the government from regulating their speech.

Direct Technique
An interest group activity that involves interaction with government officials to further the group's goals.

Indirect Technique
A strategy employed by interest groups that uses third parties to influence government officials.

TABLE 8-2

ADA Ratings for 1997

Americans for Democratic Action (ADA), a liberal political organization, tracks the votes of all senators and representatives on the set of issues that the ADA thinks is most important. The "score" for each legislator is the percentage of "correct" votes from the ADA's point of view. The "Heroes" listed below voted correctly 100 percent of the time; the "Zeroes" voted correctly 0 percent of the time.

SENATE HEROES

Boxer, B. (D., Cal.)
Durbin, R. (D., Ill.)
Kennedy, E. (D., Mass.)
Reed, J. (D., R.I.)
Sarbanes, P. (D., Md.)
Wellstone, P. (D., Minn.)

SENATE ZEROES

Allard, W. (R., Colo.)
Ashcroft, J. (R., Mo.)
Brownback, S. (R., Kans.)
Gramm, P. (R., Tex.)
Grams, R. (R., Minn.)
Helms, J. (R., N.C.)
Hutchinson, T. (R., Ariz.)
Kyl, J. (R., Ariz.)
Mack, C. (R., Fla.)
Nickles, D. (R., Okla.)
Sessions, J. (R., Ala.)
Thompson, F. (R., Tenn.)

SOURCE: Americans for Democratic Action, 1998.

1. Engaging in private meetings with public officials, including the president's advisers, to make known the interests of the lobbyist's clients. Although acting on behalf of a client, often lobbyists furnish needed information to senators and representatives (and government agency appointees) that they could not hope to obtain on their own. It is to the lobbyist's advantage to provide accurate information so that the policymaker will rely on this source in the future.

2. Testifying before congressional committees for or against proposed legislation being considered by Congress.

3. Testifying before executive rulemaking agencies—such as the Federal Trade Commission or the Consumer Product Safety Commission—for or against proposed rules.

4. Assisting legislators or bureaucrats in drafting legislation or prospective regulations. Often, lobbyists furnish legal advice on the specific details of legislation.

5. Inviting legislators to social occasions, such as cocktail parties, boating expeditions, and other events, including conferences at exotic locations. Most lobbyists feel that contacting legislators in a more relaxed social setting is effective.

6. Providing political information to legislators and other government officials. Often the lobbyists will have better information than the party leadership about how other legislators are going to vote. In this case, the political information they furnish may be a key to legislative success.

7. Supplying nominations for federal appointments to the executive branch.

The Ratings Game.   Many interest groups attempt to influence the overall behavior of legislators through their rating systems. Each year, the interest group selects those votes on legislation that it feels are most important to the organization's goals. Each legislator is given a score based on the percentage of times that he or she voted in favor of the group's position. The usual scheme ranges from 0 to 100 percent. If a legislator has a score of, for example, 90 percent on the Americans for Democratic Action (ADA) rating, it means that he or she supported that group's position to a high degree (see Table 8-2). A legislator with such a high ADA score is usually considered to be very liberal. The groups that use rating systems range from the American Conservative Union to the League of Conservation Voters (an environmental group). Each year, the latter group identifies the twelve legislators having what it sees as the worst records on environmental issues and advertises them as the "Dirty Dozen."

Campaign Assistance.   Interest groups have additional strategies to use in their attempts to influence government policies. Groups recognize that the greatest concern of legislators is to be reelected, so they focus on the legislators' campaign needs. Associations with large memberships, such as labor unions or the National Education Association, are able to provide workers for political campaigns, including precinct workers to get out the vote, volunteers to put up posters and pass out literature, and people to staff telephone banks for campaign headquarters.

In many states where membership in certain interest groups is large, candidates vie for the groups' endorsements in the campaign. Gaining those endorsements may be automatic, or it may require that the candidates participate in a debate or interview with the interest groups. Endorsements are important because an interest group usually publicizes its choices in its membership publication and because the candidate can use the endorsement in his or her campaign literature. Traditionally, labor unions such as the AFL-CIO and the Teamsters have endorsed Democratic Party candidates. Republican candidates, however, often try to persuade union locals at least to refrain from any endorsement. Making no endorsement can then be perceived as disapproval of the Democratic Party candidate.

Interest Groups: The Candidates of Choice

The 1998 elections saw the usual flurry of fund-raising activity among interest groups. Both the Democrats and the Republicans sought and received large "soft money" contributions from interest groups, corporations, and individuals. Many interest groups, however, kept a low profile during the campaign, possibly due to recent attempts to reform campaign fund-raising laws.

On election day, however, traditional interest group tactics provided a strong advantage to the Democratic ticket. The administration made an all-out effort to encourage African Americans to vote, and that effort probably led to the defeat of Republican incumbent Senator Lauch Faircloth of North Carolina. The labor unions also mounted a massive "get-out-the-vote" drive to support Democratic candidates. That effort contributed to the election of Democrats to state legislatures and, most probably, to the defeat of Republican Senator Alfonse D'Amato of New York.

PACs and Political Campaigns. In the last two decades, the most important form of campaign help from interest groups has become the political contribution from a group's **political action committee (PAC).** The 1974 Federal Election Campaign Act and its 1976 amendments allow corporations, labor unions, and other interest groups to set up PACs to raise money for candidates. For a PAC to be legitimate, the money must be raised from at least fifty volunteer donors and must be given to at least five candidates in the federal election. PACs can contribute up to $5,000 to each candidate in each election. Each corporation or each union is limited to one PAC. As you might imagine, corporate PACs obtain funds from executives in their firms, and unions obtain PAC funds from their members.

The number of PACs has grown astronomically, as has the amount they spend on elections. There were about 1,000 political action committees in 1976; by the late 1990s, there were more than 4,500 (see Figure 8–2). The total amount of

Political Action Committee (PAC)

A committee set up by and representing a corporation, labor union, or special interest group. PACs raise and give campaign donations on behalf of the organizations or groups they represent.

FIGURE 8-2

PAC Growth, 1977 to 1996

This figure shows the significant increase in PACs since 1977 as well as the large number of corporate PACs relative to PACs that are sponsored by other types of organizations.

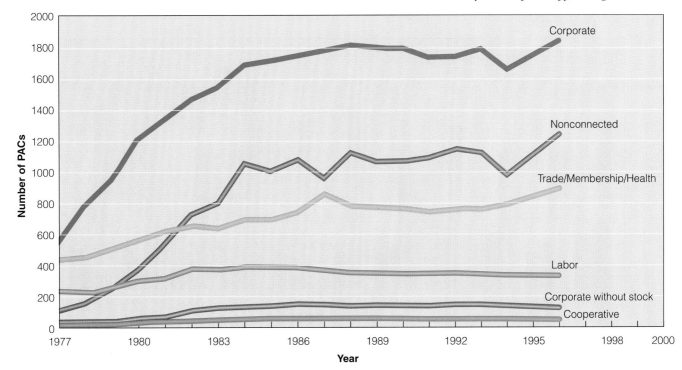

spending by PACs grew from $19 million in 1973 to an estimated $450 million in 1995–1996. Of all of the campaign money spent by House candidates in 1994, about 32 percent came from PACs.[4]

Interest groups funnel PAC money to candidates who they think can do the most good for them. Frequently, they make the maximum contribution of $5,000 per election to candidates who face little or no opposition. The summary of PAC contributions given in Figure 8–3 shows that the great bulk of campaign contributions goes to incumbent candidates rather than to challengers. Table 8–3 shows the amounts contributed by the top twenty PACs. It is clear that some PACs balance their contributions between Democratic and Republican candidates. Corporations are particularly likely to give money to Democrats in Congress as well as to Republicans, because Democratic incumbents may again chair important committees or subcommittees. Why, might you ask, would business leaders give to Democrats who may be more liberal than themselves? Interest groups see PAC contributions as a way to ensure access to powerful legislators, even though the groups may disagree with the legislators some of the time. PAC contributions are, in a way, an investment in a relationship.

The campaign-finance regulations clearly limit the amount that a PAC can give to any one candidate, but there is no limit on the amount that a PAC can spend on an independent campaign, either on behalf of a candidate or party or in opposition to one.

Indirect Techniques

Interest groups can try to influence government policy by working through third parties—who may be constituents, the general public, or other groups. Indirect techniques mask the interest group's own activities and make the effort appear to be spontaneous. Furthermore, legislators and government officials are often more impressed by contacts from constituents than from an interest group's lobbyist.

[4]Norman Ornstein, Thomas E. Mann, and Michael J. Malbin, *Vital Statistics on Congress, 1995–1996* (Washington, D.C.: Congressional Quarterly Press, 1996), p. 95.

FIGURE 8-3

PAC Contributions to Congressional Candidates, 1974 to 1996

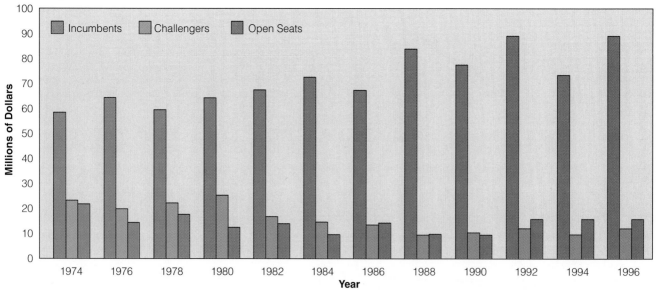

SOURCE: *Congressional Quarterly Weekly Report*, March 22, 1985, p. 657; *Federal Election Commission Report*, 1987, 1989, 1991; and *Vital Statistics on Congress, 1995–1996*.

TABLE 8-3

The Top Twenty PAC Contributors, 1995–1996 Election Cycle

RANK	CONTRIBUTOR	TOTAL	DEM %	REP %	CATEGORY
1	Teamsters Union	$2,647,165	95.8%	4.0%	Transport Unions
2	American Federation of State, County, and Municipal Employees	$2,512,821	98.0	1.6	Government Worker Unions
3	United Auto Workers	$2,475,819	99.2	0.4	Manufacturing Unions
4	American Medical Association	$2,442,576	20.1	79.7	Doctors
5	National Education Association	$2,356,006	98.8	0.8	Teachers Unions
6	National Auto Dealers Association	$2,346,925	18.2	81.7	Auto Dealers
7	Association of Trial Lawyers of America	$2,341,938	89.1	10.4	Lawyers
8	Laborers Union	$2,172,450	91.2	8.4	Building Trades
9	International Brotherhood of Electrical Workers	$2,171,262	97.6	2.1	Electrical Workers
10	National Association of Realtors	$2,099,683	31.2	68.7	Real Estate
11	United Food & Commercial Workers Union	$2,030,795	98.4	1.1	Miscellaneous Unions
12	Machinists/Aerospace Workers Union	$2,021,175	99.1	0.4	Industrial Unions
13	United Parcel Service	$1,791,147	35.3	64.7	Delivery Services
14	National Association of Letter Carriers	$1,723,228	87.5	11.9	Postal Unions
15	American Institute of CPAs	$1,690,925	32.0	67.7	Accountants
16	American Federation of Teachers	$1,619,635	98.4	1.3	Teachers Unions
17	Marine Engineers Union	$1,591,365	48.1	51.9	Sea Transport Unions
18	Carpenters Union	$1,571,466	94.6	4.9	Building Trades
19	National Rifle Association	$1,560,871	16.6	83.4	Gun Rights
20	United Steelworkers	$1,524,650	100.0	0.0	Industrial Unions

SOURCE: Center for Responsive Politics, 1998.

Generating Public Pressure. In some instances, interest groups try to produce a "groundswell" of public pressure to influence the government. Such efforts may include advertisements in national magazines and newspapers, mass mailings, television publicity, and demonstrations. The Internet and satellite links make communication efforts even more effective (see this chapter's feature *Politics Wired: Interests and the Internet* on page 264 for a discussion of this new technology). Interest groups may commission polls to find out what the public's sentiments are and then publicize the results. The intent of this activity is to convince policymakers that public opinion overwhelmingly supports the group's position.

Some corporations and interest groups also engage in a practice that might be called **climate control.** This strategy calls for public relations efforts that are aimed at improving the public image of the industry or group and are not necessarily related to any specific political issue. Contributions by corporations and groups in support of public television programs, sponsorship of special events, and commercials extolling the virtues of corporate research are examples of climate control. By building a reservoir of favorable public opinion, groups believe it less likely that their legislative goals will be met with opposition by the public.

Using Constituents as Lobbyists. One of the most effective interest group activities is the use of constituents to lobby for the group's goals. In the "shotgun" approach, the interest group tries to mobilize large numbers of constituents to write, phone, or send e-mail to their legislators or the president. Often, the group provides postcards or form letters for constituents to fill out and mail. These efforts are only effective on Capitol Hill when there is an extraordinary number of responses, because legislators know that the voters did not initiate the communications on their own. (For a perspective on a labor union leader's ability to mobilize union members for a cause, see the feature *E-Mail Messages from the Past* on page 265.)

INFOTRAC®
COLLEGE EDITION

"Grassroots Lobbying: New Standards"

Climate Control
The use of public relations techniques to create favorable public opinion toward an interest group, industry, or corporation.

POLITICS W I R E D

Interests and the Internet

The Internet may have a strong equalizing effect in the world of lobbying and government influence. The first organizations to use electronic means to reach their constituents and drum up support for action were the large economic coalitions, including the Chamber of Commerce and the National Association of Manufacturers. Groups such as these, as well as those representing a single product such as tobacco, quickly realized that they could set up Web sites and mailing lists to provide information more rapidly to their members. Members could check the Web every day to see how legislation was developing in Congress or anywhere in the world. National associations could send e-mail to all of their members with one keystroke, mobilizing them to contact their representatives in Congress.

The next interest groups to become "wired" were the large "special interests," such as the National Rifle Association, the religious right, and other groups with strongly committed members. Like the business interests, they use the Web to provide information to their members and to spur members to take action. For example, the Christian Coalition maintains a Web site that allows members to customize letters to their legislators online and send them electronically. These and other groups believe that swamping a member's office with e-mail is less burdensome to congressional staff than "snail mail" or telephone calls and just as effective in voicing their concerns.

Recently, it has become obvious that the Internet can level the playing field for small organizations. In the weeks before President Clinton designated millions of acres of Utah as the Grand Staircase–Escalante National Monument, a very small group called the Southern Utah Wilderness Alliance used its Web site to trigger thousands of letters to the White House supporting the action. Low-budget organizations that rely on volunteer time and energy can build Web sites and mailing lists that are as effective as those of large lobbying groups. E-mail is virtually free compared to standard mailing costs, and the communication link is instantaneous. As Rob Portman, a Republican member of Congress from Ohio, noted, "It's real-time. You get the message more quickly."*

*As quoted in David Hosansky, "Phone Banks to E-Mail," *Congressional Quarterly Weekly Report,* November 29, 1997, p. 2942.

Interest groups have different views on the efficacy of Internet communications. Most believe that to be effective, groups and constituents still need to make direct contact with legislators. Small groups that cannot travel to Washington view the matter differently: they now have a way to make their voices heard.

FOR CRITICAL ANALYSIS

Think about the reaction of a legislator as she tries to decide her vote on an issue. Which form of communication—e-mail, telephone calls, mail, or personal visits—would likely be most effective in swaying the legislator's vote?

A more influential variation of this technique uses only important constituents. Known as the "rifle" technique, or the "Utah plant manager's theory," the interest group contacts an influential constituent, such as the manager of a local plant in Utah, to contact the senator from Utah.[5] Because the constituent is seen as being responsible for many jobs or other resources, the legislator is more likely to listen carefully to the constituent's concerns about legislation than to a paid lobbyist.

Building Alliances.   Another indirect technique used by interest groups is to form an alliance with other groups concerned about the same legislation. Often, these groups will set up a paper organization with an innocuous name, such as the Citizens Trade Campaign, to represent their joint concerns. In this case, the alliance, comprising environmental, labor, and consumer groups, opposed the passage of North American Free Trade Agreement in 1993. Members of such an alliance share expenses and multiply the influence of their individual groups by combining their efforts. Other advantages of such an alliance are that it looks as if larger public interests are at stake, and it blurs the specific interests of the individual groups involved. These alliances also are efficient devices for keeping like-minded groups from duplicating one another's lobbying efforts.

[5]Kay Lehman Schlozman and John T. Tierney, *Organized Interests and American Democracy* (New York: Harper & Row, 1986), p. 293.

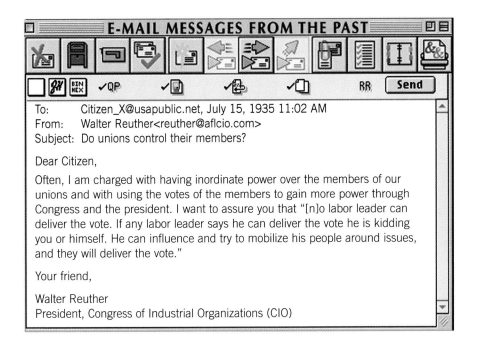

To: Citizen_X@usapublic.net, July 15, 1935 11:02 AM
From: Walter Reuther<reuther@aflcio.com>
Subject: Do unions control their members?

Dear Citizen,

Often, I am charged with having inordinate power over the members of our unions and with using the votes of the members to gain more power through Congress and the president. I want to assure you that "[n]o labor leader can deliver the vote. If any labor leader says he can deliver the vote he is kidding you or himself. He can influence and try to mobilize his people around issues, and they will deliver the vote."

Your friend,

Walter Reuther
President, Congress of Industrial Organizations (CIO)

Regulating Lobbyists

Congress made its first attempt to control lobbyists and lobbying activities through Title III of the Legislative Reorganization Act of 1946, otherwise known as the Federal Regulation of Lobbying Act. The act actually provided for public disclosure more than for regulation, and it neglected to specify which agency would enforce its provisions. The 1946 legislation defined a lobbyist as any person or organization that received money to be used principally to influence legislation before Congress. Such persons and individuals were supposed to "register" their clients and the purposes of their efforts, and report quarterly on their activities.

The legislation was tested in a 1954 Supreme Court case, *United States v. Harriss,*[6] and was found to be constitutional. The Court agreed that the lobbying law did not violate due process, freedom of speech or of the press, or the freedom to petition. The Court narrowly construed the act, however, holding that it applied only to lobbyists who were influencing federal legislation *directly.*

The result of the act was that a minimal number of individuals registered as lobbyists. National interest groups, such as the National Rifle Association and the American Petroleum Institute, could employ hundreds of staff members who were, of course, working on legislation but only register one or two lobbyists who were engaged *principally* in influencing Congress. There were no reporting requirements for lobbying the executive branch, federal agencies, the courts, or congressional staff. Approximately seven thousand individuals and organizations registered annually as lobbyists, although most experts estimated that ten times that number were actually employed in Washington to exert influence on the government.

The reform-minded Congress of 1995–1996 overhauled the lobbying legislation, fundamentally changing the ground rules for those who seek to influence the federal government. Lobbying legislation, passed in 1995, included the following provisions:

---

[6]347 U.S. 612 (1954).

1. A lobbyist is defined as anyone who spends at least 20 percent of his or her time lobbying members of Congress, their staffs, or executive branch officials.
2. Lobbyists must register with the clerk of the House and the secretary of the Senate within forty-five days of being hired or of making their first contact. The registration requirement applies to organizations that spend more than $20,000 in one year or to individuals who are paid more than $5,000 annually for their work.
3. Semiannual reports must disclose the general nature of the lobbying effort, specific issues and bill numbers, the estimated cost of the campaign, and a list of the branches of government contacted. The names of the individuals contacted need not be reported.
4. Representatives of U.S.–owned subsidiaries of foreign-owned firms and lawyers who represent foreign entities also are required to register for the first time.
5. The requirements exempt "grassroots" lobbying efforts and those of tax-exempt organizations, such as religious groups.

The 1995 law was expected to increase the number of registered lobbyists by three to ten times what it was then. It made the connections between organizations and specific issues much clearer in the reporting process. The major exemption for grass-roots campaigns, however, was expected to cause interest groups to divert major resources to organizing the folks back home so that they can exert pressure on Congress.

Concurrently with the debate on the 1995 law, both the House and the Senate adopted new rules on gifts and travel expenses: the House adopted a flat ban on gifts, and the Senate limited gifts to $50 in value and to no more than $100 in gifts from a single source in a year. There are exceptions for gifts from family members and for home-state products and souvenirs, such as T-shirts and coffee mugs. Both chambers ban all-expenses-paid trips, golf outings, and other such junkets. An exception applies for "widely attended" events, however, or if the member is a primary speaker at an event. The new gift rules stop the broad practice of taking members of Congress to lunch or dinner, but the various exemptions and exceptions undoubtedly will cause much controversy as individual cases are decided by the Senate and House Ethics Committees in future years.

Interest Groups and Representative Democracy

The significant role played by interest groups in shaping national policy has caused many to question whether we really have a democracy at all. To be sure, most interest groups have a middle-class or upper-class bias. Members of interest groups can afford to pay the membership fees, are generally fairly well educated, and normally participate in the political process to a greater extent than the "average" American. Furthermore, leaders of interest groups tend to constitute an "elite within an elite" in the sense that they usually are from a higher social class than their members. The most powerful interest groups—those with the most resources and political influence—are primarily business, trade, or professional groups. In contrast, public interest groups or civil rights groups make up only a small percentage of the interest groups lobbying Congress.

Remember from Chapter 1 that the elite theory of politics presumes that most Americans are uninterested in politics and are willing to let a small, elite group of citizens make decisions for them. Pluralist theory, in contrast, views politics as a struggle among various interest groups to gain benefits for their members. The pluralist approach views compromise among various competing interests as the

Drawing by Joseph Farris © 1994 The New Yorker Magazine, Inc.

*"A **very** special interest to see you, Senator."*

essence of political decision making. In reality, neither theory describes American politics very accurately. If interest groups led by elite, upper-class individuals are the dominant voices in Congress, then what we see is a conflict among elite groups—which would support the elitist theory, not a pluralist approach.

The results of lobbying efforts—congressional legislation—do not always favor the interests of the most powerful groups, however. In part, this is because not all interest groups have an equal influence on government. Each group has a different combination of resources to use in the policymaking process. While some groups are composed of members who have high social status and enormous economic resources, such as the National Association of Manufacturers, other groups derive influence from their large memberships. The American Association of Retired Persons (AARP), for example, has more members than any other interest group. Its large membership allows it to wield significant power over legislators. Still other groups, such as environmentalists, have causes that can claim strong public support even from those people who have no direct stake in the issue. Groups such as the National Rifle Association are well organized and have highly motivated members. This enables them to channel a stream of mail or electronic messages toward Congress with a few days' effort.

Even the most powerful interest groups do not always succeed in their demands. Whereas the National Chamber of Commerce may be accepted as having a justified interest in the question of business taxes, many legislators might feel that the group should not engage in the debate over the size of the federal budget deficit. In other words, groups are seen as having a legitimate concern in the issues closest to their interests but not necessarily in broader issues. This may explain why some of the most successful groups are those that focus on very specific issues—such as tobacco farming, funding of abortions, or handgun control—and do not get involved in larger conflicts.

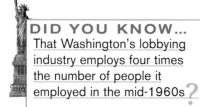

Interest Groups: Issues for the New Century

The role of interest groups in American politics has been in question since the writing of the Constitution. James Madison, among many others, worried about how to control the "mischiefs of faction" while recognizing that the very business of a democracy is to resolve the conflicts between interests. Today, the power of interest groups is probably greater than ever before: PACs sponsored by interest groups are able to raise and spend huge amounts of money to support candidates and parties; politicians admit that such support buys access, if not influence; groups use modern technology, and increasingly the Internet, to rally their members; and Congress seems unable to get beyond the adjudication of interests to write policy for the good of all.

In the future, Americans will consider whether to limit the role that interest groups can play in campaigns and elections either by reducing the financial support these groups can give or by eliminating that influence altogether through some public financing scheme. Then, all taxpayers would support campaigns rather than special groups. It is unlikely that there will be any attempt to limit severely the contact that groups have with political decision makers, because their right to access is protected by the First Amendment to the Constitution. Lobbyists could, however, be required to report every contact publicly; interest groups could be required to make public the amount that they spend on attempts to influence government; or the use of the media by specialized groups for their own interest could be regulated.

The existence of interest groups, nonetheless, has great advantages for a democracy. By participating in such groups, individual citizens are empowered to influence government in ways far beyond the ballot. Groups do increase the interest and participation of voters in the system. And, without a doubt, these groups can protect the rights of minorities through their access to all branches of the government. Thus, the future could see a continued expansion of interest groups. No doubt, numerous groups, particularly among segments of society that have been left out of the debate, will take advantage of the Internet to promote their interests at lower cost. In any case, given the structure of the government with its pluralist enticements for group struggle, it is unlikely that these political associations will disappear soon.

THE GUN CONTROL ISSUE

Is the easy availability of handguns a major cause of crime? Do people have a right to possess firearms to defend home and hearth? These questions are part of a long-term and heated battle between organized pro-firearm and anti-firearm camps. The disagreements run deeply and reflect strong sentiments on both sides. The fight is fueled by the one million gun incidents occurring in the United States each year—the murders, suicides, assaults, accidents, robberies, and injuries in which guns are involved. Proponents of gun control seek new restrictions on gun purchases—if not a ban on them entirely—while decreasing existing arsenals of privately owned weapons. Proponents of firearms are fighting back. They claim that firearms are a cherished tradition, a constitutional right, a vital defense need for individuals. They contend that the problem lies not in the sale and ownership of the weapons themselves but in the criminal use of firearms.

The National Coalition to Ban Handguns favors a total ban, taking the position that handguns "serve no valid purpose, except to kill people." The National Rifle Association of America (NRA) opposes a ban. The NRA claims, among other things, that a gun law won't reduce the number of crimes. It is illogical to assume, according to the NRA, that persons who refuse to obey laws prohibiting rape, murder, and other crimes will obey a gun law.

The debate is intense and bitter. Gun control proponents accuse their adversaries of being "frightened little men living in the pseudomacho myth." Gun control opponents brand the other side as "new totalitarians" intent on curbing individual freedom. The NRA, founded in 1871, is currently one of the most powerful single-issue groups on the American political scene, representing the seventy million gun owners in the United States.

A matter of particular concern to many Americans is the increase in crimes involving guns among younger Americans. In several incidents, teenagers or even younger children have shot other children in their schools. Many proponents of gun control insist that controlling the purchase of weapons would reduce the availability of guns to children. In response to these efforts, some states have passed laws that hold adults liable for not locking away their firearms. Some gun control proponents suggest that all guns should be sold with trigger locks to prevent accidental shootings.

In 1993, Congress passed a law instituting a five-day waiting period for all handgun purchases. Most observers saw this as a defeat for the NRA. That group, however, asserted that the law would have no effect on crime. If you agree with the NRA's position and want to get involved in its efforts in opposition to further gun control legislation, contact the NRA at the following address:

The National Rifle Association
11250 Waples Mill Rd.
Fairfax, VA 22030
703-267-1000

www.nra.org

If, however, you are concerned with the increase in gun-related crimes and feel that stricter gun laws are necessary, you can get involved through the following organizations:

Coalition to Stop Gun Violence
100 Maryland Ave. N.E.
Washington, DC 20002
202-530-0340

www.gunfree.org/

Handgun Control, Inc.
1225 I St. N.W.
Suite 1100
Washington, DC 20006
202-898-0792

www.handguncontrol.org/

Key terms

climate control 263

direct technique 259

indirect technique 259

interest group 247

labor movement 254

lobbying 247

material incentive 250

political action committee
(PAC) 261

public interest 257

purposive incentive 251

service sector 254

social movement 251

solidary incentive 250

Chapter summary

1 An interest group is an organization whose members share common objectives and who actively attempt to influence government policy. Interest groups proliferate in the United States because they can influence government at many points in the political structure and because they offer solidary, material, and purposive incentives to their members. Interest groups are often created out of social movements.

2 Major types of interest groups include business, agricultural, labor, public employee, professional, and environmental groups. Other important groups may be considered public-interest groups. In addition, special interest groups and foreign governments lobby the government.

3 Interest groups use direct and indirect techniques to influence government. Direct techniques include testifying before committees and rulemaking agencies, providing information to legislators, rating legislators' voting records, and making campaign contributions. Contributions are often made through political action committees, or PACs. Most PAC money is given to incumbents to ensure access

for the group. Indirect techniques to influence government include campaigns to rally public sentiment, letter-writing campaigns, influencing the climate of opinion, and using constituents to lobby for the group's interest.

4 The 1946 Legislative Reorganization Act was the first attempt to control lobbyists and their activities through registration requirements. The Supreme Court narrowly construed the act as applying only to lobbyists who directly seek to influence federal legislation.

5 In 1995, Congress approved new legislation requiring anyone who spends 20 percent of his or her time influencing legislation to register. Also, any organization spending $20,000 or more and any individual who is paid more than $5,000 annually for his or her work must register. Semiannual reports will include the name of clients, the bills in which they are interested, and the branches of government contacted. Grassroots lobbying and the lobbying efforts of tax-exempt organizations are exempt from the new rules.

Selected print and electronic resources

SUGGESTED READINGS

Berry, Jeffrey M. *The Interest Group Society.* 3d ed. New York: Longman, 1997. This is an excellent overview and discussion of the ways in which interest groups and lobbies participate in the political system.

Cammisa, Anne Marie. *Governments as Interest Groups: Intergovernmental Lobbying and the Federal System.* Westport, Conn.: Praeger Publishers, 1995. This book looks closely at the way state and local governments lobby Congress and the executive branch in regard to the writing of national policy that affects local governments. Housing policy, welfare policy, and child-care policy are examined with respect to the impact of state and local lobbying.

Clawson, Dan, Alan Neutstadtl, and Denise Scott. *Money Talks: Corporate PACs and Political Influence.* New York: Basic

Books, 1992. How corporations set up PACs, how they decide which candidates to support, and the goals of that support are covered in this excellent investigation.

Richan, Willard C. *Lobbying for Social Change.* 2d ed. New York: The Haworth Press, 1995. This is a handy guidebook for individuals and groups that want to begin successful lobbying efforts. It includes directions on identifying the correct political target, testifying at hearings, and using the media for the group's cause.

Wilson, James Q. *Political Organizations* (with a new introduction to the 1974 edition). Princeton, N.J.: Princeton University Press, 1995. This is one of the classic works on the formation and membership of interest groups in American society. Wilson looks closely at the motivations of a group's members and the relationship of the members to the leaders of a group.

MEDIA RESOURCES

Norma Rae–A 1979 film about an attempt by a northern union organizer to unionize workers in the southern textile industry; stars Sally Field.

Silkwood–A 1979 film focusing on the story of a nuclear plant worker who attempted to investigate safety issues at the plant and ended up losing her job; stars Meryl Streep and Cher.

Washington under the Influence–A segment of the PBS series *On the Issues,* produced in 1993, in which ABC news correspondent Jeff Greenfield follows the trail of lobbyists, press leaks, and PAC money as a corporation faces Senate hearings following allegations that the company's popular product causes injury.

Logging on

Interest groups have established literally hundreds of sites that you can investigate. A good starting point is the Web site of Internet Public Library (IPL) Associations on the Net, which provides efficient access to more than six hundred professional and trade associations. Go to

www.ipl.org/ref/AON

There are numerous Web sites on the tobacco controversy. The following site offers links to many of them:

www.tobaccoresolution.com

Gun control opponents may want to visit the National Rifle Association's site at

www.nra.org/

If you are interested in human rights worldwide, you can go to the site of Human Rights Watch at

www.hrw.org/

There are a number of sites to visit to find information concerning environmental issues. The Environmental Defense Fund's site is

www.edf.org/

You can also go to the National Resource Defense Council's site for information on environmental issues. Its URL is

www.nrdc.org/nrdc

Using the Internet for political analysis

"Today in Perspective" is a site that allows you to look at both sides of an issue. Access this site at

www.iquest.net/~gtemp

Choose an issue, and compare the information resources given for both sides of that issue. Then critique the site for

the breadth and depth of coverage on the issue. What other information might you need to form an opinion?

Political Parties

The Government Subsidized Third Parties?

BACKGROUND

AT THE PRESENT TIME, THE AMERICAN POLITICAL LANDSCAPE IS DOMINATED BY TWO MAJOR POLITICAL PARTIES. ALTHOUGH THIRD PARTIES SUCH AS THAT LED BY H. ROSS PEROT OCCASIONALLY SURFACE AND GAIN VOTES, THE TWO PARTIES CONTROL MOST ELECTIONS AND PUBLIC OFFICES. GENERALLY, THE FEDERAL ELECTION COMMISSION—THE AGENCY THAT ADMINISTERS FEDERAL ELECTION LAWS—GIVES PUBLIC FUNDS ONLY TO CANDIDATES FROM THE TWO MAJOR PARTIES. THIRD-PARTY CANDIDATES MUST DEMONSTRATE SIGNIFICANT VOTE-GETTING POWER TO RECEIVE PUBLIC FUNDING. THIRD PARTIES MUST STRUGGLE TO GET ON THE BALLOT AND FIELD CANDIDATES EVEN THOUGH MORE THAN HALF OF ALL AMERICANS BELIEVE THAT THIRD PARTIES ARE A GOOD IDEA.

WHAT IF THE GOVERNMENT SUBSIDIZED THIRD PARTIES?

Suppose that Congress, inspired by the demands of the public, rewrote campaign-finance law to provide incentives for the development and survival of third parties. Congress might enact legislation that provided for the direct reimbursement of all of the expenses that were incurred in the process of registering voters and getting candidates on the ballot. Or, the Federal Election Commission might reinterpret its regulations to encourage contributions to third parties and allow reimbursement of all of the expenses of such parties in the campaign for president.

NEW LIFE FOR ISSUES

By providing government subsidies or incentives to political parties that present different platforms and candidates than do the two major parties, the government would open the doors to a very different kind of political debate. Positions on welfare, Social Security, defense spending, and environmental or other issues that are far different from those espoused by the Democrats and Republicans could be debated publicly by candidates. If the two major parties sensed that some third-party platforms were becoming popular, the major parties might change their positions to absorb the new views.

INCREASING VOTER INTEREST

By enlarging the debate to include more points of view and more candidates, subsidized third parties might well stimulate voter interest in politics and, as a result, increase voter turnout in elections. Many scholars have suggested that voter interest has declined because the two major parties do not seem to differ much or offer much to many voters. Furthermore, general cynicism about politics seems to be increasing due to the efforts of the major parties to raise huge sums of money for campaigns. That cynicism also lowers voter turnout.

The rise of third parties that, due to government support, would be able to recruit candidates and put them on the ballot in many states would encourage more voters to take part in the process. Voters would be more likely to find a candidate who seems to reflect their interests and who might seem to be less of an "insider" to politics. For many voters, the chance to choose a candidate who actually seems to represent their viewpoint would be a real motivating factor. Political debate in general would be more open and candid if third parties had the financial strength to become participants in the public arena.

THE STRENGTH OF THE TWO-PARTY SYSTEM

Even though stronger third parties might increase voter participation, it is likely that the major parties would retain their power in government. The major parties, as noted above, would be likely to embrace any issue position put forward by a third party that seemed to win adherents. Furthermore, the best and most attractive candidates fielded by the new parties probably would be offered a place on the ticket by one of the major parties to win over their supporters. In addition, the two major parties probably would not allow subsidies to smaller parties to go unchallenged. They would demand similar assistance for themselves for protection against the newcomers. Finally, because of the constitutional requirement that a presidential candidate win a majority of the electoral votes, no "new party" is likely to ever get big enough to win that office.

FOR CRITICAL ANALYSIS

1. What kind of public pressure or political scandal might induce the government to encourage the rise of new political parties?

2. What do you think would be the most popular type of third party to be formed? Whose interests might be represented by a strong third party?

What Is a Political Party?

Around election time, the polls and the media concentrate on the state of the political parties. Every poll asks the question, "Do you consider yourself to be a Republican, a Democrat, or an independent?" Most Americans are able to answer that question, and the number of persons who identify themselves as **independents** now exceeds 30 percent. If, as was suggested in the *What If . . .* that opens this chapter, the government provided incentives for third parties, it is likely that some of these independent voters would choose a new party identification.

In the United States, being a member of a political party does not require paying dues, passing an examination, or swearing an oath of allegiance. If nothing is really required to be a member of a political party, what, then, is a political party?

A **political party** might be formally defined as a group of political activists who organize to win elections, to operate the government, and to determine public policy. This definition explains the difference between an interest group and a political party. Interest groups do not want to operate government, and they do not put forth political candidates—even though they support candidates who will promote their interests if elected or reelected. Another important distinction is that interest groups tend to sharpen issues, whereas American political parties tend to blur their issue positions to attract voters.

Political parties differ from **factions**, which are smaller groups that are trying to obtain certain benefits for themselves (see the comments on factions by James Madison in Chapter 2). Factions generally preceded the formation of political parties in American history, and the term is still used to refer to groups within parties that follow a particular leader or share a regional identification or an ideological viewpoint. The Republican Party sometimes is seen as having a northeastern "moderate" faction. The supporters of the late Robert Kennedy and Senator Edward (Ted) Kennedy might be described as a liberal faction within the Democratic Party. Factions are subgroups within parties that may try to capture a nomination or get a position adopted by the party. The key difference between factions and parties is that factions do not have a permanent organization, whereas political parties do.

Independent
A voter or candidate who does not identify with a political party.

Political Party
A group of political activists who organize to win elections, to operate the government, and to determine public policy.

Faction
A group or bloc in a legislature or political party acting together in pursuit of some special interest or position.

Supporters of Bob Dole and Jack Kemp lead the cheers for their presidential and vice-presidential candidates during the 1996 Republican National Convention.

Functions of Political Parties in the United States

Political parties in the United States engage in a wide variety of activities, many of which are discussed in this chapter. Through these activities, parties perform a number of functions for the political system. These functions include the following:

1. *Recruiting candidates for public office.* Because it is the goal of parties to gain control of government, they must work to recruit candidates for all elective offices. Often this means recruiting candidates to run against powerful incumbents or for unpopular jobs. Yet if parties did not search out and encourage political hopefuls, far more offices would be uncontested, and voters would have limited choices.

2. *Organizing and running elections.* Although elections are a government activity, political parties actually organize the voter-registration drives, recruit the volunteers to work at the polls, provide most of the campaign activity to stimulate interest in the election, and work to increase participation.

Democratic National Convention delegates in 1996 show their support for the Clinton/Gore ticket. The costumes they wear are part of the convention culture and may attract television cameras. Does the often circus-like atmosphere of national party conventions detract from the seriousness of the decisions made at these conventions?

Cadre

The nucleus of political party activists carrying out the major functions of American political parties.

3. *Presenting alternative policies to the electorate.* In contrast to factions, which are often centered on individual politicians, parties are focused on a set of political positions. The Democrats or Republicans in Congress who vote together do so because they represent constituencies that have similar expectations and demands.

4. *Accepting responsibility for operating the government.* When a party elects the president or governor and members of the legislature, it accepts the responsibility for running the government. This includes staffing the executive branch with loyal party supporters and developing linkages among the elected officials to gain support for policies and their implementation.

5. *Acting as the organized opposition to the party in power.* The "out" party, or the one that does not control the government, is expected to articulate its own policies and oppose the winning party when appropriate. By organizing the opposition to the "in" party, the opposition party forces debate on the policy alternatives.

Students of political parties, such as Leon D. Epstein, point out that the major functions of American political parties are carried out by a small, relatively loose-knit **cadre**, or nucleus, of party activists.[1] This is quite a different arrangement from the more highly structured, mass-membership party organization typical of certain European working-class parties. American parties concentrate on winning elections rather than on signing up large numbers of deeply committed, dues-paying members who believe passionately in the party's program.

A Short History of Political Parties in the United States

Political parties in the United States have a long tradition dating back to the 1790s (see Figure 9–1). The function and character of these political parties, as well as the emergence of the two-party system itself, have much to do with the unique historical forces operating from this country's beginning as an independ-

---

[1] *Political Parties in Western Democracies* (New Brunswick, N.J.: Transaction, 1980).

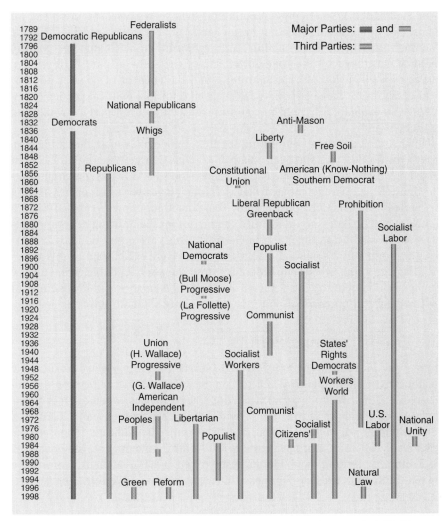

SOURCE: Congressional Quarterly, *Congressional Quarterly's Guide to U.S. Elections*, 2d ed. (Washington, D.C.: Congressional Quarterly Press, 1985), p. 224; *Congressional Quarterly Weekly Report* (1988), p. 3184; and J. David Gillespie, *Politics at the Periphery* (Columbia, S.C.: University of South Carolina Press, 1993); updated by authors.

FIGURE 9-1

American Political Parties since 1789

The chart indicates the years that parties either ran presidential candidates or held national conventions. The life span for many political parties can only be approximated, because parties existed at the state or local level before they ran candidates in presidential elections, and parties continued to exist at local levels long after they ceased running presidential candidates. Not every party fielding a presidential candidate is represented in the chart. For instance, in 1988, at least nine other parties fielded a presidential candidate in at least one state.

ent nation. Indeed, James Madison linked the emergence of political parties to the form of government created by our Constitution (see the feature *E-Mail Messages from the Past* on page 278).

Generally, we can divide the evolution of our nation's political parties into six periods:

1. The creation of parties, from 1789 to 1812.
2. The era of one-party rule, or personal politics, from 1816 to 1824.
3. The period from Andrew Jackson's presidency to just prior to the Civil War, from 1828 to 1860.
4. The post–Civil War period, from 1864 to 1892.
5. The progressive period, from 1896 to 1928.
6. The modern period, from 1932 to the present.

The Formative Years: Federalists and Anti-Federalists

The first partisan political division in the United States occurred prior to the adoption of the Constitution. The **Federalists** pushed for the adoption of the Constitution, whereas the **Anti-Federalists** were against ratification.

Federalists
The first American political party, led by Alexander Hamilton and John Adams. Many of its members had strongly supported the adoption of the new Constitution and the creation of the federal union.

Anti-Federalists
Those who opposed the adoption of the Constitution because of its centralist tendencies and attacked the failure of the Constitution's framers to include a bill of rights.

Thomas Jefferson, founder of the Democratic Republicans. His election to the presidency in 1800 was decided in the House of Representatives, because no candidate won a majority of the electoral votes.

Era of Personal Politics
An era when attention centers on the character of individual candidates rather than on party identification.

In September 1796, George Washington, who had served as president for almost two full terms, decided not to run again. In his farewell address, he made a somber assessment of the nation's future. Washington felt that the country might be destroyed by the "baneful effects of the spirit of party." He viewed parties as a threat to both national unity and the concept of popular government. Early in his career, Thomas Jefferson did not like political parties either. In 1789, he stated, "If I could not go to heaven but with a party, I would not go there at all."[2]

What Americans found out during the first decade or so after the ratification of the Constitution was that even a patriot-king (as George Washington has been called) could not keep everyone happy. There is no such thing as a neutral political figure who is so fair minded that everyone agrees with him or her. During this period, it became obvious to many that something more permanent than a faction would be necessary to identify candidates for the growing number of citizens who would be participating in elections. Thus, according to many historians, the world's first democratic political parties were established in this country. Also, in 1800, when the Federalists lost the presidential election to the Democratic Republicans (also known as the Jeffersonian Republicans), one of the first peaceful transfers of power from one party to another was achieved.

The Era of Personal Politics

From 1816 to 1828, a majority of U.S. voters regularly elected Democratic Republicans to the presidency and to Congress. Two-party competition did not really exist. This was the so-called **era of personal politics**, when attention centered on the character of individual candidates rather than on party identification. Although during elections the Democratic Republicans opposed the Federalists' call for a stronger, more active central government, they acquired the Louisiana Territory and Florida, established a national bank, enforced a higher tariff, and resisted European intrusion into the Western Hemisphere.

[2]Letter to Francis Hopkinson written from Paris while Jefferson was minister to France. In John P. Foley, ed., *The Jeffersonian Cyclopedia* (New York: Russell & Russell, 1967), p. 677.

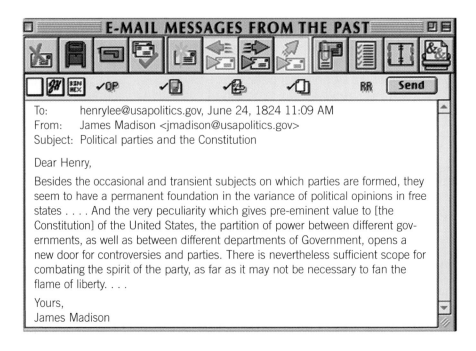

E-MAIL MESSAGES FROM THE PAST

To: henrylee@usapolitics.gov, June 24, 1824 11:09 AM
From: James Madison <jmadison@usapolitics.gov>
Subject: Political parties and the Constitution

Dear Henry,

Besides the occasional and transient subjects on which parties are formed, they seem to have a permanent foundation in the variance of political opinions in free states . . . . And the very peculiarity which gives pre-eminent value to [the Constitution] of the United States, the partition of power between different governments, as well as between different departments of Government, opens a new door for controversies and parties. There is nevertheless sufficient scope for combating the spirit of the party, as far as it may not be necessary to fan the flame of liberty. . . .

Yours,
James Madison

Because there was no real political opposition to the dominant Democratic Republicans and thus little political debate, the administration of James Monroe (1817–1825) came to be known as the **era of good feeling.**

National Two-Party Rule: Democrats and Whigs

During the era of personal politics, one-party rule did not prevent the Democratic Republican factions from competing against each other. Indeed, there was quite a bit of intraparty rivalry. Finally, in 1824 and 1828, Democratic Republicans who belonged to the factions of Henry Clay and John Quincy Adams split with the rest of the party to oppose Andrew Jackson in those elections. Jackson's supporters and the Clay-Adams bloc formed separate parties, the **Democratic Party** and the **Whig Party,** respectively. That same Democratic Party is now the oldest continuing political party in the Western world.

The Whigs were those Democratic Republicans who were often called the "National Republicans." At the national level, the Whigs were able to elect two presidents—William Henry Harrison in 1840 and Zachary Taylor in 1848. The Whigs, however, were unable to maintain a common ideological base when the party became increasingly divided over the issue of slavery in the late 1840s. During the 1850s, the Whigs fell apart as a national party.

The Post–Civil War Period

The existing two-party system was disrupted by the election of 1860, in which there were four major candidates. Abraham Lincoln, the candidate of the newly formed **Republican Party,** was the victor with a majority of the electoral vote, although with only 39.9 percent of the popular vote. This newly formed Republican Party—not to be confused with the Democratic Republicans—was created in the mid-1850s from the various groups that sought to fill the vacuum left by the disintegration of the Whigs. It took the label of Grand Old Party, or GOP. Its first national convention was held in 1856, but its presidential candidate, John C. Frémont, lost.

After the end of the Civil War, the South became heavily Democratic (the Solid South), and the North became heavily Republican. This era of Republican dominance was highlighted by the election of 1896, when the Republicans, emphasizing economic development and modernization under William McKinley, resoundingly defeated the Democratic and Populist candidate, William Jennings Bryan. The Republicans' control was solidified by winning over the urban working-class vote in northern cities. From the election of Abraham Lincoln until the election of Franklin D. Roosevelt in 1932, the Republicans won all but four presidential elections.

The Progressive Movement

In 1912, a major schism occurred in the Republican Party when former Republican president Theodore Roosevelt ran for the presidency as a Progressive. Consequently, there were three significant contenders in that presidential contest. Woodrow Wilson was the Democratic candidate, William Howard Taft was the regular Republican candidate, and Roosevelt was the Progressive candidate. The Republican split allowed Wilson to be elected. The Wilson administration, although Democratic, ended up enacting much of the Progressive Party's platform. Left without any reason for opposition, the Progressive Party collapsed in 1921.

Republican Warren Harding's victory in 1920 reasserted Republican domination of national politics until the Republicans' defeat by Franklin D. Roosevelt in 1932, in the depths of the Great Depression.

Andrew Jackson earned the name "Old Hickory" for his exploits during the War of 1812. In 1828, Jackson was elected president as the candidate of the new Democratic Party.

Era of Good Feeling
The years from 1817 to 1825, when James Monroe was president and there was, in effect, no political opposition.

Democratic Party
One of the two major American political parties evolving out of the Democratic (Jeffersonian) Republican group supporting Thomas Jefferson.

Whig Party
One of the foremost political organizations in the United States during the first half of the nineteenth century, formally established in 1836. The Whig Party was dominated by the same anti-Jackson elements that organized the National Republican faction within the Democratic (Jeffersonian) Republicans and represented a variety of regional interests. It fell apart as a national party in the early 1850s.

Republican Party
One of the two major American political parties, which emerged in the 1850s as an antislavery party. It was created to fill the vacuum caused by the disintegration of the Whig Party.

William McKinley campaigns in 1896 on a platform draped with the flag. The decorations are no different from those that candidates used a century later.

The Modern Era: From the New Deal to the Present

Franklin D. Roosevelt was elected in 1932 and reelected in 1936, 1940, and 1944. The impact of his successive Democratic administrations and the New Deal that he crafted is still with us today. Roosevelt used his enormous personal appeal to unify Democrats under his leadership, and he established direct communication between the president and the public through his radio **fireside chats.** It wasn't until 1940 that the Republicans made even a small dent in the Democratic hegemony, when Wendell Willkie reduced Roosevelt's popular vote to 54.8 percent from the 60.5 percent and the 57.4 percent of the two previous elections.

In April 1945, Roosevelt died; Vice President Harry Truman became president through succession and, in 1948, through election. The New Deal coalition, under Truman's revised theme of the Fair Deal, continued. It was not until Republican Dwight Eisenhower won the 1952 election that the Democrats lost their control of the presidency. Eisenhower was reelected in 1956.

From 1960 through 1968, the Democrats, led first by John F. Kennedy and then by Lyndon B. Johnson, held national power. Republicans again gained control of the presidency with Richard Nixon's victory in 1968 and retained it in 1972, but they lost prestige after the Watergate scandal forced Nixon's resignation on August 8, 1974. For this and other reasons, the Democrats were back in power after the presidential elections in 1976. But Democratic president Jimmy Carter was unable to win reelection against Ronald Reagan in 1980. The Republicans also gained control of the Senate in 1980 and retained it in the elections of 1982 and 1984. The 1984 reelection of Ronald Reagan appeared to some pollsters to signal the resurgence of the Republican Party as a competitive force in American politics as more people declared themselves to be Republicans than they had in the previous several decades.

The election of George Bush in 1988 may have signaled the beginning of a true era of **divided government.** Republican Bush won the presidency, but his

Fireside Chat
One of the warm, informal talks by Franklin D. Roosevelt to a few million of his intimate friends—via the radio. Roosevelt's fireside chats were so effective that succeeding presidents have been urged by their advisers to emulate him by giving more radio and television reports to the nation.

Divided Government
A situation in which one major political party controls the presidency and the other controls the chambers of Congress, or in which one party controls a state governorship and the other controls the state legislature.

Republican Party lost seats in the House and Senate to Democrats. In 1992, Democrat Bill Clinton won the presidency, with Democratic control of the House and Senate, but his party actually lost congressional seats, presaging the Democrats' debacle in 1994 when the Republicans took control of both the House and the Senate. In 1996, Bill Clinton was reelected, but the voters returned Republicans to control in Congress. Republicans also controlled most of the governorships in the states. Divided government can lead to stalemate, but to many American voters it is a way to avoid the excesses of both parties.

The Three Faces of a Party

Although American parties are known by a single name and, in the public mind, have a common historical identity, each party really has three major components. The first component is the **party-in-the-electorate.** This phrase refers to all those individuals who claim an attachment to the political party. They need not be members in the sense that they pay dues or even participate in election campaigns. Rather, the party-in-the-electorate is the large number of Americans who feel some loyalty to the party or who use partisanship as a cue to decide who will earn their vote. As discussed in Chapter 7, most Americans who actually identify with one of the parties acquired that affiliation either as a result of their family upbringing or by coming of age during the era of their party's dominance. Party membership is not really a rational choice; rather, it is an emotional tie somewhat analogous to identifying with a region or a baseball team. Although individuals may hold a deep loyalty to or identification with a political party, there is no need for members of the party-in-the-electorate to speak out publicly, to contribute to campaigns, or to vote a straight party ticket. Needless to say, the party leaders pay close attention to the affiliation of their members in the electorate.

The second component, the **party organization,** provides the structural framework for the political party by recruiting volunteers to become party leaders; identifying potential candidates; and organizing caucuses, conventions, and election campaigns for its candidates. It is the party organization and its active workers that keep the party functioning between elections, as well as make sure that the party puts forth electable candidates and clear positions in the elections. When individuals accept paid employment for a political party, they are considered party professionals. Among that group are campaign consultants; fundraisers; local, state, and national executives; and national staff members. If the party-in-the-electorate declines in numbers and loyalty, the party organization must try to find a strategy to rebuild the grassroots following.

The **party-in-government** is the third component of American political parties. The party-in-government consists of those elected and appointed officials who identify with a political party. Generally, elected officials cannot also hold official party positions within the formal organization. Executives such as the president, governors, and mayors often have the informal power to appoint party executives, but their duties in office preclude them from active involvement in the party organization most of the time.

Ties to a political party are essential to the functioning of government and the operation of the political process in the United States. Republican representatives, senators, and governors expect to receive a hearing at a Republican-controlled White House if they request it. In return, Republican presidents call on party loyalty when they ask the legislators to support their programs. Finally, the electorate at the polls is asked to judge the party-in-government by its policies and candidates. American political parties, although not nearly as ideological as many European parties, do claim to present alternative positions to the

Party-in-the-Electorate
Those members of the general public who identify with a political party or who express a preference for one party over the other.

Party Organization
The formal structure and leadership of a political party, including election committees; local, state, and national executives; and paid professional staff.

Party-in-Government
All of the elected and appointed officials who identify with a political party.

voters. If the party organization and the party-in-government are in conflict, the party-in-the-electorate is likely to look for other party leadership to articulate its preferences.

Party Organization

In theory, each of the American political parties has a standard, pyramid-shaped organization (see Figure 9–2). The pyramid, however, does not reflect accurately the relative power and strengths of the individual parts of the party organization. If it did, the national chairperson of the Democratic Party or the Republican Party, along with the national committee, could simply dictate how the organization was to be run, just as if it were Exxon Corporation or Ford Motor Company.

In reality, the formal structure of political parties resembles a layer cake with autonomous strata more than it does a pyramid. Malcolm E. Jewell and David M. Olson point out that "there is no command structure within political parties. Rather, each geographic unit of the party tends to be autonomous from the other units at its same geographic level."[3]

The National Party Organization

Each party has a national organization, the most clearly institutional part of which is the **national convention,** held every four years. The convention is used to nominate the presidential and vice presidential candidates. In addition, the **party platform** is written, ratified, and revised at the national convention. The platform sets forth the party's position on the issues and makes promises to initiate certain policies if the party wins the presidency.

After the convention, the platform frequently is neglected or ignored by party candidates who disagree with it. Because candidates are trying to win votes from a wide spectrum of voters, it is counterproductive to emphasize the fairly narrow and sometimes controversial goals set forth in the platform. The work of Gerald M. Pomper has shown, however, that once elected, the parties do try to carry out platform promises and that roughly three-fourths of the promises

---

[3]Malcolm E. Jewell and David M. Olson, *American State Political Parties and Elections,* rev. ed. (Homewood, Ill.: Dorsey Press, 1982), p. 73.

National Convention

The meeting held every four years by each major party to select presidential and vice presidential candidates, to write a platform, to choose a national committee, and to conduct party business. In theory, the national convention is at the top of a hierarchy of party conventions (the local and state conventions are below it) that consider candidates and issues.

Party Platform

A document drawn up by the platform committee at each national convention, outlining the policies, positions, and principles of the party; it is then submitted to the entire convention for approval.

FIGURE 9-2

A Theoretical Structure of the American Political Party

Each "layer" of an American political party is representative of a level of government, from local to national. Although there are linkages between the layers, each is fairly independent of the others in terms of financing, supporters, nominations, and platform. No one level of the party has real control over any other level.

National Chairperson and National Committee

National Convention and Delegates

State Chairperson/Committee

County Chairperson/Committee

Ward or Township Chairperson/Committee

Precinct Chairperson/Committee

eventually become law.[4] Of course, some general goals, such as economic prosperity, are included in the platforms of both parties.

The party convention provides the most striking illustration of the difference between the ordinary members of a party, or party identifiers, and those individuals who are party activists. As a series of studies by the *New York Times* shows, delegates to the national party conventions are quite dissimilar from ordinary party identifiers. Delegates to the Democratic National Convention, as shown in Table 9–1, are far more liberal than are ordinary Democratic voters. In the same fashion, Republican voters are not nearly as conservative as are delegates to the Republican National Convention. Why does this happen? In part, it is because a person, to become a delegate, must gather votes in a primary election from party

DID YOU KNOW...
That the political party with the most seats in the House of Representatives chooses the speaker of the House, makes any new rules it wants, gets a majority of the seats on each important committee and chooses their chairs, and hires most of the congressional staff?

[4]Gerald M. Pomper and Susan S. Lederman, *Elections in America: Control and Influence in Democratic Politics,* 2d ed. (New York: Longman, 1980).

TABLE **9-1**

Delegates and Party Voters: How They Compare on Issues and Ideology

PERCENTAGE OF . . .	DEMOCRATIC DELEGATES	DEMOCRATIC VOTERS	ALL VOTERS	REPUBLICAN VOTERS	REPUBLICAN DELEGATES
SCOPE OF GOVERNMENT					
Government should do more to . . .					
. . . solve the nation's problems	76	53	36	20	4
. . . regulate the environment and safety practices of businesses	60	66	53	37	4
. . . promote traditional values	27	41	42	44	56
SOCIAL ISSUES					
Abortion should be permitted in all cases	61	30	27	22	11
Favor a nationwide ban on assault weapons	91	80	72	62	34
Necessary to have laws to protect racial minorities	88	62	51	39	30
Affirmative action programs should be continued	81	59	45	28	9
Organized prayer should be permitted in public schools	20	66	66	69	57
INTERNATIONAL					
Trade restrictions necessary to protect domestic industries	54	65	60	56	31
Children of illegal immigrants should be allowed to attend public school	79	63	54	46	26
IDEOLOGY					
Political ideology is . . .					
. . . very liberal	15	7	4	1	0
. . . somewhat liberal	28	20	12	6	0
. . . moderate	48	54	47	39	27
. . . somewhat conservative	4	14	24	36	31
. . . very conservative	1	3	8	17	35

SOURCE: *The New York Times,* August 26, 1996.

members who care enough to vote in a primary or be appointed by party leaders. Furthermore, the primaries generally pit candidates against each other on intraparty issues. Delegates who are pledged to those candidates are also likely to hold positions on the issues that are far different from those of the other major party. Often, the most important activity for the convention is making peace between the delegates who support different candidates and helping them accept a party platform that will appeal to the general electorate.

National Committee

A standing committee of a national political party established to direct and coordinate party activities during the four-year period between national party conventions.

Choosing the National Committee. At the national convention, each of the parties formally chooses a national standing committee, elected by the individual state parties. This **national committee** is established to direct and coordinate party activities during the following four years. The Democrats include at least two members, a man and a woman, from each state, from the District of Columbia, and from the several territories. Governors, members of Congress, mayors, and other officials may be included as at-large members of the national committee. The Republicans, in addition, add state chairpersons from every state carried by the Republican Party in the preceding presidential, gubernatorial, or congressional elections. The selections of national committee members are ratified by the delegations to the national convention.

One of the jobs of the national committee is to ratify the presidential nominee's choice of a national chairperson, who in principle acts as the spokesperson for the party. Even though we have placed the national committee at the top of the hierarchy of party organization (see Figure 9–2 on page 282), it has very little direct influence. Basically, the national chairperson and the national committee simply plan the next campaign and the next convention, obtain financial contributions, and publicize the national party.

Picking a National Chairperson. In general, the party's presidential candidate chooses the national chairperson. (If that candidate loses, however, the chairperson is often changed.) The major responsibility of the chairperson is the management of the national election campaign. In some cases, a strong national chairperson has considerable power over state and local party organizations. There is no formal mechanism with which to exercise direct control over sub-

Roy Romer (left), General Chairman of the Democratic National Committee, and Jim Nicholson (right), the National Chairman of the Republican National Committee. Is the function of a national party chairman similar to the function of a chairman of a corporate board of directors?

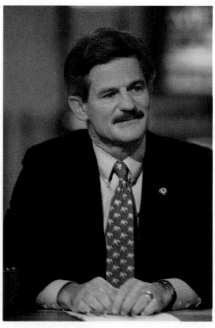

national party structures, however. The national chairperson does such jobs as establish a national party headquarters, raise and distribute campaign funds, and appear in the media as a party spokesperson.

The national chairperson, along with the national committee, attempts basically to maintain some sort of liaison among the different levels of the party organization. The fact is that the real strength and power of a national party are at the state level.

The State Party Organization

There are fifty states in the Union, plus the territories and the District of Columbia, and an equal number of party organizations for each major party. Therefore, there are more than a hundred state parties (and even more, if we include local parties and minor parties). Because every state party is unique, it is impossible to describe what an "average" state political party is like. Nonetheless, state parties have several organizational features in common.

This commonality can be described in one sentence: each state party has a chairperson, a committee, and a number of local organizations. In principle, each **state central committee**—the principal organized structure of each political party within each state—has a similar role in the various states. The committee, usually composed of those members who represent congressional districts, state legislative districts, or counties, has responsibility for carrying out the policy decisions of the party's state convention, and in some states the state committee will direct the state chairperson with respect to policymaking.

Also, like the national committee, the state central committee has control over the use of party campaign funds during political campaigns. Usually, the state central committee has little, if any, influence on party candidates once they are elected. In fact, state parties are fundamentally loose alliances of local interests and coalitions of often bitterly opposed factions.

State parties are also important in national politics because of the **unit rule**, which awards electoral votes in presidential elections as an indivisible bloc (except in Maine and Nebraska). Presidential candidates concentrate their efforts in states in which voter preferences seem to be evenly divided or in which large numbers of electoral votes are at stake.

State Central Committee
The principal organized structure of each political party within each state. This committee is responsible for carrying out policy decisions of the party's state convention.

Unit Rule
All of a state's electoral votes are cast for the presidential candidate receiving a plurality of the popular vote.

Local Party Machinery: The Grassroots

The lowest layer of party machinery is the local organization, supported by district leaders, precinct or ward captains, and party workers. Much of the work is coordinated by county committees and their chairpersons. At the end of the nineteenth century, the institution of **patronage**—rewarding the party faithful with government jobs or contracts—held the local organization together. For immigrants and the poor, the political machine often furnished important services and protections. The big-city machine was the archetypal example, and Tammany Hall, or the Tammany Society, which dominated New York City government for nearly two centuries, was perhaps the highest refinement of this political form. (See this chapter's *Politics and Ethics* on page 286.)

The last big-city local political machine to exercise a great deal of power was run by Chicago's Mayor Richard J. Daley, who was also an important figure in national Democratic politics. Daley, as mayor, ran the Chicago Democratic machine from 1955 until his death in 1976. The Daley organization, largely Irish in candidate origin and voter support, was split by the successful candidacy of African American Democrat Harold Washington in the racially divisive 1983 mayoral election. The current mayor of Chicago, Richard M. Daley, son of the

Patronage
Rewarding faithful party workers and followers with government employment and contracts.

INFOTRAC®
COLLEGE EDITION

"Demanding Patronage Appointment from Gov. James Hunt"

POLITICS and Ethics
Tammany Hall: The Quintessential Local Political Machine

The Tammany Society dominated New York City politics for nearly two centuries. Founded in 1786 with the express purpose of engaging in cultural, social, and patriotic activities, the society evolved into a major political force and became known as Tammany Hall. In the beginning, it organized and provided social services for the foreign born, who made up the bulk of the Democratic Party in New York City.

One of its more notorious leaders was William Tweed, head of the so-called Tweed ring, whose scandals were unearthed by the *New York Times* in 1871. Readers were entertained and horrified by stories of millions of dollars in kickbacks received from giving out government contracts, of how civil and criminal violations were being overlooked, and of phony leases and padded bills that were paid to members of the Tweed ring. As a result of the exposé, Tweed was imprisoned; but the other members of the ring managed to flee the country (as very wealthy men and women). Richard Crocker took over the leadership of Tammany Hall in 1886 and kept it until 1901.

Tammany Hall's influence declined when its slate of

TWEEDLEDEE AND SWEEDLEDUM.
(A New Christmas Pantomime at the Tammany Hall.)
Clown (to Pantaloon). "Let's Blind them with *this*, and then take *some more*."

candidates was defeated in a reform movement in 1901. It was not until Franklin D. Roosevelt's victory in 1932, however, that Tammany lost its political clout almost completely—but only for a couple of decades. In the 1950s, there was a short-lived resurgence in the influence of the Tammany Society. It has enjoyed no political influence in New York City politics since then.

FOR CRITICAL ANALYSIS

What kinds of organizations today provide the services that political machines did in the past?

former mayor, today heads a party organization that includes many different groups in the electorate.

City machines are now dead, mostly because their function of providing social services (and reaping the reward of votes) has been taken over by state and national agencies. This trend began in the 1930s, when the social legislation of the New Deal established Social Security and unemployment insurance. The local party machine has little, if anything, to do with deciding who is eligible to receive these benefits.

POLITICS and the Constitution

Political Patronage and the First Amendment

Traditionally, political patronage has entailed rewarding the party faithful with government jobs and contracts. It has also involved firing (or refusing to hire or award contracts to) those employees or contractors who do not support the views of a newly elected official. How, though, can firing an employee because of his or her political views be squared with the First Amendment's guarantee of free speech and expression?

In a series of decisions over the past three decades, the Supreme Court has had to grapple with the problem of how to balance these First Amendment freedoms with the tradition of political patronage. In a landmark decision in 1976, *Elrod v. Burns,** the Court held that government officials cannot discharge public employees for refusing to support a political party or its candidates unless political affiliation is an appropriate requirement for the job in question. In 1990, in *Rutan*

*427 U.S. 347 (1976).

v. Republican Party of Illinois,† the Court went even further: it ruled that not only was firing a public employee for political affiliation an impermissible infringement on the employee's First Amendment rights but so was hiring, promoting, or transferring a public employee on such a basis.

In 1996, the issue of political patronage and First Amendment rights again came before the Supreme Court. The specific issue was whether a local government could refuse to hire or to continue using the services of *independent contractors* (workers who are not classified as employees) because of their political views. The Court held that the First Amendment protections afforded to public employees against being discharged for refusing to support a political party or its candidates also extend to independent contractors.‡

†497 U.S. 62 (1990).
‡*Board of County Commissioners v. Umbehr*, 116 S.Ct. 2342 (1996); *O'Hare Truck Service, Inc. v. City of Northlake*, 116 S.Ct. 2361 (1996).

Clearly, though, political patronage itself is far from dead; and it certainly has its defenders on the Supreme Court. In the 1976 *Elrod* decision, for example, Justice William Rehnquist (now chief justice), joined by Justices Lewis Powell and Warren Burger, dissented from the majority's view and defended the patronage system. These justices could see nothing unconstitutional in conditioning public employment on political affiliation. In the 1990 *Rutan* case, Justice Antonin Scalia—joined by Chief Justice Rehnquist and Justices Anthony Kennedy and Sandra Day O'Connor—wrote a stinging dissent in which he predicted "disastrous consequences for our political system" if the view of the majority on the Court prevailed.

Again in 1996, Justice Scalia dissented from the majority's decision, this time joined by Justice Clarence Thomas. Scalia stated, "There can be no dispute that, like rewarding one's allies, the . . . act of refusing to reward

one's opponents—and at bottom both of today's cases involve exactly that—is an American political tradition as old as the Republic. This is true not only with regard to employment matters . . . but also in the area of government contracts." Scalia concluded that it was inconceivable that the protections given to public employees should extend to the "massive field" of all government contracting. "Yet amazingly, that is what the Court does. . . . It is profoundly disturbing that the varying political practices across this vast country, from coast to coast, can be transformed overnight by an institution whose conviction of what the Constitution means is so fickle."

FOR CRITICAL ANALYSIS

Justice Scalia, in his dissent from the Rutan *decision, stated that the Supreme Court justices themselves owe their appointments to political patronage. What did he mean by this?*

Local political organizations, whether located in cities, townships, or at the county level, still can contribute a great deal to local election campaigns. These organizations are able to provide the foot soldiers of politics—individuals who pass out literature and get out the vote on election day, which can be crucial in local elections. In many regions, local Democratic and Republican organizations still exercise some patronage, such as awarding courthouse jobs, contracts for street repair, and other lucrative construction contracts. (The constitutionality of awarding—or not awarding—contracts on the basis of political affiliation increasingly is subject to challenge, however. For the Supreme Court's opinion on the matter, see this chapter's *Politics and the Constitution*.) Local party organizations are also the most important vehicles for recruiting young adults into political work, because political involvement at the local level offers activists many opportunities to gain experience.

The Party and Its Members

The two major American political parties are often characterized as being too much like Tweedledee and Tweedledum, the twins in Lewis Carroll's *Through the Looking Glass*. When both parties nominate moderates for the presidency, the similarities between the parties seem to outweigh their differences. Yet the political parties do generate strong conflict for political offices throughout the United States, and there are significant differences between the parties, both in the characteristics of their members and in their platforms.

Differences between the Parties

Although Democrats and Republicans are not divided along religious or class lines to the extent that some European parties are, certain social groups are more likely to identify with each party. Since the New Deal of Franklin D. Roosevelt, the Democratic Party has appealed to the more disadvantaged groups in society. African American voters are far more likely to identify with the Democrats, as are members of union households, Jewish voters, and individuals who have less than a high school education. Republicans draw more of their support from college graduates, upper-income families, and professionals or businesspersons. In recent years, more women than men have tended to identify themselves as Democrats than as Republicans.

The coalition of minorities, the working class, and various ethnic groups has been the core of Democratic Party support since the presidency of Franklin D. Roosevelt. The social programs and increased government intervention in the economy that were the heart of Roosevelt's New Deal were intended to ease the strain of economic hard times on these groups. This goal remains important for many Democrats today. In general, Democratic identifiers are more likely to approve of social-welfare spending, to support government regulation of business, to approve of measures to improve the situation of minorities, and to support assistance to the elderly with their medical expenses. Republicans are more supportive of the private marketplace, and many Republicans feel that the federal government should be involved in fewer social programs.

Public opinion polls that ask the public which party they trust to handle certain issues reaffirm the loyalties of various groups. As shown in Figure 9–3, a majority of those polled think that Republicans are likely to do a better job on national defense, foreign affairs, balancing the budget, handling crime and the drug problem, and changing campaign-finance laws. Democrats are seen as having quite an advantage with respect to protecting Social Security and Medicare, improving the schools, protecting the environment, and helping the poor. These are the issues that are most attractive to Democratic voters.

Note that in 1998, Democrats and Republicans are viewed as about equally trustworthy on issues of keeping the economy strong and taxes low. This is a bit of a reversal from the years of Ronald Reagan and George Bush, when Republicans were perceived to have an advantage on economic issues. The strong performance of the nation's economy during the Clinton presidency apparently has increased voters' confidence in the ability of the Democratic Party to address economic issues effectively.

The Party-in-Government

After the election is over and the winners are announced, the focus of party activity shifts from getting out the vote to organizing and controlling the gov-

Question: Which political party, the Democrats or the Republicans, do you trust to do a better job on...?

FIGURE 9-3

Which Party Is Better?

	DEMOCRATS	REPUBLICANS	
Maintaining a strong national defense	37%	53%	
Foreign affairs	41%	45%	
Balancing the federal budget	41%	43%	**Advantage**
Handling the crime problem	39%	42%	**Republicans**
Reducing the problem of illegal drugs	33%	41%	
Changing the way campaigns are financed	33%	41%	
Encouraging high moral standards and values	40%	41%	
Handling the nation's economy	45%	44%	
Holding taxes down	45%	44%	
Coping with the nation's main problems*	45%	42%	
Protecting Social Security	48%	38%	
Protecting Medicare	52%	33%	
Improving education and the schools	54%	34%	**Advantage**
Providing affordable health care	54%	33%	**Democrats**
Protecting the environment	54%	31%	
Helping the middle class	57%	34%	
Helping the poor	61%	27%	

*The question posed in this case was, "Overall, which party, the Democrats or the Republicans, do you trust to do a better job in coping with the main problems the nation faces over the next few years?"

SOURCE: Survey by ABC News/*Washington Post,* January 15–19, 1998, as reported in *The Public Perspective,* April/May 1998.

ernment. As you will see in Chapter 12, party membership plays an important role in the day-to-day operations of Congress, with partisanship determining everything from office space to committee assignments and power on Capitol Hill. For the president, the political party furnishes the pool of qualified applicants for political appointments to run the government. Although it is uncommon to do so, presidents can and occasionally do appoint executive personnel, such as cabinet secretaries, from the opposition party. As we note in Chapter 13, there are not as many of these appointed positions as presidents might like, and presidential power is limited by the permanent bureaucracy. Judicial appointments, however, offer a great opportunity to the winning party. For the most part, presidents are likely to appoint federal judges from their own party.

All of these party appointments suggest that the winning political party, whether at the national, state, or local level, has a great deal of control in the American system. Because of the checks and balances and the relative lack of cohesion in American parties, however, such control is an illusion. In fact, many Americans, at least implicitly, prefer a "divided government," with the executive and legislative branches controlled by different parties. The trend toward **ticket splitting**—splitting votes between the president and members of Congress—has increased sharply since 1952. This practice may indicate a lack of trust in government or the relative weakness of party identification among many voters. Voters seem comfortable with having a president affiliated with one party and a Congress controlled by the other.

The answer to whether voters really prefer divided government seems to depend on exactly what they are asked. Generally, voters are split evenly over

Ticket Splitting
Voting for candidates of two or more parties for different offices. For example, a voter splits her ticket if she votes for a Republican presidential candidate and for a Democratic congressional candidate.

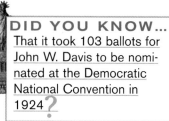

whether it is better to have a president and Congress of the same party or to have divided control; about 42 percent say the same party is preferable and 41 percent say divided government. If, however, voters are asked if they prefer to have different parties controlling Congress and the presidency to "prevent either one from going too far," 67 percent prefer divided government and only 25 percent of those polled support a government controlled by one party.[5]

Why Do We Have a Two-Party System?

Although it is difficult to imagine a political system in the United States with four, five, six, or seven major political parties, other democratic systems have three-party, four-party, or even ten-party systems. In some European nations, parties are clearly tied to ideological positions; parties that represent Marxist, socialist, liberal, conservative, and ultraconservative positions appear on the political continuum. Some nations have political parties that represent regions of the nation that have separate cultural identities, such as the French-speaking and German-speaking regions of Switzerland. Some parties are rooted in religious differences. In some Muslim nations, political parties are based on differences between factions of Islam. Parties also exist that represent specific economic interests—agricultural, maritime, or industrial—and some, such as monarchist parties, speak for alternative political systems.

The United States has a **two-party system**, and that system has been around from about 1800 to the present. Considering the range of political ideology among voters and the variety of local and state party machines, the fact that we still have just two major political parties is somewhat unusual.

There are several reasons why two major parties have dominated the political landscape in the United States for almost two centuries. These reasons have to do with (1) the historical foundations of the system, (2) the self-perpetuation of the parties, (3) the commonality of views among Americans, (4) the winner-take-all electoral system, and (5) state and federal laws favoring the two-party system.

Two-Party System
A political system in which only two parties have a reasonable chance of winning.

elections '98
Partisan Trends in the 1998 Elections

In midterm elections, the conventional wisdom suggests that the voters will most likely be faithful party identifiers who will come out to vote no matter what. The exit poll data from 1998 tended to confirm that wisdom—although there were some exceptions to the trend. The exit polls showed that 37 percent of those who voted thought of themselves as Democrats, while 36 percent identified with the Republican Party. Both of those percentages are higher than the proportion usually found in the general electorate, so it appears that party members did turn out to vote in disproportionate numbers. Many of the close elections, though, were decided by the 27 percent of the voters who declared themselves to be independents.

Generally the two major parties had different success rates depending on the local geographic area. Republicans turned out in states such as Illinois and Ohio, where most of their tickets won. In California and New York, Democrats were able to "turn out" high numbers of minority voters and union members.

---

[5]NBC News/*Wall Street Journal* poll, 1997, as reported in *The Public Perspective*, February/March 1998, p. 48.

The Historical Foundations of the Two-Party System

As we have seen, the first two opposing groups in U.S. politics were the Federalists and the Anti-Federalists. The Federalists, who remained in power and solidified their identity as a political party, represented those with commercial interests, including merchants, shipowners, and manufacturers. The Federalists supported the principle of a strong national government. The Anti-Federalists, who gradually became known as the Democratic Republicans, represented artisans and farmers. They strongly supported states' rights. These interests were also fairly well split along geographic lines, with the Federalists dominant in the North and the Democratic Republicans dominant in the South.

Two relatively distinct sets of interests continued to characterize the two different parties. During Andrew Jackson's time in power, eastern commercial interests were pitted against western and southern agricultural and frontier interests. Before the Civil War, the major split again became North versus South. The split was ideological (over the issue of slavery), as well as economic (the Northeast's industrial interests versus the agricultural interests of the South). After the Civil War, the Republicans found most of their strength in the Northeast, and the Democrats, among white voters in the Solid South. The period from the Civil War to the 1920s has been called one of **sectional politics.**

Sectional politics gave way to **national politics** as the entire nation became more urban and industrialized. (For the effects of this development on southern politics, see the feature *Politics and Ideology: The Rise of the Republican South.*)

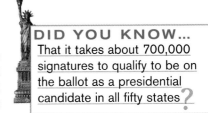

DID YOU KNOW...
That it takes about 700,000 signatures to qualify to be on the ballot as a presidential candidate in all fifty states?

Sectional Politics
The pursuit of interests that are of special concern to a region or section of the country.

National Politics
The pursuit of interests that are of concern to the nation as a whole.

Drawing by Steiner © 1994 The New Yorker Magazine, Inc.

"The euonymus likes partial shade and does equally well under Republican and Democratic Administrations."

POLITICS and Ideology

The Rise of the Republican South

As discussed in the text, the years following the Civil War saw the Republican Party controlling the northeastern and midwestern United States while the South, resentful of its defeat by the Union, became solidly Democratic. Remember from Chapter 5 that African Americans were, for the most part, denied the right to participate in southern politics until after 1965. During the late 1960s and early 1970s, the South continued to elect Democratic officeholders.

In the early 1970s, Kevin Phillips, a well-known commentator, predicted that migration from the North and the general conservative attitudes of southern white voters would lead to Republican control in that region. As the accompanying maps of the South show, the Republican Party now has control of the majority of that region's governorships, Senate seats, and House seats. Only in the state legislatures are Democrats still in control. Republicans were able to capture the national offices first because the campaigns for these offices were often statewide (for the Senate) or covered larger areas (House seats). This meant that more of the newcomers to the region

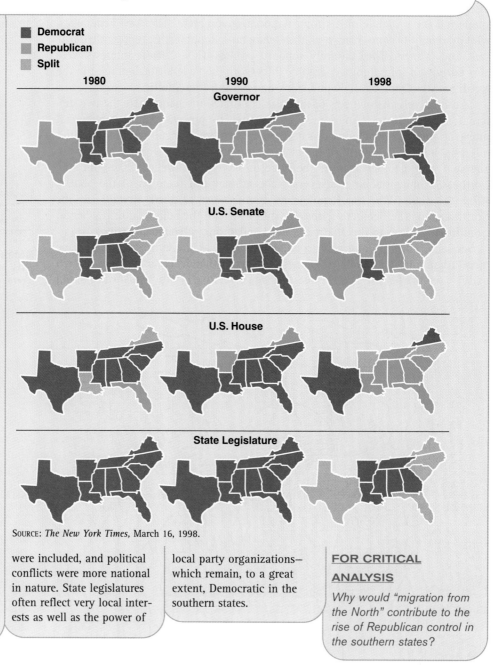

SOURCE: *The New York Times*, March 16, 1998.

were included, and political conflicts were more national in nature. State legislatures often reflect very local interests as well as the power of local party organizations—which remain, to a great extent, Democratic in the southern states.

FOR CRITICAL ANALYSIS

Why would "migration from the North" contribute to the rise of Republican control in the southern states?

Class Politics
Political preferences based on income level, social status, or both.

The contemporary period can also be described as one of **class politics,** with the Republicans generally finding support among groups of higher economic status and the Democrats appealing more to working-class constituencies and the poor.

Self-perpetuation of the Two-Party System

As we saw in Chapter 7, most children identify with the political party of their parents. Children learn at a fairly young age to think of themselves as either

Democrats or Republicans. Relatively few are taught to think of themselves as Libertarians or Socialists or even independents. This generates a built-in mechanism to perpetuate a two-party system. Also, many politically oriented people who aspire to work for social change consider that the only realistic way to capture political power in this country is to be either a Republican or a Democrat.

The Political Culture of the United States

Another determining factor in the perpetuation of our two-party system is the commonality of goals among Americans. Most Americans want continuing material prosperity. They also believe that this goal should be achieved through individual, rather than collective, initiative. There has never been much support for the idea of limiting the ownership of private property or equalizing everyone's income. Most Americans take a dim view of such proposals. Private property is considered a basic American value, and the ability to acquire and use it the way one wishes commonly is regarded as a basic American right. Thus, socialist parties have found limited support.

Another reason we have had a basic consensus about our political system and the two major parties is that we have managed largely to separate religion from politics. Religion was an issue in 1928, when Governor Alfred Smith of New York became the first Roman Catholic to be nominated for the presidency (he was defeated by Republican Herbert Hoover), and again in 1960, when John F. Kennedy was running for president. But religion has never been a dividing force triggering splinter parties. There has never been a major Catholic party or a Protestant party or a Jewish party or a Muslim party.

The major division in American politics has been economic. As we mentioned earlier, the Democrats have been known—at least since the 1920s—as the party of the working class. They have been in favor of government intervention in the economy and more government redistribution of income from the wealthy to those with lower incomes. The Republican Party has been known in modern times as the party of the middle and upper classes and commercial interests, in favor of fewer constraints on the market system and less redistribution of income.

Not only does the political culture support the two-party system, but also the parties themselves are adept at making the necessary shifts in their platforms or electoral appeal to gain new members. Because the general ideological structure of the parties is so broad, it has been relatively easy for them to change their respective platforms or to borrow popular policies from the opposing party or from minor parties to attract voter support. Both parties perceive themselves as being broad enough to accommodate every group in society. The Republicans try to gain support from the African American community, and the Democrats strive to make inroads among professional and business groups.

The Winner-Take-All Electoral System

At virtually every level of government in the United States, the outcome of elections is based on the plurality, winner-take-all principle. A plurality system is one in which the winner is the person who obtains the most votes, even if a majority is not obtained. Whoever gets the most votes gets everything. Because most legislators in the United States are elected from single-member districts in which only one person represents the constituency, the candidate who finishes second in such an election receives nothing for the effort.

The winner-take-all system also operates in the **electoral college** (see Chapter 10). In virtually all of the states, the electors are pledged to presidential candidates chosen by their respective national party conventions. During the popular

This handbill was used in the election campaign of 1860. Handbills served the same purpose as today's direct-mail advertisements, appealing directly to the voters with the candidate's message.

INFOTRAC®
COLLEGE EDITION

"The Year the GOP Went South"

Electoral College
A group of persons called electors who are selected by the voters in each state. This group officially elects the president and the vice president of the United States. The number of electors in each state is equal to the number of each state's representatives in both houses of Congress.

vote in November, in each of the fifty states and in the District of Columbia, the voters choose one slate of electors from those on the state ballot. If the slate of electors wins a plurality in a state, then usually *all* the electors so chosen cast their ballots for the presidential and vice presidential candidates of the winning party. This means that if a particular candidate's slate of electors receives a plurality of, say, 40 percent of the votes in a state, that candidate will receive all the state's electoral votes. Minor parties have a difficult time competing under such a system, even though they may influence the final outcome of the election. Because voters know that minor parties cannot succeed, they often will not vote for minor-party candidates, even if the voters are ideologically in tune with them.

Not all countries, or even all states in the United States, use the plurality, winner-take-all electoral system. Some hold run-off elections until a candidate obtains at least one vote over 50 percent of the votes. Such a system also may be used in countries with multiple parties. Small parties hope to be able to obtain a sufficient number of votes at least to get into a run-off election.

Many other nations use a system of proportional representation with multi-member districts. If, during the national election, party X obtains 12 percent of the vote, party Y gets 43 percent of the vote, and party Z gets the remaining 45 percent of the vote, then party X gets 12 percent of the seats in the legislature, party Y gets 43 percent of the seats, and party Z gets 45 percent of the seats. Because even a minor party may still obtain at least a few seats in the legislature, the smaller parties have a greater incentive to organize under such electoral systems than they do in the United States.

State and Federal Laws Favoring the Two Parties

Many state and federal election laws offer a clear advantage to the two major parties. In some states, the established major parties need to gather fewer signatures to place their candidates on the ballot than minor parties or independent candidates do. (See this chapter's *Politics and the Law* for a discussion of the widely varying signature requirements.) The criterion for determining how many signatures will be required is often based on the total party vote in the last general election, thus penalizing a new political party that did not compete in that election.

At the national level, minor parties face different obstacles. All of the rules and procedures of both houses of Congress divide committee seats, staff members, and other privileges on the basis of party membership. A legislator who is elected on a minor-party ticket, such as the Liberal Party of New York, must choose to be counted with one of the major parties to get a committee assignment. The Federal Election Commission (FEC) rules for campaign financing also place restrictions on minor-party candidates. Such candidates are not eligible for federal matching funds in either the primary or the general election. In the 1980 election, John Anderson, running for president as an independent, sued the FEC for campaign funds. The commission finally agreed to repay part of his campaign costs after the election in proportion to the votes he received.

The Role of Minor Parties in U.S. Political History

Minor parties have a difficult, if not impossible, time competing within the American two-party political system. Nonetheless, minor parties have played an important role in our political life. Frequently, dissatisfied groups have split from

POLITICS and the Law

Getting on the Ballot

Although many Americans (more than half, as of 1996) believe that it would be valuable to have a third major party contend in national elections, state laws make the task of getting a new party on the ballot very compli-cated. The state laws tend to make it easier to get a new party's presidential candidate on the ballot than to put a full slate of candidates for the House of Representatives on the ballot. If you examine the ballot requirements listed below, you will note that in Louisiana, for example, no signatures are needed to put a presidential candidate on the ballot, but 125,000 signa-tures of registered party vot-ers are needed to field an entire House slate.

FOR CRITICAL ANALYSIS

Should the federal govern-ment create regulations or enact legislation that would make it easier for third par-ties to get on the ballot?

Number of Signatures Required for a New Political Party to Get on the November 1996 Ballot

State	Presidential Candidate Only	Full Slate for U.S. House of Representatives	State	Presidential Candidate Only	Full Slate for U.S. House of Representatives
Alabama	11,991	35,973	New York	15,000	123,500
Alaska	2,586	4,753	North Carolina	51,904	51,904
Arizona	15,062	15,062	North Dakota	7,000	7,000
Arkansas	0	21,506	Ohio	33,463	33,463
California	89,006*	89,006*	Oklahoma	41,711	49,751
Colorado	0	4,800	Oregon	18,316	18,316
Connecticut	7,500	18,195	Pennsylvania	30,000†	46,351
Delaware	180*†	180*†	Rhode Island	1,000	2,000
Dist. of Columbia	3,200†	6,200†	South Carolina	10,000	10,000
Florida	65,596	196,788	South Dakota	7,792	7,792
Georgia	30,036	180,216	Tennessee	37,179	37,179
Hawaii	3,829	4,889	Texas	43,963	43,963
Idaho	9,644	9,644	Utah	300	500
Illinois	25,000	177,198	Vermont	20	20
Indiana	29,822	59,644	Virginia	16,000†	32,000†
Iowa	1,500	3,000	Washington	200	225
Kansas	16,418	16,418	West Virginia	6,837	10,904
Kentucky	5,000	7,400	Wisconsin	2,000	10,000
Louisiana	0	125,000*†	Wyoming	8,000	8,000
Maine	4,000	8,000			
Maryland	10,000	85,000†			
Massachusetts	10,000	30,000			
Michigan	30,891	30,891			
Minnesota	2,000	10,000			
Mississippi	0**	0			
Missouri	10,000	10,000			
Montana	10,471	10,471			
Nebraska	5,741	5,741			
Nevada	3,761	3,761			
New Hampshire	3,000	3,000			
New Jersey	800	2,100			
New Mexico	2,339	7,017			

*State requires voter signatories to register as members of that particular party.

**State subjectively decides whether a party is sufficiently "organized" to merit ballot access.

†Estimates.

Notes: Some signature totals are estimates because the formula for calculating the number depends on information that was not yet available (for example, the results of a November 1996 election, or the number of registered voters as of January 1, 1997). In Texas and West Virginia, primary voters cannot sign petitions for new party candidates.

Source: *Ballot Access News,* as quoted by John F. Persinos, "Voter Discontent Is Opening an Opportunity for a New Political Force," *Campaigns and Elections,* September 1995.

Eugene V. Debs was the founder of the Socialist Party and a candidate for president on that ticket five times. Despite its longevity, the party has had little impact on the American political system.

Third Party

A political party other than the two major political parties (Republican and Democratic). Usually, third parties are composed of dissatisfied groups that have split from the major parties. They act as indicators of political trends and as safety valves for dissident groups.

major parties and formed so-called **third parties,** which have acted as barometers of changes in the political mood.[6] Such barometric indicators have forced the major parties to recognize new issues or trends in the thinking of Americans. Political scientists also believe that third parties have acted as a safety valve for dissident political groups, perhaps preventing major confrontations and political unrest. Additionally, parties may be formed to represent a particular ethnic group, such as Hispanics, or groups such as gays and lesbians.

Historically Important Minor Parties

Most minor parties that have endured have had a strong ideological foundation that is typically at odds with the majority mindset. Ideology has at least two functions. First, the members of the minor party regard themselves as outsiders and look to one another for support; ideology provides tremendous psychological cohesiveness. Second, because the rewards of ideological commitment are partly psychological, these minor parties do not think in terms of immediate electoral success. A poor showing at the polls therefore does not dissuade either the leadership or the grassroots participants from continuing their quest for change in American society. Some of the notable third parties include the following:

1. The Socialist Labor Party, started in 1877.
2. The Socialist Party, founded in 1901.
3. The Communist Party, started in 1919 as the radical left wing that split from the Socialist Party.
4. The Socialist Workers' Party, formerly a Trotskyite group, started in 1938.
5. The Libertarian Party, formed in 1972 and still an important minor party.
6. The Reform Party, founded in 1996.

As we can see from their labels, several of these minor parties have been Marxist oriented. The most successful was Eugene Debs's Socialist Party, which captured 6 percent of the popular vote for president in 1912 and elected more than a thousand candidates at the local level. About eighty mayors were affiliated with the Socialist Party at one time or another. It owed much of its success to the corruption of big-city machines and to antiwar sentiment. Debs's Socialist Party was vociferously opposed to American entry into World War I, a view shared by many Americans. The other, more militant parties of the left (the Socialist Labor, Socialist Workers', and Communist parties) have never enjoyed wide electoral success. At the other end of the ideological spectrum, the Libertarian Party supports a *laissez-faire* capitalist economic program, combined with a hands-off policy on regulating matters of moral conduct.

Splinter Minor Parties

Splinter Party

A new party formed by a dissident faction within a major political party. Usually, splinter parties have emerged when a particular personality was at odds with the major party.

The most successful minor parties have been those that split from major parties. The impetus for these **splinter parties,** or factions, has usually been a situation in which a particular personality was at odds with the major party. The most famous spin-off was the Bull Moose Progressive Party, which split from the Republican Party in 1912 over the candidate chosen to run for president. Theodore Roosevelt rallied his forces and announced the formation of the Bull Moose Progressive Party, leaving the regular Republicans to support William Howard Taft. Although the party was not successful in winning the election for Roosevelt, it did succeed in splitting the Republican vote so that Democrat Woodrow Wilson won.

---

[6]The term *third party* is erroneous, because sometimes there have been third, fourth, fifth, and even sixth parties. Because it has endured, however, we will use the term here.

Theodore Roosevelt, president of the United States from 1901 to 1909, became president after William McKinley was assassinated. Roosevelt was reelected in 1904. In 1912, unable to gain the nomination of the Republican Party, Roosevelt formed a splinter group named the Bull Moose Progressive Party but was unsuccessful in his efforts to win the presidency.

Among the Democrats, there have been three splinter third parties since the late 1940s: (1) the Dixiecrat (States' Rights) Party of 1948, (2) Henry Wallace's Progressive Party of 1948, and (3) the American Independent Party supporting George Wallace in 1968. The strategy employed by Wallace in the 1968 election was to deny Richard Nixon or Hubert Humphrey the necessary majority in the electoral college. Many political scientists believe that Humphrey still would have lost to Nixon in 1968 even if Wallace had not run, because most Wallace voters would probably have given their votes to Nixon. The American Independent Party emphasized mostly racial issues, and to a lesser extent, foreign policy. Wallace received 9.9 million popular votes and 46 electoral votes.

Other Minor Parties

Numerous minor parties have coalesced around specific issues or aims. The Free Soil Party, active from 1848 to 1852, was dedicated to preventing the spread of slavery. The goal of the Prohibition Party, started in 1869, was to ban the sale of liquor.

Some minor parties have had specific economic interests as their reason for being. When those interests are either met or made irrelevant by changing economic conditions, these minor parties disappear. Such was the case with the Greenback Party, which lasted from 1876 to 1884. It was one of the most prominent farmer-labor parties that favored government intervention in the economy.

Reform Party presidential nominee Ross Perot speaks at the party's national convention in Valley Forge, Pennsylvania.

Similar to the Greenbacks, but with broader support, was the Populist Party, which lasted from about 1892 to 1908. Farmers were the backbone of this party, and agrarian reform was its goal. In 1892, it ran a presidential candidate, James Weaver, who received one million popular votes and twenty-two electoral votes. The Populists, for the most part, joined with the Democrats in 1896, when both parties endorsed the Democratic presidential candidate, William Jennings Bryan.

The Impact of Minor Parties

Minor parties clearly have had an impact on American politics. What is more difficult to ascertain is how great that impact has been. Simply by showing that third-party issues were taken over some years later by a major party really does not prove that the third party instigated the major party's change. The case for the importance of minor parties may be strongest for the splinter parties. These parties do indeed force a major party to reassess its ideology and organization. There is general agreement that Teddy Roosevelt's Progressive Party in 1912 and Robert La Follette's Progressive Party in 1924 caused the major parties to take up business regulation as one of their major issues.

Minor parties also can have a serious impact on the outcomes of an election. Although Bill Clinton may well have won the 1992 election in any case, the campaign of H. Ross Perot left its imprint on American politics. Perot was not the candidate of a third party; rather, he was antiparty, attacking both major political parties for being ineffective and beholden to special interests. Perot had a very strong appeal to young voters, to independent voters, and to disaffected party identifiers. In 1996, Perot started the Reform Party.

Perot's share of the votes in 1992 could have been divided unevenly between Bush and Clinton, thereby changing the outcome of the election. His success followed the pattern of other third parties that have polled enough votes to affect an election. In 1996, Reform Party candidate Perot received only 8 percent of the national vote. This total was enough to affect the margins of both Dole and Clinton, but because Perot drew votes from Republicans, Democrats, and independents, his campaign did not keep Clinton from being reelected.

Carol Miller, a member of the Green Party, recently won 17 percent of the vote in a special election for New Mexico's Third District congressional seat. Using a populist and environmentalist platform, the Green Party has garnered enough votes in New Mexico elections since 1994 to allow the Republicans to win three major races in a state having a Democratic majority.

Calling the U.S. system a two-party system is an oversimplification. The nature and names of the major parties have changed over time, and smaller parties almost always have enjoyed a moderate degree of success. Whether they are splinters from the major parties or expressions of social and economic issues not addressed adequately by factions within the major parties, the minor parties attest to the vitality and fluid nature of American politics.

The Uncertain Future of Party Identification

Figure 9–4 shows trends in **party identification,** as measured by standard polling techniques from 1937 to 1998. What is evident is the rise of the independent voter combined with a relative strengthening of support for the Republican Party, so that the traditional Democratic advantage in party identification is relatively small today.

In the 1940s, only about 20 percent of voters classified themselves as independents. By 1975, this percentage had increased to about 33 percent, and more recent polls show it holding steady at about that level. At times, the Democrats have captured the loyalty of about half the electorate, and the Republicans, until 1960, had more than 30 percent support. By the 1990s, the Democrats could count on less than 40 percent of the electorate and the Republicans, on about 30 percent.

Not only have ties to the two major parties weakened in the last three decades, but also voters are less willing to vote a straight ticket—that is, to vote for all the candidates of one party. The percentage of voters who engage in ticket splitting has increased from 12 percent in 1952 to more than 38 percent in the presidential election of 1996. This trend, along with the increase in the number of voters who call themselves independents, suggests that parties have lost much of their hold on the loyalty of the voters. (See this chapter's *Critical Perspective* on pages 300 and 301 for a discussion of the changing role played by political parties in the United States today.)

Party Identification
Linking oneself to a particular political party.

FIGURE 9-4

Party Identification from 1937 to 1998

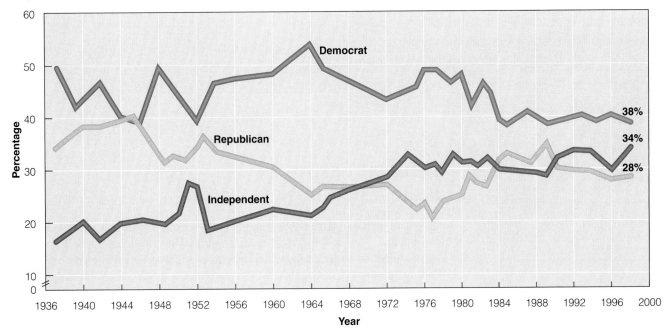

SOURCE: *Gallup Report,* August 1995; *New York Times*/CBS poll, June, 1996; *Gallup Report,* February 1998.

Critical perspective

What Role Do Political Parties Play Today?

The role of American political parties has been in doubt for the last several decades. As you can see in Figure 9–4 on page 299, the number of Americans who identify with either the Democrats or the Republicans has dropped significantly since the end of World War II. Even more importantly, the vast majority of Americans split their ballots between the parties in elections. Given the emphasis on television advertising, electronic campaigning, and the use of paid political consultants, few Americans are ever actively involved in party politics, even at the local level.

In his book entitled *Why Parties? The Origin and Transformation of Political Parties in America,** John H. Aldrich suggests that although the role of parties has undergone considerable change in recent years, they are still vital to the political process. Aldrich reviews the birth of American political parties, noting that all such structures are created to support the needs of those who pursue political office. Thus, in the first century or so, American parties were needed to get out the vote, to do the actual campaigning for office, and to provide support for the officeholders after the election. In that era, political parties may even have had the power to control the politicians—it was clearly understood that politicians were dependent on parties.

With the rise of the media campaign and political action committees (see Chapter 8), candidates for office and officeholders became much more independent of the political parties. During the years when PACs first became influential in American politics, political parties were not allowed to accept contributions in the same

*Chicago: University of Chicago Press, 1995.

way that PACs could. It became clear to politicians, party elites, and scholars that the political parties were being eclipsed by the powerful funding of the PACs. Candidates were able to ignore their parties and raise their own funds, thus lessening their loyalty to either of the major parties.

In 1979, the Federal Election Campaign Act was amended to allow contributors to give "unlimited" contributions to state and local parties for get-out-the-vote drives and other activities designed to increase participation. The intent of this legislation was to strengthen the parties by making resources available to them that candidates needed. Thus, the national party committees were allowed to raise unlimited amounts of "soft money" from individuals, corporations, and labor unions and pass the funds on to state and local parties that supported candidates.[†] In 1991, the law was further interpreted to make most of these contributions reportable, but they were still exempt from the original limits of $1,000 per person per election.

A court decision in 1996 made it legal for national and state parties to use soft money contributions to pay for television advertising, something that had been prohibited in the past. Such contributions made it possible for the Clinton-Gore campaign to collect enough funds so that long before the actual presidential campaign heated up it could begin running ads that attacked the Republicans as posing a threat to Medicare. Indeed, these amendments to the original law regulating campaign financing and the subsequent

[†]Paul Allen Beck, *Party Politics in America,* 8th ed. (New York: Longman, 1998), p. 283.

Political Parties: Issues for the New Century

American political parties face a number of issues as they look to the next decade and beyond. First and foremost is their relationship to the voters: What can the parties offer to individuals to induce them to become loyal party members? Political parties are rarely able to offer individuals the social relationship or ability to achieve political goals that they could at various times in the past.

Political parties have been weakened by the growing independence of political candidates and the ability of those candidates to raise their own funds and to run their own campaigns. If parties do not become essential to the process of

Critical perspective

What Role Do Political Parties Play Today?—continued

court decisions have made the role of the president as fund-raiser much more important.

The president, leading presidential candidates, and the leaders of Congress have always been the stars of the "chicken and green peas" circuit—the banquets and dinners that raise money for the local and state parties. Now, with the demand for soft money contributions, one of the major tasks of officeholders is to travel around the nation and raise funds through dinners that feature movie stars and better menus. It is not uncommon for the president to raise $2 million or more from one dinner, with tickets going for $10,000 each.

These changes in the law have fundamentally transformed the role of political parties in modern elections. According to Aldrich, the national political parties now are defined by the need to "serve" the political candidates, the president, and the members of Congress. The parties are the major fund-raisers and bankers for state and local parties, charged with providing funds for candidates across the nation. The Republicans demonstrated how important this fund-raising capacity can be in 1994, when they captured control of both the House and the Senate in the midterm elections. In 1996, the Democratic Party attempted to regain control of the House by raising huge amounts of funds that could be used in a national campaign. Some of these funds later had to be returned to their donors because they were given by foreign interests. The importance of the parties as fund-raisers can be illustrated by the growth in their activities. In 1991–1992, the two national political parties raised $89 million. By 1995–1996, this amount had climbed to $263 million.

What impact does this change in role have on the political parties? It may make them even more remote and out of touch from the ordinary voter who is not a campaign high roller. It probably loosens even further the parties' hold on the candidates who run on the ticket, although these same candidates need their support. Becoming a major source of funds, however, has allowed the parties to increase their national staffs and to provide services to local candidates far beyond what they could in the past. National party staffs are paid professionals who can help candidates plan their campaigns, aid in the creation of television ads, provide information and guidance on substantive issues, and supply lists of donors in the candidates' districts. The parties have become extremely proficient in developing national television ads that can be adapted to each congressional constituency. They have become, in the language of Paul Allen Beck, "service parties," dedicated to serving their candidates and officeholders.

FOR CRITICAL ANALYSIS

1. If the major role for contemporary political parties is to raise funds for candidates, why should Americans identify with a party? What does the individual citizen gain from his or her party?

2. Should political parties be able to use their fund-raising ability to influence the type of candidates who will carry the party label? Should the party be able to generate some loyalty to its positions from its candidates?

recruiting candidates to run for office and supporting them while holding office, then the parties' future is quite limited. Not only will they be unable to gain the loyalty of their officeholders, but also they will be unable to promise the voters that candidates elected on either the Republican or the Democratic ticket will behave in predictable ways on the issues.

Finally, do the political parties actually stand for different positions on the issues? The popularity of Ross Perot in 1992 and 1996 demonstrated the readiness of Americans to support a candidate on the basis of his stand against the established parties and candidates. A majority of Americans believe that a third party would be a healthful development for the nation and would give them more choices when they vote. If the political parties are not able to recruit new voters and hold their loyalty, they may be greatly weakened by the rise of new parties and the fluidity of independent voters.

TOWARD ACTIVE CITIZENSHIP

ELECTING CONVENTION DELEGATES

The most exciting political party event, staged every four years, is the national convention. Surprising as it might seem, there are opportunities for the individual voter to become involved in nominating delegates to the national convention or to become such a delegate. For both the Republican and Democratic parties, most delegates must be elected at the local level—either the congressional district or the state legislative district. These elections take place at the party primary election or at a neighborhood or precinct caucus level. If the delegates are elected in a primary, persons who want to run for these positions must file petitions with the board of elections in advance of the election. If you are interested in committing yourself to a particular presidential candidate and running for the delegate position, check with the local county committee or with the party's national committee about the rules you must follow.

It is even easier to get involved in the grassroots politics of presidential caucuses. In some states—Iowa being the earliest and most famous one—delegates are first nominated at the local precinct caucus. According to the rules of the Iowa caucuses, anyone can participate in a caucus if he or she is eighteen years old, a resident of the precinct, and registered as a party member. These caucuses, in addition to being the focus of national media attention in January or February, select delegates to the county conventions who are pledged to specific presidential candidates. This is the first step toward the national convention.

At both the county caucus and the convention levels, both parties try to find younger members to fill some of the seats. Contact the state or county political party to find out when the caucuses or primaries will be held. Then gather local supporters and friends, and prepare to join in an occasion during which political persuasion and debate are practiced at their best.

For further information about these opportunities (some states hold caucuses and state conventions in every election year), contact the state party office or your local state legislator for specific dates and regulations. Or write to the national committee for its informational brochures on how to become a delegate.

Republican National Committee
Republican National Headquarters
310 1st St. S.E.
Washington, DC 20003
202-863-8500

www.rnc.org/

Democratic National Committee
Democratic National Headquarters
430 Capital St., S.E.
Washington, DC 20003
202-863-8000

www.democrats.org/

Key terms

Anti-Federalists 277

cadre 276

class politics 292

Democratic Party 279

divided government 280

electoral college 293

era of good feeling 279

era of personal politics 278

faction 275

Federalists 277

"fireside chat" 280

independent 275

national committee 284

national convention 282

national politics 291

party identification 299

party-in-government 281

party-in-the-electorate 281

party organization 281

party platform 282

patronage 285

political party 275

Republican Party 279

sectional politics 291

splinter party 296

state central committee 285

third party 296

ticket splitting 289

two-party system 290

unit rule 285

Whig Party 279

Chapter summary

1 A political party is a group of political activists who organize to win elections, operate the government, and determine public policy. Political parties perform a number of functions for the political system. These functions include recruiting candidates for public office, organizing and running elections, presenting alternative policies to the voters, assuming responsibility for operating the government, and acting as the opposition to the party in power.

2 The evolution of our nation's political parties can be divided into six periods: (1) the creation and formation of political parties from 1789 to 1812; (2) the era of one-party rule, or personal politics, from 1816 to 1824; (3) the period from Andrew Jackson's presidency to the Civil War, from 1828 to 1860; (4) the post–Civil War period, from 1864 to 1892, ending with solid control by the modern Republican Party; (5) the progressive period, from 1896 to 1928; and (6) the modern period, from 1932 to the present.

3 A political party is composed of three components: the party-in-the-electorate, the party organization, and the party-in-government. Each party component maintains linkages to the others to keep the party strong. In theory, each of the political parties has a pyramid-shaped organization with a hierarchical command structure. In reality, each level of the party—local, state, and national—has considerable autonomy. The national party organization is responsible for holding the national convention in presidential election years, writing the party platform, choosing the national committee, and conducting party business.

4 The party-in-government comprises all of the elected and appointed officeholders of a party. The linkage of party members is crucial to building support for programs among the branches and levels of government.

5 Although it may seem that the two major American political parties do not differ substantially on the issues, each has a different core group of supporters. The general shape of the parties' coalitions reflects the party divisions of Franklin Roosevelt's New Deal. It is clear, however, that party leaders are much further apart in their views than are the party followers.

6 Two major parties have dominated the political landscape in the United States for almost two centuries. The reasons for this include (1) the historical foundations of the system, (2) the self-perpetuation of the parties, (3) the commonality of views among Americans, (4) the winner-take-all electoral system, and (5) state and federal laws favoring the two-party system. Minor parties have emerged from time to time, often as dissatisfied splinter groups from within major parties, and have acted as barometers of changes in political moods. Splinter parties, or factions, usually have emerged when a particular personality was at odds with the major party, as when Teddy Roosevelt's differences with the Republican Party resulted in formation of the Bull Moose Progressive Party. Numerous other minor parties, such as the Prohibition Party, have formed around single issues.

7 From 1937 to the present, independent voters have formed an increasing proportion of the electorate, with a consequent decline of strongly Democratic or strongly Republican voters. Minor parties have also had a serious impact on the outcome of elections. In 1992, for example, the candidacy of H. Ross Perot drew enough support to change the outcome of the presidential election.

Selected print and electronic resources

SUGGESTED READINGS

Beck, Paul Allen. *Party Politics in America.* 8th ed. New York: Longman, 1998. This excellent text covers the role of parties in the late twentieth century, the changes in campaign financing, and the role of parties in the life of the voter.

Dionne, E. J., Jr. *They Only Look Dead: Why Progressives Will Dominate the Next Political Era.* New York: Simon & Schuster, 1995. A commentary on the state of American politics by a noted *Washington Post* journalist. Dionne predicts the possible creation of a third party out of the middle class that is dissatisfied with both parties.

Hadley, Charles D., and Lewis Bowman, eds. *Southern State Party Organizations and Activists.* Westport, Conn.: Praeger, 1995. This collection of original essays examines politics in eleven southern states using data gathered from county party chairpersons.

Menendez, Albert J. *The Perot Voters and the Future of American Politics.* New York: Prometheus Books, 1995. The author analyzes state-by-state election returns to identify those groups of voters who supported Perot in 1992.

Rosenstone, Steven J., Roy L. Behr, and Edward H. Lazarus. *Third Parties in America: Citizen Response to Major Party Failure.* Princeton, N.J.: Princeton University Press, 1996. These authors look at the data on third parties in the twentieth century and suggest the conditions that make it likely for third parties to rise and for voters to choose to support them.

Shafer, Byron E., Joel H. Sibley, Michael Barone, and Charles O. Jones, eds. *Present Discontents: American Politics in the Very Late Twentieth Century.* New York: Chatham House, 1997. This collection of essays looks at the issues of divided government, the Republican revolution of 1994, and the changing politics of the South to illustrate the current state of American parties.

Wattenberg, Ben J. *Values Matter Most: How Democrats or Republicans or a Third Party Can Win and Renew the American Way of Life.* New York: Regnery Publishing, 1996. After reviewing public opinion data and other sources that reveal how Americans care about values, Wattenberg proposes strategies by which either of the parties or a third party could win the presidency and become a major party.

MEDIA RESOURCES

A Third Choice—A film that examines America's experience with third parties and independent candidates throughout American political history.

Logging on

The Democratic Party is online at

www.democrats.org/

The Republican National Committee is at

www.rnc.org/

The Libertarian Party has a Web site at

www.lp.org/lp.html

The Socialist Party in the United States can be found at

sp-usa.org/

The Pew Research Center for the American People and the Press offers survey data online on how the parties fared during the most recent elections, voter typology, and numerous other issues. To access this site, go to

www.people-press.org/

Using the Internet for political analysis

Access the home pages of both the Democratic and Republican parties using the URLs given in the *Logging On*. List at least three major differences in the policies and approaches to government of the two parties. Then look at the home page for one of the other parties—such as the Libertarian, Socialist Workers, Green, or Populist Party—and compare the policy positions you find there with those of the major parties. What other kinds of information truly differentiate the major parties from the minor ones? To what extent do the two major parties manage to ignore or minimize the importance of any other parties? How do the goals of the major parties differ from those of the minor parties?

chapter **10**

Campaigns, Candidates, and Elections

BALLOTS

BACKGROUND

THE 1974 FEDERAL ELECTION CAMPAIGN ACT SET STRICT LIMITS ON CAMPAIGN CONTRIBUTIONS: $1,000 PER ELECTION PER INDIVIDUAL AND $5,000 PER ELECTION PER POLITICAL ACTION COMMITTEE (PAC). IN ADDITION, ANNUAL GIVING LIMITS WERE ALSO ESTABLISHED. SUCH REGULATED CONTRIBUTIONS MUST BE REPORTED TO THE FEDERAL ELECTION COMMISSION AND ARE KNOWN AS "HARD MONEY." CONTRIBUTIONS THAT ARE NOT SUBJECT TO THE 1974 REGULATIONS ARE CALLED "SOFT MONEY." SOFT MONEY CONTRIBUTIONS TO STATE AND LOCAL PARTIES WERE LEGITIMIZED BY A DECISION OF THE FEDERAL ELECTION COMMISSION IN 1978 AND AN AMENDMENT TO THE LAW IN 1979.

WHAT IF "SOFT MONEY" WERE BANNED?

In the 1995–1996 federal election cycle, more than $2.7 billion was spent on campaign expenses. Of that total, about $300 million was in soft money contributions. That amounts to only one-ninth of the total. So, what would happen if all contributions to political parties and campaigns were subject to the limits of the original law?

One effect of banning soft money would be, of course, that parties and party committees would have fewer funds to spend on campaigns.

Because soft money must be spent on "party-building" activities—such as getting voters to register, encouraging turnout, and, in the case of state and local parties, preparing campaign materials—expenditures on these items would have to decline. Candidates might, in fact, be asked to share some of their own campaign funds with the parties to pay for such activities, as was the case before soft money was legalized in 1978.

WOULD THE PARTIES BE WEAKENED?

The rationale for allowing soft money was to strengthen political parties, especially at the local and state levels. The federal campaign limits were seen as being so restrictive that after individuals had exhausted their annual giving limit, they could give no additional funds to help support local activities. The national parties, needing every penny of the legal contributions, no longer were interested in helping, or able to help, state and local parties. The banning of soft money contributions would thus probably weaken local and state parties and reduce their ability to help local candidates because there would be few "big

money" sources for them to tap. Unless other sources of funding were provided to support the political parties, they would likely return to the fragmented state characteristic of the mid-1970s.

WOULD SOFT MONEY DISAPPEAR?

Even if the practice of giving unregulated contributions to political parties and campaign committees were banned, it is doubtful that unregulated expenditures would disappear from the system. There are other ways to spend money on campaigns outside the parties—ways that are protected by the courts and the First Amendment. For example, unregulated political funds can be spent freely for "issue advertising." In the 1996 campaign, both the AFL-CIO and the U.S. Chamber of Commerce developed and paid for national advertising campaigns that were supportive of their respective choices for president. Interest groups such as the tobacco industry can sponsor issue advertising, as can the Sierra Club. In fact, there are no limits on funds spent for advertising on issues so long as those expenditures are not, in the words of the Federal Election Commission, "coordinated with a candidate." If soft money were

banned, the amount of money spent on these "independent" campaign tactics would likely increase. As a result, there would be an even greater variety of voices in the political arena, and voters would find it even more difficult to identify the economic and political interests behind each advertisement.

FOR CRITICAL ANALYSIS

1. What kinds of funding could be provided to support the activities of state and local political parties that might remove the need for soft money?

2. What effect do independent expenditures of interest groups and corporations have on political debate during a campaign? How should a voter judge such independent campaigns?

3. Should the political system be concerned with providing financial support to the political parties through campaign funds? Is this an important goal for the process of campaigns and elections?

Political campaigns are at the heart of a democratic political system. When voters go to the polls and choose between candidates who have presented their views on leadership and policy, the citizens are exercising the fundamental right to choose the leadership of the nation and, thus, to direct national policy. The same process is repeated at every level of government in the United States: on election day, voters choose members of the town council, the county prosecuting attorney, state legislators, governors, and members of Congress, depending on the year in the political cycle. In each of these venues, candidates depend on their campaigns to sway the voters and win the election.

The People Who Run for Office

For democracy to work, there must be candidates for office, and for voters to have a choice, there must be competing candidates for most offices. The presidential campaign provides the most colorful and exciting look at these candidates and how they prepare to compete for the highest office in the land. In fact, soon after President Bill Clinton was reelected in 1996, men and women who wanted to be candidates in the 2000 presidential campaign began to assess their chances of winning. They faced a long and obstacle-filled path: first they needed to raise enough money to tour the nation, particularly the early primary states, to see if they had enough local supporters. Then, they needed funds to start up an organization, devise a plan to win primary votes, and win the party's nomination at the national convention. Finally, they needed funds to finance a successful campaign for president. Always, at every turn, was the question of whether they would have enough money to wage a campaign.

Why They Run

People who choose to run for office can be divided into two groups—those who are "self-starters" and those who are recruited. The volunteers, or self-starters, get involved in political activities to further their careers, to carry out specific political programs, or in response to certain issues or events. The campaign of Senator Eugene McCarthy in 1968 to deny Lyndon Johnson's renomination was

President Bill Clinton rallies voters during his 1996 presidential campaign. Such large public events are carefully staged to gain maximum television exposure for a candidate while at the same time encouraging those in the audience to vote for the candidate.

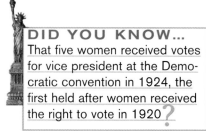

rooted in McCarthy's opposition to the Vietnam War. H. Ross Perot's runs for the presidency in 1992 and in 1996 were a response to public alienation and discontent with the major parties' candidates.

Issues are important, but self-interest and personal goals—status, career objectives, prestige, and income—are central in motivating some candidates to enter political life. Political office is often seen as the stepping stone to achieving certain career goals. A lawyer or an insurance agent may run for office only once or twice and then return to private life with enhanced status. Other politicians may aspire to long-term political office—for example, county offices such as commissioner or sheriff sometimes offer attractive opportunities for power, status, and income and are in themselves career goals. Finally, we think of ambition as the desire for ever more important offices and higher status. Politicians who run for lower offices and then set their sights on Congress or a governorship may be said to have "progressive" ambitions.[1]

We tend to pay far more attention to the flamboyant politician or to the personal characteristics of those with presidential ambitions than to their colleagues who compete for lower offices. But it is important to note that there are far more opportunities to run for office than there are citizens eager to take advantage of them. To fill the slate of candidates for election to such jobs as mosquito-abatement district commissioner, the political party must recruit individuals to run. The problem of finding candidates is compounded in states or cities where the majority party is so dominant that the minority candidates have virtually no chance of winning. In these situations, candidates are recruited by party leaders on the basis of loyalty to the organization and civic duty.

Who Is Eligible?

There are few constitutional restrictions on who can become a candidate in the United States. As detailed in the Constitution, the formal requirements for a national office are as follows:

1. *President.* Must be a natural-born citizen, have attained the age of thirty-five years, and be a resident of the country for fourteen years by the time of inauguration.

---

[1]See the discussion of this topic in Linda Fowler, *Candidates, Congress, and the American Democracy* (Ann Arbor, Mich.: University of Michigan Press, 1993), pp. 56–59.

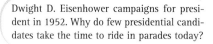

Dwight D. Eisenhower campaigns for president in 1952. Why do few presidential candidates take the time to ride in parades today?

2. *Vice president.* Must be a natural-born citizen, have attained the age of thirty-five years, and not be a resident of the same state as the candidate for president.
3. *Senator.* Must be a citizen for at least nine years, have attained the age of thirty by the time of taking office, and be a resident of the state from which elected.
4. *Representative.* Must be a citizen for at least seven years, have attained the age of twenty-five by the time of taking office, and be a resident of the state from which elected.

The qualifications for state legislators are set by the state constitutions and likewise relate to age, place of residence, and citizenship. (Usually, the requirements for the upper chamber of a legislature are somewhat higher than those for the lower chamber.) The legal qualifications for running for governor or other state office are similar.

Who Runs? In spite of these minimal legal qualifications for office at both the national and state levels, a quick look at the slate of candidates in any election—or at the current members of the U.S. House of Representatives—will reveal that not all segments of the population take advantage of these opportunities. Holders of political office in the United States are overwhelmingly white and male. Until this century, politicians were also predominantly of northern European origin and predominantly Protestant. Laws enforcing segregation in the South and many border states, as well as laws that effectively denied voting rights, made it impossible to elect African American public officials in many areas in which African Americans constituted a significant portion of the population. As a result of the passage of major civil rights legislation in the last several decades, the number of African American public officials has increased throughout the United States.

Until recently, women generally were considered to be appropriate candidates only for lower-level offices, such as state legislator or school board member. The last ten years have seen a tremendous increase in the number of women who run for office, not only at the state level but for the U.S. Congress as well. Figure 10–1 shows the increase in female candidates. (In 1998, 134 women ran for

In 1984, Geraldine Ferraro became the first woman to be nominated for vice president by a major party.

FIGURE 10-1

Women Running for Congress

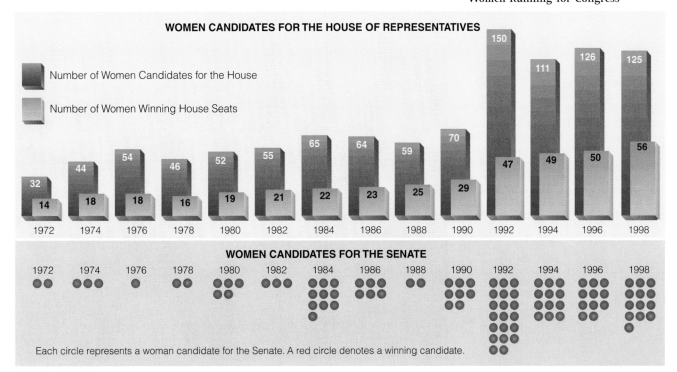

WOMEN CANDIDATES FOR THE HOUSE OF REPRESENTATIVES

Number of Women Candidates for the House

Number of Women Winning House Seats

	1972	1974	1976	1978	1980	1982	1984	1986	1988	1990	1992	1994	1996	1998
Candidates	32	44	54	46	52	55	65	64	59	70	150	111	126	125
Winning	14	18	18	16	19	21	22	23	25	29	47	49	50	56

WOMEN CANDIDATES FOR THE SENATE

1972	1974	1976	1978	1980	1982	1984	1986	1988	1990	1992	1994	1996	1998

Each circle represents a woman candidate for the Senate. A red circle denotes a winning candidate.

Congress, and 60 were elected.) Whereas African Americans were restricted from running for office by both law and custom, women generally were excluded by the agencies of recruitment—parties and interest groups—because they were thought to have no chance of winning or because they had not worked their way up through the party organization. Women also had a more difficult time raising campaign funds. Today, it is clear that women are just as likely as men to participate in many political activities, and a majority of Americans say they would vote for a qualified woman or for an African American for president of the United States.

Professional Status.   Not only are candidates for office more likely to be male and white than female or African American, but they are also likely to be professionals, particularly lawyers. Political campaigning and officeholding are simply easier for some occupational and economic groups than for others, and political involvement can make a valuable contribution to certain careers. Lawyers, for example, have more flexible schedules than do other professionals, can take time off for campaigning, and can leave their jobs to hold public office full-time. Furthermore, holding political office is good publicity for their professional practice, and they usually have partners or associates to keep the firm going while they are in office. Perhaps most important, many jobs that lawyers aspire to—federal or state judgeships, state attorney offices, or work in a federal agency—can be attained by political appointment. Such appointments most likely go to loyal partisans who have served their party by running for and holding office. Personal ambitions, then, are well served for certain groups by entering the political arena, whereas it could be a sacrifice for others whose careers demand full-time attention for many years.

The Modern Campaign Machine

American political campaigns are extravagant, year-long events that produce campaign buttons and posters for collectors, hours of film and sound to be relayed by the media, and, eventually, winning candidates who become the public officials of the nation. Campaigns are also enormously expensive; the total

These campaign workers have volunteered their time to support the candidacy of Congresswoman Loretta Sanchez, a Democrat from California. Political parties and candidates at all levels would have a difficult time conducting their campaigns without such volunteers. Volunteering for a campaign is one way to participate actively in the political process, to learn more about it, and to take advantage of one's rights as a citizen.

expenditures for 1998 were estimated to be several billion dollars for all congressional and local races in that year. Political campaigns exhaust candidates, their staff members, and the journalists covering the campaign—to say nothing of the public's patience.

The Changing Campaign

Campaigns seem to be getting longer and more excessive each year. The goal of all the frantic activity of campaigns is the same for all of them—to convince voters to choose a candidate or a slate of candidates for office. Part of the reason for the increased intensity of campaigns in the last decade is that they have changed from being centered on the party to being centered on the candidate. The candidate-centered campaign emerged in response to changes in the electoral system, to the importance of television in campaigns, to technological innovations such as computers, and to the increased cost of campaigning.

To run a successful and persuasive campaign, the candidate's organization must be able to raise funds for the effort, get coverage from the media, produce and pay for political commercials and advertising, schedule the candidate's time effectively with constituent groups and prospective supporters, convey the candidate's position on the issues, conduct research on the opposing candidate, and get the voters to go to the polls. When party identification was stronger among voters and before the advent of television campaigning, a strong party organization on the local, state, or national level could furnish most of the services and expertise that the candidate needed. Political parties provided the funds for campaigning until the 1970s. Parties used their precinct organizations to distribute literature, register voters, and get out the vote on election day. Less effort was spent on advertising for a single candidate's positions and character, because the party label communicated that information to many of the voters.

One of the reasons that campaigns no longer depend on parties is that fewer people identify with them (see Chapter 9), as is evident from the increased number of independent voters. In 1952, about 22 percent of the voters were independent voters, whereas in 1998, between 26 and 33 percent classified themselves as independents, depending on the survey. Independent voters include not only those voters who are well educated and issue oriented but also many voters who are not very interested in politics or well informed about candidates or issues. (The Internet is providing a new way of reaching both independent and partisan voters—see the feature *Politics Wired: Campaigning on the Internet.*)

The Professional Campaign

Whether the candidate is running for the state legislature, for the governor's office, for the U.S. Congress, or for the presidency, every campaign has some fundamental tasks to accomplish. What is most striking about today's campaigns is that most of these tasks are now put into the hands of paid professionals rather than volunteers or amateur politicians.

The most sought-after and possibly the most criticized campaign expert is the **political consultant,** who, for a large fee, devises a campaign strategy, thinks up a campaign theme, and possibly chooses the campaign colors and candidate's portrait for all literature to be distributed. The paid consultant monitors the campaign's progress, plans all media appearances, and coaches the candidate for debates. The consultants and the firms they represent are not politically neutral; most will work only for candidates from one party or only for candidates of a particular ideological persuasion.

Political consultants began to displace volunteer campaign managers in the 1960s, about the same time that television became a force in campaigns. Some

A volunteer campaign worker uses the telephone to collect polling information from potential voters.

Political Consultant

A paid professional hired to devise a campaign strategy and manage a campaign. Image building is the crucial task of the political consultant.

POLITICS WIRED

Campaigning on the Internet

Although political parties and government organizations have realized the importance of having a Web site for a couple of years, the Internet is just now becoming an essential part of political campaigns for individual candidates. Web sites devoted to each presidential candidate appeared for the first time in the 1996 election, along with Web sites sponsored by the candidate's opponents. There were also satirical Web sites about both presidential candidates.

The 1998 election saw the development of Web sites that served multiple purposes: giving information about the candidate and her policy preferences to voters; linking the volunteers who work for the candidate; linking the candidate to the political party; soliciting not only votes but also volunteers and donations; and providing a "town meeting" type of forum in which voters can query the candidate. Let's look at how some major functions of campaigns are enhanced by the Internet.

For one thing, the Internet provides an inexpensive and easy way for all of a candidate's campaign offices to be linked together. Volunteers can get their directions via the Internet. Imagine the difficulties in keeping a campaign organization informed

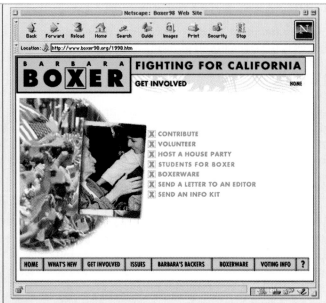

Senator Barbara Boxer's Internet site provides not only information about her candidacy, but many links that allow individuals to express their opinions or volunteer support.

in a state like Wyoming, which has only one member of Congress. In addition, the press can access any messages from the candidate immediately on the Web. To save on printing costs, campaign volunteers can download campaign materials—such as photos, brochures, and print materials—directly from the candidate's home page to distribute in their own neighborhoods.

The Internet also is the obvious replacement for direct-mail solicitations to voters for money and time,

as well as for their votes. Fund-raising can be done discreetly and privately by using the Internet. The donor must, of course, supply his or her name, Social Security number, and other information when donations are made, but the solicitation itself will be very private (on your computer at home), be less embarrassing (to both the asker and the donor), and allow donor comments to be solicited as well. In addition, the Internet is a great way to solicit volunteers, particularly among voters who are new to an area or who are not on any party mailing list.

Campaigns must be careful not to "spam" their supporters, because that's a sure way to lose votes, but an Internet home page can be a great campaign tool. Home pages should be exciting and well designed, load quickly into a user's computer, and provide for feedback from the voter. For example, a candidate running in a district that is closely contested may want to downplay partisanship, which is easy to do with a great home page. A candidate who wants to appear really open to voters' desires can set up a "chat room." Candidates can also link their home pages to other sites that their voters might like to visit. Finally, although the results would be very unscientific, the home page can be used to track public opinion among its users.

FOR CRITICAL ANALYSIS

The candidate's home page is strictly the creation of the campaign staff and consultants, so how do you know that the information posted there is accurate? How do you get additional unbiased information about the candidate?

of the first "superfirms" of consultants operated in California; Ronald Reagan engaged one of these pioneer firms, Spencer-Roberts, to organize his first campaign for governor of California. Several new generations of political consultants have succeeded these early firms. Today's most sought-after firms include those of Roger Ailes (works for Republicans), Bob Squier (Democrats), James Carville and Paul Begala (Democrats), and Bob Teeter (Republicans). Following the 1992 campaign, a documentary film about the Clinton campaign, which featured the president's consultants (Carville and Begala) and campaign staff, was released under the title *The War Room,* a reference to the center of campaign planning.

As more and more political campaigns are run exclusively by professional campaign managers, critics of the campaign system are becoming increasingly vociferous. Their worry is that political consultants are more concerned with plotting campaign strategy and developing the candidate's image than with developing positions on issues. Thomas Edmonds, a conservative consultant, believes that candidates are changing, too. He notes that "most modern candidates are more interested in sound bites [brief, memorable comments] than they are in position papers. They are more interested in how to manipulate the message than what the message really is."[2] A professional campaign manager is a public relations person. He or she may look at an upcoming election as a contest of personalities rather than as a contest between two opposing parties or opposing principles. According to critics, professional campaign managers are willing to do anything to get their candidates to win, even if this means reshaping the public image of the candidate so that it bears little relation to reality.

DID YOU KNOW...
That during Russian president Boris Yeltsin's 1996 campaign for the presidency, his campaign managers hired a team of six American political consultants?

The Strategy of Winning

The goal of every political campaign is the same: to win the election. In the United States, unlike some European countries, there are no rewards for a candidate who comes in second; the winner takes all. The campaign organization must plan a strategy to maximize the candidate's chances of winning. The basic wisdom that guides a campaign strategy in American politics is this: candidates seek to capture all the votes of their party members, to convince a majority of the independent voters to vote for them, and to gain a few votes from members of the other party. To accomplish these goals, candidates must consider their visibility, their message, and their campaign strategy.

Candidate Visibility and Appeal

One of the most important concerns is how well known the candidate is. If he or she is a highly visible incumbent, there may be little need for campaigning except to remind the voters of the officeholder's good deeds. If, however, the candidate is an unknown challenger or a largely unfamiliar character attacking a well-known public figure, the campaign must devise a strategy to get the candidate before the public.

In the case of the independent candidate or the candidate representing a minor party, the problem of name recognition is serious. There are usually a number of third-party candidates in each presidential election. Such candidates must present an overwhelming case for the voter to reject the major-party candidate. Both the Democratic and the Republican candidates use the strategic ploy of labeling third-party candidates as "not serious" and therefore not worth the voter's time.

The Use of Opinion Polls and Focus Groups

One of the major sources of information for both the media and the candidates is opinion polls. Poll taking is widespread during the primaries. Presidential hopefuls have private polls taken to make sure that there is at least some chance they could be nominated and, if nominated, elected. Also, because the party nominees depend on polls to fine-tune their campaigns, during the presidential campaign

---

[2]"The Political Campaign Industry," *Campaigns and Elections,* December/January 1994, p. 46.

The First Family aboard "The 21st Century Express" as they kick off their 1996 campaign in Huntington, West Virginia. Campaigning by train is an old American tradition, sometimes called "whistle-stopping."

Tracking Poll

A poll taken for the candidate on a nearly daily basis as election day approaches.

Focus Group

A small group of individuals who are led in discussion by a professional consultant to gather opinions and responses to candidates and issues.

itself continual polls are taken. Polls are taken not only by the regular pollsters—Roper, Harris, Gallup, and others—but also privately by each candidate's campaign organization. These private polls, as opposed to the independent public polls conducted by Gallup and others, are for the exclusive and secret use of the candidate and his or her campaign organization.

As the election approaches, many candidates use **tracking polls,** which are polls taken almost every day, to find out how well they are competing for votes. Tracking polls, by indicating how well the campaign is going, enable consultants to fine-tune the advertising and the candidate's speeches in the last days of the campaign.

Another tactic is the use of the **focus group** to gain insights into public perceptions of the candidate. Professional consultants organize a discussion of the candidate or of certain political issues among ten to fifteen ordinary citizens. The citizens are selected from certain target groups in the population—for example, working men, blue-collar men, senior citizens, or young voters. The group discusses personality traits of the candidate, political advertising, and other candidate-related issues. The conversation is videotaped (and often observed from behind a mirrored wall). Focus groups are expected to reveal more emotional responses to candidates or the deeper anxieties of voters—expressions that consultants believe often are not tapped by more impersonal telephone surveys. The campaign then can shape its messages to respond to these feelings and perceptions.

Financing the Campaign

In a book published in 1932 entitled *Money in Elections,* Louise Overacker had the following to say about campaign financing:

> The financing of elections in a democracy is a problem which is arousing increasing concern. Many are beginning to wonder if present-day methods of raising

and spending campaign funds do not clog the wheels of our elaborately constructed mechanism of popular control, and if democracies do not inevitably become plutocracies.[3]

Although writing more than sixty years ago, Overacker touched on a sensitive issue in American political campaigns—the connection between money and elections. It is estimated that over $2.7 billion was spent at all levels of campaigning in the 1995–1996 election cycle. At the federal level alone, a total of more than $478 million is estimated to have been spent in races for the House of Representatives, $288 million in senatorial races, and $600 million in the presidential campaign. Except for the presidential campaign in the general election, all of the other money had to be provided by the candidates and their families, borrowed, or raised by contributions from individuals or PACs (as discussed in Chapter 8). For the general presidential campaign, much of the money comes from the federal government.

Regulating Campaign Financing

The way in which campaigns are financed has changed dramatically in the last two and a half decades, and today candidates and political parties, when trying to increase their funding sources, must operate within the constraints imposed by complicated laws regulating campaign financing.

There have been a variety of federal **corrupt practices acts** designed to regulate campaign financing. The first, passed in 1925, limited primary and general election expenses for congressional candidates. In addition, it required disclosure of election expenses and, in principle, put controls on contributions by corporations. Numerous loopholes were found in the restrictions on contributions, and the acts proved to be ineffective.

The **Hatch Act** (Political Activities Act) of 1939 was passed in another attempt to control political influence buying. That act forbade a political group to spend more than $3 million in any campaign and limited individual contributions to a political group to $5,000. Of course, such restrictions were easily circumvented by creating additional political groups.

In the wake of the scandals uncovered after the 1972 Watergate break-in, Congress and the Supreme Court reshaped the nature of campaign financing. It was discovered during the Watergate investigations that large amounts of money had been illegally funneled to Nixon's Committee to Reelect the President (CREEP). Congress acted quickly to prevent the recurrence of such a situation.

The Federal Election Campaign Acts of 1972 and 1974

The Federal Election Campaign Act of 1972 essentially replaced all past laws and instituted a major reform. The act placed no limit on overall spending but restricted the amount that could be spent on mass-media advertising, including television. It limited the amount that candidates and their families could contribute to their own campaigns and required disclosure of all contributions and expenditures in excess of $100. In principle, the 1972 act limited the role of labor unions and corporations in political campaigns. It also provided for a voluntary $1 check-off on federal income tax returns for general campaign funds to be used by major-party presidential candidates (first applied in the 1976 campaign).

---

[3]Louise Overacker, *Money in Elections* (New York: Macmillan, 1932), p. vii.

DID YOU KNOW...
That a candidate can buy lists of all the voters in a precinct, county, or state for only about 2 cents per name from a commercial firm?

Corrupt Practices Acts
A series of acts passed by Congress in an attempt to limit and regulate the size and sources of contributions and expenditures in political campaigns.

Hatch Act
An act passed in 1939 that prohibited a political group from spending more than $3 million in any campaign and limited individual contributions to a committee to $5,000. The act was designed to control political influence buying.

Bill Clinton attends a fund-raising event in Virginia.

For many, however, the act did not go far enough. In 1974, Congress passed another Federal Election Campaign Act. It did the following:

1. *Created the Federal Election Commission.* This commission consists of six nonpartisan administrators whose duties are to enforce compliance with the requirements of the act.

2. *Provided public financing for presidential primaries and general elections.* Any candidate running for president who is able to obtain sufficient contributions in at least twenty states can obtain a subsidy from the U.S. Treasury to help pay for primary campaigns. Each major party was given $12.4 million for its national convention in 1996. The major party candidates have federal support for almost all of their expenses, provided they are willing to accept campaign-spending limits.

3. *Limited presidential campaign spending.* Any candidate accepting federal support has to agree to limit campaign expenditures to the amount prescribed by federal law.

4. *Limited contributions.* Citizens can contribute up to $1,000 to each candidate in each federal election or primary; the total limit of all contributions from an individual to all candidates is $25,000 per year. Groups can contribute up to a maximum of $5,000 to a candidate in any election.

5. *Required disclosure.* Each candidate must file periodic reports with the Federal Election Commission, listing who contributed, how much was spent, and for what the money was spent.

The 1972 act also limited the amount that each individual could spend on his or her own behalf. The Supreme Court declared the provision unconstitutional in 1976, in *Buckley v. Valeo*,[4] stating that it was unconstitutional to restrict in any way the amount congressional candidates or their immediate families could spend on their own behalf: "The candidate, no less than any other person, has a

---

[4]424 U.S. 1 (1976).

First Amendment right to engage in the discussion of public issues and vigorously and tirelessly to advocate his own election."

The 1974 act, as modified by certain amendments in 1976, allows corporations, labor unions, and special interest groups to set up PACs to raise money for candidates. For a PAC to be legitimate, the money must be raised from at least fifty volunteer donors and must be given to at least five candidates in the federal election. Each corporation or each union is limited to one PAC. As you might imagine, corporate PACs obtain funds from executives, employees, and stockholders in their firms, and unions obtain PAC funds from their members.[5]

Campaign Financing beyond the Limits

Within a few years after the establishment of the tight limits on contributions, new ways to finance campaigns were developed that skirt the reforms and make it possible for huge sums of money to be raised, especially by the major political parties.

Contributions to Political Parties. Candidates, PACs, and political parties have found ways to generate **soft money**—that is, campaign contributions to political parties that escape the rigid limits of federal election law. Although federal law limits contributions that are spent on elections, there are no limits on contributions to political parties for party activities such as voter education or voter-registration drives. This loophole has enabled the parties to raise millions of dollars from corporations and individuals. It has not been unusual for such corporations as Time Warner to give more than half a million dollars to the Democratic National Committee and for the tobacco companies to send more than a million dollars to the Republican party.[6] As shown in Table 10–1, three times as much soft money was raised in 1996 as in the 1991–1992 election cycle. The parties then spend this money for the convention, for registering voters, and for advertising to promote the general party position. The parties also send a great deal of the money to state and local party organizations, which use it to support their own tickets. (For a discussion of the use of soft money in the 1996 presidential campaign, see this chapter's feature on page 318 entitled *Politics and Economics: Financing the Presidential Campaign.*)

Independent Expenditures. Business corporations, labor unions, and other interest groups discovered that it was legal to make **independent expenditures** in an election campaign so long as the expenditures were not coordinated with those of the candidate or political party. Hundreds of unique committees and organizations blossomed to take advantage of this campaign tactic. Although a 1990 United States Supreme Court decision, *Austin v. Michigan State Chamber of Commerce*,[7] upheld the right of the states and the federal government to limit

Soft Money
Campaign contributions that evade contribution limits by being given to parties and party committees to help fund general party activities.

Independent Expenditures
Nonregulated contributions from PACs, ideological organizations, and individuals. The groups may spend funds on advertising or other campaign activities so long as those expenditures are not coordinated with those of a candidate.

---

[5]See Paul Allen Beck, *Party Politics in America*, 8th ed. (New York: Longman Publishers, 1997), p. 285.
[6]Beck, *Party Politics in America*, pp. 293–294.
[7]494 U.S. 652 (1990).

TABLE **10-1**

Soft Money Raised by Political Parties, 1992 to 1996

	1991–1992	**1993–1994**	**1995–1996**
Democratic Party	$37 million	$45.6 million	122.3 million
Republican Party	52 million	59.5 million	141.2 million
Total	89 million	106.4 million	263.5 million

SOURCE: *Congressional Quarterly Weekly Report*, September 6, 1997, p. 2065.

POLITICS and Economics

Financing the Presidential Campaign

In 1952, about $55 million was spent on the presidential campaigns. In 1996, presidential campaign expenditures were between $600 and $900 million. The exact amount will never be known because of "soft money" expenditures by the parties. Of the $453 million in regulated expenditures in 1996, the federal government financed about $211 million, including matching funding.

The reported expenditures of $453 million do not, of course, include soft money expenditures, which were estimated to be about $270 million for 1996. These funds were funneled to the political parties through the various provisions of federal election law that allow corporations, individuals, and labor unions to contribute for "party-building" activities and voter-registration drives. In addition, funds can be contributed by corporations and unions for issue-advocacy campaigns.

Not only can candidates raise funds from government sources and soft money sources, but they can also solicit individual contributions (as limited by law) and use their own funds. If you look at the accompanying table, which shows the funding sources and expenditures for the top six contenders for the presidency in 1996, you will see that two of these men used a considerable portion of their own funds for the campaign.

The two national party nominees—Bob Dole and Bill Clinton—each received the maximum in allowable primary and general election funds from the government: about $75 million. In addition, Dole raised $60 million in contributions, and Clinton raised $41 million in additional contributions.

One of the Republican candidates, Steve Forbes, spent more than $37 million of his own money and raised only $5 million in other contributions. He received no federal funds because he chose not to accept them. Ross Perot, the independent candidate, spent $8 million of his own money and received $29 million for his general election expenditures from the government. Phil Gramm, who raised more than $25 million in contributions early in the campaign, dropped out of the race very early because he was not able to win any primary elections.

What these data tell us is that running even an unsuccessful primary campaign for president can cost $20 million or $30 million. A successful campaign costs more than $200 million, counting both regulated and soft money contributions. The question is this: If the additional money available to candidates through soft money is spent on tactics that bring victory, should that money be regulated? Is it fair or good for the system for these other sources of funding to have a major effect? The impact of soft money on the presidential campaign is only one of the issues facing Congress as it considers this issue.

FOR CRITICAL ANALYSIS

Do voters approve or disapprove of a candidate who funds his or her own campaign? Are wealthy candidates at an advantage or disadvantage in a presidential campaign?

Name	Party	Net Spent	Net Receipts	Candidate Money	Federal Funds
Bob Dole	R	$131,356,423	$134,508,765	$0	$75,345,767
Bill Clinton	D	$112,622,311	$116,860,578	$0	$74,212,194
Steve Forbes	R	$42,631,277	$42,631,313	$37,394,000	$0
Ross Perot	Ind.	$37,168,218	$39,473,733	$8,201,419	$29,000,000
Patrick J. Buchanan	R	$32,311,895	$32,013,651	$0	$10,540,992
Phil Gramm	R	$31,371,253	$32,004,226	$0	$7,356,218

Source: The Center for Responsive Politics, "The Big Picture: Where the Money Came From in the 1996 Elections," www.crp.org/crpdocs/bigpicture/.

independent, direct corporate expenditures (such as for advertisements) on behalf of *candidates,* the decision did not stop business and other types of groups from making independent expenditures on *issues.*

Indeed, issue advocacy—spending unregulated money on advertising that promotes positions on issues rather than candidates—has become a prevalent tactic in recent years. Consider some examples. Prior to the 1996 campaign, Clinton's candidacy was greatly enhanced by a series of issue ads that accused the Republicans of wanting to damage Medicare if they were elected. These ads were developed and paid for by unregulated funds and were sponsored by organ-

Taiwanese Buddhist leader Hsing Yun greets Vice President Al Gore at the Hsi Lai Temple, which is the largest Buddhist monastery in the Western Hemisphere. Gore's appearance at the temple, initially characterized by him as a "community event," became a source of controversy once it was discovered that $140,000 in campaign money was raised at the event. The appearance was also sensitive because of its potentially negative impact on U.S. relations with China.

izations that were not directly connected with the president's own campaign. The Christian Coalition, which is incorporated, annually raises millions of dollars to produce and distribute voter guidelines and other direct-mail literature to describe candidates' positions on various issues and to promote its agenda. Although promoting issue positions is very close to promoting candidates who support those positions, the courts repeatedly have held, in accordance with the *Buckley v. Valeo* decision mentioned earlier, that interest groups have a First Amendment right to advocate their positions.

The Supreme Court clarified, in a 1996 decision,[8] that political parties may also make independent expenditures on behalf of candidates—as long as the parties do so *independently* of the candidates. In other words, the parties must not coordinate such expenditures with the candidates' campaigns or let the candidates know the specifics of how party funds are being spent.

Bundling. Yet another way to maximize contributions to a candidate or a party is through the practice of **bundling**—collecting $1,000 contributions from a number of individuals in the same firm or family and then sending the quite large check to the candidate of choice. While this practice is in complete compliance with the law, it makes the candidate or party more aware of the source of the funding.

The effect of all of these strategies is to increase greatly the amount of money spent for campaigns and party activities. Critics of the system continue to wonder whether the voice of the individual voter or the small contributor is drowned in the flood of big contributions. This chapter's *Critical Perspective* on page 320 discusses some of the issues that make campaign-finance reform so difficult.

Bundling
The practice of adding together maximum individual campaign contributions to increase their impact on the candidate.

---

[8]*Colorado Republican Federal Campaign Committee v. Federal Election Commission,* 116 S.Ct. 2309 (1996).

Running for President: The Longest Campaign

Presidential Primary
A statewide primary election of delegates to a political party's national convention to help a party determine its presidential nominee. Such delegates are either pledged to a particular candidate or unpledged.

"Beauty Contest"
A presidential primary in which contending candidates compete for popular votes but the results have little or no impact on the selection of delegates to the national convention, which is made by the party elite.

The American presidential election is the culmination of two different campaigns linked by the parties' national conventions. The **presidential primary** campaign lasts officially from January until June of the election year, and the final presidential campaign heats up around Labor Day.

Primary elections were first mandated in 1903 in Wisconsin. The purpose of the primary was to open the nomination process to ordinary party members and to weaken the influence of party bosses in the nomination process. Until 1968, however, there were fewer than twenty primary elections for the presidency. They were generally **"beauty contests"** in which the contending candidates for the nomination competed for popular votes, but the results had little or no

Critical perspective

Why Can't We Reform Campaign Financing?

Although the Federal Election Commission produces a number of superb brochures about the laws regulating campaign finance and provides clear assistance in print and on its Web page for citizens who seek to understand the basic law, it is clear from the activities of the last two election cycles that the law is virtually meaningless. There are enough "loopholes" in current campaign-financing law to make a screen door; among them are soft money, "independent expenditures," leadership PACs, legal defense funds, and corporate communications. If you, as the leader of a major corporation or major labor union, wish to provide hundreds of thousands of dollars to your preferred party or candidate or if you wish to "cover your bets" by supporting both major parties, there are myriad ways to do so.

Not only are there literally dozens of ways to avoid the regulations of the 1974 law, but hundreds or perhaps thousands of such instances were brought to light in the ongoing investigation of the 1996 national campaign. Barred from receiving trips or gifts by law, senators and congresspersons attended "club meetings" sponsored by party-affiliated clubs that charge "members" $25,000 apiece. Campaign contributions from foreigners and foreign contributions (banned by law) were "laundered" through American citizens' donations. Nights in the Lincoln bedroom and coffees with the president were the rewards for big donors to the Clinton campaign, while Republicans offered private dinners with the leaders of

Congress to their donors. State parties received soft money donations and then used them to pay the consulting bills for the national party campaigns. The political system seemed to be awash in campaign contributions, yet all the politicians spent endless hours raising more money.

Why Hasn't There Been Campaign-Financing Reform?

In spite of months of congressional hearings and hundreds of articles in newspapers, no campaign-finance reform legislation has yet been enacted. Cynics suggest that it is impossible for incumbent politicians to write legislation that might, in fact, disadvantage them in future elections. That is probably true, but the situation is a bit more complex than that. Both the Republicans and Democrats would support campaign-finance reform if they did not see proposals that would favor the other side. Democrats want to keep contributions from labor unions legal. Republicans want to continue to allow corporations to make donations. Both sides wish to keep funds from at least one source flowing to the national, state, and local political parties. And there is no groundswell of opinion among their constituents to pass campaign-finance reform. In fact, the majority of Americans do not believe reform measures will be passed.

impact on the selection of delegates to the national convention. National conventions were meetings of the party elite—legislators, mayors, county chairpersons, and loyal party workers—who were mostly appointed to their delegations. National conventions saw numerous trades and bargains among competing candidates, and the leaders of large blocs of delegate votes could direct their delegates to support a favorite candidate.

Reforming the Primaries

In recent decades, the character of the primary process and the make-up of the national convention have changed dramatically. The mass public, rather than party elites, now generally controls the nomination process, owing to extraordinary changes in the party rules. After the massive riots outside the doors of the 1968 Democratic convention in Chicago, many party leaders pushed for serious reforms of the convention process. They saw the general dissatisfaction with the

 Critical perspective

Why Can't We Reform Campaign Financing?—continued

What Could Campaign-Financing Reform Look Like?

Speaking from a liberal perspective, Michael Walzer suggests that the real issue is to find a way for citizens to have an equal vote in the election process. He suggests that while private funding is the best alternative, income inequalities among the American citizenry favor the rich. So, he suggests public financing of campaigns, but recognizing the public's distrust of candidates' spending government money, he also suggests that it be limited and that television time be reduced.*

There are other proponents of public financing as well, but many are concerned that public financing actually will reduce public participation in campaigns and that there will still be ways for corporations and donors to get around the laws. The courts have steadfastly supported the right of individuals and corporations to spend their own funds to support a point of view, if not a candidate.

Still another viewpoint suggests that the real issue is the tremendous cost of campaigning: the ever-increasing cost of television time, computer time, consultants, and, of course, the cost of fund-raising efforts. Some reform proposals in Congress have focused on free or discounted television time, with equal time for

all candidates. Of course, incumbents don't like the idea of free time for their challengers.

Newton Minow, former chairman of the Federal Communications Commission, supports free airtime for campaigns. He believes that Congress could prohibit broadcasters from selling any commercial time for political purposes. As he puts it, "Politicians sell access to what we own: the government. Broadcasters sell access to something we own: the public airwaves. Both do so, they tell us, in our name."†

Finally, some believe that there will always be money in politics—it is a natural occurrence. Thus, the answer is to scrap the rules, require public disclosure of every cent spent, and then allow the debate among candidates to continue. Increased spending, without the use of loopholes, might actually increase voter interest.

FOR CRITICAL ANALYSIS

1. What tools might you suggest to increase public awareness of who contributes to candidates and how much candidates spend?
2. Do you think that less time should be spent on political ads and more on informing American voters?
3. Do the current campaign-financing rules help or hinder participation in the political system by ordinary Americans?

*Michael Walzer, "Campaign Finance: Four Views," *Dissent,* Summer 1997, p. 5.

†Newton Minow, "Campaign Finance Reform: We Have Failed to Solve the Problem," *Vital Speeches of the Day,* 1997, p. 555.

Riots outside the 1968 Democratic convention in Chicago. The riots influenced the party to reform its delegate selection rules.

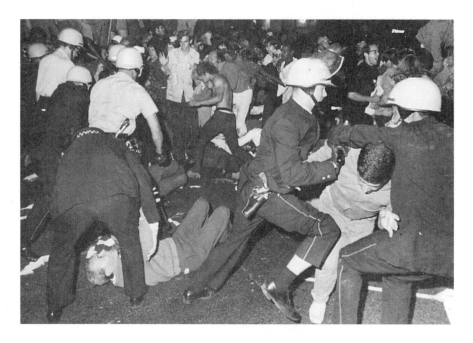

"How the Primary Schedule Favors the Rich"

Superdelegate
A party leader or elected official who is given the right to vote at the party's national convention. Superdelegates are not elected at the state level.

Caucus
A closed meeting of party leaders to select party candidates or to decide on policy; also, a meeting of party members designed to select candidates and propose policies.

Front-Runner
The presidential candidate who appears to have the most momentum at a given time in the primary season.

convention, and the riots in particular, as stemming from the inability of the average party member to influence the nomination system.

The Democratic National Committee appointed a special commission to study the problems of the primary system. Referred to as the McGovern-Fraser Commission, the group over the next several years formulated new rules for delegate selection that had to be followed by state Democratic parties.

The reforms instituted by the Democratic Party, which were imitated in most states by the Republicans, revolutionized the nomination process for the presidency. The most important changes require that most convention delegates not be nominated by the elites in either party; they must be elected by the voters in primary elections, in caucuses held by local parties, or at state conventions. (See the feature entitled *Politics and Elections: Primaries and Parties* for a description of different types of primaries.) Delegates are mostly pledged to a particular candidate, although the pledge is not always formally binding at the convention. The delegation from each state must also include a proportion of women, younger party members, and representatives of the minority groups within the party. At first, virtually no special privileges were given to elected party officials, such as senators or governors. In 1984, however, many of these officials returned to the Democratic convention as **superdelegates.**

The Primary as a Springboard to the White House

As soon as politicians and potential presidential candidates realized that winning as many primary elections as possible guaranteed the party's nomination for president, their tactics changed dramatically. Candidates such as Jimmy Carter concentrated on building organizations in states that held early, important primary elections. Candidates realized that winning early primaries, such as the New Hampshire election in February, or finishing first in the Iowa **caucus** meant that the media instantly would label the winner as the **front-runner**, thus increasing the candidate's media exposure and increasing the pace of contributions to his or her campaign fund.

The states and state political parties began to see that early primaries had a much greater effect on the outcome of the presidential election and, accordingly, began to hold their primaries earlier in the season to secure that advantage.

While New Hampshire held on to its claim as the "first" primary, other states moved to the next week. The southern states decided to hold their primaries on the same date, known as **Super Tuesday,** in the hopes of nominating a moderate southerner at the Democratic convention. When California, which had held the last primary (in June), moved its election to March, the primary season was curtailed drastically. Due to this process of **front-loading** the primaries, by 1996, the presidential nominating process was over in late March, with both Bob Dole and Bill Clinton having enough delegate votes to win their respective nominations. This meant that the campaign was essentially without news until the conventions in August, a gap that did not appeal to the politicians or the media. Both parties began to discuss whether more changes in the primary process were necessary.

On to the National Convention

Presidential candidates have been nominated by the convention method in every election since 1832. The delegates are sent from each state and are apportioned on the basis of state representation. Extra delegates are allowed to attend from states that had voting majorities for the party in the preceding elections. Parties also accept delegates from the District of Columbia, the territories, and certain overseas groups.

At the convention, each political party uses a **credentials committee** to determine which delegates may participate. The credentials committee usually prepares

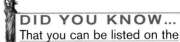
DID YOU KNOW...
That you can be listed on the New Hampshire primary ballot merely by paying a $1,000 filing fee?

Super Tuesday
The date on which a number of presidential primaries are held, including those of most of the southern states.

Front-Loading
The practice of moving presidential primary elections to the early part of the campaign, to maximize the impact of certain states or regions on the nomination.

Credentials Committee
A committee used by political parties at their national conventions to determine which delegates may participate. The committee inspects the claim of each prospective delegate to be seated as a legitimate representative of his or her state.

POLITICS and Elections

Primaries and Parties

Although most Americans assume that the presidential and congressional elections are controlled by the federal government, the only national regulations are those that affect campaign financing and set the day for the national election. States control the system of primaries and caucuses that nominate not only presidents but all candidates at the state level. In the presidential nominating process, some states use a primary election for both parties, and some prescribe a caucus system for one or both parties. The same variation exists for other types of nominations at the state level. Some state parties use the primary election, some use caucuses, and some use state-level conventions to

nominate candidates for the ticket.

Not only do the states and state parties vary in the devices they use for nominations, but they also may hold different types of primary elections. Among the most likely to be seen are the following:

■ **Closed Primary.** In a *closed primary,* the selection of a party's candidates in an election is limited to avowed or declared party members. In other words, voters must declare their party affiliation, either when they register or at the primary election. A closed-primary system tries to make sure that registered voters cannot cross over into the other party's primary in

order to nominate the weakest candidate of the opposing party or to affect the ideological direction of that party.

■ **Open Primary.** An *open primary* is a primary in which voters can vote in either party primary without disclosing their party affiliation. Basically, the voter makes the choice in the privacy of the voting booth. The voter must, however, choose one party's list from which to select candidates. Open primaries place no restrictions on independent voters.

■ **Blanket Primary.** A *blanket primary* is one in which the voter may vote for candidates of more than one party. Alaska, Louisiana, Washington, and California

all have blanket primaries. Blanket-primary campaigns may be much more costly because each candidate for every office is trying to influence all the voters, not just those in his or her party.

■ **Run-off Primary.** Some states have a two-primary system. If no candidate receives a majority of the votes in the first primary, the top two candidates must compete in another primary, called a *run-off primary.*

FOR CRITICAL ANALYSIS

If you are a candidate who has never run for office before and has not been active in the party, which type of primary election would be to your advantage?

a roll of all delegates entitled to be seated. Controversy may arise when rival groups claim to be the official party organization for a county, district, or state. The Mississippi Democratic Party split along racial lines in 1964 at the height of the civil rights movement in the Deep South. Separate all-white and mixed white and African American sets of delegates were selected, and both factions showed up at the national convention. After much debate on party rules, the committee decided to seat the pro–civil rights delegates and exclude those who represented the traditional "white" party.

Because delegates generally arrive at the convention committed to presidential candidates, no convention since 1952 has required more than one ballot to choose a nominee. Since 1972, candidates have usually come into the convention with enough committed delegates to win.

The typical convention lasts only a few days. The first day consists of speech making, usually against the opposing party. During the second day, there are committee reports, and during the third day, there is presidential balloting. On the fourth day, a vice presidential candidate is usually nominated, and the presidential nominee gives the acceptance speech.

By 1996, the outcome of the two conventions was so predictable that the national networks televised the convention proceedings for no more than two hours each evening. The convention planners concentrated on showing off the most important speeches during that prime-time period.

Delegates to the 1996 Republican National Convention in San Diego, California, nominated Bob Dole for president and Jack Kemp for vice president. Because the television networks have cut their coverage of the conventions, both parties planned their major speeches much more carefully in 1996 to maximize viewer interest.

The Electoral College

Most voters who vote for the president and vice president think that they are voting directly for a candidate. In actuality, they are voting for **electors** who will cast their ballots in the electoral college. The graphic in Figure 10-2 shows how the electoral votes are apportioned by state. Article II, Section 1, of the Constitution outlines in detail the number and choice of electors for president and vice president. The framers of the Constitution wanted to avoid the selection of president and vice president by the excitable masses. Rather, they wished the choice to be made by a few supposedly dispassionate, reasonable men (but not women).

The Choice of Electors

Each state's electors are selected during each presidential election year. The selection is governed by state laws and by the applicable party apparatus. After the national party convention, the electors are pledged to the candidates chosen. The total number of electors today is 538, equal to 100 senators, 435 members of the House, plus 3 electors for the District of Columbia (subsequent to the Twenty-third Amendment, ratified in 1961). Each state's number of electors equals that state's number of senators (two) plus its number of representatives.

The Electors' Commitment

If a **plurality** of voters in a state chooses one slate of electors, then those electors are pledged to cast their ballots on the first Monday after the second Wednesday in December in the state capital for the presidential and vice presidential

Elector
A person on the partisan slate that is selected early in the presidential election year according to state laws and the applicable political party apparatus. Electors cast ballots for president and vice president. The number of electors in each state is equal to that state's number of representatives in both houses of Congress.

Plurality
The total votes cast for a candidate who receives more votes than any other candidate but not necessarily a majority. Most national, state, and local electoral laws provide for winning elections by a plurality vote.

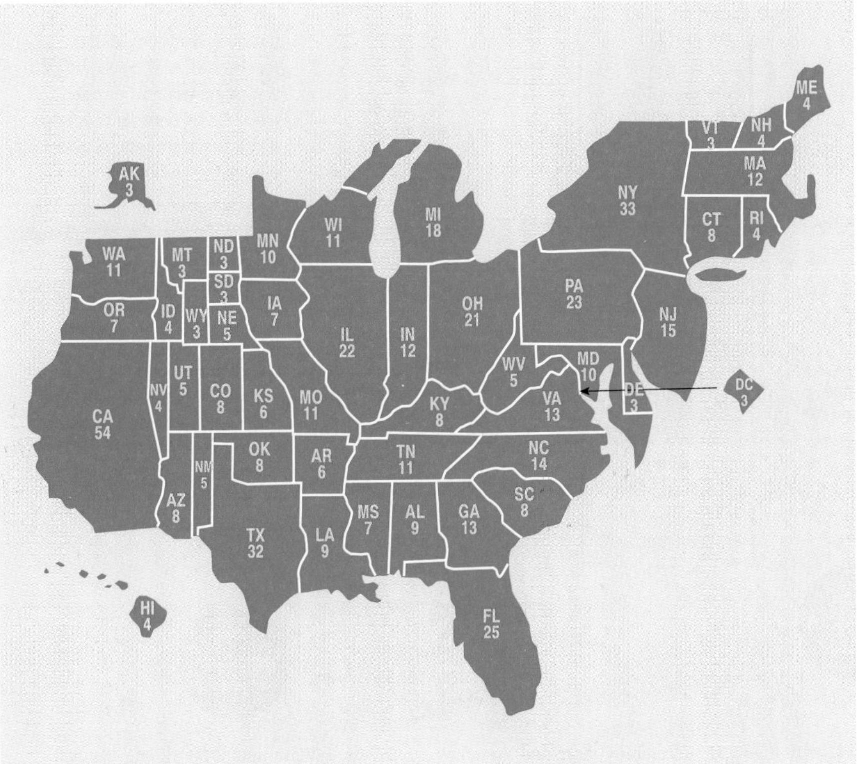

FIGURE 10-2

State Electoral Votes

The map of the United States shown here is distorted to show the relative weight of the states in terms of electoral votes. Considering that a candidate must win 270 electoral votes to be elected, the president's staff plots his visits around the nation to maximize exposure in the most important states. In the first three years of his administration, Bill Clinton, for example, visited California twenty-five times.

candidates for the winning party.[9] The Constitution does not, however, require the electors to cast their ballots for the candidate of their party.

The ballots are counted and certified before a joint session of Congress early in January. The candidates who receive a majority of the electoral votes (270) are certified as president-elect and vice president–elect. According to the Constitution, in cases in which no candidate receives a majority of the electoral votes, the election of the president is decided in the House from among the candidates with the three highest number of votes (decided by a plurality of each state delegation), each state having one vote. The selection of the vice president is determined by the Senate in a choice between the two highest candidates, each senator having one vote. Congress was required to choose the president and vice president in 1801 (Thomas Jefferson and Aaron Burr), and the House chose the president in 1825 (John Quincy Adams). The entire process is outlined in Figure 10–3.

It is possible for a candidate to become president without obtaining a majority of the popular vote. There have been numerous minority presidents in our history, including Abraham Lincoln, Woodrow Wilson, Harry S. Truman, John F. Kennedy, Richard Nixon (in 1968), and Bill Clinton. Such an event can always occur when there are third-party candidates.

Perhaps more distressing is the possibility of a candidate's being elected when the opposing candidate receives a larger share of popular vote. This occurred on three occasions—in the elections of John Quincy Adams in 1824, Rutherford B.

[9]In Maine and Nebraska, electoral votes are based on congressional districts. Each district chooses one elector. The remaining two electors are chosen statewide.

FIGURE 10-3

How Presidents and
Vice Presidents Are Chosen

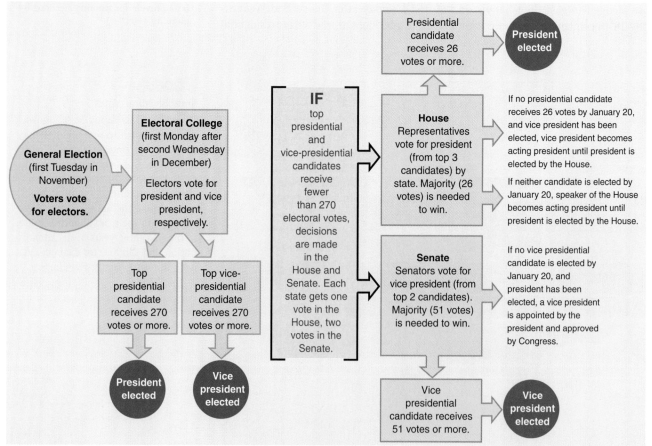

Source: Adapted from Michael J. Glennon, *When No Majority Rules: The Electoral College and Presidential Succession* (Washington, D.C.: Congressional Quarterly Press, 1993), p. 20.

Hayes in 1876, and Benjamin Harrison in 1888, all of whom won elections without obtaining a plurality of the popular vote.

Criticisms of the Electoral College

Besides the possibility of a candidate's becoming president even though his or her major opponent obtains more popular votes, there are other complaints about the electoral college. The idea of the Constitution's framers was to have electors use their own discretion to decide who would make the best president. But electors no longer perform the selecting function envisioned by the founders, because they are committed to the candidate who has a plurality of popular votes in their state in the general election.[10]

One can also argue that the current system, which gives all of the electoral votes to the candidate who has a statewide plurality, is unfair to other candidates and their supporters. The unit system of voting also means that presidential campaigning will be concentrated in those states that have the largest number of electoral votes and in those states in which the outcome is likely to be close. All of the other states generally get second-class treatment during the presidential campaign.

It can also be argued that there is something of a less-populous-state bias in the electoral college, because including Senate seats in the electoral vote total partly offsets the edge of the more populous states in the House. A state such as Alaska (with two senators and one representative) gets an electoral vote for roughly each 183,000 people (based on the 1990 census), whereas Iowa gets one vote for each 397,000 people, and New York has a vote for every 545,000 inhabitants.

Proposed Reforms

Many proposals for reform of the electoral college system have been advanced. The most obvious is to get rid of it completely and simply allow candidates to be elected on a popular-vote basis; in other words, have a direct election, by the people, for president and vice president. This was proposed as a constitutional amendment by President Jimmy Carter in 1977, but it failed to achieve the required two-thirds majority in the Senate in a 1979 vote. An earlier effort in 1969 passed the House, but a Senate vote defeated the proposed amendment due to the efforts of senators from less populous states and the South.

A less radical reform is a federal law that would require each elector to vote for the candidate who has a plurality in the state. Another system would eliminate the electors but retain the electoral vote, which would be given on a proportional basis rather than on a unit (winner-take-all) basis. This method was endorsed by President Richard Nixon in 1969.

The major parties are not in favor of eliminating the electoral college, fearing that it would give minor parties a more influential role. Also, less populous states are not in favor of direct election of the president, because they feel they would be overwhelmed by the large urban vote.

How Are Elections Conducted?

The United States uses the **Australian ballot**—a secret ballot that is prepared, distributed, and counted by government officials at public expense. Since 1888, all states have used the Australian ballot. Before that, many states used the

---

[10]Note, however, that there have been revolts by so-called *faithless electors*—in 1796, 1820, 1948, 1956, 1960, 1968, 1972, 1976, and 1988.

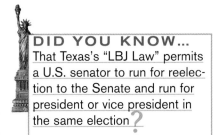

DID YOU KNOW...
That Texas's "LBJ Law" permits a U.S. senator to run for reelection to the Senate and run for president or vice president in the same election?

INFOTRAC®
COLLEGE EDITION

"Electoral College Is a Ticking Time Bomb"

Australian Ballot
A secret ballot prepared, distributed, and tabulated by government officials at public expense. Since 1888, all states have used the Australian ballot rather than an open, public ballot.

**Office-Block, or
Massachusetts, Ballot**
A form of general election ballot in
which candidates for elective office are
grouped together under the title of each
office. It emphasizes voting for the
office and the individual, rather than for
the party.

**Party-Column, or
Indiana, Ballot**
A form of general election ballot in
which candidates for elective office are
arranged in one column under their
respective party labels and symbols. It
emphasizes voting for the party, rather
than for the office or individual.

Coattail Effect
The influence of a popular or unpopular
candidate on the electoral success or
failure of other candidates on the same
party ticket. The effect is increased by
the party-column ballot, which encourages straight-ticket voting.

INFOTRAC ®
COLLEGE EDITION

**"Easy Voting: Calling Jimmy
Carter"**

A student casts his vote.

alternatives of oral voting and differently colored ballots prepared by the parties. Obviously, knowing which way a person was voting made it easy to apply
pressure to change his or her vote, and vote buying was common.

Office-Block and Party-Column Ballots

There are two types of ballots in use in the United States in general elections.
The first, called an **office-block ballot,** or sometimes called a **Massachusetts ballot,**
groups all the candidates for each elective office under the title of each office.
Politicians dislike the office-block ballot, because it places more emphasis on the
office than on the party; it discourages straight-ticket voting and encourages
split-ticket voting.

A **party-column ballot** is a form of general election ballot in which the candidates are arranged in one column under their respective party labels and symbols. It is also called the **Indiana ballot.** In some states, it allows voters to vote
for all of a party's candidates for local, state, and national offices by simply
marking a single "X" or by pulling a single lever. Most states use this type of
ballot. As it encourages straight-ticket voting, majority parties favor this form.
When a party has an exceptionally strong presidential or gubernatorial candidate to head the ticket, the **coattail effect** is increased by the use of the party-
column ballot.

Voting by Mail

Although voting by mail has been accepted for absentee ballots for many
decades, particularly for those who are doing business away from home or for
members of the armed forces, only recently have several states begun to try
offering mail ballots to all of their voters. The rationale for going to the mail
ballot is to make voting easier and more accessible to the voters, particularly in
an era when voters are likely to hold jobs and commute some distance from
home to work. The most startling result came in the spring 1996 special election
in Oregon to replace Senator Bob Packwood: turnout in the election was 66 percent, and the mail ballot saved the state more than $1 million. Another election,
held about two months later, saw nearly 54 percent of the voters participating
in a primary election that allowed mail voting.

There are arguments both for and against mail balloting across the nation.
Some commentators, including Norman Ornstein,[11] suggest that mail balloting
subverts the whole process. In part, this is because the voter casts his or her ballot at any time, perhaps before any debates or other dialogues are held between
candidates. Thus, the voter may be casting an uninformed ballot. Furthermore,
Ornstein believes that although the Oregon elections so far have shown no evidence of corruption, balloting by mail presents an exceptional opportunity for
vote fraud. Others, however, see the mail ballot as the best way to increase voter
participation in a time when many are too busy to vote or have little interest in
the process.

Vote Fraud

Vote fraud is something regularly suspected but seldom proved. Voting in the
nineteenth century, when secret ballots were rare and people had a cavalier attitude toward the open buying of votes, was probably much more conducive to
fraud than modern elections are. A recent investigation by Larry J. Sabato and

---

[11]Norman Ornstein, "Vote-by-Mail: Is It Good for Democracy?" *Campaigns and Elections,* May 1996,
p. 47.

Election judges check the registration of each voter before giving out the ballot. Most local election boards require judges from both political parties at each precinct.

Glenn R. Simpson, however, revealed that the potential for vote fraud is high in many states, particularly through the use of phony voter registrations and absentee ballots.[12]

Recent changes in the election laws of California, for example, make it very difficult to remove a name from the polling list even if the person has not cast a ballot for the prior two years. Thus, many persons are still on the rolls even though they no longer reside in California. Enterprising political activists can use these names for absentee ballots. Other states have registration laws that are meant to encourage easy registration and voting. Such laws can be taken advantage of by those who seek to vote more than once. Since the passage of the "motor voter" law in 1993, all states have been required to allow voters to register by mail. It may be necessary to develop new processes to verify that registrations or ballots sent by mail come from legitimate voters.

Voter Turnout
The percentage of citizens taking part in the election process; the number of eligible voters that actually "turn out" on election day to cast their ballots.

Voting in National, State, and Local Elections

In 1996, there were 196.5 million eligible voters. Of that number, 151.7 million, or 77 percent, actually registered to vote in the general presidential election. Of those who registered, 95.8 million actually went to the polls. The participation rate during the 1996 presidential election was only 63 percent of registered voters, down from 76 percent in 1992, and 48.8 percent of eligible voters (see Table 10–2 on the next page).

Figure 10–4 shows that the **voter turnout** in the United States compared with that of selected countries places Americans at the bottom. Figure 10–5 on page 331 shows voter turnout for presidential and congressional elections from 1896 to 1996. The last "good" year of turnout for the presidential elections was 1960, when almost 65 percent of the eligible voters actually voted. Each of the peaks in the figure represents voter turnout in a presidential election. Thus, we can also see that voting for U.S. representatives is greatly influenced by whether there is a presidential election in the same year.

FIGURE **10-4**

Voter Turnout in the United States Compared with Other Countries

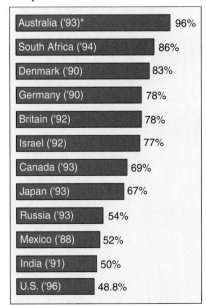

Country	Turnout
Australia ('93)*	96%
South Africa ('94)	86%
Denmark ('90)	83%
Germany ('90)	78%
Britain ('92)	78%
Israel ('92)	77%
Canada ('93)	69%
Japan ('93)	67%
Russia ('93)	54%
Mexico ('88)	52%
India ('91)	50%
U.S. ('96)	48.8%

*Year of the most recent national election.

[12]Larry J. Sabato and Glenn R. Simpson, *Dirty Little Secrets: The Persistence of Corruption in American Politics* (New York: Random House, 1996).

SOURCE: *Time* Magazine, May 23, 1994, and authors' update.

TABLE 10-2

Elected by a Majority?

Most presidents have won a majority of the votes cast in the election. We generally judge the extent of their victory by whether they have won more than 51 percent of the votes. Some presidential elections have been proclaimed *landslides,* meaning that the candidates won by an extraordinary majority of votes cast. As indicated below, however, no modern president has been elected by more than 38 percent of the total voting-age electorate.

YEAR—WINNER (PARTY)	PERCENTAGE OF TOTAL POPULAR VOTE	PERCENTAGE OF VOTING-AGE POPULATION
1932—Roosevelt (D)	57.4	30.1
1936—Roosevelt (D)	60.8	34.6
1940—Roosevelt (D)	54.7	32.2
1944—Roosevelt (D)	53.4	29.9
1948—Truman (D)	49.6	25.3
1952—Eisenhower (R)	55.1	34.0
1956—Eisenhower (R)	57.4	34.1
1960—Kennedy (D)	49.7	31.2
1964—Johnson (D)	61.1	37.8
1968—Nixon (R)	43.4	26.4
1972—Nixon (R)	60.7	33.5
1976—Carter (D)	50.1	26.8
1980—Reagan (R)	50.7	26.7
1984—Reagan (R)	58.8	31.2
1988—Bush (R)	53.4	26.8
1992—Clinton (D)	43.3	23.1
1996—Clinton (D)	49.2	23.2

SOURCE: *Congressional Quarterly Weekly Report,* January 31, 1989, p. 137; *New York Times,* November 5, 1992; and *New York Times,* November 7, 1996.

The same is true at the state level. When there is a race for governor, more voters participate both in the general election for governor and in the election for state representatives. Voter participation rates in gubernatorial elections are also greater in presidential election years. The average turnout in state elections is about 14 percentage points higher when a presidential election is held.

Now consider local elections. In races for mayor, city council, county auditor, and the like, it is fairly common for only 25 percent or less of the electorate to vote. Is something amiss here? It would seem obvious that people would be more likely to vote in elections that directly affect them. At the local level, each person's vote counts more (because there are fewer voters). Furthermore, the issues—crime control, school bonds, sewer bonds, and so on—touch the immediate interests of the voters. The facts, however, do not fit the theory. Potential voters are most interested in national elections, when a presidential choice is involved. Otherwise, voter participation in our representative government is very low (and, as we have seen, it is not overwhelmingly great even at the presidential level).

The Effect of Low Voter Turnout

There are two schools of thought concerning low voter turnout. Some view the decline in voter participation as a clear threat to our representative democratic government. Fewer and fewer individuals are deciding who wields political power in our society. Also, low voter participation presumably signals apathy about our political system in general. It also may signal that potential voters simply do not want to take the time to learn about the issues. When only a handful of people do take the time, it will be easier, say the alarmists, for an authoritarian figure to take over our government.

FIGURE 10-5

Voter Turnout for Presidential and Congressional Elections, 1896 to Present

The peaks represent turnout in presidential-election years; the troughs represent turnout in off-presidential-election years.

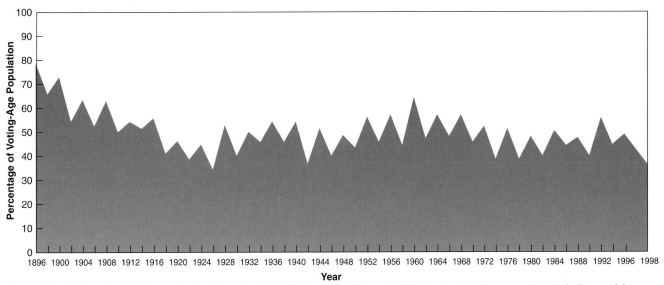

SOURCE: Historical Data Archive, Inter-university Consortium for Political and Social Research: U.S. Department of Commerce, *Statistical Abstract of the United States: 1980*, 101st ed. (Washington, D.C.: U.S. Government Printing Office, 1980), p. 515; William H. Flanigan and Nancy H. Zingale, *Political Behavior of the American Electorate*, 5th ed. (Boston: Allyn and Bacon, 1983), p. 20; *Congressional Quarterly*, various issues; and authors' update.

Others are less concerned about low voter participation. They believe that a decline in voter participation simply indicates more satisfaction with the status quo. Also, they believe that representative democracy is a reality even if a very small percentage of eligible voters vote. If everyone who does not vote believes that the outcome of the election will accord with his or her own desires, then representative democracy is working. The nonvoters are obtaining the type of government—with the type of people running it—that they want to have anyway.

Factors Influencing Who Votes

A clear association exists between voter participation and the following characteristics: age, educational attainment, minority status, income level, and the existence of two-party competition.

1. *Age.* Look at Table 10-3, which shows the breakdown of voter participation by age group for the 1996 presidential election. It would appear from these figures that age is a strong factor in determining voter turnout on election day. The reported turnout increases with older age groups. Greater participation with age is very likely due to the fact that older voters are more settled in their lives, are already registered, and have had more time to experience voting as an expected activity.

2. *Educational attainment.* Education also influences voter turnout. In general, the more education you have, the more likely you are to vote. This pattern is clearly evident in the 1996 election results, as we can see in Table 10-4. Reported turnout was over 30 percentage points higher for those who had some college education than it was for people who had never been to high school.

3. *Minority status.* Race is important, too, in determining the level of voter turnout. Whites in 1996 voted at a 56.0 percent rate, whereas the African American turnout rate was 50.6 percent.

TABLE 10-3

Voting in the 1996 Presidential Election by Age Group (in Percentage)

AGE	REPORTED TURNOUT
18–24	32.4
25–44	49.2
45–64	64.4
65 and over	67.0

SOURCE: U.S. Bureau of the Census, October 17, 1997, www.census.gov/.

TABLE 10-4

Voting in the 1996 Presidential Election by Education Level (in Percentage)

YEARS OF SCHOOL COMPLETED	REPORTED TURNOUT
8 years or less	29.9
9–11 years	33.8
12 years	49.1
1–3 years of college	60.5
4+ years of college	72.6

SOURCE: U.S. Bureau of the Census, October 17, 1997; www.census.gov/.

4. *Income levels.* Differences in income can also lead to differences in voter turnout. Wealthier people tend to be overrepresented in the electorate. In 1996, turnout among whites varied from less than 40 percent of those with annual family incomes under $15,000 to about 70 percent for people with annual family incomes of $50,000 or more.

5. *Two-party competition.* Another factor in voter turnout is the extent to which elections are competitive within a state. More competitive states generally have higher turnout rates, although the highest average percentage turnout for the past two decades has been in states in which Republicans were elected to most state offices.

The foregoing statistics reinforce one another. White voters are likely to be wealthier than African American voters, who are also less likely to have obtained a college education.

Why People Do Not Vote

For many years, political scientists believed that one reason why voter turnout in the United States was so much lower than in other Western nations was that it was so difficult to register and vote. In most states, registration required a special trip to a public office far in advance of elections. Many experts are now advancing other explanations for low U.S. voter turnout, however.

Political Withdrawal. Ruy A. Teixeira believes that the factor that has contributed most significantly to the decline in voting turnout since 1960 is not the "cost" of voting but the increasing social and political disconnectedness of American society. Teixeira's study shows that the barriers to voting have been reduced considerably since 1960, whereas turnout continues to decrease. It is true that as the population has become more educated and wealthier, turnout has increased among some groups. But with the decline of church membership, social memberships, and community identity, along with the extraordinary increase in political cynicism and distrust, fewer and fewer citizens feel close enough to government to be interested in voting.[13]

Rational Ignorance Effect
When people purposely and rationally decide not to become informed on an issue because they believe that their vote on the issue is not likely to be a deciding one; a lack of incentive to seek the necessary information to cast an intelligent vote.

The Rational Ignorance Effect. Another explanation of why voter turnout is low suggests that citizens are making a logical choice in not voting. If citizens believe that their votes will not affect the outcome of an election, then they have little incentive to seek the information they need to cast intelligent votes. The lack of incentive to obtain costly (in terms of time, attention, and so on) information about politicians and political issues has been called the **rational ignorance effect.** That term may seem contradictory, but it is not. Rational ignorance is a condition in which people purposely and rationally decide not to obtain information—to remain ignorant.

If average voters choose to remain rationally ignorant, what determines how they vote when they do vote? According to the rational ignorance theory, voters will simply rely on information that is supplied by candidates and by the mass media. Bits of information picked up from TV news and political advertising, as well as information gleaned from casual conversations with co-workers and friends, will be used as a basis for making a choice among candidates.

Why, then, do even one-third to one-half of U.S. citizens bother to show up at the polls? One explanation is that most citizens receive personal satisfaction from the act of voting. It makes them feel that they are good citizens and that

---

[13]Ruy A. Teixeira, *The Disappearing American Voter* (Washington, D.C.: Brookings Institution, 1992), p. 57.

they are doing something patriotic. But that feeling is not overriding. Even among voters who are registered and who plan to vote, if the cost of voting goes up (in terms of time and inconvenience), the number of eligible voters who actually vote will fall. In particular, bad weather on election day means that, on average, a smaller percentage of eligible voters will go to the polls.

Legal Restrictions on Voting

Legal restrictions on voter registration have existed since the founding of the nation. Most groups in the United States have been concerned with the suffrage issue at one time or another.

Historical Restrictions

In colonial times, only white males who owned property with a certain minimum value were eligible to vote, leaving a far greater number of Americans ineligible than eligible to take part in the democratic process. Because many government functions are in the economic sphere and concern property rights and the distribution of income and wealth, some of the founders of our nation felt it was appropriate that only people who had an interest in property should vote on these issues. The idea of extending the vote to all citizens was, according to South Carolina delegate Charles Pinckney, merely "theoretical nonsense."

The logic behind this restriction of voting rights to property owners was questioned seriously by Thomas Paine in his pamphlet *Common Sense:*

> Here is a man who today owns a jackass, and the jackass is worth $60. Today the man is a voter and goes to the polls and deposits his vote. Tomorrow the jackass dies. The next day the man comes to vote without his jackass and cannot vote at all. Now tell me, which was the voter, the man or the jackass?[14]

The writers of the Constitution allowed the states to decide who should vote. Thus, women were allowed to vote in Wyoming in 1870 but not in the entire

---

[14]Thomas Paine, *Common Sense* (London: H. D. Symonds, 1792), p. 28.

Voter registration is an important part of our political process. These workers are helping a citizen register to vote in the next election. The requirements for voter registration vary across states.

nation until the Nineteenth Amendment was ratified in 1920.

By about 1850, most white adult males in virtually all the states could vote without any property qualification. North Carolina was the last state to eliminate its property test for voting—in 1856.

Extension of the franchise to black males occurred with the passage of the Fifteenth Amendment in 1870. This enfranchisement was short-lived, however, as the "redemption" of the South by white racists rolled back these gains by the end of the century. As discussed in Chapter 5, it was not until the 1960s that African Americans, both male and female, were able to participate in large numbers in the electoral process. Women received full national voting rights with the Nineteenth Amendment in 1920. The most recent extension of the franchise occurred when the voting age was reduced to eighteen by the Twenty-sixth Amendment in 1971.

Current Eligibility and Registration Requirements

Registration

The entry of a person's name onto the list of eligible voters for elections. Registration requires meeting certain legal requirements relating to age, citizenship, and residency.

Voting requires **registration,** and registration requires satisfying voter qualifications, or legal requirements. These requirements are the following: (1) citizenship, (2) age (eighteen or older), and (3) residency—the duration varying widely from state to state and with types of elections. Since 1972, states cannot impose residency requirements of more than thirty days. In addition, most states disqualify people who are mentally incompetent, prison inmates, convicted felons, and election-law violators.

Each state has different qualifications for voting and registration. In 1993, Congress passed the "motor voter" bill, which requires that states provide voter-

Signs in English and Spanish encourage voters to register for the next election. The Supreme Court has ruled that registration and ballots must be available in other languages if a specified proportion of the citizens speak a language other than English.

registration materials when people receive or renew driver's licenses, that all states allow voters to register by mail, and that voter-registration forms be made available at a wider variety of public places and agencies. In general, a person must register well in advance of an election, although voters in Maine, Minnesota, Oregon, and Wisconsin are allowed to register up to, and on, election day.

Some argue that registration requirements are responsible for much of the nonparticipation in our political process. Certainly, since their introduction in the late nineteenth century, registration laws have had the effect of reducing the voting participation of African Americans and immigrants. There also is a partisan dimension to the debate over registration and nonvoting. Republicans generally fear that an expanded electorate would help to elect more Democrats.

The question arises as to whether registration is really necessary. If it decreases participation in the political process, perhaps it should be dropped altogether. Still, as those in favor of registration requirements argue, such requirements may prevent fraudulent voting practices, such as multiple voting or voting by noncitizens.

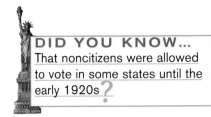

DID YOU KNOW...
That noncitizens were allowed to vote in some states until the early 1920s?

How Do Voters Decide?

Political scientists and survey researchers have collected much information about voting behavior. This information sheds some light on which people vote and why people decide to vote for particular candidates. We have already discussed factors influencing voter turnout. Generally, the factors that influence voting decisions can be divided into two groups: (1) socioeconomic and demographic factors and (2) psychological factors. (For Adlai Stevenson's views on the way voters decide, see the feature *E-Mail Messages from the Past*.)

Socioeconomic and Demographic Factors

As Table 10–5 on the next page indicates, a number of socioeconomic and demographic factors appear to influence voting behavior, including (1) education,

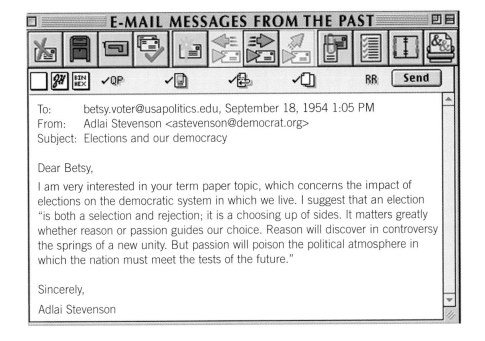

E-MAIL MESSAGES FROM THE PAST

To: betsy.voter@usapolitics.edu, September 18, 1954 1:05 PM
From: Adlai Stevenson <astevenson@democrat.org>
Subject: Elections and our democracy

Dear Betsy,

I am very interested in your term paper topic, which concerns the impact of elections on the democratic system in which we live. I suggest that an election "is both a selection and rejection; it is a choosing up of sides. It matters greatly whether reason or passion guides our choice. Reason will discover in controversy the springs of a new unity. But passion will poison the political atmosphere in which the nation must meet the tests of the future."

Sincerely,

Adlai Stevenson

TABLE 10-5

Vote by Groups in Presidential Elections since 1964 (in Percentages)

	1964		1968			1972		1976			1980		
	LBJ (DEM.)	GOLDWATER (REP.)	HUMPHREY (DEM.)	NIXON (REP.)	WALLACE (IND.)	McGOVERN (DEM.)	NIXON (REP.)	CARTER (DEM.)	FORD (REP.)	McCARTHY (IND.)	CARTER (DEM.)	REAGAN (REP.)	ANDERSON (IND.)
NATIONAL	61.3	38.7	43.0	43.4	13.6	38	62	50	48	1	41	51	7
SEX													
Male	60	40	41	43	16	37	63	53	45	1	38	53	7
Female	62	38	45	43	12	38	62	48	51	*	44	49	6
RACE													
White	59	41	38	47	15	32	68	46	52	1	36	56	7
Nonwhite	94	6	85	12	3	87	13	85	15	*	86	10	2
EDUCATION													
College	52	48	37	54	9	37	63	42	55	2	35	53	10
High school	62	38	42	43	15	34	66	54	46	*	43	51	5
Grade school	66	34	52	33	15	49	51	58	41	1	54	42	3
OCCUPATION													
Professional	54	46	34	56	10	31	69	42	56	1	33	55	10
White collar	57	43	41	47	12	36	64	50	48	2	40	51	9
Manual	71	29	50	35	15	43	57	58	41	1	48	46	5
AGE (Years)													
Under 30	64	36	47	38	15	48	52	53	45	1	47	41	11
30–49	63	37	44	41	15	33	67	48	49	2	38	52	8
50 and older	59	41	41	47	12	36	64	52	48	*	41	54	4
RELIGION													
Protestants	55	45	35	49	16	30	70	46	53	*	39	54	6
Catholics	76	24	59	33	8	48	52	57	42	1	46	47	6
POLITICS													
Republicans	20	80	9	86	5	5	95	9	91	*	8	86	5
Democrats	87	13	74	12	14	67	33	82	18	*	69	26	4
Independents	56	44	31	44	25	31	69	38	57	4	29	55	14
REGION													
East	68	32	50	43	7	42	58	51	47	1	43	47	9
Midwest	61	39	44	47	9	40	60	48	50	1	41	51	7
South	52	48	31	36	33	29	71	54	45	*	44	52	3
West	60	40	44	49	7	41	59	46	51	1	35	54	9
MEMBERS OF LABOR UNION FAMILIES	73	27	56	29	15	46	54	63	36	1	50	43	5

*Less than 1 percent.

Note: Results do not include votes for all minor-party candidates.

Socioeconomic Status
A category of people within a society who have similar levels of income and similar types of occupations.

(2) income and **socioeconomic status,** (3) religion, (4) ethnic background, (5) gender, (6) age, and (7) geographic region. These influences all reflect the voter's personal background and place in society. Some factors have to do with the family into which a person is born: race, religion (for most people), and ethnic background. Others may be the result of choices made throughout an individual's life: place of residence, educational achievement, or profession. It is also clear that many of these factors are related. People who have more education are likely to have higher incomes and to hold professional jobs. Similarly, children born into wealthier families are far more likely to complete college than children from poorer families. Furthermore, some of these demographic factors relate to psychological factors—as we shall see.

Education. Having a college education tends to be associated with voting for Republicans. An exception to the rule that more educated voters vote Republican occurred in 1964, when college graduates voted 52 percent for Democrat Lyndon

TABLE 10-5

Vote by Groups in Presidential Elections since 1964 (in Percentages)—continued

	1984		1988		1992			1996		
	MONDALE (DEM.)	REAGAN (REP.)	DUKAKIS (DEM.)	BUSH (REP.)	CLINTON (DEM.)	BUSH (REP.)	PEROT (IND.)	CLINTON (DEM.)	DOLE (REP.)	PEROT (REF.)
NATIONAL	41	59	45	53	43	38	19	49	41	8
SEX										
Male	36	64	41	57	41	38	21	43	44	10
Female	45	55	49	50	46	37	17	54	38	7
RACE										
White	34	66	40	59	39	41	20	43	46	9
Nonwhite	87	13	86	12	NA	NA	NA	NA	NA	NA
EDUCATION										
College	39	61	43	56	44	39	18	44	46	8
High school	43	57	49	50	43	36	20	51	35	13
Grade school	51	49	56	43	56	28	NA	59	28	11
OCCUPATION										
Professional	34	66	40	59	NA	NA	NA	NA	NA	NA
White collar	47	53	42	57	NA	NA	NA	NA	NA	NA
Manual	46	54	50	49	NA	NA	NA	NA	NA	NA
AGE (Years)										
Under 30	40	60	47	52	44	34	22	54	34	10
30–49	40	60	45	54	42	38	20	48	41	9
50 and older	41	59	49	50	50	38	12	48	44	7
RELIGION										
Protestants	39	61	33	66	33	46	21	36	53	10
Catholics	39	61	47	52	44	36	20	53	37	9
POLITICS										
Republicans	4	96	8	91	10	73	17	13	80	6
Democrats	79	21	82	17	77	10	13	84	10	5
Independents	33	67	43	55	38	32	30	43	35	17
REGION										
East	46	54	49	50	47	35	NA	55	34	9
Midwest	42	58	47	52	42	37	NA	48	41	10
South	37	63	41	58	42	43	NA	46	46	7
West	40	60	46	52	44	34	NA	48	40	8
MEMBERS OF LABOR UNION FAMILIES	52	48	57	42	55	24	NA	59	30	9

*Less than 1 percent.

Note: Results do not include votes for all minor-party candidates.

SOURCE: *Gallup Report*, November 1984, p. 32; *New York Times*, November 10, 1988, p. 18; *New York Times*, November 15, 1992, p. B9; *New York Times*, November 10, 1996, p. 16.

Johnson and 48 percent for Republican Barry Goldwater. Typically, those with less education are more inclined to vote for the Democratic nominee. In 1984, Democrat Walter Mondale received 43 percent and Republican Ronald Reagan, 57 percent of the vote from high school graduates, whereas those with only a grade school education voted 51 percent for Mondale and 49 percent for Reagan. The same pattern held in 1996, when 46 percent of the college graduates voted for Republican Bob Dole, compared with 28 percent of those who had not completed high school.

Income and Socioeconomic Status. If we measure socioeconomic status by profession, then those of higher socioeconomic status—professionals and businesspersons, as well as white-collar workers—tend to vote Republican more than Democratic. Manual laborers, factory workers, and especially union members are more likely to vote Democratic (but see Table 10–6). The effects of income are much the same. The higher the income, the more likely it is that a person will vote Republican. But there are no hard and fast rules. There are some very poor individuals who are devoted Republicans, just as there are some extremely wealthy supporters of the Democratic Party. In some recent elections, the traditional pattern did not hold. In 1980, for example, many blue-collar Democrats voted for Ronald Reagan, although the 1996 election showed those votes going to Bill Clinton.

Religion.   In the United States, Protestants have traditionally voted Republican, and Catholics and Jews have voted Democratic. As with the other patterns discussed, however, this one is somewhat fluid. Republican Richard Nixon obtained 52 percent of the Catholic vote in 1972, and Democrat Lyndon Johnson won 55 percent of the Protestant vote in 1964. The Catholic vote was evenly split between Democrat Jimmy Carter and Republican Ronald Reagan in 1980 but went heavily for Reagan in 1984. In 1996, Republican candidate Bob Dole obtained fewer votes from Catholics than did Democratic candidate Bill Clinton.

Ethnic Background.   Traditionally, the Irish have voted for Democrats. So, too, have voters of Slavic, Polish, and Italian heritages. But Anglo-Saxon and northern European ethnic groups have voted for Republican presidential candidates. These patterns were disrupted in 1980, when Ronald Reagan obtained much of his support from several of the traditionally Democratic ethnic groups, with the help of fundamentalist religious groups.

African Americans voted principally for Republicans until Democrat Franklin Roosevelt's New Deal in the 1930s. Since then, they have largely identified with the Democratic Party. Indeed, Democratic presidential candidates have received, on average, more than 80 percent of the African American vote since 1956.

Gender.   As discussed in Chapter 7, until relatively recently there seemed to have been no fixed pattern of voter preference by gender in presidential elections. One year, more women than men would vote for the Democratic candi-

---

TABLE **10-6**

How Democratic Are Labor Voters?

Although union members are more likely to identify themselves as Democrats than Republicans and labor organizations are far more likely to support Democratic candidates, the data below show that in seven of twelve presidential elections, Republicans have captured at least 40 percent of the votes from union households.

UNION HOUSEHOLDS VOTING REPUBLICAN FOR PRESIDENT

YEAR	CANDIDATES	PERCENTAGE
1952	Eisenhower vs. Stevenson	44%
1956	Eisenhower vs. Stevenson	57
1960	Kennedy vs. Nixon	36
1964	Johnson vs. Goldwater	17
1968	Nixon vs. Humphrey	44
1972	Nixon vs. McGovern	57
1976	Carter vs. Ford	36
1980	Reagan vs. Carter	45
1984	Reagan vs. Mondale	43
1988	Bush vs. Dukakis	41
1992	Clinton vs. Bush	32
1996	Clinton vs. Dole	30

SOURCE: *CQ Researcher*, June 28, 1996, p. 560; *The New York Times*, November 10, 1996, p. 16.

A number of factors determine how voters make decisions at the polling place. Aside from the many demographic influences that come into play, there are also psychological factors that help shape the way voters make decisions when they enter the voting booth.

date; another year, more men than women would do so. Some political analysts believe that a "gender gap" became a major determinant of voter decision making in the 1980 presidential election. Ronald Reagan obtained 15 percentage points more than Jimmy Carter among male voters, whereas women gave about an equal number of votes to each candidate. In 1984, the gender gap amounted to 9 percent nationally, with 64 percent of male voters casting their ballots for Ronald Reagan and 55 percent of female voters doing the same. In 1996, women cast 54 percent of their votes for Bill Clinton, the Democrat. The gender gap rarely appears in congressional elections.

Age.   Age clearly seems to relate to an individual's voting behavior. Younger voters have tended to vote Democratic, whereas older voters have tended to vote Republican. It was only the voters under age thirty who clearly favored Jimmy Carter during the Carter-Reagan election in 1980. This trend was reversed in 1984, when voters under thirty voted heavily for Ronald Reagan and again voted Republican in 1988. In 1992, Bill Clinton won back the young voters by 10 percentage points, a margin that expanded to 20 percentage points in 1996.

Geographic Region.   As we noted in Chapter 9, the former Solid (Democratic) South has crumbled in national elections. In 1972, Republican Richard Nixon obtained 71 percent of the southern vote, whereas Democrat George McGovern obtained only 29 percent. Ronald Reagan drew 52 percent of the southern vote in 1980, however, and 63 percent in 1984.

Democrats still draw much of their strength from large northern and eastern cities. Rural areas tend to be Republican (and conservative) throughout the country except in the South, where the rural vote still tends to be heavily Democratic. On average, the West has voted Republican in presidential elections. Except for the 1964 election between Barry Goldwater and Lyndon Johnson, and again in the 1992 and 1996 elections, the Republicans have held the edge in western states in every presidential election since 1956.

Psychological Factors

In addition to socioeconomic and demographic explanations for the way people vote, at least three important psychological factors play a role in voter decision making. These factors, which are rooted in attitudes and beliefs held by voters, are (1) party identification, (2) perception of the candidates, and (3) issue preferences.

Party Identification.   With the possible exception of race, party identification has been the most important determinant of voting behavior in national elections. As we pointed out in Chapter 7, party affiliation is influenced by family and peer groups, by age, by the media, and by psychological attachment. During the 1950s, independent voters were a little more than 20 percent of the eligible electorate. In the middle to late 1960s, however, party identification began to weaken, and by the mid-1990s, independent voters constituted over 30 percent of all voters. In 1998, the estimated proportion of independent voters was between 26 and 33 percent. Independent voting seems to be concentrated among new voters, particularly among new young voters. Thus, we can still say that party identification for established voters is an important determinant in voter choice.

Perception of the Candidates.   The image of the candidate also seems to be important in a voter's choice for president. To some extent, voter attitudes toward candidates are based on emotions (such as trust) rather than on any judgment about experience or policy. In 1996, voters' decisions were largely guided by their perceptions of who they could trust to run the economy. Bob Dole tried to reduce the voters' trust in Bill Clinton but failed to make an impact.

Issue Preferences.   Issues make a difference in presidential and congressional elections. Although personality or image factors may be very persuasive, most voters have some notion of how the candidates differ on basic issues or at least know that the candidates want a change in the direction of government policy.

Historically, economic issues have the strongest influence on voters' choices. When the economy is doing well, it is very difficult for a challenger, particularly at the presidential level, to defeat the incumbent. In contrast, increasing inflation, rising unemployment, or high interest rates are likely to work to the disadvantage of the incumbent. Studies of how economic conditions affect the vote differ in their conclusions. Some indicate that people vote on the basis of their personal economic well-being, whereas other studies seem to show that people vote on the basis of the nation's overall economic health.

Foreign policy issues become more prominent in a time of crisis. Although the parties and candidates have differed greatly over policy toward trade with China, for example, foreign policy issues are truly influential only when armed conflict is a possibility. Clearly, public dissension over the war in Vietnam had an effect on elections in 1968 and 1972.

Some of the most heated debates in American political campaigns take place over the social issues of abortion, the role of women, the rights of lesbians and gay males, and prayer in the public schools. In general, presidential candidates would prefer to avoid such issues, because voters who care about these questions are likely to be offended if a candidate does not share their views.

From time to time, drugs, crime, and corruption become important campaign issues. The Watergate affair cost the Republicans a number of congressional seats in 1974, and its aftereffects probably defeated Gerald Ford in 1976. If the president or high officials are involved in truly criminal or outrageous conduct, the issue will undoubtedly influence voters.

All candidates try to set themselves apart from their opposition on crucial issues in order to attract voters. What is difficult to ascertain is the extent to which issues overshadow partisan loyalty or personality factors in the voters' minds. It appears that some campaigns are much more issue oriented than others. Some research has shown that **issue voting** was most important in the presidential elections of 1964, 1968, and 1972, was moderately important in 1980, and was less important in the 1990s.

Issue Voting
Voting for a candidate based on how he or she stands on a particular issue.

Why Voters Voted as They Did in 1998

elections '98

The outcome of the 1998 elections was extremely difficult for candidates to predict because the electorate seemed, for most of the year, to be quite disinterested in the elections. Polls taken prior to the elections suggested that turnout would be low, that Republicans might vote in greater numbers than Democrats, and that Republicans would benefit from the historic trend of midterm losses for the president's party.

The results of the 1998 midterm elections, however, defied these predictions. First, voter turnout was close to normal levels for midterm elections. Second, Democrats were able to motivate African American and union voters to come to the polls to support their party's candidates. Finally, most elections were "local."

Exit polls showed that while voters continued to approve the president's job performance they felt that Congress had accomplished very little in the past two years. When voters were asked about their decisions with respect to members of Congress, about 30 percent said that they were voting to support the Republican majority, about 29 percent indicated that they were voting against the Republicans, and 35 percent declared that they were not motivated by either of those strategies.

Campaigns, Candidates, and Elections: Issues for the New Century

Few areas in American politics seem to be in such need of change and reform as campaigns, voting, and elections. Every four years, polls show that the majority of Americans are dissatisfied with the length of campaigns, with vicious campaign strategies, with the caliber of candidates, and with the influence of campaign contributions on the system. Yet very few serious reforms result, in part, because reforms might affect the people in office, and after the campaign fury subsides, most citizens are willing to get on with their personal business and allow the officials elected in that campaign to take office and hold political authority.

The cost of waging a national or statewide campaign continues to rise due to the need to obtain media coverage, to use new technologies, and to hire many campaign professionals. The issue of how campaigns are to be financed in the future while still preserving freedom of speech and press for all, including candidates, is one that eventually will continue to demand the attention of the American voters and politicians.

The Internet undoubtedly will play an even greater role in campaigns of the future, forcing society to deal with such issues as the truthfulness of the content of Web publications and the security of one's interactions with the Internet. In addition, the success of mail balloting in Oregon suggests that in the future, the American political system may embrace new forms of voting, such as mail voting, telephone balloting, or Internet voting, that are more in keeping with society today.

Perhaps the most important issue for the future is the increasing cynicism of the American electorate with regard to government and politics. As voter participation falls and cynicism rises, the nation will need to address the issues that have sapped the public's confidence not only in the government but also in the democratic electoral system that we use to choose our government.

TOWARD ACTIVE CITIZENSHIP

REGISTERING AND VOTING

In nearly every state, before you are allowed to cast a vote in an election, you must first register. Registration laws vary considerably from state to state, and, depending on how difficult a state's laws make it to register, some states have much higher rates of registration and voting participation than do others.

What do you have to do to register and cast a vote? Most states require that you meet minimum residence requirements. In other words, you must have lived in the state in which you plan to be registered for a specified period of time. You may retain your previous registration, if any, in another state, and you can cast an absentee vote if your previous state permits that. The minimum-residency requirement is very short in some states, such as one day in Alabama or ten days in New Hampshire and Wisconsin. No state requires more than thirty days. Other states with voter residency requirements have minimum-day requirements in between these extremes. Twenty states do not have any minimum-residency requirement at all.

Nearly every state also specifies a closing date by which you must be registered before an election. In other words, even if you have met a residency requirement, you still may not be able to vote if you register too close to the day of the election. The closing date is different in certain states (Connecticut, Delaware, and Louisiana) for primary elections than for other elections. The closing date for registration varies from election day itself (Maine, Minnesota, Oregon, and Wisconsin) to thirty days (Arizona). Delaware specifies the third Saturday in October as the closing date. In North Dakota, no registration is necessary.

In most states, your registration can be revoked if you do not vote within a certain number of years. This process of automatically "purging" the voter-registration lists of nonactive voters happens every two years in about a dozen states, every three years in Georgia, every four years in more than twenty other states, every five years in Maryland and Rhode Island, every eight years in North Carolina, and every ten years in Michigan. Ten states do not require this purging at all.

What you must do to register and remain registered to vote varies from state to state and even from county to county within a state. In general, you must be a citizen of the United States, at least eighteen years old on or before election day, and a resident of the state in which you intend to register.

Using Iowa as an example, you normally would register through the local county auditor or when you obtain your driver's license (under the "motor voter" law of 1993). If you moved to a new address within the state, you would also have to change your registration to vote by contacting the auditor. Postcard registrations must be postmarked or delivered to the county auditor no later than the twenty-fifth day before an election. Party affiliation may be changed or declared when you register or reregister, or you may change or declare a party at the polls on election day. Postcard registration forms in Iowa are available at many public buildings, from labor unions, at political party headquarters, at the county auditors' offices, or from campus groups. Registrars who will accept registrations at other locations may be located by calling your party headquarters or your county auditor.

For more information on voting registration, contact your county or state officials, party headquarters, labor union, or local chapter of the League of Women Voters. The Web site for the League of Women Voters is

www.lwv.org/

Key terms

Chapter summary

1 People may choose to run for political office to further their careers, to carry out specific political programs, or in response to certain issues or events. The legal qualifications for holding political office are minimal at both the state and local levels, but holders of political office still are predominantly white and male and are likely to be from the professional class.

2 American political campaigns are lengthy and extremely expensive. In the last decade, they have become more candidate centered rather than party centered in response to technological innovations and decreasing party identification. Candidates have begun to rely less on the party and more on paid professional consultants to perform the various tasks necessary to wage a political campaign. The crucial task of professional political consultants is image building. The campaign organization devises a campaign strategy to maximize the candidate's chances of winning. Candidates use public opinion polls to gauge their popularity and to test the mood of the country.

3 The amount of money spent in financing campaigns is steadily increasing. A variety of corrupt practices acts have been passed to regulate campaign finance. The Federal Election Campaign Acts of 1972 and 1974 instituted major reforms by limiting spending and contributions; the acts allowed corporations, labor unions, and interest groups to set up political action committees (PACs) to raise money for candidates. New techniques, including contributions to the parties, independent expenditures, and bundling, have been created to raise money.

4 Following the Democratic convention of 1968, the McGovern-Fraser Commission was appointed to study the problems of the primary system. It formulated new rules, which were adopted by all Democrats and by Republicans in many states. These reforms opened up the nomination process for the presidency to all voters.

5 A presidential primary is a statewide election to help a political party determine its presidential nominee at the national convention. Some states use the caucus method of choosing convention delegates. The primary campaign recently has been shortened to the first few months of the election year.

6 In making a presidential choice on election day, the voter technically does not vote directly for a candidate but chooses between slates of presidential electors. The slate that wins the most popular votes throughout the state gets to cast all the electoral votes for the state. The candidate receiving a majority (270) of the electoral votes wins. Both the mechanics and the politics of the electoral college have been sharply criticized. There have been many proposed reforms, including a proposal that direct elections be held in which candidates would be elected on a popular-vote basis.

7 The United States uses the Australian ballot, a secret ballot that is prepared, distributed, and counted by government officials. The office-block ballot groups candidates according to office. The party-column ballot groups candidates according to their party labels and symbols.

8 Voter participation in the United States is low (and generally declining) compared with that of other countries. Some view the decline in voter turnout as a threat to representative democracy, whereas others believe it simply indicates greater satisfaction with the status quo. There is an association between voting and a person's age, education, minority status, and income level. Another factor affecting voter turnout is the extent to which elections are competitive within a state.

9 In colonial times, only white males with a certain minimum amount of property were eligible to vote. The suffrage issue has concerned, at one time or another, most groups in the United States. Current voter eligibility requires registration, citizenship, and specified age and residency requirements. Each state has different qualifications. It is argued that these requirements are responsible for much of the nonparticipation in the political process in the United States.

10 Socioeconomic or demographic factors that influence voting decisions include (a) education, (b) income and socioeconomic status, (c) religion, (d) ethnic background, (e) gender, (f) age, and (g) geographic region. Psychological factors that influence voting decisions include (a) party identification, (b) perception of candidates, and (c) issue preferences.

Selected print and electronic resources

SUGGESTED READINGS

Bike, William S. *Winning Political Campaigns: A Comprehensive Guide to Electoral Success.* New York: Denali Press, 1998. This is a guide to politics for any aspiring officeholder or candidate.

Conway, M. Margaret, Gertrude A. Steuernagel, and David W. Ahern. *Women and Political Participation.* Washington, D.C.: CQ Press, 1997. This volume examines the changing role of women in the political system, including the increase in participation and officeholding by women.

Davis, James W. *U.S. Presidential Primaries and the Caucus-Convention System: A Sourcebook.* New York: Greenwood Press, 1997. A comprehensive source book on the history of the American electoral system, this work provides analyses of primaries, polls, and campaign-finance regulations.

Jackson, John S., III, and William Crotty. *The Politics of Presidential Selection.* New York: Longman Publishers, 1996. This account of how we elect the president and the members of Congress is based on theories of rational decision making by voters and discusses the limits to such decision making for those voters without information.

Lupia, Arthur, and Mathew D. McCubbins. *The Democratic Dilemma.* New York: Cambridge University Press, 1998. Using advances in psychology and economics to inform their work, the authors investigate the question of how citizens with little information make reasonable choices in a democratic system.

Mayer, William G., ed. *In Pursuit of the White House: How We Choose Our Presidential Nominees.* Chatham, N.J.: Chatham House Publishers, 1995. This book contains an excellent collection of articles examining the primary system, campaign financing, and independent and third-party candidates.

Simpson, Dick. *Winning Elections: A Handbook in Modern Participatory Politics.* New York: Longman Publishers, 1996. Former alderman and mayoral candidate Simpson gives advice to citizens who would like to get involved in politics at the grassroots level.

MEDIA RESOURCES

The Candidate—Starring the young Robert Redford, this 1972 film produced by Warner Brothers effectively investigates and satirizes the decisions that a candidate for the U.S. Senate must make. It's a political classic.

The War Room—Using video coverage taped throughout Bill Clinton's 1992 campaign for the presidency, this 1993 documentary shows the strategic decisions behind the scenes in the campaign. Footage shows Clinton's strategists, including James Carville and George Stephanopoulous, pulling out all the stops for their candidate.

All the King's Men—A classic film, produced in 1949 and based on a best-selling novel by Robert Penn Warren, that traces the rise to power of a southern politician (played by Broderick Crawford) and parallels the life of Huey Long, the governor of Louisiana during the Great Depression of the 1930s.

Campaigns and Elections Video Library—A series of videos, made available in 1998 by the periodical *Campaigns and Elections*, that include the best campaign ads of specific election cycles, the best overall ads, and the classic ads of all time.

Logging on

For detailed information about current campaign election laws and for the latest filings of finance reports, see the site maintained by the Federal Election Commission at

www.fec.gov/

To find excellent reports on where the money comes from and how it is spent in campaigns, be sure to view the site maintained by the Center for Responsive Politics at

www.crp.org/

You can learn about the impact of different voting systems on election strategies and outcomes at the following Web site:

www.igc.org/cvd/

Another excellent site for investigating voting records and campaign-finance information is that of Project VoteSmart. Go to

www.vote-smart.org

For a site that gives you information about political races around the nation and about controversial issues, go to ElectNet at

www.EL.com/

Using the Internet for political analysis

Point your browser at either the Federal Election Commission site (**www.fec.org/**) or the Center for Responsive Politics site (**www.crp.org/**). Choose the campaign-finance records of at least three individual candidates or members of Congress. Print out those records, and then compare the types of donors that are listed. Can you find enough information about campaign donations to have some idea of what policy positions are held by the candidates? What does the donor list tell you about each person's role and importance in Congress?

The Media

347

what if

Everyone Could Be a Broadcaster?

BACKGROUND

From the beginning of radio broadcasting until the development of cable television in the 1980s, the electronic media have been dominated by large national networks. Of course, in the early days of radio and of television, local stations were established to serve their communities. Over time, however, most of the television stations found it necessary to become "affiliates" of the national networks to have access to their news and entertainment broadcasts. With the coming of cable television, most communities that licensed cable companies required the companies to provide a number of "public access" channels, which are accessible to groups and individuals in the community. These channels continued to exist but have very small viewing audiences. The Internet, however, makes it possible for almost everyone to become a "broadcaster" on the Web.

WHAT IF EVERYONE COULD BE A BROADCASTER?

With technology already available, everyone who owns a personal computer and has an Internet connection can become a broadcaster. With a small camera and microphone attached to the personal computer, you can send pictures and sound across the Internet to anyone who tunes in to your Web site. In fact, one young American woman has been broadcasting scenes of her daily life for more than two years now. She has an international following of viewers who watch her activities in her apartment. Some suggest this is voyeurism, while others find the viewing of her personal life to be very interesting and human.

If everyone in the United States had the potential to become a broadcaster, the result would be complete freedom of speech for Americans. Anyone could comment on the news, discuss plots and conspiracies that are taking place, and publicly criticize and/or praise the president, the Supreme Court, and members of Congress. Everyone would have the opportunity to participate in public debate about the issues facing the nation and about legislation pending in Congress.

The result, of course, would be total news overload and a considerable distortion of the facts on the whole. How would the Internet "surfer" find out whether an individual "broadcasting" on the Web has any basis for his or her opinions? Are the facts that are presented true, or are they gossip? How much hate speech would be broadcast without any sort of regulation or retribution? How many politicians might see their reputations slandered? Lawyers would have a rich field of potential litigation in libel and slander cases, because the courts generally have held that the broadcaster is responsible for the material sent to the public.

WOULD THE BROADCASTING BE BIASED?

The new broadcasters would probably be people who have the leisure time and resources to dedicate to this project. Recent studies have shown that computer use and computer literacy are lower among African Americans than among the general public. Part of this is due to low incomes in many African American communities, but cultural factors may also be involved. A number of other ethnic communities in the United States place a higher value on face-to-face communication than on the anonymous communication characteristic of the Web.

Given the probable demographics of the broadcasters, certain issues would not be covered by the new newscasters. Issues such as racism, AIDS, poverty, and past slavery might be ignored. The problems of the elderly would also be less likely to be discussed. Undoubtedly, as a marketing device, corporations would provide the resources not only for their own broadcasts (as Microsoft does now) but also for broadcasts by their managers and employees. Who would sort and edit the broadcasts so that opposing voices might be heard or positions criticized?

NEW BROADCASTERS, NEW CREATIVITY

Even if the Web were flooded with Web sites and messages that were less than truthful and clearly biased, universal broadcasting would yield new voices in political debate. New positions or positions that politicians won't risk taking would be assumed. New art and new music would be made available. New forms of entertainment might arise. New conversations about the news would take place. The richness of the new voices would make a major contribution to our society.

FOR CRITICAL ANALYSIS

1. What kinds of resources might be developed to help you sort out the truth and biases generated by universal broadcasters?

2. What kind of broadcaster do you think you would want to be? What would you share with the public via the Internet?

The study of people and politics—of how people gain the information that they need to be able to choose between political candidates, to organize for their own interests, and to formulate opinions on the policies and decisions of the government—needs to take into account the role played by the media in the United States. Historically, the printed media played the most important role in informing public debate. The printed media developed, for the most part, our understanding of how news is to be reported. Today, however, more than 90 percent of all Americans use television news as their primary source of information. In the future, the Internet may become the most important source of information and political debate for Americans. If that happens, control over the gathering and sharing of news and information will be greatly changed from a system in which the media have a primary role to one in which the individual citizen may play a greater role. The chapter-opening *What If . . .* explores some of the possible consequences of such a change for the future. With that future in mind, it is important to analyze the current relationship between the media and politics.

The Media's Functions

The mass media perform a number of different functions in any country. In the United States, we can list at least six. Almost all of them can have political implications, and some are essential to the democratic process. These functions are as follows: (1) entertainment, (2) reporting the news, (3) identifying public problems, (4) socializing new generations, (5) providing a political forum, and (6) making profits. It is important to keep in mind that almost all newspapers and radio and television outlets are owned by private corporations. We will examine the growing influence of corporate giants on the media in the *Critical Perspective* presented later in this chapter.

Entertainment

By far the greatest number of radio and television hours are dedicated to entertaining the public. The battle for prime-time ratings indicates how important

Kenneth Starr, the independent counsel who investigated Bill Clinton, has been the focus of attention for the media. Indeed, one online magazine charged Starr's office with leaking information to the media from the grand jury proceedings. Following this disclosure, the White House lawyers asked the court that oversees Starr's investigation to bring charges against Starr's operation for leaking grand jury material. As the Clinton-Lewinsky scandal unfolded, the media provided the battleground for this fight over leaking news.

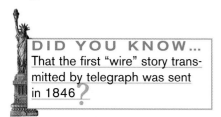

successful entertainment is to the survival of networks and individual stations.

Although there is no direct linkage between entertainment and politics, network dramas often introduce material that may be politically controversial and that may stimulate public discussion. Made-for-TV movies have focused on many controversial topics, including AIDS, incest, and wife battering.

Reporting the News

A primary function of the mass media in all their forms—newspapers and magazines, radio, television, cable, and online news services—is the reporting of news. The media convey words and pictures about events, facts, personalities, and ideas. The protections of the First Amendment are intended to keep the flow of news as free as possible, because it is an essential part of the democratic process. If citizens cannot get unbiased information about the state of their communities and their leaders' actions, how can they make voting decisions? Perhaps the most incisive comment about the importance of the media was made by James Madison, who said, "A people who mean to be their own governors must arm themselves with the power knowledge gives. A popular government without popular information or the means of acquiring it, is but a prologue to a farce or a tragedy or perhaps both."[1]

Identifying Public Problems

Public Agenda
Issues that commonly are perceived by members of the political community as meriting public attention and governmental action. The media play an important role in setting the public agenda by focusing attention on certain topics.

The power of information is important not only in revealing what the government is doing but also in determining what the government ought to do—in other words, in setting the **public agenda.** The mass media identify public issues, such as the placement of convicted sex offenders in new homes and neighborhoods. The media then influence the passage of legislation, such as "Megan's Law," which requires police to notify neighbors about the release and/or resettlement of certain offenders. American journalists also work in a long tradition of uncovering public wrongdoing, corruption, and bribery and of bringing such wrongdoing to the public's attention. Closely related to this investigative function is that of presenting policy alternatives. Public policy is often complex and difficult to make entertaining, but programs devoted to public policy increasingly are being scheduled for prime-time television. Most networks produce shows with a "news magazine" format that sometimes include segments on foreign policy and other issues.

Socializing New Generations

As mentioned in Chapter 7, the media, and particularly television, strongly influence the beliefs and opinions of all Americans. Because of this influence, the media play a significant role in the political socialization of the younger generation, as well as immigrants to this country. Through the transmission of historical information (sometimes fictionalized), the presentation of American culture, and the portrayal of the diverse regions and groups in the United States, the media teach young people and immigrants about what it means to be an American. TV talk shows, such as *Oprah,* sometimes focus on controversial issues (such as abortion or assisted suicide) that relate to basic American values (such as liberty). Many children's shows are designed not only to entertain young viewers but also to instruct them in the traditional moral values of American society. In recent years, the public has become increasingly concerned

---

[1]As quoted in "Castro vs. (Some) Censorship," editorial in the *New York Times,* November 22, 1983, p. 24.

The town meeting of yesterday gave way to the electronic town meeting of today. Here, Bill Clinton answers a question asked by a citizen in another location but whose image and voice were transmitted through video conferencing telecommunications equipment. As telecommunications that include video and voice become better and cheaper, politicians will be able to use the electronic town-meeting concept more and more.

about the level of violence depicted on children's programs and on other shows during prime time.

Providing a Political Forum

As part of their news function, the media also provide a political forum for leaders and the public. Candidates for office use news reporting to sustain interest in their campaigns, whereas officeholders use the media to gain support for their policies or to present an image of leadership. Presidential trips abroad are an outstanding way for the chief executive to get colorful, positive, and exciting news coverage that makes the president look "presidential." The media also offer a way for citizens to participate in public debate, through letters to the editor, televised editorials, or electronic mail. The question of whether more public access should be provided will be discussed later in this chapter.

Making Profits

Most of the news media in the United States are private, for-profit corporate enterprises. One of their goals is to make profits—for employee salaries, for expansion, and for dividends to the stockholders who own the companies. Profits are made, in general, by charging for advertising. Advertising revenues usually are related directly to circulation or to listener/viewer ratings. (Recent developments in the area of media ownership, particularly with respect to corporate mergers, will be discussed later in this chapter.)

Several well-known outlets are publicly owned—public television stations in many communities and National Public Radio. These operate without extensive commercials and are locally supported and often subsidized by the government and corporations.

Added up, these factors form the basis for a complex relationship among the media, the government, and the public. Throughout the rest of this chapter, we examine some of the many facets of this relationship. Our purpose is to set a foundation for understanding how the media influence the political process. (For the views of two newspaper publishers on the goals and interests of their enterprises, see the feature *E-Mail Messages from the Past* on the next page.)

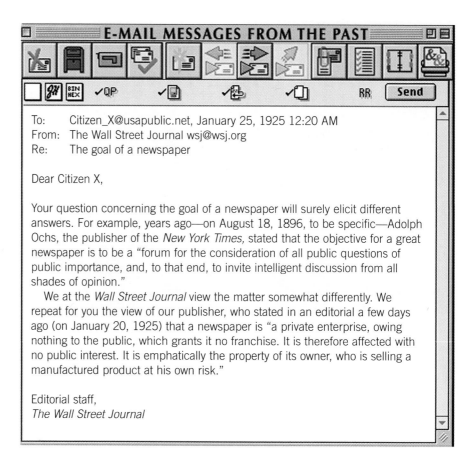

To: Citizen_X@usapublic.net, January 25, 1925 12:20 AM
From: The Wall Street Journal wsj@wsj.org
Re: The goal of a newspaper

Dear Citizen X,

Your question concerning the goal of a newspaper will surely elicit different answers. For example, years ago—on August 18, 1896, to be specific—Adolph Ochs, the publisher of the *New York Times,* stated that the objective for a great newspaper is to be a "forum for the consideration of all public questions of public importance, and, to that end, to invite intelligent discussion from all shades of opinion."

    We at the *Wall Street Journal* view the matter somewhat differently. We repeat for you the view of our publisher, who stated in an editorial a few days ago (on January 20, 1925) that a newspaper is "a private enterprise, owing nothing to the public, which grants it no franchise. It is therefore affected with no public interest. It is emphatically the property of its owner, who is selling a manufactured product at his own risk."

Editorial staff,
The Wall Street Journal

History of the Media in the United States

Many years ago Thomas Jefferson wrote, "Were it left to me to decide whether we should have a government without newspapers, or newspapers without a government, I should not hesitate a moment to prefer the latter."[2] Although the media have played a significant role in politics since the founding of this nation, they were not as overwhelmingly important in the past as they are today. For one thing, politics was controlled by a small elite who communicated personally. For another, during the early 1800s and before, news traveled slowly. If an important political event occurred in New York, it was not known until five days later in Philadelphia; ten days later in the capital cities of Connecticut, Maryland, and Virginia; and fifteen days later in Boston.

Roughly three thousand newspapers were being published by 1860. Some of these, such as the *New York Tribune,* were mainly sensation mongers that concentrated on crimes, scandals, and the like. The *New York Herald* specialized in self-improvement and what today would be called practical news. Although sensational and biased reporting often created political divisiveness (this was true particularly during the Civil War), many historians believe that the growth of the printed media played an important role in unifying the country.

---

[2]As quoted in Richard M. Clurman, "The Media Learn a Lesson," *New York Times,* December 2, 1983, p. A2.

The Rise of the Political Press

Americans may cherish the idea of a nonpartisan press, but in the early years of the nation's history, the number of politically sponsored newspapers was significant. The sole reason for the existence of such periodicals was to further the interests of the politicians who paid for their publication. As chief executive of our government during this period, George Washington has been called a "firm believer" in **managed news.** Although acknowledging that the public had a right to be informed, he felt that some matters should be kept secret and that news that might damage the image of the United States should not be published. Washington, however, made no attempt to control the press.

The Development of Mass-Readership Newspapers

Two inventions in the nineteenth century led to the development of mass-readership newspapers. The first was the high-speed rotary press; the second was the telegraph. Faster presses meant lower per-unit costs and lower subscription prices. By 1848, the Associated Press had developed the telegraph into a nationwide apparatus for the dissemination of all types of information on a systematic basis.

Along with these technological changes came a growing population and increasing urbanization. Daily newspapers could be supported by a larger, more urban population, even if the price per paper was only a penny. Finally, the burgeoning, diversified economy encouraged the growth of advertising, which meant that newspapers could obtain additional revenues from merchants who seized the opportunity to promote their wares to a larger public.

The Popular Press and Yellow Journalism

Students of the history of journalism have ascertained a change, in the last half of the 1800s, not in the level of biased news reporting but in its origin. Whereas politically sponsored newspapers had expounded a particular political party's point of view, the post–Civil War mass-based newspapers expounded whatever political philosophy the owner of the newspaper happened to have.

DID YOU KNOW...
That there are approximately 1,250 full-time radio, TV, and newspaper correspondents in Washington, D.C.?

Managed News
Information generated and distributed by the government in such a way as to give government interests priority over candor.

Reprinted with special permission of King Features Syndicate.

" INTERESTING.....IT'S LIKE A PORTABLE 500K FILE and YOU DON'T HAVE TO WAIT FOR IT TO DOWNLOAD.... AND YOU SAY IT'S CALLED A NEWSPAPER ?"

Yellow Journalism
A term for sensationalistic, irresponsible journalism. Reputedly, the term is short for "Yellow Kid Journalism," an allusion to the cartoon "The Yellow Kid" in the old *New York World*, a newspaper especially noted for its sensationalism.

Even if newspaper owners did not have a particular political axe to grind, they often allowed their editors to engage in sensationalism and what is known as **yellow journalism.** The questionable or simply personal activities of a prominent businessperson, politician, or socialite were front-page material. Newspapers, then as now, made their economic way by maximizing readership. As the *National Enquirer* demonstrates with its current circulation of more than five million, sensationalism is still rewarded by high levels of readership.

The Age of the Electromagnetic Signal

The first scheduled radio program in the United States featured politicians. On the night of November 2, 1920, KDKA-Pittsburgh transmitted the returns of the presidential-election race between Warren G. Harding and James M. Cox. The listeners were a few thousand people tuning in on very primitive, homemade sets.

By 1924, there were nearly 1,400 radio stations. But it wasn't until 8 P.M. on November 15, 1926, that the electronic media came into their own in the United States. On that night, the National Broadcasting Company (NBC) made its debut with a four-hour program broadcast by twenty-five stations in twenty-one cities. Network broadcasting had become a reality.

In a cartoon attacking yellow journalism, William Randolph Hearst (left) and Joseph Pulitzer (right) are lampooned for emphasizing scandal and gossip in news coverage.

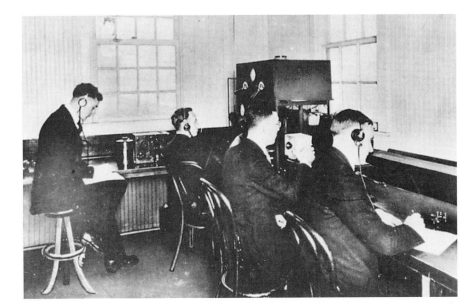

KDKA-Pittsburgh broadcast the presidential-election returns in 1920.

Even with the advent of national radio in the 1920s and television in the late 1940s, many politicians were slow to understand the significance of the **electronic media**. The 1952 presidential campaign was the first to involve a real role for television. Television coverage of the Republican convention helped Dwight Eisenhower win over delegates and secure the nomination. His vice presidential running mate, Richard Nixon, put the TV time to good use. Accused of hiding a secret slush fund, Nixon replied to his critics with his famous "Checkers" speech. He denied the attacks, cried real tears, and said that the only thing he ever received from a contributor for his personal use was his dog, Checkers. It was a highly effective performance.

Electronic Media
Broadcasting media (radio and television). The term derives from their method of transmission, in contrast to printed media.

Today, television dominates the campaign strategy of every would-be national politician, as well as that of every elected official. Politicians think of ways to continue to be newsworthy, thereby gaining access to the electronic media. Attacking the president's programs is one way of becoming newsworthy; other ways include holding highly visible hearings on controversial subjects, going on "fact-finding" trips, and gimmicks (such as a walking tour of a state). President Clinton's 1992 presidential campaign perfected the technique of "instant response," meaning that every attack was answered immediately, usually with a counterattack on the opponent.

The Revolution in the Electronic Media

Just as technological change was responsible for the end of politically sponsored periodicals, technology is increasing the number of alternative news sources today. The advent of pay TV, cable TV, subscription TV, satellite TV, and the Internet have completely changed the electronic media landscape. When there were basically only three TV networks, it was indeed a "wasteland," as former Federal Communications Commission chairman Newton Minnow once claimed. But now, with dozens of potential outlets for specialized programs, the electronic media are becoming more and more like the printed media, catering to specialized tastes. This is sometimes referred to as **narrowcasting**. Both cable television and the Internet offer the public unparalleled access to specialized information on everything from gardening and home repair to sports and religion. Most viewers are able to choose among several sources for their favorite type of programming.

Narrowcasting
Broadcasting that is targeted to one small sector of the population.

FIGURE 11-1

Network TV's Declining
Share of the Audience

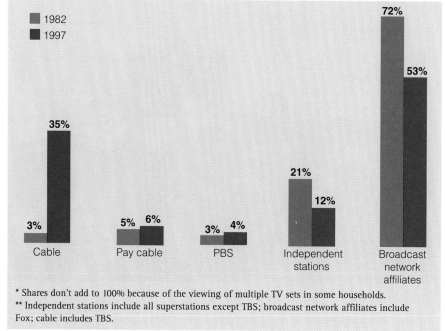

■ 1982
■ 1997

72%

53%

35%

21%

12%

3%   5% 6%   3% 4%

Cable   Pay cable   PBS   Independent   Broadcast
                                        stations   network
                                                      affiliates

* Shares don't add to 100% because of the viewing of multiple TV sets in some households.
** Independent stations include all superstations except TBS; broadcast network affiliates include
Fox; cable includes TBS.

SOURCE: *Nielsen Media Research.*

In recent years, narrowcasting has become increasingly prevalent. Consumers watch only those shows and channels that they like, and the networks' audiences are declining. As shown in Figure 11-1, between 1982 and 1997 network television's share of the audience fell from 72 percent to 53 percent. At the same time, the percentage of households having access to the Internet grew from zero to more than 40 percent, with 20 percent of all households belonging to an online service. (For some implications of news publication on the Internet, see the feature *Politics Wired: The Media and the Internet.*)

INFOTRAC®
COLLEGE EDITION

"Drudge Begrudged"

Talk-Show Politics

In the realm of politics, the multiple news outlets have given rise to literally thousands of talk shows, whether on television, radio, or the Internet. By 1997, there

TABLE 11-1

Top-Rated Radio Talk Shows in the United States

NAME	NUMBER OF STATIONS	POINT OF VIEW
Jim Bohannon	400	"Militant moderate"
Dr. Joy Brown	190	Psychologist
Alan Colmes	100	Left-of-center humorist
Bob Grant	40	Conservative
Ken Hamblin	65	Black conservative
Chuck Hardin	300	Independent
Don Imus	23*	Liberal humorist
Tom Leykis	125	Independent
S. Gordon Liddy	225	Conservative
Rush Limbaugh	660	Very conservative
Michael Reagan	100	Conservative (Ronald Reagan's son)
Dr. Laura Schlesinger	100	Psychologist
Bruce Williams	400	Fiscal conservative, social moderate

*Broadcast in 23 cities

SOURCE: "Tuning in to High-Wattage Talk Show Hosts," *USA Today,* February 1, 1995.

were more than two dozen national television talk shows; their hosts ranged from Jerry Springer, who is regarded as a sensationalist, to Larry King, whose show has become a political necessity for candidates. Ross Perot actually announced his candidacy for the presidency in the 1992 election on the *Larry King Show.*

The real blossoming of "talk" has occurred on the radio. The number of radio stations that program only talk shows has increased from about 300 in 1989 to more than 1,200 in 1998. Talk shows range from business and investment to psychology to politics. Table 11–1 shows the top-rated radio shows in the United States in 1998. There has been considerable criticism of the political talk shows, especially those hosted by Rush Limbaugh, G. Gordon Liddy, and other conservatives. Critics contend that such shows increase the level of intolerance and irrationality in American politics. The listeners to those shows are self-selected

POLITICS WIRED

The Media and the Internet

When the Internet became accessible to millions of Americans through their personal computers and the introduction of browsers that enable people to search the Web quickly, the established news media, such as the *New York Times* and *Washington Post,* were less than eager to embrace this technology. They worried that if people could read the paper free on the Internet or get online updates on sports events, they would stop buying newspapers. The three major broadcasting networks were also leery of this technology and feared that it would lure people away from television. The quick adaptation to the Web by some news outlets such as CNN, and the rapid development of electronic news resources, however, forced the major players to develop their own Web sites. In addition, the popularity of the Web became clear when, for example, millions of people around the world watched a robot vehicle scan the surface of Mars via pictures that NASA broadcast on the Internet.

Today, the media are well represented online in at least three major ways. First, the major news organizations, including the big networks— national and local radio and television stations, and national and local newspapers—have all developed Web sites. In some cases, most of a daily newspaper is available via the Internet. The major media are still struggling to figure out how to make a profit through advertising or the sale of their information on the Web.

Far more exciting is the second type of media on the Web—the purely Web-based publications. Like a crowd of rowdy children in the playyard, e-zines (magazines on the Web) are more likely to be outspoken, to have advanced graphics and interactive features, and, in some cases, to be overtly political than their print cousins are. Among the most popular are *Slate* (www.slate.com/), *Daily Muse* (www.cais.com/aschnedr/muse.htm), *Hotwired* (www.hotwired.com/), *Salon* (www.salonmagazine.com/), *news.com* (www.news.com/) and, of course, *MSNBC* (www.msnbc.

com/), and *CNN.com* (www.cnn.com/).

Of course, as soon as Congress released Independent Counsel Kenneth Starr's report on the Clinton-Lewinsky investigation, both the standard newspapers and the electronic publications provided instant access to the report on the Web. The release of the report by the *New York Times* was interrupted by hackers who replaced the front page of the Web version of the news-paper with nude photos of women. All e-zines fear such hacker invasions of their sites.

Because it is relatively simple for anyone or any organization to put up a home page or Web site, a wide variety of sites have appeared that critique the news media or give alternative interpretations of the news and the way it is presented. These sites are essential for the future usefulness of the Web for a number of reasons. For one thing, news on the Web is only made valid by its provider, and the

nation's major news organizations have a history of editing and publishing news that has been verified (Webmasters may have no such standards). Of even more importance to the phenomenon of online media is the sponsorship of Web sites by corporations. *Slate,* for example, is the creation of Microsoft Corporation. Other sites are also sponsored by corporations. How does the ordinary user know when the news provided by these online e-zines is biased toward corporate interests? How does one get access to another view of the political interests involved? In fact, the unregulated nature of the Internet has given rise to many Web sites that make it difficult to distinguish reality from fantasy in their telling of history or the news of the day.

FOR CRITICAL ANALYSIS

How can online news sites develop standards that assure the user of the authenticity of the information they provide?

INFOTRAC ®
COLLEGE EDITION

"Nets Expand to Fill News Hole"

Sound Bite
A brief, memorable comment that easily can be fit into news broadcasts.

and tend to share the viewpoint of the host. Similarly, the Internet makes it possible for a Web site to be highly ideological or partisan and to encourage chat with others of the same persuasion. One of the potential hazards of narrowcasting of this kind is that people will be less open to dialogue with those whose opinions differ from their own and that more extremism in politics may result.

The Primacy of Television

Television is the most influential medium. It also is big business. National news TV personalities such as Dan Rather may earn in excess of several million dollars per year from their TV news–reporting contracts alone. They are paid so much because they command large audiences, and large audiences command high prices for advertising on national news shows. Indeed, news *per se* has become a major factor in the profitability of TV stations. In 1963, the major networks—ABC, CBS, and NBC—devoted only eleven minutes daily to national news. By 1998, the amount of time on the networks devoted to news-type programming had increased to three hours. In addition, a twenty-four-hour-a-day news cable channel—CNN—started operating in 1980. With the addition of CNN–Headline News, CNBC, and other news-format cable channels and shows in the 1980s and 1990s, the amount of news-type programming continues to increase. News is obviously good business.

Television's influence on the political process today is recognized by all who engage in it. Its special characteristics are worthy of attention. Television news is often criticized for being superficial, particularly compared with the detailed coverage available in the *New York Times*, for example. In fact, television news is constrained by its peculiar technical characteristics, the most important being the limitations of time; stories must be reported in only a few minutes.

The most interesting aspect of television is, of course, the fact that it relies on pictures rather than words to attract the viewer's attention. Therefore, the videotapes or slides that are chosen for a particular political story have exaggerated importance. Viewers do not know what other photos may have been taken or events recorded—they note only those appearing on their screens. Television news can also be exploited for its drama by well-constructed stories. Some critics suggest that there is pressure to produce television news that has a "story line," like a novel or movie. The story should be short, with exciting pictures and a clear plot. In the extreme case, the news media is satisfied with a **sound bite,** a several-second comment selected or crafted for its immediate impact on the viewer.

It has been suggested that these formatting characteristics—or necessities—of television increase its influence on political events. (Newspapers and news magazines are also limited by their formats, but to a lesser extent.) As you are aware, real life is usually not dramatic, nor do all events have a neat or an easily understood plot. Political campaigns are continuing events, lasting perhaps two years or more. The significance of their daily turns and twists are only apparent later. The "drama" of Congress, with its 535 players and dozens of important committees and meetings, is also difficult for the media to present. What television needs is dozens of daily three-minute stories.

The Media and Political Campaigns

All forms of the media—television, newspapers, radio, and magazines—have an enormous political impact on American society. Media influence is most obvious during political campaigns. News coverage of a single event, such as the results of the Iowa caucuses or the New Hampshire primary, may be the most important factor in having a candidate being referred to in the media as the "front-runner" in presidential campaigns. It is not too much of an exaggeration to say that almost all national political figures, starting with the president, plan all public appearances and statements to snag media coverage.

Because television is the primary news source for the majority of Americans, candidates and their consultants spend much of their time devising strategies to use television to their benefit. Three types of TV coverage are generally used in campaigns for the presidency and other offices: advertising, management of news coverage, and campaign debates.

Advertising

Perhaps one of the most effective political ads of all time was a short, thirty-second spot created by President Lyndon Johnson's media adviser. In this ad, a little girl stood in a field of daisies. As she held a daisy, she pulled the petals off and quietly counted to herself. Suddenly, when she reached number ten, a deep bass voice cut in and began a countdown: "10, 9, 8, 7, 6 . . ." When the voice intoned "zero," the unmistakable mushroom cloud of an atom bomb began to fill the screen. Then President Johnson's voice was heard: "These are the stakes. To make a world in which all of God's children can live, or to go into the dark. We must either love each other or we must die." At the end of the commercial, the message read, "Vote for President Johnson on November 3."

To understand how effective this daisy girl commercial was, you must know that Johnson's opponent was Barry Goldwater, a Republican conservative candidate known for his expansive views on the role of the U.S. military. The ad's

INFOTRAC ®
COLLEGE EDITION

"Cockpit of Political Spot Post-Production"

President Lyndon Johnson's "Daisy Girl" ad contrasted the innocence of childhood with the horror of an atomic attack.

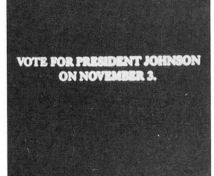

implication was that Goldwater would lead the United States into nuclear war. Although the ad was withdrawn within a few days, it has a place in political campaign history as the classic negative campaign announcement. The ad's producer, Tony Schwartz, describes the effect in this way: "It was comparable to a person going to a psychiatrist and seeing dirty pictures in a Rorschach pattern. The daisy commercial evoked Goldwater's pro-bomb statements. They were like dirty pictures in the audiences's mind."[3]

Since the daisy girl advertisement, negative advertising has come into its own. Candidates vie with one another to produce "attack" ads and then to counterattack when the opponent responds. The public claims not to like negative advertising, but as one consultant put it, "Negative advertising works." Any advertising "works" when viewers or listeners remember an ad. It is clear that negative ads are more memorable than ones that praise the candidate's virtues. Negative advertising, which supporters and independents remember longer than positive advertising, works well. No vote gain is expected anyway from members of the other party or supporters of the candidate under attack.

Too many blatantly negative ads by the candidates, of course, can alienate viewers and subject the candidates to criticism by the press and other media. Nonetheless, at least at the national level, negative ads continue to be used extensively. In fact, one study showed that 88 percent of President Clinton's ads from April to September in 1996 essentially consisted of negative messages about Bob Dole and the Republican Party.

Management of News Coverage

Using political advertising to get a message across to the public is a very expensive tactic. Coverage by the news media, however, is free; it simply demands that the campaign ensure that coverage takes place. In recent years, campaign managers have shown increasing sophistication in creating newsworthy events for journalists to cover. As Doris Graber points out, "To keep a favorable image of their candidates in front of the public, campaign managers arrange newsworthy events to familiarize potential voters with their candidates' best aspects."[4]

To take advantage of the media's interest in campaign politics, whether at the presidential level or perhaps in a Senate race, the campaign staff tries to influence the quantity and type of coverage the campaign receives. First, it is important for the campaign staff to understand the technical aspects of media coverage—camera angles, necessary equipment, timing, and deadlines—and to plan their political events to accommodate the press. Second, the campaign organization learns that political reporters and their sponsors—networks or newspapers—are in competition for the best stories and can be manipulated through the granting of favors, such as a personal interview with the candidate. Third, an important task for the scheduler in the campaign is the planning of events that will be photogenic and interesting enough for the evening news. A related goal, although one that is more difficult to attain, is to convince reporters that a particular interpretation of an event is correct.

Today, the art of putting the appropriate **spin** on a story or event is highly developed. Each presidential candidate's press advisers, often referred to as **spin doctors,** try to convince the journalists that their interpretations of the political events are correct. For example, in 1992 Bill Clinton's people tried to convince the press that he did not really expect to win the New Hampshire primary any-

Spin
An interpretation of campaign events or election results that is most favorable to the candidate's campaign strategy.

Spin Doctor
A political campaign adviser who tries to convince journalists of the truth of a particular interpretation of events.

---

[3]As quoted in Kathleen Hall Jamieson, *Packaging the Presidency: A History and Criticism of Presidential Campaign Advertising,* 3d ed. (New York: Oxford University Press, 1996), p. 200.
[4]Doris Graber, *Mass Media and American Policies,* 5th ed. (Washington, D.C.: Congressional Quarterly Press, 1997), p. 59.

way, while the Paul Tsongas camp insisted that winning the New England state was a great and unexpected victory. Journalists began to report on the different spins and on how the candidates tried to manipulate campaign news coverage.

Going for the Knockout Punch—Presidential Debates

Perhaps of equal importance to political advertisements is the performance of the candidate in a televised presidential debate. After the first such debate in 1960, in which John Kennedy, the young senator from Massachusetts, took on the vice president of the United States, Richard Nixon, candidates became aware of the great potential of television for changing the momentum of a campaign. In general, challengers have much more to gain from debating than do incumbents. Challengers hope that the incumbent may make a mistake in the debate and undermine the "presidential" image. Incumbent presidents are loath to debate their challengers, because it puts their opponents on an equal footing with them.

Three debates were held in the 1996 presidential race. The first was a formally staged and not very memorable exchange between Bill Clinton and the Republican challenger, Bob Dole. The second, also rather formal, featured the vice presidential candidates, Al Gore and Dole's Republican running mate, Jack Kemp. The two candidates engaged in relatively mild attacks on the respective presidential candidates. In the final debate, on October 16, Dole and Clinton faced off in a less formal format. They appeared together on a stage surrounded by galleries of people selected by the Gallup organization to represent a cross section of the nation. Ross Perot and Pat Choate, his running mate, were denied access to the debates by the Commission for Presidential Debate, a decision upheld by the federal courts.

The crucial fact about the practice of televising debates is that, although debates are justified publicly as an opportunity for the voters to find out how candidates differ on the issues, what the candidates want is to capitalize on the

A family watches the 1960 Kennedy-Nixon debates on television. After the debate, TV viewers thought Kennedy had won, whereas radio listeners thought Nixon had won.

In 1996, President Clinton and Bob Dole faced off in two debates. They were generally civil and respectful toward each other. Neither debate seemed to have much impact on the outcome of the 1996 elections.

INFOTRAC®
COLLEGE EDITION

"From Talking Heads to Headless Chickens"

power of television to project an image. They view the debate as a strategic opportunity to improve their own images or to point out the failures of their opponents. Candidates are very aware not only that the actual performance is important but also that the morning-after interpretation of the debate by the news media may play a crucial role in what the public thinks. Regardless of the risks of debating, the potential for gaining votes is so great that candidates undoubtedly will continue to seek televised debates.

The Media's Impact on the Voters

The question of how much influence the media have on voting behavior is difficult to answer. Generally, individuals watch television or read newspapers with certain preconceived ideas about political issues and candidates. These attitudes and opinions act as a kind of perceptual screen that filters out information that makes people feel uncomfortable or that does not fit with their own ideas.

Voters watch campaign commercials and news about political campaigns with "selective attentiveness." That is, they tend to watch those commercials that support the candidates they favor and tend to pay attention to news stories about their own candidates. This selectivity also affects their perceptions of the content of the news story or commercial and whether it is remembered. Apparently, the media are most influential with those persons who have not formed an opinion about political candidates or issues. Studies have shown that the flurry of television commercials and debates immediately before election day has the most impact on those voters who are truly undecided. Few voters who have already formed their opinions change their minds under the influence of the media.

The Role of the Media in the '98 Elections

The print and electronic media set the tone for the 1998 elections, beginning with their coverage of the Clinton-Lewinsky scandal in January of the election year. Although it was clear that most voters were very tired of the story by the time of the election, the media continued to use the scandal and the impeachment process as the theme for their election coverage.

By the time the polls closed in California, it became clear that the media had missed several of the main stories of the election. Democrats reversed electoral history by winning seats in the House of Representatives due to hard campaigning and their issue campaigns. Republicans realized that they had followed the media line instead of putting forward an issue campaign. And, to the shock of the national media, Jesse Ventura, a former professional wrestler running on the Reform Party ticket, received more votes than either the Democratic or the Republican gubernatorial candidate in Minnesota to be come governor of that state. The national media had barely noticed his participation in the campaign before election eve.

The Media and the Government

The mass media not only wield considerable power when it comes to political campaigns, but they also, in one way or another, can wield power over the affairs of government and over government officials. Perhaps the most notable example in modern times concerns the activities of *Washington Post* reporters Bob Woodward and Carl Bernstein. These two reporters were assigned to cover the Watergate break-in, and they undertook an investigation that eventually led to the resignation of President Richard Nixon.

The Media and the Presidency

A love-hate relationship clearly exists between the president and the media. During the administration of John F. Kennedy, the president was seen in numerous photos scanning the *New York Times*, the *Washington Post*, and other newspapers each morning to see how the press tallied his successes and failures. This led to frequent jocular comments about his speed-reading ability.

In the United States, the prominence of the president is cultivated by a **White House press corps** that is assigned full-time to cover the presidency. These reporters even have a lounge in the White House where they spend their days, waiting for a story to break. Most of the time, they simply wait for the daily or twice-daily briefing by the president's **press secretary.** Because of the press corps's physical proximity to the president, the chief executive cannot even take a brief stroll around the presidential swimming pool without its becoming news. Perhaps no other nation allows the press such access to its highest government official. Consequently, no other nation has its airwaves and print media so filled with absolute trivia regarding the personal lives of the chief executive and his family.

President Franklin D. Roosevelt brought new spirit to a demoralized country and led it through the Great Depression through his effective use of the media, particularly through his radio broadcasts. His radio "fireside chats" brought hope to millions. Roosevelt's speeches were masterful in their ability to forge a common emotional bond among his listeners. His decisive announcement in 1933

White House Press Corps
A group of reporters assigned full-time to cover the presidency.

Press Secretary
The individual responsible for representing the White House before the media. The press secretary writes news releases, provides background information, sets up press conferences, and so on.

President Franklin D. Roosevelt, the first president to fully exploit the airwaves for his benefit, reported to the nation through radio "fireside chats."

on the reorganization of the banks, for example, calmed a jittery nation and prevented the collapse of the banking industry, which was threatened by a run on banks, from which nervous depositors were withdrawing their assets. His famous Pearl Harbor speech, following the Japanese attack on the U.S. Pacific fleet on December 7, 1941 ("a day that will live in infamy"), mobilized the nation for the sacrifices and effort necessary to win World War II.

Perhaps no president exploited the electronic media more effectively than did Ronald Reagan. The "great communicator," as he was called, was never more dramatic than in his speech to the nation following the October 1983 U.S. invasion of the Caribbean island of Grenada. In this address, the president, in an almost flawless performance, appeared to many to have decisively laid to rest the uncertainty and confusion surrounding the event.

The relationship between the media and the president is most often reciprocal: each needs the other to thrive. Because of this co-dependency, both the media and the president work hard to exploit the other. As noted in the feature *Politics and Ethics: Reporting on Scandal,* the various news outlets made a lot

Monica Lewinsky being whisked away from reporters after she was granted transactional immunity by Kenneth Starr. Transactional immunity is the broadest form of immunity that a witness can have. It means that a witness cannot be prosecuted for anything arising from the transaction that the testimony concerns.

POLITICS and Ethics

Reporting on Scandal

Early in 1998, a news story broke that threw all of the nation's media into a maelstrom. The president of the United States, Bill Clinton, was alleged to have had an affair with a White House intern, Monica Lewinsky. The allegations were made by a friend of the intern who had taped more than twenty hours of telephone conversations with her as she talked about the president and about how, supposedly, the president encouraged her to lie about the relationship. Friends of the president were implicated in the scandal. The president responded that none of these allegations was true and that he would soon tell the public all that he knew.

In the weeks that followed, the media went into what was often called a "feeding frenzy." Eventually, even staid newspapers, such as the *New York Times*, devoted many columns to the allegations, to the potential legal charges against those involved, and to statements of Lewinsky's attorney as well as those made by White House lawyers.

Covering the Story

The news media faced several ethical issues in covering this story. First, how much of what they reported could actually be confirmed, as opposed to being secondhand information? Some news stories had to be retracted in the first few weeks. Second, did the story really justify such endless coverage? Was it really a story for the grocery store tabloids rather than the nation's leading newspapers? Editors debated whether the story was worth the effort, but because all of the others were covering it, they faced the possibility of losing sales and revenue if they stepped back from the story. In fact, all of the nation's editors and producers knew that "sex sells," and to be without this story was to lose an audience.

What to Print?

As the Clinton-Lewinsky scandal unfolded, newspaper editors were faced with other types of decisions. How graphic could the story be if it was to be read by children and discussed at home or at school? How graphic could the story be and not offend adult readers? Polls taken during 1998 showed that a majority of Americans believed that the media had acted irresponsibly in giving the scandal so much coverage, and 77 percent of those polled said that the media was more interested in "being first" with a story than in "being accurate" in their coverage.*

Competing with the Web

Any doubts that newspaper publishers had about what to print were swept aside when the House Judiciary Committee voted to publish on the Internet Independent Counsel Kenneth Starr's report on his investigation of the scandal. The committee's decision, though, posed yet

*The Gallup Organization, "The Presidential Crisis," January 28,1998.

With the Capitol in the background, members of the media watch President Clinton's videotaped grand jury testimony.

another choice for news organizations. If they posted the entire report on their Web sites, how could they deny access to the report to their print readers. What would their readers say about having such salacious material in the morning edition available to the entire family? If they did publish the report, should it be accompanied by a warning about the explicit nature of the content?

Most publishers decided to make the entire report available to the public through their Web sites and to publish in print either a summary of the report or the entire content of the executive summary in a special section. Some Internet providers, such as America Online, did post a warning to parents about the content of the report.

At least one commentator noted that the contents of the Starr report would have violated the Communications Decency Act passed by Congress two years before (see Chapter 4) if that act had not been declared unconstitutional by the Supreme Court. Others questioned whether making such materials available to the public for comment and discussion may have violated the fundamental principles of judicial process by giving public opinion too much weight in the constitutional process.

FOR CRITICAL ANALYSIS

What should be the standards for deciding what materials ought to be printed in the newspaper or posted on the Web? Who should set those standards?

of money out of the allegations about the president and White House Intern Monica Lewinsky in early 1998. According to Howard Kurtz, however, the Washington press corps was already deeply hostile toward the Clinton administration because the White House staff had so frequently attempted to "manage the news." Kurtz, in his book *Spin Cycle*,[5] describes the efforts of the White House to skirt the issues and avoid providing answers to reporters and investigators. Convinced that the administration was less than honest, the reporters, in turn, became even more critical about the president and, therefore, more likely to pursue stories by any means. According to Kurtz, each side, the press and the administration, was trying to "outspin" the other.

Setting the Public Agenda

Given that government officials have in front of them an array of problems with which they must deal, the process of setting the public agenda is constant. To be sure, what goes on the public agenda for discussion, debate, and, ultimately, policy action depends on many factors—not the least being each official's personal philosophy.

According to a number of studies, the media play an important part in setting the public agenda. Evidence is strong that whatever public problems receive the most media treatment will be cited by the public in contemporary surveys as the most important problems. Although the media do not make policy decisions, they do determine to a significant extent the policy issues that need to be decided—and this is an important part of the political process. Because those who control the media are not elected representatives of the people, the agenda-setting role of the media necessarily is a controversial one. The relationship of

[5]Howard Kurtz, *Spin Cycle: Inside the Clinton Propaganda Machine* (New York: Free Press, 1998).

the media to agenda setting remains complex, though, because politicians are able to manipulate media coverage to control some of its effects, as well as to exploit the media to further their agendas with the public.

Government Regulation of the Media

The United States has perhaps the freest press in the world. Nonetheless, regulation of the media does exist, particularly of the electronic media. Many aspects of this regulation were discussed in Chapter 4, when we examined First Amendment rights and the press.

Controlling Ownership of the Media

The First Amendment does not mention electronic media, which did not exist when the Bill of Rights was written. For many reasons, the government has much greater control over the electronic media than it does over printed media. Through the Federal Communications Commission (FCC), which regulates communications by radio, television, wire, and cable, the number of radio stations has been controlled for many years, in spite of the fact that technologically we could have many more radio stations than now exist. Also, the FCC created a situation in which the three major TV networks have dominated the airwaves.

Most FCC rules have dealt with ownership of news media, such as how many stations a network can own. Recently, the FCC has decided to auction off hundreds of radio frequencies, allowing the expansion of cellular telephone applications.

In 1996, Congress passed, and the president signed, an act that has far-reaching implications for the communications industry—the Telecommunications Act of 1996. The act ended the rule that kept telephone companies from entering the cable business and other communications markets. What this means is that a single corporation—whether AT&T or Disney—can offer long-distance and local telephone services, cable television, satellite television, Internet services, and, of course, libraries of films and entertainment. The race is on for companies to control media ownership and to develop all the needed technology. As discussed in this chapter's *Critical Perspective* on the next page, already the Disney Company has purchased ABC/Capital Cities Company, and Time Warner has acquired Turner Broadcasting. Consumers can now choose among multiple competitors for all these services delivered to the home. A single entity may own a television network; the studios that produce shows, news, and movies; and the means to deliver that content to the home via cable, satellite, or the Internet. The question to be faced in the future is how to assure competition in the delivery of the news so that citizens have access to multiple points of view from the media.

Government Control of Content

In general, the broadcasting industry has avoided government regulation of content by establishing its own code. This code consists of a set of rules developed by the National Association of Broadcasters (the lobby for the TV and radio industry) that regulate the amount of sex, violence, nudity, profanity, and so forth that is allowed on the air. (High rates of violent crime among teens have again brought the attention of Congress to media programming.) It should be noted that abiding by the code is voluntary on the part of networks and stations.

Since 1980, there has been continued public debate over whether the government should attempt to control polling and the "early calling" of presidential

Critical perspective

Bias in the Media—The Corporate Perspective

For decades, Republican politicians have complained about a liberal bias in the media, while Democratic candidates have suggested that the corporate character of newspapers makes them biased in favor of Republicans—at least in terms of endorsements on the editorial page. The recent explosion of mergers and acquisitions in the media business suggests, however, that the real source of bias in the media in the future will be corporate.

Merger Mania

Within the past five years, all of the prime-time television networks have been purchased by major American corporations and have become part of corporate conglomerates. The Turner Broadcasting/CNN network was also purchased by a major corporation, Time Warner; and Fox Television is already the child of Rupert Murdoch's publishing and media empire. In addition to these mergers and acquisitions, many of these corporations have formed partnerships with computer software makers, such as Microsoft, for joint electronic publishing ventures.

Before looking at the potential effects of these mergers, it is worth considering the scope of these corporate conglomerates. The accompanying table lists some of the components of these corporations.

Merger Bias

Each of the corporations listed in the table subscribes to the highest standards of ethics, and each has assured its network news staffs and affiliates that it respects freedom of the press. Critics are very concerned, however, that the corporations may exercise censorship over materials that might be damaging to their corporate profits and that news and information might have a bias toward their corporate business interests. One such critic, Dan Kennedy, gives evidence of corporate control in two instances: the *Jim Hightower Show*, a Texas populist talk show, was canceled soon after Disney acquired Capital Cities, presumably because Hightower had been critical of the corporate takeover on the air; and CBS's lawyers, in an attempt to avoid public and expensive lawsuits, forced *60 Minutes* to cancel an interview with a tobacco researcher who was going to talk about his research.*

Critics suggest that the corporate perspective involves very subtle forms of bias, including the suppression of news that could hurt the parent corporation, the refusal to deal with certain issues because they might potentially provoke unpopular lawsuits, and a movement toward less controversial, pure entertainment "news"—because it will offend fewer viewers. Because these major corporations control a very large percentage of local television stations, as well as other media producers (books, cable, music, movie studios), their viewpoints could become pervasive, truly limiting freedom of the press and depriving citizens of full debate on public issues.

Corporate Ownership of Media

GENERAL ELECTRIC	CBS CORPORATION (FORMERLY WESTINGHOUSE)	THE DISNEY COMPANY
GE Jet Engines	WPIC (insurance)	Movie studios
GE Appliances	Power plants	Amusement parks
GE Electrical Equipment	Waste disposal	Trade publications
GE Locomotives	Group W satellite Communication Systems	Retail stores
GE Capital Communications	Cable TV: TNN, CMT	Hockey, baseball teams
GE Lighting	Radio:	Record company
GE Medical/X-ray	21 FM stations	Home video
GE Capital (finance)	18 AM stations	Newspapers (12)
Music:	1,900 affiliates	TV/Cable:
Warner Music	TV:	Disney channel
Columbia House	CBS Network News	ESPN
Elecktra	CBS TV stations	ABC radio
NBC Network News		21 stations
NBC stations		3,400 affiliates
Cable:		ABC TV stations
CNBC		ABC Network News
Bravo,		
A & E		
History Channel		

SOURCE: "On that Chart," *The Nation*, June 3, 1996, pp. 15–27.

FOR CRITICAL ANALYSIS

1. What kinds of viewpoints might be suppressed by these corporate conglomerates?

2. How can the viewer know whether a network news broadcast is actually promoting the products or viewpoint of its owner?

*Dan Kennedy, "Merger Mania," *The Boston Phoenix*, December 5, 1995, www.bostonphoenix.com/.

elections by the television networks. On election night in 1980, before numerous states had closed their polls, the networks predicted, based on exit polls, that Ronald Reagan had been elected. The concern expressed by many was that voters on their way to vote might not bother because the victor had already been declared. It was feared that the resulting drop in turnout would particularly affect state and local races. Because some types of voters, such as factory workers, are more likely to vote late in the day, the outcomes of elections and referenda might be seriously affected.

In 1984, the networks were careful to say that they would not project winners in any state until the polling places *in that state* were closed. With the different time zones and with a concentration of population in the Northeast and Midwest, however, the networks were able to project a winner by 8 P.M. eastern time, which was 5 P.M. on the West Coast.

Some legislators and citizens have called for a ban on exit polls or on releasing them before *all* polling places in the continental United States are closed. Others have called for a federal law establishing a uniform closing time for voting so that voting would end at the same time all over the country, and thus exit polls could not be a factor. In any event, although turnout has been lower than expected in many western states, studies suggest that the early announcement of election results based on exit polls has little effect on election outcomes.

The Telecommunications Act of 1996 included two provisions that allow for some government control of the content of the media. One provision required that television manufacturers include a "V-chip" in each set. The V-chip will allow parents to block programs that include violence or sexual conduct from being viewed on their televisions. The other provision prohibited the transmission of indecent or patently offensive materials on the Internet in such a way that minors could access those materials. Responding to immediate legal challenges to this portion of the new law, two federal district courts held in 1996 that the provision blocking certain content from the Internet was unconstitutional. One court stated that this section was "profoundly repugnant" to the First Amendment's guarantee of free speech. In 1997, the Supreme Court agreed that the provision restrained too much protected adult speech and was therefore unconstitutional. Further regulation of the Internet is obviously a matter of constitutional debate (see Chapter 4).

The Public's Right to Media Access

Does the public have a right to **media access?** Both the FCC and the courts gradually have taken the stance that citizens do have a right of access to the media, particularly the electronic media. The argument is that the airwaves are public, but because they are used for private profit, the government has the right to dictate how they are used. It does so in many ways. Recall from Chapter 4 that in addition to the equal-time rule for candidates—under which broadcasters who sell airtime to political candidates must make equal time available to opposing candidates on equal terms—the FCC has also promulgated the personal attack rule. This rule allows individuals (or groups) airtime to reply to attacks that have previously been aired.

Technology is giving more citizens access to the electronic media and, in particular, to television. As more cable operators have more airtime to sell, some of that time will remain unused and will be available for public access. At the same time, the Internet makes media access by the public very easy, although not everyone has the resources to take advantage of it.

Media Access
The public's right of access to the media. The Federal Communications Commission and the courts gradually have taken the stance that citizens do have a right to media access.

Bias
An inclination or a preference that interferes with impartial judgment.

Bias in the Media

Many studies have been undertaken to try to identify the sources and direction of bias in the media, and these studies have reached different conclusions. For example, in a classic study conducted in the 1980s, the researchers found that media producers, editors, and reporters (the "media elite") had a notably liberal and "left-leaning" **bias** in their news coverage.[6] Other studies, however, have concluded that there is a pro-Republican and pro-conservative bias in the overall stance of newspapers and major networks. Still other studies assert that the press is "apolitical." For example, Calvin F. Exoo, in his study of politics in the media, suggests that journalists are neither liberal nor conservative. Rather, they are constrained by both the pro-America bias of the media ownership and the journalists' own code of objectivity. Most are more interested in improving their career prospects by covering the winning candidate and pleasing their editors to get better assignments than they are in discussing public policies.[7] Thus, the bias in the media is toward not criticizing the American system and on producing "news" that will attract viewers and readers without threatening the American way of life. This analysis would support Thomas E. Patterson's view that the real bias of the news media is to emphasize bad news and cynicism rather than any partisan position.[8]

Increasingly, the media are being criticized for their failure to provide any context—biased or not—for news events. According to one critic, the focus on the "brief now" of events tends to magnify the trivial and trivialize the important. The media convey the sense that life is just a sequence of random events in a world that "cannot be understood, shaped or controlled."[9]

The Media and Politics: Issues for the New Century

The power of the media and their impact on American society clearly are a controversial and important subject. To what extent the mass media help to clarify issues and to contribute to a more enlightened public, as opposed to distorting and oversimplifying reality, is a topic hotly debated in the United States. The increasing dependence of campaigns and candidates on the media makes this an era of symbolic politics and weakened political attachments. At the same time, the greatly expanded number of media outlets, including cable television and online services, has offered Americans more freedom to choose what they watch and read.

By 1999, the Internet had made available literally hundreds of sites allowing voters to read about candidates and "chat" with politicians, journalists, and other voters. Voters could view home pages that were advertisements for candidates and seek information about almost any topic from the great libraries of the nation. Although this interactive political forum was beyond the reach of those Americans who are not connected to the Internet, the vigor and intensity of these Internet exchanges suggest that Americans are willing and eager to express themselves in the arena of national politics. The same lesson was demonstrated

---

[6]S. Robert Lichter, Stanley Rothman, and Linda S. Lichter, *The Media Elite* (New York: Adler and Adler, 1986).

[7]Calvin F. Exoo, *The Politics of the Mass Media* (St. Paul: West, 1994), pp. 49–50.

[8]Thomas E. Patterson, *Out of Order* (New York: Knopf, 1993).

[9]James Fallows, *Breaking the News: How the Media Undermine American Democracy* (New York: Pantheon Books, 1996).

in debates in which ordinary citizens, rather than journalists, were allowed to ask the questions. At the same time, the number of partisan talk shows and cable TV channels is increasing, so Americans can choose to listen only to media outlets that support their own positions. Obviously, how to harness the potential of the mass media to allow for national debate about the good of the nation is an issue yet to be resolved.

TOWARD ACTIVE CITIZENSHIP

BEING A CRITICAL CONSUMER OF THE NEWS

Television and newspapers provide an enormous range of choice for Americans who want to stay informed. Still, critics of the media argue that a substantial amount of programming and print is colored either by the subjectivity of editors and producers or by the demands of profit making. Few Americans take the time to become critical consumers of the news, either in print or on the TV screen.

To become a critical news consumer, you must practice reading a newspaper with a critical eye toward editorial decisions. For example, ask yourself what stories are given prominence on the front page of the paper, and which ones merit a photograph. What is the editorial stance of the newspaper? Most American papers tend to have moderate to conservative editorial pages. Who are the columnists given space on the "op-ed" page, the page opposite the paper's own editorial page? For a contrast to most daily papers, occasionally pick up an outright political publication such as the *National Review* or the *New Republic* and take note of the editorial positions.

Watching the evening news can be far more rewarding if you look at how much the news depends on video effects. You will note that stories on the evening news tend to be no more than three minutes long, that stories with excellent videotape get more attention, and that considerable time is taken up with "happy talk" or human interest stories that tap the emotions of the audience.

Another interesting study you might make is to compare the evening news with the daily paper on a given date. You will see that the paper is perhaps half a day behind the news but that the print story contains far more information. Headlines must take the place of videotape in grabbing your attention.

You can also be a more active consumer by voicing your views and suggestions to the producers of television news or to the editors of newspapers and magazines through letters, by telephone, and by electronic mail. These persons are often responsive to criticism and open to constructive suggestions; you might be surprised to find them so accessible.

If you wish to obtain more information on the media and take an active role as a consumer of the news, you can contact one of the following organizations:

National Association of Broadcasters
1771 N St. N.W.
Washington, DC 20036
202-429-5300

www.nab.org

National Newspaper Association
1525 Wilson Blvd.
Arlington, VA 22209
1-800-829-4NNA
nna@as/.com

www.oweb.com/nna/

Accuracy in Media (a conservative group)
4455 Connecticut Ave. N.W., Suite 330
Washington, DC 20008
202-364-4401

www.aim.org

People for the American Way (a liberal group)
2000 M St. N.W., Suite 400
Washington, DC 20036
202-467-4999

www.pfaw.org

Key terms

bias 370

electronic media 355

managed news 353

media access 369

narrowcasting 355

press secretary 363

public agenda 350

sound bite 358

spin 360

spin doctor 360

White House press corps 363

yellow journalism 354

Chapter summary

1 The media are enormously important in American politics today. They perform a number of functions, including (a) entertainment, (b) news reporting, (c) identifying public problems, (d) socializing new generations, (e) providing a political forum, and (f) making profits.

2 The media have always played a significant role in American politics. In the 1800s and earlier, however, news traveled slowly, and politics was controlled by a small group whose members communicated personally. The high-speed rotary press and the telegraph led to self-supported newspapers and mass readership.

3 The electronic media (television and radio) are growing in significance in the area of communications. New technologies, such as cable television and the Internet, are giving broadcasters the opportunity to air a greater number of specialized programs.

4 The media wield enormous political power during political campaigns and over the affairs of government and government officials by focusing attention on their actions. Today's political campaigns use political advertising and expert management of news coverage. Of equal importance for presidential candidates is how they appear in presidential debates.

5 The relationship between the media and the president is close; each has used the other—sometimes positively, sometimes negatively. The media play an important role in investigating the government, in getting government officials to understand better the needs and desires of American society, and in setting the public agenda.

6 The media in the United States, particularly the electronic media, are subject to government regulation, although the United States has possibly the freest press in the world. Most Federal Communications Commission rules have dealt with ownership of TV and radio stations. Recent legislation has removed many rules about co-ownership of several forms of media.

7 Studies of bias in the media have reached different conclusions. Some detect a conservative bias, while others find a more liberal stance. Still other studies conclude that the media are apolitical. Recently, the media have been criticized for being biased in favor of cynicism and "bad news," as well as for not providing any context—biased or unbiased—for the events they report.

Selected print and electronic resources

SUGGESTED READINGS

Aufderheide, Patricia, ed. *Conglomerates and the Media.* New York: New Press, 1997. In this collection of essays, highly regarded scholars examine very carefully the role of corporations in the modern mass media.

Cappella, Joseph N., and Kathleen Hall Jamieson. *Spiral of Cynicism: The Press and the Public Good.* New York: Oxford University Press, 1997. The authors, after an intense examination of how the media affect voters' opinions, propose that the mass media do increase the level of cynicism in the general public through their emphasis on sound bites, exciting events, and lack of substantive reporting.

Cook, Timothy E. *Governing with the News: The News Media as Political Institution.* Chicago: University of Chicago Press, 1998. Cook reviews the history of the media and examines their position today as a powerful part of government. He looks at the interactions of the various offices and branches of government with the news media and suggests reforms to make the media more accountable in their role as a political partner in government.

Davis, Richard. *The Press and American Politics: The New Mediator.* 2d ed. Upper Saddle River, N.J.: Prentice Hall, 1996. Davis provides a historical perspective on the development of the media in the United States and their current role as the interpreter of the political scene for most citizens.

Graber, Doris A. *Mass Media and American Politics.* 5th ed. Washington, D.C.: Congressional Quarterly Press, 1997. In this new edition of a classic work, Graber gives an overview of many aspects of the mass media, including how government regulates the media, how the media decide to cover news, and how the media affect citizens' views of the world.

Jamieson, Kathleen Hall. *Packaging the Presidency: A History and Criticism of Presidential Campaign Advertising.* 3d ed. New York: Oxford University Press, 1996. This is an insightful discussion of presidential campaign advertising as it has evolved over time from printed handbills to television coverage of carefully orchestrated events.

Just, Marion H., et al. *Crosstalk: Citizens, Candidates and the Media in a Presidential Campaign.* Chicago: University of Chicago Press, 1996. The result of a lengthy study, this book analyzes how citizens respond to both the candidates' messages and the interpretations given to those messages by the media in order to form an opinion of the candidates.

Kurtz, Howard. *Spin Cycle: Inside the Clinton Propaganda Machine.* New York: Free Press, 1998. Kurtz, a member of the Washington press corps, writes about the ways that the Clinton administration tries to manipulate press coverage of its activities. Kurtz portrays the press corps as fundamentally distrustful of the president.

Mitchell, Greg. *The Campaign of the Century: Upton Sinclair's Race for Governor of California and the Birth of Media Politics.* New York: Random House, 1992. The subject of this book is the 1934 campaign of muckraking novelist Upton Sinclair, who ran for governor of California on an antipoverty platform. Frightened by his "radical" politics, the Hollywood studios and the business community hired consultants and mounted against Sinclair the first major media campaign ever, inventing the idea of political consulting.

West, Darrell M. *Air Wars: Television Advertising in Election Campaigns, 1952–1996.* Washington, D.C.: Congressional Quarterly Press, 1997. This volume examines the rise of television advertising in American campaigns, focusing particularly on the development of negative campaign ads and the efforts to keep campaign advertising truthful.

MEDIA RESOURCES

Broadcast News—A 1987 film starring Holly Hunter, Albert Brooks, and William Hurt as the members of a television news team. The film examines the ways that news broadcasts are created and satirizes the role of the handsome news anchor.

Citizen Kane—A film, based on the life of William Randolph Hearst and directed by Orson Welles, that has been acclaimed as one of the best movies ever made. Welles himself stars as the newspaper tycoon. The film also stars Joseph Cotten and Alan Ladd. Oscar-winning best film in 1941.

All the President's Men—A film, produced by Warner Brothers in 1976, starring Dustin Hoffman and Robert Redford as the two *Washington Post* reporters, Bob Woodward and Carl Bernstein, who broke the story on the Watergate scandal. The film is an excellent portrayal of the *Washington Post* newsroom and the decisions that editors make in such situations.

Logging on

The Web site of the *American Journalism Review* is a joint venture between that magazine and News Link Associates, an online research and consulting firm. This site includes features from the magazine and original content created specifically for online reading. Additionally, it provides numerous links to various publications. Go to

www.newslink.org/

The Drudge Report home page, posted by Matt Drudge, provides a handy guide to the Web's best spots for news and opinions. Its mission is one-click access to breaking news and recent columns. It provides links to specific columnists and opinion pages for magazines and major daily newspapers. Go to

www.drudgereport.com/

The Real News Web page critiques the media, promotes media activism, and calls for media reform. Its URL is

www.rain.org/~openmind/realnews.htm

To view *Slate,* the e-zine of politics and culture published by Microsoft, go to

www.slate.com/toc/FrontPorch.asp

An AP-like system for college newspapers is Uwire, offered by Northwestern University and intended to provide college papers with a reliable source of information that directly affects their readers. You can access Uwire at

www.uwire.com

The home page for the media watchdog, Accuracy in Media, has numerous links to conservative groups at

www.aim.org/

Fairness and Accuracy In Reporting (FAIR) is a national media watch group offering well-documented criticism in an effort to correct media bias and imbalance. FAIR's URL is

www.igc.org/fair/

The World News Index provides access to all news organizations that currently have Web sites at

www.stack.nl/~haroldkl/

Using the Internet for political analysis

Compare the print version of a major national newspaper—such as the *New York Times, Los Angeles Times, Wall Street Journal, Washington Post,* or *USA Today*—with its online edition from the same day. How do the two versions differ? What decisions did the editors make in regard to picture choice, headlines, placement, and length of the stories that suggest a different audience for the online edition? How does the newspaper raise revenue from each of these editions? How does the way you read the paper vary between the two editions? Which format do you think is better for generating political dialogue, and why? If you could design your own online newspaper, what features would it include?

Political Institutions

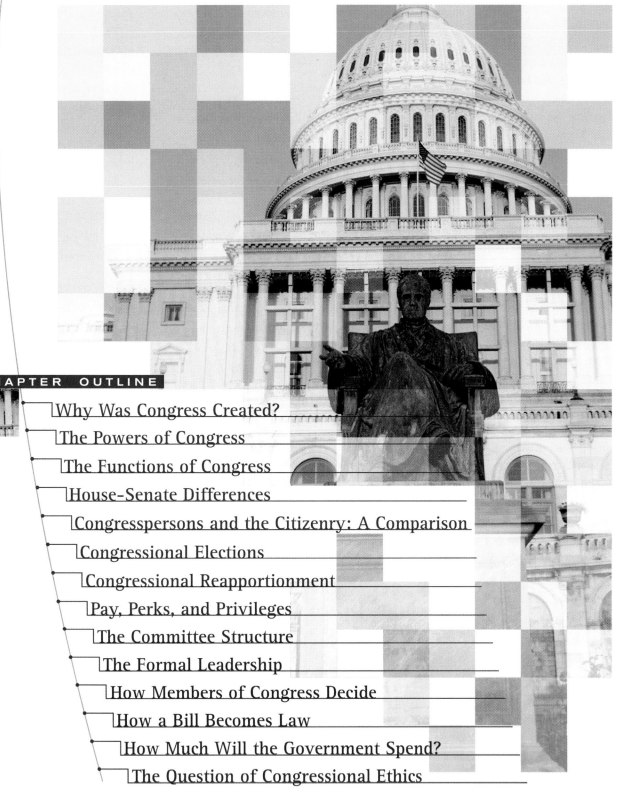

chapter **12**

The Congress

CHAPTER OUTLINE

Why Was Congress Created?

The Powers of Congress

The Functions of Congress

House–Senate Differences

Congresspersons and the Citizenry: A Comparison

Congressional Elections

Congressional Reapportionment

Pay, Perks, and Privileges

The Committee Structure

The Formal Leadership

How Members of Congress Decide

How a Bill Becomes Law

How Much Will the Government Spend?

The Question of Congressional Ethics

377

Members of Congress Were Required to Spend Six Months Each Year in Their Districts?

BACKGROUND

MEMBERS OF CONGRESS SPEND FAR MORE TIME IN WASHINGTON TALKING TO LOBBYISTS AND OTHER MEMBERS THAN THEY DO AT HOME. IN FACT, ALTHOUGH INCUMBENT MEMBERS OF CONGRESS ARE VERY DIFFICULT TO DEFEAT, A FEW OF THEM ARE CHALLENGED SUCCESSFULLY EACH ELECTION BY NEWCOMERS WHO POINT TO THE MEMBERS' WASHINGTON TOWN HOUSES AND HEAVY INVOLVEMENT WITH POLITICS "INSIDE THE BELTWAY."

SOME CONTEND THAT CONGRESSPERSONS SHOULD SPEND MORE TIME IN THEIR OWN DISTRICTS. AFTER ALL, MEMBERS OF CONGRESS ARE ELECTED TO REPRESENT THE VIEWS OF THOSE WHO ELECTED THEM—THEIR CONSTITUENTS. HOW CAN MEMBERS OF CONGRESS LEARN THEIR CONSTITUENT'S VIEWS IF THOSE MEMBERS ARE INVOLVED IN WASHINGTON POLITICS FOR MOST OF THE YEAR?

WHAT IF MEMBERS OF CONGRESS WERE REQUIRED TO SPEND SIX MONTHS EACH YEAR IN THEIR DISTRICTS?

Requiring members of Congress to be in their districts for six months each year certainly would strengthen their relationship with the voters. The voters would have far more opportunities to meet with the members and express their views. It is likely that members would be even more immersed in problem solving for ordinary citizens than they are now. It is very likely that local interests might be perceived as more powerful than they are now, and national lobbyists would have to compete with local demands. With so much time spent listening to the concerns of local workers, for example, a member of Congress might be more aware of the impact of international trade on his or her constituents.

Spending more time in the district could have the effect of reducing the legislator's tie to his or her political party. Strong state and regional interests would be likely to force the legislator to vote against the party's position if that position was contrary to constituent interests. If the legislator cultivated good constituency relations, the time spent at home probably would strengthen the power of incumbency. After all, it is much harder for voters to reject someone whom they have met and who may have helped their families or towns on an issue than it is to reject someone who is always in Washington, D.C. A new person often can get to Congress only by running for an open seat.

GETTING THE LEGISLATIVE WORK DONE

Could members of Congress complete the budget and all legislation in six months so they could go home? To be sure, most legislation could move faster than it does, particularly if members would be willing to delegate more power to committees or to the leadership. One of the problems of a speedier legislative process in Washington, D.C., however, is that not all issues might be raised or all interests considered in the process of writing legislation. Part of a representative democracy involves allowing all who have opinions to contribute to the legislative process. Shortening the time spent in Washington might reduce the amount of influence that the public has on the process. Furthermore, speeding up legislation could, in the long run, produce laws that soon would need to be reconsidered or amended. Time does allow difficult issues to be worked out.

Finally, sending members of Congress home for six months each year would transfer a great deal of power to the president and to the members of the executive branch to act without a counterbalance. While Americans might like to see more of their representatives at home, they also are unlikely to place their trust in the executive branch for six months each year.

FOR CRITICAL ANALYSIS

1. Which local interests might receive stronger representation if members spent more time at home? Which interests would be unaffected?
2. Do you think that members of Congress could transact some of their business via electronic communications systems? Is face-to-face deliberation really necessary?

Most Americans spend little time thinking about the Congress of the United States, and when they do, their opinions are frequently unflattering. For many years, the public's approval rating of Congress as a whole was about 30 percent. With the strong economy of the late 1990s, Congress's approval ratings climbed to between 40 percent and 50 percent in most polls. Most voters, however, expressed even higher approval ratings (in the range of 60 percent to 70 percent) for the members of Congress from their districts. This is one of the paradoxes of the relationship between the people and Congress. Members of the public hold the institution in relatively low regard while expressing satisfaction with their individual representatives.

Part of the explanation for these seemingly contradictory appraisals is that members of Congress spend considerable time and effort serving their **constituents.** If the federal bureaucracy makes a mistake, the senator's or representative's office tries to resolve the issue. What most Americans see of Congress, therefore, is the work of their own representatives in their home states. As suggested in this chapter's opening *What If . . .* , the tie between members of Congress and the voters might be even further strengthened if the members were at home more of the time.

Congress, however, was created to work not just for local constituents but also for the nation as a whole. Understanding the nature of the institution and the process of lawmaking is an important part of understanding how the policies that shape our lives are made.

Why Was Congress Created?

The founders of the American republic believed that the bulk of the power that would be exercised by a national government should be in the hands of the legislature. As you will recall from Chapter 2, the authors of the Constitution were strongly influenced by their fear of tyrannical kings and powerful, unchecked rulers. They were also aware of how ineffective the confederal Congress had been during its brief existence under the Articles of Confederation.

The leading role envisioned for Congress in the new government is apparent from its primacy in the Constitution. Article I deals with the structure, the powers, and the operation of Congress, beginning in Section 1 with an application of the basic principle of separation of powers: "All legislative Powers herein granted shall be vested in a Congress of the United States, which shall consist of a Senate and House of Representatives." These legislative powers are spelled out in detail in Article I and elsewhere.

The **bicameralism** of Congress—its division into two legislative houses—was in part an outgrowth of the Connecticut Compromise, which tried to balance the big-state population advantage, reflected in the House, and the small-state demand for equality in policymaking, which was satisfied in the Senate. Beyond that, the two chambers of Congress also reflected the social class biases of the founders. They wished to balance the interests and the numerical superiority of the common citizen with the property interests of the less numerous landowners, bankers, and merchants. This goal was achieved by providing in Sections 2 and 3 of Article I that members of the House of Representatives should be elected directly by "the People," whereas members of the Senate were to be chosen by the elected representatives sitting in state legislatures, who were more likely to be members of the elite. (The latter provision was changed in 1913 by the passage of the Seventeenth Amendment, which provides that senators also are to be elected directly by the people.)

The logic of separate constituencies and separate interests underlying the bicameral Congress was reinforced by differences in length of tenure. Members of the House were required to face the electorate every two years, whereas

Constituent
One of the people represented by a legislator or other elected or appointed official.

Bicameralism
The division of a legislature into two separate assemblies.

senators could serve for a much more secure term of six years—even longer than the four-year term provided for the president. Furthermore, the senators' terms were staggered so that only one-third of the senators would face the electorate every two years, along with all of the House members.

The Powers of Congress

The Constitution is both highly specific and extremely vague about the powers that Congress may exercise. The first seventeen clauses of Article I, Section 8, specify most of the **enumerated powers** of Congress—that is, powers expressly given to that body.

Enumerated Powers

The enumerated, or expressed, powers of Congress include the right to impose taxes and import tariffs; borrow money; regulate interstate commerce and international trade; establish procedures for naturalizing citizens; make laws regulating bankruptcies; coin (and print) money and regulate its value; establish standards of weights and measures; punish counterfeiters; establish post offices and postal routes; regulate copyrights and patents; establish the federal court system; punish pirates and others committing illegal acts on the high seas; declare war; raise and regulate an army and a navy; call up and regulate the state militias to enforce laws, to suppress insurrections, and to repel invasions; and govern the District of Columbia.

The most important of the domestic powers of Congress, listed in Article I, Section 8, are the rights to collect taxes, to spend, and to regulate commerce, whereas the most important foreign policy power is the power to declare war. Other sections of the Constitution give Congress a wide range of further powers. Generally, Congress is also able to establish rules for its own members, to regulate the electoral college, and to override a presidential veto.

Some functions are restricted to only one chamber. Under Article II, Section 2, the Senate must advise on, and consent to, the ratification of treaties and must accept or reject presidential nominations of ambassadors, Supreme Court

Enumerated Power

A power specifically granted to the national government by the Constitution. The first seventeen clauses of Article I, Section 8, specify most of the enumerated powers of Congress.

Representative William Jefferson, a Democrat from Louisiana, shakes hands with a constituent during a visit to his home district. Jefferson represents the Second District in Louisiana, which includes most of the city of New Orleans. After a tough fight to win his seat in 1990, Jefferson has been reelected with ease.

justices, and "all other Officers of the United States." But the Senate may delegate to the president, the courts, or department heads the power to make lesser appointments. Congress may regulate the extent of the Supreme Court's authority to review cases decided by the lower courts, regulate relations between states, and propose amendments to the Constitution.

The amendments to the Constitution provide for other congressional powers. Congress must certify the election of a president and a vice president or itself choose these officers if no candidate has a majority of the electoral vote (Twelfth Amendment). It may levy an income tax (Sixteenth Amendment) and determine who will be acting president in case of the death or incapacity of the president or vice president (Twentieth Amendment, Sections 3 and 4, and Twenty-fifth Amendment, Sections 2, 3, and 4). In addition, Congress explicitly is given the power to enforce, by appropriate legislation, the provisions of several other amendments.

The Necessary and Proper Clause

Beyond these numerous specific powers, Congress enjoys the right under Article I, Section 8 (the "elastic," or "necessary and proper," clause), "[t]o make all Laws which shall be necessary and proper for carrying into Execution the foregoing Powers [of Article I], and all other Powers vested by this Constitution in the Government of the United States, or in any Department or Officer thereof." As discussed in Chapter 3, this vague statement of congressional responsibilities set the stage for a greatly expanded role for the national government relative to the states. It also constitutes, at least in theory, a check on the expansion of presidential powers.

The Functions of Congress

The Constitution provides the foundation for congressional powers. Yet a complete understanding of the role that Congress plays requires a broader study of the functions that the national legislature performs for the American political system.

Congress, as an institution of government, is expected by its members, by the public, and by other centers of political power to perform a number of functions. Our perceptions of how good a job Congress is doing overall are tied closely to evaluations of whether and how it fulfills certain specific tasks. These tasks include lawmaking, service to constituents, representation, oversight, public education, and conflict resolution.

The Lawmaking Function

The principal and most obvious function of any legislature is **lawmaking.** Congress is the highest elected body in the country charged with making binding rules for all Americans. Lawmaking requires decisions about the size of the federal budget, about health-care reform and gun control, and about the long-term prospects for war or peace. This does not mean, however, that Congress initiates most of the ideas for legislation that it eventually considers. Most of the bills that Congress acts on originate in the executive branch, and many other bills are traceable to interest groups and political party organizations. Through the processes of compromise and **logrolling** (offering to support a fellow member's bill in exchange for that member's promise to support your bill in the future), as well as debate and discussion, backers of legislation attempt to fashion a winning majority coalition.

Lawmaking
The process of deciding the legal rules that govern society. Such laws may regulate minor affairs or establish broad national policies.

Logrolling
An arrangement in which two or more members of Congress agree in advance to support each other's bills.

Service to Constituents

Casework
Personal work for constituents by members of Congress.

Individual members of Congress are expected by their constituents to act as brokers between private citizens and the imposing, often faceless federal government. **Casework** is the usual form taken by this function of providing service to constituents. The legislator and his or her staff spend a considerable portion of their time in casework activity, such as tracking down a missing Social Security check, explaining the meaning of particular bills to people who may be affected by them, promoting a local business interest, or interceding with a regulatory agency on behalf of constituents who disagree with proposed agency regulations.

Ombudsperson
A person who hears and investigates complaints by private individuals against public officials or agencies.

Legislators and many analysts of congressional behavior regard this **ombudsperson** role as an activity that strongly benefits the members of Congress. A government characterized by a large, confusing bureaucracy and complex public programs offers innumerable opportunities for legislators to come to the assistance of (usually) grateful constituents. Morris P. Fiorina suggests somewhat mischievously that senators and representatives prefer to maintain bureaucratic confusion in order to maximize their opportunities for performing good deeds on behalf of their constituents:

> Some poor, aggrieved constituent becomes enmeshed in the tentacles of an evil bureaucracy and calls upon Congressman St. George to do battle with the dragon. . . . In dealing with the bureaucracy, the congressman is not merely one vote of 435. Rather, he is a nonpartisan power, someone whose phone call snaps an office to attention. He is not kept on hold. The constituent who receives aid believes that his congressman and his congressman alone got results.[1]

The Representation Function

Representation
The function of members of Congress as elected officials in representing the views of their constituents.

If constituency service carries with it nothing but benefits for most members of Congress, the function of **representation** is less certain and even carries with it some danger that the legislator will lose his or her bid for reelection. Generally, representation means that the many competing interests in society should be represented in Congress. It follows that Congress should be a body acting slowly and deliberately and that its foremost concern should be to maintain a carefully crafted balance of power among competing interests.

How is representation to be achieved? There are basically two points of view on this issue.

Trustee
In regard to a legislator, one who acts according to his or her conscience and the broad interests of the entire society.

The Trustee View of Representation. The first approach to the question of how representation should be achieved is that legislators should act as **trustees** of the broad interests of the entire society and that they should vote against the narrow interests of their constituents as their conscience and their perception of national needs dictate. For example, some Republican legislators supported strong laws regulating the tobacco industry in spite of the views of some of their constituents.

Instructed Delegate
A legislator who is an agent of the voters who elected him or her and who votes according to the views of constituents regardless of personal assessments.

The Instructed-Delegate View of Representation. Directly opposed to the trustee view of representation is the notion that the members of Congress should behave as **instructed delegates.** That is, they should mirror the views of the majority of the constituents who elected them to power in the first place. On the surface, this approach is plausible and rewarding. For it to work, however, we must assume that constituents actually have well-formed views on the issues that are decided in Congress and, further, that they have clear-cut preferences

---

[1]Morris P. Fiorina, *Congress: Keystone of the Washington Establishment,* 2d ed. (New Haven, Conn.: Yale University Press, 1989), pp. 44, 47.

about these issues. Neither condition is likely to be satisfied very often. Most people generally do not have well-articulated views on major issues.

In a major study of the attitudes held by members of Congress about their proper role as representatives, Roger Davidson found that neither a pure trustee view nor a pure instructed-delegate view was held by most legislators. Davidson's sampling of members of Congress showed that about the same proportion endorsed the trustee approach (28 percent) and delegate approach (23 percent) to representation. The clear preference, however, was for the **politico** position—which combines both perspectives in a pragmatic mix.[2]

The Oversight Function

Oversight of the bureaucracy is essential if the decisions made by Congress are to have any force. **Oversight** is the process by which Congress follows up on the laws it has enacted to ensure that they are being enforced and administered in the way Congress intended. This is done by holding committee hearings and investigations, changing the size of an agency's budget, and cross-examining high-level presidential nominees to head major agencies. Also, until 1983, Congress could refuse to accede to proposed rules and regulations by resorting to the **legislative veto.** This allowed one, or sometimes both, chambers of Congress to disapprove of an executive rule within a specified period of time by a simple majority vote and thereby prevent its enforcement. The legislative veto was created by 1932 legislation that directed the president to restructure the executive branch. In 1983, however, the Supreme Court ruled that such a veto violated the separation of powers mandated by the Constitution, because the president had no power to veto the legislative action. Thus, the legislative veto was declared unconstitutional.[3]

Senators and representatives increasingly see their oversight function as a critically important part of their legislative activities. In part, oversight is related to the concept of constituency service, particularly when Congress investigates alleged arbitrariness or wrongdoing by bureaucratic agencies.

The Public-Education Function

Educating the public is a function that is exercised whenever Congress holds public hearings, exercises oversight over the bureaucracy, or engages in committee and floor debate on such major issues and topics as political assassinations, aging, illegal drugs, or the concerns of small businesses. In so doing, Congress presents a range of viewpoints on pressing national questions. Congress also decides what issues will come up for discussion and decision; **agenda setting** is a major facet of its public-education function. Congressional documents are now available online at the following Web site: **thomas.loc.gov/.** Most members of Congress now have Web pages as well—see the feature *Politics Wired: Congress Goes Online* on the next page.

The Conflict-Resolution Function

Congress is commonly seen as an institution for resolving conflicts within American society. Organized interest groups and representatives of different racial, religious, economic, and ideological interests look on Congress as an access point for airing their grievances and seeking help. This puts Congress in the role of trying to resolve the differences among competing points of view by

DID YOU KNOW...
That before the Republicans reorganized House services in 1995, all members had buckets of ice delivered to their offices each day, at an annual cost of $500,000?

Politico
The legislative role that combines the instructed-delegate and trustee concepts. The legislator varies the role according to the issue under consideration.

Oversight
The responsibility Congress has for following up on laws it has enacted to ensure that they are being enforced and administered in the way in which they were intended.

Legislative Veto
A provision in a bill reserving to Congress or to a congressional committee the power to reject an action or regulation of a national agency by majority vote; declared unconstitutional by the Supreme Court in 1983.

Agenda Setting
Determining which public policy questions will be debated or considered by Congress.

---

[2]Roger Davidson, *The Role of the Congressman* (New York: Pegasus, 1969), p. 117.
[3]*Immigration and Naturalization Service v. Chadha*, 454 U.S. 812 (1983).

POLITICS W I R E D

Congress Goes Online

After the Republican victory in 1994, Speaker Newt Gingrich declared, "Information . . . [will be] available to every citizen in the country at the same moment that it is available to the highest-paid Washington lobbyist." Congress, like most institutions, did not move that quickly, but by 1999, almost all of the committees of Congress had Web sites. Many committees, in addition to posting basic schedules and agendas, posted documents and reports as soon as they were issued.

Virtually all of the senators and almost all of the representatives also now have their own Web sites. These sites, which are supported by public funds, do have some restrictions. According to the rules of both chambers, the Web sites

may not contain material that is "personal and unrelated to . . . official business." This rule, however, is difficult to interpret for many members. If a constituent seeks a senator's favorite recipe, for example, is posting that recipe personal? Representative Peter Fazio (D., Ore.) says that his constituents love the photos of his dog, his 1963 Dodge Dart, and his recipe for homebrewed beer.

Having a Web site and an e-mail address has advantages and disadvantages. Representative Ann G. Eshoo (D., Cal.) notes, "Everyone in the legislative office has total access to you 24 hours a day."*

*Jonathan Weisman, "Lawmakers Gingerly Step into the Information Age," *Congressional Quarterly Weekly Report,* November 29, 1997, p. 2935.

But a member's Web site can provide important services to constituents. The site of Representative Rick White (R., Wash.) allows constituents to apply for internships in Washington, D.C., apply for appointments to military academies, order flags, order tours of the Capitol, and register complaints electronically. Congresswoman Eshoo's "virtual office" also allows voters to send e-mail and offers forms from the Veterans Affairs Department and the Social Security Administration for constituent problem solving.

All of these electronic opportunities to reach congresspersons save time and money for both the voters and the members of Congress. Of course, such electronic access places demands on a congressperson's office staff, who must

respond to these electronic communications.

Congressional use of the Web came of age in 1998 when the House Judiciary Committee placed the entire text of Kenneth Starr's report online. A few days later, President Clinton's videotaped testimony was also on the Web. Millions of people around the world accessed the Web to view this information.

FOR CRITICAL ANALYSIS

How can a voter distinguish between straightforward information on a congressional Web site and political and partisan persuasion?

passing laws to accommodate as many interested parties as possible. To the extent that Congress meets pluralist expectations in accommodating competing interests, it tends to build support for the entire political process by all branches of government.

House-Senate Differences

Congress is composed of two markedly different—but coequal—chambers. Although the Senate and the House of Representatives exist within the same legislative institution, each has developed certain distinctive features that clearly distinguish life on one end of Capitol Hill from conditions on the other (the Senate wing is on the north side of the Capitol building, and the House wing is on the south side). A summary of these differences is given in Table 12–1.

Size and Rules

The central difference between the House and the Senate is simply that the House is much larger than the Senate. The House has 435 representatives, plus delegates from the District of Columbia, Puerto Rico, Guam, American Samoa,

TABLE **12-1**

Differences between the House and the Senate

HOUSE*	SENATE*
Members chosen from local districts	Members chosen from an entire state
Two-year term	Six-year term
Originally elected by voters	Originally (until 1913) elected by state legislatures
May impeach (indict) federal officials	May convict federal officials of impeachable offenses
Larger (435 voting members)	Smaller (100 members)
More formal rules	Fewer rules and restrictions
Debate limited	Debate extended
Less prestige and less individual notice	More prestige and more media attention
Originates bills for raising revenues	Has power to advise the president on, and to consent to, presidential appointments and treaties
Local or narrow leadership	National leadership
More partisan	Less party loyalty

*Some of these differences, such as the term of office, are provided for in the Constitution. Others, such as debate rules, are not.

and the Virgin Islands, compared with just 100 senators. This size difference means that a greater number of formal rules are needed to govern activity in the House, whereas correspondingly looser procedures can be followed in the less crowded Senate. This difference is most obvious in the rules governing debate on the floors of the two chambers.

The Senate normally permits extended debate on all issues that arise before it. In contrast, the House operates with an elaborate system in which its **Rules Committee** normally proposes time limitations on debate for any bill, and a majority of the entire body accepts or modifies those suggested time limits. As a consequence of its stricter time limits on debate, the House, despite its greater size, often is able to act on legislation more quickly than the Senate.

Debate and Filibustering

According to historians, the Senate tradition of unlimited debate, which is known as **filibustering**, dates back to 1790, when a proposal to move the U.S. capital from New York to Philadelphia was stalled by such time-wasting tactics. This unlimited-debate tradition—which also existed in the House until 1811—is not absolute, however.

Under Senate Rule 22, debate may be ended by invoking **cloture**, or shutting off discussion on a bill. Amended in 1975 and 1979, Rule 22 states that debate may be closed off on a bill if sixteen senators sign a petition requesting it and if, after two days have elapsed, three-fifths of the entire membership (sixty votes, assuming no vacancies) vote for cloture. After cloture is invoked, each senator may speak on a bill for a maximum of one hour before a vote is taken.

In 1979, the Senate extended Rule 22 to provide that a final vote must take place within one hundred hours of debate after cloture has been imposed. It further limited the use of multiple amendments to stall postcloture final action on a bill.

Rules Committee
A standing committee of the House of Representatives that provides special rules under which specific bills can be debated, amended, and considered by the House.

Filibustering
In the Senate, unlimited debate to halt action on a particular bill.

Cloture
A method to close off debate and to bring the matter under consideration to a vote in the Senate.

INFOTRAC ®
COLLEGE EDITION

"While Congress Plays Games"

Prestige

As a consequence of the greater size of the House, representatives generally cannot achieve as much individual recognition and public prestige as can members of the Senate. Senators, especially those who openly express presidential ambitions, are better able to gain media exposure and to establish careers as spokespersons for large national constituencies. To obtain recognition for his or her activities, a member of the House generally must do one of two things. He or she might survive in office long enough to join the ranks of the leadership on committees or within the party. Alternatively, the representative could become an expert on some specialized aspect of legislative policy—such as tax laws, the environment, or education. (For another difference between the House and the Senate, see the feature *Politics and the Constitution: The Power to Impeach*.)

POLITICS and the Constitution

The Power to Impeach

House Judiciary Committee Chairman Henry Hyde along with other members of the committee at a news conference after the House had voted to approve impeachment inquiry of President Clinton.

The Constitution of the United States refers to the impeachment process several times. Article II, Section 4, states as follows: "The President, Vice President and all civil Officers of the United States, shall be removed from Office on Impeachment for, and Conviction of Treason, Bribery, or other high Crimes and Misdemeanors." Article I, Sections 2 and 3, specify how the process of impeachment and conviction is to be carried out. In this process, the House and the Senate play different, but clearly defined roles.

The authority to impeach (that is, to accuse, or charge) is vested in the House of Representatives, and formal impeachment proceedings are initiated there. In the House, a representative must list the charges against the president, vice president, or other civil officer. The impeachment charges are referred either to the Judiciary Committee or to a special investigating committee. If a majority in the House votes for impeachment, then articles of impeachment are drawn up, which set forth the basis for the removal of the executive-branch officer.

The actual trial of impeachment, however, is conducted in the Senate, with all members sitting in judgment. The chief justice of the United States Supreme Court presides over the Senate trial. A two-thirds vote of the senators present is required for conviction. The only punishment that Congress can mete out is removal from office and disqualification from holding any other federal office. Of course, the convicted official is subject to further punishment according to law.

The different roles for the House and the Senate reflect the founders' views of the two chambers. Because House members were expected to represent the volatile will of the people, the founders did not give that chamber the final authority to convict and remove a federal officer. Rather, this authority was given to the Senate. The founders viewed the Senate as the more stable chamber—because of its longer terms and because it was further removed from popular influence (remember that until the passage of the Seventeenth

Amendment in 1913, senators were elected not directly by the voters but by members of the House of Representatives).

FOR CRITICAL ANALYSIS:

Do you think that the founders, by making the impeachment process so difficult and complex, were trying to neutralize the effect of partisan politics in the impeachment process?

Congresspersons and the Citizenry: A Comparison

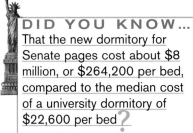

Government institutions are given life by the people who work in them and shape them as political structures. Who, then, are the members of Congress, and how are they elected?

Members of the U.S. Senate and the U.S. House of Representatives are not typical American citizens. As can be seen in Table 12–2, members of Congress are older than most Americans, partly because of constitutional age requirements and partly because a good deal of political experience normally is an advantage in running for national office. Members of Congress are also disproportionately white, male, Protestant, and trained in higher-status occupations. Lawyers are by far the largest occupational group among congresspersons, although the proportion of lawyers in the House is lower now than it was in the past.

Congressional Characteristics after the '98 Elections

elections '98

The 1998 elections did not significantly alter the make-up of Congress. The number of women in the House of Representatives increased from fifty-four to fifty-six, but the number of women in the Senate (nine) remained the same as before. Senator Carol Moseley-Braun's defeat left the Senate with no African American members, while in the House the number of African Americans remained the same at thirty-nine. The number of Hispanics also remained the same at twenty. The other characteristics of Congress listed in Table 12-2 were largely unchanged by the election outcomes.

TABLE 12-2

Characteristics of the 105th Congress (1997–1999)

CHARACTERISTIC	U.S. POPULATION (1990)	HOUSE	SENATE
Age (median)	33.0	50.9	58.4
Percentage minority	28.0	13.5	4
Religion			
Percentage church members	61.0	98	99
Percentage Roman Catholic	39.0	30	24
Percentage Protestant	56.0	63	61
Percentage Jewish	4.0	5.5	9
Percentage female	51.9	11	9
Percentage with college degrees	21.4	93	94
Occupation			
Percentage lawyers	2.8	39	54
Percentage blue-collar workers	20.1	0	0
Family income			
Percentage of families earning over $50,000 annually	22.0	100	100
Personal wealth			
Percentage of population with assets over $1 million	0.7	16	33

Congressional Elections

The process of electing members of Congress is decentralized. Congressional elections are operated by the individual state governments, which must conform to the rules established by the U.S. Constitution and by national statutes. The Constitution states that representatives are to be elected every second year by popular ballot, and the number of seats awarded to each state is to be determined by the results of the decennial census. Each state has at least one representative, with most congressional districts having about half a million residents. Senators are elected by popular vote (since the passage of the Seventeenth Amendment) every six years; approximately one-third of the seats are chosen every two years. Each state has two senators. Under Article I, Section 4, of the Constitution, state legislatures are given control over "[T]he Times, Places and Manner of holding Elections for Senators and Representatives"; however, "the Congress may at any time by Law make or alter such Regulations."

Candidates for Congressional Elections

Candidates for congressional seats may be self-selected, or, in districts where one party is very strong, they may be recruited by the local minority party leadership.[4] Candidates may resemble the voters of the district in terms of ethnicity or religion, but they are also likely to be very successful individuals who have been active in politics before. Additionally, with respect to House seats, they are likely to have local ties to their districts. Candidates most likely choose to run because they believe they would enjoy the job and its accompanying status. (For Abraham Lincoln's views on his experience in Congress, see the feature *E-Mail Messages from the Past*.) They also may be thinking about a House seat as a stepping stone to future political office as a senator, governor, or presidential candidate.

---

[4]See the work of Gary Jacobson, *The Politics of Congressional Elections*, 4th ed. (New York: Longman Publishers, 1997).

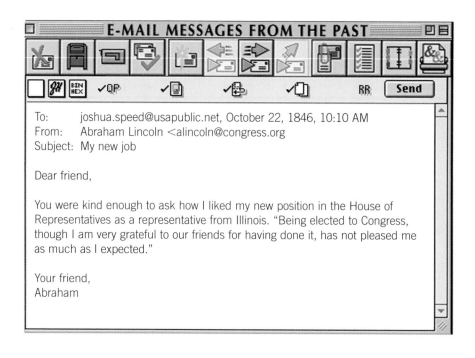

E-MAIL MESSAGES FROM THE PAST

To: joshua.speed@usapublic.net, October 22, 1846, 10:10 AM
From: Abraham Lincoln <alincoln@congress.org
Subject: My new job

Dear friend,

You were kind enough to ask how I liked my new position in the House of Representatives as a representative from Illinois. "Being elected to Congress, though I am very grateful to our friends for having done it, has not pleased me as much as I expected."

Your friend,
Abraham

Congressional campaigns have changed considerably in the past two decades. Like all other campaigns, they are much more expensive, with the average cost of a winning Senate campaign now being $4.7 million and a winning House campaign averaging more than $675,000. Campaign funds include direct contributions regulated by law (as discussed in Chapter 10), political action committee (PAC) contributions, and "soft money" funneled through the national and state party committees. Once in office, legislators spend some time almost every day raising funds for their next campaign.

Most candidates for Congress must win the nomination through a **direct primary,** in which **party identifiers** vote for the candidate who will be on the party ticket in the general election. To win the primary, candidates may take more liberal or more conservative positions to get the votes of party identifiers. In the general election, they may moderate their views to attract the votes of independents and voters from the other party.

Presidential Effects. Congressional candidates are always hopeful that a strong presidential candidate on the ticket will have "coattails" that will sweep in senators and representatives of the same party. In fact, coattail effects have been quite limited in this century, appearing only in landslide elections such as Lyndon Johnson's victory over Barry Goldwater in 1964. Members of Congress who are from contested districts or who are in their first term are more likely to experience the effect of midterm elections, which are held in the even-numbered years in between presidential contests. In these years, voter turnout falls sharply, and the party controlling the White House normally loses seats in Congress. Additionally, voters in midterm elections often are responding to incumbency issues, because there is no presidential campaign. The result is a fragmentation of party authority and a loosening of ties between Congress and the president. Table 12–3 shows the pattern for midterm elections since 1942.

Direct Primary
An intraparty election in which the voters select the candidates who will run on a party's ticket in the subsequent general election.

Party Identifier
A person who identifies with a political party.

TABLE 12-3

Midterm Losses by the Party of the President, 1942 to 1998

SEATS LOST BY THE PARTY OF THE PRESIDENT IN THE HOUSE OF REPRESENTATIVES	
1942	−45 (D.)
1946	−55 (D.)
1950	−29 (D.)
1954	−18 (R.)
1958	−47 (R.)
1962	−4 (D.)
1966	−47 (D.)
1970	−12 (R.)
1974	−48 (R.)
1978	−15 (D.)
1982	−26 (R.)
1986	−5 (R.)
1990	−8 (R.)
1994	−52 (D.)
1998	+5 (D.)

Former lieutenant governor of Ohio Nancy Hollister campaigns in Ohio's Sixth District, in southeastern Ohio. Hollister ran against Democrat Ted Strickland, who won the seat in 1992 after campaigning for it in three previous elections. This district is almost evenly divided between Republicans and Democrats, making election outcomes difficult to predict. Strickland lost his seat in 1994 but won it back again in 1996 and retained it in 1998.

The Power of Incumbency

The power of incumbency in the outcome of congressional elections cannot be overemphasized. Table 12–4 shows that the overwhelming majority of representatives and a smaller proportion of senators who decide to run for reelection are successful. This conclusion holds for both presidential-year and midterm elections. David R. Mayhew argues that the pursuit of reelection is the strongest motivation behind the activities of members of Congress. The reelection goal is

TABLE 12-4

The Power of Incumbency

	PRESIDENTIAL-YEAR ELECTIONS						**MIDTERM ELECTIONS**						
	1976	**1980**	**1984**	**1988**	**1992**	**1996**	**1974**	**1978**	**1982**	**1985**	**1990**	**1994**	**1998**
House													
Number of incumbent candidates	384	398	409	409	368	382	391	382	393	393	407	382	401
Reelected	368	361	390	402	325	359	343	358	352	385	391	347	394
Percentage of total	95.8	90.7	95.4	98.3	88.9	93.4	87.7	93.7	90.1	98.0	96.1	90.8	98.2
Defeated	16	37	19	7	43	23	48	24	39	8	16	35	8
In primary	3	6	3	1	19	2	8	5	10	2	1	1	1
In general election	13	31	16	6	24	21	40	19	29	6	15	34	7
Senate													
Number of incumbent candidates	25	29	29	27	28	21	27	25	30	28	32	26	29
Reelected	16	16	26	23	23	19	23	15	28	21	31	24	26
Percentage of total	64.0	55.2	89.6	85	82.1	90	85.2	60.0	93.3	75.0	96.9	92.3	89.6
Defeated	9	13	3	4	5	2	4	10	2	7	1	2	3
In primary	0	4	0	0	1	1	2	3	0	0	0	0	0
In general election	9	9	3	4	4	1	2	7	2	7	1	2	3

SOURCE: Norman Ornstein, Thomas E. Mann, and Michael J. Malbin, *Vital Statistics on Congress, 1993–1994* (Washington, D.C.: Congressional Quarterly Press, 1994), pp. 56–57; *Congressional Quarterly Weekly Report*, November 7, 1992, pp. 3551, 3576; and authors' update.

pursued in three major ways: by *advertising,* by *credit claiming,* and by *position taking.*[5] Advertising includes using the mass media, making personal appearances with constituents, and sending newsletters—all to produce a favorable image and to make the incumbent's name a household word. Members of Congress try to present themselves as informed, experienced, and responsive to people's needs. Credit claiming focuses on the things a legislator claims to have done to benefit his or her constituents—by fulfilling the congressional casework function or bringing money for mass transit to the district, for example. Position taking occurs when an incumbent explains his or her voting record on key issues; makes public statements of general support for presidential decisions; or indicates that he or she specifically supports positions on key issues, such as gun control or anti-inflation policies. Position taking carries with it certain risks, as the incumbent may lose support by disagreeing with the attitudes of a large number of constituents. (One way to limit the power of incumbency is by limiting the terms of members of Congress—see the feature *Politics and the Law: Legislating Term Limits* on page 392.)

[5]David R. Mayhew, *Congress: The Electoral Connection* (New Haven, Conn.: Yale University Press, 1974).

Citizens display signs that show their support for term limits for members of Congress. The movement toward establishing term limits gathered steam in the early 1990s, and by 1994 more than twenty states had passed laws imposing such limits on members of Congress elected in those states. In 1995, however, the Supreme Court held that these laws were unconstitutional. Because the Constitution did not provide for limiting the number of terms a congressperson could serve, term limits could only be established by a constitutional amendment. The Court's decision did not end the controversy over this issue, however, as this photo indicates.

POLITICS and the Law

Legislating Term Limits

Since the early 1990s, a national political movement has been under way to put term limits in place for state legislators and members of Congress. Remember that the president is limited to two terms in office by the Twenty-second Amendment to the Constitution. By 1992, fourteen states had approved term limits for their representatives to Congress, and by 1994 more than twenty states had approved such limits.

The rationale for term limits for congresspersons, as well as state legislators, is that the founders originally intended for members of Congress to be amateur politicians who took time from their farms and businesses to commit some years to public service. Holding a congressional seat was not intended to be a lifelong career.

Supporters of term limits argue that many members of Congress are "out of touch" with their constituents, too interested in the politics of Washington, D.C., and too subject to the influence of Washington lobbyists. If members of Congress were limited in their tenure, sup-porters of term limits reason, a wider variety of individuals with new ideas would be able to serve there, and no member could amass the power that comes with long incumbency.

Regardless of the wishes of the voters in the states, the Supreme Court overturned an Arkansas term-limits law for members of Congress in 1995 in *Term Limits v. Arkansas.** The Court ruled that the states could not change the terms of office that are speci-fied in the Constitution. Of course, term limits could be effected by a constitutional amendment, but this does not seem to be on Congress's agenda. There is a national organization, however, that encourages candidates for Congress to "take the pledge," meaning that they promise to serve only for some specified number of terms before they are even elected and agree to support a term-limits constitutional amendment. There is no evi-dence yet as to whether suc-cessful candidates live up to their pledge.

The issue of term limits is likely to be around for some time, although the states that have established term limits for their legislatures (see the table for the list) are seeing some adverse effects of these provisions. For example, in some states that have term limits it is clear to those who work with the legislatures that it is difficult for anyone to become a true leader and effective legislator in a short time. Additionally, in some states legislators who have little information or back-ground on the issues that confront modern govern-ments now predominate. Finally, rather than casting votes without fear of retribu-tion from the voters, some "term-limited" state legisla-tors have turned out to be highly ideological and are using their votes on princi-ples to build a reputation for their campaigns for future, higher offices.

FOR CRITICAL ANALYSIS

If a constitutional amend-ment for congressional term limits were adopted in Congress, do you think the states would ratify it? Why or why not?

*514 U.S. 779 (1995).

State Legislative Term Limits

STATE	PASSED	TERMS LIMITED TO:
Arizona	1992	8 yr in legislature
Arkansas	1992	House: 6 yr/Senate: 8 yr
California	1990	House: 6 yr/Senate: 8 yr
Colorado	1990	House: 8 yr/Senate: 8 yr
Florida	1992	House: 8 yr/Senate: 8 yr
Idaho	1994	House: 8 yr/Senate 8 yr
Louisiana	1995	House: 12 yr/Senate: 8 yr
Maine	1993	House: 8 yr/Senate: 8 yr
Michigan	1992	House: 6 yr/Senate: 8 yr
Missouri	1992	House: 8 yr/Senate: 8 yr
Montana	1992	House: 8 yr/Senate: 8 yr
Nevada	1994	House: 12 yr/Senate: 12 yr
Ohio	1992	House: 8 yr/Senate: 8 yr
Oklahoma	1990	12 yr in legislature
Oregon	1992	House: 6 yr/Senate: 8 yr
South Dakota	1992	House: 8 yr/Senate: 8 yr
Utah	1994	House: 12 yr/Senate: 12 yr
Washington	1992	House: 6 yr/Senate: 8 yr
Wyoming	1992	House: 6 yr/Senate: 12 yr

SOURCE: *U.S. Term Limits, 1998.*

The Shakeup in the 1994 Elections

The 1994 midterm elections swept the Democratic majority in both chambers of Congress out of power and brought in a Republican majority in a nationwide change of government that surprised and shocked the members of Congress and the parties themselves. According to exit polls taken on election day, Republican candidates for Congress won the votes of their own party identifiers, of the majority of independents, and of those who had voted for independent candi-

INFOTRAC®
COLLEGE EDITION

"Same as the Old Boss—Term Limits"

date H. Ross Perot in 1992, but of very few Democratic voters. Republicans captured the votes of white males, with a gender gap of about 8 percent. Republicans won 19 more seats in the South, giving them a 73–64 seat majority in that region. In Washington, the speaker of the House, Tom Foley, was defeated, the first speaker to be denied reelection since 1862. In total, the Democrats lost 53 seats, with 190 incumbents reelected and 35 defeated. All Republican incumbents in the House were reelected.

The 1994 elections resulted in a "divided" government, which was reaffirmed by the voters in 1996 and 1998. The *Critical Perspective* on the following pages discusses the issue raised by a government with no majority.

Party Control of Congress after the '98 Elections

elections '98

By the time the votes were counted on election night in 1998, it was clear that the Republicans, while retaining their majorities in both the House and the Senate, had suffered a major defeat, one which would force them into a new approach to lawmaking in the 106th Congress. The Democratic gain of the five seats in the house, which countered a long historic trend, left the Republicans with a very slim majority in that chamber: the Republicans held 223 seats; the Democrats 211 seats; and one seat was held by an independent. The Senate majority was unchanged by the elections. Republicans still held 55 Senate seats, and Democrats held 45.

This slim majority maintained by the Republicans in the House greatly decreases their chances for advancing a conservative agenda. In fact, most pundits suggested that it would be difficult to find even the 218 votes needed to vote for articles of impeachment against the president. Furthermore, the Republican Party in the House was divided between those who favored working with Democrats and the president to get legislation passed, even though the legislation might not meet their conservative goals, and those Republicans who believed that their party has not fought hard enough to further conservative ideals. In such a situation, moderate Republicans and moderate Democrats may find common ground in policymaking.

Congressional Reapportionment

By far the most complicated aspects of the mechanics of congressional elections are the issues of **reapportionment** (the allocation of seats in the House to each state after each census) and **redistricting** (the redrawing of the boundaries of the districts within each state).[6] In a landmark six-to-two vote in 1962, the Supreme Court made reapportionment a **justiciable** (that is, a reviewable) **question** in the Tennessee case of *Baker v. Carr*[7] by invoking the Fourteenth Amendment principle that no state can deny to any person "the equal protection of the laws." This principle was applied directly in the 1964 ruling, *Reynolds v. Sims,*[8] when the Court held that *both* chambers of a state legislature must be apportioned with equal populations in each district. This "one person, one vote" principle was

Reapportionment
The allocation of seats in the House of Representatives to each state after each census.

Redistricting
The redrawing of the boundaries of the congressional districts within each state.

Justiciable Question
A question that may be raised and reviewed in court.

---

[6]For an excellent discussion of these issues, see *Congressional Districts in the 1990s* (Washington, D.C.: Congressional Quarterly Press, 1993).
[7]369 U.S. 186 (1962). The term *justiciable* is pronounced juhs-*tish*-a-buhl.
[8]377 U.S. 533 (1964).

Critical perspective

Gridlock or Constitutional Balance?

By the end of George Bush's presidency, the relationship between Congress and the president was frequently described as one of gridlock. The term described the political standoff between Bush and the Democratic majority in Congress. Few of the bills that the president introduced could be passed, and he successfully vetoed a number of bills that the Democrats in Congress passed. In fact, the Democratic Party used Bush's presidential term to try to convince the electorate that it was time, after twelve years, to put a Democrat in the White House, because the Democratic-controlled Congress would work more effectively with a Democratic administration.

The relationship between the president and Congress is structured constitutionally to prevent either branch from being totally dominant. Because of checks and balances, including the veto, the veto override, the nomination and treaty processes, and the different constituencies and terms in office of members of the House and the Senate, presidential success with Congress is difficult to achieve. Some presidents of the same party as the majority in Congress have had great success after landslide elections, such as Franklin Roosevelt in 1933 and Lyndon Johnson in 1965. This happened, in part, because many new Democrats were elected with the president. Sometimes, as in Ronald Reagan's case, a president who does not control the chambers of Congress still can have great legislative success. Reagan's personal electoral victory and great popularity with the public seemed to generate congressional cooperation.

Remember that checks and balances were put into the Constitution to assure exactly what has happened–to make sure that it would not be too easy for an electoral majority, either for the president or in Congress, to make changes too quickly. In fact, opinion polls in 1997 found that 67 percent of the public approved of a divided government, believing that it kept the political parties and the government from gaining too much power.*

*Hart and Teeter poll for NBC News/*Wall Street Journal,* reported in *The Public Perspective,* February/March 1998, p. 48.

The Occurrence of Divided Government Following Presidential and Midterm Elections, 1864–1998

ELECTION YEARS	ELECTIONS RESULTING IN DIVIDED GOVERNMENT		
	% PRESIDENTIAL ELECTIONS	% MIDTERM ELECTIONS	% ALL ELECTIONS
1864–1894	25 (2/8)	75 (6/8)	50 (8/16)
1896–1966	6 (1/18)	28 (5/18)	17 (6/36)
1968–1998	75 (6/8)	88 (7/8)	81 (13/16)

Note: The numbers in parentheses are the actual number of elections in the category that resulted in divided government and the total number of presidential or midterm elections held in that period.
SOURCE: James E. Campbell, *The Presidential Pulse of Congressional Elections* (Lexington, Ky.: University Press of Kentucky, 1993), p. 212; and authors' update.

applied to congressional districts in the 1964 case of *Wesberry v. Sanders,*[9] based on Article I, Section 2, of the Constitution, which requires that congresspersons be chosen "by the People of the several States."

Severe malapportionment of congressional districts prior to *Wesberry* had resulted in some districts containing two or three times the populations of other districts in the same state, thereby diluting the effect of a vote cast in the more populous districts. This system generally had benefited the conservative populations of rural areas and small towns and harmed the interests of the more heavily populated and liberal urban areas. In fact, suburban areas have benefited the most from the *Wesberry* ruling, as suburbs account for an increasingly larger proportion of the nation's population, and cities include a correspondingly smaller segment of the population.

[9]376 U.S. 1 (1964).

Critical perspective

Gridlock or Constitutional Balance?—continued

In 1992, the voters were presented with a choice between a continuation of divided government, a Democratic-controlled government, or (in the case of H. Ross Perot) a nonpartisan presidency. Historically, there have been cycles of divided government, as shown in the accompanying table, with higher proportions before 1894 and since 1968. The question for consideration is whether a "unified" government is more likely than a "divided government" to pass legislation.

At the end of his first year in office, President Bill Clinton declared that "gridlock was over." He saluted the effectiveness of the Democratic leadership in Congress in passing his tax increase/deficit reduction plan; the family leave plan; the national service plan; and the North American Free Trade Agreement (NAFTA). The president vetoed no bills in 1993.

Scholars, however, suggest that the election of a president who is of the same party as the majority in Congress does not guarantee smooth sailing. Both David Mayhew and Roger Davidson argue that historically divided government is not related to deadlock in legislation.[†] Dwight Eisenhower, Richard Nixon, Ronald Reagan, and George Bush all were able to pass important legislation with Democratic control of one or both chambers of Congress. Democratic President Jimmy Carter, with a Democratic majority, had as much difficulty as any other president.

[†]David Mayhew, *Divided We Govern* (New Haven: Yale University Press, 1991); and Roger Davidson, "The Presidency and Three Eras of the Modern Congress," in *Divided Democracy*, ed. by James A. Thurber (Washington, D.C.: Congressional Quarterly Press, 1991).

President Bill Clinton's chance to work with a Democratic Congress ended abruptly with the 1994 election. For the first year after the election of the Republican-controlled House and Senate, the president and Congress seemed to be truly ineffective. The fight over the passage of the federal budget brought some areas of the government to a halt before the president and the congressional leadership were able to forge a deal. Actually, Clinton gained in popularity when he vetoed Republican bills that he felt he could not approve, and the Republicans in Congress gained in respect when they were able to pass major bills after compromising with their Democratic colleagues.

In 1996, the voters returned both the Democratic president and the Republican-controlled Congress to Washington. In the years of divided government, President Clinton and Congress have had major legislative accomplishments, including the restructuring of telecommunications laws and agricultural subsidies, welfare reform, and a balanced budget, which created a surplus in the federal budget in 1999 for the first time in three decades.

Along with the strong economy, this era of cooperation between the president and Congress, in spite of their partisan differences, produced an increase in job approval ratings for both Congress and the president.

FOR CRITICAL ANALYSIS
1. Who would be in favor of gridlock?
2. How did the Constitution provide for the possibility of gridlock?

Gerrymandering

Although the general issue of reapportionment has been dealt with fairly successfully by the one person, one vote principle, the **gerrymandering** issue has not yet been resolved. This term refers to the legislative boundary-drawing tactics that were used by Elbridge Gerry, the governor of Massachusetts, in the 1812 elections (see Figure 12–1 on page 396). A district is said to have been gerrymandered when its shape is altered substantially by the dominant party in a state legislature to maximize its electoral strength at the expense of the minority party. This can be achieved by either concentrating the opposition's voter support in as few districts as possible or by diffusing the minority party's strength by spreading it thinly across many districts.

In 1986, the Supreme Court heard a case that challenged gerrymandered congressional districts in Indiana. The Court ruled for the first time that redistricting for the political benefit of one group could be challenged on constitutional

Gerrymandering
The drawing of legislative district boundary lines for the purpose of obtaining partisan or factional advantage. A district is said to be gerrymandered when its shape is manipulated by the dominant party in the state legislature to maximize electoral strength at the expense of the minority party.

FIGURE 12-1

The Original Gerrymander
The practice of "gerrymandering"—the excessive manipulation of the shape of a legislative district to benefit a certain incumbent or party—is probably as old as the republic, but the name originated in 1812. In that year, the Massachusetts legislature carved out of Essex County a district that historian John Fiske said had a "dragonlike contour." When the painter Gilbert Stuart saw the misshapen district, he penciled in a head, wings, and claws and exclaimed, "That will do for a salamander!" Editor Benjamin Russell replied, "Better say a Gerrymander" (after Elbridge Gerry, then governor of Massachusetts).

SOURCE: *Congressional Quarterly's Guide to Congress,* 3d ed. (Washington, D.C.: Congressional Quarterly Press, 1982), p. 695.

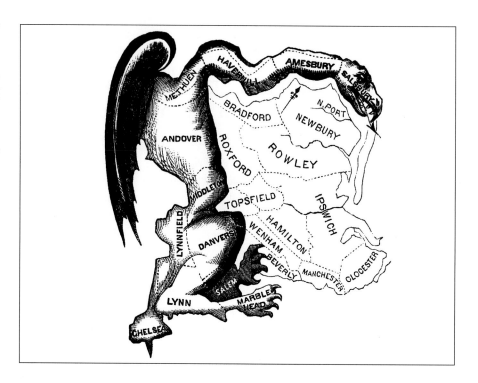

grounds. In this specific case, *Davis v. Bandemer,*[10] the Court, however, did not agree that the districts were drawn unfairly, because it could not be proved that a group of voters would consistently be deprived of its influence at the polls as a result of the new districts.

"Minority-Majority" Districts

The Supreme Court had declared as unconstitutional districts that are uneven in population or that violate norms of size and shape to maximize the advantage of one party. In the early 1990s, however, the federal government encouraged another type of gerrymandering that made possible the election of a minority representative from a "minority-majority" area. Under the mandate of the Voting Rights Act of 1965, the Justice Department issued directives to states after the 1990 census instructing them to create congressional districts that would maximize the voting power of minority groups—that is, create districts in which minority voters were the majority. One such district—the Twelfth District of North Carolina—was 165 miles long, following Interstate 85 for the most part (see Figure 12-2). According to a local joke, the district was so narrow that a car

[10]478 U.S. 109 (1986).

FIGURE 12-2

The Twelfth District of North Carolina
The Twelfth District, which was declared unconstitutional by the United States Supreme Court in 1996, was created to facilitate the election of a minority representative. It snaked through North Carolina along Interstate 85.

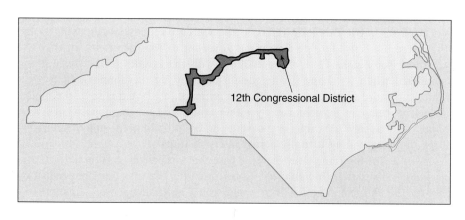

traveling down the interstate highway with both doors open would kill most of the voters in the district. Many of these "minority-majority" districts were challenged in court by citizens who claimed that to create districts based on race or ethnicity alone violates the equal protection clause of the Constitution. This issue is explored in this chapter's *Politics and the Constitution.*

Pay, Perks, and Privileges

Compared with the average American citizen, members of Congress are well paid. In 1999, annual congressional salaries were $136,700. Legislators also have many benefits that are not available to most workers.

POLITICS and the Constitution

Racial Gerrymandering

The concept of equality is a basic American value. The meaning of equality, though, depends to a great extent on how the United States Supreme Court interprets such laws as the equal protection clause of the Constitution. In the 1990s, the Supreme Court's views on equal protection clearly came into conflict with those of the Justice Department with respect to racial gerrymandering—the creation of "minority-majority" congressional districts to enhance the representation of minority groups. After the 1990 census, the Justice Department issued a directive to the states requiring them to create such districts. The motivation for this directive was a desire to ensure more equal treatment for minorities by allowing them a stronger voice in Congress.

As a result of the directive, in the early 1990s a number of states created "minority-majority" districts, some of which had extraordinarily odd shapes (see Figure 12–2, for example) so that

they could include more minority residents. Ironically, state compliance with the Justice Department's requirements resulted in several of these new districts being challenged in the courts. White plaintiffs contended that race-based districting was unconstitutional because it violated the equal protection clause. In 1993, the United States Supreme Court declared that racially gerrymandered districts were subject to strict scrutiny under the equal protection clause—which means that they can only be justified by a "compelling state interest" and must be "narrowly tailored" by the state to serve that interest.*

In 1995, the Supreme Court attacked race-based redistricting even more aggressively when it declared that Georgia's new Eleventh District was unconstitutional.

*Shaw v. Reno, 509 U.S. 630 (1993).

The district stretched from Atlanta to the Atlantic, splitting eight counties and five municipalities along the way. The Court referred to the district as a "monstrosity" linking "widely spaced urban centers that have absolutely nothing to do with each other." The Court went on to say that when a state assigns voters on the basis of race, "it engages in the offensive and demeaning assumption that voters of a particular race, because of their race, think alike, share the same political interests, and will prefer the same candidates at the polls." The Court also chastised the Justice Department for concluding that race-based districting was mandated under the Voting Rights Act of 1965: "When the Justice Department's interpretation of the Act compels race-based districting, it by definition raises a serious constitutional question."†

†Miller v. Johnson, 115 S.Ct. 2475 (1995).

In subsequent rulings, the Court affirmed its position that when race is the dominant factor in the drawing of congressional district lines, the districts are unconstitutional. In two 1996 cases, the Court ruled that the Twelfth District in North Carolina (see Figure 12–2) and three Texas districts were unconstitutional for this reason.‡ In 1997, the Court ruled Virginia's Third District unconstitutional as well, while approving a map for Georgia's Eleventh District drawn up by a three-judge panel after the Court's 1995 decision.

FOR CRITICAL ANALYSIS

Is the Supreme Court's position on racial gerrymandering consistent with its position on affirmative action programs? Why or why not?

‡Shaw v. Reno, 116 S.Ct. 1894 (1996); Bush v. Vera, 116 S.Ct. 1941 (1996).

Franking

A policy that enables members of Congress to send material through the mail by substituting their facsimile signature (frank) for postage.

Congresswoman Connie Morella of Maryland sits at her desk while speaking with her staff in her Washington, D.C., office. Congressional staff members serve as researchers, help write speeches for their legislators, answer the mail, and assist constituents in getting their problems solved. Today, staff members spend more and more of their time answering e-mail and working on their legislators' Web sites.

Special Benefits

Members of Congress benefit in many ways from belonging to a select group. They have access to private Capitol Hill gymnasium facilities; get low-cost haircuts; receive free, close-in parking at the National and Dulles airports near Washington; and get six free parking spaces per member in Capitol Hill garages—plus one free outdoor Capitol parking slot. They also avoid parking tickets because of their congressional license plates and, until 1994, were not required to comply with most labor laws in dealing with their staffs. They eat in a subsidized dining room and take advantage of free plants from the Botanical Gardens for their offices, free medical care, an inexpensive but generous pension plan, liberal travel allowances, and special tax considerations.

Members of Congress are also granted generous **franking** privileges that permit them to mail newsletters, surveys, and other letters to their constituents. The annual cost of congressional mail has risen from $11 million in 1971 to almost $60 million today. Typically, the costs for these mailings rise enormously during election years.

Permanent Professional Staffs

More than 35,000 people are employed in the Capitol Hill bureaucracy. About half of this total consists of personal and committee staff members. The personal staff includes office clerks and secretaries; professionals who deal with media relations, draft legislation, and satisfy constituency requests for service; and staffers who maintain local offices in the member's home district or state.

The average Senate office on Capitol Hill employs about thirty staff members, and twice that number work on the personal staffs of senators from the most populous states. House office staffs typically are about half as large as those of the Senate. The number of staff members has increased dramatically since 1960. With the bulk of those increases coming in assistance to individual members, some scholars question whether staff members are really advising on legislation or are primarily aiding constituents and gaining votes in the next election. Electronic communications, however, have greatly increased constituents' contacts with the legislators; staff members respond to these contacts.

Congress also benefits from the expertise of the professional staffs of agencies that were created to produce information for members of the House and Senate. The Congressional Research Service (CRS), a section of the Library of Congress, furnishes a computer-based record of the contents and current legislative status of major bills that are under consideration. This record can be reviewed by staff members using computer terminals available in most offices. The General Accounting Office (GAO) audits spending by federal agencies, investigates agency practices, and makes policy recommendations to Congress, especially concerning the financial activities of the government. The Congressional Budget Office (CBO) advises Congress on the anticipated effect on the economy of government expenditures and estimates the cost of proposed policies.

Privileges and Immunities under the Law

Members of Congress also benefit from a number of special constitutional protections. Under Article I, Section 6, of the Constitution, they "shall in all Cases, except Treason, Felony and Breach of the Peace, be privileged from Arrest during their Attendance at the Session of their respective Houses, and in going to and returning from the same; and for any Speech or Debate in either House, they shall not be questioned in any other Place." The arrest immunity clause is not really an important provision today. The "speech or debate" clause, however, means that a member may make any allegations or other statements he or she wishes in connection with official duties and normally not be sued for libel or slander or otherwise be subject to legal action.

The Committee Structure

Most of the actual work of legislating is performed by the committees and subcommittees within Congress. Thousands of bills are introduced in every session of Congress, and no single member can possibly be adequately informed on all the issues that arise. The committee system is a way to provide for specialization, or a division of the legislative labor. Members of a committee can concentrate on just one area or topic—such as taxation or energy—and develop sufficient expertise to draft appropriate legislation when needed. The flow of legislation through both the House and the Senate is determined largely by the speed with which the members of these committees act on bills and resolutions.

The Power of Committees

Commonly known as "little legislatures," committees usually have the final say on pieces of legislation.[11] Committee actions may be overturned on the floor by the House or Senate, but this rarely happens. Legislators normally defer to the expertise of the chairperson and other members of the committee who speak on the floor in defense of a committee decision. Chairpersons of committees exercise control over the scheduling of hearings and formal action on a bill. They also decide which subcommittee will act on legislation falling within their committee's jurisdiction.

Committees only very rarely are deprived of control over a bill—although this kind of action is provided for in the rules of each chamber. In the House, if a bill has been considered by a standing committee for thirty days, the signatures of a majority (218) of the House membership on a **discharge petition** can pry a bill

Discharge Petition
A procedure by which a bill in the House of Representatives may be forced out of a committee (discharged) that has refused to report it for consideration by the House. The discharge petition must be signed by an absolute majority (218) of representatives and is used only on rare occasions.

[11]The term *little legislatures* is from Woodrow Wilson, *Congressional Government* (New York: Meridian Books, 1956 [first published in 1885]).

A committee hearing on a constitutional amendment to balance the budget. Starting from the chair of the committee in the center, Democratic senators sit on the left in order of seniority, while Republicans take the seats on the right in order of seniority.

out of an uncooperative committee's hands. From 1909 to 1999, however, although over nine hundred such petitions were made, only slightly more than two dozen resulted in successful discharge efforts. Of those, twenty passed the House.[12]

Types of Congressional Committees

Over the past two centuries, Congress has created several different types of committees, each of which serves particular needs of the institution.

Standing Committees. By far the most important committees in Congress are the **standing committees**—permanent bodies established by the rules of each chamber of Congress and that continue from session to session. A list of the standing committees of the 106th Congress is presented in Table 12–5. In addition, most of the standing committees have created several subcommittees to carry out their work. In the 106th Congress, there were 68 subcommittees in the Senate and 85 in the House.[13]

Each standing committee is given a specific area of legislative policy jurisdiction, and almost all legislative measures are considered by the appropriate standing committees. Because of the importance of their work and the traditional influence of their members in Congress, certain committees are considered to be more prestigious than others. If a congressperson seeks to be influential, he or she will usually aspire to a seat on the Appropriations Committee in either chamber, on the Ways and Means Committee in the House, the House Education and Labor Committee, or the Senate Foreign Relations Committee.

Each member of the House generally serves on two standing committees, except when the member sits on the Appropriations, Rules, or Ways and Means

Standing Committee

A permanent committee within the House or Senate that considers bills within a certain subject area.

---

[12]*Congressional Quarterly's Guide to Congress,* 3d ed. (Washington, D.C.: Congressional Quarterly Press, 1982), p. 426; and authors' research.

[13]*Congressional Directory* (Washington, D.C.: U.S. Government Printing Office, various editions).

TABLE 12-5

Standing Committees of the 106th Congress, 1999 to 2001

HOUSE COMMITTEE	CHAIR	SENATE COMMITTEE	CHAIR
Agriculture	Bob Smith (R., Ore.)	Agriculture, Nutrition, and Forestry	Richard G. Lugar (R., Ind.)
Appropriations	Bob Livingston (R., La.)	Appropriations	Ted Stevens (R., Alaska)
Banking, Finance, and Urban Affairs	Jim Leach (R., Iowa)	Armed Services	Strom Thurmond (R., S.C.)
		Banking, Housing, and Urban Affairs	Phil Gramm (R., Tex.)
Budget	John Kasich (R., Ohio)	Budget	Pete V. Domenici (R., N.M.)
Commerce	Thomas Bliley, Jr. (R., Fla.)	Commerce, Science, and Transportation	John McCain (R., Ariz.)
Education and Labor	Bill Goodling (R., Pa.)		
		Energy and Natural Resources	Frank H. Murkowski (R., Alaska)
International Relations	Benjamin A. Gilman (R., N.Y.)		
Judiciary	Henry Hyde (R., Ill.)	Environment and Public Works	John H. Chafee (R., R.I.)
National Security	Floyd Spence (R., S.C.)	Finance	William V. Roth, Jr. (R., Del.)
Resources	Don Young (R., Alaska)	Foreign Relations	Jesse Helms (R., N.C.)
Rules	David Dreier (R., Calif.)	Governmental Affairs	Fred Thompson (R., Tenn.).
Science and Technology	Robert S. Walker (R., Pa.)	Judiciary	Orrin Hatch (R., Utah)
Small Business	Jan Meyers (R., Kans.)	Labor and Human Resources	James M. Jeffords (R., Vt.)
Standards of Official Conduct	Nancy L. Johnson (R., Conn.)	Rules and Administration	John W. Warner (R., Va.)
Transportation and Infrastructure	Bud Shuster (R., Pa.)	Small Business	Christopher Bond (R., Mo.)
Veterans' Affairs	Bob Stump (R., Ariz.)	Veterans' Affairs	Arlen Specter (R., Pa.)

Committee—in which case he or she serves on only that one standing committee. Each senator may serve on two major committees and one minor committee (only the Rules and Administration Committee and the Veterans' Affairs Committee are considered minor).

Select Committees. A **select committee** normally is created for a limited period of time and for a specific legislative purpose. For example, a select committee may be formed to investigate a public problem, such as child nutrition or aging. Select committees are disbanded when they have reported to the chamber that created them. They rarely create original legislation.

Joint Committees. A **joint committee** is formed by the concurrent action of both chambers of Congress and consists of members from each chamber. Joint committees, which may be permanent or temporary, have dealt with the economy, taxation, and the Library of Congress.

Conference Committees. Special types of joint committees—**conference committees**—are formed for the purpose of achieving agreement between the House and the Senate on the exact wording of legislative acts when the two chambers pass legislative proposals in different forms. No bill can be sent to the White House to be signed into law unless it first passes both chambers in identical form. Sometimes called the "third house" of Congress, conference committees are in a position to make significant alterations in legislation and frequently become the focal point of policy debates.

The House Rules Committee. Because of its special "gatekeeping" power over the terms on which legislation will reach the floor of the House of Representatives, the House Rules Committee holds a uniquely powerful position. A special committee rule sets the time limit on debate and determines whether and how a bill may be amended. This practice dates back to 1883. The Rules Committee has the unusual power to meet while the House is in session, to have its resolutions considered immediately on the floor, and to initiate legislation on its own.

The Selection of Committee Members

In the House, representatives are appointed to standing committees by the Steering and Policy Committee (for Democrats) and by the Committee on Committees (for Republicans). Committee chairpersons normally are appointed according to seniority.

The rule regarding seniority specifies that majority party members with longer terms of continuous service on the committee will be given preference when committee chairpersons—as well as holders of other significant posts in Congress—are selected. This is not a law but an informal, traditional process. The **seniority system,** although deliberately unequal, provides a predictable means of assigning positions of power within Congress.

The general pattern until the 1970s was that members of the House or Senate who represented **safe seats** would be reelected continually and eventually would accumulate enough years of continuous committee service to enable them to become the chairpersons of their committees.

In the 1970s, a number of reforms in the chairperson selection process somewhat modified the seniority system. The reforms introduced the use of a secret ballot in electing House committee chairpersons and established rules for the selection of subcommittee chairpersons that resulted in a greater dispersal of authority within the committees themselves.

Select Committee
A temporary legislative committee established for a limited time period and for a special purpose.

Joint Committee
A legislative committee composed of members from both chambers of Congress.

Conference Committee
A special joint committee appointed to reconcile differences when bills pass the two chambers of Congress in different forms.

Seniority System
A custom followed in both chambers of Congress specifying that members with longer terms of continuous service will be given preference when committee chairpersons and holders of other significant posts are selected.

Safe Seat
A district that returns the legislator with 55 percent of the vote or more.

Speaker of the House
The presiding officer in the House of Representatives. The speaker is always a member of the majority party and is the most powerful and influential member of the House.

Representative Newt Gingrich (R., Ga.), speaker of the House. Although polls showed low approval for him nationally, Gingrich easily won reelection from his Georgia district in 1998. Faced with a challenge to his leadership after the 1998 elections, Gingrich resigned from the postion of speaker.

The Formal Leadership

The limited amount of centralized power that exists in Congress is exercised through party-based mechanisms. Congress is organized by party. When the Democratic Party, for example, wins a majority of seats in either the House or the Senate, Democrats control the official positions of power in that chamber, and every important committee has a Democratic chairperson and a majority of Democratic members. The same process holds when Republicans are in the majority.

We consider the formal leadership positions in the House and Senate separately, but you will note some broad similarities in the way leaders are selected and in the ways they exercise power in the two chambers.

Leadership in the House

The House leadership is made up of the speaker, the majority and minority leaders, and the party whips.

The Speaker.   The foremost power holder in the House of Representatives is the **speaker of the House.** The speaker's position is technically a nonpartisan one, but in fact, for the better part of two centuries, the speaker has been the official leader of the majority party in the House. When a new Congress convenes in January of odd-numbered years, each party nominates a candidate for speaker. In one of the very rare instances of perfect party cohesion, all Democratic members of the House ordinarily vote for their party's nominee, and all Republicans support their alternative candidate.

The influence of modern-day speakers is based primarily on their personal prestige, persuasive ability, and knowledge of the legislative process—plus the acquiescence or active support of other representatives. The major formal powers of the speaker include the following:

1. Presiding over meetings of the House.
2. Appointing members of joint committees and conference committees.
3. Scheduling legislation for floor action.
4. Deciding points of order and interpreting the rules with the advice of the House parliamentarian.
5. Referring bills and resolutions to the appropriate standing committees of the House.

A speaker may take part in floor debate and vote, as can any other member of Congress, but recent speakers usually have voted only to break a tie.

In general, the powers of the speaker are related to his or her control over information and communications channels in the House. This is a significant power in a large, decentralized institution in which information is a very important resource. With this control, the speaker attempts to ensure the smooth operation of the chamber and to integrate presidential and congressional policies.

In 1975, the powers of the speaker were expanded when the House Democratic caucus gave its party's speaker the power to appoint the Democratic Steering Committee, which determines new committee assignments for House party members.

The election of Newt Gingrich, Republican of Georgia, as speaker in 1994 put a forceful man into an office that had not exercised much direct power, especially for Republicans. Gingrich began his term by hand-picking some of the committee chairs so they would work with him, overriding the seniority rule. On occasion, he overruled committee chairs, appointed task forces to take issues away from certain members, forced members to debate issues in the Republican caucus, and, by exercising his formal powers, kept extremely tight control of the agenda. Gingrich's strong personality, however, was unpopular with voters, and his tactics lost support among some Republican legislators. After the loss of Republican House seats in the 1998 elections, Gingrich announced that he would resign from the speaker's position rather than provoke a divisive fight within the party.

The Majority Leader.   The **majority leader of the House** is elected by a caucus of party members to foster cohesion among party members and to act as a spokesperson for the party. The majority leader influences the scheduling of debate and generally acts as the chief supporter of the speaker. The majority leader cooperates with the speaker and other party leaders, both inside and outside Congress, to formulate the party's legislative program and to guide that program through the legislative process in the House. The Democrats recruit future speakers from that position.

The Minority Leader.   The **minority leader of the House** is the candidate nominated for speaker by a caucus of the minority party. Like the majority leader, the leader of the minority party has as his or her primary responsibility the maintaining of cohesion within the party's ranks. The minority leader works for cohesion among the party's members and speaks on behalf of the president if the minority party controls the White House. In relations with the majority party, the minority leader consults with both the speaker and the majority leader on recognizing members who wish to speak on the floor, on House rules and procedures, and on the scheduling of legislation. Minority leaders have no actual power in these areas, however.

Whips.   The formal leadership of each party includes assistants to the majority and minority leaders, who are known as **whips.** The whips assist the party leaders by passing information down from the leadership to party members and by ensuring that members show up for floor debate and cast their votes on important issues. Whips conduct polls among party members about the members' views on major pieces of legislation, inform the leaders about whose vote is doubtful and whose is certain, and may exert pressure on members to support the leaders' positions.

Leadership in the Senate

The Senate is less than one-fourth the size of the House. This fact alone probably explains why a formal, complex, and centralized leadership structure is less necessary in the Senate than it is in the House.

The two highest-ranking formal leadership positions in the Senate are essentially ceremonial in nature. Under the Constitution, the vice president of the United States is the president (that is, the presiding officer) of the Senate and may vote to break a tie. The vice president, however, only rarely is present for a meeting of the Senate. The Senate elects instead a **president *pro tempore*** ("pro tem") to preside over the Senate in the vice president's absence. Ordinarily, the president pro tem is the member of the majority party with the longest continuous term of service in the Senate. The president pro tem is mostly a ceremonial position. Junior senators take turns actually presiding over the sessions of the Senate.

The real leadership power in the Senate rests in the hands of the **majority floor leader,** the **minority floor leader,** and their respective whips. The Senate majority and minority leaders have the right to be recognized first in debate on the floor

INFOTRAC ®
COLLEGE EDITION

"Seven Most Powerful Members of Congress"

Majority Leader of the House
A legislative position held by an important party member in the House of Representatives. The majority leader is selected by the majority party in caucus or conference to foster cohesion among party members and to act as spokesperson for the majority party in the House.

Minority Leader of the House
The party leader elected by the minority party in the House.

Whip
An assistant who aids the majority or minority leader of the House or the Senate majority or minority floor leader.

President *Pro Tempore*
The temporary presiding officer of the Senate in the absence of the vice president.

Majority Floor Leader
The chief spokesperson of the major party in the Senate, who directs the legislative program and party strategy.

Minority Floor Leader
The party officer in the Senate who commands the minority party's opposition to the policies of the majority party and directs the legislative program and strategy of his or her party.

and generally exercise the same powers available to the House majority and minority leaders. They control the scheduling of debate on the floor in conjunction with the majority party's Policy Committee, influence the allocation of committee assignments for new members or for senators attempting to transfer to a new committee, influence the selection of other party officials, and participate in selecting members of conference committees. The leaders are expected to mobilize support for partisan legislative initiatives or for the proposals of a president who belongs to the same party. The leaders act as liaisons with the White House when the president is of their party, try to get the cooperation of committee chairpersons, and seek to facilitate the smooth functioning of the Senate through the senators' unanimous consent. Floor leaders are elected by their respective party caucuses.

Senate party whips, like their House counterparts, maintain communication within the party on platform positions and try to ensure that party colleagues are present for floor debate and important votes. The Senate whip system is far less elaborate than its counterpart in the House, simply because there are fewer members to track.

A list of the formal party leaders of the 106th Congress is presented in Table 12-6. Party leaders are a major source of influence over the decisions about public issues that senators and representatives must make every day.

TABLE   12-6

Party Leaders in the 106th Congress, 1999–2001

POSITION	INCUMBENT	PARTY/ STATE	LEADER SINCE
House*			
Speaker	Newt Gingrich[†]	R., Ga.	Jan. 1995
Majority leader	Dick Armey	R., Tex.	Jan. 1995
Majority whip	Tom DeLay	R., Tex.	Jan. 1995
Chairperson of the Republican Conference	John Boehner	R., Ohio	Jan. 1995
Minority leader	Richard Gephardt	D., Mo.	Jan. 1995
Minority whip	David Bonior	D., Mich.	Jan. 1995
Chairperson of the Democratic Caucus	Vic Fazio	D., Calif.	Jan. 1995
Senate			
President *pro tempore*	Strom Thurmond	R., S.C.	Jan. 1995
Majority floor leader	Trent Lott	R., Miss.	June 1996
Assistant majority leader	Don Nickles	R., Okla.	June 1996
Secretary of the Republican Conference	Connie Mack	R., Fla.	Jan. 1995
Minority floor leader	Tom Daschle	D., S.Dak.	Jan. 1995
Assistant floor leader	Wendell Ford	R., Okla.	Jan. 1995
Chairperson of the Democratic Caucus	Barbara Mikulski	D., Md.	Jan. 1995

*As this book goes to press, the House Republicans are in the process of selecting new leaders.
[†]Newt Gingrich announced on November 6, 1998, that he was resigning from his position as speaker of the House.

How Members of Congress Decide

Why congresspersons vote as they do is difficult to know with any certainty. One popular perception of the legislative decision-making process is that legislators take cues from other trusted or more senior colleagues.[14] This model holds that because most members of Congress have neither the time nor the incentive to study the details of most pieces of legislation, they frequently arrive on the floor with no clear idea about what they are voting on or how they should vote. Their decision is simplified, according to the cue-taking model, by quickly checking how key colleagues have voted or intend to vote. More broadly, verbal and non-verbal cues can be taken from fellow committee members and chairpersons, party leaders, state delegation members, or the president.

Most people who study the decision-making process in Congress agree that the single best predictor for how a member will vote is the member's party membership.[15] Republicans tend to vote similarly on issues, as do Democrats. Of course, even though liberals predominate among the Democrats in Congress and conservatives predominate among the Republicans, the parties still may have internal disagreements about the proper direction that national policy should take. This was generally true for the civil rights legislation of the 1950s and 1960s, for example, when the greatest disagreement was between the conservative southern wing and the liberal northern wing of the Democratic Party.

One way to measure the degree of party unity in Congress is to look at how often a majority of one party votes against the majority of members from the other party. Table 12–7 displays the percentage of all votes in the House and the Senate when this type of party voting has occurred.

Regional differences, especially between northern and southern Democrats, may overlap and reinforce basic ideological differences among members of the same party. One consequence of the North-South split among Democrats has been the **conservative coalition** policy alliance between southern Democrats and Republicans. This conservative, cross-party grouping formed regularly on votes during the Reagan years, declined under Bush, and further weakened under Clinton, particularly with the election of large numbers of southern Republicans to Congress.

Conservative Coalition
An alliance of Republicans and southern Democrats that can form in the House or the Senate to oppose liberal legislation and support conservative legislation.

How a Bill Becomes Law

Each year, Congress and the president propose and approve many laws. Some are budget and appropriation laws that require extensive bargaining but must be passed for the government to continue to function. Other laws are relatively free of controversy and are passed with little dissension between the branches of government. Still other proposed legislation is extremely controversial and reaches to the roots of differences between Democrats and Republicans and between the executive and legislative branches.

As detailed in Figure 12–3 on page 406, each law begins as a bill, which must be introduced in either the House or the Senate. Often, similar bills are introduced in both chambers. If it is a "money bill," however, it must start in the House. In each chamber, the bill follows similar steps. It is referred to a

TABLE **12-7**

Party Voting in Congress

This table lists the percentage of all roll calls in which a majority of Democratic legislators voted against a majority of Republican legislators.

YEAR	HOUSE	SENATE
1997	50.4	50.3
1996	56.4	62.4
1995	73.0	69.0
1994	61.8	51.7
1993	65.0	67.0
1992	64.0	53.0
1991	55.0	49.0
1990	49.0	54.0
1989	55.0	35.0
1988	47.0	42.0
1987	64.0	41.0
1986	57.0	52.0
1985	61.0	50.0
1984	47.1	40.0
1983	55.6	43.6
1982	36.4	43.4
1981	37.4	47.8
1980	37.6	45.8
1979	47.3	46.7
1978	33.2	45.2
1977	42.2	42.4
1976	35.9	37.2
1975	48.4	47.8
1974	29.4	44.3
1973	41.8	39.9

Source: *Congressional Quarterly Weekly Report.*

[14]Donald Matthews and James Stimson, *Yeas and Nays: Normal Decision Making in the U.S. House of Representatives* (New York: Wiley, 1975).
[15]David Mayhew, *Party Loyalty among Congressmen* (Cambridge, Mass.: Harvard University Press, 1966).

committee and its subcommittees for study, discussion, hearings, and rewriting. When the bill is reported out to the full chamber, it must be scheduled for debate (by the Rules Committee in the House and by the leadership in the Senate). After the bill has been passed in each chamber, if it contains different provisions, a conference committee is formed to write a compromise bill, which must be approved by both chambers before it is sent to the president to sign or veto.

FIGURE 12-3

How a Bill Becomes Law

This illustration shows the most typical way in which proposed legislation is enacted into law. Most legislation begins as similar bills introduced into each chamber of Congress. The process is illustrated here with two hypothetical bills. House bill No. 100 (HR 100) and Senate bill No. 200 (S 200). The path of HR 100 is shown on the left, and that of S 200, on the right.

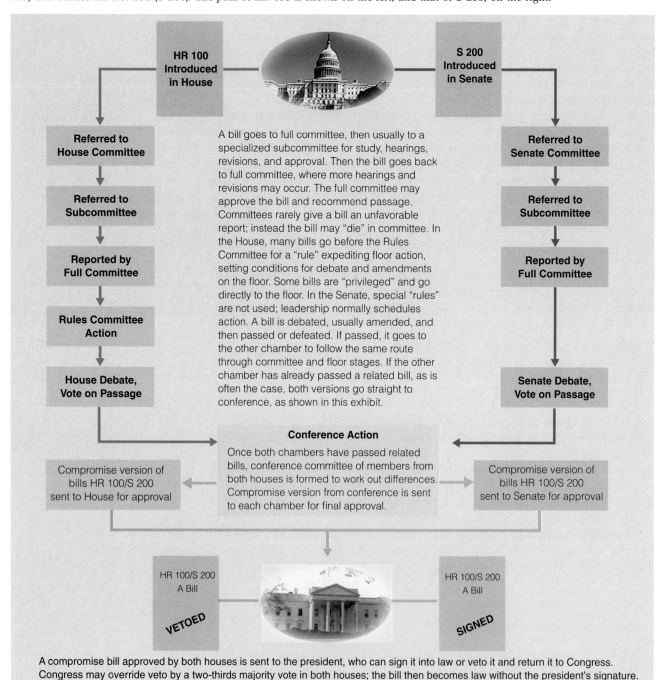

HR 100 Introduced in House

S 200 Introduced in Senate

Referred to House Committee

Referred to Senate Committee

A bill goes to full committee, then usually to a specialized subcommittee for study, hearings, revisions, and approval. Then the bill goes back to full committee, where more hearings and revisions may occur. The full committee may approve the bill and recommend passage. Committees rarely give a bill an unfavorable report; instead the bill may "die" in committee. In the House, many bills go before the Rules Committee for a "rule" expediting floor action, setting conditions for debate and amendments on the floor. Some bills are "privileged" and go directly to the floor. In the Senate, special "rules" are not used; leadership normally schedules action. A bill is debated, usually amended, and then passed or defeated. If passed, it goes to the other chamber to follow the same route through committee and floor stages. If the other chamber has already passed a related bill, as is often the case, both versions go straight to conference, as shown in this exhibit.

Referred to Subcommittee

Referred to Subcommittee

Reported by Full Committee

Reported by Full Committee

Rules Committee Action

House Debate, Vote on Passage

Senate Debate, Vote on Passage

Conference Action

Once both chambers have passed related bills, conference committee of members from both houses is formed to work out differences. Compromise version from conference is sent to each chamber for final approval.

Compromise version of bills HR 100/S 200 sent to House for approval

Compromise version of bills HR 100/S 200 sent to Senate for approval

HR 100/S 200 A Bill

VETOED

HR 100/S 200 A Bill

SIGNED

A compromise bill approved by both houses is sent to the president, who can sign it into law or veto it and return it to Congress. Congress may override veto by a two-thirds majority vote in both houses; the bill then becomes law without the president's signature.

A good example of how both chambers affect a bill and how compromises finally bring the bill to a vote is a bill signed into law by President Clinton in late 1997. The bill streamlined the procedures used by the Food and Drug Administration (FDA) to test new drugs and medical devices. The effort to speed up the testing and approval process for the sake of patients who needed the drugs was several years old by the time the bill became law.

Republicans began work on the bill to speed up FDA approval in the 104th Congress. They could not create a bill that would win support from both parties and the president, however. In the 105th Congress, the Republicans decided to use the expiration of the 1992 act that requires drug companies to pay fees to the FDA for testing as a vehicle for reforming the agency's practices. The bill began its journey in the House Commerce Committee as three separate bills: one on drug-user fees, one on medical devices, and one on food labels. The chairperson consolidated these into one bill, made a number of modifications to gain Democratic approval, and sent the bill to the floor. The House passed its version of the bill on October 7, 1997.

In the Senate, the bill had a much tougher road to travel. The bill was referred to the Senate's Labor and Human Resources Committee. Senator Edward (Ted) Kennedy (D., Mass.) fought to change a number of provisions that he felt favored the drug industry and posed some risks for patients. After several months of committee work and an extended floor debate, the Senate finally passed the bill. The House and Senate bills, however, contained differing provisions on the testing of medical devices, on the practice by pharmacists of "compounding" custom drugs, on food labels, and on asthma inhalers. The conference committee met, found compromise positions for all of these issues, and sent a new bill to both the House and the Senate for approval. The bill then went to the president for signature.

The path followed by this bill shows the importance of compromise in the legislative process. It also illustrates the power of one individual senator, Ted Kennedy, who singlehandedly held up Senate action until his concerns were satisfied. In the final analysis, the legislation that passed was acceptable not only

President Bill Clinton signs the Highway Transportation Act on June 8, 1998. Surrounding him at the signing are Democratic and Republican leaders of the House and the Senate who worked on getting the legislation passed. Even though the president had criticized the bill for some of its "pork barrel" projects, he eventually joined the bipartisan coalition that supported the legislation.

to the Republicans and Democrats in Congress but also to the FDA and the drug industry, which must follow these procedures. Whether this legislation actually proves helpful to the American people will be determined in the future.

How Much Will the Government Spend?

The Constitution is extremely clear about where the power of the purse lies in the national government: all money bills, whether for taxing or spending, must originate in the House of Representatives. Today, much of the business of Congress is concerned with approving government expenditures through the budget process and with raising the revenues to pay for government programs.

From 1922, when Congress required the president to prepare and present to the legislature an **executive budget,** until 1974, the congressional budget process was so disjointed that it was difficult to visualize the total picture of government finances. The president presented the executive budget to Congress in January. It was broken down into thirteen or more appropriations bills. Some time later, after all of the bills were debated, amended, and passed, it was more or less possible to estimate total government spending for the next year.

Frustrated by the president's ability to impound funds and dissatisfied with the entire budget process, Congress passed the Budget and Impoundment Control Act of 1974 to regain some control over the nation's spending. The act required the president to spend the funds that Congress had appropriated, frustrating the president's ability to kill programs of which the president disapproved by withholding funds. The other major accomplishment of the act was to force Congress to examine total national taxing and spending at least twice in each budget cycle.

The budget cycle of the federal government is described in the following subsections. (See Figure 12–4 for a graphic illustration of the budget cycle.)

Preparing the Budget

The federal government operates on a **fiscal year (FY)** cycle. The fiscal year runs from October through September, so that fiscal 2000, or FY00, runs from October 1, 1999, through September 30, 2000. Eighteen months before a fiscal year starts, the executive branch begins preparing the budget. The Office of Management and

Executive Budget

The budget prepared and submitted by the president to Congress.

Fiscal Year (FY)

The twelve-month period that is used for bookkeeping, or accounting, purposes. Usually, the fiscal year does not coincide with the calendar year. For example, the federal government's fiscal year runs from October 1 through September 30.

FIGURE 12–4
The Budget Cycle

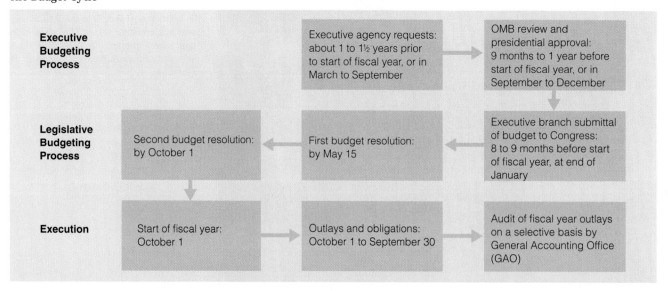

Executive Budgeting Process		Executive agency requests: about 1 to 1½ years prior to start of fiscal year, or in March to September	OMB review and presidential approval: 9 months to 1 year before start of fiscal year, or in September to December
Legislative Budgeting Process	Second budget resolution: by October 1	First budget resolution: by May 15	Executive branch submittal of budget to Congress: 8 to 9 months before start of fiscal year, at end of January
Execution	Start of fiscal year: October 1	Outlays and obligations: October 1 to September 30	Audit of fiscal year outlays on a selective basis by General Accounting Office (GAO)

Budget (OMB) receives advice from the Council of Economic Advisers (CEA) and the Treasury Department. The OMB outlines the budget and then sends it to the various departments and agencies. Bargaining follows, in which—to use only two of many examples—the Department of Health and Human Services argues for more welfare spending, and the armed forces argue for fewer defense spending cuts.

Even though the OMB has only six hundred employees, it is known as one of the most powerful agencies in Washington. It assembles the budget documents and monitors the agencies throughout each year. Every year, it begins the budget process with a **spring review,** in which it requires all of the agencies to review their programs, activities, and goals. At the beginning of each summer, the director of the OMB sends out a letter instructing agencies to submit their requests for funding for the next fiscal year. By the end of the summer, each agency must submit a formal request to the OMB.

In actuality, the "budget season" begins with the **fall review.** At this time, the OMB looks at budget requests and, in almost all cases, routinely cuts them back. Although the OMB works within guidelines established by the president, specific decisions often are left to the director and the director's associates. By the beginning of November, the director's review begins. The director meets with cabinet secretaries and budget officers. Time becomes crucial. The budget must be completed by January so that it can go to the printer to be included in the *Economic Report of the President.*

Congress Faces the Budget

In January, nine months before the fiscal year starts, the president takes the OMB's proposed budget, approves it, and submits it to Congress. Then the congressional budgeting process takes over. Congressional committees and subcommittees look at the proposals from the executive branch. The Congressional Budget Office (CBO) advises the different committees on economic matters, just as the OMB and the CEA advise the president. The **first budget resolution** by Congress is supposed to be passed in May. It sets overall revenue goals and spending targets.

During the summer, bargaining among all the concerned parties takes place. Spending and tax laws that are drawn up during this period are supposed to be guided by the May congressional budget resolution. By September, Congress is supposed to pass its **second budget resolution,** one that will set "binding" limits on taxes and spending for the fiscal year beginning October 1. Bills passed before that date that do not fit within the limits of the budget resolution are supposed to be changed.

In actuality, between 1978 and 1996, Congress did not pass a complete budget by October 1. In other words, generally, Congress does not follow its own rules. Budget resolutions are passed late, and when they are passed, they are not treated as binding. In each fiscal year that starts without a budget, every agency operates on the basis of **continuing resolutions,** which enable the agencies to keep on doing whatever they were doing the previous year with the same amount of funding. Even continuing resolutions have not always been passed on time.

Dealing with the budget is a recurring nightmare for Congress and the president. George Bush's 1990 budget battle, which forced him to raise taxes, may have cost him the presidency in 1992. President Bill Clinton won his first big budget fight in 1993 by a margin of one vote in the Senate, cast by Vice President Al Gore to break the tie, and by a single vote in the House. Clinton's deficit reduction package included large new taxes on the rich, on gasoline, and on tobacco.

The Republican sweep of 1994 changed the budget dynamics completely in the 104th Congress. The Republicans in the House, who had pledged to balance the budget as part of the Contract with America, tried to force the president to

DID YOU KNOW...
That retiring members of Congress can start collecting a pension at age fifty after twenty years of work or at age sixty after ten years of service?

Spring Review
The time every year when the Office of Management and Budget requires federal agencies to review their programs, activities, and goals and submit their requests for funding for the next fiscal year.

Fall Review
The time every year when, after receiving formal federal agency requests for funding for the next fiscal year, the Office of Management and Budget reviews the requests, makes changes, and submits its recommendations to the president.

First Budget Resolution
A resolution passed by Congress in May that sets overall revenue and spending goals for the following fiscal year.

Second Budget Resolution
A resolution passed by Congress in September that sets "binding" limits on taxes and spending for the next fiscal year beginning October 1.

Continuing Resolution
A temporary law that Congress passes when an appropriations bill has not been decided by the beginning of the new fiscal year on October 1.

accept a budget with cuts in domestic spending. President Clinton resisted the pressure. By October 1, 1995, only two of the thirteen bills needed to finance government for fiscal year 1996 had been passed. When the president and Congress could not agree on the spending bills, the government partially "shut down" twice over the next three months. Finally, after painstakingly working out the budget for each of the remaining bills, the FY96 budget was completed in April 1996, seven months after it was due.

The 1996 elections made the lessons of the budget stalemate perfectly clear: the president was reelected easily, and the Republican majority lost some of its margin in Congress. The public, according to polls, believed that Congress was more responsible for the partial government shutdowns than was the president, and the public did not approve of such tactics.

With these lessons in mind, the 105th Congress set to work on a proposal to balance the budget. After months of negotiations, the president and Congress agreed on a five-year plan to balance the budget, which included $95 billion in budget cuts and trimmed spending by more than $250 billion over five years. The agreement was made possible by two factors: the need of the Republican majority and the president to work together on the budget and the strong economy, which boosted federal tax revenues.

The Question of Congressional Ethics

Ethics is the most serious public relations problem confronting Congress today. Perhaps nothing has so tarnished the public's perception of Congress as the revelations concerning the abuse of staff members, the misuse of public funds, and the personal indiscretions and corruption of members of that institution.

Congress's response to revelations of member misconduct has been mixed. The House Democratic caucus in June 1980 voted 160 to 0 to require that chairpersons of committees or subcommittees be stripped of their posts automatically if they have been censured or indicted on a felony charge carrying a prison sentence of at least two years. This rule can be waived, however, by the same caucus.

Public financing of congressional campaigns may offer a partial solution to recurring problems of financial misconduct. Nonetheless, Congress has refused to use tax money for, or to impose spending limits on, its members' campaigns, even though it adopted such provisions for presidential campaigns in 1974. Part of the campaign-funding problem is illustrated by the former member of Congress who used leftover campaign funds to make a down payment on a fifty-five-foot houseboat in Florida and to finance a limousine carrying the congressional seal. The practice of diverting unused campaign funds to personal use was outlawed in January 1980, but members of Congress were exempted from coverage by the law until 1992. By the 1990s, the public's regard for Congress had reached an all-time low (see this chapter's *Politics and Ethics*).

The Congress: Issues for the New Century

To many voters, the House and the Senate seem like arcane institutions that spend too much time in political battles with each other and with the president. Too little legislation that matters to the people seems to be produced by Congress, and too many members of Congress seem to hold office just to satisfy their own ambitions. In addition, too much money seems to be spent in congressional cam-

POLITICS and Ethics

Congress Examines Its Own for Improprieties

Public approval of Congress as a body continues to be relatively low, in part because of the succession of ethical problems and improprieties that have become public. Both the House and the Senate have attempted to deal with the ethical lapses of their respective members through internal processes, but the public perception continues to be that many members are involved in shady dealings that the ordinary citizen finds hard to justify.

Ethical problems for elected representatives fall into several categories. The most flamboyant concern sexual misconduct involving staff members or constituents. In recent years, Representative Gus Savage of Illinois was accused of making sexual advances to a Peace Corps volunteer while on an official trip, and Representative Donald "Buz" Lukens of Ohio was convicted of having sex with a sixteen-year-old girl. Both representatives were defeated in subsequent elections. Representative Barney Frank of Massachusetts, who has acknowledged his own homosexuality, was reprimanded by the House Ethics Committee for hiring a former lover as a staff assistant and allowing that person the use of his office for personal business.

The Senate's most famous case recently has been that of Senator Robert Packwood of Oregon, who was accused of sexually harassing a number of women. Packwood admitted some of his guilt, citing abuse of alcohol as the reason for his misbehavior. Packwood resigned in September 1995, after the Senate Ethics Committee voted to expel him from the Senate.

Both the House and the Senate have also dealt with the ethical problems that arise when a member takes advantage of his or her office for personal benefit. Several House members—including Jim Wright, a former speaker, and Tony Coelho, a former Democratic whip—resigned from Congress after investigations of their personal finances. Five senators, known as the Keating Five for their association with the convicted Arizona financier Charles Keating, were reprimanded for their attempts to limit the investigation of Keating's failed savings and loans. None of the five was censured (which is a stronger action). One did not seek reelection.

In a 1994 ethics incident, Dan Rostenkowski, the one-time powerful chair of the House Ways and Means Committee, was indicted for violating House rules in the purchase of stamps and personal gifts from House stores and for misusing funds for staff and office expenses.

Even the former speaker of the House, Newt Gingrich, got into trouble in 1997. Gingrich was reprimanded by the House Ethics Committee and fined $300,000 for using money from a tax-exempt foundation to underwrite a televised college course that he taught and a televised "town hall" on politics that he led.

Ethical conduct seemed to reach a new low during the investigation of the Clinton-Lewinsky affair when various members of Congress, including Henry Hyde (R., Ill.), were accused of having had extramarital affairs. Several members confessed to having had such liaisons in order to avoid further embarassment. While these disclosures did not violate the House ethics code, there were political consequences for some of these members.

FOR CRITICAL ANALYSIS

Do you think that the public's perception of congressional behavior is influenced by media coverage?

paigns. One of the results of the public's cynical attitude toward Congress is the popularity of term limits for elected officials. Depending on how term limits are perceived to be working in the states, there could be a renewed push for a constitutional amendment to have term limits for members of Congress.

Another problem facing Congress relates to the underrepresentation of minority groups in that institution. The Supreme Court has made it clear that racial gerrymandering to increase minority representation in Congress is not an acceptable solution to this problem. Finding alternate solutions may be one of the most difficult challenges facing Congress—and American society—today.

Given the complexity of national problems and the attempts by hundreds of interest groups to influence congressional action, both the House and the Senate continue to try to meet the expectations of the people in the media age. The president continues to garner far more credit for whatever legislation is enacted, while Congress tries to find a way to balance interests and produce policies that meet modern needs. The members of Congress, however, continue to go home to their districts and, in most cases, build trusting relationships with their constituents—which helps build support for the institution as a whole.

T O W A R D   A C T I V E   C I T I Z E N S H I P

HOW TO BE AN INTERN IN WASHINGTON, D.C.

John Stuart Mill, the British political philosopher and economist, wrote in the last century, "There are many truths of which the full meaning cannot be realized until personal experience has brought it home." Hundreds of students each year flock to Washington, D.C., for a summer, a semester, or a full year to gain personal experience in one of the myriad institutions of the nation's capital. For those with "Potomac fever," an internship in Washington earning college credit while working is an extraordinary opportunity. If you are interested in a Washington experience, here are some things to keep in mind.

First, make sure that you discuss your internship plan with your faculty adviser. He or she will have useful tips. Some colleges have strict rules on who may obtain credit for internships, what preparation is necessary, in what year students are allowed to participate in internships, and other such matters. Internships are most useful if you are in your junior or senior year.

There are several ways to plan an internship. First, contact an existing program, such as the following:

The Washington Center
1101 14th St. N.W., Suite 500
Washington, D.C. 20005
1-800-486-8921
www.twc.edu/

Such an organization will assist you in finding a suitable internship in government, the private sector, foundations, and nonprofit or volunteer organizations, as well as in considering other opportunities. "Organized" internship programs will also find you housing and usually provide field trips, special seminars, internship advisers, and other support. Ask if your college or university is affiliated with a Washington program or has an internship program of its own.

Second, find your own internship. There are several avenues for identifying and pursuing opportunities. Contact the local office of your representative or senator, which is usually listed in the telephone directory under "United States Government." Many members of Congress have internship coordinators and large, well-supervised programs. Some even may be able to pay part of your expenses.

Always make sure that you explore in detail what a specific job offers. Think carefully about internships that are glorified secretarial jobs in which all you do is typing and filing. A good internship should give you an insider's view on how a profession works. It should furnish some real "hands-on" opportunities to do research, deal with the public, learn about legislation, and watch government officials in action.

Remember that most internships are nonpaying. Make sure that you understand all the costs involved. Arrange for financing through your college, a guaranteed student loan, personal savings, or family support.

Finally, keep in mind that there are also internships in most members' district offices close to home. Such jobs may not have the glamour of Washington, but they may offer excellent opportunities for political experience.

A very useful booklet with which you should start is *Storming Washington: An Intern's Guide to National Government,* by Stephen E. Frantzich. It is available from the following source:

American Political Science Association
1527 New Hampshire Ave. N.W.
Washington, DC 20036
202-483-2512
www.apsanet.org/

Key terms

agenda setting 383

bicameralism 379

casework 382

cloture 385

conference committee 401

conservative coalition 405

constituent 379

continuing resolution 409

direct primary 389

discharge petition 399

enumerated power 380

executive budget 408

fall review 409

filibustering 385

first budget resolution 409

fiscal year (FY) 408

franking 398

gerrymandering 395

instructed delegate 382

joint committee 401

justiciable question 393

lawmaking 381

legislative veto 383

logrolling 381

majority floor leader 403

majority leader of the House 403

minority floor leader 403

minority leader of the House 403

ombudsperson 382

oversight 383

party identifier 389

politico 383

president *pro tempore* 403

reapportionment 393

redistricting 393

representation 382

Rules Committee 385

safe seat 401

second budget resolution 409

select committee 401

seniority system 401

speaker of the House 402

spring review 409

standing committee 400

trustee 382

whip 403

Chapter summary

1 The authors of the Constitution, believing that the bulk of national power should be in the legislature, set forth the structure, power, and operation of Congress. The Constitution states that Congress will consist of two chambers. Partly an outgrowth of the Connecticut Compromise, this bicameral structure established a balanced legislature, with the membership in the House of Representatives based on population and the membership in the Senate based on the equality of states.

2 The first seventeen clauses of Article I, Section 8, of the Constitution specify most of the enumerated, or expressed, powers of Congress, including the right to impose taxes, to borrow money, to regulate commerce, and to declare war. Besides its enumerated powers, Congress enjoys the right to "make all Laws which shall be necessary and proper for carrying into Execution the foregoing Powers, and all other Powers vested by this Constitution in the Government of the United States, or in any Department or Officer thereof." This is called the elastic, or necessary and proper, clause.

3 The functions of Congress include (a) lawmaking, (b) service to constituents, (c) representation, (d) oversight, (e) public education, and (f) conflict resolution.

4 There are 435 members in the House of Representatives and 100 members in the Senate. Owing to its larger size, the House has a greater number of formal rules. The Senate tradition of unlimited debate, or filibustering, dates back to 1790 and has been used over the years to frustrate the passage of bills. Under Senate Rule 22, cloture can be used to shut off debate on a bill.

5 Members of Congress are not typical American citizens. They are older than most Americans; disproportionately white, male, and Protestant; and trained in professional occupations.

6 Congressional elections are operated by the individual state governments, which must abide by rules established by the Constitution and national statutes. The process of nominating congressional candidates has shifted from party conventions to the direct primaries currently used in all states. The overwhelming majority of incumbent representatives and a smaller proportion of senators who run for reelection are successful. The most complicated aspect of the mechanics of congressional elections is reapportionment—the allocation of legislative seats to constituencies. The Supreme Court's "one person, one vote" rule has been applied to equalize the populations of state legislative and congressional districts.

7 Members of Congress are well paid and enjoy other benefits, including franking privileges. Members of Congress have personal and committee staff members available to them and also benefit from a number of legal privileges and immunities.

8 Most of the actual work of legislating is performed by committees and subcommittees within Congress. Legislation introduced into the House or Senate is assigned to the appropriate standing committees for review. Select committees are created for a limited period of time for a specific legislative purpose. Joint committees are formed by the concurrent action of both chambers and consist of members from each chamber. Conference committees are special joint committees set up to achieve agreement between the House and the Senate on the exact wording of legislative acts passed by both chambers in different forms. The seniority rule specifies that longer-serving members will be given preference when committee chairpersons and holders of other important posts are selected.

9 The foremost power holder in the House of Representatives is the speaker of the House. Other leaders are the House majority leader, the House minority leader, and the majority and minority whips. Formally, the vice president is the presiding officer of the Senate, with the majority party choosing a senior member as the president

pro tempore to preside when the vice president is absent. Actual leadership in the Senate rests with the majority floor leader, the minority floor leader, and their respective whips.

10 A bill becomes law by progressing through both chambers of Congress and their appropriate standing and joint committees to the president.

11 The budget process for a fiscal year begins with the preparation of an executive budget by the president. This is reviewed by the Office of Management and Budget and then sent to Congress, which is supposed to pass a final budget by the end of September. Since 1978, Congress has not followed its own time rules.

12 Ethics is the most serious public relations problem facing Congress. Financial misconduct, sexual improprieties, and other unethical behavior on the part of several House and Senate members have resulted in a significant lowering of the public's regard for the institution of Congress. Despite congressional investigations of ethical misconduct and, in some cases, reprimands of members of Congress, the overall view of the public is that Congress has little control over the actions of its members with respect to ethics.

Selected print and electronic resources

SUGGESTED READINGS

Barone, Michael, and Grant Ujifusa. *The Almanac of American Politics, 1999.* Washington, D.C.: National Journal, 1998. This is a comprehensive summary of current political information on each member of Congress, his or her state or congressional district, recent congressional election results, key votes and ratings of roll-call votes by various organizations, sources of campaign contributions, and records of campaign expenditures.

Casey, Chris. *The Hill on the Net: Congress Enters the Information Age.* Boston: Academic Press, 1996. A staff member of Senator Edward Kennedy provides a brief history of how Congress came to embrace the Internet and gives advice on how to access information sources on Capitol Hill.

Davidson, Roger H., and Walter J. Oleszek. *Congress and Its Members.* 6th ed. Washington, D.C.: Congressional Quarterly Press, 1997. This updated classic looks carefully at the "two Congresses," the one in Washington and the role played by congresspersons at home.

Deering, Christopher J., and Steven S. Smith. *Committees in Congress.* 3d ed. Washington, D.C.: Congressional Quarterly Press, 1997. This new edition of a classic work on committees expands its coverage of reforms in Congress and now includes those that have been initiated by the Republican majority since 1995.

Fenno, Richard F., Jr. *Senators on the Campaign Trail: The Politics of Representation.* Norman, Okla.: University of

Oklahoma Press, 1996. One of the outstanding scholars of congressional elections details the relationship between senators and their constituents on the campaign trail.

Fisher, Louis. *Constitutional Conflicts between Congress and the President.* 4th ed. Lawrence, Kans.: University Press of Kansas, 1997. This is an updated version of a book that examines the issues and laws that set Congress and the president against each other.

Loomis, Burdett A. *The Contemporary Congress.* New York: St. Martin's Press, 1997. What has changed in Congress in the 1990s? This analysis looks at the 105th Congress, with its lack of leadership and individualistic membership.

Martin, Fenton S., and Robert U. Goehlert. *How to Research Congress.* Washington, D.C.: Congressional Quarterly Press, 1996. This easy-to-use guide provides information on researching bills, procedures in Congress, investigations, and the inner workings of Congress.

MEDIA SOURCES

Mr. Smith Goes to Washington—A 1939 film in which Jimmy Stewart plays the naive congressman who is quickly educated in Washington. A true American political classic.

The Seduction of Joe Tynan—A 1979 film in which Alan Alda plays a young senator who must face serious decisions about his political role and his private life.

Logging on

To find out about the schedule of activities taking place in Congress, use the following Web sites:

www.senate.gov/

http://www.house.gov/

thomas.loc.gov/

To access the congressional Internet Law Library, go to

www.law.house.gov/

The Congressional Budget Office is online at

www.cbo.gov/

The URL for the Government Printing Office is

www.access.gpo.gov/

For the real inside facts on what's going on in Washington, D.C., you can look at *RollCall*, the newspaper of the Capitol:

www.rollcall.com/

Congressional Quarterly, a publication that reports on Congress:

www.cq.com/

The Hill, which investigates various activities of Congress:

www.hillnews.com/

Using the Internet for political analysis

Point your browser to one of the general guides to Congress given at the following Web sites:

www.house.gov/

www.senate.gov/

www.congress.org/

Look up the Web pages of at least three different members of the House or the Senate. Try to pick members from each of the major parties. Compare the Web pages on the following issues:

1. Which page appears to provide the most assistance to constituents?

2. How much partisan information is included on the Web page?

3. To what extent is the member of Congress giving information about his or her policy stands?

4. To what extent is the member trying to build trust and loyalty through providing personal information and services?

chapter **13**

The Presidency

CHAPTER OUTLINE

417

The President Were Required to Answer Questions Live on Television?

BACKGROUND

EXCEPT FOR THE REQUIREMENT TO REPORT ON THE "STATE OF THE UNION" TO CONGRESS ANNUALLY, THE PRESIDENT HAS NO CONSTITUTIONAL DUTY TO REPORT TO THE PEOPLE OF THE UNITED STATES OR TO ANSWER QUESTIONS RAISED BY THE PRESS OR BY ANY BRANCH OF GOVERNMENT. PRESIDENTS ARE WELL AWARE OF THEIR ABILITY TO CONTROL THEIR MESSAGES TO THE NATION AND, DURING MOMENTS OF POLITICAL DIFFICULTY, USUALLY AVOID MEETING THE PRESS OR TAKING GENERAL QUESTIONS FROM THE MEDIA. PRESIDENT CLINTON, LIKE MANY OF HIS PREDECESSORS, MAY NOT HOLD A PRESS CONFERENCE FOR MONTHS AT A TIME.

IN CONTRAST, THE BRITISH PRIME MINISTER, AS A MEMBER OF PARLIAMENT, ANSWERS QUESTIONS DIRECTLY ON THE FLOOR OF THE HOUSE OF COMMONS IN A WEEKLY SESSION KNOWN AS THE QUESTION HOUR. ANY MEMBER MAY PUT A QUESTION TO THE PRIME MINISTER OR TO MEMBERS OF THE CABINET (ALSO PRESENT), AND IT WILL BE ANSWERED. THE SESSIONS ARE BROADCAST ON BRITISH TELEVISION (AND CAN BE SEEN ON C-SPAN).

WHAT IF . . . THE PRESIDENT WERE REQUIRED TO ANSWER QUESTIONS LIVE ON TELEVISION?

Suppose that the president of the United States were required to appear live on C-SPAN or another public television outlet to answer questions put to him by members of Congress, a panel of journalists, or even members of the public. One effect of such a requirement would be that the administration would lose some of its control over its relationship with the press. Answering questions in person reduces the ability of the president and presidential advisers to structure the situation so as to eliminate any embarrassing questions or issues. Journalists would compete for the opportunity to ask the most difficult question of the president in hopes of generating a newsmaking answer.

Spontaneous question-and-answer sessions could have advantages and disadvantages for a sitting president. John F. Kennedy used his sense of humor and extraordinary wit in frequent press conferences. Completely at ease in such a setting, President Kennedy projected assurance to the public and charmed the reporters with his ability to deal with their questions. In contrast, Dwight Eisenhower did not enjoy press conferences and preferred to make carefully worded statements or use videotaped speeches to get his point across. Presidents such as Gerald Ford and George Bush, who occasionally stumbled on words or facts, preferred not to put themselves in the press conference setting.

GETTING CLOSER TO THE VOTERS

If live question-and-answer sessions were required on a regular basis, the relationship between the president and the voters might change. People might come to have a more well-rounded view of the president if they could see the president react to unrehearsed questions in an informal setting. Although this might reduce the aura of mystery and power surrounding the presidency, it also could reduce cynicism among the public about government and politics.

Regular question periods with the president might, in addition, arouse voters' interest in the president's policies and the work of the national government. Such sessions might motivate voters to learn more about contemporary issues and to participate in politics and elections. And if the president actually took questions from the public, people might feel that they have more impact on the political process than they do now.

CHANGING THE PRESIDENCY

Presidents are not eager to engage in regular question sessions because of the possibility of being asked politically tough or embarrassing questions. Like most other activities, however, if such sessions were broadcast regularly on television, the novelty would wear off, and the administration would become better prepared to answer the questions. People would not place so much weight on any one appearance or statement by the president but rather would evaluate the president's performance over the long term.

FOR CRITICAL ANALYSIS

1. Who would be the best questioners for a presidential question hour: journalists, politicians, or the public?
2. What could be done to assure fairness and respect for the president during such question-and-answer sessions?
3. How could a president use such a process to enhance the passage of the administration's legislative program and policies?

The writers of the Constitution created the presidency of the United States without any models on which to draw. Nowhere else in the world was there a democratically selected chief executive. What the founders did not want was a king. In fact, given their previous experience with royal governors in the colonies, many of the delegates to the Constitutional Convention wanted to create a very weak executive who could not veto legislation. Other delegates, especially those who had witnessed the need for a strong leader in the Revolutionary army, believed a strong executive to be necessary for the republic. The delegates, after much debate, created a chief executive who had enough powers granted in the Constitution to balance those of the Congress.[1]

The power exercised by each president who has held the office has been scrutinized and judged by historians, political scientists, the media, and the public. Indeed, it would seem that Americans are fascinated by presidential power and by the persons who hold the office (although, as the *What If . . .* that opens the chapter suggested, there could be less mystery about the office if the president were subject to "question hours" at regular intervals). In this chapter, after looking at who can become president and at the process involved, we examine closely the nature and extent of the constitutional powers held by the president.

Who Can Become President?

The requirements for becoming president, as outlined in Article II, Section 1, of the Constitution, are not overwhelmingly stringent:

> No person except a natural born Citizen, or a Citizen of the United States, at the time of the Adoption of this Constitution, shall be eligible to the Office of President; neither shall any Person be eligible to that Office who shall not have attained to the Age of thirty-five Years, and been fourteen Years a Resident within the United States.

The only question that arises about these qualifications relates to the term "natural born Citizen." Does that mean only citizens born in the United States and its territories? What about a child born to a U.S. citizen (or to a couple who are U.S. citizens) while visiting or living in another country? Although the question has not been dealt with directly by the Supreme Court, it is reasonable to expect that someone would be eligible if his or her parents were Americans. The first presidents, after all, were not even American citizens at birth, and others were born in areas that did not become part of the United States until later. These questions were debated when George Romney, who was born in Chihuahua, Mexico, made a serious bid for the Republican presidential nomination in the 1960s.[2]

The great American dream is symbolized by the statement that "anybody can become president of this country." It is true that in modern times, presidents have included a haberdasher (Harry Truman—for a short period of time), a peanut farmer (Jimmy Carter), and an actor (Ronald Reagan). But if you examine Appendix C, you will see that the most common previous occupation of presidents in this country has been the legal profession. Out of forty-two presidents, twenty-six have been lawyers, and many have been wealthy.

Although the Constitution states that the minimum-age requirement for the presidency is thirty-five years, most presidents have been much older than that when they assumed office. John F. Kennedy, at the age of forty-three, was the youngest elected president, and the oldest was Ronald Reagan, at age sixty-nine.

Abraham Lincoln is usually classified as one of the greatest presidents because of his dedication to preserving the Union.

---

[1]Forrest McDonald, *The American Presidency: An Intellectual History* (Lawrence, Kans.: University Press of Kansas, 1994), p. 179.

[2]George Romney was governor of Michigan from 1963 to 1969. Romney was not nominated, and the issue remains unresolved.

From left to right, the first cabinet—Henry Knox, Thomas Jefferson, Edmund Randolph, Alexander Hamilton, and the first president—George Washington.

The average age at inauguration has been fifty-four. There has clearly been a demographic bias in the selection of presidents. All have been male, white, and Protestant, except for John F. Kennedy, a Roman Catholic. Presidents have been men of great stature—such as George Washington—and men in whom leadership qualities were not so pronounced—such as Warren Harding.

The Process of Becoming President

Major and minor political parties nominate candidates for president and vice president at national conventions every four years. As discussed in Chapter 10, the nation's voters do not elect a president and vice president directly but rather cast ballots for presidential electors, who then vote for president and vice president in the electoral college.

Because the election is governed by a majority in the electoral college, it is conceivable that someone could be elected to the office of the presidency without having a plurality of the popular vote cast. Indeed, in three cases, candidates won elections even though their major opponents received more popular votes. In cases in which there were more than two candidates running for office, many presidential candidates have won the election with less than 50 percent of the total popular votes cast for all candidates—including Abraham Lincoln, Woodrow Wilson, Harry S. Truman, John F. Kennedy, and Richard Nixon. In the 1992 election, Bill Clinton, with only 43 percent of the vote, defeated incumbent George Bush. Independent candidate H. Ross Perot garnered a surprising 19 percent of the vote. Remember from Chapter 10 that no president has won a majority of votes from the entire voting-age population.

On occasion, the electoral college has failed to give any candidate a majority. At this point, the election is thrown into the House of Representatives. The president is then chosen from among the three candidates having the most electoral college votes. Only two times in our past has the House had to decide on a president. Thomas Jefferson and Aaron Burr tied in the electoral college in 1800. This happened because the Constitution had not been explicit in indicating which of the two electoral votes was for president and which was for vice president. In 1804, the **Twelfth Amendment** clarified the matter by requiring the president and vice president to be chosen separately. In 1824, the House again had to make a choice, this time among William H. Crawford, Andrew Jackson, and John Quincy Adams. It chose Adams, even though Jackson had more electoral and popular votes.

Twelfth Amendment
An amendment to the Constitution, adopted in 1804, that specifies the separate election of the president and vice president by the electoral college.

The Many Roles of the President

The Constitution speaks briefly about the duties and obligations of the president. Based on a brief list of powers and the precedents of history, the presidency has grown into a very complicated job that requires balancing at least five constitutional roles. These are (1) chief of state, (2) chief executive, (3) commander in chief of the armed forces, (4) chief diplomat, and (5) chief legislator of the United States. Here we examine each of these significant presidential functions, or roles. It is worth noting that one person plays all these roles simultaneously and that the needs of these roles may at times come into conflict.

Chief of State

Chief of State
The role of the president as ceremonial head of the government.

Every nation has at least one person who is the ceremonial head of state. In most democratic governments, the role of **chief of state** is given to someone other than the chief executive, who is the head of the executive branch of government (see this chapter's *Politics and Comparative Systems*). In Britain, for example, the chief of state is the queen. In France, the prime minister is the chief executive, and the chief of state is the president. But in the United States, the president is both chief executive and chief of state. According to William Howard Taft, as chief of state the president symbolizes the "dignity and majesty" of the American people.

As chief of state, the president engages in a number of activities that are largely symbolic or ceremonial, such as the following:

■ Decorating war heroes.
■ Throwing out the first ball to open the baseball season.
■ Dedicating parks and post offices.
■ Receiving visiting chiefs of state at the White House.
■ Going on official state visits to other countries.
■ Making personal telephone calls to astronauts.
■ Representing the nation at times of national mourning, such as after the 1998 bombing of two American embassies in Africa.

Many students of the American political system believe that having the president serve as both the chief executive and the chief of state drastically limits the time available to do "real" work. Not all presidents have agreed with this

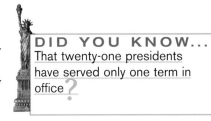

DID YOU KNOW...
That twenty-one presidents have served only one term in office?

POLITICS and Comparative Systems

Filling the Ceremonial Role

For decades, scholars have felt that the president of the United States spends far too much time on the duties of chief of state—largely ceremonial tasks, such as greeting the Super Bowl champions or receiving foreign dignitaries. In virtually every other Western nation, the chief of state is a separate position from that of the chief executive.

In the seven Western European countries headed by royalty, the monarch is considered the chief of state and plays a ceremonial role. In the United Kingdom, for example, Queen Elizabeth represents the state at ceremonial occasions, such as the opening sessions of Parliament, the christening of ships, and receptions for foreign ambassadors.

The majority of European states are not monarchies,

The President and his wife entertain the Emperor and Empress of Japan at a formal White House dinner.

but they split the duties of government between a prime minister and a president. In Switzerland, for example, the president is elected indirectly by the legislature. The president is selected from among members of a governing council, but, once chosen, assumes purely ceremonial duties.

Throughout Western Europe, the pattern is the same: presidents have ceremonial powers only. The single exception to this rule is France, which has a presidential system in which the head of state has real political power, particularly in foreign affairs.

Of course, performing ceremonial duties, such as reviewing troops or lighting the national Christmas tree, allows the U.S. president to be shown in a positive light, which might increase or shore up his popularity.

FOR CRITICAL ANALYSIS

If the United States were to create a ceremonial head of state, what duties would be given to that position? How would that help or hinder the president in performing presidential roles?

Chief Executive
The role of the president as head of the
executive branch of the government.

Civil Service
A collective term for the body of
employees working for the government.
Generally, civil service is understood to
apply to all those who gain government
employment through a merit system.

Appointment Power
The authority vested in the president to
fill a government office or position.
Positions filled by presidential appointment include those in the executive
branch and the federal judiciary, commissioned officers in the armed forces,
and members of the independent regulatory commissions.

conclusion, however—particularly those presidents who have been able to blend
skillfully these two roles with their role as politician. Being chief of state gives
the president tremendous public exposure, which can be an important asset in a
campaign for reelection. When that exposure is positive, it helps the president
deal with Congress over proposed legislation and increases the chances of being
reelected—or getting the candidates of the president's party elected.

Chief Executive

According to the Constitution, "The executive Power shall be vested in a President
of the United States of America. . . . [H]e may require the Opinion, in writing, of
the principal Officer in each of the executive Departments, upon any Subject
relating to the Duties of their respective Offices . . . and he shall nominate, and
by and with the Advice and Consent of the Senate, shall appoint . . . Officers of
the United States. . . . [H]e shall take Care that the Laws be faithfully executed."

As **chief executive,** the president is constitutionally bound to enforce the acts
of Congress, the judgments of federal courts, and treaties signed by the United
States. The duty to "faithfully execute" the laws has been a source of constitutional power for presidents. To assist in the various tasks of the chief executive,
the president has a federal bureaucracy (see Chapter 14), which currently consists of about 2.7 million federal civilian employees.

The Powers of Appointment and Removal.   You might think that the president, as head of the largest bureaucracy in the United States, wields enormous
power. The president, however, only nominally runs the executive bureaucracy,
for most government positions are filled by **civil service** employees.[3] Therefore,
even though the president has **appointment power,** it is not very extensive, being
limited to cabinet and subcabinet jobs, federal judgeships, agency heads, and
about two thousand lesser jobs. This means that most of the 2.7 million federal
employees owe no political allegiance to the president. They are more likely to
owe loyalty to congressional committees or to interest groups representing the
sector of the society that they serve. Table 13–1 shows what percentage of the
total employment in each executive department is available for political appointment by the president.

The president's power to remove from office officials who are not doing a
good job or who do not agree with the president is not explicitly granted by the
Constitution and has been limited. In 1926, however, a Supreme Court decision
prevented Congress from interfering with the president's ability to fire those
executive-branch officials whom the president had appointed with Senate
approval.[4] There are ten agencies whose directors the president can remove at
any time. These agencies include the Arms Control and Disarmament Agency,
the Commission on Civil Rights, the Environmental Protection Agency, the
General Services Administration, the Postal Service, and the Small Business
Administration. In addition, the president can remove all heads of cabinet
departments, all individuals in the Executive Office of the President, and all
political appointees listed in Table 13–1.

Harry Truman spoke candidly of the difficulties a president faces in trying to
control the executive bureaucracy. On leaving office, he referred to the problems
that Dwight Eisenhower, as a former general of the army, was going to have:
"He'll sit here and he'll say do this! do that! and nothing will happen. Poor Ike—
it won't be a bit like the Army. He'll find it very frustrating."[5]

---

[3]See Chapter 14 for a discussion of the Civil Service Reform Act.
[4]*Meyers v. United States,* 272 U.S. 52 (1926).
[5]Quoted in Richard E. Neustadt, *Presidential Power: The Politics of Leadership* (New York: Wiley,
1960), p. 9.

TABLE 13-1

Total Civilian Employment in Cabinet Departments Available
for Political Appointment by the President

EXECUTIVE DEPARTMENT	TOTAL NUMBER OF EMPLOYEES	POLITICAL APPOINTMENTS AVAILABLE	PERCENTAGE
Agriculture	102,542	439	0.42
Commerce	34,497	446	1.29
Defense	766,086	466	0.06
Education	4,540	186	4.09
Energy	17,257	433	2.50
Health and Human Services	59,378	391	0.65
Housing and Urban Development	11,094	156	1.40
Interior	70,843	240	0.33
Justice	113,881	501	0.43
Labor	15,497	188	1.21
State	24,033	1,066	4.43
Transportation	63,050	274	0.43
Treasury	156,394	231	0.14
Veterans' Affairs	243,948	315	0.12
TOTAL	1,683,040	5,332	0.31

SOURCE: *Policy and Supporting Positions* (Washington, D.C.: Government Printing Office, 1996); U.S. Office of Personnel Management, 1997.

The Power to Grant Reprieves and Pardons.   Section 2 of Article II of the Constitution gives the president the power to grant **reprieves** and **pardons** for offenses against the United States except in cases of impeachment. All pardons are administered by the Office of the Pardon Attorney in the Department of Justice. In principle, pardons are granted to remedy a mistake made in a conviction.

The Supreme Court upheld the president's power to grant reprieves and pardons in a 1925 case concerning the pardon granted by the president to an individual convicted of contempt of court. The judiciary had contended that only judges had the authority to convict individuals for contempt of court when court orders were violated and that the courts should be free from interference by the executive branch. The Supreme Court simply stated that the president could grant reprieves or pardons for all offenses "either before trial, during trial, or after trial, by individuals, or by classes, conditionally or absolutely, and this without modification or regulation by Congress."[6] In a controversial decision, President Gerald Ford pardoned former president Richard Nixon for his role in the Watergate affair before any charges were brought in court. After his defeat in the 1992 presidential election, George Bush also exercised the right of executive pardon for six former members of the Reagan administration who had been charged with various offenses relating to the Iran-*contra* affair. The affair concerned the secret sale of arms to Iran and the use of proceeds to aid insurgents (the *contras*) in Nicaragua in their struggle against that country's Communist government.

Reprieve
The presidential power to postpone the execution of a sentence imposed by a court of law; usually done for humanitarian reasons or to await new evidence.

Pardon
The granting of a release from the punishment or legal consequences of a crime; a pardon can be granted by the president before or after a conviction.

Commander in Chief

The president, according to the Constitution, "shall be Commander in Chief of the Army and Navy of the United States, and of the Militia of the several States, when called into the actual Service of the United States." In other words, the armed forces are under civilian, rather than military, control.

INFOTRAC®
COLLEGE EDITION

"Clinton Raises the Stakes in the War against Terrorism"

---

[6]*Ex parte Grossman*, 267 U.S. 87 (1925).

President Clinton talks to soldiers during a visit to Bosnia. The United States played a key role in bringing about the 1995 peace accord in this country, a former province of Yugoslavia that has been plagued by ethnic violence.

Commander in Chief

The role of the president as supreme commander of the military forces of the United States and of the state National Guard units when they are called into federal service.

Certainly, those who wrote the Constitution had George Washington in mind when they made the president the **commander in chief**. Although we no longer expect our president to lead the troops to battle, presidents as commanders in chief have wielded dramatic power. Harry Truman made the awesome decision to drop atomic bombs on Hiroshima and Nagasaki in 1945 to force Japan to surrender and thus bring to an end World War II (see the feature *E-Mail Messages from the Past*). Lyndon Johnson ordered bombing missions against North Vietnam in the 1960s, and he personally selected some of the targets. Richard Nixon decided to invade Cambodia in 1970. Ronald Reagan sent troops to Lebanon and Grenada in 1983 and ordered U.S. fighter planes to attack Libya in 1986. George Bush sent troops to Panama in 1989 and to the Middle East in 1990. Bill Clinton sent troops to Haiti in 1994 and to Bosnia in 1995, and ordered missile attacks on terrorist bases in 1998.

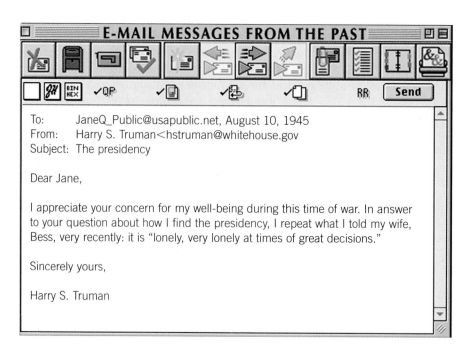

E-MAIL MESSAGES FROM THE PAST

To: JaneQ_Public@usapublic.net, August 10, 1945
From: Harry S. Truman<hstruman@whitehouse.gov
Subject: The presidency

Dear Jane,

I appreciate your concern for my well-being during this time of war. In answer to your question about how I find the presidency, I repeat what I told my wife, Bess, very recently: it is "lonely, very lonely at times of great decisions."

Sincerely yours,

Harry S. Truman

The president is the ultimate decision maker in military matters. Everywhere he goes, so too goes the "football"—a briefcase filled with all the codes necessary to order a nuclear attack. Only the president has the power to order the use of nuclear force.

As commander in chief, the president has probably exercised more authority than in any other role. Constitutionally, Congress has the sole power to declare war, but the president can send the armed forces into a country in situations that are certainly the equivalent of war. When William McKinley ordered troops into Peking to help suppress the Boxer Rebellion in 1900, he was sending them into a combat situation. Harry Truman dispatched troops to Korea as part of a "police action" in 1950. Kennedy, Johnson, and Nixon waged an undeclared war in Southeast Asia, where more than 58,000 Americans were killed and 300,000 were wounded. In none of these situations did Congress declare war.

In an attempt to gain more control over such military activities, in 1973 Congress passed a **War Powers Resolution**—over President Nixon's veto—requiring that the president consult with Congress when sending American forces into action. Once they are sent, the president must report to Congress within forty-eight hours. Unless Congress has passed a declaration of war within sixty days or has extended the sixty-day time limit, the forces must be withdrawn. The War Powers Resolution was tested in the fall of 1983, when Reagan requested that troops be left in Lebanon. The resulting compromise was a congressional resolution allowing troops to remain there for eighteen months. Shortly after the resolution was passed, however, more than 240 sailors and Marines were killed in the suicide bombing of a U.S. military housing compound in Beirut. That event provoked a furious congressional debate over the role American troops were playing in the Middle East, and all troops were withdrawn shortly thereafter.

In spite of the War Powers Resolution, the powers of the president as commander in chief are more extensive today than they were in the past. These powers are linked closely to the president's powers as chief diplomat, or chief crafter of foreign policy.

War Powers Resolution
A law passed in 1973 spelling out the conditions under which the president can commit troops without congressional approval.

President Clinton is shown here working in the Oval Office. This oval-shaped office in the White House, with its immense seal of the United States in the carpet, is often used to represent the power of the presidency and of the United States. Indeed, common references to "the Oval Office" mean specifically the president who is in power at that time.

Chief Diplomat

The Constitution gives the president the power to recognize foreign governments; to make treaties, with the **advice and consent** of the Senate; and to make special agreements with other heads of state that do not require congressional approval. In addition, the president nominates ambassadors. As **chief diplomat,** the president dominates American foreign policy, a role that has been supported numerous times by the Supreme Court.

Advice and Consent
The power vested in the U.S. Senate by the Constitution (Article II, Section 2) to give its advice and consent to the president on treaties and presidential appointments.

Chief Diplomat
The role of the president in recognizing foreign governments, making treaties, and making executive agreements.

Diplomatic Recognition
The president's power, as chief diplomat, to acknowledge a foreign government as legitimate.

Diplomatic Recognition.   An important power of the president as chief diplomat is that of **diplomatic recognition,** or the power to recognize—or refuse to recognize— foreign governments. In the role of ceremonial head of state, the president has always received foreign diplomats. In modern times, the simple act of receiving a foreign diplomat has been equivalent to accrediting the diplomat and officially recognizing his or her government. Such recognition of the legitimacy of another country's government is a prerequisite to diplomatic relations or negotiations between that country and the United States.

Deciding when to recognize a foreign power is not always simple. The United States, for example, did not recognize the Soviet Union until 1933—sixteen years after the Russian Revolution of 1917. It was only after all attempts to reverse the effects of that revolution—including military invasion of Russia and diplomatic isolation—had proved futile that Franklin Roosevelt extended recognition to the Soviet government. U.S. presidents faced a similar problem with the Chinese communist revolution. In December 1978, long after the communist victory in China, Jimmy Carter granted official recognition to the People's Republic of China.[7]

A diplomatic recognition issue that faced the Clinton administration involved recognizing a former enemy—the Republic of Vietnam. Many Americans, particularly those who believed that Vietnam had not been forthcoming in the efforts to find the remains of missing American soldiers or to find out about former prisoners of war, opposed any formal relationship with that nation. After the U.S. government had negotiated with the Vietnamese government for many years

---

[7]The Nixon administration first encouraged new relations with the People's Republic of China by allowing a cultural exchange of ping-pong teams.

The First Family, plagued by media attention at home as the Clinton-Lewinsky scandal unfolded, enjoys a private moment among the terra cotta soldiers of Xian in 1998. The president's trip to China was the first visit to that country by an American president since the Tiananmen Square uprising in 1989. That uprising, conducted by students who wanted a more democratic regime, was crushed by the government.

over the missing-in-action issue and engaged in limited diplomatic contacts for several years, President Clinton announced on July 11, 1995, that the United States would recognize the government of Vietnam and move to establish normal diplomatic relations.

Proposal and Ratification of Treaties. The president has the sole power to negotiate treaties with other nations. These treaties must be presented to the Senate, where they may be modified and must be approved by a two-thirds vote. After ratification, the president can approve the senatorial version of the treaty. Approval poses a problem when the Senate has tacked on substantive amendments or reservations to a treaty, particularly when such changes may require reopening negotiations with the other signatory governments. Sometimes a president may decide to withdraw a treaty if the senatorial changes are too extensive—as Woodrow Wilson did with the Versailles Treaty in 1919. Wilson felt that the senatorial reservations would weaken the treaty so much that it would be ineffective. His refusal to accept the senatorial version of the treaty led to the eventual refusal of the United States to join the League of Nations.

President Jimmy Carter was successful in lobbying for the treaties that provided for the return of the Panama Canal to Panama by the year 2000 and neutralizing the canal. He was unsuccessful, however, in his attempts to gain ratification of the Strategic Arms Limitation Treaty, known as SALT II. That treaty, which provided for limits on nuclear-armed long-range bombers and intercontinental ballistic missiles, encountered fierce opposition from Senate conservatives and from the subsequent Reagan administration.

President Bill Clinton won a major political and legislative victory in 1993 by persuading Congress to ratify the North American Free Trade Agreement (NAFTA). In so doing, he had to overcome opposition from Democrats and most of organized labor. In 1998, he worked closely with Senate Republicans to ensure Senate approval of the Chemical Weapons Convention (see Chapter 18).

Executive Agreements. Presidential power in foreign affairs is enhanced greatly by the use of **executive agreements** made between the president and other heads of state. Such agreements do not require Senate approval, although the House and Senate may refuse to appropriate the funds necessary to implement

DID YOU KNOW...
That President William Henry Harrison gave the longest inaugural address (8,445 words) of any American president, lasting two hours? (The weather was chilly and stormy, and Harrison caught a cold, got pneumonia and pleurisy, and died a month later.)

Executive Agreement
An international agreement made by the president, without senatorial ratification, with the head of a foreign state.

U.S. President Jimmy Carter, Egyptian President Anwar el-Sadat, and Israeli Prime Minister Menachem Begin sign the Camp David accords, bringing peace between Egypt and Israel.

them. Whereas treaties are binding on all succeeding administrations, executive agreements are not binding without each new president's consent.

Among the advantages of executive agreements are speed and secrecy. The former is essential during a crisis; the latter is important when the administration fears that open senatorial debate may be detrimental to the best interests of the United States or to the interests of the president.[8] There have been far more executive agreements (about 9,000) than treaties (about 1,300). Many executive agreements contain secret provisions calling for American military assistance or other support. For example, Franklin Roosevelt used executive agreements to bypass congressional isolationists in trading American destroyers for British Caribbean naval bases and in arranging diplomatic and military affairs with Canada and Latin American nations.

Chief Legislator

Chief Legislator
The role of the president in influencing the making of laws.

Constitutionally, presidents must recommend to Congress legislation that they judge necessary and expedient. Not all presidents have wielded their powers as **chief legislator** in the same manner. President John Tyler was almost completely unsuccessful in getting his legislative programs implemented by Congress. Presidents Theodore Roosevelt, Franklin Roosevelt, and Lyndon Johnson, however, saw much of their proposed legislation put into effect.

State of the Union Message
An annual message to Congress in which the president proposes a legislative program. The message is addressed not only to Congress but also to the American people and to the world. It offers the opportunity to dramatize policies and objectives and to gain public support.

In modern times, the president has played a dominant role in creating the congressional agenda. In the president's annual **State of the Union message**, which is required by the Constitution (Article II, Section 3) and is usually given in late January shortly after Congress reconvenes, the president as chief legislator presents his program. The message gives a broad, comprehensive view of what the president wishes the legislature to accomplish during its session. It is as much a message to the American people and to the world as it is to Congress. Its impact on public opinion can determine the way in which Congress responds to the president's agenda.

---

[8]The Case Act of 1972 requires that all executive agreements be transmitted to Congress within sixty days after the agreement takes effect. Secret agreements are transmitted to the foreign relations committees as classified information.

Each year the president presents the State of the Union message, which is required by Article II, Section 3, of the Constitution and is usually given in late January, shortly after Congress reconvenes. Because the floor of the House of Representatives is so much larger than that of the Senate, the State of the Union speech is given there. Attendees are, of course, all members of Congress, plus usually the justices of the U.S. Supreme Court, the heads of most of the executive departments, and certain others, such as the chairman of the Federal Reserve Board of Governors. The press, of course, is in attendance, too.

Getting Legislation Passed. The president can propose legislation. Congress, however, is not required to pass any of the administration's bills. How, then, does the president get those proposals made into law? One way is by exercising the power of persuasion. The president writes to, telephones, and meets with various congressional leaders; makes public announcements to force the weight of public opinion onto Congress in favor of a legislative program; and, as head of the party, exercises legislative leadership through the congresspersons of the president's party. (See the feature *Politics Wired* for an example of a current legislative proposal by the president.)

To be sure, a president whose party represents a majority in both chambers of Congress may have an easier time getting legislation passed than does a president who faces a hostile Congress. But one of the ways in which a president who faces a hostile Congress still can wield power is through the ability to veto legislation.

Saying No to Legislation. The president has the power to say no to legislation through use of the veto, by which the White House returns a bill unsigned to the legislative body with a **veto message** attached.[9] Because the Constitution requires that every bill passed by the House and the Senate must be sent to the president before it becomes law, the president must act on each bill:

Veto Message
The president's formal explanation of a veto when legislation is returned to the Congress.

---

[9]*Veto* in Latin means "I forbid."

POLITICS **W I R E D**

Should the Executive Have the Key to the Internet?

Both President Clinton and Vice President Gore have appealed to Congress to pass legislation that would prevent software manufacturers from selling their best encryption software overseas. Encryption software contains a series of mathematical codes that make it nearly impossible for someone to decode and read messages that are transmitted electronically through e-mail, within computer networks, or via the Internet.

The administration has claimed that the export of such software at the highest standard will give criminals, such as drug cartels and terrorists, protected communications and prevent the Federal Bureau of Investigation (FBI), and other agencies from

prosecuting these crimes. In addition, the administration has asked for the power to have the "key" (the ability to break the code) to all encryption software manufactured or sold in the United States. Congress has been considering such legislation for more than a year but has been unable to craft a bill that reconciles the interests of the industry and the criminal justice agencies.

Although the Clinton administration has taken a leadership role on increasing the use of technology in government and education, the software industry is opposed to the administration's position on encrypted software. Export controls damage its

business, and giving a key to the government to read its codes violates the industry's strong stand against government control of the Internet.

Certainly, criminals, terrorists, and rogue nations could use coded transmissions over the Internet to plot their activities. Yet what might happen if the executive branch had the key to read all encrypted electronic transmissions? Breaking encryption codes might enable the FBI to find terrorists before they strike or to curb child pornography on the Internet. But could an encryption key also be used to monitor a company's financial records or to monitor citizens' Internet communications and e-mail? In the wrong hands, the key could

be used to break into a company's worldwide networks for purposes of economic espionage. Finally, might encryption software keys be used for political purposes? President Nixon's close call with impeachment came, in part, from his abuse of the power of the presidency in using the FBI and the Internal Revenue Service against his enemies.

FOR CRITICAL ANALYSIS

What kind of limitations could be placed on the government's use of encryption keys? Should a court order be required before encryption keys could be used?

Pocket Veto

A special veto power exercised by the chief executive after a legislative body has adjourned. Bills not signed by the chief executive die after a specified period of time. If Congress wishes to reconsider such a bill, it must be reintroduced in the following session of Congress.

Line-Item Veto

The power of an executive to veto individual lines or items within a piece of legislation without vetoing the entire bill.

1. If the bill is signed, it becomes law.

2. If the bill is not sent back to Congress after ten congressional working days, it becomes law without the president's signature.

3. The president can reject the bill and send it back to Congress with a veto message setting forth objections. Congress then can change the bill, hoping to secure presidential approval and repass it. Or it can simply reject the president's objections by overriding the veto with a two-thirds roll-call vote of the members present in each house.

4. If the president refuses to sign the bill and Congress adjourns within ten working days after the bill has been submitted to the president, the bill is killed for that session of Congress. If Congress wishes the bill to be reconsidered, the bill must be reintroduced during the following session. This is called a **pocket veto**.

Presidents employed the veto power infrequently until the administration of Andrew Johnson, but it has been used with increasing vigor since then (see Table 13–2). The total number of vetoes from George Washington through Bill Clinton's fifth year in office was 2,513, with about two-thirds of those vetoes being exercised by Grover Cleveland, Franklin Roosevelt, Harry Truman, and Dwight Eisenhower.

After the 1994 congressional elections, Bill Clinton faced a Republican-controlled Congress. He used the veto liberally (see Table 13–2) to force Republicans to rewrite their legislative proposals to gain his approval. The Republicans, not having enough votes to overturn Clinton's veto, modified some proposals during subsequent years in order to enact them into law.

The Line-Item Veto. Ronald Reagan lobbied strenuously for Congress to give another tool to the president—the **line-item veto.** Reagan saw the ability to veto *specific* spending provisions of legislation that he was sent by Congress as the only way that the president could control overall congressional spending. In 1996, Congress passed a law providing for the line-item veto. Signed by President Clinton, the law granted the president the power to rescind any item in an appropriations bill unless Congress passed a "disapproval" bill, which could be vetoed. The law did not take effect until after the 1996 election.

President Clinton signs a law amending the federal Food, Drug, and Cosmetics Act in 1998. The law streamlined the process of approving new drugs. Present at the signing are the legislators who were the most influential in the writing of the new law.

President Clinton used the line-item veto on several occasions, beginning on August 11, 1997. While his early vetoes were of little consequence to the members of Congress, the next set of vetoes—of thirty-eight military construction projects—caused an uproar in Congress and the passage of a disapproval bill to rescind the vetoes. The act also was challenged in court as an unconstitutional delegation of legislative powers to the executive branch. In 1998, by a six-to-three vote, the U.S. Supreme Court agreed and overturned the act. The Court

TABLE 13-2

Presidential Vetoes, 1789 to Present

YEARS	PRESIDENT	REGULAR VETOES	VETOES OVERRIDDEN	POCKET VETOES	TOTAL VETOES
1789–1797	Washington	2	0	0	2
1797–1801	J. Adams	0	0	0	0
1801–1809	Jefferson	0	0	0	0
1809–1817	Madison	5	0	2	7
1817–1825	Monroe	1	0	0	1
1825–1829	J. Q. Adams	0	0	0	0
1829–1837	Jackson	5	0	7	12
1837–1841	Van Buren	0	0	1	1
1841–1841	Harrison	0	0	0	0
1841–1845	Tyler	6	1	4	10
1845–1849	Polk	2	0	1	3
1849–1850	Taylor	0	0	0	0
1850–1853	Fillmore	0	0	0	0
1853–1857	Pierce	9	5	0	9
1857–1861	Buchanan	4	0	3	7
1861–1865	Lincoln	2	0	5	7
1865–1869	A. Johnson	21	15	8	29
1869–1877	Grant	45	4	48	93
1877–1881	Hayes	12	1	1	13
1881–1881	Garfield	0	0	0	0
1881–1885	Arthur	4	1	8	12
1885–1889	Cleveland	304	2	110	414
1889–1893	Harrison	19	1	25	44
1893–1897	Cleveland	42	5	128	170
1897–1901	McKinley	6	0	36	42
1901–1909	T. Roosevelt	42	1	40	82
1909–1913	Taft	30	1	9	39
1913–1921	Wilson	33	6	11	44
1921–1923	Harding	5	0	1	6
1923–1929	Coolidge	20	4	30	50
1929–1933	Hoover	21	3	16	37
1933–1945	F. Roosevelt	372	9	263	635
1945–1953	Truman	180	12	70	250
1953–1961	Eisenhower	73	2	108	181
1961–1963	Kennedy	12	0	9	21
1963–1969	L. Johnson	16	0	14	30
1969–1974	Nixon	26*	7	17	43
1974–1977	Ford	48	12	18	66
1977–1981	Carter	13	2	18	31
1981–1989	Reagan	39	9	28	67
1989–1993	Bush	37	1	0	38
1993–1997	Clinton	17	0	0	17
TOTAL		1,473	104	1039	2,513

*Two pocket vetoes, overruled in the courts, are counted here as regular vetoes. President Clinton's line-item vetoes are not included.

SOURCE: Louis Fisher, *The Politics of Shared Power: Congress and the Executive,* 2d ed. (Washington, D.C.: Congressional Quarterly Press, 1987), p. 30; *Congressional Quarterly Weekly Report,* October 17, 1992, p. 3249; and authors' update.

stated that "there is no provision in the Constitution that authorizes the president to enact, to amend or to repeal statutes."[10]

Congress's Power to Override Presidential Vetoes.   A veto is a clear-cut indication of the president's dissatisfaction with congressional legislation. Congress, however, can override a presidential veto, although it rarely exercises this power. Consider that two-thirds of the members of each chamber who are present must vote to override the president's veto in a roll-call vote. This means that if only one-third plus one of the members voting in one of the chambers of Congress do not agree to override the veto, the veto holds. Table 13–2 tells us that it was not until the administration of John Tyler that Congress overrode a presidential veto. In the first sixty-five years of American federal government history, out of thirty-three regular vetoes, Congress overrode only one, or about 3 percent. Overall, only about 7 percent of all vetoes have been overridden.

Measuring the Success or Failure of a President's Legislative Program.   One way of determining a president's strength is to evaluate that president's success as chief legislator. A strong president may be one who has achieved much of the administration's legislative program; a weak president has achieved little. Using these definitions of strong and weak, it is possible to rank presidents according to their legislative success.

Figure 13–1 shows the percentages of presidential victories measured by congressional votes in situations in which the president took a clear-cut position. Based on this information, John Kennedy appears to have been the most successful president in recent years until Clinton, whose high success rate (86.4 percent) in the first two years of his presidency tumbled to 36 percent after the Republican victory in the 1994 elections. In the first two years of his second term, President Clinton's "success rate" hovered around 55 percent. Such data provide a statistical measure but do not indicate the importance of the legisla-

---

[10]*Clinton v. City of New York,* 118 S.Ct. 2091 (1998).

tion, the bills not introduced, or whether the president was perceived as a successful national leader regardless of this measure.

Other Presidential Powers

The powers of the president just discussed are called **constitutional powers,** because their basis lies in the Constitution. In addition, Congress has established by law, or statute, numerous other presidential powers—such as the ability to declare national emergencies. These are called **statutory powers.** Both constitutional and statutory powers have been labeled the **expressed powers** of the president, because they are expressly written into the Constitution or into law.

Presidents also have what have come to be known as **inherent powers.** These depend on the loosely worded statement in the Constitution that "the executive Power shall be vested in a President" and that the president should "take Care that the Laws be faithfully executed." The most common example of inherent powers are those emergency powers invoked by the president during wartime. Franklin Roosevelt used his inherent powers to move the Japanese living in the United States into internment camps for the duration of World War II.

Clearly, modern U.S. presidents have numerous powers at their disposal. According to some critics, among the powers exercised by modern presidents are certain powers that rightfully belong to Congress but that Congress has yielded to the executive branch—see the *Critical Perspective* for a discussion of this issue.

Constitutional Power
A power vested in the president by Article II of the Constitution.

Statutory Power
A power created for the president through laws enacted by Congress.

Expressed Power
A constitutional or statutory power of the president, which is expressly written into the Constitution or into statutory law.

Inherent Power
A power of the president derived from the loosely worded statement in the Constitution that "the executive Power shall be vested in a President" and that the president should "take Care that the Laws be faithfully executed"; defined through practice rather than through constitutional or statutory law.

The President as Party Chief and Superpolitician

Presidents are by no means above political partisanship, and one of their many roles is that of chief of party. Although the Constitution says nothing about the function of the president within a political party (the mere concept of political parties was abhorrent to most of the authors of the Constitution), today presidents are the actual leaders of their parties.

FIGURE 13-1

Presidential Support on Congressional Votes, 1953 to Present
Most presidents have their greatest successes in the first years of their terms in office.

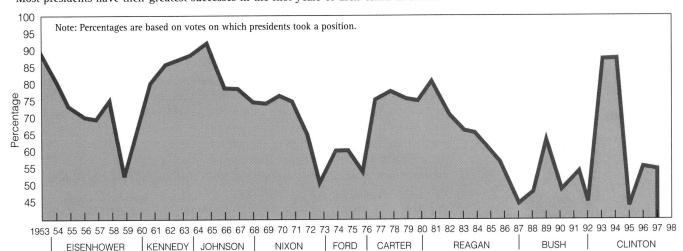

SOURCE: *Congressional Quarterly Weekly Report,* various issues.

Critical perspective

Is Congress Yielding Too Much Power to the Presidency?

When the framers crafted the U.S. Constitution more than 210 years ago, they created a balance of powers among the three branches of the national government. Today, some people claim that Congress has upset this balance of powers by yielding too many powers to the presidency that rightfully should be exercised by the legislative branch. For example, as discussed elsewhere in the chapter, critics of the Line Item Veto Act of 1996 contended that giving line-item veto power to the president essentially transferred legislative power to the executive branch. Some argue that Congress has also yielded its powers to the presidency through the passage of (1) the War Powers Resolution of 1973, (2) the acceptance of "near treaties" without Senate approval, and (3) the delegation of increasingly broad regulatory powers to the administrative branch of government.

The War Powers Resolution

Only Congress has the ability to declare war. Nevertheless, numerous presidents have sent American troops into action without a congressional declaration of war. Truman sent troops to Korea in 1950. Presidents Kennedy, Johnson, and Nixon sent hundreds of thousands of troops to Vietnam in the 1960s and 1970s. In 1973, Congress attempted to gain control over military activities by passing the War Powers Resolution. That resolution requires the president to consult with Congress when sending American troops into action. After they are sent, the president has to report to Congress within two days. Congress then has to pass a declaration of war

within sixty days or extend the sixty-day limit. Otherwise, the U.S. forces must be withdrawn.

Critics of the War Powers Resolution argue that it has had little effect on presidential use of the military throughout the world. According to some, the president today seems to take for granted the unlimited use of the military for humanitarian purposes, as when troops were sent to Somalia, Haiti, and Bosnia, for example. Political scientists Louis Fisher and David Gray Adler are particularly critical of the resolution and argue that it should be repealed. These scholars suggest that although the idea behind the resolution was to curb presidential powers, in effect, it allows the president to engage in war for up to ninety days without congressional approval. According to these authors, "Seldom has a statute misfired to such an extent on a basic purpose. The resolution does violence to the intent of the Framers and has not in any sense insured the collective judgment of Congress and the president in the use of military force."*

Near Treaties

Article II, Section 2, Clause 2, of the Constitution requires that any treaty signed by the president be ratified by a two-thirds favorable vote in the Senate to become effective. President Clinton has found a way around this constitutional requirement, according to his crit-

*Louis Fisher and David Gray Adler, "The War Powers Resolution: Time to Say Goodbye," *Political Science Quarterly*, No. 113 (Spring 1998).

The President as Chief of Party

Patronage
Rewarding faithful party workers and followers with government employment and contracts.

As party leader, the president chooses the national committee chairperson and can try to discipline party members who fail to support presidential policies. One way of exerting political power within the party is by **patronage**—appointing individuals to government or public jobs. This power was more extensive in the past, before the establishment of the civil service in 1883 (see Chapter 14), but the president still retains impressive patronage power. As we noted earlier, the president can appoint several thousand individuals to jobs in the cabinet, the White House, and the federal regulatory agencies.

Perhaps the most important role that the president has played for his party in the late 1990s is that of fund-raiser. Because of the ability of political parties to accept unregulated contributions in the form of "soft money" (see Chapter 10 for details on these contributions), the president is able to raise large amounts of money for the political party through appearances at dinners, speaking engage-

Critical perspective

Is Congress Yielding Too Much Power to the Presidency?—continued

ics, by calling what are essentially treaties by some other name. For example, an agreement signed by the president that gives Russia a voice in North Atlantic Treaty Organization (NATO) decisions whenever such decisions bear on the national security of Russia was called a "founding act" instead of a treaty. Other agreements have been titled "political agreements" or "memorandums of understanding." By not calling these agreements treaties, the president has been able to avoid the necessity of asking the Senate for its advice and consent.

At least one member of Congress, Senator Jesse Helms (R., N.C.) has argued against the legality of such "near" treaties without congressional approval. As head of the Senate Foreign Relations Committee, Helms even added a specific amendment to one treaty requiring that the president present to the Senate (for its advice and consent) any White House agreement with Russia broadening the 1972 Anti-Ballistic Missile Treaty. Helms has continued to be a vociferous critic of giving the presidency more power than the framers of the Constitution intended.

Broad Regulatory Powers

One of the duties of the president, as set forth in Article II, Section 3, of the Constitution, is to "take Care that the Laws be faithfully executed." When Congress passes laws to regulate certain practices, such as occupational safety, it falls to the administrative branch to enforce the laws.

Typically, a law passed by Congress authorizes an agency in the executive branch to "fill in the gaps" in the law by making and implementing specific rules and regulations (see Chapter 14). The Occupational Safety and Health Administration, for example, has the authority to make and implement rules to increase safety in the workplace. These rules have the force of law. Generally, the broader the language of an act, the more gaps there are to fill by agency rulemaking. Each year, administrative agency rules fill between fifty thousand and one hundred thousand pages of the *Federal Register,* the government publication in which agency rules are initially published.

Some contend that Congress, by enacting broad-brushed legislation to regulate the economy, delegates too much lawmaking authority to the executive branch. After all, the Constitution authorizes only the legislative branch to create laws. Yet administrative agencies, to which the Constitution does not specifically refer, make rules that are as legally binding as the laws passed by Congress.

FOR CRITICAL ANALYSIS

1. Senate approval is required for any treaty negotiated by the president. Should executive agreements negotiated by the president with other heads of state be subject to the same requirement? Why or why not?

2. Has Congress, by authorizing executive agencies to make legally binding rules, delegated too much of its lawmaking powers to those agencies? Do you see any reasonable alternative to delegating such authority to agencies?

ments, and other social occasions. In addition, the Clinton White House (expanding prior practice) sponsored social events in the executive mansion for prospective donors, although contributions were not directly solicited there.

Presidents have a number of other ways of exerting influence as party chief. The president may make it known that a particular congressperson's choice for federal judge will not be appointed unless that member of Congress is more supportive of the president's legislative program.[11] The president may agree to campaign for a particular program or for a particular candidate. Presidents also reward loyal supporters in Congress with funding for local projects, tax breaks for regional industries, and other forms of "pork."

---

[11]"Senatorial courtesy" (see Chapter 15) often puts the judicial appointment in the hands of the Senate, however.

Soon after his videotaped admission of a relationship with Monica Lewinsky, President Clinton visited a school in Silver Spring, Maryland, to talk about improving the nation's education system. He was met by protestors along the route.

Constituencies and Public Approval

All politicians worry about their constituencies, and presidents are no exception. Presidents, however, have numerous constituencies. In principle, they are beholden to the entire electorate—the public of the United States—even to those who did not vote. They are certainly beholden to their party constituency, because its members put them in office. The president's constituencies also include members of the opposing party whose cooperation the president needs. Finally, the president has to take into consideration a constituency that has come to be called the **Washington community.** This community consists of individuals who—whether in or out of political office—are intimately familiar with the workings of government, thrive on gossip, and measure on a daily basis the political power of the president.

All of these constituencies are impressed by presidents who maintain a high level of public approval, partly because this is very difficult to accomplish. Presidential popularity, as measured by national polls, gives the president an extra political resource to use in persuading legislators or bureaucrats to pass legislation. After all, refusing to do so might be going against public sentiment. President Reagan showed amazing strength in the public opinion polls for a second-term chief executive, as Figure 13-2 indicates, although there was a one-month drop of 20 points during the Iran-*contra* hearings. President Clinton began his term in office with a 58 percent approval rating and then saw it plummet to 38 percent six months later. By the end of his first year, his rating returned to 48 percent approving his performance, although in the following year, it dropped to 38 percent again. Before the 1996 elections, it had climbed to 51 percent, however, and it climbed to about 58 percent in 1997. To the surprise of his critics, after news of a potential scandal involving a White House intern (Monica Lewinsky) broke, President Clinton's job approval ratings improved. His ratings remained high even after he admitted publicly, in August 1998, that he had engaged in inappropriate sexual conduct with Lewinsky. The public's ratings of his moral character, however, declined steadily.

The presidential preoccupation with public opinion has been criticized by at least one scholar as changing the balance of national politics. Beginning in the early twentieth century, presidents have spoken more to the public and less to Congress. In the previous century, only 7 percent of presidential speeches were addressed to the public; since 1900, 50 percent have been addressed to the pub-

Washington Community
Individuals regularly involved with politics in Washington, D.C.

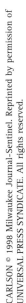

lic.[12] Samuel Kernell has proposed that the style of presidential leadership has changed since World War II, owing partly to the influence of television.[13] Presidents frequently go over the heads of Congress and the political elites, taking their cases directly to the people. This strategy, which Kernell dubbed "going public," gives the president additional power through the ability to persuade and manipulate public opinion. By identifying their own positions so clearly, presidents make compromises with Congress much more difficult and weaken the legislators' positions. Given the increasing importance of the media as the major source of political information for citizens and elites, presidents will continue to

---

[12]Jeffrey Tulis, *The Rhetorical Presidency* (Princeton, N.J.: Princeton University Press, 1987), p. 138.
[13]Samuel Kernell, *Going Public: New Strategies of Presidential Leadership,* 3d ed. (Washington, D.C.: Congressional Quarterly Press, 1997).

FIGURE 13-2

Public Popularity of Bill Clinton and His Predecessors

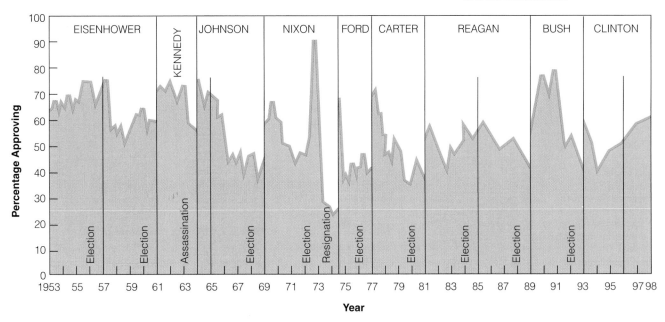

SOURCE: *Public Opinion,* February/March 1988, pp. 36–39; and Gallup Polls, March 1992 through March 1998.

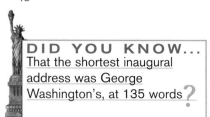

use public opinion as part of their arsenal of weapons to gain support from Congress and to achieve their policy goals.

Special Uses of Presidential Power

Presidents have at their disposal a variety of special powers and privileges not available in other branches of the U.S. government. These include (1) emergency powers, (2) executive orders, (3) executive privilege, and, until relatively recently, (4) impoundment of funds.

Emergency Powers

If you were to read the Constitution, you would find no mention of the additional powers that the executive office may exercise during national emergencies. Indeed, the Supreme Court has indicated that an "emergency does not create power."[14] But it is clear that presidents have used their inherent powers during times of emergency, particularly in the realm of foreign affairs. The **emergency powers** of the president were first enunciated in the Supreme Court's decision in *United States v. Curtiss-Wright Export Corp.*[15] In that case, President Franklin Roosevelt, without authorization by Congress, ordered an embargo on the shipment of weapons to two warring South American countries. The Court recognized that the president may exercise inherent powers in foreign affairs and that the national government has primacy in foreign affairs.

Examples of emergency powers are abundant, coinciding with real or contrived crises in domestic and foreign affairs. Abraham Lincoln's suspension of civil liberties at the beginning of the Civil War, his calling of the state militias into national service, and his subsequent governance of conquered areas and even of areas of northern states were justified by claims that such actions were essential to preserve the Union. Franklin Roosevelt declared an "unlimited national emergency" following the fall of France in World War II and mobilized the federal budget and the economy for war.

President Harry Truman authorized the federal seizure of steel plants and their operation by the national government in 1952 during the Korean War. Truman claimed that he was using his inherent emergency power as chief executive and commander in chief to safeguard the nation's security, as the ongoing steel mill strike threatened the supply of weapons to the armed forces. The Supreme Court did not agree, holding that the president had no authority under the Constitution to seize private property or to legislate such action.[16] According to legal scholars, this was the first time a limit was placed on the exercise of the president's emergency powers.

Executive Orders

Congress allows the president (as well as administrative agencies) to issue **executive orders** that have the force of law. These executive orders can do the following: (1) enforce legislative statutes, (2) enforce the Constitution or treaties with foreign nations, and (3) establish or modify rules and practices of executive administrative agencies.

An executive order, then, represents the president's legislative power. The only apparent requirement is that under the Administrative Procedure Act of

Emergency Power
An inherent power exercised by the president during a period of national crisis, particularly in foreign affairs.

Executive Order
A rule or regulation issued by the president that has the effect of law. Executive orders can implement and give administrative effect to provisions in the Constitution, to treaties, and to statutes.

---

[14]*Home Building and Loan Association v. Blaisdell,* 290 U.S. 398 (1934).
[15]229 U.S. 304 (1936).
[16]*Youngstown Sheet and Tube Co. v. Sawyer,* 343 U.S. 579 (1952).

1946, all executive orders must be published in the *Federal Register,* a daily publication of the U.S. government. Executive orders have been used to establish some procedures for appointing noncareer administrators, to implement national affirmative action regulations, to restructure the White House bureaucracy, to ration consumer goods and to administer wage and price controls under emergency conditions, to classify government information as secret, and to regulate the export of restricted items.

Executive Privilege

Another inherent executive power that has been claimed by presidents concerns the ability of the president and the president's executive officials to refuse to appear before, or to withhold information from, Congress or the courts. This is called **executive privilege,** and it relies on the constitutional separation of powers for its basis. Critics of executive privilege believe that it can be used to shield from public scrutiny actions of the executive branch that should be open to Congress and to the American public.

Limits to executive privilege went untested until the Watergate affair in the early 1970s. Five men had broken into the headquarters of the Democratic National Committee and were caught searching for documents that would damage the candidacy of the Democratic nominee, George McGovern. Later investigation showed that the break-in was planned by members of Richard Nixon's campaign committee and that Nixon and his closest advisers had devised a strategy for impeding the investigation of the crime, using the Central Intelligence Agency for illegal activities. After it became known that all of the conversations held in the Oval Office had been tape-recorded on a secret system, Nixon was ordered to turn over the tapes to the special prosecutor. Nixon refused to do so, claiming executive privilege. He argued that "no president could function if the private papers of his office, prepared by his personal staff, were open to public scrutiny." In 1974, in one of the Court's most famous cases, *United States v. Nixon,*[17] the justices unanimously ruled that Nixon had to hand over the tapes to the Court. The Court held that executive privilege could not be used to prevent evidence from being heard in criminal proceedings.

The claim of executive privilege was also raised by the Clinton administration as a defense against the aggressive investigation of Clinton's relationship with Monica Lewinsky by Independent Counsel Kenneth Starr (see the feature

---

[17]318 U.S. 683 (1974).

Federal Register
A publication of the executive branch of the U.S. government that prints executive orders, rules, and regulations.

Executive Privilege
The right of executive officials to refuse to appear before, or to withhold information from, a legislative committee. Executive privilege is enjoyed by the president and by those executive officials accorded that right by the president.

INFOTRAC®
COLLEGE EDITION

"The Problem of Privilege"

On the day after Labor Day in 1998, Independent Counsel Kenneth Starr sent his report to Congress indicating that the president may have committed impeachable offenses. Accompanying the report were thirty-six boxes of supporting material. Much more material became available in subsequent weeks.

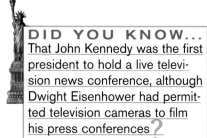
Politics and Ethics: The President and the Independent Counsel for more information on the investigation). The Clinton administration claimed executive privilege for several presidential aides who might have discussed the situation with the president. In addition, President Clinton asserted that his White House counsel did not have to testify before the Starr grand jury due to attorney-client privilege. Finally, the Department of Justice claimed that members of the Secret Service who guard the president could not testify about his activities due to a "protective function privilege" inherent in their duties.

The federal judge overseeing the case denied both the claim of protective function privilege and that of attorney-client privilege in this investigation, so both sides appealed to the Supreme Court for an expedited hearing. The Court refused to accept the case and sent it to a federal appeals court for a hearing. The appellate court upheld the lower court's decision.

POLITICS and Ethics
The President and the Independent Counsel

During the 1980s, Bill Clinton, then governor of Arkansas, and his wife, Hillary Rodham Clinton, a lawyer with a prominent Little Rock, Arkansas, law firm, invested in a real estate development called the Whitewater Development Company. Although the Clintons invested and lost only about $68,000, the irregularities surrounding that investment triggered a sequence of events starting in 1994 that has raised a number of issues about the power of special prosecutors.

The Whitewater investment had raised interest among Republicans and other opponents of the Clinton administration soon after the Clinton victory. Although the Clintons dismissed the investment as a bad family financial decision, their partner in the scheme, James McDougal, was also the owner of a failed savings and loan that was under investigation by the federal regulators in 1984. The thrift's failure cost the American taxpayers about $68 million to repay depositors.

After much delay, in January 1994, Attorney General Janet Reno named an independent counsel, Robert Fiske, who later was replaced by Kenneth Starr, to investigate the matter. As a result of Starr's investigation, James and Susan McDougal and Arkan-sas governor Jim Guy Tucker were tried for federal crimes and found guilty in 1996.

In 1998, tapes that suggested that the president might have obstructed justice by lying about an affair with an intern, Monica Lewinsky, were brought to the Justice Department. The investigation of the charges of possible obstruction of justice and perjury was given to Independent Counsel Starr by the Justice Department, a decision approved by a panel of judges.

Starr's investigation cast a wide net, issuing subpoenas to White House staff, prominent Democrats, bookstore owners, and Lewinsky's mother. It generated claims

of executive privilege and attorney-client privilege from the White House, which the federal courts refused to recognize. It included, for the first time in the nation's history, questioning a president before a grand jury. On the evening of August 17, 1998, following his appearance before the grand jury, President Clinton responded to public pressure to make a statement to the nation regarding his relationship with Monica Lewinsky. In a televised appearance, Clinton confessed that he had indeed engaged in "inappropriate" and "wrongful" conduct with Lewinsky. But he also blamed Starr for having spent more than $40 million to conduct the Whitewater investigation, with no results, and for waging what Clinton considered to be a politically motivated attack on the president.

Starr's long and seemingly political investigation prompted many to question the law that requires the appointment of an independent counsel. An outgrowth of the Watergate period, the law requires the attorney general, after receiving credi-

ble evidence of a crime being committed by one of seventy-five specified executive-branch officials, to seek the appointment of an independent counsel by a three-judge panel. The question raised by most of these investigations (and there have been at least twenty such appointments) is whether there is another way to investigate alleged crimes in the executive branch that would seem to be impartial and beyond the control of the White House. The real complaint against the Starr investigation is that there was no clear way in the law to limit the investigation or bring an end to the process.

FOR CRITICAL ANALYSIS

What kind of process could be created to provide for a fair, impartial investigation of members of the executive branch that would have the confidence of the people and Congress?

Impoundment of Funds

By law, the president proposes a budget, and Congress approves it. But there is no provision in the Constitution that requires the president, as chief executive, to *spend* all of the funds appropriated by Congress, and many presidents prior to the 1970s did not do so. The question of whether the president is required to spend all appropriated funds came to a head during the Nixon administration after a number of confrontations over this issue between the Republican president and an antagonistic, Democratic-controlled Congress. When Nixon vetoed appropriation bills, Congress often overrode his veto. In retaliation, Nixon refused to spend the appropriated funds, claiming that he wanted to reduce overall federal spending.

As part of its Budget and Impoundment Control Act of 1974, Congress required that the president spend all appropriated funds, although Congress gave the president some leeway. A president who is not going to spend all appropriated funds must tell Congress, and only if Congress agrees within forty-five days can the president withhold spending. If the president simply wishes to delay spending, this must be indicated to Congress. If Congress does not agree, it can pass a resolution requiring the immediate spending of the appropriated funds. The Supreme Court in 1975 unanimously ruled that the president had to spend money appropriated by Congress because of his constitutional obligation to "take care that the laws be faithfully executed."[18]

Abuses of Executive Power and Impeachment

Presidents normally leave office either because their first term has expired and they do not seek (or win) reelection or because, having served two full terms, they are not allowed to be elected for a third term (owing to the Twenty-second Amendment, passed in 1951). Eight presidents have died in office. But there is still another way for a president to leave office—by **impeachment.** Articles I and II of the Constitution authorize the House and Senate to remove the president, the vice president, or other civil officers of the United States for crimes of "Treason, Bribery, or other high Crimes and Misdemeanors." Remember from Chapter 12 that according to the Constitution, the impeachment process begins in the House, which impeaches (accuses) the federal officer involved. If the House votes to impeach the officer, it draws up articles of impeachment and submits them to the Senate, which conducts the actual trial. (See the feature in Chapter 12 entitled *Politics and the Constitution: The Power to Impeach* for further details.)

In the history of the United States, no president has ever been impeached and also convicted—and thus removed from office—by means of this process. President Andrew Johnson, who succeeded to the office after the assassination of Abraham Lincoln, was seen by the Radical Republicans as too lenient toward southern states. When Congress passed a law denying the president the right to remove cabinet officers, Johnson defied the law by firing his secretary of war. The House voted to impeach him and submitted eleven articles of impeachment to the Senate. After a three-month trial in the Senate, Johnson was acquitted by one vote. Seven Republicans, convinced that the impeachment articles were politically motivated, crossed party lines to vote for acquittal.

More than a century later, the House Judiciary Committee investigated President Richard Nixon for his involvement in the cover-up of the Watergate

Impeachment
As authorized by Article I of the Constitution, an action by the House of Representatives and the Senate to remove the president, vice president, or civil officers of the United States from office for crimes of "Treason, Bribery, or other high Crimes and Misdemeanors."

---

[18]*Train v. City of New York,* 420 U.S. 35 (1975).

Richard Nixon (right) leaves the White House after his resignation on August 9, 1974. Next to him are his wife, Pat, Betty Ford, and Gerald Ford, the new president.

break-in of 1972 (when Republican operatives broke into the Democratic head-quarters at the Watergate Hotel). After months of testimony, including the discovery of tapes made of presidential conversations in the Oval Office, the House committee approved three articles of impeachment against President Nixon. The charges were obstruction of justice, the abuse of power, and the failure to respond to the committee's subpoenas. Six Republicans voted with the committee's Democrats to approve the articles. Convinced that he had little hope of surviving the trial in the Senate, Nixon resigned on August 9, 1974, before the full House voted on the articles.

In both cases, charges that the process was totally political were common. The Nixon case, because of the taped evidence, became more clearly one of provable offense. In 1998, as the Republican-dominated House Judiciary Committee considered the evidence against President Clinton presented by Independent Counsel Kenneth Starr, Democrats claimed that the process was too political and that there was not enough evidence to show that President Clinton had committed any impeachable offenses.

The outcome of the November 1998 elections made it unlikely that the House could garner the necessary votes to impeach the president. The Republicans' loss of five seats in the House weakened their influence considerably. Additionally, exit polls showed that voters did not believe that the president should be impeached.

The Executive Organization

Gone are the days when presidents answered their own mail, as George Washington did. It was not until 1857 that Congress authorized a private secretary for the president, to be paid by the federal government. Woodrow Wilson typed most of his correspondence, even though he did have several secretaries. At the beginning of Franklin Roosevelt's long tenure in the White House, the entire staff consisted of thirty-seven employees. It was not until the New Deal and World War II that the presidential staff became a sizable organization.

Today, the executive organization includes a White House Office staff of about 600, including some workers who are part-time employees and others who are detailed from their departments to the White House. Not all of these employees have equal access to the president, nor are all of them likely to be equally concerned about the administration's political success. The more than 350 employees who work in the White House Office itself are closest to the president. They often include many individuals who worked in the president's campaign. These assistants are most concerned with preserving the president's reputation. Also included in the president's staff are a number of councils and advisory organizations, such as the National Security Council (NSC). Although the individuals who hold staff positions in these offices are appointed by the president, they are really more concerned with their own area than with the president's overall success. The group of appointees who perhaps are least helpful to the president is the cabinet, each member of which is the principal officer of a government department.

The Cabinet

Although the Constitution does not include the word *cabinet*, it does state that the president "may require the Opinion, in writing, of the principal Officer in each of the executive Departments." Since the time of George Washington, there has been an advisory group, or **cabinet,** to which the president turns for coun-

Cabinet

An advisory group selected by the president to aid in making decisions. The cabinet presently numbers thirteen department secretaries and the attorney general. Depending on the president, the cabinet may be highly influential or relatively insignificant in its advisory role.

sel. Originally, the cabinet consisted of only four officials—the secretaries of state, treasury, and war, and the attorney general. Today, the cabinet numbers thirteen secretaries and the attorney general. (See Table 13-1 on page 423 for the names of the cabinet departments and Chapter 14 for a detailed discussion of these units.)

The cabinet may consist of more than the secretaries of the various departments. The president at his or her discretion can, for example, ascribe cabinet rank to the National Security Council adviser, to the ambassador to the United Nations, or to others. Because neither the Constitution nor statutory law requires the president to consult with the cabinet, its use is purely discretionary. Some presidents have relied on the counsel of their cabinets more than others. Dwight Eisenhower frequently turned to his cabinet for advice on a wide range of governmental policies—perhaps because he was used to the team approach to solving problems from his experience in the U.S. Army. Other presidents solicited the opinions of their cabinets and then did what they wanted to do anyway. Lincoln supposedly said—after a cabinet meeting in which a vote was seven nays against his one aye—"Seven nays and one aye, the ayes have it."[19]

In general, few presidents have relied heavily on the advice of their cabinet members. Jimmy Carter thought he could put his cabinet to good use and held regular cabinet meetings for the first two years of his tenure. Then he fired three cabinet members and forced two others to resign, while reorganizing his "inner government." He rarely met with the members of his cabinet thereafter. In recent years, the growth of other parts of the executive branch has rendered the cabinet less significant as an advisory board to the president.

Often, a president will use a **kitchen cabinet** to replace the formal cabinet as a major source of advice. The term *kitchen cabinet* originated during the presidency of Andrew Jackson, who relied on the counsel of close friends who often met with him in the kitchen of the White House. A kitchen cabinet is a very informal group of advisers, such as Bill Clinton's Arkansas friends, who may or may not otherwise be connected with the government.

Kitchen Cabinet
The informal advisers to the president.

It is not surprising that presidents meet with their cabinet heads only reluctantly. Often, the departmental heads are more responsive to the wishes of their own staffs or to their own political ambitions than they are to the president. They may be more concerned with obtaining resources for their departments than with helping presidents achieve their goals. So there is often a strong conflict of interest between presidents and their cabinet members. It is likely that formal cabinet meetings are held more out of respect for the cabinet tradition than for their problem-solving value.

The Executive Office of the President

When President Franklin Roosevelt appointed a special committee on administrative management, he knew that the committee would conclude that the president needed help. Indeed, the committee proposed a major reorganization of the executive branch. Congress did not approve the entire reorganization, but it did create the **Executive Office of the President (EOP)** to provide staff assistance for the chief executive and to help coordinate the executive bureaucracy. Since that time, a number of agencies within the EOP have been created to supply the president with advice and staff help. These agencies are as follows:

Executive Office of the President (EOP)
Established by President Franklin D. Roosevelt by executive order under the Reorganization Act of 1939, the EOP currently consists of nine staff agencies that assist the president in carrying out major duties.

- White House Office (1939).
- Council of Economic Advisers (1946).
- National Security Council (1947).

---

[19]Quoted in Thomas E. Cronin, *The State of the Presidency,* 2d ed. (Boston: Little, Brown, 1980), p. 11.

- Office of the United States Trade Representative (1963).
- Council on Environmental Quality (1969).
- Office of Management and Budget (1970).
- Office of Science and Technology Policy (1976).
- Office of Administration (1977).
- Office of National Drug Control Policy (1988).
- Office of Policy Development (1993).

Several of the offices within the EOP are especially important, including the White House Office, the Council of Economic Advisers, the Office of Management and Budget, and the National Security Council.

The White House Office. One of the most important of the agencies within the EOP is the **White House Office,** which includes most of the key personal and political advisers to the president. Among the jobs held by these aides are those of legal counsel to the president, secretary, press secretary, and appointments secretary. Often, the individuals who hold these positions are recruited from the president's campaign staff. Their duties—mainly protecting the president's political interests—are similar to campaign functions. In all recent administrations, one member of the White House Office has been named **chief of staff.** This person, who is responsible for coordinating the office, is one of the president's chief advisers.

Employees of the White House Office have been both envied and criticized. The White House Office, according to most former staffers, grants its employees access and power. They are able to use the resources of the White House to contact virtually anyone in the world by telephone, cable, fax, or electronic mail as well as to use the influence of the White House to persuade legislators and citizens. Because of this influence, staffers are often criticized for overstepping the bounds of the office. It is the appointments secretary who is able to grant or deny senators, representatives, and cabinet secretaries access to the president. It is the press secretary who grants to the press and television journalists access to any information about the president. White House staff members are closest to the president and may have considerable influence over the administration's decisions. Often, when presidents are under fire for their decisions, the staff is accused of keeping the chief executive too isolated from criticism or help. Presidents insist that they will not allow the staff to become too powerful, but given the difficulty of the office, each president eventually turns to staff members for loyal assistance and protection.

The Council of Economic Advisers. The Employment Act of 1946 created a three-member **Council of Economic Advisers (CEA)** to advise the president on economic matters. The council's advice serves as the basis for the president's annual economic report to Congress. Each of the three members is appointed by the president and can be removed at will. In principle, the CEA was also created to advise the president on economic policy, but for the most part the function of the CEA has been to prepare the annual report.

The Office of Management and Budget. The **Office of Management and Budget (OMB)** was originally the Bureau of the Budget, which was created in 1921 within the Department of the Treasury. Recognizing the importance of this agency, Franklin Roosevelt moved it into the White House Office in 1939. Richard Nixon reorganized the Bureau of the Budget in 1970 and changed its name to reflect its new managerial function. It is headed by a director, who must make up the annual federal budget that the president presents to Congress each January for approval. In principle, the director of the OMB has broad fiscal powers in planning and estimating various parts of the federal budget, because all

---

White House Office
The personal office of the president, which tends to presidential political needs and manages the media.

Chief of Staff
The person who is named to direct the White House Office and advise the president.

Council of Economic Advisers (CEA)
A staff agency in the Executive Office of the President that advises the president on measures to maintain stability in the nation's economy; established in 1946.

Office of Management and Budget (OMB)
A division of the Executive Office of the President created by executive order in 1970 to replace the Bureau of the Budget. The OMB's main functions are to assist the president in preparing the annual budget, to clear and coordinate all departmental agency budgets, to help set fiscal policy, and to supervise the administration of the federal budget.

agencies must submit their proposed budget to the OMB for approval. In reality, it is not so clear that the OMB truly can affect the greater scope of the federal budget. The OMB may be more important as a clearinghouse for legislative proposals initiated in the executive agencies.

The National Security Council. The **National Security Council (NSC)** is a link between the president's key foreign and military advisers and the president. Its members consist of the president, the vice president, and the secretaries of state and defense, plus other informal members. The NSC has the resources of the National Security Agency (NSA) at its disposal in giving counsel to the president. (The NSA protects U.S. government communications and produces foreign intelligence information.) Included in the NSC is the president's special assistant for national security affairs. Richard Nixon had Henry Kissinger in this post; Jimmy Carter had the equally visible Zbigniew Brzezinksi. In the Reagan years, staff members of the NSC, including Lieutenant Colonel Oliver North and Admiral John Poindexter, were the focus of national media attention because of their involvement in the Iran-*contra* affair (discussed earlier in this chapter).

National Security Council (NSC)
A staff agency in the Executive Office of the President established by the National Security Act of 1947. The NSC advises the president on domestic and foreign matters involving national security.

The Vice Presidency

The Constitution does not give much power to the vice president. The only formal duty is to preside over the Senate—which is rarely necessary. This obligation is fulfilled when the Senate organizes and adopts its rules and when the vice president is needed to decide a tie vote. In all other cases, the president pro tem manages parliamentary procedures in the Senate. The vice president is expected to participate only informally in senatorial deliberations, if at all.

INFOTRAC®
COLLEGE EDITION

"Prospects for the 2000 Democratic Nomination"

The Vice President's Job

Vice presidents have traditionally been chosen by presidential nominees to balance the ticket to attract groups of voters or appease party factions. If a presidential nominee is from the North, it is not a bad idea to have a vice presidential nominee who is from the South or the West. If the presidential nominee is from a rural state, perhaps someone with an urban background would be most suitable as a running

Vice President Al Gore. Since taking office in 1993, Vice President Gore has become known for his aggressive efforts to strengthen environmental-protection policies on a global basis. He has also taken special interest in areas of emerging technology and was instrumental in providing subsidies to public schools for Internet use.

mate. Presidential nominees who are strongly conservative or strongly liberal would do well to have vice presidential nominees who are more in the middle of the political road.

Presidential nominee Bill Clinton ignored almost all of the conventional wisdom when he selected Senator Al Gore of Tennessee as his running mate in 1992. Not only was Gore close in age and ideology to Clinton, but he also came from the mid-South. The advantage gained from choosing Gore was his experience in the Senate, his strong position on issues such as the environment, and his compatibility with Clinton. Clinton and Gore and their families became a very successful campaign team whose friendship continued after the inauguration. Although Clinton's position as president has not been challenged by Gore's activity, the vice president continues to lead the administration on most environmental issues.

Vice presidents infrequently have become elected presidents in their own right. John Adams and Thomas Jefferson were the first to do so. Then Martin Van Buren was elected president in 1836 after he had served as Andrew Jackson's vice president for the previous eight years. In 1988, George Bush was elected to the presidency after eight years as Ronald Reagan's vice president.

The job of vice president is not extremely demanding, even when the president gives some specific task to the vice president. Typically, vice presidents spend their time supporting the president's activities. All of this changes, of course, if the president becomes disabled or dies in office.

Presidential Succession

An attempted assassination of Ronald Reagan occurred on March 31, 1981. In the foreground, press secretary James Brady lies seriously wounded. In the background, two men bend over President Reagan.

Eight vice presidents have become president because of the death of the president. John Tyler, the first to do so, took over William Henry Harrison's position after only one month. No one knew whether Tyler should simply be a caretaker until a new president could be elected three and a half years later or whether he

actually should be president. Tyler assumed that he was supposed to be the chief executive and he acted as such—although he was commonly referred to as "His Accidency." On all occasions since then, vice presidents taking over the position of the presidency because of the incumbent's death have assumed all of the presidential powers.

But what should a vice president do if a president becomes incapable of carrying out necessary duties while in office? When James Garfield was shot in 1881, he stayed alive for two and a half months. What was Vice President Chester Arthur's role?

This question was not addressed in the original Constitution. Article II, Section 1, says only that "in Case of the Removal of the President from Office, or of his Death, Resignation, or Inability to discharge the Powers and Duties of the said Office, the same shall devolve on the Vice President." There have been many instances of presidential disability. When Dwight Eisenhower became ill a second time in 1958, he entered into a pact with Richard Nixon that provided that the vice president could determine whether the president was incapable of carrying out his duties if the president could not communicate. John Kennedy and Lyndon Johnson entered into similar agreements with their vice presidents. Finally, in 1967, the **Twenty-fifth Amendment** was passed, establishing procedures in case of presidential incapacity.

The Twenty-fifth Amendment

According to the Twenty-fifth Amendment, when the president believes that he is incapable of performing the duties of office, he must inform the Congress in writing. Then the vice president serves as acting president until the president can resume his normal duties. When the president is unable to communicate, a majority of the cabinet, including the vice president, can declare that fact to Congress. Then the vice president serves as acting president until the president resumes his normal duties. If a dispute arises over the return of the president's ability to discharge his normal functions, a two-thirds vote of Congress is required to decide whether the vice president shall remain acting president or whether the president shall resume his duties.

Although President Reagan did not formally invoke the Twenty-fifth Amendment during his surgery for the removal of a cancerous growth in his colon on July 13, 1985, he followed its provisions in temporarily transferring power to the vice president, George Bush. At 10:32 A.M., before the operation began, Reagan signed letters to the speaker of the House and the president pro tem of the Senate directing that the vice president "shall discharge those powers and duties in my stead commencing with the administration of anesthesia to me." In the early evening of that same day, Reagan transmitted another letter to both officials announcing that he was again in charge. During this period, Vice President Bush signed no bills and took no actions as acting president. Although the Reagan administration claimed that the president's action set no precedents, most legal experts saw Reagan's acts as the first official use of the Twenty-fifth Amendment.

When the Vice Presidency Becomes Vacant

The Twenty-fifth Amendment also addresses the issue of how the president should fill a vacant vice presidency. Section 2 of the amendment simply states, "Whenever there is a vacancy in the office of the Vice President, the President shall nominate a Vice President who shall take office upon confirmation by a majority vote of both Houses of Congress." This is exactly what occurred when Richard Nixon's vice president, Spiro Agnew, resigned in 1973 because of his

Twenty-fifth Amendment
An amendment to the Constitution adopted in 1967 that establishes procedures for filling vacancies in the two top executive offices and that makes provisions for situations involving presidential disability.

Spiro Agnew was Richard Nixon's vice president from 1969 to 1973. Agnew resigned amid allegations of income tax evasion in connection with money he received when he was governor of Maryland.

TABLE 13-3

Line of Succession to the Presidency of the United States

1. Vice president
2. Speaker of the House of Representatives
3. Senate president *pro tempore*
4. Secretary of state
5. Secretary of the treasury
6. Secretary of defense
7. Attorney general
8. Secretary of the interior
9. Secretary of agriculture
10. Secretary of commerce
11. Secretary of labor
12. Secretary of health and human services
13. Secretary of housing and urban development
14. Secretary of transportation
15. Secretary of energy
16. Secretary of education
17. Secretary of veterans affairs

alleged receipt of construction contract kickbacks during his tenure as governor of Maryland. Nixon turned to Gerald Ford as his choice for vice president. After extensive hearings, both chambers of Congress confirmed the appointment. Then, when Nixon resigned on August 9, 1974, Ford automatically became president and nominated as his vice president Nelson Rockefeller. Congress confirmed Ford's choice. For the first time in the history of the country, both the president and the vice president were individuals who were not elected to their positions.

The question of who shall be president if both the president and vice president die is answered by the Succession Act of 1947. If the president and vice president die, resign, or are disabled, the speaker of the House will act as president, after resigning from Congress. Next in line is the president pro tem of the Senate, followed by the cabinet officers in the order of the creation of their departments (see Table 13–3).

The Presidency: Issues for the New Century

During the twentieth century, the responsibilities of world leadership and the growth of government led to enormous changes in the American presidency. The office changed from being that of "chief clerk" to being leader of the most powerful military in the Western world and the chief operating officer of a huge organization that affects the lives of everyone in the nation. The relationship between the president and the electorate also changed, most notably through the growth of television as the major news source for most Americans. Presidential staffs work continuously to gain favorable images and reports on television and in the other media. It may be that our nation's fixation on image and popularity keeps us from considering the substance of public policy and tackling the work of making real policy choices.

Additionally, Congress, faced with impossible tasks in regulating the huge economy and overseeing the government, has delegated much of its lawmaking power to the president. After President Clinton and the Republican Congress had tested "gridlock" through the partial shutdowns of government in 1995, both the president and the majority Republicans found that their respective standing with the public was improved by cooperation in the legislative process. Because it appears that the public approves such "divided government," presidents in the future will need to work out their relationship with the opposition in Congress to be able to pursue their policy goals.

Finally, the impact of the Clinton presidency on future presidents will only be known in the new century. In the lawsuit brought against him by Paula Jones for sexual harassment, Clinton claimed that a sitting president could not be sued for past conduct. The court held otherwise, thus setting a precedent that previously did not exist. Additionally, during Kenneth Starr's investigation of the Lewinsky affair, the president claimed various privileges in an attempt to prevent his White House counsel and members of the Secret Service from giving testimony about Clinton and his activities. It may be that President Clinton, by claiming these privileges and having them denied by the courts, has, in the long run, weakened the presidency. Future presidents may be reluctant to rely for advice on White House counsel, knowing that such communication may not be privileged. Future presidents will also face the possibility that they may be called to testify before a grand jury.

T O W A R D   A C T I V E   C I T I Z E N S H I P

COMMUNICATING WITH THE WHITE HOUSE

Writing to the president of the United States long has been a way for citizens to express their political opinions. The most traditional form of communication is, of course, by letter. Letters to the president should be addressed to:

The President of the United States
The White House
1600 Pennsylvania Avenue N.W.
Washington, D.C. 20500

If you wish to write to Hillary Rodham Clinton, letters may be sent to her at the same address. Will you get an answer? Almost certainly. The White House mail room is staffed by volunteers and paid employees who sort the mail for the president and tally the public's concerns. You may receive a standard response to your comments or a more personal, detailed response.

You can also call the White House on the telephone and leave a message for the president or First Lady. To call the switchboard, call 202-456-1414, a number publicized by former Secretary of State James Baker when he told the Israelis publicly, "When you're serious about peace, call us at . . . ." The switchboard received more than eight thousand calls in the next twenty-four hours.

The White House also has a round-the-clock comment line, which you can reach at 202-456-1111. When you call that number, an operator will take down your comments and forward them to the president's office. Again, the operators tally the calls to give the president a measurement of opinion on specific topics.

In this electronic age, the Clinton White House has been aggressive in its use of the Internet and the World Wide Web. The home page for the White House is listed in the *Logging On* feature at the end of this chapter. It is always designed to be entertaining and to convey information about the president. You can, however, easily send your comments and ideas to the White House via e-mail. Send comments to the president to

President@whitehouse.gov

Address e-mail to the First Lady at

First.Lady@whitehouse.gov

You will receive an electronic response to your mail from the White House staff. Due to the extremely heavy e-mail load, you will only receive one response per day regardless of how many messages you send.

Key terms

advice and consent 426

appointment power 422

cabinet 442

chief diplomat 426

chief executive 422

chief legislator 428

chief of staff 444

chief of state 420

civil service 422

commander in chief 424

constitutional power 433

Council of Economic Advisers (CEA) 444

diplomatic recognition 426

emergency power 438

executive agreement 427

Executive Office of the President (EOP) 443

executive order 438

executive privilege 439

expressed power 433

Federal Register 439

impeachment 441

inherent power 433

kitchen cabinet 443

line-item veto 430

National Security Council (NSC) 445

Office of Management and Budget (OMB) 444

pardon 423

patronage 434

pocket veto 430

reprieve 423

State of the Union message 428

statutory power 433

Twelfth Amendment 420

Twenty-fifth Amendment 447

veto message 429

War Powers Resolution 425

Washington community 436

White House Office 444

Chapter summary

1 The office of the presidency in the United States, combining as it does the functions of chief of state and chief executive, is unique. The framers of the Constitution were divided over whether the president should be a weak executive controlled by the legislature or a strong executive.

2 The requirements for the office of the presidency are outlined in Article II, Section 1, of the Constitution. The president's roles include both formal and informal duties. The president is chief of state, chief executive, commander in chief, chief diplomat, chief legislator, and party chief.

3 As chief of state, the president is ceremonial head of the government. As chief executive, the president is bound to enforce the acts of Congress, the judgments of the federal courts, and treaties. The chief executive has the power of appointment and the power to grant reprieves and pardons.

4 As commander in chief, the president is the ultimate decision maker in military matters. As chief diplomat, the president recognizes foreign governments, negotiates treaties, signs agreements, and nominates and receives ambassadors.

5 The role of chief legislator includes recommending legislation to Congress, lobbying for the legislation, approving laws, and exercising the veto power. The president also has statutory powers written into law by Congress. The president is also leader of his or her political party. Presidents use their power to persuade and their access to the media to fulfill this function.

6 Presidents have a variety of special powers not available to other branches of the government. These include emergency power, executive power, executive privilege, and impoundment of funds.

7 Abuses of executive power are dealt with by Articles I and II of the Constitution, which authorize the House and Senate to impeach and remove the president, vice president, or other officers of the federal government for crimes of "Treason, Bribery or other high Crimes and Misdemeanors."

8 The president gets assistance from the cabinet and from the Executive Office of the President (including the White House Office).

9 The vice president is the constitutional officer assigned to preside over the Senate and to assume the presidency in case of the death, resignation, removal, or disability of the president. The Twenty-fifth Amendment, passed in 1967, established procedures to be followed in case of presidential incapacity and when filling a vacant vice presidency.

Selected print and electronic resources

SUGGESTED READINGS

Ellis, Richard J. *Presidential Lightning Rods: The Politics of Blame Avoidance*. Lawrence, Kans.: University Press of Kansas, 1995. The author examines the tactics that presidents and their advisers use to enhance their reputations and the techniques that can be used to avoid blame for mistakes or crises.

Jones, Charles O. *The Presidency in a Separated System*. Washington, D.C.: The Brookings Institution, 1994. Rather than decrying the gridlock of Congress and the president or looking for an imperial president, Jones discusses the constitutionally required tension between the two branches of government. By looking at twenty-eight different pieces of legislation, he is able to demonstrate the many patterns of interaction and partisanship that occur in the process of lawmaking.

Kernell, Samuel. *Going Public: New Strategies of Presidential Leadership*. 3d ed. Washington, D.C.: Congressional Quarterly Press, 1997. Kernell updates his classic work on how presidents go "over the head of Congress" to the people and includes examples from the Clinton presidency.

McDonald, Forrest. *The American Presidency: An Intellectual History*. Lawrence, Kans.: University Press of Kansas, 1994. This intellectual history traces the development of the presidency and its powers from the early colonial governors through the American Revolution, the Constitutional Convention, and the early presidents.

Pfiffner, James P. *The Modern Presidency*. 2d ed. New York: St. Martin's Press, 1997. This examination of the presidency looks carefully at the importance of the White House staff, the media, and the president's role in foreign policy in the contemporary political scene.

Pious, Richard M. *The Presidency*. Boston: Allyn and Bacon, 1996. In this comprehensive look at the presidency, the author uses examples from many presidencies, including the Clinton administration, to illustrate his discussions of presidential influence.

Reich, Robert B. *Locked in the Cabinet*. New York: Random House, 1998. This memoir is a lively, anecdote-filled account of life in Washington, D.C., during Reich's four years as secretary of labor.

Thomas, Norman C., Joseph A. Pika, and Richard A. Watson. *The Politics of the Presidency*. 4th ed. Washington, D.C.: Congressional Quarterly Press, 1996. This excellent, up-to-date book covers the changing presidency as well as the relationship between the president and the other two branches of government.

Watson, Richard A. *Presidential Vetoes and Public Policy.* Lawrence, Kans.: University Press of Kansas, 1995. Watson discusses the use of the veto by presidents and its influence on lawmaking.

MEDIA RESOURCES

Sunrise at Campobello—An excellent portrait of one of the greatest presidents, Franklin Delano Roosevelt, produced in 1960 and starring Ralph Bellamy.

LBJ: A Biography—An acclaimed biography of Lyndon Johnson that covers his rise to power, his presidency, and the events of the Vietnam War, which ended his presidency; produced in 1991 as part of PBS's *The American Experience* series.

Nixon—An excellent 1995 film exposing the events of Richard Nixon's troubled presidency; Anthony Hopkins plays the embattled but brilliant chief executive.

Logging on

This is a site from which you can obtain extensive information on the White House and the presidency:

www.whitehouse.gov/WH/Welcome.html

The Library of Congress White House page is a great source of information and has numerous presidency-related links. The URL is

lcweb.loc.gov/global/

The White House archives at Texas A&M are helpful for researching documents and other academic resources. You can reach these archives at

www.tamu.edu/whitehouse/

Inaugural addresses of American presidents from Washington to Clinton can be found at

www.columbia.edu/acis/bartleby/inaugural/ index.html

Using the Internet for political analysis

Take a look at the activities of the president of the United States by clicking on the White House at

www.whitehouse.gov/

and the Government Documents site, SunSITE, at

sunsite.unc.edu/govdocs.html

Try to find the president's schedule for a day or a week, or read at least two speeches he has given within the last few months. After you have read these documents, decide which role the president was playing when he engaged in certain activities or made certain statements: commander in chief, chief legislator, and so on.

You then might want to search a site such as that of the *Congressional Quarterly* at

www.cq.com/

or AllPolitics at

www.allpolitics.com/

and look at articles from the same date as the president's speech for an alternative view of what he was proposing.

chapter **14**

The Bureaucracy

453

There Were a Freeze on Regulations?

BACKGROUND

ALTHOUGH AMERICANS BELIEVE THEM-SELVES TO BE THE FREEST OF ALL PEO-PLES, THEY NEVERTHELESS ARE SUB-JECTED TO NUMEROUS REGULATIONS IMPOSED BY GOVERNMENT AGENCIES. INDEED, RULES AND REGULATIONS DOMINATE MUCH OF THE DAILY LIFE IN THIS COUNTRY. WHEN YOU DRIVE, YOU ARE SUBJECTED TO THE "RULES OF THE ROAD," AND WHEN YOU PARK, YOU ARE SUBJECTED TO PARKING REGULATIONS. WHEN YOU ATTEMPT TO GET A JOB, PROSPECTIVE EMPLOYERS MUST ABIDE BY GOVERNMENT LAWS AND REGULA-TIONS CONCERNING HIRING DECISIONS. WHEN YOU GET A JOB, YOUR WORKING CONDITIONS ARE REGULATED BY THE FEDERAL OCCUPATIONAL SAFETY AND HEALTH ADMINISTRATION AS WELL AS BY STATE AND LOCAL AUTHORITIES.

VIRTUALLY ALL ASPECTS OF BUSI-NESS ARE REGULATED—HIRING AND FIRING DECISIONS, WORKPLACE SAFETY, PRODUCTION TECHNIQUES THAT MAY AFFECT THE ENVIRONMENT, AND SO ON. BUSINESS FIRMS TODAY HAVE FAR LESS CONTROL OVER THEIR DECISION MAKING THAN THEY DID IN THE PAST. IN FACT, JUST LEARNING ABOUT AND INTERPRETING THE MANY GOVERNMENT RULES THAT APPLY TO THEIR BUSINESSES IS DIFFICULT.

WHAT IF THERE WERE A FREEZE ON REGULATIONS?

Assume for a moment that no additional regulations whatever could be imposed on American businesses. One major area of compliance for businesses would no longer be in doubt—

pollution control. Currently, the Environmental Protection Agency (EPA) estimates that each year U.S. businesses collectively must spend at least $3 billion and 150 million hours to complete paperwork required by the EPA. Presumably, a freeze on regulations would also freeze these indirect compliance costs. In the meantime, businesses would have time to regroup. They could determine what they actually have to do for existing regulations and not have to worry about new regulations, which sometimes are issued on a monthly basis.

Regulatory language is often difficult to interpret. Recently, a federal judge commented on the regulations set forth in the Resource Conservation and Recovery Act: "The people who wrote this [act] ought to go to jail. They ought not be indicted, that is not enough." He also pointed out that EPA regulations define hazardous waste as only solid waste whereas other agency regulations define solid waste as a subset of hazardous waste.* Frank Shafrogh of the National League of Cities claims that the EPA's regulations "are written in Latin with Greek footnotes."

*Forbes, October 20, 1997, p. 174.

EMPLOYEES MIGHT BENEFIT FROM A FREEZE ON REGULATIONS

Currently, it is difficult for employees to assess what their rights are under the existing regulations. These regulations change constantly, thereby adding another layer of uncertainty. A freeze on regulations would generate more predictability in all aspects of the business world, including employment.

Finally, if regulations were frozen, the federal work force would stabilize and so, too, would the state work force, assuming that state regulations were frozen, too. Taxpayers would find fewer resources going to support federal and state bureaucracies.

THERE WOULD BE COSTS, TOO

Nothing in this world comes free of charge. A freeze on state and federal regulations might lead to additional costs to society. More environmental pollution might result because businesses could devise ways to circumvent current regulations without fear of new ones being imposed.

As new situations occur, no new regulations would be promulgated to cover those situations. This means that safety in the workplace might be com-

promised. Any work practice not currently covered by an existing regulation would not be covered by a new one. Thus, unsafe work practices that have not been identified yet by the Occupational Safety and Health Administration could continue to exist. Persons with disabilities and other protected groups might find that they have fewer guarantees if situations arise that are not covered by existing rules.

A good example of how new regulations evolve is cyberspace. Currently, Congress and the states are attempting to develop regulations for commerce and speech on the Internet. If no new regulations were possible, the Internet would essentially remain wide open and perhaps be subject to abuse.

FOR CRITICAL ANALYSIS

1. Very little of American business life was regulated in the first 150 years of this nation. Why is there so much regulation today?

2. What groups would be most against a freeze on federal and state regulations?

Virtually every modern president, at one time or another, has proclaimed that his administration was going to "fix government." As you can see in Table 14-1, all modern presidents also have put forth plans to end government waste and inefficiency. While none has come out in favor of a freeze on regulations, as this chapter's opening *What If* . . . suggested, they all have declared an intervention to reform the bureaucracy. Their success has been, in a word, underwhelming. Presidents have been generally powerless to affect the structure and operation of the federal bureaucracy significantly.

The bureaucracy has been called the "fourth branch of government," even though you will find no reference to the bureaucracy in the original Constitution or in the twenty-seven amendments that have been passed since 1787. But Article II, Section 2, of the Constitution gives the president the power to appoint "all other Officers of the United States, whose Appointments are not herein otherwise provided for." Article II, Section 3, states that the president "shall take Care that the Laws be faithfully executed, and shall Commission all the Officers of the United States." Constitutional scholars believe that the legal basis for the bureaucracy rests on these two sections in Article II.

The Nature of Bureaucracy

A **bureaucracy** is the name given to a large organization that is structured hierarchically to carry out specific functions. Generally, most bureaucracies are characterized by an organization chart. The units of the organization are divided according to the specialization and expertise of the employees.

Public and Private Bureaucracies

We should not think of bureaucracy as unique to government. Any large corporation or university can be considered a bureaucratic organization. The fact is that the handling of complex problems requires a division of labor. Individuals must concentrate their skills on specific, well-defined aspects of a problem and depend on others to solve the rest of it.

Public or government bureaucracies differ from private organizations in some important ways, however. A private corporation, such as Microsoft, has a single set of leaders, its board of directors. Public bureaucracies, in contrast, do not have a single set of leaders. Although the president is the chief administrator of the federal system, all bureaucratic agencies are subject to the desires of Congress for their funding, staffing, and, indeed, their continued existence. Furthermore, public bureaucracies supposedly serve the citizen rather than the stockholder.

One other important difference between private corporations and government bureaucracies is that government bureaucracies are not organized to make a

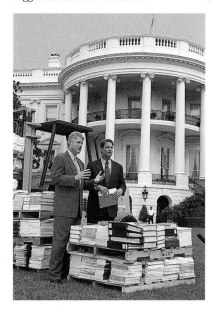

One of Vice President Gore's first tasks was to help President Clinton "change government as we know it." Gore was responsible for managing a project that became known as "reinventing government." Here, Clinton and Gore announce the publication of their program on how to reinvent government. The book and manuals surrounding them represent existing government regulations, many of which they suggested should be eliminated.

Bureaucracy
A large organization that is structured hierarchically to carry out specific functions.

INFOTRAC®
COLLEGE EDITION

"White House and Reinventing Government"

TABLE 14-1

Selected Presidential Plans to End Government Inefficiency

PRESIDENT	NAME OF PLAN
Lyndon Johnson (1963–1969)	Programming, Planning, and Budgeting Systems
Richard Nixon (1969–1974)	Management by Objectives
Jimmy Carter (1977–1981)	Zero-Based Budgeting
Ronald Reagan (1981–1989)	President's Private Sector Survey on Cost Control (the Grace Commission)
George Bush (1989–1993)	Right-Sizing Government
Bill Clinton (1993–)	"From Red Tape to Results: Creating a Government That Works Better and Costs Less"

profit. Rather, they are supposed to perform their functions as efficiently as possible to conserve the taxpayers' dollars. Perhaps it is this aspect of government organization that makes citizens hostile toward government employees when citizens experience inefficiency and red tape.

These characteristics, together with the prevalence and size of the government bureaucracies, make them an important factor in American life.

Bureaucracies Compared

The federal bureaucracy in the United States enjoys a greater degree of autonomy than do federal or national bureaucracies in most other countries. Much of the insularity that is commonly supposed to characterize the bureaucracy in this country may stem from the sheer size of the government organizations needed to implement a budget that exceeds $1.8 trillion. Because the lines of authority often are not well defined, some bureaucracies may be able to operate with a significant degree of autonomy.

The federal nature of the American government also means that national bureaucracies regularly provide financial assistance to their state counterparts. Both the Department of Education and the Department of Housing and Urban Development, for example, distribute funds to their counterparts at the state level. In contrast, most bureaucracies in European countries have a top-down command structure so that national programs may be implemented directly at the lower level. This is due not only to the small size of most European countries but also to the fact that public ownership of such things as telephone companies, airlines, railroads, and utilities is far more common in Europe than in the United States. (For a discussion of another way in which the U.S. bureaucracy differs from bureaucracies in other countries, see the feature *Politics and Comparative Systems: No More Bribes to Bureaucrats.*)

POLITICS and Comparative Systems

No More Bribes to Bureaucrats

In many foreign countries, the government exercises extensive control over trade and industry, and thus decisions on most major construction and manufacturing contracts are made by government bureaucrats. In these nations, making side payments ("gifts") to government officials in exchange for favorable business contracts is an age-old custom and, until very recently, typically was not considered unethical. Indeed, languages around the world have a word designating such payments—including "ghagshish" in the Middle East, "suborno" in South America, "dash" in West

Africa, "podkup" in Russia, and "kickbacks" in the United States.

In 1977, the U.S. Congress passed the Foreign Corrupt Practices Act (FCPA), which prohibits Americans doing business abroad from bribing foreign officials to secure advantageous contracts. In effect, the law put U.S. businesspersons at a relative disadvantage in the international marketplace. Consider that in a recent two-year period, according to the U.S. Department of Commerce, American companies lost more than one hundred inter-

national contracts, valued at $45 billion, because they (but not their competitors) were prohibited from bribing foreign officials.

For twenty years, the FCPA has been the only law of its kind in the world, despite attempts by U.S. political leaders to convince other nations to pass similar legislation. That situation is now changing, however. In 1997, the Organization for Economic Cooperation and Development, to which twenty-six of the world's leading industrialized nations belong, signed a convention (treaty) that made the bribery

of foreign public officials a serious crime. Each signatory is obligated to enact legislation within its nation in accordance with the treaty. The agreement will not only improve the ethical climate in international trade but also level the playing field for U.S. businesspersons.

FOR CRITICAL ANALYSIS

What is the difference between bribing a public official and contributing to a politician's campaign in the hope of gaining favorable treatment?

The fact that the U.S. government owns relatively few enterprises does not mean, however, that its bureaucracies are comparatively powerless. Indeed, there are numerous **administrative agencies** in the federal bureaucracy—such as the Environmental Protection Agency, the Nuclear Regulatory Commission, and the Securities and Exchange Commission—that extensively regulate private companies even though they virtually never have an ownership interest in those companies.

Theories of Bureaucracy

Several theories have been offered to help us understand better the ways in which bureaucracies function. Each of these theories focuses on specific features of bureaucracies.

The Weberian Model

The classic model, or **Weberian model,** of the modern bureaucracy was proposed by the German sociologist Max Weber.[1] He argued that the increasingly complex nature of modern life, coupled with the steadily growing demands placed on governments by their citizens, made the formation of bureaucracies inevitable. According to Weber, most bureaucracies—whether in the public or private sector—are hierarchically organized and governed by formal procedures. The power in a bureaucracy flows from the top downward. Decision-making processes in bureaucracies are shaped by detailed technical rules that promote similar decisions in similar situations. Bureaucrats are specialists who attempt to resolve problems through logical reasoning and data analysis instead of "gut feelings" and guesswork. Individual advancement in bureaucracies is supposed to be based on merit rather than political connections. Indeed, the modern bureaucracy, according to Weber, should be an apolitical organization.

[1]Max Weber, *Theory of Social and Economic Organization,* ed. by Talcott Parsons (New York: Oxford University Press, 1974).

Administrative Agency
A federal, state, or local government unit established to perform a specific function. Administrative agencies are created and authorized by legislative bodies to administer and enforce specific laws.

Weberian Model
A model of bureaucracy developed by the German sociologist Max Weber, who viewed bureaucracies as rational, hierarchical organizations in which power flows from the top downward and decisions are based on logical reasoning and data analysis.

The Department of Agriculture inspects meat-packing facilities throughout the United States, certifying the quality and condition of the meat to be sold. Why is it necessary for the U.S. government to have administrative agencies such as the Department of Agriculture?

Acquisitive Model
A model of bureaucracy that views top-level bureaucrats as seeking constantly to expand the size of their budgets and the staffs of their departments or agencies so as to gain greater power and influence in the public sector.

Monopolistic Model
A model of bureaucracy that compares bureaucracies to monopolistic business firms. Lack of competition within a bureaucracy leads to inefficient and costly operations, just as it does within monopolistic firms. Because bureaucracies are not penalized for inefficiency, there is no incentive to reduce costs or use resources more productively.

Garbage Can Model
A model of bureaucracy that characterizes bureaucracies as rudderless entities with little formal organization in which solutions to problems are based on trial and error rather than rational policy planning.

The Acquisitive Model

Other theorists do not view bureaucracies in terms as benign as Weber's. Some believe that bureaucracies are acquisitive in nature. Proponents of the **acquisitive model** argue that top-level bureaucrats will always try to expand, or at least to avoid any reductions in, the size of their budgets. Although government bureaucracies are not-for-profit enterprises, bureaucrats want to maximize the size of their budgets and staffs, because these things are the most visible trappings of power in the public sector. These efforts are also prompted by the desire of bureaucrats to "sell" their products—national defense, public housing, agricultural subsidies, and so on—to both Congress and the public.

The Monopolistic Model

Because government bureaucracies seldom have competitors, some theorists have suggested that bureaucratic organizations may be explained best by using a **monopolistic model**. The analysis is similar to that used by economists to examine the behavior of monopolistic firms. Monopolistic bureaucracies—like monopolistic firms—are less efficient and more costly to operate because they have no competitors. Because monopolistic bureaucracies are not usually penalized for chronic inefficiency, they have little reason to adopt cost-saving measures or to make more productive uses of their resources. Some economists have argued that such problems can be cured only by privatizing certain bureaucratic functions.

The Garbage Can Model

The image of a bumbling, rudderless organization is offered by proponents of the **garbage can model** of bureaucracy. This theory presupposes that bureaucracies rarely act in any purposeful or coherent manner but instead bumble along aimlessly in search of solutions to particular problems. This model views bureaucracies as having relatively little formal organization. The solutions to problems are obtained not by the smooth implementation of well-planned policies but instead by trial and error. Choosing the right policy is tricky, because usually it is not possible to determine in advance which solution is best. Thus, bureaucrats may have to try one, two, three, or even more policies before they obtain a satisfactory result.

The Size of the Bureaucracy

In 1789, the new government's bureaucracy was minuscule. There were three departments—State (with nine employees), War (with two employees), and Treasury (with thirty-nine employees)—and the Office of the Attorney General (which later became the Department of Justice). This bureaucracy was still small in 1798. At that time, the secretary of state had seven clerks and spent a total of $500 (about $5,750 in 1999 dollars) on stationery and printing. In that same year, the Appropriations Act allocated $1.4 million to the War Department (or $15.8 million in 1999 dollars).[2]

Times have changed, as we can see in Figure 14–1, which lists the various federal agencies and the number of civilian employees in each. Excluding the military, approximately 2.7 million government employees constitute the federal

[2]Leonard D. White, *The Federalists: A Study in Administrative History, 1789–1801* (New York: Free Press, 1948).

FIGURE 14-1

FIGURE 14-1

Federal Agencies and Their Respective Numbers of Civilian Employees

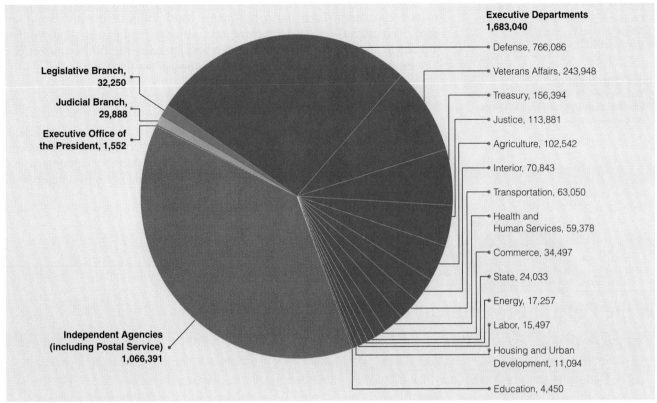

Executive Departments
1,683,040

Defense, 766,086

Veterans Affairs, 243,948

Treasury, 156,394

Justice, 113,881

Agriculture, 102,542

Interior, 70,843

Transportation, 63,050

Health and
Human Services, 59,378

Commerce, 34,497

State, 24,033

Energy, 17,257

Labor, 15,497

Housing and Urban
Development, 11,094

Education, 4,450

Legislative Branch,
32,250

Judicial Branch,
29,888

Executive Office of
the President, 1,552

Independent Agencies
(including Postal Service)
1,066,391

SOURCE: U.S. Bureau of the Census, *Statistical Abstract of the United States: 1997* (Washington, D.C.: U.S. Government Printing Office, 1997).

bureaucracy. That number has remained relatively stable for the last several decades. It is somewhat deceiving, however, because there are many others working directly or indirectly for the federal government as subcontractors or consultants and in other capacities.

The figures for federal government employment are only part of the story. Figure 14-2 shows the growth in government employment at the federal, state, and local levels. Since 1970, this growth has been mainly at the state and local levels. If all government employees are counted, then, more than 15 percent of all civilian employment is accounted for by government. (For a discussion of the "thickening" of the federal bureaucracy and how it might be curbed, see this chapter's *Critical Perspective* on pages 460–461).

The costs of the bureaucracy are commensurately high and growing. The share of the gross national product taken up by government spending was only 8.5 percent in 1929. Today it exceeds 40 percent.

The Organization of the Federal Bureaucracy

Within the federal bureaucracy are a number of different types of government agencies and organizations. Figure 14-3 (on page 462) outlines the several bureaucracies within the executive branch, as well as the separate organizations that provide services to Congress, to the courts, and directly to the president. In Chapter 13, we discussed those agencies that are considered to be part of the Executive Office of the President.

FIGURE 14-2

Government Employment at Federal, State, and Local Levels

There are more local government employees than federal and state employees combined.

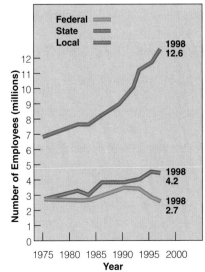

Federal
State
Local

1998
12.6

1998
4.2

1998
2.7

Number of Employees (millions)

1975 1980 1985 1990 1995 2000
Year

SOURCE: U.S. Department of Labor, Bureau of Labor Statistics, *Monthly Labor Review,* various issues. 1998 data are estimates.

Cabinet Department
One of the fourteen departments of the executive branch (State, Treasury, Defense, Justice, Interior, Agriculture, Commerce, Labor, Health and Human Services, Housing and Urban Development, Education, Energy, Transportation, and Veterans Affairs).

Line Organization
With respect to the federal government, an administrative unit that is directly accountable to the president.

The executive branch, which employs most of the bureaucrats, has four major types of bureaucratic structures. They are (1) cabinet departments, (2) independent executive agencies, (3) independent regulatory agencies, and (4) government corporations. Each has a distinctive relationship to the president, and some have unusual internal structures, overall goals, and grants of power. (For a problem facing all of these departments and agencies, see *Politics Wired: Can The Bureaucracy Meet the "Year 2000" Challenge?* on page 463.)

Cabinet Departments

The fourteen **cabinet departments** are the major service organizations of the federal government. They can also be described in management terms as **line organizations.** This means that they are directly accountable to the president and are responsible for performing government functions, such as printing money or training troops.

Critical | perspective

Is the Federal Government Becoming Top-Heavy?

In spite of the relatively recent slowdown in federal government employment, a basic question still needs to be answered: Has the federal bureaucracy become top-heavy? It is difficult for the average citizen to answer this question, for the statistics on the make-up of government employment over time are not easily digested. Paul C. Light, a professor of public affairs at the University of Minnesota, has painstakingly analyzed such statistics and come to the conclusion that, yes, the emphasis in the federal bureaucracy has shifted from lower-level workers and managers to upper-level managers. He calls this the "thickening" of government.[*]

What Actually Has Happened to the Federal Bureaucracy?

In a nutshell, Light determined that there are more layers of management between the president and the front lines of government than ever before. Further, there are more presidential appointees and senior executives in each layer than in the past. Thus, government has undergone a simultaneous vertical and horizontal thickening: more layers of management have increased the height of the federal bureaucratic hierarchy, and more appointees and executives in each layer have increased its width. This is what thickening is all about.

Thirty years ago, many of today's senior management layers did not exist. At the very top of government in 1960 there were seventeen layers of management. By the mid-1990s, there were thirty-two layers. Each time a new layer is added, the distance between the top (the president) and the bottom of government is increased. Thus, there is a greater potential for information to be distorted as it moves from the top downward. In addition, ideas for improvement also become more distorted as they move upward through more layers to the top layer. The thickening of government, according to Light, is bipartisan—it does not matter who is in the White House or who controls Congress.

What If the Trend Continues?

According to Light, if the trend continues,

the federal hierarchy may eventually resemble a circle, with very few employees at the bottom, hordes of managers, supervisors, technical analysts of one kind or another at the middle, and a vast coterie of political and career executives at the top.[†]

Government thickening seems to be inexorable. New positions are created with lofty goals in mind. Once they are created, though, they tend to spread outward. If modern presidents believe that more leaders equate to more leadership, government thickening will persist. A "copycat" phenomenon also seems to be at work. When the latest innovation in thickening occurs in the executive branch, Congress does not wait long to follow suit. Why? "Because of a simple desire by organizations within the same environment to look alike."[‡]

[†]*Ibid.,* p. 15.
[‡]*Ibid.,* p. 31.

[*]*Thickening Government: Federal Hierarchy and the Diffusion of Accountability* (Washington, D.C.: The Brookings Institution and the Government Institute, 1995).

These departments were created by Congress when the need for each department arose. The first department to be created was State, and the most recent one was Veterans Affairs, established in 1988. A president might ask that a new department be created or an old one abolished, but the president has no power to do so without legislative approval from Congress.

Each department is headed by a secretary (except for the Justice Department, which is headed by the attorney general) and has several levels of undersecretaries, assistant secretaries, and so on.

Presidents theoretically have considerable control over the cabinet departments, because presidents are able to appoint or fire all of the top officials. Even cabinet departments do not always respond to the president's wishes, though. One reason for the frequent unhappiness of presidents with their departments is that the entire bureaucratic structure below the top political levels is staffed by permanent employees, many of whom are committed to established programs or

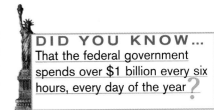

DID YOU KNOW...
That the federal government spends over $1 billion every six hours, every day of the year?

Critical perspective

Is the Federal Government Becoming Top-Heavy?—continued

In any event, the "law of increasing conservatism" is at work. According to theorist Anthony Downs, "All organizations tend to become more conservative as they get older."[§] Government agencies lose their passion, but they never go out of business. Thus, the problem is not contemporary government itself but its age. In spite of each administration's attempt at bureaucratic reform, each new administration simply adds its innovations without clearing out the old. The question is, "Can thickening be stopped?"

A Modest Proposal

Government can be "thin." A good example of a permanent thinning of government bureaucracy is Britain. It now runs with a handful of political appointees, and only about 10 percent of the bureaucracy are career executives. There are only five layers between the head of the government and the British equivalent of the deputy assistant secretary. The key to this government thinning is the British equivalent of our Office of Management and Budget (OMB). The British equivalent of the OMB establishes and monitors agency budgets. It conducts periodic reviews of the top structure of each agency as well as the number of positions. According to Light, our OMB can do the same. All that would be required in the United States is for the president and Congress to abandon their prevailing notion of what an organization should look like.

In any event, given the ease of communication through the Internet, we could collapse our federal field structure. Supervisors do not need to see their employees to supervise them. There is no longer any need to have 30,000 federal government offices spread out across the country. Light also suggests that layering could be reduced by limiting the number of times an existing position title could be extended to include other titles to a small number, such as two. If this were done, an assistant secretary title could be extended to include a deputy assistant secretary and an associate secretary, but no further. This would be part of a plan to create maximum height and width limits to any bureaucracy within the federal government.

In the last analysis, Light contends, we must change the prevailing image of effective presidential leadership. The president does not need any more help. Presidents have ample support staff and a sufficient number of political appointees, as do secretaries and members of Congress. Presidential leadership should be judged not by the thickness or thinness of government but in terms of the executive's clarity of vision, articulation of cause, and the value added by what the government does.

FOR CRITICAL ANALYSIS
1. Generally, why is it so difficult to reform the bureaucracy?
2. Is the "thickening" of government necessarily a bad thing?

[§]Anthony Downs, *Inside Bureaucracy* (Boston: Little, Brown, 1967), p. 20.

procedures and who resist change. As we can see from Table 14-2 (on page 464), each cabinet department employs thousands of individuals, only a handful of whom are under the control of the president. The table also describes the functions of each of the cabinet departments.

Independent Executive Agencies

Independent Executive Agency
A federal agency that is not part of a cabinet department but reports directly to the president.

Independent executive agencies are bureaucratic organizations that are not located within a department and report directly to the president, who appoints their chief officials. When a new federal agency is created—the Environmental

FIGURE 14-3

Organization Chart of the Federal Government

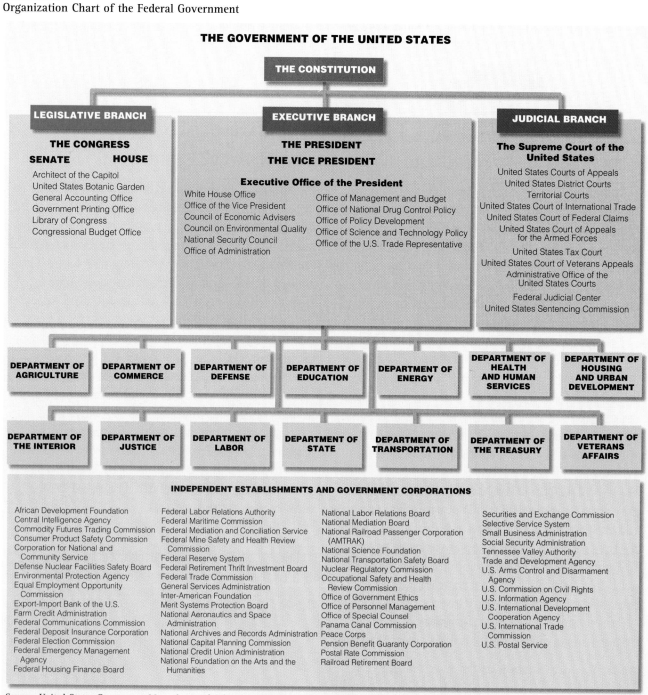

SOURCE: *United States Government Manual, 1997/98* (Washington, D.C.: U.S. Government Printing Office, 1997), p. 22.

Protection Agency, for example—Congress decides where it will be located in the bureaucracy. In this century, presidents often have asked that a new organization be kept separate or independent rather than added to an existing department, particularly if a department may in fact be hostile to the agency's creation. Table 14–3 (on page 465) describes the functions of several selected independent executive agencies.

Independent Regulatory Agencies

The **independent regulatory agencies** are typically responsible for a specific type of public policy. Their function is to make and implement rules and regulations in a particular sector of the economy to protect the public interest. The earliest such agency was the Interstate Commerce Commission (ICC), which was established in 1887 when Americans began to seek some form of government control over the rapidly growing business and industrial sector. This new form of organization, the independent regulatory agency, was supposed to make technical, nonpolitical decisions about rates, profits, and rules that would be for the benefit of all and that did not require congressional legislation. In the years that followed the creation of the ICC, other agencies were formed to regulate communication (the Federal Communications Commission), nuclear power (the Nuclear Regulatory Commission), and so on. (The ICC was abolished on December 30, 1995.)

DID YOU KNOW...
That the Commerce Department's U.S. Travel and Tourism Administration recently gave away $440,000 in so-called disaster relief to western ski resort operators because there hadn't been enough snow?

Independent Regulatory Agency
An agency outside the major executive departments charged with making and implementing rules and regulations to protect the public interest.

INFOTRAC®
COLLEGE EDITION

"Countdown to 2000"

POLITICS W I R E D

Can the Bureaucracy Meet the "Year 2000" Challenge?

In the 1990s, as the government and the nation's businesses began to be concerned about the effects of the year 2000 on computer programs, it became apparent just how "wired" our world has become. It also became evident that if existing programs and applications cannot be modified or replaced before that year begins, it could spell disaster for many government programs.

To ward off major problems, the government will need to hire armies of programmers, and it has already begun to do so. It is estimated that, all told, the year-2000 bug could cost the United States about $119 billion in lost economic output—necessitated by diverting resources to fixing the computer problem—between 1998 and 2001. And

it could cost more if the problem is not fixed.

Political leaders in Washington, D.C., are becoming increasingly worried that time is running out. Consider the work that must be completed by the Internal Revenue Service (IRS). To prepare for the year 2000, the IRS must modify 60 million lines of computer code, 88,000 separate applications programs, 80 mainframe computers, 1,000 midsize computers, 130,000 PCs, and 60,000 pieces of telecom equipment. If the system is not modified in time, tax returns would go unprocessed, refunds would be unsent, and taxpayers might be informed that they owe ninety-nine

years' interest on a disputed deduction. According to a former top IRS official, "It would shut down the entire system—everything from collections to compliance would just stop."*

Of particular concern to the government is the fact that the Federal Aviation Administration (FAA) is considerably behind schedule in repairing date-related computer glitches. According to the Transportation Department's inspector general and other experts, the FAA almost certainly will not have the necessary repairs completed by 2000. Even now, according to some observers, the FAA's technology is woefully behind the times, and on sev-

eral occasions in the last few years computer systems at vital traffic control centers have malfunctioned. Such problems may be minor in comparison to those that could occur if the year 2000 arrives before the FAA has completed the necessary repairs. Apart from safety concerns, the traffic control system is vital to our entire economy.

FOR CRITICAL ANALYSIS

Why didn't creators of computer software in the past decade make their programs adaptable to year-2000 needs?

*As quoted in *Business Week*, February 23, 1998, p. 199.

TABLE 14-2

Executive Departments

DEPARTMENT AND YEAR ESTABLISHED	PRINCIPAL FUNCTIONS	MOST IMPORTANT SUBAGENCIES
State (1789) (24,033 employees)	Negotiates treaties; develops foreign policy; protects citizens abroad.	Passport Agency; Bureau of Diplomatic Security; Foreign Service; Bureau of Human Rights and Humanitarian Affairs; Bureau of Consular Affairs.
Treasury (1789) (156,394 employees)	Pays all federal bills; borrows money; collects federal taxes, mints coins and prints paper currency; operates the Secret Service; supervises national banks.	Internal Revenue Service; Bureau of Alcohol, Tobacco, and Firearms; U.S. Secret Service; U.S. Mint; Customs Service.
Interior (1849) (70,843 employees)	Supervises federally owned lands and parks; operates federal hydroelectric power facilities; supervises Native American affairs.	U.S. Fish and Wildlife Service; National Park Service; Bureau of Indian Affairs; Bureau of Land Management.
Justice (1870)* (113,881 employees)	Furnishes legal advice to the president; enforces federal criminal laws; supervises the federal corrections systems (prisons).	Federal Bureau of Investigation; Drug Enforcement Administration; Bureau of Prisons; Immigration and Naturalization Service.
Agriculture (1889) (102,542 employees)	Provides assistance to farmers and ranchers; conducts research to improve agricultural activity and to prevent plant disease; works to protect forests from fires and disease.	Soil Conservation Service; Agricultural Research Service; Food and Safety Inspection Service; Federal Crop Insurance Corporation; Farmers Home Administration.
Commerce (1913)† (34,497 employees)	Grants patents and trademarks; conducts a national census; monitors the weather; protects the interests of businesses.	Bureau of the Census; Bureau of Economic Analysis; Minority Business Development Agency; Patent and Trademark Office; National Oceanic and Atmospheric Administration; U.S. Travel and Tourism Administration.
Labor (1913) (15,497 employees)	Administers federal labor laws; promotes the interests of workers.	Occupational Safety and Health Administration (OSHA); Bureau of Labor Statistics; Employment Standards Administration; Office of Labor-Management Standards.
Defense (1947)‡ (766,086 employees)	Manages the armed forces (army, navy, air force, and marines); operates military bases; is responsible for civil defense.	National Guard; National Security Agency; Joint Chiefs of Staff; Departments of the Air Force, Navy, Army.
Housing and Urban Development (1965) (11,094 employees)	Deals with the nation's housing needs; develops and rehabilitates urban communities; promotes improvement in city streets and parks.	Office of Block Grant Assistance; Emergency Shelter Grants Program; Office of Urban Development Action Grants; Office of Fair Housing and Equal Opportunity.
Transportation (1967) (63,050 employees)	Finances improvements in mass transit; develops and administers programs for highways, railroads, and aviation; is involved with offshore maritime safety.	Federal Aviation Administration; Federal Highway Administration; National Highway Traffic Safety Administration; U.S. Coast Guard; Federal Transit Administration.
Energy (1977) (17,257 employees)	Is involved in the conservation of energy and resources; analyzes energy data; conducts research and development.	Office of Civilian Radioactive Waste Management; Bonneville Power Administration; Office of Nuclear Energy; Energy Information Administration; Office of Conservation and Renewable Energy.
Health and Human Services (1979)§ (59,378 employees)	Promotes public health; enforces pure food and drug laws; is involved in health-related research.	Food and Drug Administration; Administration for Children and Families; Health Care Financing Administration; Public Health Service.
Education (1979)§ (4,540 employees)	Coordinates federal programs and policies for education; administers aid to education; promotes educational research.	Office of Special Education and Rehabilitation Service; Office of Elementary and Secondary Education; Office of Postsecondary Education; Office of Vocational and Adult Education.
Veterans Affairs (1988) (243,948 employees)	Promotes the welfare of veterans of the U.S. armed forces.	Veterans Health Administration; Veterans Benefits Administration; National Cemetery Systems.

*Formed from the Office of the Attorney General (created in 1789).
†Formed from the Department of Commerce and Labor (created in 1903).
‡Formed from the Department of War (created in 1789) and the Department of Navy (created in 1798).
§Formed from the Department of Health, Education, and Welfare (created in 1953).

The Purpose and Nature of Regulatory Agencies

The regulatory agencies are administered independently of all three branches of government. They were set up because Congress felt it was unable to handle the complexities and technicalities required to carry out specific laws in the public interest. The regulatory commissions in fact combine some functions of all three branches of government—executive, legislative, and judicial. They are legislative in that they make rules that have the force of law. They are executive in that they provide for the enforcement of those rules. They are judicial in that they decide disputes involving the rules they have made.

Regulatory agency members are appointed by the president with the consent of the Senate, although they do not report to the president. By law, the members of regulatory agencies cannot all be from the same political party. Presidents can influence regulatory agency behavior by appointing people of their own parties or people who share their political views when vacancies occur, in particular when the chair is vacant. Members may be removed by the president only for causes specified in the law creating the agency. Table 14–4 (on page 466) describes the functions of selected independent regulatory agencies.

Over the last several decades, some observers have concluded that these agencies, although nominally independent, may in fact not always be so. They also contend that many independent regulatory agencies have been **captured** by the very industries and firms that they were supposed to regulate. The results have been less competition rather than more competition, higher prices rather than lower prices, and less choice rather than more choice for consumers.

Deregulation and Reregulation.   During the presidency of Ronald Reagan in the 1980s, some significant deregulation (the removal of regulatory restraints—the opposite of regulation) occurred, much of which started under President Jimmy Carter. For example, President Carter appointed a chairperson of the Civil

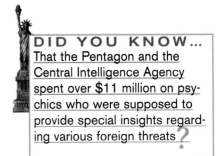

DID YOU KNOW...
That the Pentagon and the Central Intelligence Agency spent over $11 million on psychics who were supposed to provide special insights regarding various foreign threats?

Capture
The act of gaining direct or indirect control over agency personnel and decision makers by the industry that is being regulated.

INFOTRAC®
COLLEGE EDITION

"Why Deregulation Has Gone Too Far"

TABLE 14-3

Selected Independent Executive Agencies

NAME	DATE FORMED	PRINCIPAL FUNCTIONS
Central Intelligence Agency (CIA)*	1947	Gathers and analyzes political and military information about foreign countries so that the United States can improve its own political and military status; conducts activities outside the United States, with the goal of countering the work of intelligence services operated by other nations whose political philosophies are inconsistent with our own.
General Services Administration (GSA) (14,195 employees)	1949	Purchases and manages all property of the federal government; acts as the business arm of the federal government in overseeing federal government spending projects; discovers overcharges in government programs.
National Science Foundation (NSF) (1,300 employees)	1950	Promotes scientific research; provides grants to all levels of schools for instructional programs in the sciences.
Small Business Administration (SBA) (5,524 employees)	1953	Protects the interests of small businesses; provides low-cost loans and management information to small businesses.
National Aeronautics and Space Administration (NASA) (19,993 employees)	1958	Is responsible for the U.S. space program, including the building, testing, and operating of space vehicles.
Environmental Protection Agency (EPA) (17,566 employees)	1970	Undertakes programs aimed at reducing air and water pollution; works with state and local agencies to help fight environmental hazards.

*The CIA will not release information on the number of employees who work for this agency (because it is "classified information").

Aeronautics Board (CAB) who gradually eliminated regulation of airline fares and routes. Then, under Reagan, the CAB was eliminated on January 1, 1985. During the Bush administration, calls for *re*regulation of many businesses increased. Indeed, under President Bush, the Americans with Disabilities Act of 1990, the Civil Rights Act of 1991, and the Clean Air Act Amendments of 1991, all of which increased or changed the regulation of many businesses, were passed. Additionally, the Cable Reregulation Act of 1992 was passed. Under President Clinton, the Interstate Commerce Commission was eliminated, and there has been deregulation of the banking and telecommunications industries, and many other sectors of the economy. At the same time, there has been extensive regulation to protect the environment. Additionally, major attempts to institute general regulatory reform were made in Congress. So far, no significant legislation of that nature has been passed.

Government Corporations

Government Corporation

An agency of government that administers a quasi-business enterprise. These corporations are used when activities are primarily commercial. They produce revenue for their continued existence, and they require greater flexibility than is permitted for departments and agencies.

Another form of bureaucratic organization in the United States is the **government corporation.** Although the concept is borrowed from the world of business, distinct differences exist between public and private corporations.

A private corporation has shareholders (stockholders) who elect a board of directors, who in turn choose the corporate officers, such as president and vice president. When a private corporation makes a profit, it must pay taxes (unless it avoids them through various legal loopholes). It either distributes part or all of the after-tax profits to shareholders as dividends or plows the profits back into the corporation to make new investments.

A government corporation has a board of directors and managers, but it does not have any stockholders. We cannot buy shares of stock in a government cor-

| TABLE 14-4 |
Selected Independent Regulatory Agencies

NAME	DATE FORMED	PRINCIPAL FUNCTIONS
Federal Reserve System Board of Governors (Fed) (1,755 employees)	1913	Determines policy with respect to interest rates, credit availability, and the money supply.
Federal Trade Commission (FTC) (960 employees)	1914	Prevents businesses from engaging in unfair trade practices; stops the formation of monopolies in the business sector; protects consumer rights.
Securities and Exchange Commission (SEC) (2,825 employees)	1934	Regulates the nation's stock exchanges, in which shares of stocks are bought and sold; requires full disclosure of the financial profiles of companies that wish to sell stocks and bonds to the public.
Federal Communications Commission (FCC) (2,088 employees)	1934	Regulates all communications by telegraph, cable, telephone, radio, and television.
National Labor Relations Board (NLRB) (1,900 employees)	1935	Protects employees' rights to join unions and bargain collectively with employers; attempts to prevent unfair labor practices by both employers and unions.
Equal Employment Opportunity Commission (EEOC) (2,625 employees)	1964	Works to eliminate discrimination based on religion, gender, race, color, national origin, age, or disability; examines claims of discrimination.
Federal Election Commission (FEC) (310 employees)	1974	Ensures that candidates and states follow the rules established by the Federal Election Campaign Act.
Nuclear Regulatory Commission (NRC) (3,000 employees)	1974	Ensures that electricity-generating nuclear reactors in the United States are built and operated safely; regularly inspects the operations of such reactors.

poration. If the government corporation makes a profit, it does not distribute the profit as dividends. Also, if it makes a profit, it does not have to pay taxes; the profits remain in the corporation. Table 14–5 describes the functions of selected government corporations.

Staffing the Bureaucracy

There are two categories of bureaucrats: political appointees and civil servants. As noted earlier, the president is able to make political appointments to most of the top jobs in the federal bureaucracy. The president also can appoint ambassadors to the most important foreign posts. All of the jobs that are considered "political plums" and that usually go to the politically well connected are listed in *Policy and Supporting Positions,* a book published by the Government Printing Office after each presidential election. This has been informally (and correctly) called "The Plum Book." The rest of the individuals who work for the national government belong to the civil service and obtain their jobs through a much more formal process.

Political Appointees

To fill the positions listed in "The Plum Book," the president and the president's advisers solicit suggestions from politicians, businesspersons, and other prominent individuals. Appointments to these positions offer the president a way to pay off outstanding political debts. But the president must also take into consideration such things as the candidate's work experience, intelligence, political affiliations, and personal characteristics. Presidents have differed over the importance they attach to appointing women and minorities to plum positions. Presidents often use ambassadorships, however, to reward selected individuals for their campaign contributions.

Political appointees are in some sense the aristocracy of the federal government. But their powers, although appearing formidable on paper, are often exaggerated. Like the president, a political appointee will occupy his or her position

> **DID YOU KNOW...**
> That there are nineteen military golf courses around Washington, D.C., yet the Pentagon announced that it would spend over $5 million to build a new one at Andrews Air Force Base in suburban Maryland?

TABLE **14-5**

Selected Government Corporations

NAME	DATE FORMED	PRINCIPAL FUNCTIONS
Tennessee Valley Authority (TVA) (15,000 employees)	1933	Operates a Tennessee River control system and generates power for a seven-state region and for the U.S. aeronautics and space programs; promotes the economic development of the Tennessee Valley region; controls floods and promotes the navigability of the Tennessee River.
Federal Deposit Insurance Corporation (FDIC) (15,712 employees)	1933	Insures individuals' bank deposits up to $100,000; oversees the business activities of banks.
Export/Import Bank of the United States (Ex/Im Bank) (413 employees)	1933	Promotes the sale of American-made goods abroad; grants loans to foreign purchasers of American products.
National Railroad Passenger Corporation (AMTRAK) (23,000 employees)	1970	Provides a balanced national and intercity rail passenger service network; controls 23,000 miles of track with 505 stations.
U.S. Postal Service* (891,000 employees)	1970	Delivers mail throughout the United States and its territories; is the largest government corporation.

*Formed from the Office of the Postmaster General in the Department of the Treasury (created in 1789).

for a comparatively brief time. Political appointees often leave office before the president's term actually ends. The average term of service for political appointees is less than two years. As a result, most appointees have little background for their positions and may be mere figureheads. Often, they only respond to the paperwork that flows up from below. Additionally, the professional civil servants who make up the permanent civil service but serve under a normally temporary political appointee may not feel compelled to carry out their current boss's directives quickly, because they know that he or she will not be around for very long.

This inertia is compounded by the fact that it is extremely difficult to discharge civil servants. In recent years, less than one-tenth of 1 percent of federal employees have been fired for incompetence. Because discharged employees may appeal their dismissals, many months or even years may pass before the issue is resolved conclusively. This occupational rigidity helps to ensure that most political appointees, no matter how competent or driven, will not be able to exert much meaningful influence over their subordinates, let alone implement dramatic changes in the bureaucracy itself. Of course, there are exceptions. Under the Civil Service Reform Act of 1978, for example, senior employees can be transferred within their departments and receive salary bonuses and other benefits as incentives for being productive and responsive to the goals and policy preferences of their politically appointed superiors.

U.S. Postal Service employees sort the mail during the night shift at an Austin, Texas, post office. The postal service is the largest single employer in the United States.

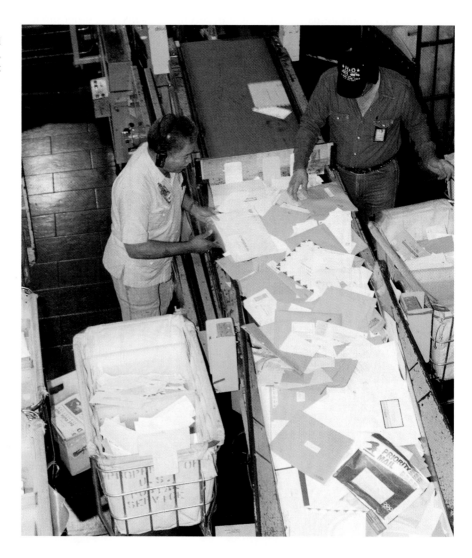

History of the Federal Civil Service

When the federal government was formed in 1789, it had no career public servants but rather consisted of amateurs who were almost all Federalists. When Thomas Jefferson took over as president, he found that few in his party were holding federal administrative jobs, so he fired more than one hundred officials and replaced them with members of the so-called **natural aristocracy**—that is, with his own Jeffersonian (Democratic) Republicans. For the next twenty-five years, a growing body of federal administrators gained experience and expertise, becoming in the process professional public servants. These administrators stayed in office regardless of who was elected president. The bureaucracy had become a self-maintaining, long-term element within government.

To the Victor Belong the Spoils.   When Andrew Jackson took over the White House in 1828, he could not believe how many appointed officials (appointed before he became president, that is) were overtly hostile toward him and his Democratic Party. The bureaucracy—indeed an aristocracy—considered itself the only group fit to rule. But Jackson was a man of the people, and his policies were populist in nature. As the bureaucracy was reluctant to carry out his programs, Jackson did the obvious: he fired federal officials—more than had all his predecessors combined. The **spoils system**—an application of the principle that to the victor belong the spoils—reigned. The aristocrats were out, and the common folk were in. The spoils system was not, of course, a Jacksonian invention. Thomas Jefferson, too, had used this system of patronage in which the boss, or patron, rewards those who worked to get him or her elected.

The Civil Service Reform Act of 1883.   Jackson's spoils system survived for a number of years, but it became increasingly corrupt. Also, the size of the bureaucracy increased by 300 percent between 1851 and 1881. Reformers began to examine the professional civil service that was established in several European countries, which operated under a **merit system** in which job appointments were based on competitive examinations. The cry for civil service reform became louder.

In 1883, the **Pendleton Act**—or **Civil Service Reform Act**—was passed, bringing to a close the period of Jacksonian spoils. The act established the principle of employment on the basis of open, competitive examinations and created the

Natural Aristocracy
A small ruling clique of a society's "best" citizens, whose membership is based on birth, wealth, and ability. The Jeffersonian era emphasized government rule by such a group.

Spoils System
The awarding of government jobs to political supporters and friends; generally associated with President Andrew Jackson.

Merit System
The selection, retention, and promotion of government employees on the basis of competitive examinations.

**Pendleton Act
(Civil Service Reform Act)**
The law, as amended over the years, that remains the basic statute regulating federal employment personnel policies. It established the principle of employment on the basis of merit and created the Civil Service Commission to administer the personnel service.

On September 19, 1881, President James A. Garfield was assassinated by a disappointed office seeker, Charles J. Guiteau. The long-term effect of this event was to replace the spoils system with a permanent career civil service, with the passage of the Pendleton Act in 1883, which established the Civil Service Commission.

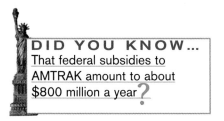

Civil Service Commission
The initial central personnel agency of the
national government; created in 1883.

Civil Service Commission to administer the personnel service. Only 10 percent of federal employees were covered initially by the merit system. Later laws, amendments, and executive orders, however, increased the coverage to more than 90 percent of the federal civil service. The effects of these reforms were felt at all levels of government, including city governments run by political machines—for example, New York's Tammany Hall. (See the feature *E-Mail Messages from the Past* for the view of Tammany Hall's George Washington Plunkitt on civil service reform.)

The Supreme Court put an even heavier lid on the spoils system in *Elrod v. Burns*[3] in 1976 and *Branti v. Finkel*[4] in 1980. In those two cases, the Court used the First Amendment to forbid government officials from discharging or threatening to discharge public employees solely for not being supporters of the political party in power unless party affiliation is an appropriate requirement for the position. Additional curbs on political patronage were added in *Rutan v. Republican Party of Illinois*[5] in 1990. The Court's ruling effectively prevented the use of partisan political considerations as the basis for hiring, promoting, or transferring most public employees. An exception was permitted, however, for senior policymaking positions, which usually go to officials who will support the programs of the elected leaders. (See the *Politics and the Constitution* in Chapter 9 for a more detailed discussion of political patronage and the First Amendment.)

The Hatch Act of 1939. The growing size of the federal bureaucracy created the potential for political manipulation. In principle, a civil servant is politically neutral. But civil servants certainly know that it is politicians who pay the bills through their appropriations and that it is politicians who decide about the growth of agencies. In 1933, when President Franklin D. Roosevelt set up his New Deal, a virtual army of civil servants was hired to staff the numerous new agencies that were created. Because the individuals who worked in these agencies owed their jobs to the Democratic Party, it seemed natural for them to campaign for Democratic candidates. The Democrats controlling Congress in the

[3]427 U.S. 347 (1976).
[4]445 U.S. 507 (1980).
[5]497 U.S. 62 (1990).

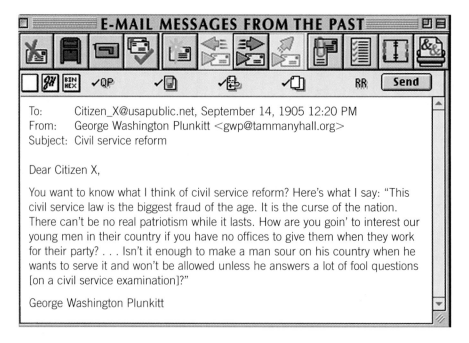

E-MAIL MESSAGES FROM THE PAST

To: Citizen_X@usapublic.net, September 14, 1905 12:20 PM
From: George Washington Plunkitt <gwp@tammanyhall.org>
Subject: Civil service reform

Dear Citizen X,

You want to know what I think of civil service reform? Here's what I say: "This civil service law is the biggest fraud of the age. It is the curse of the nation. There can't be no real patriotism while it lasts. How are you goin' to interest our young men in their country if you have no offices to give them when they work for their party? . . . Isn't it enough to make a man sour on his country when he wants to serve it and won't be allowed unless he answers a lot of fool questions [on a civil service examination]?"

George Washington Plunkitt

mid-1930s did not object. But in 1938, a coalition of conservative Democrats and Republicans took control of Congress and forced through the **Hatch Act**—or the **Political Activities Act**—of 1939.

The main provision of this act is that civil service employees cannot take an active part in the political management of campaigns. It also prohibits the use of federal authority to influence nominations and elections and outlaws the use of bureaucratic rank to pressure federal employees to make political contributions.

In 1972, a federal district court declared the Hatch Act prohibition against political activity to be unconstitutional. The United States Supreme Court, however, reaffirmed the challenged portion of the act in 1973, stating that the government's interest in preserving a nonpartisan civil service was so great that the prohibitions should remain.[6]

The Civil Service Reform Act of 1978. In 1978, the Civil Service Reform Act abolished the Civil Service Commission and created two new federal agencies to perform its duties. To administer the civil service laws, rules, and regulations, the act created the Office of Personnel Management (OPM). The OPM is empowered to recruit, interview, and test potential government workers and determine who should be hired. The OPM makes recommendations to the individual agencies as to which persons meet the standards (typically, the top three applicants for a position), and the agencies generally decide whom to hire. To oversee promotions, employees' rights, and other employment matters, the act created the Merit Systems Protection Board (MSPB). The MSPB evaluates charges of wrongdoing, hears employee appeals from agency decisions, and can order corrective action against agencies and employees.

Modern Attempts at Bureaucratic Reform

As long as the federal bureaucracy exists, there will continue to be attempts to make it more open, efficient, and responsive to the needs of U.S. citizens. The most important actual and proposed reforms in the last few years include sunshine and sunset laws, contracting out, and more protection for so-called whistleblowers.

Sunshine Laws

In 1976, Congress enacted the **Government in the Sunshine Act.** It required for the first time that all multiheaded federal agencies—about fifty of them—hold their meetings regularly in public session. The bill defined *meetings* as almost any gathering, formal or informal, of agency members, including conference telephone calls. The only exceptions to this rule of openness are discussions of matters such as court proceedings or personnel problems, and these exceptions are specifically listed in the bill. Sunshine laws now exist at all levels of government. (See the feature *Politics Wired: Should E-Mail Messages Be in the "Sunshine"?* on the next page for a recent issue concerning such laws.)

Sunset Laws

A potential type of control on the size and scope of the federal bureaucracy is **sunset legislation,** which would place government programs on a definite schedule

---

[6]*United States Civil Service Commission v. National Association of Letter Carriers,* 413 U.S. 548 (1973).

Hatch Act (Political Activities Act)
The act that prohibits the use of federal authority to influence nominations and elections or the use of rank to pressure federal employees to make political contributions. It also prohibits civil service employees from active involvement in political campaigns.

Government in the Sunshine Act
A law that requires all multiheaded federal agencies to conduct their business regularly in public session.

Sunset Legislation
A law requiring that an existing program be reviewed regularly for its effectiveness and be terminated unless specifically extended as a result of this review.

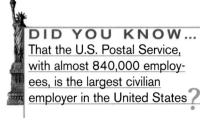

for congressional consideration. Unless Congress specifically reauthorized a particular federally operated program at the end of a designated period, it would be terminated automatically; that is, its sun would set.

The idea of sunset legislation—the first hint at the role of the bureaucracy in the legislative process—was initially suggested by Franklin D. Roosevelt when he created the plethora of New Deal agencies. His assistant, William O. Douglas, recommended that each agency's charter should include a provision allowing for its termination in ten years. Only an act of Congress could revitalize it. Obviously, the proposal was never adopted. It was not until 1976 that a state legislature—Colorado's—adopted sunset legislation for state regulatory commissions, giving them a life of six years before their suns set. Today most states have some type of sunset law.

Contracting Out

Contracting Out
The replacement of government services with services provided by private firms.

One approach to bureaucratic reform is **contracting out.** Contracting out occurs when government services are replaced by services from the private sector. For example, the government might contract with private firms to operate prisons. Supporters of contracting out argue that some services could be provided more efficiently by the private sector. Another scheme is to furnish vouchers to "clients" in lieu of services. For example, it has been proposed that instead of federally supported housing assistance, the government should offer vouchers that recipients could use to "pay" for housing in privately owned buildings.

The contracting-out strategy has been most successful on the local level. Municipalities, for example, can form contracts with private companies for such things as trash collection. Such an approach is not a cure-all, however, as there are many functions, particularly on the national level, that cannot be contracted

POLITICS WIRED

Should E-Mail Messages Be in the "Sunshine"?

State "sunshine laws" often mandate that records of any meetings among public officials be available to the public. But what if public officeholders exchange e-mail messages concerning a policy decision? Should copies of these messages be available to the public as well?

There is a growing consensus among legal experts that they should be—and this is creating problems for public officials. For example, in 1997 a lawsuit was brought against county commissioners in Sarasota, Florida, after it was discovered that the commissioners agreed via e-mail to withhold a public

vote on whether to sell a proposed library site. (The suit was dropped when the commissioners left office.) In 1998, North Dakota's attorney general ruled that the state Board of Higher Education had held illegal secret meetings and taken straw votes via e-mail on the issue of whether to fire the president of the University of North Dakota. E-mail exchanges among members of the city council of Phoenix, Arizona, also came under scrutiny recently for similar reasons.

How can public officials avoid violating state sunshine laws when communicating via e-mail? The city of Phoenix addressed the problem by upgrading its computer system so that copies of e-mail could be kept in the city clerk's office for public access. A community college in Baltimore, Maryland, took a different approach. After the county attorney told the members of the college's board that using e-mail to discuss public affairs would violate the state's open meeting law, the board decided to avoid the problem by getting rid of some $25,000 worth of

computer equipment. Generally, public officials who use e-mail will have to be careful to distinguish between communications that are primarily personal and communications that affect the public interest.

FOR CRITICAL ANALYSIS

What is the difference between private telephone conversations between public officials about public matters and private "conversations" on the same matters made via e-mail?

out in any meaningful way. For example, the federal government could not contract out all of the Defense Department's functions to a private firm.

Incentives for Efficiency and Productivity

An increasing number of state governments are beginning to experiment with a variety of schemes to run their operations more efficiently and capably. They focus on maximizing the efficiency and productivity of government workers by providing incentives for improved performance.[7]

Today, many governors, mayors, and city administrators are considering ways in which government can be made more entrepreneurial. Some of the more promising measures have included such tactics as permitting agencies that do not spend their entire budgets to keep some of the difference and rewarding employees with performance-based bonuses.

At the federal level, the Government Performance and Results Act of 1997 was designed to improve efficiency in the federal work force. The act required that all government agencies (except the Central Intelligence Agency) describe their new goals and establish methods for determining whether those goals are met. Goals may be broadly crafted (for example, reducing the time it takes to test a new drug before allowing it to be marketed) or narrowly crafted (for example, reducing the number of times a telephone rings before it is answered).

Efforts to improve bureaucratic efficiency are supported by the assertion that although society and industry have changed enormously in the past century, the form of government used in Washington, D.C., and in most states has remained the same. Some observers believe that the nation's diverse economic base cannot be administered competently by traditional bureaucratic organizations. Consequently, government must become more responsive to cope with the increasing number of demands placed on it.

Other analysts have suggested that the problem lies not so much with traditional bureaucratic organizations as with the people who run them. According to policy specialist Taegan Goddard and journalist Christopher Riback, what needs to be "reinvented" is not the machinery of government but public officials. After each election, new appointees to bureaucratic positions may find themselves managing complex, multimillion-dollar enterprises, yet they often are untrained for their jobs. According to these authors, if we want to reform the bureaucracy, we should focus on preparing newcomers for the task of "doing" government.[8]

Helping Out the Whistleblowers

The term **whistleblower** as applied to the federal bureaucracy has a special meaning: it is someone who blows the whistle on a gross governmental inefficiency or illegal action. Whistleblowers may be clerical workers, managers, or even specialists, such as scientists. The 1978 Civil Service Reform Act prohibits reprisals against whistleblowers by their superiors, and it set up the Merit Systems Protection Board as part of this protection. Many federal agencies also have toll-free hotlines that employees can use anonymously to report bureaucratic waste and inappropriate behavior. About 35 percent of all calls result in agency action or follow-up.

---

[7]See, for example, David Osborne and Ted Gaebler, *Reinventing Government: How the Entrepreneurial Spirit Is Transforming the Public Sector* (Reading, Mass.: Addison-Wesley, 1992); and David Osborne and Peter Plastrik, *Banishing Bureaucracy: The Five Strategies for Reinventing Government* (Reading, Mass.: Addison-Wesley, 1997).

[8]Taegan D. Goddard and Christopher Riback, *You Won—Now What? How Americans Can Make Democracy Work from City Hall to the White House* (New York: Scribner, 1998).

> **DID YOU KNOW...**
> That federal officials spent $333,000 building a deluxe, earthquake-proof outhouse for hikers in Pennsylvania's remote Delaware Water Gap recreation area?

Whistleblower
Someone who brings to public attention gross governmental inefficiency or an illegal action.

INFOTRAC®
COLLEGE EDITION

"Court Makes It Harder for Corporations"

Former FBI special agent Frederic Whitehurst, as he appeared on C-SPAN while making allegations of wrongdoing (evidence tampering) within the FBI's crime lab. What protections exist for employees of the federal government who "blow the whistle" on perceived wrongdoing in their agencies?

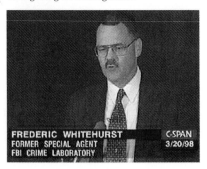

FREDERIC WHITEHURST   C-SPAN
FORMER SPECIAL AGENT   3/20/98
FBI CRIME LABORATORY

Enabling Legislation
A statute enacted by Congress that authorizes the creation of an administrative agency and specifies the name, purpose, composition, and powers of the agency being created.

Further protection against whistleblowing was provided in 1989, when Congress passed the Whistle-Blower Protection Act. That act established an independent agency, the Office of Special Counsel (OSC), to investigate complaints brought by government employees who have been demoted, fired, or otherwise sanctioned for reporting government fraud or waste.

There is little evidence, though, that potential whistleblowers truly have received more protection as a result of these endeavors. More than 40 percent of the employees who turned to the OSC for assistance in a recent three-year period stated that they were no longer employees of the government agencies on which they blew the whistle. A recent case that received wide publicity involved Frederic Whitehurst, a scientist-agent working for the crime lab at the Federal Bureau of Investigation (FBI). Whitehurst believed that the lab had been tampering with evidence to support the prosecution in several high-profile criminal cases. Immediately after Whitehurst informed the press of his conclusions, the director of the FBI suspended him from his job and barred him from entering the FBI building.

Bureaucrats as Politicians and Policymakers

Because Congress is unable to oversee the day-to-day administration of its programs, it must delegate certain powers to administrative agencies. Congress delegates the power to implement legislation to agencies through what is called **enabling legislation.** For example, the Federal Trade Commission was created by the Federal Trade Commission Act of 1914, the Equal Employment Opportunity Commission was created by the Civil Rights Act of 1964, and the Occupational Safety and Health Commission was created by the Occupational Safety and Health Act of 1970. The enabling legislation generally specifies the name, purpose, functions, and powers of the agency.

In theory, the agencies should put into effect laws passed by Congress. Laws are often drafted in such vague and general terms, however, that they provide little guidance to agency administrators as to how the laws should be put into effect. This means that the agencies themselves must decide how best to carry out the wishes of Congress.

The discretion given to administrative agencies is not accidental. Congress has long realized that it lacks the technical expertise and the resources to monitor the implementation of its laws. Hence, the administrative agency is created to fill the gaps. This gap-filling role requires the agency to formulate administrative rules (regulations) to put flesh on the bones of the law. But it also forces the agency itself to assume the role of an unelected policymaker. (For an example of a recent Environmental Protection Agency policy decision, see the feature *Politics and Economics: Who Benefits from "Environmental Justice"?*)

The Rulemaking Environment

Rulemaking does not occur in a vacuum. Suppose that Congress passes a new air-pollution law. The Environmental Protection Agency (EPA) might decide to implement the new law by a technical regulation relating to factory emissions. This proposed regulation would be published in the *Federal Register,* a daily government publication, so that interested parties would have an opportunity to comment on it. Individuals and companies that opposed parts or all of the rule might then try to convince the EPA to revise or redraft the regulation. Some parties might try to persuade the agency to withdraw the proposed regulation altogether. In any event, the EPA would consider these comments in drafting the final version of the regulation following the expiration of the comment period.

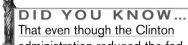

Once the final regulation has been published in the *Federal Register,* the regulation might be challenged in court by a party having a direct interest in the rule, such as a company that could expect to incur significant costs in complying with it. The company could argue that the rule misinterprets the applicable law or goes beyond the agency's statutory purview. An allegation by the company that the EPA made a mistake in judgment probably would not be enough to convince the court to throw out the rule. The company instead would have to demonstrate that the rule itself was "arbitrary and capricious." To meet this standard, the company would have to show that the rule reflected a serious flaw in the EPA's judgment—such as a steadfast refusal by the agency to consider reasonable alternatives to its rule.

In a budget package signed by the president in 1996, some regulatory relief was obtained. When an agency now issues a new rule, it has to wait sixty days (instead of only thirty days, as was previously required) before enforcing the rule. During that waiting period, businesses, individuals, and state and local governments can ask Congress to overturn the regulation rather than having to sue the agency after the rule takes effect.

> **DID YOU KNOW...**
> That even though the Clinton administration reduced the federal work force by over 200,000 people between 1994 and 1997, virtually all of the work formerly done by federal employees is now being contracted out (that is, the number of people working on federal programs has not decreased)

POLITICS and Economics

Who Benefits from "Environmental Justice"?

About 60 percent of the people who live in Covent, Louisiana, are unemployed and have low incomes. Not surprisingly, when the community learned that the Japanese-owned firm, Shintech, planned to establish a $700 million polyvinyl chloride plant in their area, many residents welcomed the prospect of the new job opportunities that would be created.

The project was approved by Louisiana's Department of Environmental Quality, and it looked as though construction would soon be under way. The Environmental Protection Agency (EPA), however, had other ideas. Concluding that blacks would suffer disproportionately from the cancer-causing emissions from the plant, in 1997 the EPA ordered that construction be delayed.

The EPA's concern with "environmental justice" began in 1993, when the agency's director, Carol Browner, created the Office

of Environmental Justice within the EPA. One of the purposes of the new office was to oversee studies on the effects of industrial pollutants on poorer, mostly black communities. In the following year, the White House supported Browner's initiative by requiring all federal administrative agencies to consider the health and environmental effects of their decisions on minority and low-income communities.

The EPA's decision with respect to the Shintech plant was applauded by a group of white, middle-class residents in Covent. But Louisiana officials, as well as the lower-income residents of Covent, were enraged at the EPA's action.

According to Louisiana's director of Economic Development, Kevin Reilly, "It is demeaning and despicable for these people to play the race card," especially when the plant would have

Carol Browner, head of the EPA.

provided economic benefits for poor people and blacks. Additionally, a study reported in the *Journal of the Louisiana Medical Society* found that the project would not have created the significant health risk that the EPA claimed it would.* Others criticized the EPA for intrud-

*Pranay Gupte and Bonner R. Cohen, "Carol Browner, Master of Mission Creep," *Forbes,* October 20, 1997, p. 175.

ing too extensively into state and local affairs.

Nevertheless, the EPA's decision, if challenged in court, will probably pass constitutional muster. Remember from Chapter 3 that under the Constitution's supremacy clause, laws and regulations of the federal government preempt conflicting state laws or regulations. With respect to environmental matters, this means that an EPA order or rule (such as an order concerning the Shintech project) will take precedence over a conflicting state action (such as Louisiana's decision to approve the Shintech plant).

FOR CRITICAL ANALYSIS

Should it matter whether those whose health may be jeopardized by an industrial plant's cancer-causing emissions are black or white?

Negotiated Rulemaking

Since the end of World War II, companies, environmentalists, and other special interest groups have challenged government regulations in court. In the 1980s and 1990s, however, the sheer wastefulness of attempting to regulate through litigation became more and more apparent. A growing number of federal agencies now encourage businesses and public interest groups to become involved directly in the drafting of regulations. Agencies hope that such participation might help to prevent later courtroom battles over the meaning, applicability, and legal effect of the regulations.

Congress formally approved such a process, which is called *negotiated rulemaking,* in the Negotiated Rulemaking Act of 1990. The act authorizes agencies to allow those who will be affected by a new rule to participate in the rule-drafting process. If an agency chooses to engage in negotiated rulemaking, it must publish in the *Federal Register* the subject and scope of the rule to be developed, the parties that will be affected significantly by the rule, and other information. Representatives of the affected groups and other interested parties then may apply to be members of the negotiating committee. The agency is represented on the committee, but a neutral third party (not the agency) presides over the proceedings. Once the committee members have reached agreement on the terms of the proposed rule, notice of the proposed rule is published in the *Federal Register,* followed by a period for comments by any person or organization interested in the proposed rule. Negotiated rulemaking often is conducted under the condition that the participants promise not to challenge in court the outcome of any agreement to which they were a party.

Bureaucrats Are Policymakers

Theories of public administration once assumed that bureaucrats do not make policy decisions but only implement the laws and policies promulgated by the president and legislative bodies. Many people continue to make this assumption. A more realistic view, which is now held by most bureaucrats and elected officials, is that the agencies and departments of government play important roles in policymaking. As we have seen, many government rules, regulations, and programs are in fact initiated by the bureaucracy, based on its expertise and scientific studies. How a law passed by Congress eventually is translated into concrete action—from the forms to be filled out to decisions about who gets the benefits—usually is determined within each agency or department. Even the evaluation of whether a policy has achieved its purpose usually is based on studies that are commissioned and interpreted by the agency administering the program.

The bureaucracy's policymaking role often has been depicted by what has been called the "iron triangle." Recently, the concept of an "issue network" has been viewed as a more accurate description of the policymaking process.

Iron Triangles.   In the past, scholars often described the bureaucracy's role in the policymaking process by using the concept of an **iron triangle**—a three-way alliance among legislators in Congress, bureaucrats, and interest groups in a given policy area. The presumption was that policy development depended on how a policy affected each component of the iron triangle.

Consider as an example the development of agricultural policy. The Department of Agriculture has over 100,000 employees working directly for the federal government and thousands of others who, directly or indirectly, work as contractors, subcontractors, or consultants to the department. Now consider that there are various interest, or client, groups that are concerned with what the federal government does for farmers. These include the American Farm Bureau Federation, the National Cattleman's Association, the National Milk Producers

Iron Triangle
The three-way alliance among legislators, bureaucrats, and interest groups to make or preserve policies that benefit their respective interests.

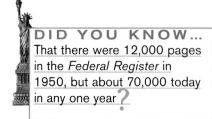

Association, the Corn Growers Association, and the Citrus Growers Association. Finally, go directly to Congress, and you will see that there are two major congressional committees concerned with agriculture–the House Committee on Agriculture and the Senate Committee on Agriculture, Nutrition, and Forestry–each of which has several subcommittees.

Clearly, it is in the Department of Agriculture's interest to support policies that enhance the department's budget and powers. Consider that the secretary of agriculture cannot even buy a desk lamp if Congress does not approve the appropriations for the department's budget. Therefore, the department will lend whatever support it can to those members of Congress who are in charge of deciding which agricultural programs should be cut, maintained, or created and what amount of funds should be allocated to the department.

Various agricultural interest groups will lobby Congress to develop policies that benefit their groups' interests. Members of Congress cannot afford to ignore the wishes of interest groups, because those groups are potential sources of voter support and campaign contributions. Therefore, the legislators involved in the iron triangle will work closely with interest group lobbyists when developing new policy. The legislators also will work closely with the Department of Agriculture, which, in implementing a policy, can develop rules that benefit–or are not adverse to–certain industries or groups.

To be sure, this is a much simplified picture of how the iron triangle works. But you can see how the interests of government agencies, legislators, and interest groups are all involved in the policymaking process. At times, iron triangles have completely thwarted efforts by the president to get the administration's programs enacted.

Issue Networks.   With the growth in the complexity of the government, including expansion in the size of the bureaucracy, the increased number of subcommittees in Congress, and the proliferation of interest groups, policymaking also has become more complex. Often, different interest groups concerned about a certain area, such as agriculture, will have conflicting demands, which makes agency decision making difficult. Additionally, government agencies often are controlled by more than one legislative group. Finally, divided government in the late 1990s has meant that departments may be pressured by the president to take one approach and by legislators to take another. Today, policymaking typically involves a complex attempt to balance many conflicting demands.

Although iron triangles still exist, often they are inadequate as descriptions of how policy is actually made. Many scholars now use the term "issue network" to describe the policymaking process. An **issue network** consists of a group of individuals or organizations that support a particular policy position on the environment, taxation, consumer safety, or some other issue. Typically, an issue network includes legislators and/or their staff members, interest groups, bureaucrats, the media, scholars and other experts, and representatives from the media. Members of a particular issue network work together to influence the president, members of Congress, administrative agencies, and the courts to change public policy on a specific issue. Each policy issue may involve conflicting positions taken by two or more issue networks.

Issue Network
A group of individuals or organizations–which may consist of legislators or legislative staff members, interest group leaders, bureaucrats, the media, scholars, and other experts–that supports a particular policy position on a given issue, such as one relating to the environment, to taxation, or to consumer safety.

Congressional Control of the Bureaucracy

Although Congress is the ultimate repository of political power under the Constitution, many political pundits doubt whether Congress can meaningfully control the federal bureaucracy. These commentators forget that Congress, as already mentioned, specifies in an agency's "enabling legislation" the powers of the agency and the parameters within which it can operate. Additionally, Congress has the power of the purse and could, theoretically, refuse to authorize or appropriate funds for a particular agency. Whether Congress would actually take such a drastic measure would depend on the circumstances. It is clear, however, that Congress does have the legal authority to decide whether to fund or not to fund administrative agencies. Congress also can exercise oversight over agencies through investigations and hearings.

Authorizing Funds

Authorization

A formal declaration by a legislative committee that a certain amount of funding may be available to an agency. Some authorizations terminate in a year; others are renewable automatically without further congressional action.

Once an agency is created by enabling legislation, Congress must authorize funds for it. The **authorization** is a formal declaration by the appropriate legislative committee that a certain amount of funding may be available to the agency. The authorization itself may terminate in a year, or it may be renewed automatically without further action by Congress. Authorizations for the National Aeronautics and Space Administration (NASA) must be periodically renewed; Social Security, in contrast, is funded through a permanent authorization. Periodic authorizations enable Congress to exercise greater control overthe spending programs of an agency, whereas permanent authorizations free Congress from the task of having to review the authorization each year. The drawback of permanent authorizations is that they can become almost impossible to control politically.

Appropriation

The passage, by Congress, of a spending bill, specifying the amount of authorized funds that actually will be allocated for an agency's use.

Appropriating Funds

After the funds are authorized, they must be appropriated by Congress. The appropriations committees of both the House and the Senate forward spending bills to their respective bodies. The **appropriation** of funds occurs when the final bill is passed. Congress is not required to appropriate the entire authorized amount. It may appropriate less if it so chooses. If the appropriated funds are substantially less than the authorized amount, however, it may signal that the agency's agenda soon may be revamped by Congress.

Investigations and Hearings

Congressional committees conduct investigations and hold hearings to oversee an agency's actions, reviewing them to ensure compliance with congressional intentions. The agency's officers and employees can be ordered to testify before a committee about the details of an action. Through these oversight activities, especially in the questioning and commenting by members of the House or Senate during the hearings, Congress indicates its positions on specific programs and issues. Congress can also ask the General Accounting Office (GAO) to investigate particular agency actions. The Congressional Budget Office (CBO) also conducts oversight studies. The results of a GAO or CBO study may encourage Congress to hold further hearings or make changes in the law. Even if a law is not changed explicitly by Congress, however, the views expressed in any investigations and hearings are taken seriously by agency officials, who often act on those views.

While the National Aeronautics and Space Administration works to build support for its programs in the future, many question the need for such an expensive public program as the space shuttle.

The Bureaucracy: Issues for the New Century

There probably will be continued attempts to reform the bureaucracy as long as we have a representative democratic form of government. The way members of the House and Senate get reelected and the way in which lobbyists fit into that process, however, practically guarantee that the bureaucracy will never be reformed completely.

This does not mean that we will not see some improvements. Indeed, competition in the private marketplace is forcing changes on some federal government institutions. For example, the efficiency of private overnight delivery services, such as FedEx, Airborne, and United Parcel Service (UPS), has forced many changes on the U.S. Postal Service. Increasingly, the use of fax machines, high-speed modems, and e-mail also has put added pressure on the U.S. Postal Service to become more efficient. Such changes are bound to continue as communications technology improves.

The actual job of the federal bureaucracy, of course, will never disappear. Federal agencies are the primary means by which the laws of Congress are put into practice. The "gap-filling" power of federal agencies gives them significant discretion to make policy. Such policymaking has certain advantages: bureaucrats are often specialists in their fields and are more knowledgeable than members of Congress about specific issues relating to the legislation passed by Congress.

DID YOU KNOW...
That each year, federal administrative agencies produce rules that fill 7,500 pages in the *Code of Federal Regulations*?

TOWARD ACTIVE CITIZENSHIP

WHAT THE GOVERNMENT KNOWS ABOUT YOU

The federal government collects billions of pieces of information on tens of millions of Americans each year. These are stored in files and gigantic computers and often are exchanged among agencies. You probably have at least several federal records (for example, those in the Social Security Administration; the Internal Revenue Service; and, if you are a male, the Selective Service).

The 1966 Freedom of Information Act requires that the federal government release, at your request, any identifiable information it has in the administrative agencies of the executive branch. This information can be about you or about any other subject. Ten categories of material are exempted, however (classified material, confidential material dealing with trade secrets, internal personnel rules, personal medical files, and the like). To request material, you must write to the Freedom of Information Act officer directly at the agency in question (say, the Department of Education). You must also have a relatively specific idea about the document or information you wish to obtain.

A second law, the Privacy Act of 1974, gives you access specifically to information the government may have collected about you. This is a very important law, because it allows you to review your records on file with federal agencies (for example, with the Federal Bureau of Investigation) and to check those records for possible inaccuracies. Cases do exist in which two people with similar or the same names have had their records confused. In some cases, innocent persons have had the criminal records of another person erroneously inserted into their files.

If you wish to look at any records or find out if an agency has a record on you, write to the agency head or Privacy Act officer, and address your letter to the specific agency. State that "under the provisions of the Privacy Act of 1974, 5 U.S.C. 522a, I hereby request a copy of (or access to) _____." Then describe the record that you wish to investigate.

If you have trouble finding out about your records or wish to locate an attorney in Washington, D.C., to help you with this matter, you can contact the following organization:

Lawyer Referral Service
Washington Bar Association
1819 H St. N.W., Suite 300
Washington, DC 20036
202-223-6600

Key terms

acquisitive model 458

administrative agency 457

appropriation 478

authorization 478

bureaucracy 455

cabinet department 460

capture 465

Civil Service Commission 470

contracting out 472

enabling legislation 474

garbage can model 458

government corporation 466

Government in the Sunshine
Act 471

Hatch Act (Political Activities
Act) 471

independent executive agency 462

independent regulatory agency 463

iron triangle 476

issue network 477

line organization 460

merit system 469

monopolistic model 458

natural aristocracy 469

Pendleton Act (Civil Service
Reform Act) 469

spoils system 469

sunset legislation 471

Weberian model 457

whistleblower 473

Chapter summary

1 Presidents have long complained about their inability to control the federal bureaucracy. There is no reference to the bureaucracy itself in the Constitution, but Article II gives the president the power to appoint officials to execute the laws of the United States. Most scholars cite Article II as the constitutional basis for the federal bureaucracy.

2 Bureaucracies are rigid hierarchical organizations in which the tasks and powers of lower-level employees are defined clearly. Job specialties and extensive procedural rules set the standards for behavior. Bureaucracies are the primary form of organization of most major corporations and universities.

3 Several theories have been offered to explain bureaucracies. The Weberian model posits that bureaucracies have developed into centralized hierarchical structures in response to the increasing demands placed on governments by their citizens. The acquisitive model views top-level bureaucrats as pressing for ever greater funding, staffs, and privileges to augment their own sense of power and security. The monopolistic model focuses on the environment in which most government bureaucracies operate, stating that bureaucracies are inefficient and excessively costly to operate because they often have no competitors. Finally, the garbage can model posits that bureaucracies are rudderless organizations that flounder about in search of solutions to problems.

4 Since the founding of the United States, the federal bureaucracy has grown from 50 to about 2.7 million employees (excluding the military). Federal, state, and local employees together make up some 15 percent of the nation's civilian labor force. The federal bureaucracy consists of fourteen cabinet departments, as well as numerous independent executive agencies, independent regulatory agencies, and government corporations. These entities enjoy varying degrees of autonomy, visibility, and political support.

5 A self-sustaining federal bureaucracy of career civil servants was formed during Thomas Jefferson's presidency. Andrew Jackson implemented a spoils system through which he appointed his own political supporters. A civil service based on professionalism and merit was the goal of the Civil Service Reform Act of 1883. Concerns that the civil service be freed from the pressures of politics prompted the passage of the Hatch Act in 1939. Significant changes in the administration of the civil service were made by the Civil Service Reform Act of 1978.

6 There have been many attempts to make the federal bureaucracy more open, efficient, and responsive to the needs of U.S. citizens. The most important reforms have included sunshine and sunset laws, contracting out, strategies to provide incentives for increased productivity and efficiency, and protection for whistleblowers.

7 Congress delegates much of its authority to federal agencies when it creates new laws. The bureaucrats who run these agencies may become important policymakers, because Congress has neither the time nor the technical expertise to oversee the administration of its laws. In the agency rulemaking process, a proposed regulation is published. A comment period follows, during which interested parties may offer suggestions for changes. Because companies and other organizations have challenged many regulations in court, federal agencies now are allowed to involve parties that will be affected by new regulations in the rule-drafting process.

8 Congress exerts ultimate control over all federal agencies, because it controls the federal government's purse strings. It also establishes the general guidelines by which regulatory agencies must abide. The appropriations process may also provide a way to send messages of approval or disapproval to particular agencies, as do congressional hearings and investigations relating to agency actions.

Selected print and electronic resources

SUGGESTED READINGS

Downs, Anthony. *Inside Bureaucracy.* Boston: Little, Brown, 1967. In this classic work on the bureaucracy, Downs provides an economist's explanation of why the bureaucracy is what it is and why bureaucrats and their agencies conduct themselves as they do.

Hill, Michael. *The Policy Process in the Modern States.* Englewood Cliffs, N.J.: Prentice-Hall, 1998. This overall view of the policymaking process includes a discussion of the role played by bureaucrats in policymaking.

Osborne, David, and Peter Plastrik. *Banishing Bureaucracy: The Five Strategies for Reinventing Government.* Reading, Mass.: Addison-Wesley, 1997. The author of *Reinventing Government* (1992), David Osborne, joined by Peter Plastrik, goes a step further in promoting an entrepreneurial model of government in which market principles are applied to government administration.

Richardson, William D. *Democracy, Bureaucracy, and Character: Founding Thought.* Lawrence, Kans.: University of Kansas, 1997. The author looks at the founders' views of how government should be administered.

Vranich, Joseph. *Derailed: What Went Wrong and What to Do about America's Passenger Trains.* New York: St. Martin's Press, 1997. The author, a former AMTRAK official, contends that the federally financed passenger railroad company is a complete waste of money and should be eliminated.

MEDIA RESOURCES

Men in Black—A 1997 science-fiction comedy about an unofficial government agency that regulates the immigration of aliens from outer space who are living on earth.

Missiles of October—A movie retelling the events of October 1962, when the Kennedy administration decided to blockade Cuba to force the Soviet Union to remove its missiles from Cuba. The 1974 film, starring William Devane and Ralph Bellamy, gives an excellent inside view of policymaking involving the State Department, the Defense Department, and the president.

1984—A 1984 adaptation of George Orwell's well-known novel about the bureaucratic world of the future, starring John Hurt and Richard Burton; a superb fable of government versus individual values.

Logging on

The National Performance Review (NPR), which was started in the early stages of the Clinton administration to "reinvent government," is now online. Go to

www.npr.gov/

Numerous links to many federal agencies and information on the federal government can be found at the Web site of Federal World. Go to

www.fedworld.gov/

The Federal Web Locator is an excellent site to access if you want to find information on the bureaucracy. Its URL is

www.law.vill.edu/Fed-Agency/fedwebloc.html

The *Federal Register,* which is the official publication for executive-branch documents, is online at

www.gpo.ucop.edu/search/fedfld.html

Another government publication that you might want to examine is the *United States Government Manual,* which describes the origins, purposes, and administrators of every federal department and agency. To access this publication online, go to

www.gpo.ucop.edu/catalog/govman.html

If you want to find telephone numbers for government agencies and personnel, you can go to

www.info.gov/fed_directory/phone.htm

"The Plum Book," which lists the bureaucratic positions that can be filled by presidential appointment, is online at

www.louisville.edu/library/ekstrom/govpubs/ federal/plum.html

Using the Internet for political analysis

Be a critical consumer of government information on the World Wide Web. Go to a government locator page, such as FedWorld (cited above), or to the Center for Information Law and Policy at

www.law.vill.edu/

and compare the Web pages of at least three federal departments or agencies. Answer the following questions for each Web page:

1. Do you get the basic information about the department or agency, including its goals, locations, size, budget, and how citizens can gain access to the agency?

2. Can you tell from the page who the primary clients of the agency are? For example, are the agency's primary clients governments, ordinary citizens, businesses, or labor unions?

3. Is the page well designed, up to date, and easy for the average citizen to use?

4. What is the most valuable information on the page for you?

The Judiciary

Federal Judges Were Elected?

BACKGROUND

THE FOUNDERS OF THIS COUNTRY ESTABLISHED A REPRESENTATIVE DEMOCRACY, IN WHICH THOSE WHO PASS LAWS AND MAKE POLICY ARE ELECTED. THEORETICALLY, AT LEAST, THEIR JOB IS TO REPRESENT THE INTERESTS OF THE PEOPLE.

IN CONTRAST, THE JUDGES (AND JUSTICES*) WHO SIT ON THE BENCHES OF THE FEDERAL COURTS ARE NOT ELECTED TO THEIR POSTS. RATHER, THEY ARE APPOINTED BY THE PRESIDENT (AND CONFIRMED BY THE SENATE). THEY ALSO HOLD THEIR OFFICES FOR LIFE, BARRING GROSS MISCONDUCT. NEVERTHELESS, THESE MEMBERS OF THE FEDERAL JUDICIAL BRANCH ARE AMONG THE MOST IMPORTANT POLICYMAKERS OF THIS NATION BECAUSE THEY DECIDE HOW THE U.S. CONSTITUTION—THE "SUPREME LAW OF THE LAND"—SHOULD BE INTERPRETED.

IN THE LAST FEW YEARS, FEDERAL JUDGES SEEM TO BE INCREASINGLY UNDER ATTACK BY THE MEDIA AND OTHER GROUPS THAT DISAGREE WITH THEIR DECISIONS. THERE IS A GROWING SENTIMENT THAT FEDERAL JUDGES OUGHT TO BE MORE ACCOUNTABLE TO THE PUBLIC FOR THEIR DECISIONS.

---

*The terms *judge* and *justice* are two designations given to judges in various courts. All members of the United States Supreme Court are referred to as justices, while those who sit on the benches of the lower federal courts typically are called judges. We use the term *judge* here to refer to all members of the federal judiciary, including the Supreme Court justices.

WHAT IF FEDERAL JUDGES WERE ELECTED?

Many contend that if federal judges were elected, they might give greater consideration to public opinion than they currently do when deciding cases. For example, assume that public opinion polls show that a majority of Americans are against laws protecting gay and lesbian rights. An elected judge about to run for reelection might be more inclined than an appointed judge to deem such laws unconstitutional.

Some argue that if federal judges were more concerned about public opinion and what the public wants, our government would be more democratic. After all, implementing the wishes of the electorate is the appropriate function of government institutions in a representative democracy.

Others point out that if federal judges were elected, they would be less able to resist the fierce winds of politics. Under the existing system, once approved by the Senate and seated on a court's bench, a judge is free to decide cases as he or she wishes. Federal judges, because they hold office for life, do not have to worry about job security.

INTEREST GROUPS AND CAMPAIGN COSTS

Federal judges, by virtue of their lifetime appointments, are immunized from the pressures brought to bear on the legislative and executive branches by various interest groups. If federal judges were elected, they certainly would lose this immunity. A person seeking election (or reelection) to a federal court might be tempted to give in to pressure to vote in accordance with a particular interest group's wishes in return for the group's political support.

POLITICAL IDEOLOGY

Humorist Finley Peter Dunne once said that "th' Supreme Court follows th' iliction returns." In other words, Democratic presidents tend to appoint liberal judges and justices to federal benches, and Republican presidents tend to appoint conservative judges and justices. Ultimately, then, the federal judiciary, including the Supreme Court, does change in response to election returns, but this process takes time. Justices on the nation's highest court, because they are at the top of the judicial career ladder, sometimes end up sitting on the Supreme Court for decades. If these justices were elected, the ideological complexion of the Court probably would change much more quickly. A voting bloc of liberal or conservative justices might be short-lived, with new alliances being formed after the next election. As a result, the decisions made by the Court, as the final interpreter of the Constitution, might not be very "final." If the next election brought in justices with different ideological views, the Court could overturn the precedents set by the Court during the previous term. Of course, staggered terms could be used, as in the Senate, to ensure more continuity in judicial decision making.

FOR CRITICAL ANALYSIS

1. Should federal judges be influenced by public opinion when making their decisions? Why or why not?

2. If Supreme Court justices were elected, would their decisions be less authoritative? Explain.

A s indicated in this chapter's opening *What If . . .* , the judges and justices of the federal court system are not elected but rather are appointed by the president and confirmed by the Senate. This fact does not mean that the federal judiciary is apolitical, however. Indeed, our courts play a larger role in making public policy than courts in any other country in the world today.

As Alexis de Tocqueville, a nineteenth-century French commentator on American society, noted, "scarcely any political question arises in the United States that is not resolved, sooner or later, into a judicial question."[1] Our judiciary forms part of our political process. The instant that judges interpret the law, they become actors in the political arena—policymakers working within a political institution. As such, the most important political force within our judiciary is the United States Supreme Court.

How do courts make policy? Why do the federal courts play such an important role in American government? The answers to these questions lie, in part, in our colonial heritage. Most of American law is based on the English system, particularly the English common law tradition. In that tradition, the decisions made by judges constitute an important source of law.

The Common Law Tradition

In 1066, the Normans conquered England, and William the Conqueror and his successors began the process of unifying the country under their rule. One of the ways they did this was to establish the king's courts, or *curiae regis*. Before the conquest, disputes had been settled according to local custom. The king's courts sought to establish a common or uniform set of rules for the whole country. As the number of courts and cases increased, portions of the more important decisions of each year were gathered together and recorded in *Year Books*. Judges settling disputes similar to ones that had been decided before used the *Year Books* as the basis for their decisions. If a case was unique, judges had to create new laws, but they based their decisions on the general principles suggested by earlier cases. The body of judge-made law that developed under this system is still used today and is known as the **common law.**

The practice of deciding new cases with reference to former decisions—that is, according to **precedent**—became a cornerstone of the English and American judicial systems and is embodied in the doctrine of ***stare decisis*** (pronounced *ster*-ay dih-*si*-ses), a Latin phrase that means "to stand on decided cases." The doctrine of *stare decisis* obligates judges to follow the precedents set previously only by their own courts or by higher courts that have authority over them.

For example, a lower state court in California would be obligated to follow a precedent set by the California Supreme Court. That lower court, however, would not be obligated to follow a precedent set by the supreme court of another state, because each state court system is independent. Of course, when the United States Supreme Court decides an issue, all of the nation's other courts are obligated to abide by the Court's decision—because the Supreme Court is the highest court in the land.

The doctrine of *stare decisis* provides a basis for judicial decision making in all countries that have common law systems. Today, the United States, Britain, and thirteen other countries have common law systems. Generally, those countries that were once colonies of Great Britain, including Australia, Canada, India, and New Zealand, have retained their English common law heritage since they

Common Law
Judge-made law that originated in England from decisions shaped according to prevailing custom. Decisions were applied to similar situations and gradually became common to the nation.

Precedent
A court rule bearing on subsequent legal decisions in similar cases. Judges rely on precedents in deciding cases.

Stare Decisis
To stand on decided cases; the judicial policy of following precedents established by past decisions.

[1]Alexis de Tocqueville, *Democracy in America* (New York: Harper & Row, 1966), p. 248.

achieved independence. The nation of Israel has a common law system also, but unlike the courts in other common law countries, the highest court in that nation is no longer obligated to apply the doctrine of *stare decisis*. (See the feature *Politics and Comparative Systems: The Americanization of Israeli Law* for a discussion of the effect of this development on Israeli law and culture.)

Sources of American Law

The body of American law is vast. It includes the federal and state constitutions, statutes passed by legislative bodies, administrative law, and case law—the legal principles expressed in court decisions.

Constitutions

The constitutions of the federal government and the states set forth the general organization, powers, and limits of government. The U.S. Constitution is the supreme law of the land. A law in violation of the Constitution, no matter what its source, may be declared unconstitutional and thereafter cannot be enforced. Similarly, the state constitutions are supreme within their respective borders

POLITICS and Comparative Systems

The Americanization of Israeli Law

As discussed in the text, the doctrine of *stare decisis* obligates courts in the United States to follow precedents. This means, for example, that the Supreme Court, when deciding new cases, must abide by decisions it made previously. Only rarely will the Court depart from this practice. In contrast, the supreme court in Israel is free to make decisions without regard to precedent. Although the lower courts continue to be obligated by *stare decisis,* the Israeli parliament released the supreme court from this obligation.

The parliament concluded that, given the nation's relative youth, cultural diversity, and the security threats it faces in the Middle East, the high court should be given more flexibility to adapt the law to changing circumstances. As a result, the

Israeli supreme court is free to turn to other nations' laws and court decisions for guidance.

Frequently, the court draws on the decisions of courts in England, Canada, Germany, France, and Australia for such guidance. Increasingly, however, the court has based its rulings on principles and legal reasoning found in U.S. jurisprudence. For example, in a recent case, the court held that Israel's all-male air force academy could not deny admission to a female applicant. The court's position was strikingly similar to that taken by U.S. courts on similar issues. In another case, which has been regarded as an Israeli version of *Marbury v. Madison,* the court declared its power to

invalidate a law passed by the Israeli parliament that conflicted with one of Israel's basic laws.

Many Israelis believe that the supreme court's importation of American law threatens their culture. Among other things, they claim that applying U.S. law promotes individualism and is contrary to those aspects of Israeli law that emphasize the rights of the community. Consider, for example, the issue of free speech. Until recently, Israel placed significant restrictions on speech, including prohibitions against "hate speech," in the interest of protecting the welfare and security of the community. In part, these limitations were imposed because Israel has a mixture of cultures, with Arabs, Christians, and Jews living side by side. Additionally,

Israeli jurisprudence relating to speech was influenced by the Holocaust and the link between that experience and Nazi anti-Jewish speech. In recent years, however, the Israeli supreme court, applying U.S. First Amendment doctrines, has tended to give the rights of individuals more weight than those of the community.

FOR CRITICAL ANALYSIS

Would the United States be better or worse off if the U.S. Supreme Court could look to other nations' laws for guidance?

(unless they conflict with the U.S. Constitution or federal laws and treaties made in accordance with it). The Constitution thus defines the political playing field on which state and federal powers are reconciled. The idea that the Constitution should be supreme in certain matters stemmed from widespread dissatisfaction with the weak federal government that had existed previously under the Articles of Confederation adopted in 1781.

Statutes and Administrative Regulations

Although the English common law provides the basis for both our civil and criminal legal systems, statutes (laws enacted by legislatures) increasingly have become important in defining the rights and obligations of individuals. Federal statutes may relate to any subject that is a concern of the federal government and may cover areas ranging from hazardous waste to federal taxation. State statutes include criminal codes, commercial laws, and laws relating to a variety of other matters. Cities, counties, and other local political bodies also pass statutes, which are called ordinances. These ordinances may deal with such things as zoning schemes and public safety. Rules and regulations issued by administrative agencies are another source of law. Today, much of the work of courts consists of interpreting these laws and regulations and applying them to circumstances in cases before the courts.

Case Law

Because we have a common law tradition, in which the doctrine of *stare decisis* plays an important role, the decisions rendered by the court also form an important body of law, collectively referred to as **case law**. Case law includes judicial interpretations of common law principles and doctrines as well as interpretations of the types of law just mentioned—constitutional provisions, statutes, and administrative agency regulations. As you learned in previous chapters, it is up to the courts, and particularly the Supreme Court, to decide what a constitutional provision or a statutory phrase means. In doing so, the courts, in effect, establish law. (We will discuss this policymaking function of the courts in more detail later in the chapter.)

Case Law
The rules and principles announced in court decisions. Case law includes judicial interpretations of common law principles and doctrines as well as interpretations of constitutional law, statutory law, and administrative law.

The Federal Court System

The United States has a dual court system. There are state courts and federal courts. Each of the fifty states, as well as the District of Columbia, has its own fully developed, independent system of courts, which we will examine in Chapter 19. Here we focus on the federal courts.

The federal court system derives its power from Article III, Section 1, of the U.S. Constitution. That section limits the **jurisdiction** (the authority to hear and decide cases) of the federal courts to cases that involve either a federal question or diversity of citizenship. A **federal question** arises when a case is based, at least in part, on the U.S. Constitution, a treaty, or a federal law. A person who claims that his or her rights under the Constitution, such as the right to free speech, have been violated could bring a case in a federal court. **Diversity of citizenship** exists when the parties to a lawsuit are from different states or (more rarely) when the suit involves a U.S. citizen and a government or citizen of a foreign country. The amount in controversy must be at least $75,000 before a federal court can take jurisdiction in a diversity case, however.

Jurisdiction
The authority of a court to decide certain cases. Not all courts have the authority to decide all cases. Where a case arises and what its subject matter is are two jurisdictional factors.

Federal Question
A question that pertains to the U.S. Constitution, acts of Congress, or treaties. A federal question provides a basis for federal jurisdiction.

Diversity of Citizenship
A basis for federal court jurisdiction over a lawsuit between (1) citizens of different states, (2) a foreign country and citizens of a state or of different states, or (3) citizens of a state and citizens or subjects of a foreign country. The amount in controversy must be more than $75,000 before a federal court can take jurisdiction in such cases.

As you can see in Figure 15-1, the federal court system is basically a three-tiered model consisting of (1) U.S. district courts and various specialized courts of limited jurisdiction (not all of the latter are shown in the figure), (2) intermediate U.S. courts of appeals, and (3) the U.S. Supreme Court.

U.S. District Courts

Trial Court
The court in which most cases usually begin and in which questions of fact are examined.

General Jurisdiction
Exists when a court's authority to hear cases is not significantly restricted. A court of general jurisdiction normally can hear a broad range of cases.

Limited Jurisdiction
Exists when a court's authority to hear cases is restricted to certain types of claims, such as tax claims or bankruptcy petitions.

Appellate Court
A court having jurisdiction to review cases and issues that were originally tried in lower courts.

The U.S. district courts are trial courts. **Trial courts** are what their name implies—courts in which trials are held and testimony is taken. The U.S. district courts are courts of **general jurisdiction,** meaning that they can hear cases involving a broad array of issues. Federal cases involving most matters typically arise in district courts. (The other courts on the lower tier of the model shown in Figure 15-1 are courts of **limited jurisdiction,** meaning that they can try cases involving only certain types of claims, such as tax claims or bankruptcy petitions.)

There is at least one federal district court in every state. The number of judicial districts can vary over time, primarily owing to population changes and corresponding caseloads. Currently, there are ninety-four federal judicial districts. A party who is dissatisfied with the decision of a district court judge can appeal the case to the appropriate U.S. court of appeals, or federal **appellate court.** Figure 15-2 shows the jurisdictional boundaries of the district courts (which are state boundaries, unless otherwise indicated by dotted lines within a state), as well as of the U.S. courts of appeals.

U.S. Courts of Appeals

There are thirteen U.S. courts of appeals. Twelve of these courts hear appeals from the federal district courts located within their respective judicial circuits (geographical areas over which they exercise jurisdiction). The Court of Appeals for the Thirteenth Circuit, called the Federal Circuit, has national appellate jurisdiction over certain types of cases, such as cases involving patent law and those in which the U.S. government is a defendant.

FIGURE 15-1
The Federal Court System

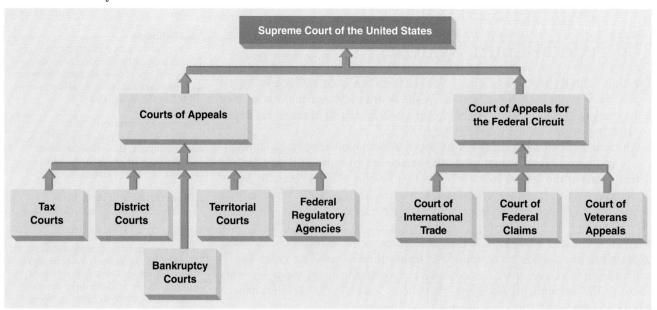

Note that when an appellate court reviews a case decided in a district court, the appellate court does not conduct another trial. Rather, a panel of three or more judges reviews the record of the case on appeal, which includes a transcript of the trial proceedings, and determines whether the trial court committed an error. Usually, appellate courts do not look at questions of *fact* (such as whether a party did, in fact, commit a certain action, such as burning a flag) but at questions of *law* (such as whether the act of flag burning is a form of speech protected by the First Amendment to the Constitution). An appellate court will challenge a trial court's finding of fact only when the finding is clearly contrary to the evidence presented at trial or when there is no evidence to support the finding.

A party can petition the U.S. Supreme Court to review an appellate court's decision. The likelihood that the Supreme Court will grant the petition is slim, however, because the Court reviews only a very few of the cases decided by the appellate courts. This means that decisions made by appellate judges usually are final.

The United States Supreme Court

The highest level of the three-tiered model of the federal court system is the United States Supreme Court. When the Supreme Court came into existence in 1789, it had five justices. In the following years, more justices were added, and since 1837 there have been nine justices on the Court.

FIGURE 15-2

Geographic Boundaries of Federal Circuit Courts of Appeals

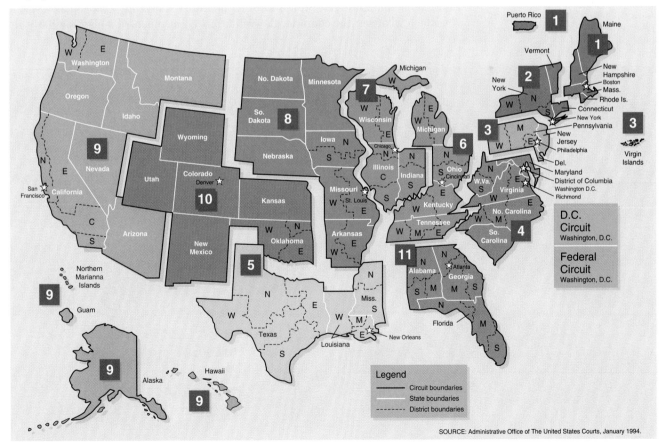

Legend
— Circuit boundaries
— State boundaries
---- District boundaries

SOURCE: Administrative Office of The United States Courts, January 1994.

Litigate
To engage in a legal proceeding or seek relief in a court of law; to carry on a lawsuit.

***Amicus Curiae* Brief**
A brief (a document containing a legal argument supporting a desired outcome in a particular case) filed by a third party, or *amicus curiae* (Latin for "friend of the court"), who is not directly involved in the litigation but who has an interest in the outcome of the case.

Class-Action Suit
A lawsuit filed by an individual seeking damages for "all persons similarly situated."

A jury is being sworn in. Most jury trials have between six and twelve jurors. Some trials are held without juries.

According to the language of Article III of the U.S. Constitution, there is only one national Supreme Court. All other courts in the federal system are considered "inferior." Congress is empowered to create other inferior courts as it deems necessary. The inferior courts that Congress has created include the federal courts of appeals and the district courts, as well as the federal courts of limited jurisdiction.

Although the Supreme Court can exercise original jurisdiction (that is, act as a trial court) in certain cases, such as those affecting foreign diplomats and those in which a state is a party, most of its work is as an appellate court. The Court hears appeals not only from the federal appellate courts but also from the highest state courts. Note, though, that the U.S. Supreme Court can review a state supreme court decision only if a federal question is involved. Because of its importance in the federal court system, we will look more closely at the Supreme Court in the next section.

Parties and Procedures

In most lawsuits, the parties are the plaintiff (the person or organization that initiates the lawsuit) and the defendant (the person or organization against whom the lawsuit is brought). There may be numerous plaintiffs and defendants in a single lawsuit. In the last several decades, many lawsuits have been brought by interest groups (see Chapter 8). Interest groups play an important role in our judicial system, because they **litigate**—bring to trial—or assist in litigating most cases of racial or gender-based discrimination, virtually all civil liberties cases, and more than one-third of the cases involving business matters. Interest groups also file ***amicus curiae*** (pronounced ah-*mee*-kous *kur*-ee-eye) **briefs,** or "friend of the court" briefs, in more than 50 percent of these kinds of cases.

Sometimes, interest groups or other plaintiffs will bring a **class-action suit,** in which whatever the court decides will affect all members of a class similarly sit-

uated (such as users of a particular product manufactured by the defendant in the lawsuit). The strategy of class-action lawsuits was pioneered by such groups as the National Association for the Advancement of Colored People (NAACP), the Legal Defense Fund, and the Sierra Club, whose members believed that the courts—rather than Congress—would offer the most sympathetic forum for their views.

Both the federal and the state courts have established procedural rules that shape the litigation process. These rules are designed to protect the rights and interests of the parties, to ensure that the litigation proceeds in a fair and orderly manner, and to identify the issues that must be decided by the court—thus saving court time and costs. Generally, these rules are rooted in the adversarial approach to justice followed in American courtrooms and determine what evidence must be disclosed by the parties to each other prior to trial, what evidence will be admissible during the legal contest between the parties, and so on. (See the feature *Politics Wired: Adversarial Justice on the Web*.)

POLITICS W I R E D

Adversarial Justice on the Web

English and American courts follow what is known as the "adversarial system of justice." In this system, parties to a lawsuit "do battle" before the court as contestants, or adversaries. Presumably, based on the evidence presented by the parties, the judge (and the jury, if it is a jury trial) will arrive at a true and just solution to the matter. In high-profile cases, typically another court is also at work—the court of public opinion. The media report both sides to the conflict, the public renders its opinion, and the media publish opinion polls summarizing the public's "verdict" in the case.

None of this is new, of course. What is new is how the World Wide Web is changing the nature and scope of this "court." For example, consider the online battle between some of the plaintiffs (those bringing lawsuits) and the defendants in the recent tobacco litigation. In its landmark case against the tobacco industry,

Minnesota's Blue Cross and Blue Shield (BC/BS) posted on its Web site (at www.mn-bluecrosstobacco.com/)

the results of laboratory studies showing the harmful effects of smoking. The tobacco industry, in turn, posted arguments and data supporting its position on its Web site (at www.tobaccoresolution.com/).

Even more significantly, BC/BS put on the Web more than thirty million pages of documents that the state of Minnesota had collected from tobacco companies. This allowed anyone with access to the Internet to view sixty years' worth of documents and data that previously had been available to only a few persons. One of the implications of this development became clear shortly after the documents were posted, as plaintiffs in tobacco suits in other nations began to use some of the documents on the BC/BS Web site to support their claims.

Some observers contend that such online legal dueling, among other things, is transforming the court of public opinion. Why? For one thing, members of the public no longer need to rely on the "filtered" version of a lawsuit presented by the press. They

can go directly to the litigants' Web sites to learn, firsthand, what the arguments in the case are and, in some cases, to find documents supporting the arguments that have been presented to the court. For another, parties with few resources can use the Internet to garner support—and contributions—for their causes. The public then can "vote" on the merits of a claim by giving or withholding contributions.

FOR CRITICAL ANALYSIS

Do you think it likely that people actually will wade through mountains of documents online to gain information about a lawsuit, rather than relying on summaries of the lawsuit provided by the press?

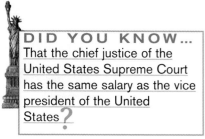

The parties must comply with procedural rules and with any orders given by the judge during the course of the litigation. When a party does not follow a court's order, the court can cite him or her for contempt. A party who commits *civil* contempt (failing to comply with a court's order for the benefit of another party to the proceeding) can be taken into custody, fined, or both, until the party complies with the court's order. A party who commits *criminal* contempt (obstructing the administration of justice or bringing the court into disrespect) also can be taken into custody and fined but cannot avoid punishment by complying with a previous order.

The Supreme Court at Work

The Supreme Court, by law, begins its regular annual term on the first Monday in October and usually adjourns in late June or early July of the next year. Special sessions may be held after the regular term is over, but only a few cases are decided in this way. More commonly, cases are carried over until the next regular session.

Of the total number of cases that are decided each year, those reviewed by the Supreme Court represent less than one-half of 1 percent. Included in these, however, are decisions that profoundly affect our lives. In recent years, the United States Supreme Court has decided issues involving capital punishment, affirmative action programs, religious freedom, assisted suicide, abortion, busing, term limits for congresspersons, sexual harassment, pornography, and numerous other matters with significant consequences for the nation. Because the Supreme Court exercises a great deal of discretion over the types of cases it hears, it can influence the nation's policies by issuing decisions in some types of cases and refusing to hear appeals in others, thereby allowing lower court decisions to stand.

Which Cases Reach the Supreme Court?

Many people are surprised to learn that in a typical case, there is no absolute right of appeal to the United States Supreme Court. The Court's appellate jurisdiction is almost entirely discretionary—the Court can choose which cases it will decide. The justices never explain their reasons for hearing certain cases and not others, so it is difficult to predict which case or type of case the Court might select. Chief Justice William Rehnquist, in his description of the selection process in *The Supreme Court: How It Was, How It Is,*[2] said that the decision of whether or not to accept a case "strikes me as a rather subjective decision, made up in part of intuition and in part of legal judgment."

Factors that bear on the decision include whether a legal question has been decided differently by two lower courts and needs resolution by the highest court, whether a lower court's decision conflicts with an existing Supreme Court ruling, and whether the issue could have significance beyond the parties to the dispute. For example, the justices very likely decided to review a case challenging the constitutionality of the Communications Decency Act of 1996 because the case involved the significant issue of the extent to which free speech on the Internet could be regulated. The justices probably decided to review the sexual-harassment case brought by Paula Jones against President Clinton (see Chapter 5) because it also involved an important question—whether a president should have to defend himself against a lawsuit while in office.

Another factor is whether the solicitor general is pressuring the Court to take a case. The solicitor general, a high-ranking presidential appointee within the

---

[2]William H. Rehnquist, *The Supreme Court: How It Was, How It Is* (New York: Morrow, 1987).

Justice Department, represents the national government in the Supreme Court and promotes presidential policies in the federal courts. He or she decides what cases the government should ask the Supreme Court to review and what position the government should take in cases before the Court. The influence wielded by solicitors general over the Court's decision making has led some to refer to the solicitor general as the "Tenth Justice."

If the Court decides to grant a petition for review, it will issue a **writ of certiorari** (pronounced sur-shee-uh-*rah*-ree). The writ orders a lower court to send the Supreme Court a record of the case for review. More than 90 percent of the petitions for writs of *certiorari* are denied. A denial is not a decision on the merits of a case, nor does it indicate agreement with the lower court's opinion. (The judgment of the lower court remains in force, however.) Therefore, denial of the writ has no value as a precedent. The Court will not issue a writ unless at least four justices approve of it. This is called the **rule of four**.[3]

Deciding Cases

Once the Supreme Court grants *certiorari* in a particular case, the justices do extensive research on the legal issues and facts involved in the case. (Of course, some preliminary research was necessary before deciding to grant the petition for

---

[3]The "rule of four" is modified when seven or fewer justices participate, which occurs from time to time. When that happens, as few as three justices can grant *certiorari*.

Writ of *Certiorari*
An order issued by a higher court to a lower court to send up the record of a case for review. It is the principal vehicle for United States Supreme Court review.

Rule of Four
A United States Supreme Court procedure requiring four affirmative votes to hear the case before the full Court.

In her chambers, Justice Ruth Bader Ginsburg works on her case load with one of her law clerks. Each justice has four law clerks, who typically are culled from the "best and the brightest" graduates from U.S. law schools. Some critics of the Supreme Court's practices argue that the clerks have too much power and influence over the Court's decision making.

Oral Arguments
The verbal arguments presented in person by attorneys to an appellate court. Each attorney presents reasons to the court why the court should rule in his or her client's favor.

INFOTRAC®
COLLEGE EDITION

"Courts Are at It Again"

Opinion
The statement by a judge or a court of the decision reached in a case tried or argued before it. The opinion sets forth the law that applies to the case and details the legal reasoning on which the judgment was based.

Affirm
To declare that a judgment is valid and must stand.

Reverse
To annul or make void a judgment on account of some error or irregularity.

Remand
To send a case back to the court that originally heard it.

Unanimous Opinion
A court opinion or determination on which all judges agree.

Majority Opinion
A court opinion reflecting the views of the majority of the judges.

Concurring Opinion
A separate opinion, prepared by a judge who supports the decision of the majority of the court but who wants to make or clarify a particular point or to voice disapproval of the grounds on which the decision was made.

Dissenting Opinion
A separate opinion in which a judge dissents from (disagrees with) the conclusion reached by the majority on the court and expounds his or her own views about the case.

review.) Each justice is entitled to four law clerks, who undertake much of the research and preliminary drafting necessary for the justice to form an opinion.[4]

The Court normally does not hear any evidence, as is true with all appeals courts. The Court's consideration of a case is based on the abstracts, the record, and the briefs. The attorneys are permitted to present **oral arguments.** The Court hears oral arguments on Monday, Tuesday, Wednesday, and sometimes Thursday, usually for seven two-week sessions scattered from the first week in October to the end of April or the first week in May. All statements and the justices' questions are tape-recorded during these sessions. Unlike the practice in most courts, lawyers addressing the Supreme Court can be (and often are) questioned by the justices at any time during oral argument.

The justices meet to discuss and vote on cases in conferences held each Wednesday and Friday throughout the term. In these conferences, in addition to deciding cases currently before the Court, the justices decide which new petitions for *certiorari* to grant. These conferences take place in the oak-paneled chamber and are strictly private—no stenographers, tape recorders, or video cameras are allowed. Two pages used to be in attendance to wait on the justices while they were in conference, but fear of information leaks caused the Court to stop this practice.[5]

Decisions and Opinions

When the Court has reached a decision, its opinion is written. The **opinion** contains the Court's reasons for its decision, the rules of law that apply, and the judgment. In many cases, the decision of the lower court is **affirmed,** resulting in the enforcement of that court's judgment or decree. If the Supreme Court feels that a reversible error was committed during the trial or that the jury was instructed improperly, however, the judgment will be **reversed.** Sometimes the case will be **remanded** (sent back to the court that originally heard the case) for a new trial or other proceeding. For example, a lower court might have held that a party was not entitled to bring a lawsuit under a particular law. If the Supreme Court holds to the contrary, it will remand (send back) the case to the trial court with instructions that the trial go forward.

The Court's written opinion sometimes is unsigned; this is called an opinion *per curiam* ("by the court"). Typically, the Court's opinion will be signed by all the justices who agree with it. Usually, when in the majority, the chief justice will write the opinion. Whenever the chief justice is in the minority, the senior justice on the majority side decides who writes the opinion.

When all justices unanimously agree on an opinion, the opinion is written for the entire Court (all the justices) and can be deemed a **unanimous opinion.** When there is not a unanimous opinion, a **majority opinion** is written, outlining the views of the majority of the justices involved in the particular case. Often, one or more justices who feel strongly about making or emphasizing a particular point that is not made or emphasized in the unanimous or majority written opinion will write a **concurring opinion.** That means the justice writing the concurring opinion agrees (concurs) with the conclusion given in the majority written opinion, but for different reasons. Finally, in other than unanimous opinions, one or more dissenting opinions are usually written by those justices who do not agree with the majority. The **dissenting opinion** is important because it often

---

[4]For a former Supreme Court law clerk's account of the role these clerks play in the high court's decision-making process, see Edward Lazarus, *Closed Chambers: The First Eyewitness Account of the Epic Struggles inside the Supreme Court* (New York: Times Books, 1998).
[5]It turned out that one supposed information leak came from lawyers making educated guesses.

forms the basis of the arguments used years later that cause the Court to reverse the previous decision and establish a new precedent.

Shortly after the opinion is written, the Supreme Court announces its decision from the bench. At that time, the opinion is made available to the public at the office of the clerk of the Court. The clerk also releases the opinion for online publication (see the *Logging On* section at the end of this chapter for Web sites that publish Supreme Court opinions). Ultimately, the opinion is published in the *United States Reports,* which is the official record of the Court's decisions.

The Selection of Federal Judges

All federal judges are appointed. The Constitution, in Article II, Section 2, states that the president appoints the justices of the Supreme Court with the advice and consent of the Senate. Congress has provided the same procedure for staffing other federal courts. This means that the Senate and the president jointly decide who shall be a federal judge, no matter what the level.

There are over eight hundred federal judgeships in the United States. Once appointed to such a judgeship, a person holds that job for life. Judges serve until they resign, retire voluntarily, or die. Federal judges who engage in blatantly illegal conduct may be removed through impeachment, although such action is extremely rare.

Nominating Judicial Candidates

Judicial candidates for federal judgeships are suggested to the president by the Department of Justice, senators, other judges, the candidates themselves, and bar associations and other interest groups. In selecting a candidate to nominate for a judgeship, the president considers not only the person's competence but also other factors, including the person's political philosophy (as will be discussed shortly), ethnicity, and gender.

The nomination process—no matter how the nominees are obtained—always works the same way. The president makes the actual nomination, transmitting the name to the Senate. The Senate then either confirms or rejects the nomination. To reach a conclusion, the Senate Judiciary Committee (operating through subcommittees) invites testimony, both written and oral, at its various hearings. In the case of federal district court judgeships, a practice used in the Senate, called **senatorial courtesy,** is a constraint on the president's freedom to appoint whomever the administration chooses. Senatorial courtesy allows a senator of the president's political party to veto a judicial appointment in his or her state.

Federal District Court Judgeship Nominations. Although the president nominates federal judges, the nomination of federal district court judges typically originates with a senator or senators of the president's party from the state in which there is a vacancy. If the nominee is deemed unqualified, as a matter of political courtesy the president will discuss with the senator or senators who originated the nomination whether the nomination should be withdrawn. Also, when a nomination is unacceptable politically to the president, the president will consult with the appropriate senator or senators, indicate that the nomination is unacceptable, and work with the senator or senators to seek an alternative candidate.

Federal Courts of Appeals Appointments. There are many fewer federal courts of appeals appointments than federal district court appointments, but they are more important. This is because federal appellate judges handle more important matters, at least from the point of view of the president, and therefore presidents

Senatorial Courtesy
In regard to federal district court judgeship nominations, a Senate tradition allowing a senator of the president's political party to veto a judicial appointment in his or her state simply by indicating that the appointment is personally not acceptable. At that point, the Senate may reject the nomination, or the president may withdraw consideration of the nominee.

INFOTRAC®
COLLEGE EDITION

"Vacancy Crisis in the Federal Judiciary"

take a keener interest in the nomination process for such judgeships. Also, appointments to the U.S. courts of appeals have become "steppingstones" to the Supreme Court. Typically, the president culls the Circuit Judge Nominating Commission's list of nominees for potential candidates. The president may also use this list to oppose senators' recommendations that may be unacceptable politically to the president.

Supreme Court Appointments.   The nomination of Supreme Court justices belongs solely to the president, as we have described. As you can see in Table 15–1, which summarizes the background of all Supreme Court justices to 1999, the most common occupational background of the justices at the time of their appointments has been private legal practice or state or federal judgeships.

TABLE   15–1

Background of Supreme Court Justices to 1999

	NUMBER OF JUSTICES (108 = TOTAL)
Occupational Position before Appointment	
Private legal practice	25
State judgeship	21
Federal judgeship	28
U.S. attorney general	7
Deputy or assistant U.S. attorney general	2
U.S. solicitor general	2
U.S. senator	6
U.S. representative	2
State governor	3
Federal executive post	9
Other	3
Religious Background	
Protestant	83
Roman Catholic	11
Jewish	6
Unitarian	7
No religious affiliation	1
Age on Appointment	
Under 40	5
41–50	31
51–60	58
61–70	14
Political Party Affiliation	
Federalist (to 1835)	13
Democratic Republican (to 1828)	7
Whig (to 1861)	1
Democrat	44
Republican	42
Independent	1
Educational Background	
College graduate	92
Not a college graduate	16
Gender	
Male	106
Female	2
Race	
Caucasian	106
Other	2

SOURCE: Congressional Quarterly, *Congressional Quarterly's Guide to the U.S. Supreme Court* (Washington, D.C.: Congressional Quarterly Press, 1996), and authors' update.

Those nine justices who were in federal executive posts at the time of their appointments held the high offices of secretary of state, comptroller of the treasury, secretary of the navy, postmaster general, secretary of the interior, chairman of the Securities and Exchange Commission, and secretary of labor. In the "Other" category under "Occupational Position before Appointment" in Table 15-1 are two justices who were professors of law (including William H. Taft, a former president) and one justice who was a North Carolina state employee with responsibility for organizing and revising the state's statutes.

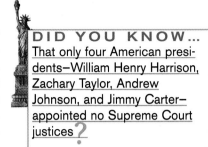

Partisanship and Judicial Appointments

Ideology plays an important role in the president's choices for judicial appointments. As a result, presidential appointments to the federal judiciary have had an extremely partisan distribution. The justices' partisan attachments have been mostly the same as those of the president who appointed them. There have been some exceptions, however. Nine nominal Democrats have been appointed by Republican presidents, three Republicans by Democratic presidents, and one Democrat by Whig president John Tyler.[6]

Presidents see their federal judiciary appointments as the one sure way to institutionalize their political views long after they have left office. By 1993, for example, Presidents Reagan and Bush together had appointed nearly three-quarters of all federal court judges. This preponderance of Republican-appointed federal judges strengthened the legal moorings of the conservative social agenda on a variety of issues, ranging from abortion to civil rights. Nevertheless, President Bill Clinton has had the opportunity to appoint about two hundred federal judges, thereby shifting the ideological make-up of the federal judiciary. Also, Clinton's appointees matched more closely the actual U.S. demographics than did the appointees of his predecessors (see Table 15-2). By the end of his first term, Clinton had appointed more women and members of minority groups to federal judgeships than any other president.

The Senate's Role

Ideology also plays a large role in the Senate's confirmation hearings, and presidential nominees to the Supreme Court have not always been confirmed. In fact,

---

[6]Actually, Tyler was a member of the Democratic Party who ran with William H. Harrison on the Whig ticket. When Harrison died, much to the surprise of the Whigs, Tyler—a Democrat—became president, although they tried to call him "acting president." Thus, some historians would quibble over the statement that Tyler was a Whig.

TABLE **15-2**

Gender and Ethnicity or Race of Appointees
to the U.S. Courts of Appeals, by Administration

GENDER/ETHNICITY	CARTER %	REAGAN %	BUSH %	CLINTON %
Gender				
Male	80.4	94.9	81.1	69.0
Female	19.6	5.1	18.9	31.0
Ethnicity/Race				
White	78.6	97.4	89.2	72.4
African American	16.1	1.3	5.4	13.8
Hispanic	3.8	1.3	5.4	10.3
Asian	1.8	—	—	3.4

SOURCE: *Judicature*, May-June 1997, p. 269.

almost 20 percent of presidential nominations to the Supreme Court have been either rejected or not acted on by the Senate. Numerous acrimonious battles over Supreme Court appointments have ensued when the Senate and the president have not seen eye to eye about political matters.

The U.S. Senate had a long record of refusing to confirm the president's judicial nominations from the beginning of Andrew Jackson's presidency in 1829 to the end of Ulysses Grant's presidency in 1877. During a fairly long period of relative acquiescence to presidential nominations on the part of the Senate, from 1894 until 1968, only three nominees were not confirmed. From 1968 through 1986, however, two presidential nominees to the highest court were rejected. Both were Nixon appointees, rejected because of questions about their racial attitudes. In 1987, two of President Ronald Reagan's nominees failed to be confirmed—Robert Bork was rejected for his views on the Constitution, and Douglas Ginsburg withdrew his nomination when it was reported that he had used marijuana in the 1970s.

President George Bush had little difficulty securing the Senate's confirmation of his nomination of David Souter to fill the void on the Court left when Justice William Brennan retired in 1989. Bush's second nominee, Clarence Thomas, underwent an extremely volatile confirmation hearing in 1991, replete with charges of sexual harassment leveled at him by his former aide, Anita Hill. Despite Hill's dramatic and televised allegations, however, Thomas's nomination was confirmed.

In 1993, President Clinton had little trouble gaining approval for his nominee to take the seat left vacant by Justice Byron White. Ruth Bader Ginsburg became the second female Supreme Court Justice. In 1994, Clinton nominated Stephen Breyer, a federal court of appeals judge, to fill the seat of retiring Supreme Court Justice Harry Blackmun. Seen by many as a consensus builder who might effectively pull together justices with divergent views, Breyer was confirmed without significant opposition.

President Clinton has found it more difficult to secure Senate approval for his judicial nominations to the lower courts, however, just as he has had difficulty with nominations to executive-branch posts. In fact, during the late 1990s the duel between the Senate and the president aroused considerable concern about the consequences of the increasingly partisan and ideological tension over federal judicial appointments. As a result of Senate delays in confirming nominations, the number of judicial vacancies mounted, as did the backlog of cases pending in the federal courts. (See this chapter's *Critical Perspective* on pages 500 and 501 for a further discussion of this issue.)

Demonstrators protest the possible confirmation of Judge Clarence Thomas in 1991, after Professor Anita Hill charged him with sexually harassing her while she was his employee. After long and difficult hearings on the subject, the Senate voted to confirm Thomas's nomination.

The Policymaking Function of the Courts

The partisan battles over judicial appointments reflect an important reality in today's American government: the importance of the judiciary in national politics. Because appointments to the federal benches are for life, the ideology of judicial appointees can affect national policy for years to come. Although the primary function of judges in our system of government is to interpret and apply the laws, inevitably judges make policy when carrying out this task. One of the major policymaking tools of the federal courts is their power of judicial review.

Judicial Review

Remember from Chapter 2 that the power of the courts to determine whether a law or action by the other branches of government is constitutional is known as the power of *judicial review*. This power of the judiciary enables the judicial branch to act as a check on the other two branches of government, in line with the checks and balances system established by the U.S. Constitution.

The power of judicial review is not mentioned in the Constitution, however. Rather, it was established by the United States Supreme Court's decision in *Marbury v. Madison*.[7] In that case (see this chapter's *Politics and the Law*), in which the Court declared that a law passed by Congress violated the Constitution, the Court claimed such a power for the courts:

---

[7]5 U.S. 137 (1803).

POLITICS and the Law

Judicial Review—*Marbury v. Madison* (1803)

In the edifice of American public law, the *Marbury v. Madison* decision in 1803 can be viewed as the keystone of the constitutional arch. The story is often told, and for a reason—it shows how seemingly insignificant cases can have important and enduring results.

Consider the facts behind *Marbury v. Madison*. John Adams had lost his bid for reelection to Thomas Jefferson in 1800. Adams, a Federalist, thought the Jeffersonian (Democratic) Republicans (Anti-Federalists) would weaken the power of the national government by asserting states' rights. He also feared the Anti-Federalists' antipathy toward business. During the final hours of Adams's presidency, he worked feverishly to "pack" the judiciary with loyal Federalists just before Jefferson took office.

All of the judicial appointments had to be certified and delivered. The task of delivery fell on Adams's secretary of state, John Marshall. Out of the fifty-nine midnight appointments, Marshall delivered only forty-two. Of course, Jefferson refused to have his new secretary of state, James Madison, deliver the remaining commissions.

William Marbury, along with three other Federalists to whom the commissions had not been delivered, decided to sue. The suit was brought directly to the Supreme Court, seeking a writ of *mandamus* (an order issued by a court to compel the performance of an act), authorized by the Judiciary Act of 1789.

As fate would have it, the man responsible for the lawsuit, John Marshall, had stepped down as Adams's secretary of state only to become chief justice. He was now in a position to decide the case for which he was responsible.* Marshall was faced with a dilemma: If he ordered the commissions delivered, the new secretary of state could simply refuse. The Court had no way to compel action, because it has no police force. Also, Congress was controlled by the Democratic Republicans. It might impeach Marshall for such an action.[†] But if Marshall simply allowed

---

*Today, any justice who has been involved in an issue before the Court would probably disqualify himself or herself because of a conflict of interest.
[†]In fact, in 1805, Congress did impeach Supreme Court Justice Samuel Chase, a Federalist, although he was not convicted. The charge was abusive behavior under the Sedition Act.

John Marshall

James Madison

Secretary of State Madison to do as he wished, the Court's power would be eroded severely.

Marshall masterfully fashioned a decision that did not require anyone to do anything but at the same time enlarged the power of the Supreme Court. He stated that the highest court did not have the power to issue a writ of *mandamus* in this particular case. Marshall pointed out that Article III of the Constitution, which spelled out the Court's original jurisdiction (its authority to decide cases brought directly to the Court instead of on appeal), did not mention writs of *mandamus*. Because Congress did not have the right to expand the Supreme Court's jurisdiction, this section of the Judiciary Act of 1789 was unconstitutional—and thus void. The decision still stands today as a judicial and political masterpiece.

FOR CRITICAL ANALYSIS

What might result if the courts could not exercise the power of judicial review?

Critical perspective

The Politicization of the Judicial Appointment Process

There used to be an implicit understanding that the president had a popular mandate to appoint as federal judges men and women whose views were compatible with those of the president. In effect, judicial appointments were part of an electoral spoils system. Although the U.S. Senate has the power of advice and consent in all federal judicial appointments, for most of this country's history the Senate did not interfere with the president's choices unless a nominee was clearly unfit to carry out the job.

Times have changed. President Clinton has accused the Republican majority in Congress of politicizing the judicial appointment process. His proof: the unfilled vacancies on the federal bench. During 1997, for example, more than one hundred federal judgeships were vacant. Thirty of those were ranked as "judicial emergencies" because they had remained empty for more than eighteen months. Nine months into that year, only nine federal judges had been approved by the Senate. Also during that year, a record wait of 183 days from nomination to confirmation occurred.

The results of these delays include significantly increased case loads for the federal bench as well as increased delays in settling cases. In some areas, the period between filing the last brief and a court hearing is two hundred days–60 percent longer than average. Additionally, there is a growing backlog of federal cases. The number of suits waiting three years or more to be heard has increased to over sixteen thousand. The federal judiciary has asked Congress for legislation to add fifty-five judgeships to the federal court system, even though Congress increased the size of the federal judiciary as recently as 1990.

Rehnquist's Report on the Federal Judiciary

By late 1997, the vacancy situation had become so bad that Chief Justice Rehnquist felt compelled to comment on it in his year-end *Report on the Federal Judiciary.* He pointed out that the scope of federal jurisdiction is increasing while at the same time judicial vacancies are aggravating the problem of "too few judges and too much work." He mentioned that in the Court of Appeals for the Ninth Circuit, over 33 percent of the seats are empty. He argued that "vacancies cannot remain at such high levels indefinitely without eroding the quality of justice that has been traditionally associated with the Federal judiciary." His plea was simple: the president should nominate candidates with reasonable promptness, and the Senate should act within a reasonable time to confirm or reject them.*

Are Partisan Republicans to Blame?

The current view seems to be that Republicans are trying to prevent President Clinton from appointing liberal activist jurists. Some Republicans have, in fact, implicitly "declared war" on Clinton's judicial choices. They have delved into everything written by Clinton judicial nominees in order to dig up evidence of liberal judicial activism.

At least one researcher, Professor Emeritus Gideon Kanner of Loyola Law School (Los Angeles), does not believe that the current politicization of Supreme Court nominees is a recent phenomenon. He goes back to the 1930s to find its roots.

"A Switch in Time That Saved Nine"

When President Franklin Roosevelt proposed numerous New Deal laws during his first few months in office, he found a hostile

*The New York Times, National Edition, January 1, 1998, p. A15.

It is emphatically the province and duty of the Judicial Department to say what the law is. Those who apply the rule to a particular case, must of necessity expound and interpret that rule. If two laws conflict with each other, the courts must decide on the operation of each.

If a federal court declares that a federal or state law or policy is unconstitutional, the court's decision affects the application of the law or policy only within that court's jurisdiction. For this reason, the higher the level of the court, the greater the impact of the decision on society. Because of the Supreme Court's national jurisdiction, its decisions can have a significant impact. For example, when the Supreme Court held that an Arkansas state constitutional amendment

Critical perspective

The Politicization of the Judicial Appointment Process—continued

Supreme Court, one that struck down many of the new laws as unconstitutional. He came up with a solution. He threatened to "pack the court" with additional judges selected on the basis of their support for his New Deal philosophy. The nine justices of the Supreme Court at that time got the message. They no longer ruled against New Deal legislation. According to Professor Kanner, from that day on, "an ideologically compliant judiciary was thus legitimized with a bang."[†]

Professor Kanner then points out that the Warren Court–the Court presided over by Chief Justice Earl Warren from 1953 to 1969–contributed greatly to the politicization of the federal judicial process in general, and therefore to the nomination process. Warren frequently would interrupt carefully legally reasoned arguments to ask, "Yes, but is it fair?" By stressing what is fair as opposed to what is law, according to Kanner, the Warren Court created among politicians and the public a dichotomous view of judges. Those who were liberal were considered to be "fair"; those who were conservative were considered to be "mean spirited." The end result is an intense scrutiny of federal judicial nominees by whichever party is in power in Congress.

Reagan, Bork, Bush, Thomas, and Senate Democrats

In our times, the most blatantly political battle over a Supreme Court justice nominee occurred during the Reagan administration.

[†]Gideon Kanner, "Don't Forget Who Brought Politics to the Bench," *The National Law Journal*, February 2, 1998, p. A20.

In 1987, Robert Bork was nominated to be on the Supreme Court. A respected legal scholar and federal circuit judge, Bork fell prey to hostile Democrats during the Senate hearings to evaluate his nomination. The proceedings were bitter, and the criticisms of Bork were often petty. Even the videos he and his wife checked out from the local rental store were mentioned. In the end, the Senate rejected his nomination.

Of course, the nationally televised spectacle of the grilling of Clarence Thomas in 1991 further cemented the notion of the legitimacy of the politicization of the federal judicial nominating process. Later, at the end of the Bush administration, 102 vacant federal judgeships were blocked by Senate Democrats. Within the Senate, those in the majority can, and do, delay scheduling of floor votes on nominations, delay scheduling of floor debates, and use floor votes of judicial nominees as bargaining chips.

Do not expect a change in the procedure very soon.

FOR CRITICAL ANALYSIS

1. Is it possible that the term "judicial activist" has no objective definition? In other words, is judicial activism in the eyes of the beholder?
2. Why are federal judicial appointments seemingly so important to both the president and the party in power in Congress?

limiting the terms of congresspersons was unconstitutional, laws establishing term limits in twenty-three other states also were invalidated.[8]

Judicial Activism and Judicial Restraint

Judicial scholars like to characterize different judges and justices as being either activist or restraintist. The doctrine of **judicial activism** rests on the conviction that the federal judiciary should take an active role in using its powers to check the activities of Congress, state legislatures, and administrative agencies when those government bodies exceed their authority. One of the Supreme Court's most activist eras was the period from 1953 to 1969 when the Court was headed

Judicial Activism
A doctrine holding that the Supreme Court should take an active role in using its powers to check the activities of Congress, state legislatures, and administrative agencies when those government bodies exceed their authority.

[8]*U.S. Term Limits v. Thornton*, 514 U.S. 779 (1995).

Judicial Restraint
A doctrine holding that the Supreme Court should defer to the decisions made by the elected representatives of the people in the legislative and executive branches.

by Chief Justice Earl Warren. The Warren Court propelled the civil rights movement forward by holding, among other things, that laws permitting racial segregation violated the equal protection clause.

In contrast, the doctrine of **judicial restraint** rests on the assumption that the courts should defer to the decisions made by the legislative and executive branches, because members of Congress and the president are elected by the people whereas members of the federal judiciary are not. Because administrative agency personnel normally have more expertise than the courts do in the areas regulated by the agencies, the courts likewise should defer to agency rules and decisions. In other words, under the doctrine of judicial restraint, the courts should not thwart the implementation of legislative acts and agency rules unless they are clearly unconstitutional.

Judicial activism sometimes is linked with liberalism, and judicial restraint with conservatism. In fact, a conservative judge can be activist, just as a liberal judge can be restraintist—and vice versa. In the 1950s and 1960s, the Supreme Court was activist and liberal. Some observers believe that the Rehnquist Court, with its conservative majority, has become increasingly activist in the 1990s.

Ideology and the Rehnquist Court

William H. Rehnquist became the sixteenth chief justice of the Supreme Court in 1986, after fifteen years as an associate justice. He was known as a strong anchor of the Court's conservative wing. With Rehnquist's appointment as chief justice, it seemed to observers that the Court necessarily would become more conservative.

This, in fact, has happened. The Court began to take a rightward shift shortly after Rehnquist became chief justice, and the Court's rightward movement continued as other conservative appointments to the bench were made during the Reagan and Bush administrations. Today, three of the justices (William Rehnquist, Antonin Scalia, and Clarence Thomas) are notably conservative in their views. Four of the justices (John Paul Stevens, David Souter, Ruth Bader Ginsburg, and Stephen Breyer) hold liberal-to-moderate views. The middle of the Court is now occupied by two moderate-to-conservative justices, Sandra Day O'Connor and Anthony Kennedy. O'Connor and Kennedy usually provide the "swing votes" on the Court in controversial cases. The ideological alignments on the Court vary, however, depending on the issues involved in particular cases.

Certainly, today's Supreme Court has moved far from the liberal positions taken by the Court under Earl Warren (1953–1969) and under Warren Burger (1969–1986). Just since 1995, the Court has issued numerous conservative rulings, many of which you have already read about in this text. Several of these rulings reflect a conservative approach to constitutional law with respect to states' rights and other federalist issues. For example, in 1995 the Court curbed—for the first time in sixty years—the national government's constitutional power under the commerce clause to regulate intrastate activities. The Court held a federal law regulating the possession of guns in school zones had nothing to do with interstate commerce, and therefore Congress had overreached its powers by attempting to regulate this activity.[9] In 1997, the Court again upheld states' rights when it invalidated portions of the federal gun control law. The Court stated that the federal government lacked constitutional authority to require state officials to perform background checks on prospective gun purchasers.[10] A further decision, rendered by the Court in 1998, concerned the constitutional separation of powers established by the framers. According to the Court, the Line Item Veto Act of

---

[9]*United States v. Lopez,* 514 U.S. 549 (1995).
[10]*Printz v. United States,* 117 S.Ct. 2365 (1997).

The Rehnquist Court

LIBERAL/MODERATE

John Paul Stevens   David Souter   Ruth Bader Ginsburg   Stephen Breyer

SWING VOTES

Sandra Day O'Connor   Anthony Kennedy

CONSERVATIVE

William Rehnquist   Antonin Scalia   Clarence Thomas

1996 (see Chapter 13) was unconstitutional because it delegated too much law-making authority from the legislative branch to the executive.[11]

In regard to civil rights issues, the Rehnquist Court's generally conservative ("strict") interpretation of the Constitution has had mixed results. In one decision, the Court refused to extend the constitutional right to privacy to include the right of terminally ill persons to end their lives through physician-assisted suicide. Therefore, a state law banning this practice did not violate the Constitution.[12] (Essentially, the Court left it up to the states to decide whether to ban—or to permit—assisted suicide; to date, only one state, Oregon, has passed a law permitting the practice.) In another decision, the Court held that a federal statute expanding

---

[11]*Clinton v. City of New York,* 118 S.Ct. 2091 (1998).
[12]*Washington v. Glucksberg,* 117 S.Ct. 2258 (1997).

religious liberties was an unconstitutional attempt by Congress to rewrite the Constitution.[13]

In regard to sexual harassment, the Court issued a series of decisions in 1998 that gave added protection to employees and employers alike. On the one hand, the Court made it easier for harassment victims (including victims of same-gender harassment) to bring claims against their employers. On the other hand, the Court made it clear that employers who were unaware of incidents of harassment in their workplaces could escape liability for those actions if they could demonstrate that they had effective antiharassment policies and procedures in place.[14]

Is the Federal Judiciary Too Powerful?

The extensive influence over national policy wielded by today's federal courts, particularly the Supreme Court, could not possibly have been foreseen by the founders. Indeed, many of the founders had few worries about judicial power. In *Federalist Paper* No. 78, Alexander Hamilton expressed the opinion that the judiciary (meaning the Supreme Court, which was the only court designated in the Constitution) was the "least dangerous branch" of government because it had no enforcement powers. If the Court rendered a decision that was unacceptable to the other branches of government or to the public, there was no way the Court itself could enforce that decision.

In its earliest years, the Court did indeed lack stature and influence. The first Supreme Court chief justice, John Jay, refused to serve a second term because he thought the Court would never play an important role in American society (see the feature *E-Mail Messages from the Past*). Jay became governor of New York instead. The next chief justice, Oliver Ellsworth, resigned his position to

---

[13]*City of Boerne v. Flores,* 117 S.Ct. 2157 (1997).

[14]*Faragher v. City of Boca Raton,* 118 S.Ct. 2275 (1998); *Burlington Industries v. Ellerth,* 118 S.Ct. 2257 (1998); *Oncale v. Sundowner Offshore Services,* 118 S.Ct. 998 (1998). These decisions are discussed more fully in Chapter 5.

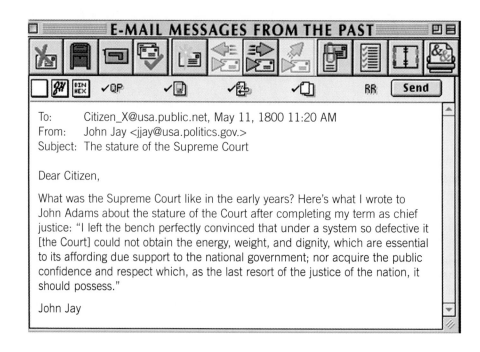

E-MAIL MESSAGES FROM THE PAST

To: Citizen_X@usa.public.net, May 11, 1800 11:20 AM
From: John Jay <jjay@usa.politics.gov.>
Subject: The stature of the Supreme Court

Dear Citizen,

What was the Supreme Court like in the early years? Here's what I wrote to John Adams about the stature of the Court after completing my term as chief justice: "I left the bench perfectly convinced that under a system so defective it [the Court] could not obtain the energy, weight, and dignity, which are essential to its affording due support to the national government; nor acquire the public confidence and respect which, as the last resort of the justice of the nation, it should possess."

John Jay

become an envoy to France. In 1801, when the federal capital was moved to Washington, somebody forgot to include the Supreme Court in the plans. As a result, the Court met in the office of the clerk of the Senate until 1935.

Some of the founders, however, were concerned about the potential danger of giving the judiciary too much power. Madison believed that to combine the powers of the judiciary with those of the legislative and executive branches was the "very definition of tyranny." Jefferson expressed concern over allowing unelected judges to be in charge of interpreting the meaning of the Constitution. In a letter to William Jarvis in 1820, Jefferson wrote, "It is a very dangerous doctrine to consider the judges as the ultimate arbiters of all constitutional questions."

A number of scholars and politicians today claim that the power of the federal courts should be curbed. Proposals for doing this include removing the judiciary's power of judicial review and giving Congress the final say on constitutional interpretation; limiting federal court jurisdiction; and impeaching "activist" federal judges who make policy based on their personal ideological preferences. Generally, federal judges have been criticized not only by Republicans in Congress but also by the media and other members of the public (see the feature *Politics and the Judiciary: Federal Judges Are under Attack*). Other groups assert that there are enough checks on the judiciary already and that the courts should be left alone.

POLITICS and the Judiciary

Federal Judges Are under Attack

Time and again during the 1990s, federal judges were criticized by members of the press, politicians, or others either for their behavior or for their decisions. Some judges were accused of accepting bribes; others, of physically assaulting defendants who made surly remarks; still others, of sexually harassing court personnel. Even more so, however, judges were attacked for their rulings. For example, the judges on the Ninth Circuit Court of Appeals, which sits in California, were widely criticized for their 1997 decision upholding the constitutionality of California's law banning state-sponsored affirmative action in that state.

A frequent criticism leveled against federal judges, particularly by certain

Republicans in Congress, is that they allow their personal views and policy preferences to dominate their decision making. A bill currently before Congress would curb what some perceive as an abuse of power by activist, liberal judges who "legislate from the bench." Supporters of the bill assert that liberal activists in the federal judiciary are threatening the separation of powers established by the Constitution because they are usurping the policy-making powers of the legislative branch.

A recent survey conducted by the American Judicature Society revealed that 73 percent of the 165 judges surveyed felt that there had been widespread attacks on

the judiciary. Eighty-seven percent believed that they are under increasing pressure to be directly accountable to public opinion. Additionally, more than half of the judges stated that they had been attacked publicly in the previous five years, and 81 percent knew of another judge who had been publicly attacked. Who was doing the attacking? According to over half of the judges, the media were the most frequent sources of public attacks, while other sources were elected officials and interest groups.

The problem for judges is that they must weather such criticism in silence. Ethical codes prevent them from explaining to the public—in the media, for example—why

it was in the interests of justice to set aside a certain jury verdict or rule a certain way on an issue. The American Bar Association recently has proposed new guidelines that might help to remedy this problem. The guidelines urge state and local bar associations to use press releases, letters to the editor, and other public forums to defend or explain judicial actions in the wake of an "unwarranted" or "unjust" attack regarding a specific case.

FOR CRITICAL ANALYSIS

Why do you suppose the legal profession considers it unethical for judges to defend their rulings publicly?

What Checks Our Courts?

Our judicial system is probably the most independent in the world. But the courts do not have absolute independence, for they are part of the political process. Political checks limit the extent to which courts can exercise judicial review and engage in an activist policy. These checks are exercised by the executive branch, the legislature, the public, and, finally, the judiciary itself.

Executive Checks

President Andrew Jackson was once supposed to have said, after Chief Justice John Marshall made an unpopular decision, that "John Marshall has made his decision; now let him enforce it."[15] This purported remark goes to the heart of **judicial implementation**—the enforcement of judicial decisions in such a way that those decisions are translated into policy. The Supreme Court simply does not have any enforcement powers, and whether a decision will be implemented depends on the cooperation of the other two branches of government. Rarely, though, will a president refuse to enforce a Supreme Court decision, as President Jackson did. To take such an action could mean a significant loss of public support, because of the Supreme Court's stature in the eyes of the nation.

More commonly, presidents exercise influence over the judiciary by appointing new judges and justices as federal judicial seats become vacant. Additionally, as mentioned earlier, the U.S. solicitor general plays a significant role in the federal court system, and the person holding this office is a presidential appointee.

Executives at the state level also may refuse to implement court decisions with which they disagree. A notable example of such a refusal occurred in Arkansas after the Supreme Court ordered schools to desegregate "with all deliberate speed" in 1955.[16] Arkansas governor Orval Faubus refused to cooperate with the decision and used the state's National Guard to block the integration of Central High School in Little Rock. Ultimately, President Dwight Eisenhower had to federalize the Arkansas National Guard and send federal troops to Little Rock to quell the violence that had erupted.

Legislative Checks

Courts may make rulings, but often the legislatures at local, state, and federal levels are required to appropriate funds to carry out the courts' rulings. A court, for example, may decide that prison conditions must be improved, but it is up to the legislature to authorize the funds necessary to carry out such a ruling. When such funds are not appropriated, the court that made the ruling, in effect, has been checked.

Courts' rulings can be overturned by constitutional amendments at both the federal and state levels. Many of the amendments to the U.S. Constitution (such as the Eleventh, Fourteenth, Sixteenth, and Twenty-sixth Amendments) check the state courts' ability to allow discrimination, for example. Proposed constitutional amendments that were created by a desire to reverse courts' decisions on school prayer and abortion have failed.

Finally, Congress or a state legislature can rewrite (amend) old laws or enact new ones to overturn a court's rulings if the legislature concludes that the court is interpreting laws or legislative intentions erroneously. For example, Congress

Judicial Implementation
The way in which court decisions are translated into action.

---

[15]The decision referred to was *Cherokee Nation v. Georgia*, 5 Pet. 1 (1831). (*Pet.* is an abbreviation of *Petrarch*, a nineteenth-century reporter of Supreme Court cases.)
[16]*Brown v. Board of Education*, 349 U.S. 294 (1955)—the second *Brown* decision.

passed the Civil Rights Act of 1991 in part to overturn a series of conservative rulings in employment-discrimination cases. In 1993, Congress enacted the Religious Freedom Restoration Act (RFRA), which broadened religious liberties, after Congress concluded that a 1990 Supreme Court ruling restricted religious freedom to an unacceptable extent.[17]

According to political scientist Walter Murphy, "A permanent feature of our constitutional landscape is the ongoing tug and pull between elected government and the courts."[18] Certainly, today's Supreme Court and the other two branches of government have been at odds on several occasions in the last decade. Consider the battle over religious rights and the RFRA. On signing the RFRA, President Clinton stated that the act was necessary to reverse the Court's erroneous interpretation of the Constitution in its 1990 decision. According to the president, the elected government's view of religious liberty was "far more consistent with the intent of the founders than [was] the Supreme Court."[19] The Supreme Court responded in kind. In 1997, it invalidated the RFRA, declaring that the act represented an unconstitutional attempt by Congress to add new rights to the Constitution.[20] The Court proclaimed horror at the prospect that "[s]hifting legislative majorities could change the Constitution."

INFOTRAC®
COLLEGE EDITION

"RFRA Coalition Frays in Wake of Ruling"

Public Opinion

Public opinion plays a significant role in shaping government policy, and certainly the judiciary is not excepted from this rule. For one thing, persons affected by a Supreme Court decision that is noticeably at odds with their views may simply ignore it. Prayers were banned in public schools in 1962, yet it was widely known that the ban was (and still is) ignored in many southern districts. What can the courts do in this situation? Unless someone complains about the prayers and initiates a lawsuit, the courts can do nothing.

The public also can pressure state and local government officials to refuse to enforce a certain decision. As already mentioned, judicial implementation requires the cooperation of government officials at all levels, and public opinion in various regions of the country will influence whether or not such cooperation is forthcoming.

Additionally, the courts themselves necessarily are influenced by public opinion to some extent. After all, judges are not "islands" in our society; their attitudes are influenced by social trends, just as the attitudes and beliefs of all persons are. Courts generally tend to avoid issuing decisions that they know will be noticeably at odds with public opinion. In part, this is because the judiciary, as a branch of the government, prefers to avoid creating divisiveness among the public. Also, a court—particularly the Supreme Court—may lose stature if it decides a case in a way that markedly diverges from public opinion. Given that it has no enforcement powers, the Court's authority is linked to its stature in the eyes of the public.

Judicial Traditions and Doctrines

Supreme Court justices (and other federal judges) typically exercise self-restraint in fashioning their decisions. In part, this restraint stems from their knowledge that the other two branches of government and the public can exercise checks on the judiciary, as previously discussed. To a large extent, however, this restraint is

---

[17]*Employment Division, Department of Human Resources of Oregon v. Smith,* 494 U.S. 872 (1990).

[18]As quoted in Neal Devins, "The Last Word Debate: How Social and Political Forces Shape Constitutional Values," *American Bar Association Journal,* October 1997, p. 48.

[19]Devins, "The Last Word Debate."

[20]*City of Boerne v. Flores,* 117 S.Ct. 2157 (1997).

mandated by various judicially established traditions and doctrines. For example, in exercising its discretion to hear appeals, the Supreme Court will not hear a meritless appeal just so it can rule on the issue. Also, when reviewing a case, the Supreme Court typically narrows its focus to just one issue or one aspect of an issue involved in the case. The Court rarely makes broad, sweeping decisions on issues. Furthermore, the doctrine of *stare decisis* acts as a restraint because it obligates the courts, including the Supreme Court, to follow established precedents when deciding cases. Only rarely will courts overrule a precedent.

Other judicial doctrines and practices also act as restraints. The courts will hear only what are called **justiciable disputes,** which are disputes that arise out of actual cases and that can be settled by legal methods. In other words, a court will not hear a case that involves a merely hypothetical issue. A party must have some stake in a real controversy before that party can bring a case before a court. Additionally, if a political question is involved, the Supreme Court often will exercise judicial restraint and refuse to rule on the matter. A **political question** is one that the Supreme Court declares should be decided by the elected branches of government—the executive branch, the legislative branch, or those two branches acting together. For example, the Supreme Court has refused to rule on the controversy regarding the rights of gays and lesbians in the military, preferring instead to defer to the executive branch's decisions on the matter. Generally, fewer questions are deemed political questions by the Supreme Court today than in the past.

Higher courts can reverse the decisions of lower courts. Lower courts can act as a check on higher courts, too. Lower courts can ignore—and have ignored—Supreme Court decisions. Usually, this is done indirectly. A lower court might conclude, for example, that the precedent set by the Supreme Court does not apply to the exact circumstances in the case before the court; or the lower court may decide that the Supreme Court's decision was ambiguous with respect to the issue before the lower court. The fact that the Supreme Court rarely makes broad and clear-cut statements on any issue facilitates different interpretations of the Court's decisions by the lower courts.

Justiciable Dispute

A dispute that raises questions about the law and that is appropriate for resolution before a court of law.

Political Question

An issue that a court believes should be decided by the executive or legislative branch.

The Judiciary: Issues for the New Century

The judiciary remains one of the most active and important institutions in American political life. Particularly at the federal level, judicial decision making through the years has affected the way all of us live and work. As the ultimate decision maker on constitutional issues, the Supreme Court will continue to play a significant policymaking role in American government. Whether the policymaking powers of the Supreme Court and other courts in the federal judiciary are too extensive and should be curbed, as some scholars and politicians suggest, remains at issue as we enter the new century.

Since the 1980s, there has been a trend toward a noticeably more conservative federal judiciary. Some have argued that this "conservative" legacy of the Reagan-Bush years will remain effective for years to come. The election of Bill Clinton, however, may have a significant effect on the ideological leanings of the federal judiciary. When he took office, over one hundred judicial openings in the lower federal courts existed. By 1997, he had already been able to appoint about two hundred federal court judges, including two Supreme Court justices. Consequently, some argue that the direction of the federal judiciary will not necessarily continue to be in a conservative direction.

A number of key constitutional issues will continue to be brought before the federal judiciary. These issues include affirmative action programs, congressional redistricting to maximize minority representation, indecent speech on the Internet, privacy rights, and a variety of other civil rights issues, as well as questions involving states' rights. The work of the judiciary in this sense will always remain unfinished. Even when an issue seems to be "resolved," it may come up again many years later. After all, the Supreme Court decision in *Roe v. Wade* appeared to have put an end to discussion about restrictions on abortion. Yet in the 1990s, the issue continues to come back to the courts and is currently being settled there, as well as through decisions and movements in public opinion. In a dynamic nation with a changing population, we can never expect issues to be resolved once and for all.

T O W A R D   A C T I V E   C I T I Z E N S H I P

CHANGING THE LEGAL SYSTEM

The U.S. legal system may seem all powerful and too complex to be influenced by one individual, but its power nonetheless depends on our support. A hostile public has many ways of resisting, modifying, or overturning statutes and rulings of the courts. Sooner or later a determined majority will prevail. Even a determined minority can make a difference. As Alexander Hamilton suggested in *The Federalist Papers,* the people will always hold the scales of justice in their hands, and ultimately all constitutional government depends on their firmness and wisdom.

One example of the kind of pressure that can be exerted on the legal system began with a tragedy. On a spring afternoon in 1980, thirteen-year-old Cari Lightner was hit from behind and killed by a drunk driver while walking in a bicycle lane. The driver turned out to be a forty-seven-year-old man with two prior drunk-driving convictions. He was at that time out on bail for a third arrest. Cari's mother, Candy, quit her job as a real estate agent to form Mothers Against Drunk Driving (MADD) and launched a personal campaign to stiffen penalties for drunk-driving convictions.

The organization now has 3.2 million members and supporters. Outraged by the thousands of lives lost every year because of drunk driving, the group not only seeks stiff penalties against drunk drivers but also urges police, prosecutors, and judges to crack down on such violators. MADD, by becoming involved, has gotten results. Owing to its efforts and the efforts of other citizen-activist groups, many states have responded with stiffer penalties and deterrents. If you feel strongly about this issue and want to get involved, contact the following organization:

MADD
511 E. John Carpenter Freeway
Suite 700
Irving, TX 75062
214-744-6233

www.madd.org/

Several other organizations have been formed by people who want to change or influence the judicial system. A few of them follow:

HALT—An Organization of Americans for Legal Reform
1612 K St. N.W., Suite 510
Washington, DC 20006
1-800-FOR-HALT

www.halt.org

National Legal Center for the Public Interest
1000 16th St. N.W.
Washington DC 20036
202-296-1683

www.nlcpi.org/

If you want information about the Supreme Court, contact the following by telephone or letter:

Clerk of the Court
The Supreme Court of the United States
1 First St. N.E.
Washington, DC 20543
202-479-3000

You can access online information about the Supreme Court at the following site:

oyez.nwu.edu

Key terms

affirm 494	judicial activism 501	precedent 485
amicus curiae brief 490	judicial implementation 506	remand 494
appellate court 488	judicial restraint 502	reverse 494
case law 487	jurisdiction 487	rule of four 493
class-action suit 490	justiciable dispute 508	senatorial courtesy 495
common law 485	limited jurisdiction 488	*stare decisis* 485
concurring opinion 494	litigate 490	trial court 488
dissenting opinion 494	majority opinion 494	unanimous opinion 494
diversity of citizenship 487	opinion 494	writ of *certiorari* 493
federal question 487	oral arguments 494	
general jurisdiction 488	political question 508	

Chapter summary

1 American law is rooted in the common law tradition, which was part of our legal heritage from England. The common law doctrine of *stare decisis* (which means "to stand on decided cases") obligates judges to follow precedents established previously by their own courts or by higher courts in their jurisdiction. Precedents established by the United States Supreme Court, the highest court in the land, are binding on all lower courts. Fundamental sources of American law include the U.S. Constitution and state constitutions, statutes enacted by legislative bodies, regulations issued by administrative agencies, and case law.

2 Article III, Section 1, of the U.S. Constitution limits the jurisdiction of the federal courts to cases involving (a) a federal question—which is a question based, at least in part, on the U.S. Constitution, a treaty, or a federal law; and (b) diversity of citizenship—which arises when a lawsuit is between parties of different states or involves a foreign citizen or government. The federal court system is basically a three-tiered model consisting of (a) U.S. district (trial) courts and various lower courts of limited jurisdiction; (b) U.S. courts of appeals; and (c) the U.S. Supreme Court. Cases may be appealed from the district courts to the appellate courts. In most cases, the decisions of the federal appellate courts are final because the Supreme Court hears only a few cases each year.

3 The Supreme Court begins its annual term on the first Monday in October and usually adjourns in late June or early July of the next year. A special session may be held, but this rarely occurs. The Court's decision to review a case is influenced by many factors, including the significance of the parties and issues involved and whether the solicitor general is pressing the Court to take the case. After a case is accepted, the justices (a) undertake research (with the help of their law clerks) on the issues involved in the case,

(b) hear oral arguments from the parties, (c) meet in conference to discuss and vote on the issue, and (d) announce the opinion, which is then released for publication.

4 Federal judges are nominated by the president and confirmed by the Senate. Once appointed, they hold office for life, barring gross misconduct. The nomination and confirmation process, particularly for Supreme Court justices, is often extremely politicized. Democrats and Republicans alike realize that justices may occupy seats on the Court for decades and naturally want to have persons appointed who share their basic views. Nearly 20 percent of all Supreme Court appointments have been either rejected or not acted on by the Senate.

5 In interpreting and applying the law, judges inevitably become policymakers. The most important policymaking tool of the federal courts is the power of judicial review. This power was not mentioned specifically in the Constitution, but John Marshall claimed the power for the Court in his 1803 decision in *Marbury v. Madison*. Judges who take an active role in checking the activities of the other branches of government sometimes are characterized as "activist" judges, and judges who defer to such activities sometimes are regarded as "restraintist" judges. The Warren Court of the 1950s and 1960s was activist in a liberal direction, whereas today's Rehnquist Court seems to be activist in a conservative direction. Several politicians and scholars argue that the policymaking powers of the federal courts should be curbed because such extensive powers were not envisioned by the founders, who entrusted Congress, an elected body, with the authority to make policy. Others contend that the courts should be left alone.

6 Checks on the powers of the federal courts include executive checks, legislative checks, public opinion, and judicial traditions and doctrines.

Selected print and electronic resources

SUGGESTED READINGS

Braum, Lawrence. *The Supreme Court*. 6th ed. Washington, D.C.: Congressional Quarterly Press, 1998. A noted judicial scholar offers a comprehensive examination of the Supreme Court.

Cheney, Timothy D. *Who Makes the Law: The Supreme Court, Congress, the States and Society*. Englewood Cliffs, N.J.: Prentice-Hall, 1998. This is an insightful examination of the Supreme Court's interactions with Congress and with the states and society.

Lazarus, Edward. *Closed Chambers: The First Eyewitness Account of the Epic Struggles inside the Supreme Court*. New York: Times Books, 1998. Lazarus, who served as a clerk to former Supreme Court Justice Harry Blackmun during the Court's 1988–1989 term, gives an eyewitness account of some of the significant ideological struggles waged within the Court, among both law clerks and the justices.

Scalia, Antonin. *A Matter of Interpretation: Federal Courts and the Law*. Ewing, N.J.: Princeton University Press, 1997. Supreme Court Justice Antonin Scalia presents his views on a number of topics, including the distinction between adjudicating and legislating. He contends that the Supreme court too often engages in making new law rather than interpreting the Constitution.

MEDIA RESOURCES

Court TV—This TV channel covers high-profile trials, including those of O. J. Simpson, the Unabomber, British nanny Louise Woodward, and Timothy McVeigh. (You can learn how to access Court TV from your area at its Web site—see the *Logging On* section below for its URL.)

First Monday in October—A 1981 movie with a light touch that centers on the appointment of the first woman to the U.S. Supreme Court.

Gideon's Trumpet—A 1980 film starring Henry Fonda as the small-time criminal, James Earl Gideon, which makes clear the path that a case takes to the Supreme Court and the importance of cases decided there.

The Magnificent Yankee—A 1950 movie, starring Louis Calhern and Ann Harding, that traces the life and philosophy of Oliver Wendell Holmes, Jr., one of the Supreme Court's most brilliant justices.

Marbury v. Madison—A thirty-minute video on this famous 1803 case that established the principle of judicial review.

Logging on

The home page of the federal courts is a good starting point if you are learning about the federal court system in general. At this site, you can even follow the "path" of a case as it moves through the federal court system. Go to

www.uscourts.gov/

Several Web sites offer searchable databases of Supreme Court decisions. You can access Supreme Court cases since 1970 at FindLaw's site:

www.findlaw.com/

The following Web site also offers an easily searchable index to Supreme Court opinions, including some important historic decisions:

supct.law.cornell.edu/supct/

You can find information on the justices of the Supreme Court, as well as their decisions, at

oyez.nwu.edu/

Court TV's Web site offers information ranging from its program schedule and how you can find Court TV in your area to famous cases and the wills of famous people. For each case it includes on the site, it gives a complete history as well as selected documents filed with the court and court transcripts. You can access this site at

www.courttv.com/

Using the Internet for political analysis

Go to one of the sites on the Web that organizes the Supreme Court's cases, such as the federal courts site or the Cornell site given above. Then look up the list of Supreme Court decisions for a recent time period—say, three months. Select three cases, and read the summary of each case. Try to categorize the federal or constitutional issue that was decided in each case. To whom is the decision important? Does the decision change the relationship between the ordinary citizen and the government? What other kinds of information would make this site more useful to you?

PART 5

Public Policy

chapter **16**

Domestic Policy

¿ what if

All Citizens Could Vote on Policy Issues?

BACKGROUND

MANY STATES ALLOW THEIR CITIZENS TO VOTE ON POLICY ISSUES BY USING THE REFERENDUM AND CITIZENS' INITIATIVE. FOR EXAMPLE, IN 1998 CALIFORNIANS PASSED A PROPOSAL TO END BILINGUAL EDUCATION PROGRAMS THAT HAD BEEN PLACED ON THE BALLOT BY A CITIZENS' INITIATIVE. IN MANY STATES, THE REFERENDUM CAN BE USED TO CHANGE OR REPEAL STATE LAWS, AND IN ALL STATES CONSTITUTIONS CAN BE AMENDED BY REFERENDA. OFTEN, THE REFERENDUM IS USED AT THE LOCAL LEVEL TO APPROVE LOCAL SCHOOL BOND ISSUES OR AT THE STATE LEVEL TO AMEND CONSTITUTIONS. ALTHOUGH THE REFERENDUM AND THE INITIATIVE REPRESENT DIRECT DEMOCRACY TO SOME EXTENT, IN A TRUE DIRECT DEMOCRACY, LIKE THAT OF ANCIENT ATHENS, ALL CITIZENS WOULD BE ABLE TO VOTE ON POLICY ISSUES AS THEY ARISE.

WHAT IF ALL CITIZENS COULD VOTE ON POLICY ISSUES?

Assume for a moment that Congress had to submit to American voters on a regular basis all major policy issues, such as those relating to welfare reform, immigration controls, changes in the tax code, and important restrictions on businesses aimed at improving the environment. Obviously, every single policy issue could not be presented to the electorate. More than twenty thousand bills are submitted in Congress each year. Thus, a

definition would be needed to determine which policy issues were "major" enough to be submitted to all citizens. Herein would lie an important policy issue in and of itself: What constitutes a major policy issue?

Additionally, congressional bills are very detailed and are often written in a way that is difficult for the average person to understand. Consequently, summaries of the bills and their implications for society would need to be given to all voters—by mail, on television, or via the Internet—so that voters would be informed. Rules would also have to be created concerning the length of the referenda submitted to the voters in elections, as well as the complexity of language used in them.

GOING TO THE POLLS MORE OFTEN

Certainly, if voters were not to be overwhelmed every couple of years with hundreds of policy issues to be decided, voting would have to occur more often. That is to say, voting on national referenda might have to take place regularly at the end of every quarter or at least twice a year. Given the poor turnouts for the elections that currently occur every two

years, is it likely that a large percentage of Americans would participate in voting on policy issues? One way to encourage more participation is to allow mail-in voting on policy issues—if a way could be found to avoid the potential fraud that mail-in voting might entail. Another alternative is to develop a system of voting through the Internet, but this would require that every eligible voter have access to the Internet and that a fraud-free identification system be devised.

A CHANGE IN HOW CONGRESS OPERATES

If major issues were presented for nationwide voting, members of Congress in favor of a given policy would have to turn to nationwide organizations to help build widespread support for that policy. Rather than trying to pressure legislators and other government officials in Washington, D.C., interest groups probably would focus their resources more on advertising, opinion polling, and other techniques used by marketing firms in creating a demand for certain products or services.

Certainly, this has happened in states that use the initiative frequently. In California, for example, interest

groups spend increasing amounts of money on advertising and other strategies to garner support for their positions on particular initiatives.

IN THE END, WOULD WE HAVE BETTER POLICIES?

In the last analysis, whether we would have better policies would depend on the extent to which citizens would actually attempt to understand the policy issues on which they would be voting. Also, the success of such a program would require, at a minimum, higher voter turnouts than we see today. If only a small percentage of Americans actually bothered to vote on national policy issues, then perhaps the results would be no better than under the current system in which all policy issues are decided by Congress, the executive branch, and the courts.

FOR CRITICAL ANALYSIS

1. What do you think the criteria should be for deciding which policy issues are "major"?
2. If all citizens voted on policy issues, including tax increases, would it ever be possible to enact laws imposing higher federal taxes?

If all citizens could vote on policy issues, as suggested in this chapter's opening *What If . . .* , certainly it would be a time-consuming process. This is because literally thousands of policy proposals are debated in the halls of Congress, in state capitols, and in municipal government halls every year. Just about any policy proposal can be subjected to a rigorous analysis. Each policy issue has numerous pros and cons, and the costs and benefits of every proposal must be analyzed carefully.

Part of the public policy debate in our nation involves domestic problems. **Domestic policy** can be defined as all of the laws, government planning, and government actions that affect each individual's daily life in the United States. Consequently, the span of such policies is enormous. Domestic policies range from relatively simple issues, such as what the speed limit should be on interstate highways, to more complex issues, such as how best to protect our environment. Many of our domestic policies are formulated and implemented by the federal government, but many others are the result of the combined efforts of federal, state, and local governments.

In this chapter we look at domestic policy issues concerned with poverty and welfare, immigration, violence and crime, and the environment. In the next chapter, we examine national economic policies undertaken solely by the federal government. Before we start our analysis, we must look at how public policies are made.

Domestic Policy
Public plans or courses of action that concern issues of national importance, such as poverty, crime, and the environment.

The Policymaking Process

How does any issue, such as a perceived need for welfare reform, get resolved? First, of course, the issue has to be identified as a problem. With respect to the welfare program, policymakers can learn that it poses a problem by looking at the cost of the federal welfare program, the overlap of the federal program with state welfare programs, the extent to which welfare programs contribute to the elimination of poverty, and nationally published statistics on other aspects of the program.

Often, policymakers simply have to open their local newspapers—or letters from their constituents—to discover that a problem is brewing. Like most Americans, however, policymakers receive much of their information from the national media. Finally, different lobbying groups provide information to members of Congress. In the area of welfare policy, for example, prior to the reform legislation passed in 1996 groups in favor of reforming welfare provided congresspersons with data showing that the existing program was not effective. Opponents of welfare reform provided members of Congress with data showing that any basic reform of the welfare program would not be in the nation's best interests.

During the 1990s, in those years when there were continuing federal budget deficits, many traditionally protected federal programs were put under the microscope. One of these programs was the welfare program. Congress and the White House gradually accepted that welfare reform was necessary. Indeed, when campaigning for his first presidential term, Bill Clinton promised that he would "change welfare as we know it."

The Role of Debate in the Policymaking Process

As just mentioned, the first step in the policymaking process is the acknowledgment that a problem exists and needs a solution. Problems and possible solutions often emerge through public debate.

The passage by Congress of the Personal Responsibility and Work Opportunity Reconciliation Act (Welfare Reform Act) of 1996 provides a good example of the

Protesters demonstrate outside the White House in August 1996 to show their opposition to the welfare reform bill then being considered by Congress. Grassroots expressions of public opinion, such as this demonstration, play a significant role in the policymaking process.

Two welfare recipients tie tourniquets as part of their training in a medical assistant program. The program will enable them to find employment.

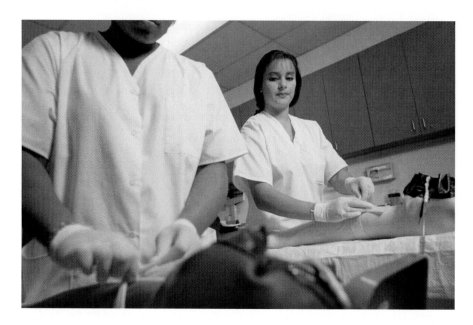

function of debate in the policymaking process. There has been debate about the welfare system since at least the 1930s, when some of the first major welfare programs were instituted. During the 1960s, when President Lyndon B. Johnson declared a "war on poverty," additional debate occurred. Finally, in the late 1980s and early 1990s, debate about the "welfare problem" intensified. Stories about second- and even third-generation welfare families abounded in the press. Knowledge that the poverty rate had not declined despite the trillions of dollars spent in welfare payments gave ammunition to those who wanted to reform welfare. Additionally, researchers pointed out that in many instances, welfare recipients actually would have less income to spend if they refused welfare and went to work. In part, this was because the Social Security and income taxes they would have to pay on their earnings would reduce their net incomes.

As far back as the 1970s, one of the key federal welfare programs, Aid to Families with Dependent Children (AFDC), came under criticism because it was designed to give aid to families in which dependent children did not have the financial support of the father—because of desertion, disability, or death. Critics argued that this "no man in the house rule" encouraged broken families.

Welfare programs were also criticized because they did not include work requirements. Under the traditional welfare system, people whose incomes were below a certain amount were simply eligible for welfare payments. Welfare recipients were not required to go to work to retain their benefits or to go off welfare after a certain period of time.

Finally, welfare spending became part of a general ongoing policy debate concerning devolution (transferring responsibilities to state governments—see Chapter 3). Many state governors argued that Washington, D.C., should give up its control over locally administered welfare programs. Groups of employees of the various welfare programs, in contrast, lobbied against devolution in this area. They feared that the states would reduce the number of eligible welfare recipients and thus the number of government employees involved in administering welfare programs.

Steps in the Policymaking Process

The passage of the Welfare Reform Act of 1996 also provides a good example of the steps involved in the policymaking process. No matter how simple or how complex the problem, those who make policy follow a number of steps. Based on observation, we can divide the process of policymaking into at least five steps.

1. **Agenda Building:** *The issue must get on the agenda.* This occurs through crisis, technological change, or mass media campaigns, as well as through the efforts of strong political personalities and effective lobbying groups. With respect to the Welfare Reform Act of 1996, members of the 104th Congress, in response to the public's concern over the then-steady federal government deficits and the perceived failure of welfare to reduce poverty rates, included welfare reform as part of their proposed legislative agenda.

2. **Agenda formulation:** *The proposals are discussed among government officials and the public.* Such discussions may take place in the printed media, on television, and in the halls of Congress. Congress holds hearings, the president voices the administration's views, and the topic may even become a campaign issue. For example, President Clinton talked about welfare reform throughout his 1992 presidential campaign. The topic was discussed during some of his "town hall meetings." It was on the agenda of the National Governors Conference for several years in a row.

3. **Agenda adoption:** *A specific strategy is chosen from among the proposals discussed.* That is, Congress must enact legislation, executive departments must write new regulations, or the courts must interpret past policies differently. Much of the congressional year prior to the passage of the Welfare Reform Act, for example, was taken up by work on that legislation. After extensive debate, a bill was passed, and the president signed it into law on August 22, 1996. The new legislation was, of course, a compromise. It attempted to meet two objectives—giving more power to the states while at the same time not being "too harsh on poor people."

4. **Agenda implementation:** *Government action must be implemented by bureaucrats, the courts, police, and individual citizens.* Although on the whole the new legislation changed the welfare landscape, some states took longer to implement changes than others. Congress also changed some of the restrictions placed on welfare payments during the two years after the act's passage.

5. **Agenda evaluation:** *Increasingly, after a policy is implemented, groups undertake policy evaluation.* Groups both inside and outside government conduct studies to show what actually happens after a policy has been implemented for a given period of time. Based on this "feedback" and the perceived success or failure of the policy, a new round of policymaking initiatives will be undertaken to correct and hopefully improve on the effort. Research groups, for example, have already studied whether the 1996 Welfare Reform Act has increased employment among those who were formally on welfare, as you will read shortly.

It is worth noting that although the flow of the policy process is well understood, there are competing models of how and for whose benefit that process works. Table 16–1 on page 520 lists a number of competing models for the policymaking process and gives a brief summary of each model.

Analyzing the Welfare Reform Act

Like all legislation, the Welfare Reform Act was a compromise. This is understandable, given that there is virtually no way to change a system that has been in effect for decades without stepping on toes. To satisfy those who wanted the states to have more authority over welfare, the act gave more control over the program to state governments. To satisfy others, the act allowed the federal government to retain some of its authority over the welfare program.

Major Provisions of the Act.   In part, the Welfare Reform Act of 1996 shifted to state governments some of the financial burden of—and control over—the welfare system. Traditionally, the federal government and the states shared the cost of welfare, but the federal government determined how the programs would be implemented and increased the funds allocated for welfare programs as the number of welfare recipients rose. Under the new system, federal and state governments continue to share the costs of welfare assistance, but the states play a greater role in establishing welfare rules (such as who will receive what type of benefits) and in managing the welfare programs.

With respect to the AFDC program, the Welfare Reform Act abolished the existing program and provided that the federal government would turn over to the states, in lump-sum grants ("block grants"—see Chapter 3), the funds that otherwise would go to the AFDC programs. The states, not the federal government, now have to meet the costs of any increased welfare spending. Although the federal government retained control over the food-stamp program (discussed later in the chapter), benefits under this program were reduced.

One of the basic aims of the act, however, was to reduce welfare spending by all governments in the long run. To do this, the bill made two significant changes in the welfare system. One change involved limiting most welfare recipients to only two years of welfare assistance. After two years, welfare payments must be discontinued unless the recipient is working, either at a public service job or in the private sector. The bill also limited lifetime welfare assistance to five years. (The federally established five-year limit can be avoided by the states, however, if they use their own funds to pay for continued welfare benefits.)

Another change involved an attempt to reduce the number of unmarried teenage mothers who receive welfare payments, because these individuals tend to stay on welfare the longest. The act discouraged illegitimate births by teenage mothers by offering "bonus payments" to states that reduce their rates of illegitimate births in this age group and by allowing the states to deny benefits to unmarried teenage mothers.

TABLE 16-1

Selected Models of the Policymaking Process

1. The Bureaucratic Politics Model. In the bureaucratic politics model, the relative power of the large bureaucracies in Washington determines which policy becomes part of the national agenda and which is implemented. This theory of American politics is based on the struggle among competing interest groups.

2. The Power Elite, or Elitism, Model. Powerful economic interests determine the outcome of policy struggles, according to the power elite, or elitism, model. The rich and those who know the rich determine what gets done. More important, the power elite decides what items do *not* get on the public agenda and which items get removed if they are already on it.

3. The Marxist Model. Closely aligned with the power elite model is the Marxist model of public policymaking, in which the ruling class institutes public policy, often at the expense of the working class. The Marxist solution is revolution and the seizure of government by the working class.

4. The Incrementalist Model. Public policy evolves through small changes or adjustments, according to the incrementalist model. Consequently, policymakers examine only a few alternatives in trying to solve national problems. A good public-policy decision is made when there is agreement among contesting interests, and agreement is obtained most easily when changes

are minimal.

5. The Rationalist Model. The rationalist model, sometimes thought of as a pure textbook abstraction, hypothesizes a rational policymaker who sets out to maximize his or her own self-interest, rather than determining what the public, or collective, interest might be. Rational policymakers will rank goals and objectives according to their benefit to the policymakers. Such a model is often viewed as an alternative to the incrementalist model. This model is sometimes known as the theory of public choice.

6. The Systems Model. The most general, and perhaps the most ambitious, approach to modeling public policymaking is a systems approach, in which policy is a product of the relationships between the institutions of government and the socioeconomic-political environment. Such a model has (a) inputs from public opinion and crises; (b) a political process including legislative hearings, debates, court deliberations, party conventions, and so on; (c) a set of policy outputs consisting of legislation, appropriations, and regulations; and (d) policy outcomes, which may provide, for example, more job security, less unemployment, more research on AIDS, and so on.

These two teenage mothers could be subject to the provisions of the 1996 welfare reform law, which limits their eligibility for federal assistance to two years. States may choose to extend assistance for a longer period of time, however. Although the goal of the law was to get people into employment, it did not provide the child-care benefits usually needed by mothers to allow them to accept jobs.

What Supporters of the Act Say. Supporters of the Welfare Reform Act maintain that it will reduce welfare spending in the long run by getting welfare recipients off welfare and into productive jobs. Supporters of the act point out that welfare rolls have indeed been cut since the passage of the act. Many former welfare recipients have been moved off welfare and into jobs, and state welfare officials have been undertaking vigorous efforts to keep people from signing up for welfare assistance. These efforts include urging welfare applicants to seek assistance from others, such as a relative, instead of the government; giving welfare applicants one-time emergency cash payments instead of longer-term welfare payments; and requiring applicants to spend a significant amount of time looking for work before they can receive welfare assistance. Nearly three-fourths of the states have implemented such "diversion" programs to keep people off welfare—people who in the past would automatically have been eligible for welfare payments. Overall, claim the act's supporters, welfare reform has resulted in a historic decline—by 27 percent nationwide—in the number of people on welfare.[1]

What the Critics Say. Many contend that the Welfare Reform Act is far from an optimal solution to the welfare problem. Senator Daniel Patrick Moynihan of New York, one of several Senate Democrats who bitterly opposed the reform bill, went so far as to say that the legislation was less "welfare reform" than "welfare repeal." Advocates for the poor and other critics of the 1996 act contend that the emerging welfare system makes it so difficult to apply for welfare assistance that many poor families are not getting the help they need. These critics worry that the new goal of keeping as many people as possible from receiving welfare may prevent welfare officials from recognizing that some families truly need assistance. They point out that even though welfare case loads have declined, there has been no significant reduction in the number of people living in poverty.

Perhaps the most criticized provisions of the act are those that deny welfare assistance to unwed teenage mothers. Critics argue that the only real effect of these provisions will be to reduce aid to poor children. They see the provisions

INFOTRAC®
COLLEGE EDITION

"A Return to the Principles of 1834"

---

[1]Barbara Vobejda and Judith Havemann, "States' Welfare Shift: Stop It before It Starts," *The Washington Post*, August 12, 1998, p. A1.

Income Transfer
A transfer of income from some individuals in the economy to other individuals. This is generally done by way of the government. It is a transfer in the sense that no current services are rendered by the recipients.

INFOTRAC®
COLLEGE EDITION

"Welfare at Groung Zero"

as a simplistic attempt to remedy a problem that is rooted deeply in social and economic factors, such as urban decay and unemployment, as well as in the disincentives to work inherent in the traditional welfare program. If a state chooses to deny benefits to unmarried teenage mothers, who will provide for the needs of illegitimate children?

Poverty and Welfare

Throughout the world, historically poverty has been accepted as inevitable. Even today, little has been done on an international level to eliminate worldwide poverty. The United States and other industrialized nations, however, have sustained enough economic growth in the past several hundred years to eliminate *mass* poverty. In fact, considering the wealth and high standard of living in the United States, the persistence of poverty here appears bizarre and anomalous. How can there still be so much poverty in a nation of so much abundance? And what can be done about it? (See the feature *E-Mail Messages from the Past* for James Madison's views on the government's role with respect to the poor.)

A traditional solution has been **income transfers.** There are methods of transferring income from relatively well-to-do to relatively poor groups in society, and as a nation, we have been using such methods for a long time. Today, a vast array of welfare programs exists for the sole purpose of redistributing income. We know, however, that these programs have not been entirely successful. Before we examine the problems posed by the welfare system, let's look at the concept of poverty in more detail and at the characteristics of the poor.

The Low-Income Population

We can see in Figure 16–1 that the number of individuals classified as poor fell rather steadily from 1959 through 1969. Then, for about a decade, the number of poor leveled off, until the recession of 1981 to 1982. The number then fell somewhat until the early 1990s, when it began to increase—until 1995. Since then, it has fallen slightly.

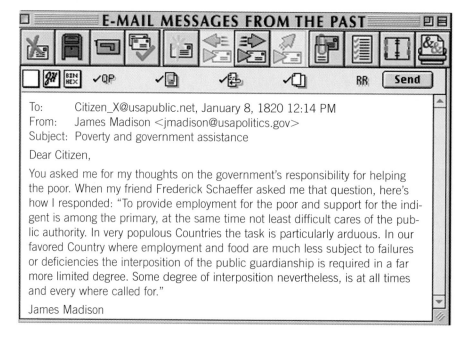

E-MAIL MESSAGES FROM THE PAST

To: Citizen_X@usapublic.net, January 8, 1820 12:14 PM
From: James Madison <jmadison@usapolitics.gov>
Subject: Poverty and government assistance

Dear Citizen,

You asked me for my thoughts on the government's responsibility for helping the poor. When my friend Frederick Schaeffer asked me that question, here's how I responded: "To provide employment for the poor and support for the indigent is among the primary, at the same time not least difficult cares of the public authority. In very populous Countries the task is particularly arduous. In our favored Country where employment and food are much less subject to failures or deficiencies the interposition of the public guardianship is required in a far more limited degree. Some degree of interposition nevertheless, is at all times and every where called for."

James Madison

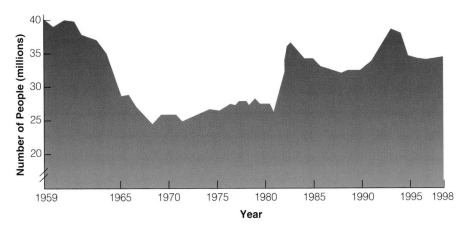

FIGURE **16-1**

The Official Number of Poor in the United States

The number of individuals classified as poor fell steadily from 1959 through 1969. From 1970 to 1981, the number stayed about the same. It then increased during the 1981–1982 recession. The number of poor then fell somewhat, until the early 1990s. After rising for a few years, the number started to fall in 1995.

Defining Poverty.   The threshold income level, which is used to determine who falls into the poverty category, was originally based on the cost of a nutritionally adequate food plan designed by the U.S. Department of Agriculture for emergency or temporary use. The threshold was determined by multiplying the food-plan cost times three, on the assumption that food expenses constitute approximately one-third of a poor family's expenditures. In 1969, a federal interagency committee examined the calculations of the threshold and decided to set new standards. Until then, annual revisions of the threshold level had been based only on price changes in the food budget. After 1969, the adjustments were made on the basis of changes in the consumer price index (CPI). The CPI is based on the average prices of a specified set of goods and services bought by wage earners in urban areas.

The low-income poverty threshold thus represents an absolute measure of income needed to maintain a specified standard of living as of 1963, with the constant-dollar value, or purchasing-power value, increased year by year in relation to the general increase in prices. For 1998, for example, the official poverty level for a family of four was about $16,500. It has gone up since then by the amount of the change in the CPI during the intervening period. (The poverty level varies with family size and location.)

Transfer Payments as Income.   The official poverty level is based on pretax income, including cash but not **in-kind subsidies**—food stamps, housing vouchers, and the like. If we correct poverty levels for such benefits, the percentage of the population that is below the poverty line drops dramatically, as can be seen in Figure 16–2 on page 524. Some economists argue that the way in which the official poverty level is calculated makes no sense in a nation that redistributed over $900 billion in cash and noncash transfers in 1998.

In-Kind Subsidy
A good or service—such as food stamps, housing, or medical care—provided by the government to lower-income groups.

Major Government-Assistance Programs

Welfare assistance to the poor traditionally has taken a variety of forms. Until 1996, the basic welfare program in the United States was known as Aid to Families with Dependent Children (AFDC). As already mentioned, this program provided aid for children who did not receive financial support from the father. With the passage of the Welfare Reform Act of 1996, the states gained more responsibility for establishing welfare rules and managing the welfare program. The AFDC program was abolished, and the U.S. government now turns over to the states, in the form of grants, funds targeted for a program called **Temporary Assistance to Needy Families (TANF)**. If a state wishes to increase the amount of payments to individuals for TANF over what the national government gives it, the state has to pay for the additional costs.

Temporary Assistance to Needy Families (TANF)
A state-administered program in which grants from the national government are given to the states, which use the funds to provide assistance to those eligible to receive welfare benefits. The TANF program was created by the Welfare Reform Act of 1996 and replaced the former AFDC program.

FIGURE 16-2

Three Measures of Poverty

The percentage of the U.S. population living in poverty depends on what one includes in the definition of income. If one looks at private money income only, the percentage of the population in poverty during the 1980s and 1990s was well above 20 percent. If one adds cash benefits paid to individuals by the government during most of the 1980s and 1990s, less than 14 percent of the U.S. population was living in poverty. Finally, if one takes account of cash benefits, in-kind benefits, and the underreporting of income, the share of the U.S. population in poverty was estimated to be about 7.9 percent in 1998.

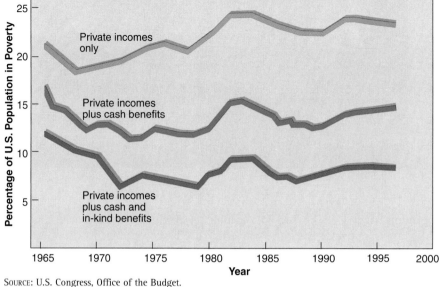

SOURCE: U.S. Congress, Office of the Budget.

**Supplemental
Security Income (SSI)**

A federal program established to provide assistance to elderly persons and disabled persons.

Food Stamps

Coupons issued by the federal government to low-income individuals to be used for the purchase of food.

**Earned-Income Tax
Credit (EITC) Program**

A government program that helps low-income workers by giving back part or all of their Social Security taxes.

The **Supplemental Security Income (SSI)** program was established in 1974 to provide a nationwide minimum income for elderly persons and persons with disabilities who do not qualify for Social Security benefits. The SSI program is one of the fastest-growing programs in the United States. When it started, it cost less than $8 billion annually. Today, that figure is close to $40 billion.

The government also issues **food stamps,** coupons that can be used to purchase food. Food stamps are available for low-income individuals and families. Recipients must prove that they qualify by showing that they do not have very much income (or no income at all). In 1964, about 367,000 Americans were receiving food stamps. In 1998, the number of those receiving food stamps was estimated at more than 26 million. The annual cost of funding food stamps jumped from $860,000 in 1964 to an estimated $23 billion in 1999. Workers on strike, and even some college students, are eligible to receive food stamps. The food-stamp program has become a major part of the welfare system in the United States, although it was started in 1964 mainly to shore up the nation's agricultural sector by distributing surplus food through retail channels.

The **earned-income tax credit (EITC) program** was created in 1975 to help low-income workers by giving back part or all of their Social Security taxes. Currently, more than 20 percent of all taxpayers claim an EITC. (For further details on this program, see the feature *Politics and Economics: The EITC—Too Much of a Good Thing?*)

Through these and other programs, hundreds of billions of dollars have been transferred to the poor over the last several decades. Nevertheless, as you can see in Figure 16-3, the poverty rate in the United States has not shown any long-run tendency to decline since about 1970.

Welfare Reform—Problems Facing the States

Although the Welfare Reform Act gave the states more control over welfare, it also created many problems for which the states must find solutions. For example, consider the state of New York. Its constitution requires the state to provide for the "aid, care and support of the needy," as determined by the state legislature. The welfare bill, by denying some benefits to legal immigrants (later modified) and imposing

POLITICS and Economics

The EITC—Too Much of a Good Thing?

If you visit the Web site of the Internal Revenue Service (IRS), you will meet Tony Chorivo, a butcher. You will see him receive a few extra dollars, compliments of the federal government's earned-income tax credit (EITC) program. The IRS points out that "[t]he meat of the matter is that if you qualify, the EITC will fatten your paycheck every month, too!" There is a lot of truth to that statement.

The EITC was created in 1975 as a way to provide rebates for Social Security taxes to low-income workers. Since then, it has grown remarkably. Current estimates show that about $23 billion a year is rebated to taxpayers through the program. The program benefits only those families earning below $28,000, which is not too far away

from the median wage. The Joint Economic Committee on Taxation estimates that by the year 2008, households earning up to $40,000 will be receiving EITC cash.

Today, the average rebate check is $1,151. To get more people to sign up for such a windfall, the IRS mails out more than ten million letters a year encouraging people "to get with the program." Currently, about 46 percent of the families in Mississippi are eligible for EITC rebates, as are 23 percent of the families in the District of Columbia. Under the Clinton administration, the program was expanded to include taxpayers without children. Families that have kids, how-

ever, profit the most. They receive up to $3,500 in EITC money, so it might not be surprising that the IRS has discovered massive rebate fraud—taxpayers "borrowing" babies to claim as their own for EITC purposes. Even after a crackdown, more than 20 percent of claims for rebates are fraudulent, and this fraud costs the government at least $5 billion a year.

According to the former chair of the president's Council of Economic Advisers, Laura Tyson, the EITC program is "a way to reward hard-working Americans who work full time." Yet, according to the General Accounting Office, the average recipient of EITC rebates works only 1,300 hours, whereas the normal

working year exceeds 2,000 hours. Moreover, the General Accounting Office claims that the EITC program has decreased the poverty rate by less than one percentage point.

FOR CRITICAL ANALYSIS

Approximately fifteen million households find that their EITC rebate offsets their entire income tax liability and gives them a cash surplus as well. How do EITC rebates differ from welfare payments?

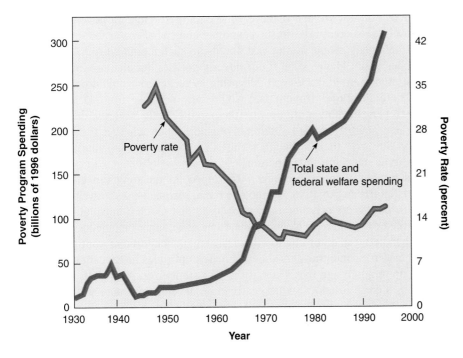

FIGURE 16–3

Welfare Spending and the Poverty Rate

Welfare spending has increased dramatically since the late 1960s. Nevertheless, the measured poverty rate has remained relatively stable.

INFOTRAC ®
COLLEGE EDITION

**"Welfare Reform Has
Severely Hurt Poor Families"**

five-year lifetime limits on welfare assistance to adults, in effect passes on the costs of providing aid to the "needy" to New York state and local governments.

Consider also a problem facing California. Providing welfare benefits to numerous immigrants in that state creates a significant burden for the state government. After the Welfare Reform Act of 1996 became effective, California attempted to address this problem by passing a law that would restrict welfare benefits to new residents. In January 1998, however, the law was held to be unconstitutional by a federal appellate court. This was the first case challenging a state's attempt to use the 1996 Welfare Reform Act to deny equal payments to all eligible residents, whether they are new or not.

Furthermore, implementing the "workfare" requirements of the bill may be costly and difficult. The concept of workfare—performing public service jobs in return for welfare benefits—is not new, and welfare reform proposals often have been couched in such terms. Many point out, though, that the work requirements of the 1996 reform bill, although they play into the public's feeling that no one should "get something for nothing," are not free. For one thing, making the state the employer of last resort adds yet another layer to the bureaucracy—those state officials who will manage the state-provided jobs. This will only add to the costs of welfare that the states must pay. According to the Congressional Budget Office, each public service job costs $3,500 a year to monitor. If it involves mothers, an additional $3,000 a year has to be paid for child-care costs. Clearly, the long-run success of the work requirements will depend on whether the states and industry can maintain their current attempts to create and monitor the millions of jobs needed to put welfare recipients to work.

Poverty's Effect on Children

F. Scott Fitzgerald once wrote that the rich "are different from you and me"; Ernest Hemingway replied, "Yes, they have more money." Are the children of low-income families the same as everyone else, except that they have less money? This has been a major policy question for years. Some have argued that children of very poor families fail in society because their parents are unlike other parents. The policy implications of this debate are crucial, for if children from poor families are just like everyone else, then reducing poverty rates will lead to higher success rates in the economic and social world for such children.

Two relatively recent studies cast doubts on such a possibility.[2] According to researcher Susan Mayer, even if our poverty policies doubled the income of the poorest 20 percent of families, childbearing by teenagers would drop only 2 percent. The high school dropout rate would only decrease from 17.3 percent to about 16 percent. Mayer argues that the parents' skills, honesty, diligence, and health may matter more to children's prospects than whether the family is in poverty. She says that "although children's opportunities are unequal, income inequality is not the primary reason."

This research has implications with respect to the long-run effects of the Welfare Reform Act of 1996. On the one hand, income losses to welfare families in the coming years may not damage children that much if unequal incomes are not at the heart of the problem. On the other hand, large income losses could be a problem because, according to other research, the children of poor parents who obtain larger income transfers show increased aptitudes in educational achievements up to about age five. Thus, if the Welfare Reform Act results in dramatic losses in income to poor families, early child development may suffer.

---

[2]Susan Mayer, *What Money Can't Buy: Family Income and Children's Life Chances* (Cambridge, Mass.: Harvard University Press, 1997); and Greg J. Duncan and Jeanne Brooks-Gunn, eds., *Consequences of Growing up Poor* (New York: Russell Sage Foundation, 1997).

Homelessness—Still a Problem

The plight of the homeless remains a problem. Indeed, some observers argue that the Welfare Reform Act of 1996 has increased the numbers of homeless persons. According to the National Alliance to End Homelessness, the number of people without a home on any given night in the United States ranges from 350,000 to as many as 600,000.

It is difficult to estimate how many people are homeless because the number depends on how the homeless are defined. There are *street people*—those who sleep in bus stations, parks, and other areas. Many of these people are youthful runaways. There are the so-called *sheltered homeless*—those who sleep in government-supported or privately funded shelters. Many of these individuals used to live with their families or friends. While street people are almost always single, the sheltered homeless include numerous families with children. Homeless families are the fastest-growing subgroup of the homeless population.

As a policy issue, how to handle the homeless problem pits liberals against conservatives. Conservatives argue that there are not really that many homeless and that most of them are alcoholics, drug users, or mentally ill. Indeed, the deinstitutionalization of the mentally ill in the 1960s and 1970s did increase our homeless population. Approximately one-fourth to one-third of the homeless are, in fact, mentally ill. In addition, one-half of all street people are alcoholics or drug abusers. Conservatives argue that these individuals should be dealt with either by the mental-health system or the criminal justice system.

In contrast, many liberals argue that homelessness is caused by a reduction in welfare benefits and by excessively priced housing. They want more shelters to be built for the homeless. During the 1980s, more shelters indeed were built. But many cities, such as New York, discovered that no matter how many shelters were built, they were always full. Many individuals and families with low incomes or no incomes who live with relatives have always taken advantage of government-provided homeless shelters.

Recently, cities have been attempting to "criminalize" homelessness. Many municipalities have outlawed sleeping on park benches and sidewalks, as well as panhandling and leaving personal property on public property. In some cities,

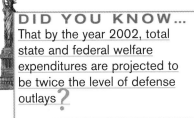

DID YOU KNOW...
That by the year 2002, total state and federal welfare expenditures are projected to be twice the level of defense outlays?

Less than one hundred yards from the White House, a homeless man sleeps, with his head on a cart containing all of his possessions. What should (or can) the government do to help the homeless?

police sweeps remove the homeless, who then become part of the criminal-justice system.

Because there is so much disagreement about the number of homeless persons, the reasons for homelessness, and the possible cures for the problem, there has been no consistent government policy. Whatever policies have been adopted usually have been attacked by one group or another.

Immigration

Immigration, like welfare, has become a political lightning rod in recent years. Although much of the debate has focused on illegal immigration and the share of welfare payments going to immigrants, the scope of the debate over immigration raises the following general question: Should *any* immigration into the United States be permitted, and if so, just who and how many individuals should be permitted to immigrate to this country?

Is Recent Immigration Greater Than in the Past?

"Sierra Club and Immigration Issues"

The immigration issue has become more important in recent years because of the upsurge in immigration rates in the last several decades, as shown in panel (a) of Figure 16–4. Currently, about 26 million foreign-born persons are living in the United States, or 9 percent of the total U.S. population (which is over 270 million), as shown in panel (b) of Figure 16–4. Although these numbers may seem impressive, when measured as a proportion of the population, immigrants are far less significant than they were in years past. For example, between 1880 and 1920, foreign-born persons constituted over 14 percent of the U.S. population, as shown in panel (b) of Figure 16–4. Subsequent legal restrictions reduced immigration sharply, leading to a forty-year decline in the proportion of the U.S.

FIGURE 16–4

Immigrants in America

Since the 1850s, immigrant arrivals peaked in the 1900–1910 period but have almost returned to that high level today, as is seen in panel (a). Nonetheless, the percentage of the U.S. population that is foreign born is still lower than it was from the 1850s to the 1920s, as is seen in panel (b).

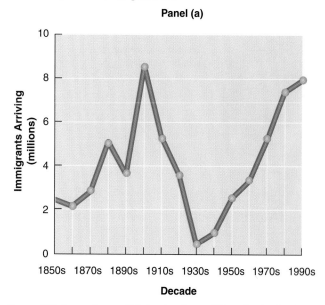

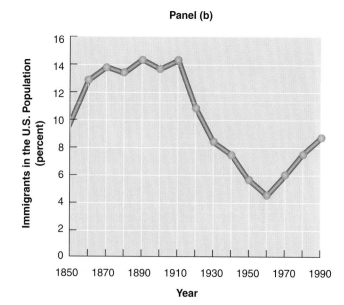

SOURCE: U.S. Census Bureau; U.S. Immigration and Naturalization Service.

population that was foreign born. Indeed, only in the last thirty or so years has the foreign-born population begun to rebound.

Changing Federal Immigration Policy

Prior to 1965, federal immigration policy favored white Europeans. Starting in 1965, that policy changed as the federal government began to make family unification the centerpiece of its immigration policy. As a result, children, spouses, and siblings poured in from around the world to join immigrants who originally had entered alone. Additionally, the flood of immigrants was stimulated by the growing sentiment that individuals fleeing persecution in then-communist countries should receive special status as political refugees. Additional entry visas were set aside for such persons, thereby pushing legal immigration totals above what they would have been otherwise.

By the mid-1990s, the public was pressing Congress to curb immigration, particularly illegal immigration, and the amount of public benefits going to noncitizen residents in the United States. In response to this pressure, Congress passed the Immigration Reform Act of 1996. To conform with the Welfare Reform Act, which had been passed earlier in the year, the act prohibited immigrants, including legal immigrants who are not yet citizens, from receiving most forms of public assistance (later modified). To stem the influx of illegal immigrants, the act also did the following:

- Doubled the number of border patrol agents.
- Increased penalties for immigrant smuggling and document fraud.
- Authorized an expedited deportation process for illegal aliens (including undocumented political refugees).
- Provided for the establishment, in five states, of pilot programs to assist employers in verifying workers' status.

A proud new U.S. citizen displays her certificate of citizenship at a ceremony on Ellis Island in New York.

I HOPE YOU GUYS REALIZE YOU'RE NOT ELIGIBLE FOR ANY WELFARE BENEFITS...

Rocks from MARS

TOLES
UNIVERSAL PRESS SYND.
©1996. FOR U.S. NEWS & WORLD REPORT

DON'T FORGET TO MENTION ABOUT SPEAKING ENGLISH

■ Provided that any person who "sponsors" an immigrant, such as a family member, must have an income of at least 125 percent of the poverty level (the poverty level in 1998 was about $16,500 for a family of four).

The 1996 act did not end the controversy over immigration. In fact, public criticism of the harshness of the act's provisions relating to public assistance to legal immigrants led the government to modify the act in the following year. Whether there is a net cost associated with immigration continues to be debated (see this chapter's *Critical Perspective* for details).

Critical perspective

Is There a Net Cost to Immigration?

Ask Bill Gates, and he will tell you: America needs more immigrants. In 1998, Senator Spencer Abraham (R., Mich.) agreed and supported a bill to increase the number of highly skilled workers given visas each year. After all, the Information Technology Association of America estimates that 340,000 skilled positions in U.S. companies are unfilled. But, ask Senator Edward Kennedy (D., Mass.), and you will hear an opposing view. He is against any permanent increase in the immigration ceiling. Kennedy is worried that Americans will be undercut by foreigners working more cheaply. The Clinton administration seems to agree. It argues that U.S. employers should be investing more in educating and training the domestic work force.

One Issue—The High-Tech Revolution

According to supporters of immigration, the high-tech revolution that is playing a key role in the U.S. economic expansion could not have happened without the creativity of gifted immigrants. They point to the founder and former chairman of Intel (Andy Grove), who was an immigrant. They point to two of the four founders of Sun Microsystems, who were also immigrants. They point to four of the ten vice presidents of Cypress Semiconductor Corporation, who are from Britain, Germany, the Philippines, and Cuba. Indeed, there are several hundred highly placed foreign-born persons in the computer and software industry. Many of them arrived as students and stayed. According to supporters of increasing the number of legal immigrants, it would be foolish to let foreigners obtain a U.S. education and then force them to leave six years later.

There is another issue. If U.S.-based companies cannot get the skilled workers they want, they will set up branches elsewhere, such as in Dublin and Kiev. This might lead to fewer jobs in the United States.

According to the U.S. Census Bureau, naturalized Americans actually earn higher incomes than native-born Americans do. In other words, resident aliens do not provide "cheap labor" forever. They eventually obtain citizenship and are paid well, because they have the skills to justify higher incomes.

There May Be a Net Cost to Immigration

Not everybody is so enthusiastic about the benefits of unlimited immigration. Certainly, opinion polls show that Americans today are less in favor of immigration than they were in the past. In California, where over one-fourth of the population is not native born, 60 percent of those polled believe that legal immigration should be reduced. A study by the Rand Corporation in Santa Monica, California, at least partially justifies their thinking.* The authors of the report argue that the benefits of immigration are diminishing because of a mismatch between economic needs and the quality of new immigrants. The U.S. economy demands more skilled and educated immigrants. Yet the latest immigrants are less well educated than those in the past, at least in California. Also, most immigrants speak little or no English today, at least initially.

The result in California, according to the Rand study, is that the native-born Californians with few skills have suffered a wage decrease and a reduction in job opportunities because of so much competition from immigrants. Additionally, the lower incomes and larger family sizes of recent immigrants have burdened state and local governments by creating an increased demand for public services, particularly in the area of education. There has been no corresponding increase in tax revenues to offset this increased burden.

*Kevin S. McCarthy and George Vernez, "Immigration and a Changing Economy: California's Experience," Rand Corporation Report, Santa Monica, Calif., November 1997.

Crime in the Twenty-first Century

The issue of crime has been on the national agenda for years now. Virtually all polls taken in the United States in the last few years show that crime is one of the major concerns of the public. Although there is some evidence that certain crime rates have fallen, on average, the public's concern has not been misplaced.

Critical perspective

Is There a Net Cost to Immigration?—continued

The Rand study concluded that legal immigration should be reduced to a "moderate range" of around 500,000 per year. Our immigration policy should also include skills and education as part of the criteria for admission.

Not Everyone Agrees

Pepperdine University researcher Gregory Rodriguez does not agree with the Rand study, at least not completely. He argues that foreign-born Hispanics have three advantages, which serve to make up for their lack of education. First, they have more wage earners per family than any other ethnic group. Second, they have the highest rate of participation in the labor force. And third, their families are more stable than native-born American families. The result, says Rodriguez, is that the households of American-born Hispanics (descendants of immigrants) have almost the same average income as Asians and whites.

While not completely supporting Rodriguez's pro-immigration stance, a study conducted jointly by the National Academy of Sciences and the National Research Council[†] concludes that the actual impact of immigration on the economy is not very great one way or the other. The authors conclude that "the costs [of immigration] to native-born workers are small, and so are the benefits. Moreover, the costs imposed are short-run costs; for in the long run, immigrants will be working hard when the baby boomers retire and extra tax dollars are required."

Overall, the authors of the report believe that although a few states, such as California, Texas, New York, and Florida, may pay a relatively high price for assimilating so many immigrants, the country as a whole benefits from immigration. Moreover, according to a study by the Organization for Economic Cooperation and Development, even if an average immigrant is a net drain on the public purse, the children of immigrants, on average, pay far more to government in taxes than they take from it.[‡]

More People, More Population?

None of the studies just cited dealt with population, land preservation, and endangered species issues. The Sierra Club, though, came close to issuing a policy statement against immigration because of three issues. In 1998, the 630,000 members of the Sierra Club voted on a measure that would have called for limits on immigration as the means of protecting the environment from overpopulation. The Wilderness Society already had officially endorsed immigration limits. Sierra Club members who pushed for an official statement by the club favoring immigration limits pointed out that in the next fifty years our population will rise from 275 million to 400 million and that recent immigrants and their children will account for the bulk of this increase. Presumably, if the population rises, there also will be more traffic and an increased demand for consumer goods. When the votes were taken, however, those in favor of the Sierra Club's maintaining a neutral position on immigration won.

FOR CRITICAL ANALYSIS

1. Are there ways to allow more immigration without increasing the burden on state budgets caused by the use of public services by new immigrants?
2. Which interest groups in America are most likely to oppose increased immigration? Why?

[‡]As reported in *The Economist,* November 29, 1997, p. 81.

[†]James P. Smith and Barry Edmonston, eds., *The New Americans: Economic, Demographic, and Fiscal Effects of Immigration* (Washington, D.C.: National Academy Press, 1997).

DID YOU KNOW...** That a University of Southern California evaluation of a gang prevention program discovered that when the program lost funding, the gang broke up and its crime rate declined?

Crime in American History

In every period in the history of this nation, people have voiced their apprehension about crime. Some criminologists argue that crime was probably as frequent around the time of the American Revolution as it is currently. During the Civil War, mob violence and riots erupted in numerous cities. After the Civil War, people in San Francisco were told that "no decent man is in safety to walk the streets after dark; while at all hours, both night and day, his property is jeopardized by incendiarism and burglary."[3] In 1886, *Leslie's Weekly* reported that "Each day we see ghastly records of crime . . . murder seems to have run riot and each citizen asks . . . 'who is safe?'" From 1860 to 1890, the crime rate rose twice as fast as the population.[4] In 1910, one author stated that "crime, especially in its more violent forms and among the young, is increasing steadily and is threatening to bankrupt the Nation."[5]

From 1900 to the 1930s, social violence and crime increased dramatically. Labor union battles and racial violence were common. Only during the three-decade period from the mid-1930s to the early 1960s did the United States experience, for the first time in its history, stable or slightly declining overall crime rates.

What most Americans are worried about is violent crime. From the mid-1980s to 1994, its rate rose relentlessly, until 1995, when it began to decline. Look at Figure 16–5, where you see the changes in violent crime rates from 1970 to 1997. Going back even further, the murder rate per 100,000 people in 1964 was 4.9, whereas in 1994 it was estimated at 9.3, an almost 100 percent increase. These nationwide numbers, however, do not tell the full story. Murder rates in some major U.S. cities are between 50 and 100 per 100,000 people. These cities include Washington, D.C.; Detroit; New Orleans; St. Louis; and Birmingham.

A disturbing element with respect to crime is the number of serious crimes committed by juveniles. As you can see in Figure 16–6, the number of violent crimes committed by juveniles increased dramatically from the mid-1980s to 1994. Since 1995, however, that number has declined somewhat. (See this chapter's *Politics and Crime* for a further examination of the problem of juvenile crime.)

The Total Cost of Crime to American Society

For the perpetrator, crime may pay in certain circumstances—a successful robbery or embezzlement, for example—but crime certainly costs the American public.

[3]President's Commission on Law Enforcement and Administration of Justice, *Challenge of Crime in a Free Society* (Washington, D.C.: Government Printing Office, 1967), p. 19.
[4]Richard Shenkman, *Legends, Lies & Cherished Myths of American History* (New York: HarperCollins, 1988), p. 158.
[5]President's Commission, *Challenge of Crime*, p. 19.

FIGURE 16–5

Changes in Violent Crime Rates from 1970 to Present

Violent crime in the United States rose from 1970 to the beginning of the 1980s. Then crime rates dropped relatively dramatically until about 1986, when they again started to climb. By 1994, they were at their highest recorded levels. Since 1995, violent crime rates have been dropping.

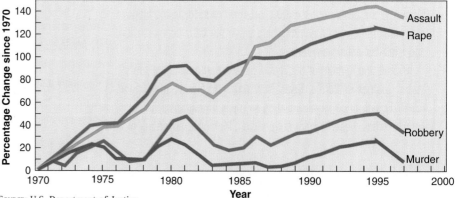

Source: U.S. Department of Justice.

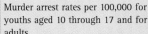

POLITICS and Crime

Attacking the Problem of Juvenile Crime

Although serious adult crimes have declined overall since 1980, those by persons aged ten through seventeen rose dramatically until 1994. As you can see in the accompanying figure, the number of arrest rates for murders committed by youths surpassed that for adults in the late 1980s—and continues to be higher. Furthermore, teenage killings with firearms quadrupled in the ten years after 1984. Currently, handguns are used in two-thirds of juvenile homicides.

The political response to this rise in serious juvenile crimes has been varied. Some cities have established juvenile curfews. Several states have begun to try more and more juveniles as adults, particularly juveniles charged with homicides. Still other states are operating juvenile "boot camps" to try to "shape up" the less violent juvenile criminals. Additionally, victims of

Police officers take fifteen-year-old Kipland Kinkel into custody following his May 23, 1998, fatal shooting spree at Thurston High School in Thurston, Oregon.

juvenile crime and victims' relatives are attempting to pry open the traditionally secret juvenile court system. Even the White House in 1996 sent to Congress a plan for federal prosecutors to try some juveniles as adults without seeking judicial permission.*

*For more details on the rights of juveniles in our legal system, see Chapter 6.

The number of youths between the ages of fifteen and seventeen will rise from about nine million today to almost thirteen million in the year 2010. It is thus understandable that there is grave concern about preventing an even worse juvenile crime problem in the years to come.

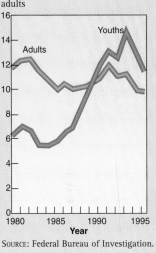

Youths and Murder

Murder arrest rates per 100,000 for youths aged 10 through 17 and for adults

SOURCE: Federal Bureau of Investigation.

FOR CRITICAL ANALYSIS

What are the pros and cons of trying more juvenile criminals as adults?

Consider one typical new home in Pico Rivera, a small city southeast of Los Angeles. The new two-story frame house has motion-sensitive floodlights, infrared alarms, video monitors, and a spiked fence topped with razor wire. The patio is surrounded by a metal cage, and every window has bars over it. In the yard are two Doberman pinschers. Private security guards patrol the community. The additional costs of building that new house in terms of crime protection are part of the nationwide cost of crime. Table 16–2 on the next page summarizes what crime is costing us every year.

The Prison Population Bomb

Virtually the instant a new prison is built, it is filled, and complaints arise about overcrowding. In 1994, for example, the state prison population was about 900,000, yet state prisons only had the capacity to hold about 500,000 inmates. The federal prison population, which is currently over 95,000, also far exceeds prison capacity. Currently, the total U.S. incarcerated population has climbed even further—to about 1.7 million in all—and is now nearly twice what it was a decade ago. (For a comparison of U.S. incarceration rates with those of other countries, see this chapter's feature entitled *Politics and Comparative Systems: Incarceration Worldwide* on page 535.)

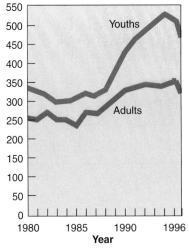

FIGURE 16–6

Arrest Rates for Violent Crime

Rates per 100,000 for youths aged 10 through 17 and for adults

SOURCE: Federal Bureau of Investigation.

TABLE　16-2

The Total Yearly Cost of Crime in America

EXPENDITURE	EXPLANATION	TOTAL COST (PER YEAR)
Criminal justice	All the spending on police, courts, and prisons at the federal, state, and local levels	$ 95 billion
Private protection	Spending on private guards, security systems, alarms, and so on	$ 70 billion
Urban decay	The cost of lost jobs and fleeing residents because of excessive crime in inner cities	$ 50 billion
Property loss	The value of stolen goods and vandalized buildings	$ 50 billion
Destroyed lives	The economic value of lost lives (death) and broken lives as a result of robberies, rapes, loss of loved ones, and so on	$175 billion
Medical care	The cost of treating victims	$ 10 billion
TOTAL		$450 billion

SOURCE: Federal Bureau of Investigation; and *Business Week,* various issues.

As the number of arrests and incarcerations in the United States increases, so does the cost of building and operating prisons. Just since 1990, 215 prisons have had to be built to house the burgeoning prison population, bringing the total number of federal and state prisons in this nation to 1,500. An additional 1,000 new prison beds are needed each week. When operational costs are included and construction costs are amortized over the life of a facility, the cost of sentencing one person to one year in jail or prison averages between $25,000 and $40,000. Thus, the annual nationwide cost of building, maintaining, and operating prisons is about $35 billion today.

When imprisonment keeps truly violent felons behind bars longer, it prevents them from committing more crimes. The average predatory street criminal commits fifteen or more crimes each year when not behind bars. But most prisoners are in for a relatively short time and are released on parole early, often because

To help ease overcrowding, inmates at the New York State Prison at Watertown are incarcerated in barracks-style prison blocks.

of prison overcrowding. Then many find themselves back in prison because they have violated parole, typically by using illegal drugs. Indeed, of the more than one million people who are arrested each year, the majority are arrested for drug offenses. Given that from twenty to forty million Americans violate one or more drug laws each year, the potential "supply" of prisoners seems virtually without limit. Consequently, it may not matter how many prisons are built; there will still be overcrowding as long as we maintain the same legislation with respect to psychoactive drugs.

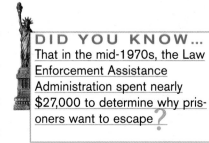

Federal Drug Laws: A Constitutional Alternative

Illegal drugs are a major source of the crisis in public safety in America. A rising percentage of arrests are for illegal drug use or drug trafficking. Violence accompanies the illegal drug trade, and one of the reasons is the "turf wars" among drug dealers to control the territories in which drugs, often crack cocaine, can be sold. A related reason is that when drug deals go bad, drug dealers cannot turn to the legal system to help them out. They turn to violence. Finally, drug addicts who do not have the income to finance their habits often turn to a life of crime—assault, robbery, and sometimes murder.

Two Frequently Mentioned Alternatives.   Two alternatives are commonly proposed for solving the drug problem in America. The first is to "get serious"

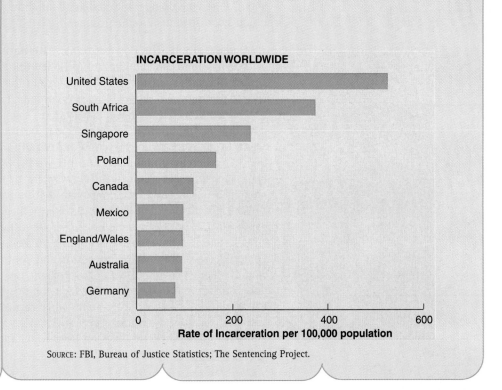

POLITICS and Comparative Systems

Incarceration Worldwide

The United States is known as "the home of the free and the land of the brave." It therefore may surprise many Americans to discover that the United States has the highest incarceration rate of any country in the world today. Just look at the figure in this feature. These data, relatively speaking, would have looked about the same ten years ago, when prison camps still existed in the former Soviet Union and when repression in South Africa was at its peak.

FOR CRITICAL ANALYSIS

Why does the U.S. prison population continue to rise even though the number of violent crimes committed each year has fallen?

INCARCERATION WORLDWIDE

Rate of Incarceration per 100,000 population

(United States, South Africa, Singapore, Poland, Canada, Mexico, England/Wales, Australia, Germany — 0, 200, 400, 600)

SOURCE: FBI, Bureau of Justice Statistics; The Sentencing Project.

about fighting illegal drug sales and use. A get-tough policy would involve major shifts in the use of government resources to fight drug trafficking and drug use. Advocates of such a policy believe that a true "war"—including use of the military—is what is needed.

At the other extreme are those who want to legalize all drugs. They argue that the prohibition against alcohol was a complete failure during this nation's "dry" period from 1920 to 1933. Under Prohibition, murder and assault rates increased, and so did the growth of organized crime. They argue that the legalization (or decriminalization) of most or all drugs would eliminate the main impetus that drives people to deal in drugs—huge profits.

Objections to These Two Alternatives.   Both of these extreme views have met with numerous objections. The get-tough policy did not work during Prohibition. Moreover, all of the increased spending on drug interdiction has had virtually no effect on overall illegal drug consumption in the United States. In fact, there is more and higher-quality cocaine available today than at any other time in the history of this country. The price of cocaine, corrected for inflation and quality increases, is about 10 percent of what it was in the early 1960s.

Mandatory sentences, which have been imposed by the federal government since the late 1980s for all federal offenses (including the sale or possession of illegal drugs), are also not an ideal solution. According to William N. Brownsberger, a researcher at Harvard Medical School, "mandatory sentencing laws are wasting prison resources on non-violent, low-level [drug-law] offenders, and reducing resources available to lock up violent offenders." Brownsberger found that more than 60 percent of those put into prison in Massachusetts for drug offenses had virtually no criminal records.[6]

An equally long list of objections to the laissez-faire view of drug legalization exists. What if nationwide legalization leads to an unprecedented increase in the use of cocaine, marijuana, heroin, and the like? Are we willing to pay the social costs of larger-scale use? If we are not, it might then be impossible for this country to revert to criminalization of drug trading and use. Also, what about those who do not want to live in a nation that allows all drugs to be freely produced, distributed, and consumed?

A Middle Ground—The Constitutional Alternative.   A middle ground has been offered by Daniel K. Benjamin and Roger LeRoy Miller in their book *Undoing Drugs: Beyond Legalization.*[7] They point out that there is a precedent for a new way of solving the drug problem. It is contained in Section 2 of the Twenty-first Amendment, which repealed Prohibition. That section states that "the transportation or importation into any State, Territory, or possession of the United States for delivery or use therein of intoxicating liquors, in violation of the laws thereof, is hereby prohibited." In other words, the repeal of Prohibition did not make alcoholic beverages legal everywhere in the United States. Rather, they remain illegal in any jurisdiction that continues to have laws against them.

Why not do the same thing with today's illegal drugs? Currently, every state has its own drug laws, which, of course, are influenced by federal legislation. All Congress would have to do, according to Benjamin and Miller, is amend the Comprehensive Drug Abuse Prevention and Control Act of 1970. This amendment would simply take the federal government out of the business of controlling drugs and leave it to the states and their subjurisdictions. The federal government still would be available to help states when requested to do so. It would still make sure that federal laws with respect to taxation were followed, much as it does today with federal excise taxes on beer, wine, and liquor.

---

[6]*National Law Journal,* December 8, 1997, p. A8.
[7]New York: Basic Books, 1993.

Benjamin and Miller predict that under their constitutional alternative, different states would undertake different ways of solving their drug problems, depending on the wishes of their electorates. Some states might devote resources to education and rehabilitation, whereas others might stress incarceration. Individuals would have the option of "voting with their feet"; they could move to those jurisdictions that have the right combination.

In essence, the Benjamin and Miller proposal is an argument in favor of federalism and devolution. The proposal suggests that the states assume police power over all psychoactive substances, just as they have over all alcoholic beverages.

What Has Caused the Decline in Crime Rates?

There is no question that crime rates have fallen since 1994. In some cities, property crime rates are half of what they were ten years ago. In 1996, reported violent crimes were 13 percent below 1992 levels. An additional 4 percent drop occurred in 1997. The trend line declines even more steeply for murder. From 1993 to 1996, the number of murders dropped by 20 percent, with an additional 9 percent reduction in 1997. In that year, Los Angeles reported the fewest murders in twenty years, and Boston had the fewest murders in thirty-six years.

Some argue that the cause for this decline in crime rates is the booming economy the United States has enjoyed since about 1993. Others claim that the $3 billion of additional funds the federal government has spent to curb crime in the last few years has led to less crime. Still others argue that an increase in the number of persons who are jailed is responsible for the reduction in crime.

Several quite novel reasons have also been offered for the declining crime rate. As more people use credit cards instead of cash, purse snatchings no longer yield much. Consequently, purse snatchings have declined. With respect to home break-ins, there seems to be a good reason why fewer are being committed: more people are staying at home. Why? The reason is the proliferation of VCRs and cable TV. Additionally, 80 percent of all new homes have closed and locked two-car garages, which protect cars and other frequently stolen items, such as bicycles.

Another reason that fewer home burglaries occur is that what is often found inside does not have much street value. Specifically, robbers used to target high-priced VCRs, stereos, and televisions. Although even more of those items are found in homes today, they are so cheap when purchased new that they have almost no value as a stolen item.

Finally, increases in violent crimes and theft have been strongly correlated with the increases in the use of crack cocaine. The crack crisis has begun to decline in big cities. The number of arrestees testing positive for cocaine has dropped dramatically. Apparently, youths have decided that crack is not cool, according to the National Development and Research Institutes in New York. As proof that crack cocaine and crime are associated, in smaller cities where crack has only recently arrived, violent crime rates are still going up.

Environmental Policy

Human actions may create unwanted side effects—including the destruction of the environment and the ecology (the total pattern of environmental relationships). Every day, humans, through their actions, emit pollutants into the air and the water. Each year, the world atmosphere receives twenty million metric tons of sulfur dioxide, eighteen million metric tons of ozone pollutants, and sixty million metric tons of carbon monoxide.

The Government's Response to Air and Water Pollution

The government has been responding to pollution problems since before the American Revolution, when the Massachusetts Bay Colony issued regulations to try to stop the pollution of Boston Harbor. In the nineteenth century, states passed laws controlling water pollution after scientists and medical researchers convinced most policymakers that dumping sewage into drinking and bathing water caused disease. At the national level, the Federal Water Pollution Control Act of 1948 provided research and assistance to the states for pollution-control efforts, but little was done. In 1952, the first state air-pollution law was passed in Oregon. The federal Air Pollution Control Act of 1955 gave some assistance to states and cities. Table 16–3 describes the major environmental legislation in the United States.

The National Environmental Policy Act. The year 1969 marked the start of the most concerted national government involvement in solving pollution problems. In that year, the conflict between oil exploration interests and environmental interests literally erupted when a Union Oil Company's oil well six miles off the coast of Santa Barbara, California, exploded, releasing 235,000 gallons of crude oil. The result was an oil slick, covering an area of eight hundred square miles, that washed up on the city's beaches and killed plant life, birds, and fish. Hearings in Congress revealed that the Interior Department did not know which way to go in the energy-environment trade-off. Congress did know, however, and passed the National Environmental Policy Act in 1969. This landmark legislation established, among other things, the Council for Environmental Quality. Also, it mandated that an **environmental impact statement (EIS)** be prepared for all major federal actions that significantly affected the quality of the environment. The act gave citizens and public-interest groups concerned with the environment a weapon against the unnecessary and inappropriate use of natural resources by the government.

Environmental Impact Statement (EIS)

As a requirement mandated by the National Environmental Policy Act, a report that must show the costs and benefits of major federal actions that could significantly affect the quality of the environment.

A number of urban areas have a landfill problem. The price of landfill has been going up in many of the major cities for many years. Nationwide, in contrast, the average per-ton price of landfill has gone down. In other words, people in many regions of the United States pay less today to dump their garbage into landfills than they did ten years ago.

The Clean Air Act of 1990.   The most comprehensive government attempt at cleaning up our environment occurred in 1990. After years of lobbying by environmentalists and counterlobbying by industry, the Clean Air Act of 1990 was passed. This act amended the 1970 Clean Air Act, which, among other things, had required a reduction of 90 percent of the amount of carbon monoxide and other pollutants emitted by automobiles. In spite of the fact that an automobile purchased in 1990 emitted only 4 percent of the pollutants that a 1970 model did, there was more overall air pollution—because so many more automobiles were being driven. The urban ground-level ozone was also as great as it was before any clean-air legislation. The 1990 Clean Air Act required automobile manufacturers to cut new automobiles' exhaust emissions of nitrogen oxide by 60 percent and the emission of other pollutants by 35 percent by 1998.

Stationary sources of air pollution were also made subject to more regulation under the 1990 act. To reduce **acid rain,** the act required 110 of the oldest coal-burning power plants in the United States to cut their emissions by 40 percent by the year 2001. Controls were placed on other factories and businesses in an attempt to reduce ground-level ozone pollution in ninety-six cities to healthful levels by 2005 (except in Los Angeles, which has until 2010 to meet the standards). The act also required that the production of chlorofluorocarbons (CFCs) be stopped completely by the year 2002. CFCs are thought to deplete the ozone

Acid Rain
Rain that has picked up pollutants, usually sulfur dioxides, from industrial areas of the earth that are often hundreds of miles distant from where the rain falls.

TABLE 16-3

Major Federal Environmental Legislation

1899 Refuse Act. Made it unlawful to dump refuse into navigable waters without a permit. A 1966 court decision made all industrial wastes subject to this act.

1948 Federal Water Pollution Control Act. Set standards for the treatment of municipal water waste before discharge. Revisions to this act were passed in 1965 and 1967.

1955 Air Pollution Control Act. Authorized federal research programs for air-pollution control.

1963 Clean Air Act. Assisted local and state governments in establishing control programs and coordinated research.

1965 Clean Air Act Amendments. Authorized the establishment of federal standards for automobile exhaust emissions, beginning with 1968 models.

1965 Solid Waste Disposal Act. Provided assistance to local and state governments for control programs and authorized research in this area.

1965 Water Quality Act. Authorized the setting of standards for discharges into waters.

1967 Air Quality Act. Established air-quality regions, with acceptable regional pollution levels. Required local and state governments to implement approved control programs or be subject to federal controls.

1969 National Environmental Policy Act. Established the Council for Environmental Quality (CEQ) for the purpose of coordinating all federal pollution-control programs. Authorized the establishment of the Environmental Protection Agency (EPA) to implement CEQ policies on a case-by-case basis.

1970 Clean Air Act Amendments. Authorized the Environmental Protection Agency to set national air-pollution standards and restricted the discharge of six major pollutants into the lower atmosphere. Automobile manufacturers were required to reduce nitrogen oxide, hydrocarbon, and carbon monoxide emissions by 90 percent (in addition to the 1965 requirements) during the 1970s.

1972 Federal Water Pollution Control Act Amendments. Set national water-quality goal of restoring polluted waters to swimmable, fishable waters by 1983.

1972 Federal Environmental Pesticide Control Act. Required that all pesticides used in interstate commerce be approved and certified as effective for their stated purpose. Required certification that they were harmless to humans, animal life, animal feed, and crops.

1974 Clean Water Act. Originally called the Safe Drinking Water Act, this law set (for the first time) federal standards for water suppliers serving more than twenty-five people, having more than fifteen service connections, or operating more than sixty days a year.

1976 Resource Conservation and Recovery Act. Encouraged the conservation and recovery of resources. Put hazardous waste under government control. Prohibited the opening of new dumping sites. Required that all existing open dumps be closed or upgraded to sanitary landfills by 1983. Set standards for providing technical, financial, and marketing assistance to encourage solid waste management.

1977 Clean Air Act Amendments. Postponed the deadline for automobile emission requirements.

1980 Comprehensive Environmental Response, Compensation, and Liability Act. Established a "Superfund" to clean up toxic waste dumps.

1990 Clean Air Act Amendments. Provided for precise formulas for new gasoline to be burned in the smoggiest cities, further reduction in carbon monoxide and other exhaust emissions in certain areas that still have dangerous ozone levels in the year 2003, and a cap on total emissions of sulfur dioxide from electricity plants. Placed new restrictions on toxic pollutants.

1990 Oil Pollution Act. Established liability for the clean-up of navigable waters after oil-spill disasters.

layer and increase global warming. CFCs are used in air-conditioning and other refrigeration units.

The Costs of Clean Air. Before the mid-1980s, environmental politics seemed to be couched in terms of "them against us." "Them" was everyone involved in businesses that cut down rain forests, poisoned rivers, and created oil spills. "Us" was the government, and it was the government's job to stop "them." Today, particularly in the United States, more people are aware that the battle lines are blurred. According to the Environmental Protection Agency (EPA), we are already spending well over $100 billion annually to comply with federal environmental rules. When the 1990 Clean Air Act is fully implemented, that amount may be as much as 50 percent higher. The government, particularly in Washington, D.C., has become interested in how to solve the nation's environmental problems at the lowest cost. Moreover, U.S. corporations are becoming increasingly engaged in producing recyclable and biodegradable products, as well as pitching in to solve some environmental problems.

Cost concerns clearly were in the minds of the drafters of the Clean Air Act of 1990 when they tackled, for example, the problem of sulfur emissions from electric power plants. Rather than tightening the existing standards, the new law simply limits total sulfur emissions. Companies have a choice of either rebuilding old plants or buying rights to pollute. The result is that polluters have an incentive to not even attempt to deal with exceptionally dirty plants. When closing down such plants, they can sell their pollution rights to those who value them more. The law is straightforward: An electric utility power plant is allowed to emit up to one ton of sulfur dioxide into the air in a given year. If the plant emits one ton of sulfur dioxide, the allowance disappears. If a plant switches to a fuel low in sulfur-dioxide, for example, or installs "scrubbing equipment" that reduces sulfur dioxide, it may end up emitting less than one ton. In this case, it can sell or otherwise trade its unused pollution allowance, or it can bank it for later use.

These rights to pollution allowances are being traded in the marketplace. Indeed, there is a well-established market in "smog futures" offered on the Chicago Board of Trade and the New York Mercantile Exchange. (For a further discussion of this topic, see the feature *Politics and the Environment: The Increasing Use of Tradable Pollution Credits.*)

There Have Been Improvements. The United States is making fairly substantial strides in the war on toxic emissions. From 1988 to 1994, the latest years for which we have data, the Environmental Protection Agency showed that the volume of chemicals released into the environment declined 37 percent. In 1988, annual toxic emissions totaled 4.848 billion pounds, and in 1994, they totaled only 3.047 billion pounds. One reason for these successes is the increased awareness of the American public of the need for environmental protection. To a large extent, this increased awareness has been brought about through the efforts of various environmental interest groups, which have also exerted pressure on Congress to take action. (If you would like to influence environmental policy, you can contact one of the environmental interest groups listed in the chapter-ending feature *Toward Active Citizenship.*)

Regulating Hazardous Waste: Superfund

In 1980, Congress passed the Comprehensive Environmental Response, Compensation, and Liability Act (CERCLA), commonly known as Superfund. The basic purpose of Superfund, which was amended in 1986 by the Superfund Amendments and Reauthorization Act, is to regulate the clean-up of leaking

POLITICS and the Environment

The Increasing Use of Tradable Pollution Credits

The Clean Air Act of 1990 allowed for open-market trading of pollution credits, and since then tradable pollution credits have become the centerpiece of federal government antipollution policy. Indeed, at the 1997 Conference on Global Warming in Kyoto, Japan, the United States stood firm about its demands—any global agreement had to include a trading scheme that would let countries buy and sell the right to pollute. Many who were attending the meeting voiced concerns that such trading would enable the richer countries to buy their way out of any commitment to reduce green-house gases. As a compromise, the Kyoto protocol allows for limited emissions trading among developed countries only. The details have yet to be ironed out.

Some political commentators, including Harvard government professor Michael J. Sandel, object to emissions trading because it removes the moral stigma that should be associated with generating pollution.* Sandel finds it reprehensible that the purchase price of pollution credits becomes just another cost

*Michael J. Sandel, *Liberalism and the Limits of Justice*, 2d ed. (New York: Cambridge University Press, 1998).

of doing business. He also believes that allowing emissions trading among countries reduces or eliminates any sense of shared responsibility that increased global cooperation requires.

The concept of tradable credits has been extended to regulations prohibiting the destruction of wetlands as well. Under the 1997 Clean Water Act, a developer normally can fill in designated wetlands (swamps) only if he or she restores acreage of a greater amount to natural wetlands or creates new ones within close proximity. Today, there are wetlands banks. Buyers and sellers of wetlands credits negotiate the price. A bank will sell wetlands credits to developers who need them to build their projects. One wetlands bank, U.S. Wetlands, has an inventory of 1,200 acres of wetlands credits available for sale in three states. These credits do not come cheaply, for the cost of converting scrub land to wetlands ranges from $15,000 to $60,000 per acre.

FOR CRITICAL ANALYSIS

Is pollution of the earth's resources primarily a political, moral, or economic problem?

hazardous waste disposal sites. A special federal fund was created for that purpose. Superfund provides that when a release or a threatened release from a site occurs, the EPA can clean up the site and recover the cost of the clean-up from (1) the person who generated the wastes disposed of at the site, (2) the person who transported the wastes to the site, (3) the person who owned or operated the site at the time of the disposal, or (4) the current owner or operator. Liability is usually assessed on anyone who might have been responsible—for example, a person who generated only a fraction of the hazardous waste disposed of at the site may nevertheless be liable for all of the clean-up costs.

By the late 1990s, less than 10 percent of the designated sites on Superfund's high-priority list had been cleaned up—at a cost of over $11 billion. Critics of the Superfund program point out that only 10 percent of the money spent by insurance companies to settle Superfund claims is used to clean up hazardous materials. According to the Rand Corporation, in Santa Monica, California, the remaining 90 percent goes to legal fees and related costs. Other critics point out that the potential benefits of such expensive toxic waste clean-ups are not worth the cost.

Domestic Policy:
Issues for the New Century

It seems strange that programs to reduce poverty are still on the domestic policy agenda. After all, the federal government started its "war on poverty" back in the early 1960s. By some estimates, we have transferred well over a trillion dollars to eliminate poverty since then. Yet poverty remains a blight on the record of one of the world's richest countries—the United States. Presidential candidate Bill Clinton claimed he would eliminate welfare "as we know it." Although the welfare reform law of 1996 is a step toward that goal, the long-term consequences of that law are unknown. Whether the state-run programs will be more successful in reducing poverty than the federal programs have been is a question for the new century.

The fact that a significant amount of public benefits goes to immigrants, particularly illegal immigrants and political refugees, has linked the domestic policy debate on welfare with the debate on immigration. Although the 1996 Immigration Reform Act authorized actions that will help to curb illegal immigration and reduce welfare spending on immigrants, certain issues—such as emergency medical services and public schooling for the children of immigrants—will continue to spark debate.

An additional domestic policy issue that certainly will continue to challenge policymakers involves crime and violence in the United States. There is little indication that this problem will be solved in the foreseeable future. The attempt to "get tough on crime" creates the further problem of how to pay for the building and maintenance of additional prisons. We probably will see continuing violence among those engaged in the illegal drug trade. No doubt, we also will hear political candidates stress that our high crime rates are a reflection of the breakdown of American values and family structure.

Finally, Congress probably will never remove environmental policy from its domestic policy agenda. Even if the United States miraculously solved many of its environmental problems, there still would be the rest of the world to worry about. Although steps have been taken toward the global coordination of environmental-protection efforts, the practical implementation of global policies remains to be achieved.

TOWARD ACTIVE CITIZENSHIP

WORKING FOR A CLEANER ENVIRONMENT

Energy undoubtedly will be among the more important domestic issues in the coming decades. Ultimately, every energy policy involves environmental questions. Not only is this issue central to our everyday lives, but also, it is argued, the fate of the planet may hang in the balance as today's policymakers make decisions about energy production and environmental protection. To make things more complicated, these parallel struggles of coping with energy problems and preserving our environment tend to work at cross-purposes. In the pursuit of secure and abundant energy, the interests of clean air, water, and land—as well as people—sometimes are sacrificed.

When objectives clash, difficult political trade-offs must be made. To a large group of environmentalists in this country, the choice is clear: if we want to improve or even preserve our quality of life, we must stop environmental degradation.

Environmental groups work on a host of issues, ranging from solar power to mass transit and from wildlife preservation to population control. If you feel strongly about these or other environmental issues and want to get involved, contact the following groups:

Environmental Defense Fund
257 Park Ave. South
New York, NY 10010
800-684-3322
www.edf.org/

National Environmental Policy Institute
1100 17th St. N.W., Suite 330
Washington, DC 20036
202-857-4784
www.nepi.org/

Friends of the Earth
1025 Vermont Ave. N.W., Suite 300
Washington, DC 20005
202-783-7400
www.foe.org/

Greenpeace USA
1436 U St. N.W.
Washington, DC 20009
202-462-1177
www.greenpeaceusa.org/

League of Conservation Voters
1707 L St. N.W., Suite 750
Washington, DC 20036
202-785-8683
www.lcv.org/

National Audubon Society
700 Broadway
New York, NY 10003
212-979-3000
www.audubon.org/nas

National Parks Conservation Association
1776 Massachusetts Ave. N.W., Suite 200
Washington, DC 20036
800-628-7275
www.npca.org/

National Wildlife Federation
8925 Leesburg Pike
Vienna, VA 22184
703-790-7000
www.nwf.org/

Natural Resources Defense Council
1200 New York Ave. N.W., Suite 400
Washington, DC 20005
202-289-6868
www.nrdc.org/

Sierra Club
85 Second St.
San Francisco, CA 94105
415-977-5500
www.sierraclub.org/

Wilderness Society
900 7th St. N.W.
Washington, DC 20006
202-833-2300
www.wilderness.org/

Key terms

acid rain 539

domestic policy 517

earned-income tax credit (EITC)
  program 524

environmental impact statement
  (EIS) 538

food stamps 524

income transfer 522

in-kind subsidy 523

Supplemental Security Income
  (SSI) 524

Temporary Assistance to Needy
  Families (TANF 523

Chapter summary

1 Domestic policy consists of all of the laws, government planning, and government actions that affect the lives of American citizens. Policies are created in response to public problems or public demand for government action. Four major policy problems now facing this nation are poverty and welfare, immigration, crime, and the environment.

2 The policymaking process is initiated when policymakers become aware—through the media or from their constituents—of a problem that needs to be addressed by the legislature and the president. The process of policymaking includes five steps: agenda building, agenda formulation, agenda adoption, agenda implementation, and agenda evaluation. All policy actions necessarily result in both costs and benefits for society.

3 In spite of the wealth of the United States, a significant number of Americans live in poverty or are homeless. The low-income poverty threshold represents an absolute measure of income needed to maintain a specified standard of living as of 1963, with the constant-dollar, or purchasing-power, value increased year by year in relation to the general increase in prices. The official poverty level is based on pretax income, including cash, and does not take into consideration in-kind subsidies (food stamps, housing vouchers, and so on).

4 The United States spends about $900 billion annually on various welfare programs. The 1996 Welfare Reform Act transferred more control over welfare programs to the states, imposed work requirements on welfare recipients, and allowed states to deny welfare benefits to unwed teenage mothers. The reform act has generated a significant amount of controversy, and its critics maintain that it is far from an optimal solution to the welfare problem.

5 Like welfare, immigration has become a controversial issue in recent years. The number of immigrants entering the United States has been rising at a rapid rate during the last several decades, and many maintain that immigration

should be limited. In response to the public backlash against immigrants, particularly illegal immigrants, Congress passed the Immigration Reform Act in 1996. The act increased the number of border patrol agents, imposed sterner penalties for document fraud and immigrant smuggling, authorized an expedited deportation process for illegal aliens, and provided for the establishment of pilot programs to help employers verify the status of job applicants. The act also prohibited immigrants from receiving many forms of public benefits.

6 There is widespread concern in this country over the high rates of violent crime, and particularly, the large number of crimes that are committed by juveniles. While the overall rate of violent crime has been declining since 1995, crime rates continue to rise in certain areas. Drug dealing and drug abusers have contributed significantly not only to escalating crime rates but also to overcrowded prisons. The prison "population bomb" presents a major challenge to today's policymakers.

7 Pollution problems continue to plague the United States and the world. Since the nineteenth century, a number of significant federal acts have been passed in an attempt to curb the pollution of our environment. The National Environmental Policy Act of 1969 established the Council for Environmental Quality. That act also mandated that environmental impact statements be prepared for all legislation or major federal actions that might significantly affect the quality of the environment. Substantial strides have been made in the war on toxic emissions, but the war has not been won. In 1980, Congress passed the Comprehensive Environmental Response, Compensation and Liability Act, commonly known as Superfund, to regulate the clean-up of leaking hazardous waste disposal sites. By the late 1990s, however, only a small percentage of the sites had been cleaned up.

Selected print and electronic resources

SUGGESTED READINGS

Benedick, Richard Elliot. *Ozone Diplomacy: New Directions in Safeguarding the Planet*. Enlarged edition. Cambridge, Mass.: Harvard University Press, 1998. The author, an experienced diplomat, gives an insider's view of some of the international efforts that have been made to address environmental issues.

Harris, Nigel. *The New Untouchables: Immigration and the New World Worker*. New York: St. Martin's Press, 1996. The author looks at the migration of workers from one country to another in the context of a changing world economy. Harris argues that fears of immigration are largely unjustified and that more immigration usually means more jobs and more income for native populations.

Miller, Roger LeRoy, et al. *The Economics of Public Issues*. 10th ed. Reading, Mass.: Addison-Wesley, 1999. Chapters 3, 4, 8, 14–18, and 24–27 are especially useful. The authors use short essays of three to seven pages to explain the purely economic aspects of numerous social problems, including the war on drugs, the environment, and poverty.

Peak, Kenneth J. *Justice Administration: Police, Courts, and Corrections Management*. 2d ed. Englewood Cliffs, N.J.: Prentice-Hall, 1997. The author, an experienced criminal-justice administrator and educator, looks closely at how the three components of the criminal-justice system—police, courts, and corrections—are administered.

MEDIA RESOURCES

America's Promise: Who's Entitled to What?—A four-part series that examines the current state of welfare reform and its impact on immigrant and other populations.

Crimes and Punishments: A History—A controversial documentary that traces the often brutal history of criminal punishment from the medieval era through today.

Young Criminals, Adult Punishment—An ABC program that examines the issue of whether the harsh sentences given out to adult criminals, including capital punishment, should also be applied to young violent offenders.

Logging on

You can find further information on most of the issues discussed in this chapter at Project VoteSmart's Web site. Go to

www.vote-smart.org/issues/

For current statistics on poverty in the United States, go to

www.census.gov/hhes/
www/poverty.html

The National Governors Association offers information on the current status of welfare reform among the various states at

www.nga.org/

The Administration for Children and Families, an agency in the Department of Health and Human Services, also provides access to publications concerning the welfare program:

www.dhhs.gov/news/welfare

The Federal Bureau of Investigation offers information about crime rates at its Web site:

www.fbi.gov

You can also find statistics and other information on crime in the United States at the Web site of the Bureau of Justice Statistics. Go to

www.ojp.usdoj.gov/bjs/

If you are interested in following a case through the criminal-justice system, you can access the Web site "Anatomy of a Murder: A Trip through Our Criminal Justice System" at

tqd.advanced.org/2760/homep.htm

You can find a large online library of materials relating to drug policy at

www.druglibrary.org/

Using the Internet for political analysis

Here's a way to think about environmental issues: Go to the Web site maintained by the Environmental Defense Fund at

www.edf.org/

Review the list of news releases and projects given at this site. Select at least one of these projects and identify the political interests that are involved in that specific environmental problem. Generally, who would be likely to support the policies discussed at this Web site? Which forces would likely oppose them?

chapter **17**

Economic Policy

¿ what if

Social Security Went Bankrupt?

BACKGROUND

OTTO VON BISMARCK, THE FIRST CHAN-CELLOR OF THE UNIFIED GERMANY THAT CAME INTO BEING IN 1861, CRE-ATED THE MODERN SOCIAL INSURANCE STATE. HE INTRODUCED GOVERNMENT TRANSFER PAYMENTS IN ORDER TO MINIMIZE WORKERS' WORRIES ABOUT THE NEW INDUSTRIAL AGE. RELATIVELY SOON THEREAFTER, MOST OF EUROPE ACCEPTED HIS IDEAS. DURING THE DEPTHS OF THE GREAT DEPRESSION IN AMERICA, CONGRESS PASSED THE SOCIAL SECURITY ACT OF 1935—OUR EQUIVALENT OF BISMARCK'S SOCIAL INSURANCE PROGRAM.

WHILE SOCIAL SECURITY WAS NEVER MEANT AS A FULL AND COM-PLETE RETIREMENT PROGRAM, IT HAS BECOME SO OVER THE YEARS FOR MANY SENIOR AMERICANS. AN INCREASING PERCENTAGE OF THE ELDERLY ARE RELYING ON SOCIAL SECURITY AS THEIR MAIN SOURCE OF INCOME AFTER THEY REACH THE AGE OF SIXTY-FIVE.

WHAT IF SOCIAL SECURITY WENT BANKRUPT?

Technically, Social Security can never really go bankrupt, for it is actually a transfer system from the young to the old. Let's assume, though, that the Social Security trust funds were depleted and that Congress refused to use general rev-enues to make payments to the more than forty-five million Americans who currently receive Social Security. There would be both immediate effects and longer-term effects.

DISASTER FOR MANY IN THE SHORT RUN

If Social Security's bankruptcy occurred with relatively little warning, millions of senior citi-zens would find themselves without sufficient income to "make ends meet." This would result in a large increase in the labor force participation rate of those over the age of sixty-five. This increase in the number of Americans seeking employment would certainly lead to an increase in the unemployment rate in the short run, an increase in unemploy-ment compensation payments, and probably a lowering of general wages.

Those seniors who could not find jobs or were too old to work would seek welfare payments. Given that since the Welfare Reform Act of 1996 the states have more control over welfare programs, the states would face an immediate financial crisis. Certainly, the federal govern-ment would have to step in to "save the day." This would increase federal government spending and thus reduce any federal government budget surplus (or increase any deficit) that would have occurred.

THE LONG-RUN EFFECTS OF SUCH A BANKRUPTCY

In the long run, we would see a much different situation. Younger Americans who are now working would plan on receiving retirement benefits only from private pension plans and other savings made during their working lives. The amount of saving in the United States consequently would increase.

Most younger Americans probably would plan on work-ing well into their late sixties and perhaps into their early seventies. Assuming that the American economy continues as it has in the 1990s, this would pose no problem for the labor market. That is to say, in the long run, the unemploy-ment rate should not be affected by the increased size of the labor force. In the last several decades, the economy has added more than thirty million new jobs, although there have been periodic ups and downs in the unemploy-ment rate.

One sector that certainly would benefit in the long run is the financial planning industry. More Americans would start planning for their retirement earlier. Their goal would be to maximize the rate of return on their savings so that they could have more funds available on retirement or so that they could retire earlier than the age currently required to receive Social Security benefits.

FOR CRITICAL ANALYSIS

1. While Social Security's bankruptcy is technically impossible, future retirement payments under the Social Security system undoubtedly will be less generous. How will this affect younger Americans' behavior?

2. How does a private pen-sion plan differ from Social Security?

As you saw in Chapter 16, public policymaking is complicated, and clear-cut answers to public-policy issues seldom are obvious. Nowhere are the principles of public policymaking more obvious than in the area of economic decisions undertaken by the federal government. The president and Congress (and to a growing extent, the judiciary) are faced constantly with questions concerning economic policy. Consider some of them:

1. Should federal income taxes be lowered, given that the federal government no longer has a budget deficit?
2. Should Social Security and Medicare taxes be raised to cover the inevitable growth in the number of recipients for those two programs?
3. Should the Federal Reserve change interest rates to counteract a possible slowing or overheating of the economy?
4. Should Congress restrict imports to improve our balance of trade?

There are no clear-cut answers to such questions. Each policy action carries with it costs and benefits, known as **policy trade-offs.** The costs are typically borne by one group and the benefits enjoyed by another group.

This chapter's opening *What If . . .* described one important federal government policy dilemma—how to handle the increasing demands placed on the Social Security system as our population ages. Whatever policy decision is made with respect to Social Security, some groups will be better off and some groups will be hurt. All economic policymaking generally involves such a dilemma. That is why policymakers do not have an easy task. We start our analysis of economic policymaking with something that affects all of us directly—taxes and subsidies.

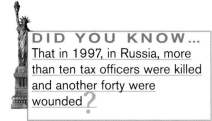
Policy Trade-Offs
The cost to the nation of undertaking any one policy in terms of all of the other policies that could have been undertaken. For example, an increase in the expenditures on one federal program means either a reduction in expenditures on another program or an increase in federal taxes (or the deficit).

The Politics of Taxes and Subsidies

Taxes are not just given to us from above. Rather, they are voted on by members of Congress. Members of Congress also vote on *subsidies,* which are a type of negative taxes that benefit certain businesses and individuals.

We begin our analysis with the premise that in the world of taxes and subsidies, the following is always true: *For every action on the part of the government, there will be a reaction on the part of the public.* Eventually, the government will react with another action, followed by the public's further reaction. The **action-reaction syndrome** is a reality that has plagued government policymakers since the beginning of this nation.

The Tax Code, Tax Rates, and Tax Loopholes

An examination of the Internal Revenue Code, encompassing thousands of pages, thousands of sections, and thousands of subsections, gives some indication that our tax system is not very simple. The 1986 Tax Reform Act was supposed to simplify it somewhat, but once you understand the action-reaction principle of taxation, you can predict that whatever simplification occurred in 1986 will be undone over time.

People are not assessed a lump-sum tax each year; each family does not just pay $1,000 or $10,000 or $20,000. Rather, individuals and businesses pay taxes based on tax rates. (Table 17–1 shows the 1998 tax rates for individuals and married couples.) The higher the tax rate—the action on the part of the government—the greater the public's reaction to that tax rate. Again, it is all a matter of costs and benefits. If the tax rate on all the income you make is 15 percent, that means that any method you can use to reduce your taxable income by one dollar saves you fifteen cents in tax liabilities that you owe the federal government. Therefore, those individuals paying a 15 percent rate have a relatively small incentive to

Action-Reaction Syndrome
For every action on the part of government, there is a reaction on the part of the affected public. Then the government attempts to counter the reaction with another action, which starts the cycle all over again.

TABLE 17-1

1998 Tax Rates for Single Persons and Married Couples

SINGLE PERSONS		MARRIED COUPLES	
MARGINAL TAX BRACKET	MARGINAL TAX RATE	MARGINAL TAX BRACKET	MARGINAL TAX RATE
$0–$23,350	15 %	$0–$42,350	15 %
$25,351–$61,400	28	$42,351–$102,300	28
$61,401–$128,100	31	$102,301–$155,950	31
$128,101–$278,450	36	$155,951–$278,450	36
$278,451 and up	39.6	$278,451 and up	39.6

Loophole

A legal method by which individuals and businesses are allowed to reduce the tax liabilities owed to the government.

avoid paying taxes. But consider individuals who were faced with a tax rate of 94 percent in the 1940s. They had a tremendous incentive to find legal ways to reduce their taxable incomes. For every dollar of income that was somehow deemed nontaxable, these taxpayers would reduce tax liabilities by 94 cents.

So, individuals and corporations facing high tax rates will always react by making concerted attempts to get Congress to add **loopholes** to the tax law that allow them to reduce their taxable incomes. When the Internal Revenue Code imposed very high tax rates on high incomes, it also provided for more loopholes. There were special provisions that enabled investors in oil and gas wells to reduce their taxable incomes. There were loopholes that allowed people to shift income from one year to the next. There were loopholes that allowed individuals to form corporations outside the United States in order to avoid some taxes completely.

These same principles apply to other interest groups. As long as one group of taxpayers sees a specific benefit from getting the law changed and that benefit means a lot of money per individual, the interest group will aggressively support lobbying activities and the election and reelection of members of Congress who will push for special tax loopholes. In other words, if there are enough benefits to be derived from influencing tax legislation, such influence will be exerted by the affected parties. (For a comment by French writer Alexis de Tocqueville on taxes in a democratic system, see the feature *E-Mail Messages from the Past.*)

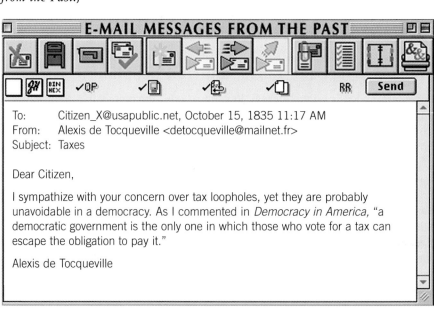

E-MAIL MESSAGES FROM THE PAST

To: Citizen_X@usapublic.net, October 15, 1835 11:17 AM
From: Alexis de Tocqueville <detocqueville@mailnet.fr>
Subject: Taxes

Dear Citizen,

I sympathize with your concern over tax loopholes, yet they are probably unavoidable in a democracy. As I commented in *Democracy in America,* "a democratic government is the only one in which those who vote for a tax can escape the obligation to pay it."

Alexis de Tocqueville

Why We Probably Will Never Have a Truly Simple Tax System

After 1986, the federal tax code was simplified for most people. But astute policymakers then predicted that it would not stay simple for long. The federal government was running large deficits in the late 1980s, and these continued until the late 1990s. When faced with the proposition of having to cut the growth of federal government spending, Congress balked. Instead, it raised tax rates. This occurred under the Bush administration in 1990 and under the Clinton administration in 1993. Indeed, at the upper end of income earners, the tax rate paid on each extra dollar earned went up from 28 percent, based on the 1986 tax reform act, to 39.6 percent after the 1993 tax bill passed. That is an increase in the effective tax rate of 41.4 percent.

In response, the action-reaction syndrome certainly went into effect. As tax rates went up, those who were affected spent more time and effort to get Congress to legislate special exceptions, exemptions, loopholes, and the like, so that the *full* impact of such tax-rate increases would not be felt by richer Americans. As a result, the U.S. tax code became as complex as, or more complicated than, it was before the Tax Reform Act of 1986. The tax code also continues to get longer. In 1997 alone, 832 pages were added to the code, which by that time had already grown to 9,400 pages in length.

The Underground Economy

Those who face higher federal income tax rates also have sought relief in the underground economy. The **underground economy** consists of individuals who work for cash payments without paying any taxes. (It also consists of individuals who engage in illegal activities, such as prostitution and drug trafficking.) As tax rates increase, individuals find a greater incentive to work "off the books."

The question, of course, is how big the underground economy is. If it is small, it is not a serious problem. Various researchers have come up with different estimates as to the size of the U.S. underground economy. These estimates range from 5 to 15 percent of total national income each year. This means that the underground economy in the United States represents anywhere from $400 billion to $1.2 trillion a year. (See Table 17–2 for estimates of the percentage of services supplied by the underground economy.) The extent of the underground economy is estimated to be even greater in some other countries. (See this chapter's feature on the next page entitled *Politics and Comparative Systems: The Worldwide Underground Economy.*)

Underground Economy
The part of the economy that does not pay taxes and so is not directly measured by government statisticians; also called the *subterranean economy* or *unreported economy.*

TABLE 17-2

Estimated Percentage of Services Supplied by the Underground Economy in the United States

Lawn maintenance	90%
Domestic help	83%
Child care	49%
Home improvements/repairs	34%
Sewing and laundry services	25%
Appliance repairs	17%
Car repairs	13%

SOURCE: U.S. Department of Labor; and the University of Michigan Institute for Social Research.

POLITICS and Comparative Systems

The Worldwide Underground Economy

As a rule, the higher the taxation rate, the bigger the underground economy (the part of the economy that does not pay taxes) will be. A country such as the United States has a smaller underground economy than Greece and Italy, where taxes are higher and hiring-and-firing laws are stricter. Both workers and employers alike have a greater incentive to go "underground."

FOR CRITICAL

ANALYSIS

Does it appear from the accompanying graph that the United States has a problem with the underground economy?

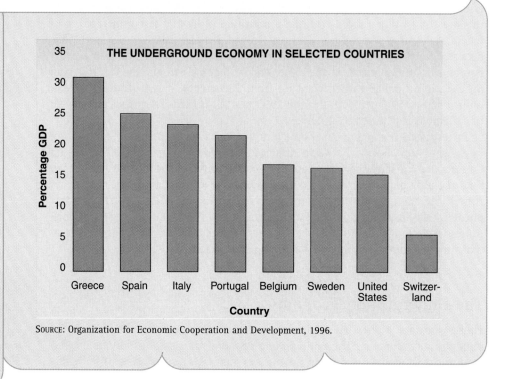

THE UNDERGROUND ECONOMY IN SELECTED COUNTRIES

Percentage GDP

Greece Spain Italy Portugal Belgium Sweden United States Switzerland

Country

SOURCE: Organization for Economic Cooperation and Development, 1996.

Social Security: How Long Will It Last?

Closely related to the question of taxes in the United States is the viability of the Social Security system, which we discussed in this chapter's *What If . . .* feature. Social Security taxes came into existence when the Federal Insurance Contribution Act (FICA) was passed in 1935. When the FICA tax was first levied, it was 1 percent of earnings up to $3,000. By 1963, the percentage rate had increased to 3.625 percent. As of 1998, a 6.2 percent rate was imposed on each employee's wages up to a maximum of $68,400 to pay for Social Security. In addition, employers must pay in ("contribute") an equal percentage. Also, there is a combined employer/employee 2.9 percent tax rate assessed for Medicare on all wage income, with no upper limit.

Social Security Is a Regressive Tax

Regressive Tax
A tax system in which tax rates go down as income goes up.

When people with higher incomes pay lower tax rates than people with lower incomes, we call it a **regressive tax.** Social Security taxes are regressive, because once individuals' incomes exceed the maximum taxable amount, they pay no more Social Security taxes. The Medicare portion of the FICA tax is no longer regressive, because it applies to all wage income, but the Social Security portion remains regressive. A person earning a million dollars in a year pays the same total Social Security taxes as a person earning $68,400.

The Grim Future of the Social Security System

In 1996, Senator Bob Kerrey (D., Neb.) stated that "we are damning our children to a very grim future if we continue to hide our heads in the sand." He was referring to the projected bankruptcy of the Social Security system sometime around the year 2010. After that date, Social Security taxes will have to be raised, Social Security benefits will have to be dramatically curtailed, or spending on other federal programs will have to be reduced. Medicare appears to be in even worse shape. As the number of Americans aged sixty-five and older increases from about thirty-three million today to forty million in the year 2010, and to seventy million in the year 2030, Medicare expenditures as a percentage of total national income are expected to grow dramatically, as can be seen in Figure 17–1.

The Real Problem

The real problem with the Social Security system is that people who pay into Social Security think that they are actually paying into a fund, perhaps with their name on it. This is what you do when you pay into a private pension plan. It is not the case, however, with the federal Social Security system. That system is basically a pay-as-you-go transfer system in which those who are working are paying benefits to those who are retired.

Currently, the number of people who are working relative to the number of people who are retiring is declining. Therefore, those who work will continue to have to pay more of their incomes in Social Security taxes in order to pay for the benefits of those who retire. In the year 2025, when the retirement of the Baby Boomer generation is complete, benefits are projected to cost almost 23 percent of taxable payroll income in the economy. Today this figure is only 14 percent. In today's dollars, that amounts to more than a trillion dollars of additional taxes annually.

As long as Congress continues to increase Social Security benefits while at the same time the labor force grows less rapidly than the number of retirees, financial strain will plague the Social Security system. Social Security also will continue to be a political issue, as well as a focal point of lobbying efforts, particularly by groups that represent older Americans.

Thinking the Unthinkable—Privatizing Social Security

Numerous proposals have been made to privatize the Social Security system. Senators Bob Kerrey (D., Neb.) and Daniel Patrick Moynihan (D., N.Y.) have come up with a compromise solution to full privatization. They want to allow individuals to take a portion—2 percentage points—of their Social Security payroll tax and invest it in stocks and bonds to build their own retirement plan. These senators point out that the typical American family of four earning $36,000 a year currently pays about twice as much in Social Security payroll taxes ($5,508) as it does in income taxes ($2,705). These senators want to reduce the payroll tax, which, as we pointed out before, is a regressive tax on labor. Given that almost 50 percent of all Americans already own some form of stocks, Americans should not have much difficulty investing part of their Social Security payroll taxes.

Politically, the Kerrey-Moynihan concept of partial privatization has been attacked by a number of groups. Those on the left of the political spectrum argue that many Americans would mismanage their additional after-tax income and not invest wisely. Indeed, several Democrats in the House of Representatives want the opposite: they have argued that the way to keep Social Security working is to *increase* the Social Security payroll tax.

Senator Kerrey points out that politicians in general are against the partial privatization of Social Security because it reduces the public's dependence on

INFOTRAC®
COLLEGE EDITION

"Genuine Social Security Reforms Appear Surprisingly Likely"

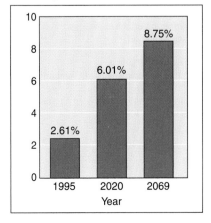

FIGURE 17–1

Medicare Expenditures as a Percentage of Total National Income

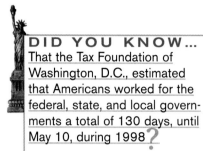

government. He believes, however, that after twenty or thirty years of building private Social Security assets, voters would become an investor class less dependent on politicians who write checks and more dependent on policies that create economic growth.

Regardless of how the Social Security problem is solved, it must be solved—because there is no way to stop the aging of the population. An even worse situation is awaiting Europeans—see the feature *Politics and Comparative Systems: Social Security Is Really in Trouble in Europe.*

The Politics of Fiscal and Monetary Policy

Fiscal Policy
The use of changes in government spending or taxation to alter national economic variables, such as the rate of unemployment.

Monetary Policy
The use of changes in the amount of money in circulation to alter credit markets, employment, and the rate of inflation.

Changes in the tax code sometimes form part of an overall fiscal policy change. **Fiscal policy** is defined as the use of changes in government expenditures and taxes to alter national economic variables, such as the rate of inflation, the rate of unemployment, the level of interest rates, and the rate of economic growth. The federal government also controls **monetary policy,** defined as the use of changes in the amount of money in circulation so as to affect interest rates, credit markets, the rate of inflation, and employment. Fiscal policy is the domain of Congress and the president. Monetary policy, as we shall see, is much less under the control of Congress and the president, because the monetary authority in the United States, the Federal Reserve System, or the Fed, is an independent agency not directly controlled by either Congress or the president.

Fiscal Policy: Theory and Reality

The theory behind fiscal policy changes is relatively straightforward: When the economy is going into a recession (a period of rising unemployment), the federal

POLITICS and Comparative Systems

Social Security Is Really in Trouble in Europe

While many Americans rely on Social Security for their retirement, most Americans also receive private pension funds that have accumulated during their working years, either through their employers or through individual investments—or a combination of the two. In contrast, in most European countries almost 100 percent of all retirement plans are paid for by the government. Very few Europeans (or Japanese, for that matter) have their own, independently arranged retirement plans.

Now consider the grim reality of the aging European (and Japanese) population. Look at the accompanying figure, which indicates the estimated percentage of the population over the age of sixty-five in the United States and other countries in the years 2010 and 2030.

What do these numbers mean? Consider one country—France. In the year 2015, France will have only two workers working and contributing taxes for each retiree. By the year 2030, a mere thirty million French workers will be expected to finance all of the pensions for almost nineteen million retirees. The situation will be worse in Germany and Japan.

Ironically, at a time when many European countries face an increasingly difficult Social Security situation, their citizens are demanding earlier retirement. When French railroad workers went on strike not too long ago, their main grievance was their desire to maintain a retirement age of fifty. This low retirement age was instituted during a period when trains ran on coal and

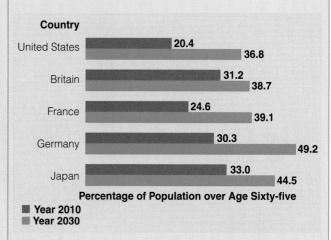

Percentage of Population over Age Sixty-five
- Year 2010
- Year 2030

those who worked in the locomotives often died before age fifty-five. Now the life expectancy of a fifty-year-old person is eighty-five years.

FOR CRITICAL ANALYSIS

With any type of "pay-as-you-go" Social Security system, an aging population spells disaster. If such a system is kept in place, how can problems be avoided as the population ages?

---

government should stimulate economic activity by increasing government expenditures, by decreasing taxes, or both. When the economy is becoming overheated with rapid increases in employment and rising prices (a condition of inflation), fiscal policy should become contractionary, reducing government expenditures and increasing taxes. That particular view of fiscal policy was first implemented in the 1930s and again became popular during the 1960s. It was an outgrowth of the economic theories of the English economist John Maynard Keynes. Keynes's ideas, published during the Great Depression of the 1930s, influenced the economic policymakers guiding President Franklin D. Roosevelt's New Deal.

Keynes believed that the forces of supply and demand operated too slowly in a serious recession and that government should step in to stimulate the economy. Such actions thus are guided by **Keynesian economics.** Keynesian economists believe, for example, that the Great Depression resulted from a serious imbalance in the economy. The public was saving more than usual, and businesses were investing less than usual. According to Keynesian theory, at the beginning of the depression, the government should have filled the gap that was created when businesses began limiting their investments. The government could have done so by increasing government spending or cutting taxes.

Keynesian Economics
An economic theory, named after English economist John Maynard Keynes, that gained prominence during the Great Depression of the 1930s. It is typically associated with the use of fiscal policy to alter national economic variables—for example, increased government spending during times of economic downturns.

Wall Street during the stock market crash of 1929. Another spectacular drop in the stock market occurred in October of 1987. Stock prices tumbled yet again in the fall of 1998.

Monetary Policy: Politics and Reality

The theory behind monetary policy, like that behind fiscal policy, is relatively straightforward. In periods of recession and high unemployment, we should stimulate the economy by expanding the rate of growth of the money supply. (The money supply is defined loosely as checking account balances and currency–see the feature *Politics Wired: Monetary Policy in the Age of Cybermoney* for a discussion of how "e-cash" presents a challenge to monetary policymakers.) An easy-money policy is supposed to lower interest rates and induce consumers to spend more and producers to invest more. With rising inflation, we should do the reverse: reduce the rate of growth of the amount of money in circulation. Interest rates should rise, choking off some consumer spending and some business investment. But the world is never so simple as the theory we use to explain it. If the nation experiences stagflation–rising inflation *and* rising unemployment–expansionary monetary policy (expanding the rate of growth of the money supply) will lead to even more inflation. Ultimately, the more money there is in circulation, the higher prices will be–there will be inflation.

The Monetary Authority–The Federal Reserve System.   Congress established our modern central bank, the Federal Reserve System, in 1913. It is governed by a board of governors consisting of seven members, including the very powerful chairperson. All of the governors, including the chairperson, are nominated by the president and approved by the Senate. Their appointments are for fourteen years.

Through the Federal Reserve System, called the Fed, and its **Federal Open Market Committee (FOMC)**, decisions about monetary policy are made eight times a year. The Board of Governors of the Federal Reserve System is independent. The president can attempt to convince the board, and Congress can threaten to merge the Fed with the Treasury, but as long as the Fed retains its independence, its chairperson and governors can do what they please. Hence, talking about "the president's monetary policy" or "Congress's monetary policy" is inaccurate. To be sure, the Fed has, on occasion, yielded to presidential pressure, and for a while the Fed's chairperson felt constrained to follow a congressional resolution requiring him to report monetary targets over each six-month period.

Federal Open Market Committee (FOMC)
The most important body within the Federal Reserve System. The FOMC decides how monetary policy should be carried out by the Federal Reserve System.

INFOTRAC ®
COLLEGE EDITION

"Who Needs the Fed"

But now, more than ever before, the Fed remains one of the truly independent sources of economic power in the government.

Monetary Policy and Lags.   Monetary policy does not suffer from the same lengthy time lags as fiscal policy does, because the Fed can, within a very short period, put its policy into effect. Nonetheless, researchers have estimated that it takes almost fourteen months for a change in monetary policy to become effective, measured from the time the economy either slows down or speeds up too much to the time the economy feels the policy change.[1] This means that by the time monetary policy goes into effect, a different policy might be appropriate.

---

[1]Robert Gordon, *Macroeconomics*, 7th ed. (New York: HarperCollins, 1996), p. 431.

POLITICS W I R E D
Monetary Policy in the Age of Cybermoney

Two British banks, National Westminster and Midland, started a plastic and silicone cash substitute called Mondex. Mondex cards are like ATM cards but carry a computer chip inside that allows consumers to use what is called *data money*. Bank customers can get data money into their cards over the phone, providing they have a "smart phone" in their home. Mondex is the beginning of the truly cashless society, but banks still play a large role.

Now there is e-money, too, which is often called digital cash. Companies other than banks have already started their own forms of electronic money, called e-cash. E-cash moves about completely outside the network of banks, checks, and paper currency. Some of the companies in the e-cash game, such as Microsoft and Xerox, are well known; others, such as CyberCash and DigiCash, are less well known. Perhaps e-cash's biggest play will be on the Internet, where electronic

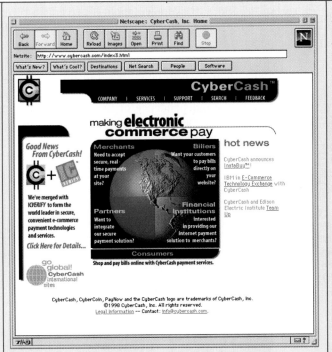

commerce is growing daily. People will be able to download money to their PCs or to palm-sized electronic wallets. People will be able to zap money to Internet merchants.

With the growth of e-cash, the traditional definition of money will certainly no longer hold. The Federal Reserve will have even less ability to control the money supply. Furthermore, e-cash may create problems if it is

stored in computer systems. What if the systems crash? Additionally, electronic counterfeiting may be a serious problem. Computer hackers who break into e-cash systems might be able to steal money from thousands or even hundreds of thousands of people all at once. Finally, e-cash may allow for an increased amount of tax evasion and money laundering.

Clearly, the concept of digital money roaming the globe at the speed of light does not bode well for the future of effective monetary policy in the United States or elsewhere. It will be difficult for our Federal Reserve System to have any control over the flows of digitally created cybermoney.

FOR CRITICAL ANALYSIS

Why should it matter whether the Federal Reserve System can or cannot regulate e-cash?

The Fed's Record.   Federal Reserve monetary policy, in principle, is supposed to be countercyclical. The economy goes through so-called business cycles, made up of recessions (and sometimes depressions) when unemployment is high, and boom times when unemployment is low and businesses are straining capacity. For the Fed to "ride against the wind," it must create policies that go counter to business activity. Researchers examining the evidence since 1914 have uniformly concluded that, on average, the Fed's policy has turned out to be pro-cyclical. That is, by the time the Fed started pumping money into the economy, it was time to do the opposite; by the time the Fed started reducing the rate of growth of the money supply, it was time for it to start increasing it. Perhaps the Fed's biggest pro-cyclical blunder occurred during the Great Depression. Many economists believe that what would have been a severe recession turned into the Great Depression in the 1930s because the Fed's action resulted in almost a one-third decrease in the amount of money in circulation. It has also been argued that the rapid inflation experienced in the 1970s was in part the result of the Fed's increasing the rate of growth of the money supply too much.

In addition, some observers of Federal Reserve policy claim that former head of the Fed Paul Volcker created one of the worst recessions since the Great Depression in 1981–1982, when he caused the Fed to engage in an extremely restrictive monetary policy. Others argue that he needed to do so to "break inflation's back." In fact, inflation did slow down to almost zero during the middle of the 1980s. It averaged about 4 percent in the early 1990s.

In the 1990s, few commentators have been able to complain about monetary policy. Inflation had almost disappeared by the end of the decade, which also saw the unemployment rate drop to its lowest level in thirty-five years by mid-1998. There used to be criticism of the Fed's actions in the financial press and even from politicians. This is not so today. There used to be discussions of eliminating the independence of the Fed and merging it with the Treasury. This is not so today. There used to be a fear that inflation was always "waiting in the wings." This is also not so today. The only real question is the following: How much longer will low unemployment and low inflation coexist?

Alan Greenspan, the chairman of the Federal Reserve. The Federal Reserve is responsible for our nation's monetary policy. Greenspan is often called to testify before various congressional committees. He finds himself frequently in the "hot seat" if interest rates are rising.

The Public Debt and
the Disappearing Deficit

Until the late 1990s, the federal government had run a deficit—spent more than it received—in every year except two since 1960. Every time a budget deficit occurred, the federal government issued debt instruments in the form of **U.S. Treasury bonds.** The sale of these bonds to corporations, private individuals, pension plans, foreign governments, foreign businesses, and foreign individuals adds to the **public debt,** or **national debt,** defined as the total amount owed by the federal government. Thus, the relationship between the annual federal government budget deficit and the public debt is clear: If the public debt is, say, $4 trillion this year and the federal budget deficit is $150 billion during the year, then at the end of the year the public debt will be $4.15 trillion. Table 17–3 shows what has happened to the net public debt over time.

It would seem that the nation increasingly has been mortgaging its future. But this table does not take into account two important variables: inflation and increases in population. In Figure 17–2, we correct the net public debt for inflation and increases in population. The per capita net public debt in so-called **constant dollars** (dollars corrected for inflation) reached its peak, as you might expect, during World War II and fell steadily thereafter until the mid-1970s. Since then, except for a slight reduction in 1980, it continued to rise until only very recently.

U.S. Treasury Bond
Evidence of debt issued by the federal government; similar to corporate bonds but issued by the U.S. Treasury.

Public Debt, or National Debt
The total amount of debt carried by the federal government.

Constant Dollars
Dollars corrected for inflation; dollars expressed in terms of purchasing power for a given year.

Is the Public Debt a Burden?

We often hear about the burden of the public debt. Some argue that the government eventually is going to go bankrupt, but that, of course, cannot happen. As

TABLE 17-3	
Net Public Debt of the Federal Government	

YEAR	TOTAL (BILLIONS OF CURRENT DOLLARS)
1940	$ 42.7
1945	235.2
1950	219.0
1960	237.2
1970	284.9
1980	709.3
1990	2,410.1
1992	2,998.6
1993	3,247.5
1994	3,432.1
1995	3,603.4
1996	3,747.1
1997	3,900.0
1998	3,870.0
1999	3,840.0*

*Estimate.

SOURCE: U.S. Office of Management and Budget.

FIGURE 17-2

Per Capita Public Debt of the United States in Constant 1992 Dollars

If we correct the public debt for intergovernmental borrowing, the growth in the population, and changes in the price level (inflation), we obtain a graph that shows the per capita net public debt in the United States expressed in constant 1992 dollars. The public debt reached its peak during World War II and then dropped consistently until about 1975. It then grew steadily—until the late 1990s.

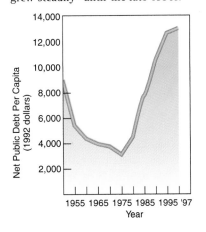

long as the government has the ability to pay the interest payments on the public debt through taxation, it will never go bankrupt. What happens is that when Treasury bonds come due, they are simply "rolled over." That is, if a $1 million Treasury bond comes due today, the U.S. Treasury pays it off and sells another $1 million bond.

What about the interest payments? Interest payments are paid by taxes, so what we are really talking about is taxing some people to pay interest to others who loaned money to the government. This cannot really be called a burden to all of society. There is one hitch, however. Not all of the interest payments are paid to Americans. A significant amount is paid to foreigners, because foreigners own over 38 percent of the public debt. This raises the fear of too much foreign control of U.S. assets. So it is no longer the case that we "owe it all to ourselves."

The Problem of "Crowding Out"

Although it may be true that we owe the public debt to ourselves (except for what is owed to foreigners), another issue is involved. A large public debt is made up of a series of annual federal government budget deficits. Each time the federal government runs a deficit, we know that it must go into the financial marketplace to borrow the money. This process, in which the U.S. Treasury sells U.S. Treasury bonds, is called **public debt financing**. Public debt financing, in effect, "crowds out" private borrowing. Consider that to borrow, say, $100 billion, the federal government must bid for loanable funds in the marketplace, just as any business does. It bids for those loanable funds by offering to pay higher interest rates. Consequently, interest rates are increased when the federal government runs large deficits and borrows money to cover them. Higher interest rates can stifle or slow business investment, which reduces the rate of economic growth. (To see how the U.S. public debt compares with that of other nations, see this chapter's feature entitled *Politics and Comparative Systems: How the U.S. Public Debt Compares with That of Other Nations.*)

Public Debt Financing
The government's spending more than it receives in taxes and paying for the difference by issuing U.S. Treasury bonds, thereby adding to the public debt.

What Happened to the "Permanent" Federal Budget Deficit?

As late as 1997, commentators frequently remarked that the federal budget deficit was a "permanent" part of our economic landscape. They argued that Congress and the president were never able to "spend within their means." Just about every year since the mid-1980s, somebody in Congress introduced a constitutional amendment to balance the federal budget.

A funny thing happened on the way to the forum—the federal budget deficit virtually disappeared by the end of 1998, and the budget actually started to show a surplus. Did this happen because Congress saw evil in its ways and therefore reduced its rate of spending increases? Hardly. Today, federal social spending is at record levels, both in inflation-corrected dollars and as a percentage of gross domestic product (GDP).

Government Spending Has Increased. In the past ten years, federal domestic expenditures, after taking inflation into account, have increased by 35 percent. In the 1960s, nondefense outlays expressed as a percentage of GDP were 10 percent, rising to 15 percent in the 1970s. Today, these expenditures constitute almost 18 percent of GDP. Certainly, the Republicans did not show themselves to be fiscal conservatives after they took control of Congress in 1995. In their first three budgets (for fiscal years 1996 through 1998), they increased domestic

POLITICS and Comparative Systems

How the U.S. Public Debt Compares with That of Other Nations

The U.S. national debt held by the public was estimated to be about $3.8 trillion in 1998, but that number alone does not tell us much. We need to compare the federal debt with a year's annual output in this country (gross domestic product, or GDP). The estimated U.S. GDP for 1998 was over $8 trillion. Therefore, the public debt expressed as a percentage of annual U.S. output was about 45 percent.

To know whether that is comparatively a low or high percentage, we need to compare the U.S. debt as a percentage of annual GDP with that of other industrialized countries. Look at the accompanying table. You will see

that relative to the public debt of most countries in the European Union (EU), the U.S. public debt is comparatively low.

In principle, the United States could catch up with Ireland, Belgium, Italy, and Greece. After all, at the beginning of the 1980s, the debt held by the public amounted to only 25 percent of annual U.S. output. By 1986, the percentage had risen to 40 percent, and it is now 45 percent.

FOR CRITICAL ANALYSIS

Why does the size of the national debt matter?

COUNTRY	NATIONAL DEBT AS A PERCENTAGE OF ANNUAL GDP
Belgium	143
Ireland	109
Italy	109
Greece	101
The Netherlands	85
Portugal	74
Denmark	72
Spain	53
France	49
Great Britain	49
United States	45
Germany	44

SOURCE: European Union, extrapolated from 1995 data.

President Clinton and Vice President Gore meet with congressional leaders to discuss how the federal government should deal with the first budget surplus in nearly three decades. The administration has suggested that the surplus be used to guarantee the Social Security system.

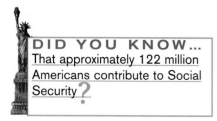

spending by $183 billion, compared to the $155 billion increase in the three years prior to the so-called Republican revolution.

In 1997, the Republicans and Democrats reached a "historic" budget deal with President Clinton's blessing. In inflation-corrected dollars, the $1.7 trillion budget for fiscal year 1999 represented more spending than the federal budgets spent *cumulatively* from 1800 to 1940.

Public perceptions of Republican-dominated congressional actions are often way off the mark. Just consider the Welfare Reform Act discussed in Chapter 16. Widespread press reports indicated that it would lead to a reduction in welfare expenditures. Looked at carefully, though, it allows welfare expenditures to rise under every program.[2] If state welfare expenditures are included, in the last ten years aggregate welfare expenditures have doubled from $190 billion to $405 billion. By 1993, aggregate government welfare expenditures exceeded total spending on national defense.

Obviously, if spending has not decreased, there is only one way to reduce or avoid a federal budget deficit—through increased taxes. That is exactly what has happened. Look at Figure 17–3. There you see that taxpayers, on average, are paying more out of their family budgets to both federal and state and local governments than ever before. Looked at from another point of view, the federal government is now collecting over 20 percent of annual GDP as taxes. This figure was matched only one time before in the history of the United States—during the height of World War II.

What to Do with the Surplus?   Politicians in Washington are now faced with a new problem—what to do with budget surpluses. In the short run, both Republicans and Democrats went on a feeding frenzy and passed a $200 billion highway transportation bill. That bill was filled with so much "pork" that it was an embarrassment to both parties. It passed nevertheless. President Clinton argued that taxes should not be lowered and that any surplus should be used to "shore up the Social Security system."

The reality is that whatever surplus occurs will not last forever. As we pointed out before, Social Security and Medicare payments are growing at an alarming rate, due for the most part to the aging of the U.S. population. Currently, Social Security and Medicare payments constitute a significant percentage of the total federal budget. As this percentage rises, if other domestic programs are not reduced, new federal budget deficits are a certainty.

FIGURE 17–3

The Budget Is Balanced through Higher Taxes

In the last three decades, the "tax bite" for the typical family budget has increased steadily.

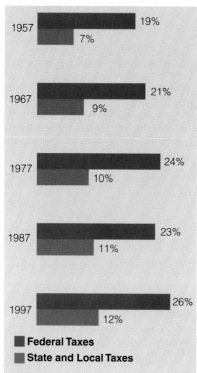

Federal Taxes

State and Local Taxes

SOURCE: The Tax Foundation, based on a 1997 study using data collected by the Internal Revenue Service, the Department of Commerce, and the U.S. Census Bureau.

Freer World Trade and the World Trade Organization

At the close of World War II, the United States was clearly the most powerful and influential nation on earth. Japan, Europe, and the Soviet Union were all in shambles. From the end of the war through most of the 1960s, America retained its economic hegemony. Over the next twenty-five years, however, U.S. dominance in the global marketplace was challenged. Japan rose from its wartime defeat to become one of the top world economic powers. Some of its Pacific Rim neighbors—Taiwan, Hong Kong, Singapore, Malaysia, and Thailand—also started to catch up.

On the other side of the world, the fifteen countries of the former European Community (EC) became one consumer market—the European Union, or EU—on December 31, 1992. For the first time in more than a hundred years, the U.S. economy slipped to second place, behind the 360-million-consumer economy of

[2]Senate Republican Policy Committee, "The Balanced Budget Reconciliation Bill," November 7, 1995.

the EU. Adding to the EU's formidable economic power is the untapped low-cost labor that is available from the former republics of the Soviet Union and from Eastern Europe, plus, of course, Latin America.

America's Current Competitive Position

It was very fashionable in the 1980s and even for much of the 1990s to argue that America had lost its competitive edge in the world economy. Numerous reports showed that we were lagging behind European countries and particularly Asian countries—such as Japan, Indonesia, Malaysia, Thailand, Hong Kong, South Korea, and Taiwan. Today, one rarely reads anything about problems with America's global competitiveness. Why? The reason is that the Asian economies went into near collapse in the late 1990s, and Europe has been stagnating. At the same time, the U.S. economy has been booming—millions of jobs have been added every year, the unemployment rate has dropped to low levels, and we are living in an era without much inflation. The economy is so strong that the United States has to import skilled laborers from other countries, particularly for the information-technology sector. (Whether our economy has been "globalized" is the topic of this chapter's *Critical Perspective* beginning on page 564.)

It is true that the United States still faces a deficit in its balance of trade. Indeed, because of failing Asian economies, the U.S. trade deficit reached record levels in 1998. But that does not mean that America has lost its global competitiveness—far from it. It simply means that the rest of the world wants to invest here. A few short years ago, only 15 percent of the net U.S. public debt was owned by foreigners, while today it is approaching 40 percent. Asians, particularly in Japan, find U.S. interest rates attractive and want to invest in our government and corporate bonds. They also want to buy real estate in the United States and stocks in U.S. companies. For every dollar of capital that foreigners invest in the United States, there has to be a dollar of trade deficit, for that is an accounting-identity requirement.

In any event, the United States remains the premier world economic power, although this position should not be taken for granted. Many countries have been economic powerhouses, only to find themselves years later way down on the ladder of developed countries.

A scene from Jakarta, Indonesia, during riots precipitated by the disastrous economic situation in 1998. Many Asian countries suffered a dramatic decline in their well-being during this period.

Critical perspective

The Global Economy: Facts and Fallacies

The term *globalization* has been used so much that almost everyone accepts globalization as a fact. After all, superfast worldwide telecommunications, the Internet, the opening of the closed economies of the former Soviet Union and its satellites, and other events all have meant that the United States no longer stands alone. For the moment, the United States is again the most powerful economic nation on earth. When the economies of Southeast Asia get back on their feet, though, this country will face an increasingly competitive global environment. In any event, the single currency (euro) market in the European Union will continue to become an important global force, requiring American companies to become more efficient.

A Voice from the Wilderness

Not all observers of the domestic and global economic scene agree that the American economy has become more globalized. According to Paul R. Krugman, an economics professor at the Massachusetts Institute of Technology, "It is a late twentieth-century conceit that we invented the global economy just yesterday."* He discovered, for example, that one hundred years ago Chicago meat packers were more acutely aware of their competition with New Zealand than they are today. At the time, railroads converged on Chicago, bringing beef and wheat that were destined for European markets. Those railroads were built with European capital. Additionally, on the eve of World War I (1914–1918), Great Britain's overseas investments were larger than its domestic investments. Krugman points out that since then, this record has never been matched by a major country.

Krugman further discovered that one hundred years ago, the chemical companies that provided Chicago residents with dyes for their fabrics and aspirin for their headaches were primarily multinational corporations headquartered in Germany. Although at that time international money transfers took a few hours instead of a split second to complete, the more serious substance of economic affairs was just as global as it is today, if not more so.

World Trade, Past and Present

World trade as a share of total world production was greater in 1913 than it was in any year until 1970. The flow of money capital around the world constituted a larger share of world savings prior to World War I than it does today. Additionally, people migrated internationally to a far greater extent prior to World War I than they have ever since.

Let's just consider the actual percentage of their income that Americans spend on imports. Today, that percentage is about 11 percent. In 1890, the corresponding figure was about 8 percent. How can this be, given that trade is so much more open today, we have cheaper modern transportation, and the communications revolution has made it possible for any one good to be manufactured in a series of steps throughout many countries? Taiwanese workers take an American microprocessor, wire it up to a disc drive made in Singapore, put the whole thing in a case made in China, and then ship it back to America. It is true that we ship manufactured goods back and forth around the world as never before—*but manufactured goods constitute a shrinking share of the things that we buy.* Since 1970, U.S. residents have decreased their spending on manufactured goods from 46 percent to around 40 percent. As a nation, we are buying more health care, entertainment, legal services, travel, restaurant meals, and so on than we did in the past. These are the kinds of services that foreigners cannot sell us very easily.

What about International Competitiveness?

Both within and outside politics, the concern about *international competitiveness* has taken on increasing proportions. There is a common view that we live in a world in which nations, like large corporations, are engaged in fierce competition for global markets. So, according to this logic, the United States competes with Japan in the same way that Pepsi competes with Coca-Cola. The United States is, in effect, in a race for the twenty-first century.

There is a basic problem, though, with the concept of international competitiveness. One can compare two corporations' profitability rates to determine which one is "winning" a competitive race. The less competitive corporation may eventually go out of business. Countries, however, do not "go out of business." They have no well-defined "bottom line." Additionally, Coke and Pepsi are true rivals. Very few of Coca-Cola's sales go to employees of Pepsi and vice versa. Thus, if Coke is successful, Pepsi is less successful.

Such is not the case with major countries, according to those who applaud the trend toward globalization. They argue that each country may sell products that compete with each other, but each

Pop Internationalism (Cambridge, Mass.: MIT Press, 1996).

Critical perspective

The Global Economy: Facts and Fallacies—continued

In Toyko, Japanese brokers trade in international commodities and in world currencies. Because of the speed of communications and the Internet, trading continues around the world long after American markets close.

country also constitutes an export market for other countries and is a supplier of useful imports to other countries. Indeed, this perspective holds that if one part of the world starts doing better economically than another part, the U.S. economy benefits—because that other part of the world simply becomes a larger market for U.S. exports. The argument is that the United States is not worse off because Europe or Asia is getting richer; in fact, the United States is better off.

Others who have examined the pattern of globalization argue that, in reality, corporations simply are trying to reduce their wage costs, reduce employee benefits, and take advantage of cheaper labor and raw materials wherever they can. Critics argue that globalization, far from providing better lives for all of those concerned, seems more likely to disrupt societies and impoverish many people. The ones who are enriched are the few who have the skills and resources to exploit such opportunities for their own advantage.

Global E-Commerce

One thing is certain about globalization: it has been affected by the increasing use of the Internet worldwide. Electronic sales, or e-commerce, are growing not only within the United States but also between countries. The governments of many nations are accepting the idea that e-commerce should not be taxed in order to encourage its growth. If the United States and other governments do not regulate the Internet, we can expect increased competition through e-commerce. This may be particularly true for services, such as finance, banking, and accounting. Already, software programmers in the United States are competing with lower-paid programmers in India and elsewhere, who can send their completed products to the United States in a split second over the Internet.

FOR CRITICAL ANALYSIS

1. Assume that there actually is increased competition from abroad. How could the U.S. economy benefit from this situation?
2. When competition from, say, Alabama causes a job loss in a competing company in Texas, the U.S. Congress normally does not react. If the same job loss occurs from increased competition in, say, Asia, however, the U.S. Congress may react. From a political perspective, what is the difference between these two situations?

Tariff
A tax on imported goods.

Opening Up World Trade—GATT and the WTO

In general, over the last decade the United States has been in the forefront of those trying to ease restrictions on international trade. In particular, the United States had been an active participant in the negotiations for reducing **tariffs** (taxes on imports) as part of the General Agreement on Tariffs and Trade, or GATT.

The origins of a worldwide trade liberalization policy date to 1947, when the initial GATT was signed. Under GATT, countries met periodically to negotiate tariff reductions that are mutually advantageous to all members. The 117 member nations of GATT account for between 85 and 90 percent of all world trade. The latest round of negotiations was called the Uruguay Round, because the meetings were held in Uruguay. The final act of the Uruguay Round was signed by over one hundred representatives in 1994. Starting in 1995, GATT ceased to exist. It was replaced by the World Trade Organization (WTO).

The ratification of the last round of GATT by the United States and the establishment of the WTO will result in a roughly 40 percent cut in tariffs worldwide. Agricultural subsidies will be reduced and eventually eliminated. Protection of patents will be extended worldwide.

The WTO raises serious political issues. Although the WTO has arbitration boards to settle international disputes over trade issues, no country has a veto. Opponents argue that a "vetoless" America will repeatedly be outvoted by the mercantile countries of Western Europe and East Asia. Some citizens' groups have warned that the unelected WTO international trade bureaucrats based in Geneva, Switzerland, might be able to weaken environmental health and consumer safety laws if such laws affect international trade flows. Indeed, some of the critics' worst fears came true in the first ruling ever by the WTO's appellate body in 1996.

Economic Policy: Issues for the New Century

The very nature of the federal government seems to be to engage in economic policymaking, and difficult trade-offs will always be involved. Certainly, the federal government will continue to grapple with questions concerning budget deficits or surpluses.

Political issues will continue to swirl around Social Security. Older Americans will continue to make Social Security a focal point of their lobbying efforts, as they have in the past, and policymakers will continue to consider alternatives to the current system.

The independence of the Federal Reserve System probably will be an issue, also. Many in Congress resent the Fed's ability to alter economic policy without consulting legislators. Debates over the effectiveness of the Fed's policies will never end, because even economists disagree.

If federal income tax rates continue to rise, another debate will become more strident. It will involve questioning whether high federal income tax rates reduce the incentives of individuals and businesses to work, save, and invest.

Certainly, the U.S. economic role in a global economy will continue to be an issue for economic policy. While the United States has become strong in the global marketplace, international trade issues continue to come to the fore. Congress and the president will always take these issues seriously.

TOWARD ACTIVE CITIZENSHIP

THE IMPORTANCE OF GOVERNMENT IN YOUR LIFE

The federal budgetary process is a complex system that has many players. The ultimate test of the effectiveness of the federal budgetary process is how it affects each individual American. One way for you to take stock of how the federal government affects your life is as follows: (1) List what you have as assets (everything that you own). (2) List what you do during the day as activities. Then note the extent to which government is involved in your life—and at what cost. The emphasis should always be on the services that must be paid for, either directly or indirectly.

Consider the following example:

1. Rode bicycle to class—highway usage. How are the highways paid for? Who pays for them?
2. Checked out book from public library. Who paid for that library? Who owns it?
3. Received student loan—a subsidy from the government. Who ultimately paid for it?
4. Went to class. On average, in the United States, taxpayers pay approximately 70 percent of the cost of higher education, and students and their families directly pay only 30 percent.
5. Got groceries. How much of the meat was government inspected?

Where else did government intervene?

Key terms

action-reaction syndrome 549

constant dollars 559

Federal Open Market Committee (FOMC) 556

fiscal policy 554

Keynesian economics 555

loophole 550

monetary policy 554

policy trade-offs 549

public debt, or national debt 559

public debt financing 560

regressive tax 552

tariff 566

underground economy 551

U.S. Treasury bond 559

Chapter summary

1 In the area of taxes and subsidies (negative taxes), policymakers have long had to contend with what is known as the action-reaction syndrome. For every action on the part of the government, there will be a reaction on the part of the public, to which the government will react with another action, to which the public will again react, and so on. In regard to taxes, as a general rule, individuals and corporations that pay the highest tax rates will react to those rates by pressuring Congress into creating exceptions and tax loopholes (loopholes allow high-income earners to reduce their taxable incomes). This action on the part of Congress results in a reaction from another interest group—consisting of those who want the rich to pay more taxes. In response, higher tax rates will be imposed on the rich, and so the cycle continues.

2 Closely related to the question of taxes is the viability of the Social Security system. As the number of people who are working relative to the number of people who are retiring declines, those who work will have to pay more Social Security taxes to pay for the benefits of those who retire.

3 Fiscal policy is the use of changes in government expenditures and taxes to alter national economic variables, such as the rate of inflation or unemployment. Monetary policy is defined as the use of changes in the amount of money in circulation so as to affect interest rates, credit markets, the rate of inflation, and employment. Fiscal policy was made popular by the English economist John Maynard Keynes, whose ideas influenced Franklin D. Roosevelt's New Deal legislation, as well as the fiscal policies of the government during the 1960s.

Keynesian fiscal policy economics usually means increasing government spending during recessionary periods and increasing taxes during inflationary boom periods. The problem with fiscal policy and monetary policy is the lag between the time a problem occurs in the economy and the time when policy changes are actually felt in the economy.

4 Whenever the federal government spends more than it receives, it runs a deficit. The deficit is met by U.S. Treasury borrowing. This adds to the public debt of the federal government. Although the public debt has grown dramatically, when corrected for increases in population and inflation, it fell from the end of World War II to the middle of the 1970s. Since then, it has increased almost to its previous level at the height of World War II. Those who oppose large increases in government spending argue that one effect of the federal deficit is the crowding out of private investment. The federal budget deficit virtually disappeared by 1998, however, and the budget actually showed a surplus.

5 As government spending continues to increase, so do taxes—to pay for the increased spending. Federal taxes, as a percentage of gross domestic product, are now as high as they were during World War II. Due to the aging U.S. population, unless the government reduces spending on other programs, increased spending on Medicare and Social Security probably will lead to further budget deficits.

6 From the end of World War II through the 1960s, the United States dominated the global marketplace. For the next thirty years, however, economic developments in Europe, Japan, and the Pacific Rim countries challenged the economic hegemony of the United States. By the late 1990s, a booming U.S. economy, as well as economic problems in Asian countries and Europe, had strengthened the U.S. competitive position in the world marketplace. The Uruguay Round of the General Agreement on Tariffs and Trade (GATT) reduced tariffs worldwide on manufactured goods and made other areas of world trade more competitive. As of January 1995, GATT ceased to exist and was replaced by the World Trade Organization (WTO). The WTO raises serious political issues, particularly in relation to its dispute-settling authority.

Selected print and electronic resources

SUGGESTED READINGS

Creedy, John. *Fiscal Policy and Social Welfare: An Analysis of Alternative Tax and Transfer Systems.* Brookfield, Vt.: Edward Edgar Publishing Co., 1996. This is an examination of alternative tax and transfer systems and their implications for social welfare and income distribution.

Friedman, Milton, and Walter Heller. *Monetary versus Fiscal Policy.* New York: Norton, 1969. This is a classic presentation of the pros and cons of monetary and fiscal policy given by a noninterventionist (Friedman) and an advocate of federal government intervention in the economy (Heller).

The President's Council of Economic Advisers. *Economic Report of the President.* Washington, D.C.: U.S. Government Printing Office, published annually. This volume contains a wealth of details concerning current monetary and fiscal policy and what is happening to the economy.

Robson, Peter. *The Economics of International Integration.* 4th ed. New York: Routledge, 1998. This revised edition of Robson's classic work addresses the latest developments in the regional integration among nation-states.

Weaver, Carolyn. *The Frayed Social Contract: Why Social Security Is in Trouble and How It Can Be Fixed.* Washington, D.C.: The American Enterprise Institute, 1998. This book offers a candid look at the future of Social Security and examines some possible alternatives.

MEDIA RESOURCES

Protectionism v. Free Trade—A 1994 film produced by the Annenberg Foundation as part of its Inside the Global Economy series; the film includes discussions of protectionist policies, including examples, and who wins and who loses by these policies.

Rollover—A 1981 film starring Jane Fonda as an ex-film star who inherits a multimillion-dollar empire when her husband is mysteriously murdered and Kris Kristofferson as a financial troubleshooter who helps her try to save the company. The film offers an insider's view of the politics of currency crises.

Logging on

You can keep up with actions taken by the Federal Reserve by checking the home page of the Federal Reserve Bank of San Francisco at

www.frbsf.org/

You can obtain information about monetary policy by accessing the home page of the Federal Reserve Bank of Minneapolis at

woodrow.mpls.frb.fed.us/info/policy/

For further information on Social Security, access the Social Security Administration's home page at

www.ssa.gov/SSA_Home.html

For information on the 1997, 1998, and 1999 budgets of the U.S. government, go to

www.gpo.ucop.edu/search/budget97.html

The annual *Economic Report of the President* is online at

www.gpo.ucop.edu/catalog/erp.ct.html

Using the Internet for political analysis

Take your turn at proposing a federal budget, balanced or not. Check out the Web site for the National Budget Simulation at

garnet.berkeley.edu:6997/

Play the game at this Web site, which allows you to simulate budget cuts by categories of spending. You will decide what should be cut and see what difference it makes in the overall budget. This site provides other budget information through the Economic Democracy Information Network.

If you would like more input into the budget, you might access the Web site for the Concord Coalition at

www.concordcoalition.org/

There, you can take part in a poll on what to do with any budget surplus in the coming years.

chapter 18

Foreign and Defense Policy

There Were No Foreign Aid?

BACKGROUND

HOW MUCH DOES THE UNITED STATES SPEND ON FOREIGN AID, AND TO WHICH NATIONS DOES IT GO? FOR FISCAL YEAR 1999, THE UNITED STATES SPENT ABOUT $8 BILLION ON FOREIGN ECONOMIC ASSISTANCE AND ABOUT $6 BILLION FOR SECURITY OR DEFENSE ASSISTANCE. IN ADDITION, THIS NATION SPENT UPWARD OF $10 BILLION ON SUBSCRIPTIONS (PAYMENTS AND CONTRIBUTIONS) TO THE WORLD BANK, THE PEACE CORPS, AND OTHER OVERSEAS PROGRAMS. ALTOGETHER, THE UNITED STATES SPENDS LESS THAN 2 PERCENT OF ITS ANNUAL BUDGET ON SUCH ASSISTANCE—LESS, IN PERCENTAGE TERMS, THAN JAPAN AND SOME OF THE EUROPEAN NATIONS.

WHAT IF THERE WERE NO FOREIGN AID?

What would be the consequences to the United States and to other nations if the United States were to cease all foreign economic assistance? Generally, economic assistance, like the Marshall Plan after World War II, has been provided to nations that need economic grants and loans to stabilize their economies—thus, the aid has been viewed as a means of promoting pro-Western institutions. In some cases, though, aid has been sent to nations that had authoritarian rulers, such as the Philippines under President Ferdinand Marcos (1965–1986), to stabilize their economies. In other cases, American aid helps small businesses start up in very poor nations or provides food assistance where agriculture is weak.

Would these nations become less democratic or their people become even poorer if American aid ceased? It is very hard to answer that question. In some areas, economic development undoubtedly would slow down. In other areas, American aid would be replaced by aid sent by other nations, which then would gain influence within the recipient nation. In many situations, the aid may be reaching more government leaders and their rich friends than poor people, so it might not be missed.

For some programs, such as Food for Peace, a cut in foreign aid would directly affect certain highly specific sectors of the American economy. In the same fashion, many economic assistance grants or loans have "strings attached" that require the money to be spent in the United States on our products, such as steam engines or bulldozers.

THE RISK TO NATIONAL SECURITY

At the end of World War II in 1945, the United States had more than seven thousand overseas bases. Today, it has only a few hundred. Some of the nations in which those bases are located receive military assistance in return. Cutting off foreign aid would mean that the United States would either lose the bases or have to pay another type of compensation to those nations for use of their property.

A far more significant question is what would happen in such nations as South Korea, Israel, Egypt, and the former Soviet republics of Ukraine and Belarus. Consider that American aid helps prop up the government of South Korea. Also, American aid supports the military programs of Israel and Egypt as a condition of their peace. And American aid will help the former Soviet republics decommission their nuclear arms.

Cutting off this stream of foreign military assistance might destabilize several regions in the world. It could lead to wars in those regions or to the emergence of governments that would be less friendly to the United States. This aid is given strictly to keep the peace and protect American interests, although few American citizens are aware of these relationships.

Finally, like foreign economic assistance, military aid often takes the form of loans at low interest that must be spent to buy armaments and training from the United States. It is, in fact, subsidized aid to American manufacturers of weapons, aircraft, and tanks. Without this aid, those industries would lose a great deal of business overseas.

FOR CRITICAL ANALYSIS

1. What are the main benefits that foreign assistance brings to the United States? Could these benefits be obtained in another way?
2. To what extent do you think that American citizens understand the goals of American aid programs?

Americans view a world that is changing so rapidly that their first response can be to turn inward and focus on domestic problems. Presidents and members of Congress also are tempted to pay less attention to foreign affairs in the post–Cold War world. The instability of world politics, however, which has been fueled by the disintegration of the Soviet Union, the rise of ethnic nationalism, the continuing threat of terrorism, and the existence of multiple regional "hot spots," presents serious threats to American security.

Without a guiding theme to foreign policy—confrontation with the Communist states—the creation and implementation of foreign policy and a national security strategy have become much more complex. The United States has lowered defense spending and concentrated on the domestic economy. Without the need to compete with the Soviet Union in different regions of the world, the United States could decide not to become engaged in regional conflicts. It could end foreign aid as a further signal that the United States is looking inward. The chapter-opening *What If . . .* suggests the consequences of cutting off such aid.

The Clinton administration, which has focused on domestic policies, including welfare reform, has been criticized for not developing an equally clearly focused foreign policy. Yet it is certainly not clear what the right policy should be toward Bosnia, Rwanda, Haiti, Pakistan, or North Korea, to name just a few trouble spots. It is clear, however, that in times of crisis, the nation still needs guiding principles for action.

INFOTRAC ®
COLLEGE EDITION

"Tab the U.S. Should Pick Up"

What Is Foreign Policy?

As the cultural, military, and economic interdependence of the nations of the world has increased, it has become even more important for the United States to establish and carry out foreign policies to deal with external situations and to carry out its own national goals. By **foreign policy,** we mean both the goals the government wants to achieve in the world and the techniques and strategies to achieve them. For example, if one national goal is to achieve stability in Eastern Europe and to encourage the formation of pro-American governments there, U.S. foreign policy in that area may be carried out using various techniques, including **diplomacy, economic aid, technical assistance,** or military intervention. Sometimes foreign policies are restricted to statements of goals or ideas, such as helping to end world poverty, whereas at other times foreign policies are comprehensive efforts to achieve particular objectives.

In the United States, the **foreign policy process** usually originates with the president and those agencies that provide advice on foreign policy matters. Foreign policy formulation often is affected by congressional action and national public debate.

National Security Policy

As one aspect of overall foreign policy, **national security policy** is designed primarily to protect the independence and the political integrity of the United States. It concerns itself with the defense of the United States against actual or potential (real or imagined) enemies, domestic or foreign.

U.S. national security policy is based on determinations made by the Department of Defense, the Department of State, and a number of other federal agencies, including the **National Security Council (NSC).** The NSC acts as an advisory body to the president, but it has increasingly become a rival to the State Department in influencing the foreign policy process. This was particularly evident when it was revealed, in November 1986, that the Reagan administration

Foreign Policy
A nation's external goals and the techniques and strategies used to achieve them.

Diplomacy
The total process by which states carry on political relations with each other; settling conflicts among nations by peaceful means.

Economic Aid
Assistance to other nations in the form of grants, loans, or credits to buy the assisting nation's products.

Technical Assistance
The sending of experts with technical skills in agriculture, engineering, or business to aid other nations.

Foreign Policy Process
The steps by which external goals are decided and acted on.

National Security Policy
Foreign and domestic policy designed to protect the independence and political and economic integrity of the United States; policy that is concerned with the safety and defense of the nation.

National Security Council (NSC)
A board created by the 1947 National Security Act to advise the president on matters of national security.

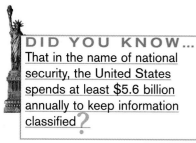

had largely bypassed the Department of State (and Congress) in using the NSC to direct sales of U.S. military equipment to Iran.

Diplomacy

Diplomacy is another aspect of foreign policy. Diplomacy includes all of a nation's external relationships, from routine diplomatic communications to summit meetings among heads of state. More specifically, diplomacy refers to the settling of disputes and conflicts among nations by peaceful methods. Diplomacy is the set of negotiating techniques by which a nation attempts to carry out its foreign policy.

Diplomacy may or may not be successful, depending on the willingness of the parties to negotiate. For example, after years of refusing to negotiate or even recognize each other's existence, Israel and representatives of the Palestine Liberation Organization (the PLO) in 1993 agreed to return control of Jericho and part of the West Bank to the Palestinians. The 1993 agreement left open the possibility of a Palestinian state.

Morality versus Reality in Foreign Policy

From the earliest years of the republic, Americans have felt that their nation had a special destiny. The American experiment in democratic government and capitalism, it was thought, would provide the best possible life for men and women and be a model for other nations. As the United States assumed greater status as a power in world politics, Americans came to believe that the nation's actions on the world stage should be guided by American political and moral principles. As Harry Truman stated, "The United States should take the lead in running the world in the way that it ought to be run."

This view of America's mission has led to the adoption of many foreign policy initiatives that are rooted in **moral idealism**, a philosophy that sees the world as fundamentally benign and other nations as willing to cooperate for the good of all.[1] In this perspective, nations should come together and agree to keep the peace, as President Woodrow Wilson (1913–1921) proposed for the League of Nations. Nations should see the wrong in violating the human rights of ethnic or religious minorities and should work to end such injustice. Many of the foreign policy initiatives taken by the United States have been based on this idealistic view of the world, but few of these actions have been very successful.

The Peace Corps, however, which was created by President John Kennedy in 1961, is one example of an effort to spread American goodwill and technology that has achieved some of its goals. The Clinton administration's actions in 1994 to return the democratically elected president of Haiti to power were rooted partly in moral conviction, although elements within the U.S. government regarded President Jean-Bertrand Aristide as unstable or left-leaning. Foreign policy based on moral imperatives often is unsuccessful because it assumes that other nations agree with American views of morality and politics.

In opposition to the moral perspective is **political realism.** Realists see the world as a dangerous place in which each nation strives for its own survival and interests. Foreign policy decisions must be based on a cold calculation of what is best for the United States without regard for morality. Realists believe that the

Moral Idealism
A philosophy that sees all nations as willing to cooperate and agree on moral standards for conduct.

Political Realism
A philosophy that sees each nation acting principally in its own interest.

---

[1] Charles W. Kegley, Jr., and Eugene Wittkopf, *American Foreign Policy, Pattern and Process,* 3d ed. (New York: St. Martin's Press, 1987), p. 73.

United States must be prepared militarily to defend itself, because all other nations are, by definition, out to improve their own situations. A strong defense will show the world that the United States is willing to protect its interests. The practice of political realism in foreign policy allows the United States to sell weapons to military dictators who will support its policies, to support American business around the globe, and to repel terrorism through the use of force. Political realism leads, for example, to a policy of not negotiating with terrorists who take hostages, because such negotiations simply will lead to the taking of more hostages.

It is important to note that the United States never has been guided by only one of these principles. Instead, both moral idealism and political realism affect foreign policymaking. Sometimes, U.S. policy blends the two, granting aid to a nation that is a major trading partner and then attaching conditions that are rooted in morality to that aid. President Clinton wrestled with the situation in Bosnia to try to find a way for the United States to practice a pragmatic policy based on moral principles. Strongly opposed to using U.S. troops to establish peace in Bosnia, the president tried to convince the warring parties–the Bosnian Serbs and the Bosnian Muslims–to negotiate and accept a cease-fire. Finally, under pressure from the United States, the warring parties hammered out an agreement to divide the territory into ethnic nations. The United States and other NATO nations guaranteed military forces to patrol the new boundaries for a period of time.

Who Makes Foreign Policy?

Is foreign policy made by the president, by the Congress, or by joint executive and congressional action? There is no easy answer to this question, because, as constitutional authority Edwin S. Corwin once observed, the U.S. Constitution created an "invitation to struggle" between the president and Congress for control over the foreign policy process. Let us look first at powers given to the president by the Constitution.

Constitutional Powers of the President

The Constitution confers on the president broad powers that are either explicit or implied in key constitutional provisions. Article II vests the executive power of the government in the president. The presidential oath of office given in Article II, Section 1, requires that the president "solemnly swear" to "preserve, protect and defend the Constitution of the United States."

In addition, and perhaps more important, Article II, Section 2, designates the president as "Commander in Chief of the Army and Navy of the United States." Starting with Abraham Lincoln, all presidents have interpreted this authority dynamically and broadly. Indeed, since the Washington administration, the United States has been involved in at least 125 undeclared wars that were conducted under presidential authority. For example, Harry Truman ordered U.S. armed forces in the Pacific to enter into North Korea's conflict with South Korea. Dwight Eisenhower threatened China and North Korea with nuclear weapons if the Korean peace talks were not successfully concluded. Bill Clinton sent troops to Haiti and Bosnia.

Article II, Section 2, of the Constitution also gives the president the power to make treaties, provided that two-thirds of the senators present concur. Presidents usually have been successful in getting treaties through the Senate. In addition to this formal treaty-making power, the president makes use of executive agreements (discussed in Chapter 13). Since World War II, executive

President Franklin D. Roosevelt signs the declaration of war against Japan on December 8, 1941.

agreements have accounted for almost 95 percent of the understandings reached between the United States and other nations.

Executive agreements have a long and important history. Significant in their long-term effects were the several agreements Franklin Roosevelt reached with the Soviet Union and other countries, especially at Yalta, during World War II. The government of South Vietnam and the government of the United States, particularly under Dwight Eisenhower, John Kennedy, and Lyndon Johnson, made a series of executive agreements in which the United States promised support. All in all, between 1946 and 1998, over eight thousand executive agreements with foreign countries were made. There is no way to get an accurate count, because perhaps as many as several hundred of these agreements have been secret.

An additional power conferred on the president in Article II, Section 2, is the right to appoint ambassadors, other public ministers, and consuls. In Section 3 of that article, the president is given the power to recognize foreign governments through receiving their ambassadors.

Informal Techniques of Presidential Leadership

Other broad sources of presidential power in the U.S. foreign policy process are tradition, precedent, and the president's personality. The president can employ a host of informal techniques that give the White House overwhelming superiority within the government in foreign policy leadership.

First, the president has access to information. More information is available to the president from the Central Intelligence Agency (CIA), the State Department, and the Defense Department than to any other governmental official. This information carries with it the ability to make quick decisions—and that ability is used often.

Second, the president is a legislative leader who can influence the amount of funds that are allocated for different programs. For example, with a large budget deficit and the end of the Cold War, President Clinton proposed large cuts in defense spending.

Third, the president can influence public opinion. President Theodore Roosevelt once made the following statement:

> People used to say to me that I was an astonishingly good politician and divined what the people are going to think. . . . I did not "divine" how the people were going to think; I simply made up my mind what they ought to think and then did my best to get them to think it.[2]

Presidents are without equal in this regard, partly because of their ability to command the media. Depending on their skill in appealing to patriotic sentiment (and sometimes fear), they can make people think that their course in foreign affairs is right and necessary. Public opinion often seems to be impressed by the president's decision to make a national commitment abroad. Presidents normally, although certainly not always, receive the immediate support of the American people when reacting to (or creating) a foreign policy crisis.

Finally, the president can commit the nation morally to a course of action in foreign affairs. Because the president is the head of state and the leader of one of the most powerful nations on earth, once the president has made a commitment for the United States, it is difficult for Congress or anyone else to back down on that commitment.

---

[2]Sidney Warren, *The President as World Leader* (New York: McGraw-Hill, 1964), p. 23.

Other Sources of Foreign Policymaking

There are at least four foreign policymaking sources within the executive branch, in addition to the president. These are (1) the Department of State, (2) the National Security Council, (3) the intelligence community and informational programs, and (4) the Department of Defense.

The Department of State. In principle, the State Department is the executive agency that is most directly concerned with foreign affairs. It supervises U.S. relations with the nearly two hundred independent nations around the world and with the United Nations and other multinational groups, such as the Organization of American States. It staffs embassies and consulates throughout the world. It has more than 24,000 employees. This may sound impressive, but it is small compared with, say, the Department of Health and Human Services with its nearly 60,000 employees. Also, the State Department had an annual operating budget of only $5.7 billion in fiscal year 1999—one of the smallest budgets of the cabinet departments.

Newly elected presidents usually tell the American public that the new secretary of state is the nation's chief foreign policy adviser. Nonetheless, the State Department's preeminence in foreign policy has declined dramatically since World War II. The State Department's image within the White House Executive Office and Congress (and even foreign governments) is quite poor—a slow, plodding, bureaucratic maze of inefficient, indecisive individuals. There is even a story about how Premier Nikita Khrushchev of the Soviet Union urged President John Kennedy to formulate his own views rather than to rely on State Department officials who, according to Khrushchev, "specialized in why something had not worked forty years ago."[3] In any event, since the days of Franklin Roosevelt, the State Department sometimes has been bypassed and often has been ignored when crucial decisions are made.

It is not surprising that the State Department has been overshadowed in foreign policy. It has no natural domestic constituency as does, for example, the Department of Defense, which can call on defense contractors for support. Instead, the State Department has what might be called **negative constituents**— U.S. citizens who openly oppose American foreign policy. One of the State Department's major functions, administering foreign aid, often elicits criticisms. Also, within Congress, the State Department is often looked on as an advocate of unpopular and costly foreign involvement. It is often called "the Department of Bad News."

Negative Constituents
Citizens who openly oppose government foreign policies.

The National Security Council. The job of the National Security Council (NSC), created by the National Security Act of 1947, is to advise the president on the integration of "domestic, foreign, and military policies relating to the national security." Its larger purpose is to provide policy continuity from one administration to the next. As it has turned out, the NSC—consisting of the president, the vice president, the secretaries of state and defense, the director of emergency planning, and often the chairperson of the joint chiefs of staff and the director of the CIA—is used in just about any way the president wants to use it.

The role of national security adviser to the president seems to fit the player. Some advisers have come into conflict with heads of the State Department. Henry A. Kissinger, Nixon's flamboyant and aggressive national security adviser, rapidly gained ascendancy over William Rogers, the secretary of state, in foreign policy. When Jimmy Carter became president he appointed Zbigniew Brzezinski

---

[3]Theodore C. Sorensen, *Kennedy* (New York: Harper & Row, 1965), pp. 554–555.

Intelligence Community
The government agencies that are involved in gathering information about the capabilities and intentions of foreign governments and that engage in activities to further U.S. foreign policy aims.

INFOTRAC®
COLLEGE EDITION

"Critical Deterrent to Bad Actors"

as national security adviser. Brzezinski competed openly with Secretary of State Cyrus Vance (who apparently had little power). In the Clinton administration, neither the national security adviser nor the secretary of state dominated the policy process.

The Intelligence Community. No discussion of foreign policy would be complete without some mention of the **intelligence community.** This consists of the forty or more government agencies or bureaus that are involved in intelligence activities, informational and otherwise. On January 24, 1978, President Carter issued Executive Order 12036, in which he formally defined the official major members of the intelligence community. They are as follows:

1. Central Intelligence Agency (CIA).
2. National Security Agency (NSA).
3. Defense Intelligence Agency (DIA).
4. Offices within the Department of Defense.
5. Bureau of Intelligence and Research in the Department of State.
6. Federal Bureau of Investigation (FBI).
7. Army intelligence.
8. Air Force intelligence.
9. Department of the Treasury.
10. Drug Enforcement Administration (DEA).
11. Department of Energy.

The CIA was created as part of the National Security Act of 1947. The National Security Agency and the Defense Intelligence Agency were created by executive order. Until recently, Congress voted billions of dollars for intelligence activities with little knowledge of how the funds were being used. Intelligence activities consist mostly of overt information gathering, but covert actions also are undertaken. Covert actions, as the name implies, are done secretly, and rarely does the American public find out about them. In the late 1940s and early 1950s, the CIA covertly subsidized anticommunist labor unions in Western Europe. The CIA covertly aided in the overthrow of the Mossadegh regime in Iran, which allowed the restoration of the shah in 1953. The CIA helped to overthrow the Arbenz government of Guatemala in 1954 and apparently was instrumental in destabilizing the Allende government in Chile from 1970 to 1973.

During the mid-1970s, the "dark side" of the CIA was at least partly uncovered when the Senate undertook an investigation of its activities. One of the major findings of the Senate Select Committee on Intelligence was that the CIA had routinely spied on American citizens domestically—supposedly, a strictly prohibited activity. Consequently, the CIA came under the scrutiny of six, and later eight, oversight committees within Congress, which restricted the scope of its activity. By 1980, however, the CIA had regained much of its lost power to engage in covert activities. In the early 1990s, as the relationships with the states of the former Soviet Union eased, the attention of the CIA and other agencies began to turn from military to economic intelligence. During the first Clinton administration, the CIA suffered damage to its reputation when a high-ranking agent, Aldrich Ames, was convicted of spying against the United States. The agency was further embarrassed in 1998 when it failed to detect India's preparations to detonate several nuclear devices. On the heels of that development and Pakistan's subsequent entry into the ranks of nuclear powers, a highly critical report highlighted the CIA's failure to gather intelligence.

The Department of Defense. The Department of Defense (DOD) was created in 1947 to bring all of the various activities of the American military establishment

The Pentagon—a five-sided building—has become the symbol of the Department of Defense. It has six million square feet of floor space and over seventeen miles of corridors.

under the jurisdiction of a single department headed by a civilian secretary of defense. At the same time, the joint chiefs of staff, consisting of the commanders of each of the military branches and a chairperson, was created to formulate a unified military strategy.

Although the Department of Defense is larger than any other federal department, it has declined in size since the fall of the Soviet Union in 1991. In the last ten years, the total number of civilian employees has been reduced by about 300,000, to the current number of 776,000. Military personnel have also been reduced from 2.1 million in 1985 to about 1.4 million today. The defense budget has decreased by about $30 billion since 1990, to $268 billion in 1998. Given the reduced budget and the cut in uniformed personnel, it is more difficult than ever for the Defense Department to maintain a high level of readiness. (For another challenge facing the Defense Department, see the feature *Politics Wired: Attacking Government Computer Systems* on the next page.)

Limiting the President's Power

A new interest in the balance of power between Congress and the president on foreign policy questions developed during the Vietnam War (1964–1975). Sensitive to public frustration over the long and costly war and angry at Richard Nixon for some of his other actions as president, Congress attempted to establish some limits on the power of the president in setting foreign and defense policy. In 1973, Congress passed the War Powers Resolution over President Nixon's veto. The act limited the president's use of troops in military action without congressional approval (see Chapter 13). Most presidents, however, have not interpreted the "consultation" provisions of the act as meaning that Congress should be consulted before military action is taken. Instead, Presidents Ford, Carter, Reagan, Bush, and Clinton ordered troop movements and then informed congressional leaders. Critics note that it is quite possible for a president to commit

POLITICS WIRED

Attacking Government Computer Systems

Although the incidents frequently are not reported in the media, attacks on the government's computer systems occur often and are sometimes extremely successful. During the Persian Gulf War, European computer hackers were able to access U.S. military computers at several dozen sites and gain information. In 1996, hackers caused mischief at the computers of the Central Intelligence Agency and the Justice Department and destroyed the Air Force's home page. In early 1998, computer hackers accessed a whole series of nonclassified sites, caused major university and National Aeronautics and Space Administration computers to crash, and defaced military base home pages. It is clear from these episodes that the electronic network used by the U.S. military and intel-

ligence organizations is quite susceptible to access by amateurs, criminals, and spies.

Military and defense sites are not the only ones targeted by hackers: perhaps even more damage could be caused by interruptions to the global economic and banking system. During 1997, a survey of banks, universities, and companies showed that more than 60 percent had been accessed "illegitimately" during that year alone.

The threat finally became so obvious to Congress that a hearing was held in 1998. The hearing featured testimony by several hackers, who informed members of Congress of the means that they used to break into government computers. One of the hackers calmly noted that

he could break into the Pentagon's computers in less than thirty minutes. Such assertions, though questioned by the government's own network personnel, caused Senator John Kyl (R., Ariz.) to say that this issue "may be the most difficult and important national security and public safety concern our nation will face in the months and years to come."*

The potential consequences of such computer break-ins are almost too great to contemplate. Among the networks that, if impaired or destroyed, could bring down the nation's activities are those that connect the military services; guide satellites for communications and

defense; launch missiles; guide submarines; and control all air traffic, credit-card transactions, interbank transactions, utility grids throughout the nation, and generally all telecommunications. What is probably most worrisome is that neither the government nor the telecommunications industry yet has a good way to prevent attacks on electronic networks.

FOR CRITICAL ANALYSIS

How can the government build up a defense system to protect against hackers without violating the privacy and rights of legitimate users of the Internet?

*As quoted in Chuck McCutcheon, "Computer-Reliant U.S. Society Faces Growing Risk of 'Information War,' " *Congressional Quarterly Weekly Report,* March 14, 1998, p. 675.

troops to a situation from which the nation could not withdraw without incurring heavy losses, whether or not Congress is consulted.

Congress also has exerted its authority to limit or deny the president's requests for military assistance to Angolan rebels and to the government of El Salvador, and requests for new weapons, such as the B-1 bomber. In general, Congress has been far more cautious in supporting the president in situations where military involvement of American troops is possible.

At times, Congress can take the initiative in foreign policy. In 1986, Congress initiated and passed a bill instituting economic sanctions against South Africa to pressure that nation into ending apartheid. President Reagan vetoed the bill, but the veto was overridden by large majorities in both the House and the Senate.

Domestic Sources of Foreign Policy

The making of foreign policy is often viewed as a presidential prerogative because of the president's constitutional power in that area and the resources of the executive branch that the president controls. Foreign policymaking is also influenced by a number of other sources, however, including elite and mass opinion and the military-industrial complex.

Elite and Mass Opinion

Public opinion influences the making of U.S. foreign policy through a number of channels. Elites in American business, education, communications, labor, and religion try to influence presidential decision making through several strategies. Some individuals, such as former secretary of state Henry Kissinger, had a long-standing interest in foreign policy and were asked to advise the president privately. Several elite organizations, such as the Council on Foreign Relations and the Trilateral Commission, work to increase international cooperation and to influence foreign policy through conferences, publications, and research.

The members of the American elite establishment also exert influence on foreign policy through the general public by encouraging debate over foreign policy positions, by publicizing the issues, and by use of the media. Generally, the efforts of the president and the elites are most successful with the segment of the population called the **attentive public.** This sector of the mass public, which probably constitutes 10 to 20 percent of all citizens, is more interested in foreign affairs than most Americans. These Americans are also likely to transmit their opinions to the less interested members of the public through conversation and local leadership.

Attentive Public
That portion of the general public that pays attention to policy issues.

The Military-Industrial Complex

Civilian fear of the relationship between the defense establishment and arms manufacturers (the **military-industrial complex**) dates back many years. During President Eisenhower's eight years in office, the former five-star general of the army experienced firsthand the kind of pressure that could be brought against him and other policymakers by arms manufacturers. Eisenhower decided to give the country a solemn and, as he saw it, necessary warning of the consequences of this influence. On January 17, 1961, in his last official speech, he said,

Military-Industrial Complex
The mutually beneficial relationship between the armed forces and defense contractors.

> In the councils of government, we must guard against the acquisition of unwarranted influence, whether sought or unsought, by the military-industrial complex. The potential for the disastrous rise of misplaced power exists and will persist. . . . Only an alert and knowledgeable citizenry can compel the proper meshing of the huge industrial and military machinery of defense with our peaceful methods and goals, so that security and liberty may prosper together.[4]

The Pentagon has supported a large sector of our economy through defense contracts. It also has supplied retired army officers as key executives to large defense-contracting firms. Perhaps the Pentagon's strongest allies have been members of Congress whose districts or states benefited from the economic power of military bases or contracts. As the Cold War ended, the defense industry looked abroad for new customers. Sales of some military equipment to China raised serious issues for the Clinton administration.

The Major Foreign Policy Themes

Although some observers might suggest that U.S. foreign policy is inconsistent and changes with the current occupant of the White House, the long view of American diplomatic ventures reveals some major themes underlying foreign policy. In the early years of the nation, presidents and the people generally agreed that the United States should avoid foreign entanglements and concentrate instead on its own development. From the beginning of the twentieth

[4]*Congressional Almanac* (Washington, D.C.: Congressional Quarterly Press, 1961), pp. 938–939.

century until today, one major theme has been increasing global involvement, with the United States taking an active role in assisting the development of other nations, dominating the world economy, and in some cases acting as a peacemaker. The major theme of the post–World War II years was the containment of communism. In the following brief review of American diplomatic history, these three themes predominate. The theme for the next century, now that there are multiple strong nations and only one superpower, has not yet emerged.

The Formative Years: Avoiding Entanglements

Foreign policy was largely negative during the formative years of the United States. Remember that the new nation was operating under the Articles of Confederation. The national government had no right to levy and collect taxes, no control over commerce, no right to make commercial treaties, and no power to raise an army (the Revolutionary army was disbanded in 1783). The government's lack of international power was made clear when the United States was unable to recover American hostages who had been seized in the Mediterranean by Barbary pirates but ignominiously had to purchase the hostages in a treaty with Morocco.

The founders of this nation had a basic mistrust of corrupt European governments. George Washington said it was the U.S. policy "to steer clear of permanent alliances," and Thomas Jefferson echoed this sentiment when he said America wanted peace with all nations but "entangling alliances with none." (For another comment by Thomas Jefferson on U.S. foreign policy, see the feature *E-Mail Messages from the Past*.) This was also a logical position at a time when the United States was so weak militarily that it could not influence European development directly. Moreover, being protected by oceans that took weeks to traverse certainly allowed the nation to avoid entangling alliances. During the 1700s and 1800s, the United States generally stayed out of European conflicts and politics.

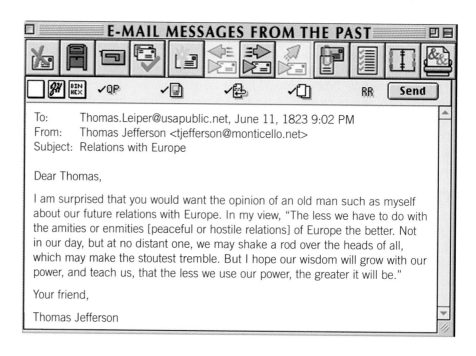

E-MAIL MESSAGES FROM THE PAST

To: Thomas.Leiper@usapublic.net, June 11, 1823 9:02 PM
From: Thomas Jefferson <tjefferson@monticello.net>
Subject: Relations with Europe

Dear Thomas,

I am surprised that you would want the opinion of an old man such as myself about our future relations with Europe. In my view, "The less we have to do with the amities or enmities [peaceful or hostile relations] of Europe the better. Not in our day, but at no distant one, we may shake a rod over the heads of all, which may make the stoutest tremble. But I hope our wisdom will grow with our power, and teach us, that the less we use our power, the greater it will be."

Your friend,

Thomas Jefferson

The Monroe Doctrine. President James Monroe, in his message to Congress on December 2, 1823, stated that this country would not accept foreign intervention in the Western Hemisphere. In return, the United States would not meddle in European affairs. The **Monroe Doctrine** was the underpinning of the U.S. **isolationist foreign policy** toward Europe, which continued throughout the nineteenth century.

In this hemisphere, the United States pursued an actively expansionist policy. The nation purchased Louisiana in 1803, annexed Texas in 1845, gained half of Mexico's territory in the 1840s, purchased Alaska in 1867, and annexed Hawaii in 1898.

The Spanish-American War and World War I. The end of the isolationist policy started with the Spanish-American War in 1898. Winning that war gave the United States possession of Guam, Puerto Rico, and the Philippines (which gained independence in 1946). On the heels of that war came World War I (1914 to 1918). In his reelection campaign of 1916, President Woodrow Wilson ran on the slogan "He kept us out of war." Nonetheless, on April 6, 1917, the United States declared war on Germany. It was evident to Wilson that without help, the Allies would be defeated, and American property and lives, already under attack, increasingly would be endangered. In the 1920s, the United States did indeed go "back to normalcy," as President Warren G. Harding urged it to do. U.S. military forces were largely disbanded, defense spending dropped to about 1 percent of total national income, and the nation entered a period of isolationism.

The Era of Internationalism

Isolationism was permanently shattered and relegated to its place in history by the bombing of the U.S. naval base at Pearl Harbor, Hawaii, on December 7, 1941. The surprise attack by the Japanese resulted in the deaths of 2,403 American servicemen and the wounding of 1,143 others. Eighteen warships were sunk or seriously damaged, and 188 planes were destroyed at the airfields. The American public was outraged. President Franklin Roosevelt asked Congress to

Monroe Doctrine
The policy statement included in President James Monroe's 1823 annual message to Congress, which set out three principles: (1) European nations should not establish new colonies in the Western Hemisphere, (2) European nations should not intervene in the affairs of independent nations of the Western Hemisphere, and (3) the United States would not interfere in the affairs of European nations.

Isolationist Foreign Policy
Abstaining from an active role in international affairs or alliances, which characterized U.S. foreign policy toward Europe during most of the nineteenth century.

This painting shows President James Monroe explaining the Monroe Doctrine to a group of government officials. Essentially, the Monroe Doctrine made the Western Hemisphere the concern of the United States.

Soviet leader Joseph Stalin, U.S. President Franklin Roosevelt, and British Prime Minister Winston Churchill met at Yalta from February 4 to 11, 1945, to resolve their differences over the shape that the international community would take after World War II.

The atomic bomb explodes over Nagasaki, Japan, on August 9, 1945.

declare war on Japan immediately, and the United States entered World War II.

This unequivocal response was certainly due to the nature of the provocation. American soil had not been attacked by a foreign power since the burning of Washington, D.C., by the British in 1814. World War II produced a permanent change in defense spending. Except for brief periods during the Civil War and World War I, defense spending had been a fairly trivial part of total national income. By the end of World War II, in 1945, however, defense spending had increased to almost 40 percent of total national income.

The United States was the only major participating country to emerge from World War II with its economy intact, and even strengthened. The Soviet Union, Japan, Italy, France, Germany, Britain, and a number of minor participants in the war were all economically devastated. The United States was also the only country to have control over operational nuclear weapons. President Harry S. Truman had personally made the decision to use two atomic bombs, on August 6 and August 9, 1945, to end the war with Japan. (Historians still dispute the necessity of this action, which ultimately killed more than 100,000 Japanese civilians and left an equal number permanently injured.) The United States truly had become the world's superpower.

The Cold War. The United States had become an uncomfortable ally of the Soviet Union after Adolf Hitler's invasion. Soon after the war ended, relations between the Soviet Union and the West deteriorated. The Soviet Union wanted a weakened Germany, and to achieve this it insisted that the country be divided in two, with East Germany becoming a buffer. Little by little, the Soviet Union helped to install Communist governments in Eastern European countries, which collectively became known as the **Soviet bloc.** In response, the United States encouraged the rearming of Western Europe. The **Cold War** had begun.[5]

In Fulton, Missouri, on March 5, 1946, Winston Churchill, in a striking metaphor, declared that from the Baltic to the Adriatic Seas "an iron curtain has descended across the [European] continent." The term **iron curtain** became even more appropriate when the Soviet Union built a wall separating East Berlin from West Berlin on August 17 and 18, 1961.

Containment Policy.   In 1947, a remarkable article was published in *Foreign Affairs.* The article was signed by "X." The actual author was George F. Kennan, chief of the policy-planning staff for the Department of State. The doctrine of **containment** set forth in the article became—according to many—the Bible of Western foreign policy. "X" argued that whenever and wherever the Soviet Union could successfully challenge Western institutions, it would do so. He recommended that our policy toward the Soviet Union be "firm and vigilant containment of Russian expansive tendencies."[6]

The containment theory was expressed clearly in the **Truman Doctrine,** which was enunciated by President Harry Truman in his historic address to Congress on March 12, 1947. In that address, he announced that the United States must help countries in which a Communist takeover seemed likely, and he proposed a Greek-Turkish aid program specifically to counter Soviet influence in the eastern Mediterranean area. Truman proposed $400 million in aid to those two countries. He put the choice squarely before Congress—it either must support those measures required to preserve peace and security abroad or risk widespread global instability and perhaps World War III.[7]

Superpower Relations

During the Cold War, there was never any direct military confrontation between the United States and the Soviet Union. Rather, confrontations among "client" nations were used to carry out the policies of the superpowers. Only on occasion did the United States directly enter into a conflict in a significant way. Two such occasions were in Korea and Vietnam.

In 1950, North Korean troops were embroiled in a war with South Korea. President Truman asked for and received a Security Council order from the United Nations (UN) for the North Koreans to withdraw their troops. The Soviet Union was absent from the council on that day, protesting the exclusion of the People's Republic of China from the UN, and did not participate in the discussion. Truman then authorized the use of American forces in support of the South Koreans. For the next three years, American troops were engaged in a land war in Asia, a war that became a stalemate and a political liability to President Truman. One of Dwight Eisenhower's major 1952 campaign promises was to end the Korean War—which he did. An armistice was signed on July 27, 1953. (American troops have been stationed in South Korea ever since, however.)

U.S. involvement in Vietnam began shortly after the end of the Korean conflict. When the French army in Indochina was defeated by the Communist forces of Ho Chi Minh and the two Vietnams were created in 1954, the United States assumed the role of supporting the South Vietnamese government against North Vietnam. President John Kennedy sent 16,000 "advisers" to help South Vietnam,

Soviet Bloc
The Eastern European countries that installed Communist regimes after World War II.

Cold War
The ideological, political, and economic impasse that existed between the United States and the Soviet Union following World War II.

Iron Curtain
The term used to describe the division of Europe between the Soviet Union and the West; popularized by Winston Churchill in a speech portraying Europe as being divided by an iron curtain, with the nations of Eastern Europe behind the curtain and increasingly under Soviet control.

Containment
A U.S. diplomatic policy adopted by the Truman administration to "build situations of strength" around the globe to contain Communist power within its existing boundaries.

Truman Doctrine
The policy adopted by President Harry Truman in 1947 to halt Communist expansion in southeastern Europe.

INFOTRAC®
COLLEGE EDITION

"The Two Presidencies"

[5]See John Lewis Gaddis, *The United Nations and the Origins of the Cold War* (New York: Columbia University Press, 1972).

[6]X, "The Sources of Soviet Conduct," *Foreign Affairs,* July 1947, p. 575.

[7]*Public Papers of the Presidents of the United States: Harry S. Truman, 1947* (Washington, D.C.: U.S. Government Printing Office, 1963), pp. 176–180.

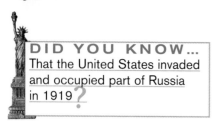

Détente

A French word meaning the relaxation
of tensions. The term characterizes
U.S.–Soviet policy as it developed under
President Richard Nixon and Secretary
of State Henry Kissinger. Détente
stressed direct cooperative dealings with
Cold War rivals but avoided ideological
accommodation.

**Strategic Arms Limitation
Treaty (SALT I)**

A treaty between the United States
and the Soviet Union to stabilize the
nuclear arms competition between the
two countries. SALT I talks began in
1969, and agreements were signed on
May 26, 1972.

and after Kennedy's death, President Lyndon Johnson greatly increased the
scope of that support. American forces in Vietnam at the height of the U.S.
involvement totaled more than 500,000 troops. More than 58,000 Americans
were killed, and 300,000 were wounded, in the conflict. The debate over U.S.
involvement in Vietnam divided the American electorate and, as mentioned previously, spurred congressional efforts to limit the ability of the president to commit forces to armed combat.

The Cuban Missile Crisis.   With the two superpowers having enough nuclear
bombs to destroy the world, a confrontation between the United States and the
Soviet Union was unthinkable. Perhaps the closest we came to such a confrontation was the Cuban missile crisis in 1962. The Soviets placed missiles
ninety miles off the U.S. coast in response to Cuban fears of an American invasion and to try to balance the American nuclear advantage. President Kennedy
and his advisers rejected the possibility of armed intervention, setting up a naval
blockade around the island instead. When Soviet vessels, apparently carrying
nuclear warheads, appeared near Cuban waters, the tension reached its height.
After intense negotiations between Washington and Moscow, the Soviet ships
turned around on October 25, and on October 28 the Soviet Union announced
the withdrawal of its missile operations from Cuba. In exchange, the United
States agreed not to invade Cuba and to remove some of its own missiles that
were located near the Soviet border in Turkey.

A Period of Détente.   The French word **détente** means a relaxation of tensions.
By the end of the 1960s, it was clear that some efforts had to be made to reduce
the threat of nuclear war between the United States and the Soviet Union. The
Soviet Union gradually had begun to catch up in the building of strategic
nuclear delivery vehicles in the form of bombers and missiles, thus balancing
the nuclear scales. Each nation acquired the military capacity to destroy the
other with nuclear weapons.

As the result of protracted negotiations, in May 1972, the United States and
the Soviet Union signed the **Strategic Arms Limitation Treaty (SALT I)**. That treaty
"permanently" limited the development and deployment of antiballistic missiles
(ABMs), and it limited for five years the number of offensive missiles each country could deploy. To further reduce tensions, under the policy of Secretary of State
Henry Kissinger and President Nixon, new scientific and cultural exchanges were
arranged with the Soviets, as well as new opportunities for Jewish emigration out
of the Soviet Union.

The policy of détente was not limited to U.S. relationships with the Soviet
Union. Seeing an opportunity to capitalize on increasing friction between the
Soviet Union and the People's Republic of China, Kissinger secretly began negotiations to establish a new relationship with that nation. President Nixon eventually visited the People's Republic of China and set the stage for the formal
diplomatic recognition of that country, which occurred during the Carter administration (1977–1981).

The Reagan-Bush Years.   President Ronald Reagan took a hard line against the
Soviet Union during his first term, proposing the strategic defense initiative
(SDI), or "Star Wars," in 1983. SDI was designed to serve as a space-stationed
defense against enemy missiles. Reagan and others in his administration argued
that the program would deter nuclear war by shifting the emphasis of defense
strategy from offensive to defensive weapons systems.

In November 1985, President Reagan and Mikhail Gorbachev, the Soviet
leader, held summit talks in Geneva. The two men agreed to reestablish cultural

President Richard Nixon signs SALT I, a Cold War agreement with the Soviet Union, in 1972. The Soviet Union dissolved in late December 1991. Consequently, do you think that the member republics of the former Soviet Union should have to abide by the SALT I agreement?

and scientific exchanges and to continue the arms control negotiations. Progress toward an agreement was slow, however.

In 1987, representatives of the United States and the Soviet Union continued work on an arms reduction agreement. Although there were setbacks throughout the year, the negotiations resulted in a historic agreement signed by Reagan and Gorbachev in Washington, D.C., on December 8, 1987. The terms of the Intermediate-Range Nuclear Force (INF) Treaty required the superpowers to dismantle a total of four thousand intermediate-range missiles within the first three years of the agreement. The verification procedures allowed each nation to keep a team of inspectors on the other nation's soil and to conduct up to twenty short-notice inspections of the disassembly sites each year. The Senate ratified the treaty in a vote of ninety-three to five on May 27, 1988, and the agreement was formally signed by Reagan and Gorbachev at the Moscow summit in 1988.

George Bush continued the negotiations with the Soviet Union after he became president. The goal of both nations was to reduce the number of nuclear weapons and the number of armed troops in Europe. The developments in Eastern Europe, the drive by the Baltic republics for independence, the unification of Germany, and the dissolution of the Soviet Union (in December 1991) made the process much more complex, however. American strategists worried as much about who now controlled the Soviet nuclear arsenal as about completing the treaty process. In 1992, the United States signed the Strategic Arms Reduction Treaty (START) with four former Soviet republics—Russia, Ukraine, Belarus, and Kazakhstan—to reduce the number of long-range nuclear weapons.

Challenges in World Politics

The end of the Cold War, the dissolution of the Soviet Union, the economic unification of Europe, and the political changes in Eastern Europe have challenged U.S. foreign policy in ways that were unimaginable a few years ago. The United States had no contingency plans for these events. Also, predicting the consequences of any of these changes for world politics is all but impossible. Furthermore, such sweeping changes mean not only that the United States must adjust its foreign policy to deal with new realities but also that it must consider adjustments in the American military and intelligence establishments.

The Dissolution of the Soviet Union

After the fall of the Berlin Wall in 1989, it was clear that the Soviet Union had relinquished much of its political and military control over the states of Eastern Europe that formerly had been part of the Soviet bloc. Sweeping changes within the Soviet Union had been proposed by Gorbachev, and talks to reduce nuclear armaments were proceeding. No one expected the Soviet Union to dissolve into separate states as quickly as it did, however. While Gorbachev tried to adjust the Soviet constitution and political system to allow greater autonomy for the republics within the union, demands for political, ethnic, and religious autonomy grew. In August 1991, the Soviet military tried to slow the process by arresting Gorbachev. Led by Boris Yeltsin, then president of Russia, the coup attempt was successfully resisted.

The result of the failed attempt to gain control by military leaders was to hasten the process of creating an independent Russian state led by Yeltsin. On the day after Christmas in 1991, the Soviet Union was officially dissolved. A few months later, the majority of the former republics had joined a loose federation called the Commonwealth of Independent States, although a few of the larger republics, including Georgia and Ukraine, refused to join.

Another uprising in Russia, this time led by anti-Yeltsin members of the new parliament who wanted to restore the Soviet Union immediately, failed in 1993. The first free elections of the new nation produced a divided parliament, with a majority of delegates who opposed Yeltsin and his programs. Yeltsin, however, won the election for president in 1996, although he appeared to be in ill health during the campaign and soon after his inauguration had heart surgery. Yeltsin's

President Bill Clinton traveled to Russia to meet with President Boris Yeltsin in September 1998. At the time, both presidents were under siege: Clinton from the Starr report and Yeltsin from attacks by a parliament that disapproved of his leadership. While the leaders did sign some agreements between their nations, those agreements were not especially significant; nor did they require approval from the two nations' respective legislatures.

presidency continued to be plagued by domestic economic problems and the uprising in Chechnya, a breakaway ethnic region.

Nuclear Proliferation

The dissolution of the Soviet Union brought a true lowering of tensions between the major powers in the world. The United States and Russia agreed to continue negotiating the dismantling of nuclear warheads and delivery systems. The problems of nuclear proliferation were far from solved, however. As shown in Table 18–1, the number of warheads known to be in stock worldwide is nearly twenty thousand; other nations do not report the extent of their nuclear stockpiles.

In 1994, North Korea defied the efforts of the International Atomic Energy Commission to inspect parts of its nuclear power plant, particularly at a time when fuel rods were to be changed. The international inspectors suspected that spent fuel would be reprocessed to make a nuclear bomb or warhead. When North Korea continued to defy international pressure to comply with inspection, the United States sought approval for sanctions on the nation from the United Nations. Former U.S. president Jimmy Carter went to North Korea in mid-1994 and negotiated a deal by which the North Koreans would give up their nuclear power plant in exchange for a new one. The new one would not have the capability to produce similar fuel rods and would be built with money loaned to North Korea by the United States. North Korea's actions continued to be a cause of concern, particularly after the United States obtained information, in the summer of 1998, that North Korea was developing an underground nuclear arms site.

Concerns over nuclear proliferation also intensified in 1998 after both India and Pakistan detonated nuclear devices within a few weeks of each other. Even though the newly elected government of India had declared its intent to pursue nuclear weapons, the American intelligence establishment did not take this declaration seriously. The Indian government proceeded to conduct two sets of tests, exploding a total of five devices. India claimed that the development of the weapons was necessary due to its long history of war with Pakistan.

After the tests, President Clinton imposed sanctions on India and then urged Pakistan not to follow suit. Two weeks later, the Pakistani government also conducted successful nuclear tests, claiming that they were necessary for its national

INFOTRAC ®
COLLEGE EDITION

"The Return of Nuclear Terror"

TABLE **18-1**

The Nuclear Club

LOCATION	KNOWN AND SUSPECTED NUMBER OF WARHEADS	
Official estimates:		
United States	8,500 (to be reduced to 3,500 by 2003)	
Former Soviet Union	9,853 (to be reduced to 3,500 by 2003)	
	In possession of:	
	Russia	8,362
	Kazakhstan	1,410
	Belarus	81
France	482	
China	284	
Britain	234	
Unofficial estimates:		
Israel	50 to 200	
India	65	
Pakistan	15 to 25	
Nations that are capable of building weapons and/or suspected of having a nuclear program:		
Algeria, Argentina, Brazil, Iran, Iraq, Libya, North Korea, South Africa, and Syria.		

SOURCE: *Newsweek,* July 24, 1995, p. 36–37; and authors' update.

While India has historically taken a neutral position in world affairs, it has engaged in military conflicts with Pakistan and China on its borders. When the new Indian government followed through on its promise to develop and test nuclear weapons, there was widespread support for that action among Indian citizens, as shown here. Nuclear testing in both India and Pakistan in 1998 caught the U.S. intelligence community off guard—it had no knowledge that the tests would be conducted.

security. Given that China has already joined the "nuclear club," the possibility of one of these three powers using a nuclear device in war seemed to the rest of the world to be a real threat.

Terrorism

Dissident groups, rebels, and other revolutionaries always have engaged in some sort of terrorism to gain attention and to force their enemies to the bargaining table. Over the last two decades, terrorism has continued to threaten world peace and the lives of ordinary citizens.

Terrorism can be a weapon of choice in domestic or civil strife. The conflict in the Middle East between Israel and the Arab states has been lessened by a series of painfully negotiated agreements between Israel and some of the other states. In recent years, Israel and the Palestinians have tried to reach agreement on some of their differences. Those opposed to the peace process, however, have continued to disrupt the negotiations through assassinations, mass murders, and bomb blasts in the streets of major cities within Israel. At this point, most of the terrorist attacks are carried out by groups (either Israeli or Arab) that reject the peace process. Similar "domestic" terrorist acts were used to disrupt talks between Britain and Ireland over the fate of Northern Ireland. The terrorist acts did not stop the peace process in Ireland, however, which culminated in a vote supporting the agreement in 1998. Terrorist acts by rebels or separatist groups have also occurred in Sri Lanka (the Tamils), Paris (Algerian extremists), Russia (Chechen rebels), and Japan (secret cults).

In other cases, terrorist acts are planned against the civilians of foreign nations to make an international statement and to frighten the citizens of a faraway land. Perhaps one of the most striking of these attacks was that launched against Israeli athletes at the Munich Olympics in 1972. Others have included ship hijackings, airplane hijackings, and the bombing of the World Trade Center in New York. In the 1990s, two other incidents brought the fear of terrorism home to Americans. In 1996, radical elements in Saudi Arabia bombed an American military compound there, killing a number of American military personnel. In 1998, terrorist bombings of two American embassies in Africa killed 257 people, including 12

In August 1998, bombs exploded virtually simultaneously in the U.S. embassies in Kenya and Tanzania. Pictured here is the embassy in Nairobi, Kenya, moments after the bombing. The administration believed that the bombs were planted by Muslim terrorists, perhaps under the direction of a Saudi millionaire who has verbally declared war on Americans. These two attacks on relatively low-security installations killed far more citizens of the two African nations than they did Americans.

Americans, and injured over 5,500 others. The United States retaliated by launching missiles against terrorist camps in Afghanistan and the Sudan.

What can nations do to prevent terrorism? Besides taking a clear stand about the consequences of such acts and punishing the perpetrators, the best defense of nations is to be vigilant. This includes stronger security measures and a commitment to intelligence gathering. The Clinton administration requested a strengthening of U.S. intelligence capabilities in 1996, but that proposal met with opposition from civil liberties groups as well as conservative Republicans. The problem that faces a democracy that upholds liberty for its citizens is how to balance the needs of increased surveillance for criminals against the rights of citizens to be free of police spying and record keeping.

The New Power: China

Since Nixon's visit to China, American policy has been to gradually engage the Chinese in diplomatic and economic relationships in the hope of turning the nation toward a more pro-Western and capitalistic system. Then, in 1992, when Chinese students engaged in extraordinary demonstrations against the government, the Chinese government crushed the demonstrations, killing a number of students and protesters and imprisoning others for political crimes.

Most-Favored-Nation Status
A status granted by an international treaty by which each member nation must treat other members at least as well as it treats the country that receives its most favorable treatment.

The Clinton administration, however, continued the policy of diplomatic outreach to the Chinese, in part because China had allowed free enterprise in many regions of the country and had the potential to be a major trading partner of the United States. China sought, and was granted, **most-favored-nation status** for tariffs and trade policy.

In 1997, China seemed to be conscious of Western concerns when it took over the government of Hong Kong in ceremonies that promised a continuation of the previous government and economic system in the former British colony. Although the new government did impose an appointed assembly, it was careful to preserve the free enterprise system of Hong Kong.

The Chinese-American connection eventually reached domestic politics in the United States when campaign-finance investigations showed that a number of Chinese Americans had made large contributions to the 1996 Clinton reelection campaign. Some of the contributions were illegal and were returned by the Democratic Party. There were also accusations that a presidential waiver given to Loral Corporation to sell technology to China was granted soon after Loral's chief executive made a major contribution to the campaign. Congressional investigations into the transfer of technology to China came at about the time that intelligence revealed China's missile technology to the world. President Clinton traveled to China for a state visit in 1998, amid protests about U.S.–China policy.

The Global Economy

Although the United States derives only about 10 percent of its total national income from world trade, it is deeply dependent on the world economy. A serious stock market crash in 1987 showed how closely other markets watch the economic situation of the United States and, conversely, how U.S. markets follow those of London and Japan. In 1997 and 1998, when several Asian economies experienced serious problems, the American business community, now dependent on Asian concerns for materials, products, and customers, showed some signs of weakness, at least for a short period of time. The Asian economies—among them South Korea and Thailand—received aid from the International Monetary Fund on the condition that they impose severe restrictions on their economies and people. In Indonesia, the failing economy brought down President Suharto, who had held that office for thirty years, and led to increased cries for reform among that nation's people.

Furthermore, since the 1980s, the United States has become a debtor nation, meaning that we owe more to foreigners than foreigners owe to us. The reason for this is a huge trade deficit and the willingness of foreign individuals and nations to finance part of the U.S. national debt by purchasing U.S. government securities. Because the United States imports more goods and services than it exports, it has a net trade deficit. These imports include BMWs, Sonys, Toshibas, and Guccis, as well as cheaper products such as shoes manufactured in Brazil and clothes from Taiwan. As Figure 18–1 shows, the biggest trade deficit is with Asian countries.

No one can predict how a unified Europe will affect world trade. With the European Union having become one economic "nation" on December 31, 1992, some expect Europe will gradually close some markets to outside economic powers. Others see a united Europe as a market opportunity for American and multinational corporations.

Regional Conflicts

The United States has played a role—sometimes alone, sometimes in conjunction with other powers—in many regional conflicts. During the 1990s, the United States has been involved in conflicts in countries and regions around the globe.

Haiti and Cuba.   The Caribbean nation of Haiti became a focal point of U.S. policy in the 1990s. The repressive military regime there ousted the democratically elected president Jean-Bertrand Aristide in 1992. The Clinton administration announced that it would support sanctions and other measures to reinstate Aristide in office. At the same time, the administration tried to stem the tide of refugees who tried to reach Florida by sea from the island nation. Although

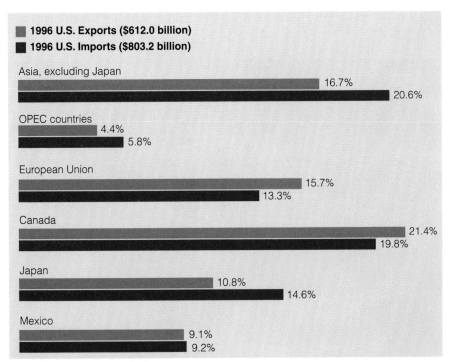

■ **1996 U.S. Exports ($612.0 billion)**
■ **1996 U.S. Imports ($803.2 billion)**

Asia, excluding Japan — 16.7% / 20.6%

OPEC countries — 4.4% / 5.8%

European Union — 15.7% / 13.3%

Canada — 21.4% / 19.8%

Japan — 10.8% / 14.6%

Mexico — 9.1% / 9.2%

SOURCE: U.S. Department of Commerce, 1997.

FIGURE 18–1

U.S. Exports and Imports, 1996
In the 1990s, the U.S. trade deficit continued to grow, reaching almost $200 billion by 1996. It is important to note, however, that Canada is the most important market for U.S. products and that Canada and Mexico together account for about 30 percent of all U.S. exports and imports. China is rapidly increasing its exports to the United States.

Clinton had promised in his campaign to admit the Haitian "boat people," he maintained the Bush policy of returning them to their native land. By 1994, he announced that the United States would at least listen to pleas for political asylum if refugees could reach Jamaica or other Caribbean islands. The Clinton administration also increased the sanctions on Haiti in 1994 and then sent troops to Haiti to assist in the reinstatement of President Aristide.

The United States continued to face problems with Cuba. In the last days of the summer of 1994, Castro threatened to "swamp" the United States with Cuban refugees. True to his word, he allowed thousands to leave the island on anything that would float. President Clinton was forced to rescind the U.S. open-door policy for Cuban refugees. He ordered the Coast Guard to return all refugees picked up at sea to the U.S. naval base at Guantanamo in Cuba. Then U.S. and Cuban authorities reached an agreement under which the United States would accept 20,000 legal Cuban immigrants a year. In exchange, Castro agreed to police Cuba's shores to prevent an exodus of Cuban refugees.

In 1996, another incident occurred. Cuban military aircraft shot down two planes flown by anti-Castro American residents who were searching for Cubans escaping by sea. The pilots were conducting the search for an anticommunist organization that had violated Cuban air space repeatedly on previous occasions. The United States, refusing to accept Cuba's explanation that the two planes were in Cuban territorial waters, retaliated by passing the Helms-Burton Act. The act, which punished owners of foreign firms (and their family members) for investing in formerly American-owned business firms that had been nationalized by Cuba, sparked international opposition.

The Middle East.   The United States has also played a role in the Middle East. As a long-time supporter of Israel, the United States has undertaken to persuade the Israelis to agree to negotiations with the Palestinians who live in the territories occupied by the state of Israel. The conflict, which began in 1948, has been extremely hard to resolve. One reason is that it requires all the Arab states in the region to recognize Israel's right to exist. Another reason is that resolution of the conflict would require Israel to make some settlement with the Palestine Liberation Organization (PLO), which has launched attacks on Israel

The Israeli-Palestinian agreements of 1993 have only partially been implemented due to continued Israeli settlements in the West Bank and continued Palestinian terrorist attacks against Israelis. In May 1998, U.S. Secretary of State Madeleine Albright met with Yasser Arafat, leader of the Palestinian Authority, in London to try to restart the negotiations between the two sides.

from within and outside its borders and which Israel has regarded as a terrorist organization. In December 1988, the U.S. began talking directly to the PLO, and in 1991, under great pressure from the United States, the Israelis opened talks with representatives of the Palestinians and other Arab states.

In 1993, the Israeli-Palestinian peace talks reached a breakthrough, with both parties agreeing to set up Palestinian territories in the West Bank and Gaza. The historic agreement, signed in Cairo on May 4, 1994, put in place a process by which the Palestinians would assume self-rule in the Gaza Strip and in the town of Jericho. In the months that followed, Israeli troops withdrew from much of the occupied territory, Palestinians assumed police duties, and many Palestinian prisoners were freed by the Israelis. During an election campaign speech, however, Israeli prime minister Yitzhak Rabin was assassinated by a right-wing Israeli student who opposed the peace process. In the election, the voters elected a new prime minister, Benjamin Netanyahu, who represented more conservative ideas. Since that time, conditions in the Palestinian areas have worsened, and it is unclear to what degree Israel will go forward with the peace process.

U.S. Response to Iraq's Invasion of Kuwait.   On August 2, 1990, the Middle East became the setting for a major challenge to the authority of the United States and its ability to buy oil from its allies there. President Saddam Hussein of Iraq initially sent more than 100,000 troops into the neighboring oil sheikdom of Kuwait, occupying the entire nation. Within less than two days, President George Bush took the position that the annexation of Kuwait must not be tolerated by the Western world and that the oil fields of Saudi Arabia must be protected. At the formal request of the king of Saudi Arabia, American troops were dispatched to set up a defensive line at the Kuwaiti border. In addition, the president announced an economic boycott of Iraq (supported by the United Nations) and sent American carrier groups to seal off the Iraqi ports, cutting off shipments of oil.

Bush continued to send troops—including reserve units called up from the United States—to Saudi Arabia. By the end of 1990, more than half a million troops were in place. After the United Nations approved a resolution authorizing

American tanks carry out maneuvers in Saudi Arabia during Operation Desert Shield. Subsequently, the United States, together with a coalition of other nations, instituted Operation Desert Storm—the Persian Gulf "hot war" that lasted for only one hundred hours on the ground, following prolonged air attacks. Such maneuvers were undertaken again in Kuwait in the fall of 1994, when Saddam Hussein moved troops close to the Kuwaiti border.

the use of force if Saddam Hussein did not respond to sanctions, the U.S. Congress reluctantly also approved such an authorization. On January 17, 1991, two days after the deadline for President Hussein to withdraw, the coalition forces launched a massive air attack on Iraq. After several weeks of almost unopposed aerial bombardment, the ground offensive began. Iraqi troops retreated from Kuwait a few days later, and the Persian Gulf War ended within another week.

After the end of the armed conflict, many Americans criticized the Bush administration for not sending troops to Baghdad, where they might have deposed Saddam Hussein. Others faulted the effort for raising the expectations of the Kurdish people that the United States would eliminate President Hussein if they revolted. The war also created an enormous environmental disaster owing to the destruction of the oil fields by the Iraqis when they retreated from Kuwait. As discussed in this chapter's *Critical Perspective,* Iraq is suspected of continuing to manufacture biological and chemical weapons.

Eastern Europe.　　Eastern Europe, a region that had been extremely stable while under Soviet domination, suddenly became an unknown quantity in U.S. policy. With the decision of the Soviet Union to allow free elections and non-Marxist

Critical | perspective

The Silent Weapons—Chemical and Biological Warfare

Between World War I, when mustard gas was last used in warfare, and the Persian Gulf War, most Americans gave little thought to the possible use of chemical and biological weapons. After U.S. troops returned from Iraq, however, Americans became aware that a number of Iraqi weapons factories were dedicated to the manufacture of chemical or biological weapons. In 1997, Iraq's refusal to accede to Western demands that inspectors be allowed to go into some buildings and sites to look for these weapons brought the United States close to another armed confrontation with Iraq. During the diplomatic stand-off, President Clinton threatened to use all necessary military force, including missile strikes, to attack some of the sites at which weapons allegedly were being manufactured.

The very threat of such an attack focused the world's attention more closely on the problem of such weapons. Iraq was accused of manufacturing a chemical weapon called VX, which attacks the nervous system. Additionally, the inspection team believed that Iraq continued to produce anthrax and botulinum toxin. The power of such weapons is astonishing. Only one gram of anthrax bacteria (the weight of two paper clips) can kill 10 million people. Botulinum is equally deadly. Producing these weapons is not extremely difficult, and obviously, because only small quantities are needed, it is possible to hide the output. What is more problematic is the delivery mechanism. Because many biological or chemical

weapons need to be inhaled, the weapons must be sprayed in a mist close to ground level. This technology is hard to achieve without notice.

Although such weapons are fairly easy to obtain and to hide, their actual use may be quite difficult, and their effectiveness depends on how they are used. It may be that, as Dr. Norton Zinder, a biologist, put it, "[a]nthrax is a terror agent, not a battlefield agent. The psychology of biological weapons is more potent than the weapons are."* Thus, the threat of using such weapons becomes a true terrorist tool with the potential of blackmailing another nation or the world community. Additionally, chemical and biological weapons hold potential for domestic terrorism. The Japanese experienced the terror of chemical weapons when a religious cult released a nerve gas in the Tokyo subway, causing several deaths and many injuries.

As part of the international community's effort to control these weapons, the U.S. Senate ratified the Chemical Weapons Convention in April 1997. Negotiated by the Reagan and Bush administrations, the treaty had been approved by seventy-nine nations before the United States ratified it. The treaty requires its signatory nations never to "develop, produce, otherwise acquire, stockpile or retain

*Nicholas Wade, "Germ Weapons: Deadly but Hard to Use," *The New York Times,* November 21, 1997, p. A13.

governments in Eastern Europe, these nations took separate paths to becoming self-governing states with mixed or market-oriented economies. Some nations immediately held elections; some struggled first to repair damaged economies; and still others attempted to deal with ethnic tensions within their populations.

It is difficult to overestimate the potential for civil disorder in these nations, particularly with regard to ethnic differences. (See this chapter's feature entitled *Politics and Ethics*.) The world watched in 1991 as Yugoslavia split into a number of independent states. As former provinces of Yugoslavia—Slovenia, Croatia, and Bosnia and Herzegovina—tried to declare independence, Serbian military and government leaders launched attacks on their neighbors. The fighting was caused by historic conflicts and by strong ethnic and religious differences.

The fighting was fiercest in the former province of Bosnia, where Serbs and Muslims launched attacks on each other's villages and cities. News reports suggested that many women were raped, and that the men were sent to camps to force their families to leave their homes. The United States and European nations forced the Serbs to withdraw their weapons from the city and to begin a process for permanent disengagement. With guarantees from the United States and other

Critical | perspective

The Silent Weapons—Chemical and Biological Warfare, Continued

U.S. troops load a missile onto a fighter plane in preparation for a confrontation with Iraq during February 1998.

chemical weapons, or transfer, directly or indirectly, chemical weapons to anyone." The treaty was opposed by conservatives, such as Senator Jesse Helms. Helms believed that the treaty would have no effect on rogue nations such as Iraq or Libya. Additionally, the treaty would create a false sense of security, with the United States being less prepared to defend itself against the use of these

weapons. Chemical manufacturers, who will bear the cost of surprise inspections, were generally neutral about the treaty because the business they would lose if the United States did not sign was likely to be greater than the cost of regulation.

Those who supported the treaty, including President Clinton and former Republican presidential nominee Bob Dole, believe that the treaty certainly will provide more security by placing severe sanctions on companies and nations that do not abide by it. Some nations that are suspected of having such weapons, including North Korea, Iraq, Iran, and Syria, did not sign it.

It is worthwhile to note that one of the first confrontations with Iraq over inspecting its sites occurred within six months after the treaty took effect. When the confrontation ended, President Clinton announced that he had set aside enough funds in the Defense Department budget to immunize all American troops against anthrax.

FOR CRITICAL ANALYSIS

1. Do you think it likely that chemical and biological weapons will be used in your lifetime? Under what circumstances might this happen?
2. How can the United States and other nations best mount a defense against the development of such weapons?

POLITICS and Ethics

The Demands of Ethnic Nationalism

The slaughter of civilians in Rwanda in 1994 and the fighting between Serbian and Moslem Bosnians is but a prelude to things to come. As new states are created from the wreckage of the Soviet Union and as postcolonial states mature, more and more people identifying with ethnic subnationalities will be claiming the right to sovereignty as new states or, at a minimum, the right to international protection for their culture and identity.

According to one commentator, the first wave of twentieth-century nationalism followed World War II, when colonial powers such as Great Britain and France allowed their former colonies to become independent states. At that time, the new states, including India, Pakistan, Vietnam, and others, fought to establish national unity against the colonial powers.*

Since that time, several more waves of ethnic nationalism have followed, as people of ethnic nationalities within these new nations (and within old nations) claim independence or the need for greater rights within the nation. The response of the world's international organizations has also changed in this century; they now support human rights in every case.

The result has been an explosion of ethnic conflicts in developing nations, in the states of the former Soviet Union, and even in the industrialized nations. A few years ago, the *Los Angeles Times* listed fifty-three separate ethnic conflicts in the

*Joane Nagel, "Ethnic Nationalism: Politics, Ideology, and the World Order," *International Journal of Comparative Sociology*, Vol. 34 (1993), p. 107.

world. Although Rwanda was mentioned, at that time, the mass killings of more than 500,000 people had not yet occurred. In India, at least twenty thousand people have been killed in violence between the Sikhs and the Hindu government. In Azerbaijan, three thousand deaths have occurred since 1988. In Sri Lanka, twenty thousand Tamils have died in their revolt against the Buddhist Sinhalese. In Iraq, persecution of the Kurds and the "marsh Arabs" continues. Within Russia, Chechen rebels successfully fended off Russian troops sent to subdue their uprising. In late 1996, ethnic strife in Rwanda again erupted into violence.

The international community faces an ethical dilemma in these situations. Should all peoples who claim an ethnic identity be protected, either by outside forces or through the creation of a separate political entity? If that is the case, what is the right of a nation as a whole to protect its sovereignty and its borders for the good of all the citizens? It cannot be correct morally to allow the oppression of one group by another, but can outsiders intervene in the domestic affairs of a nation? Finally, the solution cannot be separate states for each people. Such a solution would produce a world of nations too small to survive and would require large-scale migrations of peoples back to their homelands.

FOR CRITICAL ANALYSIS

What can the United States and other members of the world community do to curb increasing ethnic violence?

NATO allies, the warring parties began the process of establishing separate ethnic provinces and returning to their home villages. Troops from the United States and other European nations patrolled the new borders and assisted in the process. Prospects for a lasting peace after the troops leave are not great due to the degree of ethnic hatred in this region. In fact, by 1998 the situation again became violent as ethnic Albanians sought independence for the Kosovo region of Serbia.

Africa. The continent of Africa witnessed both great strides for freedom and savage civil strife during the mid-1990s. In South Africa, the first all-race elections were held—mostly in an orderly and peaceful manner—and Nelson Mandela was elected as the first president under a new constitution. Most South African constituencies took part in the election and seemed ready to support the new black-majority regime. The economic sanctions applied by the United States had helped bring the white South African government to a position of economic hardship and led, in part, to its negotiations with Mandela and his African National Congress Party.

In central Africa, another situation arose that seemed to be totally beyond the influence of the United States, France, or the United Nations. After a plane crash that killed the presidents of Rwanda and of neighboring Burundi, civil war erupted in Rwanda. The political war between the government and the rebel forces was complicated by a terrible ethnic struggle between the Hutu and Tutsi tribes. Observers estimated that more than half a million people were killed within a few weeks, with many bodies dumped in the rivers. About 250,000 refugees arrived in Uganda, setting up a small city in less than a week. Over a million others fled into neighboring Zaire. The United Nations called for troops to assist in relief efforts, but only France responded (and pulled out shortly thereafter). The United States played virtually no part in this situation until small military and civilian contingents were sent to assist with the refugee crisis. Ethnic hostilities flared up in 1996 and again in 1998, resulting in more killings.

Foreign and Defense Policy: Issues for the New Century

No president or secretary of state can predict the future of world politics. There is simply no way of knowing whether the states of the former Soviet Union will be a source of future conflicts, whether ethnic tensions will erupt in more nations, or whether the United Nations will be able to assemble an effective peacekeeping force. Nonetheless, it is necessary for U.S. leaders to try to plan for the future. The United States needs to plan a strategy for self-defense rather than a strategy for confronting Russia. Among the foreign policy issues to be considered, it is vitally important for the United States to plan an economic strategy that will increase U.S. exports and hold imports steady—in order to reduce the trade deficit. The recent severe downturns in several Asian economies showed that modern capitalist systems can experience problems.

Other issues that need to be resolved include the role that the United States sees for the United Nations, the degree to which the United States must keep a vital intelligence service, the strategies for supporting American interests in the Western Hemisphere and throughout the world, and the degree to which the United States will play an active role in the world. Without the structure of the Cold War, it is likely that foreign policy for the United States, as well as for other leading nations, will need to be much more flexible than it has been in the past to deal with changing conditions and complex situations.

As the world approaches the twenty-first century, the international experiences of the 1990s—and of the whole twentieth century—may be seen as a time of transition. The events of this century created the economic and social basis for the United States to change from a nation interested primarily in domestic policy to a major player on the world stage. The next century is likely to see that role grow, perhaps making possible a new variety of world politics.

TOWARD ACTIVE CITIZENSHIP

WORKING FOR HUMAN RIGHTS

In many countries throughout the world, human rights are not protected to the extent that they are in the United States. In some nations, people are imprisoned, tortured, or killed because they oppose the current regime. In other nations, certain ethnic or racial groups are oppressed by the majority population. In nations such as Somalia, in which civil war has caused starvation among millions of people, international efforts to send food relief to the refugee camps were hampered by the fighting among rival factions that raged within that country.

What can you do to work for the improvement of human rights in other nations? One way is to join one of the national and international organizations listed to the right that attempt to keep watch over human rights violations. By publicizing human rights violations, these organizations try to pressure nations into changing their tactics. Sometimes, such organizations are able to apply enough pressure and cause enough embarrassment that selected individuals may be freed from prison or allowed to emigrate.

Another way to work for human rights is to keep informed about the state of affairs in other nations and to write personally to those governments or to their embassies, asking them to cease these violations. Again, the organizations listed in the next column have newsletters or other publications to keep you aware of developments in other nations.

If you want to receive general information about the position of the United States on human rights viola-

tions, you could begin by contacting the State Department:

U.S. Department of State
Bureau of Democracy, Human Rights, and Labor
2201 C St. N.W.
Washington, DC 20520
202-647-4000
www.state.gov/www/global/human_rights/index.html

You can also contact the United Nations:

United Nations
777 United Nations Plaza
New York, NY 10017
212-963-1234
www.un.org/

The following organizations are best known for their watchdog efforts in countries that violate human rights for political reasons:

Amnesty International U.S.A.
322 8th Ave., Fl. 10
New York, NY 10001
212-807-8400
www.amnesty-usa.org/

American Friends Service Committee
1501 Cherry St.
Philadelphia, PA 19102
215-241-7000
www.afsc.org/

Key terms

Chapter summary

1 Foreign policy includes national goals and the techniques used to achieve them. National security policy, which is one aspect of foreign policy, is designed to protect the independence and the political and economic integrity of the United States. Diplomacy involves the nation's external relationships and is an attempt to resolve conflict without resort to arms. Sometimes U.S. foreign policy is based on moral idealism. At other times, U.S. policies stem from political realism.

2 The formal power of the president to make foreign policy derives from the U.S. Constitution, which makes the president responsible for the preservation of national security and designates the president as commander in chief of the army and navy. Presidents have interpreted this authority broadly. They also have the power to make treaties and executive agreements. In principle, the State Department is the executive agency most directly involved with foreign affairs. The National Security Council (NSC) advises the president on the integration of "domestic, foreign, and military policies relating to the national security." The intelligence community consists of forty or more government agencies engaged in intelligence activities varying from information gathering to covert actions. In response to presidential actions in the Vietnam War, Congress attempted to establish some limits on the power of the president in foreign policy by passing the War Powers Resolution in 1973.

3 Three major themes have guided U.S. foreign policy. In the early years of the nation, isolationism was the primary focus. With the start of the twentieth century, this view gave way to global involvement. From the end of World War II through the 1980s, the major goal was to contain communism and the influence of the Soviet Union.

4 During the 1700s and 1800s, the United States had little international power and generally stayed out of European conflicts and politics. The nineteenth century has been called the period of isolationism. The Monroe Doctrine of 1823 stated that the United States would not accept foreign intervention in the Western Hemisphere and would not meddle in European affairs. The United States pursued an actively expansionist policy in the Americas and the Pacific area during the nineteenth century, however.

5 The end of the policy of isolationism toward Europe started with the Spanish-American War of 1898. U.S. entanglement in European politics became more extensive when the United States entered World War I on April 6, 1917. World War II marked a lasting change in American foreign policy. The United States was the only major country to emerge from the war with its economy intact and the only country with operating nuclear weapons.

6 Soon after the close of World War II, the uncomfortable alliance between the United States and the Soviet Union ended, and the Cold War began. A policy of containment, which assumed an expansionist Soviet Union, was enunciated in the Truman Doctrine. Following the frustrations of the Vietnam War and the apparent arms equality of the United States and the Soviet Union, the United States was ready for détente. As the arms race escalated, arms control became a major foreign policy issue. Although President Ronald Reagan established a tough stance toward the Soviet Union in the first term of his administration, the second term saw serious negotiations toward arms reduction, culminating with the signing of the Intermediate-Range Nuclear Force Treaty at the Moscow summit in 1988. Negotiations toward further arms reduction continued in the Bush administration. The Strategic Arms Reduction Treaty, which limited long-range nuclear missiles, was signed in 1992 with Russia and several other states of the former Soviet Union.

7 Nuclear proliferation continues to be an issue due to the breakup of the Soviet Union and the loss of control over its nuclear arsenal, along with the continued efforts of other nations to gain nuclear warheads. The number of warheads is known to be nearly twenty thousand.

8 The United States is dependent on the world economy, as shown by the vulnerability of its stock market to world forces, its status as a debtor nation, and its significant trade deficit. The effects of a united Europe on world trade are yet to be fully realized.

9 Ethnic tensions and political instability in many regions of the world provide challenges to the United States. The nations of Central America and the Caribbean, including Haiti, require American attention because of their proximity. Negotiations have brought agreement in the Middle East and South Africa, whereas civil wars have torn apart Rwanda and Yugoslavia.

Selected print and electronic resources

SUGGESTED READINGS

Bernstein, Richard, and Ross H. Munro. *The Coming Conflict with China*. New York: Knopf, 1997. These authors take the position that it is important for the United States to be aware of the magnitude of Chinese power and to deal with China as a great nation. In their view, the rivalry between the United States and China is very natural and will require the United States to take a "containment" stance toward Chinese national goals.

Diehl, Paul F. *International Peacekeeping.* Baltimore, Md.: Johns Hopkins University Press, 1996. The author investigates the successes and failures of peacekeeping expeditions.

Haas, Richard N. *The Reluctant Sheriff: The United States after the Cold War.* New York: Council on Foreign Relations, 1997. With the end of the Cold War, the question of who polices the world is open. Haas sees the world as "unregulated" and envisions a possible role for the United States as the sheriff leading a posse of like-minded nations to keep some form of order.

Klare, Michael. *Rogue States and Nuclear Outlaws: America's Search for a Foreign Policy.* New York: Hill and Wang, 1995. The author concludes that the American military may have exaggerated the threat that lost or stolen nuclear materials will fall into the hands of terrorists in order to inflate the defense budget.

Martin, Hans-Peter, and Harald Schumann. *The Global Trap: Globalization and the Assault on Prosperity and Democracy.* New York: Oxford University Press, 1997. This analysis of globalization, written by Europeans, shows how the global companies exploit their workers and avoid the regulations of their own nations.

Miller, Judith. *God Has Ninety-Nine Names: Reporting from a Militant Middle East.* New York: Simon & Schuster, 1996. A journalist provides a lucid account of the forces at work in the Arab world of the Middle East and offers special insights into the possibilities there for terrorism and for accord.

Sagan, Scott D., and Kenneth N. Waltz. *The Spread of Nuclear Weapons: A Debate.* New York: W. W. Norton, 1995. The authors engage in a lively debate, with Waltz taking the position that nations that possess nuclear weapons are most likely to be cautious in their use, while those who do not may be reckless in war. Sagan takes the opposite view, contending that any proliferation of nuclear weapons is in itself dangerous.

Tanter, Raymond. *Rogue Regimes: Terrorism and Proliferation.* New York: Oxford University Press, 1997. A noted scholar of international relations examines the threats posed to peace and security by the so-called rogue states.

MEDIA RESOURCES

On the Beach—A film starring Gregory Peck, Ava Gardner, and Anthony Perkins that examines the lives of survivors of a nuclear holocaust living in Australia, the only nation to escape the blast.

Dr. Strangelove or How I Learned to Stop Worrying and Love the Bomb—A classic portrayal of a crazed general who is trying to start a nuclear war, produced in 1964 and starring Peter Sellers, who plays three roles; the film also stars George C. Scott and James Earl Jones.

The Mouse That Roared—An outrageous 1959 comedy that satirizes how Americans treat nations that they defeat. Peter Sellers leads the army of a very tiny nation that invades the United States in order to be defeated but ends up winning the war.

Logging on

For an overall look at the theory and practice of international relations, look at the Web site maintained by the Institute of World Politics at

www.iwp.edu/

The University of Michigan also maintains a Web site with information about regions throughout the world. Go to

henry.ugl.lib.umich.edu/libhome/Documents. center/foreign.html

The International Relations and Security Network, which is maintained by the Swiss government, contains information about human rights, national security, and other issues at

www.fsk.ethz.ch/

If you are interested in the intelligence community, you might want to look at the Web site maintained by Loyola University at

www.loyola.edu/dept/politics/intel.html

For information about visas, politics, business opportunities, and travel warnings, access the Web site maintained by the Department of State at

www.state.gov/index.html

Using the Internet for political analysis

Go to the home page maintained by the United Nations at

www.un.org/

and look over at least three of its divisions. Find out what kind of work those divisions do, and then identify the issues that might be controversial in the United States. Try to find the budget of the United Nations, and consider whether the United States should pay the back dues that it owes to this organization. Should the United States support all of the activities that you find on this Web site, or should the United States choose to support only those that are compatible with American ideals and goals?

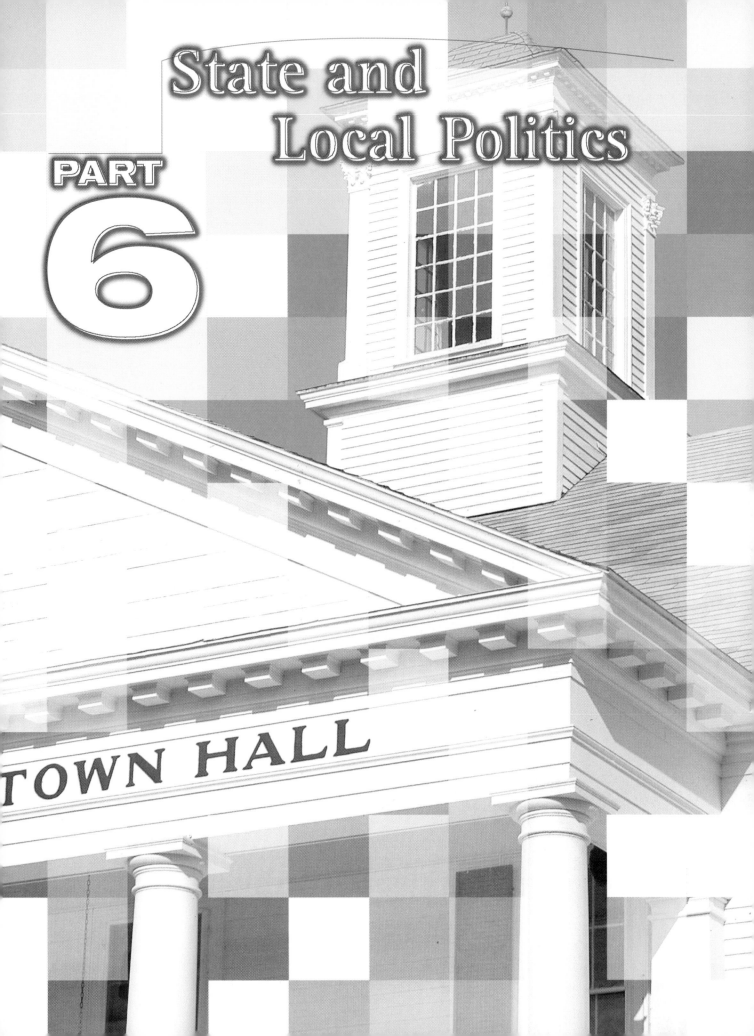

PART
6

State and
Local Politics

TOWN HALL

chapter **19**

State and Local Government

All States Allowed School Choice?

BACKGROUND

THERE IS A GROWING SENSE IN THIS COUNTRY THAT OUR EDUCATIONAL SYSTEM IS DECLINING. ROUTINELY, U.S. STUDENTS TEST POORLY IN ACHIEVEMENT, PARTICULARLY IN MATH AND SCIENCE, COMPARED TO STUDENTS IN SUCH COUNTRIES AS JAPAN, RUSSIA, AND GERMANY. NOT SURPRISINGLY, MANY OBSERVERS OF THE EDUCATIONAL SCENE BELIEVE THAT THE FAULT LIES IN OUR PUBLIC SCHOOL SYSTEM. THEY ARGUE THAT A CHANGE MUST BE MADE AND THAT THE EASIEST WAY TO MAKE SUCH A CHANGE INVOLVES SCHOOL CHOICE. CURRENTLY, PARENTS NORMALLY ARE REQUIRED TO SEND THEIR CHILDREN TO A PUBLIC SCHOOL IN THE PARTICULAR DISTRICT WHERE THE FAMILY'S PHYSICAL RESIDENCE IS LOCATED. GENERALLY, ONLY FAMILIES THAT WISH TO SPEND FROM $3,000 TO $10,000 A YEAR FOR TUITION AT PRIVATE SCHOOLS (IN ADDITION TO THE PROPERTY TAXES THEY PAY TO SUPPORT THEIR LOCAL PUBLIC SCHOOL DISTRICT) HAVE A CHOICE.

WHAT IF ALL STATES ALLOWED SCHOOL CHOICE?

The concept of school choice sometimes involves open districts, meaning that parents can choose to send their children to public schools outside their districts. The aspect of school choice that generates substantial controversy, however, usually involves giving families vouchers, representing state funds, that can be used at any school, public or private. In other words, a voucher would be worth some specified amount of money, such as $5,000, but only if it were redeemed by a bona fide public or private school. Under such a system, parents would determine where their children went to school. The children could attend the same local public school, a public school in another district, or a private school anywhere. Private schools might accept the vouchers as full payment for tuition fees or request that additional fees be paid.

COMPETITION WOULD BECOME EVIDENT

Certainly, competition for students would develop. Public schools would have to compete not only among themselves (which they currently do in areas that have open districts) but also with private schools. Private schools would have to compete with all schools, including new competitors in the educational marketplace.

Unquestionably, universal school choice would lead to a proliferation of new schools, including very small, specialized schools. For example, some small schools might arise that give special emphasis to the arts. Others might emphasize information technology, even for students at a young age. Others might emphasize foreign languages.

SOME SCHOOLS MIGHT FAIL

Because of the competitive educational environment that would be created by school choice, some public schools might not be able to retain or obtain enough students to enable the schools to survive. Unless local and state governments chose to subsidize failing public schools, they would go out of existence. (It is not surprising that virtually all public school teachers and administrators mount campaigns against any attempt in the various states to allow for school choice via the voucher system.)

Some private schools could fail also, as they already have. If they cannot compete effectively with neighboring public schools and other private schools, they, too, will close their doors. In essence, the business of education will become like other businesses, with the possibility of bankruptcy.

THE RISE OF RELIGIOUS SCHOOLING

Another possible outcome of universal school choice is the rise of religiously oriented schooling. Indeed, when a public choice initiative was put on the ballot in California a few years ago, such an argument proved extremely effective in defeating the initiative. Opponents of school choice there argued that the "religious right" would start hundreds or even thousands of new schools in California. Consequently, the state's children would run the risk of being exposed to what some perceive as "religious fanaticism." Although it is possible to start new religious schools today, virtually no public funds can be given to them. That is unlikely to be true under a voucher system that would allow parents to send their children to the schools of their choice.

FOR CRITICAL ANALYSIS

1. Why are teachers' unions, such as the National Education Association, so adamantly against school choice?

2. Is it possible that under universal school choice few, if any, new schools would be built in America's inner cities? Explain.

As you read in this chapter's *What If . . .* , it is up to the individual states to determine whether to allow school choice. There is no federal law that determines the issue, at least not yet. Within each state, even if a law allowing school choice were passed, local governments, particularly school boards, no doubt would have a large say in determining exactly how school choice would be made available in their particular areas.

This is true with respect to many state—and federal—policies. Typically, it is the local governing units in this country that give a human face to particular policies, such as welfare reform, and that deal directly with the people affected by those policies. Indeed, many people, when they think of government, think of local agencies or sets of individuals—such as city councils, city or county commissioners, school boards, libraries, zoning boards, fire and police departments, and so on—and not their state government or the federal government. Because they shape the environments in which all Americans live, the more than eighty thousand local governmental units in the United States play a vital role in our federal system.

From a practical point of view, it is impossible to understand American politics and government today without a knowledge of how state and local governments operate—the topic of this chapter. We begin by examining the constitutional powers of the states as set forth by the founders in the U.S. Constitution. As you will see, local governments were not mentioned in the Constitution. The founders left their existence in the hands of state government.

DID YOU KNOW...
That Texas's constitution declares that banks may use automated teller machines and that New York's constitution specifies the width of ski trails?

I N F O T R A C ®
COLLEGE EDITION

"Blocking the Exits"

The U.S. Constitution and the State Governments

We live in a federal system in which there are fifty separate state governments and one national government. The U.S. Constitution reserves a broad range of powers for state governments. It also prohibits state governments from engaging in certain activities. The U.S. Constitution does not say explicitly what the states actually may do. Rather, state powers are simply reserved, or residual:

Public education is one of the primary functions of state and local government. In recent years, a number of states have begun school-reform efforts, often delegating more control over local schools to parents and to the community.

Police Power
Authority to promote and safeguard the health, morals, safety, and welfare of the people.

States may do anything that is not prohibited by the Constitution or anything that is not expressly within the realm of the national government.

The major reserved powers of the states are the powers to tax, spend, and regulate intrastate commerce, or commerce within a given state. The states also have general **police power,** meaning they can impose their will on their citizens in the areas of safety (through, say, traffic laws), health (immunizations), welfare (child-abuse laws), and morals (regulation of pornographic materials).

Restrictions on state and local governmental activity are implied by the Constitution in Article VI, Clause 2:

> This Constitution, and the Laws of the United States which shall be made in Pursuance thereof; and all Treaties made, or which shall be made, under the Authority of the United States, shall be the supreme Law of the Land; and the Judges in every State shall be bound thereby, any Thing in the Constitution or Laws of any State to the Contrary notwithstanding.

In other words, it is the U.S. Constitution that is the supreme law of the land. No state or local law can be in conflict with the Constitution, with laws made by the national Congress, or with treaties entered into by the national government. Judicially, the United States Supreme Court has been the final arbiter of conflicts arising between the national government and state governments.

State Constitutions

The U.S. Constitution is a model of brevity, although at the cost of specificity. State constitutions, however, typically are excessively long and detailed. The U.S. Constitution has endured for two hundred years and has been amended only twenty-seven times. State constitutions are another matter. Louisiana has had eleven constitutions; Georgia, ten; South Carolina, seven; and Alabama, Florida, and Virginia, six. The number of amendments that have been submitted to voters borders on the absurd. For example, by 1998, the citizens of Alabama had adopted over 580 amendments to their state constitution.

Why Are State Constitutions So Long?

According to historians, the length and mass of detail of many state constitutions reflect the loss of popular confidence in state legislatures between the end of the Civil War and the early 1900s. During that period, forty-two states adopted or revised their constitutions. Those constitutions adopted before or after that period are shorter and contain fewer restrictions on the powers of state legislatures. Another equally important reason for the length and detail of state constitutions is that state constitution makers apparently have had a difficult time distinguishing between constitutional and statutory law. Does the Louisiana constitution need an amendment to declare Huey Long's birthday a legal holiday? Is it necessary for the constitution of South Dakota to authorize a cordage and twine plant at the state penitentiary? Does Article XX of the California constitution need to discuss the tax-exempt status of the Huntington Library and Art Gallery? The U.S. Constitution contains no such details. It leaves to the legislature the nuts-and-bolts activity of making specific statutory laws.

In all fairness to the states, their courts do not interpret their constitutions as freely as the United States Supreme Court interprets the U.S. Constitution. Therefore, the states feel compelled to be more specific in their own constitutions. Additionally, the framers of state constitutions may feel compelled to fill in the gaps left by the very brief federal constitution.

The Constitutional Convention and the Constitutional Initiative

Two of the several ways to effect constitutional changes are the state constitutional convention and the constitutional initiative. As of 1999, over 230 state constitutional conventions had been used to write an entirely new constitution or to attempt to amend an existing one. A major feature of the constitutions of eighteen states permits those constitutions to be amended by **constitutional initiatives.**[1] An initiative allows citizens to place a proposed amendment on the ballot without calling a constitutional convention. The number of signatures required to get a constitutional initiative on the ballot varies from state to state; it is usually between 5 and 10 percent of the total number of votes cast for governor in the last election. The initiative process has been used most frequently in California and Oregon. Relatively few initiative amendments are approved by the electorate.

Constitutional Initiative
An electoral device whereby citizens can propose a constitutional amendment through petitions signed by the required number of registered voters.

The State Executive Branch

All state governments in the United States have executive, legislative, and judicial branches. Here the similarity with the federal government ends. State governments do not always have strong executive branches.

A Weak Executive

During the colonial period, governors were appointed by the Crown and had the power to call the colonial assembly (the colonial legislative body) into session, recommend legislation, exercise veto power, and dissolve the assembly. The colonial governor acted as commander in chief of the colony's military forces and was also the head of the judiciary.

Not surprisingly, the colonies' revolt against British rule centered on the all-powerful colonial governors. When the first states were formed after the Declaration of Independence, hostility toward the governor's office ensured a weak executive branch and an extremely strong legislative branch. By the 1830s, however, the state executive office had become more important. Since Andrew Jackson's presidency, all governors (except in South Carolina) have been elected directly by the people. Simultaneously, there was an effort to democratize state government by popularly electing other state government officials as well.

Under the tenets of Jacksonian democracy, the more public officials who are elected (and not appointed), the more democratic (and better) the system will be. Even today, some states have numerous state offices with independently elected officials. The direct election of so many executive officials makes it likely that no one will have much power, because each official is working to secure his or her own political support. Only if the elected officials happen to be able to work together cohesively can they get much done.

A slight majority of the states require that the candidates for governor and lieutenant governor run for election as a team. In some states where this is not required, however, the voters have at times chosen a governor from one political party and a lieutenant governor from another. As a result, the governor may

---

[1]These states are Arizona, Arkansas, California, Colorado, Florida, Illinois, Massachusetts, Michigan, Mississippi, Missouri, Montana, Nebraska, Nevada, North Dakota, Ohio, Oklahoma, Oregon, and South Dakota.

be unwilling to leave the state in order to prevent the lieutenant governor from exerting power during the governor's travels.

Reforming the System

Most states follow the practice of electing numerous executive officials. Nonetheless, governors have exercised the authority of their office with increasing frequency in recent years. Governors have become a significant force in legislative policymaking. The governor, in theory, enjoys the same advantage that the president has over Congress in his or her ability to make policy decisions and to embody these in a program on which the state legislative body can act. How the governor exercises this ability often depends on his or her powers of persuasion. A strong personality can make for a strong executive office. Personal skill, the strength of political parties and special interest groups, and the governor's use of the media can affect how much actual power he or she has.

Reorganization of the state executive branch to achieve greater efficiency has been attempted numerous times and in many states. There are some obstacles to reorganizing state executive branches. Voters do not want to lose their ability to influence politics directly. Both the voters and the legislators fear that reorganization will concentrate too much authority in the hands of the governor. Finally, many believe that numerous governmental functions, such as control of the highway program, should remain administrative rather than political.

Despite the fragmentation of executive power and doubts about the concentration of power in an executive's hands, the trend toward modernization has increased the powers of many of the states' highest executives. Based on a governor's ability to make major appointments, formulate a state budget, veto legislation, and exercise other powers, the National Governors Association ranks the governors of at least twenty-five states as powerful or very powerful executives. Only eleven states are assessed as giving their executives little or very little power.

Moreover, state governors—as well as legislators—are playing increasingly important roles as the states assume more authority over programs, such as welfare, that for decades have been controlled by the national government. The devolutionary trend of the 1990s has allowed governors to become models of leadership on a number of issues affecting national politics, including crime, welfare, and education. A state governorship also may be a steppingstone to the U.S. presidency. Sixteen of the nation's forty-two presidents (38 percent), including three of our last four presidents (Jimmy Carter, Ronald Reagan, and Bill Clinton), served as state governors before assuming the presidential office. For these reasons, elections to state governorships tend to receive more national attention than in the past.

The Governor's Veto Power

The veto power gives the president of the United States immense leverage. Simply the threat of a presidential veto often means that legislation will not be passed by Congress. In some states, governors have strong veto power, but in other states, governors have no veto power at all. Some states give the governor veto power but allow only five days in which to exercise it. Thirteen states give the governor pocket veto power (see Chapter 13).

Item Veto
The power exercised by the governors of most states to veto particular sections or items of an appropriations bill, while signing the remainder of the bill into law.

In forty-three states, the governor has some form of **item veto** power on appropriations. If the governor in such a state does not particularly like one item, or line, in an appropriations bill, he or she can veto that item. In twelve states, the governor can reduce the amount of the appropriation but cannot reduce it to zero. Nineteen states give governors the ability to use the item veto on more than just appropriations.

The State Legislature

Although there has been a move in recent years to increase the power of governors, state legislatures are still an important force in state politics and state governmental decision making. The task of these assemblies is to legislate on such matters as taxes and the regulation of business and commerce, highways, school systems and the funding of education, and welfare payments. Allocation of funds and program priorities are vital issues to local residents and communities, and conflicts between regions within the state or between the cities and the rural areas are common.

State legislatures have been criticized for being unprofessional and less than effective. It is true that state legislatures sometimes spend their time considering trivial legislation (such as the official state pie in Florida), and lobbyists often have too much influence in state capitals. At the same time, state legislators are often given few resources with which to work. In many states, legislatures are limited to meeting only part of the year, and in some the pay is a disincentive to real service. In at least eight states, state legislators are paid less than $10,000 per year. A complete list of state legislators' salaries, as well as other characteristics of state legislatures, is given in Table 19–1 on page 612.

We have seen earlier how a bill becomes a law in the U.S. Congress. A similar process occurs at the state level. Figure 19–1 traces how an idea becomes a law in the Florida legislature. Similar steps are followed in other states (note that Nebraska has a unicameral legislature, however, so there is no second chamber process).

FIGURE 19–1

How an Idea Becomes a Law

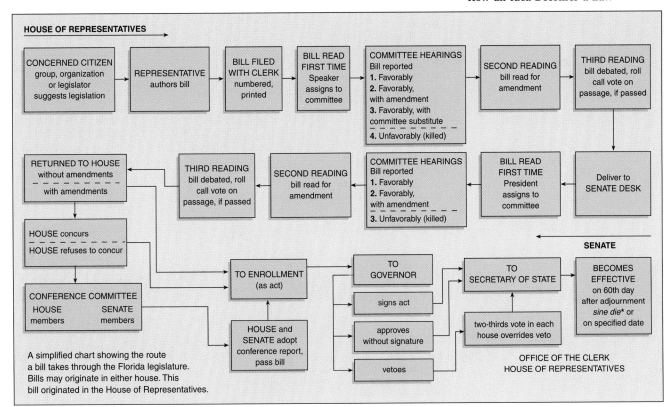

SOURCE: Allen Morris and Joan Perry Morris, Compilers, *The Florida Handbook 1997–1998*, 26th ed. (Tallahassee, Fla.: Peninsular Publishing Co., 1997).

Sine die means "without assigning a day for a further meeting."

TABLE 19-1

Characteristics of State Legislatures

	Seats in Senate	Length of Term	Seats in House	Length of Term	Years Sessions Are Held	Salary*
Alabama	35	4	105	4	Annual	$10(d)†
Alaska	20	4	40	2	Annual	24,012†
Arizona	30	2	60	2	Annual	15,000
Arkansas	35	4	100	2	Odd	12,500†
California	40	4	80	2	Even	75,600†
Colorado	35	4	65	2	Annual	17,500
Connecticut	36	2	151	2	Annual	16,760
Delaware	21	4	41	2	Annual	27,500†
Florida	40	4	120	2	Annual	24,912†
Georgia	56	2	180	2	Annual	11,348†
Hawaii	25	4	51	2	Annual	32,000†
Idaho	35	2	70	2	Annual	12,360†
Illinois	59	‡	118	2	Annual	47,039†
Indiana	50	4	100	2	Annual	11,600†
Iowa	50	4	100	2	Annual	20,120
Kansas	40	4	125	2	Annual	63(d)†
Kentucky	38	4	100	2	Even	103(d)†
Louisiana	39	4	105	4	Annual	16,800†
Maine	35	2	151	2	Even	10,500§
Maryland	47	4	141	4	Annual	29,700†
Massachusetts	40	2	160	2	Annual	46,410†
Michigan	38	4	110	2	Annual	51,895†
Minnesota	67	4	134	2	Odd	29,675†
Mississippi	52	4	122	4	Annual	10,000†
Missouri	34	4	163	2	Annual	26,803
Montana	50	4	100	2	Odd	58(d)†
Nebraska"	49	4	—	—	Annual	12,000†
Nevada	21	4	42	2	Odd	130(d)†
New Hampshire	24	2	400	2	Annual	200(b)
New Jersey	40	4	80	2	Annual	35,000
New Mexico	42	4	70	2	Annual	—†
New York	61	2	150	2	Annual	57,500†
North Carolina	50	2	120	2	Odd	13,951†
North Dakota	49	4	98	4	Odd	111(d)†
Ohio	33	4	99	2	Annual	42,427
Oklahoma	48	4	101	2	Annual	32,000†
Oregon	30	4	60	2	Odd	13,104†
Pennsylvania	50	4	203	2	Annual	57,367†
Rhode Island	50	2	100	2	Annual	10,250
South Carolina	46	4	124	2	Annual	10,400†
South Dakota	35	2	70	2	Annual	4,267#
Tennessee	33	4	99	2	Odd	16,500†
Texas	31	4	150	2	Odd	7,200†
Utah	29	4	75	2	Annual	100(d)†
Vermont	30	2	150	2	Odd	510(w)
Virginia	40	4	100	2	Annual	18,000†
Washington	49	4	98	2	Annual	28,800†
West Virginia	34	4	100	2	Annual	15,000
Wisconsin	33	4	99	2	Annual	39,211†
Wyoming	30	4	60	2	Annual	125(d)†

*Salaries annual unless otherwise noted as (d)–per day, (b)–biennium, or (w)–per week.
†Plus *per diem* living expenses.
‡Terms vary from two to four years.
§For odd year; $7,500 for even year.
"Unicameral legislature.
#For odd year; $3,733 for even year.

SOURCE: Adapted from Council of State Governments, *Book of the States, 1998–1999.*

Legislative Apportionment

Drawing up legislative districts—state as well as federal—has long been subject to gerrymandering—creative cartography designed to guarantee that one political party maintains control of a particular voting district. Malapportionment is the skewed distribution of voters in a state's legislative districts. The United States Supreme Court indicated in 1962 that malapportioned state legislatures violate the equal protection clause of the Fourteenth Amendment.[2] In a series of cases that followed, the Court held that legislative districts must be as nearly equal as possible in terms of population, and the grossest examples of state legislative malapportionment were eliminated.[3] The Burger Court, however, allowed "benevolent, bipartisan gerrymandering" in certain states. Indeed, in 1977, the Supreme Court held that a state had an obligation imposed under the 1965 Voting Rights Act to draw district boundaries to maximize minority legislative representation.[4] Thus, each decade, state and federal legislative districts must be redrawn to ensure that every person's vote is roughly equal and that minorities are represented adequately.

By the mid-1990s, however, the Supreme Court had reversed its position on what has been called "racial gerrymandering." In 1996, the Court held that voting districts that are redrawn with the goal of maximizing the electoral strength and representation of minority groups violate the equal protection clause. (See Chapter 12 for a more detailed discussion of this issue.)

Direct Democracy:
The Initiative, Referendum, and Recall

There is a major difference between the legislative process as outlined in the U.S. Constitution and the legislative process as outlined in the various state constitutions. Many states exercise a type of direct democracy through the initiative, the referendum, and the recall—procedures that allow voters directly to control the government.

The Initiative.   One technique lets citizens bypass legislatures by proposing new statutes or changes in government for citizen approval. Most states that permit the citizen **legislative initiative** require that the initiative's backers circulate a petition to place the issue on the ballot and that a certain percentage of the registered voters in the last gubernatorial election sign the petition. Twenty-two states use the legislative initiative, typically those states in which political parties are relatively weak and nonpartisan groups are strong. Legislative initiatives have involved protecting crime victims' rights, authorizing tougher penalties for certain crimes, allowing certain types of legalized gambling, limiting campaign contributions, limiting corporate spending on ballot questions, changing a state capital from one city to another, denying state services to illegal immigrants, establishing uniform state regulation of smoking, restricting the rights of homosexuals, and allowing terminally ill patients to obtain a doctor's prescription for drugs to end a life. (For a further discussion of the initiative process generally, see the feature on page 614, *Politics and the Law: Are Voter Initiatives Getting Out of Hand?*)

The Referendum.   The **referendum** is similar to the initiative, except that the issue (or constitutional change) is proposed first by the legislature and then directed to the voters for their approval. The referendum is most often used for

---

DID YOU KNOW...
That the Treasury Department recently announced that it would not oppose a plan being considered in Congress to let every state put an image of its own choosing on the back side of the quarter

Legislative Initiative
A procedure by which voters can propose a change in state or local laws by gathering signatures on a petition and submitting it to the legislature for approval.

INFOTRAC®
COLLEGE EDITION

"NRA Defeated Initiative 676 in Washington State"

Referendum
An electoral device whereby legislative or constitutional measures are referred by the legislature to the voters for approval or disapproval.

POLITICS and the Law

Are Voter Initiatives Getting Out of Hand?

The voter initiative has been around since the nineteenth century—it is a product of the grassroots politicking that was characteristic of the Progressive Era in American politics. According to some, such initiatives represent democracy at its best—citizens proposing and voting on laws tailored to the needs of their states or local regions. Voter initiatives have been particularly popular in the western states, including Arizona, California, Oregon, and Washington.

California first used the voter initiative in 1911, but it became widely popular in that state only after 1978, when Californians voted in favor of a controversial initiative referred to as Proposition 13. This proposition capped local property tax rates and cut $5 billion in taxes statewide—something that California politicians had said could not be done. In

the decade following the success of Proposition 13, the number of initiatives appearing on the California ballot doubled, and it has been rising ever since. In 1996, California voters faced a total of over twenty initiatives, many of which were controversial. The nation is still reeling from the ban on state-sponsored affirmative action created by a ballot initiative, Proposition 209, passed in that year. In 1998, Californians again faced initiatives on a number of controversial issues, including whether bilingual education programs should be ended (they were) and whether labor unions should be required to obtain permission from union members before using union dues for political activities (they were not).

Increasingly, other states (and many cities) are using

voter initiatives to put issues on the ballot. Like some recent California initiatives, those in other states are often controversial. For example, Oregon citizens recently passed an initiative legalizing physician-assisted suicide in that state—the only state to have such a law. In 1998, citizens from Alaska to Florida voted on ballot initiatives covering a wide range of issues, including tax cuts, term limits, limitations on the size of school classes, and legalization of the medical use of marijuana.

Is the initiative process getting out of hand? Some contend that it is. For one thing, say these critics, the process bypasses the traditional research and deliberation that legislators undertake before enacting new laws. In contrast, initiatives

may call for radical departures from existing law without a full exploration of their possible effects on the welfare of the state's citizens and on national-state relations. Additionally, a close examination of the initiative process reveals that it no longer represents simply grassroots politicking. On the contrary, it has come to be dominated by large, often national interest groups that funnel millions of dollars into advertising the merits (or faults) of particular initiatives and gathering the signatures necessary to get initiatives on the ballot.

FOR CRITICAL ANALYSIS

Why would a special interest group push for an initiative rather than work directly with a legislature?

approval of local school bond issues and for amendments to state constitutions. In a number of states that provide for the referendum, a bill passed by the legislature may be suspended by obtaining the required number of voters' signatures on petitions. A statewide referendum election is then held. If a majority of the voters disapprove of the bill, it is no longer valid.

The referendum was not initially intended for regular use, and indeed it was used infrequently in the past. Its opponents argue that it is an unnecessary check on representative government and that it weakens legislative responsibility. In recent years, the referendum has become increasingly popular as citizens have attempted to control their state and local governments. Interest groups have been active in sponsoring the petition drives necessary to force a referendum. Over two-thirds of the states provide for the referendum.

The Recall. The right of citizens to recall, or remove, elected officials is not exercised frequently. **Recall** is a provision written into the constitutions of fifteen states. It allows voters to remove elected state officials, including the governor, before the expiration of their terms of office. In the case of judges, the recall can terminate a lifetime appointment.

Citizens begin the recall process by circulating petitions demanding a statewide vote to remove the offending officeholder. The number of signatures required to bring about the election ranges from 10 to 40 percent of the last vote

Recall
A procedure enabling voters to remove an elected official from office before his or her term has expired.

for the office in question. If the required number of signatures is obtained, the question of whether to remove the incumbent is decided in a general election. About one-third of the states sanction the use of the recall.

The recall and the initiative are examples of "pure democracy," in which the people as a whole vote directly on important issues. Such measures are distinct in theory and in practice from the norms of "representative democracy," in which the people govern only indirectly, through their elected representatives.

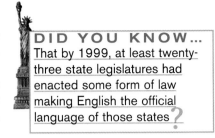

DID YOU KNOW...
That by 1999, at least twenty-three state legislatures had enacted some form of law making English the official language of those states?

The State Judiciary

Each of the fifty states, as well as the District of Columbia, has its own separate court system (which is in addition to the federal courts–see Chapter 15). Figure 19-2 shows a sample state court system. Like the federal court system, it has

FIGURE 19-2

A Sample State Court System

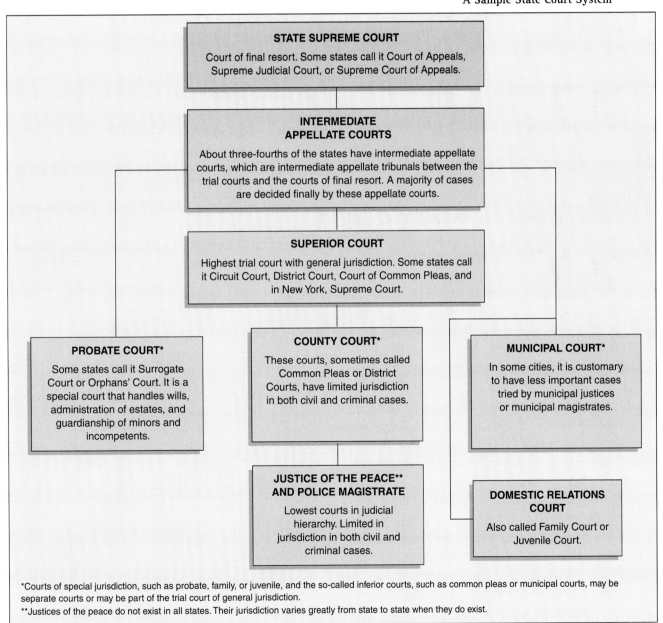

STATE SUPREME COURT

Court of final resort. Some states call it Court of Appeals, Supreme Judicial Court, or Supreme Court of Appeals.

INTERMEDIATE APPELLATE COURTS

About three-fourths of the states have intermediate appellate courts, which are intermediate appellate tribunals between the trial courts and the courts of final resort. A majority of cases are decided finally by these appellate courts.

SUPERIOR COURT

Highest trial court with general jurisdiction. Some states call it Circuit Court, District Court, Court of Common Pleas, and in New York, Supreme Court.

PROBATE COURT*

Some states call it Surrogate Court or Orphans' Court. It is a special court that handles wills, administration of estates, and guardianship of minors and incompetents.

COUNTY COURT*

These courts, sometimes called Common Pleas or District Courts, have limited jurisdiction in both civil and criminal cases.

MUNICIPAL COURT*

In some cities, it is customary to have less important cases tried by municipal justices or municipal magistrates.

JUSTICE OF THE PEACE AND POLICE MAGISTRATE**

Lowest courts in judicial hierarchy. Limited in jurisdiction in both civil and criminal cases.

DOMESTIC RELATIONS COURT

Also called Family Court or Juvenile Court.

*Courts of special jurisdiction, such as probate, family, or juvenile, and the so-called inferior courts, such as common pleas or municipal courts, may be separate courts or may be part of the trial court of general jurisdiction.
**Justices of the peace do not exist in all states. Their jurisdiction varies greatly from state to state when they do exist.

SOURCE: William P. Statsky, *Introduction to Paralegalism*, 5th ed. (St. Paul: West, 1997), p. 329.

INFOTRAC®
COLLEGE EDITION

"Odds favor More Gambling"

several tiers, including trial courts, intermediate courts of appeal, and a supreme court. Again, the trial courts are of two types: those having limited jurisdiction and those having general jurisdiction.[5] (For some jurisdictional challenges faced by state courts today, see this chapter's *Critical Perspective*.) Cases heard before these courts can be appealed to the state appellate court and ultimately to the state supreme court.

[5]See Chapter 15 for a definition of these terms.

Critical | perspective

Can States Control Betting on the Internet?

Currently, all states have laws determining the legality of gambling contracts. In most states, gambling contracts are illegal and thus void. In some states, such as Nevada, New Jersey, and Louisiana, and on some Indian reservations, casino gambling is legal. In other states, certain other forms of gambling are legal. California, for example, has not defined draw poker as a crime, although the state criminal statutes prohibit numerous other types of gambling games. Several states allow gambling at horse races, and many states have legalized state-operated lotteries, as well as lotteries (such as bingo) held for charitable purposes.

Who Can Exercise Jurisdiction?

State laws generally govern only activities within a state's borders. For example, Texas could not attempt to regulate gambling in New Jersey. In other words, Texas has no constitutional authority to regulate gambling activities in New Jersey or Nevada, or in any other state. Furthermore, no state government has jurisdiction over activities in other countries. Indeed, even the federal government has little authority concerning activities in other countries.

Likewise, the jurisdiction of state courts, the judicial branches of state governments, typically extends only to disputes involving persons within a state's borders, and not to parties in other states. In some states, however, a state court can exercise jurisdiction over out-of-state defendants who commit wrongs—such as causing automobile accidents or selling defective goods—that harm the state's residents. Additionally, as you read in Chapter 15, suits between parties of different states can be taken to the federal courts, which can exercise jurisdiction based on the diversity of citizenship between the parties.

In other words, although a state government cannot regulate the affairs of other states, the state and federal courts can and do regulate—at least to some extent—matters that might extend beyond a particular state's borders by permitting lawsuits to be brought against out-of-state defendants.

Enter the Internet

The United States, and indeed the world, is full of "netizens." They are everywhere and at the same time nowhere. Among other things, Internet users can engage in online betting. Today, for example, virtually any person, even a twelve-year-old with a credit card, can play blackjack on the Internet. Often, the gambling entity resides in some offshore location, such as the Cayman Islands or even Finland or Iceland.

Online gambling has created thorny jurisdictional issues for both state governments and the federal government. To understand why, consider an example. Assume that a resident of Missouri logs on the Internet and pulls up a gambling site. He or she then places a bet via a credit card. The home Web site server of the gambling company is on the Caribbean island of Grenada. The gambling company has a bona fide license in Grenada to operate the Web site.

One of the many Internet sites that allow individuals to engage in online gambling.

All states have major trial courts, commonly called circuit courts, district courts, or superior courts. The number of judges and their terms in office vary widely. About three-fourths of the states have intermediate appellate courts between the trial courts of original jurisdiction and the court of last resort. These are usually called courts of appeal. Salaries of state judges also vary widely, but higher pay is given to appellate and supreme court members.

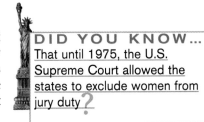

DID YOU KNOW...
That until 1975, the U.S. Supreme Court allowed the states to exclude women from jury duty?

Critical perspective

Can States Control Betting on the Internet?—continued

The interacting electronic links between the home server and the gambler would go through many different possible servers located in Africa, Asia, or anywhere.

The state of Missouri is concerned that illegal gambling transactions are occurring within its state, but what can it do? It cannot pass a law governing gambling operations in another U.S. state, let alone Grenada. It could try to bring a criminal action in court against the gambling company for conducting illegal gambling operations "within" its state, but then a jurisdictional problem arises. How can a Missouri court or even a federal court exercise jurisdiction over a foreign entity? Complicating the issue is the fact that the online transactions could have involved servers in twenty different jurisdictions. Clearly, jurisdictional concepts that have traditionally been linked to geographic borders are difficult to apply to the nonphysical landscape of the Internet.

Should the Federal Government Regulate Online Gambling?

In an attempt to regulate Internet gambling, bills have been introduced in Congress that make such actions illegal. For example, the Internet Gambling bill (S.474) introduced by Senator Jon Kyl (R., Ariz.) would do the following:

- Make bettors liable for gambling violations.
- Apply the law to Internet service providers in addition to telephone companies.
- Impose a $10,000 fine or a prison term of two years on operators of Internet gambling facilities.
- Impose a $5,000 fine on individuals who use the Internet for gambling.
- Provide federal, state, and local officials with the authority to prohibit communication facilities from transmitting betting information.

Clearly concerned that the government may place limits on its operations, the Internet gambling industry has already begun attempts at self-regulation. A code of conduct was recently put out by the Interactive Gaming Council, whose members agree to post loss limits and refer compulsive bettors to counseling organizations.

The Problem of Enforcement

Assume for the moment that a federal law is passed outlawing all online gambling. How can the law be enforced? It is impossible to keep track of what will become millions and millions of Internet Web sites. This same issue has already arisen with respect to online pornography. It is possible for anybody to access literally thousands of pornography sites. Five years from now, that number will be multiplied tenfold. No government, including the federal government, can monitor every action by every user of the Internet. Given that most Americans will be using the Internet in the next decade, "Internet watchers" would have to monitor upwards of several hundred million people. That, of course, is impossible.

Given the relative newness of the Internet, we cannot even predict how online betting operations will respond to federal (or state) laws restricting online gambling operations. Gambling site operators may just make sure that no U.S. resident has anything to do with their gambling sites. Very likely, however, because of the high profits to be made, at least some of these operators will find creative ways to circumvent the restrictions. Currently, Americans gamble over $500 billion legally (earning $50 billion in profits for the gaming industry), and we can expect online gambling to mushroom.

FOR CRITICAL ANALYSIS

1. Are jurisdictional issues a problem with the regulation of online pornography, too?
2. Which business groups in America would be in favor of making online betting illegal, and why?

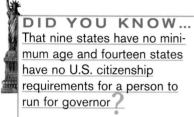

INFOTRAC®
COLLEGE EDITION

"Facing the City's Sports Future"

The state courts of last resort are usually called simply supreme courts, although they are also labeled the supreme judicial court (Maine and Massachusetts), the court of appeals (Maryland and New York), the court of criminal appeals (Oklahoma and Texas, which also have separate supreme courts for appeals in noncriminal cases), or the supreme court of appeals (West Virginia).

State court judges are either elected or appointed, depending on the state and (often) on the level of court involved—the procedures vary widely from state to state. In some states, including Delaware, the procedure is similar to the way federal judges are appointed—the judged are appointed by the governor and confirmed by the upper chamber of the legislature. In other states, all state court judges are elected, either on a partisan ballot (as in Arkansas) or on a nonpartisan ballot (as in Kentucky). In several states, judges in some of the lower courts are elected, while those in the appellate courts are appointed. Additionally, depending on the state, judges who are appointed may have to run for reelection if they wish to serve a second term. (See the feature *Politics and Elections: Is the State Judicial System Too Political?* for a discussion of some of the implications of elective judgeships.)

State courts confront severe problems of underfunding and overwork. State courts annually process more than 100 million cases per year. Almost 70 percent of those cases are traffic or other minor cases. But criminal cases account for about 13 million of the total, up by 45 percent since 1985. Short on judicial personnel and frequently delayed by complex cases with lengthy appeals, the state

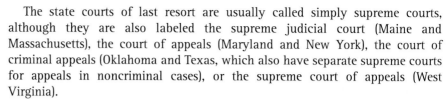

POLITICS and Elections

Is the State Judicial System Too Political?

Remember from Chapter 15 that judges in the federal courts are appointed by the president and, if confirmed by the Senate, hold office for life—unless they engage in blatantly illegal conduct. They do not have to worry about reelection and, consequently, can make rulings on specific issues without having to take public opinion into account.

Although some state judges are appointed (the procedures vary widely from state to state), in thirty-eight states at least some judges are elected. To gain (or retain) their seats, those judges typically must conduct political campaigns—and obtain funds to pay for those campaigns. In some judicial races, campaign war chests are beginning to resemble those for a

typical U.S. Senate race. Consider that in a recent Texas Supreme Court contest, candidates for the high court spent nearly $6 million. Shortly thereafter, candidates for the Alabama Supreme Court spent close to $5 million on their campaigns.

Who are the contributors? A recent study by the State Affairs Company of Reston, Virginia, showed that more than 70 percent of the contributions to judicial races come from trial lawyers, many of whom argue cases before the very judges whose campaigns they help to finance. According to Pat Rowland, executive director of a legal reform group in Arlington, Virginia, "When you look at the dollars contributed and

the time, it's obvious that the trial bar is trying to buy judgeships."*

Trial lawyers defend the practice by saying that their contributions help to level the playing field between large corporate enterprises and low-income plaintiffs. A lawyer can represent a plaintiff with few resources by charging a "contingency fee," meaning that the lawyer will get a certain percentage (usually about 30 percent) of whatever money damages are awarded in the lawsuit if the plaintiff wins. By helping to elect judges who favor high damage awards, the trial lawyers thereby lend a helping hand to the "little guy." Gary Stephens, a Houston

trial lawyer, put it this way: "We're really the only voice that the common man has."†

Nevertheless, the increasing influence of trial lawyers on state judicial elections has stirred many citizens to action. Currently, a number of groups are advocating legal reforms that include placing caps on contributions to judicial candidates.

FOR CRITICAL ANALYSIS

Would society be better off if all state court judges were appointed, as federal judges are?

†*Ibid.,* p. 20.

*As cited in "Attorneys' Rising Political Clout," *Nation's Business,* February 1998, p. 20.

This volunteer is working to make sure that a local referendum is passed in California. A referendum is an issue or constitutional change that is proposed first by the legislature and then directed to the voters for their approval. An initiative, in contrast, lets citizens bypass legislatures completely by proposing new statutes or changes in government for citizen approval.

courts are not always able to function efficiently or fairly. The consequence is all too often a resort to plea-bargained convictions or a denial of justice to plaintiffs in civil and criminal cases.

How Local Government Operates

Local governments are difficult to describe because of their great dissimilarities and because, if we include municipalities, counties, towns, townships, and special districts, there are so many of them. We limit the discussion here to the most important types and features of local governments.

The Legal Existence of Local Government

As mentioned earlier, the U.S. Constitution makes no mention of local governments. Article IV, Section 4, states that "[t]he United States shall guarantee to every State in this Union a Republican Form of Government." Actually, then, the states do not even have to have local governments. Consequently, every local government is a creature of the state. The state can create a local government, and the state can terminate the right of a local government to exist. Indeed, states often have abolished entire counties, school districts, cities, and special districts. Since World War II, almost twenty thousand school districts have gone out of existence as they were consolidated with other school districts.

Because the local government is the legal creation of the state, does that mean the state can dictate everything the local government does? For many years that seemed to be the case. The narrowest possible view of the legal status of local governments follows **Dillon's rule,** outlined by Judge John F. Dillon in his *Commentaries on the Law of Municipal Corporations* in 1811. He stated that municipal corporations may possess only powers "granted in express words . . . [that are] necessarily or fairly implied in or incident to the powers expressly

Dillon's Rule
The narrowest possible interpretation of the legal status of local governments, outlined by Judge John F. Dillon, who in 1811 stated that a municipal corporation can exercise only those powers expressly granted by state law.

Charter

A document issued by a government that grants to a person, a group of persons, or a corporation the right to carry on one or more specific activities. A state government can grant a charter to a municipality allowing that group of persons to carry on specific activities.

Cooley's Rule

The view that cities should be able to govern themselves, presented in an 1871 Michigan decision by Judge Thomas Cooley.

Municipal Home Rule

The power vested in a local unit of government to draft or change its own charter and to manage its own affairs.

Home Rule City

A city with a charter allowing local voters to frame, adopt, and amend their own charter.

General Law City

A city operating under general state laws that apply to all local governmental units of a similar type.

County

The chief governmental unit set up by the state to administer state law and business at the local level. Counties are drawn up by area, rather than by rural or urban criteria.

granted."[6] Cities governed under Dillon's rule have been dominated by the state legislature. Those communities wishing to obtain the status of a municipal corporation have simply petitioned the state legislature for a **charter.** The charter has typically been extremely narrow.

In a revolt against state legislative power over municipalities, the home rule movement began. It was based on **Cooley's rule,** derived from an 1871 decision by Michigan judge Thomas Cooley stating that cities should be able to govern themselves.[7] Since 1900, about four-fifths of the states have allowed **municipal home rule,** but only with respect to local concerns for which no statewide interests are involved. A municipality must choose to become a **home rule city;** otherwise, it operates as a **general law city.** In the latter case, the state makes certain general laws relating to cities of different sizes, which are designated as first-class cities, second-class cities, or towns. Once a city, by virtue of its population, receives such a ranking, it follows the general law put down by the state. Only if it chooses to be a home rule city can it avoid such state government restrictions. In most states, only cities with populations of 2,500 or more can choose home rule.

Local Governmental Units

There are four major types of local governmental units: municipalities, counties, towns and townships, and special districts.

Municipalities. A municipality is a political entity created by the people of a city or town to govern themselves locally. Currently, there are about nineteen thousand municipalities within the fifty states. Almost all municipalities are fairly small cities. Only about two hundred cities have populations over one hundred thousand, and only ten cities (New York, Los Angeles, Chicago, Houston, Philadelphia, San Diego, Phoenix, San Antonio, Dallas, and Detroit) have populations over a million. City expenditures are primarily for water supply and other utilities, police and fire protection, and education. About three-fourths of municipal tax revenues come from property taxes. Municipalities rely very heavily on financial assistance from both the federal and state governments.

Counties. The difference between a **county** and a municipality is that a county may not be created at the behest of its inhabitants. The state sets up counties on its own initiative to serve as political extensions of the state government. Counties apply state law and administer state business at the local level.

Counties, of which there are over three thousand within the United States, vary greatly in both size and population. San Bernardino County in California is the largest geographically, with 20,102 square miles. New York County in New York is the smallest, with less than 22 square miles. County populations range from millions of residents, as in Los Angeles County, to fewer than a hundred residents, as in Kalawao County, Hawaii.

County governments' responsibilities include zoning, building regulations, health, hospitals, parks, recreation, highways, public safety, justice, and record keeping. Typically, when a municipality is established within a county, the county withdraws most of its services from the municipality; for example, the municipal police force takes over from the county police force. County governments are extremely complex entities, a product of the era of Jacksonian democracy and its effort to bring government closer to the people. There is no easy

---

[6]John F. Dillon, *Commentaries on the Law of Municipal Corporations,* 5th ed. (Boston: Little, Brown, 1911), Vol. 1, Sec. 237.

[7]*People v. Hurlbut,* 24 Mich. 44 (1871).

way to describe their operation in summary form. Indeed, the county has been called by one scholar "the dark continent of American politics."[8]

Towns and Townships.   A unique governmental creation in the New England states is the **New England town**—not to be confused with the word *town* when used as just another name for a city. In Maine, Massachusetts, New Hampshire, Vermont, and Connecticut, the unit called the town combines the roles of city and county into one governing unit. A New England town typically consists of one or more urban settlements and the surrounding rural areas. Consequently, counties have little importance in New England. In Connecticut, for example, they are simply geographic units.

From the New England town is derived the tradition of the **town meeting,** an annual meeting at which direct democracy was—and continues to be—practiced. Each resident of a town is summoned to the annual meeting at the town hall. Those who attend levy taxes, pass laws, elect town officers, and appropriate money for different activities.

Normally, few residents show up for town meetings today unless an item of high interest is on the agenda or unless family members want to be elected to office. The town meeting takes a day or more, and few citizens are able to set aside such a large amount of time. Because of the declining interest in town meetings, many New England towns have adopted a **town manager system:** the voters simply elect three **selectpersons,** who then appoint a professional town manager. The town manager in turn appoints other officials.

Townships operate somewhat like counties. Where they exist, there may be several dozen within a county. They perform the same functions that the county would otherwise perform. Indiana, Iowa, Kansas, Michigan, Minnesota, New Jersey, New York, Ohio, Pennsylvania, and Wisconsin all have numerous townships. A township is not the same thing as a New England town, because it is meant to be a rural government rather than a city government. Moreover, it is never the principal unit of local government, as are New England towns. The boundaries of most townships are based on federal land surveys that began in the 1780s, mapping the land into six-mile squares called townships. They were then subdivided into thirty-six blocks of one square mile each, called sections. Along the boundaries of each section, a road was built.

Although townships have few functions left to perform in many parts of the nation, they are still politically important in others. In some metropolitan areas, townships are the political unit that provides most public services to residents who live in suburban **unincorporated areas.**

Special Districts.   The most numerous form of local government is the special district, which includes school districts. As of 1998, there were more than forty-four thousand special districts, including slightly less than fifteen thousand school districts, which are a type of special district (see Table 19–2). Special districts are one-function governments that usually are created by the state legislature and governed by a board of directors. Special districts may be called authorities, boards, corporations—or simply districts.

One important feature of special districts is that they cut across geographic and governmental boundaries. Sometimes special districts even cut across state lines. For example, the Port of New York Authority was established by an interstate compact between New Jersey and New York in 1921 to develop and operate the harbor facilities in the area. A mosquito control district may cut across

DID YOU KNOW...
That only 196 of the 4,200 registered voters in Peterborough, New Hampshire, turned out for a recent town meeting?

New England Town
A governmental unit that combines the roles of city and county into one unit in the New England states.

Town Meeting
The governing authority of a New England town. Qualified voters may participate in the election of officers and in the passage of legislation.

Town Manager System
A form of city government in which voters elect three selectpersons, who then appoint a professional town manager, who in turn appoints other officials.

Selectperson
A member of the governing group of a town.

Township
A rural unit of government based on federal land surveys of the American frontier in the 1780s. Townships have declined significantly in importance.

Unincorporated Area
An area not located within the boundary of a municipality.

TABLE   **19–2**

Local Governments
in the United States

Counties	3,042
Municipalities	19,205
(mainly cities and towns)	
Townships	16,691
(less extensive powers)	
Special districts	29,483
(water supply, fire protection, hospitals, libraries, parks and recreation, highways, sewers, and so on)	
School districts	14,728
Total	**83,149**

SOURCE: U.S. Bureau of the Census, *Statistical Abstract of the United States, 1997* (Washington, D.C.: U.S. Government Printing Office, 1997).

---

[8]Henry S. Gilbertson, *The County, the "Dark Continent of American Politics"* (New York: National Short Ballot Association, 1917).

A billboard in Blue Earth, Minnesota, supports a referendum to increase taxes to pay for a new school. School districts represent by far the largest share of special districts.

both municipal and county lines. A metropolitan transit district may provide bus service to dozens of municipalities and to several counties.

Except for school districts, the typical citizen is not very aware of most special districts. Indeed, most citizens do not know who furnishes their weed control, mosquito control, water, or sewage control. Part of the reason for the low profile of special districts is that most special district administrators are appointed, not elected, and therefore receive little public attention.

Consolidation of Governments

With over eighty thousand separate and often overlapping governmental units within the United States, the trend in recent years toward consolidation is understandable. **Consolidation** is defined as the union of two or more governmental units to form a single unit. Typically, a state constitution or a state statute will designate consolidation procedures.

Consolidation is often recommended for metropolitan-area problems, but to date there have been few consolidations within metropolitan areas. The most successful consolidations have been **functional consolidations**—particularly of city and county police, health, and welfare departments. In some cases, functional consolidation is a satisfactory alternative to the complete consolidation of governmental units. The most successful form of functional consolidation was started in 1957 in Dade County, Florida. The county government, called Metro-Dade, is a union of twenty-six municipalities. Each municipality has its own governmental entity, but the county government has the authority to furnish water, planning, mass transit, and police services and to set minimum standards of performance. The governing body of Metro-Dade is an elected board of county commissioners, which appoints a county manager and an attorney.

A special type of consolidation is the **council of government (COG)**, a voluntary organization of counties and municipalities that attempts to tackle areawide problems. More than two hundred COGs have been established, mainly since 1966. The impetus for their establishment was, and continues to be, federal government grants. COGs are an alternative means of treating major regional problems that

Consolidation
The union of two or more governmental units to form a single unit.

Functional Consolidation
The cooperation of two or more units of local government in providing services to their inhabitants.

Council of Government (COG)
A voluntary organization of counties and municipalities concerned with areawide problems.

various communities are unwilling to tackle on a consolidated basis either by true consolidation of governmental units or by functional consolidation.

The power of COGs is advisory only. Each member unit simply selects its council representatives, who report back to the unit after COG meetings. Nonetheless, today several COGs have begun to have considerable influence on regional policy. These include the Metropolitan Washington Council of Governments, the Supervisors' Inter-County Commission in Detroit, and the Association of Bay Area Governments in San Francisco.

How Municipalities Are Governed

We can divide municipal representative governments into four general types of plans: (1) the commission plan, (2) the council-manager plan, (3) the mayor-administrator plan, and (4) the mayor-council plan.

The Commission Plan. The commission form of municipal government consists of a commission of three to nine members who have both legislative and executive powers. The salient aspects of the commission plan are as follows:

1. Executive and legislative powers are concentrated in a small group of individuals, who are elected at large on a (normally) nonpartisan ballot.
2. Each commissioner is individually responsible for heading a particular municipal department, such as the department of public safety.
3. The commission is collectively responsible for passing ordinances and controlling spending.
4. The mayor (an office that is only ceremonial) is selected from the members of the commission.

The commission plan, originating in Galveston, Texas, in 1901, had its greatest popularity during the first twenty years of this century. It appealed to municipal government reformers. They looked on it as a type of business organization that would eliminate the problems they believed to be inherent in the long ballot and in partisan municipal politics. Unfortunately, vesting both legislative and executive power in the hands of a small group of individuals means that there are no checks and balances on administration and spending. Also, because the mayoral office is ceremonial, there is no provision for strong leadership. Not surprisingly, only about one hundred cities today use the commission plan—Tulsa, Salt Lake City, Mobile, Topeka, and Atlantic City are a few of them.

The Council-Manager Plan. In the council-manager form of municipal government, a city council appoints a professional manager, who acts as the chief executive. He or she typically is called the city manager. In principle, the manager is there simply to see that the general directions of the city council are carried out. The important features of the council-manager plan are as follows:

1. A professional, trained manager can hire and fire subordinates and is responsible to the council.
2. The council or commission consists of five to seven members, elected at large on a nonpartisan ballot.
3. The mayor may be chosen from within the council or from outside, but he or she has no executive function. As with the commission plan, the mayor's job is largely ceremonial. The city manager works for the council, not the mayor (unless, of course, the mayor is part of the council).

Today, about two thousand cities use the council-manager plan. About one-third of the cities with populations of more than 5,000 and about one-half of the cities with populations of more than 25,000 operate with this type of plan.

Only four large cities with populations of more than 500,000—Cincinnati, Dallas, San Antonio, and San Diego—have adopted this plan.

The major defect of the council-manager scheme, as with the commission plan, is that there is no single, strong political executive leader. It is therefore not surprising that large cities rarely use such a plan.

The Mayor-Administrator Plan. The mayor-administrator plan is often used in large cities where there is a strong mayor. It is similar to the council-manager plan except that the political leadership is vested in the mayor. The mayor is an elected chief executive. He or she appoints an administrative officer, whose function is to free the mayor from routine administrative tasks, such as personnel direction and budget supervision.

The Mayor-Council Plan. The mayor-council form of municipal government is the oldest and most widely used. The mayor is an elected chief executive, and the council is the legislative body. Virtually all councils are unicameral except in Everett, Massachusetts. There are typically five to nine members of the council except in very large cities, such as Chicago, which has fifty members. Council members are popularly elected for terms as long as six, but normally four, years.

The mayor-council plan can either be a strong-mayor type or a weak-mayor type. In the *strong mayor–council plan,* the mayor is the chief executive and has virtually complete control over hiring and firing employees, as well as preparing the budget. The mayor exercises strong and positive leadership in the formation of city policies. The *weak mayor–council plan* separates executive and legislative functions completely. The mayor is elected as chief executive officer; the council is elected as the legislative body. This traditional division of powers allows for checks and balances on spending and administration. (When powers are divided among too many groups, however, it may be difficult to govern a city effectively. See the feature *Politics and Local Government: The Division of Powers in Los Angeles* for an example of this problem.)

About 50 percent of American cities use some form of the mayor-council plan. Most recently, the mayor-council plan has lost ground to the council-manager plan in small and middle-sized cities.

A citizen addresses the city council of the city of Gloucester, Massachusetts. What are some of the problems facing city governments today?

Machine versus Reform in City Politics

For much of the late nineteenth and early twentieth centuries, many major cities were run by "the machine." The machine was an integrated political organization. Each city block within the municipality had an organizer, each neighborhood had a political club, each district had a leader, and all of these parts of the machine had a boss—such as William Tweed in New York (see the feature on Tammany Hall in Chapter 9), Richard Daley in Chicago, Edward Crump in Memphis, or Tom Pendergast in Kansas City. The machine became a popular form of city political organization in the 1840s, when the first waves of European immigrants came to the United States to work in urban factories. Those individuals, often lacking the ability to communicate in English, needed help; and the machine was created to help them.[9] The urban machine drew on the support of the dominant ethnic groups to forge a strong political institution that was able to keep the boss (usually the mayor) in office year after year. The machine was oiled by **patronage**—rewarding faithful party workers and followers

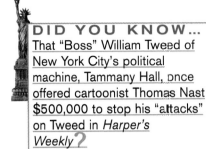

Patronage
Rewarding faithful party workers and followers with government employment and contracts.

[9]See Harvey W. Zorbaugh, *The Gold Coast and the Slum: A Sociological Study of Chicago's Near North Side* (Chicago: University of Chicago Press, 1929).

POLITICS and Local Government

The Division of Powers in Los Angeles

Since 1925, Los Angeles has operated under a weak mayor-council plan of government. Those who designed the charter apparently felt that the best way to prevent corruption was to give as much power as possible to the city council—and as little as possible to the mayor. As a result, the mayor of the second-largest city in the country, with a population almost twice the size of the entire nation in 1790, has extremely limited powers. Fred Siegel, in his recent book on American cities,[*] states that the mayor's authority "is so limited that he practically needs city council permission to attend street-naming ceremonies." Certainly, the city seems to have taken the political principle of division of powers to an extreme.

The most powerful figures in Los Angeles government are the fifteen members of the city council, who are in charge of all major city decisions, including the budget. Authority over the city's day-to-day operations, from street cleaning to policing the city's streets, is dispersed among the city's thirty-two departments, which are run by professional managers. According to Siegel, these department heads, who are protected by civil service rules, are so entrenched in the system that it is almost impossible to discipline or remove them. Powers are further dispersed among the county government (which handles social services, including welfare and hospitals) and various independent cities (including Santa Monica, Beverly Hills, and

West Hollywood). One journalist observed that in Los Angeles, "power is so widely dispersed that nobody can be held responsible for anything."[†]

According to Richard Riordan, now serving his second term as mayor of the city, the division of powers in Los Angeles institutionalizes what he calls "legal corruption"—the practice of hiring lobbyists to get action from the bureaucrats—and backroom politics. Indeed, Riordan has been able to exercise whatever authority he can over city politics only through a so-called shadow government. This behind-the-scenes group includes some of the city's wealthiest and most talented citizens. As a result, Republican Riordan has drawn criticism from the

liberal city council members as well as from others for allowing a group of "rich white men" to run the government. Riordan, who would prefer to run the city in a more accountable and direct fashion, recently appointed a commission to review the city charter and suggest changes. Not to be outdone, the city council set up a similar, rival commission.

FOR CRITICAL ANALYSIS

For all their corruption, city machines in the days of yesteryear "got things done." How can governments of large cities today manage to do likewise, yet operate democratically and avoid corruption?

[*]Frederick F. Siegel, *The Future Once Happened Here: New York, D.C., L.A., and the Fate of America's Big Cities* (New York: Free Press, 1997).

[†]*The Economist*, January 17, 1998, p. 26.

with government employment and contracts. The party in power was often referred to as the patronage party.[10]

According to sociologist Robert Merton, the machine offered personalized assistance to the needy, helped to establish local businesses, opened avenues of upward social mobility for the underprivileged, and afforded a locus of strong political authority and responsibility.[11] Others, however, viewed party machines and the behind-the-scenes government that they often involved as contrary to our principles of government (see, for example, Elihu Root's comments in the feature *E-Mail Messages from the Past*). In their classic work on city politics, Edward Banfield and James Q. Wilson also gave a critical appraisal of machine politics:

> [M]achine government is, essentially, a system of organized bribery. The destruction of machines . . . permit[s] government on the basis of appropriate motives, that is, public-regarding ones. In fact it has other highly desirable consequences—especially greater honesty, impartiality, and (in routine matters) efficiency.[12]

When the last of the big-city bosses, Mayor Richard Daley of Chicago, died in December 1976, with him died an era. The big-city machine began to be in serious trouble in the 1960s, when community activists organized to work for a more professional and efficient municipal government. Soon, a government of administrators rather than politicians began to appear. Fewer offices were elective; more were appointive.

Switching from a political to an administrative form of urban government was a way to break up the centralized urban political machine. In some cities, the results have been beneficial to most citizens. In others, decentralization has gone so far that there is no strong leader who can pull together discordant factions to create and follow a coherent policy. Consequently, in cities with a greatly decentralized government typified by numerous independent commissions and boards, a lot that should be done does not get done, particularly when an areawide problem is involved. This is an especially severe problem for less

---

[10]See, for example, Harold F. Gosnell, *Machine Politics: Chicago Model* (Chicago: University of Chicago Press, 1937).

[11]Robert Merton, *Social Theory and Social Structure* (Glencoe, Ill.: Free Press, 1957), pp. 71–81.

[12]Edward C. Banfield and James Q. Wilson, *City Politics* (New York: Vintage Books, 1963), p. 12.

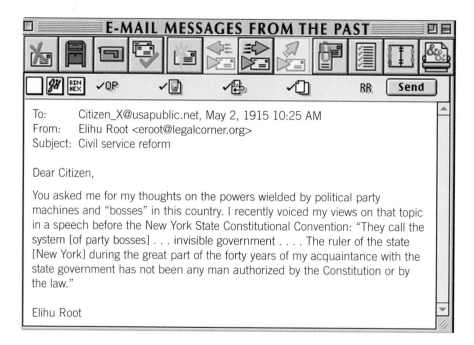

E-MAIL MESSAGES FROM THE PAST

To: Citizen_X@usapublic.net, May 2, 1915 10:25 AM
From: Elihu Root <eroot@legalcorner.org>
Subject: Civil service reform

Dear Citizen,

You asked me for my thoughts on the powers wielded by political party machines and "bosses" in this country. I recently voiced my views on that topic in a speech before the New York State Constitutional Convention: "They call the system [of party bosses] . . . invisible government . . . . The ruler of the state [New York] during the great part of the forty years of my acquaintance with the state government has not been any man authorized by the Constitution or by the law."

Elihu Root

economically privileged people, who used to be able to rely on machine-sponsored activities and on the machine's political clout to help them compete against wealthier citizens for a share of the city's services. Reform is in some ways a middle-class preoccupation, whereas the less advantaged may find themselves better served by machine politics.

Governing Metropolitan Areas

Large cities are often faced with problems that develop in part from a shrinking employment base. When employers move out of a city, there is a smaller tax base, and more people are out of work. Less tax revenue means less money to pay for schools and to meet other municipal obligations, including fighting crime and assisting those who are out of work. These developments feed on themselves, leading to more crime, more poverty, an even smaller job base, and other problems.

But crime, as well as such problems as traffic congestion and pollution, is not contained within municipal political boundaries. For this reason, solutions are sometimes sought by governing a metropolitan area as a whole. Annexation by a city of the surrounding suburbs is one solution; consolidation of city and county governments into one government is another. People who live in the suburbs often oppose such measures, however, particularly when they and the residents of a city are of different races or social classes, or have different political agendas.

A third attempt to deal with problems that spread beyond limited political boundaries is represented by a system of metropolitan government. With this method, a single entity, such as a county, concerns itself with the problems of an entire metropolitan area, and smaller entities, such as individual city governments, concern themselves with local matters. People who live in the suburbs often oppose this solution, however, for the same reasons that they oppose other measures: they want to preserve their communities and lifestyles as they are.

A fourth solution is the creation of special districts, each of which is concerned with a specific service—an area's water supply or public transportation

Concerned citizens meet with police and city council members regarding crime, drugs, and gang violence in Austin, Texas.

system, for example. Special districts are more popular than the other solutions, in part because they can deal with a single matter relatively more efficiently without concern for social issues or class conflict.

Paying for State and Local Government

Examining the spending habits of a household often gives relevant information about the personalities and priorities of the household members. Examination of the expenditure patterns of state and local governments likewise can be illuminating.

State and Local Government Expenditures

Table 19–3 shows state expenditures, expressed in percentages, for the latest fiscal year for which data are available. Table 19–4 shows the same data for local governments. There is a clear-cut pattern. State and city expenditures are concentrated in the areas of education, public welfare, highways, health, and police protection. Education is the biggest category of expenditure, particularly at the local level. Contrast this expenditure pattern with that of the federal government, which allocates only about 4 percent of its budget to education. In 1998, state and local expenditures exceeded $1 trillion.

State and Local Government Revenues

State and local expenditures have to be paid for somehow. Until the twentieth century, almost all state and local expenditures were paid for by state and local revenues raised within state borders. Starting in the twentieth century, however, federal grants to state and local governmental units began to pay some of these costs.

Figure 19–3 shows the percentages of revenues in various categories received by state and local governments. By far the most important tax at the state level is the **general sales tax**. Whereas the federal government obtains about 45 percent of its total revenues from the personal income tax, states obtain only about

General Sales Tax
A tax levied as a proportion of the retail price of a commodity at the point of sale.

TABLE 19-3	
State Expenditures (in percentages)	
Education	30.6
Public welfare	22.8
Insurance trust	10.9
Health and hospitals	7.2
Highways	6.8
Corrections	3.2
Governmental administration	3.1
Interest on general debt	3.0
Natural resources	1.5
Utilities	.9
Police	.8
Parks and recreation	.4
Liquor stores	.3
Other	8.5

Source: U.S. Bureau of the Census, 1998.

TABLE 19-4	
Local Expenditures (in percentages)	
EXPENDITURE	**PERCENTAGE**
Education	41.9
Health and hospitals	8.6
Governmental administration	5.4
Police	5.4
Public welfare	5.1
Interest on general debt	5.0
Highways	4.5
Sewerage	3.2
Housing and community development	2.8
Fire protection	2.6
Parks and recreation	2.2
Solid waste management	2.0
Corrections	1.7
Natural resources	0.4
Other	9.2

Source: U.S. Bureau of the Census, 1998.

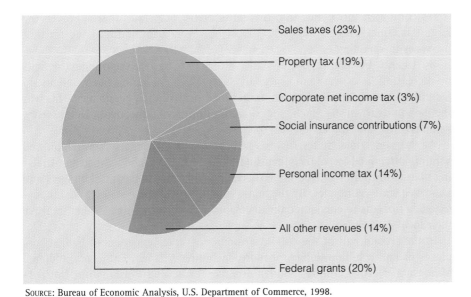

FIGURE 19-3
State and Local Government
Revenues

Sales taxes (23%)

Property tax (19%)

Corporate net income tax (3%)

Social insurance contributions (7%)

Personal income tax (14%)

All other revenues (14%)

Federal grants (20%)

Source: Bureau of Economic Analysis, U.S. Department of Commerce, 1998.

14 percent in this way. In 1998, there were still seven states that did not have a personal income tax. Other taxes assessed by states include corporate income taxes and fees, permits, and licenses at both the state and local governmental level, as well as inheritance and gift taxes at the state level. At the local level, the most important tax is the **property tax.** About 90 percent of property tax revenues are raised by local governments. Generally, the types of taxes that states levy vary widely from state to state.

A tremendous amount of variation also exists in the total amounts of state and local taxes collected. Among the states receiving the highest amounts in tax revenues are Alaska, New York, and the District of Columbia. Those levying the lowest taxes are Arkansas, Mississippi, and Alabama.

Nontax revenue includes federal grants to state and local governments. Today, federal grants to state and local governments total nearly $250 billion annually and provide about 20 percent of state government income. The grants are not always without "strings," however. Federal programs in such areas as education, highway construction, health care, and law enforcement may dispense cash subject to certain conditions. For example, the funds may be used only for a specific purpose or only if matching funds are contributed (see Chapter 3).

Profits generated by publicly operated businesses are another source of revenue for state and local governments. Publicly operated businesses include toll roads and bridges, as well as water, electric power, and mass transportation systems. More than a third of the states sell liquor through state-operated stores that earn profits. Other state-operated businesses include Washington's ferries and North Dakota's commercial banks. Some states receive lease payments for public lands, and some cities rent space in publicly owned buildings.

Other nontax revenue sources include court fines and interest on loans and investments. In the 1980s, state-run lotteries became an increasingly popular way to raise money. By 1998, nearly two-thirds of the states and the District of Columbia sponsored lotteries. It is expected that the rest of the states will soon follow.

Fiscal Policy Lessons

In the 1980s, when state budgets more than doubled, most states tried to close the gap between state income and spending by raising taxes. Many of these

Property Tax
A tax on the value of real estate. This tax is limited to state and local governments and is a particularly important source of revenue for local governments.

states continued this policy into the early 1990s. The states that approved the largest tax increases in the early 1990s, however, also approved the greatest increases in spending.

By 1999, it became clear that states' attempts to reduce their budget deficits by increasing taxes were not especially successful at lowering those deficits. In fact, many states actually harmed, rather than helped, their economies. This was the lesson learned by such states as California, Connecticut, New Jersey, Pennsylvania, and Rhode Island.

At the same time, states such as Massachusetts, Michigan, Mississippi, and Virginia attempted to balance their budgets by cutting spending instead of raising taxes. This policy proved more successful, resulting in balanced budgets and improved state economies. By the mid-1990s, many of these states were proposing state tax cuts to encourage the development of business and further improve their local economies.

In the second half of the 1990s, a number of states experienced budget surpluses of half a billion dollars or more, including Arizona, California, Indiana, Minnesota, North Carolina, South Carolina, Texas, and Washington. Not surprisingly, cries for state tax cuts were heard throughout the nation. Significant state tax cuts were enacted in over one-third of the states. While the tax cuts generally did not represent major reductions in general state revenues, they did indicate a change in the trend toward ever-increasing taxes.

State and Local Government: Issues for the New Century

The states face a broad array of problems, the solutions to which no longer can be found in Washington, D.C. Specifically, as the federal government continues to give the states more responsibilities, the states are expected to solve more problems—such as crime, education, and welfare—than they had in previous years. At the same time, some states are attempting to lure population and businesses by reducing taxes. The friction between the need to solve problems and the need to expand the business base will continue to challenge state governments for years to come.

Local governments will continue to be expected to solve the local problems of crime, pollution, congestion, and the like. Many municipalities have seen their tax bases decline as residents move to the suburbs. Nonetheless, fiscal help from the state and federal governments is less available today than ever before. Consequently, local governments must continue to seek ways to streamline the provision of public services, perhaps by more contracting out or by better management.

State and local governments also will continue to search for new ways to meet the pressing challenge of how to improve the quality of education and at the same time keep educational expenditures in check. States across the nation are experimenting with various systems, including school vouchers (discussed in this chapter's *What If . . .*), in their attempt to meet this challenge. How the states resolve the educational issues confronting them certainly will have a significant effect on America's future electorate.

T O W A R D   A C T I V E   C I T I Z E N S H I P

LEARNING ABOUT LOCAL POLITICS AND GOVERNMENT IN YOUR COMMUNITY

What government does or fails to do in the areas of education, health, employment, and crime affects you, your family, and your friends. Your sense of adventure, concern, curiosity, or injustice may urge you to take an active part in the government of a society with which you might not be particularly content. Yet getting involved on the national level may seem complicated, and national issues may not be of immediate concern. You may not even know exactly where you stand on many of those issues.

A recycling program in Portland, Oregon, is an example of a local government's successful tackling of a policy problem.

Every week, however, decisions are being made in your community that affect directly your local environment, transportation, education, health, employment, rents, schools, utility rates, freedom from crime, and overall quality of life. The local level is a good place to begin discovering who you are politically.

Many neighborhoods have formed neighborhood associations for the purposes of protecting their interests. One way to learn about issues that directly affect you (such as whether a street in your neighborhood should be widened or a park created) is to attend a local neighborhood association meeting. Another way to familiarize yourself with local political issues is to attend a city council meeting. Think about the issues being discussed. How do these issues and their outcomes concern you as an individual? What is your position on each issue?

If you are interested in education and educational reform, you can attend a school board meeting. Typically, the board will devote a substantial amount of time to budgetary decisions. Pay close attention to how the board feels school funds should be allocated. What are the board's primary concerns and priorities? Do you agree with the board's views? Find out if the school district is considering proposals to implement innovational educational programs.

Virtually all communities have groups that are working to improve the environment at the state or local level. At the local level, environmental issues may con-

cern efforts to beautify the city (by restricting billboards or yard signs, for example) or to implement recycling programs to control waste. State environmental organizations may need volunteers to go door-to-door in your community to distribute information on their lobbying efforts before the state legislature, to gather signatures for petitions, and the like. If you look in the Yellow Pages under "Environment" or "Environmental," you probably will find a listing of several local and state organizations to contact.

Getting involved in a campaign for a local or state office is another way to learn about political issues that affect your community or your state. You also can participate at the local level in campaigns by candidates seeking national office, such as candidates running for Congress. Working at the "grassroots" level for a political candidate gives you firsthand knowledge of how the politics of democracy actually work.

Finally, to observe the judicial branch of government at work, you can observe proceedings in your local courts. An important court at the local level is the small claims court. Small claims courts hear disputes involving claims under a certain amount, such as $1,000 or $2,500 (the amount varies from state to state). Lawyers are not required, and many small claims courts do not permit lawyers. Other local courts are described in Figure 19–2. For information on your local courts and on when you can attend court proceedings, call the courthouse clerk.

Key terms

Chapter summary

1 The United States has more than eighty thousand separate governmental units. State and local governments perform a wide variety of highly visible functions, such as education, police and fire protection, and so on.

2 Under the U.S. Constitution, powers not delegated expressly to the federal government are reserved to the states. The states may exercise taxing, spending, and general police powers. State constitutions are often very long, owing to the desire of their framers to include much of what we would consider statutory law because of a loss of popular confidence in state legislatures at the end of the nineteenth century. Other reasons include state courts' reluctance to interpret state constitutions as freely as the Supreme Court of the United States interprets the U.S. Constitution.

3 In colonial America, the governors of the colonies were vested with extensive powers. Following the Revolutionary War, most states established forms of government in which the governor was given extremely limited powers. After Andrew Jackson's presidency, however, all governors (except in South Carolina) were elected directly by the people. Most governors have the right to exercise some sort of veto power; some enjoy item veto power.

4 State legislatures deal with matters such as taxes, schools, highways, and welfare. They also must redraw state and federal legislative districts each decade to ensure that every person's vote is roughly equal to that of others and that minorities are adequately represented in both the state legislature and Congress. Voters may exercise some direct control over state government through the use of the initiative, referendum, and recall. Every state has its own court system. Most such systems have several levels of courts—including trial courts, intermediate courts of appeal, and a supreme court. State courts are overburdened with over 100 million cases each year, the majority of which are traffic offenses.

5 There are nearly twenty thousand municipalities in the United States, most of which are small cities. The more than three thousand counties in this country are merely extensions of state authority and apply state laws at the local level. Many of the functions of municipalities and counties are combined in towns or townships, particularly in the New England area. Municipalities may be governed by a commission consisting of members with executive and legislative powers, or they may be administered according to a council-manager, mayor-administrator, or mayor-council plan. Most major cities used to be run by political machines, which freely dispensed favors to supporters. In recent decades, however, machine politics has fallen into disfavor, particularly among the middle class.

6 State and local government spending is concentrated in the areas of education, public welfare, highways, health, and police protection. State services are funded primarily by sales taxes, whereas local services are financed by property taxes.

Selected print and electronic resources

SUGGESTED READINGS

Banfield, Edward C., and James Q. Wilson. *City Politics.* New York: Vintage Books, 1963. A classic work describing competing interests and ideas in city life.

Donahue, John D. *Disunited States: What's at Stake as Washington Fades and the States Take the Lead.* Glenview, Ill.: Basic Books, 1997. Donahue contends that the devolution of responsibilities from the national government to the states is rooted more in ideological factors than in practical needs.

Dye, Thomas R. *Politics in States and Communities*. 9th ed. Englewood Cliffs, N.J.: Prentice-Hall, 1996. This text explores the inner workings of political systems by comparing and analyzing state and local perspectives on public policy.

Siegel, Frederick F. *The Future Once Happened Here: New York, D.C., L.A., and the Fate of America's Big Cities*. New York: Free Press, 1997. The author makes a strong case as to why cities have declined, focusing particularly on the cities in the book's title.

Waste, Robert J. *Independent Cities: Rethinking U.S. Urban Policy*. Cambridge, Mass.: Harvard University Press, 1998. Public-policy specialist Robert Waste examines the problems confronting American cities and appraises solutions ranging from revamping current policies to implementing radical new approaches.

MEDIA RESOURCES

Can the States Do It Better?—A program examining devolution—shifting federal powers back to the states—and what this means for the states with respect to, among other things, school reform.

The Last Hurrah—A film based, in part, on the career of James Curley (1874-1958) of Massachusetts, who played a leading role in creating and running Boston's political machine in the first half of the twentieth century. When Curley was convicted of mail fraud and sent to prison in 1947, he refused to resign as mayor and maintained his office while in jail.

Our Town—A 1980 film based on Thorton Wilder's play about day-to-day life and politics in a small, picturesque community—Peterborough ("Grover's Corners" in the play) in New Hampshire.

Logging on

If you are interested in state law codes (statutes) and state court cases, go to

www.findlaw.com/casecode/state.html

Information on state governments, including their constitutional powers, education, and finances, can be accessed online at

www.vote-smart.org/reference/primer/

Another excellent source for information on state governments is the following Web site:

www.statesnews.org/

You can access the *Book of the States,* a biennial publication of the Council of State Governments from this site, or access it directly at

www.statesnews.org/publications/bos.html

The National Governors Association offers a wide variety of information on issues and data relating to state governments at

www.nga.org/

The National Conference of State Legislators is a good source for state information as well. Its URL is

ncsl.org/

You can find a wealth of data on state and local governments at the "Map Stats" site of the U.S. Census Bureau by simply clicking on states and counties on the maps. Go to

www.census.gov/datamap/www/index.html

Piper Resources offers a Web site with numerous links to state and local government resources. You can access this site at

www.piperinfo.com/

Using the Internet for political analysis

As you are aware, each state has its own approach to taxation, government, and the work force. Go to the home pages of several different states, and then try to find their departments of economic development. Compare how states describe their tax advantages and other virtues to try to "sell" themselves to businesses that are relocating. Seek out the sales pitches that the states make for new businesses and then compare these marketing efforts across states. Which state do you think would be most favorable to business? Which states are able to offer the best business climate? Which states have few advantages for business? How does the political climate in a state influence its business climate?

The Declaration of Independence

In Congress, July 4, 1776

A Declaration by the Representatives of the United States of America, in General Congress assembled. When in the Course of human Events, it becomes necessary for one People to dissolve the Political Bands which have connected them with another, and to assume among the Powers of the Earth, the separate and equal Station to which the Laws of Nature and of Nature's God entitle them, a decent Respect to the Opinions of Mankind requires that they should declare the causes which impel them to the Separation.

We hold these Truths to be self-evident, that all Men are created equal, that they are endowed by their Creator with certain unalienable Rights, that among these are Life, Liberty, and the Pursuit of Happiness—That to secure these Rights, Governments are instituted among Men, deriving their just Powers from the Consent of the Governed, that whenever any Form of Government becomes destructive of these Ends, it is the Right of the People to alter or to abolish it, and to institute new Government, laying its Foundation on such Principles, and organizing its Powers in such Forms, as to them shall seem most likely to effect their Safety and Happiness. Prudence, indeed, will dictate that Governments long established should not be changed for light and transient Causes; and accordingly all Experience hath shewn, that Mankind are more disposed to suffer, while Evils are sufferable, than to right themselves by abolishing the Forms to which they are accustomed. But when a long Train of Abuses and Usurpations, pursuing invariably the same Object, evinces a Design to reduce them under absolute Despotism, it is their Right, it is their Duty, to throw off such Government, and to provide new Guards for their future Security. Such has been the patient Sufferance of these Colonies; and such is now the Necessity which constrains them to alter their former Systems of Government. The History of the present King of Great-Britain is a History of repeated Injuries and Usurpations, all having in direct Object the Establishment of an absolute Tyranny over these States. To prove this, let Facts be submitted to a candid World.

He has refused his Assent to Laws, the most wholesome and necessary for the public Good.

He has forbidden his Governors to pass Laws of immediate and pressing Importance, unless suspended in their Operation till his Assent should be obtained; and when so suspended, he has utterly neglected to attend to them.

He has refused to pass other Laws for the Accommodation of large Districts of People, unless those People would relinquish the Right of Representation in the Legislature, a Right inestimable to them, and formidable to Tyrants only.

He has called together Legislative Bodies at Places unusual, uncomfortable, and distant from the Depository of their Public Records, for the sole Purpose of fatiguing them into Compliance with his Measures.

He has dissolved Representative Houses repeatedly, for opposing with manly Firmness his Invasions on the Rights of the People.

He has refused for a long Time, after such Dissolutions, to cause others to be elected; whereby the Legislative Powers, incapable of Annihilation, have returned to the People at large for their exercise; the State remaining in the mean time exposed to all the Dangers of Invasion from without, and Convulsions within.

He has endeavoured to prevent the Population of these States; for that Purpose obstructing the Laws for Naturalization of Foreigners; refusing to pass others to encourage their Migrations hither, and raising the Conditions of new Appropriations of Lands.

He has obstructed the Administration of Justice, by refusing his Assent to Laws for establishing Judiciary Powers.

He has made Judges dependent on his Will alone, for the Tenure of their offices, and the Amount and payment of their Salaries.

He has erected a Multitude of new Offices, and sent hither Swarms of Officers to harrass our People, and eat out their Substance.

He has kept among us, in Times of Peace, Standing Armies, without the consent of our Legislatures.

He has affected to render the Military independent of, and superior to the Civil Power.

He has combined with others to subject us to a Jurisdiction foreign to our Constitution, and unacknowledged by our Laws; giving his Assent to their Acts of pretended Legislation:

For quartering large Bodies of Armed Troops among us:

For protecting them, by a mock Trial, from Punishment for any Murders which they should commit on the Inhabitants of these States:

For cutting off our Trade with all Parts of the World:

For imposing Taxes on us without our Consent:

For depriving us, in many cases, of the Benefits of Trial by Jury:

For transporting us beyond Seas to be tried for pretended Offences:

For abolishing the free System of English Laws in a neighbouring Province, establishing therein an arbitrary Government, and enlarging its Boundaries, so as to render it at once an Example and fit Instrument for introducing the same absolute Rule into these Colonies:

For taking away our Charters, abolishing our most valuable Laws, and altering fundamentally the Forms of our Governments:

For suspending our own Legislatures, and declaring themselves invested with Power to legislate for us in all Cases whatsoever.

He has abdicated Government here, by declaring us out of his Protection and waging War against us.

He has plundered our Seas, ravaged our Coasts, burnt our towns, and destroyed the Lives of our People.

He is, at this Time, transporting large Armies of foreign Mercenaries to compleat the works of Death, Desolation, and Tyranny, already begun with circumstances of Cruelty and Perfidy, scarcely paralleled in the most barbarous Ages, and totally unworthy the Head of a civilized Nation.

He has constrained our fellow Citizens taken Captive on the high Seas to bear Arms against their Country, to become the Executioners of their Friends and Brethren, or to fall themselves by their Hands.

He has excited domestic Insurrections amongst us, and has endeavoured to bring on the Inhabitants of our Frontiers, the merciless Indian Savages, whose known Rule of Warfare, is an undistinguished Destruction, of all Ages, Sexes and Conditions.

In every state of these Oppressions we have Petitioned for Redress in the most humble Terms: Our repeated Petitions have been answered only by repeated Injury. A Prince, whose Character is thus marked by every act which may define a Tyrant, is unfit to be the Ruler of a free People.

Nor have we been wanting in Attentions to our British Brethren. We have warned them from Time to Time of Attempts by their Legislature to extend an unwarrantable Jurisdiction over us. We have reminded them of the Circumstances of our Emigration and Settlement here. We have appealed to their native Justice and Magnanimity, and we have conjured them by the Ties of our common Kindred to disavow these Usurpations, which, would inevitably interrupt our Connections and Correspondence. They too have been deaf to the Voice of Justice and of Consanguinity. We must, therefore, acquiesce in the Necessity, which denounces our Separation, and hold them, as we hold the rest of Mankind, Enemies in War, in Peace, Friends.

We, therefore, the Representatives of the UNITED STATES OF AMERICA, in General Congress Assembled, appealing to the Supreme Judge of the World for the Rectitude of our Intentions, do, in the Name, and by the Authority of the good People of these Colonies, solemnly Publish and Declare, That these United Colonies are, and of Right ought to be, Free and Independent States; that they are absolved from all Allegiance to the British Crown, and that all political Connection between them and the State of Great-Britain, is and ought to be totally dissolved; and that as Free and Independent States, they have full Power to levy War, conclude Peace, contract Alliances, establish Commerce, and to do all other Acts and Things which Independent States may of right do. And for the support of this declaration, with a firm Reliance on the Protection of divine Providence, we mutually pledge to each other our lives, our Fortunes, and our sacred Honor.

How to Read Case Citations and Find Court Decisions

Many important court cases are discussed in references in footnotes throughout this book. Court decisions are recorded and published. When a court case is mentioned, the notation that is used to refer to, or to cite, the case denotes where the published decision can be found.

State courts of appeals decisions are usually published in two places, the state reports of that particular state and the more widely used *National Reporter System* published by West Publishing Company. Some states no longer publish their own reports. The *National Reporter System* divides the states into the following geographic areas: Atlantic (A. or A.2d, where *2d* refers to *Second Series*), South Eastern (S.E. or S.E.2d), South Western (S.W. or S.W.2d), North Western (N.W. or N.W.2d), North Eastern (N.E. or N.E.2d), Southern (So. or So.2d), and Pacific (P. or P.2d).

Federal trial court decisions are published unofficially in *West's Federal Supplement* (F.Supp.), and opinions from the circuit courts of appeals are reported unofficially in West's *Federal Reporter* (F., F.2d, or F.3d). Opinions from the United States Supreme Court are reported in the *United States Reports* (U.S.), the *Lawyers' Edition of the Supreme Court Reports* (L.Ed.), West's *Supreme Court Reporter* (S.Ct.), and other publications. The *United States Reports* is the official publication of United States Supreme Court decisions. It is published by the federal government. Many early decisions are missing from these volumes. The citations of the early volumes of the *U.S. Reports* include the names of the actual reporters, such as Dallas, Cranch, or Wheaton. *McCulloch v. Maryland*, for example, is cited as 17 U.S. (4 Wheat.) 316. Only after 1874 did the present

citation system, in which cases are cited based solely on their volume and page numbers in the *United States Reports*, come into being. The *Lawyers' Edition of the Supreme Court Reports* is an unofficial and more complete edition of Supreme Court decisions. West's *Supreme Court Reporter* is an unofficial edition of decisions dating from October 1882. These volumes contain headnotes and numerous brief editorial statements of the law involved in the case.

State courts of appeals decisions are cited by giving the name of the case; the volume, name, and page number of the state's official report (if the state publishes its own reports); the volume, unit, and page number of the *National Reporter;* and the volume, name, and page number of any other selected reporter. Federal court citations are also listed by giving the name of the case and the volume, name and page number of the reports. In addition to the citation, this textbook lists the year of the decision in parentheses. Consider, for example, the case *United States v. Curtiss-Wright Export Co.*, 299 U.S. 304 (1936). The Supreme Court's decision of this case may be found in volume 299 of the *United States Reports* on page 304. The case was decided in 1936.

Today, many courts, including the United States Supreme Court, publish their opinions online. This makes it much easier for students to find and read cases, or summaries of cases, that have significant consequences for American government and politics. To access cases via the Internet, use the URLs given in the *Logging On* at the end of Chapter 15.

Presidents of the United States

	Term of Service	Age at Inauguration	Political Party	College or University	Occupation or Profession
1. George Washington	1789–1797	57	None		Planter
2. John Adams	1797–1801	61	Federalist	Harvard	Lawyer
3. Thomas Jefferson	1801–1809	57	Democratic-Republican	William and Mary	Planter, Lawyer
4. James Madison	1809–1817	57	Democratic-Republican	Princeton	Lawyer
5. James Monroe	1817–1825	58	Democratic-Republican	William and Mary	Lawyer
6. John Quincy Adams	1825–1829	57	Democratic-Republican	Harvard	Lawyer
7. Andrew Jackson	1829–1837	61	Democrat		Lawyer
8. Martin Van Buren	1837–1841	54	Democrat		Lawyer
9. William H. Harrison	1841	68	Whig	Hampden-Sydney	Soldier
10. John Tyler	1841–1845	51	Whig	William and Mary	Lawyer
11. James K. Polk	1845–1849	49	Democrat	U. of N. Carolina	Lawyer
12. Zachary Taylor	1849–1850	64	Whig		Soldier
13. Millard Fillmore	1850–1853	50	Whig		Lawyer
14. Franklin Pierce	1853–1857	48	Democrat	Bowdoin	Lawyer
15. James Buchanan	1857–1861	65	Democrat	Dickinson	Lawyer
16. Abraham Lincoln	1861–1865	52	Republican		Lawyer
17. Andrew Johnson	1865–1869	56	Nat/l. Union†		Tailor
18. Ulysses S. Grant	1869–1877	46	Republican	U.S. Mil. Academy	Soldier
19. Rutherford B. Hayes	1877–1881	54	Republican	Kenyon	Lawyer
20. James A. Garfield	1881	49	Republican	Williams	Lawyer
21. Chester A. Arthur	1881–1885	51	Republican	Union	Lawyer
22. Grover Cleveland	1885–1889	47	Democrat		Lawyer
23. Benjamin Harrison	1889–1893	55	Republican	Miami	Lawyer
24. Grover Cleveland	1893–1897	55	Democrat		Lawyer
25. William McKinley	1897–1901	54	Republican	Allegheny College	Lawyer
26. Theodore Roosevelt	1901–1909	42	Republican	Harvard	Author
27. William H. Taft	1909–1913	51	Republican	Yale	Lawyer
28. Woodrow Wilson	1913–1921	56	Democrat	Princeton	Educator
29. Warren G. Harding	1921–1923	55	Republican		Editor
30. Calvin Coolidge	1923–1929	51	Republican	Amherst	Lawyer
31. Herbert C. Hoover	1929–1933	54	Republican	Stanford	Engineer
32. Franklin D. Roosevelt	1933–1945	51	Democrat	Harvard	Lawyer
33. Harry S. Truman	1945–1953	60	Democrat		Businessman
34. Dwight D. Eisenhower	1953–1961	62	Republican	U.S. Mil. Academy	Soldier
35. John F. Kennedy	1961–1963	43	Democrat	Harvard	Author
36. Lyndon B. Johnson	1963–1969	55	Democrat	Southwest Texas State	Teacher
37. Richard M. Nixon	1969–1974	56	Republican	Whittier	Lawyer
38. Gerald R. Ford‡	1974–1977	61	Republican	Michigan	Lawyer
39. James E. Carter, Jr.	1977–1981	52	Democrat	U.S. Naval Academy	Businessman
40. Ronald W. Reagan	1981–1989	69	Republican	Eureka College	Actor
41. George H. W. Bush	1989–1993	64	Republican	Yale	Businessman
42. Bill Clinton	1993–	46	Democrat	Georgetown	Lawyer

*Church preference; never joined any church.
†The National Union Party consisted of Republicans and War Democrats. Johnson was a Democrat.
**Inaugurated Dec. 6, 1973, to replace Agnew, who resigned Oct. 10, 1973.
‡Inaugurated Aug. 9, 1974, to replace Nixon, who resigned that same day.
§Inaugurated Dec. 19, 1974, to replace Ford, who became president Aug. 9, 1974.

Presidents of the United States

	Religion	Born	Died	Age at Death	Vice President	
1.	Episcopalian	Feb. 22, 1732	Dec. 14, 1799	67	John Adams	(1789–1797)
2.	Unitarian	Oct. 30, 1735	July 4, 1826	90	Thomas Jefferson	(1797–1801)
3.	Unitarian*	Apr. 13, 1743	July 4, 1826	83	Aaron Burr	(1801–1805)
					George Clinton	(1805–1809)
4.	Episcopalian	Mar. 16, 1751	June 28, 1836	85	George Clinton	(1809–1812)
					Elbridge Gerry	(1813–1814)
5.	Episcopalian	Apr. 28, 1758	July 4, 1831	73	Daniel D. Tompkins	(1817–1825)
6.	Unitarian	July 11, 1767	Feb. 23, 1848	80	John C. Calhoun	(1825–1829)
7.	Presbyterian	Mar. 15, 1767	June 8, 1845	78	John C. Calhoun	(1829–1832)
					Martin Van Buren	(1833–1837)
8.	Dutch Reformed	Dec. 5, 1782	July 24, 1862	79	Richard M. Johnson	(1837–1841)
9.	Episcopalian	Feb. 9, 1773	Apr. 4, 1841	68	John Tyler	(1841)
10.	Episcopalian	Mar. 29, 1790	Jan. 18, 1862	71		
11.	Methodist	Nov. 2, 1795	June 15, 1849	53	George M. Dallas	(1845–1849)
12.	Episcopalian	Nov. 24, 1784	July 9, 1850	65	Millard Fillmore	(1849–1850)
13.	Unitarian	Jan. 7, 1800	Mar. 8, 1874	74		
14.	Episcopalian	Nov. 23, 1804	Oct. 8, 1869	64	William R. King	(1853)
15.	Presbyterian	Apr. 23, 1791	June 1, 1868	77	John C. Breckinridge	(1857–1861)
16.	Presbyterian*	Feb. 12, 1809	Apr. 15, 1865	56	Hannibal Hamlin	(1861–1865)
					Andrew Johnson	(1865)
17.	Methodist*	Dec. 29, 1808	July 31, 1875	66		
18.	Methodist	Apr. 27, 1822	July 23, 1885	63	Schuyler Colfax	(1869–1873)
					Henry Wilson	(1873–1875)
19.	Methodist*	Oct. 4, 1822	Jan. 17, 1893	70	William A. Wheeler	(1877–1881)
20.	Disciples of Christ	Nov. 19, 1831	Sept. 19, 1881	49	Chester A. Arthur	(1881)
21.	Episcopalian	Oct. 5, 1829	Nov. 18, 1886	57		
22.	Presbyterian	Mar. 18, 1837	June 24, 1908	71	Thomas A. Hendricks	(1885)
23.	Presbyterian	Aug. 20, 1833	Mar. 13, 1901	67	Levi P. Morton	(1889–1893)
24.	Presbyterian	Mar. 18, 1837	June 24, 1908	71	Adlai E. Stevenson	(1893–1897)
25.	Methodist	Jan. 29, 1843	Sept. 14, 1901	58	Garret A. Hobart	(1897–1899)
					Theodore Roosevelt	(1901)
26.	Dutch Reformed	Oct. 27, 1858	Jan. 6, 1919	60	Charles W. Fairbanks	(1905–1909)
27.	Unitarian	Sept. 15, 1857	Mar. 8, 1930	72	James S. Sherman	(1909–1912)
28.	Presbyterian	Dec. 29, 1856	Feb. 3, 1924	67	Thomas R. Marshall	(1913–1921)
29.	Baptist	Nov. 2, 1865	Aug. 2, 1923	57	Calvin Coolidge	(1921–1923)
30.	Congregationalist	July 4, 1872	Jan. 5, 1933	60	Charles G. Dawes	(1925–1929)
31.	Friend (Quaker)	Aug. 10, 1874	Oct. 20, 1964	90	Charles Curtis	(1929–1933)
32.	Episcopalian	Jan. 30, 1882	Apr. 12, 1945	63	John N. Garner	(1933–1941)
					Henry A. Wallace	(1941–1945)
					Harry S. Truman	(1945)
33.	Baptist	May 8, 1884	Dec. 26, 1972	88	Alben W. Barkley	(1949–1953)
34.	Presbyterian	Oct. 14, 1890	Mar. 28, 1969	78	Richard M. Nixon	(1953–1961)
35.	Roman Catholic	May 29, 1917	Nov. 22, 1963	46	Lyndon B. Johnson	(1961–1963)
36.	Disciples of Christ	Aug. 27, 1908	Jan. 22, 1973	64	Hubert H. Humphrey	(1965–1969)
37.	Friend (Quaker)	Jan. 9, 1913	Apr. 22, 1994	81	Spiro T. Agnew	(1969–1973)
					Gerald R. Ford**	(1973–1974)
38.	Episcopalian	July 14, 1913			Nelson A. Rockefeller§	(1974–1977)
39.	Baptist	Oct. 1, 1924			Walter F. Mondale	(1977–1981)
40.	Disciples of Christ	Feb. 6, 1911			George H. W. Bush	(1981–1989)
41.	Episcopalian	June 12, 1924			J. Danforth Quayle	(1989–1993)
42.	Baptist	Aug. 19, 1946			Albert A. Gore	(1993–　)

Federalist Papers No. 10, No. 51, and No. 78

In 1787, after the newly drafted U.S. Constitution was submitted to the thirteen states for ratification, a major political debate ensued between the Federalists (who favored ratification) and the Anti-Federalists (who opposed ratification). Anti Federalists in New York were particularly critical of the Constitution, and in response to their objections, Federalists Alexander Hamilton, James Madison, and John Jay wrote a series of eighty-five essays in defense of the Constitution. The essays were published in New York newspapers and reprinted in other newspapers throughout the country.

For students of American government, the essays, collectively known as The Federalist Papers, are particularly important because they provide a glimpse of the founders' political philosophy and intentions in designing the Constitution—and, consequently, in shaping the American philosophy of government.

We have included in this appendix three of these essays: Federalist Papers No. 10, No. 51, and No. 78. Each essay has been annotated by the authors to indicate its importance in American political thought and to clarify the meaning of particular passages.

Federalist Paper No. 10

Federalist Paper No. 10, penned by James Madison, has often been singled out as a key document in American political thought. In this essay, Madison attacks the Anti-Federalists' fear that a republican form of government will inevitably give rise to "factions"—small political parties or groups united by a common interest—that will control the government. Factions will be harmful to the country because they will implement policies beneficial to their own interests but adverse to other people's rights and to the public good.

In this essay, Madison attempts to lay to rest this fear by explaining how, in a large republic such as the United States, there will be so many different factions, held together by regional or local interests, that no single one of them will be dominate national politics.

Madison opens his essay with a paragraph discussing how important it is to devise a plan of government that can control the "instability, injustice, and confusion" brought about by factions.

Among the numerous advantages promised by a well-constructed Union, none deserves to be more accurately developed than its tendency to break and control the violence of faction. The friend of popular governments never finds himself so much alarmed for their character and fate as when he contemplates their propensity to this dangerous vice. He will not fail, therefore, to set a due value on any plan which, without violating the principles to which he is attached, provides a proper cure for it. The instability, injustice, and confusion introduced into the public councils have, in truth, been the mortal diseases under which popular governments have everywhere perished, as they continue to be the favorite and fruitful topics from which the adversaries to liberty derive their most specious declamations. The valuable improvements made by the American constitutions on the popular models, both ancient and modern, cannot certainly be too much admired; but it would be an unwarrantable partiality to contend that they have as effectually obviated the danger on this side, as was wished and expected. Complaints are everywhere heard from our most considerate and virtuous citizens, equally the friends of public and private faith and of public and personal liberty, that our governments are too unstable, that the public good is disregarded in the conflicts of rival parties, and that measures are too often decided, not according to the rules of justice and the rights of the minor party, but by the superior force of an interested and overbearing majority. However anxiously we may wish that these complaints had no foundation, the evidence of known facts will not permit us to deny that they are in some degree true. It will be found, indeed, on a candid review of our situation, that some of the distresses under which we labor have been erroneously charged on the operation of our governments; but it will be found, at the same time, that other causes will not alone account for many of our heaviest misfortunes; and, particularly, for that prevailing and increasing distrust of public engagements and alarm for private rights which are echoed from one end of the continent to the other. These must be chiefly, if not wholly, effects of the unsteadiness and injustice with which a factious spirit has tainted our public administration.

Madison now defines what he means by the term faction.

By a faction I understand a number of citizens, whether amounting to a majority or minority of the whole, who are united and actuated by some common impulse of passion, or of interest, adverse to the rights of other citizens, or the permanent and aggregate interests of the community.

Madison next contends that there are two methods by which the "mischiefs of factions" can be cured: by removing the causes of faction or by controlling their effects. In the following paragraphs, Madison explains how liberty itself nourishes factions. Therefore, to abolish factions would involve abolishing liberty—a cure "worse than the disease."

There are two methods of curing the mischiefs of faction: the one, by removing its causes; the other, by controlling its effects.

There are again two methods of removing the causes of faction: the one, by destroying the liberty which is essential to its existence; the other, by giving to every citizen the same opinions, the same passions, and the same interests.

It could never be more truly said than of the first remedy that it was worse than the disease. Liberty is to faction what air is to fire, an aliment without which it instantly expires. But it could not be a less folly to abolish liberty, which is essential to political life, because it nourishes faction than it would be to wish the annihilation of air, which is essential to animal life, because it imparts to fire its destructive agency.

The second expedient is as impracticable as the first would be unwise. As long as the reason of man continues fallible, and his is at liberty to exercise it, different opinions will be formed. As long as the connection subsists between his reason and his self-love, his opinions and his passions will have a reciprocal influence on each other; and the former will be objects to which the latter will attach themselves. The diversity in the faculties of men, from which the

rights of property originate, is not less an insuperable obstacle to a uniformity of interests. The protection of these faculties is the first object of government. From the protection of different and unequal faculties of acquiring property, the possession of different degrees and kinds of property immediately results; and from the influence of these on the sentiments and views of the respective proprietors ensues a division of the society into different interests and parties.

The latent causes of faction are thus sown in the nature of man; and we see them everywhere brought into different degrees of activity, according to the different circumstances of civil society. A zeal for different opinions concerning religion, concerning government, and many other points, as well of speculation as of practice; an attachment to different leaders ambitiously contending for pre-eminence and power; or to persons of other descriptions whose fortunes have been interesting to the human passions, have, in turn, divided mankind into parties, inflamed them with mutual animosity, and rendered them much more disposed to vex and oppress each other than to co-operate for their common good. So strong is this propensity of mankind to fall into mutual animosities that where no substantial occasion presents itself the most frivolous and fanciful distinctions have been sufficient to kindle their unfriendly passions and excite their most violent conflicts. But the most common and durable source of factions has been the various and unequal distribution of property. Those who hold and those who are without property have ever formed distinct interests in society. Those who are creditors, and those who are debtors, fall under a like discrimination. A landed interest, a manufacturing interest, a mercantile interest, a moneyed interest, with many lesser interests, grow up of necessity in civilized nations, and divide them into different classes, actuated by different sentiments and views. The regulation of these various and interfering interests forms the principal task of modern legislation and involves the spirit of party and faction in the necessary and ordinary operations of government.

No man is allowed to be a judge in his own cause, because his interest would certainly bias his judgment, and, not improbably, corrupt his integrity. With equal, nay with greater reason, a body of men are unfit to be both judges and parties at the same time; yet what are many of the most important acts of legislation but so many judicial determinations, not indeed concerning the rights of single persons, but concerning the rights of large bodies of citizens? And what are the different classes of legislators but advocates and parties to the causes which they determine? Is a law proposed concerning private debts? It is a question to which the creditors are parties on one side and the debtors on the other. Justice ought to hold the balance between them. Yet the parties are, and must be, themselves the judges; and the most numerous party, or in other words, the most powerful faction must be expected to prevail. Shall domestic manufacturers be encouraged, and in what degree, by restrictions on foreign manufacturers? Are questions which would be differently decided by the landed and the manufacturing classes, and probably by neither with a sole regard to justice and the public good. The apportionment of taxes on the various descriptions of property is an act which seems to require the most exact impartiality; yet there is, perhaps, no legislative act in which greater opportunity and temptation are given to a predominant party to trample on the rules of justice. Every shilling with which they overburden the inferior number is a shilling saved to their own pockets.

It is in vain to say that enlightened statesmen will be able to adjust these clashing interests and render them all subservient to the public good. Enlightened statesmen will not always be at the helm. Nor, in many cases, can such an adjustment be made at all without taking into view indirect and remote considerations, which will rarely prevail over the immediate interest which one party may find in disregarding the rights of another or the good of the whole.

The inference to which we are brought is that the *causes* of faction cannot be removed and that relief is only to be sought in the means of controlling its *effects*.

Having concluded that "the causes of factions cannot be removed," Madison now looks in some detail at the other method by which factions can be cured—by controlling their effects. This is the heart of his essay. He begins by positing a significant question: How can you have self-government without risking the possibility that a ruling faction, particularly a majority faction, might tyrannize over the rights of others?

If a faction consists of less than a majority, relief is supplied by the republican principle, which enables the majority to defeat its sinister views by regular vote. It may clog the administration, it may convulse the society; but it will be unable to execute and mask its violence under the forms of the Constitution. When a majority is included in a faction, the form of popular government, on the other hand, enables it to sacrifice to its ruling passion or interest both the public good and the rights of other citizens. To secure the public good and private rights against the danger of such a faction, and at the same time to preserve the spirit and the form of popular government, is then the great object to which our inquiries are directed. Let me add that it is the great desideratum by which alone this form of government can be rescued from the opprobrium under which it has so long labored and be recommended to the esteem and adoption of mankind.

Madison now sets forth the idea that one way to control the effects of factions is to ensure that the majority is rendered incapable of acting in concert in order to "carry into effect schemes of oppression." He goes on to state that in a democracy, in which all citizens participate personally in government decision making, there is no way to prevent the majority from communicating with each other and, as a result, acting in concert.

By what means is this object attainable? Evidently by one of two only. Either the existence of the same passion or interest in a majority at the same time must be prevented, or the majority, having such coexistent passion or interest, must be rendered, by their number and local situation, unable to concert and carry into effect schemes of oppression. If the impulse and the opportunity be suffered to coincide, we well know that neither moral nor religious motives can be relied on as an adequate control. They are not found to be such on the injustice and violence of individuals, and lose their efficacy in proportion to the number combined together, that is, in proportion as their efficacy becomes needful.

From this view of the subject it may be concluded that a pure democracy, by which I mean a society consisting of a small number of citizens, who assemble and administer the government in person, can admit of no cure for the mischiefs of faction. A common passion or interest will, in almost every case, be felt by a majority of the whole; a communication and concert results from the form of government itself; and there is nothing to check the inducements to sacrifice the weaker party or an obnoxious individual. Hence it is that such democracies have ever been spectacles of turbulence and contention; have ever been found incompatible with personal security or the rights of property; and have in general been as short in their lives as they have been violent in their deaths. Theoretic politicians, who have patronized this species of government, have erroneously supposed that by reducing mankind to a perfect equality in their political rights, they would at the same time be perfectly equalized and assimilated in their possessions, their opinions, and their passions.

Madison now moves on to discuss the benefits of a republic with respect to controlling the effects of factions. He begins by defining a republic and then pointing out the "two great points of difference" between a republic and a democracy: a republic is governed by a small body of elected representatives, not by the people directly; and a republic can extend over a much larger territory and embrace more citizens than a democracy can.

A republic, by which I mean a government in which the scheme of representation takes place, opens a different prospect and promises the cure for which we are seeking. Let us examine the points in which it varies from pure democracy, and we shall comprehend both the nature of the cure and the efficacy which it must derive from the Union.

The two great points of difference between a democracy and a republic are: first, the delegation of the government, in the latter, to a small number of citizens elected by the rest; secondly, the greater number of citizens and greater sphere of country over which the latter may be extended.

In the following four paragraphs, Madison explains how in a republic, particularly a large republic, the delegation of authority to elected representatives will increase the likelihood that those who govern will be "fit" for their positions and that a proper balance will be achieved between local (factional) interests and national interests. Note how he stresses that the new federal Constitution, by dividing powers between state governments and the national government, provides a "happy combination in this respect."

The effect of the first difference is, on the one hand, to refine and enlarge the public views by passing them through the medium of a chosen body of citizens, whose wisdom may best discern the true interest of their country and whose patriotism and love of justice will be least likely to sacrifice it to temporary or partial considerations. Under such a regulation it may well happen that the public voice, pronounced by the representatives of the people, will be more consonant to the public good than if pronounced by the people themselves, convened for the purpose. On the other hand, the effect may be inverted. Men of factious tempers, of local prejudices, or of sinister designs, may, by intrigue, by corruption, or by other means, first obtain the suffrages, and then betray the interests of the people. The question resulting is, whether small or extensive republics are most favorable to the election of proper guardians of the public weal; and it is clearly decided in favor of the latter by two obvious considerations.

In the first place it is to be remarked that however small the republic may be the representatives must be raised to a certain number in order to guard against the cabals of a few; and that however large it may be they must be limited to a certain number in order to guard against the confusion of a multitude. Hence, the number of representatives in the two cases not being in proportion to that of the constituents, and being proportionally greatest in the small republic, it follows that if the proportion of fit characters be not less in the large than in the small republic, the former will present a greater option, and consequently a greater probability of a fit choice.

In the next place, as each representative will be chosen by a greater number of citizens in the large than in the small republic, it will be more difficult for unworthy candidates to practice with success the vicious arts by which elections are too often carried; and the suffrages of the people being more free, will be more likely to center on men who possess the most attractive merit and the most diffusive and established characters.

It must be confessed that in this, as in most other cases, there is a mean, on both sides of which inconveniencies will be found to lie. By enlarging too much the number of electors, you render the representative too little acquainted with all their local circumstances and lesser interests; as by reducing it too much, you render him unduly attached to these, and too little fit to comprehend and pursue great and national objects. The federal Constitution forms a happy combination in this respect; the great and aggregate interests being referred to the national, the local and particular to the State legislatures.

Madison now looks more closely at the other difference between a republic and a democracy—namely, that a republic can encompass a larger territory and more citizens than a democracy can. In the remaining paragraphs of his essay, Madison concludes that in a large republic, it will be difficult for factions to act in concert. Although a factious group—religious, political, economic, or otherwise—may control a local or regional government, it will have little chance of gathering a national following. This is because in a large republic, there will be numerous other factions whose work will offset the work of any one particular faction ("sect"). As Madison phrases it, these numerous factions will "secure the national councils against any danger from that source."

The other point of difference is the greater number of citizens and extent of territory which may be brought within the compass of republican than of democratic government; and it is this circumstance principally which renders factious combinations less to be dreaded in the former than in the latter. The smaller the society, the fewer probably will be the distinct parties and interests composing it; the fewer the distinct parties and interests, the more frequently will a majority be found of the same party; and the smaller the number of individuals composing a majority, and the smaller the compass within which they are placed, the more easily will they concert and execute their plans of oppression. Extend the sphere and you take in a greater variety of parties and interests; you make it less probable that a majority of the whole will have a common motive to invade the rights of other citizens; or if such a common motive exists, it will be more difficult for all who feel it to discover their own strength and to act in unison with each other. Besides other impediments, it may be remarked that, where there is a consciousness of unjust or dishonorable purposes, communication is always checked by distrust in proportion to the number whose concurrence is necessary.

Hence, it clearly appears that the same advantage which a republic has over a democracy in controlling the effects of faction is enjoyed by a large over a small republic—is enjoyed by the Union over the States composing it. Does this advantage consist in the substitution of representatives whose enlightened views and virtuous sentiments render them superior to local prejudices and to schemes of injustice? It will not be denied that the representation of the Union will be most likely to possess these requisite endowments. Does it consist in the greater security afforded by a greater variety of parties, against the event of any one party being able to outnumber and oppress the rest? In an equal degree does the increased variety of parties comprised within the Union increase this security. Does it, in fine, consist in the greater obstacles opposed to the concert and accomplishment of the secret wishes of an unjust and interested majority? Here again the extent of the Union gives it the most palpable advantage.

The influence of factious leaders may kindle a flame within their particular States but will be unable to spread a general conflagration through the other States. A religious sect may degenerate into a political faction in a part of the Confederacy; but the variety of sects dispersed over the entire face of it must secure the national councils against any danger from that source. A rage for paper money, for an abolition of debts, for an equal division of property, or for any other improper or wicked project, will be less apt to pervade the whole body of the Union than a particular member of it, in the same proportion as such a malady is more likely to taint a particular county or district than an entire State.

In the extent and proper structure of the Union, therefore, we behold a republican remedy for the diseases most incident to republican government. And according to the degree of pleasure and pride we feel in being republicans ought to be our zeal in cherishing the spirit and supporting the character of federalists.

Publius
(James Madison)

Federalist Paper No. 51

Federalist Paper *No. 51, also authored by James Madison, is another classic in American political theory. Although the Federalists wanted a strong national government, they had not abandoned the traditional American view, particularly notable during the revolutionary era, that those holding powerful government positions could not be trusted to put national interests and the common good above their own personal interests. In this essay, Madison explains why the separation of the national government's powers into three branches—executive, legislative, and judicial—and a federal structure of government offer the best protection against tyranny.*

To what expedient, then, shall we finally resort, for maintaining in practice the necessary partition of power among the several departments as laid down in the Constitution? The only answer that can be given is that as all these exterior provisions are found to be inadequate the defect must be supplied, by so contriving the interior structure of the government as that its several constituent parts may, by their mutual relations, be the means of keeping each other in their proper places. Without presuming to undertake a full development of this important idea I will hazard a few general observations which may perhaps place it in a clearer light, and enable us to form a more correct judgment of the principles and structure of the government planned by the convention.

In the next two paragraphs, Madison stresses that for the powers of the different branches (departments) of government to be truly separated, the personnel in one branch should not be dependent on another branch for their appointment or for the "emoluments" (compensation) attached to their offices.

In order to lay a due foundation for that separate and distinct exercise of the different powers of government, which to a certain extent is admitted on all hands to be essential to the preservation of liberty, it is evident that each department should have a will of its own; and consequently should be so constituted that the members of each should have as little agency as possible in the appointment of the members of the others. Were this principle rigorously adhered to, it would require that all the appointments for the supreme executive, legislative, and judiciary magistracies should be drawn from the same fountain of authority, the people, through channels having no communication whatever with one another. Perhaps such a plan of constructing the several departments would be less difficult in practice than it may in contemplation appear. Some difficulties, however, and some additional expense would attend the execution of it. Some deviations, therefore, from the principle must be admitted. In the constitution of the judiciary department in particular, it might be inexpedient to insist rigorously on the principle: first, because peculiar qualifications being essential in the members, the primary consideration ought to be to select that mode of choice which best secures these qualifications; second, because the permanent tenure by which the appointments are held in that department must soon destroy all sense of dependence on the authority conferring them.

It is equally evident that the members of each department should be as little dependent as possible on those of the others for the emoluments annexed to their offices. Were the executive magistrate, or the judges, not independent of the legislature in this particular, their independence in every other would be merely nominal.

In the following passages, which are among the most widely quoted of Madison's writings, he explains how the separation of the powers of government into three branches helps to counter the effects of personal ambition on government. The separation of powers allows personal motives to be linked to the constitutional rights of a branch of government. In effect, rivaling personal interests in each branch will help to keep the powers of the three government branches separate and, in so doing, will help to guard the public interest.

But the great security against a gradual concentration of the several powers in the same department consists in giving to those who administer each department the necessary constitutional means and personal motives to resist encroachments of the others. The provision for defense must in this, as in all other cases, be made commensurate to the danger of attack. Ambition must be made to counteract ambition. The interest of the man must be connected with the constitutional rights of the place. It may be a reflection on human nature that such devices should be necessary to control the abuses of government. But what is government itself but the greatest of all reflections on human nature? If men were angels, no government would be necessary. If angels were to govern men, neither external nor internal controls on government would be necessary. In framing a government which is to be administered by men over men, the great difficulty lies in this: you must first enable the government to control the governed; and in the next place oblige it to control itself. A dependence on the people is, no doubt, the primary control on the government; but experience has taught mankind the necessity of auxiliary precautions.

This policy of supplying, by opposite and rival interests, the defect of better motives, might be traced through the whole system of human affairs, private as well as public. We see it particularly displayed in all the subordinate distributions of power, where the constant aim is to divide and arrange the several offices in such a manner as that each may be a check on the other—that the private interest of every individual may be a sentinel over the public rights. These inventions of prudence cannot be less requisite in the distribution of the supreme powers of the State.

Madison now addresses the issue of equality between the branches of government. The legislature will necessarily predominate, but if the executive is given an "absolute negative" (absolute veto power) over legislative actions, this also could lead to an abuse of power. Madison concludes that the division of the legislature into two "branches" (parts, or chambers) will act as a check on the legislature's powers.

But it is not possible to give to each department an equal power of self-defense. In republican government, the legislative authority necessarily predominates. The remedy for this inconveniency is to divide the legislature into different branches; and to render them, by different modes of election and different principles of action, as little connected with each other as the nature of their common functions and their common dependence on the society will admit. It may even be necessary to guard against dangerous encroachments by still further precautions. As the weight of the legislative authority requires that it should be thus divided, the weakness of the executive may require, on the other hand, that it should be fortified. An absolute negative on the legislature appears, at first view, to be the natural defense with which the executive magistrate should be armed. But perhaps it would be neither altogether safe nor alone sufficient. On ordinary occasions it might not be exerted with the requisite firmness, and on extraordinary occasions it might be perfidiously abused. May not this defect of an absolute negative be supplied by some qualified connection between this weaker department and the weaker branch of the stronger department, by which the latter may be led to support the constitutional rights of the former, without being too much detached from the rights of its own department?

If the principles on which these observations are founded be just, as I persuade myself they are, and they be applied as a criterion to the several State constitutions, and to the federal Constitution, it will be found that if the latter does not perfectly correspond with them, the former are infinitely less able to bear such a test.

In the remainder of the essay, Madison discusses how a federal system of government, in which powers are divided between the states and the national government, offers "double security against tyranny.

There are, moreover, two considerations particularly applicable to the federal system of America, which place that system in a very interesting point of view.

First. In a single republic, all the power surrendered by the people is submitted to the administration of a single government; and the usurpations are guarded against by a division of the government into distinct and separate departments. In the compound republic of America, the power surrendered by the people is first divided between two distinct governments, and then the portion allotted to each subdivided among distinct and separate departments. Hence a double security arises to the rights of the people. The different governments will control each other, at the same time that each will be controlled by itself.

Second. It is of great importance in a republic not only to guard the society against the oppression of its rulers, but to guard one part of the society against the injustice of the other part. Different interests necessarily exist in different classes of citizens. If a majority be united by a common interest, the rights of the minority will be insecure. There are but two methods of providing against this evil: the one by creating a will in the community independent of the majority—that is, of the society itself; the other, by comprehending in the society so many separate descriptions of citizens as will render an unjust combination of a majority of the whole very improbable, if not impracticable. The first method prevails in all governments possessing an hereditary or self-appointed authority. This, at best, is but a precarious security; because a power independent of the society may as well espouse the unjust views of the major as the rightful interests of the minor party, and may possibly be turned against both parties. The second method will be exemplified in the federal republic of the United States. Whilst all authority in it will be derived from and dependent on the society, the society itself will be broken into so many parts, interests and classes of citizens, that the rights of individuals, or of the minority, will be in little danger from interested combinations of the majority. In a free government the security for civil rights must be the same as that for religious rights. It consists in the one case in the multiplicity of interests, and in the other in the multiplicity of sects. The degree of security in both cases will depend on the number of interests and sects; and this may be presumed to depend on the extent of country and number of people comprehended under the same government. This view of the subject must particularly recommend a proper federal system to all the sincere and considerate friends of republican government, since it shows that in exact proportion as the territory of the Union may be formed into more circumscribed Confederacies, or States, oppressive combinations of a majority will be facilitated; the best security, under the republican forms, for the rights of every class of citizen, will be diminished; and consequently the stability and independence of some member of the government, the only other security, must be proportionally increased. Justice is the end of government. It is the end of civil society. It ever has been and ever will be pursued until it be obtained, or until liberty be lost in the pursuit. In a society under the forms of which the stronger faction can readily unite and oppress the weaker, anarchy may as truly be said to reign as in a state of nature, where the weaker individual is not secured against the violence of the stronger; and as, in the latter state, even the stronger individuals are prompted, by the uncertainty of their condition, to submit to a government which may protect the weak as well as themselves; so, in the former state, will the more powerful factions or parties be gradually induced, by a like motive, to wish for a government which will protect all parties, the weaker as well as the more powerful. It can be little doubted that if the State of Rhode Island was separated from the Confederacy and left to itself, the insecurity of rights under the popular form of government within such narrow limits would be displayed by such reiterated oppressions of factious majorities that some power altogether independent of the people would soon be called for by the voice of the very factions whose misrule had proved the necessity of it. In the extended republic of the United States, and among the great variety of interests, parties, and sects which it embraces, a coalition of a majority of the whole society could seldom take place on any other principles than those of justice and the general good; whilst there being thus less danger to a minor from the will of a major party, there must be less pretext, also, to provide for the security of the former, by introducing into the government a will not dependent on the latter, or, in other words, a will independent of the society itself. It is no less certain than it is important, notwithstanding the contrary opinions which have been entertained, that the larger the society, provided it lie within a practicable sphere, the more duly capable it will be of self-government. And happily for the republican cause, the practicable sphere may be carried to a very great extent by a judicious modification and mixture of the *federal principle*.

Publius
(James Madison)

Federalist Paper No. 78

In this essay, Alexander Hamilton looks at the role of the judicial branch (the courts) in the new government fashioned by the Constitution's framers. The essay is historically significant because, among other things, it provides a basis for the courts' power of judicial review, which was not explicitly set forth in the Constitution (see Chapters 3 and 15).

After some brief introductory remarks, Hamilton explains why the founders decided that federal judges should be appointed and given lifetime tenure. Note how he describes the judiciary as the "weakest" and "least dangerous" branch of government. Because of this, claims Hamilton, "all possible care" is required to enable the judiciary to defend itself against attacks by the other two branches of government. Above all, the independence of the judicial branch should be secured, because if judicial powers were combined with legislative or executive powers, there would be no liberty.

WE PROCEED now to an examination of the judiciary department of the proposed government.

In unfolding the defects of the existing Confederation, the utility and necessity of a federal judicature have been clearly pointed out. It is the less necessary to recapitulate the considerations there urged, as the propriety of the institution in the abstract is not disputed; the only questions which have been raised being relative to the manner of constituting it, and to its extent. To these points, therefore, our observations shall be confined.

The manner of constituting it seems to embrace these several objects: 1st. The mode of appointing the judges. 2d. The tenure by which they are to hold their places. 3d. The partition of the judiciary authority between different courts, and their relations to each other.

First. As to the mode of appointing the judges; this is the same with that of appointing the officers of the Union in general, and has been so fully discussed in the last two numbers, that nothing can be said here which would not be useless repetition.

Second. As to the tenure by which the judges are to hold their places; this chiefly concerns their duration in office; the provisions for their support; the precautions for their responsibility.

According to the plan of the convention, all judges who may be appointed by the United States are to hold their offices during good behavior; which is conformable to the most approved of the State constitutions and among the rest, to that of this State. Its propriety having been drawn into question by the adversaries of that plan, is no light symptom of the rage for objection, which disorders their imaginations and judgments. The standard of good behavior for the continuance in office of the judicial magistracy, is certainly one of the most valuable of the modern improvements in the practice of government. In a monarchy it is an excellent barrier to the despotism of the prince; in a republic it is a no less excellent barrier to the encroachments and oppressions of the representative body. And it is the best expedient which can be devised in any government, to secure a steady, upright, and impartial administration of the laws.

Whoever attentively considers the different departments of power must perceive, that, in a government in which they are separated from each other, the judiciary, from the nature of its functions, will always be the least dangerous to the political rights of the Constitution; because it will be least in a capacity to annoy or injure them. The Executive not only dispenses the honors, but holds the sword of the community. The legislature not only commands the purse, but prescribes the rules by which the duties and rights of every citizen are to be regulated. The judiciary, on the contrary, has no influence over either the sword or the purse; no direction either of the strength or of the wealth of the society; and can take no active resolution whatever. It may truly be said to have neither force nor will, but merely judgment; and must ultimately depend upon the aid of the executive arm even for the efficacy of its judgments.

This simple view of the matter suggests several important consequences. It proves incontestably, that the judiciary is beyond comparison the weakest of the three departments of power; that it can never attack with success either of the other two; and that all possible care is requisite to enable it to defend itself against their attacks. It equally proves, that though individual oppression may now and then proceed from the courts of justice, the general liberty of the people can never be endangered from that quarter; I mean so long as the judiciary remains truly distinct from both the legislature and the Executive. For I agree, that "there is no liberty, if the power of judging is not separated from the legislative and executive powers." And it proves, in the last place, that as liberty can have nothing to fear from the judiciary alone, but would have everything to fear from its union with either of the other departments; that as all the effects of such a union must ensue from a dependence of the former on the latter, notwithstanding a nominal and apparent separation; that as, from the natural feebleness of the judiciary, it is in continual jeopardy of being overpowered, awed, or influenced by its co-ordinate branches; and that as nothing can contribute so much to its firmness and independence as permanency in office, this quality may therefore be justly regarded as an indispens-

able ingredient in its constitution, and, in a great measure, as the citadel of the public justice and the public security.

Hamilton now stresses that the "complete independence of the courts" is essential in a limited government, because it is up to the courts to interpret the laws. Just as a federal court can decide which of two conflicting statutes should take priority, so can that court decide whether a statute conflicts with the Constitution. Essentially, Hamilton sets forth here the theory of judicial review—the power of the courts to decide whether actions of the other branches of government are (or are not) consistent with the Constitution. Hamilton points out that this "exercise of judicial discretion, in determining between two contradictory laws," does not mean that the judicial branch is superior to the legislative branch. Rather, it "supposes" that the power of the people (as declared in the Constitution) is superior to both the judiciary and the legislature.

The complete independence of the courts of justice is peculiarly essential in a limited Constitution. By a limited Constitution, I understand one which contains certain specified exceptions to the legislative authority; such, for instance, as that it shall pass no bills of attainder, no ex-post-facto laws, and the like. Limitations of this kind can be preserved in practice no other way than through the medium of courts of justice, whose duty it must be to declare all acts contrary to the manifest tenor of the Constitution void. Without this, all the reservations of particular rights or privileges would amount to nothing. Some perplexity respecting the rights of the courts to pronounce legislative acts void, because contrary to the Constitution, has arisen from an imagination that the doctrine would imply a superiority of the judiciary to the legislative power. It is urged that the authority which can declare the acts of another void, must necessarily be superior to the one whose acts may be declared void. As this doctrine is of great importance in all the American constitutions, a brief discussion of the ground on which it rests cannot be unacceptable.

There is no position which depends on clearer principles, than that every act of a delegated authority, contrary to the tenor of the commission under which it is exercised, is void. No legislative act, therefore, contrary to the Constitution, can be valid. To deny this, would be to affirm, that the deputy is greater than his principal; that the servant is above his master; that the representatives of the people are superior to the people themselves; that men acting by virtue of powers, may do not only what their powers do not authorize, but what they forbid.

If it be said that the legislative body are themselves the constitutional judges of their own powers, and that the construction they put upon them is conclusive upon the other departments, it may be answered, that this cannot be the natural presumption, where it is not to be collected from any particular provisions in the Constitution. It is not otherwise to be supposed, that the Constitution could intend to enable the representatives of the people to substitute their will to that of their constituents. It is far more rational to suppose, that the courts were designed to be an intermediate body between the people and the legislature, in order, among other things, to keep the latter within the limits assigned to their authority. The interpretation of the laws is the proper and peculiar province of the courts. A constitution is, in fact, and must be regarded by the judges, as a fundamental law. It therefore belongs to them to ascertain its meaning, as well as the meaning of any particular act proceeding from the legislative body. If there should happen to be an irreconcilable variance between the two, that which has the superior obligation and validity ought, of course, to be preferred; or, in other words, the Constitution ought to be preferred to the statute, the intention of the people to the intention of their agents.

Nor does this conclusion by any means suppose a superiority of the judicial to the legislative power. It only supposes that the power of the people is superior to both; and that where the will of the legislature, declared in its statutes, stands in opposition to that of the people, declared in the Constitution, the judges ought to be governed by the latter rather than the former. They ought to regulate their decisions by the fundamental laws, rather than by those which are not fundamental.

This exercise of judicial discretion, in determining between two contradictory laws, is exemplified in a familiar instance. It not uncommonly happens, that there are two statutes existing at one time, clashing in whole or in part with each other, and neither of them containing any repealing clause or expression. In such a case, it is the province of the courts to liquidate and fix their meaning and operation. So far as they can, by any fair construction, be reconciled to each other, reason and law conspire to dictate that this should be done; where this is impractable, it becomes a matter of necessity to give effect to one, in exclusion of the other. The rule which has obtained in the courts for determining their relative validity is, that the last in order of time shall be preferred to the first. But this is a mere rule of construction, not derived from any positive law, but from the nature and reason of the thing. It is a rule not enjoined upon the courts by legislative provision, but adopted by themselves, as consonant to truth the propriety, for the direction of their conduct as interpreters of the law. They thought it reasonable, that between the interfering acts of an equal authority, that which was the last indication of its will should have the preference.

But in regard to the interfering acts of a superior and subordinate authority, of an original and derivative power, the nature and reason of the thing indicate the converse of that rule as proper to be followed. They teach us that the prior act of a superior ought to be preferred to the subsequent act of an inferior and subordinate authority; and that

accordingly, whenever a particular statute contravenes the Constitution, it will be the duty of the judicial tribunals to adhere to the latter and disregard the former.

It can be of no weight to say that the courts, on the pretense of a repugnancy, may substitute their own pleasure to the constitutional intentions of the legislature. This might as well happen in the case of two contradictory statutes; or it might as well happen in every adjudication upon any single statute. The courts must declare the sense of the law; and if they should be disposed to exercise will instead of judgment, the consequence would equally be the substitution of their pleasure to that of the legislative body. The observation, if it prove anything, would prove that there ought to be no judges distinct from that body.

If, then, the courts of justice are to be considered as the bulwarks of a limited Constitution against legislative encroachments, this consideration will afford a strong argument for the permanent tenure of judicial offices, since nothing will contribute so much as this to that independent spirit in the judges which must be essential to the faithful performance of so arduous a duty.

The independence of the judges is equally requisite to guard the Constitution and the rights of individuals from the effects of those ill humors, which the arts of designing men, or the influence of particular conjunctures, sometimes disseminate among the people themselves, and which, though they speedily give place to better information, and more deliberate reflection, have a tendency, in the meantime, to occasion dangerous innovations in the government, and serious oppressions of the minor party in the community. Though I trust the friends of the proposed Constitution will never concur with its enemies, in questioning that fundamental principle of republican government, which admits the right of the people to alter or abolish the established Constitution, whenever they find it inconsistent with their happiness, yet it is not to be inferred from this principle, that the representatives of the people, whenever a momentary inclination happens to lay hold of a majority of their constituents, incompatible with the provisions of the existing Constitution, would, on that account, be justifiable in a violation of those provisions; or that the courts would be under a greater obligation to connive at infractions in this shape, than when they had proceeded wholly from the cabals of the representative body. Until the people have, by some solemn and authoritative act, annulled or changed the established form, it is binding upon themselves collectively, as well as individually; and no presumption, or even knowledge, of their sentiments, can warrant their representatives in a departure from it, prior to such an act. But it is easy to see, that it would require an uncommon portion of fortitude in the judges to do their duty as faithful guardians of the Constitution, where legislative invasions of it had been instigated by the major voice of the community.

But it is not with a view to infractions of the Constitution only, that the independence of the judges may be an essential safeguard against the effects of occasional ill humors in the society. These sometimes extend no farther than to the injury of the private rights of particular classes of citizens, by unjust and partial laws. Here also the firmness of the judicial magistracy is of vast importance in mitigating the severity and confining the operation of such laws. It not only serves to moderate the immediate mischiefs of those which may have been passed, but it operates as a check upon the legislative body in passing them; who, perceiving that obstacles to the success of iniquitous intention are to be expected from the scruples of the courts, are in a manner compelled, by the very motives of the injustice they meditate, to qualify their attempts. This is a circumstance calculated to have more influence upon the character of our governments, than but few may be aware of. The benefits of the integrity and moderation of the judiciary have already been felt in more States than one; and though they may have displeased those whose sinister expectations they may have disappointed, they must have commanded the esteem and applause of all the virtuous and disinterested. Considerate men, of every description, ought to prize whatever will tend to beget or fortify that temper in the courts; as no man can be sure that he may not be to-morrow the victim of a spirit of injustice, by which he may be a gainer to-day. Any every man must now feel, that the inevitable tendency of such a spirit is to sap the foundations of public and private confidence, and to introduce in its stead universal distrust and distress.

That inflexible and uniform adherence to the rights of the Constitution, and of individuals, which we perceive to be indispensable in the courts of justice, can certainly not be expected from judges who hold their offices by a temporary commission. Periodical appointments, however regulated, or by whomsoever made, would, in some way or other, be fatal to their necessary independence. If the power of making them was committed either to the Executive or legislature, there would be danger of an improper complaisance to the branch which possessed it; if to both, there would be an unwillingness to hazard the displeasure of either; if to the people, or to persons chosen by them for the special purpose, there would be too great a disposition to consult popularity, to justify a reliance that nothing would be consulted but the Constitution and the laws.

Hamilton points to yet another reason why lifetime tenure for federal judges will benefit the public: effective judgments rest on a knowledge of judicial precedents and the law, and such knowledge can only be obtained through experience on the bench. A "temporary duration of office," *according to Hamilton, would "discourage individuals [of 'fit character'] from quitting a lucrative practice to serve on the bench" and ultimately would "throw the administration of justice into the hands of the less able, and less well qualified."*

There is yet a further and a weightier reason for the permanency of the judicial offices, which is deducible from the nature of the qualifications they require. It has been frequently remarked, with great propriety, that a voluminous code of laws is one of the inconveniences necessarily connected with the advantages of a free government. To avoid an arbitrary discretion in the courts, it is indispensable that they should be bound down by strict rules and precedents, which serve to define and point out their duty in every particular case that comes before them; and it will readily be conceived from the variety of controversies which grow out of the folly and wickedness of mankind, that the records of those precedents must unavoidably swell to a very considerable bulk, and must demand long and laborious study to acquire a competent knowledge of them. Hence it is, that there can be but few men in the society who will have sufficient skill in the laws to qualify them for the stations of judges. And making the proper deductions for the ordinary depravity of human nature, the number must be still smaller of those who unite the requisite integrity with the requisite knowledge. These considerations apprise us, that the government can have no great option between fit character; and that a temporary duration in office, which would naturally discourage such characters from quitting a lucrative line of practice to accept a seat on the bench, would have a tendency to throw the administration of justice into hands less able, and less well qualified, to conduct it with utility and dignity. In the present circumstances of this country, and in those in which it is likely to be for a long time to come, the disadvantages on this score would be greater than they may at first sight appear; but it must be confessed, that they are far inferior to those which present themselves under other aspects of the subject.

Upon the whole, there can be no room to doubt that the convention acted wisely in copying from the models of those constitutions which have established good behavior as the tenure of their judicial offices, in point of duration; and that so far from being blamable on this account, their plan would have been inexcusably defective, if it had wanted this important feature of good government. The experience of Great Britain affords an illustrious comment on the excellence of the institution.

Publius
(Alexander Hamilton)

Justices of the U.S. Supreme Court in the Twentieth Century

Chief Justices

Name	Years of Service	State App't From	Appointing President	Age App't	Political Affiliation	Educational* Background
Fuller, Melville Weston	1888–1910	Illinois	Cleveland	55	Democrat	Bowdoin College; studied at Harvard Law School
White, Edward Douglass	1910–1921	Louisiana	Taft	65	Democrat	Mount St. Mary's College; Georgetown College (now University)
Taft, William Howard	1921–1930	Connecticut	Harding	64	Republican	Yale; Cincinnati Law School
Hughes, Charles Evans	1930–1941	New York	Hoover	68	Republican	Colgate University; Brown; Columbia Law School
Stone, Harlan Fiske	1941–1946	New York	Roosevelt, F.	69	Republican	Amherst College; Columbia
Vinson, Frederick Moore	1946–1953	Kentucky	Truman	56	Democrat	Centre College
Warren, Earl	1953–1969	California	Eisenhower	62	Republican	University of California, Berkeley
Burger, Warren Earl	1969–1986	Virginia	Nixon	62	Republican	University of Minnesota; St. Paul College of Law (Mitchell College)
Rehnquist, William Hubbs	1986–	Virginia	Reagan	62	Republican	Stanford; Harvard; Stanford University Law School

*SOURCE: Educational background information derived from Elder Witt, Guide to the *U.S. Supreme Court,* 2d ed. (Washington, D.C.: Congressional Quarterly Press, Inc., 1990) Reprinted with the permission of the publisher.

Associate Justices

Name	Years of Service	State App't From	Appointing President	Age App't	Political Affiliation	Educational* Background
Harlan, John Marshall	1877–1911	Kentucky	Hayes	61	Republican	Centre College; studied law at Transylvania University
Gray, Horace	1882–1902	Massachusetts	Arthur	54	Republican	Harvard College; Harvard Law School
Brewer, David Josiah	1890–1910	Kansas	Harrison	53	Republican	Wesleyan University; Yale; Albany Law School
Brown, Henry Billings	1891–1906	Michigan	Harrison	55	Republican	Yale; studied at Yale Law School and Harvard Law School
Shiras, George, Jr.	1892–1903	Pennsylvania	Harrison	61	Republican	Ohio University; Yale; studied law at Yale and privately
White, Edward Douglass	1894–1910	Louisiana	Cleveland	49	Democrat	Mount St. Mary's College; Georgetown College (now University)

Associate Justices (continued)

Name	Years of Service	State App't From	Appointing President	Age App't	Political Affiliation	Educational* Background
Peckham, Rufus Wheeler	1896–1909	New York	Cleveland	58	Democrat	Read law in father's firm
McKenna, Joseph	1898–1925	California	McKinley	55	Republican	Benicia Collegiate Institute, Law Dept.
Holmes, Oliver Wendell, Jr.	1902–1932	Massachusetts	Roosevelt, T.	61	Republican	Harvard College; studied law at Harvard Law School
Day, William Rufus	1903–1922	Ohio	Roosevelt, T.	54	Republican	University of Michigan; University of Michigan Law School
Moody, William Henry	1906–1910	Massachusetts	Roosevelt, T.	53	Republican	Harvard; Harvard Law School
Lurton, Horace Harmon	1910–1914	Tennessee	Taft	66	Democrat	University of Chicago; Cumberland Law School
Hughes, Charles Evans	1910–1916	New York	Taft	48	Republican	Colgate University; Brown University; Columbia Law School
Van Devanter, Willis	1911–1937	Wyoming	Taft	52	Republican	Indiana Asbury University; University of Cincinnati Law School
Lamar, Joseph Rucker	1911–1916	Georgia	Taft	54	Democrat	University of Georgia; Bethany College; Washington and Lee University
Pitney, Mahlon	1912–1922	New Jersey	Taft	54	Republican	College of New Jersey (Princeton); read law under father
McReynolds, James Clark	1914–1941	Tennessee	Wilson	52	Democrat	Vanderbilt University; University of Virginia
Brandeis, Louis Dembitz	1916–1939	Massachusetts	Wilson	60	Democrat	Harvard Law School
Clarke, John Hessin	1916–1922	Ohio	Wilson	59	Democrat	Western Reserve University; read law under father
Sutherland, George	1922–1938	Utah	Harding	60	Republican	Brigham Young Academy; one year at University of Michigan Law School
Butler, Pierce	1923–1939	Minnesota	Harding	57	Democrat	Carleton College
Sanford, Edward Terry	1923–1930	Tennessee	Harding	58	Republican	University of Tennessee; Harvard; Harvard Law School
Stone, Harlan Fiske	1925–1941	New York	Coolidge	53	Republican	Amherst College; Columbia University Law School
Roberts, Owen Josephus	1930–1945	Pennsylvania	Hoover	55	Republican	University of Pennsylvania; University of Pennsylvania Law School
Cardozo, Benjamin Nathan	1932–1938	New York	Hoover	62	Democrat	Columbia University; two years at Columbia Law School
Black, Hugo Lafayette	1937–1971	Alabama	Roosevelt, F.	51	Democrat	Birmingham Medical College; University of Alabama Law School
Reed, Stanley Forman	1938–1957	Kentucky	Roosevelt, F.	54	Democrat	Kentucky Wesleyan University; Foreman Yale; studied law at University of Virginia and Columbia University; University of Paris
Frankfurter, Felix	1939–1962	Massachusetts	Roosevelt, F.	57	Independent	College of the City of New York; Harvard Law School
Douglas, William Orville	1939–1975	Connecticut	Roosevelt, F.	41	Democrat	Whitman College; Columbia University Law School

Associate Justices (continued)

Name	Years of Service	State App't From	Appointing President	Age App't	Political Affiliation	Educational* Background
Murphy, Frank	1940–1949	Michigan	Roosevelt, F.	50	Democrat	University of Michigan; Lincoln's Inn, London; Trinity College
Byrnes, James Francis	1941–1942	South Carolina	Roosevelt, F.	62	Democrat	Read law privately
Jackson, Robert Houghwout	1941–1954	New York	Roosevelt, F.	49	Democrat	Albany Law School
Rutledge, Wiley Blount	1943–1949	Iowa	Roosevelt, F.	49	Democrat	University of Wisconsin; University of Colorado
Burton, Harold Hitz	1945–1958	Ohio	Truman	57	Republican	Bowdoin College; Harvard University Law School
Clark, Thomas Campbell	1949–1967	Texas	Truman	50	Democrat	University of Texas
Minton, Sherman	1949–1956	Indiana	Truman	59	Democrat	Indiana University College of Law; Yale Law School
Harlan, John Marshall	1955–1971	New York	Eisenhower	56	Republican	Princeton; Oxford University; New York Law School
Brennan, William J., Jr.	1956–1990	New Jersey	Eisenhower	50	Democrat	University of Pennsylvania; Harvard Law School
Whittaker, Charles Evans	1957–1962	Missouri	Eisenhower	56	Republican	University of Kansas City Law School
Stewart, Potter	1958–1981	Ohio	Eisenhower	43	Republican	Yale; Yale Law School
White, Byron Raymond	1962–1993	Colorado	Kennedy	45	Democrat	University of Colorado; Oxford University; Yale Law School
Goldberg, Arthur Joseph	1962–1965	Illinois	Kennedy	54	Democrat	Northwestern University
Fortas, Abe	1965–1969	Tennessee	Johnson, L.	55	Democrat	Southwestern College; Yale Law School
Marshall, Thurgood	1967–1991	New York	Johnson, L.	59	Democrat	Lincoln University; Howard University Law School
Blackmun, Harry A.	1970–1994	Minnesota	Nixon	62	Republican	Harvard; Harvard Law School
Powell, Lewis F., Jr.	1972–1987	Virginia	Nixon	65	Democrat	Washington and Lee University; Washington and Lee University Law School; Harvard Law School
Rehnquist, William H.	1972–1986	Arizona	Nixon	48	Republican	Stanford; Harvard; Stanford University Law School
Stevens, John Paul	1975–	Illinois	Ford	55	Republican	University of Colorado; Northwestern University Law School
O'Connor, Sandra Day	1981–	Arizona	Reagan	51	Republican	Stanford; Stanford University Law School
Scalia, Antonin	1986–	Virginia	Reagan	50	Republican	Georgetown University; Harvard Law School
Kennedy, Anthony M.	1988–	California	Reagan	52	Republican	Stanford; London School of Economics; Harvard Law School
Souter, David Hackett	1990–	New Hampshire	Bush	51	Republican	Harvard; Oxford University
Thomas, Clarence	1991–	District of Columbia	Bush	43	Republican	Holy Cross College; Yale Law School
Ginsburg, Ruth Bader	1993–	District of Columbia	Clinton	60	Democrat	Cornell University; Columbia Law School
Breyer, Stephen, G.	1994–	Massachusetts	Clinton	55	Democrat	Stanford University; Oxford University; Harvard Law School

Party Control of Congress in the Twentieth Century

CONGRESS	YEARS	PRESIDENT	MAJORITY PARTY IN HOUSE	MAJORITY PARTY IN SENATE
57th	1901–1903	T. Roosevelt	Republican	Republican
58th	1903–1905	T. Roosevelt	Republican	Republican
59th	1905–1907	T. Roosevelt	Republican	Republican
60th	1907–1909	T. Roosevelt	Republican	Republican
61st	1909–1911	Taft	Republican	Republican
62d	1911–1913	Taft	Democratic	Republican
63d	1913–1915	Wilson	Democratic	Democratic
64th	1915–1917	Wilson	Democratic	Democratic
65th	1917–1919	Wilson	Democratic	Democratic
66th	1919–1921	Wilson	Republican	Republican
67th	1921–1923	Harding	Republican	Republican
68th	1923–1925	Coolidge	Republican	Republican
69th	1925–1927	Coolidge	Republican	Republican
70th	1927–1929	Coolidge	Republican	Republican
71st	1929–1931	Hoover	Republican	Republican
72d	1931–1933	Hoover	Democratic	Republican
73d	1933–1935	F. Roosevelt	Democratic	Democratic
74th	1935–1937	F. Roosevelt	Democratic	Democratic
75th	1937–1939	F. Roosevelt	Democratic	Democratic
76th	1939–1941	F. Roosevelt	Democratic	Democratic
77th	1941–1943	F. Roosevelt	Democratic	Democratic
78th	1943–1945	F. Roosevelt	Democratic	Democratic
79th	1945–1947	Truman	Democratic	Democratic
80th	1947–1949	Truman	Republican	Democratic
81st	1949–1951	Truman	Democratic	Democratic
82d	1951–1953	Truman	Democratic	Democratic
83d	1953–1955	Eisenhower	Republican	Republican
84th	1955–1957	Eisenhower	Democratic	Democratic
85th	1957–1959	Eisenhower	Democratic	Democratic
86th	1959–1961	Eisenhower	Democratic	Democratic
87th	1961–1963	Kennedy	Democratic	Democratic
88th	1963–1965	Kennedy/Johnson	Democratic	Democratic
89th	1965–1967	Johnson	Democratic	Democratic
90th	1967–1969	Johnson	Democratic	Democratic
91st	1969–1971	Nixon	Democratic	Democratic
92d	1971–1973	Nixon	Democratic	Democratic
93d	1973–1975	Nixon/Ford	Democratic	Democratic
94th	1975–1977	Ford	Democratic	Democratic
95th	1977–1979	Carter	Democratic	Democratic
96th	1979–1981	Carter	Democratic	Democratic
97th	1981–1983	Reagan	Democratic	Republican
98th	1983–1985	Reagan	Democratic	Republican
99th	1985–1987	Reagan	Democratic	Republican
100th	1987–1989	Reagan	Democratic	Democratic
101st	1989–1991	Bush	Democratic	Democratic
102d	1991–1993	Bush	Democratic	Democratic
103d	1993–1995	Clinton	Democratic	Democratic
104th	1995–1997	Clinton	Republican	Republican
105th	1997–1999	Clinton	Republican	Republican
106th	1999–2001	Clinton	Republican	Republican

Spanish Equivalents for Important Terms in American Government

Acid Rain: Lluvia Acida
Acquisitive Model: Modelo Adquisitivo
Actionable: Procesable, Enjuiciable
Action-reaction Syndrome: Sídrome de Acción y Reacción
Actual Malice: Malicia Expresa
Administrative Agency: Agencia Administrativa
Advice and Consent: Consejo y Consentimiento
Affirmative Action: Acción Afirmativa
Affirm: Afirmar
Agenda Setting: Agenda Establecida
Aid to Families with Dependent Children (AFDC): Ayuda para Familias con Niños Dependientes
Amicus Curiae **Brief:** Tercer persona o grupo no involucrado en el caso, admitido en un juicio para hacer valer el intéres público o el de un grupo social importante.
Anarchy: Anarquía
Anti-Federalists: Anti-Federalistas
Appellate Court: Corte de Apelación
Appointment Power: Poder de Apuntamiento
Appropriation: Apropiación
Aristocracy: Aristocracia
Attentive Public: Público Atento
Australian Ballot: Voto Australiano

Authority: Autoridad
Authorization: Autorización

Bad-Tendency Rule: Regla de Tendencia-mala
"Beauty Contest": Concurso de Belleza
Bicameralism: Bicameralismo
Bicameral Legislature: Legislatura Bicameral
Bill of Rights: Declaración de Derechos
Blanket Primary: Primaria Comprensiva
Block Grants: Concesiones de Bloque
Bureaucracy: Burocracia
Busing: Transporte público

Cabinet: Gabinete, Consejo de Ministros
Cabinet Department: Departamento del Gabinete
Cadre: El núcleo de activistas de partidos políticos encargados de cumplir las funciones importantes de los partidos políticos americanos.
Canvassing Board: Consejo encargado con la encuesta de una violación.
Capture: Captura, toma
Casework: Trabajo de Caso
Categorical Grants-in-Aid: Concesiones Categóricas de Ayuda
Caucus: Reunión de Dirigentes

Challenge: Reto
Checks and Balances: Chequeos y Equilibrio
Chief Diplomat: Jefe Diplomático
Chief Executive: Jefe Ejecutivo
Chief Legislator: Jefe Legislador
Chief of Staff: Jefe de Personal
Chief of State: Jefe de Estado
Civil Law: Derecho Civil
Civil Liberties: Libertades Civiles
Civil Rights: Derechos Civiles
Civil Service: Servicio Civil
Civil Service Commission: Comisión de Servicio Civil
Class-action Suit: Demanda en representación de un grupo o clase.
Class Politics: Política de Clase
Clear and Present Danger Test: Prueba de Peligro Claro y Presente
Climate Control: Control de Clima
Closed Primary: Primaria Cerrada
Cloture: Cierre al voto
Coattail Effect: Effecto de Cola de Chaqueta
Cold War: Guerra Fría
Commander in Chief: Comandante en Jefe
Commerce Clause: Clausula de Comercio
Commercial Speech: Discurso Comercial
Common Law: Ley Común, Derecho Consuetudinario
Comparable Worth: Valor Comparable
Compliance: De acuerdo

Concurrent Majority: Mayoría Concurrente
Concurring Opinion: Opinión Concurrente
Confederal System: Sistema Confederal
Confederation: Confederación
Conference Committee: Comité de Conferencia
Consensus: Concenso
Consent of the People: Consentimiento de la Gente
Conservatism: Calidad de Conservador
Conservative Coalition: Coalición Conservadora
Consolidation: Consolidación
Constant Dollars: Dólares Constantes
Constitutional Initiative: Iniciativa Constitucional
Constitutional Power: Poder Constitucional
Containment: Contenimiento
Continuing Resolution: Resolució Contínua
Cooley's Rule: Régla de Cooley
Cooperative Federalism: Federalismo Cooperativo
Corrupt Practices Acts: Leyes Contra Acciones Corruptas
Council of Economic Advisers (CEA): Consejo de Asesores Económicos
Council of Government (COG): Consejo de Gobierno
County: Condado
Credentials Committee: Comité de Credenciales
Criminal Law: Ley Criminal

De Facto **Segregation:** Segregación de Hecho
De Jure **Segregation:** Segregación Cotidiana
Defamation of Character: Defamación de Carácter
Democracy: Democracia
Democratic Party: Partido Democratico
Dillon's Rule: Régla de Dillon
Diplomacy: Diplomácia
Direct Democracy: Democracia Directa

Direct Primary: Primaria Directa
Direct Technique: Técnica Directa
Discharge Petition: Petición de Descargo
Dissenting Opinion: Opinión Disidente
Divisive Opinion: Opinión Divisiva
Domestic Policy: Principio Político Doméstico
Dual Citizenship: Ciudadanía Dual
Dual Federalism: Federalismo Dual
Détente: No Spanish equivalent.

Economic Aid: Ayuda Económica
Economic Regulation: Regulación Económica
Elastic Clause, or Necessary and Proper Clause: Cláusula Flexible o Cláusula Propia Necesaria
Elector: Elector
Electoral College: Colegio Electoral
Electronic Media: Media Electronica
Elite: Elite (el selecto)
Elite Theory: Teoría Elitista (de lo selecto)
Emergency Power: Poder de Emergencia
Enumerated Power: Poder Enumerado
Environmental Impact Statement (EIS): Afirmación de Impacto Ambiental
Equality: Igualdad
Equalization: Igualación
Equal Employment Opportunity Commission (EEOC): Comisión de Igualdad de Oportunidad en el Empleo
Era of Good Feeling: Era de Buen Sentimiento
Era of Personal Politics: Era de Política Personal
Establishment Clause: Cláusula de Establecimiento
Euthanasia: Eutanasia
Exclusionary Rule: Regla de Exclusión
Executive Agreement: Acuerdo Ejecutivo
Executive Budget: Presupuesto Ejecutivo
Executive Office of the President (EOP): Oficina Ejecutiva del Presidente
Executive Order: Orden Ejecutivo
Executive Privilege: Privilegio Ejecutivo
Expressed Power: Poder Expresado
Extradite: Entregar por Extradición

Faction: Facción
Fairness Doctrine: Doctrina de Justicia
Fall Review: Revision de Otoño
Federalist: Federalista
Federal Mandate: Mandato Federal
Federal Open Market Committee (FOMC): Comité Federal de Libre Mercado
Federal Register: Registro Federal
Federal System: Sistema Federal
Federalists: Federalistas
Fighting Words: Palabras de Provocación
Filibuster: Obstrucción de iniciativas de ley
Fireside Chat: Charla de Hogar
First Budget Resolution: Resolució Primera Presupuesta
First Continental Congress: Primér Congreso Continental
Fiscal Policy: Politico Fiscal
Fiscal Year (FY): Año Fiscal
Fluidity: Fluidez
Food Stamps: Estampillas para Comida
Foreign Policy: Politica Extranjera
Foreign Policy Process: Proceso de Politica Extranjera
Franking: Franqueando
Fraternity: Fraternidad
Free Exercise Clause: Cláusula de Ejercicio Libre
Full Faith and Credit Clause: Cláusula de Completa Fé y Crédito
Functional Consolidation: Consolidación Funcional
Gag Order: Orden de Silencio
Garbage Can Model: Modelo Bote de Basura
Gender Gap: Brecha de Género
General Law City: Regla General Urbana
General Sales Tax: Impuesto General de Ventas
Generational Effect: Efecto Generacional

Gerrymandering: División arbitraria de los distritos electorales con fines políticos.
Government: Gobierno
Government Corporation: Corporación Gubernamental
Government in the Sunshine Act: Gobierno en la acta: Luz del Sol
Grandfather Clause: Clausula del Abuelo
Grand Jury: Gran Jurado
Great Compromise: Grán Acuerdo de Negociación

Hatch Act (Political Activities Act): Acta Hatch (acta de actividades politicas)
Hecklers' Veto: Veto de Abuchamiento
Home Rule City: Regla Urbana
Horizontal Federalism: Federalismo Horizontal
Hyperpluralism: Hiperpluralismo

Ideologue: Ideólogo
Ideology: Ideología
Image Building: Construcción de Imágen
Impeachment: Acción Penal Contra un Funcionario Público
Inalienable Rights: Derechos Inalienables
Income Transfer: Transferencia de Ingresos
Incorporation Theory: Teoría de Incorporación
Independent: Independiente
Independent Candidate: Candidato Independiente
Independent Executive Agency: Agencia Ejecutiva Independiente
Independent Regulatory Agency: Agencia Regulatoria Independiente
Indirect Technique: Técnica Indirecta
Inherent Power: Poder Inherente
Initiative: Iniciativa
Injunction: Injunción, Prohibición Judicial
Institution: Institución
Instructed Delegate: Delegado con Instrucciones
Intelligence Community: Comunidad de Inteligencia

Intensity: Intensidad
Interest Group: Grupo de Interés
Interposition: Interposición
Interstate Compact: Compacto Interestatal
In-kind Subsidy: Subsidio de Clase
Iron Curtain: Cortina de Acero
Iron Triangle: Triágulo de Acero
Isolationist Foreign Policy: Politica Extranjera de Aislamiento
Issue Voting: Voto Temático
Item Veto: Artículo de Veto

Jim Crow Laws: No Spanish equivalent.
Joint Committee: Comité Mancomunado
Judicial Activism: Activismo Judicial
Judicial Implementation: Implementacion Judicial
Judicial Restraint: Restricción Judicial
Judicial Review: Revisión Judicial
Jurisdiction: Jurisdicción
Justiciable Dispute: Disputa Judiciaria
Justiciable Question: Pregunta Justiciable

Keynesian Economics: Economía Keynesiana
Kitchen Cabinet: Gabinete de Cocina

Labor Movement: Movimiento Laboral
Latent Public Opinion: Opinión Pública Latente
Lawmaking: Hacedores de Ley
Legislative History: Historia Legislativa
Legislative Initiative: Iniciativa de legislación
Legislative Veto: Veto Legislativo
Legislature: Legislatura
Legitimacy: Legitimidad
Libel: Libelo, Difamación Escrita
Liberalism: Liberalismo
Liberty: Libertad
Limited Government: Gobierno Limitado

Line Organization: Organización de Linea
Literacy Test: Exámen de alfabetización
Litigate: Litigar
Lobbying: Cabildeo
Logrolling: Práctica legislativa que consiste en incluir en un mismo proyecto de ley temas de diversa ídole.
Loophole: Hueco Legal, escapatoria

Madisonian Model: Modelo Madisónico
Majority: Mayoría
Majority Floor Leader: Líder Mayoritario de Piso
Majority Leader of the House: Líder Mayoritario de la Casa
Majority Opinion: Opinión Mayoritaria
Majority Rule: Regla de Mayoría
Managed News: Noticias Manipuladas
Mandatory Retirement: Retiro Mandatorio
Matching Funds: Fondos Combinados
Material Incentive: Incentivo Material
Media: Media
Media Access: Acceso de Media
Merit System: Sistema de Mérito
Military-Industrial Complex: Complejo Industriomilitar
Minority Floor Leader: Líder Minoritario de Piso
Minority Leader of the House: Líder Minorial del Cuerpo Legislativo
Monetary Policy: Politica Monetaria
Monopolistic Model: Modelo Monopólico
Monroe Doctrine: Doctrina Monroe
Moral Idealism: Idealismo Moral
Municipal Home Rule: Regla Municipal

Narrow Casting: Mensaje Dirigído
National Committee: Comité Nacional

National Convention: Convención Nacional

National Politics: Politica Nacional

National Security Council (NSC): Concilio de Seguridad Nacional

National Security Policy: Politica de Seguridad Nacional

Natural Aristocracy: Aristocracia Natural

Natural Rights: Derechos Naturales

Necessaries: Necesidades

Negative Constituents: Constituyentes Negativos

New England Town: Pueblo de Nueva Inglaterra

New Federalism: Federalismo Nuevo

Nullification: Nulidad, Anulación

Office-Block, or Massachusetts, Ballot: Cuadro-Oficina, o Massachusetts, Voto

Office of Management and Budget (OMB): Oficina de Administració y Presupuesto

Oligarchy: Oligarquía

Ombudsman: Funcionario que representa al ciudadano ante el gobierno.

Open Primary: Primaria Abierta

Opinion: Opinión

Opinion Leader: Líder de Opinión

Opinion Poll: Encuesta, Conjunto de Opinión

Oral Arguments: Argumentos Orales

Oversight: Inadvertencia, Omisión

Paid-for-Political Announcement: Anuncios Politicos Pagados

Pardon: Perdón

Party-Column, or Indiana, Ballot: Partido-Columna, o Indiana, Voto

Party Identification: Identificación de Partido

Party Identifier: Identificador de Partido

Party-in-Electorate: Partido Electoral

Party-in-Government: Partido en Gobierno

Party Organization: Organización de Partido

Party Platform: Plataforma de Partido

Patronage: Patrocinio

Peer Group: Grupo de Contemporáneos

Pendleton Act (Civil Service Reform Act): Acta Pendleton (Acta de Reforma al Servicio Civil)

Personal Attack Rule: Regla de Ataque Personal

Petit Jury: Jurado Ordinario

Pluralism: Pluralismo

Plurality: Pluralidad

Pocket Veto: Veto de Bolsillo

Police Power: Poder Policiaco

Policy Trade-offs: Intercambio de Politicas

Political Action Committee (PAC): Comité de Acción Política

Political Consultant: Consultante Político

Political Culture: Cultura Politica

Political Party: Partido Político

Political Question: Pregunta Politica

Political Realism: Realismo Político

Political Socialization: Socialización Politica

Political Tolerance: Tolerancia Política

Political Trust: Confianza Política

Politico: Político

Politics: Politica

Poll Tax: Impuesto sobre el sufragio

Poll Watcher: Observador de Encuesta

Popular Sovereignty: Soberanía Popular

Power: Poder

Precedent: Precedente

Preferred-Position Test: Prueba de Posición Preferida

Presidential Primary: Primaria Presidencial

President Pro Tempore: Presidente Provisoriamente

Press Secretary: Secretaría de Prensa

Prior Restraint: Restricción Anterior

Privileges and Immunities: Privilégios e Imunidades

Privitization, or Contracting Out: Privatización

Property: Propiedad

Property Tax: Impuesto de Propiedad

Public Agenda: Agenda Pública

Public Debt Financing: Financiamiento de Deuda Pública

Public Debt, or National Debt: Deuda Pública o Nacional

Public Interest: Interes Público

Public Opinion: Opinión Pública

Purposive Incentive: Incentivo de Propósito

Ratification: Ratificación

Rational Ignorance Effect: Effecto de Ignorancia Racional

Reapportionment: Redistribución

Recall: Suspender

Recognition Power: Poder de Reconocimiento

Recycling: Reciclaje

Redistricting: Redistrictificación

Referendum: Referédum

Registration: Registración

Regressive Tax: Impuestos Regresivos

Relevance: Pertinencia

Remand: Reenviar

Representation: Representación

Representative Assembly: Asamblea Representativa

Representative Democracy: Democracia Representativa

Reprieve: Trequa, Suspensión

Republic: República

Republican Party: Partido Republicano

Resulting Powers: Poderes Resultados

Reverse: Cambiarse a lo contrario

Reverse Discrimination: Discriminación Reversiva

Rules Committee: Comité Regulador

Rule of Four: Regla de Cuatro

Run-off Primary: Primaria Residual

Safe Seat: Asiento Seguro

Sampling Error: Error de Encuesta

Secession: Secesión

Second Budget Resolution: Resolución Segunda Presupuestal

Second Continental Congress:
Segundo Congreso Continental
Sectional Politics: Política
Seccional
Segregation: Segregación
Selectperson: Persona Selecta
Select Committee: Comité Selecto
Senatorial Courtesy: Cortesia
Senatorial
Seniority System: Sistema
Señiorial
Separate-but-Equal Doctrine:
Separados pero iguales
Separation of Powers: Separación
de Poderes
Service Sector: Sector de Servicio
Sexual Harassment: Acosamiento
Sexual
Sex Discrimination:
Discriminacion Sexual
Slander: Difamación Oral,
Calumnia
Sliding-Scale Test: Prueba
Escalonada
Social Movement: Movimiento
Social
Social Security: Seguridad Social
Socioeconomic Status: Estado
Socioeconómico
Solidary Incentive: Incentivo de
Solideridad
Solid South: Súr Sólido
Sound Bite: Mordida de Sonido
Soviet Bloc: Bloque Soviético
Speaker of the House: Vocero de
la Casa
Spin: Girar/Giro
Spin Doctor: Doctor en Giro
Spin-off Party: Partido Estático
Spoils System: Sistema de
Despojos
Spring Review: Revisión de
Primavera
Stare Decisis: El principio
característico del ley comú por el
cual los precedentes
jurisprudenciales tienen fuerza
obligatoria, no sólo entre las partes,
sino tambien para casos sucesivos
análogos.
Stability: Estabilidad
Standing Committee: Comité de
Sostenimiento
State Central Committee: Comité

Central del Estado
State: Estado
State of the Union Message:
Mensaje Sobre el Estado de la
Unión
Statutory Power: Poder Estatorial
Strategic Arms Limitation Treaty
(SALT I): Tratado de Limitación de
Armas Estratégicas
Subpoena: Orden de Testificación
Subsidy: Subsidio
Suffrage: Sufrágio
Sunset Legislation: Legislación
Sunset
Superdelegate: Líder de partido o
oficial elegido quien tiene el
derecho de votar.
Supplemental Security Income
(SSI): Ingresos de Seguridad
Suplementaria
Supremacy Clause: Cláusula de
Supremacia
Supremacy Doctrine: Doctrina de
Supremacia
Symbolic Speech: Discurso
Simbólico

Technical Assistance: Asistencia
Técnica
Third Party: Tercer Partido
Third-party Candidate: Candidato
de Tercer Partido
Ticket Splitting: División de
Boletos
Totalitarian Regime: Régimen
Totalitario
Town Manager System: Sistema
de Administrador Municipal
Town Meeting: Junta Municipal
Township: Municipio
Tracking Poll: Seguimiento de
Encuesta
Trial Court: Tribunal de Primera
Truman Doctrine: Doctrina
Truman
Trustee: Depositario
Twelfth Amendment: Doceava
Enmienda
Twenty-fifth Amendment:
Veinticincoava Enmienda
Two-Party System: Sistema de
Dos Partidos

Unanimous Opinion: Opinión

Unánime
Underground Economy: Economía
Subterráea
Unicameral Legislature:
Legislatura Unicameral
Unincorporated Area: Area no
Incorporada
Unit Rule: Regla de Unidad
Unitary System: Sistema Unitario
Universal Suffrage: Sufragio
Universal
U.S. Treasury Bond: Bono de la
Tesoreria de E.U.A.

Veto Message: Comunicado de
Veto
Voter Turnout: Renaimiento de
Votantes

War Powers Act: Acta de Poderes
de Guerra
Washington Community:
Comunidad de Washington
Weberian Model: Modelo
Weberiano
Whip: Látigo
Whistleblower: Privatización o
Contratista
White House Office: Oficina de la
Casa Blanca
White House Press Corps: Cuerpo
de Prensa de la Casa Blanca
White Primary: Sufragio en
Elección Primaria/Blancos
Solamente
Writ of Certiorari: Prueba de
certeza; orden emitida por el
tribunal de apelaciones para que el
tribunal inferior dé lugar a la
apelación.
Writ of Habeas Corpus: Prueba de
Evidencia Concreta
Writ of Mandamus: Un mandato
por la corte para que un acto se
lleve a cabo.

Yellow Journalism: Amarillismo
Periodístico

Glossary

A

Acid Rain Rain that has picked up pollutants, usually sulfur dioxides, from industrial areas of the earth that are often hundreds of miles distant from where the rain falls.

Acquisitive Model A model of bureaucracy that views top-level bureaucrats as seeking constantly to expand the size of their budgets and the staffs of their departments or agencies so as to gain greater power and influence in the public sector.

Action-Reaction Syndrome For every action on the part of government, there is a reaction on the part of the affected public. Then the government attempts to counter the reaction with another action, which starts the cycle all over again.

Administrative Agency A federal, state, or local government unit established to perform a specific function. Administrative agencies are created and authorized by legislative bodies to administer and enforce specific laws.

Advice and Consent The power vested in the U.S. Senate by the Constitution (Article II, Section 2) to give its advice and consent to the president on treaties and presidential appointments.

Affirm To declare that a judgment is valid and must stand.

Affirmative Action A policy in job hiring that gives special consideration or compensatory treatment to traditionally disadvantaged groups in an effort to overcome present effects of past discrimination.

Agenda Setting Determining which public policy questions will be debated or considered by Congress.

Amicus Curiae Brief A brief (a document containing a legal argument supporting a desired outcome in a particular case) filed by a third party, or *amicus curiae* (Latin for "friend of the court"), who is not directly involved in the litigation but who has an interest in the outcome of the case.

Anarchy The condition of having no government and no laws. Each member of the society governs himself or herself.

Anti-Federalist An individual who opposed the ratification of the new Constitution in 1787. The Anti-Federalists were opposed to a strong central government.

Anti-Federalists Those who opposed the adoption of the Constitution because of its centralist tendencies and attacked the failure of the Constitution's framers to include a bill of rights.

Appellate Court A court having jurisdiction to review cases and issues that were originally tried in lower courts.

Appointment Power The authority vested in the president to fill a government office or position. Positions filled by presidential appointment include those in the executive branch and the federal judiciary, commissioned officers in the armed forces, and members of the independent regulatory commissions.

Appropriation The passage, by Congress, of a spending bill, specifying the amount of authorized funds that actually will be allocated for an agency's use.

Aristocracy Rule by the best suited, through virtue, talent, or education; in later usage, rule by the upper class.

Attentive Public That portion of the general public that pays attention to policy issues.

Australian Ballot A secret ballot prepared, distributed, and tabulated by government officials at public expense. Since 1888, all states have used the Australian ballot rather than an open, public ballot.

Authority The features of a leader or an institution that compel obedience, usually because of ascribed legitimacy. For most societies, government is the ultimate authority.

Authorization A formal declaration by a legislative committee that a certain amount of funding may be available to an agency. Some authorizations terminate in a year; others are renewable automatically without further congressional action.

B

"Beauty Contest" A presidential primary in which contending candidates compete for popular votes but the results have little or no impact on the selection of delegates to the national convention, which is made by the party elite.

Bias An inclination or a preference that interferes with impartial judgment.

Bicameral Legislature A legislature made up of two chambers, or parts. The U.S. Congress, composed of the House of Representatives and the Senate, is a bicameral legislature.

Bicameralism The division of a legislature into two separate assemblies.

Block Grants Federal programs that provide funds to state and local governments for general functional areas, such as criminal justice or mental-health programs.

Bundling The practice of adding together maximum individual campaign contributions to increase their impact on the candidate.

Bureaucracy A large organization that is structured hierarchically to carry out specific functions.

Busing The transportation of public school students from areas where they live to schools in other areas to eliminate school segregation based on residential patterns.

C

Cabinet An advisory group selected by the president to aid in making decisions. The cabinet presently numbers thirteen department secretaries and the attorney general. Depending on the president, the cabinet may be highly influential or relatively insignificant in its advisory role.

Cabinet Department One of the fourteen departments of the executive branch (State, Treasury, Defense, Justice, Interior, Agriculture, Commerce, Labor, Health and Human Services, Housing and Urban Development, Education, Energy, Transportation, and Veterans Affairs).

Cadre The nucleus of political party activists carrying out the major functions of American political parties.

Capture The act of gaining direct or indirect control over agency personnel and decision makers by the industry that is being regulated.

Case Law The rules and principles announced in court decisions. Case law includes judicial interpretations of common law principles and doctrines as well as interpretations of constitutional law, statutory law, and administrative law.

Casework Personal work for constituents by members of Congress.

Categorical Grants-in-Aid Federal grants-in-aid to states or local governments that are for very specific programs or projects.

Caucus A closed meeting of party leaders to select party candidates or to decide on policy; also, a meeting of party members designed to select candidates and propose policies.

Charter A document issued by a government that grants to a person, a group of persons, or a corporation the right to carry on one or more specific activities. A state government can grant a charter to a municipality allowing that group of persons to carry on specific activities.

Checks and Balances A major principle of the American governmental system whereby each branch of the government exercises a check on the actions of the others.

Chief Diplomat The role of the president in recognizing foreign governments, making treaties, and making executive agreements.

Chief Executive The role of the president as head of the executive branch of the government.

Chief Legislator The role of the president in influencing the making of laws.

Chief of Staff The person who is named to direct the White House Office and advise the president.

Chief of State The role of the president as ceremonial head of the government.

Civil Law The law regulating conduct between private persons over noncriminal matters. Under civil law, the government provides the forum for the settlement of disputes between private parties in such matters as contracts, domestic relations, and business relations.

Civil Rights Generally, all rights rooted in the Fourteenth Amendment's guarantee of equal protection under the law.

Civil Service A collective term for the body of employees working for the government. Generally, civil service is understood to apply to all those who gain government employment through a merit system.

Civil Service Commission The initial central personnel agency of the national government; created in 1883.

Class Politics Political preferences based on income level, social status, or both.

Class-Action Suit A lawsuit filed by an individual seeking damages for "all persons similarly situated."

Climate Control The use of public relations techniques to create favorable public opinion toward an interest group, industry, or corporation.

Cloture A method invoked to close off debate and to bring the matter under consideration to a vote in the Senate.

Cold War The ideological, political, and economic impasse that existed between the United States and the Soviet Union following World War II.

Commander in Chief The role of the president as supreme commander of the military forces of the United States and of the state National Guard units when they are called into federal service.

Commerce Clause The section of the Constitution in which Congress is given the power to regulate trade among the states and with foreign countries.

Common Law Judge-made law that originated in England from decisions shaped according to prevailing customs. Decisions were applied to similar situations and thus gradually became common to the nation.

Comparable Worth The idea that compensation should be based on the worth of the job to an employer and that factors unrelated to the worth of a job, such as the sex of the employee, should not affect compensation.

Competitive Federalism A model of federalism in which states compete with one another in the provision of goods and services so as to attract "customers"–citizens from other states.

Compliance The act of accepting and carrying out authorities' decisions.

Concurrent Powers Powers held jointly by the national and state governments.

Concurring Opinion A separate opinion, prepared by a judge who supports the decision of the majority of the court but who wants to make or clarify a particular point or to voice disapproval of the grounds on which the decision was made.

Confederal System A system of government consisting of a league of independent states, each having essentially sovereign powers. The central government created by such a league has only limited powers over the states.

Confederation A political system in which states or regional governments retain ultimate authority except for those powers they expressly delegate to a central government. A voluntary association of independent states, in which the member states agree to limited restraints on their freedom of action.

Conference Committee A special joint committee appointed to reconcile differences when bills pass the two chambers of Congress in different forms.

Consensus General agreement among the citizenry on an issue.

Consent of the People The idea that governments and laws derive their legitimacy from the consent of the governed.

Conservatism A set of beliefs that includes a limited role for the national government in helping individuals, support for traditional values and lifestyles, and a cautious response to change.

Conservative Coalition An alliance of Republicans and southern Democrats that can form in the House or the Senate to oppose liberal legislation and support conservative legislation.

Consolidation The union of two or more governmental units to form a single unit.

Constant Dollars Dollars corrected for inflation; dollars expressed in terms of purchasing power for a given year.

Constituent One of the people represented by a legislator or other elected or appointed official.

Constitutional Initiative An electoral device whereby citizens can propose a constitutional amendment through petitions signed by the required number of registered voters.

Constitutional Power A power vested in the president by Article II of the Constitution.

Containment A U.S. diplomatic policy adopted by the Truman administration to "build situations of strength" around the globe to contain Communist power within its existing boundaries.

Continuing Resolution A temporary law that Congress passes when an appropriations bill has not been decided by the beginning of the new fiscal year on October 1.

Contracting Out The replacement of government services with services provided by private firms.

Cooley's Rule The view that cities should be able to govern themselves, presented in an 1871 Michigan decision by Judge Thomas Cooley.

Cooperative Federalism The theory that the states and the national government should cooperate in solving problems.

Corrupt Practices Acts A series of acts passed by Congress in an attempt to limit and regulate the size and sources of contributions and expenditures in political campaigns.

Council of Economic Advisers (CEA) A staff agency in the Executive Office of the President that advises the president on measures to maintain stability in the nation's economy; established in 1946.

Council of Government (COG) A voluntary organization of counties and municipalities concerned with areawide problems.

County The chief governmental unit set up by the state to administer state law and business at the local level. Counties are drawn up by area, rather than by rural or urban criteria.

Credentials Committee A committee used by political parties at their national conventions to determine which delegates may participate. The committee inspects the claim of each prospective delegate to be seated as a legitimate representative of his or her state.

Criminal Law The law that defines crimes and provides punishment for violations. In criminal cases, the government is the prosecutor, because crimes are against the public order.

D

***De Facto* Segregation** Racial segregation that occurs because of past social and economic conditions and residential patterns.

***De Jure* Segregation** Racial segregation that occurs because of laws or administrative decisions by public agencies.

Democracy A system of government in which ultimate political authority is vested in the people. Derived from the Greek words *demos* ("the people") and *kratos* ("authority").

Democratic Party One of the two major American political parties evolving out of the Democratic (Jeffersonian) Republican group supporting Thomas Jefferson.

Détente A French word meaning the relaxation of tensions. The term characterizes U.S.–Soviet policy as it developed under President Richard Nixon and Secretary of State Henry Kissinger. Détente stressed direct cooperative dealings with Cold War rivals but avoided ideological accommodation.

Dillon's Rule The narrowest possible interpretation of the legal status of local governments, outlined by Judge John F. Dillon, who in 1811 stated that a municipal corporation can exercise only those powers expressly granted by state law.

Diplomacy The total process by which states carry on political relations with each other; settling conflicts among nations by peaceful means.

Diplomatic Recognition The president's power, as chief diplomat, to acknowledge a foreign government as legitimate.

Direct Democracy A system of government in which political decisions are made by the people directly, rather than by their elected representatives; probably possible only in small political communities.

Direct Primary An intraparty election in which the voters select the candidates who will run on a party's ticket in the subsequent general election.

Direct Technique An interest group activity that involves interaction with government officials to further the group's goals.

Discharge Petition A procedure by which a bill in the House of Representatives may be forced out of a committee (discharged) that has refused to report it for consideration by the House. The discharge petition must be signed by an absolute majority (218) of representatives and is used only on rare occasions.

Dissenting Opinion A separate opinion in which a judge dissents from (disagrees with) the conclusion reached by the majority on the court and expounds his or her own views about the case.

Diversity of Citizenship A basis for federal court jurisdiction over a lawsuit between (1) citizens of different states, (2) a foreign country and citizens of a state or of different states, or (3) citizens of a state and citizens or subjects of a foreign country. The amount in controversy must be more than $75,000 before a federal court can take jurisdiction in such cases.

Divided Government A situation in which one major political party controls the presidency and the other controls the chambers of Congress, or in which one party controls a state governorship and the other controls the state legislature.

Divisive Opinion Public opinion that is polarized between two quite different positions.

Domestic Policy Public plans or courses of action that concern issues of national importance, such as poverty, crime, and the environment.

Dominant Culture The values, customs, language, and ideals established by the group or groups in a society that traditionally have controlled politics and government institutions in that society.

Dual Federalism A system of government in which the states and the national government each remain supreme within their own spheres. The doctrine looks on nation and state as coequal sovereign powers. It holds that acts of states within their reserved powers are legitimate limitations on the powers of the national government.

E

Earned-Income Tax Credit (EITC) Program A government program that helps low-income workers by giving back part or all of their Social Security taxes.

Economic Aid Assistance to other nations in the form of grants, loans, or credits to buy the assisting nation's products.

Elector A person on the partisan slate that is selected early in the presidential election year according to state laws and the applicable political party apparatus. Electors cast ballots for president and vice president. The number of electors in each state is equal to that state's number of representatives in both houses of Congress.

Electronic Media Broadcasting media (radio and television). The term derives from their method of transmission, in contrast to printed media.

Elite An upper socioeconomic class that controls political and economic affairs.

Elite Theory A perspective holding that society is ruled by a small number of people who exercise power in their self-interest.

Emergency Power An inherent power exercised by the president during a period of national crisis, particularly in foreign affairs.

Enabling Legislation A statute enacted by Congress that authorizes the creation of an administrative agency and specifies the name, purpose, composition, and powers of the agency being created.

Enumerated Powers Powers specifically granted to the national government by the Constitution. The first seventeen clauses of Article I, Section 8, specify most of the enumerated powers of Congress.

Environmental Impact Statement (EIS) As a requirement mandated by the National Environmental Policy Act, a report that must show the costs and benefits of major federal actions that could significantly affect the quality of the environment.

Equal Employment Opportunity Commission (EEOC) A commission established by the 1964 Civil Rights Act to (1) end discrimination based on race, color, religion, gender, or national origin in conditions of employment and (2) promote voluntary action programs by employers, unions, and community organizations to foster equal job opportunities.

Equality A concept that all people are of equal worth.

Equalization A method for adjusting the amount of money that a state must provide to receive federal funds. The formula used takes into account the wealth of the state or its ability to tax its citizens.

Era of Good Feeling The years from 1817 to 1825, when James Monroe was president and there was, in effect, no political opposition.

Era of Personal Politics An era when attention centers on the character of individual candidates rather than on party identification.

Executive Agreement A binding international agreement made between chiefs of state that does not require legislative sanction.

Executive Budget The budget prepared and submitted by the president to Congress.

Executive Office of the President (EOP) Established by President Franklin D. Roosevelt by executive order under the Reorganization Act of 1939, the EOP currently consists of nine staff agencies that assist the president in carrying out major duties.

Executive Order A rule or regulation issued by the president that has the effect of law. Executive orders can implement and give administrative effect to provisions in the Constitution, to treaties, and to statutes.

Executive Privilege The right of executive officials to refuse to appear before, or to withhold information from, a legislative committee. Executive privilege is enjoyed by the president and by those executive officials accorded that right by the president.

Expressed Power A constitutional or statutory power of the president, which is expressly written into the Constitution or into statutory law.

F

Faction A group or bloc in a legislature or political party acting together in pursuit of some special interest or position.

Fall Review The time every year when, after receiving formal federal agency requests for funding for the next fiscal year, the Office of Management and Budget reviews the requests, makes changes, and submits its recommendations to the president.

Federal Mandate A requirement in federal legislation that forces states and municipalities to comply with certain rules.

Federal Open Market Committee (FOMC) The most important body within the Federal Reserve System. The FOMC decides how monetary policy should be carried out by the Federal Reserve System.

Federal Question A question that pertains to the U.S. Constitution, acts of Congress, or treaties. A federal question provides a basis for federal jurisdiction.

Federal Register A publication of the executive branch of the U.S. government that prints executive orders, rules, and regulations.

Federal System A system of government in which power is divided by a written constitution between a central government and regional, or subdivisional, governments. Each level must have some domain in which its policies are dominant and some genuine political or constitutional guarantee of its authority.

Federalist The name given to one who was in favor of the adoption of the U.S. Constitution and the creation of a federal union with a strong central

Federalists The first American political party, led by Alexander Hamilton and John Adams. Many of its members had strongly supported the adoption of the new Constitution and the creation of the federal union.

Feminism The movement that supports political, economic, and social equality for women.

Filibuster In the Senate, unlimited debate to halt action on a particular bill.

Fireside Chat One of the warm, informal talks by Franklin D. Roosevelt to a few million of his intimate friends—via the radio. Roosevelt's fireside chats were so effective that succeeding presidents have been urged by their advisers to emulate him by giving more radio and television reports to the nation.

First Budget Resolution A resolution passed by Congress in May that sets overall revenue and spending goals for the following fiscal year.

First Continental Congress The first gathering of delegates from twelve of the thirteen colonies, held in 1774.

Fiscal Policy The use of changes in government spending or taxation to alter national economic variables, such as the rate of unemployment.

Fiscal Year (FY) The twelve-month period that is used for bookkeeping, or accounting, purposes. Usually, the fiscal year does not coincide with the calendar year. For example, the federal government's fiscal year runs from October 1 through September 30.

Fluidity The extent to which public opinion changes over time.

Focus Group A small group of individuals who are led in discussion by a professional consultant to gather opinions and responses to candidates and issues.

Food Stamps Coupons issued by the federal government to low-income individuals to be used for the purchase of food.

Foreign Policy A nation's external goals and the techniques and strategies used to achieve them.

Foreign Policy Process The steps by which external goals are decided and acted on.

Franking A policy that enables members of Congress to send material through the mail by substituting their facsimile signature (frank) for postage.

Fraternity From the Latin *fraternus* (brother), a term that came to mean, in the political philosophy of the eighteenth century, the condition in which each individual considers the needs of all others; a brotherhood. In the French Revolution of 1789, the popular cry was "liberty, equality, and fraternity."

Front-Loading The practice of moving presidential primary elections to the early part of the campaign, to maximize the impact of certain states or regions on the nomination.

Front-Runner The presidential candidate who appears to have the most momentum at a given time in the primary season.

Functional Consolidation The cooperation of two or more units of local government in providing services to their inhabitants.

G

Garbage Can Model A model of bureaucracy that characterizes bureaucracies as rudderless entities with little formal organization in which solutions to problems are based on trial and error rather than rational policy planning.

Gender Discrimination Any practice, policy, or procedure that denies equality of treatment to an individual or to a group because of gender.

Gender Gap A term most often used to describe the difference between the percentage of votes a candidate receives from women and the percentage of votes the candidate receives from men. The term came into use after the 1980 presidential election.

General Jurisdiction Exists when a court's authority to hear cases is not significantly restricted. A court of general jurisdiction normally can hear a broad range of cases.

General Law City A city operating under general state laws that apply to all local govern-mental units of a similar type.

General Sales Tax A tax levied as a proportion of the retail price of a commodity at the point of sale.

Generational Effect A long-lasting effect of events of a particular time period on the political opinions or preferences of those who came of political age at that time.

Gerrymandering The drawing of legislative district boundary lines for the purpose of obtaining partisan or factional advantage. A district is said to be gerrymandered when its shape is manipulated by the dominant party in the state legislature to maximize electoral strength at the expense of the minority party.

Government A permanent structure (institution) composed of decision makers who make society's rules about conflict resolution and the allocation of resources and who possess the power to enforce those rules.

Government Corporation An agency of government that administers a quasi-business enterprise. These corporations are used when activities are primarily commercial. They produce revenue for their continued existence, and they require greater flexibility than is permitted for departments and agencies.

Government in the Sunshine Act A law that requires all multiheaded federal agencies to conduct their business regularly in public session.

Grandfather Clause A device used by southern states to exempt whites from state taxes and literacy laws originally intended to disfranchise African American voters. It restricted the voting franchise to those who could prove that their grandfathers had voted before 1867.

Great Compromise The compromise between the New Jersey and the Virginia plans that created one chamber of the Congress based on population and one chamber that represented each state equally; also called the Connecticut Compromise.

H

Hatch Act (Political Activities Act) The act that prohibits the use of federal authority to influence nominations and elections or the use of rank to pressure federal employees to make political contributions. It also prohibits civil service employees from active involvement in political campaigns.

Hatch Act An act passed in 1939 that prohibited a political group from spending more than $3 million in any campaign and limited individual contributions to a committee to $5,000. The act was designed to control political influence buying.

Home Rule City A city with a charter allowing local voters to frame, adopt, and amend their own charter.

Horizontal Federalism Activities, problems, and policies that require state governments to interact with one another.

Hyperpluralism A situation that arises when interest groups become so powerful that they dominate the political decision-making structures, rendering any consideration of the greater public interest impossible.

I

Ideologue An individual whose political opinions are carefully thought out and relatively consistent with one another. Ideologues are often described as having a comprehensive world view.

Ideology A comprehensive and logically ordered set of beliefs about the nature of people and about the institutions and role of government.

Impeachment As authorized by Article I of the Constitution, an action by the House of Representatives and the Senate to remove the president, vice president, or civil officers of the United States from office for crimes of "Treason, Bribery, or other high Crimes and Misdemeanors."

In-Kind Subsidy A good or service—such as food stamps, housing, or medical care—provided by the government to lower-income groups.

Income Transfer A transfer of income from some individuals in the economy to other individuals. This is generally done by way of the government. It is a transfer in the sense that no current services are rendered by the recipients.

Independent A voter or candidate who does not identify with a political party.

Independent Executive Agency A federal agency that is not part of a cabinet department but reports directly to the president.

Independent Expenditures Nonregulated contributions from PACs, ideological organizations, and individuals. The groups may spend funds on advertising or other campaign activities so long as those expenditures are not coordinated with those of a candidate.

Independent Regulatory Agency An agency outside the major executive departments charged with making and implementing rules and regulations to protect the public interest.

Indirect Technique A strategy employed by interest groups that uses third parties to influence government officials.

Inherent Power A power of the president derived from the loosely worded statement in the Constitution that "the executive Power shall be vested in a President" and that the president should "take Care that the Laws be faithfully executed"; defined through practice rather than through constitutional or statutory law.

Initiative A procedure by which voters can propose a law or a constitutional amendment.

Injunction An order issued by a court to compel or restrain the performance of an act by an individual or entity.

Institution A long-standing, identifiable structure or association that performs certain functions for society.

Instructed Delegate A legislator who is an agent of the voters who elected him or her and who votes according to the views of constituents regardless of personal assessments.

Intelligence Community The government agencies that are involved in gathering information about the capabilities and intentions of foreign governments and that engage in activities to further U.S. foreign policy aims.

Intensity The strength of a position for or against a public policy or an issue. Intensity is often critical in generating public action; an intense minority can often win on an issue of public policy over a less intense majority.

Interest Group An organized group of individuals sharing common objectives who actively attempt to influence policymakers in all three branches of the government and at all levels.

Interstate Compact An agreement between two or more states. Agreements on minor matters are made without congressional consent, but any compact that tends to increase the power of the contracting states relative to other states or relative to the national government generally requires the consent of Congress. Such compacts serve as a means by which states can solve regional problems.

Iron Curtain The term used to describe the division of Europe between the Soviet Union and the West; popularized by Winston Churchill in a speech portraying Europe as being divided by an iron curtain, with the nations of Eastern Europe behind the curtain and increasingly under Soviet control.

Iron Triangle The three-way alliance among legislators, bureaucrats, and interest groups to make or preserve policies that benefit their respective interests.

Isolationist Foreign Policy Abstaining from an active role in international affairs or alliances, which characterized U.S. foreign policy toward Europe during most of the nineteenth century.

Issue Network A group of individuals or organizations—which may consist of legislators or legislative staff members, interest group leaders, bureaucrats, the media, scholars, and other experts—that supports a particular policy position on a given issue, such as one relating to the environment, to taxation, or to consumer safety.

Item Veto The power exercised by the governors of most states to veto particular sections or items of an appropriations bill, while signing the remainder of the bill into law.

J

Joint Committee A legislative committee composed of members from both chambers of Congress.

Judicial Activism A doctrine holding that the Supreme Court should take an active role in using its powers to check the activities of Congress, state legislatures, and administrative agencies when those government bodies exceed their authority.

Judicial Implementation The way in which court decisions are translated into action.

Judicial Restraint A doctrine holding that the Supreme Court should defer to the decisions made by the elected representatives of the people in the legislative and executive branches.

Judicial Review The power of the Supreme Court or any court to declare unconstitutional federal or state laws and other acts of government.

Jurisdiction The authority of a court to decide certain cases. Not all courts have the authority to decide all cases. Where a case arises and what its subject matter is are two jurisdictional factors.

Justiciable Dispute A dispute that raises questions about the law and that is appropriate for resolution before a court of law.

Justiciable Question A question that may be raised and reviewed in court.

K

Keynesian Economics An economic theory, named after English economist John Maynard Keynes, that gained prominence during the Great Depression of the 1930s. It is typically associated with the use of fiscal policy to alter national economic variables—for example, increased government spending during times of economic downturns.

Kitchen Cabinet The informal advisers to the president.

L

Labor Movement Generally, the full range of economic and political expression of working-class interests; politically, the organization of working-class interests.

Lawmaking The process of deciding the legal rules that govern society. Such laws may regulate minor affairs or establish broad national policies.

Legislative Initiative A procedure by which voters can propose a change in state or local laws by gathering signatures on a petition and submitting it to the legislature for approval.

Legislative Veto A provision in a bill reserving to Congress or to a congressional committee the power to reject an action or regulation of a national agency by majority vote; declared unconstitutional by the Supreme Court in 1983.

Legislature A government body primarily responsible for the making of laws.

Legitimacy A status conferred by the people on the government's officials, acts, and institutions through their belief that the government's actions are an appropriate use of power by a legally constituted governmental authority following correct decision-making policies. These actions are regarded as rightful and entitled to compliance and obedience on the part of citizens.

Liberalism A set of beliefs that includes the advocacy of positive government action to improve the welfare of individuals, support for civil rights, and tolerance for political and social change.

Liberty The greatest freedom of individuals that is consistent with the freedom of other individuals in the society.

Limited Government A form of government based on the principle that the powers of government should be clearly limited either through a written document or through wide public understanding; characterized by institutional checks to ensure that government serves the public rather than private interests.

Limited Jurisdiction Exists when a court's authority to hear cases is restricted to certain types of claims, such as tax claims or bankruptcy petitions.

Line Organization With respect to the federal government, an administrative unit that is directly accountable to the president.

Line-Item Veto The power of an executive to veto individual lines or items within a piece of legislation without vetoing the entire bill.

Literacy Test A test administered as a precondition for voting, often used to prevent African Americans from exercising their right to vote.

Litigate To engage in a legal proceeding or seek relief in a court of law; to carry on a lawsuit.

Lobbying The attempt by organizations or by individuals to influence the passage, defeat, or contents of legislation and the administrative decisions of government.

Logrolling An arrangement in which two or more members of Congress agree in advance to support each other's bills.

Loophole A legal method by which individuals and businesses are allowed to reduce the tax liabilities owed to the government.

M

Madisonian Model A structure of government proposed by James Madison in which the powers of the government are separated into three branches: executive, legislative, and judicial.

Majority Floor Leader The chief spokesperson of the major party in the Senate, who directs the legislative program and party strategy.

Majority More than 50 percent.

Majority Full age; the age at which a person is entitled by law to the right to manage his or her own affairs and to the full enjoyment of civil rights.

Majority Leader of the House A legislative position held by an important party member in the House of Representatives. The majority leader is selected by the majority party in caucus or conference to foster cohesion among party members and to act as spokesperson for the majority party in the House.

Majority Opinion A court opinion reflecting the views of the majority of the judges.

Majority Rule A basic principle of democracy asserting that the greatest number of citizens in any political unit should select officials and determine policies.

Managed News Information generated and distributed by the government in such a way as to give government interests priority over candor.

Mandatory Retirement Forced retirement when a person reaches a certain age.

Matching Funds For many categorical grant programs, money that the state must provide to "match" the federal funds. Some programs require the state to raise only 10 percent of the funds, whereas others approach an even share.

Material Incentive A reason or motive having to do with economic benefits or opportunities.

Media Access The public's right of access to the media. The Federal Communications Commission and the courts gradually have taken the stance that citizens do have a right to media access.

Media The technical means of communication with mass audiences.

Merit System The selection, retention, and promotion of government employees on the basis of competitive examinations.

Military-Industrial Complex The mutually beneficial relationship between the armed forces and defense contractors.

Minority Floor Leader The party officer in the Senate who commands the minority party's opposition to the policies of the majority party and directs the legislative program and strategy of his or her party.

Minority Leader of the House The party leader elected by the minority party in the House.

Monetary Policy The use of changes in the amount of money in circulation to alter credit markets, employment, and the rate of inflation.

Monopolistic Model A model of bureaucracy that compares bureaucracies to monopolistic business firms. Lack of competition within a bureaucracy leads to inefficient and costly operations, just as it does within monopolistic firms. Because bureaucracies are not penalized for inefficiency, there is no incentive to reduce costs or use resources more productively.

Monroe Doctrine The policy statement included in President James Monroe's 1823 annual message to Congress, which set out three principles: (1) European nations should not establish new colonies in the Western Hemisphere, (2) European nations should not intervene in the affairs of independent nations of the Western Hemisphere, and (3) the United States would not interfere in the affairs of European nations.

Moral Idealism A philosophy that sees all nations as willing to cooperate and agree on moral standards for conduct.

Most-Favored-Nation Status A status granted by an international treaty by which each member nation must treat other members at least as well as it treats the country that receives its most favorable treatment.

Municipal Home Rule The power vested in a local unit of government to draft or change its own charter and to manage its own affairs.

N

Narrowcasting Broadcasting that is targeted to one small sector of the population.

National Committee A standing committee of a national political party established to direct and coordinate party activities during the four-year period between national party conventions.

National Convention The meeting held every four years by each major party to select presidential and vice presidential candidates, to write a platform, to choose a national committee, and to conduct party business. In theory, the national convention is at the top of a hierarchy of party conventions (the local and state conventions are below it) that consider candidates and issues.

National Politics The pursuit of interests that are of concern to the nation as a whole.

National Security Council (NSC) A staff agency in the Executive Office of the President established by the National Security Act of 1947. The NSC advises the president on domestic and foreign matters involving national security.

National Security Policy Foreign and domestic policy designed to protect the independence and political and economic integrity of the United States; policy that is concerned with the safety and defense of the nation.

Natural Aristocracy A small ruling clique of a society's "best" citizens, whose membership is based on birth, wealth, and ability. The Jeffersonian era emphasized government rule by such a group.

Natural Rights Rights held to be inherent in natural law, not dependent on governments. John Locke stated that natural law, being superior to human law, specifies certain rights of "life, liberty, and property." These rights, altered to become "life, liberty, and the pursuit of happiness," are asserted in the Declaration of Independence.

Necessaries In contract law, necessaries include whatever is reasonably necessary for suitable subsistence as measured by age, state, condition in life, and so on.

Negative Constituents Citizens who openly oppose government foreign policies.

New England Town A governmental unit that combines the roles of city and county into one unit in the New England states.

New Federalism A plan both to limit the national government's power to regulate and to restore power to state governments. Essentially, the new federalism is designed to give the states greater ability to decide for themselves how government revenues should be spent.

Nullification The act of nullifying, or rendering void. Prior to the Civil War, southern supporters of states' rights claimed that a state had the right to declare a national law to be null and void and therefore not binding on its citizens, on the assumption that ultimate sovereign authority rested with the several states.

O

Office of Management and Budget (OMB) A division of the Executive Office of the President created by executive order in 1970 to replace the Bureau of the Budget. The OMB's main functions are to assist the president in preparing the annual budget, to clear and coordinate all departmental agency budgets, to help set fiscal policy, and to supervise the administration of the federal budget.

Oligarchy Rule by a few members of the elite, who generally make decisions to benefit their own group.

Ombudsperson A person who hears and investigates complaints by private individuals against public officials or agencies.

Opinion The statement by a judge or a court of the decision reached in a case tried or argued before it. The opinion sets forth the law that applies to the case and details the legal reasoning on which the judgment was based.

Opinion Leader One who is able to influence the opinions of others because of position, expertise, or personality. Such leaders help to shape public opinion.

Opinion Poll A method of systematically questioning a small, selected sample of respondents who are deemed representative of the total population. Opinion polls are widely used by government, business, university scholars, political candidates, and voluntary groups to provide reasonably accurate data on public attitudes, beliefs, expectations, and behavior.

Oral Arguments The verbal arguments presented in person by attorneys to an appellate court. Each attorney presents reasons to the court why the court should rule in his or her client's favor.

Oversight The responsibility Congress has for following up on laws it has enacted to ensure that they are being enforced and administered in the way in which they were intended.

P

Pardon The granting of a release from the punishment or legal consequences of a crime; a pardon can be granted by the president before or after a conviction.

Party Identification Linking oneself to a particular political party.

Party Identifier A person who identifies with a political party.

Party Organization The formal structure and leadership of a political party, including election committees; local, state, and national executives; and paid professional staff.

Party Platform A document drawn up by the platform committee at each national convention, outlining the policies, positions, and principles of the party; it is then submitted to the entire convention for approval.

Party-in-Government All of the elected and appointed officials who identify with a political party.

Party-in-the-Electorate Those members of the general public who identify with a political party or who express a preference for one party over the other.

Patronage Rewarding faithful party workers and followers with government employment and contracts.

Peer Group A group consisting of members sharing common relevant social characteristics. These groups play an important part in the socialization process, helping to shape attitudes and beliefs.

Pendleton Act (Civil Service Reform Act) The law, as amended over the years, that remains the basic statute regulating federal employment personnel policies. It established the principle of employment on the basis of merit and created the Civil Service Commission to administer the personnel service.

Picket-Fence Federalism A model of federalism in which specific programs and policies (depicted as vertical pickets in a picket fence) involve all levels of government—national, state, and local (depicted by the horizontal boards in a picket fence).

Pluralism A theory that views politics as a conflict among interest groups. Political decision making is characterized by bargaining and compromise.

Plurality The total votes cast for a candidate who receives more votes than any other candidate but not necessarily a majority. Most national, state, and local electoral laws provide for winning elections by a plurality vote.

Pocket Veto A special veto power exercised by the chief executive after a legislative body has adjourned. Bills not signed by the chief executive die after a specified period of time. If Congress wishes to reconsider such a bill, it must be reintroduced in the following session of Congress.

Police Power The authority to legislate for the protection of the health, morals, safety, and welfare of the people. In the United States, most police power is a reserved power of the states.

Policy Trade-Offs The cost to the nation of undertaking any one policy in terms of all of the other policies that could have been undertaken. For example, an increase in the expenditures on one federal program means either a reduction in expenditures on another program or an increase in federal taxes (or the deficit).

Political Action Committee (PAC) A committee set up by and representing a corporation, labor union, or special interest group. PACs raise and give campaign donations on behalf of the organizations or groups they represent.

Political Consultant A paid professional hired to devise a campaign strategy and manage a campaign. Image building is the crucial task of the political consultant.

Political Culture The collection of beliefs and attitudes toward government and the political process held by a community or nation.

Political Party A group of political activists who organize to win elections, to operate the government, and to determine public policy.

Political Question An issue that a court believes should be decided by the executive or legislative branch.

Political Realism A philosophy that sees each nation acting principally in its own interest.

Political Socialization The process through which individuals learn a set of political attitudes and form opinions about social issues. The family and the educational system are two of the most important forces in the political socialization process.

Political Trust The degree to which individuals express trust in the government and political institutions, usually measured through a specific series of survey questions.

Politico The legislative role that combines the instructed-delegate and trustee concepts. The legislator varies the role according to the issue under consideration.

Politics According to David Easton, the "authoritative allocation of values" for a society; according to Harold Lasswell, "who gets what, when, and how" in a society.

Poll Tax A special tax that must be paid as a qualification for voting. The Twenty-fourth Amendment to the Constitution outlawed the poll tax in national elections, and in 1966 the Supreme Court declared it unconstitutional in all elections.

Popular Sovereignty The concept that ultimate political authority rests with the people.

Power The ability to cause others to modify their behavior and to conform to what the power holder wants.

Precedent A court rule bearing on subsequent legal decisions in similar cases. Judges rely on precedents in deciding cases.

President *Pro Tempore* The temporary presiding officer of the Senate in the absence of the vice president.

Presidential Primary A statewide primary election of delegates to a political party's national convention to help a party determine its presidential nominee. Such delegates are either pledged to a particular candidate or unpledged.

Press Secretary The individual responsible for representing the White House before the media. The press secretary writes news releases, provides background information, sets up press conferences, and so on.

Property Anything that is or may be subject to ownership. As conceived by the political philosopher John Locke, the right to property is a natural right superior to human law (laws made by government).

Property Tax A tax on the value of real estate. This tax is limited to state and local governments and is a particularly important source of revenue for local governments.

Public Agenda Issues that commonly are perceived by members of the political community as meriting public attention and governmental action. The media play an important role in setting the public agenda by focusing attention on certain topics.

Public Debt Financing The government's spending more than it receives in taxes and paying for the difference by issuing U.S. Treasury bonds, thereby adding to the public debt.

Public Debt, or National Debt The total amount of debt carried by the federal government.

Public Interest The best interests of the collective, overall community; the national good, rather than the narrow interests of a self-serving group.

Public Opinion The aggregate of individual attitudes or beliefs shared by some portion of the adult population. There is no one public opinion, because there are many different "publics."

Purposive Incentive A reason or motive having to do with ethical beliefs or ideological principles.

R

Ratification Formal approval.

Reapportionment The allocation of seats in the House of Representatives to each state after each census.

Recall A procedure allowing the people to vote to dismiss an elected official from state office before his or her term has expired.

Redistricting The redrawing of the boundaries of the congressional districts within each state.

Referendum An electoral device whereby legislative or constitutional measures are referred by the legislature to the voters for approval or disapproval.

Regressive Tax A tax system in which tax rates go down as income goes up.

Relevance The extent to which an issue is of concern at a particular time. Issues become relevant when the public views them as pressing or of direct concern to daily life.

Remand To send a case back to the court that originally heard it.

Representation The function of members of Congress as elected officials in representing the views of their constituents.

Representative Assembly A legislature composed of individuals who represent the population.

Representative Democracy A form of government in which representatives elected by the people make and enforce laws and policies.

Reprieve The presidential power to postpone the execution of a sentence imposed by a court of law; usually done for humanitarian reasons or to await new evidence.

Republic The form of government in which sovereignty rests with the people, who elect agents to represent them in lawmaking and other decisions.

Republican Party One of the two major American political parties, which emerged in the 1850s as an antislavery party. It was created to fill the vacuum caused by the disintegration of the Whig Party.

Reverse To annul or make void a judgment on account of some error or irregularity.

Reverse Discrimination The charge that affirmative action programs requiring preferential treatment or quotas discriminate against those who do not have minority status.

Rule of Four A United States Supreme Court procedure requiring four affirmative votes to hear the case before the full Court.

Rules Committee A standing committee of the House of Representatives that provides special rules under which specific bills can be debated, amended, and considered by the House.

S

Safe Seat A district that returns the legislator with 55 percent of the vote or more.

Sampling Error The difference between a sample's results and the true result if the entire population had been interviewed.

Secession The act of formally withdrawing from membership in an alliance; the withdrawal of a state from the federal Union.

Second Budget Resolution A resolution passed by Congress in September that sets "binding" limits on taxes and spending for the next fiscal year beginning October 1.

Second Continental Congress The 1775 congress of the colonies that established an army.

Sectional Politics The pursuit of interests that are of special concern to a region or section of the country.

Select Committee A temporary legislative committee established for a limited time period and for a special purpose.

Selectperson A member of the governing group of a town.

Senatorial Courtesy In regard to federal district court judgeship nominations, a Senate tradition allowing a senator of the president's political party to veto a judicial appointment in his or her state simply by indicating that the appointment is personally not acceptable. At that point, the Senate may reject the nomination, or the president may withdraw consideration of the nominee.

Seniority System A custom followed in both chambers of Congress specifying that members with longer terms of continuous service will be given preference when committee chairpersons and holders of other significant posts are selected.

Separate-but-Equal Doctrine The doctrine holding that segregation in schools and public accommodations does not imply that one race is superior to another; and that separate-but-equal facilities do not violate the equal protection clause.

Separation of Powers The principle of dividing governmental powers among the executive, the legislative, and the judicial branches of government.

Service Sector The sector of the economy that provides services—such as food services, insurance, and education—in contrast to the sector of the economy that produces goods.

Sexual Harassment Unwanted physical or verbal conduct or abuse of a sexual nature that interferes with a recipient's job performance, creates a hostile environment, or carries with it an implicit or explicit threat of adverse employment consequences.

Social Movement A movement that represents the demands of a large segment of the public for political, economic, or social change.

Soft Money Campaign contributions that evade contribution limits by being given to parties and party committees to help fund general party activities.

Solid South A term describing the tendency of the post–Civil War southern states to vote for the Democratic Party. (Voting patterns in the South have changed, though.)

Solidary Incentive A reason or motive having to do with the desire to associate with others and to share with others a particular interest or hobby.

Sound Bite A brief, memorable comment that easily can be fit into news broadcasts.

Soviet Bloc The Eastern European countries that installed Communist regimes after World War II.

Speaker of the House The presiding officer in the House of Representatives. The speaker is always a member of the majority party and is the most powerful and influential member of the House.

Spin An interpretation of campaign events or election results that is most favorable to the candidate's campaign strategy.

Spin Doctor A political campaign adviser who tries to convince journalists of the truth of a particular interpretation of events.

Splinter Party A new party formed by a dissident faction within a major political party. Usually, splinter parties have emerged when a particular personality was at odds with the major party.

Spoils System The awarding of government jobs to political supporters and friends; generally associated with President Andrew Jackson.

Spring Review The time every year when the Office of Management and Budget requires federal agencies to review their programs, activities, and goals and submit their requests for funding for the next fiscal year.

Stability The extent to which public opinion remains constant over a period of time.

Standing Committee A permanent committee within the House or Senate that considers bills within a certain subject area.

Stare Decisis To stand on decided cases; the judicial policy of following precedents established by past decisions.

State A group of people occupying a specific area and organized under one government; may be either a nation or a subunit of a nation.

State Central Committee The principal organized structure of each political party within each state. This committee is responsible for carrying out policy decisions of the party's state convention.

State of the Union Message An annual message to Congress in which the president proposes a legislative program. The message is addressed not only to Congress but also to the American people and to the world. It offers the opportunity to dramatize policies and objectives and to gain public support.

Statutory Power A power created for the president through laws enacted by Congress.

Strategic Arms Limitation Treaty (SALT I) A treaty between the United States and the Soviet Union to stabilize the nuclear arms competition between the two countries. SALT I talks began in 1969, and agreements were signed on May 26, 1972.

Subpoena A legal writ requiring a person's appearance in court to give testimony.

Suffrage The right to vote; the franchise.

Sunset Legislation A law requiring that an existing program be reviewed regularly for its effectiveness and be terminated unless specifically extended as a result of this review.

Super Tuesday The date on which a number of presidential primaries are held, including those of most of the southern states.

Superdelegate A party leader or elected official who is given the right to vote at the party's national convention. Superdelegates are not elected at the state level.

Supplemental Security Income (SSI) A federal program established to provide assistance to elderly persons and disabled persons.

Supremacy Clause The constitutional provision that makes the Constitution and federal laws superior to all conflicting state and local laws.

Supremacy Doctrine A doctrine that asserts the superiority of national law over state or regional laws. This principle is rooted in Article VI of the Constitution, which provides that the Constitution, the laws passed by the national government under its constitutional powers, and all treaties constitute the supreme law of the land.

T

Tariff A tax on imported goods.

Technical Assistance The sending of experts with technical skills in agriculture, engineering, or business to aid other nations.

Temporary Assistance to Needy Families (TANF) A state-administered program in which grants from the national government are given to the states, which use the funds to provide assistance to those eligible to receive welfare benefits. The TANF program was created by the Welfare Reform Act of 1996 and replaced the former AFDC program.

Third Party A political party other than the two major political parties (Republican and Democratic). Usually, third parties are composed of dissatisfied groups that have split from the major parties. They act as indicators of political trends and as safety valves for dissident groups.

Ticket Splitting Voting for candidates of two or more parties for different offices. For example, a voter splits her ticket if she votes for a Republican presidential candidate and for a Democratic congressional candidate.

Totalitarian Regime A form of government that controls all aspects of the political and social life of a nation. All power resides with the government. The citizens have no power to choose the leadership or policies of the country.

Town Manager System A form of city government in which voters elect three selectpersons, who then appoint a professional town manager, who in turn appoints other officials.

Town Meeting The governing authority of a New England town. Qualified voters may participate in the election of officers and in the passage of legislation.

Township A rural unit of government based on federal land surveys of the American frontier in the 1780s. Townships have declined significantly in importance.

Tracking Poll A poll taken for the candidate on a nearly daily basis as election day approaches.

Trial Court The court in which most cases usually begin and in which questions of fact are examined.

Truman Doctrine The policy adopted by President Harry Truman in 1947 to halt Communist expansion in southeastern Europe.

Trustee In regard to a legislator, one who acts according to his or her conscience and the broad interests of the entire society.

Twelfth Amendment An amendment to the Constitution, adopted in 1804, that specifies the separate election of the president and vice president by the electoral college.

Twenty-fifth Amendment An amendment to the Constitution adopted in 1967 that establishes procedures for filling vacancies in the two top executive offices and that makes provisions for situations involving presidential disability.

Two-Party System A political system in which only two parties have a reasonable chance of winning.

U

U.S. Treasury Bond Evidence of debt issued by the federal government; similar to corporate bonds but issued by the U.S. Treasury.

Unanimous Opinion A court opinion or determination on which all judges agree.

Underground Economy The part of the economy that does not pay taxes and so is not directly measured by government statisticians; also called the subterranean economy or unreported economy.

Unicameral Legislature A legislature with only one legislative body, as compared with a bicameral (two-house) legislature, such as the U.S. Congress. Nebraska is the only state in the union with a unicameral legislature.

Unincorporated Area An area not located within the boundary of a municipality.

Unit Rule All of a state's electoral votes are cast for the presidential candidate receiving a plurality of the popular vote.

Unitary System A centralized governmental system in which local or subdivisional governments exercise only those powers given to them by the central government.

Universal Suffrage The right of all adults to vote for their representatives.

V

Veto Message The president's formal explanation of a veto when legislation is returned to the Congress.

W

War Powers Resolution A law passed in 1973 spelling out the conditions under which the president can commit troops without congressional approval.

Washington Community Individuals regularly involved with politics in Washington, D.C.

Watergate Break-in The 1972 illegal entry into the Democratic National Committee offices by participants in Richard Nixon's reelection campaign.

Weberian Model A model of bureaucracy developed by the German sociologist Max Weber, who viewed bureaucracies as rational, hierarchical organizations in which power flows from the top downward and decisions are based on logical reasoning and data analysis.

Whig Party One of the foremost political organizations in the United States during the first half of the nineteenth century, formally established in 1836. The Whig Party was dominated by the same anti-Jackson elements that organized the National Republican faction within the Democratic (Jeffersonian) Republicans and represented a variety of regional interests. It fell apart as a national party in the early 1850s.

Whip An assistant who aids the majority or minority leader of the House or the Senate majority or minority floor leader.

Whistleblower Someone who brings to public attention gross governmental inefficiency or an illegal action.

White House Office The personal office of the president, which tends to presidential political needs and manages the media.

White House Press Corps A group of reporters assigned full-time to cover the presidency.

White Primary A state primary election that restricts voting to whites only; outlawed by the Supreme Court in 1944.

Writ of *Certiorari* An order issued by a higher court to a lower court to send up the record of a case for review. It is the principal vehicle for United States Supreme Court review.

Index

Photo Credits